strategic human resource management

3e

strategic human resource management

3e

Jeffrey A. Mello

Australia • Brazil • Japan • Korea • Mexico • Singapore • Spain • United Kingdom • United States

Strategic Human Resource Management, Third Edition
Jeffrey A. Mello

Vice President of Editorial, Business: Jack W. Calhoun

Vice President/Editor-in-Chief: Melissa Acuña

Senior Acquisitions Editor: Michele Rhoades

Developmental Editor: Daniel Noguera

Senior Editorial Assistant: Ruth Belanger

Marketing Manager: Clint Kernen

Senior Marketing Communications Manager: Jim Overly

Product Manager: Jennifer Ziegler

Content Project Management: Pre-PressPMG

Manager of Technology, Editorial: Pam Wallace

Media Editor: Rob Ellington

Production Technology Analyst: Starratt Alexander

Senior Manufacturing Buyer: Sandee Milewski

Production Service: Pre-PressPMG

Copyeditor: Pre-PressPMG

Compositor: Pre-PressPMG

Permissions Acquisition Manager/Text: Bob Kauser

Permissions Acq. Manager/Image: Don Schlotman

Senior Art Director, Cover: Tippy McIntosh

Cover Designer: Dare Porter, Real Time Design

Cover Image: © Getty Images, Digital Vision, Ryan McVay

For product information and technology assistance, contact us at
Cengage Learning Customer & Sales Support, 1-800-354-9706
For permission to use material from this text or product,
submit all requests online at **www.cengage.com/permissions**
Further permissions questions can be emailed to
permissionrequest@cengage.com

Library of Congress Control Number: 2009939687

ISBN-13: 978-0-324-78962-1

ISBN-10: 0-324-78962-9

South-Western Cengage Learning
5191 Natorp Boulevard
Mason, OH 45040
USA

Cengage Learning products are represented in Canada by Nelson Education, Ltd

For your course and learning solutions, visit **www.cengage.com**

Purchase any of our products at your local college store or at our preferred online store **www.CengageBrain.com**

Printed in the United States of America
2 3 4 5 6 7 13 12 11 10

To my daughter Logan
for making every day special and
each month more fun than the last one

BRIEF CONTENTS

CONTENTS

part two
Implementation of Strategic Human Resource Management

PREFACE

Since the publication of the second edition of this text, much has changed relative to the attention being shown to and value being placed on strategic human resource management in organizations. HR-related publications continue to thrive, while practitioner-oriented management publications—traditionally dominated by articles focused on marketing and finance—are publishing an increasingly significant number of articles on human resource management, particularly strategic aspects of HR. Within the academy, there has similarly been a significant increase in the number of HR-related articles in journals focused on general management and even those related to strategy. No longer is HR simply relegated to specialized journals that deal with HR. This significant movement toward the publication of more HR-focused articles in both the general management academic and practitioner literatures illustrates clearly that executives are realizing the role HR plays in an organization's success as well as the fact the HR is a general management responsibility and its effective practice a key to successful operating results.

Also since the publication of the second edition, the resources that have been developed and made available to those of us who teach have greatly expanded. In 2006, the Society for Human Resource Management, the world's largest HR professional association, launched its HR Education Initiative. The main components of this ongoing initiative include: 1) curriculum guidebooks and templates for both undergraduate and graduate programs; 2) dozens of cases and learning modules to assist with course design and delivery; and 3) a significant database of the latest research and position papers on critical issues in strategic HR, which allow instructors to remain very current on trends, best practices, and legislative and court activity. Much of this material is available to non-members at the SHRM website, www.shrm.org, under Resources for HR Educators, which is under the Education tab. However, the significant added benefits of SHRM membership for faculty members and students as well as practitioners far outweigh the nominal annual membership dues.

Also, in 2007, a new teaching journal, *Journal of Human Resources Education (JHRE)*, was launched under the founding editorship of my friend and colleague, Dr. Bill Heisler of Troy University. Many teaching innovations are being shared by authors in *JHRE*, and those of us who teach HR are indebted to Bill for his selfless and laborious commitment to bringing this exciting new publication to fruition.

Organization and Content

Strategic Human Resource Management, 3e is designed for: 1) graduate students enrolled in survey courses in human resource management who would benefit from a general management approach to strategic HR; 2) working professionals enrolled in specialized HR and executive programs as a capstone offering; and 3) undergraduate students enrolled in a capstone course in an HR degree program or those seeking an advanced level HR course to complement their strategy course.

The text is organized into two sections. The first section, Chapters 1–7, examines the context of strategic HR and develops a framework and conceptual model for the practice of strategic HR. The chapters in this section examine employees as "investments;" explore trends that affect human resource management practice; describe what strategic HR is, particularly in contrast to more traditional approaches to HR; and look at how both the design of work systems and relevant employment laws influence the practice of managing people in organizations. The second section, Chapters 8–14, examines the actual practice and implementation of strategic HR through a discussion of strategic issues that need to be addressed while developing specific programs and policies related to the traditional functional areas of HR. Covered within this section are strategic issues related to staffing, training, performance management, compensation, labor relations, employee separation, and managing a global workforce. Both the integrative framework that requires linkage between and consistency among these functional HR activities and the approach toward writing about these traditional functional areas from a strategic perspective distinguish the text from what is currently on the market.

Chapter Features

All chapters contain the following:

- an opening "in practice" vignette featuring a well-known organization to introduce the chapter topic as well as several additional vignettes within each chapter that illustrate pertinent chapter concepts
- three carefully selected readings that are integrated within the text discussion

Pedagogical features that appear at the end of each chapter are designed to foster the learning experience individually, in the classroom, as a group, and on the Internet. These include:

- end-of-chapter discussion questions
- experiential exercises to aid in student learning
- recommended discussion questions for each of the readings

New to the Third Edition

As the field of strategic human resource management has evolved since the second edition, this text has similarly done so in response. More than 80 percent of the end-of chapter readings (35 of 42) are new to this edition. The retained readings are those that have become "classics" and are presented alongside those that represent the latest in thinking and practice in human resource management. There are also a dozen new original exhibits that explain chapter concepts; 28 new "in practice" vignettes that describe strategic HR practices in a wide variety of organizations; and 131 new references.

There is also significant new content in each of the 14 chapters. Chapter 1 has a new section on HR metrics. Chapter 2 has greatly enhanced coverage of diversity and ethics, along with a new section on corporate social responsibility and sustainability. Chapter 3 has new sections on innovation/creativity and privatization as components of strategy. Chapter 4 has a new discussion of employee engagement as a component of HR strategy. Chapter 5 contains enhanced material on succession planning and a new section on mentoring. Chapter 6 now incorporates technology (previously contained in Chapter 2), has enhanced discussion of offshoring as well as mergers and acquisitions, and includes a new section on social networking. Chapter 7 has expanded coverage of employment-at-will, updates on the Americans with Disabilities Act and Family and Medical Leave Act, and a new section on trends in employment litigation. Chapter 8 has enhanced material on assessment as well as new section on trends in staffing and documentation of employment eligibility. Chapter 9 has a new section on organizational development. Chapter 10 has a more detailed discussion on performance feedback versus performance appraisal. Chapter 11 has additional material on executive compensation and a new section on salary compression. Chapter 12 has expanded coverage of labor history in the United States. Chapter 13 has enhanced material on retention. Chapter 14 has new sections on Canada, Mexico, India, and China.

Instructor's Resources

With this edition, we offer an Instructor's Manual and PowerPoint slides to accompany the book. These valuable assets have been prepared by Jeffrey Mello to ensure its currency to this edition, and they can be accessed visiting www.cengage.com/management/mello. The Instructor's Manual includes chapter outlines, answers to end-of-chapter content, and suggested topics for student papers, while the PowerPoint slides offers all main text concepts to encourage classroom discussion and classroom engagement.

Acknowledgments

Numerous individuals were instrumental in ensuring the success of the first two editions of this text as well as the development of this third edition. Many professional staff members of South-Western/Thomson/Cengage have displayed support and unbridled enthusiasm for this project since its inception. This project began with the belief and support of Charles McCormack, the original acquisitions editor, nearly a decade ago. Joe Sabatino served as marketing manager for the first edition and acquisitions editor for the second edition. You would not be reading this if it weren't for his talent, hard work, and support in developing and implementing the marketing plan for the first edition and seeing the potential for subsequent editions. I am grateful to him beyond what I can express in words. Mardell Glinski-Shultz (formerly Toomey) served as developmental editor *extraordinaire* (emphasis added by me) for the first two editions. She asked all the right questions and knew when to push and when to lay back. Her efforts improved this book immeasurably and are embedded in the foundation of this and all future editions. Michele Rhoades and Daniel Noguera served as acquisitions and developmental editors respectively for this edition and have brought a wonderful fresh perspective to this project. Abby Greshik of Pre-PressPMG has provided invaluable assistance with copyediting and preproduction work via mind-boggling attention to detail.

I owe a tremendous debt of gratitude to several close longtime personal friends who have careers in HR—both in academia and/or as senior executives—and have been generous with their time and expertise in allowing me to seek their advice on various ideas I have had for this project. I can't thank them enough for their ideas or their friendship. They are:

Jan Aspelund
David Balkin
Brian Brown
Deb Cohen
John Cunningham
Jeff Friant

I also wish to thank the following reviewers for the feedback and valuable recommendations they provided that greatly assisted me in the development of the third edition: Muriel Anderson, University of Buffalo; Richard Dibble, New York Institute of Technology; Michael Kendrick, David Lipscomb University; Hamid Khan, Our Lady of the Lake University; Jill Langen, Baker College; Julia Morrison, Bloomfield College; Michael Provitera, Barry University; Mark Teachout, University of the Incarnate Word; Timothy Wiedman, Doane College; and Tal Zarankin, University of Missouri.

Finally, thanks to Amy Eastwood for always keeping me laughing, Russ Boisjoly for swapping war stories and being such a great friend, Jackie Burgee for being an inspiration of courage, strength, and integrity, and Donna Edwards for 25+ years of being a partner-in-crime, best friend, and role model.

Jeffrey A. Mello

ABOUT THE AUTHOR

Jeffrey A. Mello has held faculty and administrative positions at Towson University, the George Washington University, the University of California at Berkeley, and Northeastern University, from where he received his Ph.D. He has been a recipient of the David L. Bradford Outstanding Educator Award, presented by the Organizational Behavior Teaching Society, and has received international, national, and institutional awards for his research, teaching, and service. He has authored four books and published more than 100 book chapters, journal articles, and conference papers in journals such as the *Journal of Business Ethics, Business Horizons, International Journal of Public Administration, Business & Society Review, Journal of Employment Discrimination Law, Seton Hall Legislative Journal, Journal of Individual Employment Rights, Public Personnel Management, Employee Responsibilities and Rights Journal, Labor Law Journal, Journal of Law and Business,* and the *Journal of Management Education.* He currently serves as an editor of the *Journal of Legal Studies Education* and on the editorial review boards of four leading management journals. He has also served as an editor for the *Journal of Management Education* and *Employee Responsibilities and Rights Journal.* He is a member of the Academy of Legal Studies in Business, Organizational Behavior Teaching Society, Society for Human Resource Management, and Academy of Management.

The Context of Strategic Human Resource Management

part one

An Investment Perspective of Human Resource Management

1

Learning Objectives

- Understand the sources of employee value
- Gain an appreciation of the importance of human capital and how it can be measured
- Understand how competitive advantage can be achieved through investment in employees
- Gain an appreciation of metrics, their measures, and their usefulness
- Understand the obstacles that prevent organizations from investing in their employees

Human Resources at Nordstrom

How can a retailer gain a competitive advantage in a cut-throat marketplace? Middle- and high-end retailers generally locate in close proximity to each other and often carry similar—but not identical—merchandise. Consequently, their sales and profit margins are usually in tandem. Nordstrom, however, has consistently produced above-industry-average profits and continues to be profitable when its competitors' profits are falling or flat.

The key to Nordstrom's success lies with the different way it manages its employees. Sales employees are known as "associates" and considered the organization's most valuable asset. The company's success is rooted in its strategy of providing superlative customer service. Associates are encouraged to act as entrepreneurs and build strong personal relationships with customers, or "clients." In fact, many clients shop only with a particular Nordstrom associate and call in advance to determine associate schedules or to make appointments.

Nordstrom's strategy involves a heavy investment in the organization's sales force. Nordstrom provides associates with extensive training on merchandising and product lines and offers high compensation. Its commitment to its employees is evident from the fact that the company organization chart is depicted inverse from that of a traditional retailer. Associates are at the highest level on the chart, followed by department and merchandise managers and, finally, executives. This depiction cements the organization's philosophy that the customer is king. All efforts of senior, middle, and lower-level managers should support the efforts of the sales force.

Effective organizations are increasingly realizing that of the varied factors that contribute to performance, the human element is clearly the most critical. Regardless of the size or nature of an organization, the activities it undertakes, and the environment in which it operates, its success is determined by the decisions its employees make and the behaviors in which they engage. Managers at all levels in organizations are becoming increasingly aware that a critical source of competitive advantage often comes not from having the most ingenious product design or service, the best marketing strategy, state-of-the-art technology, or the most savvy financial management but from having the appropriate systems for attracting, motivating, and managing the organizations' human resources (HR).

Adopting a strategic view of HR, in large part, involves considering employees as human "assets" and developing appropriate policies and programs as investments in these assets to increase their value to the organization and the marketplace. The characterization of employees as human assets can have a chilling effect on those who find the term derogatory because of its connotation that employees are to be considered "property." However, the characterization of employees as assets is fitting, considering what an asset actually is: something of value and worth. Effective organizations realize that their employees do have value, much as the organization's physical and capital assets have value. Exhibit 1.1 illustrates some of the value employees bring to an organization.

Adopting an Investment Perspective

The characterization of employees as human assets has important implications for the strategic management of human resources in that it allows us to consider HR from an investment perspective. Physical and capital assets in organizations, such as plant, property, machinery, and technology, are acquired and subsequently managed most effectively by

EXHIBIT 1.1 Sources of Employee Value

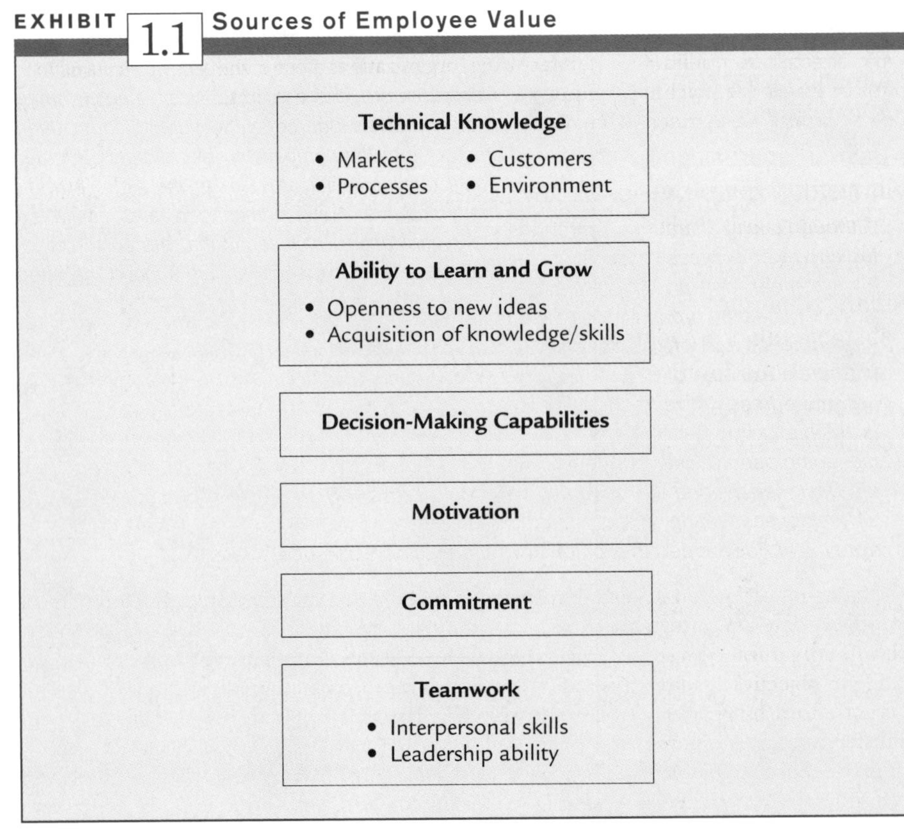

treating them as investments; the organization determines the optimal mix of high-performance, high-return assets to its strategic objectives. Analyses are made of the costs and benefits of certain expenditures, with judgments made concerning the riskiness and potential returns of such expenditures. Viewing human resources from an investment perspective, much as physical assets are viewed, rather than as variable costs of production, allows an organization to determine how to best invest in its people. Furthermore, considering the risk and return on possible expenditures related to acquiring or developing human assets allows an organization to consider how current expenditures can be best allocated to meet long-term performance goals.

In considering whether to undertake the expense of a new training program, for example, an organization needs to consider not only the out-of-pocket costs for the training but also the related opportunity costs, such as lost time on the job, and weigh these costs against the potential benefits of the training, such as enhanced performance, potential increased loyalty, and motivation. The training also needs to be assessed relative to risk because the enhanced marketability of employees makes them more desirable to competitors. Similarly, in considering compensation programs as an investment, an organization needs to consider what it is "investing" in when it pays someone (knowledge, commitment, new ideas, retention of employees from competitors). The potential return on the organization's financial outlay in compensation will determine whether its compensation system is a viable investment strategy.

Taking an investment perspective toward human resources/assets is critical considering that other physical assets, such as facilities, products and services, technologies, and markets, can be readily cloned or imitated by competitors.[1] Human assets cannot be duplicated and therefore become the *competitive advantage* that an organization enjoys in its market(s). This is becoming increasingly important as the skills required for most jobs become less manual and more cerebral and knowledge-based in nature.[2] Rapid and ongoing advances in technology have created a workplace where laborers are being replaced by knowledge workers. An organization's "technology" is becoming more invested in people than in capital. Thought and decision-making processes as well as skills in analyzing complex data are not "owned" by an organization but by individual employees. This is in stark contrast to traditional manufacturing organizations where the employer usually owns or leases the machinery and production processes, and duplication of the organization's "capital" is restricted primarily by cost considerations.

Managing Employees at United Parcel Service

Although taking a strategic approach to human resource management usually involves looking at employees as assets and considering them as investments, this does not always mean that an organization will adopt a "human relations" approach to HR. A few successful organizations still utilize principles of scientific management, where worker needs and interests are subordinate to efficiency. United Parcel Service (UPS) is a prime example of this. At UPS, all jobs from truck loaders to drivers to customer service representatives are designed around measures of efficiency. Wages are relatively high, but performance expectations are also high. This approach toward managing people is still "strategic" in nature because the systems for managing people are designed around the company's strategic objectives of efficiency. Consequently, all employee training, performance management, compensation, and work design systems are developed to promote this strategic objective of efficiency.

Managing an organization's employees as investments mandates the development of an appropriate and integrated approach to managing human resources that is consistent with the organization's strategy. As an example, consider an organization whose primary strategic objective involves innovation. An organization pursuing an innovation strategy cannot afford high levels of turnover within its ranks. It needs to retain employees and transfer among employees the new knowledge being developed in-house. It cannot afford to have its employees develop innovative products, services, and processes and then take this knowledge to a competitor for implementation. The significant investment in research and development ends up having no return. Because the outcome of this expenditure (research and development) is knowledge that employees have developed, it is critical as part of the organization's overall strategy for the organization to devise strategies to retain its employees and their knowledge bases until the "new knowledge" becomes "owned" by the organization itself (through diffusion throughout the organization) rather than by the employee.

This leads to a dilemma involving investing in human assets. An organization that does not invest in its employees may be less attractive to prospective employees and may have a more difficult time retaining current employees; this causes inefficiency (downtime to recruit, hire, and train new employees) and a weakening of the organization's competitive position. However, an organization that does invest in its people needs to ensure that these investments are not lost. Well-trained employees, for example, become more attractive in the marketplace, particularly to competitors who may be able to pay the employee more because they have not had to invest in the training that the employee has already received. Although an organization's physical assets cannot "walk," its human assets can, making the latter a much more risky investment. An organization can certainly buy or sell its physical assets because it has "ownership" of them, but it does not own its human assets. Consequently, organizations need to develop strategies to ensure that employees stay on long enough for the organization to realize an acceptable return on its investment relative to the employees' acquired skills and knowledge, particularly when the organization has subsidized the acquisition. This requires the organization to determine the actual "value" of each employee. Valuation of human assets has implications for compensation, advancement opportunities, and retention strategies as well as how much should be invested in each area for each employee.

Valuation of Assets

Five major kinds of assets or capital that organizations can leverage to aid in performance and add value to operations are financial assets/capital, physical assets/capital, market assets/capital, operational assets/capital, and human assets/capital, as shown in Exhibit 1.2. Financial assets/capital include equity, securities and investments, and accounts receivable. Physical assets/capital include plant, land, equipment, and raw materials. Market assets/capital include goodwill, branding, customer loyalty, distribution networks, product lines and patents, trademarks, and copyrights. Operational assets/capital include management practices, the structure of work, and the use of technology. Human assets/capital include employee education levels, knowledge, skills, competencies, work habits and motivation, and relationships with coworkers, customers, suppliers, regulators, and lenders.

Financial and physical assets/capital are relatively easy to measure via accounting practices. Most of these assets are tangible and have some clear market value. Market and operational assets/capital are a bit more challenging to measure, but accounting practices have been developed that can place a general subjective value on such assets. Human assets/capital, however, are very difficult to measure; attempts to do so are at the forefront of current research being conducted in human resource management. Reading 1.1, "The Hidden Leverage of Human Capital," illustrates how human assets/capital can provide a significant financial return to organizations. It explains the distinguishing features of human capital management and provides a call for an enhanced understanding among organizational leaders of the role of human capital in organizations.

Understanding and Measuring Human Capital

Given that employees and their collective skills, knowledge, and abilities represent a significant asset for organizations, a critical issue for organizations becomes measuring this value as well as its contribution to the organization's bottom line. One of the first studies that successfully demonstrated this relationship was conducted by Huselid in the

EXHIBIT 1.2 Types of Organizational Assets/Capital

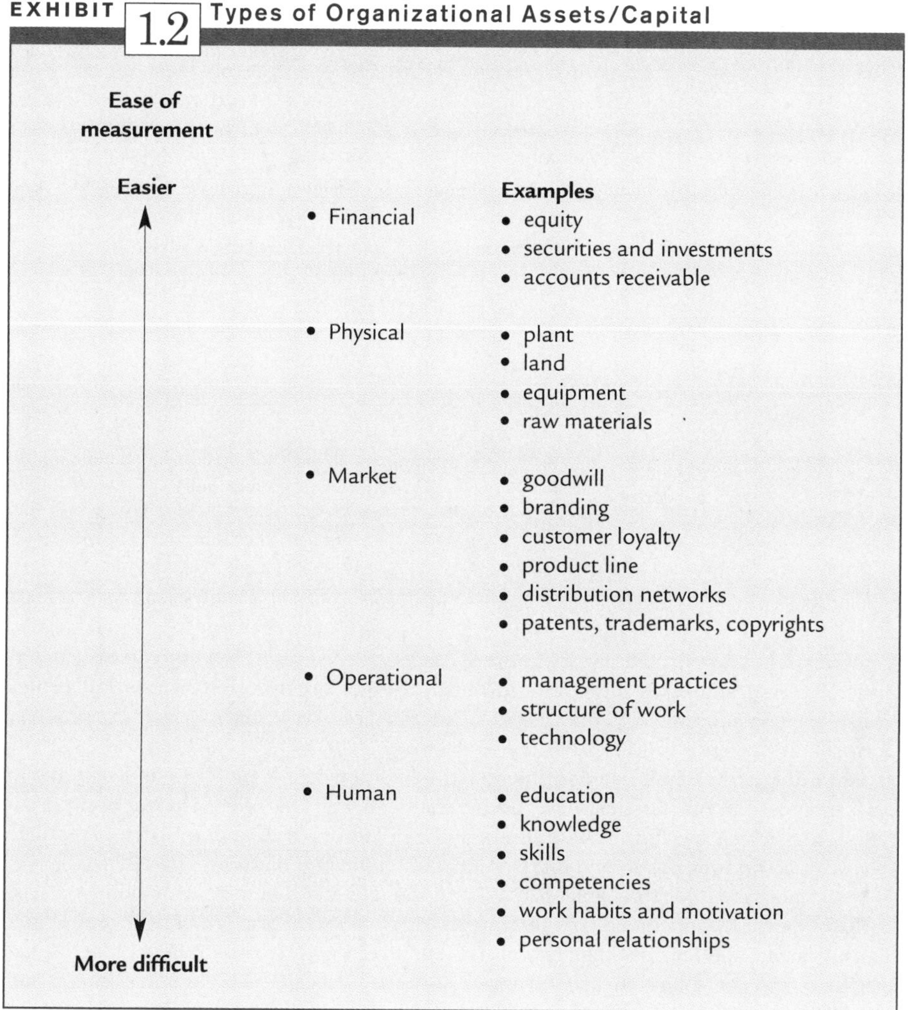

mid-1990s. This study identified what were called "high performance work systems" (HPWS) and demonstrated that integrated, strategically focused HR practices were directly related to profitability and market value.[3] A recent study by Watson Wyatt Worldwide found that the primary reason for organizational profitability is the effective management of human capital. This involves, in part, providing employees with rewards that are commensurate with their contributions and ensuring that investments in employees are not lost to competitors by actively managing employee retention.[4] Another study found that effective, integrated management of human capital can result in up to a 47 percent increase in market value.[5] A landmark study conducted by Becker, Huselid, and Ulrich that examined a variety of human resource management quality indices found that the top 10 percent of organizations studied enjoyed a 391 percent return on investment in the management of their human capital.[6]

Extending these findings, Dyer and Reeves attempted to define what can be called the HR "value chain."[7] They argued that performance could be measured via four different sets of outcomes: employee, organizational, financial and accounting, and market-based. More importantly, they proposed that these sets of outcomes had a sequential cause-and-effect relationship, as indicated in Exhibit 1.3. Each outcome fueled success in a subsequent outcome, establishing a causal link between HR practices and an organization's market value. Much of the research that has the potential to move HR practice and corresponding organizational performance forward has not been acted on and applied because it has not been effectively disseminated. Reading 1.2, "Seven Common

EXHIBIT 1.3 HR Value Chain

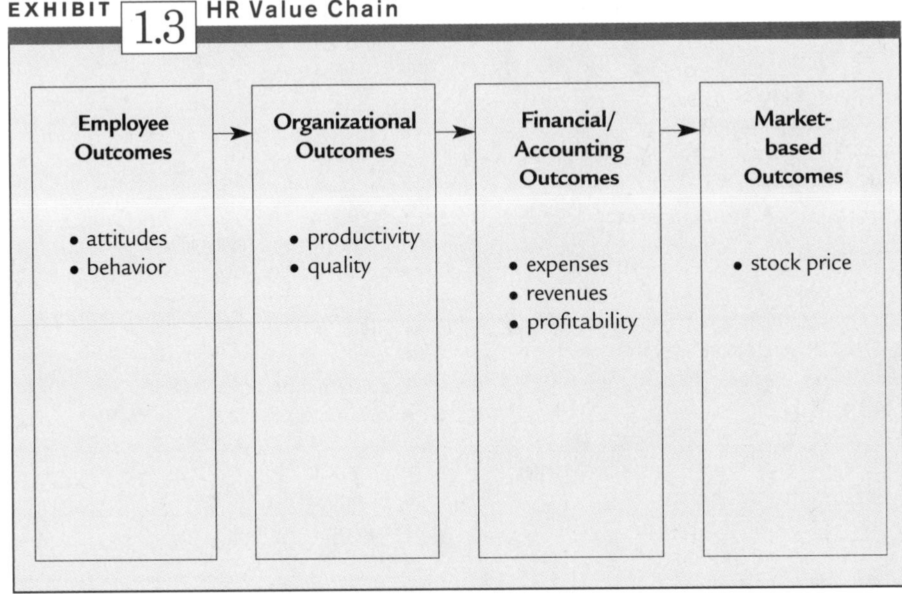

Misconceptions about Human Resource Practices: Research Findings versus Practitioner Beliefs," addresses this void and illustrates that organizations whose HR professional remain abreast of the latest academic research have superior financial performance relative to those that fail to do so.

Given this proven link between integrated and strategic HR practices and bottom-line performance, HR practitioners have been faced with the task of developing appropriate HR metrics, which specifically illustrate the value of HR practices and activities, particularly relative to accounting profits and market valuation of the organization. This task has proven to be far more complex than anticipated, given the difficulties of measuring human assets/capital. One study concluded that 90 percent of *Fortune 500* organizations in the United States, Canada, and Europe evaluate their HR operations on the basis of three rather-limited metrics: employee retention and turnover, corporate morale and employee satisfaction, and HR expense as a percentage of operational expenses.[8] Such "staffing metrics" simply document the extent to which HR performs traditional job functions without necessarily illustrating how HR impacts company profits and shareholder value. Moreover, a focus on such staffing metrics involves a demonstration of how employees can be treated as expenses rather than as assets that can be managed, invested in, and leveraged for profit.

Senior HR executives in these organizations stressed that they lacked accurate and meaningful methods that measured performance, despite the fact that human assets/capital can account for as much as 80 percent of the value of an organization.[9] One reason is that most accounting valuation methods stress the past and current value of assets. Much of the value of human assets/capital rests with the value of an organization and its ability to proactively meet challenges that lie ahead, relative to responsiveness to changing economic, political, and market conditions. As a result, valuation of human assets/capital and analysis of human capital investments can be value-laden, subjective, expensive—and, hence, ignored.

Measuring Human Assets/Capital at Dow Chemical

Dow Chemical has been a leader in forging the frontiers of measuring human capital. Dow has attempted to develop a reliable measure to help calculate each employee's current and anticipated future contribution to the financial goals of the business. A pilot project is currently being tested in a single business unit; it examines employee performance on project assignments by using two specific metrics: expected human capital return (EHCR) and actual human capital return (AHCR). EHCR involves a calculation of the break-even point of investment in an employee, above salary and additional outlays, such as recruiting and training expenses. AHCR involves a calculation of the "value created" by the employee based on the projects he or she was worked on. This metric considers the skills and knowledge of each employee relative to the net present value of a specific project. The desired outcomes of these measures are assisting managers with matching employee talents and project needs, identifying employee development opportunities, and creating a more efficient and effective means for project team staffing. Although the program is still in the pilot stage, with validation studies in progress, Dow anticipates rolling out the metrics to other business units in the very near future.[10]

Given the complex nature of measuring human assets/capital and return on such investments, where does an organization begin in assuming such an undertaking? One helpful model has been developed by Mercer that can allow those concerned with measuring HR performance and documenting the value added by specific initiatives to demonstrate to senior management the value added and bottom-line impact.[11] This model involves six steps: (1) identify a specific business problem that HR can impact; (2) calculate the actual cost of the problem to the organization; (3) choose a HR solution that addresses all or part of the problem; (4) calculate the cost of the solution; (5) 6 to 24 months after implementation, calculate the value of the improvement for the organization; and (6) calculate the specific return on investment (ROI) metric.

One caveat should be obvious from not only Mercer's approach but also that currently being employed at Dow Chemical. Unlike the returns on other types of assets/capital, the returns on investments in human assets/capital are often not realized until some point in the future. Key decision-makers need to be patient in waiting for these results, and HR also needs to subsequently take interim measures and provide status reports to senior management that illustrate preliminary beneficial results. HR needs to move away from mere data collection, however, and perform more comprehensive analysis of performance measures that relate to the critical metrics for which operating divisions are held accountable. Toward this end, HR needs to partner with chief financial officers to understand the language of investment and asset management. If HR continues to be seen as a cost center, it will be the primary target during cost-cutting operations, given that labor is the primary cost incurred in the service and information-intensive sectors that are fueling the growth in our economy. One study places the relative expenses for human capital as high as 70 percent of overall expenditures.[12] Hence, the challenge for HR is to provide senior management with value-added human capital investments backed by solid and meaningful financial metrics.

Human Resource Metrics

Many CEOs openly acknowledge the importance of effective and strategic HR management in their organization's success. Jack Welch noted in one of his last General Electric annual reports: "Developing and motivating people is the most important part of my job. I spent one-third of my time on people. We invest $1 billion annually in training to make them better. I spend most of my time on the top 600 leaders in the company. This is how you create a culture."[13] One recent study of Fortune 100 annual reports found that 14 percent of such reports contained at least one quantitative measure of human resource management, such as turnover rate, investment in training, percentage of pay that is variable, or results from an employee attitude survey.[14] Despite this, Wall Street analysts still generally fail to acknowledge human capital in their assessment of the potential worth of a company's stock or the effects which human capital measures can have on a company's stock price.

Perhaps one reason for this lack of reporting of and respect for metrics related to human capital rests with the fact that there are no universally accepted metrics for the valuation of human capital nor a standard format for measuring and reporting such data. Indeed, the Society for Human Resource Management has identified a number of common metrics for measuring the performance and value of human capital, a number of which are presented in Exhibit 1.4. These are measures that can easily be translated into bottom-line measures of performance as well as compared to industry benchmarks. Exhibit 1.5 provides examples of how five of these metrics that are often regarded as the

EXHIBIT 1.4 Common HR Metrics

Absence Rate
Cost per Hire
Health Care Costs per Employee
HR Expense Factor
Human Capital Return on Investment (ROI)
Human Capital Value Added
Labor Costs as a Percentage of Sales or Revenues
Profit per Employee
Revenue per Employee
Time to Fill
Training Investment Factor
Training Return on Investment (ROI)
Turnover Costs
Turnover Rate (Monthly/Annually)
Vacancy Costs
Vacancy Rate
Workers' Compensation Cost per Employee
Workers' Compensation Incident Rate
Workers' Compensation Severity Rate
Yield Ratio

EXHIBIT 1.5 Calculation of Human Capital Measures

Measure	Formula	Value/Use
Human Capital ROI	Revenue − (operating expenses − compensation + benefits costs) / compensation + benefits costs	Allows determination of return on human investments relative to productivity and profitability; represents pre-tax profit for amounts invested in employee pay and benefits after removal of capital expenses
Profit per Employee	Revenue − operating expenses / number of full-time equivalent (FTE) employees	Illustrates the value created by employees; provides a means of productivity and expense analysis
HR Expense Factor	Total HR expense / total operating expenses	Illustrates the degree of leverage of human capital; provides a benchmark for overall expense analysis relative to targets or budgets
Human Capital Value Added	Revenue − (operating expenses − compensation + benefits costs) / total number of FTE employees	Shows the value of employee knowledge, skills, and performance and how human capital adds value to an organization
Turnover Rate	Number of employee separations (during a given time period) / number of employees	Provides a measure of workplace retention efforts, which can impact direct costs, stability, profitability morale, and productivity; can be used as a measure of success for retention and reward programs

For a complete more list of metrics, formulas, and uses, see Society for Human Resource Management, HR Metrics Toolkit, published Nov. 15, 2007, available at http://moss07.shrm.org/hrdisciplines/Pages/CMS_005910.aspx

most prominent measures of human capital management can be calculated and utilized. Nonetheless, stock analysts are more concerned with talking with operations, accounting, and finance heads rather than those in human resources, as analysts usually have their training in and understand and are most familiar and comfortable with these areas.

Labor Supply Chain Management at Valero Energy

San Antonio-based Valero Energy is a $70 billion energy-refining and marketing company that has reinvented its staffing function through the application of principles of supply chain management. Conceptualizing the acquisition and management of talent as a supply chain, Valero scrapped its traditional staffing processes by which managers would request specific numbers of employees from human resources who, in turn, would solicit referrals from employees and contact recruiters. After an analysis of data related to hiring sources, how long new employees remained employed, performance and productivity of new hires, and "fit" with the company culture, Valero gained a sense of how to recruit the best talent at the lowest cost.

Valero's new staffing process involves forecasting three years in advance the demand for talent by both division and title. Five years of data was mined into a database, and a series of mathematical algorithms was developed for turnover trend analysis by location, position type, salary, tenure, and division. Another series of algorithms projected those trends forward for three years in line with anticipated workforce needs for future capital projects, updated systems, and anticipated new services. The result is the development of talent "pipelines," which address specific future talent needs relative to the organization's strategy and business model, allowing the development of related training and development programs and succession plans.[15]

There are no "perfect" metrics, however, as the appropriate human capital metrics would depend on the organization or business unit's strategy. Organizations concerned about minimizing costs might be most concerned with metrics related to turnover and revenue per employee. Organizations pursuing a strategy of aggressive growth might rely on metrics such as time to fill those concerned with innovation might closely monitor training costs per employee. Divisions or subsidiaries within the same organization might use totally different metrics, dependent on their unit's goals and strategies. Reading 1.3, "Maximizing Human Capital: Demonstrating HR Value with Key Performance Indicators," presents some suggestions as to how HR can develop metrics that measure some of the outcomes of its activities from a strategic perspective.

Factors Influencing How "Investment Oriented" an Organization Is

Not all organizations realize that human assets can be strategically managed from an investment perspective. As shown in Exhibit 1.6, five major factors affect how "investment oriented" a company is in its management of human resources. The first of these is management values.[16] Management may or may not have an appreciation of the value of its human assets relative to other capital assets, such as brand names, distribution channels, real estate, facilities and equipment, and information systems. The extent to which an organization can be characterized as investment-oriented may be revealed through answers to the following questions:

- Does the organization see its people as being central to its mission/strategy?
- Do the company's mission statement and strategic objectives, both company-wide and within individual business units, espouse the value of or even mention human assets and their roles in achieving goals?

EXHIBIT 1.6 Factors Influencing an Organization's Investment Orientation

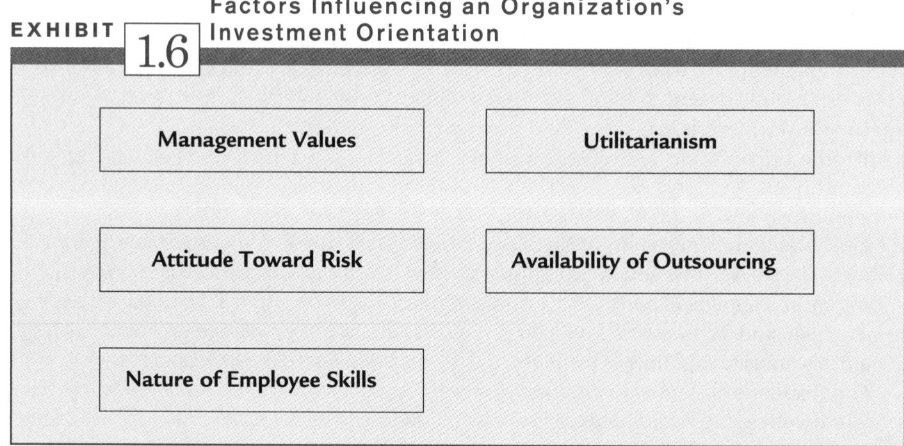

- More importantly, does the management philosophy of the organization encourage the development of any strategy to prevent the depreciation of its human assets or are they considered replicable and amortizable, like physical assets?

Senior management values and actions determine organizational investment in assets. It is critical to understand how the organization's strategy mandates the investment in particular assets relative to others. Whether management values its people is a critical factor in its willingness to invest in them.

The second factor is attitude toward risk. The most fundamental lesson in financial management is that a trade-off exists between risk and return. Higher-risk investments are generally expected to have a greater potential return; lower-risk, safer investments are generally expected to have a more modest return. For example, in financial markets, bonds are considered less-risky investments than stocks but have a limited, fixed return. Stocks, on the other hand, are considered higher-risk investments but have no limit as to their potential return.

Both personal and institutional investment strategies can be highly conservative (risk averse) or pursue unlimited returns with reckless abandon. Investments in human assets are generally far more risky for an organization than investments in physical assets: Unlike physical assets, human assets are not *owned* by the organization. An organization with risk-averse management philosophies is far less likely to make significant investments in people. Other organizations see investments in employees as necessary for their success and develop strategies to minimize the potential risk of losing their investments. An organization can attempt to gain some "ownership" of employee services through long-term employment contracts or by offering employees financial incentives, such as stock-ownership programs, as well as additional professional development opportunities.

The third factor is the nature of the skills needed by employees. Certain organizations require employees to develop and utilize very specialized skills that might not be applicable in another organization; another employer might have employees utilize and develop skills that are highly marketable. For example, if an employer has a custom-made information system to handle administrative HR functions, employees using that system might not transfer those skills to another employer. However, if an employer uses a popular software program for which there is high demand for skilled employees among competitors, the investment in employees becomes more risky.

As a result, an organization that decides to provide its employees with specialized training in skills that can be utilized by others in the marketplace has a much stronger need to develop a strong retention strategy than an organization that teaches employees skills that are less marketable. Employees with skills demanded in the marketplace become more valuable and sought-after assets by companies that choose not to make expenditures or invest in training and skill development.

The fourth factor affecting the investment orientation is the "utilitarian" mentality of the organization. Organizations that take a utilitarian, or "bottom line," perspective evaluate investments by using utility analysis, also known as *cost–benefit analysis.* Here, the costs of any investment are weighted against its benefits to determine whether the prospective investment is either profitable or, more commonly, achieves the target rate of return the organization has set for its investments. A highly utilitarian approach attempts to quantify all costs and benefits. For example, rather than just considering direct cash expenditures, this approach would also consider the cost for the time involved to develop and administer an innovative performance measurement system (by considering how much people are being paid for the time involved in the process), the cost of having larger applicant pools (by considering how much longer it would take to screen applicants), and the cost of employing more extensive employee selection procedures (again, by considering time and its monetary value).

The distinct problem many utilitarian organizations run into regarding investments in people involves the fact that many benefits of HR programs and policies are extremely difficult to quantify. If these programs and policies can be assessed quantitatively, subjectivity as to the actual value of the benefit may make consensus on the overall value difficult. This is especially true for programs that attempt to enhance performance in service organizations. As an example, consider the customer service division of your local Internet service provider. Measures of effective service are not only difficult to assess objectively, but the organization may not be able to determine how much service is necessary to prevent customers from jumping to competitors and maintain their loyalty instead. Additional investments in service may not have any direct financial benefit.

Similarly, a government organization or public utility that attempts to develop a program to enhance efficiency may have a difficult time in finding the cost justifiable. Given that no market mechanisms exist for government agencies or legal monopolies, customers have no choice among competitors. Customers may complain to regulators or officials, but there may be no incentive or benefit for the organization to enhance its efficiency from an investment perspective. On a more basic level, a program that is designed to improve employee morale can have benefits that may be very difficult to measure and quantify. A utilitarian organization is likely to reject such "soft" programs that have no quantifiable return. Hence, the more utilitarian an organization, the more likely it is to see HR programs as investments, creating a challenge for those advocating for such HR programs to find a means to show their impact on the bottom line. Some very recent studies have begun to address this issue by attempting to establish a link between HR strategies and systems and an organization's financial performance. Initial results have shown a significant impact of HR systems on both market-based and accounting-based measures of performance.[17]

The final factor impacting an organization's willingness to invest in its people is the availability of cost-effective outsourcing. An investment-oriented approach to managing an organization will attempt to determine whether its investments produce a *sustainable* competitive advantage over time. When specialists who may perform certain functions much more efficiently exist outside an organization, any internal programs will be challenged and have to be evaluated relative to such a standard. This is true for virtually any organizational function, including customer service, accounting, manufacturing, and human resource management functions.

The organization is further likely to invest its resources where key decision-makers perceive they wll have the greatest potential return. This may result in few investments in people at the expense of investment in market and product development, physical expansion, or acquisition of new technology. As an example, employers in the fast-food industry, such as at McDonald's, invest little in their people; they require minimal experience, provide little training, pay low wages, and expect high turnover because the supply of workers is excessive relative to demand. Organizations in this industry tend to invest much more in new product development, physical expansion, and marketing through competitive advertising.

Conclusion

Developing an effective strategy to manage an organization's human assets requires considering employees as investments. Such an approach helps to ensure that HR practices and principles are clearly in sync with the organization's overall strategy, forces the organization to invest in its best opportunities, and ensures that performance standards are met. As an example, employee stock-ownership programs attempt to strategically invest in the organization and its people by making employees owners of the company. Instead of having a conflict as to how profits should be allocated (bonuses to employees or reinvested in the business), both can be achieved simultaneously. In turn, this has the goal of gaining more commitment from employees and encouraging them to adopt a long-term focus toward the organization; this is often a shortcoming/deficiency of American organizations that are concerned with short-run indicators of performance. Employees who now intend to stay with the organization longer, given their vested ownership rights, provide organizations with an incentive to incur the short-term costs involved with investing in human assets for the long-term financial gains that can result from such investments.

An investment perspective of HR is often not adopted because it involves making a longer-term commitment to employees. Because employees can "walk" and because American organizations are so infused with short-term measures of performance, investments in human assets, which tend to be longer-term investments, are often ignored. Organizations performing well financially may feel no need to change their investment strategies. Those not doing well usually need a quick fix to turn things around and therefore ignore longer-term investments in people.

However, while investments in HR are longer term, once an organization gains a competitive advantage through its employees, the outcomes associated with the strategy are likely to be enduring and difficult to duplicate by competitors as such programs and values become more firmly entrenched in the organization's culture. The commitment that an organization makes to its employees through its investments in then is often rewarded with the return of employees making a longer-term commitment to the organization. Although investments in human assets may be risky and the return may take a long time to materialize, investment in people continues to be the main source of sustainable competitive advantage for organizations.

Critical Thinking

1. Why do senior managers often fail to realize the value of human assets vis-à-vis other assets?
2. Why do line managers often fail to realize the value of human assets vis-à-vis other assets?
3. Why and how might a line or an operating manager value specific metrics related to the unit's employees?
4. What can HR do to make senior and line managers take more of an investment approach to human assets?
5. Why is a competitive advantage based on a heavy investment in human assets more sustainable than investments in other types of assets?
6. Why can some organizations that fail to invest heavily in human assets still be financially successful? Why can some organizations that do invest heavily in human assets still be financially unsuccessful?
7. What challenges exist relative to the valuation of human assets and measuring human capital?

Reading 1.1

8. List all the various expenses and costs generally associated with employing workers. For each of these costs, devise strategies to leverage this expenditure into some kind of return on investment. How might you attempt to persuade senior management to adopt these strategies for investing in human capital?

Reading 1.2

9. Investigate at least two pieces of HR-related research that have recently been published in academic journals. If the authors have not already done so, determine the specific implications of this research for human resource practice and then determine how these implications might be best implemented.

Reading 1.3

10. Consider your current or most recent employer. Does the organization employ any human capital metrics or key performance indicators? If so, which ones, how are they used, and are they appropriate given the organization's strategy? If not, suggest some appropriate human capital metrics or key performance indicators given the organization's strategy.

Exercises

1. Obtain the annual report for a *Fortune 500* company of your choice. Review the material presented and the language used in the text. Write a one-page memo that assesses how investment-oriented the organization appears to be toward its human assets.
2. Arrange yourselves in small groups of four or five students and compare and contrast the similarities and differences among the organizations you investigated. Can you isolate any factors that appear to influence how an organization perceives the value of its employees?
3. How might different human resource metrics be best employed in 1) a nonprofit organization; 2) a professional sports organization; 3) a healthcare facility; 4) a small technology-based startup; and 5) a large Fortune 500 company?

Chapter References

1. Quinn, J. B., Doorley, T. L. and Paquette, P. C. "Beyond Products: Services-Based Strategy," *Harvard Business Review*, 90, (2), pp. 59–67.
2. Lawler, E. III. *The Ultimate Advantage: Creating the High Involvement Organization*, San Francisco: Jossey-Bass, 1992, p. 21.
3. Huselid, M. A. "The Impact of Human Resource Management Practices on Turnover, Productivity, Corporate Financial Performance," *Academy of Management Journal*, 38, (3), pp. 635–672.
4. Bates, S. "Study Links HR Practices with the Bottom Line," *HR Magazine*, December 2001, 46, (12), p. 14.
5. Gachman, I. and Luss, R. "Building the Business Case for HR in Today's Climate," *Strategic HR Review*, 1, (4), pp. 26–29.
6. Becker, B. E., Huselid, M.A. and Ulrich, D. *The HR Scorecard: Linking People, Strategy and Performance*. Boston: Harvard Business School Press, 2001.
7. Dyer, L. and Reeves, T. "HR Strategies and Firm Performance: What Do We Know and Where Do We Need to Go?" *International Journal of Human Resource Management*, 6, (3), pp. 656–670.
8. Bates, S. "Executives Judge HR Based on Poor Metrics, Study Finds," *HR Magazine*, September 2003, 48, (9), p. 12.
9. Ibid.
10. Bates, S. "The Metrics Maze," *HR Magazine*, December 2003, pp. 51–60.
11. Mercer, M. *Turning Your Human Resources Department into a Profit Center*. New York: AMACOM, 1989.
12. Weatherly, L. A. "Human Capital—The Elusive Assets," Society for Human Resource Management, Research Quarterly, 2003.
13. General Electric Annual Report (2005).
14. Krell, E. "Notable By Its Absence," *HR Magazine*, December, 2006, pp. 51–56.
15. Schneider, C. "The New Human-Capital Metrics," *CFO Magazine*, February 15, 2006. Available at http://www.cro.com/printable/article.cfm/5491043
16. Greer, C. R. Strategy and Human Resources: A General Manager's Perspective, Englewood Cliffs, NJ: Prentice-Hall, 1995.
17. Becker, B. E. and Huselid, M. A. "High Performance Work Systems and Firm Performance: A Synthesis of Research and Managerial Implications," *Research in Personnel and Human Resource Management*, 16, 1998, pp. 53–101.

READING 1.1

The Hidden Leverage of Human Capital

Jeffrey A. Oxman

A down economy is not the time to "slash-and-burn," but rather to ensure growth potential during the ensuing rebound. This requires a focus on strengthening key relationships, capitalizing on underutilized staff, clarifying strategic roles and forging stronger links between compensation and results.

More than 20,000 times last year in the United States, according to the Bureau of Labor Statistics, midsize and large companies responded to adversity by slashing on average about 100 staff members at a time. Considering all the news coverage about the economic downturn and the poor job market, that might, at first glance, seem like a dog-bites-man story. But that is a lot of jobs. Did circumstances always merit the drastic actions? If so, were the actions taken deliberately and carefully, with all appropriate respect toward the people involved? What sorts of provisions were made to ensure that key talent was protected? These questions are important because they go to the heart of how companies avoid lasting damage in the marketplace and build long-term value.

Trying to get a handle on the answers from publicly available data is problematic, as even a broad-based research effort would be brought to a halt at the gates of internal company performance information and organizational dynamics. But it is a safe assumption that many of these 20,000 organizations did destroy value somewhere along the way by cutting capacity that they soon had to replace, by making poor choices as to who should go and who should stay, by being careless in communicating the rationale for change and protecting the motivation levels of surviving employees, and by missing the opportunity to rethink their business model to optimize their positioning for the recovery ahead.

Organizations such as Wal-Mart Stores, Cisco, Charles Schwab and even American Airlines have recently tried to rehire laid-off employees.[1] But in so doing, the churn they generate often serves to demoralize employees and create an environmental uncertainly that compromises staff engagement, loyalty, customer service—and ultimately, company performance.

The broader issues here go well beyond layoffs. Is there a right way to manage a company through a time of challenge or tepid economic growth? What general guidelines can be discerned from the lessons of the past? And what sorts of decisions can managers make today to improve the odds that their companies will emerge as the winners of tomorrow?

Slash and Burn: Re-Engineering and Core Competencies

It used to be an article of faith that re-engineering initiatives, analytically evaluated and quickly implemented into an organization's operations, could serve as a magic bullet by helping companies realize previously unimagined efficiencies. In concert with operational streamlining, the conventional wisdom of a decade ago also advocated a devolutionary focus, whereby organizations, while earmarking core competencies for attention, at the same time took drastic steps to move outside the company those areas that didn't fall within the core.

Perhaps the exemplar of the era was the former head of Scott Paper Co., "Chainsaw" Al Dunlap. Starting in May 1994, in an effort to rebuild shareholder value, he let go more than 11,000 employees and shrank the company by selling off and outsourcing various business units and functions. Wall Street loved it for a while, as market value tripled, but ultimately it became clear that the way the restructuring had been handled rendered it difficult for the company to deliver sustained performance, and Scott Paper had to realistically evaluate its ability to survive as an independent entity. In 1995, it reached a conclusion—the company was sold to Kimberly-Clark, a longtime rival.

In this vein, while many "ruthless" organizations achieved notable efficiencies, the best re-engineering success stories—as measured by long-term company sustainability achieved—came to be viewed as those that not only emphasized a tough focus on business drivers, but also combined it with a more human touch. Jack Welch at General Electric Co., for example, while restructuring and selling underperforming units, made significant investments in management development and training, and communicated to employees the logical and rallying message that GE should be number one or two in any business in which it competed.

Similarly, Archie Norman at Asda, the U.K. supermarket group, averted bankruptcy by both flattening the organizational structure and articulating a clear long-term strategy based on everyday low pricing. In so doing, he embarked on creating an atmosphere of trust and openness.

It seemed paradoxical, but the qualities of what came to be viewed as superlative corporate leadership were best captured in a headline in the *Financial Times* that read "Wanted: Ruthless Axeman with People Skills."[2]

This context is useful as the starting point for articulating a broad-based model for management success in the current economic environment.

A Broader Leadership Model for the New Millennium

There is a sailing proverb that says, "Races are won at night and in a light wind." A quiet time, after all, is the one in which the boat can be best prepared. It's appealing to think of this quasirecessionary time as the light night wind, with people training to work better as an effective team, loads balanced, equipment optimized, communications tested to be crystal clear.

Four broad areas of preparation are critical: strengthening key relationships across customers, employees and shareholders; leveraging downtime by capitalizing on underutilized staff for innovation initiatives; refocusing staff on what's important at the company by prioritizing strategic roles and clarifying individual goals; and building return on compensation by forging stronger links between the pay people get and the results they achieve.

Strengthening Key Relationships

While strategic models of company stakeholders almost universally focus on customers, employees and shareholders, there is widespread disagreement as to where priorities lie within this list. The strongest strategies focus on all three groups of stakeholders and follow through with this approach in tough times as well as easier ones.[3]

Strengthening key relationships starts with keeping a finger on the pulse of frequently changing customer and employee needs. A good way to embark upon pulse taking is executing well-designed, customized surveys to better track the unique requirements of different customer and employee groups and how those requirements change over time. The real value of customized surveys is to help focus company resources on those customers and employees for whom company efforts yield the highest returns—whether they be key customer groups or high-performing employees whose perspectives are often obscured in more traditional, broad-based, generic questionnaires.

That said, in a challenging environment, follow-through on relationships means doing more than just surveying. Since customers and employees believe that companies reveal their true colors at a time of crisis, poor survey follow-up, or indeed any perceived mistreatment, can alienate those stakeholders permanently. Thus, what comes to the fore in relationship building—more than the newfangled concept of management—is its trusty cousin, leadership.

Leaders from Winston Churchill to Rudolph Giuliani, John F. Kennedy to Warren Buffett have a lot to impart to businesspeople with regard to building effective relationships in a crisis environment. They stood up and were visible. They didn't anticipate failure yet stuck to the facts even when the facts were dire. And for the most part, they didn't overreach. Winston Churchill's brutal honesty was combined with optimism—"blood, toil, tears and sweat" but always an upbeat feeling that England would survive "however long and hard the road may be." Former New York City Mayor Giuliani's comment that the World Trade Center death toll would be "more than we can bear" was interspersed at the same time with his steady campaign to rally a city's spirits. Mobilizing a fatigued group through a difficult time, after all, has its own historical best practices.[4]

Finally, together with leadership (perhaps, indeed, component parts of it), communication and engagement are critical to strengthening relationships. Communications across, and proactive engagement of, customers, employees and shareholders in helping to solve specific business problems go a long way toward smoothing the implementation of effective solutions.

Leveraging Downtime

In challenging times, managers are often faced with employees who suddenly find themselves with too much free time on their hands. In the old days, when this situation persisted, some of these folks would have had to be let go, due to onerous fixed-cost structures. But today's managers have a tool their predecessors lacked: variable pay.

In the last decade, many companies have been able to significantly leverage their costs by migrating to a variable-pay model, in which compensation kicks in only if company, division and/or team results dictate. The result has been increased flexibility, in a tough business environment, to keep what might in the past have been at-risk employees on staff, albeit sometimes less busy, at reduced pay levels.

Across the nation, despite the large layoff figures cited at the outset, this phenomenon has had a dramatic ameliorative effect on unemployment rates. One estimate puts the benefit at a full percentage point of employment nationally; that is, what was a 5.5% unemployment rate in fall 2001 would have been 6.5% had it not been for the new prevalence of variable pay nationwide.[5]

What does this mean for successful management in a business downturn? For starters, managers should be attuned to the risk that the good news about being able to preserve years of individual experience within company knowledge banks could be offset by unproductive employee downtime.

Almost every company, especially if it is coming out of particularly heady times, has a few areas of relative neglect to which it can now profitably allocate that downtime. These areas—most often infrastructure, marketing and operations—are ones for which experienced staff, in particular, are well positioned to offer unique insights to help the company build for the future.

Organizations should be asking some broad, basic questions and involving not just senior management, but cross-functional staff groups at all levels. Are internal company tools and procedures adding sufficient value? Have we done enough to ensure our customers fully understand how our products and services can help them be more successful? Are we optimally aligned, organizationally, to serve the customers, market segments and geographies we serve today? Strategic initiatives undertaken to tackle questions like these serve a double purpose: In leveraging the wisdom of key staff, they prepare the company optimally for the future and harvest most people's enthusiasm to play more diverse organizational roles and develop their own capabilities.

Refocusing Staff on What's Important

The question "What's most important in an organization?" can elicit surprising responses. BEA Systems, which in 2001 reached $1 billion in sales faster than any software company had previously (surpassing even Microsoft's 1980s pace), has a new CEO, Alfred Chuang, who has what some might call a ruthless perspective. "We focus on two things," he says. "Building product and selling product. I know that a lot of other functions are involved in that process, including marketing, servicing and infrastructure. But if you are not within the line of sight between the inception of the idea and delivering it to customers and making them happy, your job is not that important."[6]

BEA has a track record of success it's hard to quibble with, but it is critical for companies to go through an examination of not just employee roles, but also their people. Just as there are more strategic roles (for example, R&D in pharmaceuticals) and less strategic roles (tellers in retail banking), so there are also key people in organizations whose impact on performance can be significant, regardless of role.

How do companies determine who these people are and focus them adroitly? The key is to transform performance management from perfunctory end-of-year paper pushing to a disciplined, strategic and value-added process.

Elevating performance management starts with clearly defining and differentiating between core competencies and results—and balancing them appropriately. Some law firms, for example, rate partners exclusively on project sales and reward them for those sales through base and incentive pay. More-sophisticated law firms blend other considerations into the evaluations of a partner's results delivered—for example, sales in conjunction with profitability. But best-practice firms, when looking at a partner's longer-term contribution to the firm's sustained success, consider the extent to which he or she demonstrates competencies such as attracting and retaining an enthusiastic team of junior people, broadening firm offerings into new clients and practice areas, and enhancing client satisfaction.

The "A" partners in those firms are the ones who deliver high performance on both long-term competencies (people development, new practice areas, client satisfaction) and current results (sales, profits). This competencies/scorecard framework—viewed pictorially with competency results on one axis and scorecard results on another, with people graphically positioned at their approximate performance levels—provides a roadmap for people development that is much better supported by the long-term economics of the business.

For unfortunate cases in which job cuts are absolutely required, this methodical framework for identifying critical resources stands an organization in good stead. It makes possible a matrixed analysis of strategic jobs against priority people, which in turn yields a valuable blueprint as to what cuts should be targeted.[7]

Building Return on Compensation

If what is sometimes called "talent management," as outlined earlier, is done correctly, the foundation for wise compensation decision making is already laid. Base-pay progression can be readily and sensibly linked to competency achievement, and incentive pay to annual (or semiannual or quarterly) results. To the extent that it is tied closely to drivers of business success, built upon commonly understood criteria, and applied consistently over time, compensation—frequently viewed by managers as a sunk cost—can instead be considered an investment with a quantifiable return.

Some years ago, my colleagues and I had a team working with a subsidiary of Kodak—a photofinisher called Qualex Inc. Qualex provided overnight wholesale photofinishing services predominantly to large stores (at which retail customers had dropped off their film for developing). Every evening, Qualex would receive drop shipments of large quantities of film from the stores and (using predominantly low-wage employees) splice the film together, run rolls of negatives through the photo-development process, and by morning redistribute the pictures to the stores from which the film had come.

Across its approximately 50 locations, though, the company had a problem—significant turnover, averaging nearly 60% annually, with the added problem of spikes in turnover during the summer, just when its sales volume tended to be highest. (To make matters even worse, the company was losing the very people it could least afford to lose—the most technically proficient—as these were the people whose pay was least competitive with pay in comparable companies.) The visible business effects were shaky productivity and quality results, which, above and beyond the inherent costs, often had the secondary cost of forgone revenue because of the company's inability to meet productivity levels contractually specified in service-level agreements.

Implementation of customized rewards helped solve the problem. Rather than bring Qualex's compensation to market levels with traditional base-salary increases (historically, this had been done for years, with little operational effect), the company designed and offered to its employees generous summertime pay premiums. These premiums constituted significant rewards for employees' productivity during the period and their perseverance in the role all the way through to summer's end. Later on, new, annual group incentives tied to specific productivity and quality goals were layered into employees' pay. Because all of the new variable-pay components represented meaningful amounts, they garnered significant employee attention and had quite a noticeable effect on reducing turnover and improving operational performance.

While the costs of the new programs were significantly higher than previously awarded salary increases (about $20 million vs. $8 million), regression models linking pay to turnover to results predicted that the higher investment would demonstrate a $20 million operational return through improved productivity and quality. The historical $8 million annual salary increases, on the other hand, would have had no discernible return, because that practice would have perpetuated the old turnover, productivity and quality problems. Qualex got its expected return and wound up with more satisfied and motivated employees, working in a more positive environment and doing a better job for customers at a net lower cost.[8]

Admittedly, this type of solution is not always as straightforward to implement in environments where metrics like productivity and quality are less readily available or less appropriately measured at the individual and team level than they might be in a manufacturing or processing setting—environments such as IT architecture. However, it is safe to say that improved alignment between the value drivers in the business and the manner in which employees are rewarded is almost always possible. And given the dominance of pay as an expense-line item, such action, if implemented well, usually has a substantial, quantifiable, bottom-line effect.

Broad compensation overhauls like the one at Qualex are not always necessary to enhance return on an organization's compensation dollar. Since variable-pay plans do already exist in many companies, they often can be amended to ensure that plan payouts awarded to employees will generate return. One way to accomplish this is to ensure that plans are driven by goals over which, as closely as possible, employees have some line of sight (for example, cost management, rather than company profitability).

There are several other considerations in tailoring variable-pay programs for higher return. Shortening plan-performance periods can be helpful, especially for cases in which substandard performance occurred some time ago but within the current performance period—demotivating employees to perform now because no matter what they accomplish, they still won't receive incentives. In addition, payments for achieving stretch goals may be enhanced, and supplementing semiannual or annual payouts with spot awards can more swiftly recognize employees for special contributions.

The Real Value of Human Assets

It's become a cliché to say that the service economy revolves around human assets, but even in manufacturing and production environments, wherein traditional machinery and equipment assets loom large, the caliber of people makes an enormous difference to the inherent value of an enterprise.

It's impossible to overstate the contribution of people—especially when they are aligned with corporate goals, fully engaged in making the enterprise effective, and well suited for their individual roles. Consider that in the past 20 years the market-value-to-book-value ratio of the S&P 500 has gone from around 1:1 to around 6:1. That increase has caused many academics to begin to develop new models of company value that include human-capital components to better account for a corporation's true worth.

In good times and bad, it is critical that companies play their cards right with all their key stakeholders—including employees. The costs of failing to do so are high. A 1999 survey of more than 1,000 companies in Britain showed results that for many observers at least partially explained that country's slight lag in the marketplace. The responses of about 1,000 human-resource directors in Britain indicated that more than 60% of staff are so poorly engaged that most employers would not rehire them. And nearly a quarter of survey respondents didn't believe that their work force gave their companies a competitive edge.[9]

Whether this is a result of hiring poorly or of a failure to develop good people into appropriate roles, managers in this situation have to overcome significant obstacles to success. And managers not in that situation need to make sure they avoid it.

After all, in the United States at least, there have been nine recessions since World War II and nine recoveries: a perfect record. It's foolish not to think of this period as an opportunity to lay the groundwork for an exciting future.

Source: MIT Sloan Management Review, 43, (4), 2002, 79–88. Reprinted with permission.

ENDNOTES

1. S. Armour, "Sorry We Cut Your Job—Want It Back?" *USA Today*, Wednesday, Aug. 29, 2001, sec. B, p. 1; and I. P. Cordle, "American Back to Business in Miami," *Miami Herald*, Sunday, Feb. 3, 2002, sec. E, p. 1.
2. S. London, "Wanted: Ruthless Axeman With People Skills," *Financial Times*, Nov. 14, 2001, p. 17.
3. S. Maranjian, "Employees vs. Customers vs. Shareholders," Fool.com, Jan. 31, 2002, www.fool.com/news/foth/2002/foth020131.htm.
4. J. Useem, "What it Takes," *Fortune*, Nov. 12, 2001, 128–132.
5. D. Eisenberg, "Paying To Keep Your Job," *Time*, Oct. 15, 2001, 80–83.
6. G. Anders, "BEA Systems: A Study in Sustainability," Fast Company, March 2002: www.fastcompany.com/build/build_feature/churchill3.html.
7. "The Road to Recovery," white paper, Sibson Consulting Group, New York, November 2001, p. 2.
8. P. V. LeBlanc, J. P. Gonzalez and J. A. Oxman, "Maximize Your Compensation ROI With High-Yield Investments in Human Capital," *Compensation & Benefits Review* 30 (March–April 1998): 59–68.
9. "We Like 40% of Our Staff," Automotive Management, Aug. 13, 1999: www.mtselect.co.uk/articles/40staff.html.

READING 1.2

Seven Common Misconceptions about Human Resource Practices: Research Findings versus Practitioner Beliefs

Sara L. Rynes, Kenneth G. Brown, and Amy E. Colbert

Managers as a class are anything but stupid. But there is evidence that the job-specific knowledge bases of many, and perhaps most, executives are quite substandard. In turn, low knowledge bases may lead executives to make decisions that are less than optimal—and sometimes not even satisfactory.[1]

Considerable research demonstrates that most organizations do not employ state-of-the-art human resource (HR) practices.[2] One reason for the gap between research and practice is that very few practicing HR managers read the research literature.[3] Two major explanations have been offered as to why this is the case. The first is that HR research has become excessively technical, thus discouraging practitioners from attempting to keep up with the latest research findings.[4] This view assumes that practicing HR managers regard research findings as potentially useful, but inaccessible. The less sanguine view is that HR practitioners do not read the research because they see it as irrelevant or impractical for their needs.[5]

Whatever HR managers may feel about academic research findings, evidence is accumulating that certain HR practices are consistently related to higher individual performance, organizational productivity, and firm financial performance.[6] At least two research trends over the past two decades have increased our ability to detect relationships between HR practices and performance. The first is the development of statistical techniques which allow aggregation of many studies in order to reach more reliable conclusions about both average effects and contextual moderators.[7] The second is the emergence of the Strategic HR literature, which has stimulated much more research into the relationships between HR practices and performance at the level of the *firm* rather than the individual.[8] This last step means that we no longer have to wonder about the degree to which relationships found at the individual level are mirrored at higher levels of aggregation.

As one example of such firm-level research, a study by Welbourne and Andrews found that new companies that placed a high value on HR (as assessed by content of their prospectuses) and that included high levels of organizationally based pay-for-performance had a five-year survival rate of 92 percent as compared with 34 percent for companies that were low on both dimensions.[9] As another example, Huselid found that an increase of one standard deviation in scores on a "high-performance HR practices" scale (which included such practices as employee attitude surveying, paying for performance, formal communication programs, and use of employment tests) was associated with a 23 percent increase in accounting profits and an 8 percent increase in economic value.[10]

With research showing bottom-line effects of certain HR practices, the lack of research knowledge can clearly be costly to HR managers and their organizations. Indeed, although a direct causal link cannot be drawn, Terpstra and Rozell found that companies whose HR professionals read the academic research literature have higher financial performance than those that do not.[11]

Although the results of HR research are clearly relevant to practicing managers, not so clear is the extent to which HR managers' current beliefs are consistent (or inconsistent) with the latest findings. The areas of greatest inconsistency should dominate efforts to inform managers about HR research. We therefore conducted a survey to determine which particular areas of research findings most need more effective dissemination to practicing HR managers.

Research Findings versus Managerial Beliefs: Assessing the Gap

HR professionals are most directly responsible for acquiring and disseminating knowledge about best practices in "people management" throughout the organization. Although much of the day-to-day implementation of HR practices resides with line managers, it is the HR function's role to help executives develop a human resource strategy that is at once consistent with both the organizational business strategy and with best practices revealed by empirical research.[12]

To examine the extent to which the beliefs of HR professionals are consistent with established research findings, a 35-item questionnaire was constructed.[13] Content of the questionnaire was based on the major categories contained in the Human Resource Certification Institute's

(HRCI) Professional in Human Resources (PHR) certification exam. However, in contrast to the certification exam (which focuses heavily on definitional, legal, and procedural issues), the present survey focused on *research* findings regarding the effectiveness of particular HR practices. Items were constructed that were based on up-to-date research results. Respondents indicated whether they agreed, disagreed, or were uncertain about each item, allowing us to determine where practitioner beliefs diverge most sharply from research findings.

The survey was sent to a stratified random sample of 5,000 Society for Human Resource Management members whose titles were at the manager level and above. This sampling strategy was designed to ensure that respondents would be among the most seasoned HR professionals, with significant responsibilities for HR policy and implementation. Responses were received from 959 recipients before the cutoff date, for a response rate of 19 percent. Nearly half the respondents (49 percent) were HR managers, while 26 percent were directors, 18 percent vice presidents, and 7 percent from other functional areas. The average respondent had 14 years of experience in HR. These high levels of experience and job responsibility suggested that our respondents should be relatively well-informed members of the HR profession.

The Seven Most Common Misconceptions

For the remainder of this article, we discuss the seven HR research findings that were least believed by our responding group of HR managers. The first four of these findings pertain primarily to issues of selection (i.e., employee traits that are most strongly associated with performance and effective means of assessing them). The next two pertain to issues of effective performance management—performance appraisal and performance improvement. The final item concerns problems with relying on survey data to determine the importance of pay (and other potential motivators) in people's behavior.

1. *On average, conscientiousness is a better predictor of employee performance than intelligence.*

Although 72 percent of participants agreed with this statement, a substantial amount of research suggests that it is incorrect. A recent meta-analytic summary of nineteen different selection methods reported a predictive validity coefficient of .51 for tests of intelligence (or general mental ability, GMA), as compared with an average validity of .31 for measures of conscientiousness.[14] This means that on average, GMA explains roughly 25 percent of the variance in employee performance, while conscientiousness explains only 9 percent. The authors conclude.

> *Research evidence for the validity of GMA measures for predicting job performance is stronger than that for any other method . . . literally thousands of studies have been conducted over the last nine decades. . . . Because of its special status, GMA can be considered the primary personnel measure for hiring decisions.*[15]

Not only is GMA the single best overall predictor of likely performance, but the positive economic effects of assessing it in selection can be very substantial. For example, based on estimates derived from comparing the productivity of the most- and least-productive workers, Jack Hunter estimated that the use of rank-ordered ability scores in the federal government would increase productivity by more than $13 billion relative to simply using a minimum cutoff score at the 20th percentile. Similarly, he estimated an increase of $12 million per year for a much smaller unit, the Philadelphia police department.[16]

Given the strength of these findings, why do so many managers—especially ones trained in HR management—assume the opposite? Although many explanations are possible, we think two are particularly likely.

First, as a culture, Americans have long held negative stereotypes about highly intelligent people.[17] One such stereotype is that intelligent people are brilliant but impractical ("ivory tower intellectuals"), while a second views them as capable, but socially inept ("nerd, geek, egghead"). A third stereotype likens intelligent people to the hare in Aesop's fable—erratic performers who are brilliant on occasion but who generally underperform the "slow and steady" in the long run.[18] A final stereotype portrays intelligent people as rude, arrogant, and difficult to manage. For example, in his recent book *Working with Emotional Intelligence.* Daniel Goleman repeatedly gives examples of intelligent people with extremely negative social traits, such as being "unbelievably arrogant" or "brutally acerbic, socially awkward, with no social graces or even a social life."[19]

The resilience of such stereotypes suggests that many people hold implicit theories of intelligence that associate high levels of GMA with a variety of unattractive personal characteristics. Conscientiousness, on the other hand, is viewed positively by most people, and the stereotype of a conscientious person is nearly always good. In reality, however, intelligence is virtually uncorrelated with such personality traits as conscientiousness, agreeableness, and emotional stability.[20] Thus, for every highly intelligent introvert there is a highly intelligent extrovert; for every brilliant neurotic, there is someone who is both highly intelligent and emotionally stable.

A second (but probably less likely) reason that managers may underestimate the importance of intelligence to job performance is that people may not believe that employee intelligence varies much *within* particular job categories. For example, Goleman has argued that "in professional and technical fields the threshold for entry is typically an IQ of 110 to 120. . . . Since everyone [in these fields] is in the top 10 percent or so of intelligence, IQ itself offers relatively little competitive advantage."[21] However, in a very-large-sample study designed explicitly to test this narrow-variability-in-IQ hypothesis, the average variability of intelligence within each of 80 applicant pools for specific job categories was found to be only 10 percent less than the full variability exemplified in national norms.[22] Thus, very substantial differences in intelligence still exist among applicants for any given type of job.

There are several implications of these findings (see Table 1). The first is that because both GMA and conscientiousness are important predictors of performance in virtually all jobs, both characteristics should be assessed as thoroughly as possible in the employee selection process.[23] A second implication is that the higher the level of job complexity, the more selection should be weighted toward GMA (see Endnote 14). How might this be done?

Research suggests that the best way to assess GMA is through paper-and-pencil testing.[24] Several good paper-and-pencil tests are available for such purposes, such as the Wonderlic Personnel Test, which only takes 12 minutes to administer and which correlates very highly with more intensive methods of assessing intelligence.[25] Another point in its favor is that its items are not exotic or highly abstract but rather look like typical items from a junior high or high school exam. In addition, considerable research suggests that applicants typically view ability tests as valid means of assessment and therefore are not likely to be put off by companies that require them.[26]

Although direct assessment of ability thus has two important features to recommend it (high validity and low cost), it also has some liabilities. For example, cognitive ability tests do produce adverse impact against certain groups and, rightly or wrongly, receive a considerable amount of negative press.[27] Thus, companies that are trying to balance a number of outcomes (e.g., applicant reactions, workforce diversity) in addition to achieving validity may choose to assess GMA in less direct ways, but in ways that also have substantial validity.

For example, research has shown that structured interviews, work samples, and simulations that assess job knowledge are likely to be moderately correlated with GMA, as well as being good predictors of job performance.[28] Assessing job knowledge in these ways has the additional advantages of having very high face validity to applicants and lower levels of adverse impact against minorities, while still retaining considerable validity. The most important implication, however, is that deliberate attempts to assess and use GMA as a basis for hiring should be made for *all* jobs. Failure to do so leaves money on the table.

2. *Companies that screen job applicants for values have higher performance than those that screen for intelligence.*

A large majority of our responding SHRM managers agreed with this statement (57 percent), although available research evidence does not support it. At the outset, it should be said that there is far less research on the effects of selecting for values than there is about selecting for GMA or personality. Still, much evidence suggests that selecting for GMA leads to higher performance, and very little evidence suggests the same for values.

The available research comes in two forms. One stream focuses on values *congruence* or values *fit*. The importance of employee values has frequently been conceptualized in terms of compatibility between organizational and applicant values, rather than as a matter of positive versus negative values in an absolute sense.[29] For example, some companies focus very strongly on assessing and rewarding individual performance (e.g., Lincoln Electric or General Electric), while others motivate and reward almost entirely on the basis of group efforts and results (e.g., Southwest Airlines, Nucor). Thus, the logic goes that individualistic values would be an asset at Lincoln or GE, but a serious detriment at Southwest or Nucor.

Research has generally shown that values fit has positive consequences for employee attitudes and length of service.[30] However, there is much less evidence of a positive relationship between values fit and *performance*.[31] For example, one study found that workers who had congruent values received higher supervisory ratings when work tasks were interdependent, but *lower* evaluations when work was not interdependent.[32] Another found that workers who believed their values were congruent with the organization's displayed more citizenship behaviors but not higher task performance.[33] Thus, in distinct contrast to the research on intelligence, the limited evidence on values congruence suggests rather small and inconsistent effects on performance.

Although researchers have primarily studied the relationship between values and performance in terms of values *fit*, a second stream of research focuses on the effect of values on performance *indirectly* through research on employee personality. For example, research suggests that when managers and recruiters talk about the kinds of values they are looking for, they most often mention such characteristics as "work ethic, teamwork values, desire for improvement, liking pressure, and liking variety and change."[34] Although managers tend to describe these traits as *values*, many researchers have studied them as *personality* traits. Thus, for example, the values of "work ethic" and "desire for improvement" can be translated into the personality trait of conscientiousness, while the value of "liking variety and change" translates into openness to experience.

From this perspective, we have already seen that although some values (or personality traits) such as "work ethic" are assets to performance, they are not as important as intelligence. Thus, from either perspective (values fit or values per se), the idea that values are more important predictors of performance than intelligence is not supported by the research evidence. We would suggest, however, that more research should be done to assess this question, both at the individual and the organizational level.

3. *Although there are "integrity tests" that try to predict whether someone will steal, be absent, or otherwise take advantage of an employer, they don't work well in practice because so many people lie on them.*[35]

Only 32 percent of our responding HR managers realized that this was an inaccurate statement. Because the statement seems highly plausible on its face, analysis of the evidence concerning integrity tests requires breaking the statement into pieces.

Table 1 Common Misconceptions, Research Findings, and Implications

Research-Inconsistent Findings	What Research Shows	Ways to Implement Research
1. Conscientiousness is a better predictor of employee performance than intelligence.	The average validity coefficient is .51 for intelligence, .31 for conscientiousness. They are *both* important predictors of performance, but intelligence is relatively more important. At the very lowest levels of job complexity (unskilled work), their importance is about equal. However, as jobs increase in complexity, intelligence becomes more and more important.	• Select new employees on both intelligence (general ability, GMA) and conscientiousness. Well-validated measures of both constructs are available. • In addition to pencil-and-paper tests, GMA can also be assessed through job-knowledge tests, work samples, or simulation interview questions.
2. Companies that screen job applicants for values have higher performance than those that screen for intelligence.	Intelligence is the best single predictor of performance. Although values fit does predict employee satisfaction and retention, little evidence exists of a direct link to performance. Even if a link is shown some time in the future, it is unlikely to approach the magnitude of the effect size for intelligence.	• Even if you are interested in people's values, assess GMA and conscientiousness first. • Define what values are important to you. Then, assess them through procedures such as behavioral description interviews or accomplishment records to see whether people actually behave in ways consistent with the desired values. • Consider which personality constructs are likely to reflect the values you want; then measure personality using well-validated instruments.
3. Integrity tests don't work well in practice because so many people lie on them.	People try to make themselves look a little more ethical than they actually are. This does not seem to affect the usefulness of these tests as predictors of performance.	• Integrity tests can be used in combination with ability tests to yield very high overall predictability of job performance.
4. Integrity tests have adverse impact on racial minorities.	Racial and ethnic differences on integrity test scores are trivial. Hispanics have been found to score .14 standard deviations higher than whites; Asians, .04 standard deviations higher; Native Americans, .08 standard deviations higher, and African-Americans, .04 lower.	• Combining integrity tests with tests of GMA may reduce the amount of adverse impact in overall selection systems because minorities and whites have nearly equivalent scores on integrity tests.
5. Encouraging employees to participate in decision making is more effective for improving organizational performance than setting performance goals.	On average, performance improves 16 percent when goal-setting is implemented. The average effect from employee participation is < 1 percent. Participation can produce both positive and negative outcomes. Employees must have a clear picture of *what* they are participating *for*—that is, what they are trying to achieve—in order for participation to be successful.	• Develop goals that are inspiring, challenging, and that stretch people's capabilities. • Once goals are clearly communicated and accepted enlist broad participation, and do not shut down ideas. • Support participation and goal attainment through the reward system, such as with gain sharing or other group incentive programs.
6. Most errors in performance appraisal can be eliminated	Performance-appraisal errors are extremely difficult to eliminate. Training	• Training, practice, and feedback about how to avoid appraisal errors

by providing training that describes the kinds of errors managers tend to make and suggesting ways to avoid them.	to eliminate certain types of errors often introduces other types of errors and sometimes even decreases accuracy. The most common appraisal error is leniency, and managers often realize they are committing it. Mere training is insufficient to eliminate these kinds of errors; more systemic action is required such as intensive monitoring or forced rankings.	are necessary, but insufficient, for eliminating errors. • Eliminating errors may require alternative approaches to evaluation, such as forced distribution (e.g., General Electric). • Top managers should serve as strong role models for the performance evaluation process and attach managerial consequences to the quality of performance reviews.
7. If employees are asked how important pay is to them, they are likely to overestimate its true importance.	People tend to *understate* the importance of pay to their decisions due to social desirability considerations and lack of self-insight. Research that examines people's *behaviors* in response to pay (rather than their attitudes) tends to show very strong motivational effects.	• Recognize that employee attitude surveys are subject to a variety of cognitive biases such as social desirability and lack of self-insight. • Wherever possible, study employee *behaviors* in addition to attitudes; the two will not always converge.

First, research shows that applicants *can* distort their answers on integrity tests (and other selection devices such as resumes) in order to make themselves look better to employers.[36] In addition, many applicants probably *do* distort their answers to some extent, particularly when they believe the scores will be used for selection or promotion purposes.[37] Interestingly, however, the fact that applicants can (and probably do) distort their responses to integrity tests does *not* make them ineffective as predictors of performance.[38] In fact, the average corrected validity coefficient for integrity tests is a very respectable .41, with counterproductive behaviors such as theft, absenteeism, or violence being somewhat better predicted (.47) than overall job performance (.34).[39]

These findings raise the interesting question of why integrity tests maintain their validity, despite the potential for deliberate response distortion. One possibility is that most people distort their responses to roughly the same degree, so that the "faking factor" becomes more or less a constant (and thus a non-differentiator) in the prediction equation. Another possibility is that the extent of response distortion may be correlated with valid predictors such as conscientiousness or emotional stability.[40] Whatever the reason, to the extent that distortion is occurring, it does not appear to destroy the usefulness of integrity tests as selection devices.

It should also be noted that integrity tests work very well in conjunction with tests of GMA. This is because cognitive ability is essentially uncorrelated with the underlying dimensions tapped by integrity tests, particularly conscientiousness. Because highly intelligent people are no more (or no less) likely to be honest or conscientious than those with lesser ability, using integrity tests along with ability tests yields completely unique incremental information. In fact, the highest overall validity for any combination of two selection methods appears to be obtained by using integrity tests in conjunction with tests of GMA.[41]

4. *One problem with using integrity tests is that they have high degrees of adverse impact on racial minorities.*

Despite their validity, managers may nevertheless be nervous about using integrity tests for a variety of other reasons. One possibility is that integrity tests, while valid, may eliminate larger proportions of minority than majority candidates. Although nearly 70 percent of our respondents thought that this might be true, it is not the case.

Recent large-sample research evidence reveals that differences in integrity test scores across racial and ethnic groups are trivial (although gender differences are not).[42] Thus, another potential advantage of using integrity tests in conjunction with cognitive ability tests is that, unlike ability tests, integrity tests are unlikely to produce adverse impact. Furthermore, although evidence suggests that integrity tests are not among the best-liked selection devices, they generally are seen by applicants as an appropriate means of differentiating among candidates.[43]

5. *On average, encouraging employees to participate in decision making is more effective for improving organizational performance than setting performance goals.*

Although considerable research has shown this statement to be false, only 17 percent of respondents clearly disagreed with it. Evidence regarding this issue comes from a number of sources.

First, meta-analysis has been used by Ed Locke and his colleagues to examine the comparative effectiveness of various performance-improvement interventions.[44] This research suggests that on average, performance improves by 16 percent following goal-setting interventions, as compared with less than 1 percent for employee participation. Moreover, the effects of goal-setting appear to be positive in virtually all cases, whereas increased participation actually leads to decreases in performance in a substantial minority of cases.

The weak results for participation seem puzzling, given the number of corporate success stories that seem to have employee participation at their core (e.g., Southwest Airlines, Rosenbluth Travel, or Springfield Remanufacturing). However, other research suggests that the success of participation programs may depend on the order in which performance interventions are introduced. Specifically, it appears that in order for participative management to succeed, employees must first know *what* they are attempting to achieve through participation. In other words, goal-setting or some other means of conveying performance expectations may have to precede employee participation in order for it to be effective. As Cusumano and Selby wrote after studying Microsoft for several years: "Although having creative people in a high-tech company is important, it is often more important to *direct* their creativity."[45] For this reason. Microsoft work assignments are characterized by strong emphasis on project deadlines, multiple milestones on the path to project completion, and frequent merging of different employees' pieces of code to see how well the project is moving toward completion.

Research by McKinsey and Company on high-performing work teams also suggests the value of challenging goals for increasing the effectiveness of participation.[46] In their study of factors that distinguish high-performing teams from mediocre ones, they were surprised to find that the typical emphasis on building "teamwork" and "teamwork values" was ineffective for producing peak levels of team performance. Rather, the true distinguishing factor was the existence of a challenging, meaningful task that inspired team members and stretched their capacities. Although the concept of teamwork is different from that of participation, the pre-eminent role of a challenging goal in focusing employee efforts appears to be common to both.

In summary, participative management strategies are unlikely to be effective unless employees are clear about performance goals and objectives. However, for most employees, the major source of information about what is expected and how they are performing is the annual performance review. This is unfortunate because previous research suggests that when performance appraisal is the major vehicle for communicating information about performance, confusion about goals and objectives appears to be more common than not.[47] Therefore, other performance management strategies that incorporate both objective targets and supra-individual goals (e.g., project milestones or group incentive systems) would appear to provide a better chance of producing coordinated, effective participation (see Table 1).

6. *Most errors in performance appraisals can be eliminated by providing training that describes the kinds of errors managers tend to make and suggesting ways to avoid them.*

Although 70 percent of our HR respondents agreed with the preceding sentence, research clearly shows it to be false. A long line of research shows that performance appraisal is one of the most problematic HR practices, as well as one of the most difficult to improve.[48] In particular, rater training of the type described above (simply describing errors and suggesting ways to eliminate them) has been found to be notoriously ineffective for improving appraisal accuracy.[49] For one thing, many managers do not believe that they, personally, make the errors described by the trainer.[50] In addition, research has shown that training to reduce certain kinds of errors can actually *increase* inaccuracy by introducing other types of errors.[51]

Rather, improvement of performance appraisal appears to require a fairly intensive set of activities. These include active participation in rating videotaped performers against performance specifications, providing written justifications of their ratings, (usually) making several errors in relation to "correct" appraisal ratings, having group discussions of ways to overcome the errors, and providing further practice sessions, spaced over time.[52] Even so, it should be emphasized that studies that have shown rating improvements as a result of these methods have assessed rater accuracy by using carefully constructed videotape scenarios, where the correct rating can be known and where raters are not personally involved with the "picture-people" they are rating. Thus, it is still unclear whether managers who are able to correctly evaluate videotaped performances by unknown actors actually transfer this learnings to subsequent ratings of their own employees.

When dealing with "real employees," it is generally believed that getting rid of appraisal errors—particularly leniency—requires very substantial monitoring of appraisals and clear statements by top management that leniency or other forms of inaccuracy are not acceptable.[53] For example, General Electric found that they were unable to eliminate excessive leniency from performance appraisals until they began to insist that managers rank employees on a bell curve and attached substantial penalties to managers for failure to do so. Although this system appears to be working well at GE, it should be noted that this strong ratings differentiation is accompanied by many other supportive actions, such as three thorough performance reviews of managers each year, very aggressive career planning, highly differentiated monetary rewards linked to appraisal distributions, and refusal to promote managers who will not make the distinctions. Although one can certainly debate whether you can truly have accurate appraisals when every unit is required to rate on the same bell curve (this recently became a major issue at the Ford Motor Company), one positive feature is that measurement studies have shown that it is in fact easier to make accurate *rankings* than accurate *ratings*.[54]

7. *Surveys that directly ask employees how important pay is to them are likely to overestimate pay's true importance in employees' actual decisions.*

Although 56 percent of the HR managers responding agreed with this statement, the fact is that people are more likely to *under*-report the importance of pay than to over-report it. Moreover, this tendency has been known for quite some time. As far back as 1966, researchers cautioned that self-reports of pay importance are likely to provide underestimates due to people's tendency to answer surveys in socially desirable ways.[55] That is, people are likely to understate the importance of pay due to norms that view money as a somewhat crass source of motivation.

Evidence that people under-report pay importance comes from two different types of studies. One type compares individuals' direct self-reports of pay importance with importance as inferred from their preferences for various job descriptions. By measuring each job in terms of its underlying characteristics (i.e., different levels of pay, promotion potential, work duties, job security, and the like) and then comparing jobs with subjects' overall assessments of job attractiveness, the importance of each underlying job characteristic to overall assessments can be inferred without asking direct questions about importance. In such studies, pay has generally been found to be a substantially more important factor when inferred from participants' overall evaluations of job attractiveness than from their direct reports of pay importance.[56]

A second type of study uses the psychological principle of projection to infer how people evaluate characteristics that are heavily laden with social desirability. In the largest study of this kind, a Midwestern utility assessed the relative importance of ten job characteristics (including pay) to 50,000 applicants over a thirty-year period.[57] Based on applicants' self-reports, pay appeared to be the fifth most important characteristic to men and seventh to women. However, when asked to rate the importance of those same ten attributes to "someone just like yourself—same age, education, and gender," pay jumped to first place among both men and women.[58] In other words, people seem to believe that pay is the most important motivator to everyone except themselves.

Recognizing that employees are likely to understate the significance of pay is important, so that managers are not lulled into a false sense of complacency about their pay policies. More generally, this survey item calls attention to the broader need for managers to understand the limitations of rating and ranking survey methodologies. Although such surveys are not entirely useless as a basis for managerial decision making, they do have very serious limitations in terms of designing HR policies. For example, survey findings are likely to be highly unstable across minor variations in method, such as the number of job characteristics included, specific terminology used to describe the various characteristics (e.g., "high pay" versus "fair pay"), purpose of the survey (pure research versus policy making), and whether or not respondents are assured anonymity.[59]

For these reasons, managers are likely to benefit more from research that examines how employees actually *behave* differently under alternative employment practices than from studies of perceived importance. Studies of this type in the compensation area suggest that pay is indeed an important motivator of behavior.[60] For example, Locke and colleagues' meta-analysis found the introduction of monetary incentives to produce the largest and most reliable increases in job performance (median = 30 percent)—almost twice as large as the effects of goal setting or job enrichment. Thus, Locke et al. concluded, "Money is the crucial incentive . . . no other incentive or motivational technique comes even close to money with respect to its instrumental value."[61]

Putting Research into Practice

Previous academics and practitioners have documented a variety of reasons why research findings are not implemented in organizations.[62] However, our survey of HR managers suggests that one of the main reasons is lack of knowledge. Although this might seem unsurprising, some argue that improved mechanisms of information dissemination have made lack of knowledge a trivial problem. For example, Pfeffer and Sutton argue: "We now live in a world where knowledge transfer and information exchange are tremendously efficient, and where there are numerous organizations in the business of collecting and transferring best practices. So, there are fewer and smaller differences in what firms know than in their ability to act on that knowledge."[63]

Our results belie the assertion that knowledge transfer is "tremendously efficient." Indeed, what is particularly striking about our results is that with the exception of the research on integrity tests and values, all the other findings (i.e., regarding goal-setting, performance appraisal, intelligence, and conscientiousness) have been known for at least a decade and, in some cases, considerably longer than that. Moreover, our respondents are HR practitioners who have the most to gain from knowing this research: mid- to high-level HR managers and executives. In addition, our results also suggest that differences in knowledge across firms are likely to be large rather than small; some executives in our sample believed only 9 of the 35 research findings (26 percent), while others believed 30 of the 35 (86 percent).

One obvious solution to this problem would be for practitioners to read more of the research literature. Indeed, in our sample, practitioners who usually read academic research journals tended to agree with 23 of the research findings, as compared with the sample mean of 20—an improvement of 15 percent. However, the problem with this strategy is that very few practitioners appear to read this literature. Specifically, fewer than 1 percent of our sample indicated that they usually read the academic literature, while 75 percent reported that they *never* do so.

Thus, it appears that outlets such as *The Executive* and other efforts to disseminate research knowledge[64] to practitioners are sorely needed. In addition, very explicit attempts to turn findings into "maps for action"[65] may prove useful in helping practitioners to translate research into action. Then, as they conduct their implementation attempts, researchers can document the successes and failures via "action research."[66]

In closing, we remind the reader that what we know from a large and growing body of HR research has become considerably clearer over the past two decades. Failure to be aware of the findings from this research is likely to put one (and one's company) at a competitive disadvantage. At the same time, although enhanced knowledge can be an important asset for improving organizational performance, it is not by itself enough. Rather, improved knowledge acquisition must be paired with effective implementation. Results from our SHRM managers suggest that the transfer of knowledge from research to practice remains imperfect, even in this world of increasingly efficient markets for information.

Source: Academy of Management Executive, 16, (3), 2002, 92–103.

ENDNOTES

1. Gannon, M. J. 1983. Managerial ignorance. *Business Horizons*, May–June: 26(3).
2. Johns, G. 1993. Constraints on the adoption of psychology-based personnel practices: Lessons from organizational innovation. *Personnel Psychology*, 46(3): 569–592.
3. Terpstra, D. E., & Rozell, E. J. 1997. Attitudes of practitioners in human resource management toward information from academic research. *Psychological Reports*, 80(2): 403–412.
4. Campbell, J. P., Daft, R. L. & Hulin, C. L. 1982. *What to study: Generating and developing research questions*. Beverly Hills: Sage.
5. Oviatt, B. M., & Miller, W. D. 1989. Irrelevance, intransigence, and business professors. *The Academy of Management Executive*. 3(4): 304–312.
6. Becker, B., & Gerhart, B. 1996. The impact of human resource management on organizational performance. *Academy of Management Journal*, 39(4): 779–801.
7. Hunter, J. E., & Schmidt, F. L. 1995. *Methods of meta-analysis: Correcting error and bias in research findings*. Thousand Oaks: Sage.
8. For a good overview of this research, see the 1996 special issue of *Academy of Management Journal* edited by Becker & Gerhart, op. cit.
9. Welbourne, T. M., & Andrews, A. O. 1996. Predicting the performance of initial public offerings: Should human resource management be in the equation? *Academy of Management Journal*, 39(4): 891–919.
10. Huselid, M. A. 1995. The impact of human resource management practices on turnover, productivity, and corporate financial performance. *Academy of Management Journal*, 38(3): 635–672.
11. Terpstra, D. E., & Rozell, E. J. 1997. Sources of human resource information and the link to organizational profitability. *Journal of Applied Behavioral Science*, 33(1): 66–83.
12. Ulrich, D. 1997. *Human resource champions: The next agenda for adding value and delivering results*, Boston: Harvard Business School Press.
13. The original questionnaire had 39 items, but four items were later eliminated due to ambiguous wording or new research findings.
14. Validities are higher than .51 for more complex jobs (e.g., .58 for professional and managerial jobs) and lower for less complex jobs (e.g., .40 for semi-skilled jobs). Schmidt, F. L., & Hunter, J. E. 1998. The validity and utility of selection methods in personnel psychology: Practical and theoretical implications of 85 years of research findings. *Psychological Bulletin*, 124(2): 262–274.
15. Ibid., 264–266.
16. These figures are in 1980 dollars and thus would be considerably larger now. See Schmidt, F. L., & Hunter, J. E. 1981. Employment testing: Old theories and new research findings. *The American Psychologist*, 36(Special Issue): 1128–1137.
17. Hofstadter, R. 1996. *Anti-intellectualism in American life*. New York: Alfred A. Knopf; and Whyte, W. H. 1956. *The organization man*. New York: Touchstone Books.
18. An example can be seen in this quote from 120 years ago: "A great many of the most 'precocious' youths have dropped out of memory, while some of the plodding, but untiring and persevering ones, are holding the reins of government or guiding the counsels of school and senate." Thayer, 1882, quoted in Stross, R. E. 1997. *The Microsoft way*. Reading, MA: Addison-Wesley: 32.
19. Goleman, D. 1998. *Working with emotional intelligence*. New York: Bantam Books: 22, 35, 40.
20. Goff, M., & Ackerman, P. L. 1992. Personality-intelligence relations: Assessment of typical intellectual engagement. *Journal of Educational Psychology*, 84(4): 537–552.
21. Goleman, op. cit., 20.
22. Sackeft, P. R., & Ostgaard, D. J. 1994. Job-specific applicant pools and national norms for cognitive ability tests: Implications for range restriction corrections in validation research. *Journal of Applied Psychology*, 79(5): 680–684.
23. See also Behling, O. 1998. Employee selection: Will intelligence and conscientiousness do the job? *The Academy of Management Executive*. 12(1): 77–85.
24. Huffcutt, A. I., Conway, J. M., Roth, P. L., & Stone, N. J. 2001. Identification and meta-analytic assessment of psychological constructs measured in employment interviews. *Journal of Applied Psychology*, 96(5): 897–913.
25. The Wonderlic is available via *www.wonderlic.com*. For a review, see Murphy, K. 1984. The Wonderlic Personnel Test. In J. Hogan & R. Hogan (Eds.). *Business and industry testing: Current practices and test reviews*. Austin: Pro-Ed: 191–197.
26. Ryan, A. M., & Ployhart, R. E. 2000. Applicants' perceptions of selection procedures and decisions: A critical review and agenda for the future. *Journal of Management*, 26(3): 565–606.
27. These factors, in combination with the complexity of legal requirements, suggest that most if not all companies should get legal advice about the defensibility of their overall selection systems.
28. For example, John Hunter found job knowledge to be correlated .80 with GMA and .80 with job performance as assessed by the highly valid method of work sampling. See Hunter, J. E. 1986. Cognitive ability, cognitive aptitudes, job knowledge, and job performance. *Journal of Vocational Behavior*, 29(3): 340–362.
29. Adkins, C. L., Ravlin, E. C., & Meglino, B. M. 1996. Value congruence between co-workers and its relationship to work outcomes. *Group and Organization Management*, 21(4): 439–460; Adkins, C. L., Russell, C. J., & Werbel, J. D. 1994. Judgments of fit in the selection process: The role of work-value congruence. *Personnel Psychology*, 47(3): 605–623: and Welch, J. 2001. *Jack: Straight from the gut*. New York: Warner Business Books.
30. Chatman, J. 1991. Matching people and organizations: Selection and socialization in public accounting firms. *Administrative Science Quarterly*, 36(3): 459–484; and Meglino, B. M., & Ravlin, E. C. 1998. Individual values in organizations: Concepts, controversies, and research. *Journal of Management*, 24(3): 351–389.
31. Lauver, K., & Kristof-Brown, A. 2001. Distinguishing between employees' perceptions of person-job and person-organization fit. *Journal of Vocational Behavior* 59(3): 454–470; and Meglino & Ravlin, ibid.
32. Adkins, Ravlin, & Meglino, op. cit.
33. Lauver & Kristof-Brown, op. cit.
34. Bretz, R. D., Rynes, S. L., & Gerhart, B. 1993. Recruiter perceptions of applicant fit: Implications for individual career preparation and job search behavior. *Journal of Vocational Behavior*, 43(2): 310–327; and Kristof-Brown, A. L. 2000. Perceived applicant fit: Distinguishing

between recruiters' perceptions of person-job and person-organization fit. *Personnel Psychology*, 53(3): 643–671.

35. Integrity tests (sometimes called "honesty tests") were initially designed to predict applicant propensities to steal. Over time, they have been used to predict an increasingly broader range of behaviors, including counterproductive behaviors (e.g., absenteeism, tardiness, or violence) and even general job performance. Evidence suggests that integrity tests tap three of the "big five" personality dimensions—mostly Conscientiousness, but also Agreeableness and Emotional Stability.
36. Ryan, A. M., & Sackett, P. R. 1987. Pre-employment honesty testing: Fakability, reactions of test takers and company image. *Journal of Business and Psychology*, 1(2): 248–258.
37. Cunningham. M. R., Wong, D. T., & Barbee, A. P. 1994. Self-presentation dynamics on overt integrity tests: Experimental studies of the Reid Report. *Journal of Applied Psychology*, 79(5): 643–658.
38. Hough, L. M., Eaton, N. K., Dunnette, M. D., Kamp, J. D., & McCloy, R. A. 1990. Criterion-related validities of personality constructs and the effect of response distortion on those validities. *Personnel Psychology*, 75(5): 581–595; and Ones, D. S., Viswesvaran, C., & Reiss, A. D. 1996. Role of social desirability in personality testing for personnel selection: The red herring. *Journal of Applied Psychology*, 81(6): 660–679.
39. Ones et al., 1993, op. cit.
40. Ones et al., 1996, op. cit.
41. Schmidt & Hunter, op. cit.
42. Ones, D. S., & Viswesvaran, C. 1998. Gender, age, and race differences on overt integrity tests: Results across four large-scale job applicant data sets. *Journal of Applied Psychology*, 83(1): 35–42. Although racial and ethnic differences are trivial, women score significantly higher than men.
43. Ryan & Sackett, op. cit.
44. Locke, E. A., Feren, D. B., McCaleb, V. N., Shaw, K. N., & Denny, A. T. 1980. The relative effectiveness of four methods of motivating employee performance. In K. D. Duncan, M. M. Gruneberg, & D. Wallis (Eds.). *Changes in working life*. New York: John Wiley & Sons: 363–388.
45. Cusumano, M. A., & Selby, R. W. 1995. *Microsoft secrets*. New York: The Free Press: 10.
46. Kaizenbach, J. R., & Smith, D. K. 1994. *The wisdom of teams: Creating the high-performance organization*. New York: Harper Business.
47. Beer, M. 1997. Conducting a performance appraisal interview. Harvard Business School Case 9-497-058. Boston: Harvard Business School Press.
48. Kluger, A. N., & DeNisi, A. 1996. The effects of feedback interventions on performance. *Psychological Bulletin*, 119(2): 254–284; and Longenecker, C. O., Sims, H. P., & Gioia, D. A. 1987. Behind the mask: The politics of employee appraisal. *The Academy of Management Executive*, 1(3): 183–193.
49. Latham, G. P., & Wexley, K. N. 1980. *Increasing productivity through performance appraisal*. Reading, MA: Addison-Wesley; and Levine, J., & Butler, J. 1952. Lecture versus group decision in changing behavior. *Journal of Applied Psychology*, 36(1): 29–33.
50. Latham & Wexley, ibid.; and Wexley, K. N., Sanders, R. E., & Yuki, G. A. 1973. Training interviewers to eliminate contrast effects in employment interviews. *Journal of Applied Psychology*, 57(2): 233–236.
51. Bernardin, H. J., & Buckley, M. R. 1981. Strategies in rater training. *Academy of Management Review*, 6(2): 205–212; and Bernardin, H. J., & Pence, E. G. 1980. The effects of rater training: Creating new response sets and decreasing accuracy. *Journal of Applied Psychology*, 65(7): 60–66.
52. Latham, G. P., & Latham, S. D. 2000. Overlooking theory and research in performance appraisal at one's peril: Much done, more to do. In Cooper, C. L., & Locke, E. A. (Eds.). *Industrial and organizational psychology: Linking theory with practice*. Oxford: Blackwell: 199–215.
53. Longenecker, et al., op. cit.; and Welch, op. cit.
54. Cronbach, L. J., et al. 1972. *The dependability of behavioral measurements: Theory of generalizability of scores and profiles*, NY: John Wiley.
55. Opsahl, R. L., & Dunnette, M. D. 1966. The role of financial compensation in industrial motivation. *Psychological Bulletin*, 66(1): 94–118.
56. Feldman, D. C., & Arnold, H. J. 1978. Position choice: Comparing the importance of organizational and job factors. *Journal of Applied Psychology*, 63(6): 706–710; and Rynes, S. L., Schwab, D. P., & Heneman, H. G. 1983. The role of pay and market pay variability in job application decisions, *Organizational Behavior and Human Performance*, 31(3): 353–364.
57. Jurgensen, C. E. 1978. Job preferences (what makes a job good or bad?). *Journal of Applied Psychology*, 63(2): 267–276.
58. Jurgensen, ibid.
59. Lawler, E. E. III. 1971. *Pay and organizational effectiveness: A psychological view*. New York: McGraw-Hill.
60. Gerhart, B., & Milkovich, G. T. 1990. Organizational differences in managerial compensation and financial performance. *Academy of Management Journal*. 33(4): 663–691; and Locke et al., op. cit.
61. Ibid., 379.
62. Johns, op. cit.; and LaPointe, J. B. 1990. Industrial-organizational psychology: A view from the field. In Murphy, K. R., & Saal, F. E. (Eds.). *Psychology in organizations; Integrating science and practice*. Hillsdale, NJ: Erlbaum: 7–24.
63. Pfeffer, J., & Sutton, R. I. 2000. *The knowing-doing gap*. Boston: Harvard Business School Press: 243.
64. Examples include Locke. E. A. 2000. *The Blackwell handbook of organizational behavior*. Oxford: Blackwell; and Cooper & Locke, op. cit.
65. Argyris, C. 1985. Making knowledge more relevant to practice: Maps for action. In Lawler, E. E., Mohrman, A. M., Mohrman, S. A., Ledford, G. E., & Cummings, T. G. (Eds.). *Doing research that is useful for theory and practice*. San Francisco: Jossey-Bass.
66. Susman, G. I., & Evered, R. D. 1978. An assessment of the scientific merits of action research. *Administrative Science Quarterly*, 23(4): 582–603.

READING 1.3

Maximizing Human Capital: Demonstrating HR Value with Key Performance Indicators

Nancy R. Lockwood

Abstract

To drive value and optimize company performance, human capital—the collective knowledge, skills and abilities of people that contribute to organizational success—is an asset to be leveraged. Based on corporate culture, organizational values and strategic business goals and objectives, human capital measures indicate the health of the organization. The effective use of key performance indicators (KPIs) that measure human capital outcomes, such as talent management, employee engagement and high performance, illustrates the firm's business, financial and strategic goals, promotes partnership with senior management for organizational success and demonstrates HR value to the C-suite.

Introduction

"In order to fully value human capital, we must go beyond the view of human effort as purely individual. We, humans, affect each other profoundly, and it is the way we affect each other that determines our value to our organizations. And, it is the way that strategic human resource professionals bring this understanding to the fore of their organizations that determines HR's value at the senior management table."[1]

In 1995, the seminal study by management guru Mark Huselid linked high-performance work practices with company performance and revealed that workforce practices had an economic effect on employee outcomes such as turnover and productivity, as well as on short- and long-term measures of corporate financial performance.[2] This study marked a new era of measuring the influence of HR to promote effective organizational performance, sustainability and financial success.

As HR positions itself as a strategic business partner, one of the most effective ways to do so is to support the strategic business goals through *key performance indicators.* Key performance indicators (also known as KPIs) are defined as quantifiable, specific measures of an organization's performance in certain areas of its business. The purpose of KPIs is to provide the company with quantifiable measurements of what is determined to be important to the organization's critical success factors and long-term business goals. Once uncovered and properly analyzed, KPIs can be used to understand and improve organizational performance and overall success.[3]

Why Measure Human Capital?

The primary motivation to measure human capital is to improve the bottom line. To design better KPIs, it is essential for HR to understand what is important to the business and what key business measures exist. In addition, the drive to measure human capital reflects the change of role of human resources from administrative to that of a strategic business partner. In general, human capital measurement is a measure of effective human resource management.

Broadly stated, HR metrics measure efficiency (time and cost) and the effectiveness of certain activities. Yet mastering human capital measures can be a very complex undertaking. Today, HR professionals are expanding the "traditional" metrics, such as head count, time-to-fill and turnover, to KPIs that align with corporate objectives and create greater stakeholder value. However, KPIs often demand large amounts of data and technological support. In addition, the trial-and-error required to set appropriate and meaningful measures comes into play, as well as patience and education of those involved. Yet despite these challenges, 84% of companies expect to increase the application of human capital measures in the next few years.[4]

With a clear line of sight on workforce and organizational performance, effective use of KPIs also illustrates HR's in-depth understanding of the links to business success. KPIs help build the credibility of the HR department, demonstrate HR value and foster respect and partnership with senior management and the C-suite. For example, when an HR professional not only shows that a new recruiting program resulted in a lower time to fill positions in the organization, but can also demonstrate that the program yielded an additional amount of revenue because billable staff were able to start at client sites more quickly, he or she builds HR credibility. Credibility is increased because HR is able to link HR activities to firm performance and communicate it in financial/business terms. Additional critical reasons to measure human capital include steering human capital resource allocation, winning business cases for human capital investment, tracking human capital activities to develop human capital predictions, linking variable compensation to human capital best practices, delivering human capital information required by law and providing investors with information on human capital performance. Some firms even use KPIs to enhance their company image as a progressive employer of choice.[5]

Further, with many HR functions increasingly being outsourced, credibility is earned through activities and outcomes that result in "deliverables" that promote and lead to organizational success.[6] Consequently, it is important to select KPIs that are most meaningful to the organization. For example, logical KPIs to select are those that reflect drivers for human capital measurement, such as financial outcome measures (e.g., revenue growth and cost reduction) and performance drivers (e.g., customer satisfaction, process technology innovation, product technology innovation, globalization). Within that framework, the most common categories of people measures include turnover, productivity (revenue, profit per employee), employee satisfaction/ employee engagement, recruitment, diversity, remuneration, competencies/training, leadership, and health and safety. Most frequently measured are turnover, voluntary resignation, average compensation, average workforce age, diversity and compensation/total cost. Such KPIs will help HR professionals predict what they need to know to act in a timely and effective manner and identify ideas and areas where HR can develop new initiatives, or revisit others, to obtain stronger results.[7] Clearly, KPIs are the wave of the future for HR.

Culture, Stakeholders and KPIs

As the saying goes, "what gets measured gets managed." The company culture and corresponding values define what is measured. Therefore, when HR considers important KPIs, the first place to look is at corporate culture and what is most valued within that culture. In addition, stakeholders (both internal and external) go hand-in-hand with company culture. A stakeholder is an individual or entity with a stake in how the organization performs and/or conducts itself. Internal stakeholders are employees, line managers, senior management, C-suite and the board of directors. External stakeholders include shareholders, customers, vendors, the community and the government.

Working closely with internal stakeholders is beneficial for HR to 1) prioritize capabilities and create action plans to deliver them; 2) focus on deliverables rather than doables; 3) build relationships of trust; and 4) help resolve misconceptions of HR.[8] Different stakeholders have different criteria. The key priority is to give business partners the information they need to manage the company. For example, senior management values performance measures that predict and lead to future organizational financial success and sustainability. On the other hand, while one employee considers the availability of upward career mobility very important, another employee stays for health care benefits. As a result, training to promote opportunities to move up in the organization and informational sessions about employee benefits packages may be important. Overall, most important are KPIs that track key business indicators of human capital issues. HR must focus on KPIs that best illustrate stakeholder values that will lead to organizational success.

KPIs—A Strategic Management Tool

To think strategically about measurement and how best to use KPIs as a strategic management tool, it is essential to understand the meaning of the measurements and their purpose. This approach will not only be beneficial to help better manage the HR function, but also will naturally lead to aligning HR's goals and objectives with those of the organization.[9]

According to a recent national longitudinal study on the assessment of human resource organizations, strategy is the top high-value add for HR. However, in only 60% of companies did the HR executive see HR as a "full partner." In addition, 24% of executives outside of human resources viewed their HR counterparts as working at lower levels of strategic involvement, compared with 40% of HR executives. The study suggests that activities related to strategy provide the most high-end impact for HR to demonstrate its value (see Figure 1). In addition, the relationship between business strategy activities and HR's strategic role points to areas where HR can contribute: growth, the core business, quality and speed, information-based strategies, knowledge-based strategies, and organizational performance. The study data also reveal key strategic HR activities that link business emphases with the organization's strategic focus: 1) having a data-based talent strategy; 2) partnering with line managers to develop business strategy; 3) providing analytic support for business decision-making; 4) providing HR data to support change management; 5) driving change management; and 6) making rigorous data-based decisions about human capital management.[10] From these HR strategy activities, key performance indicators can be developed.

At the same time, when determining strategic KPIs, it is essential to consider who designs human capital measures and how they are created. Research by The Conference Board reveals key contributors to these metrics. Overall, HR designs 94% of human capital measures, often basing them on measures in the company scorecard. To create human capital measures, 77% of HR professionals meet with company business managers. For example, finance, strategic planning, outside consulting experts, business managers and IT contribute to HR measurement design. However, if HR lacks expertise with metrics, it is helpful to partner with groups such as marketing that have considerable expertise in measure design and analysis.[11]

Alignment of people metrics with organizational strategy is still at an early stage in many firms. To move human

FIGURE 1 HR Value-Added Strategic Activities

- Help identify or design strategy options.
- Help decide among the best strategy options.
- Help plan the implementation of a strategy.
- Help design the criteria for strategic success.
- Help identify new business opportunities.
- Assess the organization's readiness to implement strategies.
- Help design the organizational structure to implement a strategy.
- Assess possible merger, acquisition or divestiture strategies.
- Work with the corporate board on business strategy.
- Recruit and develop talent.

Source: Adapted from Lawler III, E. E., Boudreau, J. W., & Mohrman, S. A. (2006). *Achieving strategic excellence: An assessment of human resource organizations*. Palo Alto, CA: Stanford University Press.

capital investments forward, several key points will assist HR to better strategically align with organizational goals and garner support for human capital programs: 1) involve HR in the development of overall business strategy; 2) enlist leaders outside of HR to help develop and back KPIs; 3) collaborate with business managers to ensure KPIs link to business unit strategic goals; 4) focus more attention on links between people measures and intermediate performance drivers (e.g., customer satisfaction, innovation, engagement); 5) increase manager acceptance through training programs and concrete action plans; and 6) work with HR to simplify metric and automate data collection.[12]

In addition, benchmarking can make human capital metrics more valuable. When used wisely, benchmarking data can protect programs that are performing well, create support for organizational change and help executives in HR and other disciplines make strategic decisions that affect their organizations.[13] By focusing on internal benchmarks, customized measures may help improve the alignment of activities to HR strategy. However, caution should be used with external benchmarks due to mixing "apples and oranges"—that is, different industry sectors and underlying issues in bench-marking measures. Also, external benchmarks tend to emphasize results rather than processes. Because an external benchmark does not explain what part of the process can lead to better results, the use of external measures may not always be appropriate for internal use. In the rapid expansion of highly advanced e-learning programs, for example, different programs may deliver the same content at the same low cost, but the quality of the programs is not revealed in the benchmark itself.[14]

Overall, the top KPIs for human capital and HR effectiveness can be used by all companies, regardless of size or industry. For example, the Hay Group found that the most admired companies had effective business practices in the following areas: organizational culture, strategy implementation, attraction and retention of talent, leadership development, fostering innovation, and performance management. Successful companies assess performance by balancing profit measures with measures of shareholder value, customer satisfaction and employee satisfaction.[15] Keeping this research in the forefront will help HR develop effective and strategic KPIs for their organizations.

The Importance of Lagging and Leading Indicators

The purpose of measuring KPIs and determining what leads and what lags is to help the business make predictions. To demonstrate HR value with KPIs, it is imperative that HR has a working knowledge of lagging and leading indicators. These terms describe data regarding outcomes and/or events that affect organizational performance. Lagging and leading indicators offer a way to understand and/or predict various aspects of firm performance. However, to identify and quantify these relationships, it is essential to know more than HR is a leading variable and customer satisfaction is a lagging variable.[16] To accurately gauge the relationship between lagging and leading indicators, a sense of the magnitude of the time lag between changes in the leading indicator and subsequent changes in the lagging indicator is required. (See Figure 2 for an example of lagging and leading indicators, with turnover as the lagging indicator in response to selection and supervisory training, the leading indicators.)

To be more specific, a lagging indicator represents information that is the result of change or an event. Lagging indicators, for example, are measures of profits, sales and service levels. They reveal various aspects regarding the success or failure of a firm. Lagging indicators are particularly useful for shareholders, creditors and government agencies. Lagging indicators do not, however, help a company react quickly, show what specifically went wrong or right, or indicate exactly what needs to be done to improve. In general, lagging indicators are not useful in managing on a day-to-day basis.[17]

In contrast, a leading indicator precedes, anticipates, predicts or affects the future. For example, higher employee turnover can precede outcomes such as lower customer service scores. Of the two indicators, the leading indicator is more useful for investments or predictions. The state of

FIGURE 2 The Effects of Selection and Supervisor Training on Turnover

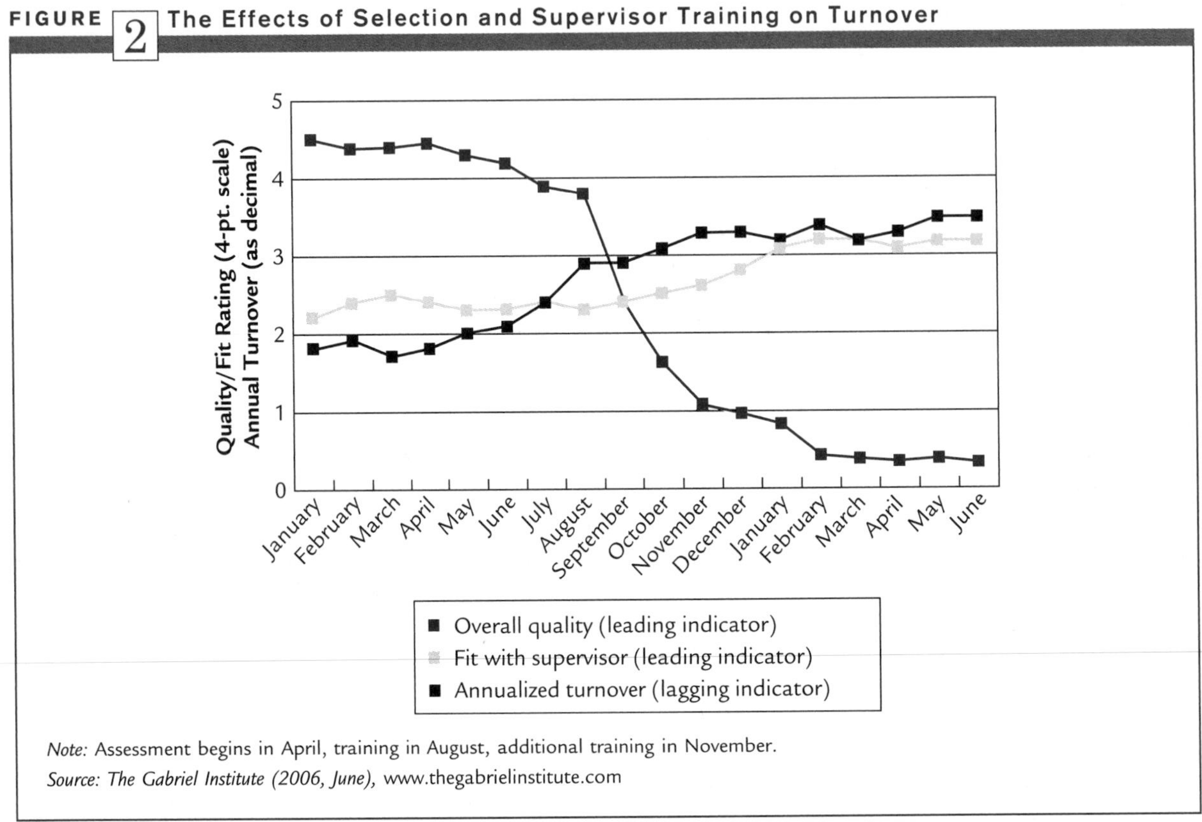

Note: Assessment begins in April, training in August, additional training in November.
Source: The Gabriel Institute (2006, June), www.thegabrielinstitute.com

the major stock markets, for example, is a leading economic indicator for the global economy. Figuring out how to measure events, practices, initiatives or outcomes helps to determine the most valuable leading indicators—that is, those indicators that may lead to clear outcomes.[18] However, part of the difficulty is clearly proving what indicators lead and with what degree of influence. For example, while the availability of talent is generally thought of as a leading indicator—as one can measure the quality of hire from it (the larger the talent pool, the more likely you are to hire more qualified people)—it is also a lagging indicator in comparison to certain political decisions. For example, consider how changes in a local taxation rate, perception of crime and ratings of school quality affect people's desire to move to a city and become part of the talent pool. Here, political decisions lead and talent availability lags. In general, the most useful measures are leading indicators, as they may predict future firm performance.

Scorecards and Dashboards

In recent years, HR scorecards and dashboards have gained popularity as a management tool. Documenting and tracking defined metrics validates human capital investments. For example, firms are increasingly tracking employee movement as a metric. Cisco Systems, Inc., the California-based communications giant, views building talent as a priority and has added to its dashboard of people measures a metric to track how many people move and the reason why, including revenue per employee. This KPI allows Cisco executives to quickly identify divisions that are creating new talent. Another firm, Valero Energy Corp. in San Antonio, developed a recruitment model using human capital metrics based on applying the supply-chain business process to labor. Scorecards help the company track the labor sources that provide the most productive employees. Using a detailed analysis of these metrics, the company can accurately forecast the demand for talent by division and title three years in advance.[19]

The HR scorecard, based on the format of the balanced scorecard, is a key management tool to strengthen HR's strategic influence in the organization. The scorecard has four perspectives—strategic, operational, financial and customer—that help organize and track areas where HR adds value: 1) the strategic perspective focuses on measurements of effectiveness of major strategy-linked people goals; 2) the operational perspective reflects the effectiveness of HR processes; 3) the financial perspective relates to financial measures of HR value to the organization; and 4) the customer perspective focuses on the effectiveness of HR from the internal customer viewpoint. Depending on the organization's business goals, these perspectives also help determine KPIs that best demonstrate HR value (see Figure 3).[20] Additional key benefits of the HR scorecard are 1) reinforcement of the distinction between HR

FIGURE 3 Examples of Key Performance Indicators for the HR Scorecard

Strategic Perspective	Organizational culture survey HR budget/actual Employee skills/competency levels Change management capability of the organization
Operational Perspective	Training cost per employee Attrition rate Time to fill vacancies Average employee tenure in the company
Financial Perspective	Compensation and benefits per employee Turnover cost Sales per employee Profit per employee
Customer Perspective	Employee perspective of human resource management Employee perspective of the company as an employer

Source: Adapted from Becker, B. E., Huselid, M. A., & Ulrich, D. (2001). *The HR scorecard: Linking people, strategy and performance.* Boston: Harvard Business School Press.

"doables" and HR "deliverables" (i.e., a policy implementation is a doable and becomes a deliverable when it creates employee behaviors that drive strategy); 2) HR's ability to control cost and create value; 3) measurement of leading indicators; 4) assessment of HR's contribution to strategy implementation and to the bottom line; 5) support of HR to manage its strategic responsibility; and 6) encouragement of flexibility and change.[21]

KPIs and Employee Engagement

Employee engagement is quickly becoming a critical success factor for competitive advantage. Using KPIs, HR can demonstrate organizational success as well as gain support for initiatives related to employee engagement. Research studies offer evidence that employee engagement is key to organizational success. In the *SHRM 2006 Job Satisfaction Survey Report,* employees identified four key aspects of job satisfaction directly linked to employee engagement: meaningfulness of job, contribution of employee's work to the firm's business goals, the work itself and variety of work.[22] Watson Wyatt's research, *The Human Capital ROI Study,* reinforces the link between employee engagement, reward systems and retaining valuable human capital.[23] A Carlson/Gallup study on employee engagement and business success shows that employees who are extremely satisfied at work are four times more likely than dissatisfied employees to have a formal measurement process in place as well as receive regular recognition. Further, 82% said recognition motivated them to improve job performance.[24] Thus, as these studies highlight, employee engagement—whether through job satisfaction indicators, reward systems, effective communication programs or succession planning initiatives—has the power not only to clearly demonstrate HR value, but more importantly, to propel human capital investment to the forefront of the C-suite agenda.

KPIs for Organizations With Small HR Departments—Mini Case Study No. 1

Not all organizations have the luxury of a dedicated HR staff to develop, track and analyze HR metrics. When an HR staff of a small organization has limited time to track all possible HR KPIs, careful choices must be made about which KPIs best serve HR's needs. This mini case study illustrates the types of KPIs selected and tracked by a small HR staff supporting a workforce of 400 employees of a firm that sells and leases health care equipment to hospitals. With only an HR director and HR assistant, this tiny HR department tracks human capital measures that reflect the state of the organization, selecting KPIs based on metrics that best reflect the company's culture and strategic goals.

In this company, certain KPIs are tracked throughout the year, while others (e.g., absenteeism) are reviewed on a quarterly basis. Overall, the HR department benchmarks progress against prior years, with the goal that the employee cost tracks favorably against revenue and profit. The primary metrics tracked are employee cost over sales revenue, employee cost over net income before taxes, turnover of full-time and part-time staff, absenteeism, time-to-fill for critical positions, and HR performance ratings. Of these metrics, four are lagging indicators: employee cost over sales revenue, employee cost over net income before taxes, turnover and performance ratings. The other two metrics—absenteeism and time-to-fill—are leading indicators. The turnover of full-time staff, for example, was 11% in 2004 and 16% in 2005, the difference reflecting the recent retirement of several long-time employees. As a result of analyzing the turnover increase, HR developed a knowledge management transfer program for employees close to retirement. Finally, to anticipate the possible effect on the next year's budget, HR reviews any changes in benefits programs against the cost of benefits per employee.

The Value of Qualitative KPIs—Mini Case Study No. 2

KPIs—as a simple tabulation of numerical indicators—do not necessarily provide management with useful information. Moving from "bean counting" to strategic HR, a more qualitative type of key performance indicator becomes essential. As this mini case study illustrates, turnover rate, as a leading indicator, is an excellent example. In a mid-size manufacturing company with 650 employees, HR, using a qualitative assessment process, asked questions to explore the true reason behind the high turnover rate of 30%. First, what was the value of the employees who left the organization? Since the turnover rate was high, for example, were the employees who left a drag on performance? If yes, then the hiring process was the next step to examine. Second, was the high turnover among valuable employees? If yes, then the next step was to examine the nature of the employee-organization interaction.

To begin, HR went back to its performance assessment process and considered people who left in each of the four categories: 4—exceeds expectations, 3—meets expectations, 2—needs improvement to meet expectations and 1—not performing even to minimal expectations. They looked at high turnover among the 3s and 4s, which represented a loss of high performers who, assuming the performance assessment was valid, were more valuable to the organization. They also considered high turnover among the 1s and 2s, a possible indication that supervisors were doing a good job of weeding out those who could not perform. Looking at turnover rates over time, HR found a need for supervisor training as well as the need to improve pre-hiring screening and the overall selection process. After tracking turnover for a year following the supervisor training initiative and improvements in the hiring process, the end result was that the savings in reduced turnover far outweighed the cost of the pre-hire assessment and supervisor training.

Role of Technology and KPIs

Today, the increasing demand for HR technology runs parallel with the growing use of workforce analytics and KPIs. HR technology systems are fast proving to be a critical vehicle for HR to contribute value to their organizations. While initially used primarily by large organizations, more small and mid-size companies now use software products to both effectively measure human capital investment and track a wide range of HR metrics. Further, there is growing evidence of cost savings in organizations that effectively use HR technology. Consequently, HR in companies of all sizes will increasingly use technology to better showcase the effects of human capital initiatives.[25]

Research by management gurus Boudreau, Lawler and Mohrman points to the critical role of technology and the corresponding strong relationship between HR and IT. Two key findings reveal that, due to technology, completely integrated HR IT systems lead to the highest level of HR effectiveness, and the effectiveness of the HR IT system is strongly related to the overall effectiveness of the HR organization. Further, the *SHRM 2005 HR Technology Survey Report* emphasizes the importance of return on investment (ROI) to build a business case to incorporate HR technology systems in the firm. The top five successes of HR technology systems are: increased accuracy of employee information; decreased cycle time for processing employee information transactions; less time spent by HR staff on administrative work; greater access by managers to employee information; and the HR department's ability to manage the workforce with the same number of HR staff. Yet, few organizations document the advantages of HR technology systems:[26]

- 65% of organizations are not measuring the ROI for HR technology systems.
- Of those that do measure the ROI, 68% measure it by determining cost savings and losses and 31% consider HR headcount.
- 10% of HR professionals do not know how the ROI is measured.

Recent Studies: Human Capital Practices Drive Performance

Increasingly, research finds that best practices around human capital can help companies successfully compete with their peer organizations. The following studies highlight the importance of human capital practices to drive organizational performance. Correspondingly, KPIs that measure these practices both validate the value of HR and advance the profession at all levels.

- Achieving Strategic Excellence: An Assessment of Human Resource Organizations[27]

This national study, the fourth in a series on the HR function in large corporations, focuses on measuring whether the HR function is changing to become more effective and, more specifically, whether HR is changing to become an effective strategic partner. The key findings show a "strong relationship between what is happening in the HR function and a company's strategic focuses." The degree to which the firm has knowledge and performance strategies is the degree to which HR is viewed as a strategic business partner. Overall, with the importance placed on talent management, the emphasis on human capital, knowledge and competencies creates a favorable environment for the HR function.

- SHRM 2006 Human Capital Benchmarking Study[28]

This executive summary provides HR professionals with key human capital measures from nearly 600 organizations on HR departments and their expenses, employment, health care, compensation, and organizational revenue and size. The key findings reveal changes and trends in the workplace. For example, of the 57% of firms that expected their HR department expenses to increase, 11% were in durable goods manufacturing. For all industries, the median for HR expense per full-time employee was $1,072. And in 2005,

FIGURE 4 Examples of Key Performance Indicators for Global HR Effectiveness

- Design and implementation of an international HR information system.
- Development of global leadership through cross-cultural assignments.
- Development of a global mindset for all employees through training and development.
- Cost reduction of expatriate assignments.
- Implementation of formal systems that improve worldwide communications.

Source: Adapted from Sparrow, P., Brewster, C., & Harris, H. (2004). *Globalizing human resource management*, London: Routledge.

organizations also increased their hiring by more than 50% from the previous year. Telecommunications, services (profit) and biotechnology industries had the top three highest medians for percentages of positions filled in 2005.

- 2006 FORTUNE Most Admired Companies: The Effectiveness of Managing Globally[29]

This study of 74 companies worldwide found that successful global organizations exploit unique knowledge and capabilities. They then effectively diffuse and adopt them worldwide to their strategic objectives, contributing to competitive differentiation. Successful global leaders, for example, take a hands-on approach to develop talent management and provide ongoing coaching to their workforce. Most admired companies have a better understanding of their talent, and consequently, positions can be filled more quickly based on required skills and career objectives.

- Maximizing the Return on Your Human Capital Investment: The 2005 Watson Wyatt Human Capital Index Report[30]

This study of 147 organizations representing all major North American industries illustrates that companies with superior human capital practices can create more shareholder value that substantially surpasses companies with average human capital practices. Excellent human capital practices—such as recruiting excellence, employee development, total rewards, turnover management and communication—make a difference, no matter the state of the economy. Key findings, for example, show that companies that filled vacancies faster reduced disruption and lost productivity from turnover. Organizations that filled positions quickly (in about two weeks) outperformed those that took longer (around seven weeks) by 48% (59% three-year total returns to shareholders versus 11%).

Using KPIs in the Global HR Function

The value of global HR is assessed by how well global HR strategy, policies and practices link with, support and forward organizational strategy (see Figure 4). In addition, global HR is often assessed by its effectiveness to deliver major organizational change. HR is often called upon, for example, to help in the design of high-level projects for major global business initiatives (e.g., talent management for expansion into new regions, a global communications program regarding new organizational values).

Yet measuring the contribution of HR on an international level becomes ever more complicated due to factors such as complexities of scope, authority level, and political, cultural and legislative barriers that directly affect the link between organizational performance and HR. Two approaches are recommended: identifying and proving the link between organizational performance and people management, and using methods of evaluation of the global HR function's contribution. The measure of the global HR function also often rests on "perceptions of effectiveness" from key stakeholders—that is, the company's worldwide employees and managers. Therefore, the ability to market HR globally as a source of competitive and strategic advantage is fundamental to measuring the contribution of the corporate global HR function.[31]

Measuring the value of international assignments, for example, is a critical success factor for global HR. Companies measure the ROI of international assignments through cost estimating, tracking and comparison. A recent global relocation trends survey, for example, found that 70% of companies required a statement of assignment objectives prior to funding assignments. In addition, to minimize expatriate turnover—a global HR KPI-64% of companies found opportunities to use international experience, with 50% of firms offering a greater choice of positions upon return and 43% offering repatriation career support.[32] However, as highlighted in an SHRM case study on repatriation, different assignments have different measures of success and, consequently, different results. A common KPI is the retention rate of expatriates following repatriation for one and/or two years. Other measures may also reflect "softer" results, such as managerial approach shifts or cultural changes. The concept behind using a variety of measures is to create a "report card" that can provide a broad view of the assignment overall.[33]

In Closing

Becoming more facile with metrics in general is a goal of many HR professionals. Further, as more HR professionals become immersed in human capital measurement, they can more effectively use key performance indicators to illustrate

Recommendations

Selecting practical KPIs requires thoughtful consideration of the message behind measures and their corresponding effect on the organization. The real-life examples below—starting at the idea stage and ending at results with meaningful measures—demonstrate HR value through KPIs.

1. Qualitative measurement is one path to assess qualitative characteristics of the workforce, such as engagement.
   Example: A public agency was experiencing high customer complaints and low staff morale. A combination of open-ended survey and focus group outputs was analyzed, and leading indicators were identified. Training was specifically designed to target the key areas, and as a result, customer complaints fell as morale improved.
2. Employee feedback provides useful perspectives on HR efficiency.
   Example: Health care costs were unusually high and customer service was very poor for the last fiscal year. Six months after a new health care provider was chosen, costs were down by 20%. The organization's HR manager developed a survey for employees to provide feedback about the new program relative to the previous one and learned that employee perception of the new program was extremely favorable.
3. Whenever possible, the impact of recruiting is best described in terms of financial gains.
   Example: An organization wanted to know the effect of its new recruiting program. The program was able to reduce time-to-fill by an average of seven days, which meant new employees could start billing sooner to client sites. Since the average daily bill rate per person was $900, the recruiting program was able to increase the firm's revenue by $6,300 per new billable employee hired.
4. Retaining older workers for future leadership roles depends on what they most value.
   Example: A survey by a multinational corporation of its older worker population in North America and Europe revealed the following top three key values: 1) support from managers: 2) ability to make one's own job-related decisions: and 3) opportunities for advancement. Leadership development programs were created to retain key talent from this group. Over a two-year period, tracking of performance, mentoring and promotions of older workers in the leadership development program found that turnover rates for older workers decreased by 28%.

the value of human capital investments through successful organizational performance at many levels. These important steps will increasingly demonstrate the high value-add required by the C-suite to be a true strategic business partner.

Acknowledgments

The author extends appreciation and thanks to members of the SHRM Human Capital/HR Metrics Special Expertise Panel (Ronald L. Adler, Crist Berry, SPHR, Bette J. Francis, SPHR, Virginia C. Hall, SPHR, Janice Presser, Ph.D.) and to Strategic Research at SHRM (John Dooney, Noël Smith and Belin Tai).

Source: Society for Human Resource Management, 2006.

ENDNOTES

1. Presser, J. (2006, February). *Approaching a metric of human capital synergy* [SHRM White Paper]. Retrieved June 10, 2006. from www.shrm.org
2. Huselid, M. (1995, June). The impact of human resource management practices on turnover, productivity and corporate financial performance. *Academy of Management Journal*, 38, 3, 635+.
3. Glossary of Human Resources Terms, www.shrm.org/hrresources/hrglossary_published
4. Schneider, C. (2006, February 15). The new human-capital metrics. *CFO Magazine*, 1+.
5. Gates, S. (2002). *Value at work: The risks and opportunities of human capital measurement and reporting*. New York: The Conference Board.
6. Ulrich, D., & Brockbank, W. (2005). *The HR value proposition.* Boston: Harvard Business School Press.
7. Gates, S. (2003). *Linking people to strategy: From top management support to line management buy-in*. New York: The Conference Board.
8. Ulrich, D., & Brockbank, W. (2005). *The HR value proposition.* Boston: Harvard Business School Press.
9. Becker, B. E., Huselid, M. A., & Ulrich, D. (2001). The *HR scorecard: Linking people, strategy and performance.* Boston: Harvard Business School Press.
10. Lawler III, E. E., Boudreau, J. W., & Mohrman, S. A. (2006). *Achieving strategic excellence: An assessment of human resource organizations*. Palo Alto, CA: Stanford University Press.
11. Gates, S. (2002). *Value at work: The risks and opportunities of human capital measurement and reporting*. New York: The Conference Board.
12. Ibid.
13. Dooney, J., & Smith, N. (2005). *SHRM human capital benchmarking study: 2005 executive summary*. Alexandria, VA: Society for Human Resource Management.
14. Gates, S. (2002). *Value at work: The risks and opportunities of human capital measurement and reporting*. New York: The Conference Board.
15. HayGroup. (2005, February). *What makes the most admired companies great?* Retrieved May 4, 2006, from www.haygroup.com
16. Becker, B. E., Huselid, M. A., & Ulrich, D. (2001). *The HR scorecard: Linking people, strategy and performance*. Boston: Harvard Business School Press.

17. Denton, D. K. (2006, March). Measuring relevant things. *Performance improvement*, 45, 3, 33–38.
18. Ibid.
19. Schneider, C. (2006, February 15). The new human-capital metrics. *CFO Magazine*, 1+.
20. Becker, B. E., Huselid, M. A., & Ulrich, D. (2001). *The HR scorecard: Linking people, strategy and performance*. Boston: Harvard Business School Press.
21. Ibid.
22. Exert, E. (2006, June). *2006 job satisfaction survey report*. Alexandria, VA: Society for Human Resource Management.
23. Watson Wyatt and Human Resource Planning Society. (2006, April). *The human capital ROI study*. Retrieved May 4, 2006, from www.watsonwyattc.org.
24. The Gallup Organization. (1998). *Employee engagement = Business success*. Retrieved March 7, 2006, from www.bcpublicservica.ca
25. Schramm, J. (2006, April). HR technology competencies: New roles for HR professionals. *SHRM Research Quarterly*, 1.
26. Collison, J. (2005, March). *2005 HR technology survey report*. Alexandria, VA: Society for Human Resource Management.
27. Lawler III, E. E., Boudreau, J. W., & Mohrman, S. A. (2006). *Achieving strategic excellence: An assessment of human resource organizations*. Palo Alto, CA: Stanford University Press.
28. Dooney, J., & Smith, N. (2006). *SHRM human capital benchmarking study: 2006 executive summary*. Retrieved June 29, 2006, from www.shrm.org
29. HayGroup. (2006, April). Leading the global organization: Structure, process, and people as the keys to success. *Hay Group Insight Selections*, 11, 1–4.
30. Watson Wyatt Worldwide. (2005). *Maximizing the return on your human capital investment: The 2005 Watson Wyatt human capital index report*. Washington, D.C.: Author.
31. Sparrow, P., Brewster, C., & Harris, H. (2004). *Globalizing human resource management*. London: Routledge.
32. GMAC Relocation Services. (2006). *Global relocation trends 2005 survey report*. Woodridge, IL: Author.
33. Society for Human Resource Management (2005, November). *Measuring the success of a repatriation program* [SHRM Case Study]. Retrieved May 9, 2006, from www.shrm.org/hrresources/casestudies_published/GlobalHR.asp

Social Responsibility and Human Resource Management

2

Learning Objectives

- Understand the challenges organizations face in managing diversity, strategies for doing so, and the critical role played by HR.
- Appreciate the importance of ethics awareness, training, and compliance the critical contributions HR can make to an ethics program.
- Gain an awareness of the movement toward corporate social responsibility/ sustainability as well as the contributions HR can make toward sustainability initiatives.

Developing Female Leaders at Safeway

Safeway is a Pleasanton, California–based Fortune 500 corporation that operates retail grocery stores around the country. In the early 2000s, Safeway realized that its competitive landscape had changed dramatically with the advent and rise of premium specialty grocers and, on the other end, from the expanded product lines of big-box hardline retailers such as Wal-Mart and Target. As a result, Safeway decided to try to position itself as an employer of choice. Realizing that 70 percent of its customer base was female and that male leadership was the norm in the retail grocery industry, Safeway decided to shift its culture and broaden its workforce in line with its customer base.

As part of its "Championing Change for Women" program, Safeway developed a Retail Leadership Development program, a formal full-time career development program that has groomed 90 percent of the company's 1,800 retail store managers. Many of these individuals started with the company as entry-level salesclerks or grocery baggers. Integral to this program, however, was the realization that women often need to coordinate their work hours with family responsibilities and that such responsibilities made frequent store relocations undesirable.

The program also involved the establishment of the Women's Leadership Network within the organizations, which provided mentoring and events, such as the Women's Road Show, which involved presentations by female executives at Safeway at locations throughout the country to facilitate learning, networking, and talent identification. Since the inception of the program, female store management has increased by 42 percent, with the number of white female store mangers increasing 31 percent and women of color in store management increasing by 92 percent. The Championing Change for Women program has been honored with the highly coveted Catalyst Award, which is presented to exemplary companies that promote the career development of women and minorities.[1]

In addition to the many challenges organizations face in abandoning traditional approaches to managing people as part of adopting an investment perspective to human resource management, they are also dealing with an increasingly diverse workforce and being increasingly called upon to be socially responsible in their operations and employment practices. This chapter examines some critical social issues—namely, diversity, ethics, and sustainability—that face organizations and the impact these issues have on human resource management.

Workforce Demographic Changes and Diversity

Demographic changes in society and the composition of the workforce are also creating a number of challenges for management of HR. Diversity has become and continues to be one of the principal buzzwords for both public and private organizations, as recognizing and promoting diversity is seen as critical for organizational success. The motivation behind diversity initiatives can vary from organization to organization. Some employers have a commitment to understanding and appreciating diversity, whereas others implement diversity initiatives simply to ensure compliance with federal, state, and local employment laws.

Congress has passed numerous laws that prohibit discrimination in employment in both private and public sector organizations. Title VII of the Civil Rights Act of 1964 prohibits discrimination based on race, color, religion, gender, and national origin. Subsequently, numerous federal laws, such as the Pregnancy Discrimination Act, the Age Discrimination in Employment Act, and the Americans with Disabilities Act, have been passed to protect employees. Each of these federal laws is discussed in Chapter 7. In addition, many individual states and municipalities have passed additional laws that protect certain groups of employees. The processes and outcomes associated with diversity initiatives that are rooted in compliance differ greatly from those that truly embrace diversity. These differences are presented in Exhibit 2.1.

One of the biggest challenges organizations face in managing diversity is overcoming some of the deep-set stereotypes that individual employees hold about certain groups in society. These stereotypes are often ingrained into individuals at a very young age and reinforced by family members, religious and educational institutions, and a local society in general. Reading 2.1, "Stereotype Threat at Work," discusses some of the challenges posed by stereotyping and proposes a means by which the consequences of stereotyping can be managed effectively in organizations.

Organization first starting paying attention to diversity in the mid 1960s, largely as a result of civil rights unrest and resultant legislation that was passed that prohibited discrimination in employment against a variety of groups. At that point, diversity was largely focused on compliance with the law and maintained that focus until the early 1980s.

EXHIBIT 2.1 Differences Between Legal Compliance and Managing Diversity

	Compliance with EEO laws	Managing Diversity
Impetus	Mandatory, forced, external	Voluntary, internal
Focus	Productivity, compliance	Understanding
Elements	Usually limited to race, gender, ethnicity	All elements of diversity
Company Culture	Fitting employees into existing culture	Creating a culture that is fluid, adaptive
Outcomes	Preferences, quotas	Equality
Time Frame	Short-term, one-shot	Continuous and ongoing
Scope	Independent of other HR activities and company strategy	Fully integrated with other HR activities and company strategy

By the mid-1980s, however, the focus of diversity training had shifted to improving working conditions by minimizing conflict between and among workers. In the mid-1990s, the focus evolved to understanding, accepting, and leveraging diversity as a means of enhancing organizational performance and remains as such to this day.[2]

The history of diversity in organizations is rooted in social justice and civil rights, but its evolution into a strategic human resource and business issue has resulted in diversity becoming somewhat of an amorphous concept. A recent Society for Human Resource Management survey conducted among HR executives revealed eight distinct definitions of diversity, with 71 percent of respondents indicating that their organizations did not have a formal definition of diversity.[3] Consequently, while many organizations embrace diversity in concept, they have not fully considered it as a strategic business issue relative to the mission and strategy of their organization. Indeed, the survey concluded with respondents identifying the needs to 1) more closely articulate the relationships between diversity initiatives and business results and 2) expand the focus away from diversity initiatives as a means of compliance with labor and employment laws.

Generational Diversity

Advances in healthcare are allowing us, as a society, to live longer, remain healthier longer, and remain in the workplace longer. Census data show 13 percent of the U.S. population is age 65 or older, with that percentage expected to grow to 20 percent, or 70 million individuals, by 2030.[4] As baby boomers continue to live longer and remain healthy, 80 percent of this group plan to continue working past age 65.[5] These "working retirements" suggest a very different type of employment relationship and a very different kind of lifestyle than that chosen by previous generations. A benefit to society is that these individuals' continued self-sufficiency may result in their being far less dependant on cash-strapped government pensions and healthcare programs. Organizations clearly benefit through the knowledge and contacts these individuals have developed through their years of professional experience.

This "graying of the workforce" can create a number of challenges, both real and perceived. Older workers are often perceived to be more resistant to change, particularly in implementing radically new programs and utilizing new technology that break from long-established ways of doing things. They may also have increased healthcare costs relative to their younger counterparts. As older workers remain in the workplace longer, fewer advancement opportunities are made available for younger workers, and in many instances, older workers command higher salaries despite the fact that they may have skills and training that are less current than those of younger workers, particularly relative to technology.

At the same time, it is important to remember that older workers can be as productive, if not more productive, than younger employees. The United States is a society that tends to devalue its older citizens, and such biases and predispositions are often found in organizational settings. However, older workers may have much more loyalty to their employers than their younger counterparts. They can also provide significant knowledge of the organization and industry as well as key contacts within their professional networks.

A number of employers have developed incentive programs for early retirement and then, in many cases, hired retirees back on a part-time basis or as consultants to take advantage of their knowledge and experience. Such programs need to be implemented carefully, however, as federal laws prohibit the setting of a mandatory retirement age in the overwhelming majority of occupations as well as using coercion to "encourage" older workers to retire.

Baby boomers—those born between 1945 and approximately 1962—are now in their mid-career years, and employers are finding that the supply of workers in this age bracket exceeds the demand for them in the middle- and senior-management-level ranks. As one moves up the management hierarchy, fewer and fewer positions are available, and the competition for senior management positions among boomers has become intense. Ironically, technology often plays a role here, as many middle- and senior-level-management positions have been eliminated because of flatter organizational structures and the increased use of information technology to perform functions previously done by middle managers. Many of these individuals will never progress beyond middle management. This can be greatly disconcerting for those who have been long-term employees of an organization and have seen their pre-boomer predecessors and coworkers rewarded and promoted for performance. Consequently, this creates a new HR challenge in managing these "plateaued" workers. Organizations need to find ways to retain them and keep them motivated despite the fact that they may have mastered their current responsibilities and aspire to advance in their careers. Slower and alternative career paths have become the norm for many of these workers. An increasing number are choosing to go out and start their own businesses.

Consequently, baby busters—those born during the declining birthrate years from approximately 1963 to the mid-1970s—also need to have lower expectations relative to the pace of their careers. The baby boomers of the previous generation have essentially created a bottleneck in the management hierarchy that baby busters find themselves behind. Until the baby boom generation has retired, there may be fewer opportunities in larger organizations for baby busters.

At the same time, this baby bust generation—which assumes low- and some mid-level-management positions—often receives higher wages than some of the baby boomers because of the forces of supply and demand. Far fewer individuals are in this lower age bracket, and in many industries, particularly rapidly growing ones—such as multimedia and the Internet—these workers have skills and training that the previous generation lacks, and they therefore command significant incomes in their early career years. In many organizations, workers in their thirties may be making as much as or more than coworkers twenty and thirty years their senior. The combination of limited supply of younger workers, high illiteracy among many new workforce entrants, and demand for skills fueled by technological change has resulted in a whole new workplace dynamic for this generation.

A different workplace dynamic is being created by what are known as Generation X employees. Generation X is those born from the mid-1960s to the late 1970s. Many of these individuals were raised in families of divorce and may have developed a tolerance for upheaval and readjustment. They witnessed firings and layoffs of family members, which may greatly influence their limited loyalty to an employer. They have also been using computers and other advanced technologies all their lives and have been exposed since birth to near-constant change in their everyday lives. More important, they bring attitudes and perceptions about work that differ significantly from those of preceding generations. These include an expectation of increased employee self-control; perceptions of themselves as independent contractors or consultants rather than as employees; less interest in job security; no expectations of long-term employment; and a demand for opportunities for personal growth and creativity.[6]

Generation Y employees, sometimes called the Baby Boom Echo, are those born after 1979. They are just beginning to enter the workforce and represent a cohort that is as large as the baby boom generation. Like the Generation X cohort, they have high comfort levels with technology but also tend to bring a more global and tolerant outlook on life to the workplace, having been raised in more culturally diverse environments and been exposed to cultural differences through the media. Twenty-five percent live in a single-parent household.[7] They are often very entrepreneurial in nature and, on average, have shorter attention spans. They also may fail to see the need to work from an office or for a particular employer, opting for more transient and variable project work.[8]

Despite some of the acknowledged and pronounced disparity among them, different generations have been found to share some commonalities. First, they all value family and are wiling to make compromises and sacrifices in support of their family members. Second, they all want respect, although different generations do not define it the same way. Older workers expect their opinions to be considered, while younger workers simply want the opportunity to be heard. Third, all generations look for trustworthiness in leaders. Fourth, all generations have some resistance to change, which has less to do with age and more to do with how an individual is personally affected by change. Fifth, all generations look for opportunities to learn, grow, and develop. And, finally, everyone in

EXHIBIT 2.2 Generations in the Workplace[10]

Generation	Percentage of Workforce	Contributions	Leadership Preferences	"Fit" sought
Traditionalists (1922–1945)	8%	Diligent, stable, loyal, detail-oriented, focused, emotionally mature	Fair, consistent, direct, respectful	Contribution (experience, balance, caring)
Baby Boomers (1946–1964)	44%	Team-oriented, experienced, knowledgeable, loyal	Equality, democratic, personable, mission-focused	Relationships (security, coworkers)
Generation X (1965–1980)	34%	Independent, adaptable, creative, non-conforming	Direct, competent, informal, flexible, supportive	Job (challenge, participation, outcomes)
Generation Y/Millennials (1981–2000)	14% (increasing)	Optimism, multi-tasking, socially responsible, diverse, tech-savvy	Positive, mentor, motivational, organized	Culture (progressive, autonomous, fast-paced)

an organization, regardless of age, appreciates feedback on what they are doing and how they are performing.[9]

Generation Y, or millennials, has received a great deal of attention recently because of the fact that they are the current new entrants to the workforce, represent its growth and evolution, and have different needs than their predecessors. Exhibit 2.2 highlights some of the differences between the generations now part of the workforce.

Sexual Orientation

Sexual orientation has been an area of diversity that increasingly has been embraced by both large and small and public and private employers. Nine of the 10 largest corporations in the United States, as well as nearly 400 of the *Fortune 500* employers, now prohibit discrimination on the basis of sexual orientation.[11] More than 200 of these employers offer full benefits for domestic partners of employees regardless of sexual orientation, although extension of benefits to domestic partners was prompted by demands from gay and lesbian employees for equality in benefits.

Sexual orientation has also provided some challenges to employers from a legal perspective beyond compliance with non-discrimination statues. At this writing, California, New Hampshire, New Jersey and Vermont and Oregon all require employers to provide the equivalent of full spousal rights to employees who are part of a same-sex couple. The District of Columbia, Hawaii, Maine and Washington each have laws that provide for some spousal rights for same-sex couples. As of April 2009, Massachusetts, Connecticut, Iowa and Vermont allow same-sex individuals to legally marry. As a result, employers need to carefully review mandates of these laws relative to the provision of employee benefits.

While no federal law exists that prohibits discrimination in employment based on sexual orientation, a number of states and municipalities have passed nondiscrimination laws and ordinances. Canadian organizations and employers that are members of European Union countries are prohibited by statute from discriminating in employment on the basis of sexual orientation. In addition to feelings about equality, some organizations are motivated to address sexual orientation issues because of the bottom line. Surveys have shown 70 percent of gay and lesbian consumers to be brand-loyal to those companies that have progressive employment policies regarding sexual orientation. This gay and lesbian consumer market is estimated at $500 billion annually.[12]

Individuals with Disabilities

Individuals with disabilities are protected from discrimination in employment under the Americans with Disabilities Act of 1990, as is discussed in Chapter 7. Nonetheless, individuals with disabilities are often not included in diversity initiatives nor have they experienced full eradication of employment discrimination. There are 54 million Americans with disabilities; of those, nearly 70 percent who are capable of working are unemployed, making individuals with disabilities the demographic group with the highest rate of unemployment in the United States.[13] Many technological innovations are increasing the ability for individuals were severe disabilities to be employed, closing the gap between physical limitations and productivity. However, the lack of employment opportunities for individuals with disabilities has less to do with ability than with the fact that many supervisors do not understand the needs of employees with disabilities, and stereotypes about disabilities believed by supervisors and coworkers prevent individuals with disabilities from being fully integrated into the workplace.[14] Hence, diversity initiatives need to pay particular attention to misperceptions surrounding individuals with disabilities.

Employees with disabilities present organizations with a challenge uncommon to other dimensions of diversity. The disabled is one minority group that any individual can join at any time in the future and often sometimes unexpectedly. Because physical and mental ability of any employee is a variable dimension of diversity, employers need to pay special attention to disability issues. As the average age of the workforce increases and employees opt to stay employed for longer periods of time, disability issues will clearly escalate for most employers, particularly given the fact that many disabilities can develop later in life. Indeed, while 13 percent of the population aged 21 to 64 has a disability, 30 percent of those from 65 to 74 and 53 percent of those 75 and older have a documented disability.[15]

Employing Workers with Disabilities at Walgreens

While many employers have policies that encourage the recruiting and hiring of individuals with disabilities, few have gone as far as Walgreens, the national largest retail drugstore chain, to employ those with disabilities. In late 2007, Walgreens opened a brand-new state-of-the art distribution facility in Windsor, Connecticut, which was designed specifically to employ individuals with disabilities. This center was designed to be a model for future distribution centers, with a goal of having at least one-third of its jobs filled by individuals with disabilities. The Windsor location has exceeded that goal with 40 percent of its employees having a disclosed physical or cognitive disability. The facility has reported 20 percent increases in efficiency in its operations since process improvements were installed as accommodations as it expands to its full capacity of 800 employees.[16]

Diversity at Hasbro

Several years ago, Pawtucket, Rhode Island–based toy manufacturer Hasbro, Inc., rolled out a diversity initiative that was offered as a half-day workshop to all of its 8,000 employees. Called "D@H5p3," which stands for "diversity at Hasbro equals people, products and productivity," the program received an award from the Society for Human Resource Management. The program involves a series of three exercises related to diversity. The first, a variation of the game show Who Wants to Be a Millionaire, *focuses on the benefits diversity can have for a business. The second, an adaptation of Hasbro's Pokeman trading card game, facilitates an understanding of how cultural and individual differences impact an organization. The third uses Hasbro-manufactured toys, such as Lincoln Logs, to illustrate community-building and an individual's place as a responsible member of his or her community. The program was designed to allow participants to better understand diversity as a business and competitive issue for Hasbro, understand each individual's frame of reference relative to diversity, and identify opportunities for development and increased effectiveness that can be achieved through diversity. The response to the program was overwhelming, with individuals asking to be involved with future workshops about diversity.*[17]

Diversity at Texas Instruments

In approaching diversity, Texas instruments (TI) eschewed the conventional strategy of bringing in external consultants for mandatory training and instead focused on an approach that attempted to embed the ideals of inclusion throughout the organization. This approach involved the establishment of "business resource groups," which include groups formed on the basis of religion, race, gender, sexual orientation, and single-parent status. These groups' distinctions relative to traditional "affinity groups" supported by other employers is that the primary function of business resource groups at TI is business rather than social. All business resource groups are open to all employees, regardless of background. The diversity within these groups helps to make them unique relative to those found in other organizations. Under the mentorship of an executive-level sponsor, the groups focus not only on career issues but also on business issues, as each group is required to contribute to the company's success in some measurable way.[18]

Other Dimensions of Diversity

One of the most notable consequences of these new workplace dynamics is that there is now an increased emphasis on the management of professionals. With fewer and fewer nonprofessional employees in organizations, situations often arise where a highly skilled/trained employee reports to a direct supervisor who is not familiar with the nature of the work being performed by subordinates. These technical workers need and want more autonomy in their responsibilities and seek greater input and participation in their work activities. In response to this, some organizations have established two separate career tracks: technical/professional and managerial/administrative. However, managers who have oversight of technical areas in which their skills are not as well developed as those of their subordinates require us to re-evaluate the nature of supervision and develop alternative strategies for managing employees.

The use of project teams helps to address this issue. Here, a technical employee often reports to a technical supervisor yet is assigned to a project team, overseen by a project or engagement manager. This model, which has been used for many years in accounting, management consulting, and advertising, often involves technical workers being responsible to both the technical and project managers and can provide enhanced opportunities for employee skill and career development. However, this dual reporting relationship can be extremely frustrating for the technical employee who may receive conflicting requests from technical and project supervisors as well as for those supervisors who do not have full authority over their subordinates.

The employees of today, both younger workers and their older peers, have values and attitudes that stress less loyalty to the company and more loyalty to one's self and one's career than those exhibited by employees in the past. This is not surprising in light of the waves of corporate downsizing and layoffs and the manner in which they have eroded employee loyalty and commitment. Workers are generally staying with employers for far shorter periods than they did previously and are moving on to other opportunities, particularly those with smaller startup organizations in the same industry or with clients. Employees with higher levels of training, education, and skills demand more meaningful work and more involvement in organizational decisions that affect them. Employees are becoming much more proactive and taking their career management into their own hands rather than leaving this responsibility with their employer. Larger employers who wish to retain the experience and skills of their employees need to develop creative retention strategies to prevent the flight of employees who may be attractive to competitors. For example, both Charles Schwab and Solectron provide employees with stock options that vest only after the employee has been with the company for a given number of years. Both of these organizations have employees who have experiences that make them highly marketable. Requiring a certain length of service in order to receive full vesting benefits allows not only better retention but facilitates human resource planning efforts; both Schwab and Solectron can anticipate dates key employees might be more likely to consider separation.

Personal and family life dynamics also continue to evolve and create challenges for organizations. The increased incidence of single-parent families and dual-career couples creates issues around child and elder care, relocation, and "parental stigma" where employees, particularly managerial employees, who devote significant time to family issues are seen as less promotable and less committed to their careers and employers. This stigma has presented particular challenges for women. Nontraditional family arrangements, where opposite or same-sex partners share their lives and living expenses, place increased pressure on organizations to offer domestic partner benefits to employees equal to those that the organization provides to employees with legal spouses. Although the provision of domestic partner benefits has increased dramatically in both large and small organizations, political and religious groups continue to lobby against and fight such efforts and to call for boycotts of companies that provide benefits to nonmarried couples.

The need for greater balance between employees' work and home lives has resulted in employee preferences and demands for policies that provide for a more optimal balance. The proliferation of dual-career households and school vacation schedules of children has resulted in difficulties in scheduling vacation time away from the office. Employees are now using paid time off in a more episodic fashion, opting for several days at a time rather than the traditional one or two weeks at a time.[19] Three- and four-day "long weekend" vacations allow more flexibility for family schedules and also provide the benefit of allowing a shorter possible period of "disengagement" from work. Few executives and even lower-level employees are willing to go a week or more without maintaining some contact from work, preventing them from full "separation" from their jobs and not allowing a true vacation. However, shorter vacation periods can allow employees the appropriate time to disengage from work and truly reap the benefits of their time away from work, benefiting both the employee and employer.

Work/life balance issues tend to affect women more disproportionately than men, given that women are often the primary caretakers for family members. While there are no easy solutions to such challenges, one model of career development for women, called the kaleidoscope, suggests that women be allowed to shift the patterns of their careers, rotating through stages where career/life issues take on different relative emphasis.[20] During the early career years, goal achievement and challenge are emphasized as a woman pursues her career interests. During the mid-career years, issues of balance and accommodation relative to family demands are the priority with the organization understanding and supporting this pursuit of balance. In late career, issues of balance have been resolved, but preferences may differ, and acknowledgement is made of an individual woman's choice as to how she wants to balance career and life at that point.

Fathers also have particular challenges in balancing work and family, as an increasing number of men desire to become more involved in the lives and upbringing of their children: 53 percent say that the benefit they most desire is a flexible work schedule, and 82 percent view employers in a more positive light if they offer a flextime benefit. However, while 58 percent of men took advantage of their employer's paternity leave option, 31 percent fear that taking time off to attend to family would hurt their careers.[21]

An increasing number of employees are opting for nontraditional work relationships, often in the form of part-time work, independent consulting, or contingent or temporary employment. Workers opting for such arrangements often seek to enjoy more flexibility in their lives as well as the opportunity to have time to pursue other endeavors. Organizations encourage these arrangements, which allow them to enjoy lower costs in employing these workers and the added ease of being able to expand or contract their workforce as necessary. These workers, however, generally receive few or no benefits and obviously have little job security. Consequently, they tend to be less loyal to their employers than permanent, full-time employees. There is a growing trend for organizations to outsource or contract certain functions or activities outside of the organization, which simultaneously creates numerous entrepreneurial opportunities for individuals. Many plateaued baby boomers have, in fact, left their organizations and then taken their former employers on as clients.

Given the changes that have been taking place in the composition of the workforce and employee values and attitudes, it is not surprising that in recent years, organizations have become much more concerned about managing diversity. Understanding and appreciating diversity is critical for organizations, as the increasing proportions of various ethnic and minority groups in the American consumer population make it imperative for organizations to understand the needs and wants of these groups if they hope to effectively market goods and services to them. Consider the following U.S. Census Bureau predictions:

- By 2050, close to 50 percent of the U.S. population will be non-Caucasian.
- By 2005, the ethnic minority share of the workforce will be 28 percent, up from 22 percent in 1990 and 18 percent in 1980.
- By 2025, African-Americans will represent 14 percent of the population, up from 12 percent in 1994.
- By 2025, Hispanics will represent 17 percent of the population, up from 10 percent in 1994.
- By 2025, Asians and Pacific Islanders will represent 8 percent of the population, more than doubling from 3 percent in 1994.[22]

Diversity Initiatives at Intel

Intel, one of the world's leading manufacturers of computer chips, understands the importance of diversity in the workplace. In an industry where demand for trained professionals greatly exceeds supply, Intel has developed a creative program for recruiting and developing minority employees.

To assist with recruiting, Intel hired a leading consulting firm to assist it in identifying the ten colleges and universities with the highest minority enrollments in the field of circuitry design. Intel has also established an undergraduate minority scholarship fund that awards in excess of $1 million annually to undergraduate students. Although recipients are not required to work for Intel after graduation, a significant number of them opt to do so.

Intel has also established a college internship program whereby students are identified as high-potential employees as early as their sophomore year. Interns receive employment and are matched with mentors for their entire college careers. Those who choose to stay onboard after graduation are assigned to supervisors who provide specific training that will allow their proteges to develop a variety of skills that can be applied to different jobs within the organization and will willingly allow employees to transfer within the company in order to retain their services. As a result, Intel has seen the proportion of ethnic minorities in management positions jump from 13 to 17 percent in a four-year period, despite efforts by its competitors to recruit its talent away.[23]

There is probably no better way to understand and market to these groups than to have them represented as employees at all levels of the organization. In addition to this, diversity initiatives help to ensure that personal differences that have nothing to do with job performance are less likely to impact hiring, promotion, and retention decisions. Intense competition and tight labor market conditions make it imperative that such decisions result in the hiring and promotion of the most qualified individuals.

One popular strategy organizations are using for recruiting and retaining diverse talent is the support of employee network or affinity groups. Affinity groups can be formed around any commonality shared by employees, including ethnicity, age, disability, family status, religion, sexual orientation, and usually have some association with a culture or perspective that has faced challenges in either society or the organization. Employee networks or affinity groups can provide the organization with a number of benefits, including: 1) aiding in the recruiting and retention of employees from the affinity group; 2) gaining broader perspectives on the organization's employment practices and business strategy; and 3) assisting an organization with its consumer awareness and reach in the marketplace. Affinity groups can provide the organizations with heightened insights into the culture, perceptions, and needs and wants of various consumer groups as well as bridge gaps between the organizations and various potential consumer groups worldwide.

Managing Diversity at PepsiCo

PepsiCo has been one of the corporate leaders in promoting diversity among its employees, and its commitment to diversity includes holding senior executives themselves personally accountable for diversity. Each of PepsiCo's CEO's direct reports has responsibility for working with a specific group of employees in understanding the workplace issues each group, including white males, black employees, Latinos, gay and lesbian employees, and employees with disabilities, faces. However, each group's executive comes from outside the group being overseen and mentored. Executives identify high-performing, high-potential individuals within their groups, communicate the needs of each group to each other, and are held accountable for addressing the concerns of their assigned group. This level of executive commitment and accountability greatly distinguishes PepsiCo from its corporate peers relative to diversity.[24]

Affinity Groups at Frito-Lay and PepsiCo

The Frito-Lay snack food division of PepsiCo has enjoyed tremendous success as a result of the work of one of its affinity groups. The Latino Employee Network, known as Adelante, provided invaluable assistance during the development of Doritos' guacamole-flavored tortilla chips. Members of the group were actively involved in product development decisions related to taste and packaging to ensure that the product would be seen as authentic in the Latino community. The participation of Adelante in the development of guacamole-flavored Doritos resulted in one of the most successful new product launches in the company's history, with first-year sales in excess of $100 million.[25]

Corporate parent PepsiCo used an affinity group to push boundaries in creating awareness. During the 2008 Super Bowl telecast, PepsiCo purchased a multimillion-dollar advertising slot and aired an ad completely void of sound. The ad was created by and featured PepsiCo employees who are part of the employee group EnAble, which attempts to promote understanding and inclusion of individuals with disabilities. The ad featured two friends driving to the house of a third friend to watch a football game. Communicating only in American Sign Language, the two friends lamented the fact that they could not remember the house number of the third friend's home. They then proceed to drive slowly down the street, honking their horn repeatedly as lights flashed on in each house but one—the only one apparently undisturbed by the noise. The ad was designed not to sell a product but to create awareness with broad appeal and clearly displays PepsiCo's commitment to diversity.[26]

While affinity groups were traditionally found in only larger organizations, they are becoming increasingly popular in small to medium-sized organizations, aided by the fact that they require little to no expense to start up and maintain.[27] They are best aided when organization provides them with a structure, including a formal application process for recognition, complete with a mission, goals, and a leadership plan. They also tend to function best when encouraged to focus on solutions rather than problems.[28]

As a result, diversity management programs have become quite popular. In fact, an entire industry has developed around helping organizations manage diversity. However, many diversity initiatives are ill-conceived, not integrated with the organization's mission and objectives, and can create additional challenges above those for which they were designed to respond. Key decision-makers in organizations need to ask themselves what benefits diversity specifically provides their organization. There are numerous ways to implement diversity initiatives and different levels on which to understand diversity. There is no one best way to manage diversity in organizations; the optimal way is contingent on the organization, its people, its mission, and its culture. Diversity initiatives also have to make the critical decisions about where to draw the line, meaning which elements of diversity are incorporated into the initiative and which are excluded.

Diversity initiatives can present organizations with a complicated mosaic. Exhibit 2.3 presents a model of some of the individual dimensions of diversity. Both work-related and personal sources of diversity are presented. While most diversity initiatives cover some combination of personal dimensions, managers must remain cognizant of the work-related dimensions of diversity in ensuring that workers are managed and given job assignments that allow for both maximum satisfaction and productivity.

EXHIBIT 2.3 Individual Dimensions of Diversity

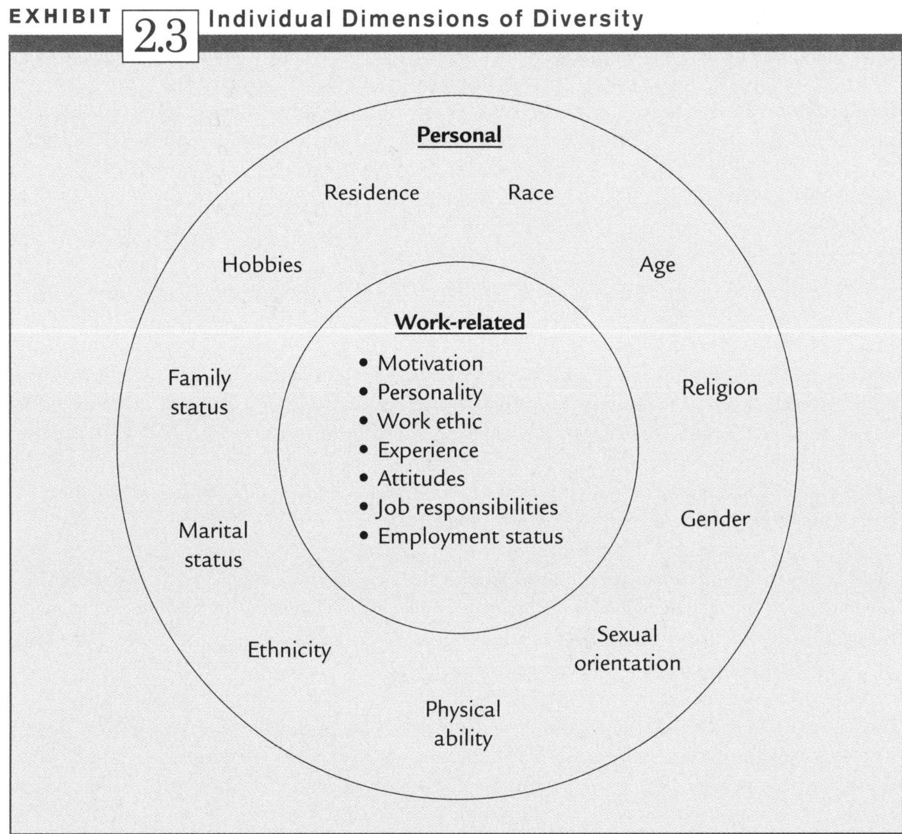

EXHIBIT 2.4 The Strategic Management of Diversity

1) Determine why diversity is important for the organization.
2) Articulate how diversity relates to the mission and strategic objectives of the organization.
3) Define diversity and determine how inclusive its efforts will be.
4) Make a decision as to whether special efforts should be extended to attract a diverse workforce.
5) Assess how existing employees, customers, and other constituencies feel about diversity.
6) Determine specific types of diversity initiatives that will be undertaken.

An understanding of and appreciation for diversity is both necessary and desirable for all organizations. However, it is important that those responsible for diversity initiatives realize that diversity can be a double-edged sword. Prior to undertaking any diversity issues, an organization needs to strategize its approach in dealing with diversity. This involves consideration of six issues, as illustrated in Exhibit 2.4.

Ethical Behavior

The recent series of corporate bankruptcies, scandals, and business meltdowns has reinvigorated the discussion and debate about ethical behavior in organizations. Ethics, however, go far beyond issues related to financial reporting and disclosure. Many areas of operations, as well as aspects of how employees are treated, leave a tremendous amount of discretion for employers relative to their practices and policies. Many executives report that an organization's reputation is a paramount concern in deciding whether to accept an offer of employment. A recent survey found that 65 percent of executives reported that they would thoroughly investigate the culture and value system of any prospective employer.[29] This same survey found that 40 percent of executives had resigned from an organization at least once because of the employer's perceived unethical business practices. Of this group, 75 percent reported that they did not expose the behavior at the time but 33 percent stated that, given recent corporate scandals, they would disclose and report the behavior if faced with the situation again.

While many organizations have long had ethics and social responsibility as central components of their mission and operating standards, the first federal government action related to ethics in organizations was the Federal Sentencing Guidelines for Organizations (FSGO) of 1991. The FSGO set minimum voluntary standards for employers in the areas of implementation of a code of ethical conduct, ethics training for officers and employees, high-level internal oversight of ethics and periodic measurement of the effectiveness of ethics initiatives. Compliance with the FSGO would result in lesser penalties if the case organizational misconduct. A 2004 amendment to the FSGO provides more specific and strict guidance for ethics training and also emphasizes the responsibility of the organization to create a company culture that embraces ethics, rather than just piecemeal compliance with FSGO guidelines.

There are numerous dimensions of the employment relationship where ethical decisions need to be made by senior management. The challenge faced by these individuals rests with the fact that ethics are not universally defined but rather subject to personal values and convictions. Ethical behavior is subjectively assessed as right or wrong, appropriate or inappropriate, and, in some cases, moral or immoral.

One area of ethical concern for HR is employee off-duty behavior. Winn-Dixie Stores, Inc., faced a very challenging situation when it terminated a truck driver with a 20-year history of exemplary service and performance when it was discovered he was a cross-dresser in his private life. The truck driver, dressed as a woman and assuming a female identity, accompanied his wife and family in public. Concerns about the company image caused Winn-Dixie to terminate his employment. He sued on the grounds that he was terminated for something that had nothing to do with his employment and job performance, but there is no law that universally protects employee's off-duty behavior. Winn-Dixie did win in court, but may have lost significantly in the court of public opinion. The story generated tremendous media attention that provided a good deal of support for the driver, from both the general public and his Winn-Dixie coworkers.[30]

The Winn-Dixie's example pertains to only one area of off-duty conduct. Employers also face dilemmas about off-duty behavior involving tobacco, alcohol and drug use, political and religious activity, and prior arrests and/or convictions. The majority of jobs are considered to be "at-will," which will be discussed in depth in Chapter 7, and employees have very limited protection at the federal level from arbitrary dismissal from their jobs. However, there has been a movement toward providing greater protection for employees in regard to their off-duty behavior. At this juncture, four states—New York, California, North Dakota, and Colorado—protect all off-duty, legal activity of employees.

Another increasingly important area of ethical consideration for employers is ownership of work. Given that a good deal of employee work in a knowledge economy involves the application of knowledge and skills in the development of new and improved products, services, and processes, conflicts have arisen concerning intellectual property rights. Employers have used nondisclosure and noncompete agreements to ensure that the work developed by its employees stays with the employer when employees leave. This is serious business for large and small employers alike. It is estimated that *Fortune 1000* organizations incur losses exceeding $45 billion annually from trade-secret theft.[31] Technology has made it much easier for such confidential information to be transmitted. No longer are documents stored in locked file cabinets in secure rooms; now they are contained on hard drives and diskettes that can be accessed more easily.

A related ethical dilemma is the "fairness" of noncompete clauses, which may address the employee going to work for a competitor or starting her or his own business. When accountants, consultants, attorneys, physicians, or other trained professionals decide to start their own business, do they have a right to bring clients with them and/or actively recruit former clients? Noncompete agreements have received mixed reviews in the courts. Some courts have found them to be binding legal contracts and hold former employees to their obligations. Other courts have found them to be invalid and unnecessarily restrictive of free enterprise and the right to compete. The ethical concern involves balancing the rights of employers to "own" work that was done for compensation by employees versus the rights of individuals to work for whom they chose, including themselves.

Intrapreneurship at Intel

One very unique approach to balancing ownership rights has been developed by Intel. Given the demand for services and products provided in Intel's markets, many employees have opted to start their own businesses, which then have competed against Intel. In lieu of requiring that employees sign noncompete agreements, Intel created a New Business Initiative (NBI) division that actively solicits new business proposals from its employees. The NBI functions as a kind of internal venture capital operation. It operates autonomously: Its staff receives proposals from employees and makes recommendations for start-up funding for those ventures it deems worthy. NBI has proven to be a highly successful retention tool and has afforded Intel the opportunity to avoid the often antagonistic work environment that results from noncompete agreements.[32]

In response to the accounting scandals that rocked the U.S. economy in the early part of the decade, Congress passed the Sarbanes-Oxley Act of 2002. The act was passed to eliminate both deception in accounting and management practices by increasing government oversight of financial reporting and holding senior executives more directly responsible for violations. As a result, organizations need to respond seriously to, and investigate, employee complaints of possible wrongdoing or fraud. Much of the responsibility will fall with HR to create policies and procedures to communicate anonymous, confidential concerns and to establish a review mechanism for such reports.[33]

An important provision of Sarbanes-Oxley is the protection it provides to "whistle-blowers," employees who provide information and/or assistance to investigators that assists in the review of potential violations of federal laws related to fraud against shareholders. Such whistle-blowers are protected only when information is provided to one of three sources: a federal regulatory or law enforcement agency; any member or committee of Congress; and a person with supervisory authority over the employee who has the authority to investigate such allegations. Reporting such activity to the media or even an HR manager may fall outside of the protection offered by the act. An employee is protected as long as he or she "reasonably believes" that the reported conduct is a violation, regardless of the outcome of any investigation. The Sarbanes-Oxley Act further mandates that all publically traded organizations disclose whether a code of ethics for senior officers has been adopted.

Given the increased concern for ethical behavior and accountability, it is clearly in an organization's best interest to establish some kind of Code of Ethics. Currently, more than 90 percent of Forbes 500 organizations have such codes and more than 82 percent have recently revised them.[34] Exhibit 2.5 presents the Code of Ethical and Professional Standards in Human Resource Management developed by the Society for Human Resource Management for its members and profession. Such industry-specific standards can greatly assist executives in developing an in-house code, but an organization's formal code needs to address a variety of issues specific to the organization. Frank Ashen, executive vice president for Human Resources at the New York Stock Exchange, has developed some guidelines for an organization's Code of Ethics that are presented in Exhibit 2.6.[35]

History has shown that the majority of organizations that undertake ethic awareness and training initiatives do so as a means of complying with legal mandates in attempting to minimize potential liability.[36] However, there is increasing evidence that ethics training and the creation and maintenance of a culture that stresses ethics has a positive impact on employee recruitment, morale, and retention. One survey of employees conducted by Deloitte and Touche found that the indicators of ethics sought by applicants and employees were the behaviors of supervisors and officers relative to giving proper credit for work performed, honesty in dealing with employees and coworkers, and treating people in a fair and just manner without showing preferential treatment.[37]

EXHIBIT 2.5 Society for Human Resource Management Code of Ethical and Professional Standards in Human Resource Management

Society for Human Resource Management
CODE PROVISIONS

Professional Responsibility

Core Principle

As HR professionals, we are responsible for adding value to the organizations we serve and contributing to the ethical success of those organizations. We accept professional responsibility for our individual decisions and actions. We are also advocates for the profession by engaging in activities that enhance its credibility and value.

Intent

- To build respect, credibility and strategic importance for the HR profession within our organizations, the business community, and the communities in which we work.
- To assist the organizations we serve in achieving their objectives and goals.
- To inform and educate current and future practitioners, the organizations we serve, and the general public about principles and practices that help the profession.
- To positively influence workplace and recruitment practices.
- To encourage professional decision-making and responsibility.
- To encourage social responsibility.

Guidelines

1. Adhere to the highest standards of ethical and professional behavior.
2. Measure the effectiveness of HR in contributing to or achieving organizational goals.
3. Comply with the law.
4. Work consistent with the values of the profession.
5. Strive to achieve the highest levels of service, performance, and social responsibility.
6. Advocate for the appropriate use and appreciation of human beings as employees.
7. Advocate openly and within the established forums for debate in order to influence decision-making and results.

PROFESSIONAL DEVELOPMENT

Core Principle

As professionals we must strive to meet the highest standards of competence and commit to strengthen our competencies on a continuous basis.

Intent

- To expand our knowledge of human resource management to further our understanding of how our organizations function.
- To advance our understanding of how organizations work ("the business of the business").

Guidelines

1. Pursue formal academic opportunities.
2. Commit to continuous learning, skills development and application of new knowledge related to both human resource management and the organizations we serve.
3. Contribute to the body of knowledge, the evolution of the profession and the growth of individuals through teaching, research, and dissemination of knowledge.
4. Pursue certification such as CCP, CEBS, PHR, SPHR, etc. where available, or comparable measures of competencies and knowledge.

ETHICAL LEADERSHIP

Core Principle

HR professionals are expected to exhibit individual leadership as a role model for maintaining the highest standards of ethical conduct.

Intent

- To set the standard and be an example for others.
- To earn individual respect and increase our credibility with those we serve.

Guidelines

1. Be ethical; act ethically in every professional interaction.
2. Question pending individual and group actions when necessary to ensure that decisions are ethical and are implemented in an ethical manner.
3. Seek expert guidance if ever in doubt about the ethical propriety of a situation.
4. Through teaching and mentoring, champion the development of others as ethical leaders in the profession and in organizations.

FAIRNESS AND JUSTICE

Core Principle

As human resource professionals, we are ethically responsible for promoting and fostering fairness and justice for all employees and their organizations.

Intent

To create and sustain an environment that encourages all individuals and the organization to reach their fullest potential in a positive and productive manner.

Guidelines

1. Respect the uniqueness and intrinsic worth of every individual.
2. Treat people with dignity, respect, and compassion to foster a trusting work environment free of harassment, intimidation, and unlawful discrimination.
3. Ensure that everyone has the opportunity to develop their skills and new competencies.
4. Assure an environment of inclusiveness and a commitment to diversity in the organizations we serve.
5. Develop, administer, and advocate policies and procedures that foster fair, consistent, and equitable treatment for all.
6. Regardless of personal interests, support decisions made by our organizations that are both ethical and legal.
7. Act in a responsible manner and practice sound management in the country(ies) in which the organizations we serve operate.

CONFLICTS OF INTEREST

Core Principle

As HR professionals, we must maintain a high level of trust with our stakeholders. We must protect the interests of our stakeholders as well as our professional integrity and should not engage in activities that create actual, apparent, or potential conflicts of interest.

Intent

To avoid activities that are in conflict or may appear to be in conflict with any of the provisions of this Code of Ethical and Professional Standards in Human Resource Management or with one's responsibilities and duties as a member of the human resource profession and/or as an employee of any organization.

Guidelines

1. Adhere to and advocate the use of published policies on conflicts of interest within your organization.
2. Refrain from using your position for personal, material, or financial gain or the appearance of such.
3. Refrain from giving or seeking preferential treatment in the human resources processes.
4. Prioritize your obligations to identify conflicts of interest or the appearance thereof; when conflicts arise, disclose them to relevant stakeholders.

USE OF INFORMATION

Core Principle

HR professionals consider and protect the rights of individuals, especially in the acquisition and dissemination of information while ensuring truthful communications and facilitating informed decision-making.

Intent

To build trust among all organization constituents by maximizing the open exchange of information, while eliminating anxieties about inappropriate and/or inaccurate acquisition and sharing of information.

Guidelines

1. Acquire and disseminate information through ethical and responsible means.
2. Ensure only appropriate information is used in decisions affecting the employment relationship.

3. Investigate the accuracy and source of information before allowing it to be used in employment-related decisions.
4. Maintain current and accurate HR information.
5. Safeguard restricted or confidential information.
6. Take appropriate steps to ensure the accuracy and completeness of all communicated information about HR policies and practices.
7. Take appropriate steps to ensure the accuracy and completeness of all communicated information used in HR-related training.

EXHIBIT 2.6 Guidelines For Developing a Code of Ethics/Conduct

- Need for Personal Integrity—a statement about dealing with individuals both inside and outside of the organization
- Compliance and Laws—addressing intolerance for violating employment, labor, or any other laws that affect the organization
- Political Contributions and Activity—a statement concerning the employer's policy in this domain, including solicitation of personal and/or financial support
- Confidential Information—a statement that identifies what is considered confidential and how such information should be treated, including a statement on employee expectations of privacy
- Conflicts of Interest—a statement that employees are expected to act in the employer's interests in carrying out their job duties along with disclosure requirements
- Books and Records—a statement stressing the practice of using accurate and accepted standards for financial reporting, as well as a prohibition against falsification
- Employment Policies—a general statement on how employees are to be treated, including issues of fairness, discrimination, and safety
- Securities Transactions—a statement on any restrictions that might exist relative to the purchase or sale of stock, as well as a statement and policy directed at insider trading
- Use of Company Assets—a statement that assets will be used only for business, rather than personal interests and needs
- Gifts, Gratuities, and Entertainment—a statement about such relationships and exchanges with clients, with further guidance provided for employees who deal with individuals from other countries where customs, laws, and business practices may differ from those domestically
- The Environment—a statement about the organization's relationship to its environment, if the area of business has an impact on the environment
- Compliance—a statement concerning how the Code of Ethics is to be communicated, certified, implemented, and enforced

Codes of ethics/conduct can be effective only if communicated to all employees and reinforced through the behaviors of senior managers and the organization's reward system. Codes that are developed, then exist, isolated from specific business practices and rewards are likely to have little impact on employees' behavior. Senior managers need to lead by example, modeling the kinds of behaviors expected of employees at all levels of the organization. Finally, such codes can succeed only if a mechanism exists to enforce compliance with their terms, including follow-up and corrective action.

Ethics training programs should not be developed in a piecemeal manner but rather tied in to, if not fully integrated with, the organization's mission and strategy. Only once this critical link has been established and communicated can an ethics training program be developed that truly has the potential to be effective. The ideal components of an ethics training program include: 1) mandatory attendance for all employees, including senior managers and officers; 2) a strict code of ethics that sets standards for behavior in areas such as responsibility, respect, fairness, and honesty—at a minimum; 3) presentations of relevant laws related to the organization's business and operations; 4) decision-making models that present questions employees can ask themselves when faced with ethical dilemmas (such as the possible repercussions of the decision); 5) in-house resources for questions related to ethics or for reporting perceived violations; and 6) role-playing scenarios that present possible ethical dilemmas an employee in an organization might face or a re-enactment of situations that have already taken place.[38]

The establishment of a code of ethics and ethics training program are critical components of an organization's ethics program, but unless there is ongoing communication concerning and oversight of ethics initiatives, continued attention to and compliance with ethics becomes less likely. In response to this, an increasing number of organizations are creating the position of ethics officer. This role is sometimes contained within the HR function, with compliance responsibility ultimately resting with the head of HR. However, most organizations prefer to have an ethics officer who has an accounting and/or legal background, given the proliferation of regulations related to financial reporting and compliance.[39] Particularly since the passage of Sarbanes-Oxley, HR members usually do not have the specialized knowledge and technical skills to understand the intricacies of financial compliance.

Regardless of whether HR oversees the organization's ethics program, HR and its staff face their own ethical dilemmas on a regular basis in the conduct of their own work. Ensuring that immigrant workers have proper documentation; classifying employees appropriately under the Fair Labor Standards Act; ensuring that hiring, performance management, and compensation systems are free from bias; and investigating charges of discrimination and harassment are just a few of the areas in which HR functions as the organization's ethical "compass." An HR officer frequently finds him or herself in a situation in which he or she is at odds with his or her own ethical standards and/or the ethical standards of the profession and the expectations or demands of senior managers or owners of the business.[40] Reading 2.2, "The Ethics of Human Resource Management," explores many of the ethical dilemmas that HR professionals face on a continuous basis in carrying out their job responsibilities.

Corporate Social Responsibility/Sustainability

While ethics programs focus on behavior and decision-making, corporate social responsibility (CSR) is more macro-focused and looks at how the organization's operations interface with and affect the larger society and world. The World Business Council for Sustainable Development defines CSR as "contributing to sustainable development by working to improve quality of life with employees, their families, the local community and stakeholders up and down the supply chain." CSR is often operationalized relative to what has been called the "triple bottom line," where considerations are paid simultaneously to profits (economic bottom line), people (social bottom line), and the planet (environmental bottom line). Organizations who successfully and simultaneously invest in all three areas vie for inclusion in the Dow Jones Sustainability World Index (DJSWI), which includes 250 worldwide organizations based on their successes relative to economic, environmental, and social performance. There is considerable debate as to whether the costs of being a social responsible organization and employer exceed the benefits, as outlined in Reading 2.3, "Does It Pay to Be Green? A Systematic Overview." However, since its inception, the DJSWI has outperformed the Standard & Poor 500 Index by 15 percent, according to PricewaterhouseCoopers.[41]

From an HR perspective, CSR initiatives have been found to have a direct positive impact on enhanced recruitment, retention of top performers and increased productivity.[42] A recent survey of North American business students revealed that 70 percent would not apply for a position with an employer they deemed to be socially irresponsible, and 68 percent responded that salary was less important than working for a socially responsible employer. Another survey found that MBA graduates would sacrifice an average of $13,700 in annual salary to work for a socially responsible employer.[43] An additional survey found that 81 percent of employees prefer to work for a company that has a good reputation for social responsibility, 92 percent of students and entry-level hires would be more inclined to work for environmentally friendly employers, and 80 percent of young professionals seek employment with organizations that have a net positive impact on the environment.[44]

Sustainability at General Electric

GE CEO Jeffrey Immelt launched the multibillion dollar Ecomagination initiative at GE in 2005 to enhance financial and environmental performance simultaneously in driving company growth. Consistent with the GE corporate citizenship philosophy—"make money, make it ethically, make a difference"—Ecomagination is designed to invest in clean technology research and development, introduce environmentally friendly products for consumers, and reduce GE's own gas emissions. Every dimension of the initiative, however, is drive by employees.

GE regularly sponsors employee contests to solicit ideas to reduce the use or waste of energy as well as engage employees in the design of environmentally friendly products and processes. To date, these have included energy-efficient appliances, compact fluorescent lighting, and wind turbine power. The company has developed an internal certification process that quantifies the environmental impacts and benefits of each new product or process on a scorecard, which are externally verified by an external source. The "bottom line" results are startling. From 2004 to 2009, GE's investment in "green" technologies doubled from $750 million to $1.5 billion. During the same period, its revenues from certified "green" technologies similarly doubled from $10 billion to $20 billion.[45]

Offshoring at Gap, Inc.

American apparel manufacturers have been subjected to great criticism in recent years over the offshoring of their manufacturing operations to less-developed countries and the corresponding deplorable working conditions and wages found in such "sweatshops." San Francisco–based Gap, Inc. was one of the first apparel manufacturers to take action in this area with the establishment of its Global Compliance program. Initially started in 1992, the program sets standards for labor, environmental, and health and safety standards for all of the organization's third-party manufacturers. The initial program has evolved into a full company function of more than ninety full-time employees, called vendor compliance officers, who work strictly on ensuring compliance with the standards. These employees are based globally and represent twenty-five different countries of origin, with most working in countries or communities to which they are native. They conduct inspections of all existing as well as prospective facilities that may enter into manufacturing contracts with Gap, Inc. Since 2003, Gap, Inc. has been publicly releasing a biannual Social Responsibility Report that outlines the company's efforts and successes in ethical outsourcing and labor relations and standards as well as its collaborative and partnership initiatives with all stakeholders. These include the development of an "integrated sourcing scorecard," which provides reports of each factory's compliance history and production standards relative to measures such as quality, innovation, cost, and speed to market.[46] *Such transparency in the apparel manufacturing industry is unprecedented and sets the benchmark for others relative to both CSR and reporting of success and initiatives.*

Organizational benefits of sustainability initiatives include improved public opinion and enhanced customer and government relations.[47]

HR usually plays a central role in any sustainability initiatives. While often strategic and operational in nature, they involve the need to communicate with and train employees as well as shape the organization's culture around issues of sustainability and CSR. Given the desire of many members of the workforce to be employed in socially responsibility organizations, such initiatives may also form the basis for the employment branding of an organization. Indeed, of the seventy-nine indicators of performance identified by the Amsterdam-based Global Reporting Initiative, which produces the generally accepted framework for corporate reporting on sustainability, twenty-four of these relate to human resource management. Performance management and compensation systems, whose design and oversight is usually under the purview of HR, can be revamped to provide incentives for sustainability and CSR initiatives. These are presented in Exhibit 2.7.[48]

Much as many employers are designating chief ethics officers, many are similarly designating chief sustainability officers. This trend reflects the fact that sustainability has become

EXHIBIT 2.7 Global Reporting Initiatives That Pertain to Human Resource Management[51]

Labor and Decent Work

1. Total workforce by employment type, employment contract, and region.
2. Total number and rate of employee turnover by age group, gender, and region.
3. Benefits provided to full-time employees not provided to temporary or part-time employees.
4. Percentage of employees covered by collective-bargaining agreements.
5. Minimum notice periods regarding significant operational changes, including whether specified in collective agreements.
6. Percentage of total workforce represented in joint management/worker/health and safety committees that help monitor and advise on occupational health and safety programs.
7. Rates of injury, lost days, and absenteeism and the total number of work-related fatalities by region.
8. Education, training, counseling, prevention, and risk-control programs in place to assist workforce members, their families, or community members regarding serious diseases.
9. Health and safety topics covered in formal agreements with trade unions.
10. Average hours of training per year per employee.
11. Programs for skills management and lifelong learning that support the continued employability of employees and assist them in managing career endings.
12. Percentage of employees receiving regular performance and career development reviews.
13. Composition of governance bodies and breakdown of employees per category according to gender, age group, minority group membership, and other indicators of diversity.
14. Ratio of basic salary of men to women by employee category.

Human Rights

15. Total hours of employee training on policies and procedures concerning aspects of human rights relevant to operations.
16. Total number of incidents of discrimination and actions taken.
17. Operations identified in which the right to exercise freedom of association and collective bargaining may be at significant risk and actions taken to support these rights.
18. Operations identified as having significant risk for incidents of child labor and measures taken to contribute to the elimination of child labor.
19. Operations identified as having significant risk for incidents of forced or compulsory labor and measures to contribute to the elimination of forced or compulsory labor.
20. Total number of incidents of violations involving rights of indigenous people and actions taken.

Social

21. Nature, scope, and effectiveness of any programs and practices that assess and manage the impacts of operations on communities, including entering, operating, and exiting.

Economic

22. Coverage of the organization's defined benefit plan obligations.
23. Range of ratios of standard entry-level wage compared to local minimum wage at significant locations of operation.
24. Procedures for local hiring and proportion of senior management hired from the local community at significant locations of operation.

a key business issue and strategic focus for many organizations. It has been argued that we are fast approaching the day when an organization's "carbon statement" will be as prominent as its financial statements.[49] Indeed, pension funds, state controllers, institutional investors, and even investment bankers are already pressuring organizations to be responsive to environmental issues.[50] Despite a focus on environmental issues that began in the early 1990s, Mitsubishi International, Corp. did not designate a chief sustainability officer until early 2008. Mitsubishi's approach, however, is not piecemeal. The focus of its sustainability office is to look holistically at the effects of climate change, resource depletion, and energy uses and prices on the organization from a strategic planning standpoint rather than simply a compliance standpoint. This trend will undoubtedly accelerate in the near future.

Conclusion

The contexts in which HR is managed in today's organizations are constantly changing. The larger environments in which organizations operate can be in a state of constant change. Nowhere is this more evident than in the areas of technology, ethics, workforce composition, and globalization. Organizations of the twenty-first century cannot expect to be successful without an understanding of and response to these trends and changes. No longer do organizations utilize one set of manufacturing processes, employ a homogeneous group of loyal employees for long periods of time, or develop one set way of structuring how work is done and supervisory responsibility is assigned. Constant if not continuous changes in who organizations employ and what these employees do require HR practices and systems that are well-conceived and effectively implemented to ensure high performance and continued success.

More importantly, HR practices must constantly be reviewed and evaluated to allow an organization to respond to changes taking place in its environment. Nothing should be accepted as a "given." Failure to allow HR to assess and drive change initiatives can greatly compromise an organization's ability to remain competitive in an ever-changing marketplace and society.

Critical Thinking

1. What are the most important societal trends affecting HR today?
2. What are the most important workplace trends affecting HR today?
3. How well do you feel HR as a profession responds to these trends?
4. Predict societal changes that you believe might take place within the next ten years. What challenges will these changes present to organizations?
5. Predict workplace changes that you believe might take place within the next ten years. What challenges will these changes present to organizations?
6. How will HR be impacted by these changes? How can HR help organizations become more effective in meeting the challenges these changes present?

Reading 2.1

7. Should managers promote open discussion of stereotypes as part of a strategy for managing diversity? What risks and potential advantages and disadvantages are inherent with such a strategy?

Reading 2.2

8. What involvement should HR have with organization-wide ethics initiatives? What organizational decisions or policies might challenge the professional ethics of an HR professional? What day-to-day challenges do line managers face relative to HR-related ethical issues?

Reading 2.3

9. Identify obstacles that may prohibit the potential "win-win" outcomes (the simultaneous better environmental and financial performance) associated with sustainability. Should HR be involved with sustainability issues? Identify the benefits, costs, and challenges with such involvement.

Exercises

1. In small groups, identify and discuss the significant trends related to diversity, ethics and sustainability that impact your college, university, or employer. What challenges do these trends present? What initiatives have been established thus far to meet these challenges?
2. List various groups who are often stereotyped in society or school (i.e., members of religious and racial groups, individuals with disabilities, athletes, sexual minorities, etc.), the stereotypes associated with each group, and the basis for the formation of these stereotypes. For individuals who belong to one of these groups, share how it feels for you to be stereotyped and judged as such.
3. Visit the Web site of the U.S. Bureau of Labor Statistics (http://www.bls.gov). What trends do you see taking place in the data presented? What information at the site is most useful for organizations in assessing workforce trends?

Chapter References

1. Pomeroy, A. "Cultivating Female Leaders" *HR Magazine*, 52, (4), April, 2007, 44–50.
2. Anand, R. and Winters, M. "A Retrospective View of Corporate Diversity Training from 1964 to the Present" *Academy of Management Learning & Education*, 7, (3), 356–372, 2008.
3. Society for Human Resource Management. 2007 State of Workplace Diversity Management. Alexandria, VA: Society for Human Resource Management. 2008.
4. Society for Human Resource Management, *Workplace Visions*, No. 4, 2001.
5. Ibid.
6. Harvey, B. H. "Technology, Diversity and Work Culture–Key Trends in the Next Millennium," *HR Magazine*, 45, (7), July, 2000, p. 59.
7. Society for Human Resource Management, *Workplace Visions*, No. 2, 2001.
8. Robinson, K. "Get Ready to Mediate among Generations, Speakers Advise," *HR News*, December 2002.
9. Deal, J. *Retiring the Generation Gap: How Employees Young & Old Can Find Common Ground.* San Francisco: Jossey-Bass, 2006.
10. Compiled from AARP, Leading A Multigenerational Workforce. Washington, DC 2007; Sabatini, F., Hartmann, D. and McNally, K. "The Multigenerational Workforce: Management Implications and Strategies for Collaboration. Boston: Boston College Center for Work & Family, 2008; Tyler, K. The Tethered Generation. *HR Magazine*, May, 2007, 41–46; Zemke, R., Raines, C. and Filipczak, B. Generations At Work: Managing the Clash of Veterans, Boomers Xers and Nexters in Your Workplace. New York: American Management Association, 2000; Eisner, S. Managing Generation Y. *SAM Advanced Management Journal*, 70, (4), 4–15, Autumn 2005.
11. Human Rights Campaign Workplace Project. www.hrc.org
12. Cadrain, D. "Equality's Last Frontier," *HR Magazine*, 48, (3), March 2003, pp. 64–68.
13. Cohen, S. "High-Tech Tools Lower Barriers for the Disabled," *HR Magazine*, October 2002, pp. 60–65.
14. Gray, C. "Employees A-Plenty: The Emerging Workforce of People with Disabilities," Society for Human Resource Management, *Mosaics*, 8, (1), 2002.
15. Wells, S. "Counting on Workers with Disability" *HR Magazine*, 53, (4), April, 2008, 45–49.
16. Wells, S. "Counting on Workers with Disability" *HR Magazine*, 53, (4), April, 2008, 45–49.
17. Leonard, B. "Reflecting the Wide World of HR," *HR Magazine*, July 2002, pp. 50–56.
18. Frase-Blunt, M. "Thwarting the Diversity Backlash," *HR Magazine*, June 2003, pp. 137–143.
19. Gurchiek, K. "Workers Opt for Long Weekends Over Big Vacations" *Society for Human Resource Management, article 021719*, published at www.shrm.org/hrnews_/published/articles/CMS_021719.asp May 31, 2007.
20. Mainiero, L. and Sullivan, S. "Kaleidoscope careers: An alternate explanation for the "opt-out revolution" *Academy of Management Executive*, 19, (1), 106–123 (2005).
21. Gurchiek, K. "Providing Work/Life Benefits for Dads Can Give Employers an Edge" *Society for Human Resource Management, article 021880.* published at www.shrm.org/hrnews_/published/articles/CMS_021880.asp June 15, 2007.
22. Minehan, M. "The Fastest Growing U.S. Ethnic Groups," *HR Magazine*, 42, (5), May 1997.
23. Adams, M. "Diversity: Building a Rainbow One Stripe at a Time," *HR Magazine*, 43, (8), August 1998.
24. Rodriguez, R. "Diversity Finds Its Place" *HR Magazine*, 51, (8), August 2006, 56–61.
25. Rodriguez, R. "Diversity Finds Its Place" *HR Magazine*, 51, (8), August 2006, 56–61.
26. Hastings, R. "Pepsi Listens to Employees, Airs 60 Seconds of Silence" *Society for Human Resource Management, article 24468*, published at www.shrm.org/hrnews_/published/articles/CMS_24468.asp January 31, 2008.
27. Arnold, J. "Employee Networks" *HR Magazine*, 51, (6), June 2006, 145–152.
28. Arnold, J. "Employee Networks" *HR Magazine*, 51, (6), June 2006, 145–152.
29. Leonard, B. "Corporate Scandals Will Slow the Pace of Executive Recruitment," *HR Magazine*, October 2002, pp. 27–28.
30. Hirschman, C. "Off Duty, Out of Work," *HR Magazine*, February 2003, pp. 51–56.
31. Society for Human Resource Management, *Workplace Visions*, No. 5, 2001, p. 4.
32. Ibid.
33. Fitzgerald, P. W., Warren, S., Bergman, J., Teeple, M. and Elrod, G. B. "Employment Law Implications of the Sarbanes-Oxley Act of 2002: What Should Human Resource Managers Do Now?" Paper presented at the Academy of Legal Studies in Business Annual Meeting. Nashville, TN, 2003.
34. Ashen, F. Z. "Corporate Ethics–Who Is Minding the Store?" *Society for Human Resource Management White Paper.* www.shrm.org/hrresources/whitepapers_published/CMS_00248.asp
35. Ibid.
36. Tyler, K. "Do the Right Thing" *HR Magazine*, 50, (2), February, 2005, 99–102.
37. Gurchiek, K. "Report Lines Work/Life Balance to Ethical Behavior" *Society for Human Resource Management, article 021322*, published at www.shrm.org/hrnews_/published/articles/CMS_023659.asp, April 23, 2007.
38. Tyler, K. "Do the Right Thing" *HR Magazine*, 50, (2), February, 2005, 99–102.
39. Buss, B. "Corporate Compass" *HR Magazine*, 49, (6), June 2004, 127–132.
40. Pomeroy, A. "The Ethics Squeeze" *HR Magazine*, 51, (3), March, 2006, 48–55.
41. Fox, A. "Corporate Social Responsibility Pays Off" *HR Magazine*, 52, (8), August, 2007, 43–48.
42. Willard, B. The Sustainability Advantage: Seven Business Case Benefits of a Triple Bottom Line. New Society Publishers, 2002.
43. Fox, A. "Corporate Social Responsibility Pays Off" *HR Magazine*, 52, (8), August, 2007, 43–48.
44. Fox, A. "Getting in the Business of Being Green" *HR Magazine*, 53, (6), June 2008, 45–50.
45. Fox, A. "Corporate Social Responsibility Pays Off" *HR Magazine*, 52, (8), August, 2007, 43–48.
46. Ansett, S. "Labor Standards in the Supply Chain: The Steep Climb to Sustainability" *Perspectives on Work*, Winter 2006, 9, (2), 11–13.
47. Fox, A. "Getting in the Business of Being Green" *HR Magazine*, 53, (6), June 2008, 45–50.
48. Fox, A. "Getting in the Business of Being Green" *HR Magazine*, 53, (6), June 2008, 45–50.
49. Woodward, N. "New Breed of Human Resource Leader" *HR Magazine*, 53, (6), June 2008, 52–56.
50. Fox, A. "Getting in the Business of Being Green" *HR Magazine*, 53, (6), June 2008, 45–50.
51. Fox, A. "Getting in the Business of Being Green" *HR Magazine*, 53, (6), June 2008, 45–50.

READING 2.1

Stereotype Threat at Work

Loriann Roberson and Carol T. Kulik

Executive Overview

Managing diversity in organizations requires creating an environment where all employees can succeed. This paper explains how understanding "stereotype threat"—the fear of being judged according to a negative stereotype—can help managers create positive environments for diverse employees. While stereotype threat has received a great deal of academic research attention, the issue is usually framed in the organizational literature as a problem affecting performance on tests used for admission and selection decisions. Further, articles discussing stereotype threat usually report the results of experimental studies and are targeted to an academic audience. We summarize 12 years of research findings on stereotype threat, address its commonplace occurrence in the workplace, and consider how interventions effective in laboratory settings for reducing stereotype threat might be implemented by managers in organizational contexts. We end the paper with a discussion of how attention to stereotype threat can improve the management of diversity in organizations.

Ongoing demographic trends (increasing percentages of African Americans, Hispanics, and Asians in the American workforce, an aging population, expanding female labor force participation) have made diversity a fact of organizational life. When these trends were first identified in the mid-1980s, they were heralded as an opportunity for organizations to become more creative, to reach previously untapped markets, and in general to achieve and maintain a competitive advantage (Cox, 1994; Robinson & Dechant, 1997; Thomas & Ely, 1996).

However, employee diversity does not *necessarily* boost creativity, market share, or competitive advantage. In fact, research suggests that left unmanaged, employee diversity is more likely to damage morale, increase turnover, and cause significant communication problems and conflict within the organization (Jackson et al., 1991; Jehn, Neale, & Northcraft, 1999; Tsui, Egan, & O'Reilly, 1992; Zenger & Lawrence, 1989). Thus, "managing diversity" has become a sought-after managerial skill, and concerns about effective diversity management have spawned an industry of diversity training programs, diversity videos, and diversity consultants. But despite several decades of effort and millions of dollars invested, the evidence suggests that organizations continue to do a poor job of managing diversity. A recent comprehensive report concluded that organizations rarely are able to leverage diversity and capitalize on its potential benefits (Hansen, 2003; Kochan et al., 2003). What's the problem? Are we missing a key piece of the diversity management puzzle?

Most of the attention in the diversity management literature has been focused on the organizational decision maker—the manager who is prejudiced against certain groups and who allows these prejudices to influence how he or she treats employees. These individual-level prejudices become institutionalized—meaning, they become embodied in organizational policies and practices that systematically disadvantage some employees. In their efforts to reduce discrimination, organizations are increasingly concerned about hiring non-prejudiced managers, redesigning biased selection, appraisal, and promotion procedures, and generally eradicating stereotypes from managerial decision making (Greengard, 2003; Rice, 1996). If we eliminate stereotypes from organizational decision making, the logic goes, we'll create an organization where all employees can flourish and advance.

Unfortunately, even if an organization were successful in hiring only non-prejudiced managers and eliminating stereotypes from its formal decision making, stereotypes would still exist in broader society. As a result, every employee walking through the door of the organization knows the stereotypes that might be applied to him or her and wonders whether organizational decision makers and co-workers will endorse those stereotypes. Here, we discuss the effects of these stereotypes, and highlight an important aspect of diversity management that has not received much attention by diversity or management scholars: stereotype threat, the fear of being judged and treated according to a negative stereotype about members of your group (Steele, Spencer, & Aronson, 2002). Research on stereotype threat has shown that societal stereotypes can have a negative effect on employee feelings and behavior, making it difficult for an employee to perform to his or her true potential. Research has also indicated that stereotype threat can result in employees working harder, but not better. When stereotype threat is present, performance declines. Therefore, a non-prejudiced manager who uses objective performance indicators as a basis for decision making risks underestimating the employee's true ability. When an organizational context contains the conditions that create stereotype threat, nontraditional employees experience additional barriers to success despite the good intentions of everyone involved. Therefore, stereotype threat places certain demands on the manager of diverse employees—demands to create conditions that minimize the occurrence of stereotype threat, so that all employees can perform effectively.

Stereotype threat has been discussed almost exclusively as an issue for high stakes testing, particularly in educational arenas. For example, we're all familiar with the opportunities that hang on scores from tests such as the Scholastic Aptitude Test (SAT), the Graduate Record Examination (GRE) and the Graduate Management Achievement Test (GMAT): without the "right" scores, a student won't be able to get into the best college for his or her chosen field. In 1999, PBS aired a documentary concluding that stereotype threat was suppressing the standardized test performance of African American students (Chandler, 1999). These effects on high stakes tests are important, but stereotype threat is not limited to African-American students taking large-scale standardized academic tests. It is also present in the everyday, routine situations that are a part of all jobs. Thus, knowledge of stereotype threat and its corrosive effects on performance is needed to understand the work experience of members of stereotyped groups and to manage diversity more effectively in the organization. In this article, we answer the following questions: What is stereotype threat and what are its effects? How can stereotype threat be reduced?

We begin with a short review of the concept and the research evidence. We then describe the conditions that increase the risk of stereotype threat. Because these conditions regularly occur in the workplace, stereotype threat is also likely to be a common part of many people's work experience. Finally, we present strategies for reducing stereotype threat from the academic research literature, and consider if and how those strategies might be applied in organizations. We also discuss how attention to stereotype threat adds value to current organizational approaches to managing diversity.

Stereotype Threat at Work

Every job involves being judged by other people, whether you are giving a sales presentation to clients, representing your work team at a meeting, or showing your boss your work for some informal feedback. Being evaluated can raise anxieties for anyone. Apprehension in these kinds of situations is a common phenomenon, and in fact, a little anxiety can even boost performance (Cocchiara & Quick, 2004; Reio & Callahan, 2004; Yerkes & Dodson, 1908). But anxieties can be heightened for those employees who are members of a negatively stereotyped group, especially when they are performing a kind of task on which, according to the stereotype, members of their group do poorly. Consider these statements by people who are members of stereotyped groups:

> *From a marketing manager: "You can see in someone's eyes when you are first introduced that you're dead in the water just because you're seen as old." Many older workers refer to "the look" on someone's face as they are introduced. A 57 year old accounts supervisor recounted that on meeting someone face to face for the first time, she was told with a tone of disappointment, "Oh, you have such a young voice on the phone" (Blank & Shipp, 1994).*
>
> *From a White loan officer (concerned about being perceived as racist or sexist): "I'm always worried about how I was heard. How will I be interpreted? Did I say the wrong thing?" (Blank & Shipp, 1994).*
>
> *From a Black manager: "I felt Whites had a lot of negative ideas about Blacks. I felt evaluated when I asked questions. Asking questions became painful for me" (Dickins & Dickins, 1991).*
>
> *From an overweight worker: "... I work extra hard because I know the stereotype, and I feel I need to prove myself. I work harder than most of my coworkers who do the same job. Yet my (skinny, size-10) boss continually talks about me behind my back to my coworkers - she says that I'm lazy and that I don't take any initiative, and who knows what else. She sees me for maybe half an hour out of the work week, which is hardly enough time to judge me on my work ... It doesn't matter that I know the job inside-out, or that my customer-service skills are topnotch. It doesn't matter that I'm on time and do any stupid little task that I'm asked. All that matters is the width of my ass" (Personal blog, 2005).*

The individuals quoted here are members of different identity groups, but they all voice a common concern: the fear of being seen and judged according to a negative stereotype about their group, and the concern that they might do something that would inadvertently confirm the negative stereotype (Steele, 1997; Steele et al., 2002). These individuals are experiencing "stereotype threat."

Stereotype threat describes the psychological experience of a person who, while engaged in a task, is aware of a stereotype about his or her identity group suggesting that he or she will not perform well on that task. For example, a woman taking a math test is familiar with the common stereotype that "girls aren't good at math." Or a Black faculty member preparing his case for promotion is aware that some people believe that Blacks are intellectually inferior. This awareness can have a disruptive effect on performance—ironically resulting in the individual confirming the very stereotype he or she wanted to disconfirm (Kray, Thompson, & Galinsky, 2001). Anyone can experience anxiety while performing a task with important implications (a test to get into graduate school or a presentation to a big client), but stereotype threat places an *additional* burden on members of stereotyped groups. They feel "in the spotlight," where their failure would reflect negatively not only on themselves as individuals, but on the larger group to which they belong. As singer and actress Beyoncé Knowles said in an interview with *Newsweek* in 2003: "It's like you have something to prove, and you don't want to mess it up and be a negative reflection on black women" (quoted in Smith, 2004, p. 198).

In the first (and now classic) study on stereotype threat, Claude Steele and Joshua Aronson (1995) asked Black and White students to take a very difficult test. The test was composed of items from the verbal section of the Graduate Record Examination, and it was deliberately designed to tax students' ability. For some students, this test was described simply as a laboratory problem-solving task. However, for other students, the test was described as a "genuine test of your verbal abilities and limitations." The important difference between these two descriptions was that race stereotypes were irrelevant in the "laboratory task" version—there was no reason for a Black participant to expect race to impact his or her performance, or to think that other people might expect race to have an impact. However, in the scenario where the test was described as a genuine test of abilities and limitations (the stereotype threat condition), the racial stereotype (that Blacks lack intellectual ability) *was* relevant, and the researchers predicted that Black participants would be both aware of the stereotype and want to avoid confirming it.

When Steele and Aronson examined the results, they found that White students' performance was largely unaffected by the test instructions—the White students performed about equally well whether the test had been described as an ability test or as a laboratory problem-solving task. However, the instructions made a big difference in the performance of Black students. They performed less well in the ability test condition than in the problem-solving condition—even though the test was equally difficult in both conditions. In fact, after Steele and Aronson controlled for pre-study differences in ability (measured by the students' SAT scores), they found that Black and White students in the laboratory problem-solving condition performed about the same—but Black students underperformed relative to Whites in the ability test condition (Steele & Aronson, 1995).

This basic experimental design, in which researchers compare the performance of two groups (one group is negatively stereotyped, the other is not) in two task conditions (one condition presents the task as stereotype-relevant, the other does not), has been replicated many times over the last twelve years with consistent results. The negatively stereotyped group underperforms when the stereotype is seen as relevant to the task. This research is summarized in Table 1.

As the table shows, the stereotype threat phenomenon has been documented in a large number of groups, across a wide range of diversity dimensions, and in many different performance domains. In the top (unshaded) part of the Table, the "Who was affected?" column includes the people we generally think of as disadvantaged in the workplace due to negative stereotypes—racial and ethnic minorities, members of lower socio-economic classes, women, older people, gay and bisexual men, and people with disabilities. The academic literature sometimes describes members of these groups as "stigma conscious" (Aronson et al., 1999). That means that members of these groups can be very aware of the social stereotypes other people associate with their group. Since the relevant stereotype is very likely to come to mind, concerns about stereotype confirmation are easily aroused. As a result, very subtle contextual variations (a slight wording difference in the way a test is described, for example) may be enough to make the stereotype salient and disrupt performance.

But research has shown that this phenomenon does not apply only to people in disadvantaged groups. In fact, the bottom (shaded) part of Table 1 shows that even members of high status groups can experience stereotype threat. For example, we don't normally think of White men as being disadvantaged in the workplace. White men generally enjoy more hiring opportunities, higher salaries, and more organizational status than women or members of racial minority groups with comparable education and ability (Hite, 2004; Parks-Yancy, 2006). However, even high status groups have some negative stereotypes associated with them, and one of the stereotypes most strongly associated with the White group is the belief that Whites are racist (Frantz et al., 2004). The research suggests that many Whites are chronically concerned with not appearing racist (and inadvertently confirming the stereotype). Therefore, task situations that are described as dependent on racial attitudes can trigger stereotype threat in Whites (and result in participants looking more prejudiced than they might actually be) (Frantz et al., 2004).

Further, members of any group may experience stereotype threat when their identity group is negatively compared with another group. For example, comparative stereotypes suggest that Whites have less mathematical ability than Asians, men are less effective in processing affective (emotional) information than women, and White men have less athletic prowess than Black men. These negative comparisons can induce stereotype threat, and members of the target group demonstrate the short-term performance detriments associated with stereotype threat, as the studies listed in the table have found. One conclusion that can be drawn from looking at the table is that stereotype threat can affect all of us because each of us is a member of at least one group about which stereotypes exist. If you think about the stereotypes that could be applied to your own social group, you might recall situations where you personally experienced stereotype threat. If you think about the stereotypes that could apply to your employees, you can also identify the situations where they might be vulnerable to stereotype threat.

The research referred to in the table has decisively shown that stereotype threat has a negative impact on short term performance. But an unresolved question is why does stereotype threat have this negative impact? Researchers have suggested several different answers to this question

Table 1 Examples of Stereotype Threat[1]

Who Was Affected?	How Did the Researchers Create Stereotype Threat?	What Stereotype Was Activated?	What Happened?
Black students	Told the students that they were about to take a very difficult test that was a "genuine test of your verbal abilities and limitations"	"Blacks lack intellectual ability"	The students performed less well on the test
Latino students	Told the students that they were about to take a very difficult mathematical and spatial ability test that would provide a "genuine test of your actual abilities and limitations"	"Latinos lack intellectual ability"	The students performed less well on the test
Low socio-economic status (SES) students	Asked the students to provide background information including their parents' occupation and education, then told them they were about to take a difficult test that would "assess your intellectual ability for solving verbal problems"	"Low SES students lack intellectual ability"	The students attempted to solve fewer problems and had fewer correct answers on the test
Women	Reminded the women that "previous research has sometimes shown gender differences" in math ability, then asked them to take a test that "had shown gender differences in the past"	"Women have weak math ability"	The women performed more poorly on the math test
Older individuals (60 years and older)	Gave the older people a series of memory tests and presented them with a list of "senile" behaviors ("can't recall birthdate") too quickly for conscious awareness. Then researchers gave the older people the memory tests a second time	"Older people have bad memory"	The older people had a significant decline in memory performance from pretest to posttest
Gay and bisexual men	Asked the men to indicate their sexual orientation on a demographic survey, then videotaped the participants while they engaged in a "free play" activity with children	"Gay men are dangerous to young children"	Judges rated the men as more anxious and less suitable for a job at a daycare center
People with a head injury history	Told participants that a "growing number" of neuropsychological studies find that individuals with head injuries "show cognitive deficits on neuro psychological tests," then gave participants a series of tests assessing memory and attention	"Persons with a head injury history experience a loss of cognitive performance"	The participants performed worse on tests of general intellect, immediate memory, and delayed memory
Whites	Told participants that a "high proportion of Whites show a preference for White people" before asking them to complete the IAT (implicit attitude test) that would measure their "unconscious racial attitudes toward Blacks and Whites"	"Whites are racist"	The participants had a larger IAT effect (the difference in response time between incompatible and compatible trials), suggesting a preference for White faces
White students	Gave the students a packet of newspaper articles emphasizing a "growing gap in academic performance between Asian and White students" before asking them to take a very challenging math test	"White students have less mathematical ability than Asian students"	The students solved fewer problems on the math test

Table 1 Continued

Who Was Affected?	How Did the Researchers Create Stereotype Threat?	What Stereotype Was Activated?	What Happened?
Men	Reminded participants that "it is a well-known fact that men are not as apt as women to deal with affect ... and to process affective information as effectively" then asked them to indicate whether a series of words were "affective" or not	"Men are less capable than women in dealing with affective (emotional) information"	The men made more errors on the task
White men	Told the men that they would be engaged in a golf task that measured their "natural athletic ability." The men completed a demographic survey that included a question about their racial identity, then took the test	"White men have less athletic prowess than Black men"	The men made more strokes (performed worse) on the golf task

[1]The research summarized in this table include the following articles: Steele, C. M., & Aronson, J. (1995). Stereotype threat and the intellectual test performance of African Americans. *Journal of Personality and Social Psychology*, 69, 797–811; Gonzales, P. M., Blanton, H., & Williams, K. J. (2002). The effects of stereotype threat and double-minority status on the test performance of Latino women. *Personality and Social Psychology Bulletin*, 28, 659–670; Croize, J., & Claire, T. (1998). Extending the concept of stereotype threat to social class: The intellectual underperformance of students from low socioeconomic backgrounds. *Personality and Social Psychology Bulletin*, 24, 588–594; Spencer, S. J., Steele, C. M., & Quinn, D. M. (1999). Stereotype threat and women's math performance. *Journal of Experimental Social Psychology*, 35, 4–28; Bosson, J. K., Haymovitz, E. L., & Pinel, E. C. (2004). When saying and doing diverge: The effects of stereotype threat and self-reported versus non-verbal ability. *Journal of Experimental Social Psychology*, 40, 247–255; Suhr, J. A., & Gunstad, J. (2002). "Diagnosis threat": The effect of negative expectations on cognitive performance in head injury. *Journal of Clinical and Experimental Neuropsychology*, 24, 448–457; Frantz, C. M., Cuddy, A. J. C., Burnett, M., Ray, H., & Hart, A. (2004). A threat in the computer: The race implicit association test as a stereotype threat experience. *Personality and Social Psychology Bulletin*, 30, 1611–1624; Aronson, J., Lustina, M. J., Good, C., Keough, K., Steele, C. M., & Brown, J. (1999). When White men can't do math: Necessary and sufficient factors in stereotype threat. *Journal of Experimental Social Psychology*, 35, 29–46; Leyens, J., Desert, M., Croizet, J., & Darcis, C. (2000). Stereotype threat: Are lower status and history of stigmatization preconditions of stereotype threat? *Personality and Social Psychology Bulletin*, 26, 1189–1199; Stone, J., Lynch, C. I., Sjomeling, M., & Darley, J. M. (1999). Stereotype threat effects on Black and White athletic performance. *Journal of Personality and Social Psychology*, 77, 1213–1227.

(the literature calls these answers "mediating" explanations), but there is no consensus on which is the "right" answer. The dominant explanation has to do with anxiety (Aronson, Quinn, & Spencer, 1998), but there is still some disagreement over how anxiety affects performance. One argument suggests that anxiety increases a person's motivation and effort. Stereotype threatened participants are very motivated to perform well, and sometimes they try too hard or are too cautious in performing (Cadinu et al., 2003). For example, Steele and Aronson (1995) found that the Black participants in their research spent too much time trying to answer a small number of problems. They worked too hard on getting the right answer, and they disadvantaged themselves by not answering enough questions. Another argument proposes the opposite—that anxiety decreases a person's motivation and effort (Cadinu et al., 2003). The explanation is that stereotype threatened participants lose confidence that they can perform well, and in a self-fulfilling way this undermines performance. Given that the evidence thus far is still mixed and unclear, we will have to wait for further research to provide a more definitive answer to the why question. However, research has clearly identified the conditions under which stereotype threat is more and less likely to occur. This brings us to the next section of our paper.

Conditions for Stereotype Threat

We've seen that the content of stereotypes about groups includes beliefs about the abilities of group members to perform certain kinds of tasks. Stereotype threat will only occur for those tasks associated with the stereotype. But simply being *asked* to perform a stereotype-relevant task is not enough to create stereotype threat. Research has identified two additional conditions needed for stereotype threat to emerge: task difficulty and personal task investment. In addition, the context can influence the perceived relevance of the stereotype for performance of the task or job. We have diagrammed these conditions, and the stereotype threat process, in Figure 1.

Stereotype Relevance of the Task: What Does it Take to Perform Well?

Stereotype threat is situation specific, felt in situations where one can be "judged by, treated and seen in terms of, or self-fulfill a negative stereotype about one's group" (Spencer, Steele, & Quinn, 1999, p. 6). These situations occur when doing well on the task requires an ability on which, according to the stereotype, the person performing the task has a deficit. In the studies we have reviewed, the stereotype relevance of the task has often been created by telling

FIGURE 1 The stereotype threat process

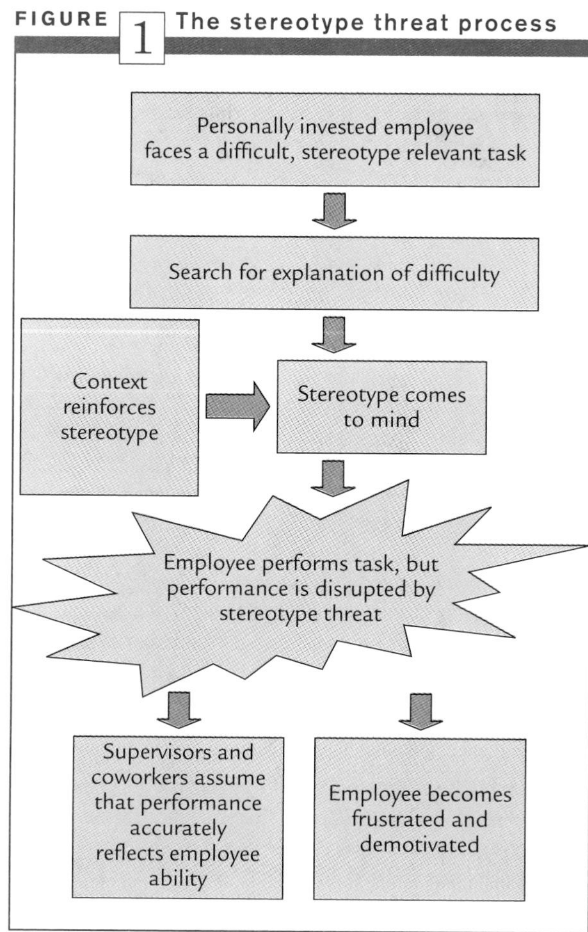

participants that the task is a direct "test" of the stereotyped ability. So, for example, math tests have been used to create a stereotype relevant task for women and verbal or cognitive ability tests used to create stereotype relevant tasks for African Americans and Hispanics. But stereotype relevance isn't limited to standardized tests. Laura Kray and her colleagues surveyed participants to show that negotiation tasks are stereotype relevant for women. The researchers found that people believed that good negotiators were "assertive and concerned with personal gain" and that "men are more likely to be assertive than women" (Kray, Galinsky, & Thompson, 2002). Therefore, it logically follows that "men are better negotiators than women."

Research has shown that in our society many people believe successful managers have attributes more similar to those of men and Whites than to those of women, Hispanics, or African Americans (Chung-Herrera & Lankau, 2005; Heilman, Block, Martell, & Simon, 1989; Tomkiewicz, Brenner, & Adeyemi-Bello, 1998). But beliefs about the traits necessary for jobs can also be organization specific. The potential for stereotype threat exists any time employees' beliefs about the particular traits needed for good job performance are linked to stereotypes about groups.

Task Difficulty: Why is this so Hard?

Stereotype threat is most likely to influence performance on very difficult tasks—those that are at the limits of a person's abilities (Steele et al., 2002). On easier tasks, stereotype threat doesn't have much negative effect. According to psychologist Claude Steele, experiencing frustration with task accomplishment is an important trigger for stereotype threat (Steele et al., 2002). On a simple task there is little frustration—the person is doing well and knows it. But with a difficult task, progress is not so smooth. People who experience frustration with a task try to explain their difficulty to themselves: "Why is this so hard? Is this job just impossible? Am I not working hard enough? Am I having a bad day?" They also think about how others (co-workers, supervisors) will explain their difficulty: "Will they think I'm not working hard enough?" But when the person is a member of a stereotyped group, the stereotype is also likely to come to mind as a potential explanation that others might use: "Will they think the stereotype is true? It's going to look like the stereotype is true."

A negative dynamic operates between task difficulty and stereotype threat. When a task is difficult, stereotype threat evokes concern over performance. But this concern also has a greater impact on the performance of difficult tasks. Difficult jobs require concentration and focus; all of one's cognitive/mental resources must be directed toward accomplishing the work. If some of those resources are diverted towards worrying about one's skills and how one will be viewed by others, performance decrements occur (Beilock & Carr, 2005; Verbeke & Bagozzi, 2000). Thus, difficult tasks trigger stereotype threat, and also are most affected by it.

In work settings then, difficult, complex, and challenging tasks are where stereotype threat is most likely to occur. This creates a dilemma for managers. Task difficulty is not just a fact in many (especially professional) jobs, it is a desired condition. For years, job design experts have recommended that every job contain some challenging aspects to increase job involvement and avoid boredom and skill atrophy (Greenberg, 1996; Hackman & Oldham, 1980). In fact, giving demanding assignments to new hires is sometimes recommended as a good way to develop employees. Early demanding experiences predict later career success (Habermas & Bluck, 2000). In many organizations, "stretch" assignments (assignments for which an employee is not yet fully qualified, "stretching" the employee's skills and abilities) (McCauley, Eastman, & Ohlott, 1995) are used as developmental tools throughout a person's tenure (Noe, 1999). Stretch assignments are needed for skill development, but managers must be aware of the extra potential for stereotype threat these assignments might involve for stereotyped employees, and counteract this risk. (We discuss how managers might do this later in the paper.)

In addition, tasks that are new and unfamiliar to the person performing them may be more at risk for stereotype threat than routine, familiar ones. New employees in particular are likely to find task accomplishment challenging as they learn their responsibilities. Thus, managers also must be aware of the higher potential for stereotype threat for their new hires.

Personal Task Investment: How Important is this to Who I Am?

Personal task investment refers to how important doing well on the task is to the individual's self esteem and identity. Some employees strongly identify with a particular skill or competency as a part of who they are. We often hear people say, "I'm good with people," or "I'm a techie." For these people, the skill is a part of how they define themselves. For such invested people, doing well in that task domain is important for their self-esteem and for feeling good about themselves. Researchers have argued that people who are personally invested in the task would be most influenced by stereotype threat because they are the ones who really care about their performance (Steele, 1997; Steele et al., 2002). If you want your work performance to say something about you personally, then the prospect of being viewed in terms of a negative stereotype is most disturbing. Studies have consistently confirmed this. Those invested in the task are more negatively affected by stereotype threat than those without such personal task investment.

What does this mean, practically? People tend to be invested in tasks they are good at (Steele, 1997). So the heavy impact of stereotype threat on the personally invested means that "the most capable members of stereotyped groups tend to be the most adversely affected in their performance by stereotype threat" (Kray et al., 2002, p. 388). This carries an important reminder for managers: the employees who care about their work and really want to do well are generally the ones that a manager is least likely to worry about since they are the ones he or she thinks will succeed on their own, and thus don't need coaxing, coaching, or extra attention. Yet, these are the people most likely to be affected by stereotype threat, and therefore, most in need of a manager's efforts to address and reduce it. For example, a manager might think that because the talented Hispanic salesperson graduated at the top of his class, he's already proven that stereotypes don't apply to him and isn't bothered by them. Or that the efficient accountant who earned her CPA despite caring for four children no longer worries about not being taken seriously by male managers. But it's exactly these employees, the ones who have made a big investment in their work, who might be most likely to suffer the effects of stereotype threat.

The Context: Is this a Place Where Stereotypes Operate?

We've seen that the most important condition for stereotype threat is stereotype relevance: stereotype threat only occurs when the stereotype seems relevant to performing the task (Steele et al., 2002). In the academic research described earlier, stereotype relevance was created by the way the researchers described the tasks in a laboratory setting. In work settings, the relevance of the stereotype for performance can also be signaled and reinforced by the diversity (or the lack of diversity) of people who are currently performing the job. Rosabeth Moss Kanter used the term "token" to describe individuals who are different from others on a salient demographic dimension—race, sex, or age (Kanter, 1977). Kanter and others have shown that tokens feel very "visible"—that they stand out from the rest of the group. In addition, those in the majority are more likely to view tokens in terms of their distinguishing characteristic: as *the* woman or *the* Asian. Because everyone (the tokens and the tokens' colleagues) is more aware of group memberships under these conditions, associated stereotypes are more likely to come to mind (Niemann & Dovidio, 1998). In addition, the numerical differences reinforce the relevance of the stereotype for performance in the setting. Consider the solitary woman in a team of software engineers. Being the "only one" suggests that the stereotype about women lacking quantitative skills is true, and therefore sex is relevant to job performance. After all, the reasoning goes, if "those people" were good at this kind of job, wouldn't we see more of them performing it? Two studies have provided evidence of the link between token status and stereotype threat. In one, laboratory experimenters found that token women showed lower performance than non-tokens only on a math task (a stereotyped domain) and not on a verbal task (a non stereotyped domain) (Inzlicht & BenZeev, 2003). In the other, field researchers found that Black managers who were tokens in their work group reported higher levels of stereotype threat than non-tokens (Roberson, Deitch, Brief, & Block, 2003).

Thus, group representation can raise the relevance of the stereotype for performance. Work situations involving lone members of a social or demographic group are common. For example, in the field research described above, 18% of the Black managers were tokens in their work group (Roberson et al., 2003). Managers need to be aware of this effect of the environment and find ways to neutralize it.

In summary, these conditions make stereotype threat more likely for members of negatively stereotyped groups:

- The employee is invested in doing well, on:
- A difficult, stereotype relevant task, where:
- The context reinforces the stereotype

When stereotype threat occurs, performance is disrupted. But the effects of stereotype threat go beyond short-term performance decrements. The Black managers who experienced stereotype threat in the field research said that they spent more time monitoring their performance (for example, by comparing themselves to peers) and were more likely to discount performance feedback that they received from the organization (Roberson et al., 2003). So, for example, a Black employee who is regularly exposed to stereotype threat about his intellectual ability might dismiss performance feedback from his White manager that would have helped him to meet organizational performance expectations and get on the promotion "fast track."

But maybe these responses are functional. If your manager holds a negative stereotype about you, maybe you should discount feedback from that person (or at least, take it with a large grain of salt). If you can't trust your manager, monitoring the performance of your peers might yield more credible information with which to assess your performance. And if stereotype threat causes people to work harder, couldn't that be a positive benefit? Earlier, we quoted Beyoncé Knowles as feeling like she had "something to prove." Beyoncé has clearly been able to channel those feelings in a positive way in order to become a successful performer. Maybe a strong motivation to disprove a negative stereotype about your group can increase persistence and determination to succeed. Research on achievement goals has shown that a desire to prove one's ability can be a powerful form of motivation (Elliott & Harackiewicz, 1996), most effective in improving performance and persistence on simple tasks that are familiar to the performer (Steele-Johnson, Beauregard, Hoover, & Schmidt, 2000; Vandewalle, 2001). If you know *how* to perform a task, this kind of motivation can help you to perform better. But remember the Black students in Steele and Aronson's research—the ones who spent a lot of time answering very few questions? Those students were very motivated, but they were working on very complex, challenging problems and their efforts did not pay off. This kind of motivation often works for you, but it can work against you.

Questions about whether employee responses to stereotype threat can be functional or potentially beneficial indicate that we need to know a lot more about the long-term consequences of repeated exposure to stereotype threat. To answer these questions, research has to study stereotype threat over time in real-world organizational settings. So far, the research suggests that repeated exposure to stereotype threat may have serious, and primarily negative, side effects. Stereotype threat is accompanied by physiological reactions such as an increase in blood pressure, leading researchers to speculate that long-term exposure to stereotype threat conditions might contribute to chronic health problems such as hypertension (Blascovich, Spencer, Quinn, & Steele, 2001). Stereotype threat is also associated with lower job satisfaction (Niemann & Dovidio, 1998; Roberson et al., 2003). Researchers have further suggested that repeated, regular exposure to stereotype threat may lead a person to disengage (or "disidentify") with the performance domain (Steele, 1997). That solo female in your engineering group may begin to think that an alternative career path might be preferable. This leads one to wonder whether long-term exposure to stereotype threat could be one cause of turnover for women and racial/ethnic minorities in professional and managerial jobs. Indeed, some studies have found that members of these groups leave jobs at a higher rate than White men (Horn, Roberson, & Ellis, 2007).

Fortunately, research on the conditions under which stereotype threat is most likely to occur also provides information about reducing the risk of stereotype threat. Recent studies have directly examined ways to reduce or eliminate stereotype threat by changing the conditions that produce the effect—in essence, interrupting the process. These studies are important because they point to some steps that can be taken by managers to lessen the possibility that stereotype threat operates for their employees. We now turn to specific strategies for reducing the likelihood of stereotype threat.

Interrupting the Stereotype Threat Process

Strategies for Reducing Stereotype Threat

We have mentioned that stereotype threat effects are strongest for people who are highly identified with the task domain. Researchers fear that over time, stereotyped people may find one way to reduce stereotype threat themselves—by disidentifying with the affected task domain. In other words, they break the psychological connection between their performance and their self-esteem so that doing well on that kind of task is less important. This is the only solution under the individual's control, but it is also perhaps the worst solution, costly for both the individual who gives up a valued part of the self, and for the organization that loses an engaged and motivated employee. Here we describe some alternatives to this worst case scenario—other strategies for reducing stereotype threat. These strategies, demonstrated to be effective in laboratory studies, all involve changing the conditions for stereotype threat. The strategies, and the points in the process at which they intervene, are shown in Figure 2.

Provide a Successful Task Strategy

We know that stereotype threat influences people only on very difficult tasks—those at the outer limits of ability and skill. Evidence suggests that stereotype threatened people seek to distance themselves from the stereotype by acting opposite to it (Aronson, 2002). They often put their noses to the grindstone, work harder and longer to prove the stereotype wrong—to show it does not apply to them. In the original study by Steele and Aronson, stereotype threatened Black students worked harder and more diligently at the task, expending more effort than the unthreatened. Unfortunately, working harder and more carefully didn't increase performance. The task they were working on was extremely difficult, right at the outer limit of their abilities. Effort *alone* couldn't boost performance—what the students needed was an effective strategy for solving the problems.

A recent study provided stereotype threatened participants with a strategy to successfully counteract the stereotype. In a negotiation task, women were explicitly told about gender stereotypes suggesting that women are less assertive than men and tend not to act in their own self-interest; these characteristics reduce their effectiveness in negotiations. The women in the study were able to counteract the stereotype by acting particularly assertively when making opening offers to their partners, and this strategy improved their performance in the negotiation. However, the women acted this way only when they were *explicitly* told about gender's effect on negotiation. The women already knew how to act assertively—all they needed to perform successfully was a cue that this context was one in which acting assertively was a good strategy (Kray et al., 2001).

FIGURE 2 Interrupting the stereotype threat process

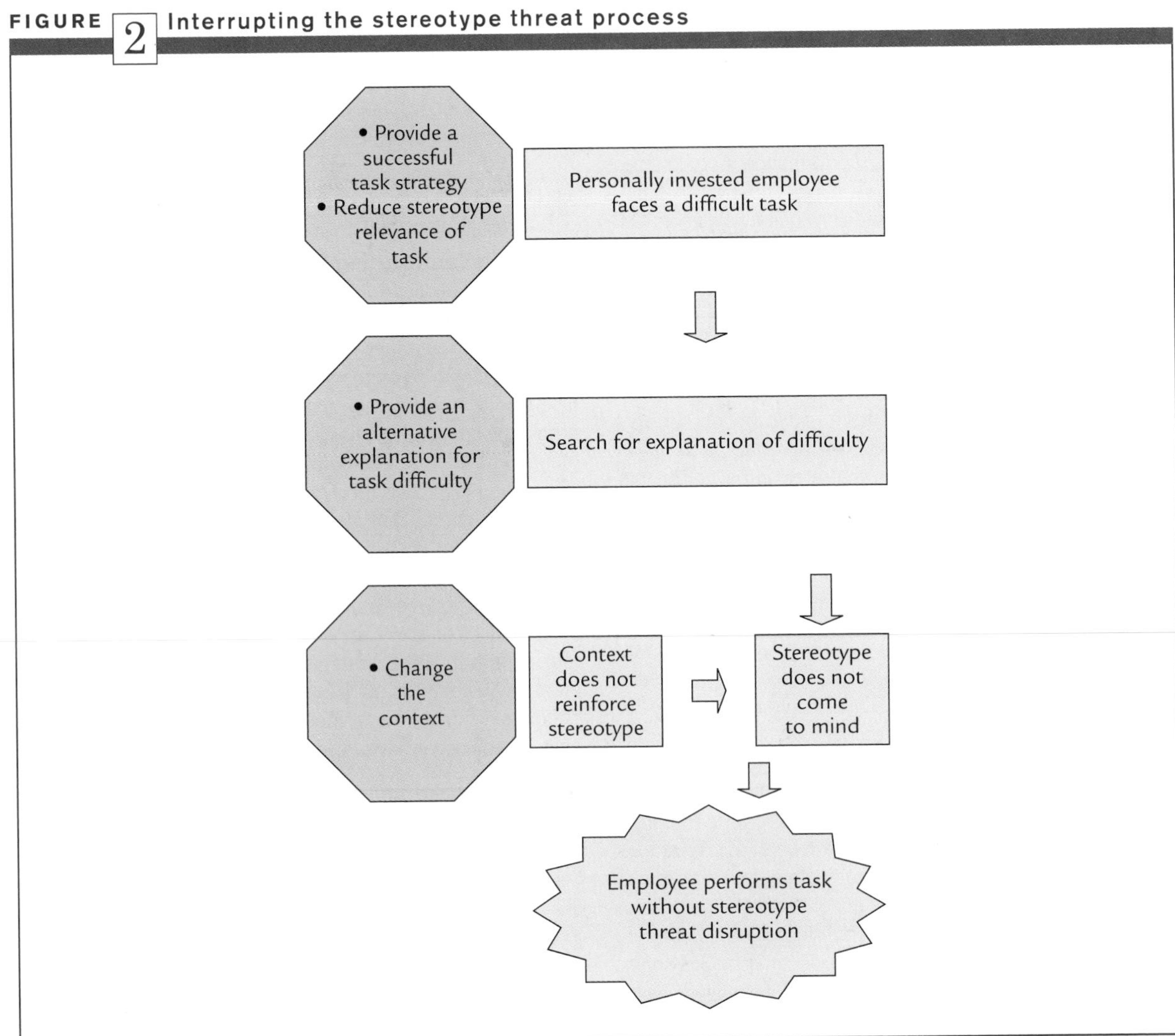

This research suggests that one way to reduce stereotype threat is to teach affected employees behavioral strategies for improving performance and counteracting negative stereotypes. This intervention addresses task difficulty—one of the conditions for stereotype threat. Having good strategies available to cope with challenges makes the task seem less difficult and less frustrating. This research suggests that when using stretch assignments, managers should set goals, and also help employees develop strategies towards attaining them. The "sink or swim" attitude toward stretch assignments common in many organizations can be particularly detrimental for stereotype threatened individuals. If managers discuss and suggest task strategies to employees, stereotype threat should be reduced.

Reduce the Stereotype Relevance of the Task

We also know that stereotype threat happens when the stereotype is relevant to the task; when performance on a task is believed to reflect an ability or trait that differentiates stereotyped and nonstereotyped groups (e.g., women and men; Blacks and Whites). Several studies have eliminated stereotype threat effects by refuting or diminishing the stereotype relevance of the task. In one study, researchers asked men and women to take a difficult math test composed of items from the GRE exam. All participants were told that they were taking the math test as part of an effort to develop new testing procedures for the university. Half of the participants were also informed that this particular test had been shown not to produce gender differences—that men and women performed equally well. The other half were not given any information about gender differences. The researchers predicted that stereotype threat would operate when there was no information given about gender differences, because when labeled simply as a "math test," the gender stereotype that "women can't do math" would be relevant. However, being told explicitly that there were no gender differences would reduce the relevance of the stereotype to the task, and hence reduce stereotype threat. By presenting the test as one with no gender differences, the stereotype would be irrelevant to interpreting performance on the test. These results were confirmed: women underperformed relative to men in the "no information" (stereotype relevant) condition, but performed equally to men in the "no gender difference" (stereotype irrelevant) condition (Spencer et al., 1999).

Another study reduced the stereotype relevance of the task in a slightly different way, by emphasizing characteristics shared by both groups. Male and female college students participated in a negotiation exercise. For half of the participants, researchers made gender stereotypes relevant by saying that the most effective negotiators are "rational and assertive" rather than "emotional and passive" (cueing gender stereotypes). For the other half, researchers eliminated the relevance of the gender stereotype for performance. They told this half of the participants that "rational and assertive" people do better than "emotional and passive" individuals. But then they added, "people who are in competitive academic environments, like you, do exceptionally well in the negotiation. This is true for men and women alike." This description highlighted characteristics important for performance that are shared by both men and women, diminishing the stereotype relevance of the task. This strategy was also successful in decreasing stereotype threat and gender differences in performance (Kray et al., 2001).

These studies show that reducing the stereotype relevance of the task—one of the conditions for stereotype threat—is effective in removing stereotype threat. But is this a realistic strategy in organizations? In the laboratory, it is possible to label an unfamiliar task as one showing group differences or not. It is easy to manipulate participants' beliefs about whether a task reflects group differences when those participants have no prior experience with the task. The situation is different with real world tasks or jobs where employees and co-workers may have strong opinions about the types of people who do well in various jobs or roles. Consider technical or mathematical tasks. Belief in gender differences on such tasks is widespread (Brown & Josephs, 1999), so when faced with a technical or mathematical task, a woman may not believe a manager who says it does not reflect gender differences. It might be more effective for managers instead to use the strategy in the second experiment. For example, rather than try to discredit gender differences, one could make gender differences irrelevant by stressing *common* characteristics of employees that are relevant for performing the task. This could be done by identifying characteristics important for task success that are unlinked to group stereotypes. Perhaps a manager could inform all employees that they were hired precisely because they have the skills needed to do well. For example, "We have such good hiring procedures—the people who we bring in, both men and women, have the skills to perform well."

Provide an Alternative Explanation for Task Difficulty

Task difficulty is a trigger for stereotype threat because people try to explain their difficulty to themselves: on a stereotype relevant task, where the context reinforces the stereotype, they are more likely to think of the stereotype as a potential explanation. The resulting anxiety and distress then disrupts performance. Several studies have shown that by giving an explanation for task difficulty *besides* the stereotype, stereotype threat can be reduced.

In one study, men and women students who came to the laboratory were told they would take a math test being developed by the psychology department for placement purposes. Immediately after this general description, half of the students were asked to begin the test, and were given 20 minutes to complete 20 problems. The other half were told that there would be a practice session before the test, administered on a computer. The experimenter explained that this would help them to "warm up," allowing a better assessment of their true ability level on the actual test. However, when the experimenter turned on the computer, the screen was unreadable (the computer had been rigged). After fiddling with the knobs and controls to no avail, the experimenter then announced that the students would have to take the test without the benefit of warming up, and this extenuating circumstance would be noted on their answer sheets. The researchers designed this study because they reasoned that being denied the "warm up" opportunity would provide a viable alternative to the gender stereotype as an explanation for any experienced task difficulty, reducing stereotype threat effects for women. Results confirmed this: men's performance was not affected by the test conditions. However, the performance of women was greatly affected. Women performed better on the math test when they were denied their "warm up" opportunity (Brown & Josephs, 1999).

In another study, researchers induced stereotype threat for White men by heightening the salience of the stereotype that Whites have less natural athletic ability than Blacks. The researchers then informed half of these participants that the lab space where they would perform athletic tasks had recently been renovated, and that the lab administration wanted "to know if the new changes made research participants feel tense or uneasy." Because of this concern, the participants would be asked to rate the lab space and its effects on their emotions after the experiment (Stone, Lynch, Sjomeling, & Darley, 1999). This information provided participants with another explanation (the renovated lab space) for any anxiety they experienced during the task. White men who received this alternative explanation for poor performance performed better than those who did not.

Again, however effective these manipulations are in the laboratory, their feasibility for the work setting may be limited. Managers certainly shouldn't lie to their employees (as in the first study) to give them an excuse for task difficulty and poor performance. But managers could remind employees about real-life factors that might be constraining their performance (e.g., a difficult client, limited resources, or a tight deadline). Another feasible strategy for providing an alternative explanation comes from a third study. The experimenters induced stereotype threat for women using the usual setup—telling participants that they would be completing a standardized math test for a study of gender differences. One group received just these instructions. With another group, in addition to these instructions, the experimenters described the phenomenon of stereotype threat and said, "... if you are feeling anxious while taking this test, this anxiety could be the result of these negative [gender] stereotypes that are widely known in society and have nothing to do with your actual ability to do well" (Johns, Schmader, & Martens, 2005: 176). These instructions had a positive effect on test performance. Women underperformed on the math test relative to men when given only the "math test" description. When stereotype threat was explained and offered as a possible cause of their anxiety, the performance of men and women was similar.

Telling people who might be affected by stereotype threat about the phenomenon has some advantages. Stereotype threat is real, and its effects on performance are well-documented. You might think that explicitly raising the issue of stereotype threat with a potentially affected employee might make matters worse by drawing attention to the stereotype—better to keep quiet and act like it doesn't exist. But instead the opposite appears to be true. Telling employees that you know stereotype threat can happen, and that they should be aware of it, gives them a different attribution for their difficulty and anxiety (it's not the stereotype, it's the stereotype *threat*).

Change the Context

The context is another condition that can affect the likelihood of stereotype threat. We discussed how one aspect of the context—the diversity of people performing the job—can reinforce or diminish the relevance of stereotypes. The research showing that tokens are more likely to experience stereotype threat also suggests a way to reduce stereotype threat: change the context by removing people from token situations.

This strategy may work in the laboratory, but how can managers realistically achieve this goal? In organizations, the composition of work groups is already constrained by employee skills, task interdependence, and other factors. Managers can't shuffle employees around based on their demographics to avoid token situations. However, several studies have changed the context using another strategy that does not involve changing the demographic make-up of the work group: presenting a role model who contradicts the stereotype. In one study, participants were administered a difficult math test by either a male or female experimenter. The experimenters gave identical instructions designed to accomplish two goals: 1) induce stereotype threat in the women by presenting the test as diagnostic of ability; and 2) create perceptions of the experimenter's competence in math. Scores on the math test showed that women underperformed relative to men only when the test was administered by a male experimenter. A follow-up study revealed that it was not the physical presence of the female experimenter, but rather her perceived competence that protected the women from stereotype threat. Seeing a woman who was competent in the math domain boosted women's beliefs in their own mathematical abilities and maintained their performance (Marx & Roman, 2002).

Other researchers found similar results when role models were presented in a different way. One study asked participants to read and critique four biographical essays. Half of the participants read essays concerning successful women in a variety of fields such as medicine and law. The other half read essays concerning successful corporations. Then all the participants completed a math test administered by a male experimenter. Results indicated that the role model manipulation reduced stereotype threat: Women scored worse than men on the test when they had read about successful corporations, but women scored at the same level as men when they had read about successful women (McIntyre, Paulson, & Lord, 2003).

These studies suggest that managers may be able to change the context for stereotyped employees by boosting the salience and visibility of role models. Note that in the "essay" study, the physical presence of a role model was not necessary—what was important was that the competence of the role model was salient. This strategy could be feasibly implemented in organizations. Managers can increase access to role models by encouraging employee participation in mentoring programs, professional associations, and employee network groups (Friedman & Holtom, 2002; Friedman, Kane, & Cornfield, 1998). If managers maintain a diverse network of associates themselves, they can be more aware of potential role models for all of their employees, and attempt to connect people.

Implications for Diversity Management

Would a greater focus on reducing stereotype threat add anything new to diversity management? We think it would. Existing diversity management programs tend to have two major objectives (Kellough & Naff, 2004): One goal is to change managers' *attitudes*—to reduce negative attitudes, stereotypes, and prejudice against members of different groups. Much diversity training is geared toward this goal. A second related goal is to change managers' *behaviors*—how they select, appraise, and develop employees (Brief & Barsky, 2000). For example, managers are encouraged, and often required, to specify explicit behavioral and performance standards for promotion or advancement, and to adhere to these in making decisions. These are important objectives. However, these objectives ignore two realities. First, changing attitudes and reducing stereotypes is a long term endeavor. Stereotypes are embedded in the culture, and reinforced outside of the work setting (Brief, 1998). Until society changes, stereotypes about different groups will remain. Even if a particular manager is unprejudiced, others in the workgroup may not be, and employees may still feel stereotype threat. While we need to try to reduce stereotypes, in the foreseeable future we have to deal with existing attitudes, and try to reduce the *impact* of stereotypes on affected employees. Second, while increasing the objectivity of measurement and decisions is necessary, the presence of stereotype threat means that performance *itself* may convey biased information about a person's true ability. So the well-intentioned manager who relies on objective performance data without understanding the impact of stereotype threat will still unfairly underestimate performance. Focusing on stereotype threat takes these realities into account, and highlights two principles that are currently downplayed in most diversity management efforts:

1. Acknowledge stereotypes and address them directly. Unfortunately, the goal of eliminating stereotypes from organizational decision making sometimes leads organizational members to deny their existence. People sometimes confuse stereotype awareness with stereotype endorsement (Adler, 2002). Yet research has shown that even unprejudiced people are familiar with the content of common stereotypes and can easily describe what prejudiced people believe about members of certain groups (Devine, 1989). Putting our strategies into action means that a manager has to honestly acknowledge the stereotypes that exist. The manager who acknowledges the existence and potential impact of stereotypes does not have to endorse or support those stereotypes. Only a manager who acknowledges stereotypes can acknowledge the opportunity for stereotype threat and take corrective action.

The strategies for reducing stereotype threat further imply that managers should talk explicitly about stereotypes with their potentially threatened employees (Kray et al., 2001). Rarely are stereotypes directly named and described—particularly to the affected parties. Although many people (managers and subordinates alike) might see this as a risky step, explicit discussion about stereotypes can be useful in reducing their impact. If supervisors and subordinates trust one another, it can be a good strategy. David Thomas' comparison of successful and plateaued non-White executives demonstrated that successful executives found mentors early in their careers who were able to talk directly about race and the challenges it presented (Thomas, 2001; Thomas & Gabarro, 1999). Such openness about the existence of stereotypes and stereotype threat provides employees with alternative explanations for task difficulty and also may decrease concerns that they will be judged in light of the stereotype. Many managers would shy away from such a frank discussion, but the evidence says that evasion is not always helpful. Honest engagement of the problem and an exploration of action strategies to counteract perceptions can increase trust, reduce stereotype threat, and improve performance. How can managers be encouraged to take these risks? Perhaps diversity training should focus on providing managers with the skills and confidence to talk about stereotypes with their employees.

2. Shift the focus from the manager to the environment. Diversity management programs tend to focus on the manager as the target of change. Diversity training programs, for example, are designed to change managerial attitudes and behavior (Bendick, Egan, & Lofhjelm, 2001). In contrast, the strategies for reducing stereotype threat focus on the *environment* as the target of change. In other words, changing the conditions that lead to stereotype threat. Managers need to attend to managing the environment and reducing the cues that signal to employees that stereotypes are operating.

Effective diversity management has always meant creating an environment where all can succeed (Cox, 1994; Thomas, 1991). Knowledge of stereotype threat increases our understanding of what that really means. It is more than being personally nonprejudiced and unbiased. It means actively reducing cues that limit the contributions of *all* employees. Only in this way can the benefits of diversity be realized.

Source: Academy of Management Perspectives, 21, (2), 2007, 24–40.

REFERENCES

Adler, N. J. (2002). *International dimensions of organizational behavior,* Fourth Edition. Cincinnati OH: South-Western Publishing.

Aronson, J. (2002). Stereotype threat: Contending and coping with unnerving expectations. In J. Aronson (Ed.) *Improving academic achievement: Impact of psychological factors on education* (pp. 279–301). San Francisco: Elsevier.

Aronson, J., Lustina, M. J., Good, C., Keough, K., Steele, C. M., & Brown, J. (1999). When White men can't do math: Necessary and sufficient factors in stereotype threat. *Journal of Experimental Social Psychology, 35,* 29–46.

Aronson, J., Quinn, D. M., & Spencer, S. J. (1998). Stereotype threat and the academic underperformance of minorities and women. In Swim, J. K., & Stangor, C. (Eds.), *Prejudice: The target's perspective* (pp. 83–103). New York: Academic Press.

Beilock, S. L., & Carr, T. H. (2005). When high-powered people fail: Working memory and "choking under pressure" in math. *Psychological Science, 16,* 101–105.

Bendick, M., Egan, M. L., & Lofhjelm, S. M. (2001). Workforce diversity training: From anti-discrimination compliance to organizational development. *Human Resource Planning, 24,* 10–36.

Blank, R., & Shipp, S. (1994). *Voices of diversity: Real people talk about problems and solutions in a workplace where everyone is not alike.* New York: AMACOM.

Blascovich, J., Spencer, S. J., Quinn, D., & Steele, C. (2001). African Americans and high blood pressure: The role of stereotype threat. *Psychological Science, 12,* 225–229.

Brief, A. P. (1998). *Attitudes in and around organizations.* Thousand Oaks, CA: Sage.

Brief, A. P., & Barsky, A. (2000). Establishing a climate for diversity: The inhibition of prejudiced reactions in the workplace. *Research in Personnel and Human Resources Management, 19,* 91–129.

Brown, R. P., & Josephs, R. A. (1999). A burden of proof: Stereotype relevance and gender differences in math performance. *Journal of Personality and Social Psychology, 76,* 246–257.

Cadinu, M., Maass, A., Frigerio, S., Impagliazzo, L., & Latinotti, S. (2003). Stereotype threat: The effect of expectancy on performance. *European Journal of Social Psychology, 33,* 267–285.

Chandler, M. (1999, October 4). *Secrets of the SAT* (FRONTLINE, #1802). New York and Washington, D.C.: Public Broadcasting Service.

Chung-Herrera, B. G., & Lankau, M. J. (2005). Are we there yet? An assessment of fit between stereotypes of minority managers and the successful-manager prototype. *Journal of Applied Social Psychology, 35*, 2029–2056.

Cocchiara, F. K., & Quick, J. C. (2004). The negative effects of positive stereotypes: Ethnicity-related stressors and implications on organizational health. *Journal of Organizational Behavior, 25*, 781–785.

Cox, T. H. Jr. (1994). *Cultural diversity in organizations: Theory, research, and practice*. San Francisco, CA: Berrett-Koehler.

Devine, P. G. (1989). Stereotypes and prejudice: Their automatic and controlled components. *Journal of Personality and Social Psychology, 56*, 5–18.

Dickins, F., & Dickens, J. B. (1991). *The Black manager: Making it in the corporate world*. New York: AMACOM.

Elliott, A. J., &. Harackiewicz, J. M. (1996). Approach and avoidance achievement goals and intrinsic motivation: A mediational analysis. *Journal of Personality and Social Psychology, 70*, 461–475.

Frantz, C. M., Cuddy, A. J. C., Burnett, M., Ray, H., & Hart, A. (2004). A threat in the computer: The race implicit association test as a stereotype threat experience. *Personality and Social Psychology Bulletin, 30*, 1611–1614.

Friedman, R. A., & Holtom, B. (2002). The effects of network groups on minority employee turnover intentions. *Human Resource Management, 41*, 405–421.

Friedman, R. A., Kane, M., & Cornfield, D. B. (1998). Social support and career optimism: Examining the effectiveness of network groups among Black managers. *Human Relations, 51*, 1155–1177.

Greenberg, J. (1996). *Managing behavior in organizations: Science in service to practice*. Upper Saddle River, NJ: Prentice Hall.

Greengard, S. (2003). Gimme attitude. *Workforce, 82*, 56–60.

Habermas, T., & Bluck, S. (2000). Getting a life: The emergence of the life story in adolescence. *Psychological Bulletin, 12*, 748–769.

Hackman, J. R., & Oldham, G. R. (1980). *Work redesign*. Reading, MA: Addison-Wesley.

Hansen, F. (2003). Diversity's business case doesn't add up. *Workforce, 82*, 28–32.

Heilman, M. E., Block, C. J., Martell, R. F., & Simon, M. C. (1989). Has anything changed? Current characterizations of men, women, and managers. *Journal of Applied Psychology, 74*, 935–942.

Hite, L. M. (2004). Black and White women managers: Access to opportunity. *Human Resource Development Quarterly, 15*, 131–146.

Horn, P. W., Roberson, L., & Ellis, A. D. (2007). *Challenging conventional wisdom about who quits: Revelations from corporate America*. Manuscript submitted for publication, Arizona State University.

Inzlicht, M., & Ben Zeev, T. (2003). Do high-achieving female students underperform in private? The implications of threatening environments on intellectual processing. *Journal of Educational Psychology, 95*, 796–805.

Jackson, S. E., Brett, J. F., Sessa, V. I., Cooper, D. M., Julin, J. A., & Peyronnin, K. (1991). Some differences make a difference: Individual dissimilarity and group heterogeneity as correlates of recruitment, promotions, and turnover. *Journal of Applied Psychology, 76*, 675–689.

Jehn, K. A., Neale, M., & Northcraft, G. (1999). Why differences make a difference: A field study of diversity, conflict, and performance in workgroups. *Administrative Science Quarterly, 44*, 741–763.

Johns, M., Schmader, T., & Martens, A. (2005). Knowing is half the battle: Teaching stereotype threat as a means of improving women's math performance. *Psychological Science, 16*, 175–179.

Kanter, R. (1977). *Men and women of the organization*. New York: Basic Books.

Kellough, J. E., & Naff, K. C. (2004). Responding to a wake up call: An examination of Federal Agency Diversity Management Programs. *Administration & Society, 36*, 62–91.

Kochan, T., Bezrukova, K., Ely, R., Jackson, S., Joshi, A., Jehn, K., Leonare, J., Levine, D., & Thomas, D. (2003). The effects of diversity on business performance: Report of the diversity research network. *Human Resource Management, 42*, 3–21.

Kray, L. J., Galinsky, A. D., & Thompson, L. (2002). Reversing the gender gap in negotiations: An exploration of stereotype regeneration. *Organizational Behavior and Human Decision Processes, 87*, 386–409.

Kray, L. J., Thompson, L., &. Galinsky, A. (2001). Battle of the sexes: Gender stereotype confirmation and reactance in negotiations. *Journal of Personality and Social Psychology, 80*, 942–958.

Marx, D. M., & Roman, J. S. (2002). Female role models: Protecting women's math test performance. *Personality and Social Psychology Bulletin, 28*, 1183–1193.

McCauley, C., Eastman, L., & Ohlott, P. (1995). Linking management selection and development through stretch assignments. *Human Resource Management, 34*, 93–115.

McIntyre, R. B., Paulson, R. M., & Lord, C. G. (2003). Alleviating women's mathematics stereotype threat through salience of group achievements. *Journal of Experimental Social Psychology, 39*, 83–90.

Niemann, Y. F., & Dovidio, J. F. (1998). Relationship of solo status, academic rank, and perceived distinctiveness to job satisfaction of racial/ethnic minorities. *Journal of Applied Psychology, 83*, 55–71.

Noe, R. A. (1999). *Employee training and development*. Boston: Irwin McGraw-Hill.

Parks-Yancy, R. (2006). The effects of social group membership and social capital resources on career. *Journal of Black Studies, 36*, 515–545.

Personal blog. (2005, June 3). Available at: http://www.big fatblog.com/archives/001607.php.

Reio, Jr., T. G., & Callahan, J. L. (2004). Affect, curiosity, and socialization-related learning: A path analysis of antecedents to job performance. *Journal of Business and Psychology, 19*, 3–22.

Rice, F. (1996). Denny's changes its spots. *Fortune, 133*, 133–138.

Roberson L., Deitch, E., Brief, A. P., & Block, C. J. (2003). Stereotype threat and feedback seeking in the workplace. *Journal of Vocational Behavior, 62*, 176–188.

Robinson, G., & Dechant, K. (1997). Building a business case for diversity. *Academy of Management Executive, 11*, 21–31.

Smith, J. L. (2004). Understanding the process of stereotype threat: A review of mediational variables and new performance goal directions. *Educational Psychology Review, 16*, 177–206.

Spencer, S. J., Steele, C. M., & Quinn, D. M. (1999). Stereotype threat and women's math performance. *Journal of Experimental Social Psychology, 35*, 4–28.

Steele, C. M. (1997). A threat in the air: How stereotypes shape intellectual identity and performance. *American Psychologist, 52*, 613–629.

Steele, C. M., & Aronson, J. (1995). Stereotype threat and the intellectual test performance of African Americans. *Journal of Personality and Social Psychology, 85*, 440–452.

Steele, C. M., Spencer, S. J., & Aronson, J. (2002). Contending with group image: The psychology of stereotype and social identity threat. *Advances in Experimental Social Psychology, 34*, 379–440.

Steele-Johnson, D., Beauregard, R. S., Hoover, P. B., & Schmidt, A. M. (2000). Goal orientation and task demand effects on motivation, affect, and performance. *Journal of Applied Psychology, 85*, 724–738.

Stone, J., Lynch, C. L., Sjomeling, M., & Darley, J. M. (1999). Stereotype threat effects on Black and White athletic performance. *Journal of Personality and Social Psychology, 77*, 1213–1227.

Thomas, D. A. (2001). The truth about mentoring minorities: Race matters. *Harvard Business Review, 79*, 98–107.

Thomas, D. A., & Ely, R. J. (1996). Making differences matter: A new paradigm for managing diversity. *Harvard Business Review, 74*, 79–91.

Thomas, D. A., & Gabarro, J. J. (1999). *Breaking through: The making of minority executives in corporate America.* Boston, MA: Harvard Business School Press.

Thomas, R. R. Jr. (1991). *Beyond race and gender: Unleashing the power of your total work force by managing diversity.* NY: AMACOM.

Tomkiewicz, J., Brenner, O. C., & Adeyemi-Bello, T. (1998). The impact of perceptions and stereotypes on the managerial mobility of African Americans. *Journal of Social Psychology, 138*, 88–92.

Tsui, A. Egan, T., & O'Reilly, C. (1992). Being different: Relational demography and organizational attachment. *Administrative Science Quarterly, 37*, 549–579.

Verbeke, W., & Bagozzi, R. (2000). Sales call anxiety: Exploring what it means when fear rules a sales encounter. *Journal of Marketing, 64*, 88–102.

Vandewalle, D. (2001). Goal orientation: Why wanting to look successful doesn't always lead to success. *Organizational Dynamics, 30*, 162–171.

Yerkes, R. M., & Dodson, J. D. (1908). The relation of strength of stimulus to rapidity of habit formation. *Journal of Comparative Neurology, 18*, 459–482.

Zenger, T., & Lawrence, B. (1989). Organizational demography: The differential effects of age and tenure distributions on technical communications. *Academy of Management Journal, 32*, 353–376.

READING 2.2

The Ethics of Human Resource Management

Elizabeth D. Scott

In a time when most organizations claim that "our employees are our most important [most valuable, greatest] asset," the ethical challenge to human resource (HR) managers is clear: How do we avoid treating employees merely as *means*? The term "human resources" may be relatively new, but viewing employees as something to be used is as old as the Roman days, when the tools of production were classified as "dumb tools" (used of plows, shovels), "semi-speaking tools" (used of animals), and "speaking tools" (used of slaves). While many employees would prefer to be referred to as an asset rather than as an expense or liability, the phrase "human resources" still rankles among those who see it as evidence that employers have not changed over the millennia. Assuming, *arguendo*, that we are discussing HR managers who wish to be ethical, one of their main challenges is to belie their titles. That is, they must manage humans not as resources but as autonomous individuals with legitimate rights and interests.

Ethical Theories

Elsewhere in this volume, others describe ethical theories in depth. I will not repeat those theories, save to suggest that each has something to say about how HR managers do their jobs. HR managers face the Kantian ethical question of how to ensure that their treatment of employees, applicants, and former employees respects the autonomy of those constituents. Stakeholder ethics also requires that the HR manager consider the interests of employees, applicants, and former employees, at least if we are to accept Clarkson's definition that "stakeholders are persons or groups that have or claim ownership, rights, or interests in a corporation and its activities, past, present, or future" (1995:106). HR managers who judge ethics by fairness or justice must apply them to employees, applicants, and former employees, and they may even be required by Rawls's (1971) conception of justice to ensure that the least well off are not disadvantaged by the policies they implement and also have a voice in decision-making processes.

Utilitarian HR managers must consider the outcomes of their decisions on everyone, including employees, applicants, and former employees. And virtue ethics would recommend developing habits that contribute to the flourishing of humans, as individuals and in community. While there might be special situations in which a particular ethical theory would prescribe behavior different from that prescribed by other theories, my interest is not in ferreting out those exceptions but in illustrating the claims these theories make on HR managers desiring to be ethical in performing their functions. Therefore, where I use such words as "fairness," "stakeholder," and "duty," I intend to invoke principles of ethics derived from the theories discussed elsewhere.

Types of Ethical Issues Addressed

Three different types of ethical problems face HR managers. The first type is the need for discernment—determining the right thing to do in very complex situations. The HR manager has both authority and the support of management to make and implement decisions, but he or she still must weigh options and make decisions with incomplete information. The second type of problem is a conflict between the HR manager's professional judgment of what is right and the responsibility as an agent of the employer to do what the employer asks. The third type of problem involves conflict of interest—or *appearance* of conflict of interest—when the HR manager's personal interest differs from the responsibility as an agent of the employer. The first type of problem has the potential to turn into the second or third type once the HR manager determines the appropriate course of action.

The common challenge with all three problems is recognizing them (Rest 1976). Often, in the day-to-day requirements of running a human resources operation, the manager does not have time to reflect on the ethical implications of an action (Moberg 2000). The more obviously "ethical" situations involve virtue or moral courage—the HR manager simply has to refuse to do that which is not right and choose to do what is. For example, an HR manager who looks the other way or even helps falsify the paperwork when a hiring manager uses slave labor is not facing an ethical issue but rather simply failing to do right. There are many cases, though, where HR managers do not know all of the facts, do not think about the implications of a decision, or do not see themselves as moral agents in the decision and thus do not recognize it as a moral issue.

One challenge, then, to HR managers who wish to behave ethically, is to find ways to increase their abilities to recognize moral issues. They can do this by setting time aside to reflect, by talking with other managers about issues, by reading journals and newspaper columns devoted to discussion of ethics, and by listening carefully to employees who voice concerns. The allocation of resources to this effort becomes an ethical issue in itself. How much time can an HR manager devote to better recognizing ethical issues before being guilty of neglecting other duties? Is once a year enough? Is every day too often? The more HR managers develop their moral sensitivities, though, the more difficult it may be to learn of ethical issues, because other employees in the organization may go out of their way to hide information. There may be a counterbalancing tendency of wronged individuals to seek out the HR manager known to be ethical (Trevino, Hartman, and Brown 2000), but since many of those wronged may be outside of the organization, they may never learn of the HR manager's reputation. HR managers wishing to behave ethically thus must also increase their abilities to discover hidden motives and activities.

Even after recognizing a moral issue, obtaining facts and determining right action is still difficult. Not all facts are available, and many that are cannot be obtained in a timely (or fiscally responsible) manner. Taking incomplete information, considering it, and making decisions are what managers do. Some decisions are just more difficult to make than others, especially when several different duties or interests are opposed and the information gap is large.

Problems related to fetal protection can fall in this category. While adults may be able to evaluate incomplete scientific data and determine whether the risks of working in a particular environment are worth the other benefits of engaging in that work, they may not be in a position to make those decisions for their future offspring. The HR manager must consider both interests as well as the interests of the firm and its stockholders and the firm's ability to mitigate potential harms, all in an environment where data are incomplete and the HR manager's power is limited. Knowing the history of industries where scientists withheld information about harm to consumers, such as the tobacco industry, the HR manager may be very skeptical of the scientific data that *are* available.

"Right action," once discerned by the HR manager, is sometimes translated into policy and procedure, to provide guidance to other managers and information to employees. Policies and procedures help HR managers ensure fairness by making the decision-making process more consistent and transparent. However, policies and procedures can also detract from HR managers' recognizing some ethical issues, because policy may be applied without regard for changes over time or for individual situations. One approach to that dilemma is to set up systems whereby employees review HR policies and practices regularly (Kochan 2002).

HR managers can also turn to their professional associations for guidance. Codes of ethics established by professional associations of human resource managers require certain levels of integrity, obedience to the letter and spirit of the law, contribution to the organization and the profession, loyalty, and confidentiality (Wiley 2000). A more skeptical view of these codes' usefulness has been expressed by Scoville (1993).

This chapter does not address the ethical issues faced by HR managers as managers dealing with their subordinates. Instead, it addresses their responsibilities with respect to the organization's policies and procedures and the special role of HR manager. This chapter also does not discuss the legal requirements affecting HR managers. It assumes that the HR manager has an obligation to obey the law unless the law itself is immoral. The chapter does address, however, ethical issues faced by HR managers when others violate laws, when laws are immoral, and when the letter and spirit of the law do not coincide.

Functions of an HR Manager

HR managers are taught that they have four basic functions with respect to employees: to recruit, to train, to motivate, and to retain. A fifth function, terminating, is also performed by HR managers, albeit usually after failing somehow at one of the other four functions. All of these functions are aimed at achieving the goals of the organization, and each has the potential for all three kinds of ethical issues. Some responsibilities (e.g., compensation, benefits, labor relations, record-keeping) cross several functions. For example, compensation is used to recruit applicants and to motivate and retain employees. Labor relations (addressed in another chapter) affect recruiting, training, motivating, retaining, and terminating employees. Practices in organizations vary widely, so not all of the descriptions of issues here will apply to every organization.

Recruitment

HR managers know all too well that, despite organizational rhetoric, they are not looking for *the* best qualified person for each job. They are looking for someone who can do the job well and, in some cases, for someone who shows promise for being promoted. To this end, HR managers are expected to outline minimum qualifications, set an entry salary range, advertise the position, refer applicants to hiring managers, and review selection decisions in a way that balances the organization's resources with the likelihood of finding a well-qualified person. The ethical challenge is to balance individuals' expectations of (and rights to) equal opportunities with the organization's obligation of resource stewardship.

Minimum Qualifications To recruit employees, an HR manager needs a clear idea of qualifications needed to perform job duties. Before advertising a vacancy, the HR manager usually establishes the minimum knowledge, skills, and abilities a person must have to be considered for the position. Setting minimum qualifications is an ethical decision, but it is often approached as merely a strategic one. The strategic decision is certainly important. Setting the minimum qualifications too high will result in applicants unwilling to accept either the position or the salary offered. Setting the minimum qualifications too low will result, at best, in applications from so many people that extensive secondary screening procedures will be required and, at worst, in signaling to the most desirable applicants that they need not apply because they will be judged overqualified.

In addition, however, the HR manager is often faced with special requests—such as ensuring that the qualifications don't exclude the hiring manager's preselected favorite candidate—that further complicate the process of determining what qualifications to require. Ever since the days of *(Griggs v. Duke Power* 1971:424), it has been evident that managers can use minimum qualifications to exclude people who are perfectly capable of doing a job. While the *Griggs* decision outlawed these exclusions where they distinguish on the basis of race, sex, or other legally defined classification, there is no similar protection when the minimum qualifications exclude individuals who cannot claim "adverse impact" under *Griggs*. However, ethical principles would still require fairness.

It is sometimes difficult for the HR manager to discern why a hiring manager insists on a particular qualification that does not seem necessary for performance of the job duties. Sometimes the HR manager does not fully understand the job duties, but other times the hiring manager wants to avoid having to consider a particular employee. The hiring manager may have good reason not to want this employee, but manipulating the minimum qualifications is not the way to achieve that end. The HR manager has an ethical obligation to try to eliminate such managerial behavior—both because it can be disastrous for the employer and because it singles out individuals for unfair treatment. A typical example occurs when a hiring manager prefers a relatively new employee over more senior candidates. Observing that the more senior candidates have no college degrees, the hiring manager requests that a degree be one of the minimum qualifications—erroneously believing that in the end this will appear to be an "objective" reason why the junior person obtained the job and thus head off internal bickering. Unfortunately for the manager, the other internal applicants are not usually so easily fooled. Depending on the HR manager's authority within the situation, he or she may be able to refuse the hiring manager's request outright or may have to pursue another avenue (e.g., internal whistleblowing) to eliminate this kind of behavior.

Entry Salary Range HR managers must balance several consideration in setting appropriate salary ranges. First, there is the question of what the current labor market demands. This is mainly a practical consideration. If the labor market demands more than the employer is willing to pay, it may be foolish to spend resources to recruit applicants. However, there are also ethical considerations associated with internal equity. If the current labor market demands more than it once did, employers may find themselves paying new employees more than long-term employees doing the same job. This fact may not always be apparent to the existing employees, who may not realize that they could command higher salaries elsewhere and may not have direct contact with other employees doing the same work. The ethical consideration for the HR manager then becomes whether to take steps to increase the salaries of the existing employees or change the job classifications of the new employees. If there are real differences between the skills and abilities of those in the external labor market and the existing employees, changing the job classification of the vacant position may be the appropriate action. The change may take the form of a higher classification for people with greater skills and abilities or of a lower classification to attract trainees who do not yet have the skills and abilities necessary. If there are no real differences, the ethical HR manager will address the question of internal equity before advertising the job, developing a plan to ensure that existing employees are not penalized with lower salaries for failing to seek jobs elsewhere.

The second question regarding entry salary levels relates to what has been called "comparable worth." If applicants would be hireable at lower salaries due to generalized discrimination against members of the labor market, does the employer have an ethical obligation to pay on the basis of the contribution made to the organization? An HR manager with limited resources is unlikely to conduct studies assessing the "worth" of jobs, but failing to do so because one wants to avoid legal liability would be, in Kantian term, not produced by a "good will."

The third question is whether to advertise the salary range for the position and, if so what portion. Omitting a salary or salary range may simply be an effort to save on advertising costs. However, when it is done to enable employers to negotiate lower salaries for those most desperate for work, it violates the Rawlsian principle of setting up systems that protect the least advantaged. Similarly, advertising just the top of the salary range when most employees achieve only a small percentage of it is dishonest. When the vast majority of employees in a particular job make minimum wage, advertisements that claim employees can earn huge bonuses and commissions, even if true, mislead potential applicants to believe they *will* earn significantly more than is true.

Advertising A position can be advertised very narrowly, such as by handing a vacancy announcement to one person, or very broadly, by putting a sign in the window, a link on a web page, an ad in the paper, or a commercial on television. The decision about how broadly to advertise has both strategic and ethical components. When the position would represent a promotion (or even a more desirable career path) for current employees, the strategic component involves considering the costs and benefits of going outside the organization. Possible costs include monetary expense for ads, lost productivity during the recruiting period, and turnover by disappointed employees. There also may be adverse effects caused by creating new vacancies and encouraging complacency by promoting from within. Organizations wishing to encourage employee loyalty often require posting positions internally first and going outside the organization only after all internal candidates have been rejected. Other organizations, hoping to encourage creativity and internal competition, routinely recruit outside. This assessment of costs and benefits remains in the strategic realm as long as the HR manager's concern is to maximize the welfare of the organization, but as the concern broadens to include maximizing the welfare of society, the analysis enters the realm of utilitarian ethics.

One of the ethical balancing acts an HR manager must perform regarding advertising is between fulfilling promises (or psychological contracts) regarding career advancement and providing legitimate opportunities for those outside the organization to obtain employment. Hiring managers sometimes request advertisements with no intention of considering anyone beyond a particular individual. Such pro forma advertisements waste applicants' time, energy, money, and hope, and they either encourage favored candidates to believe it is acceptable to mislead others or they cause favored candidates to feel insecure about jobs they have already been promised. Often the advertisement is placed at the behest of the HR manager, who insists that the position be advertised to provide equal employment opportunities. But since advertising does not ensure that the hiring manager will be any more open to considering all applicants, the HR manager's goal would be better served by establishing a procedure under which hiring managers can request exemption from any requirement to advertise vacancies by providing evidence that forgoing advertisement is appropriate in the particular case.

With a decision to advertise outside the organization made, the HR manager should consider the organization's stated values and choose methods that reflect them. Word-of-mouth advertising, for example, is most likely to generate applicants similar to current employees. If the organization claims to value diversity but is not already diverse, this form of recruitment would call into question the truth of the organization's claim. Similarly, website advertising may create a bias in favor of wealthier and younger applicants. If computer skills are not important to the job, such advertising diminishes the integrity of the process. The HR manager's job is to consider cost-effective outlets where qualified candidates are most likely to see or hear a vacancy announcement. In choosing among those outlets, the HR manager's ethical obligation is, foremost, not to bias the pool unfairly and, second, not to bias it in ways that conflict with the organization's stated values. (If the values themselves are unfair, the HR manager has no obligation to ensure that they are enacted in advertising positions.)

Adhering to the organization's stated values is, in ethical terms, promise keeping. If the organization promises in its stated values to promote from within, an initial advertisement beyond the bounds of the organization would violate that promise. The more difficult problem for the HR manager is determining when the inevitable bias caused by the choice of advertisements is significant enough to render the process unfair. One important consideration is the intentionality of the bias (Kant's notion of a "good will"). For example, it is impossible to ensure that no employee is on leave when a vacancy is announced, but if a hiring manager waits until a particular employee's vacation week to advertise a vacancy because the manager wants to avoid considering the person, that bias is unfair. A second important consideration is the potential effect of the choice of advertisement on society. Ethical theories put varying degrees of emphasis on the outcomes of an action, but they would suggest considering whether the bias caused by the advertising benefited those least well off in society, whether there was more good than harm done by the bias, and whether important stakeholders were considered in the decision. The advertisement of any particular vacancy is probably unlikely to affect society in an appreciable way, but a policy or practice of a large corporation to, for example, post all entry-level vacancies with the local employment service office or in shelters for battered women has the potential to affect local economies.

The HR manager sometimes faces the question of whether to recruit applicants from competitors, suppliers, customers, or regulators. HR managers should not encourage among potential or actual employees disloyalty, dishonesty, or violation of "noncompete" agreements that have been legitimately negotiated (i.e., by knowledgeable participants with relatively equal power). But they should also respect the autonomy of potential employees to choose to leave another employer. Whether an applicant has slighted, or even breached a duty to, a current employer is difficult for the HR manager to monitor, because such information is not always available. HR managers have a duty to scrutinize any decisions to hire people who have had prior dealings with the organization as employees of another organization, especially if the prior dealings resulted in unusually advantageous decisions for the hiring organization. And, since violations are so hard to find, those that are found should be punished sufficiently harshly to transmit the message that the behavior is contrary to any employer's values.

An issue currently in the forefront or business ethics is outsourcing. In order to determine the ethical stance in this discussion, an HR manager must clearly understand the anticipated outcomes regarding all of the stakeholders: employees, potential employees, local communities, external communities, and stockholders (Arnold and Bowie 2003).

The manager also needs to clearly understand all of the contracts, both actual and psychological, surrounding the relationships with current employees.

Selection The final step in the recruitment process is to select from among the applicants for a position. Selection is so important that it is sometimes listed as a separate function of HR managers. However, it is often performed by the hiring manager, after the HR department has collected applications and eliminated the people who clearly don't qualify. The HR manager establishes policies and procedures to be followed but may have little control over what occurs in the actual selection process.

Screening of applicants can be performed by HR staff. They may add a set of preferred qualifications that are more stringent than the minimum qualifications posted in the advertisement. They may use written or performance tests. In both of these cases, the HR manager has to worry not only about being fair but also about appearing fair. Tests or screening criteria that do not have face validity appear unfair to applicants, even when the employer knows that they are valid through extensive studies linking test scores with job success. One threat to test validity exists if applicants who take a test multiple times can do better on that specific test, but not necessarily on the job, just because they have practiced the test (Huasknecht, Trevor, and Farr 2002). If there are practice effects that are not related to on-the-job performance, to preserve fairness HR managers should consider whether to implement rules limiting the number of times an applicant can take the same test.

HR staff may conduct recruiting or screening interviews, and surely every HR manager has experienced having a CEO or other senior staff member send people to be interviewed "as a favor." In these cases, HR's role is to represent the organization well and to become familiar enough with the applicant's qualifications to help locate vacancies in the organization that might prove fruitful. The ethical HR representative must be careful not to overpromise to the applicant or to misread the degree of assistance promised by the senior staff member.

After the applicant pool is narrowed through evaluating preferred qualifications and testing, there is often a small set of applicants presented to the hiring manager for interviews and the selection decision. The HR manager bears some responsibility for training the hiring manager in interviewing technique and for reviewing the process to ensure that interviews are conducted and evaluated fairly. Many organizations are moving toward establishing work teams, with the team empowered to select its members. There is some evidence that teams are more likely to pick people like themselves, demographically, and thus engage in unlawful discrimination as agents of the employer (Goins and Mannix 1999). The HR manager has an obligation to create mechanisms that reduce this tendency.

An ethical issue associated with the interviewing process is the amount of privacy protection due applicants. Depending on the applicant's power in the situation, various ethicists have recommended eliminating all questions aimed at determining attitudes, motivations, and beliefs, arguing that applicants have a right to keep this information to themselves. Others see this position as paternalistic (Nye 2002). The HR manager's job is to discern the appropriate amount of privacy protection due applicants and convey this to hiring managers.

As genetic screening tests become available, employers face the possibility of having information that could be relevant to long-term employment decisions. Knowing that a particular employee has a greater likelihood of developing a serious disease can tempt an employer to pass over that person for promotions or for training requiring long-term investment. HR managers have a responsibility to ensure that these records are not available to anyone but the employee and that such data are not collected without the employee's knowledge and consent.

Many HR managers in industries with very low-wage jobs find themselves in the position of not knowing whether their employees are legally allowed to work—for example, because they are aliens, because they are below a minimum age, or because they have not obtained required licenses. In some cases, line managers obtain forged supporting documents (birth certificates, passports, etc.) proving eligibility to work. While lack of participating in the forgery may exempt the HR manager from legal liability, he or she still has an ethical obligation to take reasonable steps to ensure that neither line managers nor new employees violate laws that are themselves ethical. Random checks of original documents may eliminate widespread violations, but there may be no way to thwart the determined violator. Internal whistleblowing by the HR manager may be necessary to bring violations to the attention of someone with the power to enact sanctions. Clear and relatively harsh consequences for employees who are complicit in hiring illegally may be the only way to convey the organization's lack of support for such behavior.

Violating hiring laws would generally fall in the area of unethical behavior. However, HR managers sometimes must discern whether the law, various regulations, or court decisions are ethical. For example, organizations considering employing persons with disabilities whose conditions pose a threat to their own health and safety on the job but not the health and safety of others faced conflicting Equal Employment Opportunity Commission (EEOC) regulations and court decisions. The EEOC allowed employers to refuse employment on this basis, but the 9th Circuit Court of Appeals did not. While this controversy has been resolved by the U.S. Supreme Court, in favor of the EEOC regulations, it illustrates a case where the HR manager must balance concern for the health and welfare of the prospective employee against employees' rights to make decisions about their own health and welfare (Reed 2003). Similarly, HR managers of multinational corporations during apartheid in South Africa made decisions to violate local laws requiring separation of the races.

A common complaint from applicants is that they submitted applications and "never heard back" from the employer.

This contributes to a perception of unfairness, and it may actually inhibit the freedom of an applicant who waits to hear about an employment application rather than go on vacation or accept other employment. At the conclusion of the selection process, the ethical HR manager will ensure that unsuccessful applicants are notified promptly and kindly of rejection decisions.

Successful Applicants Having identified successful applicants, HR managers face several ethical challenges. The HR manager must carefully explain the employment contract. Some ethicists argue that "at will" contracts are not morally permissible (Werhane 1983; Radin and Werhane 2003; McCall 2003), while others argue simply that the employer should not sugarcoat the nature of the relationship (Roehling 2003). If a union represents the prospective employee's position, the collective bargaining contract must be provided to the applicant. While there is pressure on the HR manager to "woo" successful applicants, the ethical manager will provide an accurate picture of the job and the organization. There may also be pressure to negotiate the lowest possible salary, but ethics require that the manager not take advantage of applicants' vulnerabilities (Brenkert 1998), and fairness requires equal pay for equal work.

Determining the point at which to check references requires balancing the need to protect applicants' privacy against the need to obtain relevant information. In many industries, employees are fired if their employers learn they are even applying for other jobs. Reference checking is especially important in jobs where the incumbent will have unsupervised responsibility for children or elderly persons or access to large quantities of cash. If the applicant is internal, the HR manager must decide what information gained from within is appropriate to transmit to the hiring manager and what information is irrelevant to the hiring decision. If the applicant is external, an HR manager often draws upon personal or professional contacts to obtain reference information about an applicant. In this case, the HR manager has an obligation to balance the discretion due the informant and the fair hearing due the applicant.

Conflict of Interest The recruitment function is not fraught with large conflicts of interest for HR managers. There may be a temptation to use the power of the position to provide jobs to friends or relatives or to ensure that recruiting trips include the HR manager's alma mater, but since there is usually a separation between functions of the HR and the hiring managers, the HR manager may find efforts to place family and friends thwarted.

Training and Development

Typically, training is divided into two types: general training, which will make an employee more flexible and adaptable within the organization and more marketable outside it, and specific training, which is unique to the organization or even the position. Employee development involves examining an employee's career prospects and offering support in his or her career path. The ethical challenge to HR managers is to devise systems of providing training and development opportunities that are fair to all employees.

General Training Organizations are often reluctant to provide general training, because they see themselves as paying for training that an employee can then take to a competitor and use against them. There is no ethical obligation to promote general training programs, but doing so is one way to treat employees as more than a means to an end. One financial safeguard used by some employers is to require employees to sign agreements to repay the cost of their training if they leave within a certain period. The ethical issue facing the HR manager drafting such an agreement is to ensure that it is clearly explained and does not take unfair advantage of the employee.

Safety Training While HR managers may have no ethical obligation to provide general training, they are obliged to ensure that all employees are aware of any safety hazards associated with their jobs or their work environments. Beyond simply providing safety warnings, HR managers have an ethical obligation to ensure that the warnings are clearly understood by employees, particularly those who may not be able to read the language of the warning or who otherwise may not understand the danger being identified in the warning. Literacy training may be a necessary precursor to safety training.

A special case of safety training involves protection against potentially contagious diseases, such as AIDS and hepatitis. When possible, safety training should be designed to prevent or reduce transmission of disease, whether or not the infection status of a person is known. Gloving, hand washing, and proper instrument disposal are all techniques that can be taught to employees. However, employees understandably want to be informed whenever their risk level increases. They expect employers to provide them with the identities of infected co-workers, clients, or customers. The HR manager must balance the likelihood that an employee will become infected against the infected person's right to privacy. In this balancing, the HR manager must consider that knowing the identities of some but not all people who are infected may actually put employees at a higher risk, because it will give them a false sense of security with any others who are infected but not known to be.

A second special case of safety training is balancing an employee's right to make decisions about undertaking risk and the employer's responsibility to protect others from harm. When an employee's job involves risk to bystanders if done incorrectly, an employer cannot stop after providing training and assume that the employee will bear the ethical burden of keeping others safe. The employer has an obligation to ensure that the job is performed as taught and that the employee is not provided with incentives to take unnecessary risks. Again, while the burden of legal liability may be on someone else, an ethical HR manager will implement systems to monitor the transfer of the training to the workplace and will build incentive systems that encourage safety.

Values Training Some employees resent being required to attend values training because they see it as an attempt to indoctrinate them into a particular religion or to brainwash them. The HR manager, who presumably shares the organization's values, should ensure clear consistency both between values addressed in training and those supported by the organization and between these values and the organization's reward and discipline systems. The training should also recognize that new employees may intend to be ethical but may be less sophisticated than experienced employees in evaluating the implications of various behaviors (Stevens 2001).

There should also be some provision for employees to opt out of training they consider morally objectionable. However, enough such requests should give the HR manager pause. It could be simply the method of training and not the core value that is in question, but it could also be time to reexamine the underlying values or the employee selection methods. Ever since Weber (1930) described how religious beliefs can fuel corporate profits, employers have sought to select employees with some set of religious or quasireligious beliefs or to create it in them. The Kantian idea of a categorical imperative can guide HR managers trying to ensure that all employees accept certain values. Some values, such as participative management, tolerance, and diversity, create internal inconsistencies when organizations attempt to require them as "rules for all." Requiring all managers to use participative management, for example, does not allow managers to participate in the decision to use it. Requiring tolerance of all employees is intolerant of those who are themselves intolerant. Embracing diversity means embracing even those who do not embrace diversity. Rules that the HR manager either does not want applied universally or cannot imagine applying universally should not be implemented. The HR manager should periodically review values-training programs to ensure that they are consistent with all of the organization's values, not simply the one or ones being addressed in that particular session.

Employers have occasionally been required by law or court order to train employees in certain values, such as diversity. In these cases, the HR manager is faced with following the law, advocating for a change in the law, breaking the law, or resigning. Deciding among these options requires considering one's personal position and the organization's position. If they are not in concert, and neither party is convinced by the other to change, an ethical HR manager will resign. This is because ethical HR managers cannot abrogate their responsibilities to their employers by acting on behalf of an employer to violate a law the employer would have them follow or to follow a law the employer would have them violate. However, ethical HR managers also cannot abrogate responsibility to themselves by following a law they believe to be immoral or violating one they believe to be moral. If the HR manager and the organization are in concert, they can devise an approach together. Where the organization, the HR manager, and the law are all in concert, the decision-making process is relatively simple: the law is followed. Decision making becomes complex where the law differs from what the HR manager and organization believe. An organization should not take lightly the decision to violate a law or court order. Avenues of appeal and legislative influence should be exhausted first, but where the law is immoral (not simply inconvenient or costly for the employer to implement), the organization can ethically engage in civil disobedience. Laws or court orders that require employers to trample on employees' freedoms should give HR managers great pause. Some managers who have been too quick to follow such laws or too enthusiastic in sanctioning employees who object to the training have found that courts subsequently overturned the laws in question.

Conflict of Interest Building a training staff large enough to provide any kind of training for the organization can contribute to the HR manager's personal influence and even compensation level. Being able to select from among consultants can give HR managers opportunities to assist friends or family in the consulting firm or to receive gifts or favors from the consultants. Both situations represent conflicts of interest that the ethical HR manager will avoid. Decisions should be made on the basis of the HR manager's professional judgment, not personal interests.

Career Development Many organizations use mentoring programs to foster career development, pairing new (or at least junior) employees one-on-one with employees with significant experience. What was once an informal practice has become much more formal in many organizations. Mentors can take advantage of their positions of power with respect to the employees they are mentoring, so the HR manager's ethical responsibility is to ensure that abuses of power are minimized (Moberg and Velasquez 2004).

A typical career development program includes succession planning, in which the organization identifies employees who are prepared (or have the potential to be prepared) to step into vacancies as key staff retire, are promoted, or otherwise leave their positions. The organization provides training to prepare the designated employees for eventual vacancies and does not provide such training to those deemed not promotable. To ensure that such planning does not treat employees unfairly, HR managers should develop procedures that, at a very minimum, allow employees to indicate their interests in being promoted and notify those deemed not promotable of the decision. Employees remain with organizations with the belief that they will have a chance to compete for future vacancies on a level playing field. If a determination is made to give the inside track to certain employees, in terms of both training offered and preference for assignments, then the employees deemed not promotable should not be deceived into thinking that, if they are loyal employees, their tenure will be rewarded with promotions. They should be provided with clear feedback that enables them to consider whether they want to remain with the current organization without being promoted or to try their chances at another. If current trends continue, such that employees have reduced expectations that they will remain with the same employer for life, this may become less of an ethical issue (Cappelli 1999).

Motivation

In designing motivation systems, HR managers seek to align employees' goals with those of the organization. This can be done coercively or by convincing employees of the worthiness of the organization's goals and the value of employee contributions to them. Designing effective motivation systems is difficult; ensuring that they have no coercive element is almost impossible. The HR manager's ethical challenge is to consider the amount of coercion used and discern whether it is reasonably balanced against the employee's power in the situation and whether it serves the goals and values articulated by the employee. Taking the car keys away from a drunk would-be driver is coercive, but it properly considers other stakeholders as well as the values the driver has when sober. Similarly, docking the salary of an employee who fails to follow safety regulations is a coercive way to change behavior, but it can also be an ethical way to motivate a recalcitrant employee. On the other hand, offering huge sums of money to employees to work in dangerous environments may be an unethical form of coercion, especially if the technology exists to make the environment less dangerous. The problem of discernment for an HR manager wishing to behave ethically is determining the point at which "hazardous duty pay" stops being a reasonable recognition of risk freely undertaken by an employee and becomes an offer the employee truly *couldn't* refuse. Coercion removes the employee's freedom to choose, thus abridging the right to liberty (Greenwood 2002).

Systems to motivate employees are developed both by HR managers and by direct supervisors. While supervisory intervention may have the most significant effect on employee motivation, tools that the HR manager provides can make supervisors more effective. These tools can include compensation systems, performance appraisal systems, employee monitoring systems, organizational climate, charitable contribution campaigns, job design, work teams, progressive disciplinary systems, and others. Line supervisors can use the tools ethically or unethically; the HR manager's ethical responsibility is to design tools that are not easily used unethically and to develop procedures to monitor their use.

Compensation Though compensation systems are designed to align the interests of employee and employer, they can also create conflicts of interest. Commission compensation systems can provide incentives to salespeople to disregard the interests of customers in order to obtain the highest commission (Robertson and Anderson 1993; Kurland 1999). Insurance agents, stock brokers, and real estate buyers' agents, for example, may urge clients to purchase a more expensive product to increase commissions. Supervisors who receive bonuses for number of days without a lost-time accident may pressure employees not to seek treatment for injuries. Managers whose performance is measured by staff productivity may require subordinate employees to work "off the clock" or to skip their breaks. In each of these cases, the organization motivates employees to perform well using some proxy (seniority, supervisor's assessment, hours worked, quantity of output) to estimate the value of the employee's contribution. There is nothing inherently unethical about any of these compensation systems, but other parts of the organization must be operated ethically in order for the compensation systems not to create conflicts of interest. Using seniority as a method of determining pay, for example, is often criticized as unfair. However, this criticism may arise because seniority no longer operates as a proxy for performance on the job. This could occur for one or a number of reasons: because employees who should have been fired were not, because technology has changed and long-term employees were not trained, because the selection system used in the past was faulty, because the cumulative effect of a number of years of working for the employer decreases employees' abilities. The HR manager has the responsibility to ensure that every compensation system contains effective mechanisms to reduce conflicts of interest.

HR managers face a personal conflict of interest in implementing and administering compensation systems. They might be tempted to implement systems that benefit them financially. For example, if the system establishes pay caps for jobs based on market analysis, the manager may be tempted to recommend eliminating caps as he or she approaches the limit, based on the desire to earn more money rather than professional judgment about the caps. The ethical obligation is to ignore such temptation and instead continue to develop a system that is best for the employer, administer it impartially, and build in checks and balances.

HR managers' problem of discernment requires determining a compensation system that is fair and just, and this may differ within and between organizations. Issues include the appropriate difference between pay for the CEO and for rank-and-file employees, systems for paying line versus staff employees, comparable worth, merit-based pay, team-based pay, power differences in salary negotiations, coercively high pay, unpaid work, paid breaks, travel pay, overtime pay, vacation pay, holiday pay, and sick pay, among many others. In some jurisdictions, local and national laws govern the treatment of some of these issues, and the problem becomes more complex in multistate and multinational organizations (Graham and Trevor 2000; Donaldson 2001).

Much of the current controversy regarding compensation addresses executive compensation, especially for CEOs in publicly held firms (Hannafey 2003). Decisions on executive compensation are almost always outside of the HR manager's job, though the manager may be able to use informal influence and earned authority to affect these decisions. In cases where the HR manager cannot create a fair compensation system because of decisions made by senior managers or the board of directors, the only ethical recourse may be to resign.

Performance Appraisal Systems Performance appraisals are almost universally dreaded. Despite this, HR managers argue, at least publicly, that appraisals are valuable because they know that feedback is important to smooth organizational functioning and that informal feedback, while essential, is not remembered the same by both parties. At their best, performance appraisals motivate employees to continue the things they are doing well, to improve at things they are doing poorly, and to cease things they should not be doing at all. At their worst, they are used to attack or protect employees based on managers' likes and dislikes. Ethics dictate that the HR manager not create a system so complex, cumbersome, or unmonitored that supervisors ignore it or use it improperly.

Employee Monitoring Many employers have systems of monitoring employees—to measure productivity, to prevent theft, or to protect others (Hoffman and Hartman 2003)—through videotaping, capturing keystrokes, reviewing e-mail, tapping telephones, collecting specimens for drug testing, or tracking locations (Mishra 1998). In all cases, the HR manager must weigh the employee's right to privacy against the reason for the monitoring. Some ethicists argue that monitoring systems offend against employees' freedoms and that the legitimate ends of monitoring can be achieved in less intrusive ways (Mishra 1998).

Climate and Culture There is evidence that the organizational climate and subunit climate can motivate employees to engage in ethical or unethical behavior (VanSandt 2003; Weber, Kurke, and Pentico 2003). Insofar as the HR manager has control over climate, there is an ethical obligation to ensure that it is ethical. However, even when the HR manager cannot control climate, especially in subunits, he or she may set up systems to monitor climate and provide training or advice to managers on how to improve it.

Charitable Contribution Campaigns Many employers seek to motivate employees by projecting an image as a caring, socially responsible organization. Some sponsor campaigns to encourage employees to contribute to charitable organizations, including, in the cases of qualified organizations, the employer itself. This practice, when carried out without coercion, can contribute to employees' sense that their employer does good, especially when the employer matches employee contributions. However, some employers pressure employees for contributions, eliminating the strategic purpose of motivation and reducing the overall good done by the organization. HR managers are usually removed from the solicitation activity, giving them freedom to lessen pressure on employees by reminding both solicitors and those solicited that contributions are truly voluntary. They should remind management, in particular, to discourage campaigns seeking 100% participation and to recognize employee charitable activities not connected with the organization's campaign.

Job Design The HR literature argues that jobs need to be intrinsically rewarding to be motivating. Hackman and Oldham's classic set of factors is still used today (Hackman, Oldham, Janson, and Purdy 1975). Jobs must have skill variety, task identity, task significance, autonomy, and feedback to have the potential to be motivating. Some ethicists suggest that employers have an obligation to ensure that jobs are intrinsically rewarding. Others suggest that it is an obligation to design jobs in a way that makes them more accessible to people with disabilities. HR managers should consider such arguments in writing job descriptions. Similarly, there is considerable debate over the number of hours a week a person is expected to work. Flexibility in hours worked makes jobs more accessible to people with lower levels of stamina, with competing home responsibilities, or with restrictions on the income they can earn. Determining that a job is "part-time" has significant implications for most benefits contracts. Many organizations provide reduced or no benefits to people in part-time positions.

Teams and Quality Circles Teams can make employees happier with their jobs and more likely to stay (Hunter, Macduffie, and Doucet 2002), and they have been used to motivate employees by giving them more control over their jobs. However, teams have also been shown to be related to increases in injuries (Brenner and Fairris 2004). HR managers have an ethical obligation to monitor the behavior of teams to ensure that the increased motivation is not misdirected toward activities that endanger team members.

Progressive Discipline HR policies usually include a range of disciplinary actions that can be taken to motivate employees when more positive reinforcement fails, including such things as warnings, reprimands, docking pay, demotion, suspension, and firing. The HR manager's ethical challenge is to ensure internal equity in the selection of appropriate disciplinary action and to ensure that the person disciplined is treated with respect. For example, the Minnesota Department of Corrections failed to ensure internal equity when it reprimanded some employees for reading religious texts during training but did not reprimand others for reading magazines, doing paperwork, or sleeping (*Altman & Minnesota Department of Corrections* 2001).

Disciplinary action is often taken without consultation with the HR manager. An ethical manager will use mechanisms such as employee handbooks, training, and newsletters to provide notice of policies and performance requirements. It is especially important to provide such notice when it is not obvious that a behavior is proscribed. An HR manager need not provide notice to employees regarding the employer's objection to punching a supervisor, but organizations with rules against accepting tips or holding secondary employment have an obligation to put employees on notice. Consequently, much of the mechanism to ensure fairness must be incorporated in policy and supervisory training. If disciplinary actions are regularly overturned by arbitration panels or courts, HR managers should take steps to correct problems quickly. Otherwise, some actions warranting discipline may go unchecked because a supervisor does not want to go through the process of a disciplinary action only to be overturned. This would result in inequities in implementing discipline (and therefore even more decisions overturned) and might also result in employees suffering harassment or other abuse at the hands of co-workers because supervisors believe it is impossible to discipline anyone successfully. Some supervisors are very concerned about the effects of their actions on subordinates and their families, to the point where HR managers should be alert to instances where employees without families receive harsher discipline than those with families (Butterfield, Trevino, and Ball 1996).

Retention

The origin of many HR departments can be traced to Henry Ford's efforts to maintain a stable, trained workforce. He paid employees more money and offered them long-term benefits, such as retirement, that made it very difficult for them to quit. The first ethical challenge for HR managers is to examine the measures used to retain employees and to ensure that they do not make it so difficult to quit that employees will not leave or confront the organization even when put in untenable ethical positions. Do the on-site child care, company-subsidized mortgage, stock-option incentive pay, and family-friendly health plan tie employees so closely to the company that they are afraid to quit or to report irregularities? Even if the HR manager determines that the benefits offered have enough portability not to bind employees too closely, there are ethical issues surrounding the specific programs implemented and the amount of choice given employees.

Benefits The negotiating power that a large employer has in providing benefits for employees helps drive the costs lower than they would be if they were purchased individually by the employees. However, HR managers must consider the ethical implications of reducing costs for their own full-time employees while increasing them for their part-time employees, the unemployed, and persons employed in the secondary labor market. This is probably irrelevant for some of the more trendy benefits, such as on-site dry cleaning and fitness centers, but for retirement and health insurance, the reflective HR manager whose ethical concern goes beyond the organization's boundaries must consider these implications. I do not mean to suggest that any individual HR manager has the power to reverse the dominant U.S. model for providing health benefits to employees. In fact, were any organization to cut its benefits significantly, it might be violating its duty to keep promises to employees unless it made arrangements for the same benefits to be provided through another source. HR managers in multinational firms, however, would do well to consider whether adding U.S.-style benefits might begin a trend to undermine functioning national systems.

The most common method of providing benefits to employees of large organizations is to offer them an array from which they can choose. In some cases, employees are given a fixed sum of benefit dollars to spend; in others, they are given the option to use part of their salary to purchase the benefit. Many benefits are available through salary reduction, which shields part of the employee's salary from income taxes.

Even where there is a choice in benefits, the HR manager must decide which benefits will be included and, usually, which carrier will provide them. An ethical issue facing HR managers in this arena is the potential for conflict of interest. It can take two forms. First, the HR manager, as an employee, can be tempted to select programs for the benefit smorgasbord that are personally appealing. Second, since large revenues hinge upon these decisions, insurance carriers can be tempted to offer kickbacks or other incentives for the HR manager to select them. In both cases, the HR manager has a clear ethical obligation not to allow personal considerations to affect professional choices.

HR managers also have to balance the welfare of employees against the cost of benefit plans, and they have to make decisions about the amount of choice employees can reasonably be given. Obviously, companies could go bankrupt offering employee benefits. The strategy of offering benefits thus must take into account the likelihood that offering a particular benefit will help the employer attract better employees, retain desirable employees at lower overall cost, and motivate employees to devote more hours to productive work. The strategic question is not easily answered by a formula. Some benefits have a very short half-life on the employee-motivation scale, after which they become minimum requirements. By offering "cafeteria" plans of benefit choice, employers reduce the need to up the benefit ante every year, but they also increase administrative costs and decrease their purchasing power. So even within their obligation to be good stewards of employer resources, HR managers have real choices to make that have ethical implications.

Over the past half century, the costs of benefits have skyrocketed, with health insurance costs accounting for a large portion of the increase. The introduction of health maintenance organizations (HMOs) and preferred provider organizations (PPOs) to the Mix slowed the rise for some time, but some of the limitations imposed by these plans created very real problems for employees. HR managers were faced with angry employees, who felt that their psychological contract with the employer had been violated

(Lucero and Allen 1994). As demand for lifting the restrictions increased, so did costs. In response, some companies are cutting benefits or increasing the portion of the costs paid by employees. The ethical implications of cutting benefits or increasing co-payments mean that even when employers offer benefits, many lower-paid employees (Rawls's "least advantaged") are unable to purchase them.

The amount of choice provided to employees can be overwhelming. HR managers can provide a real service by examining plans carefully and providing information to employees making choices. The problem of discernment the HR manager faces is determining when the restriction of choice infringes on employee freedoms.

Balance There is considerable current research on the effects on workers of trying to balance work with "family" or "life" or "nonwork" activities. Organizations seeking to retain employees have instituted "work–family" benefits, including such things as on-site day care, work–family training, day-care referral programs, elder care assistance, and flexible schedules (Osterman 1995). These programs have generally been hailed by the business ethics literature as virtuous (Marchese, Bassham, and Ryan 2002), but the HR manager must address the issue of fairness, as employees with fewer dependents may begin to complain that they are shouldering more than their share of the work or receiving disproportionately fewer benefits.

Compensation Systems Compensation systems are also important to retention (Gerhart and Trevor 1996). HR managers must ensure that employees perceive their jobs as being worth at least as much as any alternative employment available to them. Some ethicists suggest that employers who receive higher-than-average profits in an industry have a moral obligation to pay their employees higher-than-average wages for that industry (Koys 2001). Turnover is related not only to the amount of compensation but also to the growth of compensation over time (Trevor, Gerhart, and Boudreau 1997). Certain compensation systems are designed as "golden handcuffs" that force employees to stay even when they wish to leave. Stock options that don't mature for years, longevity salary increases, and other devices intended to link the long-term interests of the organization with the employee's interests can become coercive if they represent a sufficient percentage of the employee's compensation.

Employee Complaint Mechanisms Hirschman (1970) suggests that people given the opportunity to voice complaints will be less likely to choose "exit" as their strategy. Many organizations have employee complaint procedures, administered through the HR department. Typically, they allow an employee to bring a formal complaint first to the supervisor or manager accused of wrongdoing, then to successively higher levels of management. One of the challenges facing HR managers is to ensure that the power differential between managers and employees does not quash complaints that should be heard. Unfortunately, one of the few ways to ensure this is to allow the expression of complaints that shouldn't be heard, taking up valuable staff time. An independent complaint investigator may lend credibility to the procedure. There is some evidence that having decision makers who are not part of management increases the number of grievances (Colvin 2003). However, even if the typical system is used, it is important for managers to receive training that enables them to see the employees' side of issues (Moberg 2003). An ethical HR manager will encourage legitimate grievances, will have them heard in a just platform, and will seek meaningful resolutions.

Termination

Not mentioned in the core responsibilities of HR managers but still a very real part of their jobs are employee dismissals, layoffs, resignations, and retirements. Employees who violate the organization's rules or fail to meet the standards established for their employment are dismissed. Those whose jobs are no longer needed, due to changes in organizational structure, goals, or finances, are laid off, The main difference between the two is that dismissal is person specific while layoff is job specific. In either case, the person affected is often devastated, and the HR manager has the ability to make the process less distressing. While the law in some places allows an employer to fire an employee for "a good reason, a bad reason, or no reason at all," Kant ([1785] 1981) would suggest that only actions done for good reasons can be good.

Dismissal Dismissals for rule violations are different from dismissals for poor performance: the first is willful, while the second may not be. The distinction has implications for how an HR manager addresses dismissals. "Fault" and "blame" should not be ascribed to people who are unable to achieve the standards of the organization, especially if they have been able to achieve those standards for years or are new employees. In the first case, it is likely declining capabilities that cause the inability to meet standards, and blaming a person for a natural process is cruel. In the second case, the HR manager is perhaps more blameworthy, having assessed the person's qualifications and determined that he or she could perform the job duties. However, in cases where the employee has chosen not to meet standards or has intentionally violated a rule, the HR manager may take pains to explain that the dismissal was within the employee's control.

HR managers have an obligation to make sure that systems of dismissing employees for rule violations are fairly designed and administered and clearly articulated. While employees whose productivity is high may be given special dispensation to violate rules (for example, to come to work late), it is important for HR managers to ascertain that all similarly situated employees receive the same dispensation. It is easy to look at an individual's record and say, "Of course that person deserves to be fired," but fairness cannot be determined until the HR manager has compared that record to the records of those who are not being considered for firing. The manner in which the employee is informed of the dismissal, as well as treatment after the notice has been provided, must respect the dignity of the employee and the safety of co-workers. Cases where disgruntled people take up arms and attack former supervisors or co-workers are rare enough to make front-page news, but the HR manager's ethical responsibility is to take steps to make sure they stay rare.

Layoffs When there are insufficient funds or orders to justify the size of the workforce, workers are laid off, either temporarily (until business picks up) or permanently. Layoffs are sometimes conducted under very strict rules, requiring people to be dismissed in reverse order from their hiring and providing "bumping rights" to people to return to previously held positions, forcing the incumbents to be laid off instead. The first job of the ethical HR manager is to provide alternatives to layoffs, outsourcing, or downsizing to the other managers considering the action. This requires clearly understanding the anticipated outcomes in terms of what might happen to all of the stakeholders: employees, potential employees, local communities, external communities, and stockholders (Arnold and Bowie 2003). The HR manager must also clearly understand all of the contracts, both actual and psychological, surrounding the relationships with current employees.

Assuming that a layoff does occur, the second job of the ethical HR manager is to provide notice, placement assistance, and recommendations for those being laid off. The specifics for each of these depend on the situation. The ethical HR manager should focus on looking out for those least advantaged by the decision. The third job is to provide for the emotional reactions of the "survivors," both rank-and-file co-workers and managers in the affected unit (Dewitt, Trevino, and Mollica 2003).

Resignation Employees who quit their jobs sometimes leave because they haven't found an outlet where they can voice their complaints. One way an HR manager can help these employees is to provide exit interviews, which, though not completely satisfying, may at least help the employees to feel as if their departure could help those left behind. Assuming the HR manager investigates and acts on complaints voiced in these interviews, other employees can be helped by subsequent reforms. One practice prevalent in some industries is to process all resignations immediately, despite any employee attempts to give notice. Unless there is a compelling reason to do otherwise, HR managers should encourage practices that reward giving notice rather than punish it.

Death Employees who die while employed leave family members in vulnerable positions with respect to the employer. The ethical HR manager can smooth the way for survivors by providing prompt and clear information on final paychecks, life insurance, continuation of health coverage, and other benefits that might be useful. Similarly, the HR manager can provide support for co-workers, including notices of the death and funeral arrangements and time off to attend the funeral, and can work with the direct supervisor to ensure smooth transitions.

Conclusion

Having been an HR practitioner for more than a decade, I have special sympathy for the pressures HR managers live under. It is rare that they can sit back and reflect on the many ethical issues involved in every decision they make. It is even rarer that they find other managers in the organization who are attuned to HR issues from an ethical perspective. While it may be easy for those removed from the situation to point to all of the ethical lapses of HR managers, I would hope that industrial relations and HR faculty would recognize their great potential to assist current practitioners and influence the behavior of future practitioners.

Teaching faculty can stress strategic or ethical considerations in their HR courses. Stressing ethical considerations would be one way to help develop an ethical sense among future practitioners. Faculty can make a course in ethics a prerequisite for their own HR courses and then address ethics regularly in relation to the topics they cover. They can invite ethicists to give guest lectures and local HR managers to talk about ethical issues they face. A few of the available HR textbooks address ethics in almost every chapter—choosing those over textbooks that ignore ethics or relegate it to a paragraph or two would be one way to underscore that students should consider ethics in all that they do. In "HR for the non-HR manager" courses, faculty can give other managers an appreciation for the multiplicity of ethical issues involved in their interactions with employees and with the HR department.

Research faculty have the opportunity to do considerably more work in the area of HR ethics. They have examined HR practices alone and in "bundles" to determine whether there are any that characterize more productive organizations. The consensus seems to be that there are "bundles" of best practices, but they are industry- or organization-specific (Macduffie 1995; Hunter 2000). That is, HR practices must work together toward the achievement of the organizational goal. How the ethics of human resources fits into this picture is not clearly understood. Researchers have yet to add what they know about ethics to what they know about bundles of practices. Similarly, researchers could examine the human costs of various HR practices.

In the end, though, the burden is on each individual HR manager to be reflective, always alert to the potential that what appears to be a routine decision may actually be a chance to do right.

Source: In The Ethics of Human Resources and Industrial Relations. Budd, J. and Scoville, J. (eds.) Labor and Employment Relations Association (2005), 173–201. Reprinted by permission.

REFERENCES

Altman v Minnesota Department of Corrections, 251 F.3d 1199 (8th Cir., 2001).

Arnold, Denis G., and Norman E. Bowie. 2003. "Sweatshops and Respect for Persons." *Business Ethics Quarterly*, Vol. 13, no. 2 (April), pp. 221–43.

Brenkert, George G. 1998. "Marketing and the Vulnerable," *Business Ethics Quarterly, The Ruffin Series [Special issue]*, No. 1, pp. 7–20.

Brenner Mark, and David Fairris. 2004. "Flexible Work Practices and Occupational Safety and Health: Exploring the Relationship Between Cumulative Trauma Disorders and Workplace Transformation." *Industrial Relations*, Vol. 43, no. 1 (January), pp. 242–67.

Butterfield, Kenneth D., Linda Klebe Trevino, and Gail A. Ball. 1996. "Punishment from the Manager's Perspective: A Grounded Investigation and Inductive Model." *Academy of Management Journal*, Vol. 39, no. 6 (December), pp. 1479–1512.

Cappelli, Peter. 1999. "Career Jobs Are Dead." *California Management Review*. Vol. 42, no. 1 (Fall), pp. 146–67.

Clarkson, Max E. 1995. "A Stakeholder Framework for Analyzing and Evaluating Corporate Social Performance." *Academy of Management Review*, Vol. 20, no. 1 (January), pp. 92–118.

Colvin, Alexander J. S. 2003. "The Dual Transformation of Workplace Dispute Resolution." *Industrial Relations*, Vol. 42, no. 4 (October), pp. 712–36.

Dewitt, Rocki-Lee, Linda Klebe Trevino, and Kelly A. Mollica. 2003. "Stuck in the Middle: A Control-Based Model of Managers' Reactions to Their Subordinates' Layoffs." *Journal of Managerial Issues*, Vol. 15, no. 1 (Spring), pp. 32–49.

Donaldson, John, 2001. "Multinational Enterprises, Employment Relations, and Ethics," *Employee Relations*, Vol. 23. no. 6 (November), pp. 627–42.

Gerhart, Barry, and Charlie O. Trevor. 1996. "Employment Variability Under Different Managerial Compensation Systems." *Academy of Management Journal*, Vol. 39, no. 6 (December), pp. 1692–712.

Goins, Sheila, and Elizabeth A. Mannix. 1999. "Self-Selection and Its Impact on Team Diversity and Performance." *Performance Improvement Quarterly*. Vol. 12, no. 1, pp. 127–47.

Graham, Mary E., and Charlie O. Trevor. 2000. "Managing New Pay Program Introductions to Enhance the Competitiveness of Multinational Corporations." *Competitiveness Review*, Vol. 10, no. 1, pp. 136–54.

Greenwood, Michelle R. 2002. "Ethics and HRM: A Review and Conceptual Analysis." *Journal of Business Ethics*, Vol. 3, no. 3 (March), pp. 261–78.

Griggs v. Duke Power 401 U.S. 424 (1971).

Hackman, J. Richard, Greg Oldham, Robert Janson, and Kenneth Purdy. 1975. "A New Strategy for Job Enrichment." *California Management Review*, Vol. 17, no. 4 (Summer), pp. 57–71.

Hannafey, Francis T. 2003. "Economic and Moral Criteria of Executive Compensation." *Business and Society Review*, Vol. 108, no. 3 (Fall), pp. 405–15.

Hirschman, Albert O. 1970, *Exit, Voice, and Loyalty : Responses to Decline in Firms, Organizations, and States*. Cambridge, MA: Harvard University Press.

Hoffman, W Michael, and Laura P. Hartman. 2003. "You've Got Mail ... and the Boss Knows: A Survey by the Center for Business Ethics of Companies' Email and Internet Monitoring." *Business and Society Review*, Vol. 108, no. 3 (Fall), pp. 285–307.

Huasknecht, John P., Charlie O. Trevor, and James L. Farr. 2002. "Retaking Ability Tests in a Selection Setting: Implications for Practice Effects, Training Performance, and Turnover." *Journal of Applied Psychology*, Vol. 87, no. 2 (April), pp. 243–54.

Hunter, Larry W. 2000. "The Adoption of Innovative Work Practices in Service Environments." *International Journal of Human Resource Management*, Vol. 11, no. 3 (June). pp. 477–97.

Hunter, Larry W., John Paul MacDuffie, and Lorna Doucet. 2002. "What Makes Teams Take? Employee Reactions to Work Reforms." *Industrial and Labor Relations Review*, Vol. 55, no. 3 (April), pp. 448–73.

Kant, Immanuel. [1785]. 1981. *Groundings for the Metaphysics of Morals*. Indianapolis: Hackett.

Kochan, Thomas A. 2002. "Addressing the Crisis in Confidence in Corporations: Root Causes. Victims, and Strategies for Reform." *Academy of Management Executive*, Vol. 16. no. 3 (August), pp. 139–42.

Koys, Daniel J. 2001. "Integrating Religious Principles and Human Resource Management Activities," *Teaching Business Ethics*. Vol. 5. no. 2 (May), pp. 121–39.

Kurland, Nancy. 1999. "Ethics and Commission." *Business and Society Review*, Vol: 104, no. 1 (Spring). pp. 29–33.

Lucero, Margaret A., and Robert E. Allen 1994. "Employee Benefits: A Growing Source of Psychological Contract Violations." *Human Resource Management*, Vol. 33, no. 3 (Fall). pp. 425–46.

MacDuffie, John Paul. 1995. "Human Resource Bundles and Manufacturing Performance: Organizational Logic and Flexible Production Systems in the Automobile Industry." *Industrial and Labor Relations Review*., Vol. 48, no. 2 (January), pp. 197–222.

Marchese, Marc C., Gregory Bassham, and Jack Ryan. 2002. "Work–Family Conflict: A Virtue Ethics Analysis." *Journal of Business Ethics*, Vol. 40, no. 2 (October), pp. 145–54.

McCall, John J. 2003. "A Defense of Just Cause Dismissal Rules." *Business Ethics Quarterly*. Vol. 13, no. 2 (April), pp. 151–76.

Mishra, Jitendra M. 1998. "Employee Monitoring: Privacy in the Workplace?" *S.A.M. Advanced Management Journal*. Vol. 63. no. 3 (Summer), pp. 4–15.

Moberg, Dennis J. 2000. "Time Pressure and Ethical Decision-Making: The Case for Moral Readiness." *Business and Professional Ethics Journal*, Vol. 19, no. 2 (Summer), pp. 41–67.

_______. 2003. "Managers as Judges in Employee Disputes: An Occasion for Moral Imagination." *Business Ethics Quarterly*, Vol. 13, no. 4 (October), pp. 453–78.

Moberg, Dennis, and Manuel Velasquez. 2004. "The Ethics of Mentoring." *Business Ethics Quarterly*, Vol. 14. no. 1 (January), pp. 95–133.

Nye, David. 2002. "The Privacy in Employment Critique: A Consideration of Some of the Arguments for Ethical HRM Professional Practice." *Business Ethics: A European Review*, Vol. 11, no. 3 (July), pp. 224–33.

Osterman, Paul. 1995. "Work/Family Programs and the Employment Relationship." *Administrative Science Quarterly*, Vol. 40, no. 4 (December), pp. 681–701.

Radin, Tara J., and Patricia H. Werhane. 2003. "Employment-at-Will, Employee Rights, and Future Directions for Employment." *Business Ethics Quarterly*, Vol. 13. no. 2 (April), pp. 113–30.

Rawls, John. 1971. *A Theory of Justice*. Cambridge, MA: Belknap Press.

Reed, Lisa J. 2003. "Paternalism May Excuse Disability Discrimination: When May an Employer Refuse to Employ a Disabled Individual Due to Concerns for the Individual's Safety?" *Business and Society Review*. Vol. 108, no. 3 (Fall), pp. 417–24.

Rest, James R. 1976. "New Approaches in the Assessment of Moral Judgment." In Thomas Lickona, ed., *Moral Development and Behavior Theory, Research, and Social Issues*. New York: Holt, Rinehart and Winston, pp. 198–218.

Robertson, Diana C., and Erin Anderson, 1993. "Control Systems and Task Environment Effects on Ethical Judgment: An Exploratory Study of Industrial Salespeople." *Organization Science*, Vol. 4, no. 4 (November), pp. 617–44.

Roehling, Mark V. 2003. "The Employment-at-Will Doctrine: Second Level Ethical Issues said Analysis." *Journal of Business Ethics*, Vol. 47, no. 2 (October), pp. 115–25.

Scoville, James G. 1993. "The Past and Present of Ethics in Industrial Relations." *Proceedings of the Forty-Fifth Annual Meeting* (Anaheim, CA, January 5–8, 1993). Madison, WI: Industrial Relations Research Association, pp. 198–206.

Stevens, Betsy. 2001. "Hospitality Ethics: Responses from Human Resource Directors and Students to Seven Ethical Scenarios." *Journal of Business Ethics*, Vol. 30, no. 3 (April), pp. 233–42.

Trevino, Linda Klebe, Laura Pincus Hartman, and Michael Brown. 2000. "Moral Person and Moral Manager: How Executives Develop a Reputation for Ethical Leadership." *California Management Review*, Vol. 42, no. 4 (Summer), pp. 128–42.

Trevor, Charlie O., Barry Gerhart, and John W Boudreau. 1997. "Voluntary Turnover and Job Performance: Curvilinearity and the Moderating Influences of Salary Growth and Promotions." *Journal of Applied Psychology*, Vol. 82, no. 1 (February), pp. 44–61.

VanSandt, Craig V. 2003. "The Relationship Between Ethical Work Climate and Moral Awareness." *Business and Society*, Vol. 42, no. 1 (March), pp. 144–52.

Weber, James, Lance B. Kurke, and David W. Pentico. 2003. "Why Do Employees Steal?" *Business and Society*, Vol. 42, no. 3 (September), pp. 359–80.

Weber, Max. 1930. *The Protestant Ethic and the Spirit of Capitalism*. London: Allen & Unwin.

Werhane, Patricia. 1983. "Individual Rights in Business." In Tom Regan, ed., *Just Business*. Philadelphia, PA: Temple University Press. pp. 100–29.

Wiley, Carolyn. 2000. "Ethical Standards for Human Resource Management Professionals: A Comparative Analysis of Five Major Codes." *Journal of Business Ethics*, Vol. 25, no. 2 (May), pp. 93–114.

READING 2.3

Does It Pay to Be Green? A Systematic Overview

Stefan Ambec and Paul Lanoie

Executive Overview

The conventional wisdom concerning environmental protection is that it comes at an additional cost imposed on firms, which may erode their global competitiveness. However, during the last decade, this paradigm has been challenged by a number of analysts (e.g., Porter & van der Linde, 1995), who have argued basically that improving a company's environmental performance can lead to better economic or financial performance, and not necessarily to an increase in cost. The aim of this paper is to review empirical evidence of improvement in both environmental and economic or financial performance. We systematically analyze the mechanism involved in each of the following channels of potential revenue increase or cost reduction owing to better environmental practices: (a) better access to certain markets; (b) differentiating products; (c) selling pollution-control technology; (d) risk management and relations with external stakeholders; (e) cost of material, energy, and services; (f) cost of capital; and (g) cost of labor. In each case, we try to identify the circumstances most likely to lead to a "win-win" situation, i.e., better environmental and financial performance. We also provide a diagnostic of the type of firms most likely to reap such benefits.

Since the publication of the Brundtland Report in 1987 and the subsequent Earth Summits in Rio de Janeiro (1992) and Johannesburg (2002), sustainable development has become one of the foremost issues facing the world. It is recognized that natural systems can be especially vulnerable to human activity because of limited adaptive capacity, and some of these systems may undergo significant and irreversible damage. Furthermore, recurrent smog alerts, acid rain, holes in the ozone layer, global warming, and the loss of biodiversity are among the growing evidence that such a calamity is indeed possible—and occurring faster, in many cases, than scientists originally thought. That is why environmentalists in particular, and the general population more broadly, believe that a business-as-usual approach is worrying. This kind of concern is likely to become more pressing in the future as young generations become even more sensitive to these issues.

Managers have long associated environmental protection with additional costs imposed by government, which in turn erode a firm's global competitiveness. This view relies on a basic paradigm: In general, markets work well to reach optimal use of scarce resources, so that government intervention is useful only for redistributing revenues, or when markets are no longer fulfilling their role effectively. This is precisely what occurs in the case of environmental problems. One of the prerequisites for the adequate functioning of markets is the existence of well-defined ownership rights. In the case of environmental resources available to all, such as clean air and water, these rights are very difficult to assign. Therefore, because air and water belong to no one (or to everyone), economic agents may use them at zero cost, whereas the actual cost of this use for society as a whole is certainly greater. Polluters receive the wrong signal and, because they use these resources without paying the true price, they are encouraged to do so to excess. Left alone, the market mechanism generates too much pollution, and government intervention is legitimate to reduce it to a tolerable threshold. To that end, government has at its disposal a panoply of instruments, such as regulations, taxation, and pollution permits,[1] that may result in the polluters' receiving the right signal, once confronted with the true cost of their actions. In short, from this perspective, consideration of the environment is necessarily associated with a cost increase for companies that have used environmental resources with impunity. Indeed, the prevailing wisdom is that environmental concerns divert managers from their main responsibility, which should be the maximization of profit (see Friedman, 1970).

However, during the last decade, this paradigm has been challenged by a number of analysts (Gore, 1993; Porter, 1991; Porter & van der Linde, 1995). In particular, Porter argued that pollution is often associated with a waste of resources (material, energy, etc.), and that more stringent environmental policies can stimulate innovations that may offset the costs of complying with these policies. In fact, there are many ways that improving a company's environmental performance can lead to better economic or financial performance, and not necessarily to an increase in cost. To be systematic, it is important to look at both sides of the balance sheet: increasing revenues and reducing costs.

In the literature, one can find conceptual or theoretical arguments outlining seven opportunities (described in detail below) companies can make use of to either increase revenues or reduce costs while at the same time being responsible with the earth's resources (Lankoski, 2000, 2006; Reinhardt, 2000). However, to our knowledge, there has been no systematic effort to provide empirical evidence supporting the existence of these opportunities and assess their scope. In this paper, for each of the opportunities we have identified, we present the economic reasoning involved and provide a systematic review of the empirical evidence available. Furthermore, in each case, we try to identify the circumstances most likely to lead to a "win-win" situation (i.e., better environmental and financial performance) and describe the types of firms most likely to enjoy such benefits. The objective of the paper is not to show that a reduction of pollution is *always* accompanied by better financial performance, but rather to show that, in many cases, the expenses incurred to reduce pollution can partly or completely be offset by gains made elsewhere.

The rest of the paper is organized as follows: First, we sketch our basic analytical framework. Second, we review the opportunities available for improving a company's environmental performance while increasing its revenues. Third, we present the categories of cost that can be reduced through better environmental performance. Finally, we conclude with a summary and a discussion of future research.

Analytical Framework

Firms are facing growing pressure to become greener. Various stakeholders (consumers/purchasers, investors, bankers, NGOs, and so on) press companies to reduce their negative impact on the environment. This is now seen as firms' social responsibility, what businesspeople often refer to as "corporate social responsibility" (Friedman, 1970; May et al., 2007). In various industries, firms must try to cope with these pressures while staying competitive. Management studies (e.g., Aupperle et al, 1985; Folger & Nutt, 1975; Levy, 1995) have argued that environmental corporate social responsibility is generally associated with a reduction in competitiveness. Yet firms can try to reduce their environmental impacts without hurting their economic performance by implementing an ambitious innovation strategy. Such an approach would include one or more of seven strategies that could result in increased revenues or reduced costs.

First, better environmental performance can lead to an increase in revenues through three channels: (a) better access to certain markets; (b) differentiating products; and (c) selling pollution-control technology. Second, better environmental performance can lead to reductions in cost in four categories: (a) risk management and relations with external stakeholders; (b) cost of material, energy, and services; (c) cost of capital; and (d) cost of labor. These mechanisms are summarized in Figure 1.

Interestingly, opportunities to increase revenues or reduce costs can reinforce each other, leading to the arrows between both sets of opportunities. For instance, producing greener products through a differentiation strategy may enhance workers' commitment toward a company, and this could facilitate recruiting and retaining workers. In the same vein, reducing the material or energy costs of a product may facilitate the incorporation of environmental features into the product, helping to develop a differentiation strategy.

Increased Revenues

Better Access to Certain Markets

Better environmental performance may facilitate access to certain markets. First, generally speaking, reducing pollution and other environmental impacts may improve the overall image or prestige of a company, and thus increase customers' loyalty or support sales efforts. Although this argument seems pretty straightforward, it is difficult to find strong empirical evidence that customers are influenced by a company's "green" image. Consumers may be aware of a company's environmental performance through its offer of green products, but they are less likely to be familiar with its environmental performance as measured by its emissions to water or the atmosphere.

Second, more specifically, purchasing policies of public and private organizations may reward green suppliers. It is becoming increasingly common for public administrations to include environmental performance as a criterion for choosing suppliers of goods or services. This phenomenon is known as green public purchasing (GPP). As an illustration, Kunzik (2003) reported that, in general, the central U.K. government, in its Greening of Government Operations policy, aims to:

- Encourage manufacturers, suppliers, and contractors through specifications to develop environmentally preferable goods and services at competitive prices.
- Ensure that any products derived from wildlife, such as timber, plants, and leather goods, are from sustainable sources ... (p. 194).

More specifically, for instance, the U.K. Department of Environment, Transport, and Regions has the following objectives:

- Buy a minimum of 10% of electricity from renewable sources.
- Purchase sustainably produced timber products by, for example, specifying that suppliers provide independently verifiable documentary evidence that their timber has been lawfully obtained from sustainable forests managed "to prevent harm to other ecosystems and any indigenous people" (p. 197).

FIGURE 1 **Positive Links Between Environmental and Economic Performance**

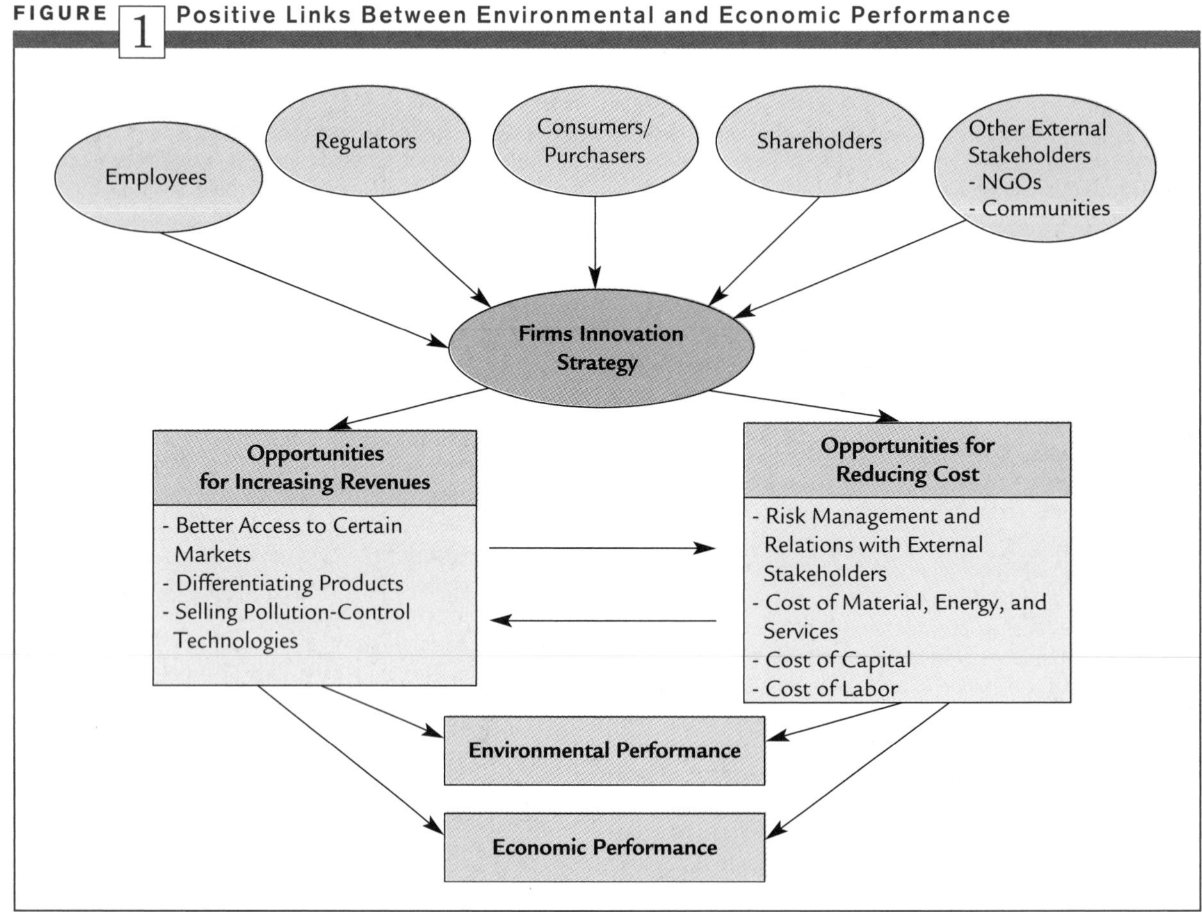

In the United States, the Federal Acquisition Regulations provide a detailed code of rules governing procurement by all federal agencies. For instance, these rules specify that "the Environmental Protection Agency (EPA) has to prepare guidelines on the availability, sources, and potential uses of recovered materials and associated products, including solid waste management services; and require federal agencies themselves to develop and implement affirmative procurement programs for EPA-designated products" (Kunzik, 2003, p. 203).

Overall, public purchasing is fairly important in the economy. In 1998, it was estimated that government-sector expenditures for consumption and investment were responsible for 20% of GDP in OECD member countries, 9% when subtracting compensation for employees (Johnstone & Erdlenbruch, 2003).[2] It can be argued that green public purchasing "can spur innovation by increasing the competitive advantage of greener products in the market, which can then be followed by larger commercialization and diffusion. In particular, public demand may provide "demonstration" effects, giving valuable information to other actors in the economy about potential benefits of newer untried green technologies and products" (p. 12).

In addition, private companies have taken steps to "green" their supply chains. Presumably, all plants with ISO 14001 certification pay attention to their suppliers' environmental performance, as this is one of the criteria to be fulfilled to obtain the certification (Barla, 2007).[3] Furthermore, a recent survey of the OECD, covering more than 4,000 facilities in seven countries, showed that 43% of them assess their suppliers' environmental performance (Johnstone et al., 2007).

Some companies' policies regarding their suppliers' green performance have been well documented in case studies. For instance, before choosing a supplier, IBM asks potential candidates to do a self-evaluation of their environmental performance, and for those that have a satisfactory score on the self-evaluation, there is an on-site evaluation of practices (Herren et al., 1998). In the same vein, since 1992 Body Shop International has had a strict evaluation system for its suppliers' environmental performance, the Supplier Environmental Star-Rating Scheme (Wycherley, 1999).

Wal-Mart has developed incentive plans and "commonsense" scorecards for its merchandise buyers to encourage innovation and environmentally preferable products.[4]

Beyond these laudable efforts by companies, is there any research or empirical evidence showing that it pays firms to incur extra expense to improve their environmental performance in order to have better access to certain markets? In other words, is it profitable to be green? There is little evidence to that effect. At best, we can rely on the recent study of Hamschmidt and Dyllick (2006) who provided, to our knowledge, the first cost-benefit analysis of an implementation of ISO 14000. In many cases, companies are making the effort to comply with the ISO 14000 requirements in order to improve their image and reach extra customers (Hess et al., 1999). For their sample of 158 certified Swiss firms, they found that the average payback period of the adoption of ISO 14000 was 2.2 years.

Given that most public administrations are now involved in GPP, and that a large percentage of private firms are also paying attention to their suppliers' environmental performance, it seems that firms selling to governments or other businesses (as opposed to consumers) can actually obtain better access to certain markets by improving their environmental performance.

Differentiating Products

Along the same lines, it is possible that better environmental performance through greener products or services can allow companies to use a differentiation strategy so as to exploit niches in environmentally conscious market segments. In this case, even if green products or services are more expensive to produce, the extra cost can likely be transferred to consumers who are willing to pay more for more environmentally friendly products or services.[5]

Ecolabeling can make information about the environmental features of a product or service more credible. The popularity of ecolabeling is increasing, especially in Europe. In particular, sales of products with the European ecolabel went from €51 million in 2000 to €644 million in 2004.[6] Consumers' willingness to buy green products in general is important, although the actual amounts devoted to such purchases may be less impressive. For example, 80% of French adults say they favor the purchase of ecoproducts, while 10% say they actually make such purchases regularly (Guilloux, 2006).[7]

Specific examples of enterprises that have adopted this differentiation approach are numerous. For some companies, it even became a core strategy. Among the classic examples is Patagonia, an American sport garments company, which in the 1990s launched new lines of clothing made of recycled PET (polyethylene terephthalate) and organic cotton. This was a commercial success in spite of the higher price of these products (Reinhardt, 2000). Swiss chemical company Ciba Geigy in the mid-1990s created a new type of bioreactive dye, Cibacron LS. This new dye had a higher fixation rate, which meant that less dye was required to color textiles. In turn, this meant that rinsing was simpler and less expensive, and that firms' wastewater treatment costs could be lower. In other words, this dye helped Ciba's clients reduce their environmental cost. Ciba protected this new dye via a patent. The dye was a commercial success despite its higher price (Reinhardt, 1999).

The development of the "biofood" industry (organic food producers and retailers) serves as another example of the success of this strategy, although in this case one can argue that, when buying these products, consumers are also looking at their health attributes.[8] This industry is becoming sizable; for instance, the world market for biofood products doubled between 2003 and 2006. This represents almost 8% of the world food market.[9] In Europe, the market share for biofood is estimated at 10%. Similarly, sales of organic cotton (produced without chemical fertilizers or pesticides) soared worldwide, from $245 million in 2001 to an estimated $1 billion in 2006.[10]

It is also becoming more common to see companies emerging in the "green energy" market, i.e., companies that have access to the grid to sell energy from renewable sources, such as biomass, wind, and solar. A well-documented example is the Dutch enterprise PNEM, which generates electricity from a biomass-fired power plant (Hofman, 2005).

Here again, we can ask the question: Is it worthwhile for firms to adopt this strategy? There is little empirical evidence available. FGCAQ (2004) and Parsons (2005) studied the profitability of farms producing organic milk compared with that of farms producing regular milk, and they concluded that there is no significant difference between the two groups in terms of profits.

From these examples, it seems that a differentiation strategy is more likely to work when[11] (a) the information about the environmental features of the product is credible (e.g., an ecolabel), (b) consumers are willing to pay for extra environmental features (this is more difficult with low-end products), and (c) there is a barrier to imitation from competitors (such as the patent obtained by Ciba). The variety of the examples available leads us to believe that a wide range of enterprises can actually achieve better environmental performance and obtain more revenues by using this strategy. Even firms producing fairly homogeneous goods that are usually difficult to differentiate, such as agricultural products or energy, can do so.

Selling Pollution-Control Technology

For decades, solving environmental problems has become a business opportunity for companies that specialize in this area—what we can refer to as the ecoindustry. A detailed description of this industry and its market structure lies beyond the scope of this paper.[12] Rather, we are interested in firms that, in their search for better environmental performance, are led to do research and development in the area of pollution-control technologies, so as to optimize their manufacturing or waste management processes. This can lead to technological breakthroughs that potentially can be attractive for others. Companies adopting such a strategy may also enjoy a "first-mover" advantage, and may eventually lobby governments for stricter regulations.

For example, as mentioned above, Ciba Geigy patented its new Cibacron LS dye that could be sold to other companies under licensing agreements. Indeed, following its experience with the new dye and wastewater treatment, Ciba in 1998 bought Allied Colloids Group, a U.K. manufacturer of water treatment additives. This was the first step in creating its environmental division. Another example of a large company that has diversified its activity by opening an "environment" division is General Electric. Its Ecomagination division includes 32 clean-technology products, such as wind turbines, and had revenues of $10 billion in 2005 and is forecasting $20 billion in 2010.[13]

In the same vein, the major aluminum producer Alcan has developed and tested a spent potlining (SPL)[14] treatment, the Low Caustic Leaching and Liming (LCLL) process. Up to now, SPL was considered a hazardous waste that had to be stored or landfilled very carefully. With its new process, Alcan will be able to recycle a large part of this waste. The company is building a new plant in Canada to treat its own and eventually other companies' SPL.

Selling pollution-control technology, as one way to turn an environmental problem into an increase in revenues, is probably not a widespread phenomenon. The three examples we found suggest that firms must already have research facilities and a large amount of resources to eventually sell a pollution-control technology they have developed for themselves.

Cost Reductions

Risk Management and Relations With External Stakeholders

Better environmental performance may make the relations between the firm and its external stakeholders (e.g., government, ecological groups, media, communities) easier and reduce the risk associated with these relations. In particular, as suggested by Lankoski (2006), less pollution means lower liability costs, avoiding potentially costly litigation and fines. As a concrete example, El Bizat (2006) showed, through a survey of Canadian jurisprudence, that the implementation of a proper environmental management system (EMS), such as that recognized by ISO 14001, can be useful in proving due diligence in court in cases of illegal spills or other environmental accidents.

Better environmental performance may also allow a firm to anticipate and reduce the risk associated with future regulation. Firms could even push for tighter standards in order to enjoy a strategic first-mover advantage. For instance, it is well documented that, in the 1980s, Dupont lobbied to ban CFCs and other ozone-depleting substances, because it had the leadership in the research for substitutes (Reinhardt, 2000).

In the same vein, firms with a better environmental performance may find it easier to deal with other external stakeholders. For instance, goods that are more environmentally friendly are less likely to suffer from a boycott campaign orchestrated by ecological groups and carried out in the media. Similarly, firms with better environmental performance may obtain approvals from the government and the community more rapidly to extend the size of a new plant or build a new one. Risk management is again facilitated. Finally, learning to deal well with environmental stakeholders may have positive spillover with nongreen stakeholders such as unions or authorities responsible for workers' safety and health.

The companies most likely to benefit from these cost reductions are those that are heavily regulated and scrutinized by the public. One can include in this category firms with toxic emissions, such as the chemical and metallurgic industries, and firms with substantial pollutant emissions, such as the pulp and paper industry and the energy sector.

Cost of Material, Energy, and Services[15]

As mentioned in the introduction, Porter has suggested that pollution is generally associated with a waste of resources, raw material not being fully used, or lost energy. "Pollution is a manifestation of economic waste and involves unnecessary or incomplete utilization of resources.... Reducing pollution is often coincident with improving productivity with which resources are used" (Porter & van der Linde, 1995, p. 99). From this reasoning, Porter argued that more stringent and flexible environmental regulations, such as taxes and tradable permits, would be fruitful for the economy, stimulating innovations that might offset the cost of complying with these policies. This is known as the Porter hypothesis (PH). In particular, this line of reasoning implies that reducing pollution can generate a reduction of expenditures on raw material, energy, or services.

In the economic literature, the PH has been criticized for its lack of theoretical foundation (Palmer et al., 1995). It rests on the idea that firms systematically ignore profitable opportunities, in contradiction of the standard assumption of profit-maximizing firms subject to competitive market pressure. There are no reasons why regulation would actually be needed for firms to adopt profit-increasing innovations. Walley and Whitehead (1994) argued that, although win-win situations might exist by chance, they are very rare, and, given the magnitude of some investment for regulation compliance, the financial return is likely to be negative.

Recent papers have provided a basis for the PH by introducing a market failure (in addition to failure owing to pollution). Environmental regulations, which are devoted to solving the market failure resulting from the pollution externality, prove to mitigate the other market failure to the benefit of the regulated firms. Examples of such market failures include market power (Greaker, 2003; Simpson & Bradford, 1996), specific investments with contractual incompleteness (Ambec & Barla, 2005), asymmetric information within firms

(Ambec & Barla, 2002), and spillovers in knowledge (Ambec & Barla, 2005; Jaffe et al., 2004) or learning-by-doing (Mohr, 2002). For instance, learning how to use energy more efficiently or exploit waste and by-products in one production plan might benefit other production plants and improve managerial expertise and, therefore, might entail knowledge spillovers among a firm's divisions (Clemens & Douglas, 2006; Rosen, 2001). Yet such innovation policy might not have been implemented without regulation, owing to organizational failures such as asymmetric information between divisions.

Given the objective of this paper, it is relevant to review the rapidly growing empirical literature on the PH. We distinguish between two broad sets of studies. A first set estimates the impact of environmental regulations on the firm's innovation policy and technological choice measured by investment in R&D or in capital and new technologies or by successful patent applications. These studies test the first premise of the PH that more stringent environmental regulations enhance innovation. Yet more innovation is a necessary but not sufficient condition for the PH. Therefore, they can only invalidate or provide some support for the mechanism underlying the PH without directly testing it. In the second set of studies, the impact of environmental regulations is estimated on measures of firms' performance, such as productivity and costs. The aim is to test whether more stringent environmental policies can be beneficial to the firms. Yet those papers are silent on the process that leads to higher productivity. Ambec and Lanoie (2007) summarized several empirical papers that fit into these two sets.

In the first set of papers, Jaffe and Palmer (1997) estimated the relationship between total R&D expenditures (or the number of successful patent applications) and pollution abatement costs (a proxy for the stringency of environmental regulations). They found a positive link with R&D expenditures (an increase of 0.15% in R&D expenditures for a pollution abatement cost increase of 1%), but no statistically significant link with the number of patents. Restricting themselves to environmentally related successful patents, Brunnermeier and Cohen (2003) found a positive but small relationship with environmental regulations. Both studies suggest a weak but positive link between better environmental performance (through better compliance with regulations) and the firm's innovation policy.

For the firm's technological choices, Nelson et al. (1993) found that air pollution regulations significantly increased the age of capital in U.S. electric utilities in the 1970s. Gray and Shadbegian (1998) found that more stringent air and water regulations have a significant impact on paper mills' technological choice in the U.S. However, their results suggest that this tends to divert investment from productivity to abatement, consistent with the standard paradigm.

The second set of studies has a long tradition in the economic literature (see Jaffe et al., 1995, for a review). Most papers reviewed in Jaffe et al. (1995) highlighted the negative impact of environmental regulations on productivity. For instance, Gollop and Roberts (1983) estimated that SO_2 regulations[16] slowed productivity growth in the U.S. in the 1970s by 43%. More recent papers find more positive results. For example, Berman and Bui (2001) reported that refineries in the Los Angeles area enjoyed significantly higher productivity than other U.S. refineries despite more stringent air pollution regulations in the area. Similarly, Alpay et al. (2002) estimated that the productivity of the Mexican food processing industry was increasing under pressure from environmental regulations. They therefore suggested that more stringent regulations are not always detrimental to productivity.[17]

Relying on an extensive survey from OECD, Lanoie et al. (2007) tested the full causality chain of the PH (from environmental regulations to R&D, and then to business performance). They found that environmental regulation stringency affects R&D spending positively. Yet it has two impacts on business performance: a negative direct impact and a positive indirect impact through environmental R&D, in the spirit of the PH. The net impact of environmental regulations on business performance is nevertheless negative.

Although the mentioned studies tend to reject the PH, one cannot conclude that being green harms the firm. Concerning this research, two caveats are worth mentioning. First, it may be argued that previous studies have not properly allowed for the dynamic dimensions of the PH. Porter argued that more stringent environmental policies will lead to innovations to reduce inefficiencies, and this in turn will eventually reduce costs. This process may take some time. In previous studies on the determinants of productivity, researchers have regressed productivity at time 0 on proxies of environmental regulation stringency at time 0 as well, which allows no time for the innovation process to occur. By introducing lags of three or four years between changes in the severity of environmental regulations and their impact on productivity, Lanoie et al. (2008) found that more severe regulations led to modest gains in productivity in a sample of 17 Quebec manufacturing sectors. Furthermore, they showed that this effect is greater in industries highly exposed to outside competition.

Second, most studies rely on command-and-control regulatory instruments, such as pollution standards, while environmental regulations are moving to more efficient "market-based" instruments, such as tradable emission permits. The economic theory predicts that emission markets reduce compliance costs by assigning those costs where they are lower. In contrast to standards (that might not be binding after a while), market-based instruments provide constant incentives to innovate. The PH is therefore more likely to be satisfied in industries regulated with the new market-based instruments, especially tradable emission permits.

In this vein, Burtraw (2000) provided evidence that the 1990 switch in environmental regulation of SO_2 emissions in the U.S. from a technological standard with emission caps to an allowance trading program considerably reduced compliance cost (40% to 140% lower than projection). It indeed not only enhanced innovation, but also fostered organizational change and competition on the upstream input market. The program left enough flexibility for the firms to select the best strategy for reducing emissions, including a switch to coal with lower sulfur content. The industry also experienced innovation in fuel blending and in the scrubber market.[18] In addition, the switch from a technological standard to tradable emission allowances led to a transfer of responsibility from engineers or chemists, typically in charge of environmental issues, to top executives such as financial vice presidents, who are trained to treat SO_2 emissions allowances as financial assets.

Even if the PH cannot be generalized to the "whole" economy, it is clear that some firms have been able to reduce emissions and costs at the same time. Let us mention a few examples. First, Dow Chemicals is well known for its WRAP (Waste Reduction Always Pays) Award program, which was implemented in 1986. "Since the program began, Dow has given the WRAP Award to 395 projects. Worldwide, the projects account for the reduction of 230,000 tons of waste, 13 million tons of wastewater, and 8 trillion BTUs of energy. The (net) value of all these projects totals roughly $1 billion."[19] Second, when implementing ISO 14001, the authorities of GM's Flint, Michigan, plant realized that they were using a lot of energy during weekends when the machines were stopped (448,918 kWh during the 1999 Thanksgiving holiday). Shutdown efforts were made very systematically so as to generate savings of approximately $250,000 per year (174,299 kWh were used during the same holiday two years later) (El Bizat, 2006). Third, examples can be found even in the services industry; five changes have been made recently at the headquarters of Adobe Systems (ranging from automatic faucets to motion sensors), which involved an initial investment of around $250,000 for annual savings of around $246,000 (*Fortune*, 2006). Fourth, Kats (2003) showed with a sample of 33 green buildings that the financial benefits of green design are more than 10 times the additional cost associated with building green. Currently, there is a movement toward "eco-efficiency," which implies that many changes can be both economical and ecological at the same time.[20] Lanoie has collected more than 50 examples over the last eight years of companies that were able to reduce both pollution and the cost of resources, energy, and services (Lanoie & Tanguay, 2000, 2004). These companies are very diversified in terms of size, origin, and industry. The actions taken to reach these win-win outcomes are also fairly diversified (reuse of waste, use of waste as a source of energy, more efficient production technology, more efficient energy use, etc.), and this suggests that the set of potential opportunities is fairly broad.

It is not always possible to reduce both pollution and the cost of energy, material, and services, but the set of opportunities to do so seems relatively large. These opportunities are more likely to emerge in firms where the production process is flexible, and in industries where market-based instruments (such as pollution taxes and tradable permits) are implemented.

Cost of Capital

It is also possible that better environmental performance can be associated with a lower cost of financial capital. First, it is becoming quite clear that greener firms have easier access to capital markets through the proliferation of all the green (or ethical) mutual funds.[21] Through these funds, green investors can be sure that their money will be invested in firms that meet certain criteria, such as the existence of a proper environmental management system (EMS) or the absence of environmental litigation. Socially responsible investment (SRI) is becoming an important phenomenon. Assets in U.S. socially screened funds increased by 258% between 1995 and 2005, a rate of growth faster than the average of other professionally managed U.S. funds. In France, the increase was 92% between 2002 and 2006. In 2005, nearly one out of every 10 dollars (9.4%) under professional management in the U.S. was involved in SRI (10% to 15% in Europe).[22] Portfolio analysis allows one to compare the performance of these socially screened funds with that of conventional funds, as we will see below.

Second, firms with better environmental performance can borrow more easily from banks. Most banks now have a team of experts to evaluate the environmental performance of possible borrowers, in particular the size of potential liabilities owing to contaminated assets.[23] Furthermore, about 40 international banks have now adopted the Equator Principles to make sure that the projects they finance are developed in a socially responsible manner and reflect sound environmental management practices.[24]

Third, shareholders in general may be influenced by information on the environmental performance of companies, and their reactions can be perceptible on the stock market. These movements may in turn influence the cost of capital. A large number of empirical studies have tried to identify the stock market reaction to news on environmental performance. Three main approaches are dominant in that literature: (a) portfolio analyses, (b) event studies, and (c) long-term studies using regression analysis. In each case, we will present the methodology used, the main conclusions, and the limitations.

Portfolio Analysis[25] Portfolio analysis is used to examine whether SRI funds (or indices) exhibit different performance from funds in a more general investment context. Such analysis compares the economic performance of portfolios consisting of companies with a higher environmental or social performance with portfolios of companies that have not been screened with these criteria. The comparison is done using such indicators as Jensen's alpha and Sharpe and Treynor ratios.[26] In general, it is expected that ethical funds will underperform over the long run because fund managers are constrained to a subset of the market portfolio.

We came across 16 studies of this type, which are summarized in Ambec and Lanoie (2007).[27] Eleven of them came to the conclusion that there is no statistically significant difference between the performance of SRI funds and conventional ones, while five of them showed results confirming that SRI funds outperform conventional ones. However, the weaknesses of these studies should be noted. First, the financial success of existing funds depends heavily on the ability of fund management. Portfolio studies cannot easily separate these management effects from social or environmental performance effects. Second, in these analyses, only the average performances of funds are compared. Consequently, the specific form of the influence of environmental performance on economic performance can hardly be separated from other influences such as management of the fund, capitalization, and regional peculiarities. The identification of specific effects requires econometric methods that include all control variables besides the variable of interest (environmental performance).[28]

Event Studies The event-study methodology is based on the assumption that the capital market is sufficiently efficient to reflect the impact of all new information (events) on the future expected profits of firms (see Fama et al., 1969). The reaction to the announcement of an event is obtained by predicting a "normal" return for each firm during an "event window" (usually the day prior to the event, the day of the event, and a few days after the event), and then subtracting this predicted normal return from the actual return observed on those days of the event window. If there is a significant difference between the predicted return and the observed return (i.e., an abnormal return), one can conclude that the event had a significant influence on the stock price. Normal returns are usually predicted using a version of the Capital Asset Pricing Model (CAPM).

Many researchers have examined the effects of environmental "events" on stock market performance. The events considered generally have the character of negative news, such as information about illegal spills, prosecutions, fines, or the emission data related to the American Toxics Release Inventory (TRI). Only a few studies consider the effects of positive news, such as information on environmental awards (Klassen & McLaughlin, 1996; Yamashita et al., 1999). Some authors, such as Blacconiere and Patten (1994), Jones et al. (1994), and White (1996), have considered only one major event, such as the Bhopal explosion or the Exxon Valdez oil spill. We surveyed 14 event studies, which are summarized in Ambec and Lanoie (2007).[29] All of them show that stock markets react significantly to good or bad environmental news. Actually, the average daily abnormal returns for bad news represents a loss of 2.22%.

Event studies offer strong econometric results of causality when they are limited to one or at most five trading days after the event to ensure that news of confounding events does not interfere with the effect of interest. Can we conclude from such results that poor environmental performance leads to an increase in the cost of capital? The potential reaction of capital markets to new information on companies' environmental impact can actually be explained by two basic scenarios.[30] In the first one, new information on liabilities (potential litigation or fine) or cleanup costs enters the market at time t, causing the stock price to drop because investors expect reduced earnings and dividend payments. The return is unchanged if the fundamentals of the company do not change. This is the cash flow news effect, and its existence can be tested using the event-study methodology.

Such a short-run negative price movement does not, however, mean that the price of capital is going up. Such price changes do not provide enough substance to formulate buy/sell strategies unless we believe environmental performance to be a matter for day traders constantly arbitraging. We can thus turn to the second scenario, the "green investor effect"[31] that may come about through SRI. Learning about bad environmental news, these investors may worry about the quality of the management of the companies involved and decide to sell "dirty" stocks, which reduces their price. Investors' green preferences are likely to be more long-lived, and thus require multiperiod analyses to be well investigated (using panel data and regression analysis for instance). In this second scenario, as the price of "dirty" stocks falls, investors will demand compensation with a higher return; therefore, the cost of capital for such companies will increase, and it will be more difficult to raise new funds. In the context of our discussion on the impact of better environmental performance on the cost of capital, it will be crucial to find out which of these two scenarios dominates.[32]

Long-Term Studies Using Regression Analysis In these studies, investigators examine, through regression analysis, the relationship between certain characteristics of companies (including their environmental performance) and their financial performance. In contrast to event studies, the analysis concentrates on characteristics of companies and not on specific news about the companies. In contrast to portfolio analysis, researchers examine not a portfolio of stocks, but single stocks. We identified 12 studies in this category, which are summarized in Ambec and Lanoie (2007).[33] Different measures of economic performance (Tobin's Q,[34] return on assets, return on sales, return on equity) and environmental performance (TRI emissions, ISO 14001 certification, the adoption of other international environmental standards) were used in the various studies. Nine studies showed that better environmental performance is associated with better economic performance. Two studies showed no impact, while one concluded that a negative relationship exists. Generally speaking, one can say that these results suggest that bad environmental performance is associated with lower economic performance on a long-term basis, and this implies an increase in the cost of capital.

Overall, what can we conclude from this extensive literature regarding the impact of better environmental performance on the cost of capital? It seems clear that a large majority of the portfolio analyses, event studies, and long-term studies show that better environmental performance is associated with better financial performance (or at least not worse). As we have discussed, the long-term studies are the most reliable, and they offer converging evidence to support the hypothesis that lower environmental performance leads to lower financial performance, and thus to a higher cost of capital.

Furthermore, it is clear that, in day-to-day life, banks (and insurers) examine the environmental performance of their clients and adjust lending conditions according to that performance. It is also evident that green or ethical mutual funds are becoming more popular, and this is providing green firms with better access to capital. Thus, we can conclude that there is strong evidence that better environmental performance does not lead to an increase in the cost of capital. In fact, there is some relatively convincing evidence that better environmental performance leads to a reduction in the cost of capital. Large firms with shares exchanged on the stock markets are more likely to benefit from these gains.

Cost of Labor

Some authors have also argued that better environmental performance can lead to a reduction in the cost of labor. As stated by two Ciba Geigy managers: "An improved image of the company results in an improved atmosphere in the workplace and hence in higher productivity.... People who feel proud of the company for which they work not only perform better on the job, but also become ambassadors for the company with their friends and relatives, enhancing goodwill and leading to a virtuous circle of good repute. Of course, this is impossible to quantify, but it seems clear that it is true.... This is especially important in recruiting talented young scientists, managers, and engineers, many of whom ... simply would not work for a company with a poor social and environmental reputation.... No one wants to work for a dodgy company, and the brightest people obviously have a choice" (Reinhardt, 1999, p. 11). Similarly, De Backer (1999) provided anecdotal evidence that ISO 14001 has significant effects on employees' morale and productivity, much more than ISO 9000 certification.

If this is the case, better environmental performance can indeed reduce the cost of labor by reducing the cost of illnesses, absenteeism, recruitment, and turnover. A few analysts (e.g., Lankoski, 2006) have put forward this argument in favor of labor cost reduction. Even if the argument is fairly compelling, to our knowledge there is no direct empirical evidence supporting it. However, indirect evidence exists from surveys indicating that companies are aiming at better environmental performance to improve the satisfaction of their employees and unions. For instance, Henriques and Sadorsky (2007) found that workers' pressure is a significant determinant of a firm's commitment toward a better environment (e.g., implementation of an EMS). Grolleau et al. (2009) showed that improving human resource management is a significant motivation behind the decision to obtain the ISO 14000 certification.

What types of companies could potentially achieve labor cost reductions associated with better environmental performance? Basic intuition suggests the following: (a) companies whose emissions can affect their workers' health; (b) companies that seek to attract young, well-educated workers, such as scientists, MBAs, and engineers; and (c) companies located in areas where sensitivity to environmental concerns is more acute (e.g., the West Coast of North America).

Conclusion

The conventional wisdom about environmental protection is that it is an extra burden imposed on companies by government. However, during the last decade, this paradigm has been challenged by a number of analysts who have suggested ways in which improving a company's environmental performance can be associated with better economic performance. The objective of this paper was not to show that a reduction of pollution is *always* accompanied by better economic performance, but rather to show that the expenses incurred to reduce pollution can be partly or completely offset by gains made elsewhere. Through a systematic examination of all the possibilities, we also tried to identify the circumstances most likely to lead to a "win-win" situation. These circumstances are summarized in Table 1, in which we introduce examples for each of the seven opportunities to illustrate our point.

Table 1 allows us to have in mind a taxonomy of the firms most likely to benefit from better environmental performance. For instance, an energy company located on the West Coast of the United States and selling part of its production to public authorities is very likely to make a financial gain from an improvement in its environmental performance. However, farms, which in general are less scrutinized by regulators, sell homogeneous products, are not on the stock market, and have few employees, may be less likely to benefit from better environmental performance (Lanoie & Llerena, 2007).

Implications for Future Research

As we have seen, there has been significant recent research on the topic of green profitability. However, in many areas, extra effort would certainly be welcome. Regarding opportunities to increase revenues while improving environmental performance, more cost-benefit analyses from a company point of view of strategies to differentiate products are needed. Are the extra costs of producing greener products worth the benefits of reaching new niches of environmentally conscious consumers? Furthermore, we found very few examples of firms being able to sell pollution-control technologies that they developed for their own purposes. More empirical work, digging into licensing agreements for instance, would help provide a clearer picture of this issue.

Regarding opportunities to reduce costs, impacts of better environmental performance on the cost of capital and the

Table 1 Summary of Positive Links Between Environmental and Economic Performance

Opportunities for Increasing Revenues	Circumstances Making This Possibility More Likely	Examples
1) Better access to certain markets	More likely for firms selling to the public sector (construction, energy, transportation equipment, medical products, and office equipment) and to other businesses.	The Quebec government now cares about the environmental performance of all vehicles it buys, not only about the price.
2) Differentiating products	More likely when there is: a) Credible information about the environmental features of the product b) Willingness-to-pay by consumers c) Barrier to imitation. Wide range of possibilities.	Toyota has announced that all its models will be available with hybrid engines in 2012.
3) Selling pollution-control technologies	More likely when firms already have R&D facilities.	Alcan has patented a process to recycle its own spent pot lining, and that of other companies.
Opportunities for Reducing Costs		
4) Risk management and relations with external stakeholders	More likely in industries that are highly regulated and scrutinized by the public, such as chemical, energy, pulp and paper, metallurgy, etc.	Statoil injects 1 million tons of CO_2 a year beneath the seabed of the North Sea, thus avoiding the Norway carbon tax.
5) Cost of materials, energy, and services	More likely when: a) Firms have a flexible production process b) Firms are in highly competitive industries where optimization of resources is important c) Firms are in industries where market-based environmental policies are implemented d) Firms already have R&D facilities.	BP has reduced its emissions of GHGs 10% below their level in 1990 at no cost by implementing an internal tradable permit mechanism (see Reinhardt, 2001).
6) Cost of capital	More likely for firms with shares exchanged on stock markets.	The stock value of Exxon went down by $4.7 billion following the wreck of the Exxon Valdez.
7) Cost of labor	More likely for: a) Firms whose emissions may affect their workers' health b) Firms that seek to attract young, well-educated workers c) Firms located in areas where sensitivity to environmental concerns is important.	A 2004 survey of Stanford MBAs found that 97% of them were willing to forgo 14% (on average) of their expected income to work for an organization with a better reputation for corporate social responsibility.

cost of labor should be better investigated. For instance, one difficulty with the studies on the link between environmental performance and financial performance is determining the direction of the causality. A first plausible mechanism is that environmental performance leads to changes in financial performance, as postulated in the studies discussed above. Second, the direction of the causality may be reversed; profitable enterprises can afford to invest in environmental performance. Third, there may be another omitted factor, influencing both environmental and economic performance, that is responsible for the apparent statistical relationship. Apart from Wagner et al. (2002), very few attempts have been made to tackle the question with simultaneous equation models. Another possible criticism is the common use of the TRI as an indicator of environmental performance. In particular, TRI does not provide any information about emissions of nontoxic substances (such as carbon dioxide), or through energy or material use.

To provide empirical evidence of labor cost reductions associated with less pollution, one would need a database including observations on proxies of labor cost, such as turnover rates and absenteeism, and data on environmental performance. We are not aware of any database that includes all of these elements, so a new survey would have to be designed to test this hypothesis. Such an exercise would certainly be helpful.

Lastly, from a sustainable development perspective that is oriented toward a triple bottom line (economic, environmental, and social), it would also be interesting to examine the social performance of firms and its relationship to economic performance.[35] We have deliberately tried to avoid mixing environmental and social performance, although in certain areas, such as ethical mutual funds, this is almost impossible. This is a difficult topic, since there is no clear consensus on the measurement of social performance, but, given the importance of sustainable development in the minds of politicians, NGOs, and academics, it is certainly worth making the effort.

Source: Academy of Management Perspectives, 22, (4), 2008, 45–62. Reprinted by permission.

ENDNOTES

1. In general, it is considered that "market-based" instruments, such as green taxes and pollution permits, should be preferred over regulation, because they provide incentives for abatement cost minimization and continuous innovation.
2. According to Marron (2003), the largest private suppliers of public administration are in the following sectors: construction, energy services, transportation equipment, transportation services, shipbuilding, medical equipment, military equipment (including paper), office equipment, electrical machinery, and clothing.
3. As of January 1, 2006, there were 103,583 plants worldwide that were ISO 14001 certified (http://www.ecology.or.jp/isoworld/english/analy14k.htm).
4. http://www.treehugger.com/files/2006/11/walmart_introdu.php.
5. This differentiation strategy is related to ecodesign, which refers to all the actions taken and activities carried out originating from the incorporation of environmental performance requirements in a product development project. See Johansson et al. (2001), who reported 10 ecodesign-related commercial success stories. Ecodesign can sometimes also reduce certain types of expenditures, such as the quantity of raw material used, packaging, or transportation.
6. http://www.abgs.gov.tr/tarama/tarama_files/27/SC27EXP_EU%20Eco-label.pdf.
7. See also Carlson et al. (1996) and Willard (2005) on the differences between "intentions" and "actions."
8. Bonny (2006) showed that environmental attributes are almost as important as health attributes in the decision to purchase biofood in European Union countries (EU-I5).
9. http://seme.cer.free.fr/index.php?cat=filiere-bio.
10. *Les Échos*, November 21, 2006.
11. See also Reinhardt (2000) for more discussion.
12. Ecoindustries are industries that produce goods and services to measure, prevent, limit, minimize, or correct environmental damage to water, air, and soil, as well as problems related to waste, noise, and ecosystems. This includes cleaner technologies, products, and services that reduce environmental risk and minimize resource use. In 2005, it was estimated that ecoindustries represented revenues of €180 billion and 500,000 jobs (http://ec.europa.eu/research/briefings/sustain-devel_en.html).
13. http://ge.ecomagination.com/site/.
14. "Spent potlining (SPL) is the main waste residue generated by the electrolysis process in the smelters producing aluminium. It consists of the internal lining of the pots, which is replaced after five to seven years of use. SPL is classified as hazardous waste by many jurisdictions worldwide due to its toxicity and explosive nature" (http://www.publications.alcan.com/sustainability/2005/en/pdf/alcan_sr05_web_releases.pdf).
15. The services we have in mind here are mainly wastewater treatment, garbage collection, and use of recycling facilities.
16. The regulations implemented to reduce sulfur dioxide emissions from coal power plants (see Burtraw, 2000, for details).
17. In the same vein, Hoglund Isaksson (2005) looked at the impact of a charge on nitrogen oxide emissions introduced in Sweden in 1992 on 114 combustion plants. Her findings suggest that extensive emission reductions took place at zero or very low cost, and that effects of learning and technological development in abatement were present during the period analyzed.
18. The former "command and control" did not provide incentives to increase SO_2 removal by scrubbers from more than the 90% (for high-sulfur coal) or 70% (for low-sulfur coal) standard. With the new program, the incentives are such that upgrading of existing scrubbers through improvements is likely to occur.
19. http://www.dow.com/commitments/studies/wrap.htm.
20. According to the World Business Council for Sustainable Development, there are seven principles for eco-efficiency: (a) reduce the material intensity of goods and services, (b) reduce the energy intensity of goods and services, (c) reduce toxic dispersion, (d) enhance material recyclability, (e) maximize sustainable use of renewable resources, (f) extend product durability, and (g) increase the service intensity of goods and services. See http://www.wbcsd.org/plugins/DocSearch/details.asp?type=DocDet&ObjectId=MTgwMjc, or Orsato (2006).
21. In general, environmental performance is one of the criteria used to select firms in an ethical mutual fund.
22. http://www.socialinvest.org/resources/sriguide/srifacts.cfm.
23. For instance, the French bank BNP Paribas has a team of 120 professionals in the area of sustainable development (http://www.bnpparibas.com/en/sustainable-development). Similarly, the American Citibank reported that, in 2004 and 2005, more than 1,500 of its employees were trained on environmental issues (http://www.aeca.es/comisiones/rsc/biblioteca_memorias_rsc/informes_empresas_extranjeras_4/citigroup_2005.pdf).
24. www.equator-principles.com. One can also refer to the Enhanced Analytics Initiative (EAI), in which members agree to use part of their budget to reward brokers who publish research on extrafinancial issues such as climate change or brand management (http://www.enhancedanalytics.com).
25. See also the discussion in Rennings et al. (2006) and Plinke and Knorzer (2006).
26. For more details, see Bauer et al. (2005).
27. http://www.hec.ca/iea/cahiers/2007/iea0704_planoie.pdf. See page 17 for a summary table.
28. Bauer et al. (2005, 2007) partly overcame this difficulty through the use of Carhart's (1997) multifactor performance attribution approach. They also concluded that "any performance differential between ethical mutual funds and their conventional peers is insignificant."
29. http://www.hec.ca/iea/cahiers/2007/iea0704_planoie.pdf. See page 21 for a summary table.
30. This part of the presentation is based on Koehler (2006).
31. Heinkel et al. (2001) demonstrated that the number of green investors is key to affecting stock prices as in the second scenario. They designed an equilibrium model of capital markets assumed

to be efficient with two types of risk-averse investors: neutral investors with low sensitivity to environmental concerns and green investors. These investors were faced with opportunities to buy more or fewer "dirty" stocks. After conducting sensitivity analysis on various parameters, they found that a key determinant of the environmental performance of companies is the fraction of green investors. They concluded that it is necessary to have at least 25% green investors to change corporate environmental investment strategy.

32. Other limitations of the event-study methodology have been recognized. For instance, McWilliams and Siegel (1997) and McWilliams et al. (1999) have noted various methodological concerns. They criticized the use of the CAPM model, which is often chosen to predict normal returns. They also questioned the assumption of investors' rational expectations, arguing that investors could be biased.
33. http://www.hec.ca/iea/cahiers/2007/iea0704_planoie.pdf. See page 25 for a summary table.
34. Tobin's Q is the ratio of the market value of a firm divided by its replacement cost.
35. See in particular Margolis and Walsh (2001) and UNEP (2001).

REFERENCES

Alpay, E., Buccola, S., & Kerkvliet, J. (2002). Productivity growth and environmental regulation in Mexican and U.S. food manufacturing. *American Journal of Agricultural Economics, 84*(4), 887–901.

Ambec, S., & Barla, P. (2002). A theoretical foundation of the Porter hypothesis. *Economics Letters, 75*(3), 355–360.

Ambec, S., & Barla, P. (2007). Quand la réglementation environnementale profite aux pollueurs. Survol des fondements théoriques de l'hypothèse de Porter. *L'Actualitié économique, 83*(3), 399–414.

Ambec, S., & Barla, P. (2006). Can environmental regulations be good for business? An assessment of the Porter hypothesis. *Energy Studies Review, 14*(2), 42–62.

Ambec, S., & Lanoie, P. (2007). When and why does it pay to be green? (Discussion Paper No. IEA-07-04). Montreal: HEC. Retrieved October 23, 2008, from http://www.hec.ca/iea/cahiers/2007/iea0704_planoie.pdf.

Arimura, T., Hibiki, A., & Johnstone, N. (2007). An empirical study of environmental R&D: What encourages facilities to be environmentally-innovative? In Johnstone, N. (Ed.), *Environmental policy and corporate behaviour.* Cheltenham, UK: Edward Elgar, in association with OECD.

Aupperle, K. E., Carroll, A. B., & Hatfield, J. D. (1985). An empirical examination of the relationship between corporate social responsibility and profitability. *Academy of Management Journal, 28*(2), 446–463.

Barla, P. (2007). ISO 14001 certification and environmental performance in Quebec's pulp and paper industry. *Journal of Environmental Economics and Management, 53*(3), 291–306.

Bauer, R., Derwall, J., & Otten, R. (2007). The ethical mutual fund performance debate: New evidence from Canada. *Journal of Business Ethics, 70*(2), 111–124.

Bauer, R., Koedijk, K., & Otten, R. (2005). International evidence on ethical mutual fund performance and investment style. *Journal of Banking and Finance, 29*, 1751–1767.

Berman, E., & Bui, L. T. M. (2001). Environmental regulation and productivity: Evidence from oil refineries. *The Review of Economics and Statistics, 83*(3), 498–510.

Blacconiere, W. G., & Patten, D. M. (1994). Environmental disclosures, regulatory costs, and changes in firm value. *Journal of Accounting and Economics, 18*(3), 357–377.

Bonny, S. (2006). *L'agriculture biologique en Europe: Situation et perspective.* Paris: European Union.

Brunnermeier, S. B., & Cohen, M. A. (2003). Determinants of environmental innovation in US manufacturing industries. *Journal of Environmental Economics and Management, 45*(2), 278–293.

Burtraw, D. (2000). Innovation under the tradable sulfur dioxide emission permits program in the U.S. electricity sector. (Discussion Paper No. 00-38). Washington, DC: Resources for the Future.

Carhart, M. M. (1997). On persistence in mutual fund performance. *The Journal of Finance, 52*(1), 57–82.

Carlson, L., Grove, S. J., Laczniak, R. N., & Kangun, N. (1996). Does environmental advertising reflect integrated marketing communications? An empirical investigation. *Journal of Business Research, 37*(3), 225–232.

Clemens, B., & Douglas, T. (2006). Does coercion drive firms to adopt voluntary green initiatives? Relationships among coercion, superior firm resources, and voluntary green initiatives. *Journal of Business Research, 59*(4), 483–491.

Cram, D. P., & Koehler, D. A. (2000). *Pollution as news: Controlling for contemporaneous correlation of returns in event studies of toxic release inventory reporting.* Cambridge: MIT Sloan School of Management & Harvard School of Public Health.

De Backer, P. (1999). *L'impact économique et l'efficacité environnementale de la certification ISO 14001/EMAS des entreprises industrielles.* (ADEME Consulting Report). Accessed on October 29, 2008, from http://213.41.254.7/DocumentPrint.htm?numrec=031917080919980.

El Bizat, K. (2006). *EMS and ISO 14001 selected topics for discussion.* Mimeo, HEC Montreal.

Elkington, J. (1994). Towards the sustainable corporation: Win-win-win business strategies for sustainable development. *California Management Review, 36*(2), 90–100.

Fama, E. F., Fisher, L., Jensen, M. C., & Roll, R. (1969). The adjustment of stock prices to new information. *International Economic Review, 10*(1), 1–21.

FGCAQ Fédération des groupes conseils agricoles du Québec (2004). *Analyse de groupe provinciale-Lait biologique 2003.* Mimeo.

Fogler, H. R., & Nutt, F. (1975). A note on social responsibility and stock valuation. *Academy of Management Journal, 18*(1), 155–160.

Fortune (2006, October 16). It's easy and cheap being green, p. 26.

Friedman, M. (1970, September 13). The social responsibility of business is to increase its profits. *New York Times Magazine*, p. 33.

Gollop, F. M., & Roberts, M. J. (1983). Environmental regulations and productivity growth: The case of fossil-fuelled electric power generation. *Journal of Political Economy, 91*(4), 654–674.

Gore, A. (1993). *Earth in the balance: Ecology and the human spirit.* NewYork: Penguin.

Gray, W. B., & Shadbegian, R. J. (1998). Environmental regulation, investment timing, and technology choice. *The Journal of Industrial Economics, 46*(2), 235–256.

Greaker, M. (2003). Strategic environmental policy: Ecodumping or a green strategy? *Journal of Environmental Economics and Management, 45*(3), 692–707.

Grolleau, G., Mzoughi, N., & Thomas, A. (2009). What drives agro-food firms to seek a certified environmental management system? *European Review of Agricultural Economics*, forthcoming.

Guilloux, G. (2006). Les produits éco-conçus – Vers une consommation durable. Oral presentation at the *Biennale du design de St-Étienne, November 27th*, St-Étienne, France.

Hamschmidt, J., & Dyllick, T. (2006). ISO 14001: Profitable? Yes! But is it eco-effective? In Schaltegger, S., & Wagner, M. (Eds.), *Managing the business case for sustainability* (pp. 554–568). Sheffield: Greenleaf Publishing.

Heinkel, R., Kraus, A. & Zechner, J. (2001). The Effect of Green Investment on Corporate Behavior. *Journal of Finance and Quantitative Analysis, 36*(4), 431–449.

Henriques, I., & Sadorsky, P. (2007). Environmental management and practices: An international perspective. In N. Johnstone (Ed.), *Environmental policy and corporate behaviour.* Cheltenham UK: Edward Elgar in association with OECD.

Herren, N., Major, F., Milot, A., Provost, M., & Dubé, R. (1998). *IBM Bromont, les exigences d'un donneur d'ordres en matière environnementale.* (HEC Case Study). Montreal: HEC.

Hess, J., Kaouris, M., & Williams, J. (1999). What ISO 14000 brings to environmental management and compliance. In G. Crognale (Ed.), *Environmental management strategies: The 21st century perspective* (pp. 317–352). Upper Saddle River, NJ: Prentice Hall.

Hoffman, A. J. (2000). *Competitive environmental strategy: A guide to the changing business landscape.* Washington, DC: Island Press.

Hofman, P. S. (2005). Becoming a first mover in green electricity supply: Corporate change driven by liberalisation and climate change. In K. Begg, F. Van der Woerd, & D. Levy, (Eds.), *The business of climate change: Corporate responses to Kyoto.* Sheffield, UK: Greenleaf Publishing.

Isaksson, L. H. (2005). Abatement costs in response to the Swedish charge on nitrogen oxide emissions. *Journal of Environmental Economics and Management, 50*(1), 102–120.

Jaffe, A. B., Peterson, S. R., Portney, P. R., & Stavins, R. N. (1995). Environmental regulation and the competitiveness of U.S. manufacturing: What does the evidence tell us? *Journal of Economic Literature, 33*(1), 132–163.

Jaffe, A. B., & Palmer, K. (1997). Environmental regulation and innovation: A panel data study. *The Review of Economics and Statistics, 79*(4), 610–619.

Jaffe, A. B., Newell, R. G., & Stavins, R. N. (2004). A tale of two market failures: Technology and environmental policy. (Discussion Paper No. DP 04-38). Washington, DC: Resources for the Future.

Johansson, G., Widheden, J., & Bergendahl, C. G. (2001). *Green is the colour of money–commercial success stories from eco-design.* Green-Pack Report 2001-02, Nordic Industrial Fund. See authors for source material.

Johnstone, N., & Erdlenbruch, K. (2003). *The environmental performance of public procurement: Issues of policy coherence* (pp. 9–15). Paris: OECD.

Johnstone, N., Serravalle, C., Scapecchi, P., & Labonne, J. (2007). Public environmental policy and corporate behaviour: Project background, overview of the data and summary results. In N. Johnstone (Ed.), *Environmental policy and corporate behaviour.* Cheltenham, UK: Edward Elgar in association with OECD.

Jones, J. D., Jones, C. L., & Phillips-Patrick, F. (1994). Estimating the costs of the Exxon Valdez oil spill. *Research in Law and Economics, 16,* 109–150.

Kats, G. H. (2003). *Green building costs and financial benefits.* Boston: Technology Collaborative, p. 10. Accessed October 23, 2008, from http://www.mtpc.org/renewableenergy/green_buildings/GreenBuildingspaper.pdf.

King, A., & Lenox, M. (2001). Does it really pay to be green? Accounting for strategy selection in the relationship between environmental and financial performance. *Journal of Industrial Ecology, 5*(1), 105–116.

Klassen, R. D., & McLaughlin, C. P. (1996). The impact of environmental management on firm performance. *Management Science, 42*(8), 1199–1214.

Koehler, D. A. (2006). Capital markets and corporate environmental performance: Research in the United States. In S. Schaltegger, & M. Wagner (Eds.), *Managing the business case for sustainability* (pp. 211–231). Sheffield: Greenleaf Publishing.

Kunzik, P. (2003). National procurement regimes and the scope for the inclusion of environmental factors in public procurement. In OECD (Ed.), *The environmental performance of public procurement: Issues of policy coherence* (pp. 193–220). Paris: OECD.

Lankoski, L. (2000). *Determinants of environmental profit: An analysis of the firm-level relationship between environmental performance and economic performance.* Espoo: Helsinki University of Technology, Institute of Strategy and International Business.

Lankoski, L. (2006). Environmental and economic performance: The basic links. In S. Schaltegger, & M. Wagner (Eds.), *Managing the business case for sustainability* (pp. 32–46). Sheffield: Greenleaf Publishing.

Lanoie, P., & Tanguay, G. (2000). Factors leading to green profitability: Ten case studies. *Greener Management International, 31,* 39–50.

Lanoie, P., & Tanguay, G. (2004). Dix exemples de rentabilité verte. *Risque et management international, 3,* 85–106.

Lanoie, P., Patry, M., & Lajeunesse, R. (2008). Environmental regulation and productivity: Testing the Porter hypothesis. *Journal of Productivity Analysis, 30,* 121–128.

Lanoie, P., Johnstone, N., Lucchetti, J., & Ambec, S. (2007). *Environmental policy, innovation and performance: New insights on the Porter hypothesis.* (GAEL Working Paper No. 2007-07). Accessed October 23, 2008, from http://www.grenoble.inra.fr/Docs/pub/A2007/gael2007-07.pdf.

Lanoie, P., & Llerena, D. (2007). *Des billets verts pour des entreprises agricoles vertes?* (GAEL Working paper No. 2007-08). Accessed October 23, 2008, from http://www.grenoble.inra.fr/Docs/pub/A2007/gael2007-08.pdf.

Les Échos (2006, November 21). *Les distributeurs s'emballent pour le cotton biologique et equitable,* p. 35.

Levy, D. L. (1995). The environmental practices and performance of transnational corporations. *Transnational Corporations, 4*(1), 44–67.

Margolis, J. D., & Walsh, J. P. (2001). *Misery loves companies: Whither social initiatives by business?* (Working Paper No. 01-058). Cambridge: Harvard Business School.

Marron, D. (2003). Greener public purchasing as an environmental policy instrument. In OECD (Ed.), *The environmental performance of public procurement: Issues of policy coherence* (pp. 21–48). Paris: OECD.

May, S. K., Cheney, G., & Roper, J. (2007). *The debate over corporate social responsibility.* Oxford University Press.

McWilliams, A., & Siegel, D. (1997). Event studies in management research: Theoretical and empirical issues. *The Academy of Management Journal, 40*(3), 626–657.

McWilliams, A., Siegel, D., & Teoh, S. H. (1999). Issues in the use of the event study methodology: A critical analysis of corporate social responsibility studies. *Organisational Research Methods, 2*(4), 340–365.

McWilliams, A., & Siegel, D. (2000). Corporate social responsibility and financial performance: Correlation or misspecification? *Strategic Management Journal, 21*(5), 603–609.

Mohr, R.-D. (2002). Technical change, external economies, and the Porter hypothesis. *Journal of Environmental Economics and Management, 43*(1), 158–168.

Nelson, R. A., Tietenberg, T., & Donihue, M. R. (1993). Differential environmental regulation: Effects on electric utility capital turnover and emissions. *The Review of Economics and Statistics, 75*(2), 368–373.

Orsato, R. J. (2006). Competitive environmental strategies: When does it pay to be green? *California Management Review, 48*(2), 126–142.

Palmer, K., Oates, W. E., & Portney, P. R. (1995). Tightening environmental standards: The benefit-cost or the no-cost paradigm? *Journal of Economic Perspectives, 9*(4), 119–132.

Parsons, R. (2005). *Rentabilité comparée des fermes laitières biologiques du Nord-Est.* Mimeo, University of Vermont.

Plinke, E., & Knorzer, A. (2006). Sustainable investment and financial performance: Does sustainability compromise the financial performance of companies and investment funds? In S. Schaltegger, & M. Wagner (Eds.), *Managing the business case for sustainability* (pp. 232–241). Sheffield: Greenleaf Publishing.

Porter, M. (1991). America's green strategy. *Scientific American, 264*(4), 168.

Porter, M., & Van der Linde, C. (1995). Toward a new conception of the environment-competitiveness relationship. *Journal of Economic Perspective, 9*(4), 97–118.

Reinhardt, F. L. (1999). *Ciba specialty chemicals.* (Harvard Business School Case Study No. 9-799-086). Cambridge: Harvard Business School.

Reinhardt, F. L. (2000). *Down to earth: Applying business principles to environmental management.* Cambridge: Harvard Business School Press.

Reinhardt, F. L. (2001). *Global climate change and BP Amoco.* (Harvard Business School Case Study No. 9-700-106). Cambridge: Harvard Business School.

Rennings, K., Schröder, M., & Ziegler, A. (2006). The economic performance of European stock corporations: Does sustainability matter? In S. Schaltegger & M. Wagner (Eds.), *Managing the business case for sustainability* (pp. 196–210). Sheffield: Greenleaf Publishing.

Rosen, C. M. (2001). Environmental strategy and competitive advantage: An introduction. *California Management Review, 43*(3), 8–17.

Schaltegger, S., & Synnestvedt, T. (2002). The link between green and economic success: Environmental management as the crucial trigger between environmental and economic performance. *Journal of Environmental Management*, *65*(4), 339–346.

Schaltegger, S., & Wagner, M. (2006). Managing and measuring the business case for sustainability. Capturing the relationship between sustainability performance, business competitiveness and economic performance. In S. Schaltegger & M. Wagner (Eds.), *Managing the business case for sustainability* (pp. 1–27). Sheffield: Greenleaf Publishing.

Simpson, D., & Bradford, R. L. (1996). Taxing variable cost: Environmental regulation as industrial policy. *Journal of Environmental Economics and Management*, *30*(3), 282–300.

United Nations Environment Programme – UNEP (2001). *Buried treasure: Uncovering the business case for corporate sustainability.* London: SustainAbility. Accessed on October 23, 2008, from http://www.sustainability.com/researchandadvocacy/reports_article.asp?id=141.

Wagner, M., Schaltegger, S., & Wehrmeyer, W. (2001). The relationship between the environmental and economic performance of firms: What does theory propose and what does empirical evidence tell us? *Greener Management International*, *34*, 95–108.

Wagner, M., Nguyen Van, P., Azomahou, T., & Wehrmeyer, W. (2002). The relationship between the environmental and economic performance of firms: An empirical analysis of the European paper industry. *Corporate Social Responsibility and Environmental Management*, *9*, 133–146.

Walley, N., & Whitehead, B. (1994). It's not easy being green. *Harvard Business Review, 72*(3), 46–52.

White, M. A. (1996). *Investor response to the Exxon Valdez oil spill.* (Working Paper No. WHI003). Charlottesville: McIntire School of Commerce, University of Virginia.

Willard, B. (2005). *The next sustainability wave: Building boardroom buy-in.* Gabriola Island, Canada: New Society Publishers.

Wycherley, I. (1999). Greening supply chains: The case of the Body Shop International. *Business Strategy and the Environment*, *8*(2), 120–7.

Yamashita, M., Sen, S., & Roberts, M. C. (1999). The rewards for environmental conscientiousness in the U.S. capital markets. *Journal of Financial and Strategic Decisions*, *12*(1), 73–82.

Strategic Management 3

Learning Objectives

- Understand the differences between the two traditional models of strategy and the strengths and weaknesses of each
- Explain the steps in the strategic management process and the interrelatedness of its sequence of steps
- Appreciate the different corporate and business unit strategies and the HR challenges inherent with each
- Understand the different HR-related challenges in private and publicly held organizations

Strategic Management at Costco

Costco is an international chain of membership retail warehouse stores that offers brand-name merchandise at prices lower than those of other retailers. Costco has effectively utilized a strategy that has allowed it to produce stellar financial results relative to competitors. Although Sam's Club, another warehouse retailer and chief competitor, has 42 percent more members and 70 percent more stores, Costco's annual sales exceed those at Sam's by $1 billion. This is particularly impressive, given that Sam's is affiliated with Walmart stores.

Costco's strategy involves having a lower overhead by utilizing warehouse space and buying in bulk, both of which drive their costs down. Perhaps more important, Costco only carries approximately 4,000 SKUs (stock-keeping units) of inventory as opposed to the typical supermarket, which carries about 30,000 SKUs, or the typical discount retailer, which carriers about 40,000 SKUs. Consequently, the consumer is not overwhelmed at Costco, as the organization does the comparison shopping for its customers through its buying process and selection of merchandise. Costco also employs very limited staff outside of the functions of buying and merchandising products, further eliminating unnecessary overhead.

Costco realizes a need among busy consumers who not only want value but also want convenience. Costco's streamlined operations and willingness to accept lower profit margins on merchandise than its competitors allow them to offer goods at very competitive prices. Costco also offers convenience to time-sensitive customers by offering a variety of products, including electronics, clothing, food, furniture, jewelry, and appliances, under one roof. Clearly, Costco knows its customers' needs, and its strategy is effective, as it is been rewarded with increased sales and customer loyalty, reflected in its 97 percent member renewal rate.[1]

The central idea behind strategic human resource management is that all initiatives involving how people are managed need to be aligned with and in support of the organization's overall strategy. No organization can expect to be successful if it has people management systems that are at odds with its vision and mission. Many organizations suffer from the syndrome of seeking certain types of behaviors and performance from employees but have human resource management programs, particularly those related to performance feedback and compensation, that reward the opposite behaviors.[2] As a prerequisite for understanding how to strategically manage human resources (HR), it is necessary to understand the process of strategic management.

Strategic management is the process by which organizations attempt to determine what needs to be done to achieve corporate objectives and, more important, *how* these objectives are to be met. Ideally, it is a process by which senior management examines the organization and the environment in which it operates and attempts to establish an appropriate and optimal "fit" between the two to ensure the organization's success. Strategic planning is usually done over three- to five-year time horizons by senior management, with a major review of the strategic plan on an annual basis or when some significant change impacts the organization, such as a merger or acquisition, or its environment.

Models of Strategy

Two major models outline the process of what strategy is and how it should be developed. The first is the industrial organization (I/O) model. This "traditional" model formed the basis of strategic management through the 1980s.[3] The I/O model argues that the primary determinant of an organization's strategy should be the external environment in which the organization operates and that such considerations have a greater influence on performance than internal decisions made by managers.[4] The I/O model assumes that the environment presents threats and opportunities to organizations, that organizations within an industry control or have equal access to resources, and that these resources are highly mobile between firms.[5] The I/O model argues that organizations should choose to locate themselves in industries that present the greatest opportunities and learn to utilize their resources to suit the needs of the environment.[6] The model further suggests that an organization can be most successful by offering goods and services at a lower cost than its competitors or by differentiating its products from those of competitors such that consumers are willing to pay a premium price.

The second major model is the resource-based model, sometimes referred to as the resource-based view (RBV) of the firm. The resource-based model argues that the organization's resources and capabilities, rather than environmental conditions, should be the basis for organizational decisions.[7] Included among these resources are an organization's human resources.[8] Organizations hence gain competitive advantage through the acquisition and value of their resources. This approach is consistent with the investment perspective of human resource management. Reading 3.1, "Human Resources and the Resource-Based View of the Firm," further illustrates how the resource-based view of the firm has formed the foundation for strategic human resource management. An understanding of this theoretical foundation is indispensable when attempting to implement the concepts of strategic HR management in the workplace.

The RBV challenges the assumptions of the I/O model. The resource-based view assumes that an organization will identify and locate key valuable resources and, over time, acquire them.[9] Hence, under this model, resources may not be highly mobile across organizations because once they are acquired by a particular organization, that organization will attempt to retain those resources that are of value.[10] However, resources are only of value to an organization when they are costly to imitate and nonsubstitutable.[11]

In contrasting the two approaches, the I/O model suggests that an organization's strategy is driven by external considerations; the RBV argues that strategy should be driven by internal considerations. The I/O model argues that strategy will drive resource acquisition;

the RBV argues that strategy is determined by resources. Interestingly enough, research has provided support for both positions.[12]

Sarasota Memorial Hospital

Why would a nurse pass up a job paying $2 more per hour than her current position with an employer whose facility she drives past on her way to work? For nurses at Florida's Sarasota Hospital, the answer is simple. Sarasota Hospital's strategic plan centers around a "pillars of excellence" concept, adopted after a benchmarking study that included hospitals from across the United States. Sarasota developed its five pillars of excellence—service, people, quality, finance, and growth—then did all strategic planning around them. A performance management system was designed to support the pillars; HR was given the directive to establish a strategic plan under the "people" pillar. It created a set of cross-functional team leadership development; service recovery; measurement; reward and recognition; inpatient, outpatient, and ER patient satisfaction; and physician satisfaction. Each team engaged in process mapping and eliminated duplicated steps. Next to be cut were steps that did not add value, followed by nonessential, "sacred cow" steps. The outcome? Both customer and employee satisfaction have increased dramatically, and operations have become far more efficient. Customer satisfaction rose from the 43rd to the 97th percentile in one year. During this time, staff turnover decreased from 24 percent to 16 percent, with the current rate this year further reduced to 9 percent. The culture of the organization—and the ability of each employee to see her or his contribution to it—helps explain why employees are willing to drive further to work for lower pay at Sarasota Memorial.[13]

While the I/O and RBV models present contrasting philosophies as to whether strategy should be developed from internal or external perspectives, they are not the only perspectives on strategy. Indeed, both perspectives have found support in both research and practice, but more important is the fact that strategy is a dynamic field of study with new theories, models, and perspectives constantly being advanced. Strategy itself has become somewhat ill-defined and a catch-all term for a variety of organizational activities. Reading 3.2, "Are You Sure You Have A Strategy?" presents an alternative framework for the design of strategy by considering strategy as an overarching integrative concept with five distinct components.

The Process of Strategic Management

Our examination of strategy, for the purposes of understanding the relationship between HR and strategy, will consider the premises of both the I/O and RBV models. In line with this, the process of strategic management is presented as a series of five distinct steps, as outlined in Exhibit 3.1.

I: Mission Statement

The first stage of strategic management is for the organization to establish or examine, if it currently has one, its mission statement. Virtually all organizations have a mission statement that explains in very simple terms the organization's purpose and reason for existence. Mission statements are usually very broad and generally limited to no more than a couple of sentences. Although the statement appears to be simple, it is often very difficult to construct because it serves as the foundation for everything that the organization does. It requires those formulating it to have a clear and articulated understanding and vision of the organization and to be in consensus on what the organization is all about and why it exists in the first place.

Exhibit 3.2 presents the mission statement for Solectron. Established in 1977, Solectron is the world's largest electronics manufacturing services organization, offering supply-chain management systems for many of the world's leading electronics equipment

EXHIBIT 3.1 The Process of Strategic Management

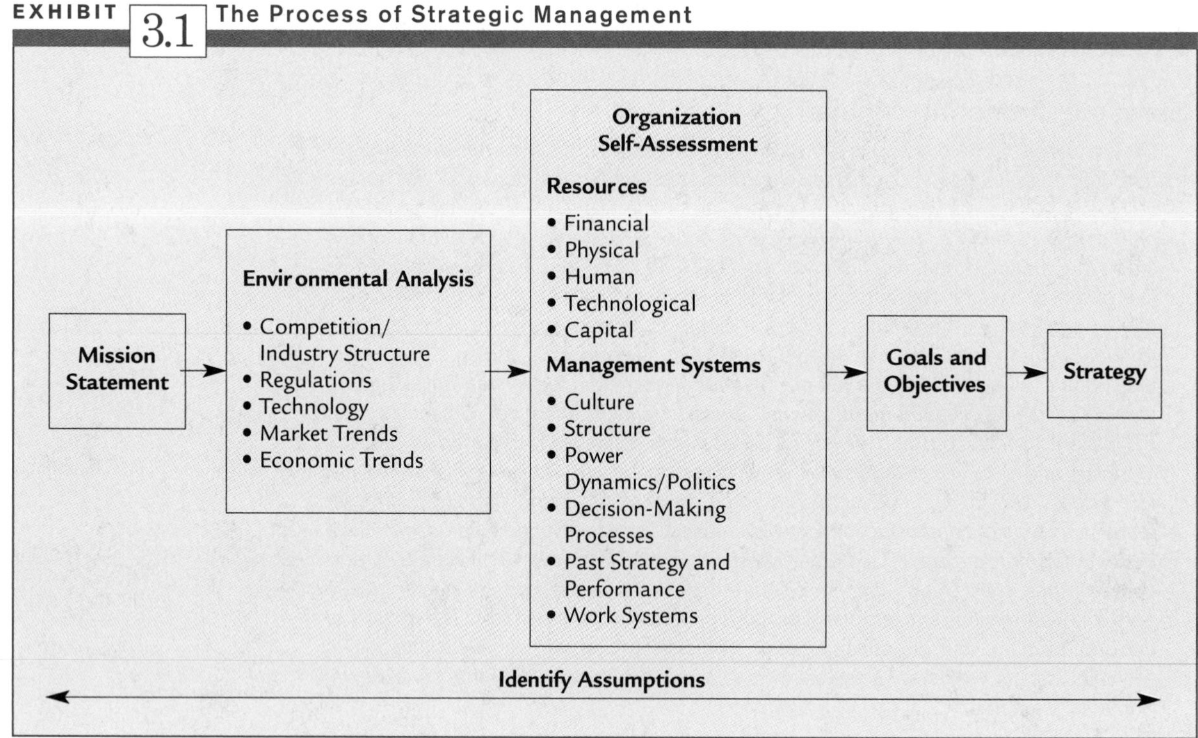

EXHIBIT 3.2 Solectron Mission Statement

"Our mission is to provide worldwide responsiveness to our customers by offering the highest quality, lowest total cost, customized, integrated, design, supply-chain and manufacturing solutions through long-term partnerships based on integrity and ethical business practices."

manufacturers. Solectron has received more than 200 quality and service awards and was the first company to win the Malcolm Baldrige National Quality Award twice.[14]

II: Analysis of Environment

Upon establishing a mission statement, the next step is to analyze the external environment in which the organization operates consistent with the I/O model of strategic management. Decision-makers need to analyze a variety of different components of the external organization, identify key "players" within those domains, and be very cognizant of both threats and opportunities within the environment. Among the critical components of the external environment are competition and industry structure, government regulations, technology, market trends, and economic trends as indicated in Exhibit 3-1.[15]

In examining competition and industry structure, critical issues that need to be identified include who the chief competitors are, the means by which they compete, where "power" lies within the industry, barriers to entry, opportunities to acquire and merge with other organizations, critical success factors within the industry, and industry "maturity level." In addition, consideration must be paid to industries that produce complementary or substitute goods or services that may impact the demand for the organization's output.

In examining government regulation, critical issues that need to be identified include the scope of laws and regulations that may impact what the organization does. This involves everything from federal laws regulating the industry and the employment relationship to local zoning ordinances that may affect the size, scope, and location of operations. A significant number of strategic human resource management decisions that must be made have to be done within the context of federal, state, and local labor laws. Similarly, organizations need to establish beneficial relationships with agencies that enforce these laws and legislators who propose, pass, amend, and repeal such laws.

The technological sector of the environment involves looking at automation processes, new materials and techniques for producing goods and services, and improved products and special features. It also involves an assessment of how to obtain new technology and the decision as to whether the organization wants to pioneer new technology or allow others to do so and then attempt to copy it.

Analyzing market trends involves examining who existing customers are, their needs and wants, and how well satisfied they are. It also involves looking at potential customers who do not utilize the product or service and determining how existing products and services can be adopted or modified to address the needs of different target groups of consumers and developing strategies to increase the rate or level of usage by current customers. It also involves examining demographic, psychographic, and lifestyle issues among consumers, such as family status, age, interests, residence, education, and income level and determining shifts that are taking place in society relative to these areas.

Analyzing economic trends involves forecasting the condition and direction of the national and local economy. Although it is critical to remember that any kind of forecasting isn't an exact science and that no one can accurately predict the future, organizations need to plan for what may happen in the economy that can have a significant impact on operations. Interest rates, levels of inflation and unemployment, international exchange rates, fiscal and monetary policy, and levels of GNP and economic growth will impact what an organization can accomplish; these need to be factored in to any assessment of future direction of the firm.

The analysis of an organization's environment can be a complex undertaking. Some organizations operate in a highly complex environment where a large number of often interrelated factors impact the organization. Some organizations also operate in volatile environments where the elements that impact the organization are dynamic and often in a state of near-constant change. Reading 3.3, "Strategic and Organizational Requirements for Competitive Advantage," presents a model of environmental analysis that indentifies four different types of industry environments and the suggested corresponding strategies for organizations that find themselves in each of the different environment typologies.

III: Organization Self-Assessment

Once an organization has scanned and assessed its external environment and identified any threats and opportunities, it then turns to the third stage of strategic management: assessing the internal environment of the organization. In this stage, the key outcome is for decision-makers to identity the organization's primary strengths and weaknesses and find ways to capitalize on the strengths and improve or minimize the weaknesses, as espoused by the resource-based view of strategic management. This requires the organization to examine both its resources and its internal management systems as indicated in Exhibit 3-1.

Resources

Financial resources can significantly affect an organization's competitive advantage. An organization that has the ability to generate internal funds and/or borrow significant sums is able to convert these funds into other assets. Virtually all components of an organization's business can be purchased, so the presence or absence of financial resources can have a significant impact on an organization's performance.

Physical resources include the actual equipment and machinery owned or leased as well as the location of the business and its proximity to customers, labor, raw materials, and transportation. Physical location is clearly a more important resource in some industries than others. A large manufacturing facility has far different choices and considerations with its physical resources than does a small electronic-commerce business.

Human resources includes not only the sum of technical knowledge of employees but also their personal traits, including commitment, loyalty, judgment, and motivation. An organization is only as strong or as weak as its employees, and the skills, backgrounds, and motivation these employees bring to their jobs will therefore be a key factor in the organization's overall performance. The organization also needs to consider the kinds of obligations it has to employees in the form of contracts or agreements to continue to employ them and the extent that it wishes to enter into such agreements in the future.

Technological resources include the processes by which the organization produces its goods and services. The technology used by an organization can be a major influence on its cost structures and measures of efficiency. A large number of organizations leverage this resource to their advantage by obtaining patents, trademarks, or copyrights. The extent to which an organization is able to safeguard its production processes can be a tremendous resource.

Capital resources include all other items of value, including brand names, reputations with customers, relationships with key constituents in the environment, and goodwill. Many items that can be grouped here are intangibles that do not show up on an organization's financial statements. It has been argued that the more unobservable or intangible a resource is, the more sustainable an advantage it might supply.[16]

Management Systems

In assessing culture, an organization needs to understand the core values and philosophies that guide its day-to-day activities. Many aspects of culture are covert and not clearly articulated but rather assumptions that individuals in the organization make about the company. As part of the strategic planning process, it is critical that elements of culture be identified and that an understanding be achieved about how these elements of culture influence behavior and impact overall performance.

No standard type of organization structure or way to draw up an organization chart exists. However, certain types of structural configurations may be more suited to certain types of conditions than others.[17] Organization structure has a significant impact on how work is carried out, how groups and departments interact with each other, and where accountability for performance lies. Certain types of structures are also most conducive to certain strategic objectives. Essentially, an organization's structure can act as a catalyst for achieving certain strategic objectives or as an impediment to performance.

Assessing power dynamics and politics allows an organization to see who *really* controls what happens in an organization. Power is not necessarily related to hierarchical position; those in low-level positions can often obtain significant amounts of power and influence behaviors and activities of others in organizations. Politics is a process by which people utilize the power they have in order to influence outcomes in a manner that they desire. How power and politics are utilized in an organization can allow it to achieve its objectives or be self-serving obstacles to success.

Decision-making processes can be a competitive advantage to an organization or a weight that inhibits timely, effective action. In assessing decision-making, one needs to look at whether decisions are made by individuals or groups; who gets involved in decision-making; how information is collected, distributed, and made available to which individuals in the organization; how long it takes for decisions to be made; and the information criteria that are employed in reaching decisions. These assessments can allow the organization to see whether its decision-making processes promote or inhibit effective performance as defined by the organization's strategic objectives.

An examination of the organization's past strategy and performance is critical to understanding its internal environment. By looking at past strategic initiatives and measuring the organization's success in meeting them, an organization can attempt to determine how and why it was or was not successful in the past, re-examine the processes that facilitated or hindered its success, and take action that attempts to capitalize on its successes and remedy its shortcomings.

Finally, it is critical to examine the organization's work systems. Work systems involve the design of jobs and allocation of responsibilities to assist an organization in meeting its objectives. Considerations that need to be addressed include the "fit" between job requirements and employee skills and the extent to which changes in how work is done can be met by either providing current employees with further training or seeking applicants from outside the organization. The organization needs to ensure that it is designed work systems in an optimal manner to allow the organization to pursue its current and future objectives.

IV: Establishing Goals and Objectives

Once the organization has established and articulated its mission, assessed its external environment, and identified internal resources and management systems that affect its performance, it is then ready to establish its goals and objectives for the next time period. Goals should be specific and measurable; in fact, at the same time they are established, decision-makers should also identify *how* performance toward these goals will be measured and evaluated. In the planning process, measurement of goals is often overlooked. It serves little purpose to set goals and subsequently have no means to measure performance toward them.

Goals also need to be flexible. Because the whole process of setting goals involves dealing with the future and anticipating what might or might not happen, realistic goals should *not* be "carved in stone." What will actually happen in the external environment may likely be different from that which was assumed or anticipated when the goals were set. To maintain goals that were set under assumed conditions that have not materialized is unrealistic and impractical. Goals can be adjusted upward as well as downward in response to how events in the environment have unfolded. For this reason, some organizations, particularly those that operate in highly volatile environments, rely more on a strategic vision for the organization over the longer term. Visions are generally less detailed and formal than strategic plans but can still guide managers at all levels in their day-to-day decision-making.

V: Setting Strategy

Once goals have been defined, an organization is then ready to determine its strategy. Strategy, very simply, is *how* the organization intends to achieve its goals. The means it will use, the courses of action it will take, and how it will generally operate and compete constitute the organization's strategy.

The strategic choices an organization makes then need to be incorporated into a general human resource strategy, which will be discussed in subsequent chapters. Ideally, this HR strategy will serve as a framework by which the organization can develop a consistent and aligned set of practices, policies, and programs that will allow employees to achieve the organization's objectives. Ideally, HR strategy will serve to ensure a "fit" between corporate strategy and individual HR programs and policies. It is important to remember that there is no one "model" way to manage human resources strategically because every organization is different. One organization should not necessarily copy the management systems of another organization—even a successful organization that operates in the same industry. Every organization is unique, and any "best practices" that are considered or even adopted should be evaluated within the context of the specific organization in which they are being implemented.

First Tennessee National Corp.

Eyebrows were raised when First Tennessee National, a bank holding company and financial service organization, hired an executive who had a background in finance to head its HR function. HR was given the directive to not only maximize financial performance but to also demonstrate to shareholders the value-added benefits of HR programs and policies. This decision resulted in a strategic partnership between HR and finance that has greatly aided the profitability of First Tennessee. Studies were undertaken that aligned the organization's reward system with business strategy. Several years of data were mined that related HR activities to employee performance, retention, market share, profitability, customer value, and loyalty. Relationships between tenure, retention, and team performance were established. As a result, more visible career paths for high-potential and high-performing employees were established to aid in retention and, ultimately, profitability.[18]

Corporate Strategies

Different types of organization strategies require different types of HR programs. In essence, there are three different generic organization strategies,[19] and each would require a significantly different approach to managing people.

The first strategy is growth. Growth can allow an organization to reap the benefits of economies of scale, to enhance its position in the industry vis-à-vis its competitors, and to provide more opportunities for professional development and advancement to its employees. Growth can be pursued internally or externally. Growth can be achieved internally by further penetrating existing markets, developing new markets, or developing new products or services to sell in existing and/or new markets. Chief strategic HR issues associated with a growth strategy involve adequate planning to ensure that new employees are hired and trained in a timely manner to handle market demand, alerting current employees about promotion and development opportunities, and ensuring that quality and performance standards are maintained during periods of rapid growth.

External growth comes from acquiring other organizations. This is commonly done with competitors or with other organizations that might supply raw materials or be part of the organization's distribution chain (called *vertical integration*). There are two key strategic HR issues associated with external growth. The first involves merging dissimilar HR systems from different organizations. It is probable that two different systems existed for staffing, compensation, performance management, and employee relations, and the appropriate new system may or may not be one of the previous systems or even a hybrid of such. The process may involve starting from scratch and establishing an entirely new HR strategy for the "new" organization. The key factor to be considered here is whether the organization's overall strategy has changed as a result of the merger or acquisition and how this strategy changes.

The second strategic HR issue involves the fact that mergers and acquisitions usually result in the dismissal of employees. Critical decisions will need to be made concerning who is retained and who is let go, and a well-developed retention program should be developed that is cognizant of all legal obligations to employees that the organization might have.

The second organizational strategy involves stability or simply "maintaining the status quo." An organization pursuing this strategy may see very limited opportunities in its environment and decide to continue operations as is. The critical strategic HR issue for this type of organization would be the fact that an organization that is not growing will also be limited in the opportunities it is able to offer to its employees. There may be fewer opportunities for upward mobility, and employees may decide to leave and pursue opportunities with other employers. Hence, it is critical for the employer to identify key employees and develop a specific retention strategy to assist in keeping them.

The third type of overall strategy is a turnaround or retrenchment strategy. Here, the organization decides to downsize or streamline its operations in an attempt to fortify its basic competency. Often, a large organization will grow to the point where it becomes inefficient, particularly relative to smaller competitors, and finds itself unable to respond quickly to changes in the marketplace. Decision-makers may see the environment as offering far more threats than opportunities and the organization's weaknesses as exceeding its strengths. Therefore, the organization tries to retool itself to capitalize on its existing strengths and - remain solvent. In a retrenchment strategy, a key issue that needs to be addressed is cost-cutting; in many organizations, particularly service organizations, payroll is the chief expense. As with an acquisition strategy, the organization must be careful to adhere to all laws that regulate the employment relationship in selecting individuals to be terminated.

At the same time, the organization also needs to develop a strategy to manage the "survivors." This is, without question, one of the most neglected aspects of downsizing in organizations. It is often assumed by managers that those whose jobs are spared will be relieved that their employment is maintained and will consequently be grateful and return to their jobs motivated and productive. However, the opposite is often true. Many organizations announce the intention to lay off employees well in advance of the actual notification of individually affected employees. As a result, many of these "survivors" may have been working for several months in fear that their employment was in jeopardy. When their jobs are retained, they then find many friends and coworkers, with whom they may have worked alongside for many years, gone. They are often asked to assume additional job responsibilities of those who have departed, generally without any additional compensation. Furthermore, they may feel that during any subsequent layoffs, they may not be as "fortunate" and lose their jobs. Boosting the morale of these employees is a significant HR challenge. Many are demoralized, depressed, significantly stressed, and less loyal to their employer. However, the organization now depends on these employees for high performance more than it ever did. Consequently, these individuals will directly affect whether the organization stays in business.

Business Unit Strategies

There is a significant and growing trend for larger organizations to break their operations into smaller, more manageable, and more responsive units. Subdivisions are often established by product or service, customer group, or geographic region. In addition to the general, corporate-level strategies explained earlier, many individual business units or product, service, or customer divisions develop a more specific strategy to fit the circumstances of their marketplace and competitive environment. Consequently, there are three different business unit strategies that require correspondingly different strategic approaches to HR.[20]

The first of these business unit strategies is cost leadership. An organization pursuing this strategy attempts to increase its efficiency, cut costs, and pass the savings on to the consumer. It assumes that the price elasticity of demand for its products is high—or, in other words, that a small change in price will significantly affect customer demand. It also assumes that consumers are more price-sensitive than brand-loyal—or, in other words, they see the product or service of each organization as being non-distinguishable. Suave has successfully utilized this strategy in the shampoo market. Knowing that a large segment of consumers are price-sensitive in shampoo purchase decisions has allowed Suave to compete quite successfully in a very competitive industry.

This type of organization would center its HR strategy around short-term, rather than long-term, performance measures that focused on *results*. Because efficiency is the norm, job assignments would be more specialized, but employees might be cross-trained during slack or downtime periods. Cost-cutting measures might also result in developing incentives for employees to leave the organization, particularly higher-salaried managerial employees.

The second business unit strategy is differentiation. An organization pursuing this strategy distinguishes its product or service from those of competitors or, at least, attempts to make consumers *perceive* that there are differences. This allows the organization to demand a premium price over the price charged by competitors and attempts to gain the loyalty of consumers toward a particular brand. Nike has successfully utilized this strategy to gain tremendous loyalty among its customers. Whether there are actual or perceived performance benefits for athletes or some status identification with the brand name, many consumers will not wear any other brand of athletic footwear.

With this type of strategy, creativity and innovation in product design or service delivery are important in developing such a distinction. Consequently, this type of strategy would involve the organization offering incentives and compensation for creativity. Measures for performance might be more long term in establishing and building brand names. Staffing may focus more on external hiring and recruiting individuals who bring a fresh, unique, outside perspective to the organization rather than being bound by existing ways of doing things.

The third business unit strategy is a focus strategy. An organization pursuing this strategy realizes that different segments of the market have different needs and attempts to satisfy one particular group. For example, this might involve a restaurant that targets families, a clothing store that targets larger individuals, or a retail business that targets a particular ethnic group. Big 'N' Tall clothing stores for men and Dress Barn for women have successfully used this strategy to gain a loyal following among an often-neglected group of consumers.

The key strategic HR issue here is ensuring that employees are very aware of what makes the particular market unique. Training and ensuring customer satisfaction are critical factors in this strategy. An organization often attempts to hire employees who are part of the target market and therefore are able to empathize with customers. A large woman would probably be more comfortable dealing with a salesperson in a clothing store who was also large than one who was slim and svelte.

Another framework developed for examining business unit strategy depicts strategies by "logics of control" and identifies three separate strategies: an investment logic, an inducement logic, and an involvement logic.[21] An investment logic is adopted by organizations concerned with adaptability to changing market conditions. Consistent with the I/O model, it bases strategic decisions on external considerations and utilizes very loose control of day-to-day operations. A minimum of formal rules and procedures facilitates adaptability and change in response to the organization's environment. Jobs and responsibilities are broadly defined, and compensation programs encourage and reward initiative and creativity.

An inducement logic is adopted by organizations concerned largely with cost containment and efficiency. Day-to-day management decisions are governed by tight control mechanisms in the form of budgets and special reports. Job responsibilities are narrowly defined to promote maximum efficiency in operations. Loyalty and commitment are rewarded to discourage excessive amounts of turnover.

An involvement logic is adopted by organizations that have a dual strategy of cost containment and innovation. This type of organization tends to adopt management practices that have some consistency with both the investment and inducement logics, as illustrated in Exhibit 3.3. Some systems are consistent with those of the investment logic, while others are consistent with those of the inducement logic.

Innovation and Creativity as Components of Strategy

One theme that often cuts across many of the strategies noted above is innovation. Indeed, innovation is one of the drivers of growth and can even be a critical component of a turnaround or retrenchment strategy as the organization attempts to find new ways of conducting its business in order to survive. Cost leadership, differentiation, and focus are all strategies that can involve if not mandate innovation. Innovation is often referred to as a strategy itself, yet it tends to be more of a driver or means of carrying out one of the previously mentioned strategies. Indeed, Proctor & Gamble, which is known for producing a large number of innovations in its various businesses, considers innovation to be a competency that it seeks and attempts to measure among its new employee recruits.[22] One leading management consultant has argued that in the future, "no company is going to be able to opt out of business innovation," given the pace of change in our world.[23]

EXHIBIT 3.3 Dyer and Holder's Typology of Strategies

Logics			
Goals	**Investment**	**Inducement**	**Involvement**
Contribution	High initiative and creativity; high performance expectations; some flexibility	Some initiative and creativity; very high performance standards; modest flexibility	Very high initiative and creativity; very high performance expectations; high flexibility; self-managed
Composition	Comfortable head count (core and buffer); high skill mix; moderate staff	Lean head count (core and buffer); low skill mix; minimal staff	Comfortable head count; protected core; high skill mix; minimal staff
Competence	High	Adequate	Very high
Commitment	High; identification with company	High; instrumental	Very high; strong identification with work, team, and company
Practices			
Staffing	Careful selection, extensive career development; some flexibility; minimal layoffs	Careful selection; few career options, use of temps; minimal layoffs	Very careful selection; some career development; extreme flexibility; minimal (or no) layoffs
Development	Extensive; continuous learning	Minimal	Extensive, continuous learning
Rewards	Tall structure; competitive, fixed, job based, merit, many benefits	Flat structure; high, variable, piece rate; profit sharing; minimal benefits	Flat structure, high, partially variable, skill- and competency-based; gain sharing; flexible benefits
Work systems	Broad jobs; employee initiative; some groups	Narrow jobs; employee paced; individualized	Enriched jobs; self-managed work teams
Supervision	Extensive, supportive	Minimal, directive	Minimal, facilitative
Employee relations	Much communication; high voice; high due process; high employee assistance	Some communication; some voice; egalitarian	Open and extensive communication; high voice; some due process; egalitarian, some employee assistance
Labor relations	Nonissue	Union avoidance or conflict	Union avoidance and/or cooperation
Government relations	Overcompliance	Compliance	Compliance

Source: Dyer and Holder (1988, pp. 1–21).

Innovation at Whirlpool

Whirlpool Corp, the Michigan-based industry leader in the home appliance industry, has always embraced risk-taking and innovation as a means of maintaining its dominant position in the marketplace. Employee teams—consisting of engineers, industrial designers, and marketers—conduct field research by going into homes and observing how consumers live and use their products. These observations have resulted in numerous product innovations with greatly reduced development time. Because innovation is a core competency for Whirlpool, all company employees are required to be trained and company-certified at an appropriate proficiency level in innovation. The level depends on the individual employee job. HR is centrally involved in developing training and proficiency measures for certification as well as developing a compensation program that reflects the organization's commitment to innovation. The organization maintains an intranet to view all ideas currently in the "idea pipeline" at any given moment so employees can contribute to development.[24]

A critical question related to innovation is how it can be promoted and nurtured within an organization. Clearly, an organization's culture and reward system can either encourage or discourage creativity and risk-taking. One of the world's most successful creative organizations has developed a blueprint for encouraging creativity among its workers, which can be applied to any organization.

Creativity at Cirque du Soleil

Cirque du Soleil, the world-renowned troupe of performance artists, began in 1984 as a small group of street performers in Montreal. Using a circus tent provided by the Quebec government, the group began performing in Quebec and Ontario. In 1987, they began touring the United States and secured a permanent performance space in Las Vegas in 1992. Cirque du Soleil has produced more than a dozen full-length feature shows and currently employs more than 4,000 employees.[25] *To entice creativity within the organization, the company employs seven different tools, which it calls "doors": 1) setting expectations that tap into the creativity that everyone has within them; 2) encouraging employees to trust their senses and intuitions; 3) seeking open-minded risk takers who feel no boundaries or constraints in their lives; 4) creating and maintaining a nurturing environment to encourage productivity, creativity, personal growth, and teamwork; 5) acknowledging constraints and using such constraints to fuel further resourcefulness and creativity; 6) enhancing risk-tasking through acknowledging employee credibility gained through learning from mistakes; and 7) encouraging continuous feedback through the value of shared creativity.*[26]

The Privatization Decision as Part of Strategy

Although not a strategy, one critical strategic business decision that many organizations are currently facing is the decision whether to remain a publicly held company or revert to private ownership. This question actually reverses the typical evolution of the majority of for-profit organizations. Starting out as privately held entrepreneurial endeavors, successful organizations usually reach a critical point in their development when they decide to provide an initial public offering (IPO) of stock for sale. At this point, the owners seek a significant infusion of outside ownership capital to fuel the continued growth of the organization. IPOs are often greatly anticipated and significant newsworthy events for both the financial community and the general public.

More recently, there has been a pronounced trend in reversing this process whereby publicly held and traded organizations are taken private. There are a number of reasons for this. In some instances, executives and board members tire of attempting to gain the support and goodwill of Wall Street analysts and feel that reports on the organization's stock have it undervalued. Second, the significantly increased costs of compliance associated with the Sarbanes-Oxley Act (discussed in Chapter 2) have lessened the desirability of maintaining public status. One estimate puts the cost of post Sarbanes-Oxley compliance at double that incurred prior to its passage and implementation, with the greatest costs increases incurred from director and officer liability insurance.[27]

Third, corporate governance and disclosure requirements for publicly traded companies can be significant and provide information that the organization would prefer to keep from its competitors. Finally, long-term strategic initiatives can be pursued more easily in a privately held organization that is not under pressure for short-term quarterly results sought by Wall Street and the investment community. This latter issue was a key factor in the decision to privatize Dole Food, Co., the world's largest producer of fruits and vegetables, in 2003.

HR plays a critical role in the success or failure of any decision to take a publicly traded company private. From the perspective of recruiting, prospective employees might be less attracted to an employer whose stock is not publically traded on a stock exchange because of lessened perceptions of the prestige of the organization. On the other hand, a privately held company may be less susceptible to a buyout or takeover, which could result in layoffs. Compensation issues can be affected dramatically in a decision to take an organization private. Without the performance-based incentives of stock grants or options, employers need to devise a way to allow employees to fully share in the financial success of the organization once it becomes privately held. This is particularly true when the employer previously offered those forms of compensation that were lost with the decision to go private. Many younger workers still dream of initially working for a small, private startup with a low salary but generous stock options that could make them wealthy in the event of an initial public offering. In addition, stock options are a relatively low-cost form of compensation, so any substitute form of performance-based compensation is likely to be more costly because of direct out-of-pocket expenses for employers. In attempting to address these issues in retaining top performers during a privatization decision, HR has at least as critical a role in the success of the initiative as any other department or function within the organization.

Conclusion

Many organizations have difficulty achieving their strategic objectives because employees don't really understand what these are or how their jobs contribute to overall organizational effectiveness. Less than 50 percent of employees understand their organization's strategy and the steps that are being taken toward fulfilling the organization's mission. Furthermore, only 35 percent see the connection between their job performance and their compensation. Effective strategic management requires not only that the organization's strategic objectives be communicated to employees but that there be a link between employee productivity—relative to these objectives—and the organization's reward system, as is discussed in Chapter 10. Organizations that communicate their objectives to employees and tie in rewards with objectives-driven performance have much higher shareholder rates of return than organizations that do not.[28]

A critical lesson to be learned is that the development of an organization's strategy is a process unique to every individual organization. The factors identified in Exhibit 3.1 can vary dramatically from one organization to another. Even organizations in the same industry can have radically different strategies.

The process of setting an organization's strategy should be the driving force in the establishment of all HR policies, programs, and practices. A strategic approach to HR provides an organization with three critical benefits: (1) It facilitates the development of a high-quality workforce through its focus on the types of people and skills needed; (2) it facilitates cost-effective utilization of labor, particularly in service industries where labor is generally the greatest cost; and (3) it facilitates planning and assessment of environmental uncertainty and adaptation to the forces that impact the organization, as is further discussed in Chapter 4.

Critical Thinking

1. Compare and contrast the premises and assumptions of the industrial organization and resource-based models of strategic planning. What benefits does each model offer that aid in strategic planning?
2. Identify the HR challenges associated with each of the three major corporate strategies.
3. Identify the HR challenges associated with each of the three major business unit strategies.
4. Critique the model presented in Exhibit 3.1. What benefits can be gained from this process? What shortcomings exist within the model?
5. Examine your current organization's process of strategic management. How effective is this process relative to the organization's performance? What factors contribute to its effectiveness or ineffectiveness?

Reading 3.1

6. Trace the development of strategic human resource management from the resource-based view of the firm. How does the resource-based view of the firm facilitate and inhibit the actual practice of strategic human resource management?

Reading 3.2

7. Explain how the five elements of strategy portrayed in the reading relate to either the I/O or RBV traditional models of strategy.

Reading 3.3

8. Examine each of the four different types of environments an organization might face. Are there any other factors that might influence the classification of an organization's environment? What particularly HR challenges are inherent with each strategy that corresponds to each environment?

Exercises

1. Obtain a copy of a publicly held organization's most recent annual report. To what is its performance for the past year attributed? What strategy does it seem to be following and how integrated with this strategy do the operating units appear to be?
2. Select an organization of your choice and apply the five major elements of strategy from the Hambrick reading to explain its success, failure, or stagnation.
3. Apply the I/O and RBV models of planning to your college or university. What are the key factors in the environment that impact the school's performance? What are its key resources, and how can they best be deployed?
4. Select four organizations of your choosing, not discussed in the Lei and Slocum reading, that correspond to each of the environments described in the article. Provide evidence that they have or have not adopted the corresponding strategies suggested by the authors.
5. Select a particular industry (i.e., pharmaceuticals, shipping, auto, or manufacturing) and identify at least three major competitors in that industry. Visit their Web sites and identify key strategic issues within the industry as well as key strategic issues for the individual firms.

Chapter References

1. Hitt, M. A., Ireland, R. D., and Hoskisson, R. E. "Costco Companies, Inc.: The Retail Warehouse Store Revolution," *Strategic Management*, 3d ed., Cincinnati: South-Western College Publishing, 1999.
2. For a discussion of this, see Kerr, S. "On the Folly of Rewarding A, While Hoping for B," *Academy of Management Journal*, 18, 1975, pp. 769–783.
3. Barney, J. B. "Firm Resources and Sustained Competitive Advantage," *Journal of Management*, 17, 1991, pp. 99–120.
4. Schendel, D. "Introduction to Competitive Organizational Behavior: Toward an Organizationally Based Theory of Competitive Advantage," *Strategic Management Journal*, 15 (2), Special Winter Issue, 1994.
5. Seth, A. and Thomas, H. "Theories of the Firm: Implications for Strategy Research," *Journal of Management Studies*, 31, 1994, pp. 165–191.
6. Hitt, M. A., Ireland, R. D. and Hoskisson, R. E. *Strategic Management: Competitiveness and Globalization*, 3d ed., Cincinnati: South-Western College Publishing, 1998, 19.
7. Cool, K. and Dierckz, I. "Commentary: Investments in Strategic Assets; Industry and Firm-Level Perspectives," in Shrivastava, P., Huff, A., and Dutton, J. (eds.), *Advances in Strategic Management* 10A, Greenwich, CT: JAI Press, 1994, pp. 35–44.
8. Barney, op. cit.; Hitt et al., op. cit., pp. 1–41.
9. Barney, op. cit., pp. 113–115.

10. Hitt et. al., op. cit., p. 21.
11. Barney, op. cit.
12. McGahan, A. M. and Porter, M. E. "How Much Does Industry Matter, Really?" *Strategic Management Journal*, 18, 1997, Special Summer Issue, pp. 15–30; Henderson, R. and Mitchell, W. "The Interactions of Organizational and Competitive Influences on Strategy and Performance," *Strategic Management Journal*, 18, Special Summer Issue, 1997, pp. 5–14.
13. Heuring, L. H. "Patients First," *HR Magazine*, July 2003, pp. 65–69.
14. Taken from http://www.solectron.com.
15. For an excellent discussion of the components of an organization's external environment, see Hitt, op. cit., Chapter 2, pp. 42–81.
16. Godfrey, P. C. and Hill, C. W. L. "The Problem of Unobservables in Strategic Management Research," *Strategic Management Journal*, 16, 1995, pp. 519–533.
17. For a complete discussion of the different forms of organization structure and their appropriateness, see Daft, R. L. *Organization Theory*, 6th ed., Cincinnati: South-Western College Publishing, 1998, pp. 200–233.
18. Bates, S. "First Tennessee—Talking to the People," *HR Magazine*, 48, (9), September 2003, p. 48.
19. This typology was developed by Michael E. Porter. *Competitive Strategy*, New York: Free Press, 1980.
20. This typology was developed by William F. Glueck. *Business Policy: Strategy Formulation and Management Action*, New York: McGraw-Hill, 1976.
21. Dyer, L. and Holder, G. W. "A Strategic Perspective of Human Resources Management," in Dyer, L. and Holder, G. W. (eds.), *Human Resources Management: Evolving Roles and Responsibilities*, Washington, DC: American Society for Personnel Administration, 1988, pp. 1–45.
22. Pomeroy, A. "Cooking Up Innovation," *HR Magazine*, 49, (11), November, 2004, 46–53.
23. Hamel, G. "Leading the Revolution," *How to Thrive in Turbulent Times by Making Innovation a Way of Life*. Plume Books, 2002.
24. Pomeroy, A. "Cooking Up Innovation" *HR Magazine*, 49, (11), November, 2004, 46–53.
25. Smith, J. "Promoting Creativity Is Cirque du Soleil's Business Strategy" Society for Human Resource Management, article 025197, published at www.shrm.org/hrnews_/published/articles/CMS_025197.asp April 3, 2008.
26. Bacon, J. *Cirque du Soleil: The Spark - Igniting the Creative Fire that Lives within Us All*. Doubleday, 2006.
27. Ladika, S. "Going Private" *HR Magazine*, 49, (12), December, 2004, 50–54.
28. Bates, S. "Murky Corporate Goals Can Undermine Recovery," *HR Magazine*, November 2002, p. 14.

READING 3.1

Human Resources and the Resource-Based View of the Firm

Patrick M. Wright, Benjamin B. Dunford, and Scott, A. Snell

1. Introduction

The human resource function has consistently faced a battle in justifying its position in organizations (Drucker and Stewart). In times of plenty, firms easily justify expenditures on training, staffing, reward, and employee involvement systems, but when faced with financial difficulties, such HR systems fall prey to the earliest cutbacks.

The advent of the sub field of strategic human resource management (SHRM), devoted to exploring HR's role in supporting business strategy, provided one avenue for demonstrating its value to the firm. Walker's (1978) call for a link between strategic planning and human resource planning signified the conception of the field of SHRM, but its birth came in the early 1980s with Devanna, Fombrum and Tichy's (1984) article devoted to extensively exploring the link between business strategy and HR. Since then, SHRM's evolution has consistently followed (by a few years) developments within the field of strategic management. For example, Miles and Snow's (1978) organizational types were later expanded to include their associated HR systems (Miles & Snow, 1984), Porter's (1980) model of generic strategies was later used by SHRM researchers to delineate the specific HR strategies that one would expect to observe under each of them (Jackson & Schuler, 1987; Wright & Snell, 1991).

Though the field of SHRM was not directly born of the resource-based view (RBV), it has clearly been instrumental to its development. This was largely because of the RBV shifting emphasis in the strategy literature away from external factors (such as industry position) toward internal firm resources as sources of competitive advantage (Hoskisson, Hitt, Wan & Yiu, 1999). Growing acceptance of internal resources as sources of competitive advantage brought legitimacy to HR's assertion that people are strategically important to firm success. Thus, given both the need to conceptually justify the value of HR and the propensity for the SHRM field to borrow concepts and theories from the broader strategy literature, the integration of the RBV of the firm into the SHRM literature should surprise no one.

However, two developments not as easily predicted have emerged over the past 10 years. First, the popularity of the RBV within the SHRM literature as a foundation for both theoretical and empirical examinations has probably far surpassed what anyone expected (McMahan, Virick & Wright, 1999). Second, the applications and implications of the RBV within the strategy literature have led to an increasing convergence between the fields of strategic management and SHRM (Snell, Shadur & Wright, 2001). Within the strategic literature, the RBV has helped to put "people" (or a firm's human resources) on the radar screen. Concepts such as knowledge (Argote; Grant and Liebeskind), dynamic capability (Eisenhardt and Teece), learning organizations (Fiol and Fisher), and leadership (Finkelstein; Norburn and Thomas) as sources of competitive advantage turn attention toward the intersection of strategy and HR issues.

The purpose of this paper is to examine how the RBV has been applied to the theoretical and empirical research base of SHRM, and to explore how it has provided an accessible bridge between the fields of strategy and HR. To accomplish this, we will first review the specific benchmark articles that have applied the RBV to theoretical development of SHRM. We will then discuss some of the empirical SHRM studies that have used the RBV as the basis for exploring the relationship between HR and firm performance. Finally, we will identify some of the major topic areas that illustrate the convergence of the fields of strategy and HR, and propose some future directions for how such a convergence can provide mutual benefits.

2. Applying the RBV to SHRM

While based in the work of Penrose (1959) and others, Wernerfelt's (1984) articulation of the resource-based view of the firm certainly signified the first coherent statement of the theory. This initial statement of the theory served as the foundation that was extended by others such as Rumelt and Barney, and Dierickx and Cool (1989). However, Barney's (1991) specification of the characteristics necessary for a sustainable competitive advantage seemed to be a seminal article in popularizing the theory within the strategy and other literatures. In this article he noted that resources which are rare, valuable, inimitable, and nonsubstitutable can provide sources of sustainable competitive advantages.

Although debates about the RBV continue to wage (e.g., whether the RBV is a theory, whether it is tautological, etc. Priem; Priem and Barney) even its critics have acknowledged the "breadth of its diffusion" in numerous strategic research programs (Priem & Butler, 2001a, p. 25–26). With its emphasis on internal firm resources as sources of competitive advantage, the popularity of the RBV in the SHRM literature has been no exception. Since Barney's (1991) article outlining the basic theoretical model and criteria for sources of sustainable competitive advantage, the RBV has become by far, the theory most often used within SHRM, both in the development of theory and the rationale for empirical research (McMahan, Virick & Wright, 1999).

3. RBV and SHRM Theory

As part of *Journal of Management*'s Yearly Review of Management issue, Wright and McMahan (1992) reviewed the theoretical perspectives that had been applied to SHRM. They presented the RBV as one perspective that provided a rationale for how a firm's human resources could provide a potential source of sustainable competitive advantage. This was based largely on what was, at the time a working paper, but later became the Wright, McMahan and McWilliams (1994) paper described later.

Almost simultaneously, Cappelli and Singh (1992), within the industrial relations literature, provided an examination of the implications of the RBV on SHRM. Specifically, they noted that most models of SHRM based on fit assume that (1) a certain business strategy demands a unique set of behaviors and attitudes from employees and (2) certain human resource policies produce a unique set of responses from employees. They further argued that many within strategy have implicitly assumed that it is easier to rearrange complementary assets/resources given a choice of strategy than it is to rearrange strategy given a set of assets/resources, even though empirical research seems to imply the opposite. Thus, they proposed that the resource-based view might provide a theoretical rationale for why HR could have implications for strategy formulation as well as implementation.

Shortly thereafter, two articles came out arguing almost completely opposite implications of the potential for HR practices to constitute a source of sustainable competitive advantage. Wright et al. (1994), mentioned above, distinguished between the firm's human resources (i.e., the human capital pool) and HR practices (those HR tools used to manage the human capital pool). In applying the concepts of value, rareness, inimitability, and substitutability, they argued the HR practices could not form the basis for sustainable competitive advantage since any individual HR practice could be easily copied by competitors. Rather, they proposed that the human capital pool (a highly skilled and highly motivated workforce) had greater potential to constitute a source of sustainable competitive advantage. These authors noted that to constitute a source of competitive advantage, the human capital pool must have both high levels of skill and a willingness (i.e., motivation) to exhibit productive behavior. This skill/behavior distinction appears as a rather consistent theme within this literature.

In contrast, Lado and Wilson (1994) proposed that a firm's HR practices could provide a source of sustainable competitive advantage. Coming from the perspective of exploring the role of HR in influencing the competencies of the firm, they suggested that HR systems (as opposed to individual practices) can be unique, causally ambiguous and synergistic in how they enhance firm competencies, and thus could be inimitable. Thus, whereas Wright et al. (1994) argued for imitability of individual practices, Lado and Wilson noted that the system of HR practices, with all the complementarities and interdependencies among the set of practices, would be impossible to imitate. This point of view seems well accepted within the current SHRM paradigm (Snell, Youndt & Wright, 1996).

Boxall (1996) further built upon the RBV/SHRM paradigm, suggesting that human resource advantage (i.e., the superiority of one firm's HRM over another) consists of two parts. First, human capital advantage refers to the potential to capture a stock of exceptional human talent "latent with productive possibilities" (p. 67). Human process advantage can be understood as a "function of causually ambiguous, socially complex, historically evolved processes such as learning, cooperation, and innovation." (p. 67). Boxall (1998) then expanded upon this basic model presenting a more comprehensive model of strategic HRM. He argued that one major task of organizations is the management of mutuality (i.e., alignment of interests) to create a talented and committed workforce. It is the successful accomplishment of this task that results in a human capital advantage. A second task is to develop employees and teams in such a way as to create an organization capable of learning within and across industry cycles. Successful accomplishment of this task results in the organizational process advantage.

Most recently, Lepak and Snell (1999) presented an architectural approach to SHRM based at least partly in the RBV. They proposed that within organizations, considerable variance exists with regard to both the uniqueness and value of skills. Juxtaposing these two dimensions, they built a 2×2 matrix describing different combinations with their corresponding employment relationships and HR systems. The major implication of that model was that some employee groups are more instrumental to competitive advantage than others. As a consequence, they are likely to be managed differently. While the premise of an architectural perspective is rooted in extant research in HR (cf., Baron; Osterman and Tsui) and strategy (cf., Matusik & Hill, 1998). Lepak and Snell (1999) helped SHRM researchers recognize that real and valid variance exists in HR practices within the organization, and looking for one HR strategy may mask important differences in the types of human capital available to firms (cf. Truss & Gratton, 1994).

In essence, the conceptual development within the field of SHRM has leveraged the RBV to achieve some consensus on the areas within the human resource architecture in

FIGURE 1 A Model of the Basic Strategic HRM Components

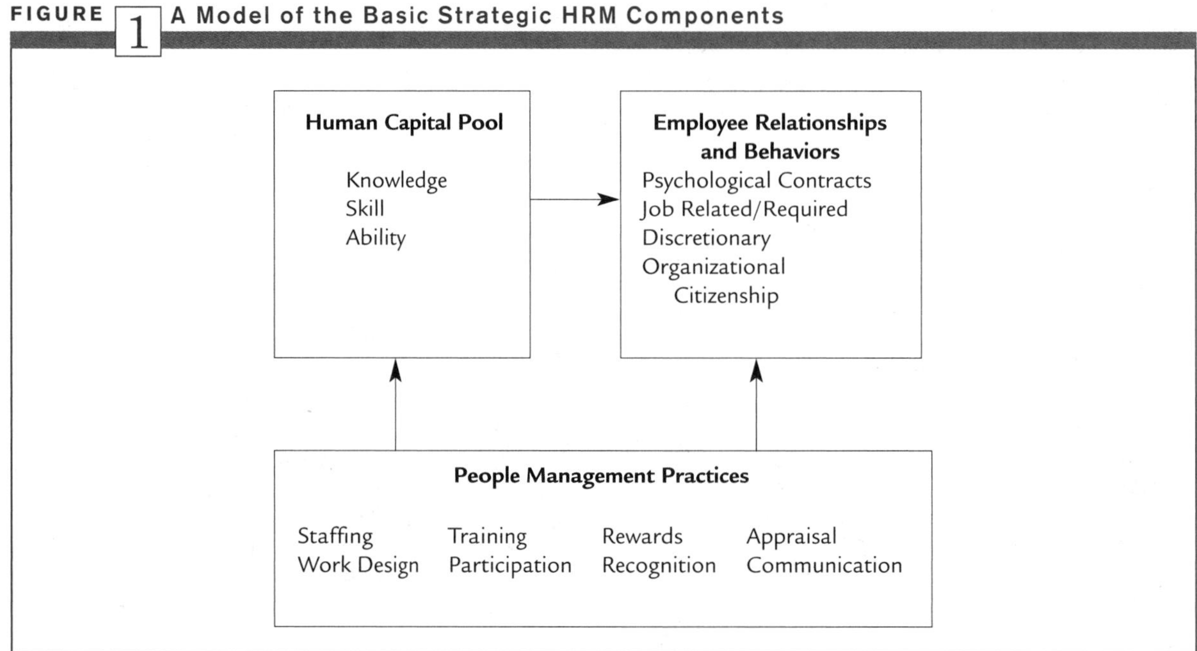

which sustainable competitive advantage might be achieved. Figure 1 depicts these components.

First, the human capital pool refers to the stock of employee skills that exist within a firm at any given point in time. Theorists focus on the need to develop a pool of human capital that has either higher levels of skills (general and/or firm specific), or achieving a better alignment between the skills represented in the firm and those required by its strategic intent. The actual stock of human capital can and does change over time, and must constantly be monitored for its match with the strategic needs of the firm.

Second, an increasing consensus is emerging among researchers that employee behavior is an important independent component of SHRM. Distinct from skills of the human capital pool, employee behavior recognizes individuals as cognitive and emotional beings who possess free will. This free will enables them to make decisions regarding the behaviors in which they will engage. This is an important, if subtle, distinction. A basic premise of human capital theory is that firms do not own it; individuals do. Firms may have access to valuable human capital, but either through the poor design of work or the mismanagement of people, may not adequately deploy it to achieve strategic impact. For example, MacDuffie (1995) focuses on the concept of discretionary behavior. Discretionary behavior recognizes that even within prescribed organizational roles, employees exhibit discretion that may have either positive or negative consequences to the firm. Thus, a machine operator who hears a "pinging" has discretion to simply run the machine until something breaks or to fix the problem immediately, and thus save significant downtime. Similar to March and Simon's (1958) concept of "the decision to contribute" SHRM's focus on discretionary behavior recognizes that competitive advantage can only be achieved if the members of the human capital pool individually and collectively choose to engage in behavior that benefits the firm.

Finally, while many authors describe HR practice or High Performance Work Systems, a broader conceptualization might simply be the people management system. By using the term *system*, we turn focus to the importance of understanding the multiple practices that impact employees (Wright & Boswell, in press) rather than single practices. By using the term *people*, rather than HR, we expand the relevant practices to those beyond the control of the HR function, such as communication (both upward and downward), work design, culture, leadership, and a host of others that impact employees and shape their competencies, cognitions, and attitudes. Effective systems for managing people evolve through unique historical paths and maintain interdependence among the components that competitors cannot easily imitate (Becker & Huselid, 1998). The important aspect of these systems is that they are the means through which the firm continues to generate advantage over time as the actual employees flow in and out and the required behaviors change because of changing environmental and strategic contingencies. It is through the people management system that the firm influences the human capital pool and elicits the desired employee behavior. This dynamic process, while not depicted in the figure, will be taken up later in the paper.

The implications of our figure and this model are that while a firm might achieve a superior position in any one of the three, sustainable competitive advantage requires superior positions on all three.

This is because of three reasons. First, the value that skills and behaviors can generate requires that they be paired together (i.e., without skills, certain behaviors cannot be exhibited, and that the value of skills can only be realized through exhibited behavior). Second, it is difficult to conceive of a firm's human capital pool containing both the highest levels of skills and exhibiting optimal behaviors in the absence of an aligned people management system. Finally, the effects of the people management systems are subject to time compression diseconomies (Dierickx & Cool, 1989). While these systems might be immediately imitated, a significant time lag will occur before their impact is realized, thus making it costly or difficult for competitors to imitate the value generated by the human capital pool. We will later build upon this model to explore how this fits within the larger organization.

3.1. Summary of RBV-Based Conceptual Literature

In summary, the RBV has proven to be integral to the conceptual and theoretical development of the SHRM literature. Our brief review demonstrates how the RBV-based SHRM research has evolved in the last decade. This evolution began when HR researchers recognized that the RBV provided a compelling explanation for why HR practices lead to competitive advantage. Ensuing scholarly debate about the specific mechanics of this relationship advanced the SHRM literature to its current state. The net effect has been a deeper understanding of the interplay between HRM and competitive advantage. The model depicted in Fig. 1 demonstrates that sustained competitive advantage is not just a function of single or isolated components, but rather a combination of human capital elements such as the development of stocks of skills, strategically relevant behaviors, and supporting people management systems. Although there is yet much room for progress it is fair to say that the theoretical application of the RBV has been successful in stimulating a substantial amount of activity in the SHRM arena. Having summarized the conceptual development, we now turn to the empirical research.

4. RBV and Empirical SHRM Research

In addition to the many applications of the RBV to theoretical developments within SHRM, this perspective also has emerged as one of the more popular foundations for exploring empirical relationships within SHRM. In fact, one is hard pressed to find any SHRM empirical studies conducted over the past few years that do not at least pay lip service to the RBV. In the interest of brevity, we will cover a sample of such studies that illustrate the application of RBV concepts to empirical SHRM research. We chose these studies either because they specifically attempt to build on resource-based theory or because they tend to be most frequently cited within the SHRM literature and at least tangentially rely on resource-based logic.

In an early application, Huselid (1995) argued at a general level that HR practices could help create a source of competitive advantage, particularly if they are aligned with the firm's competitive strategy. His study revealed a relationship between HR practices (or High Performance Work Systems) and employee turnover, gross rate of return on assets, and Tobin's Q. That study received considerable attention because it demonstrated that HR practices could have a profound impact on both accounting and market-based measures of performance.

Koch and McGrath (1996) took a similar logic in their study of the relationship between HR planning, recruitment, and staffing practices and labor productivity. They argued that "...a highly productive workforce is likely to have attributes that make it a particularly valuable strategic asset" (p. 335). They suggested firms that develop effective routines for acquiring human assets develop a stock of talent that cannot be easily imitated. They found that these HR practices were related to labor productivity in a sample of business units, and that this relationship was stronger in capital intensive organizations.

Boxall and Steeneveld (1999) conducted a longitudinal case study of participants in the New Zealand engineering consultancy industry. They suggested that one of the firms in the industry had achieved a superior competitive position because of its human resource advantage in 1994, but that by 1997 two of the competitors had caught up in the competitive marketplace. They posited that this could mean that either the two competitors had been able to successfully imitate the former leaders' human resource advantage, or that the former leader has developed an advantage about which there is presently uncertainty, but which will be exploited in the future.

Diverging from the focus on HR practices, Wright, McMahan and Smart (1995) studied NCAA Men's basketball teams using an RBV framework. They focused on the skills of the team members and experience of the coach, and examined how a fit between skills and strategy impacted the team's performance. They found that the relationship between certain skills and team performance depended upon the strategy in which the team was engaged. In addition, their results indicated that teams whose coaches who were using a strategy different from their preferred strategy performed lower than teams where the coach was able to use his preferred strategy.

Recent empirical studies using the RBV build on Lepak and Snell's (1999) architectural framework discussed above. Lepak and Snell (in press) asked executives to describe the HR systems that existed for jobs that represented particular quadrants of their model. They found considerable support for the idea that the value and uniqueness of skills are associated with different types of HR systems within the same organization. These results were mostly consistent with the Lepak and Snell (1999) model, and supported the basic proposition that diverse HR strategies exist within firms. A follow up study (Lepak, Takeuchi & Snell, 2001) indicated that a combination of knowledge work and contract labor was associated with higher firm performance. This finding not only raises some interesting ideas about the development of valuable human resources, but also highlights the importance of combinations of various types used in conjunction with one another.

In another example of examining the human capital pool, Richard (2001) used resource-based logic to examine the impact of racial diversity on firm performance. He argued that diversity provides value through ensuring a variety of perspectives, that it is rare in that very few firms have achieved significant levels of diversity, and that the socially complex dynamics inherent in diversity lead to its inimitability. He found in a sample of banks that diversity was positively related to productivity, return on equity, and market performance for firms engaged in a growth strategy, but negatively related for firms downsizing.

In an effort to look beyond human capital pool alone, Youndt and Snell (2001) studied the differential effects of HR practices on human capital, social capital, and organizational capital. They found that intensive/extensive staffing, competitive pay, intensive/extensive training and promotion from within policies were most important for distinguishing high levels of human capital in organizations. In contrast, broad banding, compressed wages, team structures, socialization, mentoring, and group incentives distinguished those with high social capital (i.e., relationships that engender knowledge exchange) but had very little effect on human capital itself. Finally, organizational capital (i.e., knowledge embedded in the organization's systems and processes) was established most through lessons learned databases and HR policies that reinforced knowledge capture and access.

4.1. Summary of RBV-Based Empirical Research: Limitations and Future directions

Recent debate about the usefulness of the RBV provides an interesting commentary about the current state of SHRM research (Barney and Priem). In response to claims that the RBV is tautological and does not generate testable hypotheses, Barney recognizes that most research applying the RBV has failed to test its fundamental concepts. Rather, he notes that much of the existing research has used the RBV to "establish the context of some empirical research—for example that the focus is on the performance implications of some internal attribute of a firm—and *are not really direct tests of the theory developed in the 1991 article*." (Barney, 2001, p. 46, emphasis added).

Much of the existing SHRM research falls into this category. Although the empirical application of the RBV has taken a variety of forms, ranging in focus from High Performance Work Systems and stocks of talent, to the fit between employee skills and strategy it has employed a common underlying logic: Human resource activities are thought to lead to the development of a skilled workforce and one that engages in functional behavior for the firm, thus forming a source of competitive advantage. This results in higher operating performance, which translates into increased profitability, and consequently results in higher stock prices (or market values) (Becker & Huselid, 1998). While this theoretical story is appealing, it is important to note that ultimately, most of the empirical studies assess only two variables: HR practices and performance.

While establishing such a relationship provides empirical evidence for the potential value of HR to firms, it fails to adequately test the RBV in two important ways. First, no attempt has yet been made to empirically assess the validity of the proposition that HR practices (or HPWS) are path dependent or causally ambiguous, nor whether they are actually difficult to imitate. While intuitively obvious and possibly supported by anecdotal data, the field lacks verifiable quantitative data to support these assertions. In fact, Boxall and Steeneveld's (1999) findings might suggest that HR systems are more easily imitated (or at least substitutable) than SHRM researchers previously believed. Certainly, efforts such as King and Zeithaml's (2001) study assessing causal ambiguity of competencies could be replicated with regard to SHRM issues. These authors asked managers to evaluate their firm's competencies and the generated measures of causal ambiguity based on these responses. While ambiguity was negatively related to firm performance in their study, they provide an example of how one might attempt to measure some of the variables within the RBV.

Second, few attempts have been made to demonstrate that the HR practices actually impact the skills or behaviors of the workforce, nor that these skills or behaviors are related to any performance measures. Arthur (1994) and Huselid (1995) did find a relationship between HR practices and turnover. Wright, McCormick, Sherman and McMahan (1999) found that appraisal and training practices were related to executives' assessment of the skills and that compensation practices were related to their assessments of workforce motivation. However, as yet no study has demonstrated anything close to a full causal model through which HR practices are purported to impact firm performance.

In short, a major step forward for the SHRM literature will be to move beyond simply the application of RBV logic to HR issues toward research that directly tests the RBV's core concepts. In fairness, this state of affairs does not differ from attempts to study competitive advantage within the strategy literature. As noted by Godfrey and Hill (1995), it is impossible to assess the degree of unobservability of an unobservable, and inimitable resources are often purported to be unobservable. Thus, strategy researchers are often left to using proxy variables that may not be valid for measuring the underlying constructs (Hoskisson, Hitt, Wan & Yiu, 1999).

However, given the single respondent, cross-sectional, survey designs inherent in much of this research, one cannot rule out alternative explanations for the findings of empirical relationships. For example, Gerhart, Wright, McMahan and Snell (2000) and Wright, Gardner, Moynihan, Park, Gerhart and Delery (in press) both found that single respondent measures of HR practices may contain significant amounts of measurement error. Gardner, Wright and Gerhart (2000) also found evidence of implicit performance theories suggesting that respondents to HR surveys might base their descriptions of the HR practices on their assessments of the organization's performance. This raises the possibility that research purporting to support the RBV through demonstrating a relationship between HR and performance may result from spurious relationships, or even reverse causation

(Wright & Gardner, in press). The point is not to discount the significant research that has been conducted to date, but rather to highlight the importance of more rigorous and longitudinal studies of HR from a RBV perspective.

Taking a deeper understanding the resource-based view of the firm into empirical SHRM research entails focusing primarily on the competencies and capabilities of firms and the role that people management systems play in developing these. It requires recognizing that the inimitability of these competencies may stem from unobservability (e.g., causal ambiguity), complexity (e.g., social complexity), and/or time compression diseconomies (e.g., path dependence). This implies that rather than simply positing a relationship between HR practices and sustainable competitive advantage, one must realize that people management systems might impact this advantage in a variety of ways.

For instance, these systems might play a role in creating cultures or mindsets that enable the maintenance of unique competencies (e.g., the safety record of DuPont). Or, these systems may promote and maintain socially complex relationships characterized by trust, knowledge sharing, and teamwork (e.g., Southwest Airlines' unique culture). Finally, these systems might have resulted in the creation of a high quality human capital pool that cannot be easily imitated because of time compression diseconomies (e.g., Merck's R&D capability). Whichever the case, it certainly calls for a more complex view of the relationship between HR and performance than is usually demonstrated within the empirical literature.

In addition to a more complex view, such grounding would imply different strategies for studying HR and competitive advantage. For instance, recognizing time compression diseconomies implies more longitudinal or at least historical approaches to examining competitive advantage as opposed to the more popular cross-sectional studies. Focusing on causal ambiguity and social complexity might suggest more qualitative approaches than simply asking subjects to report via survey about the HR practices that exist. In sum, strategic HRM research more strongly anchored in the RBV of the firm would look significantly different than what currently exists. However, such research would shed light on both HR and strategy issues.

Extending this further, strategists who embrace the RBV point out that competitive advantage (vis core competence) comes from aligning skills, motives, and so forth with *organizational systems, structures, and processes* that achieve capabilities at the organizational level (Hamel; Peteraf and Teece). Too frequently, HR researchers have acted as if organizational performance derives solely from the (aggregated) actions of individuals. But the RVB suggests that strategic resources are more complex than that, and more interesting. Companies that are good at product development and innovation, for example, don't simply have the most creative people who continually generate new ideas. Product development capabilities are imbedded in the organizational systems and processes. People execute those systems, but they are not independent from them. So while core competencies are knowledge-based, they are not solely human. They are comprised of human capital, social capital (i.e., internal/external relationships and exchanges), and organizational capital (i.e., processes, technologies, databases) (Snell, Youndt & Wright, 1996).

That doesn't negate the importance of HR; it amplifies it and extends it. The RVB provides a broader foundation for exploring the impact of HR on strategic resources. In this context, HR is not limited to its direct effects on employee skills and behavior. Its effects are more encompassing in that they help weave those skills and behaviors within the broader fabric of organizational processes, systems and, ultimately, competencies.

Notwithstanding a great deal of room for development, it is clear from the preceding review that the conceptual and empirical application of the RBV has led to considerable advancement of the SHRM literature. In a broader sense, the RBV has impacted the field of HRM in two important ways. First, the RBV's influence has been instrumental in establishing a macro perspective in the field of HRM research (Snell et al., in press). This macro view has provided complimentary depth to a historically micro discipline rooted in psychology. Relatedly, a second major contribution of the RBV has been the theoretical and contextual grounding that it has provided to a field that has often been criticized for being atheoretical and excessively applied in nature (Snell et al., 2001).

5. The Convergence of RBV and SHRM: Potential Mutual Contributions

Thus far, we have discussed how the RBV has contributed to the field of SHRM. As noted before, however, that the RBV has also effectively put "people" on the strategy radar screen (Snell et al., in press). In the search for competitive advantage, strategy researchers increasingly acknowledge human capital (Hitt, Bierman, Shimizu & Kochar, 2001), intellectual capital (Edvinsson & Malone, 1997) and knowledge (Grant; Liebeskind and Matusik) as critical components. In so doing, the RBV has provided an excellent platform for highlighting the importance of people to competitive advantage, and thus, the inescapable fact that RBV strategy researchers must bump up against people and/or HR issues.

In fact, recent developments within the field of strategy seem to evidence a converging of that field and SHRM (Snell et al., in press). It seems that these areas present unique opportunities for interdisciplinary research streams that provide significant leaps forward in the knowledge base. We will discuss the concept of core competencies, the focus on dynamic capabilities, and knowledge-based views of the firm as potential bridges between the HR and strategy literatures. We choose these concepts because of both their popularity within the strategy literature and their heavy reliance on HR related issues.

6. Core Competencies

Prahalad and Hamel (1990) certainly popularized the core competency concept within the strategy literature. They stated that core competencies are "...the collective learning in the organization, especially how to coordinate diverse production skills and integrate multiple streams of technologies" (p. 64), and that they involve "many levels of people and all functions" (p. 64). While the distinctions between core competencies and capabilities (Stalk, Evans & Schulman, 1992) seems blurred, one can hardly conceptualize a firm capability or competency absent the people who comprise them nor the systems that maintain them.

For example, competencies or capabilities refer to organizational processes, engaged in by people, resulting in superior products, and generally these must endure over time as employees flow in, through and out of the firm. Numerous researchers within the strategy field focus on firm competencies (e.g., King; Leonard and Leonard). These researchers universally recognize the inseparability of the competence and the skills of the employees who comprise the competence. In addition, some (e.g., Leonard-Barton, 1992) specifically also recognize the behavioral aspect of these employees (i.e., their need to engage in behaviors that execute the competency) and the supportive nature of people management systems to the development/maintenance of the competency. However, often these treatments begin quite specifically when examining the competency and its competitive potential within the marketplace. However, they then sometimes become more generic and ambiguous as they delve into the more specific people-related concepts such as knowledges, skills, abilities, behaviors, and HR practices.

This illustrates the potential synergy that might result from deeper integration of the strategy and strategic HRM literatures. To deeply understand the competency one must examine (in addition to the systems and processes that underlie them) the people who engage in the process, the skills they individually and collectively must possess, and the behavior they must engage in (individually and interactively) to implement the process. In addition, to understand how such a competency can be developed or maintained requires at least in part examining the people management systems that ensure that the competency remains as specific employees leave and new employees must be brought in to replace them. This again exemplifies the interaction of people and processes as they comprise competencies.

Focusing on the people-related elements of a core competency provides a linking pin between the strategy and HR literatures. Traditional HR researchers refer to a "competence" as being a work-related knowledge, skill, or ability (Nordhaug, 1993) held by an individual. This is not the same as the core competencies to which strategy researchers refer. Nordhaug and Gronhaug (1994) argue that firms possess individuals with different competences that they refer to as a portfolio of competences. They further propose that a core (or distinctive) competence exists when a firm is able to collaboratively blend the many competences in the portfolio, through a shared mindset, to better perform something than their competitors. For SHRM researchers, this implies a need to develop an understanding of firms, the activities in their value chains, and the relative superiority in value creation for each of these activities. For strategy researchers, it suggests a need to more deeply delve into the issues of the individuals and groups who comprise the competency, and the systems that develop and engage them to exhibit and maintain the competency. Lepak and Snell's (1999) model provides one tool for making this link between the firm's competency, the people that comprise it, and the systems that maintain it.

7. Dynamic Capabilities

The RBV has frequently focused on resources or competencies as a stable concept that can be identified at a point in time and will endure over time. The argument goes that when firms have bundles of resources that are valuable, rare, inimitable, and nonsubstitutable, they can implement value creating strategies not easily duplicated by competing firms (Barney; Conner; Peteraf; Wernerfelt and Wernerfelt).

However, recent attention has focused on the need for many organizations to constantly develop new capabilities or competencies in a dynamic environment (Teece, Pisano & Schuen, 1997). Such capabilities have been referred to as "dynamic capabilities" which have been defined as:

> *The firm's processes that use resources—specifically the processes to integrate, reconfigure, gain, and release resources—to match and even create market change. Dynamic capabilities thus are the organizational and strategic routines by which firms achieve new resource reconfigurations as markets emerge, collide, split, evolve, and die (Eisenhardt & Martin, 2000).*

Such dynamic capabilities require that organizations establish processes that enable them to change their routines, services, products, and even markets over time. While in theory, one can easily posit how organizations must adapt to changing environmental contingencies, in reality changes of this magnitude are quite difficult to achieve, and the difficulty stems almost entirely from the human architecture of the firm. The firm may require different skill sets implying a release of some existing employees and acquisition of new employees. The change entails different organizational processes implying new networks and new behavioral repertoires of employees. The new skills and new behaviors theoretically must be driven by new administrative, (i.e., HR) systems (Wright & Snell, 1998).

This implies the centrality of HR issues to the understanding and development of dynamic capabilities. This centrality is well articulated by Teece et al. (1997) who note:

> *"Indeed if control over scarce resources is the source of economic profits, then it follows that such issues as skill acquisition, the management of*

knowledge and know how and learning become fundamental strategic issues. It is in this second dimension, encompassing skill acquisition, learning and accumulation of organizational and intangible or invisible assets that we believe lies the greatest potential for contributions to strategy" (pp. 514–515).

8. Knowledge-Based Theories of the Firm

Unarguably, significant attention in the strategy literature within the RBV paradigm has focused on knowledge. Efforts to understand how firms generate, leverage, transfer, integrate and protect knowledge has moved to the forefront of the field (Hansen; Hedlund; Nonaka; Svieby and Szulanski). In fact, Grant (1996) argues for a knowledge-based theory of the firm, positing that firms exist because they better integrate and apply specialized knowledge than do markets. Liebeskind (1996) similarly believes in a knowledge-based theory of the firm, suggesting that firms exist because they can better protect knowledge from expropriation and imitation than can markets.

Interestingly, knowledge-centered strategy research inevitably confronts a number of HR issues. Knowledge management requires that firms define knowledge, identify existing knowledge bases, and provide mechanisms to promote the creation, protection and transfer of knowledge (Argote; Henderson and Liebeskind). While information systems provide a technological repository of knowledge, increasingly firms recognize that the key to successful knowledge management requires attending to the social and cultural systems of the organization (Conference Board, 2000).

Knowledge has long been a topic within the HR literature, whether the focus was on testing applicants for job-related knowledge (Hattrup & Schmitt, 1990), training employees to build their job-related knowledge (Gephart, Marsick, Van Buren & Spiro, 1996), developing participation and communication systems to transfer knowledge (Cooke, 1994), or providing incentives for individuals to apply their knowledge (Gerhart, Milkovich & Murray, 1992). The major distinctions between the strategy and HR literatures with regard to knowledge has to do with the focus of the knowledge and its level. While the HR literature has focused on job-related knowledge, the strategy literature has focused on more market-relevant knowledge, such as knowledge regarding customers, competitors, or knowledge relevant to the creation of new products (Grant and Liebeskind).

In addition, while HR literature tends to treat knowledge as an individual phenomenon, the strategy and organizational literatures view it more broadly as organizationally shared, accessible, and transferable (cf. Argyris; Brown and Snell). Knowledge can be viewed as something that characterizes individuals (i.e., human capital), but it can also be shared within groups or networks (i.e., social capital) or institutionalized within organization processes and databases (organizational capital).

These distinctions represent something of a departure for HR researchers. However, the processes of creation, transfer, and exploitation of knowledge provide common ground across the two fields, again highlighting their potential convergence within the RBV paradigm. Although theorists such as Argyris and Schon (1978) argue that all learning begins at the individual level, it is conditioned by the social context and routines within organizations (Nonaka & Takeuchi, 1995). Coleman (1988), for example, noted that social capital has an important influence on the creation of human capital. What seems clear is that these different "knowledge repositories" complement and influence one another in defining an organization's capabilities (Youndt & Snell, 2001).

But there are substantial differences between HR systems that support individual learning and those that support organizational learning. Leonard-Barton (1992), for example, noted that organizational learning and innovation were built on four inter-related processes and their related values: (1) owning/solving problems (egalitarianism), (2) integrating internal knowledge (shared knowledge), (3) continuous experimentation (positive risk), and (4) integrating external knowledge (openness to outside). Each of these processes and values works systemically with the others to inculcate organizational learning and innovation. Each process/value combination is in turn supported by different administrative (HR) systems that incorporate elements of staffing, job design, training, career management, rewards, and appraisal. Again, the concept of knowledge brings together the fields of strategy and HR. But a good deal more work needs to be done to integrate these research streams. Strategy theory and research provides the basis for understanding the value of knowledge to the firm and highlights the need to manage it. The HR field has lacked such a perspective, but has provided more theory and research regarding how knowledge is generated, retained, and transferred among individuals comprising the firm.

9. Integrating Strategy and SHRM within the RBV

We have discussed the concepts of core competencies, dynamic capabilities, and knowledge as bridge constructs connecting the fields of strategy and SHRM. We proposed that both fields could benefit greatly from sharing respective areas of expertise. In fact, at the risk of oversimplification, the strategy literature has generated significant amounts of knowledge regarding who (i.e., employees/executives or groups of employees/executives) provides sources of competitive advantage and why. However, absent from that literature are specific techniques for attracting, developing, motivating, maintaining, or retaining these people. SHRM, on the other hand has generated knowledge regarding the attraction, development, motivation, maintenance, and retention of people. However, it has not been particularly successful yet at identifying who the focus of these systems should be on and why.

The strategy literature has also highlighted the importance of the stock and flow of knowledge for competitive advantage. However, it has not explored in great detail the role that individuals as well as their interactions with others contribute to this. Conversely SHRM has missed much of the organizational view of knowledge, but can provide significant guidance regarding the role that individuals play.

This state of affairs calls for greater integration between these two fields. Figure 2 illustrates this potential integration. Overall, the figure depicts people management systems at the left, core competencies at the right, intellectual capital and knowledge management as the bridge concepts between the two, and dynamic capability as a renewal component that ties all four concepts over time.

Note that the basic constructs laid out in Fig. 1 still appear in this expanded model, yet with a much more detailed set of variables. At the right- hand side of the model we place the people management systems construct. This placement does not imply that all competitive advantage begins with people management systems, but rather, that this represents the focus of the HR field. We suggest that these people management systems create value to the extent that they impact the stock, flow, and change of intellectual capital/knowledge that forms the basis of core competencies.

Rather than simply focusing on the concepts of "skills" and "behavior" we propose a more detailed analysis with regard to the stock and flow of knowledge. To this end we suggest that the "skill" concept might be expanded to consider the stock of intellectual capital in the firm, embedded in both people and systems. This stock of human capital consists of human (the knowledge skills, and abilities of people), social (the valuable relationships among people), and organizational (the processes and routines within the firm). It broadens the traditional HR focus beyond simply the people to explore the larger processes and systems that exist within the firm.

The "behavior" concept within the SHRM literature can similarly be reconceptualized as the flow of knowledge within the firm through its creation, transfer, and integration. This "knowledge management" behavior becomes increasingly important as information and knowledge play a greater role in firm competitive advantage. It is through the flow of knowledge that firms increase or maintain the stock of intellectual capital.

At the right-hand side of the model we place the core competence, one of the major foci of the strategy literature. We propose that this core competence arises from the combination of the firms stock of knowledge (human, social, and organizational capital embedded in both people and

FIGURE 2 A Model for Integration Strategy and Strategic HRM

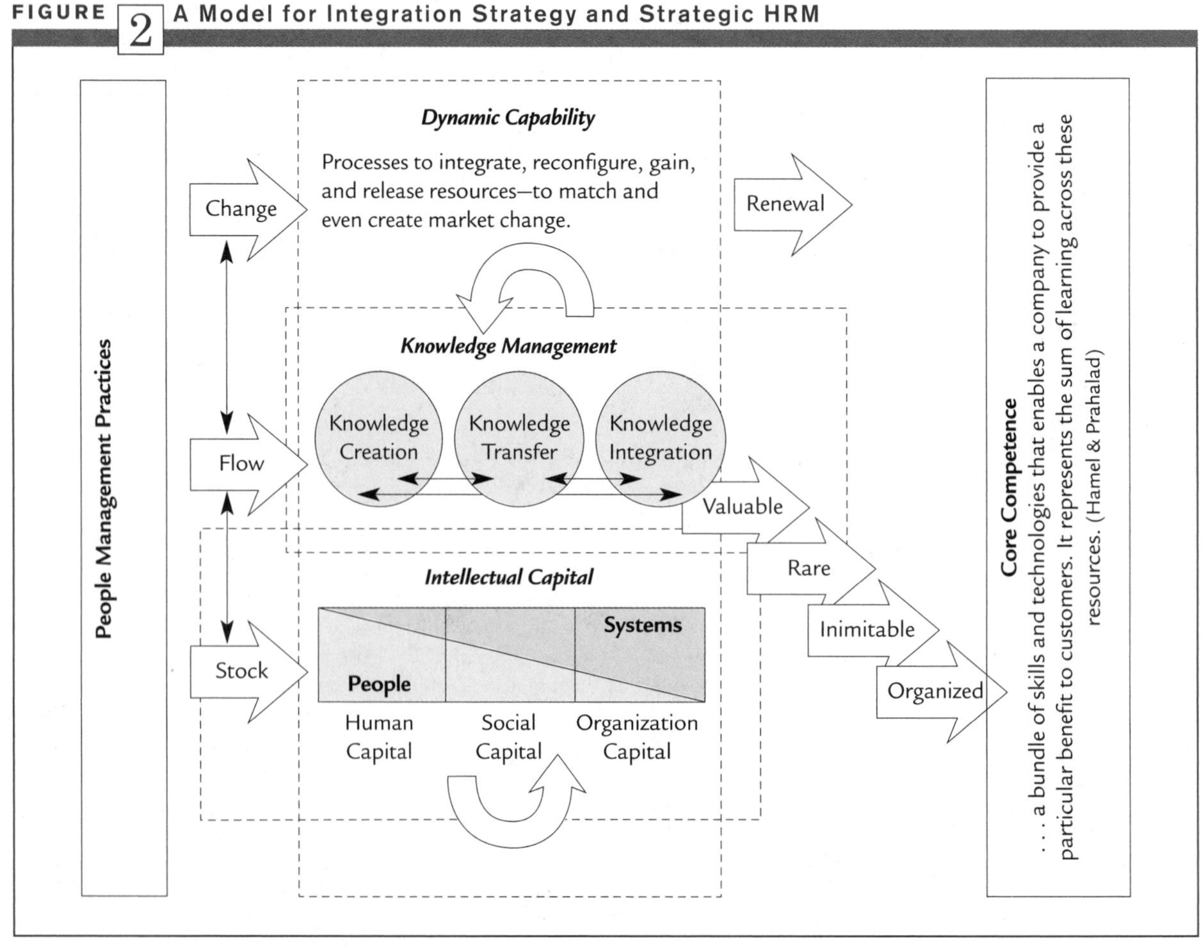

systems) and the flow of this knowledge though creation, transfer, and integration in a way that is valuable, rare, inimitable, and organized. This provides a framework for more specifically exploring the human component to core competencies, and provides a basis for exploring the linkage between people management systems and core competencies through the management of a firm's stock and flow of knowledge.

Finally, the dynamic capability construct illustrates the interdependent interplay between the workforce and the core competence as it changes over time. It represents the renewal process that organizations must undergo to remain competitive. Dynamic capability requires changing competencies on the part of both the organization and the people who comprise it. It is facilitated by people management systems that promote the change of both the stock and flow of knowledge within the firm that enable a firm to constantly renew its core competencies.

This model by no means serves as a well-developed theoretical framework, but rather simply seeks to point to the areas for collaboration between strategy and SHRM researchers. These two fields share common interests in issues and yet bring complementary skills, knowledge, and perspectives to these issues. The RBV highlights these common interests and provides a framework for developing collaborative effort.

10. Conclusion

The RBV has significantly and independently influenced the fields of strategy and SHRM. More importantly, however, it has provided a theoretical bridge between these two fields. By turning attention toward the internal resources, capabilities and competencies of the firm such as knowledge, learning, and dynamic capabilities (Hoskisson et al., 1999), it has brought strategy researchers to inescapably face a number of issues with regard to the management of people (Barney, 1996). We would guess that few strategy researchers are well versed in the existing research base regarding the effectiveness of various specific HR tools and techniques for managing people, and thus addressing these issues with necessary specificity.

This internal focus also has provided the traditionally atheoretical field of SHRM with a theoretical foundation from which it can begin exploring the strategic role that people and HR functions can play in organizations (Wright & McMahan, 1992). In addition to the lack of theory, this literature has also displayed little, or at least overly simplistic views of strategy, thus limiting its ability to contribute to the strategy literature (Chadwick & Cappelli, 1998). The RBV provides the framework from which HR researchers and practitioners can better understand the challenges of strategy, and thus be better able to play a positive role in the strategic management of firms.

We propose that both fields will benefit from greater levels of interaction in the future. This interaction should be deeper than simply reading each other's literature, but rather organizing conferences aimed at promoting face-to-face discussions of the common issues and challenges. In fact, we believe that future interdisciplinary research studies conducted jointly by strategy and SHRM researchers would exploit the unique knowledge and expertise of both fields, and synergistically contribute to the generation of new knowledge regarding the roles that people play in organizational competitive advantage (Jackson et al., 1989).

Source: Journal of Management, 27, 2001, 701–721.

SELECTED BIBLIOGRAPHY

L. Argote and P. Ingram, Knowledge transfer: A basis for competitive advantage in firms. *Organizational Behavior and Human Decision Processes* **82** 1 (2000), pp. 150–169.

C. Argyris and D. A. Schon, *Organizational learning: A theory of action perspective*, Addison-Wesley, Reading, MA (1978).

J. B. Arthur, Effects of human resource systems on manufacturing performance and turnover. *Academy of Management Journal* **37** 3 (1994), pp. 670–687.

J. N. Baron, A. Davis-Blake and W. T. Bielby, The structure of opportunity: How promotion ladders vary within and among organizations. *Administrative Science Quarterly* **31** (1986), pp. 248–273.

J. Barney, Firm resources and sustained competitive advantage. *Journal of Management* **17** 1 (1991), pp. 99–120.

J. Barney, The resource-based theory of the firm. *Organizational Science* **7** (1996), p. 469.

J. Barney, Is the resource-based view a useful perspective for strategic management research? Yes. *Academy of Management Review* **26** (2001), pp. 41–56.

B. E. Becker and M. A. Huselid, High performance work systems and firm performance: A synthesis of research and managerial applications. *Research in Personnel and Human Resources Management* **16** (1998), pp. 53–101.

J. S. Brown and P. Duguid, Organizational learning and communities-of-practice: Toward a unified view of working, learning, and innovation. *Organizational Science* **2** (1991), pp. 40–57.

P. F. Boxall, The Strategic HRM debate and the resource-based view of the firm. *Human Resource Management Journal* **6** 3 (1996), pp. 59–75.

P. F. Boxall, Human resource strategy and industry-based competition: A conceptual framework and agenda for theoretical development. In P. M. Wright, L. D. Dyer, J. W. Boudreau and G. T. Milkovich (Eds.), Research in personnel and human resources management (Suppl. 4, pp. 1–29). Madison, WI: IRRA (1998).

P. F. Boxall and M. Steeneveld, Human resource strategy and competitive advantage: A longitudinal study of engineering consultancies. *Journal of Management Studies* **36** 4 (1999), pp. 443–463.

P. Cappelli and H. Singh, Integrating strategic human resources and strategic management. In: D. Lewin, O. S. Mitchell and P. D. Sherer (Eds.), *Research frontiers in industrial relations and human resources*, IRRA, Madison, WI (1992), pp. 165–192.

C. Chadwick, & P. Cappelli, Alternatives to generic strategy typologies in strategic human resource management. In P. M. Wright, L. D. Dyer, J. W. Boudreau & G. T. Milkovich (Eds.), *Research in personnel and human resources management* (Suppl. 4, pp. 1–29). Greenwich, CT: JAI Press, Inc. (1998).

J. S. Coleman, Social capital in the creation of human capital. *American Journal of Sociology* **94** (1988), pp. s95–s120.

Conference Board. *Beyond knowledge management: New ways to work*. Research Report 1262–00RR (2000).

W. Cooke, Employee participation programs, group-based incentives, and Company performance: A union-nonunion comparison. *Industrial and Labor Relations Review* **47** (1994), pp. 594–609.

K. R. Conner and C. K. Prahalad, A resource-based theory of the firm: Knowledge versus opportunism. *Organization Science* **7** (1996), pp. 477–501.

M. A. Devanna, C. J. Fombrun, & N. M. Tichy, A Framework for Strategic Human Resource Management. *Strategic Human Resource Management* (Chapt. 3, pp. 33–51). New York: Wiley (1984).

I. Dierickx and K. Cool, Asset stock accumulation and sustainability of competitive advantage. *Management Science* **35** (1989), pp. 1504–1511.

P. Drucker *The practice of management.* Harper, New York (1954).

L. Edvinsson and M. Malone *Intellectual capital.* Harvard Business School Press, Cambridge, MA (1997).

K. M. Eisenhardt and J. A. Martin, Dynamic capabilities: What are they? *Strategic Management Journal* **21** (2000), pp. 1105–1121.

C. M. Fiol and M. A. Lyles, Organizational learning. *Academy of Management Review* **10** (1985), pp. 803–813.

S. Finkelstein and D. Hambrick, *Strategic leadership: Top executives and their effects on organizations.* West Pub. Co, Minneapolis/St. Paul (1996).

S. R. Fisher and M. A. White, Downsizing in a learning organization: Are there hidden costs? *Academy of Management Review* **25** 1 (2000), pp. 244–251.

T. M. Gardner, P. M. Wright, & B. Gerhart, The HR-Firm performance relationship: Can it be in the mind of the beholder? Working Paper, Center for Advanced Human Resource Studies, Cornell University (2000).

B. Gephart, M. Marsick, V., Van Buren, M., & M. Spiro, Learning Organizations come alive. *Training and Development,* **50** (1996), pp. 34–35.

B. Gerhart, G. Milkovich and B. Murray, Pay, performance and participation. In D. Lewin, O. Mitchell and P. Sherer (Eds.), *Research frontiers in industrial relations and human resources,* IRRA, Madison, WI (1992).

B. Gerhart, P. M. Wright, G. C. McMahan and S. A. Snell, Measurement error in research on human resources and firm performance: How much error is there and how does it influence effect size estimates? *Personnel Psychology* **53** (2000), pp. 803–834.

P. C. Godfrey and C. W. L. Hill, The problem of unobservables in strategic management research. *Strategic Management Journal* **16** (1995), pp. 519–533.

R. M. Grant, Toward a knowledge-based theory of the firm. *Strategic Management Journal* **17** Winter Special Issue (1996), pp. 108–122.

G. Hamel and C. K. Prahalad, Competing for the future. *Harvard Business Review* **72** 4 (1994), pp. 122–129.

M. T. Hansen, The search-transfer problem: The role of weak ties in sharing knowledge across organization sub units. *Administrative Science Quarterly* **44** March (1999), pp. 82–111.

G. Hedlund, A model of knowledge management and the N-form corporation. *Strategic Management Journal* **15** (1994), pp. 73–90.

K. Hattrup and N. Schmitt, Prediction of trades apprentices' performance on job sample criteria. *Personnel Psychology* **43** (1990), pp. 453–467.

R. Henderson and I. Cockburn, Measuring competence? Exploring firm effects in pharmaceutical research. *Strategic Management Research* **15** (1994), pp. 63–84.

M. A. Hitt, L. Bierman, K. Shimizu and R. Kochhar, Direct and moderating effects of human capital on the strategy and performance in professional service firms: A resource-based perspective. *Academy of Management Journal* **44** (2001), pp. 13–28.

R. E. Hoskisson, M. A. Hitt, W. P. Wan and D. Yiu, Theory and research in strategic management: Swings of a pendulum. *Strategic Management Journal* **25** 3 (1999), pp. 417–456.

M. A. Huselid, The impact of human resource management practices on turnover, productivity, and corporate financial performance. *Academy of Management Journal* **38** 3 (1995), pp. 635–672.

S. E. Jackson, R. S. Schuler and J. C. Rivero, Organizational characteristics as predictors of personnel practices. *Personnel Psychology* **42** (1989), pp. 727–786.

A. W. King and C. P. Zeithaml, Competencies and firm performance: Examining the causal ambiguity paradox. *Strategic Management Journal* **22** (2001), pp. 75–99.

M. J. Koch and R. G. McGrath, Improving labor productivity: Human resource management policies do matter. *Strategic Management Journal* **17** (1996), pp. 335–354.

A. A. Lado and M. C. Wilson, Human resource systems and sustained competitive advantage: A competency-based perspective. *Academy of Management Review* **19** 4 (1994), pp. 699–727.

D. Leonard-Barton, The factory as a learning laboratory. *Sloan Management Review* **34** 1 (1992), pp. 23–38.

D. Leonard-Barton, *Wellsprings of Knowledge.* Harvard Business School Press, Boston (1995).

D. P. Lepak and S. A. Snell, The human resource architecture: Toward a theory of human capital allocation and development. *Academy of Management Review* **24** (1999), pp. 31–48.

D. P. Lepak, & S. A. Snell, Examining the human resource architecture: The relationships among human capital, employment, and human resource configurations. *Journal of Management* (in press).

D. P. Lepak, R. Takeuchi, & S. A. Snell, An empirical examination of employment mode use and firm performance. Working paper, University of Maryland (2001).

J. P. Liebeskind, Knowledge, strategy, and the theory of the firm. *Strategic Management Journal* **17** Winter Special Issue (1996), pp. 93–107.

J. March and H. Simon, *Organizations.* Wiley, New York (1958).

J. P. MacDuffie, Human resource bundles and manufacturing performance: Organizational logic and flexible production systems in the world auto industry. *Industrial & Labor Relations Review* **48** 2 (1995), pp. 197–221.

S. F. Matusik and C. W. L. Hill, The utilization of contingent work, knowledge creation, and competitive advantage. *Academy of Management Review* **23** (1998), pp. 680–697.

G. C. McMahan, M. Virick, & P. M. Wright, Alternative theoretical perspective for strategic human resource management revisited: progress, problems, and prospects. In P. M. Wright, L. D. Dyer, J. W. Boudreau, & G. T. Milkovich (Eds.), *Research in personnel and human resources management* (Suppl. 4, pp. 99–122). Greenwich, CT: JAI Press, Inc. (1999).

R. E. Miles and C. C. Snow, *Organizational strategy, structure and process.* McGraw-Hill, New York (1978).

R. E. Miles, & C. C. Snow, Designing strategic human resources systems. *Organizational Dynamics,* Summer, (1984), pp. 36–52.

I. Nonaka, The knowledge creating company. *Harvard Business Review* **69** 6 (1991), pp. 96–104.

I. Nonaka and H. Takeuchi, *The knowledge-creating company: How Japanese companies create the dynamics of innovation.* Oxford Press, New York (1995).

D. Norburn and S. Birley, The top management team and corporate performance. *Strategic Management Journal* **9** (1988), pp. 225–237.

O. Nordhaug, *Human capital in organizations: Competence, training and learning.* Scandinavian University Press/Oxford University Press, Oslo/London (1993).

O. Nordhaug and K. Gronhaug, Competences as resources in firms. *The International Journal of Human Resource Management* **5** 1 (1994), pp. 89–106.

P. Osterman, Choice of employment systems in internal labor markets. *Industrial Relations* **26** 1 (1987), pp. 48–63.

M. A. Peteraf, The cornerstones of competitive advantage: A resource based view. *Strategic Management Journal* **14** (1993), pp. 179–191.

E. T. Penrose, *The theory of the growth of the firm,* Wiley, New York (1959).

M. E. Porter, *Competitive strategy.* New York: Free Press, pp. 34–46 (1980).

C. K. Prahalad, & G. Hamel, The core competence of the corporation. *Harvard Business Review*, May/June (1990), pp. 79–91.

R. L. Priem and J. E. Butler, Is the resource based "view" a useful perspective for strategic management research? *Academy of Management Review* **26** 1 (2001), pp. 22–40.

R. L. Priem and J. E. Butler, Tautology in the resource based view and the implications of externally determined resource value: Further comments. *Academy of Management Review* **26** 1 (2001), pp. 57–66.

O. C. Richard, Racial diversity, business strategy, and firm performance: A resource-based view. *Academy of Management Journal* **43** 2 (2001), pp. 164–177.

R. Rumelt, Toward a strategic theory of the firm. In R. Lamb (Ed.), *Competitive strategic management* Prentice-Hall, Englewood Cliffs, NJ (1984), pp. 556–570.

S. A. Snell, M. A. Shadur, & P. M. Wright, The era of our ways. In M. A. Hitt, R. E. Freeman, & J. S. Harrison (Eds.), *Handbook of strategic management* (pp. 627–629). Oxford: Blackwell Publishing (2001).

S. A. Snell, D. Stueber, & D. P. Lepak, Virtual HR departments: Getting out of the middle, In: Robert L. Heneman & David B. Greenberger, *Human resource management in virtual organizations*. Information Age Publishing (2001).

S. A. Snell, M. A. Youndt, & P. M. Wright, Establishing a framework for research in strategic human resource management: Merging resource theory and organizational learning. In G. Ferris (Ed.), *Research in personnel and human resources management* (Vol. 14, pp. 61–90), (1996).

G. Stalk, P. Evans and L. Schulman, Competing on capabilities: The new rules of corporate strategy. *Harvard Business Review* **70** (1992), pp. 57–69.

T. A. Stewart, Human resources bites back. *Fortune*, May, (1996). pp. 175.

K. E. Svieby *The new organizational wealth: Managing and measuring knowledge based assets*. Berrett-Koehler, San Francisco (1997).

G. Szulanski, Exploring internal stickiness: impediments to the transfer of best practice within the firm. *Strategic Management Journal* **17** Winter Special Issue (1996), pp. 27–43.

D. J. Teece, G. Pisano and A. Shuen, Dynamic capabilities and strategic management. *Strategic Management Journal* **18** 7 (1997), pp. 509–533.

A. B. Thomas, Does leadership make a difference in organizational performance? *Administrative Science Quarterly* **33** (1988), pp. 388–400.

C. Truss and L. Gratton, Strategic human resource management: A conceptual approach. *International Journal of Human Resource Management* **5** (1994), pp. 663–686.

A. S. Tsui, J. L. Pearce, L. W. Porter and A. M. Tripoli, Alternative approaches to the employee-organization relationship: Does investment in employees pay off? *Academy of Management Journal* **40** (1997), pp. 1089–1121.

J. Walker, Linking human resource planning and strategic planning. *Human Resource Planning* **1** (1978), pp. 1–18.

B. Wernerfelt, A resource-based view of the firm. *Strategic Management Journal 5* (1984), pp. 171–180.

B. Wernerfelt, The resource based view of the firm: Ten years after. *Strategic Management Journal* **16** (1995), pp. 171–174.

P. M. Wright, & W. Boswell, Desegregating HRM: A Review and Synthesis of Micro and Macro Human Resource Management Research. *Journal of Management* (in press).

P. M. Wright, & T. M. Gardner, Theoretical and empirical challenges in studying the HR practice-firm performance relationship. In D. Holman, T. D. Wall, C. Clegg, P. Sparrow, & A. Howard (Eds.), *The new workplace: People technology, and organization*. New York: John Wiley and Sons (in press).

P. M. Wright, T. M. Gardner, L. M. Moynihan, H. Park, B. Gerhart, & J. Delery, Measurement error in research on human resources and firm performance. Additional data and suggestions for future research. *Personnel Psychology* (in press).

P. M. Wright, B. McCormick, W. S. Sherman and G. C. McMahan, The role of human resources practices in petro-chemical refinery performance. *The International Journal of Human Resource Management* **10** (1999), pp. 551–571.

P. M. Wright and G. C. McMahan, Theoretical perspectives for strategic human resource management. *Journal of Management* **18** 2 (1992), pp. 295–320.

P. M. Wright, G. C. McMahan and A. McWilliams, Human resources and sustained competitive advantage: A resource-based perspective. *International Journal of Human Resource Management* **5** 2 (1994), pp. 301–326.

P. M. Wright, D. L. Smart and G. C. McMahan, Matches between human resources and strategy among NCAA basketball teams. *Academy of Management Journal* **38** 4 (1995), pp. 1052–1074.

P. M. Wright and S. A. Snell, Toward an integrative view of strategic human resource management. *Human Resource Management Review* **1** 3 (1991), pp. 203–225. *Abstract*

P. M. Wright and S. A. Snell, Toward a unifying framework for exploring fit and flexibility in strategic human resource management. *Academy of Management Review* **23** 4 (1998), pp. 756–772.

M. A. Youndt, & S. A. Snell, Human resource management, intellectual capital, and organizational performance. Working Paper, Skidmore College (2001).

READING 3.2

Are You Sure You Have a Strategy?

Donald C. Hambrick and James W. Fredrickson

Executive Overview

After more than 30 years of hard thinking about strategy, consultants and scholars have provided an abundance of frameworks for analyzing strategic situations. Missing, however, has been any guidance as to what the product of these tools should be—or what actually constitutes a strategy. Strategy has become a catchall term used to mean whatever one wants it to mean. Executives now talk about their "service strategy," their "branding strategy," their "acquisition strategy," or whatever kind of strategy that is on their mind at a particular moment. But strategists—whether they are CEOs of established firms, division presidents, or entrepreneurs—must have a strategy, an integrated, overarching concept of how the business will achieve its objectives. If a business must have a single, unified strategy, then it must necessarily have parts. What are those parts? We present a framework for strategy design, arguing that a strategy has five elements, providing answers to five questions—arenas: where will we be active? vehicles: how will we get there? differentiators: how will we win in the marketplace? staging: what will be our speed and sequence of moves? economic logic: how will we obtain our returns? Our article develops and illustrates these domains of choice, particularly emphasizing how essential it is that they form a unified whole.

Consider these statements of strategy drawn from actual documents and announcements of several companies:

> *"Our strategy is to be the low-cost provider."*
> *"We're pursuing a global strategy."*
> *"The company's strategy is to integrate a set of regional acquisitions."*
> *"Our strategy is to provide unrivaled customer service."*
> *"Our strategic intent is to always be the first-mover."*
> *"Our strategy is to move from defense to industrial applications."*

What do these grand declarations have in common? Only that none of them is a strategy. They are strategic threads, mere elements of strategies. But they are no more strategies than Dell Computer's strategy can be summed up as selling direct to customers, or than Hannibal's strategy was to use elephants to cross the Alps. And their use reflects an increasingly common syndrome—the catchall fragmentation of strategy.

After more than 30 years of hard thinking about strategy, consultants and scholars have provided executives with an abundance of frameworks for analyzing strategic situations. We now have five-forces analysis, core competencies, hypercompetition, the resource-based view of the firm, value chains, and a host of other helpful, often powerful, analytic tools.[1] Missing, however, has been any guidance as to what the product of these tools should be—or what actually constitutes a strategy. Indeed, the use of specific strategic tools tends to draw the strategist toward narrow, piecemeal conceptions of strategy that match the narrow scope of the tools themselves. For example, strategists who are drawn to Porter's five-forces analysis tend to think of strategy as a matter of selecting industries and segments within them. Executives who dwell on "co-opetition" or other game-theoretic frameworks see their world as a set of choices about dealing with adversaries and allies.

This problem of strategic fragmentation has worsened in recent years, as narrowly specialized academics and consultants have started plying their tools in the name of strategy. But strategy is not pricing. It is not capacity decisions. It is not setting R&D budgets. These are pieces of strategies, and they cannot be decided—or even considered—in isolation.

Imagine an aspiring painter who has been taught that colors and hues determine the beauty of a picture. But what can really be done with such advice? After all, magnificent pictures require far more than choosing colors: attention to shapes and figures, brush technique, and finishing processes. Most importantly, great paintings depend on artful combinations of *all* these elements. Some combinations are classic, tried-and-true; some are inventive and fresh; and many combinations—even for avant-garde art—spell trouble.

Strategy has become a catchall term used to mean whatever one wants it to mean. Business magazines now have regular sections devoted to strategy, typically discussing how featured firms are dealing with distinct issues, such as customer service, joint ventures, branding, or e-commerce. In turn, executives talk about their "service strategy," their "joint venture strategy," their "branding strategy," or whatever kind of strategy is on their minds at a particular moment.

Executives then communicate these strategic threads to their organizations in the mistaken belief that doing so will help managers make tough choices. But how does knowing that their firm is pursuing an "acquisition strategy" or a "first-mover strategy" help the vast majority of managers do their jobs or set priorities? How helpful is it to have new initiatives announced periodically with the word strategy tacked on? When executives call everything strategy, and end up with a collection of strategies, they create confusion and undermine their own credibility. They especially reveal that they don't really have an integrated conception of the business.

Many readers of works on the topic know that strategy is derived from the Greek *strategos,* or "the art of the general." But few have thought much about this important origin. For example, what is special about the general's job, compared with that of a field commander? The general is responsible for multiple units on multiple fronts and multiple battles over time. The general's challenge—and the value-added of generalship—is in orchestration and comprehensiveness. Great generals think about the whole. They have a strategy; it has pieces, or elements, but they form a coherent whole, Business generals, whether they are CEOs of established firms, division presidents, or entrepreneurs, must also have a strategy—a central, integrated, externally oriented concept of how the business will achieve its objectives. Without a strategy, time and resources are easily wasted on piecemeal, disparate activities; mid-level managers will fill the void with their own, often parochial, interpretations of what the business should be doing; and the result will be a potpourri of disjointed, feeble initiatives.

Examples abound of firms that have suffered because they lacked a coherent strategy. Once a towering force in retailing, Sears spent 10 sad years vacillating between an emphasis on hard goods and soft goods, venturing in and out of ill-chosen businesses, failing to differentiate itself in any of them, and never building a compelling economic logic. Similarly, the once-unassailable Xerox is engaged in an attempt to revive itself, amid criticism from its own executives that the company lacks a strategy. Says one: "I hear about asset sales, about refinancing, but I don't hear anyone saying convincingly, 'Here is your future.'"[2]

A strategy consists of an integrated set of choices, but it isn't a catchall for every important choice an executive faces. As Figure 1 portrays, the company's mission and objectives, for example, stand apart from, and guide, strategy. Thus we would not speak of the commitment of the *New York Times* to be America's newspaper of record as part of its strategy. GE's objective of being number one or number two in all its markets drives its strategy, but is not strategy itself. Nor would an objective of reaching a particular revenue or earnings target be part of a strategy.

Similarly, because strategy addresses how the business intends to engage its environment, choices about internal organizational arrangements are not part of strategy. So we should not speak of compensation policies, information systems, or training programs as being strategy. These are critically important choices, which should reinforce and support strategy; but they do not make up the strategy itself.[3] If everything important is thrown into the strategy bucket, then this essential concept quickly comes to mean nothing.

We do not mean to portray strategy development as a simple, linear process. Figure 1 leaves out feedback arrows and other indications that great strategists are iterative, loop thinkers.[4] The key is not in following a sequential process, but rather in achieving a robust, reinforced consistency among the elements of the strategy itself.

The Elements of Strategy

If a business must have a strategy, then the strategy must necessarily have parts. What are those parts? As Figure 2 portrays, a strategy has five elements, providing answers to five questions:

- Arenas: where will we be active?
- Vehicles: how will we get there?
- Differentiators: how will we win in the marketplace?
- Staging: what will be our speed and sequence of moves?
- Economic logic: how will we obtain our returns?

This article develops and illustrates these domains of choice, emphasizing how essential it is that they form a unified whole. Where others focus on the inputs to strategic thinking (the top box in Figure 1), we focus on the output—the composition and design of the strategy itself.

Arenas

The most fundamental choices strategists make are those of where, or in what arenas, the business will be active. This is akin to the question Peter Drucker posed decades ago: "What business will we be in?"[5] The answer, however, should not be one of broad generalities. For instance, "We will be the leader in information technology consulting" is more a vision or objective than part of a strategy. In articulating arenas, it is important to be as specific as possible about the product categories, market segments, geographic areas, and core technologies, as well as the value-adding stages (e.g., product design, manufacturing, selling, servicing, distribution) the business intends to take on.

For example, as a result of an in-depth analysis, a biotechnology company specified its arenas: the company intended to use T-cell receptor technology to develop both diagnostic and therapeutic products for battling a certain class of cancers; it chose to keep control of all research and product development activity, but to outsource manufacturing and a major part of the clinical testing process required for regulatory approvals. The company targeted the U.S. and major European markets as its geographic scope. The company's chosen arenas were highly specific, with products and markets even targeted by

FIGURE 1 Putting Strategy in Its Place

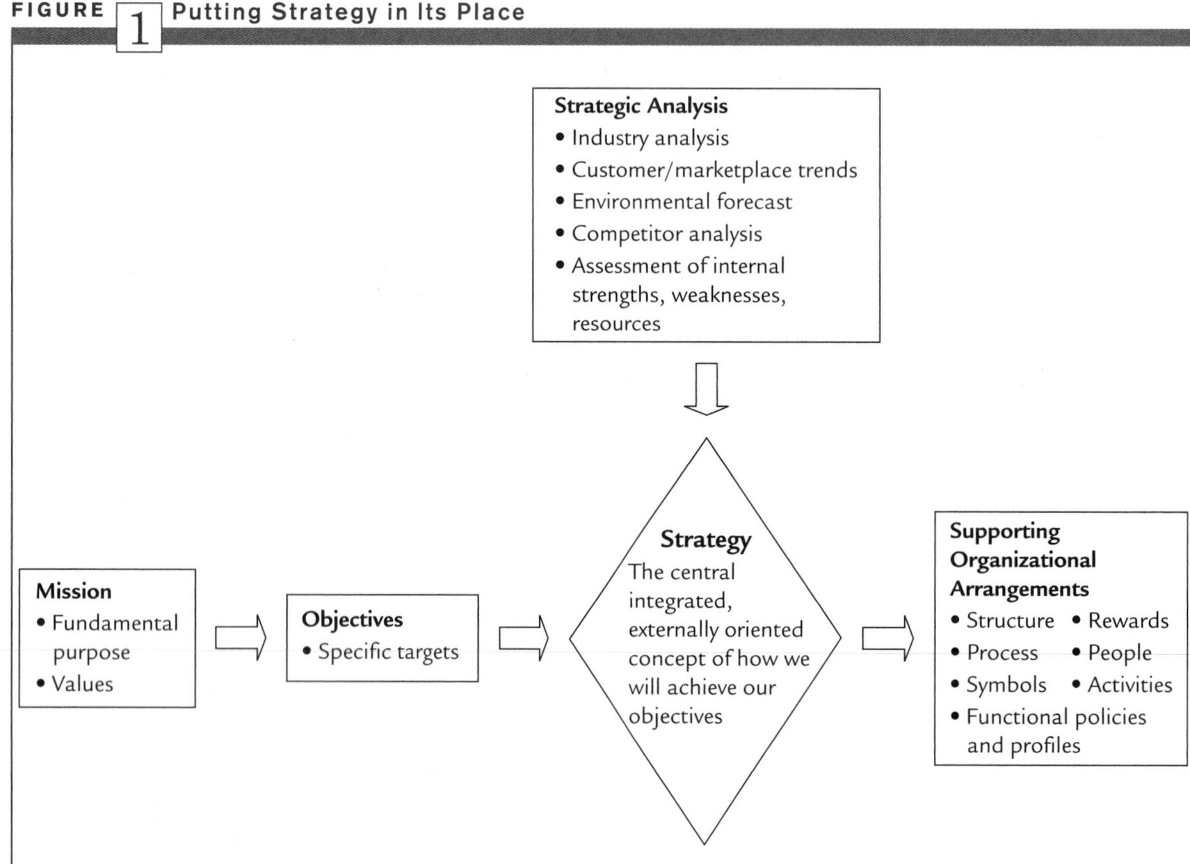

name. In other instances, especially in businesses with a wider array of products, market segments, or geographic scope, the strategy may instead reasonably specify the classes of, or criteria for, selected arenas—e.g., women's high-end fashion accessories, or countries with per-capita GDP over $5,000. But in all cases, the challenge is to be as specific as possible.

In choosing arenas, the strategist needs to indicate not only where the business will be active, but also how much emphasis will be placed on each. Some market segments, for instance, might be identified as centrally important, while others are deemed secondary. A strategy might reasonably be centered on one product category, with others—while necessary for defensive purposes or for offering customers a full line—being of distinctly less importance.

Vehicles

Beyond deciding on the arenas in which the business will be active, the strategist also needs to decide how to get there. Specifically, the means for attaining the needed presence in a particular product category, market segment, geographic area, or value-creation stage should be the result of deliberate strategic choice. If we have decided to expand our product range, are we going to accomplish that by relying on organic, internal product development, or are there other vehicles—such as joint ventures or acquisitions—that offer a better means for achieving our broadened scope? If we are committed to international expansion, what should be our primary modes, or vehicles—green-field startups, local acquisitions, licensing, or joint ventures? The executives of the biotechnology company noted earlier decided to rely on joint ventures to achieve their new presence in Europe, while committing to a series of tactical acquisitions for adding certain therapeutic products to complement their existing line of diagnostic products.

The means by which arenas are entered matters greatly. Therefore, selection of vehicles should not be an afterthought or viewed as a mere implementation detail. A decision to enter new product categories is rife with uncertainty. But that uncertainty may vary immensely depending on whether the entry is attempted by licensing other companies' technologies, where perhaps the firm has prior experience, or by acquisitions, where the company is a novice. Failure to explicitly consider and articulate the intended expansion vehicles can result in the hoped-for entry's being seriously delayed, unnecessarily costly, or totally stalled.

There are steep learning curves associated with the use of alternative expansion modes. Research has found, for instance, that companies can develop highly advantageous, well-honed capabilities in making acquisitions or in managing joint ventures.[6] The company that uses various vehicles on an

FIGURE 2 The Five Major Elements of Strategy

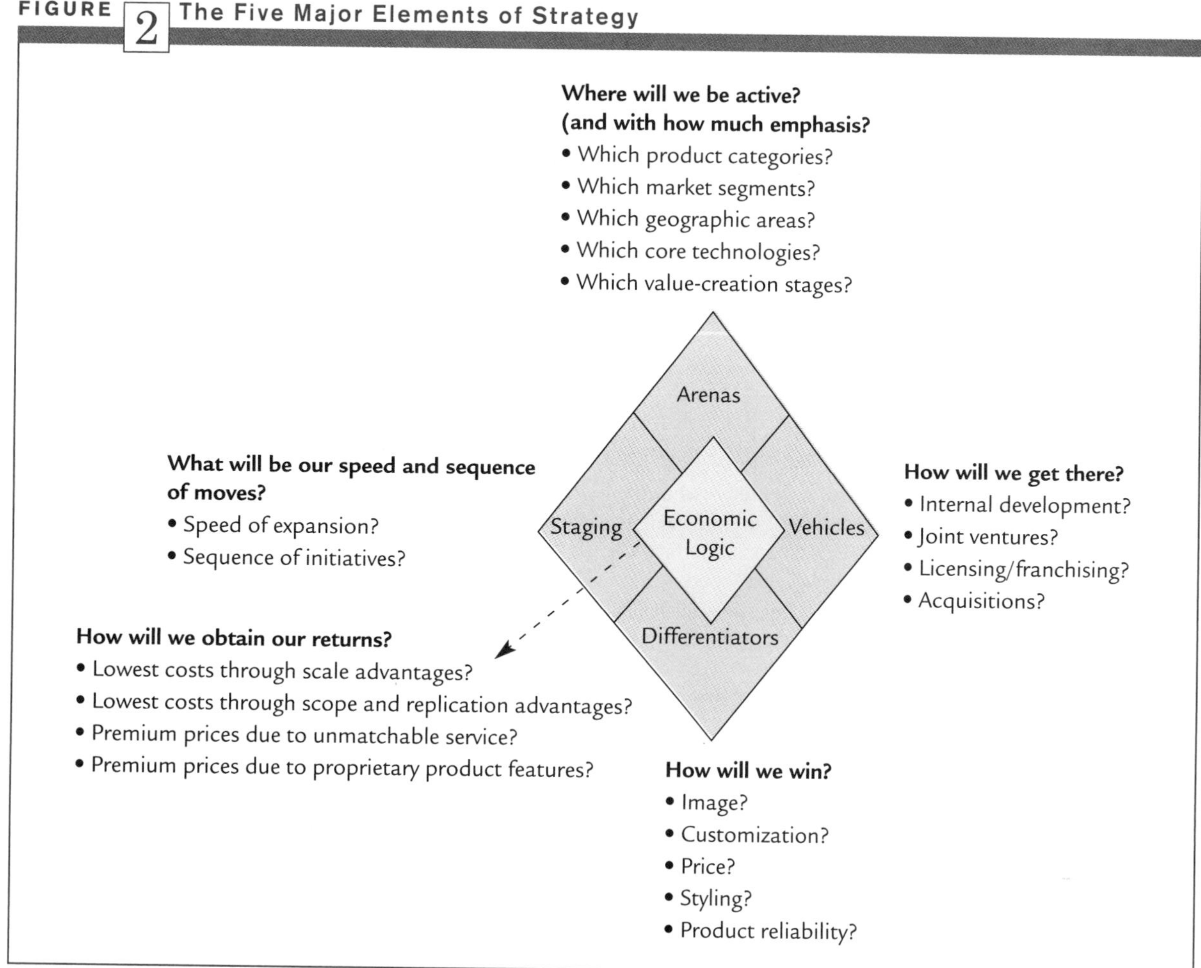

ad hoc or patchwork basis, without an overarching logic and programmatic approach, will be at a severe disadvantage compared with companies that have such coherence.

Differentiators

A strategy should specify not only where a firm will be active (arenas) and how it will get there (vehicles), but also how the firm will win in the marketplace—how it will get customers to come its way. In a competitive world, winning is the result of differentiators, and such edges don't just happen. Rather, they require executives to make upfront, conscious choices about which weapons will be assembled, honed, and deployed to beat competitors in the fight for customers, revenues, and profits. For example, Gillette uses its proprietary product and process technology to develop superior razor products, which the company further differentiates through a distinctive, aggressively advertised brand image. Goldman Sachs, the investment bank, provides customers unparalleled service by maintaining close relationships with client executives and coordinating the array of services it offers to each client. Southwest Airlines attracts and retains customers by offering the lowest possible fares and extraordinary on-time reliability.

Achieving a compelling marketplace advantage does not necessarily mean that the company has to be at the extreme on one differentiating dimension; rather, sometimes having the best combination of differentiators confers a tremendous marketplace advantage. This is the philosophy of Honda in automobiles. There are better cars than Hondas, and there are less expensive cars than Hondas; but many car buyers believe that there is no better value—quality for the price—than a Honda, a strategic position the company has worked hard to establish and reinforce.

Regardless of the intended differentiators—image, customization, price, product styling, after-sale services, or others—the critical issue for strategists is to make up-front, deliberate choices. Without that, two unfortunate outcomes loom. One is that, if top management doesn't attempt to create unique differentiation, none will occur. Again, differentiators don't just materialize; they are very hard to achieve. And firms without them lose.

The other negative outcome is that, without up-front, careful choices about differentiators, top management may seek to offer customers across-the-board superiority, trying simultaneously to outdistance competitors on too broad on array of differentiators—lower price, better service, superior styling, and so on. Such attempts are doomed, however, because of their inherent inconsistencies and extraordinary resource demands. In selecting differentiators, strategists should give explicit preference to those few forms of superiority that are mutually reinforcing (e.g., image and product styling), consistent with the firm's resources and capabilities, and, of course, highly valued in the arenas the company has targeted.

Staging

Choices of arenas, vehicles, and differentiators constitute what might be called the substance of a strategy—what executives plan to do. But this substance cries out for decisions on a fourth element—staging, or the speed and sequence of major moves to take in order to heighten the likelihood of success.[7] Most strategies do not call for equal, balanced initiatives on all fronts at all times. Instead, usually some initiatives must come first, followed only then by others, and then still others. In erecting a great building, foundations must be laid, followed by walls, and only then the roof.

Of course, in business strategy there is no universally superior sequence. Rather the strategist's judgment is required. Consider a printing equipment company that committed itself to broadening its product line and expanding internationally. The executives decided that the new products should be added first, in stage one, because the elite sales agents they planned to use for international expansion would not be able or willing to represent a narrow product line effectively. Even though the executives were anxious to expand geographically, if they had tried to do so without the more complete line in place, they would have wasted a great deal of time and money. The left half of Figure 3 shows their two-stage logic.

The executives of a regional title insurance company, as part of their new strategy, were committed to becoming national in scope through a series of acquisitions. For their differentiators, they planned to establish a prestigious brand backed by aggressive advertising and superb customer service. But the executives faced a chicken-and-egg problem: they couldn't make the acquisitions on favorable terms without the brand image in place; but with only their current limited geographic scope, they couldn't afford the quantity or quality of advertising needed to establish the brand. They decided on a three-stage plan (shown in the right half of Figure 3): 1) make selected acquisitions in adjacent regions, hence becoming a super-regional in size and scale; 2) invest moderately heavily in advertising and brand-building; 3) make acquisitions in additional regions on more favorable terms (because of the enhanced brand, a record of growth, and, they hoped, an appreciated stock price) while simultaneously continuing to push further in building the brand.

Decisions about staging can be driven by a number of factors. One, of course, is resources. Funding and staffing every envisioned initiative, at the needed levels, is generally not possible at the outset of a new strategic campaign. Urgency is a second factor affecting staging; some elements of a strategy may face brief windows of opportunity, requiring that they be pursued first and aggressively. A third factor is the achievement of credibility. Attaining certain thresholds—in specific arenas, differentiators, or vehicles—can be critically valuable for attracting resources and stakeholders that are needed for other parts of the strategy. A fourth factor is the pursuit of early wins. It may be far wiser to successfully tackle a part of the strategy that is relatively doable before attempting more challenging or unfamiliar initiatives. These are only some of the factors that might go into decisions about the speed and sequence of strategic initiatives. However, since the concept of staging has gone largely unexplored in the strategy literature, it is often given far too little attention by strategists themselves.

FIGURE 3 Examples of Strategic Staging

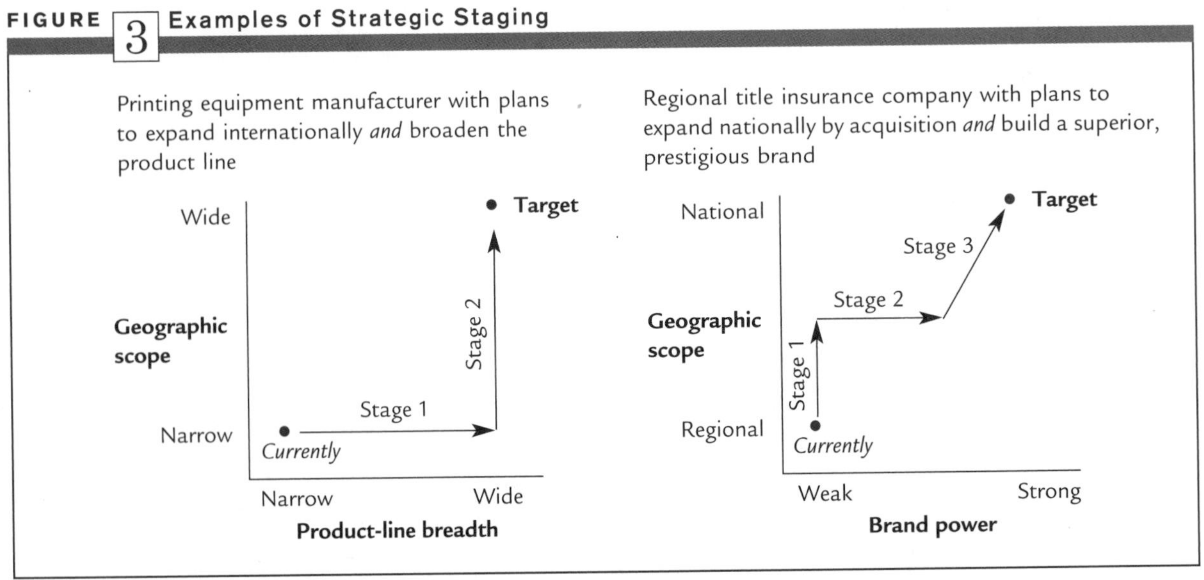

Economic Logic

At the heart of a business strategy must be a clear idea of how profits will be generated—not just some profits, but profits above the firm's cost of capital.[8] It is not enough to vaguely count on having revenues that are above costs. Unless there's a compelling basis for it, customers and competitors won't let that happen. And it's not enough to generate a long list of reasons why customers will be eager to pay high prices for your products, along with a long list of reasons why your costs will be lower than your competitors'. That's a sure-fire route to strategic schizophrenia and mediocrity.

The most successful strategies have a central economic logic that serves as the fulcrum for profit creation. In some cases, the economic key may be to obtain premium prices by offering customers a difficult-to-match product. For instance, the *New York Times* is able to charge readers a very high price (and strike highly favorable licensing arrangements with on-line information distributors) because of its exceptional journalistic quality; in addition, the *Times* is able to charge advertisers high prices because it delivers a large number of dedicated, affluent readers. ARAMARK, the highly profitable international food-service company, is able to obtain premium prices from corporate and institutional clients by offering a level of customized service and responsiveness that competitors cannot match. The company seeks out only those clients that want superior food service and are willing to pay for it. For example, once domestic airlines became less interested in distinguishing themselves through their in-flight meals, ARAMARK dropped that segment.

In some instances, the economic logic might reside on the cost side of the profit equation. ARAMARK—adding to its pricing leverage—uses its huge scale of operations and presence in multiple market segments (business, educational, healthcare, and correctional-system food service) to achieve a sizeable cost advantage in food purchases—an advantage that competitors cannot duplicate. GKN Sinter Metals, which has grown by acquisition to become the world's major powdered-metals company, benefits greatly from its scale in obtaining raw materials and in exploiting, in country after country, its leading-edge capabilities in metal-forming processes.

In these examples the economic logics are not fleeting or transitory. They are rooted in the firms' fundamental and relatively enduring capabilities. ARAMARK and the *New York Times* can charge premium prices because their offerings are superior in the eyes of their targeted customers, customers highly value that superiority, and competitors can't readily imitate the offerings. ARAMARK and GKN Sinter Metals have lower costs than their competitors because of systemic advantages of scale, experience, and know-how sharing. Granted, these leads may not last forever or be completely unassailable, but the economic logics that are at work at these companies account for their abilities to deliver strong year-in, year-out profits.

The Imperative of Strategic Comprehensiveness

By this point, it should be clear why a strategy needs to encompass all five elements—arenas, vehicles, differentiators, staging, and economic logic. First, all five are important enough to require intentionality. Surprisingly, most strategic plans emphasize one or two of the elements without giving any consideration to the others. Yet to develop a strategy without attention to all five leaves critical omissions.

Second, the five elements call not only for choice, but also for preparation and investment. All five require certain capabilities that cannot be generated spontaneously.

Third, all five elements must align with and support each other. When executives and academics think about alignment, they typically have in mind that internal organizational arrangements need to align with strategy (in tribute to the maxim that "structure follows strategy"[9]), but few pay much attention to the consistencies required among the elements of the strategy itself.

Finally, it is only after the specification of all five strategic elements that the strategist is in the best position to turn to designing all the other supporting activities—functional policies, organizational arrangements, operating programs, and processes—that are needed to reinforce the strategy. The five elements of the strategy diamond can be considered the hub or central nodes for designing a comprehensive, integrated activity system.[10]

Comprehensive Strategies at IKEA and Brake Products International

IKEA: Revolutionizing an Industry

So far we have identified and discussed the five elements that make up a strategy and form our strategy diamond. But a strategy is more than simply choices on these five fronts: it is an integrated, mutually reinforcing set of choices—choices that form a coherent whole. To illustrate the importance of this coherence we will now discuss two examples of fully elaborated strategy diamonds. As a first illustration, consider the strategic intent of IKEA, the remarkably successful global furniture retailer. IKEA's strategy over the past 25 years has been highly coherent, with all five elements reinforcing each other.

The arenas in which IKEA operates are well defined: the company sells relatively inexpensive, contemporary, Scandinavian-style furniture and home furnishings. IKEA's target market is young, primarily white-collar customers. The geographic scope is worldwide, or at least all countries where socioeconomic and infrastructure conditions support the concept. IKEA is not only a retailer, but also maintains control of product design to ensure the integrity of its unique image and to accumulate unrivaled expertise in designing for efficient manufacturing. The company, however, does not manufacture, relying instead on a host of long-term suppliers who ensure efficient, geographically dispersed production.

As its primary vehicle for getting to its chosen arenas, IKEA engages in organic expansion, building its own wholly owned stores. IKEA has chosen not to make acquisitions of existing retailers, and it engages in very few joint ventures. This reflects top management's belief that the company needs to fully control local execution of its highly innovative retailing concept.

IKEA attracts customers and beats competitors by offering several important differentiators. First, its products are of very reliable quality but are low in price (generally 20 to 30 percent below the competition for comparable quality goods). Second, in contrast to the stressful, intimidating feeling that shoppers often encounter in conventional furniture stores, IKEA customers are treated to a fun, non-threatening experience, where they are allowed to wander through a visually exciting store with only the help they request. And third, the company strives to make customer fulfillment immediate. Specifically, IKEA carries an extensive inventory at each store, which allows a customer to take the item home or have it delivered the same day. In contrast, conventional furniture retailers show floor models, but then require a 6- to 10-week wait for the delivery of each special-order item.

As for staging, or IKEA's speed and sequence of moves, once management realized that its approach would work in a variety of countries and cultures, the company committed itself to rapid international expansion, but only one region at a time. In general, the company's approach has been to use its limited resources to establish an early foothold by opening a single store in each targeted country. Each such entry is supported with aggressive public relations and advertising, in order to lay claim to the radically new retailing concept in that market. Later, IKEA comes back into each country and fills in with more stores.

The economic logic of IKEA rests primarily on scale economies and efficiencies of replication. Although the company doesn't sell absolutely identical products in all its geographic markets, IKEA has enough standardization that it can take great advantage of being the world's largest furniture retailer. Its costs from long-term suppliers are exceedingly low, and made even lower by IKEA's proprietary, easy-to-manufacture product designs. In each region, IKEA has enough scale to achieve substantial distribution and promotional efficiencies. And each individual store is set up as a high-volume operation, allowing further economies in inventories, advertising, and staffing. IKEA's phased international expansion has allowed executives to benefit, in country after country, from what they have learned about site selection, store design, store openings, and ongoing operations. They are vigilant, astute learners, and they put that learning to great economic use.

Note how all of IKEA's actions (shown in Figure 4) fit together. For example, consider the strong alignment between its targeted arenas and its competitive differentiators.

FIGURE 4 IKEA's Strategy

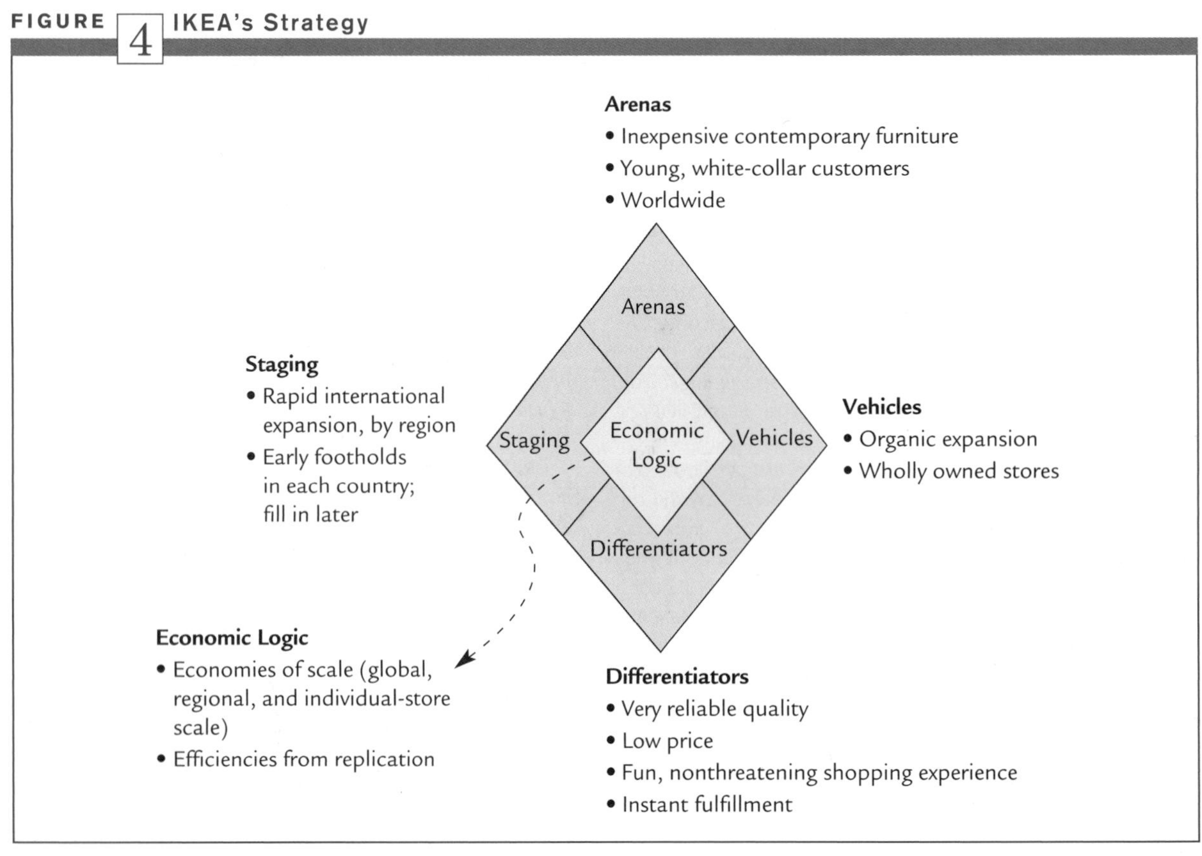

An emphasis on low price, fun, contemporary styling, and instant fulfillment is well suited to the company's focus on young, first-time furniture buyers. Or consider the logical fit between the company's differentiators and vehicles—providing a fun shopping experience and instant fulfillment requires very intricate local execution, which can be achieved far better through wholly owned stores than by using acquisitions, joint ventures, or franchises. These alignments, along with others, help account for IKEA's long string of years with double-digit sales growth, and current revenues of $8 billion.

The IKEA example allows us to illustrate the strategy diamond with a widely familiar business story. That example, however, is admittedly retrospective, looking backward to interpret the company's strategy according to the framework. But the real power and role of strategy, of course, is in looking forward. Based on a careful and complete analysis of a company's environment, marketplace, competitors, and internal capabilities, senior managers need to craft a strategic intent for their firm. The diamond is a useful framework for doing just that, as we will now illustrate with a business whose top executives set out to develop a new strategy that would allow them to break free from a spiral of mediocre profits and stagnant sales.

Brake Products International: Charting a New Direction The strategy diamond proved very useful when it was applied by the new executive team of Brake Products International (BPI), a disguised manufacturer of components used in braking and suspension systems for passenger cars and light trucks. In recent years, BPI had struggled as the worldwide auto industry consolidated. Its reaction had been a combination of disparate, half-hearted diversification initiatives, alternating with across-the-board expense cuts. The net result, predictably, was not good, and a new management team was brought in to try to revive performance. As part of this turnaround effort, BPI's new executives developed a new strategic intent by making critical decisions for each of the five elements—arenas, vehicles, differentiators, staging, and economic logic. We will not attempt to convey the analysis that gave rise to their choices, but rather (as with the IKEA example) will use BPI to illustrate the articulation of a comprehensive strategy.

For their targeted arenas, BPI executives committed to expanding beyond their current market scope of North American and European car plants by adding Asia, where global carmakers were rapidly expanding. They considered widening their product range to include additional auto components, but concluded that their unique design and manufacturing expertise was limited to brake and suspension components. They did decide, however, that they should apply their advanced capability in antilock-braking and electronic traction-control systems to develop braking products for off-road vehicles, including construction and farm equipment. As an additional commitment, executives decided to add a new service, systems integration, that would involve bundling BPI products with other related components, from other manufacturers, that form a complete suspension system, and then providing the carmakers with easy-to-handle, preassembled systems modules. This initiative would allow the carmakers to reduce assembly costs significantly, as well as to deal with a single suspension-system supplier, with substantial logistics and inventory savings.

The management team identified three major vehicles for achieving BPI's presence in their selected arenas. First, they were committed to organic internal development of new generations of leading-edge braking systems, including those for off-road vehicles. To become the preferred suspension-system integrator for the major auto manufacturers, executives decided to enter into strategic alliances with the leading producers of other key suspension components. Finally, to serve carmakers that were expanding their operations in Asia, BPI planned to initiate equity joint ventures with brake companies in China, Korea, and Singapore. BPI would provide the technology and oversee the manufacturing of leading-edge, high-quality antilock brakes; the Asian partners would take the lead in marketing and government relations.

BPI's executives also committed to achieving and exploiting a small set of differentiators. The company was already a technology leader, particularly in antilock-braking systems and electronic traction-control systems. These proprietary technologies were seen as centrally important and would be further nurtured. Executives also believed they could establish a preeminent position as a systems integrator of entire suspension assemblies. However, achieving this advantage would require new types of manufacturing and logistics capabilities, as well as new skills in managing relationships with other component companies. This would include an extensive e-business capability that linked BPI with its suppliers and customers. And finally, as one of the few brakes/suspension companies with a manufacturing presence in North America and Europe—and now in Asia—BPI executives concluded that they had a potential advantage—what they referred to as "global reach"—that was well suited to the global consolidation of the automobile industry. If BPI did a better job of coordinating activities among its geographically dispersed operations, it could provide the one-stop, low-cost global purchasing that the industry giants increasingly sought.

BPI's executives approached decisions about staging very deliberately. They felt urgency on various fronts, but also realized that, after several years of lackluster performance, the firm lacked the resources and credibility to do everything all at once. As is often the case, decisions about staging were most important for those initiatives where the gaps between the status quo and the strategic intent were the greatest. For example, executives decided that, in order to provide a clear, early sign of continued commitment to the major global auto manufacturers, a critical first step was to establish the joint ventures with brake manufacturers in Asia. They felt just as much urgency to gain a first-mover advantage as a suspension-system integrator. Therefore, management committed to promptly establish alliances with a select group of manufacturers of other suspension components, and to experiment with one pilot customer. These two sets of initiatives constituted stage one of BPI's strategic intent. For stage two, the executives planned to launch the full versions of the systems-integration and global-reach concepts, complete with aggressive marketing. Also in this second stage, expansion into the off-road vehicle market would commence.

BPI's economic logic hinged on securing premium prices from its customers, by offering them at least three valuable, difficult-to-imitate benefits. First, BPI was the worldwide technology leader in braking systems; car companies would pay to get access to these products for their new high-end models. Second, BPI would allow global customers an economical single source for braking products; this would save customers considerable contract administration and quality-assurance costs—savings that they would be willing to share. And third, through its alliances with major suspension-component manufacturers, BPI would be able to deliver integrated-suspension-system kits to customers—again saving customers in purchasing costs, inventory costs, and even assembly costs, for which they would pay a premium.

BPI's turnaround was highly successful. The substance of the company's strategy (shown in Figure 5) was critically important in the turnaround, as was the concise strategy statement that was communicated throughout the firm. As the CEO stated:

> *We've finally identified what we want to be, and what's important to us. Just as importantly, we've decided what we don't want to be, and have stopped wasting time and effort. Since we started talking about BPI in terms of arenas, vehicles, differentiators, staging, and economic logic, we have been able to get our top team on the same page. A whole host of decisions have logically fallen into place in support of our comprehensive strategic agenda,*

FIGURE 5 BPI's Strategy

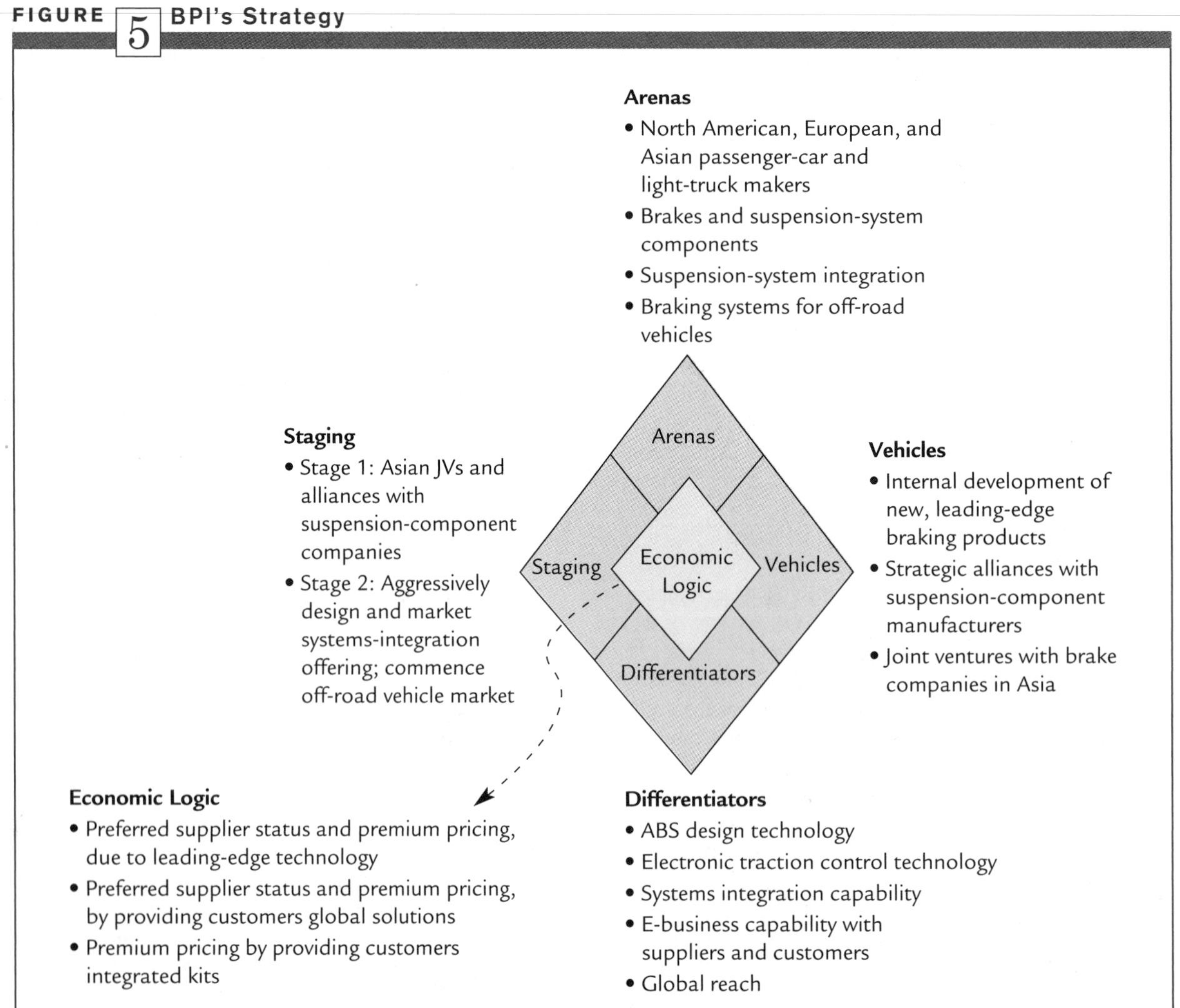

Of Strategy, Better Strategy, and No Strategy

Our purpose in this article has been elemental—to identify what constitutes a strategy. This basic agenda is worthwhile because executives and scholars have lost track of what it means to engage in the art of the general. We particularly hope to counter the recent catchall fragmentation of the strategy concept, and to remind strategists that orchestrated holism is their charge.

But we do not want to be mistaken. We don't believe that it is sufficient to simply make these five sets of choices. No—a business needs not just a strategy, but a *sound* strategy. Some strategies are clearly far better than others. Fortunately, this is where the wealth of strategic-analysis tools that have been developed in the last 30 years becomes valuable. Such tools as industry analysis, technology cycles, value chains, and core competencies, among others, are very helpful for improving the soundness of strategies. When we compare these tools and extract their most powerful central messages, several key criteria emerge to help executives test the quality of a proposed strategy. These criteria are presented in Table 1.[11] We strongly encourage executives to apply these tests throughout the strategy-design process and especially when a proposed strategy emerges.

There might be those who wonder whether strategy isn't a concept of yesteryear, whose time has come and gone. In an era of rapid, discontinuous environmental shifts, isn't the company that attempts to specify its future just flirting with disaster? Isn't it better to be flexible, fast-on-the-feet, ready to grab opportunities when the right ones come along?

Some of the skepticism about strategy stems from basic misconceptions. First, a strategy need not be static: it can evolve and be adjusted on an ongoing basis. Unexpected opportunities need not be ignored because they are outside the strategy. Second, a strategy doesn't require a business to become rigid. Some of the best strategies for today's turbulent environment keep multiple options open and build in desirable flexibility—through alliances, outsourcing, leased assets, toehold investments in promising technologies, and numerous other means. A strategy can help to intentionally build in many forms of flexibility—if that's what is called for. Third, a strategy doesn't deal only with an unknowable, distant future. The appropriate lifespans of business strategies have become shorter in recent years. Strategy used to be equated with 5- or 10-year horizons, but today a horizon of two to three years is often more fitting. In any event, strategy does not deal as much with preordaining the future as it does with assessing current conditions and future likelihoods, then making the best decisions possible today.

Strategy is not primarily about planning. It is about intentional, informed, and integrated choices. The noted strategic thinkers Gary Hamel and C. K. Prahalad said: "[A company's] leadership cannot be planned for, but neither can it happen without a grand and well-considered aspiration."[12] We offer the strategy diamond as a way to craft and articulate a business aspiration.

Source: Academy of Management Executive, 19, (4), 2005, 51–62. Reprinted by permission.

Table 1 Testing the Quality of Your Strategy

Key Evaluation Criteria

1. **Does your strategy fit with what's going on in the environment?**
   Is there healthy profit potential where you're headed? Does your strategy align with the key success factors of your chosen environment?

2. **Does your strategy exploit your key resources?**
   With your particular mix of resources, does this strategy give you a good head start on competitors? Can you pursue this strategy more economically than competitors?

3. **Will your envisioned differentiators be sustainable?**
   Will competitors have difficulty matching you? If not, does your strategy explicitly include a ceaseless regimen of innovation and opportunity creation?

4. **Are the elements of your strategy internally consistent?**
   Have you made choices of arenas, vehicles, differentiators, and staging, and economic logic? Do they all fit and mutually reinforce each other?

5. **Do you have enough resources to pursue this strategy?**
   Do you have the money, managerial time and talent, and other capabilities to do all you envision? Are you sure you're not spreading your resources too thinly, only to be left with a collection of feeble positions?

6. **Is your strategy implementable?**
   Will your key constituencies allow you to pursue this strategy? Can your organization make it through the transition? Are you and your management team able and willing to lead the required changes?

Acknowledgments

We thank the following people for helpful suggestions: Ralph Biggadike, Warren Boeker, Kathy Harrigan, Paul Ingram, Xavier Martin, Atul Nerkar, and Jaeyong Song.

ENDNOTES

1. Porter, M. E. 1980. *Competitive strategy.* New York: The Free Press, provides an in-depth discussion of the five-forces model. Hypercompetition is addressed in D'Aveni, R. A. 1994. *Hypercompetition.* New York: The Free Press. The resource-based view of the firm is discussed in Barney, J. 1991. Firm resources and sustained competitive advantage. *Journal of Management,* 17: 99–120. See Brandenburger, M., & Nalebuff, R. J. 1995. The right game: Use game theory to shape strategy. *Harvard Business Review,* July-August: 57–71, for a discussion of co-opetition.
2. Bianco, A., & Moore, P. L. 2001. Downfall: The inside story of the management fiasco at Xerox. *BusinessWeek,* 5 March 2001.
3. A widely applicable framework for strategy implementation is discussed in Galbraith, J. R., & Kazanjian, R. K. 1986. *Strategy implementation: Structure, systems and process,* 2nd ed. St. Paul: West Publishing. A similar tool is offered in Hambrick, D. C., & Cannella, A. 1989. Strategy implementation as substance and selling. *The Academy of Management Executive, 3(4)*: 278–285.
4. This observation has been made for years by many contributors, including Quinn, J. B. 1980. *Strategies for change: Logical incrementalism.* Homewood, IL: Richard D. Irwin Publishing: and Mintzberg, H. 1973. Strategy making in three modes. *California Management Review,* 15: 44–53.
5. Drucker, P. 1954. *The practice of management.* New York: Harper & Row.
6. Haleblian, J., & Finkelstein, S. 1999. The influence of organizational acquisition experience on acquisition performance: A behavioral learning perspective. *Administrative Science Quarterly,* 44: 29–56.
7. Eisenhardt, K. M., & Brown, S. L. 1998. Time pacing: Competing in markets that won't stand still. *Harvard Business Review,* March-April: 59–69, discusses "time pacing" as a component of a process of contending with rapidly changing environments.
8. The collapse of stock market valuations for Internet companies lacking in profits—or any prospect of profits—marked a return to economic reality. Profits above the firm's cost of capital are required in order to yield sustained or longer-term shareholder returns.
9. Galbraith & Kazanjian, op. cit., and Hambrick & Cannella, op. cit.
10. Porter, M. E. 1996. What is strategy? *Harvard Business Review,* November–December: 61–78.
11. See Tilles, S. 1963_ How to evaluate strategy. *Harvard Business Review,* July–August: 112–121, for a classic, but more limited, set of evaluative tests.
12. See Hamel, G., & Prahalad, C. K. 1993. Strategy as stretch and leverage. *Harvard Business Review,* March–April: 84–91.

READING 3.3

Strategic and Organizational Requirements for Competitive Advantage

David Lei and John W. Slocum, Jr.

Executive Overview

Formulating an effective business strategy for a firm is a complex task. How best to compete in an industry is one of the major determinants that influence managers' choices of business strategy. The life cycle stages of the industry and the rate of technological change are two drivers that have significant impact on industry evolution. We develop a typology of four types of industry environments: Fast Growth; Wild, Wild West; Steady Evolution; and Creative Destruction. Each of these generates a different set of strategic imperatives for managers. To operate effectively in each type of industry environment, managers may select among four business strategies: Concept Drivers, Pioneers, Consolidators, and Concept Learners. We present the various strengths and challenges posed by each strategy and how managers can overcome these.

Although successful organizations are less unified than living organisms, they too constitute configurations of mutually supporting parts that are organized around stable themes or strategies. These themes or strategies may be derived from leaders' visions, the influence of powerful departments/divisions, or the state of the industry. Once a stable theme or strategy emerges, a whole infrastructure emerges to support it. The firm perpetuates and amplifies one type of design and suppresses all mutations. That is, senior managers choose a set of goals and values and champion these above all others.

In this article, we will point out that managers need to understand the nature of their industry's life cycle and the rate of technological change and their impact on the strategies and organization designs they craft to compete in their industry. In addressing the nature of changing environments, we examine the broad nature of industry transformation in the first part of our article. Industries are economic complex adaptive systems that evolve through states of birth, growth, maturity, and death at their own rates. These systems are also impacted by the rate of technological change that can redefine the nature of firms' offerings to their respective markets. The second part of our article examines how four archetypes of firms – Concept Drivers, Pioneers, Consolidators, and Concept Learners—can redefine their strategies and organization designs to respond to these different types of change. We consider the impact of industry change on how firms are likely to adapt to faster changing environments in the future.

Industry Ecosystems and Change

Industries can be viewed as economic examples of a complex adaptive system. This is a concept that has been used to describe the evolution that occurs in living ecosystems (e.g., forests, climates, creation of new species). Although firms in an industry ecosystem compete with one another for customers, they are also highly interdependent in the sense that they share the same changes that affect an industry over time. The parallel growth and decline of semiconductor, telecommunications, and even Internet-based "dot.com" firms during the late 1990s reveals to an amazing degree the shared fate that tied these firms together within their respective industry ecosystems. The slump in the demand for broadband communications technology used to power the Internet precipitated a massive decline in demand for personal computers and other related equipment. In turn, this cascaded into one of the roughest downturns ever for the semiconductor industry. Major changes in an industry ecosystem can dramatically reshape the industry's structure, and define the context of the competitive strategies used by firms to build new sources of competitive advantage.[1] In addressing changing environments, firms in some industries have engaged in proactive actions to help mold the structure of their industry and to render the underlying competitive setting more advantageous for them. However, as the competitive environment continues to evolve over time, it is often quite difficult for firms to manage every aspect of their industry ecosystem. For example, in the early 1990s, a consortium of firms (AT&T, RCA, Philips, Zenith, General Instrument, and NBC) worked together to develop the current standards of high-definition television (HDTV) to help define an entirely new technology for consumer electronics. Although their efforts were highly successful in shaping today's broadcasting standards, the ensuing development of the technologies used to make HDTV sets followed much of the same progression that defined the earlier generations of analog color television sets and other consumer electronics products. Likewise, the nature of competition among firms can influence the value received by customers, as well as how closely firms work in conjunction with their suppliers. For example, the symbiotic relationship between Wal-Mart and Procter & Gamble has redefined the role of the supplier in the massive retailing industry. The accumulation of their responses (and their subsequent effects) shaped the overall competitive structure of this industry.

Two defining characteristics of an economic complex adaptive system are: (1) the existence of a life cycle that guides evolution within the system; and (2) the rate of technological change that can dramatically reshape the configuration of the system itself.[2] We will use these two underlying tenets of complex adaptive systems to aid our understanding of industry change.

If industries are viewed from this perspective, we need to be able to demonstrate how organizations respond to changing environments. First, it is important to delineate the nature of life cycle-based evolution within an industry. The early stage of the life cycle, characterized by rapid growth, proliferation of firms, and low barriers to entry, witnesses many firms attempting to get their innovative products accepted by customers. As the overall size of the market expands, it attracts a large number of competitors. This growth provides considerable economic ferment that enables different firms to craft strategies to compete in the industry, often by developing highly differentiated products that lead to a wide spectrum of value propositions for customers. Over time, however, customers become more knowledgeable and competing products become more similar to one another. Declining differences between products of competing firms generally leads to similar pricing, and also compressed margins. This results in much slower revenue growth, and potentially lower economic returns to many firms. As the industry becomes highly mature, a dominant industry-wide paradigm becomes established. At this time, firms become highly specialized and cost efficiency becomes important in determining profitability. The evolution of products and technologies in most industries tends to exhibit strong life cycle characteristics. Recent examples of industries that have undergone such a progression include cell phones, digital cameras, and managed health care plans.

In adaptive systems, rate of technological change refers to the extent to which new products and technologies evolve in ways and patterns that are completely different from their predecessors. On the one hand, all industries undergo a constant, steady evolution in which technologies slowly improve over time. Change is often gradual and highly predictable as product and process technologies follow a well-defined progression. However, industries are subject to periods of "disruption," when new technologies can redefine an industry's structure in unpredictable ways. Disruptive technologies can "shake up" a dominant design (i.e., way of conceiving and commercializing a product/service offering) and established firms to such an extent that an entire industry can be transformed in a short time.[3] For example, the latest advances in medical technology have raised considerable hope that entirely new forms of treatments and less-invasive surgical procedures will be developed shortly. These technologies would provide entirely new treatment regimens that represent bold opportunities for the rise of new firms. Similarly, the advent of wireless Internet capabilities and their impact on traditional telecommunications firms relying on land-line modes of transmission would represent another avenue to create entirely new service offerings as well.

The creation of new core technologies to design products for a set of customers in one industry may serendipitously open up new avenues to exploit the technology in other markets. More often than not, a new technology destabilizes the industry's pre-existing equilibrium and a transformed industry ecosystem replaces it. In recent years, for example, this pattern has emerged numerous times within several different industries, such as photography, telecommunications, and financial services. Indeed, most industries periodically face the prospect of substantial technological change, when an entirely new method, product design, or value proposition dramatically redefines the strategies and market positions of competing firms. The competitive environment in these industries will become significantly more intense.[4]

The presence of life cycle dynamics, combined with the prospect for technological change provides the basis for understanding how firms can rapidly adapt to a variety of contexts. Our characterization of industries enables us to develop a framework that captures the strategic and organizational imperatives that are likely to guide firm behavior. Figure 1 presents an overlay of life cycle dynamics with the levels of industry technological change to highlight the different sets of ecosystems.

Quadrant One: Fast Growth

In quadrant one, a new product concept or idea becomes the basis for fast industry growth. Firms will try to stake out and expand key portions of the market by offering their own distinctive value proposition for customers. Often, firms compete with highly differentiated product offerings that not only seek to capture market share, but also to create a product concept or design that cannot easily be replicated throughout the industry.[5] The underlying technology or method used to create new products and service concepts evolves in a predictable manner. Eventually, an industry "shakeout" displaces weaker rivals and industry growth abates as buyers become more knowledgeable about how the product/service adds value for them. However, there is still room for a number of strong rivals to continue offering their own unique value propositions, since the underlying product or service concept has either attracted a loyal following, or created high switching costs that lock in the buyer.

FIGURE 1 Industry Ecosystems

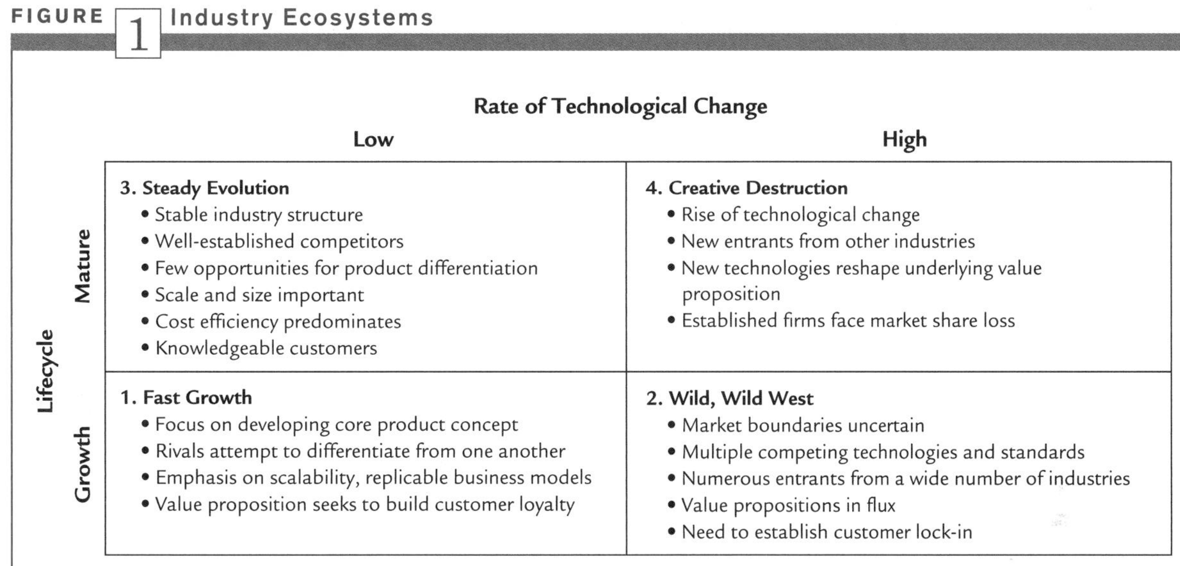

Many product and service concepts fit this industry setting. For example, the rapid growth in chain restaurants, specialty retailing, laboratory diagnostics, auto service centers, hair-styling salons, and video games have followed well-defined trajectories in which a core product concept was successfully tested and replicated throughout the industry. In the restaurant industry, a highly innovative product concept (e.g., Corner Bakery) or service approach (e.g., Sonic Drive-Ins) has enabled a variety of competing firms to thrive, even when they serve a similar menu line. This has enabled firms in many different technology and service-based industries to grow rapidly by following a highly replicable and distinctive business model. Even certain high-technology products, such as software and specialized chemical agents, have followed a similar development path, where leading companies have built a strong lock-in with their buyers.

Quadrant Two: Wild, Wild West

In quadrant number two, a combination of fast growth and technological ferment attracts numerous upstarts who bring novel ideas and new technologies to a highly dynamic setting. As the number of new firms increases, so does the potential range of technologies and concepts that firms will use to stake out their market positions. Rivals face a highly dynamic, fluid industry environment that is not only fast-growing, but also ripe for numerous competing, emerging, and breakthrough technologies. Market boundaries are unstable, since customer expectations and value propositions are changing so quickly that firms choose not to commit to a standard technology or product platform.[6] Customers may flock to a given product or service in one time period, and then embrace a completely new version later. It is difficult for any firm to "command the high ground" in the industry, since there are so many different types of technologies that could be used to create new products and services. The technologies themselves are highly unstable and subject to rapid change or substitution from newer innovations, mostly from within the industry. This industry segment witnesses a high rate of firm entry and exit as new product and technology concepts are developed and tested. Moreover, these technologies are often so new or different that it is impossible for any given firm to define an industry-wide standard early on.

Industries that fit this characterization include many aspects of biotechnology, medical devices and instrumentation, fuel cells, and even digital home electronics. Consider, for example, some of the recent developments that firms have pioneered to create alternative sources of fuels for automobiles.[7] A wide range of battery technologies based on nickel-metal hydrides, lithium derivatives, and hydrogen cells compete for attention and investment funds by large automotive firms for the development of advanced systems to power new generations of cars. These technologies are themselves subject to fast-changing innovations that promise even more reliable sources of power and ease of manufacture. In the biotechnology field, dozens of new entrants compete with one another to create treatment regimens for a variety of ailments and diseases. They employ a broad range of techniques from molecular biology, genetic engineering, and even nanotechnology-based electronic devices that can regulate body functions. More recently, a number of firms have begun to offer a fully digital home entertainment system (e.g., Samsung, Sony, Intel) in which a central computer or networking device controls everything from the television to washing machines and even Internet access.[8]

Quadrant Three: Steady Evolution

In quadrant number three, industry maturity is characterized by a stable industry structure, where large firms enjoy significant market shares. Market share for competitors has become well-established, making it essential for firms to capture and sustain cost-driven efficiencies. Opportunities for product differentiation may still exist, but they are more difficult to pursue because buyers are knowledgeable about competing firms' products (e.g., the airline industry). As a result, products from competing firms often exhibit a marked tendency to utilize standardized technologies, platforms, and operating systems.[9] Consequently, the pursuit of substantial economies of scale—large size, integrated supply chains, and continuous improvements in process technologies—drives firms in this environment. As the industry continues to mature, many firms will seek to lower their cost structures even further, often by working more closely with key suppliers to outsource some of their high fixed-cost activities. In order to further stabilize industry-wide pricing and to gain even greater economies of scale, some firms will seek to acquire their rivals in order to gain even stronger bargaining power over their suppliers and buyers.

Industries such as personal computers, memory chips, automobiles, chemicals and even managed health care populate quadrant three. The automotive and memory chip industries have begun to consolidate in recent years as firms needed to become larger in order not only to gain additional scale, but also to amortize the costs of capital-intensive product and process development. Even in such high-technology fields as information technology and consulting, numerous firms (e.g., Deloitte Consulting, EDS, IBM) have begun to outsource some of their data processing operations to India and China. This trend has occurred throughout the globe, as established firms seek ways to further lower their operational costs.

Quadrant Four: Creative Destruction

In quadrant four, firms in highly mature industries face the onslaught of new technologies and other technological changes from outside their industry that promise to transform the very essence of their survival. Although a single technology or external event may provide the trigger for industry-wide change, over time the cumulative effect results in an ecosystem-wide phenomenon.[10] Creative destruction is the hallmark of quadrant four, as new technologies or ways of serving a customer dramatically redefine the nature of the product or service offered to customers. The previous ways of creating value crumble under the weight of a new technology that dramatically changes the performance and/or pricing of previous offerings. In many situations, the new entrant will set a new standard for customers' expectations regarding product/service design, price, convenience, and speed; newly designed products that build on a superior value proposition accelerate the displacement and substitution of older products. Established firms face enormous tradeoffs as they attempt to adapt to the new paradigm, since they must respond in ways that denigrate the value of their current business models and invested assets.[11]

Industries such as entertainment, photography, financial services, travel agencies, telecommunications, semiconductor capital equipment, and even certain medical devices and procedures have recently faced significant forces of creative destruction that have completely transformed how firms create value for their customers. For example, the rapid creation and dissemination of MP3 and other formats in the entertainment industry reveal the extent to which new products (and strategic requirements) are completely different from the capabilities of established firms. They have also served to create the basis for an entirely new method of reaching customers, as music and eventually video offerings are distributed through the Internet and other mobile technology platforms.

Strategic Requirements for Competing in Different Ecosystems

As the industry ecosystem changes, firms must be able to learn, develop, and adjust their core competencies in ways that respond quickly to external developments. Strategies and organization designs that seem well-suited for a particular stage of an industry's life cycle may not translate into competitive advantage or success in another stage.

Competitive advantage depends upon a firm's ability to craft a coherent strategy that integrates several core pillars of delivering a successful value proposition. Using a unified strategic framework developed by Hambrick and Fredrickson, we build upon their set of core strategic pillars, which include: (1) arenas, (2) vehicles, (3) distinguishing features, (4) economic logic, and (5) staging of actions to highlight some possible combination of strategies that enable firms to compete effectively.[12] Arenas focus on what businesses the firm will be in, product categories, geographic areas, core technologies, as well as the value-adding stages (e.g., product design, manufacturing, or logistics). Besides specifying these arenas, strategists need to determine the relative importance that will be placed on each arena. Vehicles are the ways that strategists need to choose among to enter the arena(s). That is, how is the firm going to accomplish entry into an arena: licensing agreements, joint ventures, acquisitions, and/or internal development are all vehicles for entering an arena. A strategy should not only specify what arenas the firm will be active in and how it will get there, but how the firm will distinguish itself in the marketplace. That is, how will the firm compete—through styling, price, product features, and quality. Economic logic refers to how firms will capture returns that exceed their cost of capital. That is, will these be achieved through low costs and scale advantages, scope, replication, or will it charge premium prices because it will offer superior service or develop proprietary product features? While these choices have been referred to as the pillars of a firm's business strategy, there is some judgment needed about the staging or sequencing of these choices. Staging of actions refers to the sequencing of choices related to the first four strategic pillars, since the actions taken by any given firm will depend on its unique circumstances.

Archetypes and Industry Ecosystems

The four types of ecosystems we illustrated in Figure 1 place different demands on the organization to respond. We present four different archetypes that correspond to the four different ecosystems. Consolidators, Concept Learners, Concept Drivers, and Pioneers are each viable to operate in different ecosystems, albeit at different levels of effectiveness. These strategic archetypes focus at the line of business level within the firm. Unlike other strategic typologies that have been developed, we focus on industry life cycle and technological change as the major drivers of industry ecosystem evolution.[13] For example, firms facing an ecosystem characterized by steady evolution are driven towards crafting business strategies that align with our consolidators in Figure 2. They have developed a broad line of standard products for customers and focus primarily on cost reduction and scale. Conversely, pioneers that aggressively pursue new technologies and strive to be first-movers in the marketplace tend to dominate the Wild, Wild West quadrant of Figure 1. For example, Ampex (a pioneer) developed the first video recorder, but JVC and Sony (both consolidators) eventually mass produced it. Similarly, Bowmar (a pioneer) created the first pocket calculator, but Texas Instruments (consolidator) captured the mass market because of its distinctive manufacturing competency. While each archetype tends to be focused on doing one thing extremely well, each firm positions itself to exploit an ecosystem. That is, they create competencies and complementary assets to take advantage of their strategy. While it is impossible to specify a universally superior set of pillars that will apply to each firm, there are some compelling patterns and differences that exist across the four ecosystems. Even though these strategic pillars will vary in their importance across the ecosystems, each firm must build upon its own internally consistent set to produce firm-specific competitive advantage. Figure 2 presents four strategic archetypes that overlay the general properties that shape these five core pillars across the four environmental states.

Quadrant One: Concept Drivers

Concept drivers are firms competing in fast-growth industries that create a value proposition which is highly differentiated from those of its rivals to sustain high profitability.

FIGURE 2 Archetypes and Strategies

Rate of Technological Change

Lifecycle	Low		High	
Mature	**3. Consolidators**		**4. Concept Learners**	
	Arenas:	Broad-line markets/wide product lines	Arenas:	Mature markets impacted by disruption
	Vehicles:	Long-term supplier relationships, selective mergers & acquisitions	Vehicles:	"Skunkworks," incubation of new businesses, strategic alliances with related firms
	Distinguishing Features:	Low cost, standardized offerings	Distinguishing Features:	New product introduction, ease-of-use by customers
	Staging:	Outsourcing to reduce backward integration	Staging:	Sequencing is difficult due to cannibalization
	Economic Logic:	Attain maximum scale to reduce costs; strive for industry leadership	Economic Logic:	Premium prices based on new products or low cost to serve large markets
Growth	**1. Concept Drivers**		**2. Pioneers**	
	Arenas:	New market entry based on core product concept	Arenas:	New products, new core technologies
	Vehicles:	Internal development of product concepts; related acquisitions	Vehicles:	Internal development and external licensing to larger firms
	Distinguishing Features:	Customization, fast innovation, branding	Distinguishing Features:	First-to-market, fast innovation, patents
	Staging:	Penetration and development of related products and neighboring geographic markets	Staging:	Quick speed of expansion into niche markets; develop sequential new technologies in R&D
	Economic Logic:	Superior pricing through customer loyalty or proprietary features	Economic Logic:	Generate high royalties from proprietary technology/patents; premium pricing from niched products

Brinker International and Discount Tire are examples of concept drivers that have created and shaped a core product concept that enables them to achieve a competitive advantage. These firms invest heavily in market research and product R & D to craft a product or service design that is highly replicable or "scalable" across markets. As a result, the *arenas* of concept drivers are typically new markets they can enter easily with a well-developed and easily replicable business model. Core value-adding activities (e.g., human resources, merchandising, accounting, logistics) are often centralized to achieve uniformity and consistency of operations. Brinker's acquisition of The Corner Bakery was synergistic because it had operations, such as Chili's, On The Border, and Romano's Macaroni Grill. Brinker was able to replicate its supply chain, logistics systems, hiring practices, market research capabilities, and other competencies to service this new arena.[14] To sustain this strategy, concept drivers frequently experiment and innovate new product offerings that borrow upon and expand their core product/service. They often acquire rivals that enable them to enter new product or geographic markets quickly. Thus, their primary *vehicles* for building and extending their competitive advantage are through internal development and related acquisitions to complement their existing product lines.

A concept driver must continue to focus its new product development initiatives that reinforce and build upon its core product expertise and knowledge, and test new markets to ensure a workable fit. As a result, these firms are likely to evaluate new market opportunities through a carefully *staged* process. Many concept drivers invest heavily in new process technologies that enable them to engage in product customization and provide customer intimacy. These skills enable them to build strong barriers to imitation from their rivals. Concept drivers seek to build strong customer loyalty or customer lock-in by virtue of a highly desirable offering or a proprietary technology. This effort to secure a strong customer lock-in serves as the foundation for an *economic logic* predicated on either the possession of proprietary technology or the delivery of superior product or service features. Branding is a vital tool to help fast shapers reduce buyers' perceived risk when introducing new products.

Concept drivers rely on organization designs that support fast innovation, creativity, and flexibility within a division.[15] This places a high premium on fast communication and information flow across functions within a division. Concept drivers must also cultivate and develop their own talent internally, since these firms rely heavily on experience and tacit knowledge that are further refined with each subsequent product innovation.

Discount Tire appears to be setting the industry standard for providing replacement tires.[16] Unlike other auto repair firms that offer a wide range of other services, Discount Tire relies on a simple formula of only providing ultra-courteous fast tire repair, rotation, and installation at all of its stores. Discount Tire also offers a generous mileage-based warranty program that enables the customer to lower the lifetime cost and risk of tire ownership by allowing for free tire replacement in case of road hazard or other circumstances at any Discount store. By focusing exclusively on providing fast turnaround and lower-risk tire ownership, Discount Tire has created a distinctive value proposition. This $1.4 billion privately held firm has expanded rapidly from its Arizona roots to serve customers in 20 states across the country. Everyone from managers to technicians are trained to examine customers' tires, assess the need for repair or replacement, write up the purchase, and install the new tires within a very short time. This cross-functional approach to customer service enables Discount Tire to slice the waiting time that customers face in their tire maintenance needs.

Quadrant Two: Pioneers

Pioneers are risk-takers that thrive in highly uncertain, dynamic environments where barriers to entry and exit are often quite low.[17] In addition, pioneers face a high degree of uncertainty regarding customer expectations. These firms are often small and possess a deep knowledge about leading-edge technologies. Typically, they possess the seeds of a breakthrough technology that can transform or even create entirely new products. Pioneers rely on agility and speed of product development to create bold new product ideas that keep competitors from copying their initiative. They cannot count on the presence of a large customer base to amortize their investment costs. Customers who buy pioneers' products tend to be technology enthusiasts who want the "new toy." It is the functionality of the product that attracts customers. Unlike consolidators, they often confine their *arenas* to very specialized technological niches that could lead to breakthrough products. The only way to innovate successfully is to be intimately familiar with specific technologies and with exact needs of a particular set of customers. Too broad a range of product offerings works against the sharp focus so necessary for pioneers to survive. If a pioneer develops an end product, it likely meets the needs of a specialized niche, rather than a mass market. More often, pioneers seek to aggressively develop and license their technologies to other firms that may be better positioned to assume the risks of full-fledged market development. For example, Chicopee Mills first introduced the disposable diaper in 1932. By 1956 only one percent of the market was buying them. The main reason was cost–around $.09 per diaper In 1962, Procter & Gamble acquired the company. Through their efficient marketing and manufacturing capabilities, P & G drastically reduced the cost to less than $.03 per diaper. Today, Pampers commands a 15 percent market share of this $19 billion market.

A combination of internal technology development and external licensing represent important strategic *vehicles* for pioneers. Pioneers need to keep their R & D wellsprings full with a continuous flow of new ideas and emerging technologies to create opportunities for application in numerous product markets by other firms. Pioneers seek to *distinguish* themselves from other rivals through faster innovation, better designs, or advanced technologies. Overall, pioneers can survive only to the extent they are effective in developing new technologies and protecting them from rapid competitor imitation. The combination of developing new technology with a marked tendency to rely on licensing it to other partners means that the *economic logic* of pioneers rests on securing a steady stream of profits generated by strong proprietary features.[18] Pioneers often gain the needed financial support from private financiers. Unless the product has the necessary technical features, financiers will not back it.

Pioneers depend on organizational routines that promote fast learning, experimentation, and encouragement of internal debate. Because they license their technologies to other firms, they must also be able to use these strategic alliances as a vehicle to better understand market developments and customer evolution, since they are unlikely to possess these capabilities on their own. Pioneers are particularly attractive acquisition candidates for established firms seeking to learn and to build entirely new core competencies, like P & G did with Chicopee Mills. However, they often represent a difficult cultural and organizational fit with the management practices and routines that are embedded in an established firm's organization.

Pioneers tend to populate those fast-moving industries driven by high levels of R&D spending and fast product innovation. In recent years, pioneer-type firms have charted new techniques and methods to dramatically lower the cost of telecommunications, despite this industry's massive downturn. Companies such as Vonage, 8×8, and others have begun offering Voice-over-Internet-Protocol (VoIP) technology that enables savvy users to place long-distance calls over the Internet through personal computers and other access devices.[19] Although many large corporate buyers are already heavy users of VoIP technology, Vonage and 8×8 are directly challenging established long-distance firms, such as AT&T and MCI, with their dramatically lower costs and ease of network installation. While it is unlikely that these small firms will become telecom giants in their own right because of current industry over-capacity, they have started discussions to form marketing and technology development alliances with Regional Bell Operating Companies to learn more about users' needs. Other pioneer-type firms active in the Internet and telecommunications industries have focused on new applications such as data encryption and audio/video streaming.

Quadrant Three: Consolidators

Consolidators are firms competing in mature life cycles that seek to capture the benefits of consolidating their industries in the midst of slow growth.[20] Consolidators are those firms that seek to maximize the benefits of cost and process efficiencies in their attempt to garner industry-wide economies of scale. Wal-Mart and CVS in the retailing industry, and Lenovo in electronics and PC manufacturing in China are examples of consolidators.[21] As a result, their typical choice of *arenas* is to focus on gaining access to a wide scope of markets that enables them to leverage their fixed costs. Consolidators move into pioneers' markets by shifting the basis of competition from technical performance to such attributes as quality and price (e.g., in microwave ovens, from Litton to Samsung; in 35 mm cameras, from Leica to Canon). This makes the product attractive to the mass market and facilitates a change in the product's life cycle from growth to maturity. Carefully honed marketing campaigns, distribution networks, and customer service are essential to capture value by consolidators. Consolidators that are cost leaders are not known for major technological innovations in their product lines. Even though consolidators often introduce incremental technological improvements to extend the range and longevity of a product, their motto, "Do not be first, be the best" captures the zeitgeist of these firms.

Consolidators actively search for ways to reduce their high capital intensity. They frequently attempt to work closely with their core suppliers to share the risks of future product development and new market entry. At the same time that consolidators narrow the scope of their activities through outsourcing, many also seek to become larger by merging and acquiring competitors in order to attain even greater benefits of scale and size. Hence, they primarily rely on such *vehicles* as long-term supply and co-production/sourcing arrangements, as well as selective mergers to help reinforce their scale-based advantages and negate rivals' moves to gain market share. In particular, consolidators in many cases look to their suppliers not only as a provider of necessary inputs, but also as an outsourcing platform in which the supplier takes on a greater role (and cost) in the firm's overall value creation process (e.g., Wal-Mart and Procter & Gamble). Consequently, as consolidators over time become more specialized in their activities, they also must become adept at an important *staging* skill – that of sequentially orchestrating and managing an expansive web of suppliers that are becoming important sources of process technologies in their own right. The move to outsource a broader range of value-creating activities to key suppliers enables the consolidator to become more focused on what it considers to be its future core competencies. Accordingly, these firms generally avoid products that require a high degree of customization in favor of mass production and distribution of more standardized products that facilitate low cost operations. Managing distribution channels to buyers is also an important skill.

Many companies in recent years have already surfaced to play important consolidator roles in their respective industries. For example, in the automobile industry, new car designs are based increasingly on shared platforms and components that are found across a manufacturer's entire line of product offerings. Core components, such as safety glass, fuel tanks, braking systems, engine sealants, automotive seats, and dashboards made of advanced composites are designed for similar manufacture and use for cars at the upper, middle and entry price points. As a result, automotive companies need to maximize the potential scale economies and cost efficiencies that accompany the development of shared technologies and components across all product lines.

Quadrant Four: Concept Learners

Concept learners are firms that successfully acquire new knowledge and competencies as well as harness change to create new value propositions. In a mature industry that faces a high rate of technological change, firms must adapt quickly to create new products and services based on a rapidly evolving technology or new means of serving a customer.[22] In many cases, established firms have not been able to adjust their strategies and organization designs rapidly enough to learn the new requirements to revitalize themselves successfully. However, a growing number of firms in a wide range of industries will face the challenge of meeting and adapting to the imperatives that accompanies technological change.

Concept learners actively seek knowledge about emerging technologies and developments in other industries to redefine their core products. Successful concept learners not only have the capability to rapidly absorb new technologies, but are also willing to "unlearn" pre-existing core competencies that can become core rigidities in the creative destruction of their ecosystem. Change will compel concept learners to reconfigure themselves in any number of different *arenas,* but the primary realignment occurs in the firm's core technology base. This base is confronted with rapid obsolescence from a more vibrant or more cost-effective substitute.[23] As a result, a change in the core technology will certainly make itself felt in the type of new products introduced in subsequent periods. Many concept learners approach product development by attempting to "incubate" a variety of technological "seeds" that lay the foundation for different product designs. By fostering an internal corporate race to assess which product design is ultimately accepted, this "parallel" approach builds on a *vehicle* that promotes risk-taking and knowledge-sharing which is valuable for future idea generation. Joint ventures and strategic alliances represent important complementary vehicles for concept learners, especially with partners that are likely to possess important related technologies. These learning-based alliances enable the firm not only to reduce some the internal costs and risks of going-it-alone, but also to gain important insight into a potential competitor's market direction. Concept learners need to regain the initiative by introducing bold new products quickly into the marketplace, but face a critical tradeoff when they start cannibalizing their older product offerings. Thus, these firms are faced with significant difficulties concerning the speed of *staging* of their product introductions. Long-term, their economic viability will depend on how well they can learn and assimilate sources of change as part of their renewal.

The medical devices industry confronts the challenge of harnessing new forms of technology with increasing frequency.[24] For example, the development of next-generation pacemakers, telemedicine products, minimally invasive surgical tools, and self-regulating pumps has incorporated many technology developments, processes, and ideas that were originally conceived outside the industry by other firms. The need to carefully monitor chronic disease conditions has provided the innovative ferment that now makes possible proactive disease management programs and products through the Internet and even wireless technologies.

Medtronic, a leading medical device firm, has incorporated telecommunications-based technologies to create a wireless pacemaker that automatically and quietly dials for assistance in advance of a cardiac event. Previous pacemakers designed by Medtronic and other firms did not offer this instantaneous, immediate response capability, and the patient had to be aware of his/her imminent condition to seek help on his/her own. Medtronic also began to investigate and learn how to develop wireless applications for other body-monitoring products. To create new types of advanced self-regulating pumps that help diabetic patients manage their disease, Medtronic has also invested heavily in new types of servomechanics-based competencies that mimic the human body's endocrine regulatory feedback system. In late 2001, Medtronic bought Mini-Med, a small leading-edge developer of miniaturized insulin pumps. This acquisition complements Medtronic's growing core competencies in working with advanced microelectronics, as well as enables the firm to learn even newer drug-delivery methodologies that will likely reshape other disease treatment regimens in the future.[25]

Potential Organizational Issues and Challenges

Each of the strategic archetypes represents a way of competing, creating value, and adjusting to its environment. Yet, as a firm adapts to the economic and strategic requirements necessary to build competitive advantage, it also faces a series of important tradeoffs — many of which are embedded in the design of the firm's organizational structure. Figure 3 captures some of the more salient strengths and weaknesses that confront firms in each strategic archetype.

Quadrant One: Concept Drivers

Concept drivers face a number of important organizational challenges as they pursue high-growth market opportunities. To remain innovative and agile, they are organized by product, with each line of business formulating a product- or market-specific strategy. Although this provides the benefit of fast response to meeting customers' needs, this design also delimits the firm's ability to promote internal resource sharing and cooperation among business units.[26] Centralization of key processes, such as merchandising, logistics, inventory management, purchasing, and human resources is important to achieve consistency of operations. As a result, a strong product focus may sometimes reward managers for becoming overly focused on their individual units' performance at the expense of that of the overall firm. In turn,

FIGURE 3 Strengths and Weaknesses of Strategic Archetypes

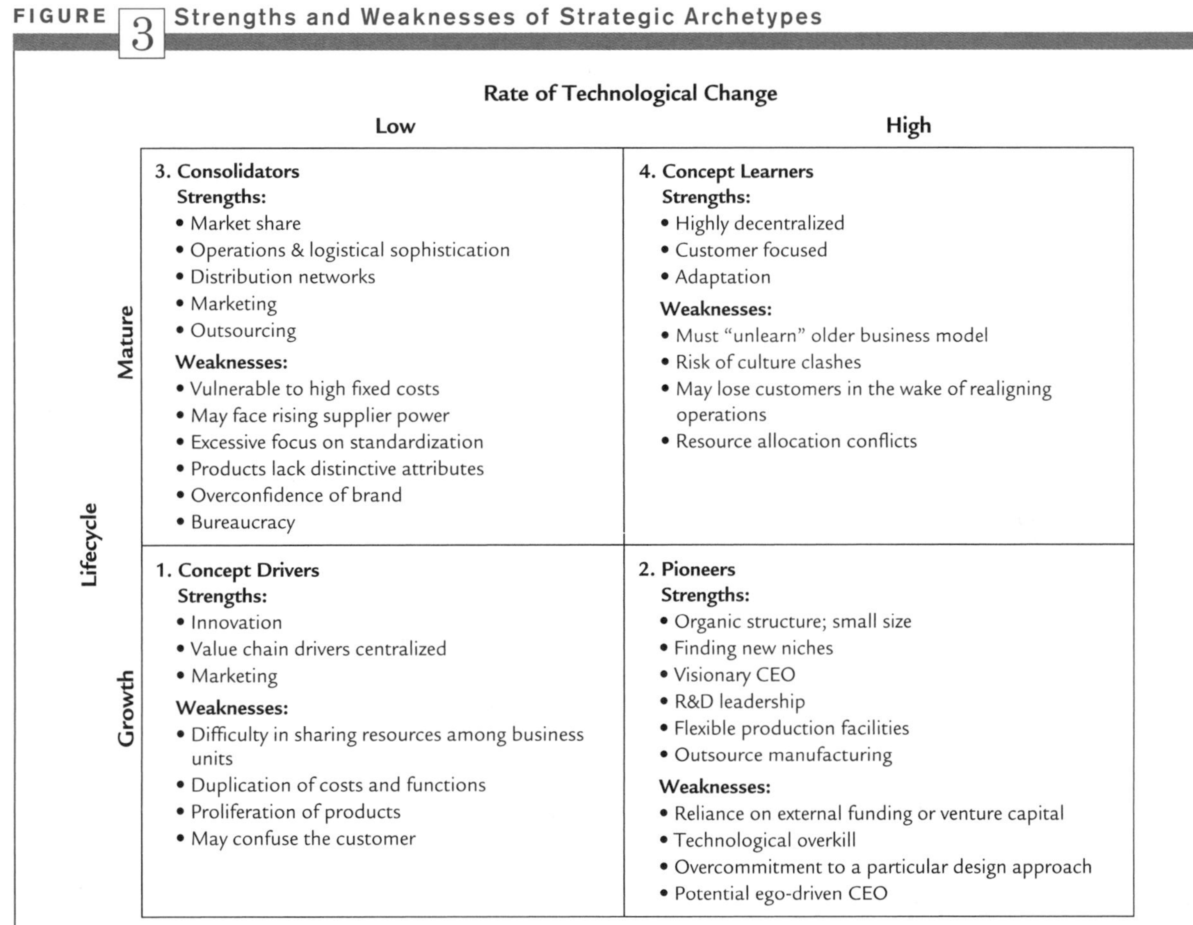

concept drivers are likely to have high cost structures, particularly as business units duplicate important functional activities as they expand into new products or markets. If growth and expansion are not carefully managed, there is a high risk of excessive product proliferation that may actually confuse the customer, cannibalize the unit's offerings, and bring out products that are not needed.

For example, many financial services firms (e.g., Citigroup, Fidelity Investments) that offer one-stop shopping, such as brokerage, banking, and insurance offerings to their customers have recently confronted some important organizational challenges. In the early 1990s, different divisions within Merrill Lynch attempted to sell high-return funds, fixed-income securities, annuities, and insurance to their customers. Although Merrill encouraged each division to promote its offerings aggressively (and rewarded its managers for doing so), many customers were often confused by the message they received. Clients wanting the benefits of more stable, secure investments received a very different message from account representatives who wanted to steer them towards higher-risk products, such as stocks and growth-oriented funds.[27] In a similar vein, the specialty retailer Gap now faces the challenge of sustaining high growth without diluting the core message, marketing strategy, and retailing approach of each of its three divisions. Composed of three different divisions—The Gap, Banana Republic, and Old Navy—this company has thrived by providing highly fashionable clothing to young adults and children looking for the right blend of design elegance, comfort, and versatility. In particular, the Banana Republic focuses on trendy but elegant clothing, The Gap is oriented more towards active wear, while Old Navy offers a full array of fashionable clothing at slightly lower prices targeted towards teenagers and college students. Even though the company has begun to share some ordering and logistics functions across its three divisions, the company still faces the potential risk of cannibalizing its own revenues if expansion is not carefully managed.

Quadrant Two: Pioneers

Pioneers thrive by engaging in fast innovation of breakthrough technologies and products. With organic structures, R&D-driven cultures, and few manufacturing capabilities, these firms can accelerate the pace and scope of their product innovations. These firms by their very nature are risk takers and have been founded by entrepreneurs whose technical and engineering competencies allow them to translate a certain technology into a new product. Yet, they are also potentially vulnerable to a series of organizational issues. First, because pioneers tend to focus on leading-edge technologies whose ultimate market applications are unknown, they face the risk of "technological overkill." Consequently, these firms often have few marketing competencies. In some cases, pioneers can find themselves refining a technology beyond the point (and cost) that would meet the needs of customers or firms. Because most pioneers are young and small, they are also unable to dedicate the resources to monitor highly intricate accounting, human resources, and other "infrastructure" related tasks. Many pioneer firms are highly dependent on venture capital or external funding from established firms that are their alliance partners to sustain their growth. Leadership in pioneer firms is highly dependent on a singular-focused CEO who may become overly "wedded" to a particular technology or product design at the risk of ignoring other developments or trends in the industry. Steve Jobs' promotion of Lisa at Apple Computer, Edwin Land's vision for Polaroid cameras, and Fred Smith's zap mail at Federal Express (now FedEx) were all major technological projects that customers eventually rejected.

Quadrant Three: Consolidators

In their continuing search for greater economies of scale, consolidators strive to achieve a high degree of product and process standardization. Known for their low cost operations, consolidators stay ahead of their competition by devising ever more economical means of service or manufacturing to lead the race down the cost curve. Consolidators are run by strong leaders who crafted tightly knit cultures. These cultures ensure that the company's values are inextricably linked to its goals. Sam Walton at Wal-Mart Stores, Meg Whitman at eBay, and Liu Chuanzhi at Lenovo all fostered cultures that infused employees with day-to-day behaviors consistent with the firms' goals. They face very high fixed costs that make it difficult to change quickly. Likewise, consolidators must have the organizational capability to manage vast webs of suppliers and distributors to serve mass markets. Consolidators face a number of important issues within their respective industries. First, they are highly dependent on their suppliers because of the increased reliance on outsourcing. If a consolidator's set of suppliers were to merge and consolidate among themselves, they would yield considerable supplier power. Their margins will erode as suppliers charge higher prices. Second, the large size of consolidators means they are likely to become highly risk-averse, bureaucratic, and smother innovation. The cumbersome reporting relationships and growing bureaucracy can breed decision-making that is slow, cautious, and inflexible. Hence even those consolidators who invest heavily in product innovation are likely to be slower than a concept driver or pioneer in racing to market. Finally, the standardization of products, components, and technologies strongly suggests that consolidators will have difficulty appealing to many different market segments with a compelling value proposition for each.

Quadrant Four: Concept Learners

Concept learners face a vast array of organizational challenges as they attempt to adapt to change in their creative destruction ecosystem. Concept learners compete in highly mature markets that are ripe for change, but they must be able to learn new technologies or ways of serving their customers quickly. One of the biggest organizational challenges for concept learners is how best to reposition themselves to learn about new customers and developments beyond their immediate focal market or industry. Thus, concept learners face a much more complex set of organizational challenges than pioneers, consolidators, or concept drivers. Concept learners must investigate and invest in new technologies because they are often very different from their existing core technology. Concept learners in turn must manage two different mindsets and possibly two or more different perspectives that shape how managers view their customers. Concept learners also face numerous internal resource allocation issues as they try to find ways to invest in new customers and technologies. In particular, they must be able to reinvest the cash generated by mature businesses into promising new opportunities.

Managerial Implications

When competing in their industry ecosystems, firms need to develop important sources of competitive advantage that build upon their own unique strengths, core competencies, and complementary assets. As firms jockey for stronger market position, they will seek to develop strategies that best match their vision of the industry with the resources at hand. Yet, some general strategic patterns of behavior are exhibited across the four cells.

For concept drivers, they need to focus their strategies on defining a unique product or service concept that enables them to expand the range of markets they serve. Concept drivers need to engage in a high degree of marketing and innovation to sustain the cutting-edge feel to their products or services. Developing a replicable business model that erects strong barriers to imitation (especially by way of branding, service delivery, or product design) from rivals is central to the concept driver's future prosperity. Centralization of decision-making in key value-adding activities is needed to achieve consistency of operations, as well as to capture important sources of scale economies. For retailing firms such as Gap Stores, Tiffany & Co., and Chico's FAS, distinctive product offerings allow these companies to define the leading edge of fashion in clothing, exquisite jewelry and specialty women's clothing respectively. Similarly, Starbucks has been able to redefine the notion of what customers should expect from their morning coffee. By creating exciting new flavors in both hot and cold formats, Starbucks has been able to greatly expand the number of outlets in the

United States and increasingly abroad over the past ten years.

Careful experimentation and market testing of new product ideas can help the concept driver stake out an attractive position in its industry's ecosystem to sustain profitable growth. To do this, the concept driver should focus on creating or acquiring small, highly autonomous units whose purpose is to test market boundaries to capture new customers. For example, in 2002 Tiffany & Co. acquired Little Switzerland, a jewelry retailer that serves tourists in the Caribbean, Alaska, the Florida Keys, and sells to customers mostly through duty-free stores that are near cruise-ship destinations. Little Switzerland will operate under its own trade name and will offer jewelry and renowned brand-name watches and other items. At the same time, Tiffany has also taken a major investment position in Temple St. Clair, a leading gem designer that has debuted new boutiques in high-end shopping malls such as southern California's South Coast Plaza. Little Switzerland helps Tiffany expand its reach into new tourist markets, while Temple St. Clair enables the firm to reach upscale female customers who prefer to purchase jewelry for themselves. In 2004, Tiffany & Co. will begin selling a new line of pearls that complement its diamond and traditional jewel-based offerings.

Can you name the company that created online book retailing? If your answer is Amazon.com, you're wrong. The idea originated with Charles Stack, an Ohio-based bookseller in 1991. Amazon, under CEO Jeff Bezos, did not enter the market until 1995. Who created the first safety shaving razor? The natural answer would be Gillette, but in reality, the first safety razor was created by Henry Gaisman, founder of the AutoStrop Safety Razor Corporation in 1928. In 1930, Gillette bought AutoStrop and its safety razor patent. These examples highlight a key point. Oftentimes, the companies that create radically new products are not necessarily those that succeed in the mass market. Pioneers are rarely able to explore new technologies quickly enough and to create an organization design that can serve the mass market.

There are several implications for pioneers. First, new products do not automatically translate into a successful business model. Initial products frequently do not satisfy a well-articulated need, and therefore adoption rates are often slow. To survive in this ecosystem, pioneers must have a deep knowledge of technology, strong financial backing, and be interested in pushing the envelope. These firms are serial risk takers because they are willing to bet on the results of new products that extend beyond the current state of knowledge. Second, pioneers need to create organic management systems so they can quickly respond to the developments of new technologies. Learning new technological skills and information is prized and rewarded. Their competitive advantage stems from their ability to remain flexible and to hit a moving target. Customers of pioneers often share an enthusiasm for technology and value a pioneer's performance much like investors do.[28] Third, effective pioneers must be ready to leap into a new market when a dominant technology is about to become standardized because they rarely have the capabilities to craft an organization design that can distribute and serve a large customer base. Since pioneers do not have the cultures necessary to compete in mature markets, they should spend their time developing new markets for their cutting-edge technologies.

For consolidators, these firms need to focus on refining key value-creating activities such as manufacturing, logistics, and reaching a large customer base. Although Procter & Gamble has attained dominance in the disposable diaper market by dramatically improving both product quality and cost, there are instances where consolidators have captured large market share gains even with a product whose features do not match those offered by a pioneer. Particularly in high-technology markets, consolidators can often seize large market share by creating a product that is good enough for the vast majority of users. When they are able to do this at a much lower price, consolidators can transform the ecosystem to make it much more advantageous for them to compete. For example, Apple Computer created the Newton hand-held communication device in 1993. Palm followed three months later with the Zoomer. Both products flopped a short time later. In 1995, Palm was acquired by U.S. Robotics, a leading manufacturer of modems and other communication devices. Palm's product was technologically less sophisticated than Apple's Newton, but U.S. Robotics' stronger financial position and distribution-based competencies enabled it to capture more than 70 percent of the market by producing a product for less than $300, compared to the Apple's $700 Newton line.

Consolidators can also change distribution channels to better complement their low-cost, operational competencies. In the 1960s, most potato chips in the United Kingdom were sold in pubs. All major competitors established distributors to supply pubs around the country. Golden Wonder, a Scotland-based division of Imperial Tobacco, changed the target market and began marketing chips as a snack for women. The company developed competencies in distribution channels most appropriate for its target customers — supermarkets and other retail outlets — by training sales people to sell products to retailers, arrange shop displays, and provide point-of-sale promotional materials. Golden Wonder also invested in new technology to improve the product's quality and to reduce manufacturing costs. In a ten-year period, its percentage of sales of chips in pubs went from 75 percent to 25 percent, while sales at supermarkets surged from 25 percent to 65 percent. Selling at convenience outlets made up the other 10 percent of sales.

Concept learners face a difficult balancing act. The advent of rapid technological change in mature markets means that concept learner firms are compelled to develop entirely new competencies and even mindsets in order to adapt. Creative destruction in an industry means that winning products quickly become dinosaurs as new technologies lay the groundwork for next-generation innovations. Concept learners must continue to scan the environment to learn about new technologies and other developments that could trigger massive disruption in their industry. On the other hand, they must simultaneously wean themselves from excessively depending on highly mature products for their long-term profitability. Once the period of creative destruction in an industry ends, concept learners will need to develop new sets of core competencies that will enable them to recast themselves as either concept drivers or consolidators to compete in a later time period. This is because the industry has evolved to a more steady state (thus requiring a consolidator strategy), or to fast growth (thus requiring a concept driver strategy).

Creating an entirely new business unit to learn and to experiment with emerging technologies is essential for concept learners. Ideally, managers and technical personnel in these units should not report to existing lines of businesses, but directly to the CEO so that they can develop their own innovative cultures. When managers charged with learning about a new technology must report to senior management through the pre-existing organizational arrangement (usually a large, well-established unit), they will be unable to "break free" from the constraints and core rigidities that will likely be imposed on them by managers who are still thinking about today's current line of products. Instead, they should be thinking about designing new products for tomorrow's potential customers. For example, only now after a dozen restructurings do managers at Eastman Kodak have greater freedom to pursue a full-blown digital imaging strategy. In the past, managers who wanted to develop next-generation filmless cameras and other technologies still had to report to superiors who viewed these products from the perspective of chemical-based imaging and not through the lens of more advanced technologies. Also, concept learners need to build a web of strategic alliances to learn about new technologies from multiple partners, particularly before committing to an emerging product or technical standard, since forecasting market demand will likely remain uncertain for an extended period.

Managers operating in highly diversified firms need to formulate business unit strategies that best match the industry in which each small business unit (SBU) resides. As a practical matter, highly diversified firms will likely have a mix of businesses that will transcend all four cells of Figure 2. To provide overall coherence of a corporate strategy, senior management should evaluate each SBU's strategy within the context of its particular industry. Even though the SBU is part of a larger corporation, it needs to develop the competencies and resources that will enable it to perform most effectively in its competitive setting.[29]

Acknowledgments

This research was sponsored by the Division of Research, Edwin L. Cox School of Business, Southern Methodist University, Dallas, Texas and the OxyChem Corporation of Dallas, TX. Portions of this paper were presented at the 21st Pan-Pacific Conference, Anchorage, Alaska, May 26, 2004. The authors would like to thank Anita Bhappu, Mel Fugate, Don Hellriegel, Peter Heslin, Roger Kerin, Bharath Rajagopolan, and Don VandeWalle for their constructive comments on an earlier draft of this manuscript.

Source: Academy of Management Executive, 19, (1), 2005, 31–45. Reprinted by permission.

ENDNOTES

1. D'Aveni, R. 1994. *Hypercompetition.* New York: Free Press; Iansiti, M., & Levien, R. 2004. Strategy as ecology. *Harvard Business Review,* 82(3): 68–81.
2. Zimmerman, B., Plsek, P., & Lindberg, C. 1998. *Edgeware: Insights from complexity science for health care leaders.* Dallas: VHA, Inc.
3. Christensen, C. M. 1997. *The innovator's dilemma.* Boston, MA: Harvard Business School Press. Also see Adner, R. 2002. When are technologies disruptive: A demand-based view of the emergence of competition. *Strategic Management Journal,* 23(8): 667–688.
4. See Anderson, P., & Tushman, M. L. 1990. Technological discontinuities and dominant designs: A cyclical model of organizational change. *Administrative Science Quarterly,* 35: 606–633. Also see Christensen, op. cit. and Dosi, G. 1992. Technological paradigms and technological trajectories. *Research Policy,* 11: 147–162. Also see Porter, M. E. 2001. Industry transformation. Case Number 9-701-008.
5. Tushman, M., & Murmann, J. P. 1998. Dominant designs, technology cycles, and organizational outcomes. *Research in organizational behavior.* Greenwich, CT: JAI Press, 20.
6. Evans, P. B., & Wurster, T. S. 1997. Strategy and the new economics of information. *Harvard Business Review,* 75(6): 71–82. Also see Cheng, Y. T. and Van de Ven, A. H. 1996. Learning the innovation journey: Order out of chaos. *Organization Science,* 7(6): 593–614; Markides, C., & Geroski, P. 2003. Colonizers and consolidators: The two cultures of corporate strategy. *Strategy + Business,* 32: 46–55.
7. See, for example, Ball, J. 2004. Car makers split over timing of hydrogen-powered vehicles. *The Wall Street Journal,* 26 February 2004.
8. Lei, D. 2003. Competitive strategy and the rise of new organizational forms in the semiconductor industry. *Review of the Electronic and Industrial Distribution Industries,* 2: 116–142.
9. Christensen, op. cit. Also see Morris, C. R., & Ferguson, C. H. 1993. How architecture wins technology wars. *Harvard Business* Review, 71(2): 86–97.
10. The original landmark work that pioneered the notion of creative destruction is Schumpeter, J. A. 1939. *Business cycles: A theoretical, historical and statistical analysis of the capitalist process.* New York and London: McGraw-Hill. More recent works that further develop the creative destruction concept include Foster, R., & Kaplan, S. 2001. *Creative destruction.* New York: Currency and Doubleday. Also see Kodama, F. 1995. *Emerging patterns of innovation.* Boston: Harvard Business School Press.
11. Jones, N. 2003. Competing after radical technological change: The significance of product line management strategy. *Strategic Management Journal,* 24: 1265–1288. A classic leading work in this area is Leonard-Barton, D. 1992. Core capabilities and core rigidities: A paradox in managing new product development. *Strategic Management Journal,* 13: 111–25. Also see Tripsas, M. 1997. Surviving radical technological change through dynamic capability: Evidence from the typesetter industry. *Industrial and Corporate Change,* 3: 341–377; Henderson, R. M., & Clark, K. B. 1990. Architectural innovation: The reconfiguration of existing product technologies and the failure of established firms. *Administrative Science* Quarterly, 35: 9–30.
12. Hambrick D. C., & Fredrickson, J. W. 2001. Are you sure you have a strategy. *Academy of Management Executive,* 15(4): 48–59.

13. Some of the more prominent strategic typologies developed in the strategic management field include those of Miles, R. E., & Snow, C. C. 1978. *Organizational strategy, structure and process.* New York: McGraw-Hill; Miller, D. 1990. *The Icarus Paradox: How exceptional companies bring about their own downfall.* New York: Harper Business; Treacy, M., & Wiersema, F. 1995. *The discipline of market leaders.* Reading, MA: Addison-Wesley.
14. Conversation with Jean Birch, President, Corner Bakery, Dallas, Texas, February 10, 2004.
15. See, for example, Galbraith, J. R. 2002. *Designing organizations.* San Francisco: Jossey-Bass; Grant, R. M. 1996. Prospering in dynamically competitive environments: Organizational capability as knowledge integration. *Organization Science*, 7: 375–387; Slocum, J. W., McGill, M. E., & Lei, D. 1994. The new learning strategy: Anytime, anything, anywhere. *Organizational Dynamics*, 23(2): 33–48.
16. A discussion of Discount Tire's strategy is found in a strategic typology presented in Lei, D., & Greer, C. R. 2003. The empathetic organization. *Organizational Dynamics*, 32: 142–164.
17. Markides, C., & Geroski, P. 2004. The art of scale. *Strategy + Business,* 35, Summer, 50–59.
18. Ibid.
19. Latour, A., & Grant, P. 2004. PC users an now make long-distance calls free. *The Wall Street Journal*, 9 October 2003. Also see Drucker, J. 2004. Vonage, TI plan a web-phone deal. *The Wall Street Journal*, 9 January 2004; Drucker, T. 2004. Big-name mergers won't ease crowding in cellphone industry. *The Wall Street Journal*, 13 February 2004.
20. Porter, M. E., 1985. *Competitive advantage: Creating and sustaining superior performance.* New York: Free Press; Scherer, F. M., & Ross, D. 1990. *Industrial market structure and economic performance.* Boston: Houghton-Mifflin. Also see Dobrev, S. D., & Carroll, G. R. 2003. Size (and competition) among organizations: Modeling scale-based selection among automobile producers in four major countries. *Strategic Management Journal*, 24: 541–558. At the business unit level, see Anderson, C. R., & Zeithaml, C. P. 1984. Stages of the product life cycle, business strategy, and business performance. *Academy of Management Journal*, 27(4): 5–24.
21. Biediger, J., DeCicco, T., Green, T., Hoffman, G., Lei, D., Mahadevan, K., Ojeda, J., Slocum, J. W. Jr., & Ward, K. 2005. Strategic action at Lenovo. *Organizational Dynamics*, in press.
22. Christensen, op. cit.
23. See Lei, D. 2000. Industry evolution and competence development: The imperatives of technological convergence. *International Journal of Technology Management*, 19(7): 699–738.
24. See, for example, Wysocki, B. 2004. Robots in the *OR. The Wall Street Journal*, 26 February 2004.
25. Medtronic to buy MiniMed and Medical Research. 2001. *The Wall Street Journal*, 31 May 2001.
26. Govindarajan, V., & Fisher, J. 1990. Strategy, control systems and resource sharing. *Academy of Management Journal*, 33(2): 259–285.
27. See Retail financial services in 1998. Harvard Business School Case 9-799-051.
28. Markides & Geroski, op. cit.
29. See, for example, Chandler, A. D. 1990. *Scale and scope: The dynamics of industrial capitalism.* Cambridge, MA: Harvard University Press.

The Evolving/Strategic Role of Human Resource Management

4

Learning Objectives

- Understand the fundamental differences between traditional and strategic HR
- Explain why some organizations still fail to deliver HR strategically
- Describe the outcomes and benefits of strategic HR
- Understand how different company strategies might result in the need for HR to assume different primary roles

Strategic HR at Yahoo!

Since its founding in 1994, Yahoo has grown to 8,700 employees, with $3.6 billion in annual revenue and $840 million in annual profit. With a mission of being the most essential global internet service for both consumers and businesses, Yahoo has been a magnet for job applicants who seek to work in a dynamic, high-growth organization with a lauded company culture. Yahoo's approach to HR is the utilization of a six-faceted circular talent management process which fuels the organization's strategy and performance.

The first dimension is planning the type and number of employees Yahoo needs. With the goal of being an employer of choice and acquiring top talent faster and better than its competitors, the planning function works continuously in tandem with the development of the organization's strategy.

The second dimension is attracting desirable employees. Yahoo uses its growth to persuade potential employees that it has the ability to provide constantly changing and evolving career paths. Yahoo has branded itself in the marketplace to conjure up images of free-thinkers and talented technicians.

The third dimension is recruiting potential employees. Because the demand for talent in the market in which Yahoo engages often exceeds supply, qualified individuals who are not actively looking for a job must be recruited. Yahoo uses some of its high-profile networked employees as "talent magnets," who are responsible for directly recruiting individuals outside of the organization. Current employees are also provided bonuses for recruiting new employees.

The fourth dimension is assessing qualifications of job applicants. Here, Yahoo attempts to determine who can add value to the organization while simultaneously fitting with the organization's culture. To determine the latter, extensive interviewing is utilized, with an average of 12 hours of interviews conducted for each new hire.

The fifth dimension is developing employees to ensure that the skills sets of employees are updated and developed in tandem with the evolving talent needs of the organization.

Finally, the sixth dimension is retaining top performers. Here, Yahoo ensures that employees are continuously motivated by their work and compensated accordingly.

Even though these six dimensions of talent management form a sequence of human resource activities, they are not delivered sequentially. In a strategic mindset, the processes are fluid and all occur simultaneously and continuously.[1]

The role of human resource management in organizations has been evolving dramatically in recent years. The days of human resources as the "personnel department"—performing recordkeeping, paper pushing, file maintenance, and other largely clerical functions—are over. Any organization that continues to utilize its HR function solely to perform these administrative duties does not understand the contributions that HR can make to an organization's performance. In the most financially successful organizations, HR is increasingly being seen as a critical strategic partner and assuming far-reaching and transformational roles and responsibilities.

Taking a strategic approach to human resource management involves abandoning the mindset and practices of "personnel management" and focusing more on strategic issues than operational issues. Strategic human resource management involves making the function of managing people the most important priority in the organization and integrating all human resource programs and policies within the framework of a company's strategy. Strategic human resource management realizes that people make or break an organization because all decisions made regarding finance, marketing, operations, or technology are made by an organization's people.

Strategic human resource management involves the *development of a consistent, aligned collection of practices, programs, and policies to facilitate the achievement of the organization's strategic objectives.* It considers the implications of corporate strategy for all HR systems within an organization by translating company objectives into specific people management systems. The specific approach and process utilized will vary from organization to organization, but the key concept is consistent; essentially all HR programs and policies are integrated within a larger framework facilitating, in general, the organization's mission and, specifically, its objectives.

Probably the single-most important caveat of strategic human resource management is that there is no one best way to manage people in any given organization. Even within a given industry, HR practices can vary extensively from one organization to another, as seen in Reading 4.1, "Distinctive Human Resources Are Firms' Core Competencies," and In any organization, a critical prerequisite for success is people management systems that clearly support the organization's mission and strategy.

Establishing a strong HR strategy that is clearly linked to the organization's strategy is not enough. HR strategy needs to be communicated, practiced, and—perhaps most important—spelled out and written down. A recent study by global consulting firm PricewaterhouseCoopers found that those organizations with a written HR strategy tend to be more profitable than those without one.[2] It appears that writing down an organization's HR strategy facilitates the process of involvement and buy-in on the parts of both senior executives and other employees. The study found that organizations with a specific written HR strategy had revenues per employee that are 35 percent higher than organizations without a written strategy and that those organizations with a written strategy 12 percent less employee absenteeism and lower turnover.[3]

Strategic HR at General Electric

With revenues exceeding $100 billion annually, GE operates in more than 100 countries, employing more than 290,000 people, including 155,000 in the United States. A key component to GE's success is the belief that the HR function is a critical factor in driving its performance, worldwide. The importance of GE's people to the attainment of its corporate objectives is echoed at even the highest levels of the organization. Former GE CEO Jack Welch, in his annual letter to shareholders, refers to GE as "evolving to a company of 'A' products and 'A' services delivered by 'A' players."

Susan Peters, vice president of HR at GE Appliances, has noted that at GE, the human resource function is "truly a value-added business partner who is a fully participating member of the business decision-making team." At GE, HR executives are expected to have a keen understanding of the factors that are critical to the success of the business, including finance, marketing, and operations issues. Top management feels that it would otherwise not be possible to develop HR programs and policies that support business goals.

To support this need, newly hired HR professionals attend a comprehensive Human Resources Leadership Program (HRLP), designed to allow them to assume this critical role as a strategic partner. Those who enroll in the HRLP commit to an extensive period of training, conducted over a 2-year period. During this time, they develop skills through a combination of hands-on rotational assignments and training seminars. These assignments include working both in HR as well as in non-HR operating divisions to allow enrollees to develop an understanding of the numerous factors that impact the success of the individual business units. In addition to recruiting talent from top business schools across the country, GE also recruits internally from other functions within GE. These individuals receive specialized training in HR that augments the operating experience they have within GE. In both cases, GE ensures that its HR professionals have technical HR knowledge as well as a keen understanding of the business in which they work to allow them to meet expectations and fully contribute to their business as a true strategic partner.[4]

Strategic HR Versus Traditional HR

Strategic HR can be contrasted to the more traditional administrative focus of HR through an examination of four different roles that HR can play in an organization. Ulrich developed a framework, presented in Exhibit 4.1, that proposes an entirely new role and agenda for HR that focuses less on traditional functional activities, such as compensation and staffing, and more on outcomes.[5] In this scenario, HR would be defined not by what it does but rather by what it delivers. Ideally, HR should deliver results that enrich the organization's value to its customers, its investors, and its employees. This can be accomplished in four ways: (1) by HR becoming a partner with senior and line managers in strategy execution; (2) by HR becoming an expert in the way that work is organized and executed; (3) by HR becoming a champion for employees, working to increase employee contribution and commitment to the organization; and (4) by HR becoming an agent of

EXHIBIT 4.1 Possible Roles Assumed by the HR Function

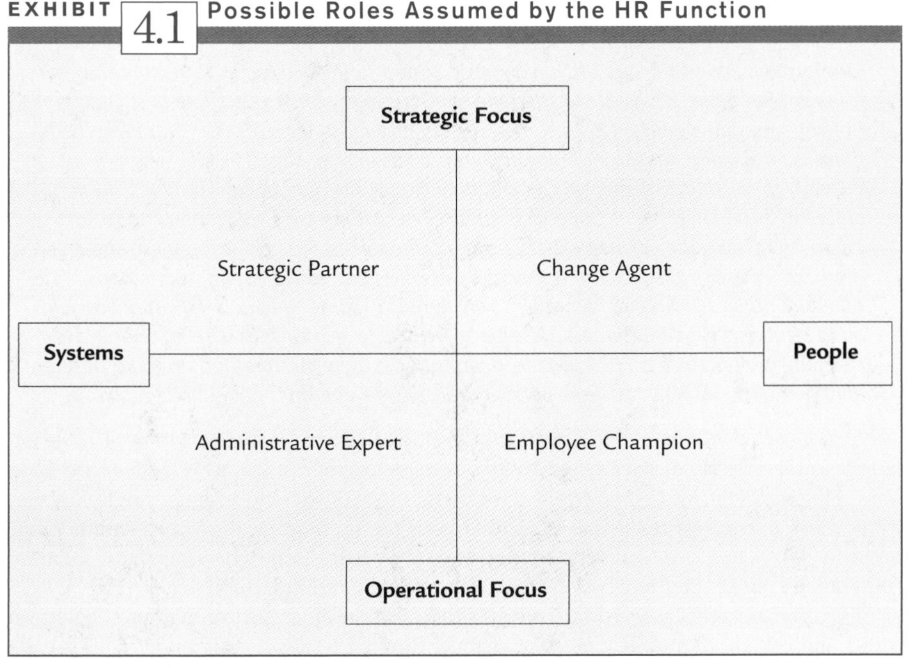

continuous transformation that shapes processes and culture to improve an organization's capacity for change.

The first role involves becoming a partner in strategy execution. Here, HR is held responsible for the organizational architecture or structure. HR would then conduct an organizational audit to help managers identify those components that need to be changed to facilitate strategy execution. HR should then identify methods for renovating the parts of the organizational architecture that need it. Finally, HR would take stock of its own work and set clear priorities to ensure delivery of results. These activities require HR executives to acquire new skills and capabilities to allow HR to add value for the executive team with confidence.

For decades, HR professionals have fulfilled an administrative function within their organizations. In the administrative expert role, these individuals would shed their image of rule-making police while ensuring that the required routine work still gets done effectively and efficiently. This requires improving or "rethinking" a number of traditional HR functions, such as benefits and selection, which now can be automated by using technology and therefore be more cost-efficient. Such streamlining of functions would help HR professionals become strategic partners in their organizations and enhance their credibility.

An organization cannot thrive unless its employees are committed to and fully engaged in the organization and their jobs. In the new role of employee champion, HR professionals are held accountable for ensuring that employees are fully engaged in and committed to the organization. This involves, in part, partnering with line management to enhance employee morale and training line managers to recognize—and avoid—the causes of low morale, such as unclear goals, unfocused priorities, and ambiguous performance management. It also involves acting as an advocate for employees, representing them and being their voice with senior management, particularly on decisions that impact them directly.

The pace of change experienced by organizations today can be dizzying. As a change agent, HR has to be able to build the organization's capacity to embrace and capitalize on new situations, ensuring that change initiatives are defined, developed, and delivered in a timely manner. HR also needs to help the organization plan for and overcome any resistance to change that might present itself. Particularly challenging are any efforts to alter the organization's culture.

HR Roles at Mercantile Bank

One organization that has effectively redesigned its HR function to assume all four roles is Mercantile Bank. Headquartered in St. Louis, Mercantile Bank is a multibank holding company, with $131 billion in assets and more than 10,000 employees. The bank strategically redesigned its HR function during the 1990s, when it went through more than 39 mergers and acquisitions. As part of this process, Mercantile's HR function moved beyond traditional recordkeeping and compliance to become more strategic in nature. This transformation happened through streamlining work processes, eliminating unnecessary activities, reevaluating technology, and outsourcing nonstrategic functions. Furthermore, some retained HR functions remain centralized at headquarters; others are deployed to operating divisions. Consequently, Mercantile's HR function is able to assume the roles of strategic partner, change agent, administrative expert, and employee champion simultaneously.[6]

A number of other models have been developed relative to the portfolio of roles that HR can and/or should play in becoming a strategic partner in the knowledge-based economy. Lengnick-Hall and Lengnick-Hall found that for HR to build strategic credibility, new roles needed to be assumed that expanded both the methods and processes traditionally used in HR.[7] These roles include human capital steward, knowledge facilitator, relationship builder, and rapid deployment specialist, as illustrated in Exhibit 4.2.

The human capital steward role involves the creation of an environment and culture in which employees voluntarily want to contribute their skills, ideas, and energy. This is based

EXHIBIT 4.2 HR Roles in a Knowledge Based Economy

- Human capital steward
- Knowledge facilitator
- Relationship builder
- Rapid deployment specialist

on the premise that unlike raw materials, plant, and equipment, human capital is not "owned" by the organization; it can move freely from organization to organization at the employee's whim. A competitive advantage can be maintained only when the best employees are recruited, duly motivated, and retained.

The knowledge facilitator role involves the procurement of the necessary employee knowledge and skill sets that allow information to be acquired, developed, and disseminated, providing a competitive advantage. This process can succeed only as part of a strategically designed employee development plan, whereby employees teach and learn from each other and sharing knowledge is valued and rewarded.

The relationship builder role involves the development of structure, work practices, and organizational culture that allow individuals to work together, across departments and functions. To ensure competitiveness, networks need to be developed that focus on the strategic objectives of the organization and how synergies and teamwork that lead to outstanding performance are valued and rewarded.

The rapid deployment specialist role involves the creation of an organization structure and HR systems that are fluid and adaptable to rapid change in response to external opportunities and threats. The global, knowledge-based economy changes quickly and frequently, and success in such an environment mandates flexibility and a culture that embraces change.

In addition to these models, a study sponsored by the Society for Human Resource Management (SHRM) and the Global Consulting Alliance found that HR's success as a true strategic business partner was dependent on five specific competencies being displayed by HR,[8] as illustrated in Exhibit 4.3. These competencies are radically different from those required in the past, when HR played a more administrative role. The first, strategic contribution, requires the development of strategy, connecting organizations to external constituents, and implementing systems that align employee performance with company strategy. The second, business knowledge, involves understanding the nuts and bolts of the organization's operations and leveraging this knowledge into results. The third, personal credibility, requires that measurable value be demonstrated in programs and policies implemented. The fourth, HR delivery, involves serving internal customers through effective and efficient programs related to staffing, performance management, and employee development. The fifth, HR technology, involves using technology to improve the organization's management of its people.

Whereas the SHRM study identifies a set of competencies that all HR executives will need, others conclude that HR roles may need to become more highly specialized. One set of roles identifies five competencies that might easily become areas of specialization.[8] The first role is "chief financial officer" for HR, an individual who is an expert at metrics,

EXHIBIT 4.3 SHRM Critical HR Competencies

- Strategic contribution
- Business knowledge
- Personal credibility
- HR delivery
- HR technology

financial analysis, and can argue the cost-effectiveness of various HR programs. The second role is "internal consultant," an individual who trains and empowers line managers to assume much of the day-to-day responsibility for managing employees and understanding the legal aspects of the employment relationship. The third role is "talent manager," an individual who focuses on finding, developing, and retaining the optimal mix of employees to facilitate the organization's strategic objectives. The fourth role is "vendor manager," an individual who determines which functions can be better handled internally or externally and assumes the responsibility for sourcing and selecting vendors as well as managing vendor relations. The fifth role is "self-service manager," an individual who oversees the technology applications of human resource management, including all aspects of e-HR.

So far, our discussion has focused on roles that HR needs to assume and competencies that need to be demonstrated to ensure that HR be seen as a true strategic partner as well as to facilitate high performance. This discussion has ignored the fact that different organizations engage in different types of employment in pursuing their strategies. To better understand these employment models, a system was developed by Lepak and Snell that identifies four different employment models and examines the types of HR systems required by each.[9]

Lepak and Snell first analyzed the characteristics of human capital by using two dimensions. The first is its *strategic value,* or the extent of its potential to improve efficiency, effectiveness, exploit market opportunities, and/or neutralize potential threats. The authors found that as the strategic value of human capital increased, the greater the likelihood that the organization would employ it internally rather than externally. The second is its *uniqueness,* or the degree to which it is specialized and not widely available. The authors found that the more unique an organization's human capital, the greater potential source of competitive advantage it would provide. These two dimensions form the matrix, presented in Exhibit 4.4, that identifies the four types of employment modes.

Quadrant 1 illustrates knowledge-based employment, human capital that is unique and has high strategic value to the organization. This type of employment requires *commitment-based* human resource management. Commitment-based HR involves heavy investment in training and development, employee autonomy and participation,

EXHIBIT 4.4 Lepak and Snell's Employment Models

Uniqueness	Strategic Value: *Low*	Strategic Value: *High*
High	**Quadrant 4:** Alliances / Partnerships Collaborative-Based HR Configuration	**Quadrant 1:** Knowledge-Based Employment Commitment-Based HR Configuration
Low	**Quadrant 3:** Contractual Work Arrangements Compliance-Based HR Configuration	**Quadrant 2:** Job-Based Employment Productivity-Based HR Configuration

employment security, and compensation systems that are long-term (i.e., stock options) and knowledge-based.

Quadrant 2 illustrates job-based employment, human capital that has limited uniqueness but is of high strategic value to the organization. This type of employment requires *productivity-based* human resource management. Less investment will be made in employees, and the organization will seek to acquire individuals with the requisite skills rather than provide training in skills that are generic. Shorter time frames will be established for performance and rewards, and jobs will be more standardized.

Quadrant 3 illustrates contractual employment, human capital that is not unique nor of strategic value to the organization. This type of employment requires *compliance-based* human resource management. Structure and direction would be provided for employees and systems established to ensure that employees comply with rules, regulations, and procedures. Workers would receive little discretion, and any training, performance management, and compensation would be based on ensuring compliance with the set work structures.

Quadrant 4 illustrates alliance/partnership employment, human capital that is unique but of limited strategic value to the organization. This type of employment requires *collaborative-based* human resource management. Much of the work would be outsourced to an outside vendor based on the sharing of information and establishment of trust. The organization would select alliance partners who are committed to the relationship as well as the organization's success. Performance standards and incentives would be established that mutually benefit both partners.

Strategic Human Resource Management at Southwest Airlines

Southwest Airlines (SWA) was one of the most successful airline companies in the 1990s. Throughout the decade, it was the only major domestic airline to turn a profit, and it consistently outperformed its competitors in customer service. A key factor in the success of SWA has been its unique corporate culture and the human resource management practices that have been developed as part of this culture. These practices are integrated with each other and directly developed under founding CEO Herb Kelliher and maintained as part of Southwest's competitive strategy of delivering both low costs and superior service. These human resource practices create shareholder value through employees via low turnover and high productivity and allow employees to experience significant job satisfaction.

Southwest's success centers around a "value cycle": Southwest first creates value through its HR practices for employees; this value is then converted, in part, to customer value via the design of specific operating processes and then captured through the provision of low costs and superior service relative to competitors. This cycle of creating, converting, and capturing value is unique among not only airlines but labor-intensive organizations in general. Other airlines have traditionally competed by creating barriers to entry via the development of hub and spoke networks and by sophisticated customer segmentation and information processing via computer reservation systems.

Southwest sees its competition not as other airlines but rather the automobile. Most of its flights are "short-haul" (less than 90 minutes) and involve quick turnaround of planes at the gate and the use of less congested airports. The company also restricts its growth relative to the rate at which it can hire and train new employees who fit with the company culture.

Southwest practices an alternative strategy called value analysis. Here, a value chain is created for the buyer, firm, and supplier. SWA does this by increasing its passengers' willingness to pay, decreasing the price passengers are charged, decreasing its own costs, and reducing employees' opportunity cost. SWA increases its passengers' willingness to pay by providing a higher level of service than its competitors, offering more frequent departures, and amusing its passengers, which makes the end of a long workday more entertaining. SWA also attempts to offer the lowest airline fare in a specific market. This allows SWA to differentiate itself from competitors that offer a relatively generic service.

Personnel is one of the most significant costs an airline incurs. At SWA, however, employees are more productive than at other major airlines. Most SWA employees are directly involved in moving passengers from departure to destination as gate agents, ramp agents, baggage handlers, flight attendants, or pilots. The result? An average airplane takes 45 minutes to turnaround: SWA averages only 17 minutes.

SWA can turn around its aircraft in 17 minutes for three reasons. First, it uses standardized aircraft—737s only. Second, no meals are provided on flights, enhancing efficiency and reducing costs. Finally, the airline has designed its work systems to allow cross-functional coordination by all its employees. From the moment a SWA flight touches down until the minute it clears the gate, every member of the flight and ground crews does everything necessary to get the next flight segment out on time.

Southwest has a culture that stresses "LUV" and "FUN." "LUV" refers to one of the company's core values, involving respect for individuality and a genuine concern for others. "FUN" refers to the company's philosophy of employees enjoying themselves at work and creating an atmosphere that allows customers to also have fun. FUN and LUV are critical elements of SWA's culture and are embedded in the hiring process, with prospective employees being asked to describe their most embarrassing moment. FUN and LUV are also critical components of SWA's compensation system. Actual salaries are at the industry average, but most employees consider SWA's work environment to be a form of nonmonetary compensation.

SWA uses a variety of HR practices to create its unique labor force. Starting with a rigorous selection process, employees are paid an average compensation, combined with significant nonmonetary awards. Employees treat one another well, and there is a focus on ongoing training and development. Employees' suggestions are also constantly solicited. The nurturing, ongoing development of the organizational culture is critical to Southwest's competitive advantage.[10]

Strategic HR differs radically from traditional HR in a number of ways, as illustrated in Exhibit 4.5. In a traditional approach to HR, the main responsibility for people management programs rests with staff specialists in the corporate HR division. A strategic approach places the responsibility for managing people with the individuals most in contact with them: their respective line managers. In essence, strategic HR would argue that any

EXHIBIT 4.5 Traditional HR Versus Strategic HR

	Traditional HR	Strategic HR
Responsibility for HR	Staff specialists	Line managers
Focus	Employee relations	Partnerships with internal and external customers
Role of HR	Transactional change follower and respondent	Transformational change leader and initiator
Initiatives	Slow, reactive, fragmented	Fast, proactive, integrated
Time horizon	Short-term	Short, medium, long (as necessary)
Control	Bureaucratic–roles, policies, procedures	Organic–flexible, whatever is necessary to succeed
Job design	Tight division of labor, independence, specialization	Broad, flexible, cross-training, teams
Key investments	Capital, products	People, knowledge
Accountability	Cost center	Investment center

individual in an organization who has responsibility for people is an HR manager, regardless of the technical area in which he or she works.

Traditional HR focuses its activities on employee relations, ensuring that employees are motivated and productive and that the organization is in compliance with all necessary employment laws, as illustrated in the operational quadrants in Exhibit 4.1 on page 157. A strategic approach shifts the focus to partnerships with internal and external constituent groups. Employees are only one constituency that needs to be considered. The focus on managing people is more systemic, with an understanding of the myriad factors that impact employees and the organization and how to manage multiple relationships to ensure satisfaction at all levels of the organization. Critical partners in the process include employees, customers, stockholders/owners, regulatory agencies, and public interest groups.

Traditional HR assumes a role of handling transactions as they arise. These may involve compliance with changing laws, rectifying problems between supervisors and subordinates, recruiting and screening applicants for current needs, and basically responding to events after they happen. Strategic HR is much more transformational and realizes that the success of any initiatives for growth, adaptation, or change within the organization depend on the employees who utilize any changes in technology or produce any changes in the organization's product or service. HR therefore plays more of a transformational role in assisting the organization in identifying and meeting the larger challenges it faces in its external environment by ensuring that the internal mechanisms that facilitate change are in place.

Similarly, any initiatives for change coming from traditional HR are usually slow and fragmented, piecemeal, and not integrated with larger concerns. Strategic HR is more proactive and systemic in change initiatives. Rectifying a specific employee discipline problem or moving to a new sales commission system are examples of the former approach. Strategic HR is flexible enough to consider the various time frames (short, medium, and/or long-run) as necessary to facilitate the development of programs and policies that address the critical strategic challenges being faced by the organization. At the same time, these strategically conceived initiatives must be developed and implemented in concert with other HR systems.

As an example, the HR systems at Mercantile Bank were not developed independent of each other. As the HR function evolved with subsequent mergers and acquisitions, HR initiatives were developed in tandem with other HR programs and policies. For example, job analysis procedures developed competencies that formed the basis for recruiting, testing, performance feedback, and compensation programs. The performance feedback program was developed in tandem with a succession planning program and incentive programs for high performers. These types of integrated initiatives are one of the principle differences between traditional and strategic human resource management.

The traditional approach to HR manifests itself in bureaucratic control through rules, procedures, and policies that ensure fair treatment of employees and predictability in operations. Indeed, Exhibit 4.1 notes the role of HR as administrative expert in developing and enforcing rules and standards of behavior for employees. Strategic HR, on the other hand, realizes that such an approach limits an organization's ability to grow and respond to a rapidly changing environment. Strategic HR utilizes control that is much more "organic," or loose and free-flowing, with as few restrictions on employee actions and behaviors as possible. Flexibility in work processes and job responsibilities are common and is discussed in Chapter 6. Rather than being bound by excessive rules and regulations, operations are controlled by whatever is necessary to succeed, and control systems are modified as needed to meet changing conditions.

Traditional HR grew out of principles of scientific management and job specialization to increase employee efficiency. A tight division of labor with independent tasks allowed employees to develop specific skills and maintain a focus on their specific job responsibilities. A strategic approach to HR allows very broad job design, emphasizing flexibility and a need to respond as change takes place in the external environment. Specialization is replaced by cross-training, and independent tasks are replaced by teams and groups—some of which are permanent, some of which are temporary, and many of which are managed autonomously by the workers themselves.

The traditional approach to HR sees an organization's key investments as its capital, products, brand name, technology, and investment strategy. Strategic HR sees the organization's key investment as its people and their knowledge and abilities. This approach realizes that competitive advantage is enjoyed by an organization that can attract and retain "knowledge workers" who can optimally utilize and manage the organization's capital resources. In the long run, people are an organization's only sustainable competitive advantage.[11]

Finally, accountability for HR activities in the traditional approach considers functions, including HR, as cost centers with an emphasis on monitoring expenditures and charging overhead to fiscal units. An investment approach considers returns as well as expenditures, with attention paid toward the "value added" by HR activities.

As the above discussion illustrates, traditional HR is largely focused on administrative oversight and process. Strategic HR, on the other hand, focuses on deliverables, quantifiable results, and value creation. One conceptualization of strategic HR sees HR adding value with the effective management of four "flows": 1) the flow or people; 2) the flow of performance; 3) the flow of information; and 4) the flow of work.[12] The flow of people considers how employees enter, move through, and eventually leave the organization. The flow of performance considers the development of standards and rewards that are consistent with the interests of stakeholders. The flow of information considers how employees are made aware of priorities and activities and provided feedback. The flow of work considers the processes in which employees engage and the appropriate responsibility for these processes.

As noted in Chapter 1, organizations are increasingly utilizing metrics to illustrate the value of HR activities and processes and their resultant impact on organizational performance. However, such an approach is of value to small organizations as well as larger ones. One recent study of HR practices in small businesses found a direct correlation between three key HR strategies and organizational performance.[13] The first strategy is ensuring that selection strategies for the organization focus on person-organization fit rather than person-job fit. Hiring to ensure a fit with company culture is far more critical than ensuring that an individual has the necessary experience and skills to do a job. The second strategy is allowing employee autonomy, providing workers with discretion to decide how to schedule and complete their work rather than constantly monitoring employee activities. This allows employees to be more involved in decision-making, suggest new and better ways to complete their jobs, and become more involved with the work of their team. The third strategy is motivating and rewarding employees through a family-like atmosphere rather than individualized monetary rewards. Employers who create a social dimension to the job provide employees with a kind of compensation that is difficult for competitors to replicate. While other employers can match and even exceed levels of pay and benefits, each organization can create a unique culture that might make employees less likely to leave. The study found that employers who utilized all three strategies experienced 22 percent higher sales growth, 23 percent higher profits, and 67 percent less attrition that those who did not. Even employers who implemented only one of the three strategies still saw significant improvements in their financial performance.

The question remains, though, as to how to create a culture that promotes employee engagement to ensure that the organizations benefits from improved sales and profitability and lower attrition. A variety of specific HR programs can be developed around an overall HR strategy that attempts to increase employee engagement and commitment, as discussed in Reading 4.2, "Employee Engagement and Commitment: A Guide to Understanding, Measuring and Increasing Engagement in Your Organization."

Employee Engagement at Aetna Corp.

Hartford, Connecticut–based Aetna found itself in serious trouble at the turn of the millennium. Despite more than 150 years in business, the company found itself performing poorly as its diversified multinational multibusiness strategy had the company on *the verge of bankruptcy. The decision to downsize and focus solely on Aetna's core businesses of health insurance and employee benefit products wasn't enough, as even the downsized organization was still losing more than $1 million per day. However, by 2007 Aetna had completed one of the most lauded turnarounds in American corporate history, turning a $2.5 billion annual loss into a $1.7 billion profit and increasing market valuation from $3.3 billion to $29 billion in just six years.*

The journey began with the new CEO asking all employees to provide input as to what they wanted the organization to be. This yielded a company values statement of integrity, quality service, excellence and accountability, and employee engagement. Every year, employees complete a 70-question online "climate survey," which provides feedback about employee beliefs concerning values and vision. Employee engagement is assessed via four questions: 1) I would recommend Aetna as a good place to work; 2) I rarely think about looking for a new job with another company; 3) I am proud I work for Aetna; and 4) Overall, I am extremely satisfied with Aetna as a place to work.

HR facilitates much of this engagement through a succession planning program where top executives identify the "top 200" employees who are being groomed for future leadership. This process is facilitated by a $50 million automated system called Talent Manager, which contains data about Aetna's 34,000 employees. The system contains information about jobs held and correlated skills and competencies. Employees and supervisors access and update records where both parties provide performance feedback and ratings. Solid performers, at-risk employees, and "mismatches" are identified through this system to assist with planning and engagement. The system has not only improved financial performance, but since its implementation, employee retention has held steady at 90 percent annually.[14]

Barriers to Strategic HR

Although the concept of strategic HR may make sense logically and intuitively, many organizations have a difficult time taking a strategic approach to HR. A number of reasons contribute to this. The first is that most organizations adopt a short-term mentality and focus on current performance. Performance evaluations and compensation throughout organizations tend to be based on current performance. This is not surprising given the emphasis by most shareholders and Wall Street on short-term organizational performance in terms of quarterly measures of profitability and return on investments. CEOs need to focus on short-term quarterly financial performance in order to retain their jobs. Several consecutive "down" quarters will often result in dismissal. This philosophy then trickles throughout the organization. Rewards are not provided for laying plans that may (or may not) provide significant gain three or five years in the future. Most owners and investors do not take a longer-term view of their investments; they expect to see quarterly progress in wealth-building. There are few, if any, clear incentives for managers to think long term in making their decisions. Consequently, although many organizations desire management decisions that will benefit the organization in the long run, rewards are based on short-term performance.[15]

A second barrier to strategic HR is the fact that many HR managers do not think strategically, given their segmented understanding of the entire business. Human resource management is a complex and ever-changing function, requiring a tremendous amount of technical knowledge. HR managers often have insufficient general management training to understand the entire organization and the issues and challenges being experienced in the finance, operations, and marketing departments. Consequently, their ability to think strategically may be impaired, and their ability to influence colleagues in other functions may be limited. Unless senior HR managers can appreciate these functional issues and speak the language of these disciplines, they can not fully contribute to the organization in a strategic manner nor gain the support of managers in these areas.

A third barrier is that most senior managers lack appreciation for the value of HR and its ability to contribute to the organization from a strategic perspective. Many simply understand the traditional or operational function of HR and fail to realize the contributions HR can make as a strategic partner. Managers throughout the organization often see the HR function as providing unnecessary bureaucracy to their work and being more of an adversary than an ally. Their perception of HR is that it is inflexible and rules-oriented—"You can't do this. You have to do that."—and that it delays their ability to do their jobs (taking time to get job descriptions written and approved, postings, delays, procedures). Although a key function of HR is ensuring compliance with laws that regulate the employment relationship, many managers see the HR function as detracting from their ability to do their jobs because of the perceived added administrative work required by HR.

A fourth barrier is that few functional managers see *themselves* as HR managers and are concerned more with technical aspects of their areas of responsibility than the human aspects. Regardless of the function or technical specialty of a manager, any individual who has responsibility for people is an HR manager. Although a controller, chief financial officer, or information technology manager might not consider him or herself to be an HR manager, any individual responsible for the performance of other employees is, in fact, an HR manager. The role of HR as a strategic partner involves line managers assuming more responsibility for day-to-day operational issues, with HR providing internal support or assistance for employee relations rather than assuming full and sole responsibility for it.

A fifth barrier to strategic HR is the difficulty in quantifying many of the outcomes and benefits of HR programs. With competitive pressures making organizations more bottom-line oriented, programs that may not have any direct quantifiable benefit—such as team building—may be disregarded or shelved. Senior HR managers consistently find resistance toward resources being allocated to programs that have less tangible, measurable benefits than those that do.

Another barrier to strategic HR is the fact that human assets are not owned by organizations and, therefore, are perceived as a higher risk investment than capital assets. Particularly in highly competitive industries where key executives may be recruited from competitors, there is an incentive to invest less in employees than in technology and information, which are more proprietary. Organizations adopting this mindset fail to realize that it is the people who utilize the technology and information that provide an organization with stellar performance and a competitive advantage; investments in these individuals can be more critical than corresponding investments in technology and information. Although technology and information constantly need to be replaced because of depreciation in their value, an organization's human resource hold their value and can have this value enhanced by minimal investments in them.

Finally, strategic HR may be resisted because of the incentives for change that might arise. Taking a strategic approach to HR may mean making drastic changes in how work is organized; how employees are hired, trained, and developed; how performance is measured; how employees are compensated; standards of performance; and relations between employees and supervisors and among employees themselves. Because people tend to be creatures of habit and enjoy maintaining the status quo—particularly older workers and those with less training and skills—organizations often find resistance to any change initiatives. Such significant changes can be very risky for those responsible for implementation if such efforts fail. An organization that "punishes" those responsible for unsuccessful change efforts instead of looking at such endeavors as learning experiences provides disincentives for change. Exhibit 4.6 summarizes these barriers to change.

Most of these barriers are rooted in the culture of an organization. As noted, the organization's history, values, and management practices can act as disincentives for any change initiative. The question remains concerning if and how an organization's HR systems can promote or encourage change initiatives.

EXHIBIT 4.6 Barriers to Strategic HR

- Short-term mentality/focus on current performance
- Inability of HR to think strategically
- Lack of appreciation of what HR can contribute
- Failure to understand general manager's role as an HR manager
- Difficulty in quantifying many HR outcomes
- Perception of human assets as higher-risk investments
- Incentives for change that might arise

Outsourcing and Revamping HR

One critical strategic decision that many organizations are facing relative to their HR operations is whether to outsource some components or all of it. A strategic approach to HR moves the HR function and staff away from administrative "transactional" kinds of responsibilities toward those that create value and provide a clear return. However, those administrative functions—including enrolling employees for benefits, managing payroll, counseling employees, testing and background checks for applicants, and creating and maintaining a database—still need to be performed. The past two decades have seen proliferation of entrants into the HR services industry, where organizations provide specialized or packaged HR services administration for employers.

The benefits of outsourcing include: 1) allowing the organization to reduce its HR staff (and possibly save money); 2) enhancing the quality of HR services provided; 3) freeing up HR staff to focus on more strategic, value-added activities; and 4) frequent reduction in the costs of outsourced services through economies of scale "bundling" of services with other employers. It involves a shift in the culture of the organization relative to the roles and expectations for in-house HR professionals and certainly allows HR to display its understanding of the needs of the organization and how it can deliver value from a strategic perspective.

Rather than outsource some or all of the HR function, an organization may decide that it needs to totally reinvent its HR programs and systems in response to a change in strategy and/or the environment in which the organization operates. The decision to centralize the HR function at headquarters provides economies of scale but not responsiveness to individual business needs and locations. Decentralized HR provides responsiveness relative to the needs and differences of different operational locations but often produces duplication of effort and inefficiencies. Reading 4.3, "Remodeling HR at Home Depot," provides a case study of how the entire HR function at the organization has evolved in response to the organization's strategy and business needs.

Conclusion

Recognizing that a strategic approach to human resource management needs to be undertaken within the context of a specific organization is paramount to successful implementation: What works for one organization will not necessarily work for another. This point is well-illustrated by looking at how two large organizations revamped their HR functions. One did so by making HR more centralized, whereas the other did so by making HR more decentralized. Both efforts were successful because they were designed and implemented within the context of the organization's strategy.

Strategic Reorganization of the HR Function at General Motors

We might logically assume that larger and older organizations would be less prone to dramatic changes in their operating practices; however, one of the most venerable corporations in the United States has been among the most innovative in its HR practices. General Motors, like other domestic automakers, watched its market share shrink as Japanese, German, and Korean competitors captured the American consumer's dollar. When Rick Wagoner became CEO in the late 1990s, one of his primary objectives was to shake up the status quo at the organization through its HR practices. Wagoner had the head of HR join the senior management team and pushed HR into a more strategic role. At the time, the HR function at GM was totally "siloed," with a highly decentralized structure in which every GM facility administered HR in its own way. Each plant had its own HR staff, which operated with near total autonomy. Wagoner brought in Kathleen Barclay to head HR, which she revamped through a strategy she called the 3Ts: technology, talent, and transformation.

Technology was used to overhaul HR by creating an effective and accessible corporate intranet and transforming that site into a full-service HR portal. This system is described more fully in Chapter 2. The focus on talent resulted in the development of GM University, one of the largest corporate education and training programs in the world. The university has 15 separate colleges that develop training and curricula tailored to the professional needs of and challenges faced by the organization's employees. The transformation component has standardized operations, resulting in greater efficiency, improved communications and interaction, and tighter coordination of operations. The "siloed" nature of GM has been replaced by an organization that now operates as a true global entity.[16]

Strategic Reorganization of the HR Function at Wells Fargo Bank

San Francisco–based Wells Fargo Bank has 185 branches, more than 3,000 employees, five separate division presidents, and does more than $20 billion in business annually. In such a large organization, HR had performed many of its traditional administrative roles. To become more competitive, Wells Fargo saw the need to move to a more strategic approach to human resource management. Line managers needed specific HR solutions to help them improve their operations and impact the bottom line, but HR was unable to deliver this under its existing administrative structure. That structure was highly centralized, with all HR consultants and staffing managers assigned to separate divisions but working out of headquarters. That was changed to create a new structure in which HR staff worked at the branch level to become more integrated with operations and support local management.

To facilitate this process, an outside trainer was brought in to work with the HR staff to refocus their responsibilities and skills. HR professionals were trained in facilitation and consultation, technical issues, and strategizing and partnering by using a four-phase consultative methodology that ranged from the creation of work agreements, problem identification, data analysis and implementation, and follow-up. The transformation occurred over a year and has reduced turnover by 19% and pay problems by 99%. By centralizing some generic administrative duties, the organization was able to save close to $1 million annually. New hire time was reduced from fourteen days to seven. The end result is that the reorganization has allowed managers to reach their strategic and business goals by moving HR closer to these managers and creating value-added processes.[17]

Top management in most organizations does not realize the contribution that HR can make to overall organizational performance because they still perceive HR in more traditional ways. A contributing factor to this is that senior HR managers themselves may not understand how they can contribute to their organizations strategically. Without a holistic understanding of the organization, HR managers have limited ability to contribute to high-level strategic thinking. Until HR managers take the initiative to gain technical knowledge about their organizations, products and services, competition, and markets and learn how to work politically with other senior managers, their organizations will not be able to fully integrate HR strategy with corporate strategy and will continue to operate at less-than-optimal levels of performance and efficiency.

The key to achieving this is for HR managers to realize that strategic HR can provide three critical outcomes: increased performance, enhanced customer and employee satisfaction, and enhanced shareholder value, as outlined in Exhibit 4.7. These outcomes can be accomplished through effective management of the staffing, retention, and turnover processes; selection of employees that fit with both the organizational strategy and culture; cost-effective utilization of employees through investment in *identified* human capital with the potential for high return; integrated HR programs and policies that clearly follow from corporate strategy; facilitation of change and adaptation through a flexible, more dynamic organization; and tighter focus on customer needs, key and emerging markets, and quality.

A model that illustrates how this can be accomplished is presented in Exhibit 4.8. This model provides the framework for the remainder of this book. At this point, we have discussed how corporate and business unit strategies are formed as well as organizational and external environment factors that need to be considered when developing strategy. The next two chapters, 5 and 6, focus on the HR strategy component of the model, examining human resource planning and the design of jobs and work systems. The remaining chapters focus on how each of the functional areas of HR can be derived from this strategy. Finally, Chapter 14 will conclude by examining strategic human resource management from an international perspective.

EXHIBIT 4.7 Outcomes of Strategic HR

EXHIBIT 4.8 A Model of Strategic Human Resource Management

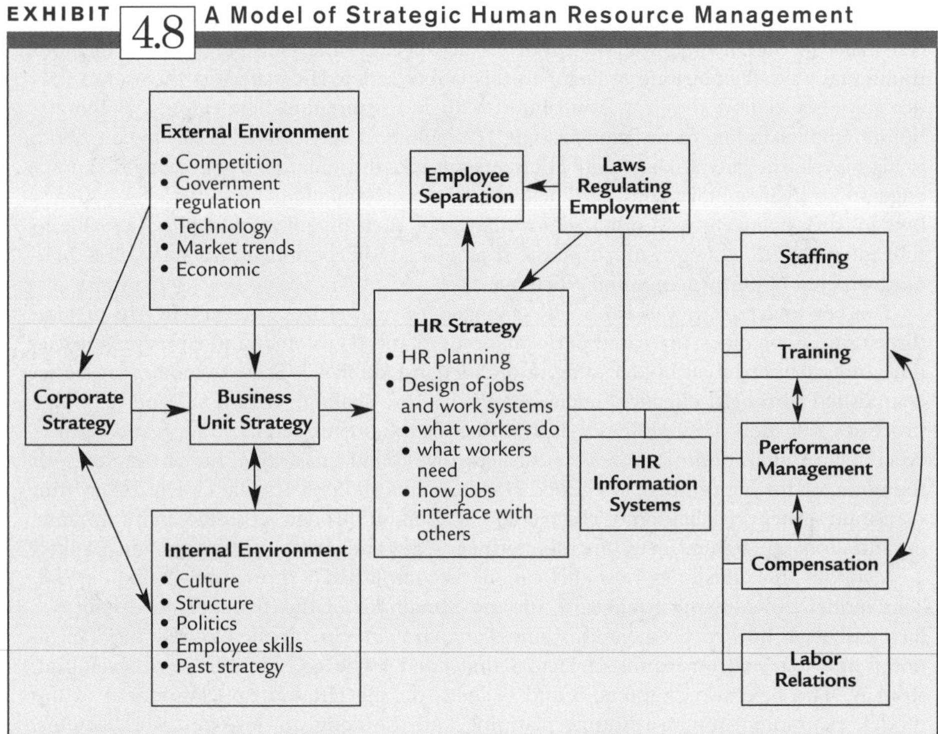

Critical Thinking

1. Compare and contrast traditional and strategic HR. In what types of organizations might traditional HR still be appropriate?
2. What are the main barriers that prevent an organization from taking a more strategic approach to HR? Why do they exist, and how can they be overcome?
3. What is the role of HR in your current organization? What could it be? What should it be? Why does HR assume the role that it does?
4. Analyze the four HR roles presented by the Lengnick-Halls. How might the criticality of each of these roles be impacted by different strategies?
5. To be a true strategic partner, does HR need to take on a more generalized or specialized approach to its work? Why?

Reading 4.1

6. Examine each of the pairs of organizations the authors discuss. Determine whether their strategies are based on I/O or RBV assumptions. What does this imply about strategic planning in general?

Reading 4.2

7. What kinds of employment practices encourage employee engagement? What are the benefits of enhanced engagement?

Reading 4.3

8. Assess the pros and cons of Home Depot's revamping of its HR function. What dimensions of the retail industry make Home Depot's delivery of HR desirable or undesirable?

Exercises

1. Assume the position of a consultant hired to assess the approach toward human resource management taken by a client organization. What factors might you evaluate in determining whether an organization uses a traditional or strategic approach to managing its human resource? Develop specific questions that need to be answered and determine which key decision-makers in an organization should be asked these questions.
2. Select a local organization and investigate these factors by interviewing selected key decision-makers.

3. Visit the Web site for the Society for Human Resource Management (http://www.shrm.org). SHRM is the largest professional association for HR practitioners in the world. Determine whether this organization encourages HR professionals to approach HR from a traditional or strategic standpoint. Print examples of pages that support your conclusion, and be prepared to present them to the class.

Chapter References

1. Fegley, S. and Lockwood, N. "Staffing Research: Talent Management," Society for Human Resource Management, 2006.
2. Bates, S. "Written HR Strategy Pays Off," *HR Magazine*, April 2003, p. 12
3. Ibid.
4. Stockman, J. "Building a Quality HR Organization at GE," *Human Resource Management,* Summer 1999, Vol. 38, No. 2, pp. 143–146.
5. Ulrich, D. *Human Resource Champions: The Next Agenda for Adding Value and Delivering Results*, Boston: Harvard Business School Press, 1997.
6. Forbringer, L. R. and Oeth, C. "Human Resources at Mercantile Bankcorporation, Inc.: A Critical Analysis," *Human Resource Management*, 37, (2), pp. 177–189.
7. Lengnick-Hall, M. and Lengnick-Hall, C. *Human Resource Management in the Knowledge Economy*, Berrett Koehler, 2003.
8. Meisinger, S. "Adding Competencies, Adding Value," *HR Magazine*, July 2003, p. 8.
9. Lepak, D. P. and Snell, S. A. "Examining the Human Resource Architecture: The Relationships among Human Capital, Employment and Human Resource Configurations," *Journal of Management*, 28, (4), pp. 517–541.
10. Hallowell, R. "Southwest Airlines: A Case Study Linking Employee Needs Satisfaction and Organizational Capabilities to Competitive Advantage," *Human Resource Management*, 35, (4), pp. 513–534.
11. Pfeffer, J. *Competitive Advantage Through People: Problems and Prospects for Change*, Boston: Harvard Business School Press, 1994.
12. Ulrich, D. and Brockbank, W. *The HR Value Proposition*, Harvard Business School Press, 2005.
13. Collins, C.
14. Grossman, R. "Steering a Business Turnaround" *HR Magazine*, 53, (4), April 2008, pp. 73–80.
15. Kerr, S. "On the Folly of Rewarding A, While Hoping for B," *Academy of Management Journal* (18), 1975, pp. 769–783.
16. Leonard, B. "GM Drives HR to the Next Level," *HR Magazine*, March 2002, pp. 47–50.
17. Fox, A. "HR Makes Leap to Strategic Partner," *HR Magazine*, July 2003, p. 34.

READING 4.1

Distinctive Human Resources Are Firms' Core Competencies

Peter Cappelli and Anne Crocker-Hefter

Find a firm with a reputation for excellence in some function, copy its practices, and your company, too, will excel. Advice such as this, under the rubric of "best practices" or "benchmarking," has flooded the popular business literature. Each article implicitly extends the argument that superior management practices are readily identifiable and can be transferred across organizations.

The best practices advocates, however, must contend with a discomforting reality: *Many firms—some very successful—stubbornly refuse to adopt those practices.* Are we to assume, perhaps, that competition drives out firms that do not adopt the most efficient techniques—and that the intractable companies will ultimately fail? Hardly the case.

To understand what is happening, we need to look at a counterpoint to the best practices approach. When it comes to explaining how and why certain firms have carved out competitive advantages, attention increasingly focuses on unique, *differentiating* resources—the notion of "core competencies" being perhaps the best known of these resource arguments.

We believe that the notion of a single set of "best" practices may, indeed, be overstated. As we illustrate below, there are examples in virtually every industry of highly successful firms that have very distinct management practices. We argue that these distinctive human resource practices help to create unique competencies that differentiate products and services and, in turn, drive competitiveness. Indeed, product differentiation is one of the essential functions of strategic management, and distinctive human resource practices shape the core competencies that determine how firms compete.

The argument that there should be a "fit" between human resource practices and business strategies can be traced back to manpower planning and is certainly not new in management circles. What is new here is the argument that people management practices are the *drivers*—the genesis of efforts to create distinctive competencies and, in turn, business strategies.

We illustrate this point by examining pairs of successful organizations competing in the same industry. We chose the paired companies by asking analysts, consultants, and other industry experts to help us identify successful organizations in their industry that appeared to have very different employee management practices. We began our investigation with financial reports and other publicly available information on the organizations, including stories in the business press over the past five years. We also contacted each organization for information and in most cases visited them. The most revealing sources of information, however, tended to be competitors and former employees. The competitors in particular, typically the other member of an industry "pair," had a keen sense for what was truly distinctive in each organization. Former employees also have a clear sense about what actually happens inside organizations, as opposed to what the written practices say.

With the help of industry experts and competitors, we then identified the distinctive competencies and competitive advantages of each organization. There was remarkably little variance across respondents in what they believed these competencies to be. In most cases, competencies were clearly associated with particular employee groups—customer service, for example, or marketing.

The next step was to describe the employment practices associated with the relevant employee group. In cases where practices have recently changed, we describe the longstanding practices that were in place when the distinctive competencies were developed. In our final step, we compared the distinctive competencies for each organization with the employment practices for the relevant employee group to suggest how these competencies were created.

When Employees Are the "Product"

The link between people management practices and the way organizations compete is most direct in industries where employees, by themselves, create what the organization sells—where the "product" is a service provided directly by employees interacting with customers. Consider the following cases.

Professional Sports

Professional sports are obviously big-businesses in their own right, and it's easy to see how "employee performance" matters in this arena. The rules governing each sport standardize the equipment, playing fields, and time limits for all competitors. Within those parameters, each club must deliver its services—an event that attracts an audience.

Sports are idiosyncratic in other ways as well. The fact that there is no "open" labor market and that teams tend to control hiring through drafts may make it easier to align organizations and employees than in other industries. Financial success and the success of the team in its sport are not always related, which may reduce somewhat the financial incentives to seek out the most effective strategies and employee matches on the field.

The San Francisco 49ers and Oakland Raiders have been among the most successful teams in American sports, yet they represent very distinct models of player management. The 49ers have succeeded by using a strategy of long-term player development—recruiting through college drafts rather than through trades, developing talent within the team, and then holding on to the best players by keeping them happy. Their salaries are among the most generous in the league, and more than in other clubs, the 49ers players have some influence on team decisions and feel that they are a part of the organization.

On the field, the club relies on experienced athletes who have worked with their coaches for years and who act as team leaders. (The coaches and management staff also have long tenure with the team.) They have a reputation for playing as a precise, well-disciplined unit. Long-tenure players also help create long-term relationships with fans, helping cement their loyalty to the club. If production language could be applied to sports, this is a "high commitment" organization that operates as a "quasi-autonomous team" on the field. The approach has apparently paid off—the 49ers have won at least ten games a year every year since 1983.

The Raiders, in contrast, do not as a rule develop their own players, but instead use trades to scoop up talented players who fail or do not fit in elsewhere. The club has a very high player turnover and a reputation as a collection of individuals who often do not fit together well. As an organization, the Raiders are not known for treating players especially well, or for letting them have much influence on team decisions. The team, which has been called "an organizational anomaly," has an autocratic owner who is personally involved in coaching and personnel decisions. No employee participation here.

On the field, the Raiders are known for their individual performances and wide-open playing style, a style that makes good use of their pool of individual talent. The players are not known for their personal discipline either, having "swashbuckled through Bourbon Street" during Super Bowl week, for example, and recovered by game day.

The practices of these two clubs create reputations that contribute to some self-selection of players, reinforcing their systems; those comfortable working in disciplined systems go to the 49ers while players who bridle at the constraints such systems impose go to the Raiders. It makes sense for the 49ers to staff their team with inexperienced players from the college draft in order to better "stamp" them with their own system; players from other pro teams are more likely to come in with expectations and playing habits that might be incompatible with the 49ers' system. Similarly, the fact that the Raiders hire experienced players who bring disparate attitudes and reputations that are not easily blended helps create their more individualistic playing style.

To some extent, football teams compete for fans the same way that firms compete for customers, and having distinct styles of play may help build a national audience. A distinctive and unusual style may be useful on the field as well, in that it demands unusual responses from the other side that may be difficult to master.

How Do Management Practices Help Build Distinct Competencies?

Employee selection, i.e., the selection of employees with distinctive capabilities, provides the most obvious example of how management practices create distinct competencies. Moreover, a company's reputation for certain employment practices may attract employees and thus push the process along, aligning individual and organizational attributes. In practice, this is an imperfect mechanism. It requires that both employers and prospective employees have accurate information about each other and it assumes stable characteristics and mobility between organizations. But there is considerable evidence that this matching process between organizations and employee characteristics does occur.

In addition, each organization has its own training programs, rewards systems, and work organization, and these systems develop skills and behaviors that help an organization create distinctive competencies for attacking markets.

Retailing: Sales as the Service

Sears and Nordstrom are both legends in the retailing industry.

Sears was the world's largest retailer for generations and has outlasted all of its historical competitors. During the 1980s, Nordstrom set service and growth standards for the industry. Although Sears stumbled in this period—as did most department stores—it has recently reorganized with improved performance.

Sears and Nordstrom are very different companies, with different employment practices, especially with reference to sales positions—the key job in retailing. Yet each company's practices make sense for its operations.

Sears has been and remains one of the pioneering firms in the science of employee selection. It relies on some of the most sophisticated selection tests in American industry. The company has refined these tests over time to achieve extremely high predictive power. Once hired, employees receive extensive training in company practices. Management also keeps track of employee attitudes and morale through frequent and rigorous employee surveys.

Two practices are especially noteworthy in the management of sales representatives. The first is intensive training in Sears products, operating systems, and sales techniques. The second is the pay program: a great many sales employees work on straight salary—not commissions—and the commissions that are paid at Sears are modest. (They have recently been cut to one percent of sales.)

Nordstrom operates with virtually none of the formal personnel practices advanced by Sears. Indeed, its practices appear downright primitive in comparison. Nordstrom's hiring is decentralized and uses no formal selection tests. Managers look for applicants with experience in customer contact—not necessarily prior retailing experience (which is often seen as a drawback). The important qualities are a pleasant personality and motivation. The company has only one rule in its personnel handbook: "Use Your Best Judgment at All Times." Individual sales clerks run their areas almost as if they were private stores.

Nordstrom maintains a continuous stream of programs to motivate employees toward the goal of providing intensive service, but it offers very little of what could be thought of as training. The pay system is leaded toward commissions, which makes it possible for clerks to earn sizable incomes. Nordstrom sales personnel are also ranked within each department according to their monthly sales: the most successful are promoted (virtually all managers are promoted from within) and the least successful let go.

In Nordstrom's fashion-oriented retail business, the service that customers demand is not detailed knowledge of the products, but personal contact. The clerk's emotional energy is important—and hustle, running across the store to match an item, remembering an individual customer's tastes, etc. Impulse purchases are more important in fashion than in other segments of retailing, and the clerk's effort can be especially important in such sales.

The Nordstrom employment system fuels an intense level of personal motivation and customer contact. The commissions, internal competition, and motivation programs provide the drive, while autonomy and the absence of rules allow it to be exercised. Many new hires do not survive—Nordstrom's turnover ranks among the highest in the industry. But because the investment in each employee is relatively small, such turnover is not a real problem.

Sears is also in the retail business, of course, and service is part of what it sells. But it is service of a different kind, in part because housewares, rather than fashion, dominate its product line. Customers buying home appliances or hardware want information about the products and how they are used. Sears also sells financing and warranties, reasonably complicated services that require some background knowledge. As evidenced by its marketing ("The Name You Can Trust"), Sears trades, in part, on a reputation for steering the customer in the right direction.

With this strategy, training is important, and turnover is costly—hence the emphasis on selection. Salary pay systems, as opposed to commissions, create no incentives to push products irrespective of customer needs or to cut back on "non-selling time" associated with providing information. Personal relationships with customers also help build a reputation for honest and reliable service. Sears customer satisfaction data finds that the stores with the lowest employee turnover and the least temporary help have the highest satisfaction ratings. (Interestingly, Sears' problem with fraud in its automotive business a few years ago provides an exception that proves the rule—automotive managers operated on commissions and quotas that provided the incentives to encourage repairs that in many cases were apparently not needed.)

The restructuring of Sears during the past two years smashed its no-layoff policy, but left other principles of employment intact. In fact, the amount of training for sales representatives has increased and the limited commission-based pay reduced further.

Professional Service Firms: Information and Advice as the Product

Boston Consulting Group (BCG) and McKinsey & Company are among the world's leading strategic consulting firms. Both have world-wide operations, and their reputations for thoughtful leadership and quality service to management are comparable. Both firms hire from the best undergraduate and MBA programs and compete for the top students. Both have rigorous selection procedures and exceptional compensation. Yet the characteristics of the people the two firms hire, and the way each firm manages people, differ in important ways. Again, the practices relate to the companies' approaches to their markets.

BCG tends to attract candidates with very broad perspectives on business. Some have started their own businesses, and others leave BCG to found new companies. BCG also maintains something of a "revolving door" with academia, hiring business school professors as consultants and sometimes losing consultants to faculty positions in business schools. Once hired, consultants jump right into work, albeit closely supervised, and the formal training they receive is likely to be from outside courses.

BCG has an entrepreneurial environment—an expectation that each project team will come up with its own innovative approach. Each office is seen as having a slightly different culture. BCG pays less than many of its competitors, but offers more individualized incentive pay, reinforcing the entrepreneurial culture.

While BCG has some standard "products" such as time-based competition and capabilities-based strategies, these are not the source of its competency. Indeed, some products, such as the "Growth-Share" matrix, are well-publicized and basically given away. The value-added comes from the customized application to the client's situation. Many of

BCG's projects do not even start with these products but rather with a "clean sheet of paper" approach. What clients buy, therefore, are original solutions and approaches to their problems. And these approaches begin with consultants whose varied backgrounds and entrepreneurial spirit help produce a unique product.

McKinsey, on the other hand, has historically taken virtually all of its new hires from on-campus recruiting and rarely hires from other employers. It tends to prefer candidates with technical backgrounds, such as engineering and computer science, who have depth in some functional business area. The new entrants vary less in terms of their management experience and come in as "blank slates" in terms of their consulting ideas. If McKinsey consultants leave, they are more likely to take senior line management positions in corporations than entrepreneurial positions.

McKinsey provides new consultants with extensive training in the company's method of project execution and management, even though this is highly tailored to each client's situation. McKinsey's size—3,000 consultants compared to 800 at BCG—may create scale economies in training new entrants that make it easier for the firm to provide such programs itself. The firm expects the career path to the highest position, senior partner, to take approximately 12 years (versus six to eight at BCG), which gives the consultants a long period to learn how to fit in.

The company is known for the "McKinsey way." McKinsey believes that it is important to provide its clients with consistent services; the client knows what to expect from the project teams whose products and techniques are regarded as proprietary and are not publicized. The firm's core competency, therefore, is in the consistent products and techniques that constitute the "McKinsey way." This standardization is especially notable given the far-flung nature of McKinsey's empire. Half of its senior partners are abroad, and 27 of the 33 offices it has opened since 1980 are outside the U.S.

Business Schools

A similar pattern of employment practices applies across business schools. And because these schools serve as supply channels for business, the pattern also influences the relationships with firms that recruit at those schools.

As an employer, the Harvard Business School represents the end of the spectrum associated with internal development of skills. Harvard is well-known for identifying bright young academics who, in many cases, come from fields largely unrelated to business. Harvard hires them as assistant professors and turns them into business experts. Harvard is also known for a faculty with unique skills and abilities: a deep and practical knowledge of business problems typically acquired through clinical methods, and the ability to teach "cases" using the Socratic method. Compared with other schools, Harvard is organized more by problem areas and teaching responsibilities than by traditional academic fields.

Several personnel practices support the development of these skills. Until recently, a system of post-doctoral fellowships specifically for Ph.D.s in non-business fields helped them learn about business. The best of these fellows were then hired as assistant professors. A second practice is a longer tenure clock than at many schools—nine years—which makes it easier for candidates to make the significant investment in Harvard-specific methods and for the institution to observe who is really fitting in. The tenure evaluation is more likely to stress factors specific to Harvard, such as course development, and to rely on evaluations from internal faculty. Finally, Harvard has been much more inclined than most schools to hire its own students as faculty, providing a more direct way of ensuring that the faculty "fit" into the organization.

The Wharton School exemplifies the other end of the continuum. It seeks faculty whose work is recognized as excellent. in academic fields such as finance, accounting, and management. Like most business schools, Wharton hires its faculty from the network of Ph.D. programs and competitor schools with similar departments that make up the academic labor market. It is extremely rare that Wharton will hire one of its own Ph.D. students. Indeed, a majority of the tenured professors have been hired away from a faculty position elsewhere. The tenure decision is based largely on evaluations from faculty at other schools as a way of ensuring that successful candidates truly have skills recognized elsewhere. And a shorter tenure clock makes it easier to move faculty in and out, making use of the outside market.

What Wharton gets from its faculty, then, are skills oriented toward academic functional areas. Within the school, departments are organized according to academic fields. And the fact that it is the largest of the major business schools ensures that each department has considerable depth.

Given these different orientations, it is not surprising that the two schools produce different "products"—MBA students with different strengths. Harvard graduates are known for their general management orientation and superior discussion skills, while Wharton graduates have superior analytic skills associated with functional areas. It makes sense, therefore, that companies interested in general talent like McKinsey prefer Harvard's MBAs while those interested in specific skills, like the investment banks, prefer Wharton graduates. In 1992, for example, 26 percent of the Harvard MBA class went into consulting compared with 20 percent at Wharton, while 27 percent of the Wharton class went into commercial and investment banking compared with only 18 percent at Harvard.

Financial Services

The property and casualty section of the insurance industry is based, perhaps more directly than other businesses, on knowledge and skills. The ability to identify and assess risk in unique situations, for example, is the central issue in the business, so it may not be a surprise that employees and the practices used to manage them are at the heart of competencies in this industry.

Yet we find a very wide range of people management practices and policies in the property and casualty business, a range that once again appears to result from different competitive strategies that are driven by different competencies. The two property and casualty firms exemplifying the most marked difference with respect to people management are Chubb and American International Group (A.I.G.). Yet both are among the most profitable firms in the entire insurance business.

Chubb, often described by competitors as the "Cadillac" of its industry, is successful by being the best at what it does. Chubb does not create new markets or drive the ones that it is in through low prices. Instead, in the property business, it tries to find the very best risks that will provide a high return on its premiums. Chubb often goes after customers of other firms who it believes are good risks, identifies "gaps" or problems in their coverage, and offers them superior insurance protection. For both businesses and individuals, Chubb also looks for customers who are willing to pay a premium for superior service that is manifested by intensive customer contact. It has a reputation for being the "insurer of choice" for the very wealthy who are willing to pay a premium for superior service and customer contact.

In short, Chubb earns above-market profits by targeting those customers who will pay some premium for superior products and service and by identifying particularly good risks not spotted by competitors. These competencies—superior underwriting and service—are generated by Chubb's employee management practices.

Chubb makes a substantial investment in its employees, beginning with recruitment. Historically, it has recruited graduates, regardless of major, from the most prestigious undergraduate schools. These candidates, often from the liberal arts, come with the interpersonal and communication skills upon which insurance-specific skills can be built. The recruiters seek out applicants who "look like" Chubb's customers—i.e., who have personal contacts in the monied class and are comfortable with potential customers in that social stratum. New hires participate in several months of intensive training and testing before going to the branch into which they were hired. For the next 6 to 12 months, they work alongside established underwriters in an apprentice-like system.

With this substantial investment in skills, the company goes to great lengths to ensure that the new workers (and their skills) stay around long enough for the investment to be recouped. First, Chubb keeps its underwriters from the boredom of desk jobs, which often produces turnover elsewhere, by making them agents. The fact that underwriters go to the field to do the selling is a key factor in creating Chubb's competency. It eliminates communication problems that might otherwise exist between the sales and underwriting functions. The underwriter gets better information for assessing risks, and also provides customers with better service, including better information about their risks. The superior abilities of the underwriter/agents make it possible to combine these two roles.

Second, Chubb fills vacancies internally, moving people frequently and retraining them for new jobs. The pace of work eventually pushes some people out of the organization, but they rarely go to other insurance companies and more typically become independent agents, helping to expand the network for Chubb's business. And this turnover expands what would otherwise be very limited opportunities for career development in a reasonable stable organization.

American International Group (A.I.G.) achieves its high level of profitability in a different way, but one that also relies on its human resources. A.I.G. is a market maker. It identifies new areas of business, creates new products, and benefits from "first mover" advantages. It was the first insurer allowed into communist China and has recently entered the Russian market. A.I.G. thrives by finding markets where it has little competition, often high-risk operations that competitors avoid. Once companies that compete on price enter its markets, A.I.G. might well move on to another product.

The company's competencies, therefore, are in marketing—identifying new business areas—and in the ability to change quickly. It pursues change with a set of policies that are virtually the mirror opposite of Chubb's. Operating in a highly decentralized manner by creating literally hundreds of subsidiary companies, each targeted to a specific market, it creates new companies to attack new markets and staffs them by hiring experts with industry skills from other firms. It has been known to hire away entire operations from competitors, typically for much higher pay. For example, it hired the head and seven other members of Drexel Burnham Lambert's interest rate swap department in 1987 as part of its move into capital markets.

A.I.G. has little interest in developing commonalities across its companies. The executives in each company are managed through a series of financial targets—with generous rewards for meeting the targets—and are otherwise given considerable autonomy in running the businesses. When a market dries up or tough competition enters the picture, A.I.G. may close shop in that arena. For example, the company's top executives forced out most of the original management team at A.I.G. Global Investors after determining that the profit potential in that market was no longer there. The fact that the company changes markets so quickly would make it difficult to recoup an investment in developing employees with market-specific skills itself, so it relies on the outside labor market instead.

The advantages of speed in attacking markets effectively make other ways of competing difficult. For example, hiring experienced employees away from competitors without offering any real job security means that A.I.G. is paying top dollar to get them, an expense that would make it difficult to compete as a low-cost provider. The reverse argument could be made about Chubb, that the investment in people required to develop the competencies needed to exploit existing markets would be too slow and expensive for attacking new markets as they emerge.

Beyond Direct Services

The link between employees and product market strategy is sometimes less direct when one moves away from services. But there are still relationships between the way employees are managed, the competencies employees help produce, and the way companies compete. Let's consider two examples, one from a service industry that relies heavily on technology, the other from food and beverage manufacturing.

The Shipping Business

It is difficult to find two companies with people management systems that are more different than those at Federal Express and United Parcel Service. FedEx has no union, and its work force is managed using most of the "hot" concepts in contemporary human resource management. The company has pay-for-suggestions systems, quality-of-worklife programs, and a variety of other arrangements to "empower" employees and increase their involvement. The most important of these may be its "Survey-Feedback-Action" program that begins with climate surveys and reviews by subordinates and ends with each work group developing a detailed action plan to address the problems identified by the surveys and reviews.

Employees at FedEx play an important role in helping to design the work organization and the way technology is used, and employee hustle and motivation have helped make FedEx the dominant force in the overnight mail business. As evidence that initiatives paid off, FedEx claimed the honor of being the first service company to win the Malcolm Baldrige National Quality Award.

One of the goals at FedEx is that every employee should be empowered to do whatever is necessary to get a job done. Decentralized authority and the absence of detailed rules would lead to a chaotic pattern of disorganized decisions in the absence of a strong set of common norms and values. FedEx achieves those with an intensive orientation program and communication efforts that include daily information updates broadcast to each of its more than 200 locations. Empowering individual employees also requires that they have the information and skills to make good decisions. FedEx requires that employees pass interactive skills tests every six months. The tests are customized to each location and employee, and the results are tied to a pay-for-skill program.

UPS, on the other hand, has none of these people management practices. Employees have no direct say over work organization matters. Their jobs are designed in excruciating detail, using time-and-motion studies, by a staff of more than 3,000 industrial engineers. Drivers are told, for example, how to carry packages (under their left arm) and even how to fold money (face up). The company measures individual performance against company standards for each task, and assesses employee performance daily. There are no efforts at employee involvement other than collective bargaining over contract terms through the Teamsters' Union. The union at UPS does not appear to be the force maintaining this system of work organization. The initiative on work organization issues has been with management, which has shown little interest in moving toward work systems such as FedEx champions. Indeed, the view from the top of the company has been that virtually all of the company's problems could be addressed by improving the accountability of employees—setting standards for performance and communicating them to workers.

The material rewards for working at UPS are substantial and may, in the minds of employees, more than offset tight supervision and the low level of job enrichment. The company pays the highest wages and benefits in the industry, and it also offers employees gainsharing and stock ownership plans. UPS remains a privately held company owned by its employees. In contrast to FedEx, virtually all promotions (98 percent) are filled from within, offering entry-level drivers excellent long-term prospects for advancement. As a result of these material rewards, UPS employees are also highly motivated and loyal to the company. The productivity of UPS's drivers, the most important work group in the delivery business, is about three times higher (measured by deliveries and packages) than that at FedEx.

Why might it make sense for UPS to rely on highly engineered systems that are generally thought to contribute to poor morale and motivation, and then offset the negative effects with strong material rewards, especially when FedEx offers an alternative model with high levels of morale and motivation and lower material rewards? Differences in technology do not explain it. FedEx is known for its pioneering investments in information systems, but UPS has recently responded with its own wave of computerized operations. Yet the basic organization of work at UPS has not changed.

The employment systems in these two companies are driven by their business strategies. FedEx is much the smaller of the two companies, operating until recently with only one hub in Memphis, and focusing on the overnight package delivery service as its platform product. UPS, in contrast, has a much wider range of products. While its overnight delivery volume is only 60 percent of FedEx's, its total business is nine times as large (11.5 million deliveries per day versus 1.2 million at FedEx).

The scale and scope of UPS's business demand an extremely high level of coordination across its network of delivery hubs, coordination that may be achievable only through highly regimented and standardized job design. The procedures must be very similar, if not identical, across operations if the different delivery products are to move smoothly across a common network that links dozens of hubs.

The highly integrated system at UPS parallels the experience with assembly line production, where workers are closely coupled to each other by the line. The elimination of "buffers" or inventory stocks between work stations associated with just-in-time systems increases the coupling and dictates that the pace at which work flows be the same across all groups, substantially eliminating the scope for autonomy within groups and increasing the need for coordination across groups. The delivery business is like an extreme version of a just-in-time system in that there can be no buffers. A package arrives late from another hub, and it misses its scheduled delivery—clearly a worse outcome even than a temporary break in the flow of an assembly line. And the more points of interchange, the more the need for coordination. Changes in practices and procedures essentially have to be system-wide to be effective. Such coordination is incompatible with significant levels of autonomy of the kind associated with shop floor employee decision making. It is compatible with the system-wide process of collective bargaining, however.

In short, the scale and scope of UPS's business demand a level of coordination that is incompatible with individual employee involvement and a "high commitment" approach. UPS substitutes a system of unusually strong material rewards and performance measurement to provide alternative sources of motivation and commitment. Having historically one hub at FedEx meant that there were fewer coordination problems, allowing considerable scope for autonomy and participation in shaping work decisions at the work group level and more of a "high commitment" approach.

History as Influence

What determines the investments in particular employment practices in the first place is a fascinating question. Often, the differences in practices seem to be associated with the period when the organization was formed. UPS for example, was founded in 1907 when the scientific management model for effective work organization was in full bloom. Federal Express, in contrast, was founded in 1971 when job enrichment and work reform programs were the innovations taught in every major business school. Similarly, companies like Sears (founded in 1886) grew up in the period where top-down, command-and-control systems of work organization dominated American industry. While Nordstrom began as a shoe store in 1901, it did not sell apparel until 1966 and became a major organization some time later, when more decentralized management structures became popular.

In the pairs discussed here, the older companies are the ones with employment practices that invest in their employees. Whether the different practices of the newer member of the pair resulted simply from growing up in a different period (i.e., Federal Express) or from a need to differentiate itself from the more established competitor (i.e., Pepsi), or both is an open question.

Food and Beverages

Few products appear to be more similar than soft drinks, yet "The Cola Wars" that marked the product market competition between Coke and Pepsi show how even organizations with highly similar products can be differentiated by their business strategies.

Coke is the most recognized trademark in the world. First marketed some 70 years before Pepsi, Coke has been a part of American history and culture. In World War I, for example, Coca-Cola set up bottling plants in Europe to supply the U.S. forces. With such enormous market recognition, Coke's business strategy centers on maintaining its position and building on its carefully groomed image. Compared with other companies its size, Coca-Cola owns and operates few ventures besides Coke (especially now that its brief fling with Columbia Pictures is over) and has relatively few bottling franchises with which to deal. Indeed, the largest franchisee, which controls 45 percent of the U.S. market, is owned by Coca-Cola itself.

Given its dominance, the Coke trademark is akin to a proprietary technology, and Coca-Cola's business strategy turns on subtle marketing decisions that build on the trademark's reputation. This is not to suggest that running Coke's business strategy is easy. Rather, the decisions are highly constrained within a framework of past practices and reputation. (One of the reasons that "New Coke" was such a debacle, it can be argued, was that it broke away from the framework represented by Coke's tradition.)

Managing Coca-Cola therefore requires a deep firm-specific understanding and a "feel" for the trademark that cannot be acquired outside the company—or even quickly inside it. What Coke does, then, is build an employment system that both creates those skills and hangs onto them. Coke typically hires college graduates—often liberal arts majors and rarely MBAs—with little or no corporate experience and provides them with intensive training. Jobs at Coke are very secure. Adequate performers can almost count on lifetime employment, and a system of promotion-from-within and seniority-based salary increases provides the carrot that keeps employees from leaving. The internal company culture is often described as family-like. Decision making is very centralized and there is little autonomy and a low tolerance for individual self aggrandizement: No one wants an unsupervised, low-level decision backfiring on the trademark. To reinforce the centralized model, performance is evaluated at the company or division level.

Coca-Cola slowly steeps its new employees in the company culture—in this case, an understanding of the trademark's image. The people management system then ensures that only career Coke managers who have been thoroughly socialized into worrying about the company as a whole get to make decisions affecting the company.

Perhaps the main point in understanding Pepsi is simply that it is not Coke. Pepsi has prospered by seeking out the market niches where Coke is not dominant and then differentiating itself from Coke. From its early position as a price leader ("Twice as Much for a Nickel") to contemporary efforts at finding a "New Generation" of consumers, Pepsi cleans up around the wake left by the Coke trademark.

Pepsi has found new markets by becoming highly diversified. Its fast food operations—Taco Bell, Pizza Hut, Kentucky Fried Chicken—provide proprietary outlets for Pepsi soft drinks. Pepsi markets more aggressively to institutional buyers like hotels and restaurants than does Coke, which is focused on individual consumers. Pepsi also has many more bottling franchises that operate with some autonomy.

Given this strategy of operating in many different markets, Pepsi faces a much more diversified and complicated set of management challenges. It relies on innovative ideas to identify market niches, and it needs the ability to move fast. Its people management system makes this possible. Pepsi hires employees with experience and advanced degrees—high-performing people who bring ideas with them. In particular, Pepsi brings in more advanced technical skills. Once in the company, Pepsi fosters individual competition and a fast-track approach for those who are successful in that competition. The company operates in a much more decentralized fashion with each division given considerable autonomy, and performance is evaluated at the operating and individual levels. The recent restructuring has moved toward further decentralization and introduced the "Sharepower" stock option program designed to push entrepreneurial action down to individual employees.

Pepsi employees have relatively little job security, which is accentuated by the absence of a strong promotion-from-within policy. One Pepsi insider commented: "Whenever anybody is either over 40 or has been in the same Pepsi job for more than four or five years, they tend to be thought of as a little stodgy." In part because of higher turnover, Pepsi employees have significantly less loyalty to the company than do their counterparts at Coke. Indeed, the main issue that unites them, some say, is their desire to "beat Coke."

What Pepsi gets from this system is a continuous flow of new ideas (e.g., from experienced new hires), the ability to change quickly (e.g., hiring and firing), and the means for attacking many different markets in different ways (e.g., decentralized decision making with individual autonomy).

Conclusions

Our paired comparisons uncover clear patterns in the relationships between business strategies and employment practices. Organizations that move quickly to seize new opportunities compete through flexibility and do not develop employee competencies from within. It does not pay to do so. Instead, these organizations rely on the outside market to take in new competencies, individualism to sustain performance, and the outside market to get rid of old competencies. Organizations that compete through their dominance in an established market or niche, on the other hand, rely on organization-specific capabilities developed internally and group-wide coordination.

EXHIBIT 1 HR Competencies and Business Strategies

Business Strategies	HR Competencies: "Outside" Development	HR Competencies: "Inside" Selection
Flexibility	Raiders BCG A.I.G. Pepsi	–
Established Markets/ Niches	–	49ers McKinsey Chubb Coke

Exhibit 1 illustrates the relationship between the way in which human resource competencies are generated and the business strategies that flow from them. The "flexibility" dimension is associated with "prospectors"—companies that seek first-mover advantages in attacking new markets or quick responses to changing customer preferences. The "established markets" category is linked to classifications like "defenders," firms that maintain stable market niches. The most interesting part of the chart is the absence of cases in the off-diagonal quadrants. It is difficult to think of companies with a tradition of internal development that are known for their flexibility in response to markets or ones with reputations for outside hiring that have the kind of proprietary competencies associated with established products and market.

There may well be a natural equilibrium in the marketplace between the flexible and established market firms. Companies like Pepsi and A.I.G. exist in part because they have competitors like Coke and Chubb that do not (perhaps cannot) adapt quickly to new opportunities; similarly, companies like McKinsey succeed because their competitors cannot easily match the depth of competencies and long-term investments that they have established.

One factor that helps sustain this equilibrium is the difficulty in changing strategies. Historical investments in a particular approach create considerable inertia and reputations that, in turn, affect employee selection long after those investments have been exhausted. Going from an "inside" employment strategy to a market or "outside" approach, and in turn from the "established market" to the "flexibility" quadrant in business strategy, can probably be done more easily than the reverse (i.e., discarding the firm-specific assets and going to the market for new ones).

General Electric under Jack Welch may represent one of the more successful attempts to make such a change in HR competencies and in business strategy, and even there it has taken about a decade. It is very difficult, however, to find examples of mature firms that have gone from a market approach to an inside employment strategy. Start-up firms and those that are growing rapidly have no choice but to rely on a market approach to get staff, and some of these firms eventually switch to an inside strategy. But that is not the same as the transition from outside to inside for mature firms.

The fact that employment practices are so difficult to change and transfer helps explain the basic notion that core competencies should drive business strategy and not vice versa: It may be easier to find a new business strategy to go with one's existing practices and competencies than to develop new practices and competencies to go with a new strategy.

Companies that secure skills and competencies in the outside market, on the other hand, are pursuing a strategy that is not difficult to reproduce. And if these competencies are in fact available to everyone on the open market, how can they generate a unique competency and competitive advantage for any one firm? One answer is that a firm may be better at spotting talent on the open market or at managing that talent than are those competitors that are also trying to secure skills and competencies directly from the market. The Raiders' player management, for example, has been particularly good at incorporating and accommodating talented players who have trouble playing effectively under other systems. The fact that BCG is able to hire new consultants at salaries somewhat below those of its leading competitors suggests a competency in recruiting—an ability to identify underpriced talent and/or job characteristics that substitute for salary.

The Need for Change

The increase in the need for flexibility and change, pressures that virtually all firms feel, may be exacting a toll on employers that develop their own competencies. Competitive pressures may be pushing more of them toward the "outside"/"flexibility" quadrant. UPS, for example, did not mount an overnight delivery business until 1982, despite 10 years of lessons from FedEx that customers would pay almost twice as much for it. It also delayed automating its operations until 1986. It was also slow to develop modern computer and information systems because it did not have the skills in-house to build them and no experience in getting such skills on the outside.

A portion of IBM's recent troubles has been attributed to its inability to respond to changing markets, due in part to a lack of new talent and ideas from the outside. Sears' high-quality but high-cost sales force became a disadvantage when it confronted competition from low-cost discounters that sold reliable brand-name products. Its delay in restructuring its operations despite a decade of decline has been attributed in part to inbred management. Companies like Coca-Cola and McKinsey have begun to take in more talent from the outside, and schools like Wharton that traditionally supplied functional skills have changed curricula to ensure that their graduates are broader and more flexible. The increased need for flexibility may erode the market niches mined by firms with high competencies and specific skills like Chubb. Perhaps these firms will find lower cost ways of creating the necessary competencies in the future, possibly assembling them from the outside market.

Whether firms with highly skilled, broadly trained employees can be more flexible in their product markets than firms that hire-and-fire to change their competencies is an important empirical question. The former may well be better at creating flexibility within their current product market (e.g., "quick response" or customized production) although the latter may achieve more flexibility in moving across product markets.

Public policy discussions about changing employment practices in the nation as a whole—increased levels of employer investment in skills or introducing "high performance" systems of work organization—must be thought through very carefully in light of the above arguments. Mandated changes in employment practices could well alter the competencies of organizations and their business strategies. Some might argue that changing business strategies is a desirable outcome. The constraints on dismissing employees in European countries, for example, encourage investments in existing employees and, it is argued, shift production toward the higher quality (and higher cost) markets that make use of higher skills. But they may also drive out of business firms that rely on first-mover advantages based on very high levels of internal flexibility. The fact that distinctive ways of competing appear to be driven by competencies and capabilities that are created by unique sets of employee management practices helps explain the long-standing puzzle noted earlier: Why is there so much variance in management practices? Even practices that appear to have been demonstrated to be "best" in some firms never seem to sweep over the business community as a whole.

None of this suggests, of course, that all practices are equally good. For practices that are not central to an organization's core competency, there may indeed be best practices that clearly cut across firms; for companies with similar business strategies, hence similar core competencies, it may also be possible to identify management practices that dominate others—"lean production" among auto assemblers, for example. But it should come as no surprise that variety in employment practices, as in other aspects of life, can be a source of distinctiveness and competitive advantage.

Source: Organizational Dynamics, Winter 1996, pp. 7–22.

SELECTED BIBLIOGRAPHY

Resource-based arguments in the strategy field suggest that the source of competitive advantage lies within the firm, not in how it positions itself with respect to the market. See Robert M. Grant, "The Resource-Based Theory of Competitive Advantage: Implications for Strategy Formation," *California Management Review*, Vol. 33, 1993. Among the most influential of the resource-based arguments has been C. K. Prahalad and G. Hamel, "The Core Competence of the Corporation," *Harvard Business Review*, May–June 1990, which suggests that the key resource of a firm lies on the procedural side. Several articles document differences in human resource practices among otherwise similar firms. One of the most interesting of these sees the differences as relating to business strategies: Jeffrey B. Arthur, "The Link Between Business Strategy and Industrial Relations Systems in American Steel Minimills," *Industrial and Labor Relations Review*, Vol. 45, 1992.

Among more behaviorally oriented research, many studies find that the process of selection may create distinctive organizational characteristics. See Ben Schneider, "The People Make the Place," *Personnel Psychology*, Vol. 40, 1987.

Evidence about the organizations described in this article often included published material. Interesting evidence explaining the link between employment strategies and business needs at Sears is reported in Dave Ulrich, Richard Halbrook, Dave Meder, Mark Stuchlik, and Steve Thorpe, "Employee and Customer Attachment: Synergies for Competitive Advantage," *Human Resource Planning*, Vol. 41, 1992. Complete references for the company material presented in this paper are available from the authors.

READING 4.2

Employee Engagement and Commitment

Robert J. Vance

Employee Engagement First

[No] company, small or large, can win over the long run without energized employees who believe in the [firm's] mission and understand how to achieve it. That's why you need to take the measure of employee engagement at least once a year through anonymous surveys in which people feel completely safe to speak their minds.

Jack and Suzy Welch

Employees who are engaged in their work and committed to their organizations give companies crucial competitive advantages—including higher productivity and lower employee turnover. Thus, it is not surprising that organizations of all sizes and types have invested substantially in policies and practices that foster engagement and commitment in their workforces. Indeed, in identifying the three best measures of a company's health, business consultant and former General Electric CEO Jack Welch recently cited employee engagement first, with customer satisfaction and free cash flow coming in second and third, respectively.[1] "Reaping Business Results at Caterpillar" and "Engagement Pays Off at Molson Coors Brewing Company" show two examples of companies that benefited from enhancing engagement and commitment.

Reaping Business Results at Caterpillar

Construction-equipment maker Caterpillar has garnered impressive results from its employee engagement and commitment initiatives, including:

- $8.8 million annual savings from decreased attrition, absenteeism and overtime (European plant)
- a 70% increase in output in less than four months (Asia Pacific plant)
- a decrease in the break-even point by almost 50% in units/day, and a decrease in grievances by 80% (unionized plant)
- a $2 million increase in profit and a 34% increase in highly satisfied customers (start-up plant)

Engagement Pays Off at Molson Coors Brewing Company

At beverage giant Molson Coors, engaged employees were five times less likely than nonengaged employees to have a safety incident and seven times less likely to have a lost-time safety incident. Moreover, the average cost of a safety incident for engaged employees was $63, compared with an average of $392 for nonengaged employees. By strengthening employee engagement, the company saved $1,721,760 in safety costs during 2002. Engagement also improved sales performance at Molson Coors: Low-engagement teams fell far behind engaged teams in 2005 sales volumes. In addition, the difference in performance-related costs of low- vs. high-engagement teams totaled $2,104,823.

But what are employee engagement and commitment, exactly? This report examines the ways in which employers and corporate consultants define these terms today, and offers ideas for strengthening employee engagement. Though different organizations define *engagement* differently, some common themes emerge. These themes include employees' satisfaction with their work and pride in their employer, the extent to which people enjoy and believe in what they do for work and the perception that their employer values what they bring to the table. The greater an employee's engagement, the more likely he or she is to "go the extra mile" and deliver excellent on-the-job performance. In addition, engaged employees may be more likely to commit to staying with their current organization. Software giant Intuit,[2] for example, found that highly engaged employees are 1.3 times more likely to be high performers than less engaged employees. They are also five times less likely to voluntarily leave the company.

Clearly, engagement and commitment can potentially translate into valuable business results for an organization. To help you reap the benefits of an engaged, committed workforce at your organization, this report provides guidelines for understanding and measuring employee engagement, and for designing and implementing effective engagement initiatives. As you will see, everyday human resource practices such as recruitment, training, performance management and workforce surveys can provide powerful levers for enhancing engagement.

Employee Engagement: Key Ingredients

"Employee Engagement Defined" shows examples of engagement definitions used by various corporations and consultancies. Clearly, definitions of employee engagement vary greatly across organizations. Many managers wonder how such an elusive concept can be quantified. The term does

Employee Engagement Defined

CORPORATIONS

Caterpillar

Engagement is the extent of employees' commitment, work effort, and desire to stay in an organization.

Dell Inc.

Engagement: To compete today, companies need to win over the MINDS (rational commitment) and the HEARTS (emotional commitment) of employees in ways that lead to extraordinary effort.

Intuit, Inc.[3]

Engagement describes how an employee thinks and feels about, and acts toward his or her job, the work experience and the company.

CONSULTANTS and RESEARCHERS

Corporate Leadership Council

Engagement: The extent to which employees commit to something or someone in their organization, how hard they work and how long they stay as a result of that commitment.

Development Dimensions International

Engagement is the extent to which people enjoy and believe in what they do, and feel valued for doing it.

The Gallup Organization

Employee engagement is the involvement with and enthusiasm for work.

Hewitt Associates

Engagement is the state of emotional and intellectual commitment to an organization or group producing behavior that will help fulfill an organization's promises to customers - and, in so doing, improve business results.

Engaged employees:

- Stay - They have an intense desire to be a part of the organization and they stay with that organization;
- Say - They advocate for the organization by referring potential employees and customers, are positive with co-workers and are constructive in their criticism;
- Strive - They exert extra effort and engage in behaviors that contribute to business success.

Institute for Employment Studies[4]

Engagement: A positive attitude held by the employee toward the organization and its values. An engaged employee is aware of business context, and works with colleagues to improve performance within the job for the benefit of the organization. The organization must work to develop and nurture engagement, which requires a two-way relationship between employer and employee.

Kenexa

Engagement is the extent to which employees are motivated to contribute to organizational success, and are willing to apply discretionary effort (extra time, brainpower and effort) to accomplishing tasks that are important to the achievement of organizational goals.

Towers Perrin

Engagement is the extent to which employees put discretionary effort into their work, beyond the required minimum to get the job done, in the form of extra time, brainpower or energy.

encompass several ingredients for which researchers have developed measurement techniques. These ingredients include the degree to which employees fully occupy themselves in their work, as well as the strength of their commitment to the employer and role. Fortunately, there is much research on these elements of engagement—work that has deep roots in individual and group psychology. The sections following highlight some of these studies.

Occupying the Job

Psychologist William Kahn[5] drew on studies of work roles[6] and organizational socialization[7] to investigate the degrees to which people "occupy" job roles. He used the terms "personal engagement" and "personal disengagement" to represent two ends of a continuum. At the "personal engagement" end, individuals fully occupy themselves—physically, intellectually and emotionally—in their work role. At the "personal disengagement" end, they uncouple themselves and withdraw from the role.

How do people become personally engaged in their work activities? Why do they become more engaged in some activities than others? Scholars have proposed answers to these questions based on their studies of the psychology of commitment.

Committing to the Work and the Company

Some experts define *commitment* as both a willingness to persist in a course of action and reluctance to change plans, often owing to a sense of obligation to stay the course. People are simultaneously committed to multiple entities, such as economic, educational, familial, political and religious institutions.[8,9] They also commit themselves to specific individuals, including their spouses, children, parents and siblings, as well as to their employers, co-workers, supervisors and customers.

Commitment manifests itself in distinct behavior. For example, people devote time and energy to fulfill their on-the-job responsibilities as well as their family, personal, community and spiritual obligations. Commitment also has an emotional component: People usually experience and express positive feelings toward an entity or individual to whom they have made a commitment.[10] Finally, commitment has a rational element: Most people consciously decide to make commitments, then they thoughtfully plan and carry out the actions required to fulfill them.[11]

Because commitments require an investment of time as well as mental and emotional energy, most people make them with the expectation of reciprocation. That is, people assume that in exchange for their commitment, they will get something of value in return—such as favors, affection, gifts, attention, goods, money and property. In the world of work, employees and employers have traditionally made a tacit agreement: In exchange for workers' commitment, organizations would provide forms of value for employees, such as secure jobs and fair compensation. Reciprocity affects the intensity of a commitment. When an entity or individual to whom someone has made a commitment fails to come through with the expected exchange, the commitment erodes.

Dramatic changes in the global economy over the past 25 years have had significant implications for commitment and reciprocity between employers and employees—and thus for employee engagement. For example, increasing global competition, scarce and costly resources, high labor costs, consumer demands for ever-higher quality and investor pressures for greater returns on equity have prompted organizations to restructure themselves. At some companies, restructuring has meant reductions in staff and in layers of management.

Employee Engagement Survey Items: Samples

DELL

- Even if I were offered a comparable position with similar pay and benefits at another company, I would stay at Dell.
- Considering everything, Dell is the right place for me.

DEVELOPMENT DIMENSIONS INTERNATIONAL

- My job provides me with chances to grow and develop.
- I find personal meaning and fulfillment in my work.
- I get sufficient feedback about how well I am doing.

INSTITUTE FOR EMPLOYMENT STUDIES[12]

- A positive attitude toward, and pride in, the organization.
- A willingness to behave altruistically and be a good team player.
- An understanding of the bigger picture and a willingness to go beyond the requirements of the job.

INTUIT[13]

- I am proud to work for Intuit.
- I would recommend Intuit as a great place to work.
- I am motivated to go "above and beyond" what is expected of me in my job.

TOWERS PERRIN

- I am willing to put in a great deal of effort beyond what is normally expected to help my organization succeed.
- I understand how my role in my organization is related to my organization's overall goals, objectives and direction.
- My organization inspires me to do my best work.

Although restructuring helps organizations compete, these changes have broken the traditional psychological employment "contract" and its expectations of reciprocity. Employees have realized that they can no longer count on working for a single employer long enough to retire. And with reduced expectations of reciprocity, workers have felt less commitment to their employers. Many companies, having broken both formal and psychological employment agreements, are struggling to craft effective strategies for reviving employees' commitment and thereby revitalizing their engagement.

10 Common Themes: How Companies Measure Engagement

Employers typically assess their employees' engagement levels with company-wide attitude or opinion surveys. (See "Employee-Engagement Survey Items: Samples" on page 5.) A sampling of the criteria featured in such instruments reveals 10 common themes related to engagement:

- Pride in employer
- Satisfaction with employer
- Job satisfaction
- Opportunity to perform well at challenging work
- Recognition and positive feedback for one's contributions
- Personal support from one's supervisor
- Effort above and beyond the minimum
- Understanding the link between one's job and the organization's mission
- Prospects for future growth with one's employer
- Intention to stay with one's employer

This broad array of concepts has come to be labeled *employee engagement* by virtue of *linkage research*, which relates survey results to bottom-line financial outcomes. (See "About Linkage Research.") Workforce surveys will be covered in greater detail later in this report.

About Linkage Research

Psychologist Benjamin Schneider and colleagues in 1980 developed linkage research to show that employee perceptions of service to customers correlate highly with customers' evaluations of service quality.

Linkage analysts:

- Aggregate employee-opinion survey responses at the business-unit level (summarizing by averaging across survey respondents)
- Statistically correlate aggregated employee-opinion survey responses with measures of business outcomes, such as sales volume, profitability, customer loyalty, employee safety, attendance and retention.

Employee-engagement survey items are those having the strongest correlations with business results.

The Link Between Employer Practices and Employee Engagement

How does an engaged workforce generate valuable business results for an organization? The process starts with employer practices such as job and task design, recruitment, selection, training, compensation, performance management and career development. Such practices affect employees' level of engagement as well as job performance. Performance and engagement then interact to produce business results. Figure 1 depicts these relationships.

FIGURE 1 Employer Practices Ultimately Influence Business Results

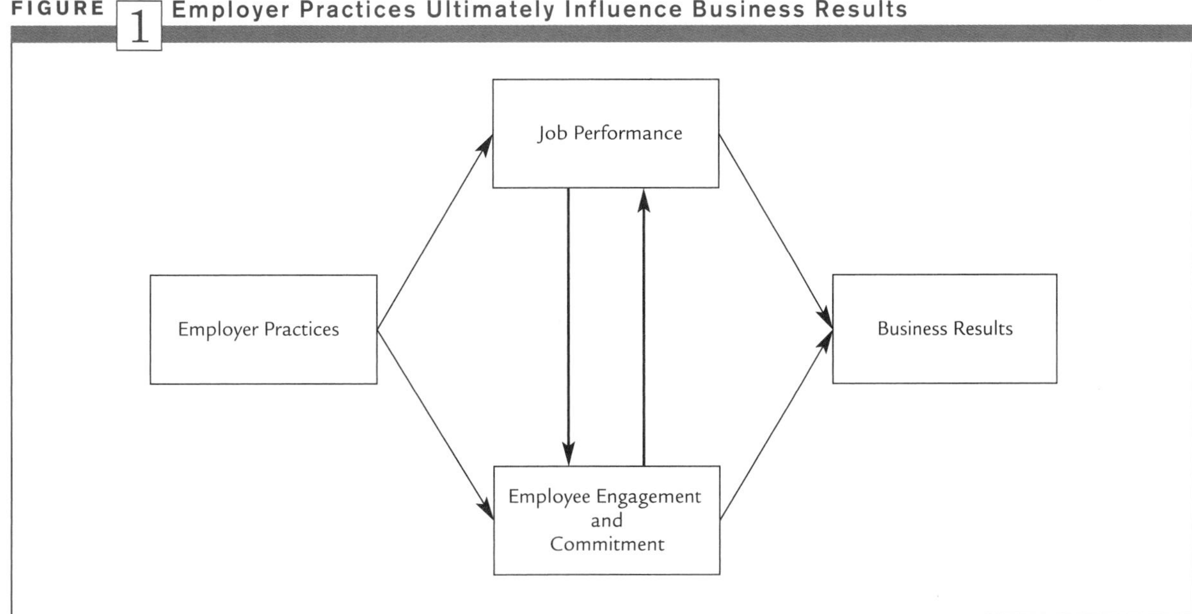

Think about what engagement and commitment mean in your own organization. To help you get started, review the questions in "Food for Thought" below.

Food for Thought

Employee Commitment

- How do you and other managers in your organization define commitment?
- Are some employees in your company engaged in their work but not committed to the organization? Committed to staying with your firm but not exactly engaged in their work? Both engaged and committed?
- To whom are your organization's employees committed? The company? Their supervisor? Co-workers? Team members? Customers?
- What business results has commitment from employees created for your organization? For example, has commitment reduced turnover and, therefore, decreased recruitment, hiring and training costs?
- What does your company do to reciprocate employees' commitment? Is the organization living up to its side of the bargain?

Employee Engagement

- How do you and other managers in your organization define employee engagement?
- How do you know that certain employees in your company are engaged? Do they relish their jobs? Enjoy specific responsibilities or tasks? Willingly "go the extra mile"?
- In teams, departments or business units in your company that have a large number of engaged employees, what business results are you seeing? Higher productivity? Lower costs? Greater revenues? More efficiency? Lower turnover? Higher product or service quality?
- Conversely, how do disengaged employees behave, and what are the consequent costs for their teams, unitsand your entire company?

To engage workers as well as to benefit from that engagement, your organization must invest in its human resource practices. But just like other investments, you need to consider potential return—that is, to devote resources to the HR practices you believe will generate "the biggest bang" for your investment "buck." You must weigh how much engagement and commitment your company wants—and at what cost. Below, we review employer practices that affect employee engagement and commitment and examine ways to manipulate these "levers" to influence engagement or commitment or both.

To shed light on the ways in which employer practices affect job performance and engagement, Figure 2 presents a simple job performance model.[14]

As Figure 2 suggests, a person possesses attributes such as knowledge, skills, abilities, temperament, attitudes and personality. He or she uses these attributes to accomplish work behaviors according to organization-defined procedures, by applying tools, equipment and/or technology. Work behaviors, in turn, create the products and services that make an organization successful. We classify work behaviors into three categories: those required to accomplish duties and tasks specified in a job description (*prescribed* behaviors), "extra" behaviors that an employee contributes for the good of the organization (*voluntary* behaviors), and behaviors prohibited by an employer (*proscribed* behaviors, including unexcused absenteeism, stealing and other counterproductive or illegal actions).[15] Of course, job performance occurs in an organizational context, which includes elements such as leadership, physical setting and social setting.

Employers naturally want to encourage workers to perform prescribed and voluntary activities while avoiding proscribed ones. To achieve these goals, organizations use a number of HR practices that directly affect the person, process and context components of job performance. Employees' reactions to these practices determine their levels of engagement and commitment. Next we examine several such practices in greater detail.

Job and Task Design

Over the past 250 years, the nature of work and employment has evolved through a series of stages. Initially, craftspeople and laborers worked on farms and in workshops. Then cottage industries arose, in which suppliers assembled goods and products for companies that marketed them. Later, people worked for companies in increasingly formalized employment relationships. And today, the world of work is characterized by flat and agile organizations that outsource production of goods and services on a global scale.[16]

Likewise, the nature of job and task design also has evolved.[17] For example, with the advent of mass production in the early part of the 20th century, many American companies adopted the "scientific management" approach to work design. Through scientific management, companies simplified tasks to be performed by highly specialized, narrowly trained workers.[18] Though this system enhanced efficiency, it also exacted costs: Workers—unhappy with routine, machine-paced jobs that afforded little personal control or autonomy—felt dissatisfied with their work, were often absent, and left employers in search of more meaningful employment.[19] In short, fitting jobs to efficient production systems disengaged employees and eroded their commitment.

Workers' negative responses to job design in early 20th century America spurred organizational scientists to examine the human component of work more closely. By the 1950s, several theories of job satisfaction and work motivation had emerged that related to job design, particularly the beneficial effects of *job enlargement* (broadening the scope of job tasks)

FIGURE 2 A Job Performance Model

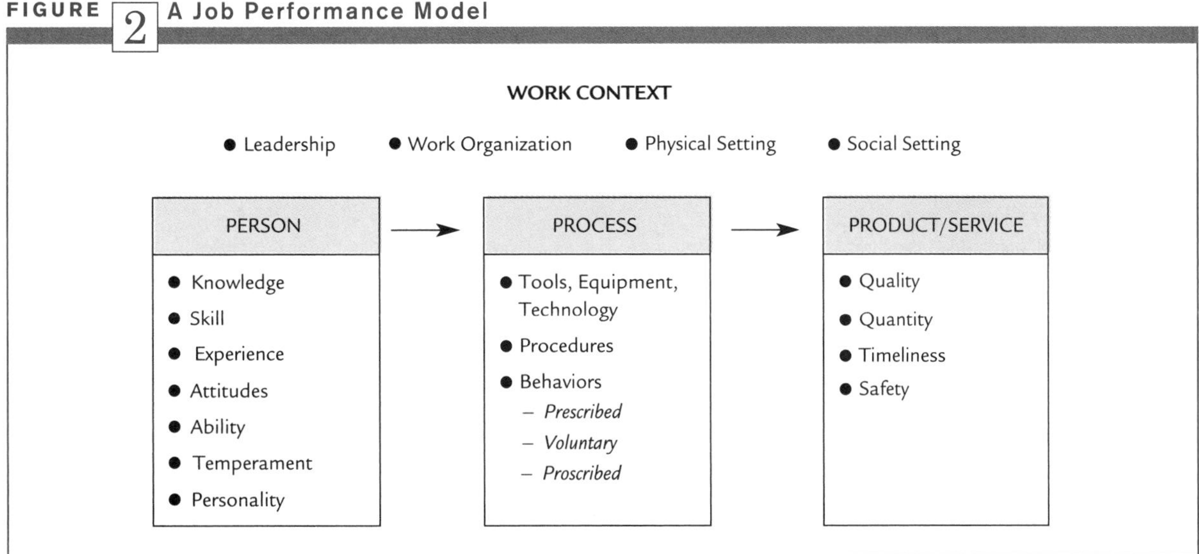

and *job enrichment* (providing more complex and challenging tasks).[20]

With publication of the *job characteristics* model in the early 1970s, interest in the impact of job design on worker motivation and productivity intensified.[21] This model proposed five "core" or motivational job characteristics: skill variety, task identity, task significance (which collectively contribute to a sense of work meaningfulness), autonomy and performance feedback.[22] Jobs that have these characteristics promote internal motivation, personal responsibility for performance and job satisfaction—in short, engagement. The job characteristics model became so widely accepted by management scientists that comparatively few studies of work design and motivation have been published in recent years.[23]

As employers broadened the scope of job responsibilities in flatter organizations with less management oversight, researchers also began looking at the social characteristics of work, including interdependence of job roles, feedback from others and opportunities to get advice and support from coworkers.[24] Analysis of work-design research revealed that social characteristics strongly influence both employee engagement and commitment.

In addition, researchers have recently begun investigating job enrichment's relationship to proactive work behaviors—those self-initiated "extra" contributions noted in many engagement definitions.[25,26] Findings show that managers who provide enriched work (jobs that are high in meaningfulness, variety, autonomy and co-worker trust) stimulate engagement and enthusiasm in their employees. In turn, engagement and enthusiasm encourage employees to define their work roles broadly. Broad definition of job roles then enhances workers' willingness to take ownership of challenges that lie beyond their immediate assigned tasks. These challenges inspire people to innovate and to solve problems proactively. Thus, job enrichment promotes engagement in both prescribed *and* voluntary work activities. Although somewhat preliminary, these studies shed valuable light on how your organization might design work to inspire employee engagement and commitment. "The Power of Job Enrichment" captures key lessons from this research.

The Power of Job Enrichment

TO INCREASE ENGAGEMENT

Imbue jobs with:

- meaningfulness
- variety
- autonomy
- co-worker support

With job enrichment, employee performance on prescribed tasks improves. Workers define their role more broadly—and willingly take on tasks outside their formal job description.

TO ENHANCE COMMITMENT

Demonstrate reciprocity by providing employees with opportunities for personal development.

Increasing
- knowledge
- skills
- experience
- expertise

BUILDS

Increasing
- self-efficacy
- self-esteem
- employer commitment

Recruiting

The messages your organization conveys while seeking to attract job applicants also can influence future employees' engagement and commitment. If your firm has designed jobs specifically to engage employees, then you'll want to ensure that recruiting ads extol these positions' attractive features—such as challenging work assignments, a highly skilled team environment or minimal supervision. Applicants who notice and respond to these ads will more likely be motivated by these features.

Also consider how you might best seek candidates from inside your organization. When you recruit existing employees for desirable jobs, you enhance their engagement (by maximizing the person-job fit) *and* commitment (by providing growth and advancement opportunities to employees in return for their loyalty). If you recruit from outside when qualified internal candidates are available, you may unwittingly suggest to current employees that your company is not willing to reciprocate their commitment. Existing staff may then begin questioning their own commitment to your firm.

By contrast, you recruit external candidates to both the job and your organization. For these candidates, ensure that recruiting messages highlight attractive job features, organizational values and commitment reciprocity. That is, in return for performance and dedication, your company offers competitive pay and benefits, flexible work hours and learning and career advancement opportunities.

Also remember that prospective employees have multiple commitments: You will inevitably have to compete with those commitments as you try to attract candidates to your firm. Most people find it easier to make a new commitment when it is compatible with their other obligations. For example, you boost your chances of recruiting a highly qualified candidate who is a single parent if you offer flexible work hours, family health benefits and on-site day care. "Recruiting for Engagement and Commitment" captures some of the principles discussed above.

Recruiting for Engagement and Commitment

TO INCREASE ENGAGEMENT

Target qualified applicants likely to find the work interesting and challenging.

Send recruiting messages that:

- Extol attractive job features to enhance person-job fit.
- Encourage those who are not suited to the work to self-select out.

TO INCREASE COMMITMENT

For internal candidates

Send recruiting messages that:

- Emphasize possibilities of movement/promotion to more desirable jobs, to signal commitment reciprocity.

For external candidates

Send recruiting messages that:

- Highlight the employer side of the exchange relationship-pay and benefits, advancement opportunities, flexible work hours.
- Recognize and address commitment congruence (e.g., work-family balance.)
- Encourage those who are not suited to the organization to self-select out.

Employee Selection

Once your recruiting efforts produce a pool of promising job candidates, you select among them to fill available positions. When you select the right individuals for the right jobs, your new hires carry out their work more smoothly and experience fewer performance problems.[27] The result? Greater enjoyment of—and engagement in—the job. (For more information on implementing formal assessments, see the SHRM Foundation's "Selection Assessment Methods"[28] by Elaine Pulakos.)

To enhance engagement through your selection of employees, identify those candidates who are best-suited to the job *and* your organization's culture. Also use candidate-assessment methods that have obvious relevance to the job in question—for example, by asking interviewees what they know about the role and having them provide work samples. Most candidates will view these techniques more positively than tests with less apparent relevance, such as personality and integrity assessments.[29] Successful candidates feel good about having "passed the test," and see your company as careful and capable for having selected them. A positive initial impression of an employer encourages growth of long-term commitment. "Effective Employee Selection" summarizes lessons from this section.

Effective Employee Selection

TO INCREASE ENGAGEMENT

Select the right individuals for the right jobs.

Choose candidates most likely to:

- Perform prescribed job duties well.
- Contribute voluntary behaviors.
- Avoid proscribed activities

TO INCREASE COMMITMENT

- Present selection hurdles that are relevant to the job in question. Successful candidates will feel good about surmounting such hurdles to land the job.
- Create a positive first impression of your company's competence. You will set the stage for growth of long-term commitment.

Training and Development

Training and development can serve as additional levers for enhancing engagement and commitment. For new hires, training usually begins with orientation. Orientation presents several important opportunities—including explaining pay, work schedules and company policies. Most important, it gives you a chance to encourage employee engagement by explaining how the new hire's job contributes to the organization's mission. Through orientation, you describe how your company is organized, introduce the new employee to his or her co-workers, give the person a tour of the area where he or she will be working and explain safety regulations and other procedural matters. In short, you foster person-organization fit—vital for developing productive and dedicated employees.

Through training, you help new and current employees acquire the knowledge and skills they need to perform their jobs. And employees who enhance their skills through training are more likely to engage fully in their work, because they derive satisfaction from mastering new tasks. Training also enhances employees' value to your company as well as their own employability in the job market. In addition, most companies offer higher wages for skilled workers, to compensate them for their greater value and to discourage turnover.

If your company is reluctant to invest in training, consider demonstrating to executives the links between training investments, employee engagement and measurable business results.

To get the most from your training investments, also explore how you might leverage digital technology and the Internet. Whereas companies once had to deliver training to employees in the same place at the same time, you can now use technology to offer self-paced and individualized instruction for employees in far-flung locations. Such training not only reduces your company's travel expenses; it also helps employees to manage their other commitments, such as family obligations. Consequently, their commitment to your organization increases.

"Training and Development" summarizes key lessons from this section.

Compensation

Like the HR practices discussed above, compensation can powerfully influence employee engagement and commitment. Some compensation components encourage commitment to employers, while others motivate engagement in the job. It is possible to stimulate one and not the other, though it's generally better to foster both. For example, a company that offers a strong performance incentive system but no retirement plan will probably realize exceptional engagement from its workers; however, they may eventually commit themselves to another company that does offer a good retirement plan. Meanwhile, an organization that offers generous retirement benefits but a traditional seniority-based pay grade system may have committed employees; however, these workers might deliver pedestrian performance as they bide their time until retirement. In designing compensation plans, you therefore need to consider employee engagement and commitment strategically.

Compensation consists of financial elements (pay and benefits) but may also include nonfinancial elements or perks, such as on-site day care, employee assistance programs, subsidized cafeterias, travel discounts, company picnics and so on. The most effective compensation plans support your organization's strategic objectives. For example, if your company's strategy hinges on innovation, then your compensation system should encourage and reward risk-taking. A well-designed compensation plan gives your organization a competitive advantage. How? It helps you attract the best job candidates, motivate them to perform to their maximum potential and retain them for the long term.

Training and Development

TO INCREASE ENGAGEMENT

Provide employee orientation to establish:

- The employer-employee exchange relationship.
- Understanding of how the job contributes to the organization's mission.

Offer skill development to enhance:

- Performance.
- Satisfaction.
- Self-efficacy.

Provide training to encourage prescribed and voluntary performance.

TO ENHANCE COMMITMENT

Signal commitment reciprocity by:

- Your investments in training.
- Modes of training delivery that accommodate employees' other commitments.

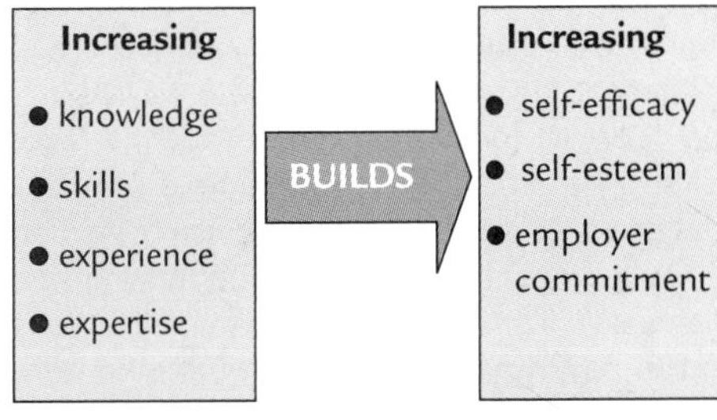

Incentive pay, also known as pay-for-performance, can directly influence employees' productivity (and thus their engagement) as well as their commitment to your organization (as workers learn to trust that they will be rewarded for good performance). Piecework, annual bonuses, merit raises and sales commissions are familiar examples of incentive pay that rewards individual performance. You can also tie incentive pay to team or work group performance, and to organization-wide results through profit sharing, gain-sharing, and employee stock ownership plans. Most employees are motivated by financial incentives and will exert greater effort to produce more if the incentives your company offers make it worthwhile to do so.

The caveat with incentive plans, of course, is that you must first define and measure performance and then decide which aspects of performance you will tie to pay. Because incentive-plan programs can present a heavy administrative burden, many companies opt to reward performance that is easiest to quantify. But this approach can have unintended—and undesirable—consequences. For example, if you pay people based on how many units of a product they assemble per hour, you may encourage quantity at the expense of quality: Employess assemble the units as fast as they can in order to get the incentive pay, regardless of whether they're making mistakes along the way. The challenge in using incentive plans is to reward the results most important to your organization—even if those results are relatively difficult to quantify. You also need to encourage employees' willingness to "go the extra mile" rather than just doing the minimum to reap a reward. To that end, you may want to combine financial incentives and recognition-based awards to foster the full range of performance your organization needs to stay competitive.

You might also consider competency-based (or skill-based) pay, which has grown more popular in recent years. Through competency-based pay, you reward employees not only for mastering job-relevant knowledge and skills but also for using those abilities to produce results that your organization values. This type of pay can increase engagement by fostering employees' pride in their new mastery. And it can enhance commitment because workers learn that the company is willing to help them burnish their employability.

Many companies also offer retirement plans as part of their compensation package. Although these plans are usually available to all full-time employees, the specific plans offered may depend on job, year hired, number of years employed, highest salary achieved and so on. As we've seen, well-designed and secure retirement plans can encourage long-term commitment to your organization.

In designing financial forms of compensation, consider employees' sensitivity to equity. Will they perceive compensation as commensurate with their contributions? As fair compared to pay earned by co-workers performing the same or similar jobs? Fair compared to what other jobs in the organization pay? Reasonable given what other employers are paying for the same work? Perceived inequity can cause employees to disengage and reexamine their commitment to your firm. They may ask for a raise, seek employment elsewhere or stop striving so hard to deliver top-notch results. And none of these outcomes benefits your organization.

"Strategic Compensation" distills some of the key points from this section.

Strategic Compensation

TO INCREASE ENGAGEMENT:

- **Equitable exchange:** Motivates willingness to contribute prescribed and voluntary performance, and to avoid proscribed behaviors.
- **Pay-for-performance:** Focuses employees' attention on incentivized behaviors—but be careful how you define performance.
- **Competency-based pay:** Fosters acquisition of knowledge and skill and enhance employees' performance, satisfaction and self-efficacy.

TO ENHANCE COMMITMENT:

- **Competitive pay:** Attracts qualified job candidates.
- **Equitable exchange:** Signals commitment reciprocity.
- **Flexible benefits and perks:** Facilitates commitment congruence (e.g., work-family balance matched to stage of life).
- **Retirement and seniority-graded pay plans:** Fosters long-term commitment and identification with your company.

Performance Management

The right performance management practices also can enhance employee engagement and commitment. (See the SHRM Foundation's report on "Performance Management"[30] by Elaine Pulakos for information on creating an effective system.) To design your performance management system, begin by linking job objectives to organizational objectives. What are your organization's priorities, and how will each employee help to achieve them? What results does your organization expect employees to produce? How might you help managers throughout your organization to communicate performance expectations and goals to their direct reports?

Encourage managers to include employees in the goal-setting process. This technique helps to ensure that workers understand the goals. It also promotes acceptance of challenging objectives, because people generally feel more committed to goals they have helped define.

In addition, consider how you and other managers will recognize and encourage contributions that exceed expectations. For example, when a piece of equipment malfunctions, Joe finds other ways to maintain production rather than merely shutting down the machine and waiting for the maintenance staff to fix it. Or when a less experienced co-worker encounters a new task, Sally offers friendly coaching, instead of standing by and waiting for the inevitable mistakes to crop up.

Performance management processes operate on a continuous basis. Therefore, they provide perhaps the best ongoing opportunities for employers to foster employee engagement and commitment. For example, managers can use routine discussions about performance and feedback sessions to learn which aspects of the job hold the most interest for each employee and which tasks are most challenging. During such discussions, managers also can define what "going above and beyond the call of duty" looks like and generate ideas for rewarding such contributions.

An employee's aspirations and career goals can receive careful attention during performance appraisal meetings. Without inquiring into an employee's personal life, a supervisor can nevertheless explore ways to enhance the compatibility between the worker's commitment to your organization and the employee's other life commitments. Through such means, the organization personalizes its relationship to each employee and provides support, while also expressing appreciation for their contributions—key drivers of engagement and commitment.

To further engage employees and win their commitment through your performance management programs, consider how to treat your organization's most experienced employees. In many cases, these employees understand the intricacies of a job better than their supervisors or managers do. By virtue of long identification with your organization, they may be deeply committed to high-level goals. They use their expertise to contribute in ways that newer employees simply cannot match. But many of them also may be planning to retire soon, especially if they are from the "Baby Boomer" generation. How will you transfer their knowledge to younger workers? Design a performance management system that recognizes and rewards proactive sharing of knowledge and expertise among co-workers. For example, create knowledge repositories or learning histories that can be stored in databases that employees can access, and then create incentives for people who contribute to and use these repositories.

Of course, effective performance management systems also identify employees who are not meeting expectations. Failing to address problem performance can erode other employees' engagement and commitment, as their workloads increase and they conclude that the company is willing to tolerate poor performance. If feedback, coaching and remedial training are of little avail, the manager may need to move the person to a different position within the company where he or she can make a more valuable contribution, or let the individual go if there is no good match elsewhere in the organization.

"Effective Performance Management" lists key points from this section.

Effective Performance Management

TO INCREASE ENGAGEMENT:

Provide:

- Challenging goals that align with your company's strategic objectives.
- Positive feedback and recognition for accomplishments.
- Recognition and appreciation for extra voluntary contributions.

TO ENHANCE COMMITMENT:

Manage performance to:

- Enable employees to experience success over the long term.
- Facilitate congruence between employee commitment to your organization and other life commitments.
- Value the expertise of experienced employees.

A Closer Look at Workforce Surveys

Many organizations use workforce surveys to gauge the intensity of employee engagement and assess the relationships between engagement and important business results. Findings from such surveys can shed light on which investments in engagement initiatives are paying off, which are not and how you might change your engagement-related HR practices and investment decisions.

Today's employee surveys are often shorter, more narrowly focused and more frequently administered than traditional instruments. In many cases, respondents also fill out the surveys online rather than using paper and pencil. Survey questions or statements now explicitly link employee attitudes to business objectives; for example, "I can see a clear link between my work and Dell's objectives."

Engagement surveys conducted by research firms across many organizations typically give rise to empirically grounded engagement models. Consider this example from the Corporate Leadership Council (CLC).[31] Based on extensive surveys of more than 50,000 employees of 59 global organizations representing 10 industries and 27 countries, the CLC model identifies 300-plus potential "levers of engagement" (specific employer practices that drive employee engagement). These levers collectively influence employees' rational and emotional commitment to their jobs, teams, managers and company, which in turn influences employees' discretionary efforts and intentions to remain with their employers. "Going the extra mile" and planning to stay with a company then lead to improved performance and retention, respectively.

To date, much employee engagement research has been conducted by consulting firms. Owing to their proprietary status, these studies validating engagement models have yet to appear in refereed scientific journals. Most of this research is unavailable to detailed outsider scrutiny. Nevertheless, numerous linkage research studies have been published. Based on these studies, there is evidence that aggregated employee opinions relate fairly strongly to important business outcomes.[32] But does engagement cause business outcomes to improve? Are business units profitable because their employees are engaged, or are employees engaged because they work for profitable units?[33] Do they say they hope to remain indefinitely because they wish to stick with a winner? Recent evidence suggests that the causal direction is not so straightforward.[34] It is important to understand the cause-and-effect relationships involved given the considerable cost and effort associated with organizations' attempts to improve employee engagement. One way to determine the causal direction is to conduct research specifically designed to answer these important questions in your own organization.

A summary model (Figure 3) by Jack Wiley, cofounder of Gantz Wiley Research (now part of Kenexa) shows how employer leadership practices, employee results of those practices, customer results of leadership and work practices and business performance are interrelated.[35] The model is cyclical, showing that, over time, business performance also influences leadership practices. In addition, this model suggests particular variables within each factor that may affect employee engagement.

Aside from learning how engagement is affecting business results in your organization, surveying employee opinions and attitudes—in itself—can enhance engagement and commitment. For example, by asking employees for their opinions and then taking constructive action based on survey results, you signal that the organization values them and takes their feedback seriously. This enhances engagement. Surveying employees also reinforces a two--way employer-employee relationship, strengthening commitment to your firm.

FIGURE 3 The High Performance Model

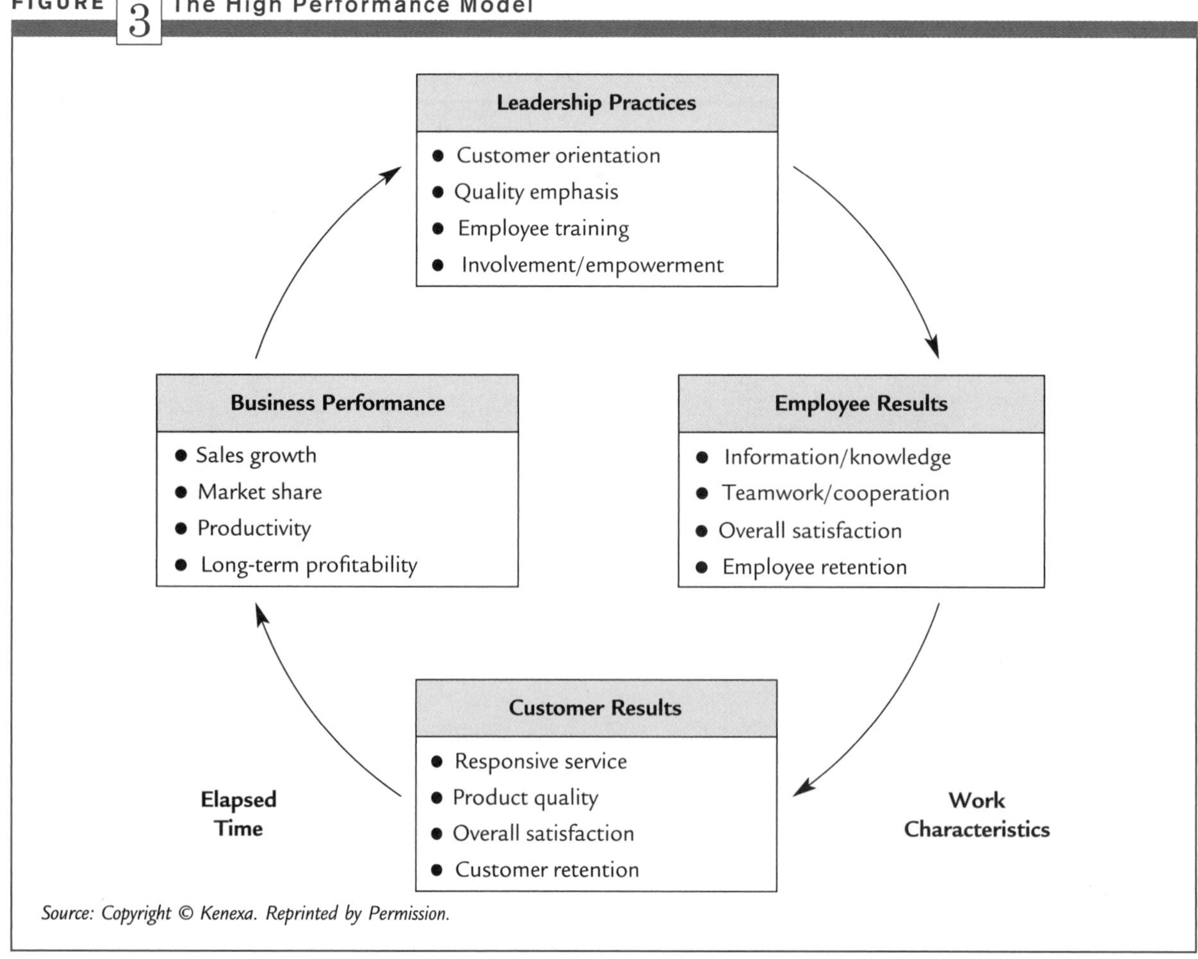

Source: Copyright © Kenexa. Reprinted by Permission.

Designing Engagement Initiatives: Guidelines to Consider

The HR practices discussed above—job design, recruitment, employee selection, training and development, compensation and performance management—are just some of the practices you can leverage to improve engagement and commitment in your organization. As you consider adopting or changing these practices, keep the following guidelines in mind.

Make Sound Investments

Think strategically about how your organization currently uses its human resource practices. Which of these merit greater investment to improve engagement or commitment? What's more important to your organization—employees who are engaged in their work, or those who feel a strong sense of commitment to the organization? Or are both equally important? How much is your organization willing to invest in specific HR practices designed to foster engagement, commitment or a combination of these?

Given your organization's objectives, in some cases you may want to use specific HR practices to foster engagement in work but not commitment to your organization. In others, your goal may be employee engagement and short-term commitment. In still others, it may be maximum engagement and long-term commitment. For example, if your HR strategy relies on increasing the use of contingent workers in order to cut costs and create more flexible staffing, you'll want to take steps to enhance not only contingent workers' engagement but also their short-term commitment. "Matching Engagement and Commitment Strategies to Business Conditions" shows additional examples.

Craft compelling Business Cases for Improving Engagement and Commitment

To gain the funding needed to invest in engagement and commitment initiatives, you may need to apply your powers of persuasion. Creating a compelling business case for these initiatives can increase your chances of success. How might you make the business case for such investments to your supervisor or members of the executive team? Show how these investments have paid off for your organization or for other organizations by generating measurable business results. "Employee Engagement Drives Results at Intuit" and "Employee Engagement Drives Customer Satisfaction at a State Transportation Department" provide examples of effective business cases.

Matching Engagement and Commitment Strategies to Business Conditions

If You Are Facing This Business Condition...	Change Your HR Practices In These Ways...	To Enhance...
Restructuring to flatter organization with broader job responsibilities	• Align job/work design to new roles/responsibilities. • Recruit, select, train, compensate and manage accordingly. • Outsource or automate simple or routine work.	• Engagement • Short-term commitment • Long-term commitment
Changing technology	• If technology increases job complexity, train and compensate accordingly. • If technology simplifies work, enlarge jobs or outsource.	• Engagement
Increasing customer focus, emphasis on quality	• Recognize and reward voluntary contributions and proactive work behaviors. • Redefine performance expectations. • Provide supervisor/performance management support.	• Engagement • Short-term commitment • Long-term commitment
Increasing reliance on contingent and contract workers	Core employees: • Increase job complexity and job security. Contingent employees: • Emphasize pay-for-performance. • Provide results-based incentives. • Increase task identity.	• Engagement • Long-term commitment • Engagement • Short-term commitment
Broken employment contracts resulting from merger, acquisition or bankruptcy	• Confront the question, Commitment to whom? • Earn credibility with realistic promises, avoiding promises that can't or won't be kept.	• Engagement • Short-term commitment

Employee Engagement Drives Results at Intuit[36]

PROBLEM

Between 2003 and 2004, engagement levels among employees of Intuit's Contact Centers dropped significantly. These employees, who make up 40% of the company's workforce, provide service and assistance to customers. Intuit's engagement survey findings pointed to several areas for possible action.

SOLUTIONS

With understandable urgency, the company conducted a Six Sigma process analysis to identify the root causes of the engagement problem. Remedies initiated in 2004 targeted front-line leadership training, to provide supervisors with better coaching skills, and Intuit's performance measurement and incentive system, which the company revised to give employees greater flexibility in determining how to provide the best customer service.

RESULTS

Within two years of implementing these initiatives, Contact Center engagement scores (percent favorable) increased by 16%. There was a corresponding steady increase in the number of new-business referrals by satisfied customers. Revenue growth for 2006 rebounded and grew to 15%-the best growth rate in four years. Intuit stock rose almost 300% over this period, outperforming the Dow Jones Industrial Average, the S&P 500 and the NASDAQ Composite.

Consider Unintended Consequences

In weighing options for redesigning HR practices to foster engagement and commitment, be sure to think about the possible unintended consequences that revised policies can bring. For example, suppose you want to add flextime to your organization's overall work policies. If employee demographics differ across business units (by age, gender and so forth), the new flextime policy may generate more engagement and commitment in units populated primary by, say, single parents with young children than in units with different demographics.

Keep in mind that employees are individuals. Each one may value something different about the organization's work experience and benefits. When you plan a change to your policies or benefits, take time to consider the impact of that change on employees with different life situations—married, single, older, children at home, childless and so forth. Then be sure the change is a net positive for the majority of your workforce. If you expect that some groups of employees will not like the change, be prepared to address this honestly and directly. If possible, consider making several changes at once that benefit different groups. That way no one will feel left out.

Employee Engagement Drives Customer Satisfaction at a State Transportation Department

PROBLEM

A county highway maintenance unit of a state department of transportation was plagued with low morale and a disengaged workforce. At just 36% favorable (indicating very low engagement), scores on the annual employee engagement survey were among the lowest in the state. The department had recently begun a customer-focus initiative, and customer satisfaction scores for ride quality and road maintenance were falling in this county.

SOLUTIONS

The "old school" county manager retired. His successor, a former assistant manager in another county, was selected because he demonstrated skills in employee- and customer-focused management. He proved much more open than the previous manager in his communication with employees-inviting their participation in decision-making and encouraging teamwork. Employee survey scores for each of these dimensions steadily improved by more than 50 percentage points favorable over the next three years. The new manager also encouraged innovation. Scores on process improvements and use of new equipment and technology increased from 19% to 85% favorable.

RESULTS

County employees responded well to the new management approach. Engagement scores showed steady improvement-from 36% favorable just before the change of manager to 84% favorable three years later. An important payoff was a corresponding increase in customer satisfaction, from 51% favorable to 66% percent favorable.

Ground Investment Decisions in Sound Data

It is important to ground decisions about engagement and commitment initiatives in sound data. Linkage research conducted within an organization yields customized advice that highlights specific HR practices likely to produce the best results. Outcomes of this research may include short lists of the highest-impact engagement levers and actionable survey items that differentiate top-performing units in your

Linking Customer Satisfaction to Employee Opinions

	Average 3 Best Units*		Store 2-1	
Employee Opinion Items Customer Service	Agree (% Positive)	Disagree (% Negative)	Agree (% Positive)	Disagree (% Negative)
In my work unit, a frequent topic of discussion is how well we satisfy our customers' needs.	62.7%	16.9%	27.6%	29.3%
My work unit responds to customer complaints by providing prompt resolution.	67.1%	26.1%	42.7%	21.0%
My work unit obtains reliable information about customer satisfaction.	64.8%	14.4%	22.7%	28.6%

*Average 3 Best Units: The 3 stores having the best Customer Satisfaction scores from Customer Pulse Survey.

At one retailer, employees at the three stores with the best customer satisfaction scores expressed different opinions in a survey than employees from other, lower-performing stores (e.g., Store 2-1). The differences in employee opinions across stores suggest differences in engagement levels and may stimulate ideas for changing workplace practices in stores with lower customer satisfaction scores.

company from less successful units. "Linking Customer Satisfaction to Employee Opinions" shows an example.

To develop sound investment decisions, be sure to measure employee engagement at least once a year. Choose a survey consulting firm to adapt a standard engagement survey to your organization by linking survey items to the organization's performance measures, which support its business strategy. Performance measures may include profitability, productivity, efficiency, quality, safety, employee attendance, employee retention, customer satisfaction and customer loyalty—and may differ for each business unit depending on that unit's role in supporting the high-level organizational strategy.

For example, if your company's strategy calls for increasing customer loyalty, you might set a goal to raise employee retention in all customer-facing departments. Since longstanding employees are more likely to establish more enduring relationships with customers, it follows that they will provide higher-quality service. You also can create your own engagement survey. If you decide to go this route, include actionable survey items (topics over which management has some control) that explicitly link employee opinions to your organization's business objectives.

Using your engagement survey results, identify top levers of engagement and drivers of measurable results for each business unit. Determine which aspects of engagement are most important for business success. Then work with unit managers to create an Employee Engagement Action Plan for each unit. Determine ownership and accountability for each action item in these plans. "Owners" may include organizational policy and executive decision-makers, unit managers and teamsupervisors. Also identify the resources—personnel, time, funding, space, equipment—that you will need to put each plan into action.

Create an Engagement Culture

Establish a receptive foundation for your engagement initiatives by creating an "engagement culture." Communicate the value of employee engagement through your company mission statement and other executive communications. For example, look through the "Sample Mission Statements" from three different organizations, and think about how they emphasize the importance of engaged employees for organizational success. Follow up and ensure that all units execute their engagement action plans. Monitor progress on engagement-improvement efforts, and adjust your strategies and plans as needed. Equally important, be sure to recognize and celebrate progress and results.

Conclusion

Engaged employees can help your organization achieve its mission, execute its strategy and generate important business results. This report has highlighted ways in which different HR practices, including job design, recruitment, selection, training, compensation and performance management can enhance employee engagement. But these examples also show that employee engagement is more complex than it may appear on the surface. Organizations define and measure engagement in a variety of different ways, suggesting there is no one "right" or "best" way to define or stimulate engagement in your workforce. The decision to invest in strengthening engagement or commitment (or both) depends on an organization's strategy and the makeup of its workforce.

Sample Mission Statements

STARBUCKS COFFEE COMPANY

Establish Starbucks as the premier purveyor of the finest coffee in the world while maintaining our uncompromising principles while we grow.

The following six guiding principles will help us measure the appropriateness of our decisions:

- Provide a great work environment and treat each other with respect and dignity.
- Embrace diversity as an essential component in the way we do business.
- Apply the highest standards of excellence to the purchasing, roasting and fresh delivery of our coffee.
- Develop enthusiastically satisfied customers all of the time.
- Contribute positively to our communities and our environment.
- Recognize that profitability is essential to our future success.

Source: http://www.starbucks.com/aboutus/environment.asp, October 12, 2006

BRIGHT HORIZONS FAMILY SOLUTIONS

The Bright Horizons Family Solutions mission is to provide innovative programs that help children, families and employers work together to be their very best.

We are committed to providing the highest-quality child care, early education and work/life solutions in the world. We strive to:

- Nurture each child's unique qualities and potential.
- Support families through strong partnerships.
- Collaborate with employers to build family-friendly workplaces.
- Create a work environment that encourages professionalism, growth and diversity.
- Grow a financially strong organization.

We aspire to do this so successfully that we make a difference in the lives of children and families and in the communities where we live and work.

Source: http://www.brighthorizons.com/Site/pages/mission.aspx, October 12, 2006.

WD-40 COMPANY

We are a global consumer products company dedicated to building brand equities that are the first or second choice in their respective categories.

Our mission is to leverage and build the brand fortress of WD-40 Company by developing and acquiring brands that deliver a unique high value to end users and that can be distributed across multiple trade channels in one or more areas of the world.

We strive to cultivate a learning culture based on our corporate values. We have a healthy discomfort with the status quo. We reward those who take personal responsibility in getting results to increase the profitability and growth of our business.

Source: http://www.wd40.com/AboutUs/our_philosophy.html, October 12, 2006.

For these reasons, it is vital to consider your own organization's view of engagement, as well as its strategy and workforce composition when deciding which HR practices will receive scarce investment dollars. The research, guidelines and examples provided in this report—as well as the annotated bibliography—can help you begin to weigh the options and to craft an investment plan that will best suit your organization's unique circumstances.

Source: Alexandria, VA: Society for Human Resource Management Foundation (2006).

REFERENCES

1. Welch, J., & Welch, S. (2006, May 8). Ideas the Welch way: How healthy is your company? *Business Week*, 126.
2. Ramsay, C. S., & Finney, M. I. (2006). *Employee engagement at Intuit.* Mountain View, CA: Intuit Inc.
   Ramsay, C. S. (2006, May). Engagement at Intuit: It's the people. In J. D. Kaufman (Chair), *Defining and measuring employee engagement: Old wine in new bottles?* Symposium conducted at the Society for Industrial and Organizational Psychology 21st Annual Conference, Dallas, Texas.
3. See note 2 above.
4. Robinson, D., Perryman, S., & Hayday, S. (2004). *The drivers of employee engagement.* IES Report No. 408. Brighton, UK: Institute for Employment Studies.
5. Kahn, W. A. (1990). Psychological conditions of personal engagement and disengagement at work. *Academy of Management Journal*, *33*, 692–724.
6. Katz, D., & Kahn, R. L. (1978). *The social psychology of organizations* (2nd ed). New York: John Wiley & Sons.
7. Van Maanen, J. (1976). Breaking in: Socialization to work. In R. Dubin (Ed.), *Handbook. of work, organization, and society* (pp. 67–130). Chicago: Rand McNally & Co.
8. Abrahamson, M., & Anderson, W. P. (1984). People's commitments to institutions. *Social Psychology Quarterly*, *47*, 371–381.
9. Cohen, A. (2003). *Multiple commitments in the workplace: An integrative approach.* Mahwah, NJ: Lawrence Erlbaum Associates.
10. Meyer, J. P., & Allen, N. J. (1991). A three-component conceptualization of organizational commitment. *Human Resource Management Review*, *1*, 61–89.
11. Meyer, J. P., Becker, T. E., & Vandenberghe, C. (2004). Employee commitment and motivation: A conceptual analysis and integrative model. *Journal of Applied Psychology*, *89*, 991–1007.
12. Robinson, D., Perryman, S., & Hayday, S. (2004). *The drivers of employee engagement.* IES Report No. 408. Brighton, UK: Institute for Employment Studies.
13. See note 2.
14. Vance, R. J. (2006). Organizing for customer service. In L. Fogli (Ed.), *Customer service delivery: Research and best practices* (pp. 22–51). San Francisco, Calif.: Jossey-Bass.
15. Vance, R. J. (2006). Organizing for customer service. In L. Fogli (Ed.), *Customer service delivery: Research and best practices* (pp. 22–51). San Francisco, Calif.: Jossey-Bass.
   Organ, D. W., & Ryan, K. (1995). A meta-analytic review of attitudinal and dispositional predictors or organizational citizenship behavior. *Personnel Psychology*, *48*, 775–802.
   Borman, W. C., & Motowidlo, S. J. (1997). Task performance and contextual performance: The meaning for personnel selection research. *Human Performance*, *10*, 99–110.
16. Barley, S. (1996). *The new world of work.* London: British-North American Research Committee.
17. Humphrey, S. E., Nahrgang, J. D., & Morgeson, F. P. (2006). *Integrating social and motivational models of work design: A meta-analytic summary and theoretical extension of the work design literature.* Paper presented at the annual conference of the Society for Industrial and Organizational Psychology, Dallas, Texas.
18. Taylor, F. W. (1911). *The principles of scientific management.* New York: W. W. Norton.
19. Hackman, J. R., & Lawler, E. E. (1971). Employee reactions to job characteristics. *Journal of Applied Psychology Monograph*, *55*, 259–286.
20. Georgopoulos, B. A., Mahoney, G. M., & Jones, M. W. (1957). A path-goal approach to productivity. *Journal of Applied Psychology*, *41*, 345–353.
   Herzberg, F., Mausner, B., & Snyderman, B. B. (1959). *The motivation to work.* New York: Wiley.
   Ford, R. N. (1969). *Motivation through the work itself.* New York: American Management Association.
21. See note 19 above.
22. Hackman, J. R., & Oldham, G. R. (1980). *Work redesign.* Reading, Mass. Addison-Wesley.
23. Humphrey, S. E., Nahrgang, J. D., & Morgeson, F. P. (2006). *Integrating social and motivational models of work design: A meta-analytic summary and theoretical extension of the work design literature.* Paper presented at the annual conference of the Society for Industrial and Organizational Psychology, Dallas, Texas.
   Fried, Y., & Ferris, G. R. (1987). The validity of the job characteristics model: A review and meta-analysis. *Personnel Psychology*, *40*, 287–322.
24. Morgeson, F. P., & Humphrey, S. E. (2006). The Work Design Questionnaire (WDQ): Developing and validating a comprehensive measure for assessing job design and the nature of work. *Journal of Applied Psychology.*
25. Parker, S. K., Williams, H. M., & Turner, N. (2006). Modeling the antecedents of proactive behavior at work. *Journal of Applied Psychology*, *91*, 636–652.
26. Parker, S. K. (2006). *A broaden-and-build model of work design: How job enrichment broadens thought-action repertoires via positive affect.* Paper presented at the annual conference of the Society for Industrial and Organizational Psychology, Dallas, Texas.
27. Vance, R. J., & Colella, A. (1990). The utility of utility analysis. *Human Performance*, *3*, 123–139.
28. Pulakos, E. D. (2005). *Selection assessment methods: A guide to implementing formal assessments to build a high-quality workforce.* Alexandria, Va.: SHRM Foundation.
29. Hausknecht, J. P., Day, D. V., & Thomas, S. C. (2004). Applicant reactions to selection procedures: An updated model and meta-analysis. *Personnel Psychology*, *57*, 639–683.
30. Pulakos, E. D. (2004). *Performance management: A roadmap for developing, implementing and evaluating performance management systems.* Alexandria, Va.: SHRM Foundation.
31. Corporate Leadership Council (2004). *Driving performance and retention through employee engagement.* Washington, DC: Corporate Executive Board.
32. Schneider, B., Parkington, J. J., & Buxton, V. M. (1980). Employee and customer perceptions of service in banks. *Administrative Science Quarterly*, *25*, 252–267.
   Schneider, B., Hanges, P. J., Smith, B., & Salvaggio, A. N. (2003). Which comes first: Employee attitudes or organizational financial and market performance? *Journal of Applied Psychology*, *88*, 836–851.
   Schneider, B., White, S. S., & Paul, M. C. (1998). Linking service climate and customer perceptions of service quality: Test of a causal model. *Journal of Applied Psychology*, *83*, 150–163.
   Ryan, A. M., Schmit, M. J., & Johnson, R. (1996). Attitudes and effectiveness: Examining relations at an organizational level. *Personnel Psychology*, *49*, 853–882.
   Dietz, J., Pugh, S. D., & Wiley, J. W. (2004). Service climate effects on customer attitudes: An examination of boundary conditions. *Academy of Management Journal*, *47*, 81–92.
   Harter, J. K., Schmidt, F. L., & Hayes, T. L. (2002). Business-unit-level relationship between employee satisfaction, employee engagement, and business outcomes: A meta-analysis. *Journal of Applied Psychology*, *87*, 268–279.

33. Schneider, B., Hanges, P. J., Smith, B., & Salvaggio, A. N. (2003). Which comes first: Employee attitudes or organizational financial and market performance? *Journal of Applied Psychology, 88*, 836–851.

34. See note 33.

35. Brooks, S. M., Wiley, J. W., & Hause, E. L. (2006). Using employee and customer perspectives to improve organizational performance. In L. Fogli (Ed.), *Customer service delivery: Research and best practices* (pp. 52–82). San Francisco, Calif.: Jossey-Bass. Wiley, J. W. (1996). Linking survey results to customer satisfaction and business performance. In A. I. Kraut (Ed.), *Organizational surveys: Tools for assessment and change* (pp. 330–359). San Francisco, Calif.: Jossey-Bass Publishers.

36. Ramsay, C. S., & Finney, M. I. (2006). *Employee engagement at Intuit*. Mountain View, CA: Intuit Inc.
Ramsay, C. S. (2006, May). Engagement at Intuit: It's the people. In J. D. Kaufman (Chair), *Defining and measuring employee engagement: Old wine in new bottles?* Symposium conducted at the Society for Industrial and Organizational Psychology 21st Annual Conference, Dallas, Texas.

READING 4.3

Remodeling HR at Home Depot

Robert J. Grossman

Home Depot's announcement last April that it was slicing 1,200 human resource positions—more than 50 percent of its HR staff—by eliminating HR managers from each of its nearly 1,970 U.S. stores sent chills through the HR community.

With the housing market in the doldrums and the economy teetering on recession, the world-leading hardware and home improvement retailer had to make tough decisions. Ten percent of the 5,000 staffers at headquarters in Atlanta had already been let go.

But this broadside at human resources was different and, to some observers, counterintuitive. With more than 330,000 associates and 2,254 stores worldwide, Home Depot continues to face daunting challenges in retention and gaps in worker training and expertise. Its customer service ratings significantly lag those of competitors such as Lowe's. In addition, Chief Executive Officer Frank Blake must heal wounds remaining from the cultural upheaval wrought by his predecessor Robert Nardelli.

Seven years ago, the company had assigned HR managers to each store to work as business partners with store managers. Now, its leaders have concluded that an HR presence is a luxury they can no longer afford. How could Home Depot expect to address its human capital issues by decimating the HR ranks, eliminating the professionals trained to focus on them?

Where were the HR executives when all this came down? Were they outside the loop while others determined their fate? It turns out they were initiators of and prime advocates for the plan.

Partnership carries responsibilities, and, in this case, HR executives were resolute that they could "take one for the team." They are now convinced they can run HR companywide equally well or better with their streamlined organization, freeing salaries for more sales associates. Today at Home Depot, HR professionals are strategic business partners, sharing decision-making at the highest level.

The Nardelli Regime

No doubt, HR professionals at the company would not be prime movers in shaping their destiny and the future direction of Home Depot had it not been for Nardelli, now CEO at Chrysler. Their ascension began in 2001 when the board put outsider Nardelli in command. It cost $39.7 million in annual salary to snare him from General Electric (GE) after he fell short in the competition to replace GE's outgoing CEO Jack Welch.

The Nardelli era was anything but dull. In his seven-year tenure, he grew the company, adding stores in the U.S., Mexico, Canada and China. He committed to establishing a wholesale business that some observers thought was drawing attention and resources away from Home Depot's fundamental retail operations.

Along the way, he wreaked havoc with the philosophy that founders Arthur Blank and Bernie Marcus espoused in 1979. Press-the-flesh retailers who understood the importance of customers and the associates that serve them, they advocated bottom-up, consultative management centered on customers and store employees. They promoted entrepreneurism and creativity in the ranks and offered financial rewards and recognition for sales performance, even stock benefits. They portrayed their philosophy as an inverted pyramid, with customers at the top followed by store employees and the CEO at the bottom.

Nardelli turned the pyramid upside down. Imposing rigorous controls and metrics, he focused on containing costs and cutting or reducing benefits associates had come to expect. He called the shots, shipping directives through an authoritarian command-and-control structure. "Bob was like the stepfather that made you be a disciplined teenager," says Teresa Duren, vice president for Home Depot's 780-store Southern Division. "We needed some discipline and process; it made us stronger."

Store Managers: Lords of the Manor

No question, Nardelli inherited an enterprise in dire need of order, direction and discipline. Blank and Marcus built the Home Depot empire by empowering store managers. Typically, store managers employ 150 to 300 associates and oversee "boxes" that each average $38 million in annual revenue. They enjoyed exceptional autonomy as long as they reached revenue targets. In effect, they did their own HR work, relying on district HR managers responsible for supporting as many as 30 stores.

"We didn't have much of an HR established practice," observes Duren, who has been with the company since 1996.

Nardelli could see, however, that there were potential problems and liabilities that could be addressed only by developing better systems and controls. With his exposure to HR at General Electric—where human capital is a top priority—Nardelli knew Home Depot's laissez-faire approach was not sustainable in the long run.

Nardelli recruited Dennis Donovan from General Electric to be executive vice president for HR. Donovan came aboard with a compensation package unparalleled for HR executives—and influence to match. Nardelli's right-hand man, he ushered HR into the C-suite, giving it an active voice in strategic management. "These were great times to be in HR," Duren recalls.

Lacking retail experience himself, Donovan assembled a core of senior HR executives with strong backgrounds in retailing, establishing credentials that the company now seeks in all HR appointments. "For example, the fact that Mike Buskey, our senior vice president of HR, U.S. store operations, knows the business—seasonal, inventory, hurricanes, underperforming [stores]—is what makes him so effective," explains Paul Raines, who was executive vice president, U.S. stores, before leaving Home Depot this August.

Buskey oversees HR in Home Depot's 1,964 U.S. stores. Raines like Buskey's assertiveness. "He's an invite-yourself-to-the-party kind of executive," Raines says. "The key to success in HR is you've got to get in the foxhole with the other people. That's what it takes."

The line experience makes executives more relevant, agrees Carole Pietak, vice president for the 480-store Western Division. "You have to understand the culture of retail—the hours, the high pace—and be able to juggle."

Human Resources to the Fore

Donovan re-engineered HR operations, installed an extensive array of metrics and moved quickly to create a full-time, exempt HR presence in each store. "You don't want 1,300 store managers hiring and firing on their own," Duren says. Ideally, candidates for the position would have at least three years of experience in HR and experience in a retailing area similar to Home Depot's.

And Donovan expected that they would develop into true business partners, providing important perspective for each store manager. "If a particular department isn't doing well, the merchant will look at the merchandise, the operator will look at the execution. It's up to the HR person to focus on staffing—the numbers, the quality, ask if we're scheduling to the peak times. Are we getting bogged down in transactional activities? Do we have the product knowledge we need?" Pietak says.

In January 2006, Nardelli resigned to mixed reviews. He had doubled sales and increased earnings per share, and the wholesale business was showing a profit. But the stock price remained flat, disappointing shareholders and Wall Street. He had become a lightning rod for critics, including share-holder activists, who objected to his compensation package.

One month later, Donovan bowed out, walking away with a cash settlement of $2.96 million and stock valued at $17 million but leaving his HR blueprint and executive team as his legacy.

Blake Changes Course

Home Depot's board tapped Vice Chairman Blake to succeed Nardelli. A lawyer, former diplomat and assistant U.S. secretary of energy, Blake also had come from General Electric and had no prior retail experience.

Early on, it became clear that Blake was cut from a different cloth than Nardelli. He is open, consultative and accessible. He listens and learns. "We're back to our old-school approach preached by co-founder Bernie Marcus," says Raines, interviewed before leaving Home Depot. "All of us are out there. Never go 48 hours without being on the floor of a store."

According to Duren, "Blake, is reaffirming our focus on our core values. It's been a welcome message. The culture has shifted back to realizing we are a retail company that needs to focus on customers."

In February 2007, Blake, staying in-house, promoted Tim Crow as executive vice president of HR to replace Donovan. Crow had been vice president of organization, talent and performance systems. Donovan had hired him in 2002 from KMart, where he was senior vice president for HR.

Crow sits on Blake's six-person Executive Leadership Team, meets alone with Blake daily and travels with him on store visits. He staffs the board of director's Leadership Development & Compensation Committee. "I'm involved with everything," he says.

The contrast between Crow's leadership style and his predecessor's is as striking as the differences between Nardelli and Blake. Whereas Donovan had no prior retail experience and rarely strayed from the Atlanta headquarters, Crow, a seasoned retailer, lives the business and constantly rubs elbows with associates and managers.

With Crow, "The pyramid is upside down again; we're back to being associate- and customer-centered," says Leslie Joyce, vice president and chief learning officer. "Under Dennis, we decided what was best for stores. Now it's more a matter of us asking questions and responding to their needs."

With Crow pushing the agenda, benefits Nardelli took away to cut costs came back and new practices have been adopted to enhance recognition and a sense of ownership and pride, Buskey says. "Even though the economy is tough, we're doubling the amount of money we give our supervisors when they make their revenue targets. Last year, the average associate got $200" when stores made their targets. "We've given our assistant store managers a restricted stock grant when the rest of the world is going the other way."

Home Depot

Ownership: Publicly traded on New York Stock Exchange. Symbol HD.

2007 annual revenue: $77 billion.

Top managers: Frank Blake, chief executive officer; Tim Crow, executive vice president of HR.

Employees: 330,000.

Locations: 2,254 worldwide, 206 warehouses and distribution centers.

Connections: www.homedepot.com

Tough Times Continue

But while the change in attitude and approach to customers has received praise from some critics, Home Depot's stock and financials continue to falter, exacerbated by the poor economy and housing crisis. When Blake took control in January 2007, a share of stock sold for $39. By this summer, it was trading in the $20s. The company reported that its net earnings for the first half of fiscal 2008 (through Aug. 3) plunged 41 percent compared to the first half of 2007.

Also, customer satisfaction, which in retailing tends to correlate with stock performance, is below par. Home Depot's score of 67 in the fourth quarter of 2007 put it dead last in the American Customer Satisfaction Index within the grouping that includes Circuit City, Best Buy, Sam's Club and Lowe's.

"They're getting the equivalent of a C-," says Claes G. Fornell, a professor and head of the index at the University of Michigan in Ann Arbor. Lowe's, in comparison, earned a rating of 75 for the same quarter.

Human Resources Steps Up

As a result, Blake faced a vexing problem: How could he improve customer service, boost staff morale and revitalize Home Depot's culture while revenues were declining? In November 2007, he announced an initiative called "Aprons on the Floor," aimed at spending $180 million to increase the number and quality of associates in each store. He challenged his senior leadership team to come up with cost-cutting strategies that would raise the money. "This is about an environment forcing change on an organization and people rallying around a back-to-basics message and facing tough decisions," Raines says.

Crow took the challenge to his team. "We began looking at ways to contribute and began to explore ways to provide HR services for less money," says Pietak. Donovan's HR store managers (HRMs) had been in place for seven years. It was time to take a closer look at how they were faring.

On paper, HRMs' portfolios included recruitment, staffing, training, career development, associate relations and community relations. Celia Scanlon, now a district HR manager in Fairfax County, Va., describes her former role as HRM at a store in Dale City, Va., as doing everything from A to Z: "I was the right-hand person to the manager. We did everything together from hiring, interviewing, job fairs, performance management, coaching, counseling, training and helping managers write up discipline notes." Sounds good. But those relationships created some issues. Among them:

Dual Reporting "You had a dotted line to a district human resource manager whose portfolio covered up to 30 stores and a solid line to the store manager who wrote your review," recalls Ismay Czarniecki, an HRM in Wappingers Falls, N.Y., from 2001–06, who has also worked in HR at Target and Lowe's. She says store managers wanted to keep any compliance violations or employee relations issues in-house. "Once your realize how things work, if you want to survive, you go native, giving your loyalty to your store manager."

Keeping accurate records of associate training was especially problematic. Store managers were supposed to allocate time for associates to train, but training took them off the selling floor, says George Marron, one of the first HRM hires in Chandler, Ariz., and now professor of HR management at Marist College in Poughkeepsie, N.Y. "Headquarters staff was always wondering why their programs didn't roll out on time; the store managers wouldn't allow us to run them because they kept aprons off the floor," he says.

High Attrition and Culture Clash Many HRMs had difficulty adjusting to Home Depot's rough-and-tumble environment. "It's a demanding position," Buskey says. "This is the toughest retail you'll see; the jobs are not easy, and the people work hard. We're not moving pillows and sheets; these are warehouses—drafty and cold."

Czarniecki adds, "They hired professional HR people who expected they'd have a secretary and an office, and it just wasn't so. Walking into Home Depot, if you see something that needs to be done, you do it. If you don't know how it's done, you find out. That's the culture.... Some people fit, and some did not."

Taxing Workload Some HRMs were working as many as 55 hours each week. "They wanted us to find out what people think, but you can't get people to talk unless they trust you, and they won't trust you with harassment and discrimination complaints, for example, unless they know you," Czarniecki says. "You get to know the players by being there—that means you have to be there sometimes until closing, at nights when there are evening crews and on weekends."

It was hard to stay in control and head off problems, recalls Marron. "Every time you turned around, an assistant department manager was saying the wrong thing. There were safety issues and complaints. It went on and on."

Mountains of Mundane HRMs were spending too much time on routine, daily paperwork. "We expected them to be thinking into the future while the store manager worries about the here and now. But it wasn't happening," says Pietak. "They were engaged in the transactional stuff."

The Decision Is Made

In consultation with his senior HR team, Crow weighed his options, crafted the reorganization proposal, and presented it to Blake and the executive leadership team. Crow believed he could revamp the HR operation and plow the savings into the stores. After the April 1 announcement, changes were implemented May 1.

"It was my decision; there was no pressure from Frank Blake or other non-HR executives," Crow says emphatically. His rationale: Transaction processing in stores was inefficient; centralizing it would "free HR people to become business partners." And, he concludes, "We'd be better off with a district team that's more strategic."

Under the reorganization, 230 HR district teams oversee six to 10 stores. District managers have three HR generalists (DHRMs) reporting to them. The generalists each carry responsibility for a function—staffing and development, associate relations, and performance management. "These jobs, without the transactional baggage, are better jobs from an HR perspective," Crow says. "And the store managers haven't lost an HR manager; they've gained three."

Crow expects he'll receive more accurate and timely feedback: "With one HR person in a store, you might miss what's going on. Now, I have four sets of eyes and ears rotating through each store."

Releasing HR professionals from reporting to store managers may be an improvement, Czarniecki says. "There are so many legal violations in terms of safety, security and employee relations that HR needs to be removed from the stores in order to approach the situation as a consultant who won't be influenced by not getting a good review."

The remaining HR transactional activities—like putting people on and off the payroll and transferring them between departments—have been insourced to a 220-person HR phone-access services center in Atlanta staffed by customer service representatives.

Potential savings are substantial: The company is striving to add three associates to the floor of each store by year's end. The savings from 1,200 HR positions should provide about two-thirds of the resources. "Two full-time associates could replace an HR person," Czarniecki projects.

Some observers question whether the absence of HR onsite in stores will end up costing more in legal and compliance mistakes than the revenue generated by new sales associates.

Based on his experience as an HRM in Phoenix, Marron, who also was a longtime manager at CVS, is wary because the reorganization appears to place more HR responsibilities on store managers. "Unless they've made an improvement in the quality of the management since I left in 2004, I'd be concerned," he says. "The managers in the stores were so poorly trained, had so little understanding about dealing with people, it was scary."

Buskey voices confidence that store managers are accomplished enough to function without HR managers continuously by their side. Although store managers are rated primarily by their revenue numbers, he says they're qualified to handle human capital issues. "Our managers have learned how to integrate the HR functions into their styles," he says.

"If I felt there was a risk that managers would cut corners, I wouldn't have proposed the change," Crow insists.

The fired HRMs received two months of severance pay and were offered an opportunity to apply for the new district positions or other openings. Many were successful. "We've whittled the number of displaced workers down to about 800, but still we've lost some really good people," Buskey says.

From the Field

Mike Leith, PHR, formerly an HR manager at a Home Depot store in Beaverton Ore., emerged from the reorganization as a district HR manager for associate relations in District 24. When the news filtered down, he was "shocked." Still, he understood the rationale.

Previously, Leith enjoyed the relationship he had with his store manager and being part of a leadership team. He likes his new job even more. "I get more perspective, a more global view of what's going on. Your store can be isolated. I'm touching more, and it feels good. What's great about the new role is that if you're good at what you can do, you can do it for several managers."

Leith's HR team covers 10 stores around Portland, Ore. "It's great to be on a team that's focused on HR–partnering with the store managers to drive the business," he says. "This structure has the potential to unlock a lot of energy. Managers and associates may not have an interaction with HR every day, But when they do, it will be positive."

Leith says some store managers were worried about losing their in-store HR manager but are adjusting. "We've been very visible in the stores, and they seem pleased." He spends a half day each week in his "home store office." Otherwise, he's on the road. "My laptop and BlackBerry are my good friends."

Celia Scanlon, now a district manager in Fairfax County, Va., says she's still helping store managers make key decisions, but now she's helping six instead of one. Constantly on the move, she uses her car as an office. "I have three HR partners who help me out with reviews, performance management, coaching and leadership skills," she says.

So far, the reorganization looks like a win-win for the company and HR. "I've been doing round tables with district HR managers and the three who support them," Crow says. "They love it. They say, 'This is a fun job. I can make an impact on the business more than before.' And the store managers like it as well. They've gone from having one HR partner to a team of four."

The service center staffed by customer service people and former store associates is meeting expectations. "We have daily metrics to monitor the call volume, how the calls are being handled, as well as feedback from store managers and district HR managers," Duren says.

How Home Depot Compares

Some retailers, such as Target and Lowe's, continue to find that a full-time HR presence at the store level remains important. Others, such as Sears, do not.

Ed Lawler, professor of business and director of the Center for Effective Organizations at the University of Southern California in Los Angeles, says that while stand-alone businesses the size of a typical Home Depot store would have an HR person, many retail chains get by with a manager assigned to handle administration and scheduling. Lawler says moving the HRMs out should not affect HR's strategy role, explaining "There are no strategy issues in the stores—administrative, business and compliance issues are front and center."

In moving routine HR transactions to a service center, Home Depot is in step with many large retailers who outsource or insource this work. Target and Wal-Mart, for example, have service centers. This trend is likely to continue in retailing, suggesting that the number of transactional HR jobs will continue to decline significantly but that remaining jobs will be more influential and will require greater sophistication and business acumen.

Ideally, district HR team jobs at Home Depot will be these kinds of jobs. DHRMs and their managers should have greater opportunities to distinguish themselves and develop leadership skills. "You'll make more decisions in a day than you'll make in a week elsewhere," says Tim Hourigan, vice president of performance management. "If you don't like being involved with the business and being counted on to make tough decisions, this is not the place for you."

In the end, metrics will make or break the case for the reorganization. Crow is looking for growth in sales and improved reports from surveys that ask customers if they would recommend Home Depot to others and if they found associates attentive and responsive. Buskey will be providing data from his HR scorecard that will help round out the picture. "We have four buckets to measure: staffing, learning, performance management and associate relations," he says.

Meanwhile, despite the savings plowed back into sales, there are lingering doubts about the move. "We didn't want to take the HRMs out of the stores; we knew we were giving something up," Raines concedes. "Do we gain back more through this reinvestment in associates, and will we recover some of what we've sacrificed in the stores with the district-level teams?"

Time will tell. IR

Source: HR Magazine, 53, (11), 67–72 (2008). Reprinted by permission.

Human Resource Planning 5

Learning Objectives

- Understand the objectives and benefits of human resource planning
- Explain the link between an organization's strategy and its human resource plan
- Gain an appreciation for the need for and value of succession planning
- Appreciate the role that mentoring can play in succession planning

Developing Talent at Proctor & Gamble

Consumer goods conglomerate Proctor & Gamble has had a long, successful history based on hiring at the entry level and developing and promoting its managers and executives from within. The key to this success is the organization's Build from Within program, which tracks the performance of every manager within the organization relative to his or her potential and next area for development. Each of the organization's top 50 jobs consistently has three internal replacement candidates lined up and ready to assume responsibility. Loyalty of employees is paramount to ensuring the success of such a program, and P&G's history of grooming and training its employees promotes such loyalty. Fewer than 5 percent of the organization's non-entry-level hires come from outside the organization, and its rigorous and competitive screening process, in which fewer than 5 percent of applicants are hired, ensures that P&G hires those best suited for the organization and its culture. P&G's 138,000 employees are tracked via monthly and annual performance reviews in which managers discuss business goals, personal goals. and how they've trained others to assume responsibility. The latter is a key factor in the upward mobility of any manager. P&G prides itself in being able to fill any opening internally "in an hour." All executives are required to teach in the organization's training programs, and the CEO assumes direct responsibility for the development of the organization's top 150 employees.[1]

Once the corporate and business unit strategies have been established, then the human resource strategy can begin to be developed. The HR strategy involves taking the organization's strategic goals and objectives and translating them into a consistent, integrated, complementary set of programs and policies for managing employees.

This does not imply, however, that strategic HR is reactive in nature. Although it is derived from corporate and/or business unit strategies, HR strategy is developed in a proactive manner, with HR staff attempting to design and develop appropriate HR systems to meet the anticipated conditions under which the organization will operate. The senior HR professional, as a vital member of the top management team, should also be heavily involved in corporate or business unit strategic planning so that the top management team can include human resource management concerns in its overall planning. HR needs to inform the top management team of the skills and capabilities of the organization's workforce and how they might impact strategic plans.

The first component of human resource management strategy is human resource planning. The second component, the design of work systems, is covered in Chapter 6. All other functional HR activities, such as staffing, training, performance management, compensation, labor relations, and employee separation, are derived and should flow from the human resource planning process. When undertaking human resource planning, the organization considers the implications of its future plans on the nature and types of individuals it will need to employ and the necessary skills and training they will require. The organization will also need to assess its current stock of employees as well as those available for employment externally. The key facet of human resource planning is that it is a *proactive* process. It attempts to plan and anticipate what might happen in the various domains of the organization's internal and external environments and to develop plans to address these events prior to their actually happening. Rather than react to changes in the industry, marketplace, economy, society, and technological world, human resource planning ensures that the organization can adapt in tandem with these changes and maintain the fit between the organization and its environment. HR planning is particularly important during periods of organizational turbulence, such as during a merger or acquisition, when labor market conditions are tight, or when unemployment is high.

Because human resource planning involves making assumptions about the future, particularly the status of the economy, competition, technology, regulation, and internal operations and resources, it is critical that all human resource planning initiatives be flexible. If events and circumstances materialize differently from how they are anticipated, then the organization should not be bound by prior and existing plans. Changes to any planning initiatives should not be viewed as a weakness in the planning process. Rather, they should be a positive sign that the organization is carefully monitoring its external environment and responding appropriately to any changes taking place.

In order to facilitate this flexibility, it is critical that key decision-makers in the organization *clarify and write down* all assumptions they make about the external environment and the organization when developing the human resource plan. If the organization has difficulty achieving its strategic objectives despite following a carefully wrought human resource plan, there is a very good chance that inaccurate assumptions were made about what might happen in the future or when expectations failed to materialize.

Clarifying and writing down these assumptions make subsequent intervention and corrective action much easier. Many interventions become complicated and time-consuming because when decision-makers revisit the process, the strategy seems to flow logically from the process outlined in Chapter 3. However, as previously noted, much of the assessment of the external environment involves assumptions that various conditions of the economy, technology, marketplace, competition, and regulatory environment will remain the same or change. These assumptions are often held by key decision-makers but not verbalized. As a result, corrective action may be stymied because of an inability to identify the key problem.

Human resource planning goes far beyond simple hiring and firing. It involves planning for the deployment of the organization's human capital in the most effective and efficient ways, in line with the organization and/or business unit strategy. In addition to hiring and/or separation, human capital management may involve reassignment, training and development, outsourcing, and/or using temporary help or outside contractors. Modern organizations need as much flexibility as possible in how they utilize human talent in the pursuit of their strategic goals.

Human Resource Planning at Drexel Heritage Furnishings

Drexel Heritage Furnishings is a North Carolina–based, century-old manufacturer of premium quality furniture. To plan its workforce needs in such a competitive, volatile, and seasonally cyclical industry, the organization carefully monitors a variety of internal and external indicators. The vice president of HR carefully tracks incoming orders to monitor and project volume over the coming quarter. In addition, the Purchasing Managers Index, a monthly measure of nationwide business activity, is tracked. This index is a gauge of consumer sentiment about the economy and is based on new orders, prices, inventories, and backlogs. Additional indicators such as real estate activity—including construction activity, mortgage rates, relocations, and market prices—are also monitored by HR, as these factors can be tied to demand for home furnishings. Finally, trends in employee compensation, including bonuses and stock options, are considered, as such "add-on" compensation may be used as discretionary income for the purchase of home furnishings.[2]

The need to carefully monitor human resource planning activities will become even more acute in the coming years. The U.S. Bureau of Labor Statistics estimates that during the current decade, the civilian labor force will increase by only 1 percent and that after that, the retirement of baby boomers will slow the growth to only two-tenths of a percent until the year 2025.[3] Probably nowhere is this creating more challenges than with the federal workforce. Recent reports published by the U.S. Merit Systems Protection Board (MSPB) have determined that the federal government's recruiting processes greatly hamper its ability to hire needed employees. With an average age of approximately 50 years, between one-half million and one million federal employees are expected to retire by 2010. Because little concerted effort is being made to replace such workers or to provide training for those who will remain after these retirements, the future looks grim. In addition, the process for hiring new employees has been found to be so cumbersome that many qualified workers are discouraged from applying for federal jobs.[4] However, one federal employer, the U.S. Postal Service, has developed a model for human capital management that is exemplary for government agencies.

Human Capital Management at the United States Postal Service

With more than 800,000 employees, the U.S. Postal Service (USPS) has the second-largest workforce in the country. The 230-year-old post service has an operating budget of $65 billion and has been under increased competitive pressure from organizations such as Federal Express, United Parcel Service, and Internet service providers, all of whom have eroded market share and offered alternatives to the traditional monopoly enjoyed by the USPS. Current projections are that 85 percent of its executives, 74 percent of its managers and supervisors, and 50 percent of its career workforce will be eligible to retire by 2010.

The postal service has developed a strategy to ensure that it attracts the right people and then deploys them effectively to where they are most needed. To ensure that the best employees are retained, performance management and leadership development programs have been created to motivate and reward them. At the center of its human capital management plan are four key strategies: (1) aggressive recruitment of future leaders; (2) building of an effective, motivated workforce in which individuals and teams are recognized through a performance-based pay system; (3) establishment and maintenance of a good work environment, based on cooperative working relationships between unionized employees and management; and

(4) creation of a flexible workforce that can be readily adjusted as conditions change and new needs arise.

To facilitate these goals, back-office functions have been reorganized and consolidated into 85 separate "performance clusters." Each cluster has its own HR staff that applied re-engineering principles and technology tools to repetitive transactional service work to create more self-service transactions for employees and managers. Performance management is being integrated into virtually every organizational initiative to ensure that rewards are commensurate with productivity. Succession planning and corresponding training and development initiatives have been established to ensure that vital skills are identified and transferred to up-and-coming employees. The Advanced Leadership Program has been developed as a premier program for high-potential future executives that trains them to understand the strategic challenges being faced by the organization and to develop the skills that allow participants to creatively address those challenges.[5]

Objectives of Human Resource Planning

There are five major objectives of HR planning, as outlined in Exhibit 5.1. The first is to prevent overstaffing and understaffing. When an organization has too many employees, it experiences a loss of efficiency in operations because of excessive payroll costs and/or surplus production that cannot be marketed and must be inventoried. Having too few employees results in lost sales revenue because the organization is unable to satisfy existing demand of customers. Moreover, the inability to meet current demand for products or services due to understaffing can also result in the loss of future customers who turn to competitors. Human resource planning helps to ensure that operations are not only efficient but also timely in response to customer demand.

The second objective is to ensure that the organization has the right employees with the right skills in the right places at the right times. Organizations need to anticipate the kinds of employees they need in terms of skills, work habits, and personal characteristics and time their recruiting efforts so that the best employees have been hired, fully trained, and prepared to deliver peak performance exactly when the organization needs them. Specific techniques for accomplishing this will be discussed in Chapter 8. Nonetheless, the planning process needs to consider myriad factors, including skill levels, individual employee "fit" with the organization, training, work systems, and projected demand, and then integrate these factors as a critical component of its HR strategy.

The third objective is to ensure that the organization is responsive to changes in its environment. The human resource planning process requires decision-makers to consider a variety of scenarios relative to the numerous domains in the environment. For example, the economy might grow, remain stagnant, or shrink; the industry might remain the same or become either more or less competitive; government regulation may remain the same, be relaxed, or become more stringent; technology may or may not be further developed. Human resource planning forces the organization to speculate and assess the state of its eternal environment. Anticipating and planning for any possible changes rather than passively reacting to such conditions can allow the organization to stay one step ahead of its competitors.

EXHIBIT 5.1 Key Objectives of Human Resource Planning

- Prevent overstaffing and understaffing
- Ensure the organization has the right employees with the right skills in the right places at the right times
- Ensure the organization is responsive to changes in its environment
- Provide direction and coherence to all HR activities and systems
- Unite the perspectives of line and staff managers

The fourth objective is to provide direction and coherence to all human resource activities and systems. Human resource planning sets the direction for all other HR functions, such as staffing, training, and development, performance measurement, and compensation. It also ensures that the organization takes a more systemic view of its human resource management activities by understanding the interrelatedness of the HR programs and systems and how changes in one area may impact another area. A coherent human resource plan will ensure, for example, that the areas in which employees are being trained are being incorporated into their performance measurements and that these factors are additionally considered in compensation decisions.

The fifth objective is to unite the perspectives of line and staff managers. Although human resource planning is usually initiated and managed by the corporate HR staff, it requires the input and cooperation of all managers within an organization. No one knows the needs of a particular unit or department better than the individual manager responsible for that area. Communication between HR staff and line managers is essential for the success of any HR planning initiatives. Corporate HR staff needs to assist line managers in the planning process but simultaneously acknowledge the expertise of and responsibility assigned to individual line managers in considering their input to the planning process.

Types of Planning

Planning is generally done on two different levels. *Aggregate planning* anticipates needs for groups of employees in specific, usually lower-level jobs (the number of customer service representatives needed, for example) and the general skills employees need to ensure sustained high performance. *Succession planning* focuses on key individual management positions that the organization needs to make sure remain filled and the types of individuals who might provide the best fit in these critical positions.

Aggregate Planning

The first step in aggregate planning is forecasting the demand for employees. In doing so, the organization needs to consider its strategic plan and any kinds and rates of growth or retrenchment that may be planned. The single greatest indicator of the demand for employees is demand for the organization's product or service. It is imperative when forecasting the demand for employees to clarify and write down any assumptions that might affect utilization of employees (new technology that might be developed or acquired, competition for retention of existing employers, changes in the production of a product or provision of a service, new quality or customer service initiatives, or redesign of work systems).

Although there are several mathematical methods, such as multiple regression and linear programming, to assist in forecasting demand for employees, most organizations rely more on the judgments of experienced and knowledgeable managers in determining employee requirements. This may be done through unit forecasting (sometimes called *bottom-up planning*), top-down planning, or some combination of both.

In unit forecasting, each individual unit, department, or branch of the organization estimates its future needs for employees. For example, each branch of a bank might prepare its own forecast based on the goals and objectives each branch manager has for the particular office. These estimates are then presented to subsequent layers of management, who combine and sum the totals and present them to senior management for approval.

This technique has the potential for being the most responsive to the needs of the marketplace because it places responsibility for estimating employee needs at the "point of contact" in service provision or product production. However, unless there is some mechanism for control and accountability for allocating resources, such a technique can easily lead managers to overestimate their own unit needs. Without accountability and control measures for costs and productivity, this technique can become quite inefficient as lower-level managers attempt to hoard employees without regard as to whether these human assets might better be deployed in another division of the organization.

Consequently, any system of unit forecasting needs to have an accompanying program of accountability for performance based, at least in part, on headcount. This underscores the need for having integrated HR systems and programs.

Top-down forecasting involves senior managers allocating a budgeted amount for employee payroll expenditures and then dividing the pool at subsequent levels down the hierarchy. Each manager receives a budget from her/his supervisor and then decides how to allocate these funds down to the next group of managers. This technique is similar to sales and profit plans in many organizations, whereby each unit is assigned a budgeted amount and then required to make decisions on deploying those resources in the manner most consistent with business objectives. Although this technique may be efficient, as senior management allocates HR costs within a strict organization-wide budget, there is no guarantee that it will be responsive to the needs of the marketplace. Allocations are based solely on what the organization can afford, without regard to input concerning demand and marketplace dynamics.

Unit forecasting promotes responsiveness to customers and the marketplace; top-down forecasting promotes organizational efficiency in resource allocation. Consequently, an organization can choose a planning technique that is consistent with its overall strategy. An organization whose key strategic objectives involve cost minimization can opt for top-down forecasting. An organization more concerned with change and adaptability can opt for unit or bottom-up forecasting. However, if an organization has objectives of both responsiveness and efficiency, it is possible to use both forms of forecasting and have middle levels of management responsible for negotiating the differences between the two techniques.

In addition to the demand for actual headcount of employees, the organization also needs to consider the demand for specific skills that it will require of its employees as part of the HR planning process. Changes in workplace demographics are having a significant impact on the skills that job applicants bring to an organization. Technology is also having an impact on the skills required of employees. Assessment of the demand for employees needs to consider not only numbers but also the kinds of workers who will best fit with the organization relative to personal characteristics, work habits, and specific skills.

Once demand for employees has been forecasted, the organization then has to plan for an adequate supply of employees to meet this demand. This process involves estimating the actual number of employees and determining the skills that these employees must have and whether their backgrounds, training, and career plans will provide a sufficient fit for the organization's future plans. This chapter focuses on the internal supply of labor. Chapter 8 expands the discussion to consider external labor markets.

One way to assess the abilities, skills, and experiences of existing employees is by using a skills inventory. In the past, these inventories were usually compiled and processed manually, but skills inventories are now usually computerized databases that are part of the organization's overall human resource information system. Each employee provides information on his or her experience, education, abilities, job preferences, career aspirations, and other relevant personal information. This allows an organization to gain a collective sense of who their employees are and what capabilities they have. Skills inventories must be constantly updated to be of any value to an organization. Changing employee backgrounds and preferences mandate that the skills inventory be updated at least annually.

Estimates of the existing supply of human resource relative to quantity is not a static measure; rather, it is dynamic. In the majority of medium and large organizations, employees change positions and job levels constantly or leave the organization. Consequently, any attempt to assess the supply of employees needs to assess mobility within the organization as well as turnover rates. This can be done through a mathematical technique known as *Markov analysis*, which describes the probability of employees staying with the job in any job category, moving to another job, or leaving the organization over a given time period, usually one year. It uses a transition probability matrix that is established based on historical trends of mobility. Markov analysis can also be utilized to allow managers to identify problem departments within an organization or positions that appear to be less desirable as reflected in high rates of turnover or low rates of retention. A sample Markov analysis is illustrated in Exhibit 5.2.

EXHIBIT 5.2 Transition Probability Matrix for a Restaurant

		One Year From Now			
		Servers	**Hosts**	**Buspersons**	**Exit**
	Servers	.80	.10	0	.10
Current Year	Hosts	.10	.70	0	.20
	Buspersons	.15	.05	.40	.40

Analysis of Matrix

		Retention Levels
	Servers	80%
	Hosts	70%
	Buspersons	40%

		Forecasted Levels			
Incumbents		**Servers**	**Hosts**	**Buspersons**	**Exit**
60	Servers	48	6		6
10	Hosts	1	7		2
20	Buspersons	3	1	8	8
	Total	52	14	8	16

The top portion of this exhibit presents a sample transition probability matrix. For the sake of simplicity, we will assume that there are three job classifications in the restaurant: servers, hosts, and buspersons. Horizontal readings show the movement anticipated during the coming year for each job classification based on historic trends. For example, 80 percent of the current staff of servers would be expected to remain employed in that capacity one year from now; 10 percent will become hosts; none will become buspersons; and 10 percent will leave the organization.

The bottom half of the exhibit first shows retention levels, followed by a forecast of the supply of employees expected in each position. To calculate these values, we take the number of incumbents and multiply them by the percentages from the transition probability matrix. Summing each of the columns that pertain to job classifications allows us to determine, given normal movement, expected supply levels of employees one year from now.

After reliable estimates have been made for both supply and demand of employees, programs can be implemented to address any anticipated surplus or shortage of employees in a particular job category. In planning for anticipated shortages, the organization first needs to consider whether the shortage is expected to be temporary or indefinite. This has implications for whether the organization should hire temporary or permanent employees or even consider subcontracting work to an outside vendor. If permanent employees are to be hired, the plan needs to be comprehensive and consider the types of employees that should be recruited, whether they should be recruited internally or externally, how long they will need for training to perform at acceptable levels, and how long the recruiting process has historically taken. Issues and strategies for addressing these concerns are discussed in Chapter 8.

Another important consideration is whether the individuals will need the latest skills or whether the organization requires more hands-on practical experience. The former strategy would suggest recruiting younger employees directly out of formal schooling or training programs; the latter strategy would suggest recruiting from competitors or possibly having older workers postpone retirement or work on a contract or part-time consulting basis.

If a surplus of employees is anticipated, a critical strategic issue that must be addressed is whether this surplus is expected to be temporary or permanent. The most extreme action to

EXHIBIT 5.3 Strategies for Managing Employee Shortages and Surpluses

Strategies for Managing Shortages	Strategies for Managing Surpluses
• Recruit new permanent employees • Offer incentives to postpone retirement • Rehire retirees part-time • Attempt to reduce turnover • Work current staff overtime • Subcontract work out • Hire temporary employees • Redesign job processes so that fewer employees are needed	• Hiring freezes • Do not replace those who leave • Offer early retirement incentives • Reduce work hours • Voluntary severance, leaves of absence • Across-the-board pay cuts • Layoffs • Reduce outsourced work • Employee training • Switch to variable pay plan • Expand operations

Adapted from Fisher, Schoenfeldt, and Shaw. Human Resource Management, *4d, 1999.*

reduce a surplus is to lay off employees. Layoffs should usually be conducted only as a last resort, given the effects they can have on the morale of remaining employees as well as the significant economic costs that often result from large-scale layoffs. Surpluses can also be addressed through early retirement programs, transfer and retraining of existing employees, and/or an across-the-board reduction in salaries or working hours. Exhibit 5.3 summarizes some strategies for managing employee shortages and surpluses. Shortages are discussed in more depth and detail in Chapter 8, while surpluses are discussed in Chapter 13.

Succession Planning

Succession planning involves identifying key management positions that the organization can not afford to have vacant. These are usually senior management positions and/or positions that the organization has traditionally had a very difficult time filling. Succession planning serves two purposes. First, it facilitates transition when an employee leaves. It is not unusual to have a departing employee work alongside his or her successor for a given period prior to departure to facilitate the transition. Succession planning aids in this process. Second, succession planning identifies the development needs of high-potential employees and assists with their career planning. By identifying specific individuals who might be asked to assume high-level responsibilities, the organization can attempt to develop key skills in these individuals that might be needed in subsequent assignments.

Although succession planning programs are relatively easy to understand in concept, actual practice shows that even though organizations realize how critical the processes are, they may fail to implement succession planning effectively. One criticism of existing succession planning models is that their timing often does not remain in synch with ongoing and evolving business needs, resulting in constant shortages or surpluses of talent. Reading 5.1,"Talent Management for the Twenty-First Century," briefly examines the history of talent management programs in organizations and then suggests that the process of balancing supply and demand of talent in organizations can be improved through the application of principles of operations and supply chain management.

Succession Planning at K. Hovanian Enterprises

Red Bank, New Jersey–based K. Hovanian Enterprises is one of the nation's largest homebuilders. The $2.6 billion company was recently cited by Fortune *as the nation's fifteenth-fastest-growing company. As it has acquired seven other homebuilding companies within a three-year period, senior management saw the need to develop a succession planning committee to select and approve candidates who had high potential to move the organization ahead. In assessing candidates, data is collected in confidence on each candidate that consists of detailed feedback provided by twelve to fourteen direct reports, colleagues, and senior managers. This* *data is used to assess leadership ability and potential. After a candidate is accepted by the committee, that person is notified, and he or she creates a plan for personal development that reflects his or her experience and background. Employees are expected to devote 10–20 percent of their time to their personal development plan. The company has reported successful results to date. One hundred percent of the employees who have completed the program have been promoted, whereas those hired from the outside have a promotion success rate of only 50 percent.*[6]

Traditional succession planning utilizes a relatively simple planning tool called a replacement chart. Replacement charts identify key positions, possible successors for each of these positions, whether each potential successor currently has the background to assume the job responsibilities, or the expected amount of time it will take for the potential successor to be ready. Replacement charts are easily derived from the organizational chart and are often part of the human resource information system: They can narrow in on one key position and the subordinates reporting to the individual holding that position. A sample replacement chart is presented in Exhibit 5.4.

In this example, Smith is the vice president of marketing and has three direct reports: Jones, Williams, and Anderson. Beneath the three reports' job titles is the expected period of additional time each will need to be ready to assume the vice president responsibilities. The assessments of time are generally not objective. They are usually based on the opinions and recommendations of higher-ranking managers. In this example, Smith may have provided the time estimates for the three subordinates based on subjective personal assessments.

Some organizations, however, are much more systematic about their succession planning. Their replacement charts may contain specific skills, competencies, and experiences rather than subjective estimates of time-readiness. This may help to overcome problems associated with personal bias and ensure that the most qualified individuals are promoted. Moreover, it allows an organization to provide its high-potential employees with more specific feedback regarding developmental needs. Such an approach might ensure that women and minorities have equal access to high-level management positions.

Clearly, the more volatile competitive organizations of the twenty-first century may need to develop much larger pools of talent with very broad sets of skills. Consequently, many organizations are beginning to embrace the development of succession planning strategies that are based more on organization-needed competencies and flexibility than focusing on subjective assessment of "readiness."

Succession planning has traditionally been very limited in scope, focused on senior executives within the organization. One estimate is that a typical organization's succession planning process involves no more than 2 percent of the organization's workforce.[7] Much of the process of succession planning has involved CEOs and other executives secretly identifying their chosen successors from among the ranks of existing employees.[8] Wall Street analysts also consider and weigh in on likely successors and their identities

EXHIBIT 5.4 Sample Replacement Chart

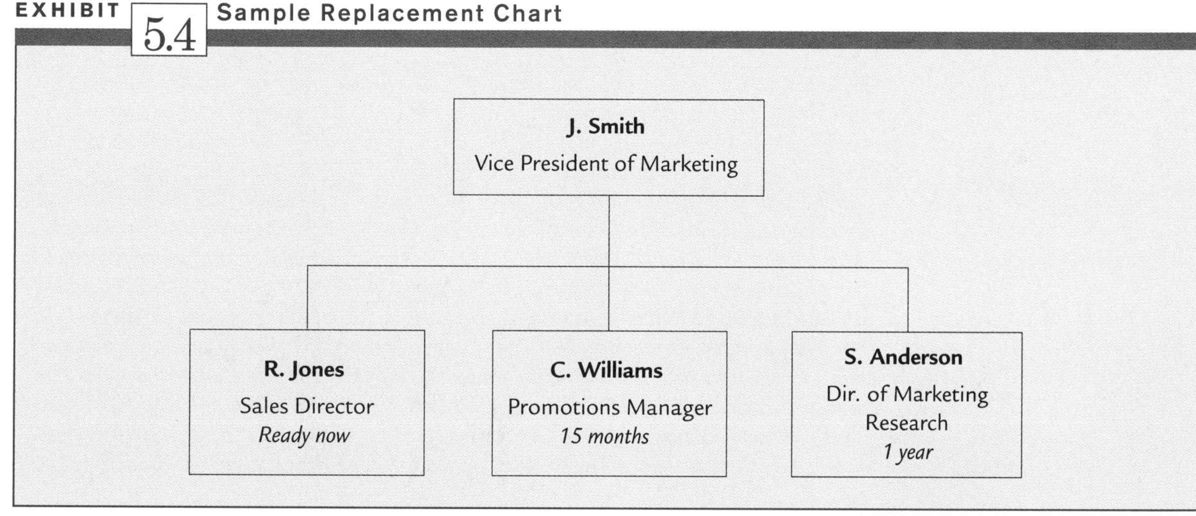

in assessing an organization's ongoing potential and value. In more recent years, however, succession planning has been taking place throughout the managerial and technical ranks of organizations and become seen increasingly as a critical component of an organization's talent management and development process. While individual high-potential employees are still identified and targeted for development, many organizations now take a broader approach and focus on pools of talent to ensure depth of employee skill development throughout the organization and the development of successors for a wide range of positions than just those at the senior executive ranks.

Some guidelines for effective succession planning are presented in Exhibit 5.5. First, succession planning efforts should be tied into an organization's strategy relative to projected needs and competencies over the coming five years. It is critical that the organization modify the plan accordingly as the organization responds to unanticipated events and revamps its strategy. Second, organizations should monitor the progress of succession planning initiatives and measure outcomes as frequently as financial performance is measured (preferably quarterly). This helps to ensure that targeted efforts are producing results. Third, succession planning efforts needs to ensure that all HR functions that impact the succession plan (hiring, training and development, compensation, and retention) are integrated and working in tandem. Typically, succession planning and these other areas are siloed without any coordination.[9] Planning efforts are a critical part of the organization's HR strategy and ideally function as a blueprint for all the various HR activities. Fourth, the organization needs to ensure that there is some centralized coordination of succession planning effort to ensure that top performers are not being coveted by different executives as a possible successor, potentially setting managers against each other in cannibalizing talent. Finally, succession planning efforts need to engage and involve managers throughout the organization. While HR can coordinate the process, effective succession planning requires "multiple owners" of the process. In-depth interviews with managers of business units are as critical as—if not more important than—any computer-generated information. Managers need to see the benefits of succession planning and be willing to partner with HR in developing plans for their workforce.

EXHIBIT 5.5 Guidelines for Effective Succession Planning

- Tie into organization's strategy (and modified accordingly)
- Monitor the progress and measure outcomes of succession planning initiatives
- Ensure that all HR functions that impact the succession plan are iterated and working in tandem
- Ensure centralized coordination of succession planning
- Engage and involve managers throughout the organization

Succession Planning at Eli Lilly

Eli Lilly and Co. is a global manufacturer and seller of pharmaceuticals. Based in Indianapolis, the organization employs more than 38,000 worldwide. Lilly first started using succession planning in 1957 but in 2002 moved its succession planning efforts online in an attempt to allow every employee with the company to apply for any job for which he or she feels qualified. The system is assessed by several metrics, including the skill level of talent in the pipeline and the number of positions for which there is a "ready" candidate. Three potential successors are named for each senior position within the organization. Roughly 3,800 positions have been identified as "key" positions—those that will cause disruption to operations if left unstaffed and not filled in a timely manner. Managers within the organizations can query the system to identify existing positions worldwide, those candidates being groomed for any such position, and skill gaps that might adversely impact the ability to fill the position. Whenever no candidates are available for succession, the system identifies new potential trainees and proposes individual development plans. Similarly, the system detects hidden "vulnerabilities," where individuals are part of more than three separate succession tracks. Individual employees who have been targeted for succession are not informed of the organization's sense of their potential for advancement in an attempt to alleviate stress and prevent breakdowns in communication and cooperation because of perceived competition.[10]

Succession planning not only helps to ensure that key management positions remain filled, but it also helps to identify critical training and development needs of both individual managers and the organization as a whole. Succession planning clearly involves taking an investment-oriented approach toward employees. Although the benefits of a well-developed succession planning program can be significant, such programs can also come at a significant cost to an organization. An employer should ensure that there is at least one individual able to assume every critical position if something prevents the incumbent from continuing in it; however, the more prepared an individual is for a promotion that he or she does not receive, the greater the possibility that he or she might seek such a position elsewhere. This is particularly true for succession planning programs built around defined management competencies. The end result of this process is the organization invests in an individual and a competitor receives the return on that investment. Succession planning initiatives aimed at key managers need to be coupled with a specific retention strategy designed for potential successors.

One key issue that organizations must address in their succession planning is the extent to which these efforts will be public and whether those targeted for grooming for higher-level assignments are informed of their "high-potential" status. These questions have been the subject of ongoing debate, as outlined in Exhibit 5.6. Telling employees that they have been identified as key potential players in the organization's future plans might reinforce these employees' decision to stay with the organization for a longer period of time in light of alternative career opportunities. At the same time, it may create expectations for these employees that advancement is guaranteed and/or imminent. In addition, it could create a kind of implied contract to workers that they are guaranteed continued employment, eroding the employment-at-will doctrine, which is discussed in Chapter 7. Not telling employees has the benefit of the employer "not committing" to employees and allows some flexibility in changing the mix of employees as business needs and the skill sets and experiences required to run the business change. On the other hand, if individuals are not aware that they have been targeted as "high potential," they may be more receptive to opportunities with other employers or consider going out on their own. One recent survey found that 37.5 percent of employers tell employees that they have been targeted; another found that 64 percent did so.[11] There is clearly no consensus as to whether such information should be kept confidential among the senior management team, and each organization should weigh the pros and cons presented in Exhibit 5.6 when deciding its strategy.

EXHIBIT 5.6 Pros and Cons of Disclosing Succession Planning

	Disadvantages	Advantages
Do Not Tell	High performers may leave the organization, unsure of their future	Allows flexibility as business needs change
Tell	Unrealistic expectations and implied contracts	Retention strategy

Succession Planning at Dole Food

California-based Dole Food Company, Inc., which produces and markets fruits, vegetables, and flowers, has more than 61,000 employees in more than 90 countries, with annual revenues of more than $4.6 billion. As the company grew from its humble origins, a decentralized structure was kept in place that allowed each unit to remain flexible relative to local market conditions. However, as Dole has become a worldwide conglomerate, this structure has inhibited the effective management of human capital at the executive level. To facilitate the global deployment of human capital, Dole instituted a succession planning model that revolves around four strategic competencies: accountability, business acumen, multifunctionality (cross-training), and vision/originality. Conducted entirely online, the program allows top managers access via a password. Employees provide a résumé and fill out personal data, including career interests and mobility restrictions, and assess themselves on the four competencies. The information is then made available to managers who can assess the data for promotability as well as identify those employees for whom a special retention strategy should be developed. The data is then used to create a career development plan for each employee and to keep executives informed about those internal candidates who might be best suited for an opening. The system also allows Dole to identify those areas where it has a "talent gap" so development opportunities might be provided, candidates sourced externally, or both, until those competencies are fully contained in-house.[12]

Succession planning efforts for the top executive spots have taken on more importance in recent years. With increasing pressure from boards and shareholders for continual profitability, the job of CEO has become far less attractive, particularly as the economy slows. Approximately 20 percent of the CEOs of America's 200 largest corporations were replaced in a recent year, and the average CEO tenure is currently less than three years.[13] Even more startling is the number of high-profile CEOs who have departed after 18 months or less on the job, either by resignation or ouster, including the CEOs of Procter & Gamble, Mattel, Gillette, and Maytag.[14] Although turnover at the CEO level can be beneficial for an organization, it can also be highly disruptive. Consequently, organizations need to pay special attention to planning at the CEO level.

CEO Succession Planning at General Electric

When legendary General Electric (GE) CEO Jack Welch announced his pending retirement, there was not as much concern among GE stakeholders as might be expected. In keeping with GE's reputation as one of the best organizations at grooming senior management, Welch had planned his succession for more than six years prior to his public announcement. Within one month of Jeffrey Immelt being named president and chairman-elect of GE as Welch's successor, two other top GE executives were named CEOs of Minnesota Mining and Manufacturing (3M) and Home Depot, Inc., affirming that GE is known for its superb training of senior executives for the chief executive's role.

GE's plan is relatively simple. Managers and executives are rotated from job to job every two to three years, with each new assignment being carefully designed to build experience and skills, creating a knowledgeable and experienced team of managers who have been exposed to a range of the giant corporation's divisions. Each new assignment involves a specific set of goals and expectations that must be met to ensure further advancement. The model is relatively simple and easy to duplicate, yet it takes a tremendous amount of time, energy, and commitment to make it succeed. At GE, the model is firmly ingrained in the corporate culture and creates a highly competitive system of performance management in which only the best and brightest executive will ultimately succeed.[15]

Mentoring

One key tool often used in succession planning is mentoring, whereby an individual executive or manager assumes responsibility for the development of an individual employee. Mentoring programs ideally mesh the needs of individual employees and those

EXHIBIT 5.7 Model of an Effective Mentoring Program

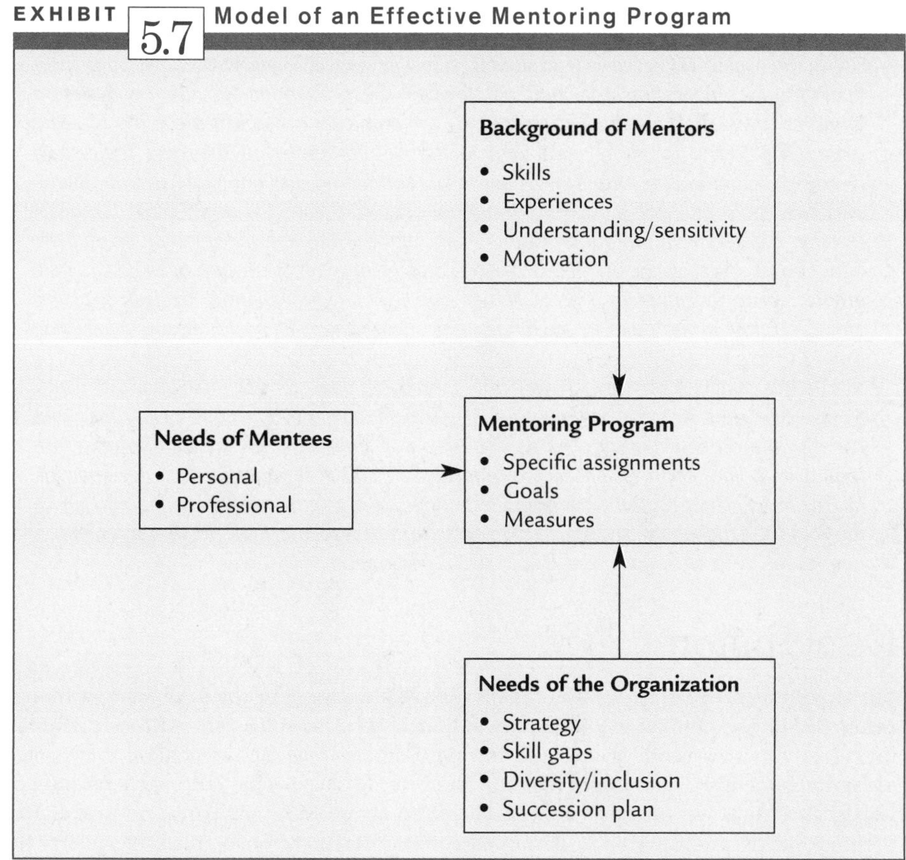

of the organization under the stewardship of a responsible individual senior to the individual being mentored. Exhibit 5.7 presents a model of an effective mentoring program.

In selecting individuals to be mentored, an organization will usually select an individual who has proven high levels of performance and/or is high potential in the case of a new hire. Mentoring should be holistic in nature and consider the needs of the individual being mentored, or mentee, from both personal and professional perspectives. Mentors should be selected who have the appropriate skill and experience to guide the mentee but, equally important, have a genuine interest in mentoring and some sensitivity toward the needs of the mentee. The mentoring program should be designed around specific organizational needs, considering the organization's strategy, identified skill gaps that need to be addressed and developed, and diversity and inclusion initiatives. To be effective, a mentoring program should have specific goals and measures of success identified prior to its inception. On a micro level, these might involve performance levels and skills development of individual employees. On a macro level, these might involve retention, knowledge transfer, and development and promotion of targeted minority groups.

Mentoring programs may be formal or informal. Informal mentoring programs have been criticized as being less effective because individual employees are prone to seeking out mentors who are like themselves, relative to demographic factors such as race, gender, ethnicity, and/or religion.[16] Organizations that have little diversity in the executive and managerial ranks may find that informal mentoring does little to alleviate this shortage. One criticism of succession planning programs is that many have perpetuated the development and succession of white males (or majority employees) at the expense of others, particularly in organizations where the demographic makeup of the executive team does not reflect the overall diversity of employees or percentage of employees from different groups in the organization's overall workforce. Reading 5.2, "Diverse Succession Planning: Lessons from the Industry Leaders," addresses this issue and presents suggestions as to how succession planning and diversity programs can work in tandem with each other.

Mentoring at Raytheon Vision Systems

Raytheon Vision Systems is a Goleta, California–based national defense contractor that produces detection and imaging devices. Several years ago, the organization came to the realization than 35 percent of its employees would be eligible to retire within five years. In many instances, potential retirees were the only individuals within the organization who knew how to do something, as they were the ones who had invented a product or process. In response to this potential talent drain, the organization created a mentoring program called Leave-A-Legacy, in which older employees who had vital, proprietary knowledge were paired with high-potential subordinate employees to facilitate transfer of knowledge. Knowledge sharing involves activities such as bringing mentees to meetings, introducing them to customers and involving them in the proposal or design stages of product development, and is facilitated by third-party coaches who work with the employee pairs to set individualized plans. Pending retirees report that the program gives them a strong sense of purpose and value to the organization as well as ensuring that their legacies are carried on. Mentees have higher commitment to the organization and a stronger interest in remaining at Raytheon. The program is a potential model for any organization concerned about the loss of experience, skills, and contacts from a resulting large-scale retirement of employees who are part of the Baby Boom generation.[17]

Conclusion

Effective human resource planning is the first key component for developing a human resource strategy. Human resource planning involves translating corporate-wide strategic initiatives into a workable plan for identifying the people needed to achieve these objectives; simultaneously, planning serves as a blueprint for all specific HR programs and policies. It is critical for the success of smaller, rapidly growing companies to ensure that their growth is properly managed and focused. Human resource planning allows the HR function to contribute to an organization's effectiveness by laying a foundation for proactive management that is strategically focused. Reading 5.3, "The Annual HR Strategic Planning Process: Design and Facilitation Lessons from Corning Incorporated Human Resources," provides a case study example that illustrates the relationship between HR planning and overall strategic planning for the organization.

More specifically, human resource planning facilitates a number of key processes within an organization. First, it facilitates leadership continuity through succession planning. It ensures that there will be no—or, at most, minimal—disruption of day-to-day operations because of unplanned departures.

Second, it facilitates strategic planning by examining the future availability of employees and their skill sets. Although human resource planning follows from the strategic plan, the information collected in the human resource planning process contributes to the assessment of the internal organization environment done in subsequent strategic planning.

Third, it facilitates an understanding of shifts and trends in the labor market through an examination of job requirements and employee capabilities. By assessing demographics, skills, and knowledge of employees and applicants vis-à-vis job requirements, the organization can remain ahead of its competitors in understanding the changing labor force.

Fourth, it facilitates employee development by determining the skills that are needed to achieve strategic objectives as well as to ensure future career success in the organization. Ideally, this can serve as a catalyst for investing in employees through targeted training and development programs.

Fifth, it facilitates budget planning and resource allocation by determining needs for employees in response to the organization's strategic plan. This is particularly important in labor-intensive service industries where a significant portion of the budget is assumed by direct and indirect payroll expenditures.

Sixth, it facilitates efficiency by estimating future employee surpluses and shortages. Costs of overstaffing and understaffing can be significant and are minimized by the human resource planning process, allowing organizations to maintain a more competitive cost structure.

Finally, it facilitates the organization's adaptation to its environment. By assessing the external factors that can affect the organization against existing employee skills and background, the organization is better able to maintain an appropriate fit with its environment by ensuring that it has the in-house talent to manage its relationship with its environment.

Critical Thinking

1. What are the major objectives of human resource planning? Why is each of these objectives critical for an organization's success? What benefits are provided by each that can result in a competitive advantage?
2. Why are aggregate and succession planning of critical importance? How might failures in these areas impact an organization's ability to compete?
3. What role might human resource planning play in each of the following organizations?
   - A small, rapidly growing technology company
   - A medium-sized nonprofit
   - A state government agency social services agency
   - A professional sports franchise
   - A company planning on acquiring or merging with a key competitor
4. Discuss the implications and pros and cons for managing surpluses and shortages by using the various strategies presented in Exhibit 5.3.
5. Discuss the pros and cons of informing employees that they have been targeted as part of the organization's succession planning process. What particular business conditions and/or strategy might make telling or not telling the more advantageous option?
6. Identify the steps you might take in consulting with the federal government about human resource planning. What factors would you suggest senior managers examine, and what obstacles to implementing change might exist?
7. Select three organizations in which a new CEO has assumed responsibility during the past year. Identify via news sources factors that may have led to the change at the top of the organization. What appears to be the reason for the succession, and what was the general reaction to the succession?
8. What problems are demographic shifts and layoff practices causing for succession planning? What role do competencies play in the succession planning initiatives of leading organizations?
9. Identify the positions within your school for which you feel succession planning is critical, such as deans, program directors, or department chairs. What critical skills or competencies are needed to perform these jobs? Design a succession planning program that is consistent with the strategic objectives of your school, utilizing the four phases of the succession model presented in the reading.
10. What are the advantages and disadvantages of establishing cross-cultural mentoring relationships?

Reading 5.1

11. What potential problems or limitations are possible in applying principles of supply chain management to the deployment of human capital?

Reading 5.2

12. Should special succession planning programs directed toward minorities be established? Discuss the pros and cons of identifying "best" and "best minority" candidates in succession planning, as is done at Proctor & Gamble and Motorola.

Reading 5.3

13. Explain the process used for human resource planning at Corning. What obstacles might exist to implementing such a process in another organization?

Exercises

1. Explain how the dean of your school would employ techniques of HR planning to decide how many faculty and staff to employ in the coming academic year and which specific employees to retain, reassign, or release. What critical pieces of information would the dean need in order to arrive at these decisions?
2. Visit the Web site for the Human Resource Planning Society, a professional organization of those who are involved with HR planning, at http://www.hrps.org. Identify the programs that they offer that might be of value to various organizations.

Chapter References

1. Kimes, M. "P&G's Leadership Machine," *Fortune*, 159, (7), p. 22 (April 13, 2009).
2. Wells, S. J. "Keeping Watch: Tracking the Evidence," *HR Magazine*, April 2002, pp. 34–35.
3. Wells, S. J. "Catch a Wave," *HR Magazine*, April 2002, pp. 31–37.
4. Leonard, B. "Study Shows U.S. Government Needs to Restructure Recruiting, Training Tactics," *HR Magazine*, June 2003, p. 36.
5. Staisey, N., Treworgy, D., and Shiney, M. "Managing for the Future: Human Capital Strategies at the United States Postal Service," *The Business of Government*, Spring 2002, pp. 47–50.
6. Ibid.
7. Webster, L. "Leaving Nothing to Chance," *T + D*, 62, (2), 56–61 (2009).
8. Kirchhoff, J. "Objective Measurement in Succession Planning. Society for Human Resource Management," article 016356, published at www.shrm.org/hrnews_/published/articles/CMS_016356.asp, May 2006.
9. Cooper, J. "Succession Planning: It's Not Just for Executive Anymore," *Workspan*, 49, (2), 44–47 (2006).
10. Olson, S. "Lilly Relying on Technology to Spot Management Talent," *Indianapolis Business Journal*, 29, (53), p. 16 (March 2, 2009).
11. Wells, S. J. "Who's Next?" *HR Magazine*, November 2003, pp. 45–50.
12. Roberts, B. "Matching Talent With Tasks," *HR Magazine*, November 2002, pp. 91–96.
13. Leonard, B. "Turnover at the Top," *HR Magazine*, May 2001, pp. 46–52.
14. Ibid.
15. Ibid.
16. Tyler, K. Cross-Cultural Connections. *HR Magazine*. 52, (10), pp. 77–83, October 2007.
17. Tyler, K. "Training Revs Up," *HR Magazine*, 50, (4), pp. 58–63, April, 2005.

READING 5.1

Talent Management for the Twenty-First Century

Peter Cappelli

Failures in Talent Management are an ongoing source of pain for executives in modern organizations. Over the past generation, talent management practices, especially in the United States, have by and large been dysfunctional, leading corporations to lurch from surpluses of talent to shortfalls to surpluses and back again.

At its heart, talent management is simply a matter of anticipating the need for human capital and then setting out a plan to meet it. Current responses to this challenge largely fall into two distinct – and equally ineffective – camps. The first, and by far the most common, is to do nothing: anticipate no needs at all; make no plans for addressing them (rendering the term "talent management" meaningless). This reactive approach relies overwhelmingly on outside hiring and has faltered now that the surplus of management talent has eroded. The second, common only among large, older companies, relies on complex and bureaucratic models from the 1950s for forecasting and succession planning – legacy systems that grew up in an era when business was highly predictable and that fail now because they are inaccurate and costly in a more volatile environment.

It's time for a fundamentally new approach to talent management that takes into account the great uncertainty businesses face today. Fortunately, companies already have such a model, one that has been well honed over decades to anticipate and meet demand in uncertain environments – supply chain management. By borrowing lessons from operations and supply chain research, firms can forge a new model of talent management better suited to today's realities. Before getting into the details, let's look at the context in which talent management has evolved over the past few decades and its current state.

How We Got Here

Internal development was the norm back in the 1950s, and every management development practice that seems novel today was commonplace in those years – from executive coaching to 360-degree feedback to job rotation to high-potential programs.

Except at a few very large firms, internal talent development collapsed in the 1970s because it could not address the increasing uncertainties of the marketplace. Business forecasting had failed to predict the economic downturn in that decade, and talent pipelines continued to churn under outdated assumptions of growth. The excess supply of managers, combined with no-layoff policies for white-collar workers, fed corporate bloat. The steep recession of the early 1980s then led to white-collar layoffs and the demise of lifetime employment, as restructuring cut layers of hierarchy and eliminated many practices and staffs that developed talent. After all, if the priority was to cut positions, particularly in middle management, why maintain the programs designed to fill the ranks?

The older companies like PepsiCo and GE that still invested in development became known as "academy companies": breeding grounds for talent simply by maintaining some of the practices that nearly all corporations had followed in the past. A number of such companies managed to ride out the restructurings of the 1980s with their programs intact only to succumb to cost-cutting pressures later on.

The problems faced by Unilever's Indian operations after 2000 are a case in point. Known as a model employer and talent developer since the 1950s, the organization suddenly found itself top-heavy and stuck when business declined after the 2001 recession. Its well-oiled pipeline saddled the company with 1,400 well-trained managers in 2004, up 27% from 2000, despite the fact that the demand for managers had fallen. Unilever's implicit promise to avoid layoffs meant the company had to find places for them in its other international operations or buy them out.

The alternative to traditional development, outside hiring, worked like a charm through the early 1990s, in large measure because organizations were drawing on the big pool of laid-off talent. As the economy continued to grow, however, companies increasingly recruited talent away from their competitors, creating retention problems. Watching the fruits of their labors walk out the door, employers backed even further away from investments in development. I remember a conversation with a CEO in the medical device industry about a management development program proposed by his head of human resources. The CEO dismissed the proposal by saying, "Why should we develop people when our competitors are willing to do it for us?" By the mid-1990s, virtually every major corporation asserted the goal of getting better at recruiting talent away from competitors while also getting better at retaining its own talent – a hopeful dream at the individual level, an impossibility in the aggregate.

Outside hiring hit its inevitable limit by the end of the 1990s, after the longest economic expansion in U.S. history absorbed the supply of available talent. Companies found they were attracting experienced candidates and losing experienced employees to competitors at the same rate. Outside searches became increasingly expensive, particularly when they involved headhunters, and the newcomers blocked prospects for internal promotions, aggravating retention problems. The challenge of attracting and retaining the right people went to the very top of the list of executives' business concerns, where it remains today.

The good news is that most companies are facing the challenge with a pretty clean slate: Little in the way of talent management is actually going on in them. One recent study, for example, reports that two-thirds of U.S. employers are doing no workforce planning of any kind. The bad news is that the advice companies are getting is to return to the practices of the 1950s and create long-term succession plans that attempt to map out careers years into the future – even though the stable business environment and talent pipelines in which such practices were born no longer exist.

That simply won't work. Traditional approaches to succession planning assume a multiyear development process, yet during that period, strategies, org charts, and management teams will certainly change, and the groomed successors may well leave anyway. When an important vacancy occurs, it's not unusual for companies to conclude that the candidates identified by the succession plan no longer meet the needs of the job, and they look outside. Such an outcome is worse in several ways than having no plan. First, the candidates feel betrayed – succession plans create an implicit promise. Second, investments in developing these candidates are essentially wasted. Third, most companies now have to update their succession plans every year as jobs change and individuals leave, wasting tremendous amounts of time and energy. As a practical matter, how useful is a "plan" if it has to be changed every year?

Talent management is not an end in itself. It is not about developing employees or creating succession plans, nor is it about achieving specific turnover rates or any other tactical outcome. It exists to support the organization's overall objectives, which in business essentially amount to making money. Making money requires an understanding of the costs as well as the benefits associated with talent management choices. The costs inherent to the organization-man development model were largely irrelevant in the 1950s because, in an era of lifetime employment and a culture in which job-hopping was considered a sign of failure, companies that did not develop talent in-house would not have any at all. Development practices, such as rotational job assignments, were so deeply embedded that their costs were rarely questioned (though internal accounting systems were so poor that it would have been difficult to assess the costs in any case).

That's no longer true. Today's rapid-fire changes in customers' demands and competitors' offerings, executive turnover that can easily run to 10%, and increased pressure to show a financial return for every set of business practices make the develop-from-within approach too slow and risky. And yet the hire-from-without models are too expensive and disruptive to the organization.

A New Way to Think About Talent Management

Unlike talent development, models of supply chain management have improved radically since the 1950s. No longer do companies own huge warehouses where they stockpile the components needed to assemble years' worth of products they can sell with confidence because competition is muted and demand eminently predictable. Since the 1980s, companies have instituted, and continually refined, just-in-time manufacturing processes and other supply chain innovations that allow them to anticipate shifts in demand and adapt products ever more accurately and quickly. What I am proposing is something akin to just-in-time manufacturing for the development realm: a talent-on-demand framework. If you consider for a moment, you will see how suited this model might be to talent development.

Forecasting product demand is comparable to forecasting talent needs; estimating the cheapest and fastest ways to manufacture products is the equivalent of cost-effectively developing talent; outsourcing certain aspects of manufacturing processes is like hiring outside; ensuring timely delivery relates to planning for succession events. The issues and challenges in managing an internal talent pipeline – how employees advance through development jobs and experiences – are remarkably similar to how products move through a supply chain: reducing bottlenecks that block advancement, speeding up processing time, improving forecasts to avoid mismatches.

The most innovative approaches to managing talent use four particular principles drawn from operations and supply chain management. Two of them address uncertainty on the demand side: how to balance make-versus-buy decisions and how to reduce the risks in forecasting the demand for talent. The other two address uncertainty on the supply side: how to improve the return on investment in development efforts and how to protect that investment by generating internal opportunities that encourage newly trained managers to stick with the firm.

PRINCIPLE 1 – Make *and* Buy to Manage Risk

Just as a lack of parts was the major concern of midcentury manufacturers, a shortfall of talent was the greatest concern of traditional management development systems of the 1950s and 1960s, when all leaders had to be homegrown. If a company did not produce enough skilled project managers, it had to push inexperienced people into new roles or give

Operations Principles Applied to Talent Management

A supply chain perspective on talent management relies on four principles, two that address the risks in estimating demand and two that address the uncertainty of supply.

PRINCIPLE 1

Make *and* Buy to Manage Risk

A deep bench of talent is expensive, so companies should undershoot their estimates of what will be needed and plan to hire from outside to make up for any shortfall. Some positions may be easier to fill from outside than others, so firms should be thoughtful about where they put precious resources in development: Talent management is an investment, not an entitlement.

PRINCIPLE 2

Adapt to the Uncertainty in Talent Demand

Uncertainty in demand is a given, and smart companies find ways to adapt to it. One approach is to break up development programs into shorter units: Rather than put management trainees through a three-year functional program, for instance, bring employees from all the functions together in an 18-month course that teaches general management skills, and then send them back to their functions to specialize. Another option is to create an organization-wide talent pool that can be allocated among business units as the need arises.

PRINCIPLE 3

Improve the Return on Investment in Developing Employees

One way to improve the payoff is to get employees to share in the costs of development. That might mean asking them to take on additional stretch assignments on a volunteer basis. Another approach is to maintain relationships with former employees in the hope that they may return someday, bringing back your investment in their skills.

PRINCIPLE 4

Preserve the Investment by Balancing Employee-Employer Interests

Arguably, the main reason good employees leave an organization is that they find better opportunities elsewhere. This makes talent development a perishable commodity. The key to preserving your investment in development efforts as long as possible is to balance the interests of employees and employer by having them share in advancement decisions.

up on projects and forgo their revenue. Though forecasting was easier than it is today, it wasn't perfect, so the only way to avoid a shortfall was to deliberately overshoot talent demand projections. If the process produced an excess of talent, it was relatively easy to park people on a bench, just as one might put spare parts in a warehouse, until opportunities became available. It may sound absurd to suggest that an organization would maintain the equivalent of a human-capital supply closet, but that was extremely common in the organization-man period.

Today, a deep bench of talent has become expensive inventory. What's more, it's inventory that can walk out the door. Ambitious executives don't want to, and don't have to, sit on the bench. Worse, studies by the consulting firm Watson Wyatt show that people who have recently received training are the most likely to decamp, as they leave for opportunities to make better use of those new skills.

It still makes sense to develop talent internally where we can because it is cheaper and less disruptive. But outside hiring can be faster and more responsive. So an optimal approach would be to use a combination of the two. The challenge is to figure out how much of each to use.

To begin, we should give up on the idea that we can predict talent demand with certainty and instead own up to the fact that our forecasts, especially the long-range ones, will almost never be perfect. With the error rate on a one-year forecast of demand for an individual product hovering around 33%, and with nonstop organizational restructurings and changes in corporate strategy, the idea that we can accurately predict talent demand for an entire company several years out is a myth. Leading corporations like Capital One and Dow Chemical have abandoned long-term talent forecasts and moved toward short-term simulations: Operating executives give talent planners their best guess as to what business demands will be over the next few years; the planners use sophisticated simulation software to tell them what that will require in terms of new talent. Then they repeat the process with different assumptions to get a sense of how robust the talent predictions are. The executives often decide to adjust their business plans if the associated talent requirements are too great.

Operations managers know that an integral part of managing demand uncertainty is understanding the costs involved in over- or underestimation. But what are the costs of developing too much talent versus to little? Traditionally, workforce planners have implicitly assumed that both the costs and the risks even out: that is, if we forecast we'll need 100 computer programmers in our division next year and we end up with 10 too many or 10 too few, the downsides are the same either way.

In practice, however, that's rarely the case. And, contrary to the situation in the 1950s, the risks of overshooting are greater than those of undershooting, now that workers can leave so easily. If we undershoot, we can always hire on the outside market to make up the difference. The cost per hire will be greater, and so will the uncertainty about employees' abilities, but those costs pale in comparison to retention costs. So, given that the big costs are from overshooting, we will want to develop fewer than 100 programmers and expect to fall somewhat short, hiring on the outside market to make up the difference. If we think our estimate of 100 is reasonably accurate, then perhaps we will want to develop only 90 internally, just to make sure we don't overshoot actual demand, and then plan to hire about 10. If we think our estimate is closer to a guess, we will want to develop fewer, say 60 or so, and plan on hiring the rest outside.

Assessing the trade-offs between making and buying include an educated estimation of the following:

- How long will you need the talent? The longer the talent is needed, the easier it is to make investments in internal development pay off.
- How accurate is your forecast of the length of time you will need the talent? The less certainty about the forecast, the greater the risk and cost of internal development — and the greater the appeal of outside hires.
- Is there a hierarchy of skills and jobs that can make it possible for candidates who do not have the requisite competencies to learn them on the job, without resorting to specialized development roles or other costly investments? This is particularly likely in functional areas. The more it is so, the easier it will be to develop talent internally.
- How important is it to maintain the organization's current culture? Especially at the senior level, outside hires introduce different norms and values, changing the culture. If it is important to change the culture, then outside hiring will do that, though sometimes in unpredictable ways.

The answers to these questions may very well be different for different functional areas and jobs within the same company. For instance, lower-level jobs may be easily and cheaply filled by outsiders because the required competencies are readily available, making the costs of undershooting demand relatively modest. For more highly skilled jobs, the costs of undershooting are much higher, requiring the firm to pay for an outside search, a market premium, and perhaps also the costs related to integrating the new hires and absorbing associated risks, such as misfits.

PRINCIPLE 2 – Adapt to the Uncertainty in Talent Demand

If you buy all of your components in bulk and store them away in the warehouse, you are probably buying enough material to produce years of product and therefore have to forecast demand years in advance. But if you bring in small batches of components more often, you don't have to predict demand so far out. The same principle can be applied to shortening the time horizon for talent forecasts in some interesting, and surprisingly simple, ways.

Consider the problem of bringing a new class of candidates into an organization. At companies that hire directly out of college, the entire pool of candidates comes in all at once, typically in June. Let's assume they go through an orientation, spend some time in training classes, and then move into developmental roles. If the new cohort has 100 people, then the organization has to find 100 developmental roles all at once, which can be a challenge for a company under pressure, say, to cut costs or restructure.

But in fact many college graduates don't want to go directly to work after graduation. It's not that difficult to split the new group in half, taking 50 in June and the other 50 in September. Now the program only needs to find 50 roles in June and rotate the new hires through them in three months. The June cohort steps out of those roles when the September cohort steps into them. Then the organization need find only 50 permanent assignments in September for the June hires. More important, having smaller groups of candidates coming through more frequently means that forecasts of demand for these individuals can be made over shorter periods throughout their careers. Not only will those estimates be more accurate but it will be possible to better coordinate the first developmental assignments with subsequent assignments — for instance, from test engineer to engineer to senior engineer to lead engineer.

A different way to take advantage of shorter, more responsive forecasts would be to break up a long training program into discrete parts, each with its own forecast. A good place to start would be with the functionally based internal development programs that some companies still offer. These programs often address common subjects, such as general management or interpersonal skills, along with function-specific material. There is no reason that employees in all the functions couldn't go through the general training together and then specialize. What used to be a three-year functional program could become two 18-month courses. After everyone completed the first course, the organization could reforecast the demand for each functional area and allocate the candidates accordingly. Because the functional programs would be half as long, each forecast would only have to go out half as far and would be correspondingly more accurate. An added advantage is that teaching everyone the general skills together reduces redundancy in training investments.

Another risk reduction strategy that talent managers can borrow from supply chain managers is an application of the principle of portfolios. In finance, the problem with holding only one asset is that its value can fluctuate a great deal, and one's wealth varies a lot as a result, so investment advisers remind us to hold several stocks in the same portfolio. Similarly, in supply chain management it can be risky to rely on just one supplier.

For a talent-management application, consider the situation in many large and especially decentralized organizations where each division is accountable for its own profit and loss, and each maintains its own development programs. The odds that any one division will prepare the right number of managers to meet actual demand are very poor. Some will end up with a surplus, others a shortfall. If, however, all of these separate programs were consolidated into a single program, the unanticipated demand in one part of the company and an unanticipated shortfall in another would simply cancel out, just as a stock portfolio reduces the volatility of holding individual stocks. Given this, as well as the duplication of tasks and infrastructure required in decentralized programs, it is a mystery why large organizations continue to operate decentralized development programs. Some companies are in fact creating talent pools that span divisions, developing employees with broad and general competencies that could be applied to a range of jobs. The fit may be less than perfect, but these firms are finding that a little just-in-time training and coaching can help close any gaps.

PRINCIPLE 3 – Improve the Return on Investment in Developing Employees

When internal development was the only way to produce management talent, companies might have been forgiven for paying less attention than they should have to its costs. They may even have been right to consider their expensive development programs as an unavoidable cost of doing business. But the same dynamics that are making today's talent pool less loyal are presenting opportunities for companies to lower the costs of training employees and thereby improve the return on their investment of development dollars, as they might from any R&D effort.

Perhaps the most novel approach to this challenge is to get employees to share in the costs. Since they can cash in on their experience on the open market, employees are the main beneficiaries of their development, so it's reasonable to ask them to contribute. In the United States, legislation prevents hourly workers from having to share in the costs of any training required for their current job. There are no restrictions, however, even for hourly workers, on contributing to the costs of developmental experiences that help prepare employees for future roles.

People might share the costs by taking on learning projects voluntarily, which means doing them in addition to their normal work. Assuming that the candidates are more or less contributing their usual amount to their regular job and their pay hasn't increased, they are essentially doing these development projects for free, no small investment on their part. Pittsburgh-based PNC Financial Services is one of several companies that now offer promising employees the opportunity to volunteer for projects done with the leadership team, sometimes restricting them to ones outside their current functional area. They get access to company leaders, a broadening experience, and good professional contacts, all of which will surely help them later. But they pay for it, with their valuable time.

Employers have been more inclined to experiment with ways to improve the payoff from their development investments by retaining employees longer, or at least for some predictable period. About 20% of U.S. employers ask employees who are about to receive training or development experiences to sign a contract specifying that if they leave the business before a certain time, they will have to pay back the cost. As in the market for carbon credits, this has the effect of putting a monetary value on a previously unaccounted for cost. This practice is especially common in countries like Singapore and Malaysia: Employees often leave anyway, but typically the new employer pays off the old one.

A more interesting practice is to attempt to hang on to employees even after they leave, making relatively small investments in maintaining ties. Deloitte, for example, informs qualified former employees of important developments in the firm and pays the cost of keeping their accounting credentials up-to-date. Should these individuals want to switch jobs again, they may well look to the place where they still have ties: Deloitte. And because their skills and company knowledge are current, they will be ready to contribute right away.

PRINCIPLE 4 – Preserve the Investment by Balancing Employee-Employer Interests

The downside of talent portability, of course, is that it makes the fruits of management development perishable in a way they never were in the heyday of the internal development model. It used to be that managers and executives made career decisions for employees, mating individuals and jobs. In the organization-man period, the company would decide which candidates were ready for which experience, in order to meet the longer-term talent needs of the organization. Employees had little or no choice: Refusing to take a new position was a career-ending move.

Today, of course, employees can pick up and leave if they don't get the jobs they want inside – and the most talented among them have the most freedom to do so. In an effort to improve retention, most companies – 80% in a recent survey by applicant-tracking company Taleo – have moved away from the chess-master model to internal job boards that make it easy for employees to apply for openings and so change jobs within the organization. Dow Chemical, for example, cut its turnover rate in half when it moved its vacancies to such internal boards.

These arrangements have effectively turned the problem of career management over to employees. As a result, employers have much less control over their internal talent. Employees' choices may not align with the interests of the employer, and internal conflicts are increasing because half of the employers in the U.S. no longer require that employees seek permission from their supervisors to move to new positions.

So it has become imperative for companies to find more effective ways to preserve their management development investment. The key is to negotiate solutions that balance the interests of all parties. McKinsey's arrangement for associates relies not only on how they rank their preferences for projects posted online but also on how the principals running the projects rank the associates. The final decision allocating resources is made by a senior partner who tries to honor the preferences of both sides while choosing the assignment that will best develop the skill set of each associate. Bear, Stearns established an office of mediation, which negotiates internal disputes between managers when an employee wants to move from one job to another in the firm.

...

The talent problems of employers, employees, and the broader society are intertwined. Employees want the skills they need when they need them, delivered in a manner they can afford. Employees want prospects for advancement and control over their careers. The societies in which they operate and the economy as a whole need higher levels of skills – particularly deeper competencies in management – which are best developed inside companies.

Those often-conflicting desires aren't addressed by existing development practices. The language and the frameworks of the organization-man model persist despite the fact that few companies actually employ it; there simply aren't any alternatives. The language comes from engineering and is rooted in the idea that we can achieve certainty through planning – an outdated notion. But before an old paradigm can be overthrown there must be an alternative, one that describes new challenges better than the old one can. If the language of the old paradigm was dominated by engineering and planning, the language of the new, talent-on-demand framework is driven by markets and operation-based tools better suited to the challenges of uncertainty. Talent on demand gives employers a way to manage their talent needs and recoup investments in development, a way to balance the interests of employees and employers, and a way to increase the level of skills in society.

Source: Harvard Business Review, March, 2008, 74–81. Reprinted by permission.

READING 5.2

Diverse Succession Planning: Lessons From the Industry Leaders

Charles R. Greer and Meghna Virick

Although practitioners and academics alike have argued for succession planning practices that facilitate better talent identification and creation of stronger "bench strength," there has been little attention to the incorporation of gender and racial diversity with succession planning. We discuss practices and competencies for incorporating diversity with succession planning and identify methods for developing women and minorities as successors for key positions. Improvements in strategy, leadership, planning, development, and program management processes are suggested. Recommendations for process improvement are developed from the diversity and succession planning literatures and interviews of 27 human resource professionals from a broad range of industries.

Those being positioned as future leaders tend to look and act an awful lot like people in those top positions ... It simply reflects an adherence to traditional methods of succession planning. (Tom McKinnon, Novations Group)

An emerging body of empirical evidence (e.g., Richard, 2000; Wright, Ferris, Hiller, & Kroll, 1995) indicates positive performance effects for diversity, and there are increasing indicators of the strategic importance of diversity to the success of companies. PepsiCo's previous CEO, Steve Reinemund, has said, "I believe that companies that figure out the diversity challenge first will clearly have a competitive advantage" (Terhune, 2005). A leading insurer, Allstate, also has embraced diversity and sees it as a source of competitive advantage, particularly in terms of expanding the number of minority policyholders (Crockett, 1999). Cosmetics maker L'Oreal attributes its global success in developing and marketing cosmetics to marketing initiatives that have drawn on international diversity (Salz, 2005).

Aside from the impact of competitive forces, some of the recent interest in succession planning may be attributed to the more active role of boards of directors in response to the Sarbanes-Oxley Act of 2002 and other regulatory developments. We see striking examples of succession planning successes and failures in organizations. For instance, GE's former CEO Jack Welch placed great emphasis on succession planning. One of his legacies was a process that allows the company, which is a veritable CEO greenhouse, to develop and promote talent from within the organization (Gale, 2001). Companies such as Bank of America, Dell, Dow Chemical, and Ely Lilly also have developed bench strength for their top positions by closely linking leadership development with succession planning (Conger & Fulmer, 2003; Karaevli & Hall, 2003). McDonald's provides an unusual example of preparedness in that the company was able to quickly designate a permanent replacement within six hours of CEO Jim Cantalupo's death, compared to the typical timetable of several months (Gibson & Gray, 2004; Hymowitz & Lublin, 2004). A few months later, when Cantalupo's successor, Charlie Bell, resigned because of terminal illness, McDonald's was able to immediately appoint Jim skinner as CEO (Gray, 2004; McGuirk, 2005).

While there have been note-worthy successes with succession planning, companies have had disappointments. At Coca-Cola, for example, Douglas Ivester replaced the late Robert Goizueta but lasted only two-and-a-half difficult years (Conger & Fulmer, 2003). While such failures may be attributed to flawed external searches, internal succession is often not an attractive option in the absence of succession planning and development. Some well-managed firms, such as Hewlett-Packard, Lincoln Electric, Southwest Airlines, and Whole Foods Markets, place heavy emphasis on promotion from within (Pfeffer, 1998) and treat succession planning as a critical process. Improved practices and competencies are needed for succession planning to meet the challenges posed by environmental turbulence, shortage of talent, and globalization (Karaevli & Hall, 2003).

Although these examples concern high-profile CEO succession, our broader approach involves succession to key managerial and professional positions and incorporates diversity initiatives. While failures in diversity are reflected in enduring underrepresentation of women and minorities in key positions, the combined effects of diverse succession planning have received little attention. Nonetheless, companies such as Allstate are using succession planning to increase diversity in key positions and women now occupy 40% of Allstate's executive and managerial positions, with 21% being held by minorities (Kim, 2003). Succession planning has also been critical to Harley-Davidson's accomplishments in diversity, as 17% of its vice presidents are women (PR Newswire, 2004).

Although we are unaware of any empirical evidence on the combined effects of diverse succession planning, the importance placed on both diversity and succession planning by several leading companies makes the topic relevant for consideration. Recent survey data also have called attention to the importance of diversity practices for increased organizational competitiveness (Esen, 2005). The significance of linking diversity management with succession planning is that more robust succession plans are produced and thus provide a strategic focus for the development of a diverse workforce. With such linkage, the planned succession of diverse talent provides more options for strategy formulation, such as the pursuit of growth in diverse and global markets or innovation-based strategies, while strategy implementation and operations benefit from the flexibility provided by a deeper talent pool.

Practitioners and academics alike have argued for succession planning practices that facilitate better talent identification and create stronger bench strength, yet there has been little attention paid to the incorporation of gender and racial diversity with succession planning. As companies attempt to revitalize their succession planning, it is a good time to address a major challenge for these efforts—specifically, integrating diversity with succession. This article addresses these concerns by identifying practices and competencies that can facilitate such integration. We draw on results of interviews with human resource professionals along with findings from the literature to identify suggestions for integrating the two processes.

Performance Effects of Diverse Succession Planning

While little research has focused on the performance effects of succession planning, some aspects of succession systems are related to financial performance (Friedman, 1986). Success factors include CEO involvement, rewards for developing subordinates, "earnestness" of performance reviews, forecasting the need for talent, and individual values consistent with organizational values (Friedman, 1986). Succession planning also has indirect impacts on measures of firm performance such as productivity and gross returns on assets (Huselid, Jackson, & Schuler, 1996). Indirect evidence of effective succession planning also is provided by the lower failure rates of insider CEOs (Charan, 2005) and the infrequency in which some very successful companies search beyond the firm to fill vacant CEO Positions. A landmark study of visionary companies found that poor succession planning caused gaps in internal supplies of leadership talent, as described in the following statement:

> *We found evidence that only two visionary companies (11.1 percent) ever hired a chief executive directly from outside the company, compared to thirteen (72.2 percent) of the comparison companies. Of 113 chief executives for which we have data in the visionary companies, only 3.5 percent came directly from outside the company, versus 22.1 percent of the 140 CEOs at the comparison companies. (Collins & Porras, 1994, p. 172)*

Promotion-from-within policies, which require some level of sophistication in succession planning, also are positively associated with measures of organizational performance (Delaney & Huselid, 1996). In fact, researchers have concluded that external successors are likely to be effective in more limited circumstances, such as when they are brought in to help with poorly performing firms (Wei & Cannella, 2002).

The future of many organizations is likely to depend on their mastery of diverse succession planning given that building bench strength among women and minorities will be critical in the competitive war for talent. For example, the U.S. Department of Labor predicts that women and minorities will account for 70% of the new participants in the labor force in 2008 (McCuiston, Wooldridge, & Pierce, 2004). Furthermore, women account for an increasing proportion of the well-educated workforce and are forecasted to receive 60% of all bachelor's degrees, 60% of all master's degrees, and 48% of all doctoral degrees by 2014 (U.S. Department of Education, 2005). Moreover, organizations lacking effective diversity management programs often experience excessive turnover and high replacement costs, loss of investments in training, brand image problems, poor employer image, and litigation (Hubbard, 2004). Absence of diversity programs also may result in strategic opportunity costs such as unrealized market access or lack of awareness (D. A. Thomas & Ely, 1996). Indeed, if the performance impact of diversity problems is approached in terms of litigation and related costs alone, the costs for some leading companies such as Coca-Cola ($102.5 million) and State Farm ($250 million) have been breathtaking (Hubbard, 2004).

The integration of diversity with succession planning requires an appropriate approach. Typically, organizations have adopted one of three approaches to managing diversity: an assimilation view that downplays differences; an access view that focuses on building diversity in order to gain access to ethnic consumer groups; and an integrated view that emphasizes uniform performance standards, personal development, openness, acceptance of constructive conflict, empowerment, egalitarianism, and a nonbureaucratic structure that encourages challenges to the status quo (D. A. Thomas & Ely, 1996). We argue that an integrated approach and a culture of inclusiveness are critical for diverse succession planning. Next we describe the methods used to examine the interface between diversity and succession planning.

Data Sources and Analysis

Our investigation was based on a review of the succession planning and diversity literature and on 27 interviews of HR professionals from 25 different organizations in the United States and one in Canada. Interviews were conducted using a semistructured format based on a set of seven questions that were revised as other issues became evident. Questions such as the following were used for the initial inquiries:

"What are some of the things that (your organization) does in terms of the succession planning of women and minorities?"; "Are there any practices that link the management of diversity to succession planning?"; and "Are there methods for increasing nominations of diverse professionals for admission to the pool of potential successors?"

Notes taken during the interviews were reviewed to identify practices or themes and then transferred to electronic files for analysis with computer search routines. Because we were concerned with identifying a broad range of practices we used qualitative "editing" and "template" analytical approaches (King, 1994; Miller & Crabtree, 1992). These approaches provide a search for meaningful content segments (Miller & Crabtree, 1992), and a codebook is compiled from the categories or themes that are created from an initial examination of the data or on an a priori basis. The codebook is then revised as themes emerge from continued searches of the data (King, 1994).

We identified several themes such as communication related to program strategy, values driving the process, and leadership involvement. Computer search routines were then used to refine the organization of content according to the themes and to reconcile the content with the narrative of our findings. We will discuss the practices that facilitate the integration of diversity with succession planning, beginning with the organization's business strategy. Information on interviewee demographics, job titles, and industries of their organizations is provided in Table 1. As indicated in Table 1, there was substantial diversity in our group of interviewees.

Practices and Competencies

Our discussion of practices and competencies follows a sequence of five processes that reflect the order of succession planning. We begin with a discussion of integration of strategy and planning. Figure 1 illustrates this integration with a feedback loop of diverse talent influencing strategy formulation. Next, we discuss leadership practices and then move on to critical planning practices. We then focus on systematic approaches to development and mentorship competencies, with special attention to paradoxes and challenges. Finally, we address program management practices and issues.

Business Strategy

The integration of diversity with business and human resource strategies, reflected in Figure 1, lays the foundation for identifying the range of competencies and for designing the developmental experiences required for succession. This integration process should be continuous and flexible, because the competencies for key personnel are likely to change in the future (McCall, 1998). The example of GE (Hymowitz & Lublin, 2004; Karaevli & Hall, 2003) demonstrates the critical role of alignment with business strategy. In GE's continuous process of succession planning, the CEO first sets objectives for the various business units. The process of setting objectives includes succession planning as a key part of the decision framework and involves attention to such issues as staffing, backups for key slots, global issues, technical workforce development, and diversity (Liebman, Bruer, & Maki, 1996). Motorola, PepsiCo, and IBM provide examples of other companies that integrate human resource development processes with business strategy (Childs, 2005; McCall, 1998). One of our interviewees stressed the importance of communication about strategy and goals of diversity initiatives. Without such communication, individuals targeted for development have no basis for comparing developmental requirements with their aspirations or for making informed decisions about program participation (Cespedes & Galford, 2004).

Leadership

Commitment and direct involvement by the CEO and the senior leadership team are clear threshold requirements for diverse succession planning. A recent comparison by Hewitt Associates of 20 top companies, including such companies as 3M, GE, IBM, Medtronic, Pitney Bowes, and Procter & Gamble, found that 100% of the CEOs in the top group (defined as companies that have built a sustainable pipeline of future leaders) were involved with leadership development relative to only 65% of other companies (Salob & Greenslade, 2005). Colgate-Palmolive, ranked among the best companies in diversity, devotes four sessions each year to developing plans for high-potential minorities (Sherwood & Mendelsson, 2005). The relevance of senior leadership involvement is revealed as follows:

> *... bringing attention to diversity into succession planning processes [requires that] ... that possible successors for key jobs are diversity-competent. Unfortunately, only a small percentage of companies take this seriously ... CEOs and others who are committed to changing the culture of their organizations to be better at welcoming and using diversity must make sure that the people most likely to replace them are strong on managing diversity. (Cox, 2001, p. 123)*

Leadership support for diverse succession planning is also reflected in reporting relationships. A recent survey of 1,700 HR executives found that a relatively small percentage of the companies for which the respondents worked (30%) had direct reporting relationships between their diversity officers and their CEOs (Alleyne, 2005). On the other hand, positions for chief diversity officers (CDOs) or vice presidents for diversity have been created at such companies as Abbott Labs, Boeing, Colgate-Palmolive, Johnson Controls, Lockheed Martin, PricewaterhouseCoopers, and Starbucks. Approximately 20% of our interviewees noted the importance of top leadership involvement in various capacities. One interviewee emphasized the importance of a direct reporting relationship to the CEO and noted that she had power to influence inclusion of women and minorities in succession planning solely by virtue of access to the CEO. Aside from the leadership provided by CEOs and diversity officers, management of diversity should be embraced by the entire leadership team and not perceived as the exclusive domain of the HR function (Childs, 2005).

Table 1 Architecture for Intangibles

Gender	Interviewees		
Men	18		
Women	9		
Race	**Interviewees**		
Caucasian	18		
African American	6		
Hispanic	2		
Asian	1		
Job Titles	**Interviewees**	**Job Titles**	**Interviewees**
President	2	Director of Diversity Council	1
Executive Vice President	1	Senior Human Resource Manager	1
Senior Vice President	3	Training Manager	1
National Managing Partner	1	Workforce Diversity Manager	1
Vice President	2	Human Resource Manager	1
Partner	1	Inspector—Career Development	1
Assistant Vice President	1	Human Resource Business Partner	1
Plant Manager	1	Human Resource Generalist	1
Senior Executive and Director	1	Senior Sourcing Specialist	1
Senior Director	1	Account Manager for College Relations and Recruitment	1
Director	3		
Industries		**Industries**	
Computer Manufacturing		Gift Manufacturing	
Commercial Real Estate		Pharmaceuticals	
Convenience Retailing		Public Administration	
Consulting Services		Railway Transportation	
Distilling		Semiconductor Manufacturing	
Electronics Manufacturing		Specialty Retailing	
Financial Services		Specialty Services	
Food Manufacturing		Telecommunications	
General Manufacturing		Wholesaling	

Note: Interviewees' organizations included nine Fortune 500 publicly traded companies, with the remainder being foreign-held companies, smaller publicly traded companies, privately held companies, small and large consulting firms, and one public-sector organization. One of the interviewees had retired from his executive position to become a consultant and educator.

In organizations that emphasize the use of succession planning for development, managerial accountability becomes important (McCall, 1998). This may take the form of mentoring. One interviewee, who led her company's diversity efforts, noted top-level involvement through the requirement for senior executives to personally mentor a woman or minority. She also stressed the frequency of succession planning, noting that they had a biannual succession planning exercise involving the CEO and the company's top 15 executives. In contrast, an interviewee from another company with a fairly comprehensive succession planning program indicated that until recently, the company had only addressed gender diversity in a reactive manner by asking, during the process of compiling lists of high potentials, whether any women candidates ought to be considered. Slow progress on diversity issues points to the importance of having more responsive leadership.

FIGURE 1 Diverse Succession Planning Practices and Competencies

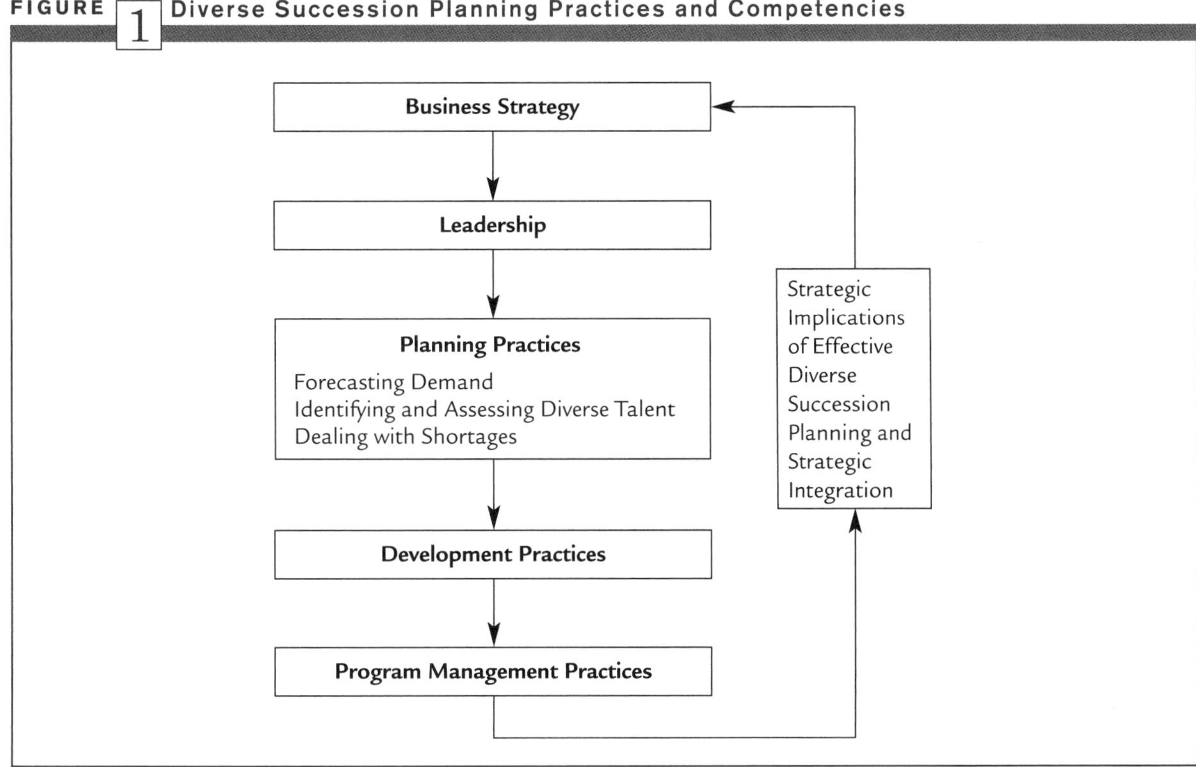

Planning

Forecasting Demand Although the demand for talent is driven by business strategy and the approach to diversity, the talents and behavioral competencies identified as requirements for future executive positions are likely to change (Charan, 2005; McCall, 1998). One of the paradoxes of planning is that with more turbulent conditions, planning is more difficult but it also becomes more valuable (Greer, 2001; Niehaus, 1988). Given the long developmental time horizons and the associated uncertainty, flexibility is best obtained with talent pool approaches to succession planning as opposed to more position-specific targeted approaches, typically referred to as replacement planning (Carnazza, 1982).

Talent Identification and Assessment Early identification of talent is important for the development of broad range of experiences needed to fill executive positions (McCall, 1998), and our interviewees stressed the need to reach deeper into the organization. Fortunately, our understanding of early talent identification is improving, especially the role of learning and learning agility, which are critical indicators of success in senior leadership positions (Lombardo & Eichinger, 2000). McCall and his colleagues have identified several learning-oriented dimensions that are helpful for early identification such as "seeks opportunities to learn," "is committed to making a differences," "has the courage to take risks," "seeks and uses feedback," and "learns from mistakes" (McCall, 1998, pp. 128–129). Measures of learning ability, defined as the ability and willingness to learn from experience, or the ability to learn as conditions change, also are available (Eichinger & Lombardo, 2004; Lombardo & Eichinger, 2000). The common problem of negative bias in performance evaluations for minorities makes measures of learning agility particularly relevant to the issue of diverse succession planning. One of our interviewees noted her company's reliance on a measure of learning agility in the use of data and on a measure of results orientation toward both deadlines and goals.

One of the most heavily utilized approaches for identifying talent for succession planning involves performance evaluations. This approach has problems, given evidence of negative bias in performance evaluations of minority managers (Kilian, Hukai, & McCarty, 2005). Companies leading the way in developing minority executives take a different approach by emphasizing results, relying on objective indicators of competency, and focusing on measurable track records to identify talent (Thomas & Gabarro, 1999). One interviewee mentioned the use of an anecdotal profile of potential successors as an important component of assessment. Another interviewee stressed the importance of objective standards of potential and readiness for promotion to offset unconscious biases against women. Assessment-center procedures are also used for succession planning and have potential for diversity initiatives (Conger & Fulmer, 2003; Klimoski, 1997; Yeung, 1997).

Additional recommendations deal with formalization, involving more decision makers, and the degree to which decisions on participation should be centralized. More specifically, it has been recommended that organizations should keep the list of high potentials subject to revision while another recommendation is to allow for self-nominations (Conger & Fulmer, 2003). An interviewee noted the value of his company's human resource inventory system in identifying employees who are ready for opportunities. Leaders in succession planning such as Eli Lilly, Hewlett-Packard, Citigroup, and the U.S. Army have adopted group approaches that have the advantage of utilizing more than one individual's perceptions of potential (Karaevli & Hall, 2003). Along this line, Deloitte & Touche has changed its succession process from one in which the departing manager selected a successor to a more centralized approach. When vacancies arise in the top ranks, senior managers across the country review short lists of candidates keeping diversity objectives in mind (Armour, 2003).

A variant of this approach, noted by one interviewee, was to have decentralized identification of high potentials, along with some centralized oversight with interwoven diversity objectives. This approach was considered to be the key to her company's success in succession planning, and is consistent with organizations such as Lockheed-Martin. When oversight reveals that women and minorities are not represented in developmental programs, managers are asked to provide explanations. The manager of organizational effectiveness has the authority to promote developmental opportunities, even if it means changing succession plans (Bogan, 2002). Replacement lists are also monitored at companies such as IBM and Dow Corning (Salomon & Schork, 2003), and several interviewees told us that their companies will not fill some jobs without conversations aimed at having a diverse slate of candidates.

Another concern for talent identification is related to the residual effects of differences in past assignments. Current successors to top-level positions often have benefited from prior advantageous developmental assignments and have sometimes been selected simply due to their similarity to past incumbents in terms of work experiences and demographic characteristics of gender, race, and age (Frase-Blunt, 2003). Such similarity biases are more likely to occur in the absence of formal succession planning (Rothwell, 2001). This heightens the need for defining competencies for senior-level positions in terms of specific behaviors with the purpose of making the process more transparent and acceptable (McKinnon, 2003).

Certain technical planning practices are also relevant to diverse succession. At Procter & Gamble, top-level managers designate three successors: an "emergency" replacement, who is typically a peer who could fill the position very quickly; a "planned" successor, who will be prepared to fill the position after some period of time if provided with the correct developmental experiences; and a potential "diversity" successor (Himelstein & Forest, 1997). In a similar vein, Motorola attempts to identify three successors: an immediate replacement, someone who could fill the position with three to five years of development, and the best qualified woman candidate beyond any already identified for the first two categories. Four years after the program's implementation, the company increased the number of minority women vice presidents from one to eleven (Caudron, 1999; Himelstein & Forest, 1997).

Dealing with Shortages One approach for dealing with shortages of diverse talent when there is no time for longer-term development is referred to as "priming the pump." This approach encourages early promotions or brings in diverse talent from the outside. The following account of a presentation to Boeing employees by James Bell, Boeing's CFO and president, provides perspective on the need for rapid progress:

> *When high-potential young people from diverse backgrounds look at Boeing's organization chart—or [those of] any of a thousand large publicly traded companies—more often than not, they're seeing a picture that doesn't appropriately reflect their experience." He argued that that reality simply must change in order for Boeing to maintain its market leadership. ... (Orenstein, 2005, p. 234)*

Some interviewees noted the importance of developing a culture of inclusiveness as employees look upward in the hierarchy to see if there are people who look like them. Minority employees are likely to ask, "Is the environment accepting of me?" Quick-fix approaches that bypass developmental time, or methods based on expediency, can produce ill-prepared successors and cause problems in morale and turnover (Rothwell, 2001). As such, they should be viewed with caution. As Charan (2005, p. 81) noted, "A quick infusion of talent may be a company's only course, but it is no way to run a railroad." Nonetheless, we found that some organizations obtain quick infusions of talent by bringing in senior-level women and minorities from the outside or by relying on early promotions. One of our interviewees noted the symbolic importance of success stories and reported successful use of judicious pump priming with the early promotion of a high-potential woman who improved the environment for women engineers in his company.

Development

Systematic Approaches Evidence indicates that companies with good reputations for developing people, such as Colgate-Palmolive, Emerson Electric, General Electric, Johnson & Johnson, Procter & Gamble, and Sherwin-Williams (Charan, 2005), have been both systematic and persistent over a long period of time before having obtained results (Carnazza, 1982; Charan, 2005; Conger & Fulmer, 2003). Succession planning at the American Red Cross includes talented women and minorities in special developmental programs and emphasizes communication and individual career development plans (Frase-Blunt, 2003). The key to development lies in providing challenging assignments to high potentials with accountability for profit and loss and close evaluation of performance in these roles (Cappelli & Hamori, 2005; Cespedes & Galford, 2004; Charan, 2005). Women's inexperience with profit-and-loss responsibility is one of the reasons for their slow progress in obtaining senior-level jobs (Catalyst, 2003). Many leading companies have recognized and are addressing this issue. Lateral moves are especially important in large complex companies dominated by engineering or other technical work (Flynn, 1998), since many key professional positions are not on the vertical career track.

Contact and visibility with senior leaders is also important. The Hewitt study cited earlier found that 95% of the companies in the top group create such opportunities for high potentials (Salob & Greenslade, 2005). One of our interviewees emphasized the critical importance of positioning succession planning programs so that they focus on developing high potentials rather than on diversity per se. His approach was to ensure diversity in the succession pool, with the overall emphasis being the creation of a "leadership pipeline full of good people." Special programs for women and minorities may be hindered by the stigma of special treatment (Murrell & James, 2001), and may not conform to the special consideration test proposed by Roosevelt Thomas because they are not open to everyone (R. Thomas, 1990). As Thomas has stated, "Does this program or policy give special consideration to one group? If so, it won't solve your problem—and may have caused it" (R. Thomas, 1990). Other observers (Liff, 1997) and some of our interviewees also cautioned against special succession planning programs for women and minorities. One interviewee, in reference to women and minorities in leadership ranks, stated that "the way they got there is more important than the fact that they got there." Interviewees also noted that programs championed by only a few senior leaders are unlikely to be successful in the long term because of the lack of organizational support and the absence of a systematic approach. After the champions are gone, the programs often fail.

Nonetheless, it has been argued that in the absence of special programs that are targeted specifically toward women and minorities, very little is likely to change. Special programs have had an impact in some organizations, such as GE and shell (Reinhold, 2005), Deloitte & Touche (Anderson, 2005), and IBM (D. Thomas, 2004). However, such programs reflect the reality of constrained resources that prevent unlimited access for all employees. Special programs also address the problem of small numbers. As one interviewee pointed out, if women and minorities are simply given the same assignments as everyone else, some will get interesting assignments while others will not. Because of smaller numbers, when women and minorities leave as a result of uninteresting or unchallenging assignments, there are serious problems for diversity objectives. We sometimes encountered contradictions in that interviewees initially noted the inadvisability of special programs but later mentioned that their companies provided such programs for women and minorities.

Special challenges often occur in professional settings when there are small proportions of women or minorities. In these circumstances, they are visible because of their uniqueness and isolated because they have few diverse peers (Estlund, 2003). Interestingly, when women comprise a small proportion in a professional setting, those in early-career stages may not perceive senior women as role models because they view such women as lacking in power or behaving more like men than women (Ely, 1994; Murrell & James, 2001).

Women employed in industries that rely heavily on operations face such challenges. One interviewee told us that women sometimes faced so much difficulty in gaining acceptance in operations that they simply concluded it was not worth their effort to pursue a career in the area. Another interviewee told us that the old guard would conclude that a woman might not be suited for a position because it was a "tough job" involving 24/7 operations or unions. Other interviewees reported difficulties in obtaining representation of women in technology areas, such as chip design and manufacturing. These experience gaps are critical, because operations voids in the skill portfolios of women reduce their opportunities to move into senior executive ranks.

Mentorship Scholars have found differences in mentoring experiences when different races and genders are involved (Noe, Greenberger, & Wang, 2002; Wanberg, Welsh, & Hezlett, 2003). For example, when women are mentored by women, they are likely to learn more about overcoming barriers to promotion and methods for achieving career and family balance (Noe et al., 2002; Ragins & McFarlin, 1990). With same-race mentorship relationships, there also tends to be more psychological or social support (Noe et al., 2002; D. Thomas, 1990). However, because of the scarcity of women and minorities in senior positions, cross-gender and cross-race mentoring relationships are prevalent (Noe et al., 2002; Ragins & Cotton, 1991; Wanberg et al., 2003). Nonetheless, cross-gender mentoring relationships can add value because they enable men and women to gain insights and perspectives about how the other gender handles workplace issues (Clawson & Kram, 1984; Noe et al., 2002).

PepsiCo, which has been cited as a leader in diversity (Sherwood & Mendelsson, 2005; Terhune, 2005), views cross-race mentorship as more than a substitute for same-race or same-gender mentoring. Its former CEO, Steve Reinemund encouraged mentoring across race and gender lines. More specifically, Reinemund required his direct reports to serve as sponsors for diversity across race and gender lines. An African American serves as the sponsor for white men, a white man sponsors African Americans, and a white woman sponsors Latinos (Terhune, 2005). PepsiCo's current CEO, Indra Nooyi, has said that the company wants its managers to be "'comfortable being uncomfortable' so they're willing to broach difficult issues in the workplace" (Terhune, 2005, p. B1).

Nonetheless, cross-race relationships require that mentors have diversity skills. With cross-gender mentoring relationships, there also can be problems unless mentors and protégés maintain appropriate levels of admiration, informality, respect, and trust, and act in a manner that does not create public image problems (Clawson & Kram, 1984). Not all mentors perform well in such roles, but some are truly exceptional. One interviewee told us that his company made this discovery when it asked approximately 100 of its minority and women employees about their experiences with mentors. When asked "Who was there for you in your darkest hour?" the group identified a very small number of mentors, and the same person was identified by as many as 20 to 25 individuals. Thus, efforts to identify exceptional mentors and leverage their skills should be a priority. Another interviewee emphasized the importance of training mentors and the value for basic guidelines such as advising mentors to avoid discussions of sensitive issues like race until the parties have established a strong relationship. Good match-ups are always important, but are critical when high-level executives are involved. One interviewee told us that she personally makes the high-level match-ups and lags the notification to mentors by several days so that mentees have an opportunity to anonymously decline a mentor.

The retention of women and minorities, which is critical for program success, is being addressed with a number of different practices. A number of companies have been using affinity groups to provide informal guidance and networking assistance. For example, Nike now has such groups for African Americans, lesbians, gays, and other minorities (Jung, 2005). One interviewee told us that a great deal of coaching is needed in order to retain minorities and that the senior executive in charge of diversity needs to be heavily involved in these efforts, while another observed that succession planning is closely related to retention, but only when the company follows through with development. Another interviewee noted dramatically that organizations need to "throw their arms around women and minorities" in order to retain them and that coaching and mentoring are key for their retention. He also reported that his organization is reaching down to minority professionals, even at entry level, to help them discover the hidden messages that are critical to development in the organization's culture.

Program Management

Reward Systems Some companies are using reward systems to motivate diverse succession. Senior executives at Denny's have a strong incentive to be responsive to diversity because the representation of minorities and women in their divisions accounts for 25% of executives' bonuses (Brathwaite, 2002). At Hyatt, where 52% of the company's managers are women, diversity goals account for 15% of bonuses (Prince, 2005). When retention levels for high potentials drop below 90% at Colgate-Palmolive, top-level managers lose money. Some companies have also implemented rewards for mentors. One interviewee told us that his company initially used only recognition as a reward for mentors who performed well, but that over time the company began to include such contributions in the performance-appraisal process and linked financial rewards to these efforts. On the other hand, intrinsic rewards may be very powerful, particularly for minority mentors who mentor other minorities (Noe et al., 2002; Ragins, 1997a, 1997b).

Confidentiality and Transparency Trade-offs As with some other issues in diverse succession planning, there are differing views on transparency. The Hewitt study noted earlier found that 68% of the top companies in leadership development informed employees of their status as high potentials while only approximately 53% in the comparison group of companies provided such information (Salob & Greenslade, 2005). With transparency, the career objectives of the candidate may be considered in developmental planning. On the other hand, complete transparency may interfere with teamwork and demotivate those not included on the list (Conger & Fulmer, 2003; Yeung, 1997). Informing employees of their readiness for promotion is a related issue. We saw varying levels of transparency. Whereas some of our interviewees stressed the importance of transparency and informing employees of their readiness in succession, other interviewees advocated the use of partial transparency, where individuals are told that they are making a contribution but are not explicitly told that they are high potentials to avoid raising expectations.

Measurement and Evaluation Ideally, evaluations should draw on both qualitative and quantitative measures. Qualitative measures may include factors such as satisfaction with the process at multiple levels of the managerial hierarchy and across gender and racial groups, as well as perceptions of fairness and usefulness. Such measures could include perceived smoothness of succession and the perceived quality of the talent pool. Quantitative metrics may include measures such as the percentage of diverse successors obtained internally, waiting time or ratios of "ready now" potentials to incumbents, and reservoirs of cross-functional or international experience, as well as attrition rates for diverse high potentials (Conger & Fulmer, 2003). One of our interviewees emphasized the importance of setting diversity targets in anticipation of the future racial composition of the United States. His pragmatic justification of his organization's adoption of special programs was that "you are not going to be successful by osmosis." Another interviewee, who stressed the importance of measuring the impact of such programs with more than one indicator, noted that her company uses 14 different measures of program effectiveness, including retention, advancement, hiring, and development. A different interviewee's company conducts periodic "pulse surveys" of employees to determine satisfaction with their career succession. Whatever the metric or diversity scorecard used, it is important to allow sufficient time, perhaps four to five years, for the effects to be evident before a program is evaluated and potentially disbanded (Carnazza, 1982).

Implications for Practitioners Industry leaders such as PepsiCo and Allstate provide examples of companies that have made diversity a part of their competitive strategies while others, such as GE, Eli Lilly, and Dell Computer provide examples of companies that are very skilled at developing talent through succession planning. We have identified a number of competencies and practices being used by industry leaders to increase diversity through the succession planning process. Those who wish to excel in this area will benefit from the knowledge of industry leaders that we have attempted to convey in this article. As we have noted, some leading companies recognize the performance effects to be gained from excellence in managing diversity and the value that may be created through such initiatives. The persuasion of others to support the development of organizational competencies in diverse succession planning requires a clear understanding of the business strategy and communication of how the process will provide a source of competitive advantage. Nonetheless, despite the rapid successes of a few leading organizations, senior leaders who seek to persuade their colleagues on the importance of diverse succession planning should understand and communicate to others that success in this area involves a longterm commitment.

Several practices appear to be important for success in this area, and a summary of these practices and competencies is provided in Table 2.

Table 2 Suggestions for Diverse Succession Planning

Strategic Integration
- Obtain alignment between business strategy and diverse succession planning.
- Frame programs with emphasis on developing "high potentials."
- Communicate the strategy and goals of the program.

Leadership
- Establish a values basis for diverse succession.
- Obtain commitment of top executives to personally mentor diverse successors.
- Include diversity goals in performance evaluations of executives and managers.
- Establish close contact between the CEO and the chief diversity officer.
- Establish authority and accountability for diverse succession goals.
- Involve the chief diversity officer in all succession decisions.

Planning Processes
- Identify behavioral competencies for the future while recognizing that these may change.
- Disseminate descriptions of specific behavioral competencies required for top positions.
- Conduct deep internal searches for diverse high potentials.
- Rely on assessments from credible mentors.
- Evaluate recruiting programs for their impact on diversity.
- Use valid objective testing where feasible to offset unconscious bias in assessment.
- Use valid objective indicators of performance, competence, and potential where possible.
- Use valid learning-oriented early identifiers of executive ability.
- Use valid measures of results orientation to identify high potentials.

Development Practices
- Develop behavioral competencies for training, development planning, and evaluations.
- Focus on the advantages of same-race/gender or cross-race/gender mentorship.
- Provide anonymous procedures for mentees to decline pairing with potential mentors.
- Provide opportunities for diverse high potentials to gain exposure with senior executives.
- Create critical masses of diverse talent to prevent tokenism and related effects.
- Use "pump priming" where appropriate to signal commitment and opportunity.

Program Management Practices
- Monitor flows of diverse successors into core areas as opposed to periphery functions.
- Identify effective mentors and leverage their skills.
- Include diverse succession in executive performance evaluation and reward systems.
- Inform high potentials of their inclusion in succession plans and obtain their inputs.
- Monitor succession and high-potential programs for representation of diversity.
- Evaluate diverse succession planning with multiple metrics such as retention, development, advancement, and size of the "ready now" talent pool.

In summary, we need to understand how organizations can implement the guidance we received from one of our interviewees, that organizations should "throw their arms around women and minorities." We were deeply impressed by the passion and commitment of our interviewees, many of whom shared deep feelings with us. We point to the passion and persuasiveness of champions of diversity and talented mentors as a means of selling the importance of the process to others in the organization. Nonetheless, we acknowledge that diverse succession planning is a sensitive area in many organizations since future opportunities and limited numbers of developmental assignments are at stake, particularly where greater progress in diversity is needed. Although it is sometimes difficult to obtain candid answers about diverse succession planning practices, there is much to learn in most organizations about this issue and much to be gained in terms of competitive advantage. Further investigation of questions, such as one posed by one of our interviewees, would seem to add value. The surprising answer to his question, "Who did you turn to in your darkest hour?" indicates that there is much to learn in most organizations.

Those organizations that excel at managing diversity will need to be creative in developing programs that reduce the negative side effects of special programs for women and minorities. Such programs pose a paradox, because while the conventional wisdom is that they should not be adopted, they appear to be necessary for progress.

Acknowledgments

The authors would like to acknowledge questions posed by Shannon Ryan, executive vice president, Stagen Leadership, Inc., which provided focus for our inquiry. In addition, they would also like to express their appreciation for insights provided by John Baum, Jim Combs, John Delaney, Mark Huselid, Shirley Rasberry, Lynn Wooten, and two anonymous reviewers.

Source: Human Resource Management, 47, (2), 351–367 (2008). Reprinted by permission.

REFERENCES

Alleyne, S. (2005). But can you walk the walk. Black Enterprise, 35(2), 100–106.

Anderson, R. (2005). Welcome to the diversity and inclusion initiative. Deloitte & Touche USA LLP. Retrieved February 29, 2008, from http://www.deloitte.com/dtt/article/

Armour, S. (2003, November 24). Playing the succession game. USA Today, p. 3B.

Bogan, C. (2002). Best practices in career path definition and succession planning. Chapel Hill, NC: Best Practices, L.L.C. (revised 2005).

Brathwaite, S. T. (2002). Denny's: A diversity success story. Franchising World, 34(5), 28–29.

Cappelli, P., & Hamori, M. (2005). The new road to the top. Harvard Business Review, 83(1), 25–23.

Carnazza, J. (1982). Succession/replacement planning programs and practices. New York: Center for Research in Career Development, Columbia Business School, Columbia University.

Catalyst. (2003). Women in U.S. corporate leadership: 2003. New York: Author.

Caudron, S. (1999). The looming leadership crisis. Workforce, 78(9), 72–79.

Cespedes, F. V., & Galford, R. M. (2004). Succession and failure. Harvard Business Review, 82(6), 31–42.

Charan, R. (2005). Ending the CEO succession crisis. Harvard Business Review, 83(2), 72–81.

Childs, J. T., Jr. (2005). Managing workforce diversity at IBM: A global HR topic that has arrived. Human Resource Management, 44, 73–77.

Clawson, J. G., & Kram, K. E. (1984). Managing cross-gender mentoring. Business Horizons, 27(3), 22–32.

Collins, J. C., & Porras, J. I. (1994). Built to last: Successful habits of visionary companies. New York: HarperCollins.

Conger, J. A., & Fulmer, R. M. (2003). Developing your leadership pipeline. Harvard Business Review, 81(12), 76–84.

Cox, T., Jr. (2001). Creating the multicultural organization: A strategy for capturing the power of diversity. San Francisco, CA: Jossey-Bass.

Crockett, J. (1999, May). Winning competitive advantage through a diverse workforce. HR Focus, pp. 9–10.

Delaney, J. T., & Huselid, M. A. (1996). The impact of human resource management practices on perceptions of organizational performance. Academy of Management Journal, 39, 949–969.

Eichinger, R. W., & Lombardo, M. M. (2004). Learning agility as a prime indicator of potential. Human Resource Planning, 27, 12–15.

Ely, R. J. (1994). The effects of organizational demographics and social identity on relationships among professional women. Administrative Science Quarterly, 39, 203–238.

Esen, E. (2005). 2005 workplace diversity practices: Survey report. Alexandria, VA: Society for Human Resource Management.

Estlund, C. (2003). Working together: How workplace bonds strengthen a diverse democracy. New York: Oxford University Press.

Flynn, G. (1998). Texas Instruments engineers a holistic HR. Workforce, 77(2), 26–30.

Frase-Blunt, M. (2003). Moving past 'mini-me': Building a diverse succession plan means looking beyond issues of race and gender. HR Magazine, 48(11), 95–98.

Friedman, S. D. (1986). Succession systems in large corporations: Characteristics and correlates of performance. Human Resource Management, 25, 191–213.

Gale, S. F. (2001). Bringing good leaders to light. Training, 38, 38–42.

Gibson, R., & Gray, S. (2004, April 20). Death of chief leaves McDonald's facing challenges. Wall Street Journal, pp. Al, A16.

Gray, S. (2004, November 24). Naming Skinner CEO, McDonald's shows its executive depth. Wall Street Journal, p. B2.

Greer, C. R. (2001). Strategic human resource management: A general managerial approach (2nd ed.). Upper Saddle River, NJ: Prentice Hall.

Himelstein, L., & Forest, S. A. (1997, February 17). Breaking through. Business Week, p. 64.

Hubbard, H. E. (2004). The diversity scorecard: Evaluating the impact of diversity on organizational performance. Oxford, UK: Elsevier Butterworth-Heinemann.

Huselid, M. A., Jackson, S. E., & Schuler, R. S. (1996). Technical and strategic human resource management effectiveness as determinants of firm performance. Academy of Management Journal, 40, 171–188.

Hymowitz, C., & Lublin, J. S. (2004, April 20). McDonald's CEO tragedy holds lessons. Wall Street Journal, pp. B1, B8.

Jung, H. (2005, April 21). Few women, minorities in top positions at Nike. The Oregonian, p. B01.

Karaevli, A., & Hall, D. T. (2003). Growing leaders for turbulent times: Is succession planning up to the challenge? Organizational Dynamics, 32, 62–79.

Kilian, C. M., Hukai, D., & McCarty, C. E. (2005). Building diversity in the pipeline to corporate leadership. Journal of Management Development, 24, 155–168.

Kim, S. (2003). Linking employee assessments to succession planning. Public Personnel Management, 32, 533–547.

King, N. (1994). The qualitative research interview. In C. Cassell & G. Symon (Eds.), Qualitative methods in organizational research: A practical guide (pp. 14–36). London: Sage.

Klimoski, R. (1997). Assessment centers. In L. H. Peters, C. R. Greer, & S. A. Youngblood (Eds.), Blackwell encyclopedic dictionary of human resource management (pp. 10–12). Oxford, UK: Blackwell.

Liebman, M., Bruer, R. A., & Maki, B. R. (1996). Succession management: The next generation of succession planning. Human Resource Planning, 19, 16–29.

Liff, S. (1997). Two routes to managing diversity: Individual differences or social group characteristics. Employee Relations, 19, 11–26.

Lombardo, M. M., & Eichinger, R. W. (2000). High potentials as high learners. Human Resource Management, 39, 321–329.

McCall, M. W. (1998). High flyers: Developing the next generation of leaders. Boston: Harvard Business School Press.

McCuiston, V. E., Wooldridge, B. R., & Pierce, C. K. (2004). Leading the diverse workforce: Profit, prospects and progress. Leadership and Organizational Development Journal, 25, 73–91.

McGuirk, R. (2005, January 17). Cancer claims ex-McDonald's CEO Bell at 44. Associated Press Newswires.

McKinnon, T. (2003). Building a diversity succession plan you can really use. Presentation at the American Society for Training and Development, ASTD 2003 International Conference and Exposition. San Diego, CA.

Miller, W. L., & Crabtree, B. F. (1992). Primary care research: A multimethod typology and qualitative road map. In B. F. Crabtree & W. L. Miller (Eds.), Doing qualitative research (pp. 3–28). Newbury Park, CA: Sage.

Murrell, A. J., & James, E. H. (2001). Gender and diversity in organizations: Past, present, and future directions. Sex Roles, 45, 243–257.

Niehaus, R. (1988). Models for human resource decisions. Human Resource Planning, 11, 95–107.

Noe, R. A., Greenberger, D. B., & Wang, S. (2002). Monitoring: What we know and where we might go. In G. R. Ferris & J. J. Martocchio (Eds.), Research in personnel and human resources management (Vol. 21, pp. 129–173). Greenwich, CT: JAI Press.

Orenstein, E. G. (2005). The business case for diversity. Financial Executive, 21(4), 22–25.

Pfeffer, J. (1998). The human equation: Building profits by putting people first. Boston: Harvard Business School Press.

PR Newswire. (2004, January 15). General Electric, Harley-Davidson, and Shell Oil Company earn prestigious Catalyst Award for efforts to advance women employees.

Prince, C. J. (2005). Doing diversity. Chief Executive, 207, 46–49.

Ragins, B. R. (1997a). Antecedents of diversified mentoring relationships. Journal of Vocational Behavior, 51, 90–109.

Ragins, B. R. (1997b). Diversified mentoring relationships in organizations: A power perspective. Academy of Management Review, 22, 482–521,

Ragins, B. R., & Cotton, J. L. (1991), Easier said than done: Gender differences in perceived barriers to gaining a mentor. Academy of Management Journal, 34, 939–951.

Ragins, B., & McFarlin, D. (1990). Perceptions of mentor roles in narcissistic self-esteem management in cross gender mentoring relationships. Journal of Vocational Behavior, 37, 321–339.

Reinhold, B. (2005). Smashing glass ceilings: Why women still find it tough to advance to the executive suite. Journal of Organizational Excellence, 24, 43–55.

Richard, O. C. (2000). Racial diversity, business strategy, and firm performance: A resource-based view. Academy of Management Journal, 43, 164–177.

Rothwell, J. J. (2001). Effective succession planning: Ensuring leadership continuity and building talent from within (2nd ed.). New York: American Management Association.

Salob, M., & Greenslade, S. (2005), How the top 20 companies grow great leaders, 2005 Research Highlights: Hewitt Associates LLC. Retrieved February 29, 2008, from http://was4.hewitt.com/hewitt/resource/

Salomon, M. F., & Schork, J. M. (2003). Turn diversity to your advantage, Research Technology Management, 46, 37–44.

Salz, P. A. (2005, May 2). A vital building block in attaining that competitive edge calls for the creation of a unique corporate anatomy. Wall Street Journal, p. A8.

Sherwood, S., & Mendelsson, M. (2005, October). Marriott goes far beyond the numbers. Diversity Inc., pp. 29–34.

Terhune, C. (2005, April 19). Pepsi, vowing diversity isn't just image polish, seeks inclusive culture. Wall Street Journal, p. B1,

Thomas, D. (1990). The impact of race on managers' experiences of developmental relationships (mentoring and sponsorship): An intra-organizational study. Journal of Organizational Behavior, 11, 479–492.

Thomas, D. (2004). Diversity as a strategy. Harvard Business Review, 82(9), 98–108.

Thomas, D. A., & Ely, R. J. (1996). Making differences matter: A new paradigm for managing diversity. Harvard Business Review, 74(5), 79–90.

Thomas, D. A., & Gabarro, J. J. (1999). Breaking through: The making of minority executives in America. Boston: Harvard Business School Press.

Thomas, R. (1990). From affirmative action to affirming diversity. Harvard Business Review, 68(2), 107–117.

U.S. Department of Education. (2005). Projections of education statistics to 2014. Retrieved from http://nces.ed.gov/programs/projections/projections2014/index.asp

Wanberg, C. R., Welsh, E. T., & Hezlett, S. A. (2003). Mentoring research: A review and dynamic process model. In J. J. Martocchio & G. R. Ferris (Eds.), Research in personnel and human resources management (Vol. 22, pp. 39–124). Greenwich, CT: JAI Press.

Wei, S., & Cannella, A., Jr. (2002). Power dynamics within top management and their impacts on CEO dismissal followed by inside succession. Academy of Management Journal, 45, 1195–1206.

Wright, P., Ferris, S. P., Hiller, J. S., & Kroll, M. (1995). Competitiveness through management of diversity: Effects on stock price valuation. Academy of Management Journal, 38, 272–287.

Yeung, A. K. (1997). Succession planning. In L. H. Peters, C. R. Greer, & S. A. Youngblood (Eds.), Blackwell encyclopedic dictionary of human resource management (pp. 340–341). Oxford, UK: Blackwell.

READING 5.3

The Annual HR Strategic Planning Process: Design and Facilitation Lessons from Corning Incorporated Human Resources

Debbie Bennett, and Matthew Brush

Abstract

This article presents an internal perspective on the Annual HR Strategic Planning Process Corning's HR team uses to prioritize HR investments and deliver services aligned with business requirements. Over three years, this process has integrated inputs from a Human Capital Planning process, the HR function's transformation goals, and other corporate initiatives into a one-page Annual Operating Plan with supporting objectives. The authors share process, meeting design and facilitation lessons learned from their work with their clients.

Corning Corporate History

From a shatter-proof lens for railroad lanterns and a glass envelope for Edison's new light bulb filament, to premium quality LCD glass substrates and highly engineered optical fiber, Corning has established a 150-plus year legacy of technological innovation.

Through the early 1990s, Corning maintained a diverse portfolio of businesses that typically generated $4 billion to $5 billion in annual revenues; the sale of its well known consumer business (Corelle dishes, Visions cookware, etc.) funded a massive investment in the telecommunications sector and explosive growth, followed by a major retrenchment. All of which, of course, had significant impact on the HR function as well as the company overall.

Corning Human Resources History

The HR function can be described as having a sterling legacy of constructive union labor relations, innovative corporate Centers of Excellence (COEs), and responsive generalists in the business – all three of which were managed separately for a number of years until they were consolidated under a single senior vice president in April 2002. This fragmented approach caused a disconnect between the COEs and the businesses. This created dynamic tension between centralization and decentralization of strategy as the COE specialists and the business unit generalists struggled in regard to their roles relative to strategy development and deployment. When businesses were ascendant, the pendulum swung toward decentralization and the businesses set the agenda for what HR needed to focus on; when the businesses were not performing as well, as during the telecom downturn in 2001, the pendulum swung toward centralization as a way of controlling costs and focusing the HR function on the most important work. Developing a robust Annual Operating Plan (AOP) process and applying the human capital planning process to the HR function has helped Corning HR to step out of the pendulum dynamic and better balance multiple sources of input regarding the work that HR should be doing.

Corning's HR AOP Process

This paper will examine the creation and evolution of Corning's Annual HR Strategic Planning Process – the Process that Corning's HR team uses to prioritize HR investments and deliver services aligned with business requirements. We will examine how this process has blended the inputs from an innovative Human Capital Planning process, the HR function's transformation goals, and other corporate initiatives into a one-page Annual Operating Plan with supporting objectives. These objectives are woven into our compensation programs and are used to track our progress toward our goals. Where practical, we will examine the process, meeting design, and facilitation lessons we have learned from our work with our clients – the senior leaders in Corning Human Resources.

It is important to note that the current Human Capital Planning process was built from foundational conversations with John Boudreau and Peter Ramstad (Boudreau, et al, 2003) that were then operationalized for Corning in partnership with Sibson Consulting.

Corning Human Resources – Business Context

As Corning's telecommunications businesses grew rapidly in the late 1990s, the human resources function had to change. HR was supporting explosive growth in an environment of plentiful resources. The HR leadership team developed four transformation goals (Figure 1) to guide that growth. We had to build a better connection between HR function strategy and business strategy, support growth globally, deliver scalable solutions and still manage to reach our broad cost targets.

FIGURE 1 Corning Human Resources Transformation Goals

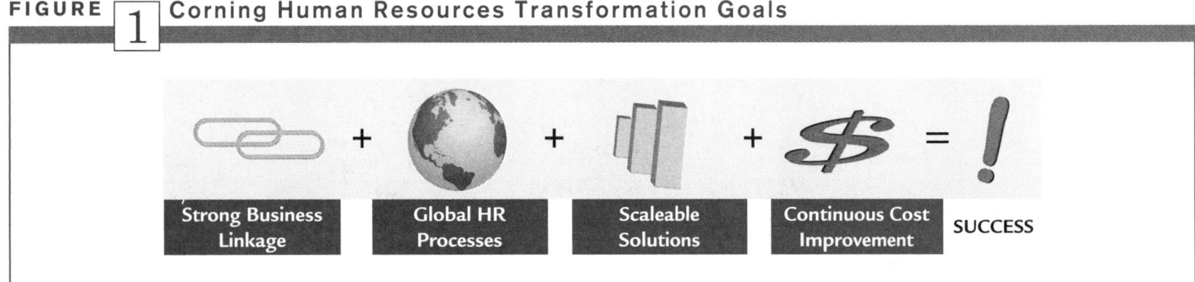

Then, the telecommunications businesses started to contract dramatically. Although the transformation goals still made sense, the emphasis changed completely. Suddenly, it was primarily a "cost game" – with a target of spending no more than 1% of revenue on the global HR function – and scalability became focused on becoming *smaller* instead of *bigger*. The Senior Vice President of HR, Kurt Fischer, challenged his team to still deliver the global mindset and processes, as well as a strategy process that linked with the client businesses, but faster, and on a much tighter budget.

Decentralization v. Centralization

The tension between centralization and decentralization is new to no one in the organizational development field. How it played out in Corning HR was fairly classic. The field generalists were part of the business unit and the business unit provided direction, funding, appraisal and rewards. The COE folks were part of 'corporate' and their direction came primarily from large corporate initiatives emanating from the Senior Management Team or HR Function Strategy. COEs had some input from the business units but it was fragmented and often driven by whichever business happened to be the current "king of the hill". This created a situation in which the unspoken job of the generalist was often to protect the business from the COEs. The field generalists were accused of "going native" and the COE specialists were accused of not knowing what was really going on, what was really needed by the people who generated revenue.

That is not to say that no collaboration or cooperation occurred, but rather, that it was situation dependent. Then the telecommunications bust forced us to look at how ineffective and inefficient this approach had become. Accepting the fact that both centralization and decentralization have advantages and disadvantages, the question before us was how we could better balance the two. Part of the answer came in the form of our AOP Planning Process.

Human Capital Planning as Transformation Accelerator

Realizing that the first transformation goal, linking HR strategy effectively with business strategy, represented a powerful tool for driving change in the global HR function, Fischer commissioned a next-generation Human Capital Planning process using a combination of internal and external consultants. The result was a four step process (Figure 2) that gave business unit generalists shared tools and language for deconstructing client business strategy into actionable steps for talent development, and gave the HR function as a whole a way of identifying and prioritizing needs across businesses and COEs.

Steps 1 through 3 of the process enable the identification of the talent that will *most impact* the success of business strategy, and the talent that will be *most impacted by* the success of the business strategy, enabling a multi-year look at the number, type and timing of critical talent requirements supported by rigorous gap analysis that drives staffing actions. Step 4 delivers powerful organizational effectiveness diagnostic tools and a prioritization process that balances competing inputs from the business unit HR team members.

As part of successive years of continuous improvement efforts, Corning has managed to build in opportunities for robust input from corporate COEs (compensation and benefits, workforce development and learning, talent management, and employee relations) and the regional HR leads outside the U.S. These inputs ensure that the division HR leads have an understanding of issues that will impact their global businesses, including HR technical and regulatory changes as well as regional dynamics that will impact one or more businesses that operate in greater China, Japan and Europe.

The COEs and the corporate HR leadership team have found it valuable to receive spreadsheets that consolidate the outputs from each business, allowing them to see all of the major initiatives to be undertaken by HR resources within the businesses on one sheet, and all the work being requested of the COEs by the businesses on another. This facilitates the identification of common requests across businesses that might otherwise go unidentified or might not make the final prioritized list, and forms one of the inputs for the AOP discussion.

Our annual strategic planning process (Figure 3) for HR brings together several key components including: (a) corporate strategy and the implications of that strategy for HR, (b) HR function strategy including the strategic direction for each of the COEs, and (c) the outputs of the Human Capital Planning process for each of the business units, which is essentially the HR implications of each of their business strategies. As all of these involve "strategy," they all encompass a three to five year planning process. These three

FIGURE 2 Corning's Human Capital Planning Process

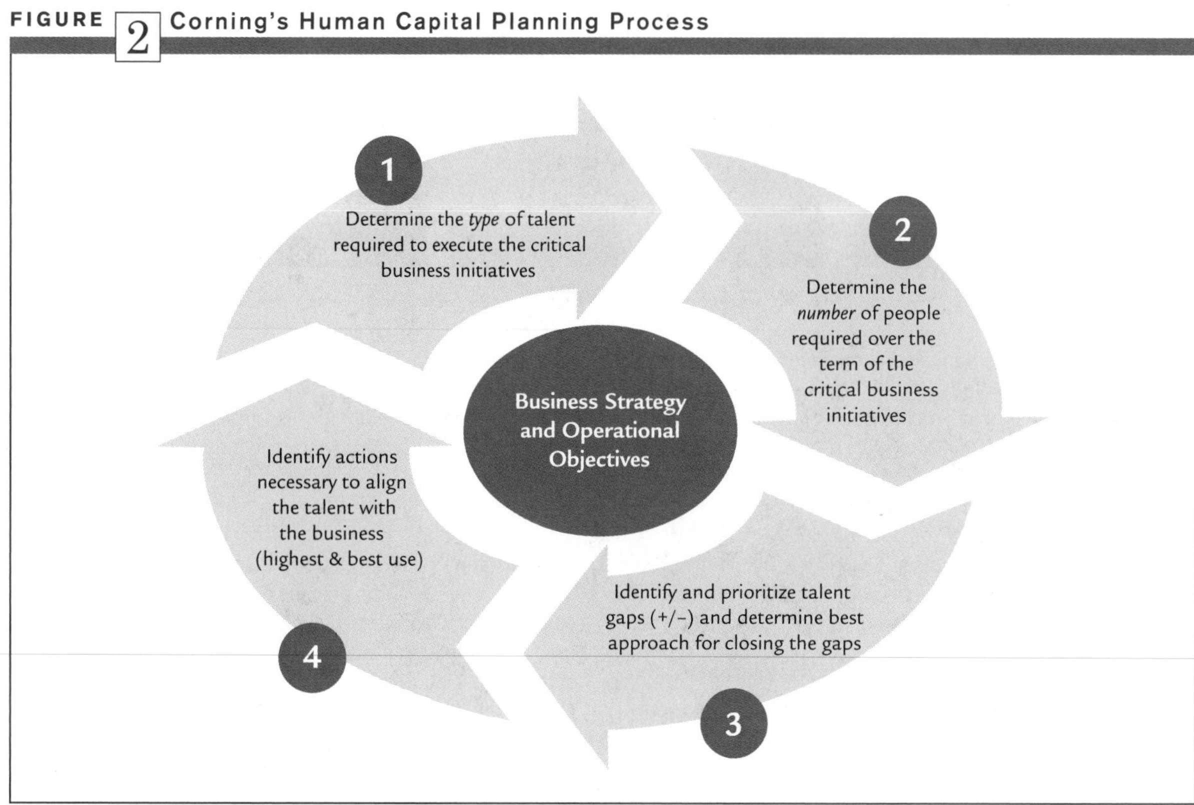

FIGURE 3 Annual Strategic Planning Process

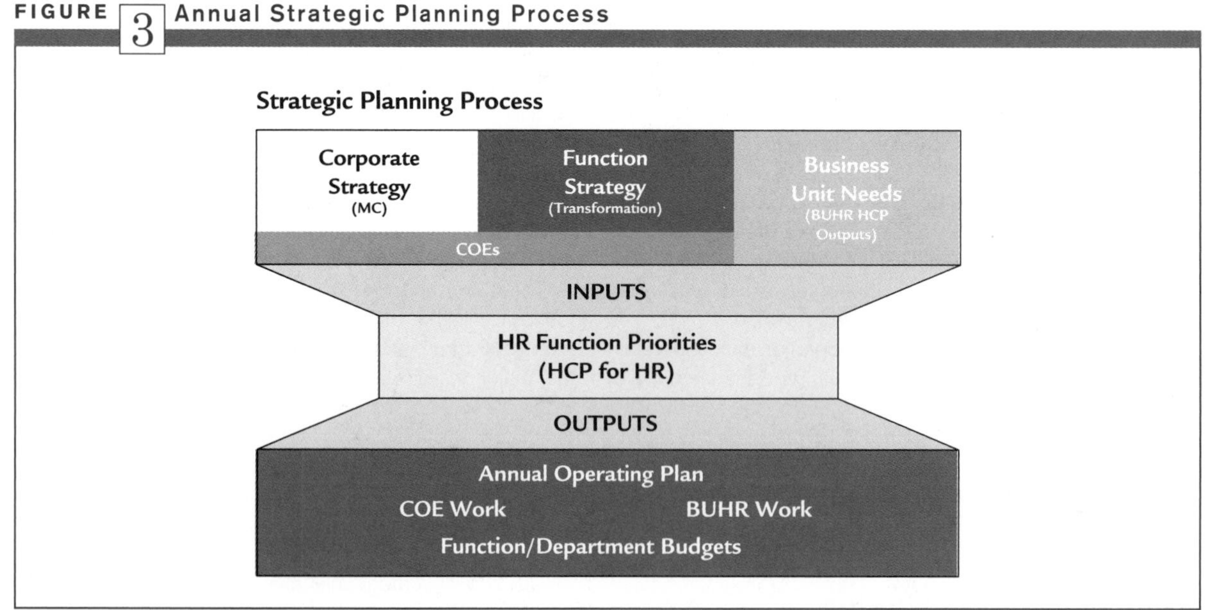

discrete inputs are brought together at an annual offsite meeting of the direct reports to the senior vice president of HR, plus several facilitators, usually in October, where we further develop and build alignment around the Human Capital Planning process for HR and develop the Annual Operating Plan.

AOP Offsite – Preparation and Meeting Design

Prior to the annual offsite to develop the HR Annual Operating Plan (AOP), each of these components are analyzed for "must have's", common themes, clear conflicts in the data, and key outliers (e.g. those things that may not show up as a theme but are highly probable and will have a high impact). The senior HR leadership team owners of each component dialogue with their teams so that when they come to the HR AOP offsite they are ready to present the real core of the work. Several years ago much of this work was done during the offsite itself. We have since found that doing much of this in preparation for the offsite allows for broader participation, more ownership as the constituents are helping to provide prioritization, and a more efficient, more focused AOP session. In 2006 we actually "took our own medicine" by following the HCP Process for the HR Function as the funnel to synthesis the key inputs prior to the offsite (Figure 3).

The HR AOP offsite meeting is attended by the HR function staff, the chief of staff for business unit HR, and two internal facilitators. We have the group arrive at the off-site location the night before and have a group dinner and some team activity to help them let go of the day-to-day, often role-specific work they were focused on and get them refocused, as a team, on their function leadership role.

The first day begins with a review of the agenda, groundrules for the session and the boundary conditions. The boundary conditions are essential as no work is done in a vacuum. For our purposes the boundary conditions include our HR governance statements which include our corporate values and core deliverables; our budget for the upcoming year, the HR transformation goals (the strategic goals for the HR function) and HR HCP outputs. Throughout the process we check our work against these boundary conditions to ensure that we remain on target. That is not to say that we never go outside the boundaries, but if we do, it is in a very explicit way. For example, if we have a large initiative that will go beyond regular budget boundaries, it must be demonstrated how we can show the plan for funding that work, what is the likelihood of funding, what are the trade-offs with other projects that are then less likely to be resourced, etc.

Next, each staff member presents the pre-work they completed with their staff. During these presentations each staff member explains the objectives that they are proposing be included in the upcoming year's plan and why. The focus at this point is on understanding what conclusions were reached by the staff members, and how they were reached. This is done through facilitated dialogue and, as these are the main ingredients to success, we ensure that the tough questions and important challenges are brought out. Throughout these discussions the facilitators are capturing and testing changes so that by the time this section is complete we have a reasonable draft of the AOP. Hence this is a highly interactive and iterative session, as changes in one section often cause us to go back and revisit a previous section. Day one does not end until the group has agreed on the main elements of the AOP.

On the second day, following an evening of relaxation, we break the leadership team into sub-teams. The objectives agreed to on the previous day are divided up and the subteams' task is to articulate how we will measure each objective in the context of the Corning incentive compensation payout scheme by setting 50%, 100%, and 150% performance targets for each. This exercise serves several purposes including (a) providing another cross-check of the objectives themselves, often helping us to calibrate scope, complexity, timing etc., (b) tightening up our language. Having to determine how to measure something lends a lot of clarity to the goals, and (c) forces even more clarity regarding what work will be required to deliver on these objectives.

The last day of the AOP offsite has two components. Considerable time is devoted to planning the communication of the finished AOP to business unit leaders and all HR employees. The balance of the day focuses on the creation of a global HR function calendar for the following year, capturing key function activities like deployment meetings, staff meetings, communication meetings, HCP process deadlines, etc.

The outputs of the AOP offsite include: a final one-page Annual Operating Plan summary, the detailed goals behind the AOP, an understanding of the required work from both the COEs and business unit HR. While budgets are used as a boundary condition at the offsite, a follow-up staff meeting includes the reconciliation of the AOP with the relevant department budgets.

Strategy Elements in the Larger Context – Pulling It All Together

To put the various elements in context, Figure 4 illustrates the annual cycle of human capital planning, the human resources annual operating plan process, and the corporate strategy process (as discussed previously in this paper) on

FIGURE 4 Human Capital Planning and Annual Operating Plan Integrated Timeline

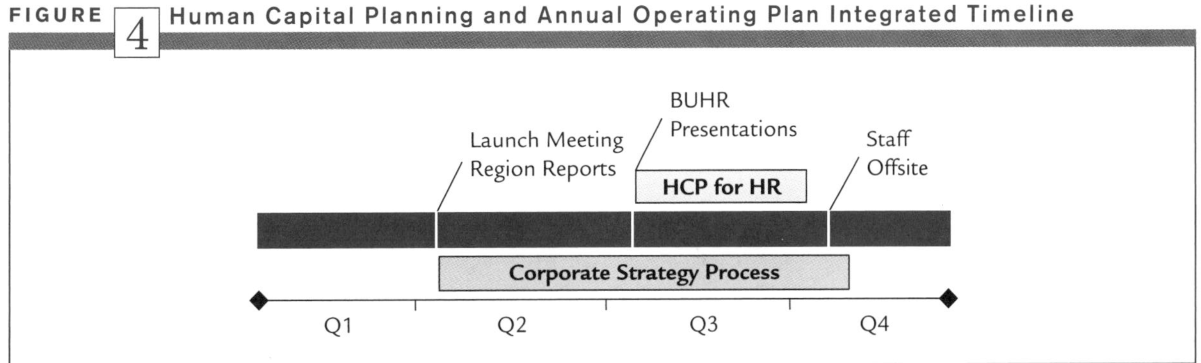

a single timeline. The business unit human capital planning process runs in parallel with the business unit portion of the corporate strategy process, and the two inform each other. HR completes its human capital planning process on itself using the output of the business units' work.

Lessons Learned & Continuous Improvement Opportunities

As with many HR processes, the AOP process is based on an annual cycle and the year-on-year improvements are best understood by considering each year in turn.

We have implemented the annual AOP process for each of three years. Each year, we have learned new lessons that enable us to continually improve the process. In the first year, the COE presentations were made at the April kick-off meeting. The process did not include an opportunity for the region HR leaders to provide a global perspective. Additionally, the business unit HR output was not formally prioritized before the offsite, resulting in a mix of "wish list" and duplicate requests.

Relative to the AOP offsite itself, in the first year there was no pre-agreement on what the AOP would look like or what the framework would be. As a result, this work took up considerable time in the meeting. The summary page was ultimately organized by a framework that included the following three main headings: Improve Cost Performance, Deliver Quality and Continuous Improvement, and Drive for Talent Management Excellence. While the specific objectives under these headings have changed from year to year, the headings have remained viable.

In the second year, we kept the COE presentations at the April kick-off meeting, and added time for the regional HR leads to provide input. The business unit HR team prioritized their requests in a single meeting prior to the AOP offsite, which resulted in a more coherent set of requests. The process was also modified to provide formal opportunity for COE leaders to work with their staffs on the business unit HR requests for support before coming to the offsite.

In developing the AOP itself, we re-used the framework developed in year one, saving considerable meeting time. We felt that consistency was more important than change for change's sake. This meeting went considerably smoother from facilitation standpoint, as the participants were on more familiar ground.

In pursuit of efficiency in the HCP process, we made an overcorrection in the third year by having the COE presentations done virtually, via a page on the intranet rather than during a live meeting. This was a mistake, as it sent a message to the COEs that their input was undervalued and it allowed some business unit HR people to under value the COE input. The prioritization of BUHR input was dramatically improved by facilitating a senior HR staff debrief dinner directly following the business unit HR HCP presentations in July and facilitating a business unit HR cross-business prioritization process and identifying common threads.

With regard to the annual offsite, we broke the three days into two sessions; one day for HCP for HR, and two days for the AOP. This made the work more manageable and resulted in more focused sessions with the senior staff. The strength of the AOP framework that we developed in year one, and retained in year two, was validated in year three when we kept the main headings consistent but were able to make accommodation for a major new initiative.

Meeting Facilitation – Basics Reconfirmed

The following points, while focused on Corning's experience with this particular set of meetings, and perhaps basic to the seasoned facilitator, have added value in our process:

- The meeting structure and overall process design must permit individuals with different work styles to process the information effectively, and to engage with their staffs as appropriate before group meetings.
- The meeting facilitators have to seek a balance between efficiency and effectiveness as the meeting unfolds – there is no substitute for frank dialog regarding thorny issues. Likewise the facilitators must provide pre-work material while resisting the urge to over-process that material for the participants. This means cleaning up the inputs without trying to do the work for the team.
- As with any leadership team working through a difficult process, facilitation was key. We found value in using someone outside the intact staff – which allows all the staffers to participate and improves facilitator independence. In addition, we found that a two person facilitation team added significant value in managing both the group dynamics and the meeting content. Using the same team year on year allowed the facilitators to develop a feel for when to push for closure and when to back off.
- Our facilitation was further improved by our ability to process the content live in the room on a computer and projector, rather than on flipcharts. Having immediate visual turnaround of the feedback greatly improved meeting effectiveness and efficiency.
- By including in the meeting design opportunities for max-mix sub teams to do break-out work and present it to the rest of the participants, we found that more issues got raised in the room and resolved productively.

Continuous Improvement Opportunities

There are still many opportunities for us to improve our strategic planning process in total. While most of the HR generalists have now embraced the human capital planning process, there are still some that struggle with the concepts and corrective action is now appropriate. As the generalists who do understand the process drive it further into their client business' strategic planning process, we expect to draw more general managers into the mid-year report-out sessions. As the HR leadership team gets more comfortable with and confident in the process, we have an opportunity to make greater distinctions between the requests from the different businesses, driving more prioritization of projects and work requests based on their impact to the requesting business. This will drive better portfolio management decisions and help HR to achieve its goal of containing cost while delivering value to the organization.

As we transition to a new facilitation team for the annual offsite, we have articulated clear concerns about how much work the facilitator can do in preparation for the meeting without undermining the leadership team. In some departments, facilitators can save time and add value by creating "straw person" proposals that interpret the source data. However, our recommendation has been to resist that temptation and to allow the team to work directly with the raw data. This experience with the raw inputs gives them greater familiarity with the details and helps them to arrive at a shared point of view. Over-processing the inputs might save time in the meeting, but at the risk of losing the alignment of the participants.

General Conclusions

Working together, the human capital planning and annual operating plan processes reviewed in this paper have helped to build a more coherent global HR function for Corning by creating a shared understanding across the COEs and the business unit HR groups of the many client business' situations and needs, and of the technical and strategic advances in each of the COEs. While the details of such processes must differ from company to company, the creation of such integrated, structured, and repeatable processes appear to add considerable value for HR professionals and their clients. Anecdotal evidence for the value of this work has come from the number of requests from other companies to benchmark Corning on this subject.

Critical elements of a successful AOP process include a number of mechanisms for gathering input; corporate strategy input from senior management, function-specific direction from the senior leadership of the function, and business-specific input from each of the businesses supported by the HR function. The more diverse the lines of business that the company is pursuing, the more important a robust planning process similar to Corning's HCP process becomes.

The process for developing the AOP is important as well. While a certain amount of pre-work is desirable, there is no substitute for a well-facilitated meeting of the senior team where options can be identified, ideas can be discussed and alignment can be gained on the agreed-upon actions.

Finally, alignment of the HR strategy process with the corporate and discrete business unit strategy processes increases HR's ability to align the services it offers, and the way it delivers them, with the needs of businesses.

Acknowledgements

As with many Corning HR programs, the Annual Operating Plan (AOP) process originated in one of the businesses – in this case, in a best practice developed in the then Optical Fiber business. The calendar and AOP templates were introduced within Corning by Christy Pambianchi, who currently serves as Division Vice President of Business Unit HR. The current process incorporates the feedback of numerous Corning HR colleagues received by the authors in the last three years, but most importantly from the members of Kurt Fischer's staff, for whom this work was commissioned. The Human Capital Planning process that Corning has been using in its current form since 2004 has roots in the HC BRidgetm work of Dr. John Boudreau and Peter Ramstad. This work has also benefited greatly from the practical consulting approach of Don Ruse of Sibson Consulting.

Authors' Reflection

As Director of Human Capital Planning for Corning Inc., my mission was to develop, deploy and manage a process for identifying the talent implications of the business strategy each business was pursuing. Working directly for the SVP of HR, I was asked to co-develop and co-facilitate an Annual Operating Plan process with Debbie Bennett, a senior member of the in-house OD team.

As with any senior leadership team, a major challenge was to develop a process that would focus on a specific outcome – a clear, measurable plan – that would effectively balance the differing personalities and perspectives of the senior HR leadership team. Being an internal consultant was beneficial, because my co-facilitator and I were familiar with each team member's style, strengths, and weaknesses. Our ongoing relationships with the team allowed us to push the team in ways that an external consultant would not have been able to easily accomplish.

Beyond the reflections contained in our paper, we would encourage any internal consultant to carefully consider the balance between completing some of the framework of the plan prior to any working offsite meeting to maximize the effectiveness of the session for all participants, and leaving sufficient work to be done by the group in person to ensure meaningful dialog between the participants and full ownership of the final project.

Source: Organization Development Journal, 25, (3), 87–93 (2007).

REFERENCES

Boudreau, J.W., Ramstad, PM & Dowling, PJ, (2003). "Global Talentship; Toward a Decision Science Connecting Talent to Global Strategic Success." In W. Mobley and P. Dorfman (Eds.), Advances in Global Leadership (Volume 3). JAI Press/Elsevier Science, 63–99.

Brush, M.C., Ruse, DH, (2005). "Driving Strategic Success Through Human Capital Planning; How Corning Links Business and HR Strategy to Improve the Value and Impact of Its HR Function." Human Resource Planning (Volume 28.1). 49–60.

Design and Redesign of Work Systems

6

Learning Objectives

- Understand the individual and organizational factors that affect job design
- Gain an appreciation of the need for "fit" between individuals and jobs and how such fit can be achieved
- Understand the reasons why organizations outsource and/or offshore and the pros and cons of utilizing alternative work location strategies
- Gain an appreciation of the role of HR in mergers and acquisitions
- Understand the impact that technology has on the design of jobs and work

Work Design at Johnsonville Sausage

Johnsonville Sausage is a family-owned business headquartered in Kohler, Wisconsin. Founded in 1944, the company has designed its workplace to facilitate employee involvement in all aspects of the business. Johnsonville hires "members," as opposed to employees, and supervisors are referred to as coaches or team leaders, with work units organized as teams rather than departments. From the time of hire, all members are required to learn about the entire business. During the first six months of employment, all members are required to attend a series of four 4-hour workshops that introduce them to company history and culture, teamwork, diversity, and financial management, including how the work of teams affects cash flow and profits. Production teams hold daily meetings prior to the beginning of their shifts to discuss issues of concern. The organization's "culture of empowerment" gives members the authority to shut down the production line at any time if they observe something that does not appear to be correct. Member involvement in all aspects of Johnsonville's business is reinforced with monthly bonuses that are tied to the month's production goals and profitability. Employee involvement in the business has resulted in an annual turnover rate of 8 percent at Johnsonville, which is significantly than the 20 percent average in the meatpacking industry.[1]

The second component in the development of human resource management strategy, in addition to human resource planning, is the design of work systems. The organization must consider the implications of its future plans on how tasks and responsibilities should be assigned to individuals and groups within the organization and decide how to redesign existing work systems. A model for the design of work systems is presented in Exhibit 6.1.

Design of Work Systems

In Exhibit 6.1, three primary considerations are presented that decision-makers need to consider in designing jobs: what workers do, what workers need, and how jobs interface with other jobs within the organization.

What Workers Do

One of the more challenging tasks in organizations is allocating specific tasks and job responsibilities to employees. Those who assign responsibilities need to ensure that employees are not overwhelmed by their jobs yet at the same time ensure that employees have sufficient work to keep them both productive and motivated. In addition, job titles and content serve as an important basis of comparison for employees within the organization relative to status, power, and appropriateness of compensation.

There are various strategies for the design of individual jobs. Those responsible for designing jobs and work systems need to fully assess the skills, knowledge, and abilities required by the organization both currently and in the future and consider both existing and possible future technologies. As noted in Chapter 5, a critical component of human resource planning is anticipating changes in the organization's environment. Work systems need to be constantly assessed and evaluated to ensure that the organization has assigned workers tasks and responsibilities that assist in achieving organizational objectives.

Early approaches to work system design focused on individual employees' jobs. In the late nineteenth and early twentieth centuries, industrial engineering prescribed work systems with jobs that had very narrow task assignments, thus giving rise to the term *job specialization.* These systems attempted to promote efficiency in industrial operations by allowing workers to specialize in particular tasks and gain high levels of competence in their work. Jobs had a limited number of tasks assigned that required little thought but precise execution. Not surprisingly, although these efforts toward simplified, specialized jobs provided efficiency, they also resulted in creating jobs that were boring and

EXHIBIT 6.1 A Model for the Designs of Work Systems

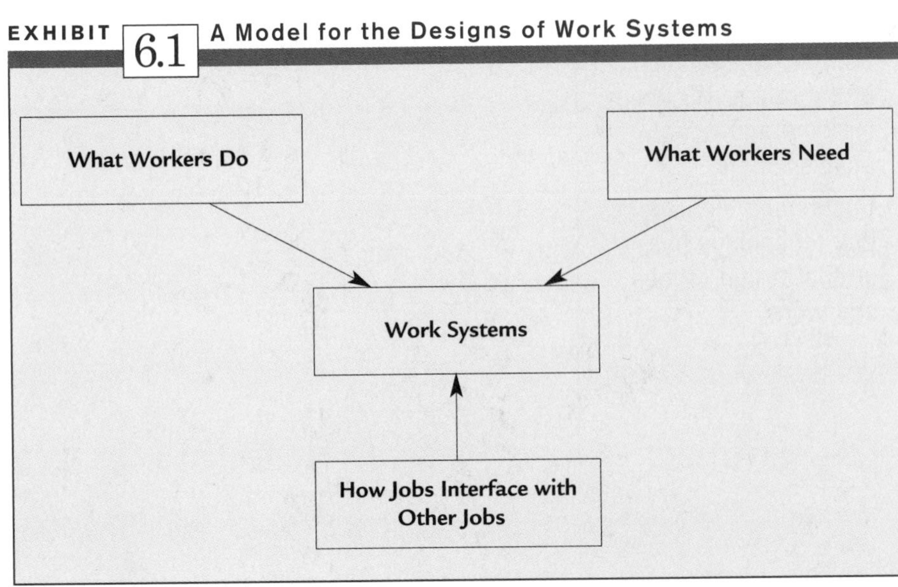

monotonous for employees. Because employees were not encouraged to go beyond a basic robotic function in most of their work, they were consequently unable to contribute to the organization in any meaningful way. This does not mean, however, that job specialization is inappropriate or never works. In fact, United Parcel Service, as discussed in Chapter 1, uses techniques of job specialization extensively. Job specialization can be a viable strategy for the design of work systems in organizations that require high levels of efficiency and cost minimization in order to compete effectively. It can also be appropriate for organizations that employ workers who do not seek to grow and be challenged in their careers.

Initial efforts to relieve this boredom and design more stimulating work for employees focused on providing them with tasks outside the scope of their previously narrowly defined jobs. *Job enlargement* provides some variety by increasing the number of tasks, activities, or jobs to help alleviate the boredom of highly specialized work. A variation of job enlargement is *job rotation*, where workers rotate across different specialized positions within the organization. Both techniques of designing jobs rest with providing employees with more variety in the tasks they perform. However, although these approaches add variety to tasks, they don not necessarily involve giving employees more responsibility. This does not mean that efforts to allow or require workers to perform additional tasks are necessarily useless. Employees who assume responsibility for additional tasks can have their understanding of organizational production processes enhanced and have a greater appreciation of how their specialized job contributes to the overall organization. Several studies have documented the success of both job enlargement and job rotation. Shortly after World War II, IBM instituted a job enlargement program and found a significant increase in product quality and a reduction in down or idle time.[2] Pharmaceutical company Eli Lilly utilized a popular job rotation program that allowed employees to qualify for salary increases and promotions while enhancing career development opportunities.[3]

Job rotation has become increasingly popular in recent years as a key tool by which employees are developed through exposure to different roles and functions within an organization. This is particularly true for HR professionals. In order for HR to be a true strategic partner, HR executives must understand fully not only the functional aspects of human resource management but also the nature of the organization's business. One of the best ways to obtain this understanding is to work within the organization in an operating division outside the HR function. Ironically, for many years, HR has developed programs that rotate employees across functions such as marketing, finance, operations, and accounting, providing those in rotation with a better grasp of the entire organization and an appreciation for how individual functions contribute to overall strategy. HR executives, however, are usually not part of such programs because of the traditional "administrative" role that HR played. In order to participate in an organization's success at the highest levels, HR executives need to avail themselves of opportunities to "learn the business" by actually participating in and learning about the entire organization and its various units. Until they do so, they can not contribute to the organization as a true strategic partner.

Job Rotation at General Electric

General Electric (GE) has always been a leader in employee development among large organizations. For many years, entry-level HR managers have been placed in a two-year job rotation program on joining the organization. New hires spend three 8-month rotations within the HR function. Although they might end up in different business units or divisions, these rotations were still within the HR domain and confined to areas such as labor relations, compensation, staffing, and benefits. The goal of this program was to develop strong HR generalists who could eventually become senior HR executives within GE. In the mid-1990s, GE added cross-functional rotations to the mix, whereby individuals would leave HR for at least one rotation, working in areas such as audit, marketing, finance, or operations. This rotation program can continue throughout the employee's career as new skills, competencies, experiences, and knowledge bases are sought. HR executives in GE now have far greater credibility among their non-HR peers given this experience and are also better able to understand the business and develop HR solutions to key business challenges faced by divisions.[4]

Job enrichment initiatives involve going beyond merely adding tasks to employees' jobs. Job enrichment involves increasing the amount of responsibility employees have. Work is designed so employees have significant responsibility for their own work. In many cases, the employee becomes more accountable for his or her own performance because responsibilities for quality and productivity that were previously assigned to the employee's supervisor are redirected to the employee. This process of reassigning what were formerly supervisory responsibilities to employees is commonly referred to as *vertical loading*.

To assist organizations in designing enriched jobs, a model was developed that illustrated the relationships between redesigned jobs and ultimate performance and behavioral outcomes.[5] The Job Characteristics Model is presented in Exhibit 6.2. This model suggests that five core job characteristics can impact certain employee psychological states that will impact certain work-related outcomes. These five core job characteristics are: 1) skill variety, the extent to which the work allows an employee to use a variety of acquired skills; 2) task identity, the extent to which the work allows an employee to complete a "whole" or "identifiable" piece of work; 3) task significance, the extent to which the employee perceives that his or her work is important and meaningful to those in the organization or those outside of the organization; 4) autonomy, the extent to which the employee is able to work and determine work procedures at her or his own discretion, free of supervision; and 5) feedback, the extent to which the work allows the employee to gain a sense of how well job responsibilities are being met. The model argues that work systems can be designed to enhance motivation, performance, and satisfaction and reduce absenteeism and turnover.

Frequently, the job characteristics model can be utilized to allow workers to assemble an entire product or provide a wider range of services to customers. For example, at Motorola's Communications Division, individual employees assemble, test, and package paging devices, whereas previously these tasks were performed on an assembly line with

EXHIBIT 6.2 The Job Characterstics Model

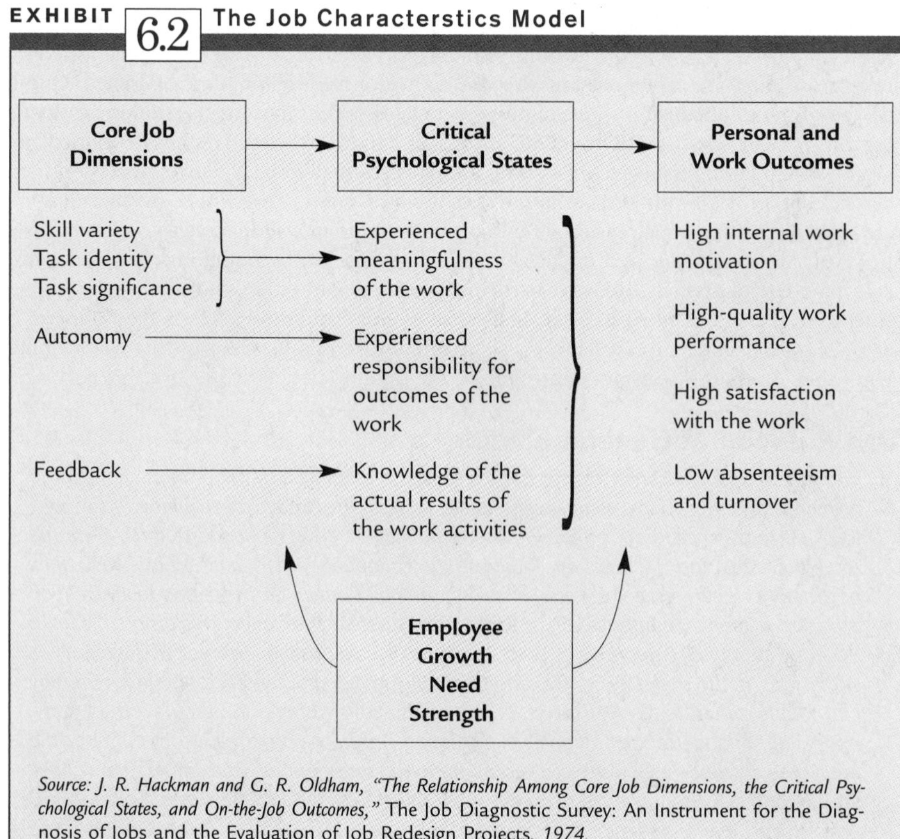

Source: J. R. Hackman and G. R. Oldham, "The Relationship Among Core Job Dimensions, the Critical Psychological States, and On-the-Job Outcomes," The Job Diagnostic Survey: An Instrument for the Diagnosis of Jobs and the Evaluation of Job Redesign Projects, *1974.*

100 workers performing 100 different steps.[6] Similarly, the job responsibilities of a group of employees may be enriched by allowing the work group the autonomy to complete an entire range of tasks in a manner determined by the group.

What Workers Need

The design of work systems also needs to consider what workers need and want in order to carry out their job responsibilities. Certainly, all employees don not work for the same reasons nor do they expect the same things from their employers. However, employers must consider a number of important universal considerations in designing work systems to ensure that workers are motivated, productive, and happy.

The first of these considerations is the changing demographics and lifestyles of the labor market. As noted in Chapter 2, there are some significant differences in the composition of the twenty-first century workforce. No longer are the majority of employees married white males who are considered the breadwinners of their families. In fact, white males now make up less than 50 *percent* of the U.S. workforce. Organizations need to realize that employees no longer have generic needs. Employees expect their employers to understand their needs and respect them as individuals. Worker needs will vary among and between those of different age groups, genders, races, religions, physical abilities, sexual orientations, and marital and family status. In order to perform at peak levels, employees need to remain free from bias or prejudice in hiring, treatment, performance management, compensation, and advancement decisions and programs. This diversity of worker needs creates a significant challenge for allocating work in organizations.

Organizations also need to be more aware of employee needs for work/life balance. All employees, but particularly younger employees, are far less loyal to their employers than they were a generation ago. Employers who design work systems that do not allow employees to have the balance they desire in their life activities will find workers who not only are less committed to the organization but who may also suffer from burnout and perform at less than optimal levels. An increasing number of employers are establishing stress management programs as well as physical health and wellness programs and are contracting with outside employee assistance programs to ensure that employees retain an essential balance among their life activities. In response to the particularly stressful work environments in which many high-technology executives find themselves, the Growth and Leadership Center of Mountain View, California, was established to work with executives from nearby Silicon Valley. Leading employers such as Sun Microsystems, Intel, and Netscape sent employees at risk for burnout to the center for weekly coaching sessions.[7] A typical 10-week program costs $12,000 per employee. Such excessive costs can be avoided through the development of work systems that are strategically designed to allow the organization's employees to retain the right balance in their life activities and can be a key catalyst to high performance.

A third consideration in determining what employees want is ensuring that employees have some form of representation, or "voice." More highly skilled and trained workers do not expect to be micromanaged. They expect to use their training and experience to make a contribution to the organization, and they expect the organization to listen to their concerns. Systems for employee input are not only motivational to employees, but they also allow the organization to fully utilize its existing human capabilities by encouraging employees to get involved in work-related issues that impact them. Work systems need to be designed so employees have sufficient voice to allow them to contribute their perspectives and expertise.

In unionized organizations, employee voice is formalized and centralized. However, less than 20 *percent* of the U.S. workforce is unionized. Unions also restrict the individual employee's right to have an independent voice, apart from the majority. In the absence of and even with a formal union, employers need to design their work systems to ensure that employees are able to communicate their needs and concerns in a constructive manner within an atmosphere of mutual respect. Both employees and the organizations win when this is accomplished.

One final consideration that needs to be incorporated in work system design under worker needs is workplace safety. The United States has established numerous guidelines for employers, administered by the Occupational Safety and Health Administration (OSHA), which oversees the Occupational Safety and Health Act. The act largely addresses employer liability for on-the-job injuries and occupationally acquired diseases. In addition to the traditional concerns of hazardous products or waste and unsafe physical conditions, increasing attention is being paid to safety issues regarding technology. Ergonomics is a relatively new science that explores the relationship between injuries and physical office working conditions. The National Institute for Occupational Safety and Health reported that in 1997, musculoskeletal disorders related to the neck, shoulders, elbow, hand, wrist, and back generated more than $13 billion in worker compensation claims.[8] Consequently, OSHA has been developing national standards related to ergonomics.

The near-constant use of computers with video display monitors has ignited debate concerning radiation hazard and the potential long-term effects of sustained gazing at video display monitors on an individual's vision. Because many employees also spend significant amounts of time at their desks or workstations, concern is also being addressed toward the ergonomics of worksites. Work systems and jobs need to be designed to be consistent with employees' physical capabilities and allow them to perform their jobs without any undue risks.

How Jobs Interface with Other Jobs

The final component of designing jobs is an understanding of how individual jobs may have interdependencies with other jobs as well as how individual jobs can or should interface with others. There are three traditional types of task interdependence: pooled, sequential, and reciprocal.

Pooled interdependence is where individual employees can work independently of each other in performing their tasks but utilize some coordination of their activities. Bank loan officers utilize this kind of work system. Each loan officer works independently of peers, yet the work of each officer is coordinated within the rules and procedures outlined by the bank for lending. In addition, experienced loan officers may often assist newer officers with specific tasks or questions they might have.

Sequential interdependence refers to work that flows from one individual to another, where one individual depends on the timely completion of quality work from another coworker. Mass-production assembly line workers utilize this kind of work system. Here, the output of one employee becomes the input for the next employee. Timely completion of work to be "passed on" is essential to avoid any slack or downtime, which creates inefficiencies and may strain relations between coworkers.

Reciprocal interdependence occurs when the workflow is not linear (as in sequential interdependence) but random. Employees can process work so that its flow is not necessarily predictable and often spontaneous to suit an immediate situation. Teammates on a basketball or hockey team utilize reciprocal interdependence, as would the different departments within a hospital. Employees in a reciprocal interdependence need to be flexible and are often configured as a team, with joint and shared responsibility.

When the work of one employee interfaces with another, concern must be paid to designing the work system to allow as efficient a flow as possible. Higher levels of interdependence require higher levels of coordination and attention. In designing work systems, organizations need to consider the implications that the levels of interdependence have for management practices that facilitate control of processes and communication among the interdependent tasks. For example, higher levels of interdependence might require more frequent meetings between employees, regular status reports, and more careful monitoring of performance and processes by management.

The design of organizational work systems is not an easy task. Allocation of tasks and responsibilities must be balanced with worker needs. Consideration must also be paid to the need for interdependencies among workers. Because changes in technology and changes in workforce composition continue to present ongoing challenges, the design of work systems is not a static activity.

Teams at Dow Chemical

Michigan-based Dow Chemical has been a leader in the use of employee teams since it began the practice in Europe in 1994. The large, bureaucratic organization felt that it was not using the skills and talent of its employees as well as it might, which led to a restructuring of plant operations. Work processes, from budgeting to actual production, were examined, and a three-tiered system was developed for rating the degree of autonomy each team displayed. With the goal of removing day-to-day control and responsibility from a supervisor and giving it to a team—allowing individuals to contribute more fully to the organization—Dow developed audit systems that assessed teams and their independence. Rewards were developed commensurate with team performance and autonomy. The teams have saved Dow more than $1 billion in their first ten years of operation. The process also has allowed Dow staff engineers to spend more time on improving plant processes rather than its operations.[9]

The key strategic challenge in designing and staffing jobs is ensuring an optimal "fit" between the needs of employees and the needs of the organization. Ironically, employers are often very unaware of the needs and concerns of their own employees. A *2008 Job Satisfaction Survey Report*, prepared by the Society for Human Resource Management, surveyed the top needs of employees as well as the perceptions of HR professionals as to employees' top needs. Of the top four employee needs—which, in order, were job security, benefits, compensation and safety—only benefits appeared on the list of responses of HR professionals. The consequences of poor "fit" between employees and employers can be significant in terms of productivity, motivation, and willingness to remain in the organization. Reading 6.1, "The Mismatched Worker: When People Don't Fit Their Jobs," examines the nature of poor fit or mismatches and its consequences and implications.

Work at Best Buy

In the mid-2000s, Minneapolis-based consumer electronics retailer Best Buy adopted a new program that allowed most of its 4,000 corporate staff employees to work off-site without restriction. The Results-Only Work Environment (ROWE) has since been rolled out to the 100,000 employees who work in Best Buy's retail stores. The program attempts to provide employees with better work/life balance and allows employees to complete their work whenever and wherever they choose. The program has required significant time and training for managers in an attempt to move the company culture from the management of people to the management of results. The program has resulted in productivity increases averaging 35 percent and voluntary turnover decreases as much as 90 percent in the divisions in which ROWE has been implemented. In one procurement division alone, turnover dropped from 36.6 percent to less than 6 percent in one year. Initially developed as a "guerrilla" operation, unknown to and unsanctioned by management and focused strictly on flextime, the early pilot run illustrated that flextime was an oxymoron and actually required much additional work to track employee's time, but, more importantly, flextime enhanced employee communication and teamwork by transcending the traditional eight-hour workday. ROWE's success is based on the three key commandments ingrained into the system: 1) There are no work schedules; 2) every meeting is optional; and 3) employees should render no judgment as to how coworkers spend their time. Best Buy has found that ROWE enhances their ability to recruit new employees and retain existing employees and has allowed the organization to refocus its performance management system on goal-setting and outcomes-based measures. The team-based nature of Best Buy's work environment ensures that employees who fail to abide by the system are pressured by their team members and eventually select out of Best Buy. The program has also resulted in significant cost savings relative to real estate and employee retention, as desktop computers and offices have been replaced with laptops, cell phones, and PDAs.[10]

Redesign of Work Systems

The redesign of work systems represents one of the most radical yet common changes taking place in organizations from an HR perspective. Traditional work systems that stressed individualized jobs that were specialized and hierarchical have inhibited organizations and hindered performance. Current and future work systems are becoming much more broadly defined and stress designing jobs not solely around technical measures for efficiency but around strategic choices made by management. The greater the volatility in an organization's environment, the greater the need for more flexible, adaptive work systems. In fact, a new model for organizational effectiveness requires organizations to be agile or infinitely adaptable.[11] Although redesign efforts may initially be a very time-consuming process, well-designed flexible work systems can provide an organization with the ongoing ability to respond quickly to a changing environment.

Although key decision-makers can and do approach work redesign from a more macro, holistic perspective, individual employees' main concerns usually involve their individual jobs. This is not to say that employees are not concerned about larger, systemic types of organizational change; understandably, individuals have the greatest concern about changes that directly impact their careers and livelihoods. Many of the most significant change initiatives being undertaken in contemporary organizations involve job design—notably, what workers do, what workers are given and need in terms of resources, how jobs interface with each other, and skills requirements. Changes in these areas may be referred to in a number of ways, particularly re-engineering, but the bottom line is that employees' jobs are changing faster than they ever have before, particularly in light of how information-processing technology is impacting the nature of work.

The trend toward re-engineering has resulted in numerous changes in the fundamental ways in which work is carried out. Unnecessary activities that add no value are eliminated; tasks are outsourced; work is consolidated; and divisions are restructured in the interest of increased efficiency and enhanced performance. These efforts often result in the establishment of cross-functional teams that have a very high potential for conflict as areas of responsibility are redefined and positions are eliminated. At the same time, these changes can have a negative impact on employee motivation and morale, as workers may feel some threat to their job security. Therefore, management needs to consider and plan for those possible effects prior to implementation, when redesign initiatives are initially being considered.

The increased use of teams and project groups in organizations has also created a number of challenges. Because U.S. culture is so highly individualistic, there is some discomfort as to the role that teams and group decision-making should play vis-à-vis individual initiative. Employees who have been brought up in such an individualistic culture need training to be effective team members. In some instances, teams function more effectively than individuals, but in others, they do not. Although teams are becoming more prevalent, organizations still struggle with how to effectively manage them.

In designing motivating and challenging work for employees, it is critical to remember that as employees become more proficient at their jobs, they will seek new challenges and opportunities for growth and development. A model that addresses the stages of a typical employee "life cycle" is presented in Exhibit 6.3. While typical time frames associated with each life cycle stage of this model are presented, individual employees may move through these stages at varying rates. Hence, it is important to be alert to any signs of potential boredom or disengagement on the part of employees, communicate with employees, and consider alternatives in light of the employee's needs and the needs and strategy of the organization and work unit.

Strategic Work Redesign in Action

Outsourcing and Offshoring

Developing an organization's strategy involves, in part, an assessment of the organization's strengths and weaknesses, as discussed in Chapter 3. This process increasingly forces senior management to consider how best to leverage these strengths and minimize weaknesses.

EXHIBIT 6.3 The Employee life cycle

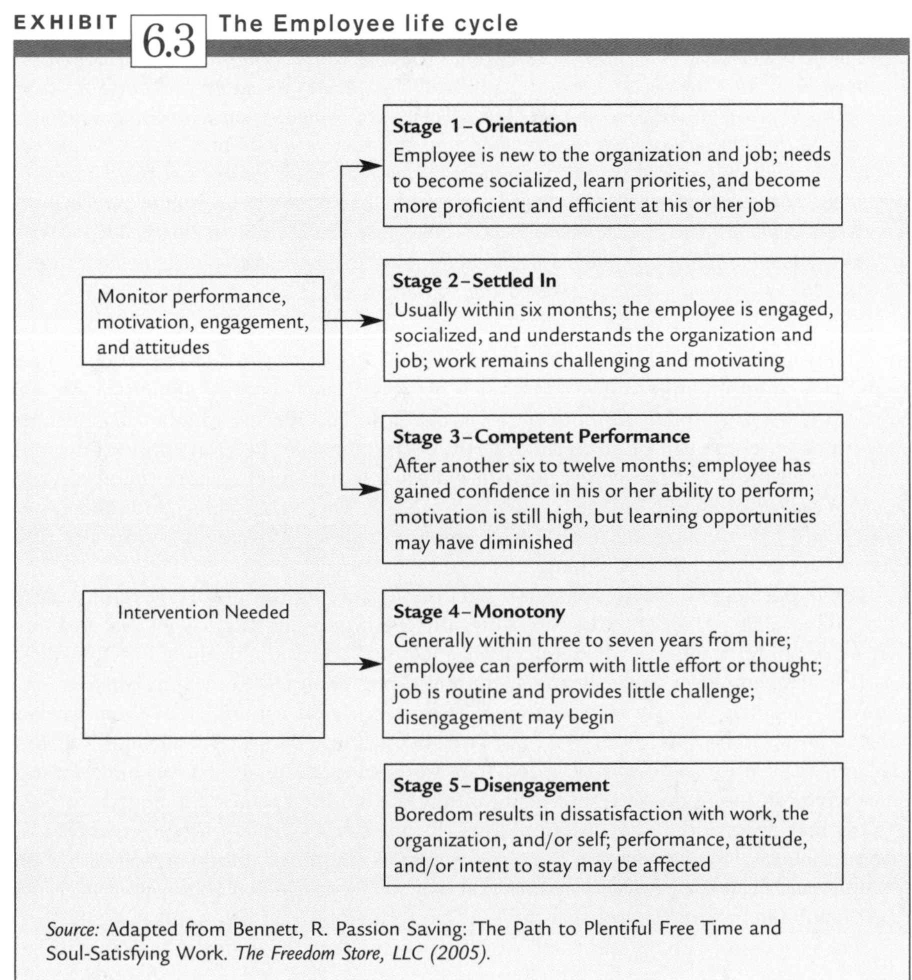

Source: Adapted from Bennett, R. Passion Saving: The Path to Plentiful Free Time and Soul-Satisfying Work. *The Freedom Store, LLC (2005).*

Frequently, the result is the decision to outsource some of the work being done by in-house employees. While outsourcing originated with larger organizations, it has now become a popular practice in organizations of all sizes. Reading 6.2, "Using Outsourcing for Strategic Competitiveness in Small and Medium-Sized Firms," illustrates how outsourcing can provide strategic advantages for smaller organizations, which may allow them to compete more effectively with their larger rivals.

Outsourcing involves contracting some of the organization's noncore work activities to outside specialists who can do the job more effectively, often for less than it costs the organization to do such work in-house. Once an organization identifies its core competencies—the things that it does better than its competitors—anything remaining may be expendable. A simple cost-benefit analysis can allow managers to determine the efficacy of outsourcing a particular function. Within HR, payroll and benefits are two areas that are frequently outsourced. Technological support is often outsourced because of the high costs involved with keeping an organization's technology support systems from becoming obsolete. Training and capital investment in this area often provide limited return because of the rate of change in the application of information technology in organizations. Such work is often better handled by outsourced specialists, usually at a lower cost to the organization.

Outsourcing by Federal and State Governments

The popularity of outsourcing is not limited to for-profit organizations. In late 2002, President Bush announced plans to put out for bid up to 850,000 federal jobs, close to half of the non-postal civilian positions within the federal government. One *successful outsourcing bid involved the merging of 22 separate payroll systems into only two systems, at a projected savings of more than $1 billion over the coming decade. Florida has been a leader in outsourcing, taking its entire HR function for 189,000 state employees and elected officials and outsourcing it under a seven-year, $280 million contract. This action is anticipated to save the state an average of $24 million annually, in addition to the $65 million to $90 million it avoided having to spend to update its antiquated software system. The contractor operates "employee care service centers" in Jacksonville and Tallahassee to handle administrative work, and remaining HR employees with the state now focus on strategic issues such as collective bargaining and specialized training and staffing.*[12]

One recent study showed that more than 75 *percent* of organizations outsource at least one HR function.[13] A particular benefit for HR in outsourcing is that the assignment of transactional and administrative work, such as payroll and benefits administration, can free up HR staff to focus on more strategic issues. In considering whether to outsource any function, either within or outside of HR, decision-makers need to consider not only costs but also whether the contractor can deliver a higher level of performance; where control and responsibility will lie, particularly in areas where compliance with laws is necessary; and how outsourcing might affect employees whose jobs might be lost as well as the morale of remaining employees.

The importance of the compliance aspect of outsourcing can not be overemphasized. In October 2003, Wal-Mart made headlines not for increasing its sales, profits, and market share but for the raids by federal agents at 60 of its stores that rounded up 250 illegal workers. The employees were cleaners, employed by a contractor to whom Wal-Mart outsourced this area of its retail operations. Two weeks later, a number of these workers turned around and sued both Wal-Mart and the cleaning contractor, alleging that they did not receive overtime pay to which they were entitled and that taxes and workers' compensation premiums were not being withheld from their wages. Employers who outsource may be considered "joint employers" if they exert a certain level of control over these employees. An organization can give contractors complete latitude in their hiring and compensation practices, but the organization may still face legal liability if a court finds that the organization exerts control over the work performed by the subcontractor's staff.

Decisions to outsource some or all of the work being done in an organization are usually driven by projected cost savings. Employers in our information and services-based economy frequently have labor as their chief expense. While many domestic outsourcing contractors can provide cost savings relative to labor, they are often limited by laws that mandate minimum wages and/or by the forces of supply and demand relative to the market value of certain skills and competencies. As a result, many organizations are taking outsourcing one step further by using a practice known as "offshoring." Offshoring involves the exporting of tasks and jobs to countries where labor costs are significantly less than comparable costs in the United States. Offshoring was once considered a threat only to manufacturing and assembly jobs that required relatively low levels of skill and education. Many domestic workers in these jobs were unionized, with correspondingly high wages, particularly relative to those that could be earned in less-developed countries. Because these jobs required basic manual skills that were easily taught, organizations began to enjoy significant cost savings when they exported such jobs to Mexico and underdeveloped areas in Central America and Asia. More recently, many white-collar, professional jobs have been the target of offshoring, and decisions by organizations to engage in such practice have been controversial.

Chief among the jobs that are offshored are those in the information technology sector, computer programming, back-office accounting, and customer service call centers.[14] India remains the largest market for offshoring, accounting for as much as 90 *percent* of the industry.[15] The workforce there is largely fluent in English and highly educated, with approximately 2 million university graduates annually, many with science and engineering backgrounds.[16] Most important to organizations, however, is the fact that wages for these workers—at approximately 10 *percent* of those that would be paid for the same work done in the United States—are considered good by local standards.[17] Oracle Corporation recently offshored more than 2,000 software development jobs to India. China, Russia, and Ireland are also popular locations for the offshoring of white-collar jobs.

Offshoring has presented an unprecedented challenge to organizations via the means of managing virtual global teams. The projected cost savings that can be realized by offshoring some work can be lost if employees from different regions of the world fail to work together effectively. A nonstop, 24-hour work environment creates a dispersed global team with sequential and reciprocal interdependence. Managers responsible for such dispersed teams need to exercise tight organizational and operational control to ensure coordination and communication. The challenge of managing virtual work teams is addressed in Reading 6.3, "Leading Virtual Teams."

Offshoring is certainly a controversial practice, as was seen in January 2004, when an IBM company memo was leaked to the *Wall Street Journal.* Meant for internal consideration, the memo reported that IBM could save $168 million annually by offshoring programming jobs to China, where the going wage rate was 20 *percent* of that in the United States.[18] Offshoring has been criticized for a number of reasons, but its proponents argue not only its merit but its necessity if domestic organizations are to continue to be successful and build the U.S. economy. These pros and cons are illustrated in Exhibit 6.4.

The chief advantage of—and often motivating factor behind—the decision to offshore is the savings that can be realized through reduced labor costs. It has been argued that this can make the U.S. economy more efficient and competitive and is necessary to allow domestic organizations to compete with their foreign counterparts who already enjoy such reduced labor costs. In addition, offshoring can extend the workday around the clock. This can be particularly beneficial for functions such as software development, allowing production time to be reduced considerably as the work is transferred across time zones. Call center operations can also claim enhanced 24-hour customer service through offshoring. The biggest criticism of offshoring involves the fact that offshored jobs usually result in job loss for domestic workers, hampering our domestic economy. In addition, offshoring often involves the transfer of technical knowledge overseas, developing the workforces of other countries rather than benefitting domestic employees. Job losses through offshoring can also be detrimental to the morale and loyalty of employees who remain, fearing that their jobs might next be exported. Finally, because offshoring can be viewed as unpatriotic, organizations who offshore have to be concerned about their public image and take steps to maintain the loyalty of their customers, the public, and government agencies and officials who have decried the practice of offshoring.

However, at the same time many jobs are being offshored, negative outcomes associated with offshoring are causing many employers to consider alternatives to sending jobs abroad. Complaints from customers concerning language and communication barriers as well as the inability of call center employees to be responsive to their needs and the corresponding loss of business associated with this dissatisfaction have resulted in many organizations "reshoring" their customer services operations. In many instances, customer service operations are being handled by contract employees who work from their homes. This reshoring trend reverses the movement of jobs overseas and is expected to involve more than 300,000 jobs by 2010 as organizations such as Office Depot, J. Crew, Wyndham Hotels, Sears, and Victoria's Secret, among others, return customer service operations domestically.[19] In these and other organizations, domestic call center staff usually work as independent contractors, receiving few or no benefits, and provide their own technology, which can reduce employer costs by as much as 80 *percent* over those associated with offshoring. Because these individuals work from their own homes, this

EXHIBIT 6.4 Advantages and Disadvantages of Offshoring

Advantages	Disadvantages
• Cost savings	• Loss of domestic jobs
• Extend workday to 24 hours (continuous)	• Transfer of technical knowledge
	• Demoralizing
	• Public image/loyalty concerns

practice is sometimes referred to as "homeshoring" and expands an employer's potential labor pool by allowing individuals to work who otherwise might not have the opportunity to do so. These workers also tend to be better educated, as 70–80 *percent* of home-based call center employees have college degrees, compared with 30–40 *percent* who work in conventional call centers.

Homeshoring at JetBlue Airlines

JetBlue Airlines has utilized home-base call center employees since the organization's inception in 2000. These individuals are full employees of JetBlue, receiving all company benefits, and live in the greater Salt Lake City area, where JetBlue bases its reservations operations. JetBlue employs more than 1,500 agents who work from their homes, 70 percent of whom are stay-at-home mothers. Seventy percent of these agents work part-time, and JetBlue strives to maintain the ratio of 70 percent / 30 percent part-time/full-time staff because part-timers have a higher retention rate. The system provides JetBlue with a competitive advantage in its service operations, as employees can still be "on the job" during periods of severe weather, when customer service needs increase greatly.[20]

Mergers and Acquisitions

Throughout the 1990s and into the twentieth century, merger and acquisition activity in the United States has grown at a frenetic pace. An increasing number of domestic organizations are merging and/or being acquired by both domestic and international partners. While most merger activity is fairly well-planned relative to financial, product line, and operational decisions, the human element of mergers and acquisitions is often ignored. In a study of merger activity in the banking industry, the International Labour Organization found that neglecting human resource activities in merger and acquisitions results in a much higher risk of failure.[21] It found that mergers are pursued for a variety of reasons, including economies of scale in operations, consolidation in saturated markets, and improving competitive position through a larger asset base. Employees, however, often first gain knowledge of pending merger and acquisition activity through the news media rather than from their employers. This lack of communication erodes trust and loyalty, resulting in increased job insecurity and workplace stress. The ILO report states that a full two-thirds of mergers fail to achieve their objectives, largely because of the inability to merge cultural and other human factors into the combined enterprise or a blatant failure to even consider such issues.

Consistent with international findings in the banking industry and despite the proliferation of high-profile domestic M&A activity in recent years, three out of four M&As undertaken in the United States fail to achieve the targeted strategic and financial goals sought through with combination.[22] M&A activity creates uncertainty among customers, suppliers, creditors, the financial community, and, most of all, employees because of the uncertainty surrounding the future of their employment. It has been argued that the management of people's expectations, fears, and concerns is the most important job a CEO can perform during M&A activity.[23] Ideally, the new organization created by the merger or acquisition should involve a mission and vision that encompasses the best parts of the separate organizations and the creation of a new organization that builds on strengths and synergies that allows it to be stronger than either of the separate organizations. In order to accomplish this, however, focus needs to be placed on the similarities of the cultures of the separate organizations rather than their differences. The key challenge for success is retaining and continuing to motivate good employees and creating a human resource strategy that addresses employee needs as well as the mission and vision of the new organization.

The Human Side of Creating AOL Time Warner

The $162 billion merger of America Online (AOL) with Time Warner was the largest in corporate history. Whereas much has been written about the strategic and financial

EXHIBIT 6.5 HR's Role in Mergers/Acquistions

	Stage of Merger/Acquisition			
	Pre-deal	**Due Diligence**	**Integration Planning**	**Implementation**
HR Roles	• Identifying people related issues • Assessing individual's fit with new needs • Assessing "cultural fit" between organizations • Educating top management on HR aspects of transaction	• Estimating employee related costs • Estimating employee-related savings • Assessing cultural issues as potential challenges	• Developing communication strategies • Designing talent retention programs • Planning for overcoming resistance	• Managing employee communication • Aligning rewards with organizational needs • Monitoring the new culture and employee dynamics

aspects of the merger, little insight has been shared as to the role that HR played in the merger to ensure its success. HR focused on five critical areas in attempting to merge the organizations as seamlessly as possible. First, HR restructured itself. Some operating units didn't need a full-time HR presence, so HR managers divided their time among units as necessary. Routine administrative work was outsourced to allow HR to focus on strategic and human resource planning. Second, the foreign HR staff was flown to corporate headquarters to collaboratively work on global strategy. Foreign operations were centralized in London, Paris, and Hong Kong to speed up both production and communication. Third, talent profiles were developed for 300 key executives to assist with the most efficacious deployment of talent worldwide. Fourth, recruiting practices were redesigned to facilitate an expedited review process as well as the sharing of applicant information across the different business units. Finally, an Internet tutorial, AOL Time Warner 101, was developed that explained the reasons for the merger as well as the benefits that it could provide to employees. As one of the most closely watched business transactions ever undertaken, the AOL Time Warner merger has been facilitated by the involvement of HR as a true strategic partner from the initial stages of merger planning onward.[24]

Successful merger and acquisition activity has been described as progressing through four distinct stages.[25] The first is the pre-deal, or selection of the target organization. The second is due diligence, during which time the parties meet and disclose all information relevant to the merger or, in the case of a hostile takeover, the acquiring company gathers its information on its own. The third is integration planning, or pre-merger activity just prior to the formal launch. The fourth is the actual implementation. HR plays a critical role in each of these stages, as identified in Exhibit 6.5.

Impact of Technology

One of the most significant trends affecting HR and people in organizations is technology. Simply defined, an organization's technology is the process by which inputs from an organization's environment are transformed into outputs.[26] Technology includes tools, machinery, equipment, work procedures, and employee knowledge and skills. All organizations, be they manufacturing or service, public or private, large or small, employ some form of technology to produce something for the open marketplace or for a specific group of constituents.

With constant advances in technology and work processes, organizations are under increased competitive pressure to implement, if not develop on their own, more efficient means of operations. However, the financial considerations of whether to adopt a new technology must be balanced with a number of strategic issues and, more specifically,

EXHIBIT 6.6 Issues for Integrating New Technologies

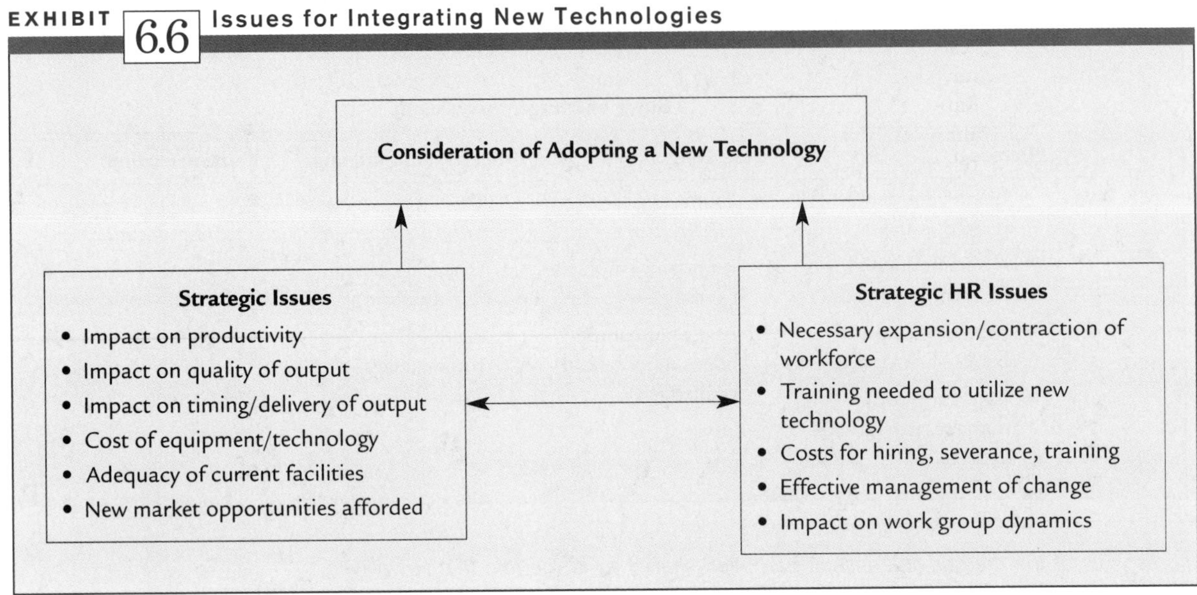

a number of specific strategic HR issues, as shown in Exhibit 6.6. The specifics of these issues are discussed in greater detail in Chapter 6 but are presented here to give the reader a sense of how technological initiatives need to be considered from a holistic perspective that transcends the sole consideration of economic costs. At this juncture, we will address three ways in which work is changing, as illustrated in Exhibit 6.7.

As newer technologies are developed and implemented, the skills and work habits required of employees also change. There is a much greater need to continue to upgrade existing employee skills today than there has ever been at any time in the past. Gone are the days when employees utilized the same skills and equipment to perform their jobs for decades at a time.

At the same time that technological change is creating demand for workers with more sophisticated training and skills, a significant number of new workforce entrants have limited technical skills and, in some cases, little or no training beyond basic literacy. For at least the first decade of the twenty-first century, immigrants will represent the largest increase in the workforce in the United States.[27] This is compounded by the fact that the growth in our economy and the greatest number of jobs being created are in the

EXHIBIT 6.7 Impact of Technology on Organizations

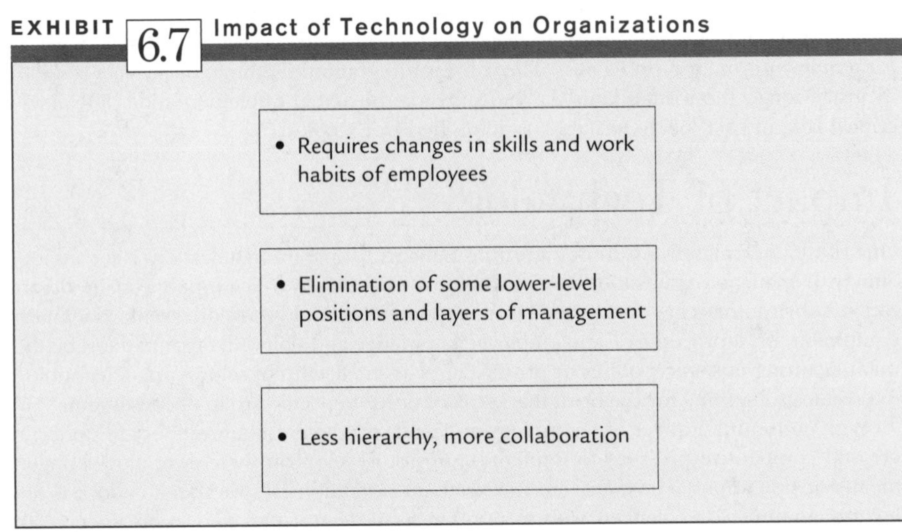

service sector, particularly services related to information processing. Service organizations are relatively easy to establish and expand, and they provide significant entrepreneurial opportunities. However, service sector employees need different skills than those utilized in manufacturing.[28] Rather than manual dexterity, service sector employees need strong interpersonal and communication skills as well as the ability to be flexible in handling a variety of problems related to serving clients. Customers of service organizations need much more "customized" or individualized output. For example, the clients of a real estate brokerage do not all wish to purchase the same kind of housing. However, many organizations are finding it quite challenging to bridge the gap between the skills new workforce entrants possess and those required in the marketplace in an expeditious, efficacious manner.

The implementation of advanced technologies has also resulted in many organizations eliminating lower-level positions held by employees who performed tasks that can now be accomplished through automation. This has resulted in reduced employee headcounts, with those remaining employees having higher levels of training and skills. Automated technologies require more technically trained employees who act as troubleshooters to repair, adjust, or improve existing processes.[29] Consequently, organizations have been able to reduce and, in some cases, eliminate layers of management and move toward "flatter" organization structures with fewer levels in the hierarchy. At the same time, because these technical workers have advanced training, the power bases in many organizations have been rearranged from management to technical workers. It is not uncommon today for managers to have limited understanding of the technical dimensions of their subordinates' work. This is a dramatic departure from traditional supervision and creates unprecedented challenges for managers.

Technological change has resulted in hierarchical distinctions being blurred and more collaborative teamwork where managers, technicians, and analysts work together on projects. This, in part, is reflected in the growing trend for organizations to offer total quality management (TQM) initiatives for employees that focus on collaborative attempts to improve organizational processes to ensure continual improvement in the quality of the organization's product or service. Similarly, technology has created more flexible, dynamic organization structures that facilitate change and adaptation to changes in the organization's environment. These alternative structures take the form of unbundled corporations, autonomous groupings or subsidiaries, or smaller, streamlined units designed to be more responsive to changing customer needs and competitive pressures.[30]

HR Issues and Challenges Related to Technology

In addition to impacting how work is organized and organization structure, technology has created three new areas of concern for HR and organizations: telecommuting, workplace monitoring and surveillance, and e-HR.

Telecommuting

Telecommuting, the process by which employees work from home, is increasing dramatically in popularity in both small and large organizations. The key factors that have facilitated this trend are the advances taking place in information processing and telecommunications technologies. Telecommuting involves more than merely an agreement between employees and supervisors that the subordinate can work at home. It involves a management system that allows employees a tremendous amount of discretion as to how they fulfill their job responsibilities.

The number of Americans working from home at least part of the workweek grew from 3.4 million in 1990 to 19.6 million by the beginning of 2000. Two-thirds of Fortune 100 companies currently have telecommuting programs, half of which were implemented over the past three years. Of the remaining Fortune 100 organizations, 60 *percent* are planning to implement a telecommuting program.

Telecommuting programs can provide a number of benefits. Stringent environmental regulations, such as the Clean Air Act, have put pressure on many urban areas to reduce employee commuting on roadways. It is estimated that if 5 *percent* of Los Angeles commuters worked from home once a week, 9.5 million gallons of gasoline would be saved annually and 94 million fewer tons of pollutants would be dumped into the atmosphere. Telecommuting can be used as a retention aid, as a more flexible work environment can allow an employee to balance multiple roles. Telecommuting can help employers to retain their investment in employees in situations where the employee needs to relocate for personal reasons as well as when the organization needs to relocate and the employee is unable to do so. Telecommuting also creates flexibility in recruiting and allows employers to hire from a broader prospective applicant pool. Organizations can gain significant savings relative to real estate costs, which are often high in larger urban areas. Additional studies also show that telecommuting can significantly increase productivity.

Despite these benefits, there is often strong resistance to telecommuting from direct supervisors of workers who would telecommute, primarily over the issue of measuring performance and monitoring progress of employees who are working remotely. Although the criteria for performance and accountability standards need not be different for those who telecommute vis-à-vis those employees who do not, the fact that there is no face-to-face contact is disconcerting to many supervisors.

A clear performance measurement system is the key component of a successful telecommuting program. The telecommuting employee should have a clearly defined set of measurable objectives, which can be integrated into a telecommuting agreement. Organizations such as Hewlett-Packard and Cisco Systems have successfully implemented objectives-based performance management programs that have facilitated telecommuting arrangements.

A second issue is deciding how many and which employees are offered participation in the telecommuting program. Care has to be exercised to avoid creating resentment or morale problems among nonparticipants. A key factor to be considered is the extent to which an individual's job responsibilities can be performed effectively away from the office. Attention also must be paid to individual employee characteristics. Telecommuting generally requires employees to have strong organizational and time management skills as well as be self-motivated.

Another consideration is the expense of purchasing equipment for the employee's home office. Similarly, liability for injuries incurred while working at home must be factored in. Because the home workspace is considered an extension of the company, the liability for job-related injuries continues to rest with the employer.

A final issue is that many managers are just not comfortable having their direct reports away from the office. Unfortunately, this is because of the fact that many managers have had no prior telecommuting experience themselves. Training programs aimed at both telecommuters and those who supervise such employees that cover issues such as goal setting, time management, and project reporting could help mitigate some of these concerns.

Attention also needs to be paid to the investment that a networking system will require and the capacity of that system to support the volume of remote access from telecommuters. A technological feasibility assessment is as important as ensuring that the appropriate employees are allowed to participate in the program.

One study has shown that a well-designed and implemented telework program can reduce turnover by an average of 20 *percent*, boost productivity by up to 22 *percent*, and reduce absenteeism by nearly 60 *percent*.[31] More recently, telecommuting has been used to aid succession planning, particularly in cases of high potential, high performing employees whose services the employer does not want to lose but who are unable or unwilling to relocate for career advancement. In such cases, employees may periodically commute to company headquarters or some other site while primarily working off-site.[32]

Telecommuting at the U.S. Patent and Trademark Office

Most federal government agencies are slow to adapt to changes, particularly changes in how work is performed. However, the U.S. Patent and Trademark Office (USPTO) has been a leader among federal agencies in the use of telecommuting as a central *component of its business strategy. Its program, involving the participation of more than 40 percent of the agency's 3,600 employees, was designed to promote higher productivity, efficiency, and performance, reduce traffic congestion and air pollution around the nation's capital, and reduce real estate costs. The agency started its telecommuting program as a pilot and saw that productivity and retention were immediately impacted in a positive way. Because the nature of trademark examination work lends itself to ease of reporting and documentation, performance for employees who telecommute is easily measurable. The agency has determined that its program saves more than 613,000 gallons of gasoline consumption and $1.8 million in fuel costs annually.*[33]

Telecommuting at Merrill Lynch

Financial services giant Merrill Lynch did not rush into the decision to offer its employees the option to telecommute. The program was the product of four years of study, research, and planning that resulted in a well-designed, strategized approach to telecommuting that fits the organization's strategic objectives and culture. A 21-page managers' guide was developed that explained the nature and benefits of alternative work arrangements. Workshops are required in which employees and managers confront issues that could be affected by telecommuting, including productivity measurement, time management, coworker communication, and career planning. Prior to allowing an employee to start telecommuting, a two-week "simulation lab" experience is required, during which prospective telecommuters work in isolation from their managers and coworkers. During that time, communication is allowed by phone or e-mail only, as it would be if the employee were working at home. Employees also receive training in troubleshooting problems with computer hardware and software that will be used at home. During the first year of the program, productivity among telecommuters increased 15–20 percent, turnover declined by 6 percent, and fewer sick days were used by telecommuters. The program has also been used effectively as a recruiting tool and allowed the organization to retain many workers it would have lost when it moved its headquarters.[34]

Employee Surveillance and Monitoring

Most employers and employees agree that technology, particularly access to the Internet, has enhanced employees' abilities to do their jobs: The dizzying array of information available on demand on the Internet allows more comprehensive and faster data collection when addressing issues and problems at work. Online technology also makes it far easier for employees to work at home via either telecom-muting or on the employee's own time. As employees perform more of their job responsibilities on "nonwork" time, they may feel much more free to take care of their personal needs during work hours, as long as their job responsibilities are being fulfilled. One study found that 90 *percent* of employees admitted to visiting non-work-related Web sites while at work, spending an average of more than two hours per week taking care of personal work and needs.[35] Much of this activity centers around banking, bill paying, and shopping, but there is also significant employee visits to adult Web sites, chat rooms, daring sites, and gaming sites during the working day.

In response, an increasing number of employers have implemented electronic monitoring of their employees, using software to track employee Internet use. More than 80 *percent* of large employers are now utilizing such technology, which can monitor not only Internet usage but also e-mails, computer files, and voice mail and telephone usage. Such monitoring raises serious concerns about employee rights to privacy and can also have a detrimental effect on employee morale and loyalty. As heightened job demands require employees to spend more and more time at the office and to do work-related business at home, the line between work and personal life blurs. Hence, employers have to balance the need for employee productivity with employees' rights to privacy and their need to maintain a balance between work and personal life.

Employees actually have very limited privacy rights in the area of workplace monitoring. The Electronic Communications Privacy Act (ECPA), passed in 1986, is the only federal law that addresses employer monitoring of electronic communications in the workplace. While the ECPA prohibits the intentional interception of employees' oral, wire, and electronic communications, it contains two important workplace exceptions. The first is the "business purpose exception," which allows the monitoring and interception of employee communications as long as the employer can show a legitimate business reason for doing so. The second is the "consent exception," which allows for monitoring of employee communications when employees have provided the employer with their permission to do so, thereby relinquishing employee claims for invasion of privacy.

The ECPA also provides that employers may monitor oral telephone communications if they normally do so within the course of their business. This is important for telemarketing and customer service operations where employers have particular concerns related to professionalism, productivity, and quality control. However, the ECPA requires that employers refrain from listening to employee telephone conversations the moment they determine that such calls are personal in nature.

Because many employers have taken punitive action against employees for their use of technology for personal purposes during working hours, there is the potential for increased tension between employees and employers surrounding the use of telecommunications technology. Employers who chose to monitor employee use of telecommunications equipment should implement a clear and succinct policy and communicate this policy to all employees. Monitoring should be kept to a minimum and be consistent with "business necessity" or with performance problems or deficiencies dealt with as part of the employer's performance management system. As employee loyalty continues to decline, employers need to ensure that their policies do not create additional distrust on the part of their employees.

In addition to surveillance and monitoring of employee computer usage, maintaining the security of information obtained by employers is a critical concern that organizations must address. As an increasing amount of employee personal information is collected and stored in automated databases, organizations have a heightened responsibility to ensure that reasonable measures of security have been put in place to prevent access to and leakage of employee information, particularly to those outside the organization. With incidents of identity theft on the rise, inappropriate access to employee personal information contained in employment records could cause tremendous harm to both employees and the employer. Leakage of such information can result in a loss of employee and consumer confidence, harm the organization's reputation, and expose the organization to legal liability.[36] While the body of case law in this domain is still under development, an increasing number of state legislatures are passing laws that hold employers responsible for safeguarding all employee information and records.[37]

e-HR

Technological advances have also provided HR with an incredible opportunity to deliver many of its transactional types of services online, freeing HR staff to work on more strategic issues. Payroll, employee benefits, scheduling, recruiting, training, and career development are just some of the areas that are being delivered in a self-service format to employees. While there are many examples of how various employers are using e-HR to benefit both employees and the organization, the examples provided here illustrate the range of HR activities that are being delivered electronically as well as the scope of how "deep" such delivery can go.

Time Warner Cable, Inc., in Houston has more than 1,660 employees, spread out over 27 locations. The majority of these employees work a great distance from any HR office or staff. In response to the mandate for better delivery of HR services, Time Warner installed kiosks at its remote locations to provide better service to installers and service center personnel in these locations. Initially designed to facilitate the delivery of HR programs and services, many other departments in the organization soon wanted to become a part of the communications vehicle. Employees can now do everything from participate in open enrollment for benefits to learn about the activities of the public affairs department via the kiosks.[38]

In 2003, the city of Dallas stopped issuing paychecks to its employees. This was not because of the inability of the city to pay its employees but rather was a result of the full elimination of paper paychecks. Many employees had been receiving their pay through direct deposit, but for those without bank accounts, the city began issuing debit cards. The distribution of paper paychecks was expensive and time-consuming for the city; the move to "electronic pay" resulted in a $150,00 annual savings, in addition to the freed-up time of human resource staff. Payroll debit cards can be used to obtain cash at automated teller machines as well as purchase goods from most retailers. In addition to the Dallas city government, employers such as Little Caesars pizza, Sears, Office Depot, and Chicago's public school system have eliminated the use of paper paychecks in lieu of plastic.[39]

American Airlines, Inc., was one of the early pioneers in using the Internet for customer service. It has since expanded its use of online technology for managing its more than 100,000 employees worldwide. American has a highly mobile workforce, with more than 25 *percent* in the air at any time and more than 50 *percent* with no office. Consequently, it needed an effective means to communicate with employees at a time and place that was convenient for each employee. A program was launched to assist employees with the purchase of low-cost personal computers to facilitate the implementation of American's "jetnet" program. Under this program, employees and retirees can complete benefits enrollment and book travel. Pilots and flight attendants, who bid for monthly flight schedules through a preference system, saw the time required for this activity reduced from four to five hours monthly to less than thirty minutes. jetnet has allowed American to not only greatly reduce costs but to also provide its mobile workforce with a tremendous added time-saving convenience.[40]

One of the most comprehensive examples of electronic delivery of human resource services can be seen at General Motors. GM sees itself not as the world's largest manufacturer of automobiles but rather as an e-commerce organization that just happens to manufacture cars. A special unit of GM, e-GM, has been created to produce consumer Web sites and business-to-business portals and to deliver e-HR services. The delivery of e-HR, through GM's "Employee Service Center," is designed to allow HR to move away from transactional issues and focus more on strategic issues. The ESC allows different information to be displayed to different employee groups, in line with each group's needs. Access to the center is not u8limited to the workplace; employees can access it anywhere via the Internet. The site receives more than 15 million hits per month and allows employees to enroll in classes online, develop a career development plan that can be reviewed with their supervisor, view job postings, manage their benefits, and review their employment history. GM has rolled out its ESC to its international divisions and sees the project as continuous, with an updated re-release of the site planned every six months.[41]

Social Networking

As Internet-based social networking sites have proliferated and their membership mushroomed, employers have begun to see the benefits that online social networking can have for the workplace. Some smaller employers have embraced existing sites, such as Facebook, and encouraged their employees to join and use their membership as a means of getting to know co-workers, particularly those who work at different locations, and to promote the organization and its business.[42] However, while many employers favor bringing dispersed workers closer together virtually, the idea of having the organization co-opt with a large general public provider may be unappealing. Many employers have developed their own in-house corporate network that would permit social networking among employees but maintain oversight of the site under the command-and-control features of the organization's firewall. Dow Chemical has developed its own social networking site as a critical means of maintaining contact with former employees and retirees. Given the episodic, temporary, project-based nature of work at Dow, the site is used to recruit back retirees for temporary projects as well as stay in touch with and recruit back former employees for permanent employment. Use of the site for recruiting has significantly reduced recruited and hiring costs.[43]

Social Networking at Capital One

Capital One, a 26,500 employee banking and financial services organization based in McLean, Virginia, has long maintained its own employee intranet, called Oneplace. Oneplace was largely a depository of materials related to basic HR services, such as benefits information and forms, training schedules, and the employee handbook. Realizing that the workplace was not as collaborative as senior management wished, the organization decided to add a social networking site to Oneplace in 2008. Employees are allowed to post personal profiles, photographs, and information about their jobs and areas of expertise and interest. Bulletin boards allow communication about any area of interest, regardless of whether it is work-related or personal. Contained within Oneplace is a feature called "communities of practice," where employees can post tips or seek advice on various aspects of their jobs. While the site is new and no measures of its success are yet available, 96 percent of Capital One employees visit the site at least once a month, and the typical employee visits 14 different days during the month, accessing 85 pages of content.[44]

Understanding Change

The pressure to change can be a constant force in many organizations. Small organizations try to grow to gain the economic and market advantages that come with larger size. At the same time, larger organizations try to become smaller—either by streamlining operations or dividing into smaller subsidiaries—to increase efficiency and responsiveness to marketplace changes. Multinational organizations try to change to adapt to different economic, political, social, and market conditions faced in various locations around the world.

Despite the need for and pressure to change, any change initiatives in organizations are often met with resistance. There are several reasons for such resistance. One is the real or perceived costs of change. Change involves disrupting the status quo and entering areas of uncertainty. It also generally involves commitment of resources (financial, time, capital, human) that could be deployed otherwise. Particularly when there is a mentality of "If it ain't broke, don't fix it," the opportunity cost of the resources being committed to an uncertain change initiative may be questioned. If employees fail to see any real need to change the design of work systems, they are less likely to support changes in their job or work environment, particularly if they enjoy things as they are.

Resistance to change can also be found when those involved with and impacted by the change efforts fail to perceive any benefits for themselves. Rank-and-file employees, in particular, may have no incentive to do things differently, be retrained, or have their jobs restructured if they see no personal benefit. Employees may adopt the attitude that the organization is trying to get them to do more without compensating them for their efforts. This can be particularly problematic in union settings where union representatives often reject any initiatives that may alter the collective bargaining agreement in spite of benefits they may provide.

A third barrier to change involves risk and the uncertainty inherent in doing something differently. There is no assurance that the change initiatives will result in higher performance, greater efficiency, better working conditions, or improved morale. Older workers with greater tenure in an organization are more likely to be creatures of habit and find the risk to greatly outweigh any return they or the organization might receive. Employees who question the utilization of and need for new technology or distrust team-based responsibility may be particularly resistant to work redesign.

Finally, poor coordination and communication often undermine change initiatives. Managers are well aware that change initiatives are often met with some resistance, and therefore, they may refrain from informing workers about new projects and programs that are being considered or developed. Unfortunately, the organization's grapevine invariably gets a sense that something may be happening and often produces exaggerated and/or more threatening rumors than what is actually being planned. Although senior managers may wish to develop change initiatives in a vacuum, that vacuum always has leaks. Misinformation unrefuted by managers can result in the departure of employees who may sense a threat to their jobs.

Managing Change

The management challenge then becomes how to overcome resistance to change. First, organizations need to plan to promote and implement change so it provides benefits to the users—those who will be most affected by the change. This might be in the form of incentives to learn, an understanding of how it will make a job easier or more enjoyable, enhanced marketability of skills, an upgrading of a position, or some form of "gain sharing" of the results for employees. Work redesign strategies need to consider the employee perspective as to how the changes will improve work and organizational life for them.

Second, those responsible for change initiatives need to promote and invite participation. Employees will generally be much more committed to any course of action they have been consulted on and agreed to than one that is forced upon them. In addition, the organization stands to benefit from the most fundamental rule of managing people in organizations: No one knows a job better than the person doing it. An employee who "lives" with a job day in and day out can provide far keener insights as to how to improve the job, working conditions, or efficiency than virtually anyone else. Consider how many senior managers in organizations know what it is like to work in a mailroom day after day, week after week, year after year; how many have ever worked swing shifts, cleaning the offices after everyone has left; how many have ever worked at a fast-paced reception desk/switchboard all day long. An individual does not need an advanced degree in management to be able to make significant recommendations and contributions relative to work design based on their own *real* experiences in living with a job.

Finally, change is facilitated by open, two-way communication. In addition to seeking input from those affected by change, managers also need to keep all employees informed of what is being considered and planned. This is particularly true when nothing has yet been decided. A lack of any information at all can cause employees to suspect that something significant may be in the works. Again, the informal rumor mill will often manufacture scenarios that are far more threatening than anything that might be under consideration. Employees who are apprehensive and have dubious perceptions of what management might be planning will be more stressed and less productive. Seeking employee input is not only motivating and beneficial for the organization in soliciting relevant expertise, but communicating with employees also fosters an atmosphere of trust and allows the organization to determine where resistance might lie prior to implementation of change rather than after.

Conclusion

The changing nature of work requires organizations to strategically manage change processes as part of work design and redesign. Redesigning work to create more flexible, responsive organizations is probably the biggest unmet need in modern organizations and a key, ongoing strategic issue for organizations of all sizes, in all industries, and in all locations.

Restructuring an organization is a risky undertaking and provides no guarantee of success. One 18-year study of Standard and Poor's 500 companies found no correlation between an organization's decision to downsize and its profitability.[45] To optimize performance, organizations need to determine the factors that distinguish successful reorganizations and restructurings from those that are less successful. Cascio has identified the practices that correlate with successful restructuring as:

- Skills training and continuous learning
- Increased employee participation in the design and implementation of work processes

- Flattened organizational structures
- Labor-management partnerships
- Compensation linked to organizational performance[46]

Clearly, HR plays a critical role in the success of any restructuring efforts. In partnering with senior executives on strategic objectives and how the organization's human capital might best be deployed toward those objectives, HR can facilitate the effective implementation of change that accompanies restructuring decisions and increase the probability that such efforts will be successful.

A strategic approach to human resource management involves HR acting as a change agent to drive, facilitate, and strategize change in organizations. Although some areas and functions, notably marketing, may respond to and/or drive change external to the organization, no other area drives change within the organization as the human resource function does.

Critical Thinking

1. Obtain the job description for your current or most recent job (prepare one yourself if one does not exist). Redo this description by using the job characteristics framework presented in Exhibit 6.2. Design a job that would be more interesting, challenging, and enjoyable for you.
2. What are the critical factors to consider in the design of work systems? What particular role does technology play in the design of work systems?
3. Compare and contrast job enlargement, rotation, and enrichment. How are they similar to and different from each other?
4. What barriers to change exist in most organizations, and how can they be overcome?
5. Describe a successful and unsuccessful attempt at job redesign that you have experienced or observed. What factors contributed to the success or failure of the change initiative? How could the unsuccessful attempt have been managed better?
6. Debate how offshoring might impact the U.S. economy. Do you feel that it will cause domestic organizations to become more competitive in the global marketplace through increased efficiency and reduced costs or will it simply result in higher unemployment and an erosion of the consumer segment of our economy?

Reading 6.1

7. Devise specific HR strategies or programs that address each of the seven types of mismatches.

Reading 6.2

8. How might the HR function be affected by outsourcing decisions in small and medium-sized organizations? What roles can and should HR play in such decisions?

Reading 6.3

9. What specific HR strategies and programs can be developed to improve the performance of virtual teams?

Exercises

1. Apply the job characteristics model in Exhibit 6.2 to the following positions:
   - an order-taker at McDonald's
   - an usher in a movie theater
   - a receptionist
   - a manager of an auto rental company
   - a computer programmer
   - an insurance salesperson
2. Visit the Web site for Kaiser Permanente health maintenance organization (HMO) at http://www.kaiserpermanente.org. If you are a member, go to Kaiser Permanente Online. This site allows the organization to extend member services to the Web by allowing community members to interact with one another and with physicians in moderated sessions. Members can also research their own healthcare needs as well as arrange appointments. The goal of this site is to improve outcomes and lower operating costs by fostering preventive care. This form of "redesigning" the work of healthcare enables Kaiser to get feedback that can be used to improve the delivery of services.

Chapter References

1. Pomeroy, A. "Great Places, Inspired Employees," *HR Magazine*, 49, (7), pp. 46–54, July 2004.
2. Walker, C. R. "The Problem of the Repetitive Job," *Harvard Business Review*, 28, 1950, pp. 54–58.
3. Campion, M. A., Cheraskin, L., and Stevens, M. J. "Career-Related Antecedents and Outcomes of Job Rotation," *Academy of Management Journal*, 37, 1994, pp. 1518–1542.
4. Grossman, R. J. "Putting HR in Rotation," *HR Magazine*, March 2003, pp. 51–57.
5. Hackman, J. R. and Oldham, G. R. "The Job Diagnostic Survey: An Instrument for the Diagnosis of Jobs and the Evaluation of Job Redesign Projects," *Technical Report No. 4*, New Haven, CT: Department of Administrative Sciences, Yale University, 1974.
6. Gomez-Meija, L. R., Balkin, D. B., and Cardy, R. L. *Managing Human Resources*, 3 ed., Upper Saddle River, NJ: Prentice Hall, 2001.
7. "Tough Love for Techie Souls," *Business Week*, November 29, 1999, p. 164.
8. Gomez-Meija, L. R., Balkin, D. B., and Cardy, R. L. *Managing Human Resources*, 3 ed., Upper Saddle River, NJ: Prentice Hall, 2001.
9. Bates, S. "Accounting for People," *HR Magazine*, October 2002, pp. 31–37.
10. Jossi, F. "Clocking out," *HR Magazine*, 52, (6), pp. 47–50, June 2007.
11. Shafer, R. A. "Only the Agile Will Survive," *HR Magazine*, July 2000, pp. 50–51.
12. Overman, S. "Federal, State Governments Fishing for Business Process Outsourcing Bounties," *HR Magazine*, September 2003, p. 32.
13. Pomeroy, A. "Telecom Leaders Share HR Outsourcing Tips," www.shrm.org/hrnews_published/articles/CMS_003846.asp.
14. "Job You Like May Be Going Overseas Soon," *Baltimore Sun*, December 30, 2002, p. 14D.
15. Babcock, P. "America's Newest Export: White-Collar Jobs," *HR Magazine*, April 2004, pp. 50–57.
16. Schramm, J. "Offshoring," *Workplaces Visions*, Society for Human Resource Management, 2004, No. 2.
17. "Job You Like May Be Going Overseas Soon," *Baltimore Sun*, December 30, 2002, p. 14D.
18. Babcock, P. "America's Newest Export: White-Collar Jobs," *HR Magazine*, April 2004, pp. 50–57.
19. Frase-Blunt, M. "Call Centers Come Home," *HR Magazine*, 52, (1), pp. 85–89.
20. Ibid.
21. "Financial Sector Workforce Hit by Mergers and Acquisitions," "'Human Factor' is Key Element in Success Rates for Merged Companies," International Labour Organization, www.ilo.org/public/english/burea/inf/pr/2001/06.htm.
22. Marks, M. and Mirvis, P. "Making Mergers and Acquisitions Work: Strategic and Psychological Preparation," *Academy of Management Executive*, 15, (2), pp. 80–92 (2001).
23. Carey, D. and Ogden, D. *The Human Side of M&A*, New York: Oxford University Press, 2004.
24. Adams, M. "Making a Merger," *HR Magazine*, March 2002, pp. 52–57.
25. Schmidt, J. A. "The Correct Spelling of M&A Begins with HR," *HR Magazine*, June 2001, pp. 102–108.
26. Perrow, C. "A Framework for the Comparative Analysis of Organizations," *American Sociological Review*, 32 (1967), pp. 194–208; Rousseau, D. M. "Assessment of Technology in Organizations: Closed versus Open Systems Approaches," *Academy of Management Review*, 4, (1979), pp. 531–542.
27. Harvey, B. H. "Technology, Diversity and Work Culture—Key Trends in the Next Millennium," *HR Magazine*, 45, (7), July 2000, p. 59.
28. Bowen, D. E. and Lawler, E. III. "The Empowerment of Service Workers: What, Why, How and When," *Sloan Management Review*, Spring 1992, pp. 31–39.
29. Daft, R. L. *Organization Theory and Design*, 6th ed., Cincinnati: South-Western College Publishing, 1998, pp. 126–130.
30. Ibid.
31. Wells, S. J. "Two Sides to the Story," *HR Magazine*, October 2001, p. 41.
32. Yost, C. *Work + Life: Finding the Fit That's Right for You*, Riverhead/Penguin Group, 2005.
33. Overman, S. "Most Federal Agencies Don't Measure Telework Program Results," Society for Human Resource Management, article 023659, published at www.shrm.org/hrnews_/published/articles/CMS_023659.asp, November 2007.
34. Wells, S. J. "Making Telecommuting Work," *HR Magazine*, October 2001, pp. 34–45.
35. Society for Human Resource Management, *Workplace Visions*, No. 5, 2001, p. 5.
36. Caterinicchia, D. "Safeguarding HR Information" *HR Magazine*, 50, (11), November 2005, pp. 55–59.
37. Cadrian, D. "Liability for Employee Identity Theft Is Growing" *HR Magazine*, 50, (6), June, 2005, pp. 35–40.
38. Robb, D. "Kiosks Bring HR Services to All Employees," *HR Magazine*, October 2002, pp. 109–114.
39. Demby, E. R. "Plastic Paychecks," *HR Magazine*, April 2003, pp. 89–94.
40. Roberts, B. "Portal Takes Off," *HR Magazine*, February 2003, pp. 95–99.
41. Jossi, F. "Taking the E-HR Plunge," *HR Magazine*, September 2001, pp. 96–103.
42. Roberts, B. "Social Networking at the Office" *HR Magazine*, 53, (5), May 2008, pp. 81–83.
43. Ibid.
44. Zeidner, R. "Employee Networking" *HR Magazine*, 53, (11), November, 2008, pp. 58–60.
45. Cascio, W. *Responsible Restructuring*, San Francisco: Berrett-Koehler, 2002.
46. Ibid.

READING 6.1

The Mismatched Worker: When People Don't Fit Their Jobs

Arne L. Kalleberg

Executive Overview[1]

When people's jobs match their needs, preferences, and abilities, they are likely to be relatively happy and satisfied with their work and lives, and workplaces are apt to function fairly smoothly and effectively. On the other hand, when there is a mismatch, or lack of fit, a variety of difficulties are likely to result for workers and their families as well as for employers and society. Mismatches have become more common in the United States in the past several decades, due in large part to the pressures on companies to be more competitive, increased skill requirements, and the growing diversity of the labor force. Here we look at some of the major changes in labor markets that have led to seven types of mismatches between workers and jobs in the U.S. and discuss their implications.

Matching people to jobs successfully has always been problematic in industrial societies, due to the complexity of jobs and the diversity among people. However, mismatches have become more common in the United States in the past several decades: There are a growing number of serious imbalances between today's workforce and workplace and the institutions and policies that support and govern them. The escalation in mismatches stems primarily from changes (or lack of changes) in the institutional structure and the workplace that have not kept pace with some of the main trends in work and the labor force: *globalization* (which leads to pressure on businesses to become more competitive), *growth of information technology and technological innovation* (which increases skill requirements), the *geographic dispersion* of workers, and the growing *diversity* of the labor force.

The concept of mismatch calls to mind the extensive literature in industrial/organizational and personnel psychology on "person-environment fit." Psychologists studying industries and organizations have long been concerned with the nature and consequences of a lack of fit between an individual's ability, interests, preferences, personality, or beliefs and the corresponding requirements of jobs (e.g., Edwards, 1991; Holland, 1973; Wilk, Desmarais, & Sackett, 1995) or between an individual's beliefs and perceptions and the organization's culture (e.g., Kristof, 1996; O'Reilly, Chatman, & Caldwell, 1991). (For recent reviews of the literature on person-environment fit, see Cable & Edwards, 2004, and Walsh, 2006.) Psychologists generally focus on the micro aspects of these fits, however, and rarely assess how mismatches are linked to changes in the institutional context and workplace.

By contrast, institutional economists and sociologists have emphasized macro-level changes in institutions, organizations, and the characteristics of the labor force that might produce conflicts between workers' interests and the characteristics of jobs (e.g., Sullivan, 1978). Economists, for example, study how discrepancies between the supply of workers and the demand for employees in labor markets may create mismatches and the economic consequences that arise when workers' skills and qualifications do not fit those required by the jobs that are available (e.g., Tyler, Murnane, & Levy, 1995). A recent assessment concluded that:

> *"The result of these changes is a fundamental mismatch between labor market institutions and the deployment of the work force. There is also a mismatch between individuals' commitments to the labor market and their responsibilities to their families. Also mismatched are the structures of social insurance, job security, family benefits, and career advancement" (Osterman et al., 2001, p. 9).*

Unfortunately, economists and sociologists rarely assess the noneconomic outcomes of mismatches and their impacts on workers' psychological states. The concept of mismatch provides common ground that allows a multidisciplinary look at the literature from both macro and micro perspectives. Mismatches between the institutional structures governing work (such as labor laws, workplace organization, and labor-management relations) and characteristics of the workforce (such as workers' family responsibilities) generate poor fits between persons and jobs at the individual level. Understanding how the dynamics of institutions and the labor force lead to mismatches and their consequences is valuable for managers and policy makers as they seek to address issues related to human resources.

This article provides an overview of how changes in labor markets and the workforce have led to seven types of mismatches or conflicts between workers and jobs within the United States. I also present illustrative data on some of these kinds of mismatches. I finally discuss a few implications of mismatches for individuals and organizations, and suggest some strategies that may improve the fit between them.

Creating Mismatches

Mismatches result from the interplay between some combination of people's needs, interests, values, and expectations on the one hand and the characteristics and rewards associated with their jobs and organizations on the other. Jobs and people differ in many ways, so many kinds of mismatches may occur in an industrial society.

First, let's look at jobs. Jobs are work tasks that require particular skills and qualifications. How most jobs are done is affected by their relationships to other jobs within a particular workplace. Jobs differ in terms of their timing, which is often governed by the requirements of product or service delivery. For example, an increasing number of jobs in the economy involve serving customers (such as in restaurants, hotels, convenience stores, and supermarkets), and the needs of customers may increasingly require that these jobs be performed on a "24/7" basis. Jobs also differ in the extent to which they provide people with intrinsic rewards, such as opportunities for personal gratification, as well as extrinsic benefits, such as money, chances for advancement, and health insurance.

People, like jobs, vary in a number of ways. Workers vary in their skills and abilities, family situations, life stages and experiences, and cultural backgrounds. People have different preferences for the number of hours they work and for when these hours are; some are "morning" people, while others prefer to work at night. People also diverge in the importance they place on the various kinds of benefits jobs provide: Some people attach highest value to having a challenging or secure job; others focus more on the economic rewards of work. These individual differences produce diversity in what people want, need, and expect from their jobs with regard to characteristics such as pay, challenge, and working hours.

Combining the characteristics of people and jobs identifies categories of possible mismatches. In this article, I discuss five mismatched situations (leading to seven kinds of mismatches), as people and jobs may have poor fits with regard to:

1. Skills and qualifications (*overqualification* and *underqualification*).
2. Geographical or spatial location.
3. Temporality and time preferences (*overworking* and *underworking*).
4. Inadequate earnings.
5. Conflicts between work and family lives.

These types of mismatches are based on several criteria. The psychology (and organizational behavior) literature emphasizes ability and preferences as the basic dimensions of fit, suggesting mismatches such as over- or underqualification (based on proxies for ability) and over- and underworking (which may reflect preferences). Economists (and industrial relations researchers) have focused on conflicts between workers and their employers with regard to such things as money, and have been concerned with mismatches that might be called "inadequate earnings." Sociologists have concentrated on jobs that make it difficult for people to take care of their family obligations. And geographers and sociologists have studied mismatches between workers' home and work locations. In all these mismatches, persons are unable to satisfy their needs or preferences through their jobs.

Mismatches Are Contextual

In order to conclude that a worker and job are mismatched, we must evaluate the person's skills, needs, and preferences *in relation* to the requirements or benefits available from the job. Two people in the same job may or may not be mismatched depending on their preferences, interests, and needs. For example, whether a person is considered to be overworked depends on his or her needs and preferences as well as on the demands of the job. Some people might like to work 80 to 90 hours a week, while others feel overworked if they have to work even 20 hours a week. Whether a job that pays a minimum wage is inadequate for a person's economic needs depends in part on her or his family situation and life stage: A teenager who has dropped out of high school and who lives at home and works full time may feel that a minimum-wage job fulfills her needs for spending money; someone who has been employed for many years and has a family to support is likely to experience a mismatch if he is forced to work a job that pays poorly.

The notion of a mismatch is also shaped by cultural understandings of what is considered "normal" and the conditions under which a job might reasonably be expected to be a "good fit." In France, for instance, people who work more than 35 hours a week may feel overworked, while in the United States such levels of work effort are considered common. These cultural norms also change over time within a country. In the Depression era of the 1930s in the United States, for example, people were happy to have a job at all, despite oppressive working conditions, inadequate health and safety protections, and lack of health and retirement benefits. Workers generally sought to satisfy only fairly basic needs through their jobs, such as earning a living wage. Those who were lucky to have jobs at all were not apt to be overly concerned that those jobs might not make full use of their skills or qualifications, required them to work too many hours, or left them little time to spend with their families. While we might consider people who had jobs that did not fit their skills or time preferences in this period to be mismatched, they probably did not.

Needs are subjective, though, and the range of needs and wants people seek to fulfill through their paid work in the early 21st century has expanded considerably. What's more, people increasingly expect their jobs to provide challenging work and meaningful social relationships, in addition to economic success. This may be due to the greater availability of information about the kinds of jobs that exist, making it easier for people to compare their jobs to others and to assess the relative "goodness" of their jobs. As a result, there are likely to be more cases where people feel that there is a mismatch between their needs and the rewards their jobs provide. Add in declines in the real value of wages, fewer opportunities for advancement, absence of health insurance, and so on and the sources of complaints and negative feelings on the part of workers and their families begin to multiply.

Most, if not all, of the mismatches discussed here have increased, sometimes substantially, in the United States in recent years. Work-family conflict and overworking, for example, are more common now than ever before due primarily to the greater participation of women in the labor market, which has not made the kinds of accommodations that would help men and women better balance their work and family lives. Pressures on organizations to "do more with less" have made it harder for some workers to avoid having to work more hours (and working more intensely during those hours) than they would like.

Interrelations Among Mismatches

These mismatches do not occur independently; they may be related in several ways (see also Jansen & Kristof-Brown, 2006).

First, one mismatch may cause others. For example, geographical mismatches may account for other kinds of mismatches. Some people may not be able to find jobs that fit their skills, preferences, or needs because they are geographically constrained and are not able to move to areas where they might find jobs that better fit their needs. This is often the case for "trailing spouses," who may be overqualified or may not be able to work as much as they would like because they are unable to find suitable employment in the area where their wives or husbands are working. Also, immigrants who have recently arrived in the United States, like minorities who live in inner-city areas, are often not competitive for jobs that exist in their geographical area largely because of their lack of skills and qualifications; they may also not have the resources to travel to other areas to search for jobs for which they might be more qualified. In addition, firms may make strategic choices to move jobs to areas with plentiful and cheap labor, perhaps improving matches between persons and jobs in the new area but creating mismatches in the areas they vacate.

Moreover, work-family conflicts may be both a cause and a consequence of other mismatches. People may forgo a better job in order to have flexible work hours for childcare, creating a skills mismatch. On the other hand, people who feel they are overworked may experience conflict between their work and family lives.

Second, some kinds of mismatches may coexist because they result from similar processes, such as from a disharmony between labor supply and employment demand. Thus, a labor shortage can coexist with high underemployment. For example, some jobs may lie vacant due to a lack of applicants with the requisite education and training (e.g., high school math and physics teachers), while some college graduates work as bartenders. Additionally, hours in the labor market are often poorly distributed, so some workers may feel overworked at the same time others are seeking more hours, reflecting the polarization that exists with regard to temporal mismatches (Jacobs & Gerson, 2004).

Third, some kinds of mismatches may be mutually exclusive and negatively related to each other. Obtaining a job that avoids one type of mismatch may thus lead to another type, and it may be difficult if not impossible to achieve good fits on all dimensions. For example, obtaining a high-skilled job that fits with one's qualifications and pay preferences may require the person to work more hours than he or she desires. Alleviating work-family conflict may require that people obtain more flexible jobs that do not fully utilize their educational qualifications or that do not pay as much as they would like. The negative relationships among some mismatches suggest that people may be forced to trade off obtaining good matches on some dimensions in order to avoid being mismatched on others.

Types of Mismatches

In this section, I provide an overview of the different types of mismatches, and in some cases provide some illustrative data on their incidence.

Skills Mismatches

Skills mismatches denote a lack of fit between people's skills or qualifications and their jobs' skill requirements. There are two general kinds of skill mismatches: overqualification,[2] where people's skills (often equated with their education and perhaps other work-related qualifications) exceed the skills that are objectively required to perform the job, and underqualification, where people do not have the skills necessary to carry out job duties adequately. Over- and underqualification reflect disconnects between the distribution of workers' qualifications and jobs' requirements at any point in time.

The extent to which overqualification or underqualification attracts greater interest by social scientists and the media has changed over time. In the 1970s, sociologists and economists focused mainly on the causes and likely consequences of overqualification, as the rapid increase in the number of college graduates in the 1960s and early 1970s was generally believed to exceed the growth in high-skilled jobs. By contrast, concern in the 1980s and 1990s shifted to the problem of underqualification and its relationship to rapid technological change and increased competitiveness in the world economy. This led some observers to conclude that the nature of skills mismatch had changed and that "the skills glut seemed to have turned rapidly into a skills shortage" (Handel, 2003, p. 137).

Overqualification The estimates[3] in Table 1 indicate that about one in five full-time workers in the United States was overqualified in the years from 1993 to 2002. This percentage represented an increase from previous years and was about twice as large as in the years from 1972 to 1982.

Women were slightly less likely than men to be overqualified, though the gender gap in overqualification has appeared to narrow slightly during the 30-year period from 1972 to 2002. Non-whites were more apt to be overqualified for their jobs than whites in each of the three periods. Younger workers were more likely to be overqualified than older workers in the years from 1972 to 1992, though this age gap had virtually disappeared in the most recent period. College-educated workers were more likely to be overqualified than workers with less education, as we would expect. More than half of workers with more than a college education were overqualified in the period 1993 to 2002, which represents a marked increase from earlier years.

Overqualification is likely to continue to grow into the future, as the Bureau of Labor Statistics projects that by 2010, only 20.7% of all jobs will require a college degree or more (Tufekci, 2004). A quarter of the U.S. population already has this level of education, and this percentage will undoubtedly continue to increase.

It is not surprising that overqualification occurs frequently. One explanation is the operation of firm internal labor markets. A person who is really qualified for job Z must start at job X, a lower-level one, as that is the entry point to the organization. Doing well in job X will lead to job Y, which may then lead to job Z – but the person is qualified for job Z all along and thus is overqualified in jobs X and Y. This process may not be illogical if matching on some other dimensions (e.g., cultural fit) is important; for example, the firm may want to screen out employees who don't "mesh" well with the organization.

Underqualification Table 2 presents estimates of the extent to which people in the United States are underqualified for their jobs.

Table 1 Estimates of Overqualification[a] among U.S. Workers, by Selected Demographic Characteristics, 1972–2002[b]

	% Overqualified (3 or more years)		
	1972–1982	1983–1992	1993–2002
Gender			
Males	11.6	16.1	20.3
Females	9.4	14.5	19.8
Race			
White	10.4	15.0	19.4
Non-white	14.0	17.8	22.6
Education			
Less than H.S. (0–11 years)	0.4	0.6	1.3
High school graduate	5.5	4.7	6.0
Some college (13–15 years)	12.5	15.0	17.1
College graduate	17.7	25.7	29.8
College + (17–20 years)	39.7	45.3	51.0
Age			
25–34	13.9	16.1	20.8
35–44	11.0	17.8	19.0
45–54	9.2	13.3	20.1
55–65	6.6	10.1	18.9

[a]Overqualification is defined as having an educational attainment that is three or more years greater than the educational requirements of the job.

[b]Source: General Social Survey data, reported in Stephen Vaisey (2006), Table 2 (p. 845).

Table 2 Estimates of Underqualification[a] among U.S. Workers, by Selected Demographic Characteristics, 1972–2002[b]

	% Underqualified (3 or more years)		
	1972–1982	1983–1992	1993–2002
Gender			
Males	19.9	11.8	7.2
Females	11.9	9.5	6.7
Race			
White	16.9	10.4	6.9
Non-white	18.4	13.1	7.4
Education			
Less than H.S. (0–11 years)	51.0	47.1	41.2
High school graduate	8.4	7.8	7.0
Some college (13–15 years)	4.4	2.8	2.5
College graduate	5.5	3.3	2.2
College + (17–20 years)	1.5	1.2	0.6
Age			
25–34	9.0	7.8	5.5
35–44	14.6	7.8	6.4
45–54	23.8	14.0	7.4
55–65	27.5	22.1	11.4

[a]Underqualification is defined as having an educational attainment that is three or more years less than the educational requirements of the job.

[b]Source: General Social Survey data, analyzed by Stephen Vaisey (personal communication).

These estimates indicate that about 20% of men and 12% of women in the United States were underqualified for their jobs in the period from 1972 to 1982. The gender gap in under-qualification has narrowed since then, and the percentage of both men and women who have at least three fewer years of education than that required by their jobs has decreased over time; in the years from 1993 to 2002, only about 7% of men and slightly less than that of women were underqualified by this measure. The declining gender gap reflects in part the relatively greater growth in educational attainment among women. Non-whites are more likely to be underqualified than whites, but the gap is relatively small and has also narrowed in the most recent decade.

Underqualification is more apt to characterize workers with a high school degree or less, as shown in Table 2. The percentage of underqualified workers with at most a high school diploma has declined over time, from nearly six out of ten workers in the years from 1972 to 1982 to slightly less than 50% in the decade from 1993 to 2002. These estimates suggest that underqualification is concentrated among those with a high school diploma or less, similar to the way that overqualification is highest among college graduates (see Table 1).

By contrast, relatively small percentages of workers who have attained a college degree or more are underqualified by these measures. This illustrates a "ceiling" effect: The more education people have, the less likely it is that their jobs will require more education than they have.

Underqualification also appears to be most prevalent among older workers. Nearly a quarter of workers aged 45 to 54 and over a quarter of workers aged 55 to 65 were underqualified in the years from 1972 to 1982;[4] the percentages of these groups who were underqualified from 1993 to 2002 were about 7% and 11%, respectively. By contrast, relatively small proportions of the youngest workers were underqualified (fewer than 10% in the years from 1972 to 1982 and fewer than 6% in the period from 1993 to 2002).

Taken as a whole, these results do not support arguments that underqualification is increasing in the United States. The percentages in every demographic group have declined over time, suggesting that concerns about a "coming skills shortage" are likely to have been exaggerated, perhaps by employers not willing to invest in training for their workers (see Cappelli, 1999).

Geographical Mismatches

Geographical mismatches occur when geographic or spatial barriers prevent people from obtaining jobs for which they are qualified or that meet their needs.

One type of geographical mismatch occurs when jobs move from one area to another, leaving behind workers who neither are able to move nor have the skills to fill the jobs that remain in the area. This is illustrated by the shift of manufacturing industries from the Midwest or Northeast regions of the United States to the South and West; "de-industrialization" was a prominent concern in the U.S. in the 1980s (e.g., Bluestone & Harrison, 1982). These geographical movements of jobs also reflect the shift to a service economy from one based on manufacturing. Geographical mismatches are also created by the movement of jobs out of the United States altogether; such offshoring of both high-skill and low-skill jobs reflects the increasing globalization of the economy.

Another type of geographical mismatch is the lack of fit between jobs and people located in cities and suburbs. Most cities in America started with an urban-industrial core with people living within walking distance of their jobs. As cities (and transportation) evolved, more affluent people moved away from the city core to create the suburbs. Later the jobs followed, leaving low-income, minority residents behind in an often hollowed-out urban core. The resulting geographical mismatch is frequently studied by social scientists in terms of the "spatial mismatch" hypothesis. This idea posits that discrimination and other constraints, in housing markets have denied minorities access to homes in suburban areas where the jobs for which they may be qualified have migrated. As a result of these limits on geographical mobility, minorities in particular have been forced to live in inner-city areas where there are insufficient jobs that make use of their qualifications. Their lack of access is compounded because minorities often have difficulty commuting to places where suitable jobs are located; the jobs in these locations don't pay well enough to support both a family and the commute.

Temporal Mismatches

People differ in the number of hours they prefer to work. Their preferences depend on factors such as the centrality of work to their identity and the extent to which they have non-work interests or family responsibilities. People also vary as to whether they need to work a relatively large or small number of hours in order to earn a certain level of income or to satisfy career objectives. For workers who are paid by the hour, their income is directly linked to the number of hours they work, though salaried workers are often able to vary their hours (at least in the short run) without affecting their income.

There are two main kinds of temporal mismatches: overworking, in which a person works more hours than he or she wants (or, alternatively, works harder than he or she prefers within a fixed number of hours), and underworking, in which a person works fewer hours than he or she wants. Overworking is often (though not always) associated with relatively high-paying, high-status, professional jobs and self-employment. These jobs place relatively high demands on workers, especially early in their careers, but they also provide workers with opportunities for high earnings and often advancement to higher paying and even better jobs. On the other hand, underworking is usually related to economic hardship and often does not lead to better jobs in the future. In both cases, people are not able to work the amount of time they prefer or that meets their needs. Despite their differences, both of these types of temporal mismatches are likely to lead to stress and may contribute to other problems, such as work-family conflict.

Overworking There are several ways to obtain information about whether someone works more hours than he or she wants. One set of questions focuses on the *number of hours* one wants to work; a second set asks about the *intensity* of work during those hours.

One approach to assessing whether one works too many hours is to ask the worker to indicate the actual number of hours he or she works at his or her main job during an average week and then to inquire: "Ideally, how many hours, in total, would you like to work each week?" Workers whose actual number of hours worked exceed their ideal number are considered to be overworked. The first set of rows in Table 3 presents information obtained in this way, from the 1997 National Study of the Changing Workforce (for a description of this study, see Bond, Galinsky, & Swanberg, 1998).

In the late 1990s, about six out of ten men and women in the United States wanted to work fewer hours per week than they actually did. Men typically desired to work full time and women typically preferred somewhat less than full time. For men, the average difference between actual hours per week worked (47.3) and ideal number of hours (37.5) was 9.8 hours. For women, the difference was 9.3 hours.

The vast majority of those who wanted to work fewer hours said they preferred to work at least five hours fewer than they actually worked. And about half of the 60% of workers who reported that they wanted to work fewer hours (about three in ten in the overall labor force) said they would prefer to work at least 20 fewer hours than they actually worked.

The gaps between actual and ideal hours were greatest for highly educated workers, those in managerial and professional occupations, workers in the middle age range (36 to 55 years old), and married workers. For women, the biggest gap was for those who were married to an employed spouse (Jacobs & Gerson, 2004, Table 3.2); dual-earner couples are most likely to experience a "time squeeze" or "leisure pinch."

Another way to assess whether people work more hours than they prefer is to ask respondents generally if they want to spend more, less, or the same amount of time at work, if they could decide this. The General Social Survey asked workers this question in 1998, as well as whether they preferred to have a full-time or a part-time job. The second set of rows in Table 3 presents the percentages of wage-and-salaried full-time and part-time male and female workers who were classified as overworked on the basis of these questions (see Reynolds, 2003).

Table 3 Extent of Overworking in the United States[a]

	Men	Women
Actual hours worked > ideal hours[b]		
Total hours usually worked (all jobs)	47.3	41.4
Ideal hours	37.5	32.1
Difference (actual − ideal)	9.8	9.3
Actual hours > ideal hours	60.2	60.1
Actual hours at least 5 hours > ideal hours	58.4	58.6
Actual hours at least 10 hours > ideal hours	47.4	48.8
Actual hours at least 20 hours > ideal hours	28.3	27.9
Want to spend less time on paid work[c]		
Full-time wants fewer hours	22	15
Full-time wants part-time	9	21
Part-time want fewer hours	2	3
Want to work fewer hours and earn less money[d]		
Work fewer hours and earn less (1998)	5.6	5.3
Work fewer hours and earn less (1998)	7.6	12.2

[a]Percentages.

[b]Source: National Study of the Changing Workforce, 1997. Reported in Jacobs and Gerson, *The Time Divide* (2004), Table 3.1.

[c]Source: General Social Survey, 1998. Reported in Reynolds (2003), Table 2.

[d]Source: General Social Surveys, 1989, 1998. Author's calculations.

These figures reveal somewhat smaller proportions of overworked workers than those suggested by the first measure. Women are more likely to report being overworked compared to men on this indicator: 22% of men and 15% of women who work full time would like to work fewer hours; an additional 9% of men and 21% of women who work full time would like to change their status to part time. In addition, 2% of men and 3% of women who work part time would like to work fewer hours. Adding these percentages together yields 33% of men and 39% of women classified as "overworked."

The figures from the General Social Survey also indicated that workers with higher levels of education (especially a college degree or more) were more apt to report that they were overworked, whites were more likely to say they were overworked than blacks, and workers who were aged 40 to 59 were more apt to prefer to work fewer hours than younger or older workers.

Both of these measures of overwork may tend to encourage wishful thinking, as they do not take into account the reality that working fewer hours means a person may earn less money and perhaps lose health benefits. (For many salaried workers, this trade-off may not be all that relevant, as the number of hours worked is typically not tied directly to one's earnings; see Reynolds, 2003, pp. 1182–1183.)

The General Social Survey also asked a question that tapped this potential trade-off between time and money. The bottom two rows of Table 3 reports the percentage of men and women in 1989 and 1998 who said they would prefer to work fewer hours, even if this meant earning less. Much lower proportions of workers say they are willing to work fewer hours if it means earning less money, though these percentages have increased over time: from 6% to 8% among men; and from 5% to 12% among women. The higher rates among women may reflect a hidden cost of women's full-time careers, which may produce conflicts with family roles. The percentage of people who are overworked as judged by the "trade-off" criterion is also substantially higher among whites; parents of young children; those who work many hours per week; and managerial, professional, and technical workers (Golden, 2003).[5]

A second set of indicators of overwork asks about *work intensity*, or the amount of time pressure workers experience on the job. The empirical evidence indicates that the proportion of Americans who feel under high time pressure has increased in recent decades. For example, the percentage of adults (aged 18 to 64) who say that they "always feel rushed" on the job has increased from 24% in 1965 to 38% in 1992 (though this percentage declined slightly, to 33%, in 1995) (Robinson & Godbey, 1997, p. 232).

Another measure of work intensity is the extent to which people say they *feel* overworked. This is likely to be directly related to the number of hours people work. In 1997, for example, 37% of full-time workers and 19% of part-timers felt that they were overworked (Galinksy, Kim, & Bond, 2001). Among those working 50 or more hours a week, 45% said they were overworked, compared to 6% of those who worked between 1 and 19 hours a week. About a quarter of those who worked the same or fewer hours than they preferred (26%) said they felt overworked, compared to 44% of those who worked more hours than they preferred.

People who work a large number of hours are thus more likely to feel overworked. However, workers who work relatively few hours in a week—and even fewer hours than they prefer—may still feel they are overworked. This is consistent with the idea that people may be "overworked" and "underworked" at the same time (see Bluestone & Rose, 1997).

In addition to how much or how hard people work, they may not be able to work at the times they prefer. This "work-schedule" mismatch is a third type of temporal mismatch and is illustrated by people who must work nonstandard shifts such as weekends or evenings (as opposed to a standard work schedule of 9 a.m. to 5 p.m., Monday through Friday), even though such schedules may conflict with their family or other responsibilities. About two-fifths of all employed Americans worked such nonstandard shifts in the late 1990s. Many of these jobs requiring nonstandard schedules are likely to expand greatly in the next few years and are apt to be disproportionately held by women and minorities; these occupations include registered nurses and nurse's aides, cashiers, and retail sales clerks (Presser, 2003).

Underworking The three survey questions used to assess overworking can also be used to estimate the percentage of workers who would like to work more hours than they currently work. The percentages of labor force members who are underworked according to these three measures are presented in Table 4.

In the late 1990s, about 19% of men and women in the United States said the ideal number of hours they wanted to work in a week was greater than the number of hours they actually worked. This is only about a third of the number of workers who said their ideal number of hours was less than the number of hours they actually worked (about 60%; see Table 3).

When the question was changed slightly to ask whether workers wished to spend more or less time in paid work, a higher percentage of male workers (25%) and the same percentage of women (about 19%) said they would prefer to work more hours. The majority of workers classified as "under-worked" by this last measure were full-time workers who wanted to work even more hours.

Finally, when workers were asked whether they would like to work more hours and earn more money, the percentages classified as underworked were much greater: About 37% of men and about 28% of women in both 1989 and 1998 said they would like to work more hours if this meant they would be able to earn more money.

Earnings Mismatches

Some people are unable to earn enough money from their jobs to meet their needs and those of their families. Earnings mismatches could in principle occur regardless of how much money a person earns: Even highly paid CEOs may feel that the amount they earn does not meet their "needs" for private airplanes, yachts, and summer homes in exotic locales; such high earners are not what we normally think of when we consider earnings mismatches and reflect runaway expectations rather than the kinds of mismatches associated with inadequate work.

I focus here mainly on earnings mismatches that occur at lower levels, such as the working poor. This group may be defined as those who work full time at a wage rate that is not sufficient to provide for their families' needs, which is often equated with the federal government's poverty threshold (an amount that depends on family size).[6] In addition to

Table 4 Extent of Perceived Underworking in the United States[a]

	Men	Women
Actual hours worked < ideal hours[b]	19.3	18.5
Want to spend more time on paid work[c]		
Full-time wants more hours	18	10
Part-time wants more hours	2	4
Part-time wants full-time	5	5
Want to work fewer hours and earn more money[d]		
Work more hours and earn more (1989)	37.2	27.5
Work more hours and earn more (1998)	37.5	28.3

[a]Percentages.

[b]Source: National Study of the Changing Workforce, 1997. Reported in Jacobs and Gerson, *The Time Divide* (2004), Table 3.1.

[c]Source: General Social Survey, 1998. Reported in Reynolds (2003), Table 2.

[d]Source: General Social Surveys, 1989, 1998. Author's calculations.

the working poor, many middle-class workers may also experience an earnings mismatch. Such workers have seen their earnings stagnate and decline in the past several decades, and many have experienced an "income squeeze." This has made it necessary for both spouses in a household to work—and work for more hours—in order to be able to afford to send their children to college, to live in a good neighborhood, to drive a nice car, and to obtain other amenities of a middle-class lifestyle.

Closely related to earnings mismatches is the situation in which people work in jobs that do not provide benefits such as health insurance. In the United States, people generally acquire health insurance through their employers, not from the government as a benefit of citizenship, as is the case in most other industrial countries. More than 46 million Americans (about 16% of the population) lacked health insurance in 2005, and the number continues to rise. Low-wage jobs generally do not provide health insurance, though many workers on the margins of the working poor will take jobs that pay poorly if they come with benefits.

Table 5 provides an overview of some basic characteristics of low-wage workers in the United States in 2005 (first column) and compares these to characteristics of the labor force as a whole in that year (second column). Nearly a quarter (24.7%) of the U.S. labor force was classified as "low-wage" in 2005, accounting for slightly over 29 million workers.

Low-wage workers shared certain individual characteristics. More than half were women (58%), even though women constituted less than half of the labor force, and they were disproportionately non-white. They were more likely than workers as a whole to have relatively little education: Nearly a quarter did not graduate from high school (compared to about 11% of the labor force), and six in ten low-wage workers had a high school diploma or less. On the other hand, nearly a quarter (24.5%) of low-wage workers had some college education (compared to about 20% of the labor force as a whole), and 9% were college graduates (compared to nearly 30% of all workers). These results do not support the view that all members of the working poor lack higher education, since about a third had at least some college. Some of the attributes of the working poor (especially low education and being non-white) are similar to those characteristics that are associated with being underqualified and underworked. Indeed, these three types of mismatches tend to overlap considerably.

Moreover, the working poor were more likely to be concentrated in certain kinds of work settings. Only 6.3% of low-wage workers belonged to a union; this is less than half of the percentage in the overall labor force who were union members (14%). The working poor are much more likely to be in service occupations: More than a third (35.3%) worked in a service occupation, more than twice the representation of these kinds of occupations in the labor force as a whole. Low-wage workers are also overrepresented in sales occupations, which include jobs in the retail sector, including the "big box" stores such as Wal-Mart and Target. By contrast,

Table 5 Characteristics of Low-Wage Workers in the United States (compared to total labor force), 2005[a]

Share of workforce	24.5%	100.0%
Number	29,275,894	119,587,366
Average hourly wage	$7.36	$18.07
Female	57.5%	47.8%
Race/ethnicity		
White	56.5%	68.6%
African American	15.3	11.2
Hispanic	22.4	13.9
Asian	3.7	4.3
Other	2.2	1.8
Education		
Less than high school	22.9%	10.4%
High school	36.7	30.1
Associate degree	6.9	9.8
Some college	24.7	20.1
College degree or more	8.8	29.6
Union member	6.3%	14.0%
Occupations		
Managers/professionals	11.3%	34.2%
Admin/office support	14.1	15.0
Blue-collar	21.9	23.5
Services	35.3	16.1
Sales	15.6	10.4
Other occupations	1.8	0.7
Industries		
Construction	4.6%	6.9%
Manufacturing	8.8	12.7
Durable	4.8	8.1
Non-durable	3.9	4.6
Trade	21.3	14.8
Wholesale	2.1	3.3
Retail	19.2	11.6
Transportation and utilities	3.2	5.4
Financial and information services 5.5	5.5	9.6
Services	52.4	43.8
Government	2.3	5.3
Other industries	2.0	1.3

[a]Source: Table 6.14 in Mishel, Bernstein & Allegretto (2007), *State of Working America 2006/2007*, pp. 305–6.

low-wage workers are underrepresented in managerial and professional occupations. These occupational differences are reflected in the kinds of industries in which low-wage workers are more likely to be employed. The working poor are most apt to be found in the service sector of the economy (more than half of low-wage workers work in service industries) and in retail trade industries. Low-wage workers are less likely to work in manufacturing industries (especially durable manufacturing such as automobiles and steel), financial and information services, and the government sectors.

Work-Family Mismatches

People's experiences in non-work roles may either deplete their energies or enrich them (see, e.g., Rothbard, 2001). Work-family mismatches occur when people's jobs deplete them or conflict with their performance in other roles such as their family (and vice versa). There are three general situations that may lead to work-family mismatch or conflict (Greenhaus & Beutell, 1985):

1. *Time-based conflict* exists when the time commitments associated with performing one role make it difficult for people to fulfill their obligations in another role. This is illustrated by people who are overworked in their jobs and thus do not have enough time to take care of their family-related obligations.
2. *Strain-based conflict* occurs when fatigue or frustrations produced in one role affect performance in another role. For example, people who are worried, tired, or tense as a result of what happens at work may find it difficult to achieve a positive family life, and vice versa.
3. *Behavior-based conflict* results when the expectations regarding behavior in one role conflict with behavior in another role. Thus, both men and women may be expected to be aggressive and objective in their dealings with coworkers or customers on the job, but be encouraged to be warm, emotional, and vulnerable to members of their family at home.

Work-family mismatches are likely to be especially problematic for women, who are generally expected by our society to play a larger role in parenting and other caregiving and household activities than men. Rothbard (2001), for example, found that work was more likely to be depleting for family life among women, but not men. Nevertheless, an increasing number of men are facing this kind of mismatch as well.

Table 6 presents estimates of the proportion of men and women in the United States in 2002 who reported that they

Table 6 Work-Family Conflict in the United States, 2002[a]

	Men		Women	
	No Kids	Kids	No Kids	Kids
Work-family conflict				
"How much do your job and your family life interfere with each other?" ("a lot" and "somewhat").[c]	32	48	34	42
"How easy or difficult is it for you to manage the demands of your work and your personal or family life?" ("very difficult," "difficult," "sometimes easy and sometimes difficult")[c]	48	58	50	62
Impact of family life on work				
"How often does family life interfere with job?" ("often" and "sometimes")[b]	25	37	25	45
"How often has your family or personal life kept you from doing as good a job at work as you could?" ("very often," "often," and "sometimes")[c]	21	24	22	27
Impact of work on family life				
"How often does job interfere with family life?" ("often" and "sometimes")[b]	36	57	33	45
"How often has your job kept you from concentrating on important things in your family or personal life?" ("very often," "often," and "sometimes")[c]	37	42	34	36

[a]Percentages.

[b]Source: General Social Survey, 2002. Author's calculations.

[c]Source: National Study of the Changing Workforce, 2002. Author's calculations.

experienced various kinds of mismatches between their work and family lives, expressed as some sort of conflict between these two roles. These estimates are based on data from two national surveys of the labor force: the 2002 General Social Survey (GSS) and the 2002 National Survey of a Changing Workforce (NSCW).

Table 6 reports the percentages of workers who responded that they have some degree of conflict between their work and family lives, separately for men and women and by whether or not the person has children.[7] Workers with children are expected to be generally more likely to experience conflict between their work and family lives, as their family responsibilities are likely to be greater than for those workers without children.

The responses to these questions suggest that a substantial number of Americans report having some difficulty in balancing their work and family lives and that these difficulties are greater for workers with children. For example, 44% of men and 40% of women overall say that their job and family life interfere with each other "a lot" or "somewhat" (results for the overall samples of men and women are not presented in Table 6). Workers with children are substantially more likely to say that work interferes with their family life: Nearly half of the men (48%) and 42% of women with children say that there is "a lot" or "some" interference between their work and family lives, compared to only about a third of men and women without children.[8]

These surveys also included questions about the directionality of this work-family conflict: that is, whether workers' families had a negative impact on their work or whether work negatively affected their family lives. The results in Table 6 indicate that work generally has a stronger negative impact on family life than vice versa, at least for men. This is especially true for men and for women without children. For example, both men and women without children are more likely to say that their work interferes with their family activities "often" or "sometimes" than they are to say that their family life interferes with their job (36% vs. 25% for men, 33% vs. 25% for women). That work interferes with family more than vice versa is a consistent finding in the literature on work-family conflict; it is generally assumed that the organization's demands are given primacy over family issues because of the often essential economic contribution paid work provides to the family (Greenhaus & Parasuraman, 1999).

Consequences of Mismatches

Each of these mismatches is problematic for some people and their families. They are also detrimental for many employers and society more generally. All of these parties would benefit if workers were able to have jobs that met their work-related preferences and needs.

Mismatches are likely to have widespread negative consequences for individuals. Each mismatch produces dissatisfaction with the job and is apt to encourage individuals to change the work situation to improve the match or, if possible, to leave the job in the hopes of finding one that fits better (see, for example, Edwards & Shipp, 2007). Some mismatches are particularly likely to produce stress and other negative psychological and physical outcomes that may often spill over to nonwork situations. Overworking, work-family conflict, and working in low-wage jobs have been shown repeatedly to lead to high stress. These mismatches are also liable to have adverse consequences for the welfare and well-being of the family and so are likely to be particularly difficult for workers who are primarily responsible for supporting their families.

Some of these mismatches also have negative consequences for employers and organizations. In particular, the underutilization of our workforce is a serious issue that costs billions of dollars in lost productivity. Workers who are overqualified for their jobs or unable to work as much as they would like are denied the opportunity to fully employ their talents and abilities; this may reduce an organization's competitive advantage, which increasingly relies on the full utilization of human resources (e.g., Pfeffer, 1994). Workers who are overworked or experience work-family mismatches are unlikely to put forward their best efforts on behalf of the organization, harming its productivity and performance.

In addition, the consequences of mismatches cost the nation billions of dollars each year for social services such as hospitals and family support to help people cope with the undesirable consequences of earnings mismatches and the stress produced by overwork and related mismatches.

Reducing Mismatches

The growing incidence of mismatches between workers and jobs has made it urgent that we seek to alleviate them and their consequences. All of the mismatches discussed here are shared by relatively large groups of people: They are not "personal troubles" but "public issues" (Mills, 1959) that are rooted in structural disjunctures between labor market institutions and the nature and composition of the labor force. Thus, reducing mismatches cannot rely solely or even primarily on the actions of individuals and their families; these actions are insufficient to make a difference on a large scale. Rather, as these mismatches are structural in nature, alleviating them requires institutional and structural solutions; we "need to update the institutional structures to match the new reality" (Osterman et al., 2001, p. 5).

Reducing mismatches requires varying strategies, depending on what we see as their basic underlying cause. Mismatches related to skills and abilities (overqualification and underqualification), for example, and to some extent to preferences (overwork and underwork) are likely to require a person to change jobs to improve fit. Thus, these mismatches could be reduced by better sorting of workers to jobs. On the other hand, mismatches related to overwork or underwork might be alleviated by the person changing his or her expectations or referents—without necessarily changing jobs—if these preferences are not rooted in basic economic requirements or firmly held career objectives. Finally, other types of mismatches—such as inadequate earnings—are more about conflicts of interest than about poor sorting in that employees want or need higher earnings than employers are willing to pay. Such conflicts over money cannot be solved by joint gain interventions; power needs to be shifted to employees in order to lessen these conflicts of interest.[9]

What complicates matters considerably is that the different kinds of mismatches involve matching workers and jobs on multiple dimensions, and it's unlikely that good fits can be achieved in all aspects at the same time. For example, raising the skill requirements associated with jobs may help reduce the extent to which workers are overqualified, but may exacerbate the problem of underqualification. Giving workers more education and training may lead to more overqualification if there is not a sufficient supply of available high-skilled jobs. Lowering the number of hours a person is allowed to work may reduce the incidence of overworking, but is not likely to address mismatches associated with underworking.

Better Sorting of Workers to Jobs

There is little reason to assume that labor market matching mechanisms, left unfettered, will operate efficiently to reduce mismatches between workers and jobs. Markets don't operate freely, as they are created by social actors according to a set of rules embedded in other social institutions such as labor laws, collective bargaining agreements, and families (see Massey, 2005). This underscores the need for social policies that shape the operation of labor markets so as to alleviate mismatches and temper their consequences.

The potential for more efficient job-person matching is enhanced by advances in information technology. Employers are now able to specify in great detail the requirements of their job vacancies, and workers can get a better sense of whether these jobs meet the needs and preferences they seek to satisfy through paid work. Job seekers can post their résumés and qualifications on the Web, and employers can judge whether potential job candidates have the appropriate qualifications to perform the jobs.

Formal sorting mechanisms such as those used to assign residency placements to medical students illustrate possible ways to improve the outcomes of matching processes. So too might databases on the careers of executives around the world maintained by the larger executive recruiting companies (Cappelli, 1999) or social networks that transmit information about job seekers and employers to each other. The explosive growth in recent years of the temporary help industry has also created new opportunities for employers and workers to learn about each other on a trial basis before committing to a more permanent relationship.

Social Policies

Other industrial countries, notably those in Europe, have done better than the United States in avoiding certain kinds of mismatches. The working time policies of Scandinavian countries, for example, have made overworking less likely and provided workers with attractive part-time work options. Parental leave and child care policies adopted by a number of European countries have helped their workers achieve a better balance between their work and family lives. Vocational training regimes in countries such as Germany have helped workers avoid being underqualified. And so on.

It is unlikely that governments in the United States will ever adopt a Scandinavian social model, or reduce the full-time working week. Nevertheless, there are a number of things that governments might do to address some mismatches, such as alleviating the plight of the working poor. Governmental social and economic policies—along with private business strategies—need to accomplish two main goals to alleviate mismatches and their consequences.

First, we must create better jobs. The proliferation of low-wage, often low-skilled jobs and the disappearance of middle-class jobs in recent years have contributed to the rise in earnings and benefits mismatches, along with underworking, overqualification, and geographical mismatches. Social policies and business strategies are needed to reverse these trends toward bad jobs; we must create jobs that require higher skill levels, provide living wages, and allow workers to have more flexibility over their working time.

Second, it is necessary to build a "safety net" to protect people from the negative consequences of mismatches. It is inevitable that some mismatches will occur in a dynamic industrial society, and some people will always be more vulnerable than others to experiencing earnings and geographical mismatches, work-family conflicts, and temporal and skill mismatches. Therefore, social policies must focus on protecting workers from the negative consequences associated with these mismatches. The government has a responsibility to provide all its citizens with basic protections such as health insurance, and not to leave the distribution of such benefits up to the benevolence and economic success of particular employers.

Improving the fit between people and jobs will remain an ongoing challenge for managers and social policy makers in the United States. It is important that we continue to seek ways to reduce the kinds of mismatches discussed here.

Source: Academy of Management Perspectives, 22, (1), 24–40 (2008). Reprinted by permission of the Copyright Clearance Center.

REFERENCES

Autor, D. H., Levy, F., & Murnane, R. J. (2003). The skill content of recent technological change: An empirical exploration. *Quarterly Journal of Economics, 118*, 1279–1334.

Bluestone, B., & Harrison, B. (1982). *The deindustrialization of America: Plant closings, community abandonment, and the dismantling of basic industry.* New York: Basic Books.

Bluestone, B., & Rose, S. (1997). Overworked and underemployed. *The American Prospect, 31*, 58–69.

Bond, J. T., Galinksy, E., & Swanberg, J. E. (1998). *The 1997 national study of the changing workforce.* New York: Families and Work Institute.

Cable, D. M., & Edwards, J. R. (2004). Complementary and supplementary fit: A theoretical and empirical integration. *Journal of Applied Psychology, 89*(5), 822–834.

Cappelli, P. (1999). *The new deal at work: Managing the market-driven workforce.* Boston: Harvard Business School Press.

Edwards, J. R. (1991). Person-job fit: A conceptual integration, literature review and methodological critique. *International Review of Industrial/Organizational Psychology* (Vol. 6, pp. 283–357). London: Wiley.

Edwards, J. R., & Shipp, A. J. (2007). The relationship between person-environment fit and outcomes: An integrative theoretical framework.

In C. Ostroff & T. A. Judge (Eds.), *Perspectives on organizational fit* (pp. 209–258). San Francisco: Jossey-Bass.

Galinksy, E., Kim, S., & Bond, J. (2001). *Feeling overworked: When work becomes too much.* New York: Families and Work Institute.

Golden, L. (2003). *Overemployed workers in the U.S. labor market.* Paper presented at the Industrial Relations Research Association (IRRA) ASSA conference, San Diego, CA.

Greenhaus, J. H., & Beutell, N. J. (1985). Sources of conflict between work and family roles. *Academy of Management Review, 10*(1), 76–88.

Greenhaus, J. H., & Parasuraman, S. (1999). Research on work, family, and gender. In Gary N. Powell (Ed.), *Handbook of gender and work* (pp. 391–412). Thousand Oaks, CA: Sage Publications.

Handel, M. J. (2003). Skills mismatch in the labor market. *Annual Review of Sociology, 29,* 135–165.

Holland, J. L. (1973). *Making vocational choices: A theory of careers.* Englewood Cliffs, NJ: Prentice-Hall.

Jacobs, J. A., & Gerson, K. (2004). *The time divide: Work, family, and gender inequality.* Cambridge, MA: Harvard University Press.

Jansen, K. J., & Kristof-Brown, A. (2006). Toward a multi-dimensional theory of person-environment fit. *Journal of Managerial Issues, 28,* 193–212.

Kalleberg, A. L. (2007). *The mismatched worker.* New York: W. W. Norton.

Kalleberg, A. L., & Sørensen, A. B. (1973). The measurement of the effects of overtraining on job attitudes. *Sociological Methods and Research, 2*(2), 215–238.

Kristof, A. L. (1996). Person-organization fit: An integrative review of its conceptualizations, measurement and implications. *Personnel Psychology, 49,* 1–49.

Livingstone, D. W. (1998). *The education-jobs gap: Under-employment or economic democracy.* Boulder, CO: West-view Press.

Massey, D. S. (2005). *The return of the "L" word: A liberal vision for the new century.* Princeton, NJ: Princeton University Press.

Mills, C. W. (1959). *The sociological imagination.* London: Oxford University Press.

Mishel, L., Bernstein, J., & Allegretto, S. (2007). *The state of working America 2006/2007.* Ithaca, NY: Cornell University Press.

O'Reilly, C., Chatman, J., & Caldwell, D. (1991). People and organizational culture: A profile comparison approach to assessing person-organization fit. *Academy of Management Journal, 34,* 487–516.

Osterman, P., Kochan, T. A., Locke, R. M., & Piore, M. J. (2001). *Working in America: A blueprint for the new labor market.* Cambridge, MA: MIT Press.

Pfeffer, J. (1994). *Competitive advantage through people: Unleashing the power of the work force.* Boston: Harvard Business School Press.

Pleck, J. H. (1977). The work-family role system. *Social Problems, 24*(4), 417–427.

Presser, H. B. (2003). *Working in a 24/7 economy: Challenges for American families.* New York: Russell Sage Foundation.

Reynolds, J. (2003). You can't always get the hours you want: Mismatches between actual and preferred work hours in the U.S. *Social Forces, 81*(4), 1171–1199.

Robinson, J., & Godbey, G. (1997). *Time for life: The surprising way Americans use their time.* University Park, PA: Pennsylvania State University Press.

Rothbard, N. P. (2001). Enriching or depleting? The dynamics of engagement in work and family roles. *Administrative Science Quarterly, 46,* 655–684.

Rumberger, R. W. (1981). *Overeducation in the U.S. labor market.* New York: Praeger.

Smith, H. L. (1986). Overeducation and underemployment: An agnostic review. *Sociology of Education, 59* (April), 85–99.

Sullivan, T. A. (1978). *Marginal workers, marginal jobs: The underutilization of American workers.* Austin, TX: University of Texas Press.

Tufekci, Z. (2004, January 25). They can point and click, but still end up painting walls. *The Washington Post,* p. B4.

Tyler, J., Murnane, R. J., & Levy, F. (1995). Are more college graduates really taking "high school" jobs? *Monthly Labor Review, 118,* 18–27.

Vaisey, S. B. (2006). Education and its discontents: Overqualification in America, 1972–2002. *Social Forces, 85*(2), 835–864.

Walsh, W. B. (2006). Person-environment psychology and work: Theory, implications, and issues. *The Counseling Psychologist, 34*(3), 443–456.

Wilk, S. L., Desmarais, L. B., & Sackett, P. R. (1995). Gravitation to jobs commensurate with ability: Longitudinal and cross-sectional tests. *Journal of Applied Psychology, 80*(1), 79–85.

ENDNOTES

1. This article is based on Arne L. Kalleberg, *The Mismatched Worker* (New York: W. W. Norton, 2007).
2. Others have called this phenomenon "over-education" (Rumberger, 1981), "overtraining" (Kalleberg & Sorensen, 1973), "occupational mismatch" (Smith, 1986), "skill underemployment," "underutilization," and the "education-jobs" gap (Livingstone, 1998).
3. The estimates of overqualification were taken from Vaisey (2006). He obtained the measures of educational requirements of jobs from the *Dictionary of Occupational Titles* (see Autor, Levy, & Murnane, 2003). Education, of course, is an imperfect measure of skills, as it is also likely to reflect processes such as credentialism. The criterion used to define overqualification (i.e., people's years of schooling are at least three years greater than the educational requirements of their jobs) leads to fairly conservative estimates of the extent to which individuals' educational attainments exceed their jobs' educational requirements. (This is the mirror image of the criterion used in Table 2 to measure underqualification.)
4. This underscores the problem with using years of education as the sole measure of skills: Many of these older workers have accrued job-specific skills and work experience that make them more valuable to their employers and able to perform jobs that are seemingly "too much" in terms of educational qualifications. Their failure to achieve a college education is primarily an artifact of being in the generation when college degrees were not as widespread.
5. Other studies that ask about trading off hours for money have found higher percentages of workers classified as overworked than the figures reported in the bottom two rows of Table 3 (Jacobs & Gerson, 2004). There are also important career issues (e.g., "mommy track," "off-ramping") that play a role in the decisions and the outcomes of decisions about how much to work.
6. Low-wage workers are defined here as those earning no more than $9.60 an hour in 2005; which is the hourly wage required to lift a family of four above the poverty threshold, given full-time, full-year work. While this is an admittedly arbitrary definition, it is useful as a point of departure because it is utilized by the government to collect statistics on the working poor and is often the basis for deciding whether one is eligible for financial and other forms of government aid.
7. The measure of children in the NSCW data is whether the respondent is the parent or guardian of children of any age, while in the GSS data it is whether the respondent has children 18 years of age or younger living in the home.
8. Overall, 13% of men and 11% of women say that their job and family life interfere with each other "a lot." Among workers with children, 15% of men and 12% of women say there is "a lot" of interference between their work and family lives, compared to 8% of men and women without children.
9. While sorting may help ease these conflicts to some extent—for example, when low-wage jobs are matched to teenagers or retirees, or when family-unfriendly jobs are matched to workers in traditional families or those without children—it is unlikely that low-wage and family-unfriendly jobs would meet the needs of most people.

READING 6.2

Using outsourcing for strategic competitiveness in small and medium-sized firms

B. Elango

Introduction

Outsourcing of activities which started largely in the manufacturing sector to secure lower cost supplies is also growing widely throughout the service sector. Its growing importance has made it a major concern for industry, government and the public at large. The consequences of outsourcing in today's business landscape cannot be ignored. The global outsourcing market is estimated at $386 billion and is estimated to be growing at a rate of 25 percent (Tagliabue, 2007). It is estimated that almost 80 percent of *Fortune* 500 firms are involved in some form of outsourcing already and continue to be involved in more outsourcing work. This pattern in outsourcing is also reflected in Europe where the offshore practices of European firms are predicted to grow about 30–40 percent during the years 2003–2008 (Kshetri, 2007). The growth of newer communication and computing technologies which facilitate outsourcing in the service sector, coupled with globalization, seem to be driving this growth in outsourcing services.

While many firms have used outsourcing effectively to achieve important cost saving, additional potential to exploit outsourcing still exists. While cost reduction is important, one time cost reduction does not offer sustained competitive advantage for firms only till rivals catch up. For instance, about 97 percent of companies report cost reduction to be a big motivation in a survey of companies involved in outsourcing conducted by Lewin and Peeters (2006). A much lower percentage of companies cited strategy to be the factor driving their outsourcing decision. This paper seeks to contribute to managerial practice by showing that outsourcing of certain activities within the core of the company can potentially lead to strategic innovation.

In particular, one untapped arena is where outsourcing can be effectively exploited by small and medium-sized firms to enhance their competitive advantage through strategic innovation. Based on an outsourcing matrix, this paper explains how outsourcing can facilitate strategic innovation, apart from the traditional roles played by outsourcing, namely enhancing operational efficiency and flexibility. In particular, this approach gives small and medium-sized firms an option to become more creative in strategy innovation (i.e. creation of newer services and products), potentially leveling the playing field with larger rivals. Using the financial services industry as a context for illustration, this paper presents various options of outsourcing based on the outsourcing matrix and suggests steps a company should take to achieve strategic innovation. This paper is structured into six sections inclusive of this introductory section. The second section presents the methodological approach used in this paper, and the third contain outlines the conceptual overview of the matrix. In the following section, the outsourcing matrix is presented and elucidated using a case study. This section also presents suggestions as to how the matrix may be implemented for strategic innovation. The final two sections present the managerial implications of this paper and conclude with suggestions for future research.

Methodological Approach

The methodological approach followed in this study is of an explanatory case study (Yin, 1993, 2003). This approach tries to understand the casual structure of the specific phenomenon to provide a basis of new theory generation or new understanding of the event studied. This approach is in contrast to explorative and descriptive case studies common in the literature, where the motivation is to develop a grounded theory. According to Yin, in an exploratory case study the goal is "analytic generalization." This approach fits well with the goals for this paper, as it allows for us to build upon and understand the typology presented. Therefore, we present the conceptual underpinnings of the typology, follow it with the background of the industry and integrate the case study in illustrating the model's logic. For this case study, we use secondary as well as primary data from several interviews with the founders of the firm and industry experts to present the underlying logic of the matrix. The combination of the two sources of data ensured a certain level of convergence and completeness in our explanations. However, considering the strategic importance of this topic to the firm as well as the political sensitivity of this topic, it should be noted the interviews were offered under strict conditions of anonymity and confidentially. In fact, one of the interviewees let it be known that any breach in the agreement would lead to prompt legal action by his firm. Hence, all names or any identifying information is deliberately obscured.

Conceptual Overview

In management literature, outsourcing has been defined as moving activities that had previously been performed within the organization externally (Parkhe, 2007). In this paper, we use the term outsourcing in instances of the outsourcing activity done locally (within a country's borders) and in other countries. We make this point to clarify to the reader that even though in the popular press there is a tendency to use offshoring and outsourcing interchangeably, it should be noted that offshoring can also be done within the company;, i.e. captive outsourcing (UNCTAD, 2004). Traditionally, in strategy literature, the outsourcing decision was viewed within the transaction cost framework (Grant, 2008). Under this framework, the focus was on optimizing the costs/risks given the tradeoffs between conducting the activity internally or externally. This perspective usually applies to firms who outsource activities which were deemed non-core (i.e. non-critical), such as payroll maintenance. While not challenging the importance and usefulness of this transaction cost view, it brings in firm resources to show how a firm can expand the concept of outsourcing by further differentiating its core activities into supplementary and complementary activities. By doing so, firms are able to transform themselves by redefining their business strategies. In the literature, others have referred to such changes as third generation outsourcing (Brown and Wilson, 2005) or transformational outsourcing (Linder, 2004). While the suggestions presented in this paper are applicable to small and large-sized firms, it is more critical for smaller firms, as they do not have the choice of captive offshoring. In this type of offshoring, large corporations can internalize some of the benefits of outsourcing through the establishment of foreign affiliates. For instance, firms like IBM have restructured themselves as a globally integrated enterprise. In such cases, firms locate operations and functions anywhere in the world – based on the right cost, the right skills and the right business environment, integrating those operations horizontally (Palmisano, 2006). Considering the fact that larger firms have capitalized on the information revolution, wherein the flow of information has expanded the scope of tradable services (Blinder, 2006), small and medium-sized firms need to "rethink" more effective ways to compete (Ali, 2006).

Outsourcing Matrix

The goal of this matrix is to allow firms to link outsourcing decisions with strategic planning rather than using them just as a means of cost reduction. Understanding this link is critical, as one of the major reasons for failure of outsourcing projects is the failure to clarify the strategic objectives of the onset of the project (Robinson and Kalakota, 2005). While the process of outsourcing involves moving internal activities externally, the outcomes achieved by a firm through outsourcing vary, based on the particular activity outsourced. To explain the varied outcomes and the implications for competitive advantage, this paper presents an outsourcing matrix (Figure 1). The following paragraphs discuss each of the three outcomes (Cell A: efficiency, Cell B: synergy

FIGURE 1 Outsourcing Matrix

		Strategic Importance	
		Non-Core	Core
Outsourcing Role	Supplementary	Cell 1 Efficiency (*e.g., Record-Keeping, Web-Site Maintenance*)	
	Complementary	Cell 2 Synergy & Legitimacy (*e.g., Joint Marketing, Financial Reporting*)	Cell 3 Core-Enhancing (*e.g., Research*)

and legitimacy, and Cell C: core-enhancing) of outsourcing. The fourth cell (shaded in grey) will not be discussed, as this option represents strategic suicide for a firm.

The vertical axis of the matrix represents the generic role played by outsourcing based on similar articulation on information strategy literature (Elango, 2000). When outsourcing leads to replacement of one or more of the value activities currently done by the firm internally, we call this role supplementary. Examples of such activities include tasks such as building maintenance, payroll processing and payments, web site maintenance, etc. to external parties. In a situation where outsourcing leads to supporting a value activity within a firm, causing it to be done more effectively, we call this role complementary. Examples of such roles could include accounting or marketing activities. For instance, the usage of professional accounting firms or advertising firms is the norm in many firms. In these cases, while the services of these external firms are used, it does not mean that these activities are eliminated within the firm. Typically, what we see happening is that some activities where the firm does not have expertise (i.e. expert knowledge) are done outside and some activities are carried inside where the firm is more effective in accomplishing the task.

The horizontal axis of the matrix represents degree of strategic importance of a particular value activity. Here, we split activities into two groups: core and non-core activities. Core activities refer to value activities which fall within the core-competence of a firm and non-core activities refer to activities outside it. Core competence is the collective learning in an organization and refers to the ability to integrate diverse streams of knowledge (Barney and Hesterly, 2008). Further differentiation of core vs non-core activities are presented in subsequent sections. Within the two axes presented, the outsourcing matrix consists of four cells, three of which offer viable outsourcing options. Each of these three cells offers specific options for firms to pursue, and these roles will be expanded with examples from the case study from the financial services sector following a presentation of the context of the industry studied.

Contextual Background

The examples used in this paper are based on a medium-sized investment firm called Boutique Asset Management (BAM) in the financial services industry. This firm operates in the Portfolio Management (NAICS code: 52392) segment of this industry. In this industry, the prime source of revenue for firms is fees or commissions received for managing the assets of others. The activities of firms in this industry include management of mutual funds, pension funds, portfolio funds, and investment trusts. It is estimated that this industry employs around 200,000 individuals, has a combined revenue of $84 billion and industry gross product of $44.5 billion, and grew about 7.7 percent in 2005 (IBISWorld, 2006). It is estimated there are 7,977 mutual funds holding around $8905 billion worth of assets (US Census Bureau, 2007). In this industry, about 62 percent of firms have outsourcing arrangements and about 31 percent say they will be increasing their outsourcing in the next two years (Maxey, 2007). Estimates of the services outsourcing by the financial services industry is about $40 billion.

BAM was started in 1997 by two friends Sammie Bjiorshein (henceforth referred to as Sam) and Raja Tamil (henceforth referred to Raj). They initially met in a required financial modeling class as they were working on their PhDs in Economics and Business, respectively, at the City University of New York. Raj, who had extensive background and contacts in financial markets, felt there existed a market for mutual fund firms whose stock picking strategy was based on econometric models infused with neural networks. He was also very impressed by Sam's capabilities in advanced mathematical models incorporating complexity theory by virtue of skills he had developed earlier while getting his PhD in Mathematics. The usage of complexity theory with neural networks allowed Sam's models to infuse technical and fundamental modeling concepts seamlessly. So, he broached the idea to Sam that starting a firm could make them rich. To his surprise, Sam jumped at the offer. Both of them dropped out of the PhD program to start BAM. Within eight months, they completed the regulatory requirements along with the certification exams required to operate in this industry and secured seed capital. BAM was born in the basement of a multistory building near Wall Street, with two state-of-the-art computers and Raj's wife as part-time secretary without pay. The initial startup capital of $130,000 was raised with contributions from family members, while investments (i.e. assets) were secured from wealthy friends and contacts in the industry.

After going through initial start-up pains, BAM prospered due to its ability to produce consistently high returns for its initial investors. BAM quickly become a favorite among investors who sought this type of stock-picking methodology. BAM' reputation for consistency improved significantly in a short time, as its returns were not even affected by the 2000 and 2003 market meltdowns. The consistency and market-leading performance of BAM led to a short article in one of the country's largest newspapers, wherein BAM was noted for being the "best" in its niche. Soon thereafter, investors were pouring money into BAM. However, this also invited new competition in its product segment.

By late 2006, there were about 20 direct competitors and an equal number of indirect competitors (ETFs) compared to only one or two during its initial days in 1997. Moreover, some of the newer competitors were broad financial conglomerates with interests in banking and insurance. Raj and Sam felt the pressure to reduce management fees (the prime source of revenue) as well as a demand for additional services (e.g. web-based access). On the cost side, they found their expenses continuing to increase. Over the last nine years, they had added about 46 members to their firm. Additionally, the salaries for good business graduates in New York City had gone up by 80 percent during the same time period. While BAM was doing well by most industry metrics, the risks of competing with larger conglomerates worried both partners. BAM was already one of the pioneers in using outsourcing, having begun as early as 1996, which allowed it to keep its costs low. Both partners felt there was a need for them to plan for the reinvigoration of the firm. Raj came across an article titled "Global sourcing" by Forbath and Brooks (2007). This article claimed the next wave of outsourcing would lead to "non-financial" benefits like faster time-to-market, ancillary revenue streams, and process improvement. This convinced Sam and Raj that maybe there were other options in outsourcing which would allow them to chart a better future for their firm. Given this situation, they hired a former PhD colleague (who was also a professor) to conduct strategic analysis and offer suggestions for BAM on outsourcing options.

Outsourcing Matrix Applied

In this sub-section, we apply the outsourcing matrix to BAM to show potential options of outsourcing and its varied outcomes.

Cell 1. This cell represents non core-activities wherein the external service provider supplements (i.e. replaces) a value activity that is done internally. The activities in the cell do not represent the core of the firm and, coupled with ability of a firm to achieve cost savings along with reduced administrative burden, makes their outsourcing a logical choice for most firms. Examples of this type of outsourced activity include record-keeping, data warehousing, development of web pages, etc. The prime driver of this type of outsourcing is efficiency. BAM, as mentioned earlier, had outsourced these activities, because Raj and Sam felt these activities consumed too much time and attention. They felt it was more cost-effective to secure services from outside firms rather than keep them internally.

Cell 2. This cell represents non core-activities wherein the external service provider complements a value activity within a firm. In these activities, firms do not have the scale, legitimacy, or synergy to get the task done internally. Therefore, firms use outside providers to complement their services. Examples of this type of outsourced activity include marketing, computer infrastructure maintenance and auditing services. The driver of this type of outsourcing is synergy and legitimacy. For instance, to promote its products, a firm needs a distribution network. BAM, being a smaller firm, did not have the scale to run its own distribution network. Therefore, it had secured the services of a large financial service firm to market its products along with several firms on a fee/commission basis.

As is the case with many firms, BAM had already exploited the options (efficiency and synergy and legitimacy) provided by Cells 1 and 2. These two cells represent traditional outsourcing space and have been well exploited by firms for several decades. The exploitation of these two cells is also referred to as the first and second wave of outsourcing (Brown and Wilson, 2005). However, a key limitation of these two cells is that once similar cost reductions are achieved by rivals, they do not offer any strategic advantage. Therefore, the key focus of this paper is Cell 3, wherein firms seek to enhance their strategic core by outsourcing to generate strategic innovations.

Cell 3. This cell represents core-activities of the firm which can be complemented by outsourcing. Conventional logic on outsourcing dictates that value activities within this cell should be conducted within the company, as these activities are of strategic importance. While this paper concurs with the notion that the core competence of an organization should be protected, we believe some fine tuning of this notion will allow greater benefits to small and medium-sized organizations.

To illustrate this point, in the case of BAM, its core competence (*raison d'etre*) is the ability to pick the "right" stocks based on specific requirements of its portfolio models and customer mix. Therefore, BAM should not outsource this activity (i.e. strategic suicide). However, what BAM can do is look for activities outside its core which will enable it to pick stocks. For instance, to sustain this core competence, BAM needs a continuous stream of stock market research to be conducted on firms both within and outside its portfolio. Such research costs are estimated to comprise about 30–40 percent of operating costs in this industry. If BAM can outsource its research activities more efficiently and effectively than its current operations, it will enhance its core, allowing for strategy innovation. Obviously, BAM, through outsourcing, gains cost parity with larger rivals who may be conducting such activities internally. Therefore, outsourcing may allow BAM to tap specialized knowledge and processing capabilities at a reasonable cost which might not have been possible before.

As mentioned earlier, such options are critical for small and medium-sized firms. This is because when large firms face twin pressures to reduce costs and conduct these activities internally, they typically internationalize operations through captive offshoring, as they have the resources to buy out local firms or set up greenfield operations on their own. For instance, according to the *Wall Street Journal* (Kelly, 2007), Merrill Lynch & Co. has taken minority stake in the research firm Copal Partners to create "deal books" for corporate mergers and acquisitions. For firms such as BAM, choosing to offshore operations internally is usually not viable in terms of scale and costs. Moreover, smaller firms do not have the resources or capabilities to set up ventures in foreign countries, unlike large firms. Therefore, this matrix offers small and medium-sized firms new options with outsourcing of Cell 3 activities to enhance their strategic innovation.

Exploiting Strategic Innovation

In this sub-section, we explain how Cell 3 activities can be used for enhancing strategic innovations. Let us assume that BAM uses outsourcing firms for stock and market research activities. Through these firms, BAM can contract CAs in India (equivalent of CPAs in the USA) with about five to ten years' experience to conduct financial analysis. Currently, the cost for such services in Indian outsourcing markets is between $20,000 and $30,000 (inclusive of benefits and other costs). For comparison, this is about $20,000 to 30,000 lower than the starter compensation package an average business undergraduate would receive in the USA. Hiring CPAs in the USA with comparable experience could cost three times as much as outsourcing. While there have been increases in hiring costs for such professionals in India and elsewhere, it should be noted they are typically in offshoring hubs such as Bangalore or Moscow (Farrell, 2006). It is estimated that more than 90 percent of such people are located in less well-known cities like Coimbatore in India or Zlin in the Czech Republic. Therefore, this option not only allows for operational cost reductions (even relative to lesser qualified talent secured locally), but also provides for a significant upgrade in BAM's capabilities. For instance, BAM can use the Indian CAs to conduct scenario-forecasting on tax policies based on accounting principles. While these services are available in the USA, for BAM the fees and costs are unviable, forcing senior management to make judgment calls based on heuristics. By outsourcing Cell 3, BAM has access to new research at about 50 percent of the current costs (Kentouris, 2005) endowed with greater skills, allowing for BAM to innovate strategically by finding new competitive positions against rivals.

Porter (1996) suggests new competitive positions (need, access, and variety based) can help firms draw new customers into the market or draw customers from rivals. The various strategic options BAM could consider include:

- offering additional personalized services which were previously unviable for its "medium network" clients (i.e. need-based position);
- reducing its entry point for its clients from, say, $1 million to a much lower figure (i.e. access-based position); and
- increasing its scope of operations, for instance, BAM may have kept itself out of BRIC countries due to the high cost of information collection in these emerging markets.

However, lower operational costs and newer capabilities will allow it to add a market segment which was not possible before (i.e. variety-based position). Without outsourcing these activities, BAM's strategic options were limited to broad segments which were not too specialized, in which larger firms operate. The key notion being advanced here is that outsourcing Cell 3 activities allows BAM' to avail itself of cutting-edge services at a low cost, thereby creating an arsenal of new options for strategic innovation.

Therefore, Cell 3 allows BAM to exploit capabilities outside the organization to leverage its own ability to offer newer services and products, improve quality, speed and responsiveness and achieve operational scale previously impossible. In this approach BAM, rather than being boxed in a corner by newer rivals, can compete by offering newer services and products which are hard for rivals to replicate. At the least, it creates a level playing field. While the earlier example focused on research activities to explicate the benefits of Cell 3 outsourcing, other activities for BAM to consider for outsourcing include fund accounting and management reports, statutory accounting and compliance audits, investor reporting and investor relations.

Managerial Implications

This section of the paper offers suggestions for managers implementing core-enhancing outsourcing. First, while Cell 3 represents an opportunity for strategic innovation, differentiating value activities of the core suitable for outsourcing is critical. Any wrong choice in identifying the elements to outsource will result in a diminished strategic position for the firm. In order to differentiate core activities that can be outsourced, firms may want to question if the knowledge required to complete the outsourced task is explicit or implicit (Polanyi, 1967; Szulanski, 2003). Explicit knowledge is knowledge about a particular concept or phenomenon which is explainable, whereas implicit knowledge is tacit and cannot be explained, usually characterized by understanding of insights and acquired through experience. Explicit knowledge is conducive to transfer from one person to another through formal languages, manuals, blueprints, etc. and therefore can be outsourced. Moreover, since the underlying principles are usually well-understood, the firm is unlikely to face any additional strategic threat through outsourcing. Implicit knowledge, on the other hand, is embedded knowledge within the firm and involves factors which cannot and should not be articulated, as this can result in strategic risk for the firm.

Again, using BAM as an example, let us apply this concept of explicit and implicit knowledge. Assume that BAM has several proprietary stock selection models for stock screening and selection. BAM would be faced with minimal competitive risk if it outsourced and asked CAs from India to review financial reports of firms around the world and to generate input information for its stock selection model or generate reports. There are several reasons for this. First, this is a case of explicit knowledge wherein most individuals with financial analysis training would be aware of such models. Training a few more individuals does not pose an additional strategic threat. Moreover, information generated through outsourcing by itself is not proprietary, as it is based on information which can be acquired by others. However, in the case of implicit knowledge the reverse will hold true. Therefore, BAM should not outsource the running or refinement of its proprietary stock selection models, nor share any insight into the specifics of its outsourcing model, such as weighting criteria of input parameters. In fact BAM should make efforts to "wall-off" (Hamel *et al.*, 1989) such knowledge, by building institutional barriers between personnel, records and processes within BAM and outsourcing firms.

Second, while there are many risks to outsourcing, activities in Cell 3 have relatively higher risks compared to those in Cells 1 and 2. Therefore, firms may need to be careful to avoid these pitfalls. First, if a firm outsources part of its core activities, specific guarantees need to be sought that information collected will not shared with (i.e. resold to) others. Therefore, apart from careful screening of vendors, specific safeguards should be negotiated and protected through legal means. For instance, BAM should demand that outsourcing work be carried out in a facility that is not shared and that information generated by employees in the facility is secured. Second, monitoring the quality of the outsourcing supplier is much more difficult in activities related to Cell 3. For instance, non-systemic errors in research reports cannot be identified easily and the consequences of such errors are significantly high. Therefore, firms need to be careful to identify supplier firms who have good reputations. Additionally, firms should also use an in-house employee to institute random quality control checks. Despite these risks, small and medium-sized firms may find it worthwhile to exploit this opportunity of outsourcing, not as a means for cost reduction alone, but also as a means for enhancing their core competencies, thereby serving as a tool of strategic innovation.

Third, managers of core-enhancing outsourcing need to careful not to create a "hollow corporation." Firms should not completely lose in-house capabilities of core related activities. For instance, BAM should always retain some capability in research however effective the outsourced partner is in providing research services. This will allow BAM an exit strategy (Lorber, 2007) to rebuild such operations in-house if needed.

Fourth, managers should not forget that core-enhancing outsourcing is more costly in terms of managerial time and commitment relative and requires different approaches compared to the options presented in Cells 1 and 2. For instance, each of the five costs of outsourcing (Kelly and Jude, 2005): cost of knowledge transfer; cost of contracting; cost of communications; cost of quality; and cost of change will be higher for Cell 3.

Finally, managers need to recognize that a collaborative approach is needed with core enhancing outsourcing to get its full benefits. Firms need to find partners who have higher operation and ethical standards, reputation, trust, and competence, as an agnostic attitude does not work for Cell 3 initiatives. Failure of managers to adapt to this requirement increase the possibility of firms failing in Cell 3 outsourcing despite successful experience in Cells 1 and 2 outsourcing previously. Therefore, firms need to make realistic commitment of resources and refinement of strategies to ensure the plans of such outsourcing are achieved.

Conclusion

In this section, we conclude by offering suggestions for future research. This paper's primary goal was to develop an outsourcing matrix to illustrate how outsourcing can be used by small and medium-sized firms to gain competitive advantage. To this extent, a typology was presented and supported through the explanatory case study. We believe this paper offers practicing managers of medium and small businesses a tool for using outsourcing as a means to compete effectively with large firms. Additionally, compared to the outsourcing literature's traditional focus on large firms, this paper is one of the few which posits the perspective of the small or medium sized firm.

While we hope this paper serves as a foundation for future work and theory building on this topic, we believe this paper suffers from the inherent limitations due to the case study methodology employed. Therefore, we also offer two fruitful avenues for researchers working on this topic. The choice for the case study was made considering the newness in the execution of the particular option of outsourcing suggested in this paper. Therefore, replication of the matrix at a later date using broader samples may offer needed refinements to the model presented. Second, in order to implement core-enhancing outsourcing strategies, we believe much work is needed on the topic of services outsourcing risk management. Our review of the literature found that, while academic work on this nascent topic of outsourcing is emerging, work on implementing risk management programs (Whitmore, 2006) during outsourcing in service firms seems to be rather scarce. This topic needs attention, as the typical contractual risk mitigating mechanisms commonly used in outsourcing (McIvor, 2005) may not work in a knowledge-based transaction. In this regard, we hope this paper serves as a foundation for future scholars working on implementing outsourcing strategies.

Source: Competitiveness Review, 18, (4), 322–332 (2008). Reprinted by permission of the Copyright Clearance Center.

REFERENCES

Ali, A. (2006), "Rethinking competition," *Competitiveness Review*, Vol. 16, pp. 171–2.

Barney, J.B. and Hesterly, W.S. (2008), *Strategic Management and Competitive Advantage*, Pearson Prentice-Hall, Upper Saddle River, NJ.

Blinder, A. (2006), "Offshoring: The next industrial revolution?," *Foreign Affairs*, Vol. 85, pp. 113–28.

Brown, D. and Wilson, S. (2005), *The Black Book of Outsourcing: How to Manage the Changes, Challenges, and Opportunities*, Wiley, New York, NY.

Elango, B. (2000), "Do you have an internet strategy?," *Information Strategy*, Vol. 17, pp. 32–8.

Farrell, D. (2006), "Smarter offshoring," *Harvard Business Review*, June, pp. 85–92.

Forbath, T. and Brooks, P. (2007), "Global service providers: outsourcing's next wave," *Financial Executive*, April, pp. 21–4.

Grant, R.M. (2008), *Contemporary Strategy Analysis*, Blackwell, Malden, MA.

Hamel, G., Doz, Y. and Prahalad, C.K. (1989), "Collaborate with your competitors – and win," *Harvard Business Review*, January/February, pp. 133–9.

IBISWorld (2006), *Industry Report: Portfolio Management in the US: 52392*, IBISWorld, New York, NY.

Kelly, K. (2007), "Mergers' India connection: Merrill joins rivals in outsourcing grunt work," *Wall Street Journal*, June 16, p. C3.

Kelly, M. and Jude, M. (2005), "Making the outsourcing decision," *Business Communication Review*, December, pp. 28–31.

Kentouris, C. (2005), "New outsourcing target: private equity funds," *Securities Industry News*, January 9, p. 11.

Kshetri, N. (2007), "Institutional factors affecting offshore business process and information technology outsourcing," *Journal of International Management*, Vol. 13, pp. 38–56.

Lewin, A. Y. and Peeters, C. (2006), "Growth strategies: the top-line allure of offshoring," *Harvard Business Review*, March, pp. 22–4.

Linder, J.C. (2004), "Transformational outsourcing," *Supply Chain Management Review*, Vol. 8, pp. 54–61.

Lorber, L. (2007), "An expert's dos and don'ts for outsourcing technology," *Wall Street Journal*, May 7, p. B8.

McIvor, R. (2005), *The Outsourcing Process: Strategies for Evaluation and Management*, Cambridge University Press, Cambridge.

Maxey, D. (2007), "Fund's outsourcing may be boon to investors," *Wall Street Journal*, May 29, p. C2.

Palmisano, S. (2006), "The globally integrated enterprise," *Foreign Affairs*, Vol. 85, pp. 127–36.

Parkhe, A. (2007), "International outsourcing of services: introduction to the special issue," *Journal of International Management*, Vol. 13, pp. 3–6.

Polanyi, M. (1967), *The Tacit Dimension*, Anchor Books, Garden City, NY.

Porter, M. (1996), "What is strategy?," *Harvard Business Review*, November/December, pp. 61–78.

Robinson, M. and Kalakota, R. (2005), *Offshore Outsourcing: Business Models, ROI and Best Practices*, Mivar Press, Inc., Alpharetta, GA.

Szulanski, G. (2003), *Sticky Knowledge: Barriers to Knowing in the Firm*, Sage, London.

Tagliabue, J. (2007), "Eastern Europe becomes a center for outsourcing," *The New York Times*, April 19, p. B2.

UNCTAD (2004), *World Investment Report*, United Nations, New York, NY.

US Census Bureau (2007), *Statistical Abstract of the United States: 2000*, Department of Commerce, Washington, DC.

Whitmore, H.B. (2006), "You've outsourced the operation, have you outsourced the risk?," *Financial Executive*, November, pp. 41–3.

Yin, R.K. (1993), *Application of Case Study Research*, Sage, Newbury Park, CA.

Yin, R.K. (2003), *Case Study Research: Design and Methods*, Sage, London.

READING 6.3

Leading Virtual Teams

Arvind Malhotra, Ann Majchrzak and Benson Rosen

Executive Overview

Virtual teams, whose members are geographically dispersed and cross-functional yet work on highly interdependent tasks, present unique leadership challenges. Based on our observations, interviews, and survey data, we identify six leadership practices of effective leaders of virtual teams. Specifically, we elaborate how leaders of successful virtual teams: 1) establish and maintain trust through the use of communication technology; 2) ensure that distributed diversity is understood and appreciated; 3) manage virtual work-life cycle (meetings); 4) monitor team progress using technology; 5) enhance visibility of virtual members within the team and outside in the organization; and 6) enable individual members of the virtual team to benefit from the team. These practices of virtual team leaders can be used to establish a foundation for training and developing future virtual team leaders.

Virtual teams are teams whose members are geographically distributed, requiring them to work together through electronic means with minimal face-to-face interaction. Often, virtual teams consist of cross-functional members working on highly interdependent tasks and sharing responsibility for team outcomes. More and more, the deployment of virtual teams in organizations requires some level of team-based innovation to leverage and integrate diverse expertise (e.g., functional/organizational/regional expertise) and to generate an innovative product, process, or business strategy (Lipnack & Stamps, 2000; Duarte & Snyder, 1999; & Townsend, DeMarie, & Hendrickson, 1998). Individuals placed on virtual teams are invaluable in terms of their expertise to the organization (locally as well as globally), and thus are on multiple teams simultaneously (many of which are geographically co-located). Consequently, travel even for short face-to-face team meetings is counterproductive as it takes the member away from the local constituency they need to consult for decisions and information.

Thus, while the term virtual team can apply to any team of geographically distributed people—even if they are working on routine problems and can travel often for face-to-face team meetings—we are interested in that subset of virtual teams whose objective is innovation without collocation. We believe that it is with these teams that the huge challenge of leadership is particularly acute because the leader has the joint challenge of geographic dispersion and innovative problem-solving.

Much has been written about how virtual teams differ from face-to-face teams in terms of coordination, communication, and collaboration (Rol & O'Connor, 2005; Saunders, Van Slyke, & Vogel, 2004; Gibson & Cohen, 2003; Majchrzak, Malhotra, Stamps, & Lipnack, 2004; Furst, Reeves, Rosen, & Blackburn, 2004; Jarvenpaa, Shaw, & Staples, 2004; Maznevski & Chudoba, 2000; Kirkman, Rosen, Gibson, Tesluk, & McPherson, 2002). Considerable attention has also focused on the communication technologies needed to facilitate virtual work and enable knowledge sharing (Malhotra & Majchrzak, 2004, 2005; Cascio, 2000; Zigurs, 2003; & Davis, 2004). However, the special skills needed to lead teams that have both geographic dispersion and innovative problem-solving challenges have received limited attention in research.

Some researchers have begun to uncover the nature of virtual leadership in experimental laboratory settings (Kayworth & Leidner, 2001/2002). Others have outlined strategies for virtual team leaders (Malhotra & Majchrzak, 2006). However, a large-scale field study of how virtual team leaders manage the joint challenges of dispersion and innovative problem-solving is yet to be reported.

Over the past seven years, we have collected survey and interview data from virtual team leaders, members, and sponsors. We began our research by following a virtual team at Boeing-Rocketdyne though its life-cycle from inception to project completion (Malhotra, Majchrzak, Carmen, & Lott, 2001). In a follow-up large-scale research study, we interviewed team members and team leaders and attended virtual team meetings of 55 successful virtual teams in 33 different companies to make observations of leadership practices in action (see Appendix A for a complete description of our research methodology). In this paper we present results of our research. We highlight six practices used by virtual team leaders that help manage the joint challenge of innovative problem-solving while being dispersed.

Leadership Practices of Virtual Team Leaders

Leaders of *all* teams—dispersed or collocated—that are engaged in innovative problem-solving have a number of responsibilities that they must discharge. These include articulating a vision for the team, communicating the vision with passion, setting an execution plan so the vision can be accomplished, forming coalitions of believers, aligning others behind the vision, and shaping a team culture by articulating operating values. All leaders carry out these responsibilities by selecting and motivating the right members for the teams, establishing the right norms of behaviors, encouraging social events, building trust, setting goals, preparing the team to anticipate and cope with novel situations, fostering internal communications, and recognizing contributions.

Leaders of successful virtual teams engaged in innovative problem-solving are no different. Leaders of virtual teams spend time mentoring the team members, enforcing norms, and recognizing and rewarding members and the team. However, some of these responsibilities are difficult to exercise without the benefit of physical presence. Leaders of collocated teams can physically observe when the team is getting sluggish, when the team needs a social event to rebuild momentum, when the team needs focus and direction, and when the team needs resources. The leaders of virtual teams don't have the same powers of physical observation, and have to be creative in setting up structures and processes so that variations from expectations can be observed virtually. Leaders of virtual teams cannot assume that members are prepared for virtual meetings. Virtual team leaders have to sense when "electronic" silence means acquiescence rather than inattention. Leaders also have to ensure that the unique knowledge of each distributed person on the virtual team is being fully utilized. Now we look at the six leadership practices—identified in our research—that leaders of successful teams use to overcome the unique challenges of managing virtual teams.

Establish and Maintain Trust Through the Use of Communication Technology

In virtual teams, trust is often based on actions, rather than goodwill (Jarvenpaa & Leidner, 1999). Because goodwill is hard to observe virtually, expectations about actions and the actions themselves need to be made as explicit as possible for all others to see. This is done first by focusing on the norms regarding how information will be communicated during the course of their virtual work. Several of the teams we studied struggled initially because they lacked a common set of procedures or way of doing things. In the absence of communication norms, team members resorted to using the practices prevalent in their local setting. This often led to each team member communicating in her/his own way, and thus not adequately sharing information with other team members. The result was a lack of cohesion and difficulty in integrating the work of different team members.

Virtual teams need norms that describe how communication technology will be used. These norms describe how often to check the team's knowledge repository, how to ensure that the repository is a "living" team room (to encourage active electronic discussions and ensure that the latest versions of evolving documents are maintained) rather than a place to store old documents. Norms also need to be established regarding what to post (to avoid information overload), when to post (to support work coordination), how to comment (to ensure documents stay current), who owns documents for revisions (to support version control), how to inform other members of their whereabouts (to help establish virtual co-presence), etiquette for electronic communication (e.g., use of all capitals only to express urgency), and audio-conferencing (e.g., prefacing verbal comments with team member's name to avoid confusion over who is talking).

Trust within a team can be harmed by breaches in confidentiality outside of the team. As breaches cannot be physically observed (given that members are not collocated), an important norm for the team concerns what should be shared outside the team. One team had an external communication norm that restricted team members from conveying negative information to anyone outside the team. Another team had a norm that limited access to the team's virtual workspace to team members, "locking out" managers. Most teams had an "external-facing" website where they would put documents to be shared with outside team members. Discussions were typically needed among all team members to confirm that a document was ready to be shared externally.

Not only must team norms be established for the use of communication technology, but they must be repeatedly revisited. The virtual team leaders we observed did this through "virtual-get-togethers" in which members would use the time to reexamine norms and renew their sense of purpose and shared identity. These get-togethers were called various names including team tuning sessions, rejuvenation, yearly strategic meetings, team development sessions, and in-process self-evaluations. Sometimes these "virtual-get-togethers" were annual, sometimes on an as-needed basis. All shared the objective of helping the team to evaluate their process and reinvigorate their identity and direction as a team.

The leaders of the most effective virtual teams developed a "virtual" sense about when these interventions were needed to reenergize their teams. They were sensitive to clues such as participation lapses in asynchronous electronic discussions, and terse and potentially divisive electronic communications among some members. Such electronic clues indicated that the virtual team needed an opportunity to "*clear the virtual air and get back on the same page.*"

Ensuring that everyone "suffered" equally from working in a geographically distributed world also created trust. The team leaders rotated the times at which weekly audio-conferences were held so that everyone (at some point in

Table 1 Practices of Effective Virtual Team Leaders

Leadership Practices of Virtual Team Leaders	How do Virtual Team Leaders do it?
1. Establish and Maintain Trust Through the Use of Communication Technology	• Focusing the norms on how information is communicated • Revisiting and adjusting the communication norms as the team evolves ("virtual get-togethers") • Making progress explicit through use of team virtual workspace • Equal "suffering" in the geographically distributed world
2. Ensure Diversity in the Team is Understood, Appreciated, and Leveraged	• Prominent team expertise directory and skills matrix in the virtual workspace • Virtual sub-teaming to pair diverse members and rotate sub-team members • Allowing diverse opinions to be expressed through use of asynchronous electronic means (e.g. electronic discussion threads)
3. Manage Virtual Work-Cycle and Meetings	• All idea divergence between meetings (asynchronous idea generation) and idea convergence and conflict resolution during virtual meetings (synchronous idea convergence) • Use the start of virtual meeting (each time) for social relationship building • During meeting—ensure through "check-ins" that everyone is engaged and heard from • End of meeting—ensure that the minutes and future work plan is posted to team repository
4. Monitor Team Progress Through the Use of Technology	• Closely scrutinize asynchronous (electronic threaded discussion and document postings in the knowledge repository) and synchronous (virtual meeting participation and instant messaging) communications patterns • Make progress explicit through balanced scorecard measurements posted in the team's virtual workspace
5. Enhance External Visibility of the Team and its Members	• Frequent report-outs to a virtual steering committee (comprised of local bosses of team members)
6. Ensure Individuals Benefit from Participating in Virtual Teams	• Virtual reward ceremonies • Individual recognition at the start of each virtual meeting • Making each team member's "real location" Boss aware of the member's contribution

the team's life cycle) would experience the pain of a late night or early morning meeting. Making explicit the task progress based on agreed-upon timelines also helped to create virtual team trust. Leaders of successful virtual teams required their members to regularly post their work outputs in the team repository and electronically link it to action item lists and project timelines. These postings also helped to create competency-based trust among team members as other members could "virtually" observe the contributions being made.

In sum, one insightful virtual team leader from an international computer technology company pointed out that it was critical for the virtual team members to trust the leader and trust each other. *"The quickest ways to build trust in a virtual team,"* he noted, *"was to play fair and deliver on your promises."*

Ensure That Diversity in the Team is Understood, Appreciated, and Leveraged

Virtual teams are composed of individuals representing a rich diversity of stakeholders, experiences, functions, organizations, decision-making styles, and interests. The team's ability to successfully innovate is in large part based on how well this diversity is understood, appreciated, and leveraged.

A common way leaders of virtual teams ensure that diversity is understood and appreciated is to develop an explicit "expertise directory" at the onset of the team. The directory can include a photo of each member along with information about his or her training, experience, previous assignments, and professional association affiliations. A virtual team leader in the petroleum industry noted that collaboration between virtual team members started once members knew more about the background and expertise of each team member. He said, *"Face-to-face teams would learn what they needed to know for good collaboration over dinner and drinks, but the virtual team members will just have to settle for the electronic directory."* Other team leaders placed a skills matrix of the team in a visible location on the team's virtual workspace to remind everyone on the team of the *"deep local domain expertise"* that each member brought to the team. The expertise directory and the skills matrix are both means to understand diversity and sow the seeds for building competency-based trust.

Since members of the virtual teams we studied had rarely worked with one another in the past, most didn't know what the others knew or their working styles. So team leaders often assigned pairs of individuals to complete a task, picking the pairs based on who could benefit the most by learning from each other. These pairs are often geographically distributed and functionally diverse (e.g., pairing a design engineer in Brazil with a marketing expert in Sweden). Such combinations would not be possible in a collocated team. Once the task is accomplished, the individuals can be redistributed to new tasks to avoid the ingroup-outgroup fault lines often observed in virtual teams. When the virtual pairs (sub-teams) are composed of culturally diverse members, the close working relationship proved an excellent way to break down cultural stereotypes and overcome communications barriers. According to one leader in the international travel and relocation business, *"The virtual bonding that took place within the pairs and sub-groups seemed to endure and carry over to the full team, contributing to greater collaboration and team cohesiveness."*

Most successful virtual team leaders establish a synchronous as well as an asynchronous collaboration rhythm. In most traditional face-to-face collaborations (and even some unsuccessful virtual teams), team members wait until face-to-face or synchronous (such as all-team audio conferencing) meetings to brainstorm and make progress on the innovation task. On the other hand, successful virtual teams use the time between meetings to asynchronously (through use of electronic discussion threads and annotation of documents in the repository) generate and evaluate ideas. By working asynchronously virtual team members can pick and choose when they can make their contributions. This allows team members with diverse backgrounds to have a different rhythm and pace of generating their own ideas and digesting others' ideas. Leaders also use asynchronous discussion threads to identify areas of disagreements because the discussion threads give members with different language capabilities time to share their thoughts in their non-native languages in ways that they find difficult in synchronous (fast-paced audio-conference) sessions.

Manage Virtual Work-Cycle and Meetings

There have been some that say virtual brain-storming is not possible, that when you can't see the "whites of one's eyes" it is hard to judge the confidence that others have in what they are suggesting or what you are proposing. Yet, the team leaders have to be able to facilitate virtual brainstorming. How do they do it?

A large majority of team leaders in our studies reported that regular all-team audio-conferences were the "life-blood" of the team, even when tasks were distributed among all the team members. The meetings were structured, though, not just for reporting and coordination, but also for discussions. In order to "keep everyone in the loop" it was often mandated that all team members attend these audio-conference sessions (some were as frequent as once every week).

Virtual team leaders use meetings as the way to keep members engaged, excited about the work, and aligned with each other. Virtual team meetings (especially the ones that involved all team members) are "premium" activities. Team leaders need to ensure that a clear agenda is set out for these meetings and communicated in advance. Such meetings have a tendency to get off-track (or as a leader put it, "hijacked"). Team leaders have to ensure that the agenda is adhered to and that the "attention-span" at virtual meetings is optimized. Because members can be easily distracted in a virtual meeting, meetings should be treated not simply as a semi-structured activity in which members share, but rather as an opportunity to instill creativity, focus, and enthusiasm. For a meeting to capitalize on this opportunity, it must be managed carefully as a highly choreographed event. Several practices were used to turn meetings into choreographed events. These practices can be categorized as stages in an event lifecycle:

Pre-meeting Practices

As one leader commented to us: *"We found that planning out a meeting poorly for a collocated team is OK; but in a virtual environment, team pre-planning is critical. Otherwise nothing gets done and bridge meetings are required to fill in the gaps."* In order to ensure that the work is accomplished, between virtual meetings, a large majority of team leaders we observed follow these practices:

- Begin electronic discussion threads about the team's current work activities prior to all-team audio-conference meetings. (Posting draft documents in the virtual workspace and asking team members to comment on them often started these discussion threads. The comments posted on the discussion threads were examined and summarized a few days before the virtual meeting took place. To ensure that the virtual meetings were productive, only those areas of *disagreement* that were identified from the discussion thread were raised at the meeting.)

- Ensure that all team meetings have clear written agendas with time allocations circulated in advance so that members know when they should attend during a meeting.
- Request that members post their progress (using draft documents, memos, drawings, spread-sheets, analysis results, PowerPoint slides, etc.) on the repository linking them to project timelines, action item lists, and responsibility charts prior to the meeting.

Start of Meeting Practice

Virtual team leaders often report feeling the need to have members "reconnect" at the start of a meeting. As is often the case, virtual team members have only been in touch with each other asynchronously and most of their electronic communications are almost exclusively task related. Virtual team leaders feel that it is helpful to have team members reconnect with the "human" side of each individual, which helps to remind each member of their similarities, as well as provide them "boundary objects" or common metaphors to work from during the meeting. To reconnect, team leaders start their meetings in various ways:

- Have each member share a personal story about an event that happened to them over the last week.
- Ask each member to share a hobby they were working on.
- Focus on major events in one or two of the members' lives. For example, one team member lived in a Washington, D.C. suburb near the 2002 sniper attacks, which became the focus of the beginning of one meeting.

During Meeting Practices

Most team leaders we interviewed find it critical to keep members engaged throughout a meeting. They maintain this engagement by having members "check-in" throughout the meeting process, sometimes using voting tools as check-in devices. For example, one team leader used the voting tool on the net conferencing technology to have members vote on whether or not an issue being discussed was resolved to their satisfaction and should continue to be discussed. Increasingly, team leaders are using Instant Messaging to stay checked-in during meetings and engage those not participating actively.

End of Meeting Practices

Virtual meetings are the primary mechanism for creating commitment toward forward movement. Therefore, ending each meeting with a list of action items that are then posted in the team repository is a key practice in virtual teams. Action items include assignments of individuals to tasks and assignment of due dates for task completion.

In addition to action items, several team leaders we interviewed use a "minutes-on-the-go" practice, where minutes are logged during the meeting and appear immediately on the virtual workspace screen. The minutes are then posted to the repository immediately after the meeting. The minute-taking responsibility is often rotated among members, supported by development of norms for minute-taking. In one team, norms require that minutes be taken during the meeting on a Word document opened and displayed in the shared workspace for all to see. The norm also dictates that only results of discussion (i.e., decision and rationale) be captured to reduce the burden on the note-taker. Team members summarize what should be said in the minutes, and the minutes are posted immediately after the meeting.

Between Meeting Practices

Leaders understand that virtual team members may easily forget that they are members of a team when the team isn't actually in a virtual meeting session. Therefore, the team leaders work hard to keep the members engaged as a team between meetings. They use a variety of techniques including electronic discussion threads, instant messaging (e.g., to see who's available to discuss a problem immediately), making spontaneous announcements on the team's website (e.g., to share some recent good news with the team), and automatic notifications of recent postings to the website to keep members abreast of progress of team members.

In sum, by orchestrating virtual team meetings carefully, virtual team leaders are able to reinforce the team's mission, increase team commitment and participation, leverage the team's collective expertise, and reinforce the value of virtual team membership. As one virtual team leader pointed out, "*The challenge was to command member attention and focus in an era of multi-tasking.*"

Monitor Team Progress Through the Use of Technology

While all leaders monitor team progress, virtual team leaders have the opportunity to monitor progress online; the most successful leaders we observed leveraged this opportunity. Virtual team leaders can scrutinize asynchronous (electronic threaded discussion and document postings in the knowledge repository) and synchronous (virtual meeting participation and Instant Messaging sessions) communications patterns to determine who is participating in team activities and who needs support and prompting for further participation. Virtual team leaders can also monitor how the communication technology is used and offer coaching and training for those team members who underutilize their electronic communication and collaboration resources. This monitoring is done in a variety of ways. Leaders track the usage of the team's knowledge repository on a regular basis, emailing members who do not contribute to or use the repository regularly. Other leaders examine repository log data to determine who is using the team repository and how often.

Team leaders also assign a "facilitator" to keep track of tool usage and report problems to the team leader. The leaders check for the possibility of "social loafing" or "coasting" when some members fail to meet deadlines or follow work protocols. In these cases, virtual leaders waste no time investigating problems and confronting under-performers.

Virtual team leaders also diligently monitor progress in the use of information technology to support team processes as well. Virtual teams rarely began with their teams having all the technologies in place from the onset. Instead, team leaders instill an attitude of: *"Let's try and work together virtually and find the tools we need to do our job."* This attitude of experimentation means that the teams are not unduly frustrated by failure (i.e., when the technology doesn't work), accept some responsibility to make it work (i.e., by asking questions if they don't understand the technology and finding the right resources to help them), and are interested in making something work regardless of how elegant or complete the technology solution. Team leaders allow for flexibility in the usage of information technology tools as the needs of the team evolve, and as the technology itself evolves. In sum, leaders closely monitor tools that work and allow for technology evolution over time. In the words of one team leader: *"Our technology use evolved over time. Our database [of services and clients] matured. We initially had a discussion database. Then we added IM. Then we added Change Request capability. Then we added a Call Tracking database. Then we added an Issue Log. Then we created a view called "Management View" with schedule, costs spent to date and project status. Then we added a Working Section view just for the team. We tried videoconferencing but stopped using it when the team did not find it useful."*

Enhance External Visibility of the Team and its Members

Leading a virtual team requires parallel processing skills. While team building requires an internal focus, virtual team leaders must especially also remain sensitive to the needs of various external stakeholders including project sponsors local executives, and both internal and external customers of the virtual team's output. When it comes to external (specifically local bosses of the virtual team members) the phrase "out of sight, out of mind" is all the more a challenge. Therefore, leaders often develop "balanced scorecards" for the team indicating what each manager expects from the team as a whole and from the member who is reporting to that manager. To develop this balanced scorecard, the virtual team leaders work with each member's primary local manager to ensure that expectations for each member are clear. Once established, the balanced scorecard provides a relatively objective and standardized basis for the allocation of team-level rewards.

Virtual team leaders often have multiple people to report to—each of the team members local managers, as well as senior executives of the organization. The virtual team leaders we studied used a variety of approaches for external reporting; all, however, had the underlying goal of continuously and clearly representing the "virtual work" of their team and its members. One team leader, for example, organized a steering committee of managers from the various departments and client organizations represented, and conducted formal status briefings with this steering committee. A virtual team in the electronics testing industry was required to report the team's outcomes and accomplishments to a steering committee. The steering committee was designed in a way that it had a representative (senior level executive) from every location where there was a team member present. This senior level executive provided the aegis under which his/her local team member worked on the virtual team. They were also responsible for periodically ensuring that their local team member remained at a high motivation level.

In an alternative approach, the team leader expected each member to "report out" to the sponsoring manager closest to the functional, geographical, or business unit that the individual member represented. The choice of the approach depends on the preferences of management, the type of tasks the team is performing, and the abilities of the team members. Regardless of the approach selected, leaders often instill a norm whereby all reports intended for managers be approved first by all team members so that they feel a part of the report-out process.

In addition to report-outs to management, virtual team leaders often find themselves in the position of explaining to managers the value of a member to the team. In one case, the team leader worked with each member's manager to create and sign a "certificate of contribution" which clarified how the individual's contribution to the team would help the manager's own division.

Many leaders of face-to-face teams attest to the difficulty of providing individuals and teams with the recognition that they deserve. Recognizing and rewarding virtual team work is even more complex and even more important. By keeping virtual team members in the corporate spotlight, the rewards and recognition follow.

Ensure Individuals Benefit from Participating in Virtual Teams

For team members to contribute, they must believe that they personally benefit from the team. We asked team leaders how they ensured that individuals personally benefited from the team. Team leaders reported conducting the following activities:

- Virtual reward ceremonies, such as having gifts delivered to each individual and then having a virtual party.
- Starting each virtual meeting with recognition of specific successes. A leader of a virtual team in the high-tech industry used the practice of giving members a "gold star" for work well done. This award afforded the members recognition in the organization and could be parlayed for future promotions.

- Praising a manager for having a great employee. Team leaders often had the entire team or subteam brief executives (often virtually). When an executive was pleased with the briefings, the team leaders would suggest that the executive inform each member's manager about the great work that the members were doing.

Importantly, leaders of successful virtual teams realize that team members are often in high demand by others (their local responsibilities). Regardless of how much upfront negotiation occurs over time commitments, team members generally gravitate to those commitments that give them the greatest benefits: in terms of intellectual growth, visibility, and fun. Virtual team leaders understand this and often structure team meetings to capitalize on these benefits by including mini-lectures on a topic related to the team's work which might be provided by an expert, short online appearances by executives giving members an opportunity to enter into a virtual dialogue about an issue related to the team's work, and fun activities such as sharing hobbies, sharing catered lunches, Internet-based scavenger hunts, and virtual celebrations.

In short, the most effective virtual team leaders enhance the team experiences for each of their members by ensuring that each has an opportunity to learn, grow, contribute, and feel an integral part of the team.

Final Words On Leadership of Virtual Teams

We noted at the onset that leading a virtual team requires all the leadership and project management skills needed for leading a collocated team and *more.* As one of the team leaders we spoke with said: *"Synchronizing the efforts of a geographically, culturally, and technically diverse virtual team does not happen magically.... My first priority is to build the kinds of working relationships where team members will freely share knowledge, leverage members' collective expertise, anticipate each others' actions, and feel confident that all team members are making a full-fledged contribution to the team's success."*

Virtual team leaders must overcome coordination barriers associated with working across distance and time, cross cultural and language barriers, trust and team cohesion barriers created when team members have very limited opportunities to identify common values, and numerous other challenges associated with virtual work. Our virtual team leaders emphasized the additional challenges of fighting for each team member's commitment to the virtual project, given the local demands for their special expertise.

In addition, virtual team leaders have to overcome member feelings of isolation, build team cohesion, establish norms of collaboration and knowledge sharing, and motivate team members to make a major commitment to the team's mission. To do so required the development of new leadership skills. As one virtual team leader noted, *"I must be a diplomat to help teams overcome cultural differences, an ambassador to keep sponsors around the world updated on the team's progress, a psychologist to provide a variety of rewards to a diverse and often isolated group of team members, an executive, a coach, and a role model all at the same time."* Another noted, *"Leadership in my book comes down to communication. But communicating in person and communicating electronically are not the same. It is darn hard to motivate and inspire from long distance. Even telephone conversations fall short of actual meetings. So, for me to lead virtually, I have to learn to be clear and concise, but also to communicate a passion for the assignment and a caring for my people. Communicating virtually is a work in progress for me."*

Given the challenges associated with leading a virtual project team, the payoffs need to be substantial for an organization to embrace this relatively new way of working. Because virtual teams have access to specialized expertise across geographical boundaries, they are poised to develop better-informed and more creative solutions to complex, often global organizational problems. For instance, one of the teams in our sample was developing collaborative technologies that would be used in different regions of Europe. By including team members from 15 European countries, the team was able to create a solution that was customized for the different regions, yet had 70% commonality. This "think global, act local" solution reflects the creative capacity of virtual teams.

When firms become virtual, the need to change work and leadership practices is imperative. In the years ahead, we would expect greater organizational efforts to prepare future leaders of virtual teams. Recent research indicates that only a small number of organizations have created specialized training programs to prepare virtual team leaders and virtual team members (Rosen, Furst, & Balckburn, 2006). Among those organizations that have training programs in place, an even smaller number rate them as effective. And, some organizations report that while virtual team training is available, it is often ignored.

Similarly, we would expect business schools to focus more on developing the critical competencies needed to lead project teams from a distance. For example, in the context of a project management course, students could be assigned to work virtually with other students taking similar courses at universities in various parts of the world. The experience of working cross-culturally and virtually introduces students to both the potential and the challenges of working in virtual teams. Instructors can use these assignments to coach teams at the "teachable moments" when they encounter project management issues.

The adage that "forewarned is forearmed" rings particularly true when it comes to virtual leadership and management. Organizations that appreciate the value in developing virtual team leaders are likely to see substantial benefits from their investments.

REFERENCES

Cascio, W. F. (2000). Managing a virtual workspace. *Academy of Management Executive, 14*(3), 81–90.

Davis, D. D. (2004). The Tao of leadership in virtual teams. *Organizational Dynamics, 33*(1), 47–62.

Duarte, D. L., & Snyder, N. T. (1999). *Mastering virtual teams: Strategies, tools, and techniques that succeed.* San Francisco: Jossey-Bass.

Fiol, C. M., & O'Connor, E. J. (2005). Identification in face-to-face, hybrid and pure virtual teams: Untangling the contradictions. *Organization Science, 16*(1), 19–32.

Furst, S. A., Reeves, M., Rosen, B., & Blackburn, R. S. (2004). Managing the life-cycle of virtual teams. *The Academy of Management Executive, 18*(2), 6.

Gibson, C. B., & Cohen, S. G. (Eds.). (2003). *Virtual teams that work: Creating conditions for virtual team effectiveness.* San Francisco: Jossey-Bass.

Jarvenpaa, S. L., & Leidner, D. E. (1999). Communication and trust in global virtual teams. *Organization Science, 10*(6), 791–815.

Jarvenpaa, S. L., Shaw, T. R., & Staples, D. S. (2004). Toward contextualized theories of trust: The role of trust in global virtual teams. *Information Systems Research, 15*(3), 250–267.

Kayworth, T. R., & Leidner, D. E. (2001/2002). Leadership effectiveness in global virtual teams. *Journal of Management Information Systems, 18*(3), 7–40.

Kirkman, B. L., Rosen, B., Gibson, C. B., Tesluk, P. E., & McPherson, S. O. (2002). Five challenges to virtual team success. *Academy of Management Executive, 16*(3), 67–79.

Lipnack, J., & Stamps, J. (2000). *Virtual teams: People working across boundaries with technology.* NY: John Wiley & Sons.

Majchrzak, A., Malhotra, A., Stamps, J., & Lipnack, J. (2004). Can absence make a team grow stronger? *Harvard Business Review*, May, 137–144.

Maznevski, M. L., & Chudoba, K. M. (2000). Bridging space over time: Global virtual-team dynamics and effectiveness. *Organization Science, 11*, 473–492.

Malhotra, A., &, Majchrzak, A. (2004). Enabling knowledge creation in global virtual teams: Best practices for IT support and knowledge sharing. *Journal of Knowledge Management, 8*(4), 75.

Malhotra, A., & Majchrzak, A. (2005). Virtual workspace technologies: Enabling virtual teams. *Sloan Management Review, 46*(2), 11–14.

Malhotra, A., & Majchrzak, A. (2006, March 31). Teams across borders. *Financial Times*, p. 11.

Malhotra, A., Majchrzak, A., Carmen, R., & Lott, V. (2001). Radical innovation without collocation: A case study at Boeing Rocketdyne. *MIS Quarterly, 25*(2), 229–249.

Rosen, B., Furst, S., & Blackburn, R. (2006). Training for virtual teams: An investigation of current practices and future needs. *Human Resource Management, 45*(2), 229–247.

Saunders, C., Van Slyke, C., & Vogel, D. (2004). My time or yours? Managing time visions in global virtual teams. *Academy of Management Executive, 18*(1), 19.

Townsend, A. M., DeMarie, S. M., & Hendrickson, A. R. (1998). Virtual teams: Technology and workspace of the future. *Management Executive, 12*(3), 17–29.

Zigures, I. (2003). Leadership in virtual teams: Oxymoron or opportunity? *Organizational Dynamics, 31*(4), 339–351.

Appendix A: Research and Data Collection Methodology

In order to understand the leadership practices in successful virtual teams we collected data in two phases. In the first phase, we followed one virtual team at Boeing-Rocketdyne through its life cycle (from inception to project completion) (see Jarvenpaa, Shaw, & Staples, 2004). We interviewed the team members and leaders at different points in the life-cycle and attended the virtual meetings of the virtual teams to observe leadership practices "in-action."

In the second phase, we solicited participation from several hundred virtual teams and screened them based on stringent criteria to determine whether they fit our notion of virtual teams. Over the course of six months we identified 54 "successful" virtual teams from the several hundred teams that responded to our call. These were categorized as successful based on the independent assessment of an executive familiar with the team. Executives who were knowledgeable about the team but were not members of the team were asked to complete a short ten-item assessment of the team's outputs to-date, including assessments of the team's efficiency, quality of innovations, adherence to schedule and budget, and work excellence.

The 54 virtual teams that were identified represented 33 different companies from 14 different industries. The teams in the study represented a range of outputs for which they were responsible: new product development, pure research and development, best practice identification, knowledge management, information systems support, mergers, strategy development, new technology development, development of employee training, and benchmarking analysis.

The teams ranged in size from a low of 2 (not including the team leader) to a high of 50, with the teams having 12 members on average. Among the teams, 43% were tasked with innovation-oriented tasks while 33% were involved in operational services tasks. Teams were at diverse phases of their life-cycles, with 25% already completing their tasks and 20% just starting. Half of the teams included more than one company and more than 50% included more than one function. Finally, 75% of the teams included members from more than one national culture, with 60% including members at 3 or more time zones apart or with different native languages.

To collect data on the teams, we first interviewed each team leader. The interviews, which lasted about 40 to 60 minutes, addressed such questions as: the purpose of the team; why it was structured as a distributed team; what practices the leader established in the team for cohesiveness, trust-building, and shared understanding; any adjustments made to the team during its lifecycle; and the use of technology by the team. Team members were contacted (either by us directly or by the team leader) and asked to complete a web-based survey that we prepared. We guaranteed confidentiality of all responses. In all, 269 individuals from 54 teams completed our survey. Members were asked about the intellectual capital they had acquired on the team and their views of such team management issues as trust, leadership, cohesiveness, and personal benefits from the team.

Source: Academy of Management Perspectives, 21, (1), 60–70 (2007). Reprinted by permission of the Copyright Clearance Center.

Employment Law

7

Learning Objectives

- Describe the doctrine of employment-at-will and its impact on the employment relationship
- Understand the provisions and enforcement of federal laws that impact the employment relationship
- Understand the positions and arguments in favor of and against affirmative action
- Gain an appreciation of the issues surrounding the management of sexual harassment in organizations
- Gain an awareness of trends in employment litigation and the challenges they present to employers

Racial Harassment at Lockheed Martin

In January 2007, the Equal Employment Opportunity Commission announced a settlement with Lockheed Martin, the Bethesda, Maryland–based Fortune 100 corporation and world's largest military contractor. As part of the settlement, Lockheed paid $2.5 million to an employee who had complained about racial discrimination and harassment and terminated four coworkers and the supervisor who were alleged to have participated in the harassment. The employee who brought the charges had been a field service worker who was called the "N-word" and physically threatened while working on military aircraft on team assignments in Florida, Washington, and Hawaii. The only black worker on the team, the complainant was subjected to weekly mock "newsletters" in the employee break room for Ku Klux Klan meetings, racist graffiti in restrooms, threatened with lynching, told how easy it would be to make him disappear on the isolated worksites, and subjected to coworkers repeatedly circling the block by his home late at night. After complaining to Lockheed's human resources office, the harassment escalated and the complaining employee was kept on the same team as the harassing coworkers. When the complaining employee filed his allegations with the EEOC, corporate HR became angry and told him "We're Lockheed Martin. We never lose." upon firing him. In addition to the monetary award and firings, Lockheed was required to provide annual antidiscrimination training to all employees and report annually to the EEOC as to whether any new claims of discrimination had been levied and what actions had been taken in response.[1]

The increasing scope, complexity, and ambiguity of federal laws that regulate the employment relationship have contributed to making employment law more of a critical strategic issue for employers than it has been in the past. Organizations that knowingly or unknowingly violate these laws can be saddled with significant litigation costs, negative press and public relations, and lowered employee morale, even if the organization is eventually cleared of the allegations. When employers are found to have violated laws, the consequences can be even more severe.

Employment law can have a significant impact on an organization's cost structure. The establishment and maintenance of internal mechanisms, such as training and reporting systems, to ensure compliance with laws can be time-consuming and costly. Violations of the law can result in significant monetary penalties and damage an organization's name and reputation.

Several federal laws protect individuals from unfair treatment in the workplace. Congressional intent in passing these laws is to ensure that all Americans receive equal access to and treatment in employment. In other words, all Americans should enjoy equal opportunity in employment. From an organizational perspective, there are two reasons why it makes sense to be an equal opportunity employer. First, federal laws provide for a variety of penalties for organizations that violate such laws. Second it is in an organization's best interest to hire the most qualified applicant for any job or to promote the most qualified individual, regardless of factors that do not impact the individual's ability to perform the job in question.

A critical component of the strategic management of human resources involves attracting, developing, and retaining the highest quality workforce. Decisions regarding staffing, compensation, and other HR programs and policies are mitigated by laws regulating employment, as noted in Chapter 4. Employment law has a significant impact on an organization's ability to implement strategic human resource management for two reasons. First, any strategic HR initiatives must be tempered and structured within the context of applicable laws that regulate the employment relationship. Second, there is a significant cost to organizations for noncompliance with these laws. Pretrial costs to defend an allegation of illegal employment discrimination can exceed $1 million. These costs are incurred regardless of whether the complaints are judged to be valid. Additional costs include the impact of litigation and publicity on the organization's reputation with customers and prospective employees as well as on the morale and productivity of current employees.

Employment-at-Will

Contrary to popular belief, most employees in the United States receive very limited protection against unfair treatment at work. The reason for this is the fact that the doctrine of "employment-at-will" is applied to the employment relationship. Originally developed as part of British common law, employment-at-will argues that the employment relationship should allow either an employer or employee the right to terminate their relationship at any time, without giving the other party prior notice. Even in the 21st century, employment-at-will remains the fundamental rule on which employment and job security are based. Cursory "two-week notices" that employees often give to employers are not required by law nor does the employer need to give an employee any advance notice about the termination of employment under employment-at-will.

The only exceptions to employment-at-will are: 1) conditions specified in a collective-bargaining agreement (union contract), which is discussed in Chapter 12; 2) express written contracts between an employee and employer that are not part of a collective-bargaining agreement; 3) terms of implied contracts between an employer and employees; 4) judicially determined "public policy exceptions" to employment-at-will; and 5) and federal and state statutes that expressly prohibit the discrimination against individuals who are members of certain "protected classes."

Express employment contracts are often used for middle and executive-level management positions to ensure these individuals some degree of security with their employment and income. Middle and executive-level managers often give up positions of significant responsibility and income with other employers to assume a position with a new organization and consequently usually receive some form of written guarantee that their employment and/or income will be guaranteed for a given time period. Implied contract exceptions are the most widely recognized exceptions to pure employment-at-will. Implied contracts involve some reassurance to an employee or group of employees that their employment can not be terminated at-will. Implied contracts are usually based on terms found in an organization's employee handbook or policy manual or through some oral promise or representation by a supervisor that employment is something other than at-will. Public policy exceptions to employment-at-will are generally judicially manufactured and usually based on state law. The doctrine of public policy exceptions to employment-at-will is based on the belief that an employer should not be allowed to terminate an employee for engaging in some activity that, while detrimental to the employer, is beneficial to public welfare. The most frequently acknowledged activity covered under this doctrine is "whistleblowing," where the employee reports the employer's actions to a law enforcement or regulatory agency, but also included in the protections of public policy are refusal to commit an illegal or unethical act, exercising legal rights (such as filing a worker's compensation or sexual harassment claim), good-faith assistance of a coworker who has filed a claim against the employer, and the performance of a legal, civic duty (such as military service or jury duty). Specific laws that regulate the employment relationship are discussed below.

Scope of Laws

Laws passed by Congress at the federal level are binding on each of the 50 United States as well as the U.S. territories. Individual states can pass their own additional, supplemental laws as long as these laws do not violate or contradict federal laws. These state laws are then binding on all cities, towns, and municipalities in that state. Individual municipalities can also pass their own laws that extend state laws, as long as the municipal laws do not contradict or violate state and, consequently, federal laws. For example, no federal law currently prohibits discrimination in employment on the basis of sexual orientation. Although such a bill has been proposed in Congress, it has not received sufficient support to be passed into law at this writing. However, ten individual states have decided to offer this protection at the state level. California is one such state. One municipality within California, San Francisco, has decided to extend this protection under the law even further and prohibit discrimination based on gender orientation or that directed at transgendered individuals. In this example, each lower level of government has exercised the freedom to extend or supplement the laws that have been passed by higher legislative bodies.

An organization that operates in multiple states or even within multiple municipalities within a single state may find that it needs to comply with different legal requirements in different locations. This would require the employer to have separate HR programs and policies at different locations or one blanket policy that covers all locations and considers state and local laws in all locations in which it operates.

The process of selecting applicants for positions requires employers to discriminate in their selection decisions. The process of discrimination, in and of itself, is not an illegal action. To discriminate simply means "to make or note a distinction." Employers do this all the time; they discriminate, for example, regarding the number of years' prior experience and levels of education applicants have. Discrimination becomes illegal, however, when it is directed at groups that Congress has decided to protect under federal law. Groups that enjoy protection against illegal job discrimination are referred to as "protected classes."

Federal Antidiscrimination Laws

The first law passed by Congress that impacted the employment relationship was the Civil Rights Act of 1866. This law literally gave all citizens the right to enter into contracts as "white citizens." Although this terminology may sound racist, it is important to interpret this language within its historical context. The year 1865 marked the end of the Civil War and the abolition of slavery. Congress' intent in passing this law was to ensure that the former slaves enjoyed freedom in their lives and were able to obtain gainful employment on an equal basis with Caucasians. Congress, however, was a bit naive in assuming that just because it passed a law, employers would comply. No remedies for unjust treatment were provided in this law when it was passed. Not surprisingly, racial discrimination did not end upon passage of the law; however, those discriminated against had no recourse. Consequently, Congress passed the Civil Rights Act of 1871, which gave individuals the right to sue if they felt that they had been deprived of their rights under the Civil Rights Act of 1866.

Equal Pay Act

Nearly a century passed before Congress ratified another law aimed at protecting workers from discrimination in employment. In 1963, Congress passed the Equal Pay Act, which prohibits wage discrimination based on sex or gender for jobs that require equal skill, effort, and responsibility and are performed under similar working conditions. In short, it states that women cannot be paid less than men for doing the same jobs. However, more than 35 years have passed since the passage of this act, and women still make, on average, somewhere around 70 to 75 cents on the dollar of what men make.

One reason for this discrepancy is that Congress provided four exceptions, or exclusions, to the law. If satisfied, these conditions allow an employer to legally pay women less than men. The first exception is a bona fide seniority system. When compensation is based on seniority and men have held jobs longer than women, pay differentials are legitimate. Throughout American labor history, Congress and the courts have readily embraced the idea of seniority as a legitimate criterion in making employment-related decisions because it is an objective standard. The term "bona fide" in describing a seniority system refers to the fact that the seniority system must not be self-serving as a means of facilitating wage discrimination. It must be an existing, legitimate, and enforced system of managing various aspects of employee relations.

The second exclusion to the Equal Pay Act is differences in quality of performance. If the employer can show that men perform at higher levels than women, then the pay differential is justified. This, however, can be problematic, as most assessments of performance are highly subjective in nature. Organizations need to ensure that any merit-based pay system does not intentionally or inadvertently discriminate against women. This is discussed in greater detail in the chapter on performance management systems.

The third exception to the law is pay plans that are based on quantity of output. Traditionally called "piece-rate" systems in manufacturing organizations, compensation is based on how much an individual produces. This is somewhat analogous to commission-based sales in today's organizations or wages based on the number of transactions completed or customers serviced.

The final exception is for "factors other than sex." Although this term is often treated with cynicism, Congress realized when passing the law that it could not anticipate every possible contingency that might arise in establishing a basis of equity in pay. Therefore, it allowed this exclusion to give employers some latitude if they had some other means of compensation that resulted in gender-based pay differentials that did not take gender into account. This is one of many laws that Congress has passed that has included a provision allowing somewhat of an open option for employers to articulate a legitimate, nondiscriminatory means for treating employees as it does.

Civil Rights Act of 1964

The following year, Congress passed the Civil Rights Act of 1964, which is often regarded as being the single-most important piece of social legislation of the 20th century. The act is broken into a number of different sections, called *titles*; Title VII pertains to employment. As a result, when referring to this particular act, most employers, policymakers, and members of the legal and judiciary communities simply refer to it as "Title VII."

Title VII prohibits discrimination in employment based on race, color, religion, sex, and national origin. Conditions of employment included under Title VII include hiring, firing, promotion, transfer, compensation, and admission to training programs. Title VII applies to all private employers with 15 or more employees as well as state and local governments, colleges and universities, and employment agencies and labor unions.

The law also established the Equal Employment Opportunity Commission (EEOC), which was charged with overseeing Title VII. Prior to the passage of this law, employees who felt that they had been discriminated against had no means by which to pursue their complaints outside of hiring a private attorney. Because many employees could not afford the kind of costly legal counsel that their employers could, the playing field was hardly level. Consequently, Congress saw a need to establish a federal agency to enforce federal labor laws and receive employee complaints. In addition to Title VII, the EEOC is also charged with oversight of the Equal Pay Act of 1963 and all other federal labor laws subsequently discussed in this chapter.

Racial Discrimination at Coca-Cola

In late 2000, Coca-Cola made the largest settlement in history related to a race discrimination case. The organization agreed to pay $192.5 million to a group of African-American employees and former employees and also agreed to institute significant changes in its employment practices relative to the ways it manages and promotes minority employees. The lawsuit began when four employees came forward with their allegations; the case escalated into a highly publicized event as 45 current and former employees traveled from Coke's Atlanta headquarters to Washington, D.C., on a "bus ride for justice." Reverend Jesse Jackson joined the fray by calling for a consumer boycott of the company and its products.

In addition to paying the monetary settlement, Coke created a panel of outside monitors to perform independent audits of the organization's performance on diversity issues as well as to mandate changes in HR practices. The panel's recommendations are binding on the organization, unless Coke can prove in court that they are financially impossible to implement. In addition to the panel, Coke's board of directors also agreed to establish a Public Issues and Diversity Review Committee to oversee corporate equal employment opportunity programs and devise a strategy for tying executive compensation to successful EEO efforts.[2]

Age Discrimination in Employment Act of 1967

The Age Discrimination in Employment Act of 1967 prohibits employment discrimination against employees who are age 40 or older and prohibits the setting of mandatory retirement ages (although mandatory retirement ages are allowed in some occupations that deal with public safety). This act was amended in 1990 by the Older Workers Protection Act, which prohibits employers from discriminating based on age when providing benefits to employees or from asking older workers to sign waivers of any future age discrimination claims when being laid off. The EEOC—as well as the federal government—has oversight of this law, which applies to all employers covered under Title VII in addition to the federal government.

Rehabilitation Act of 1973

The Rehabilitation Act of 1973 prohibits discrimination by organizations with federal contracts against applicants or employees who are handicapped. It should be noted that by requiring compliance only by federal contractors, the majority of private employers are not covered under this act. The act has a three-pronged definition of what constitutes an individual with a handicap: (1) an individual with a physical or mental impairment that substantially limits one or more major life activities; (2) an individual with a history or record of such impairment; (3) an individual regarded as having such an impairment. The act requires individuals with these conditions to be "otherwise qualified" to perform job responsibilities (in spite of their handicap) in order to receive protection against discrimination and also requires employers to provide "reasonable accommodation" to such qualified individuals with handicaps. The Supreme Court has ruled that "reasonableness" of an accommodation would be determined on a case-by-case basis relative to the specific facts of the case, including the cost of the accommodation, the resources of the employer, the nature of the job, workplace safety issues, and any relevant collective-bargaining provisions.

Pregnancy Discrimination Act of 1978

The Pregnancy Discrimination Act of 1978 prohibits employers from discriminating against pregnant employees by requiring employers to allow pregnant employees to take leave for pregnancy and childbearing, as it would for any other medical condition. In short, the law requires the employer's existing policy on disability leave to be extended to include pregnancy. This act does not require the employer to reinstate the employee in the same job upon return from leave and does not allow the employer to determine the dates of leave. It further prohibits employers from refusing to hire or promote because of pregnancy or from providing health insurance plans that do not cover pregnancy.

Americans with Disabilities Act of 1990

The Americans with Disabilities Act (ADA) of 1990 greatly extends the protection first offered under the Rehabilitation Act. The act covers all public and private employers with 15 or more employees and utilizes much of the same language as the Rehabilitation Act. The ADA's definition of disability is adapted from the Rehabilitation Act, and the ADA retains the Rehabilitation Act provisions for being "otherwise qualified" and providing "reasonable accommodation."

The extension of the coverage of the Rehabilitation Act under the ADA to so many additional Americans with disabilities has resulted in a flood of litigation. The courts have found many of the provisions of the ADA to be quite ambiguous and open to interpretation. For example, there is some concern as to whether certain medical conditions really are impairments and whether they limit any major life activity. This is particularly problematic when a condition can be controlled by medication or some prosthetic device. Courts have issued ambiguous rulings in this regard related to a number of medical conditions, including diabetes, epilepsy, asthma, HIV, hypertension, and lymphoma. They have also disagreed as to whether any major life activities other than earning a living are relevant to consider in employment discrimination cases.

The courts have ruled that "otherwise qualified" and "reasonable accommodation" need to be determined on a case-by-case basis. Some courts have been sympathetic to those with disabilities by granting great latitude to employees or applicants stating a claim; others have been very strict in their interpretations of the provisions of the ADA in ruling for employers. Similarly, some courts have granted wide latitude as to what constitutes a disability. In certain instances, aspects of physical appearance, including weight and poor dental health, have been considered disabilities under the third prong of the definition in the statute. Although the ADA has provided the more than 43 million Americans with disabilities wide protection against discrimination in employment and in other areas of their lives, the statute as it stands is very vague, flexible, and open to the interpretation and whim of the courts.

Employees with Disabilities at IBM

Since 1995, Armonk, New York–based IBM has sponsored an employee disabilities taskforce. One of eight diversity task forces within IBM, this group was asked first to address four issues. The first is what IBM could do to make employees with disabilities feel welcome and valued. The second was what IBM could do to maximize disabled employees' productivity. The third was what IBM could do to maximize business opportunities with consumers with disabilities. The fourth was an inquiry as to what community organizations employees would like to see IBM participate in. The task force was designed with a dual purpose: to assist in the recruiting and retention of employees with disabilities and to capitalize on new market opportunities. As part of its initiatives, IBM has created a partnership with the American Association for the Advancement of Science, which recruits and screens undergraduate students with disabilities to receive training in math- and science-related disciplines for positions at IBM. It is also allowed IBM to develop a number of products that make workplace and home technology more accessible to individuals with disabilities.[3]

In response to some controversial Supreme Court rulings under the ADA, Congress amended the ADA through passage of the ADA Amendments Act of 2008 (ADAAA). The terms of the ADAAA went into effect January 1, 2009, and greatly expand the protection offered for individuals with disabilities as well as expand coverage to individuals whose protection was not provided or ambiguous under the original ADA. The ADAAA has five major provisions that expand on the ADA. First, the ADAAA specifies that an impairment must be evaluated without the consideration of mitigating measures, such as medication, hearing aids, or other devices. This provision was in direct response to a Supreme Court decision that found that mitigating measures should be considered in assessing whether an impairment limited a major life activity. Second, the ADAAA specifies that impairments that are episodic or in remission are to be considered disabilities. Hence, individuals who have had cancer, mental illness, diabetes, epilepsy, or any other condition that is not currently "active" are covered. Third, the ADAAA expressly identifies major life activities to include "eating, sleeping, walking, standing, lifting, bending, reading, concentrating, thinking and communicating" as well as all bodily functions. Fourth, the ADAAA lowers the standard in determining whether an individual is "regarded" as having a disability by not requiring that the perceived condition limit any major life activity. Finally, the ADAAA directs the EEOC to reinterpret its equation of the ADA terms "substantially limits" to "significantly restricts." Congress found this language too limiting and asked the EEOC for a broader interpretation of "substantially limits."

Remaining intact under the ADAAA is the requirement that an employee be able to perform the essential duties of her/his job, which are to be determined by the employer. The ADAAA also left unchanged the requirement that an individual not pose a safety threat to themselves or others in order to receive protection under the statute. The employee is also required to cooperate with employers as part of an interactive process that attempts to determine any reasonable accommodation that can be provided by the employer. The net effect of the ADAAA is the shifting of the main issue in ADA litigation from whether an employee is covered under the ADA to whether the employer engaged in an interactive process with the employee who attempted to find a reasonable accommodation. The express expanded coverage of what constitutes a "disability" under the ADA will leave little subjectivity as to whether an individual employee is protected under the ADA.

Civil Rights Act of 1991

Congress extended the rights of individuals protected under Title VII when it passed the Civil Rights Act (CRA) of 1991. This law has four specific provisions that amend the coverage of Title VII: (1) It extends the protection of Title VII to federal government employees; (2) it allows litigants to sue for compensatory and punitive damages, in addition to back pay, benefits, and attorney's costs; (3) it requires a heavier "burden of proof" on the part of employers in rebutting claims of unlawful discrimination; and (4) it provides for "extraterritorial enforcement" of federal labor laws, protecting U.S. employees on overseas assignments unless compliance would violate laws of the foreign country where the employee is on assignment. The additional protection and benefits offered to employees under the CRA of 1991 have resulted in a dramatic increase in Title VII filing with the EEOC.

Family and Medical Leave Act of 1992

The Family and Medical Leave Act (FMLA) of 1992 requires employers to provide up to 12 weeks unpaid leave for the birth, adoption, or serious illness of a child, family member, or the employee during any 12-month period. It only covers organizations with 50 or more employees. In order to receive protection, an employee has to have been employed a minimum of 25 hours per week for one year, or 1,250 hours in total. Employees whose salaries are among the highest 10 percent of the employer's workforce do not receive FMLA protection.

The employer is required to continue the employee's group health insurance during the leave, and the employee must be allowed to return to the same job or an equivalent position upon returning to work. The employer may require that the employee utilize any accrued vacation or sick time as part of the leave. It is important to remember that this law sets a minimum federal standard for compliance. Any organization is obviously free to provide more generous options, such as longer leave, paid leave, or other accommodations, such as working at home when the leave time period has been completed.

Interestingly enough, when President Clinton signed the Family and Medical Leave Act into law, its passage was hailed as a major victory for families and parents. It had taken a number of years and several congressional revisions of the act before it was finally passed. Although an earlier version had been passed by Congress, it had been vetoed by President George H. W. Bush. However, despite its family-friendly provisions, the FMLA provides far less extensive coverage than comparable laws of other industrialized countries. European countries, for example, tend to be far more generous in both the length of the leave that they provide as well as the compensation and benefits offered to employees. Sweden offers up to one full year parental leave for either parent, with the first 38 weeks at 90 percent salary, with guaranteed job security. Italy provides mothers with up to 40 weeks, with 100 percent salary for the first 22 weeks, with guaranteed job security. Finland provides either parent 35 weeks of leave at 100 percent salary, with guaranteed job security. It is worth noting, however, that citizens of these countries are taxed at a significantly higher rate than those in the United States. However, these European countries share a philosophy that children are a "national resource" to be properly nurtured and developed and that the future of the nation depends on proper childrearing. The United States, on the other hand, considers children to be the "personal property" of parents, with responsibility for childrearing resting with the parents rather than the state, unless the state can find abusive treatment of the child.

While the terms of the FMLA are relatively straightforward, implementation of the provisions of the statute are quite challenging because of the fact that most individual states have their own leave laws, many of which provide more generous coverage than the FMLA. The FMLA expressly states that its terms do not supersede any terms of comparable state or local laws that pertain to employee leave. Consequently, if a state provides more generous leave than the FMLA, the state statute requirements must be met as long as they are not in violation of any terms of the FMLA.

The most common areas of disparity between state leave laws and the FMLA are those involving coverage; namely, which employers are covered, which employees are protected, and what specific types of leave are covered. Usually, state law provides more generous coverage than the FMLA in one or more of these areas. For example, some states, such as Hawaii, Massachusetts, and Oregon, provide leave for employees after 6 months rather than 12 months, while others, such as Connecticut, New Jersey, Wisconsin, and the District of Columbia, provide leave after only 1,000 hours rather than 1,250 hours. Eight states and the District of Columbia provide leave for the care of a parent-in-law or domestic partner, which is not included in the FMLA. Many state statutes also cover smaller employers, with Kansas, Minnesota, Montana, and the District of Columbia covering employers with as few as one employee, Iowa covering those with at least four employees, Maine and Vermont covering those with 15 or more employees and Louisiana and Oregon covering those with 25 or more employees. Connecticut and the District of Columbia each provide up to 16 weeks leave over a 24-month period.

Complicating this mosaic even further, it is not uncommon for an employer to have to provide separate consecutive leaves to an employee, first providing FMLA leave and then upon the end of the FMLA leave, giving additional leave under state law for a condition that is not covered under the FMLA. Leave may run concurrently when the applicable terms and conditions of the FMLA and relevant state statute are identical; however, this is frequently not the case. As an example, the New Jersey Family Leave Act (NJFLA) does not provide leave for an employee's own medical condition. Hence, an employee in New Jersey in a given year could take 12 weeks leave for her/his own medical condition under the FMLA and another 12 weeks under the NJFLA for any other reason provided in the NJFLA, including one that might also be covered under the FMLA. Even without considering state law, it is possible for an employee to be granted 24 consecutive weeks of leave under the FMLA, depending on how the employer determines the 12-month period. Such a process is calling "stacking." As an example, if an employer uses a simple calendar year approach in the determination of the 12 month period, it is possible for an employee to take leave for the last 12 weeks of one calendar year and the first 12 weeks of the subsequent calendar year. The FMLA allows employers to determine how the 12-month period is calculated, including: 1) calendar year; 2) any other "fixed" year (such as an employee's date of hire); 3) a "forward" year (in which leave is calculated from the first day an employee takes leave); or 4) a "backward" year (in which leave is calculated backward from each date the employee uses leave). While the first two methods are easiest, they also allow for the potential of employees to "stack" leave and have a single leave extend past 12 weeks. Some states have weighed in on this issue and require that the leave period be calculated in a specified manner. Rhode Island requires the use of a calendar year, while California requires a forward-year calculation. Needless to say, FMLA compliance is greatly complicated given the variance, scope, and inconsistencies between individual state laws related to leave.

Enforcement of Federal Laws Under the EEOC

As previously mentioned, Title VII created the EEOC to oversee and enforce federal labor laws. Any individuals who feel that their rights under Title VII have been violated may file a complaint with the EEOC in an attempt to remedy the situation. The procedures that are followed in an EEOC investigation are outlined in Exhibit 7.1.

The first requirement is that the charge be filed within 180 days of the alleged discriminatory act. The charge can be filed with the federal EEOC office or a state or local agency responsible for overseeing claims of employment discrimination. If charges are initially filed with a state or local agency and the complainant is dissatisfied with the outcome, the individual may refile the charge with the EEOC within 30 days of the initial decision.

The EEOC will then investigate the complaint to determine if there is reasonable cause to believe that discrimination has occurred. If no cause is found, the complaint will be dismissed, although the complainant still retains the right to hire a private attorney. If cause is found, the EEOC will notify the employer of the charge and attempt to mediate the dispute with the employer on behalf of the complainant. The EEOC will first meet with the complainant to determine what would constitute a satisfactory settlement and then attempt to have the employer sign a conciliation agreement. If the employer refuses, the EEOC may file suit on behalf of the complainant or issue the complainant a "right to sue" letter.

In proving illegal discrimination, the burden of proof first falls with the employee or applicant to establish a prima facie case. *Prima facie* means "on the surface" or "at first look," and prima facie status is established by showing either disparate treatment or disparate impact. It should be noted that disparate treatment/impact is sometimes referred to as *adverse treatment/impact.*

Disparate or adverse treatment happens when an employee is treated differently from others based on some dimension of protected-class status, such as age, race, sex, religion,

EXHIBIT 7.1 EEOC Complaint Process

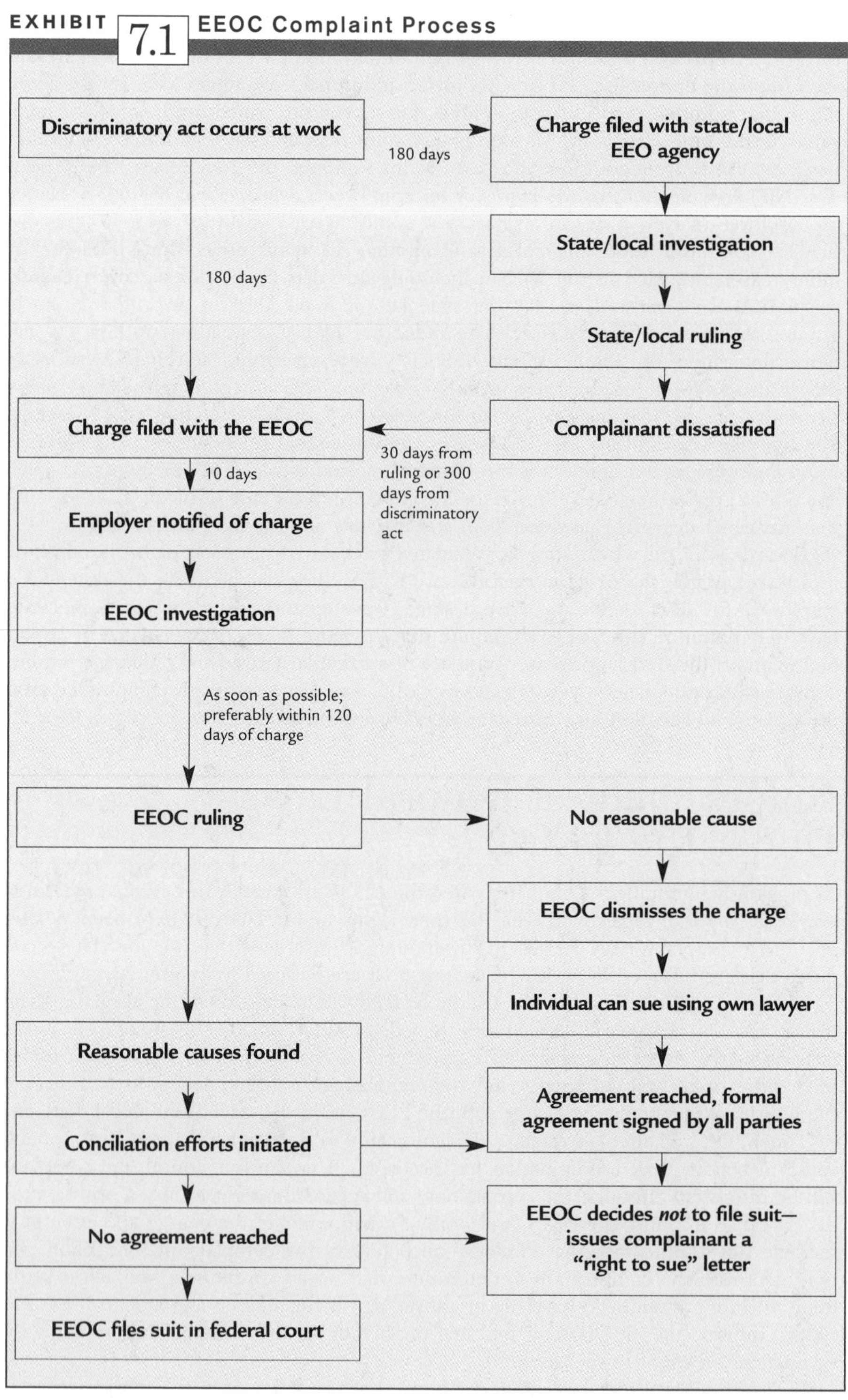

national origin, or disability. Disparate or adverse impact is a bit more subtle. Here, the same standards and treatment are applied to all workers, but the outcomes or consequences of this treatment are different for different groups. For example, a requirement that all employees be a certain height might result in adverse impact for an applicant who uses a wheelchair. Similarly, an employment test in which individuals from one ethnic or religious background consistently score higher than individuals from other backgrounds would establish adverse impact. Disparate impact is usually illustrated statistically by using the four-fifths rule. Under this, if the selection rate for a protected group is less than 80 percent of the selection rate for a majority group, then adverse impact is established. For example, if an employment test resulted in 20 out of 100 males being qualified, then at least 16 out of 100 (16 being four-fifths of 20) females should be assessed similarly to refute the fact that the test results in disparate impact.

Once the complainant has established disparate treatment or impact, the burden of proof then shifts to the employer to provide a legally justifiable, nondiscriminatory reason for the action. There are essentially four ways in which an employer can rebut a prima facie case.

The first is through showing job-relatedness. To do this, the employer illustrates that the criteria utilized to select applicants is essential for performance of the job. Proving job-relatedness is not easy; employers usually have to perform validation studies of tests or other criteria used to screen applicants or provide performance data of past employees to support their contentions.

The second means is by claiming a bona fide occupational qualification (BFOQ) defense. This defense requires the employer to explain why it is essential for the employee to be a member of a certain group. This defense has been utilized most frequently in gender and religious discrimination cases. It would be legitimate, for example, to deny a woman a job as a men's locker room attendant. Customer preferences for a certain "type" of individual do not support the BFOQ defense. When an airline refused to hire male flight attendants, claiming that being female was a BFOQ because of "customer preferences," they were found in violation of Title VII.

The third defense is a bona fide seniority system. As previously discussed, courts support the use of seniority in employment decisions because of the objectivity of seniority. As long as the system is bona fide, meaning it was not set up to discriminate or perpetuate discrimination, seniority systems are a justifiable defense. When the city of Memphis used seniority as the criterion to lay off firefighters, African-American firefighters who had been hired under an affirmative action program were disproportionately affected. Because the department had traditionally used seniority in making other personnel decisions, the criterion was upheld, even though it had significant adverse impact on a protected class.

The final defense is "business necessity." This defense requires the employer to show that the criteria used are essential to the safe and efficient operation of the enterprise. However, the courts have rejected business necessity claims that were based on profitability or other economic concerns of the business owners. Instead, this condition applies more to factors related to the safety of employees and customers. For example, a postal worker who was of short stature sued the U.S. Postal Service when it refused to provide him with a reasonable accommodation in the form of a stepstool so he could reach mail slots that were beyond the reach of his arms. The postal service successfully argued that having an employee constantly climbing up and down a stepstool would be unsafe for the employee and coworkers around him.

Although the EEOC has broad oversight of federal antidiscrimination laws, it does not serve as a judiciary authority and has limited power over employers. It is empowered by Congress to perform only a conciliatory role between employers and those who file discrimination charges and relies on the federal court system to enforce charges it brings against employers. Currently, the EEOC has a backlog of tens of thousands of cases because it is being called upon to play a different role than that envisioned by Congress when it passed Title VII. This backlog is severely undermining Congress' intentions to have discrimination-free workplaces. Under a new chair, the EEOC has recently taken a very aggressive stance in attempting to reduce the backlog of cases on its docket. Over 95,000 private sector charges were filed in 2008 and the average time to process these complaints declined to 171 days, despite the increased caseload.[4] To assist with the resolution of claims, the EEOC Web site now has a special page that assists employers with investigations. Much of the EEOC's success can be attributed to its strategic plan, which

EXHIBIT 7.2 Strategic Plan of the Equal Employment Opportunity Commission

- Prevent discrimination through education and partnerships with other like-minded organizations.
- Efficiently track and resolve charges of discrimination, evaluate data, and report trends to employers.
- Develop efficient working relationships between attorneys and investigators for more strategic enforcement and litigation.
- Expand the mediation program and increase use of external mediators.
- Become a model workplace and an example for the private sector to follow.

provided much-needed direction to agency activities and initiatives. This plan is presented in Exhibit 7.2.

Perhaps the EEOC initiative that has had the most impact on resolving discrimination charges against employers has been its voluntary mediation program. While the program has been in existence since the early 1990s, it really had not had a tremendous impact until the new chair decided to emphasize its use. Mediation involves the employee and employer attempting to resolve their differences outside of a courtroom through the assistance of an EEOC mediator. The process is designed to be fair, impartial, and unbiased and has met with resounding success. Ninety-six percent of employers and 91 percent of employees who engaged in EEOC-assisted mediation reported that they would do so again. However, when offered mediation services by the EEOC, only 30 percent of employers agreed to mediation, as opposed to 83 percent of employees.[5] Despite the fact that the EEOC uses what it calls "facilitative mediation," many employers initially view EEOC-assisted mediation with some skepticism because the EEOC was established to ensure compliance with federal laws as well as to assist employees with their claims. Employers may also reject mediation when they are certain that the claims against them will eventually be judged unfounded after an investigation. Also, by refusing mediation, employers may force the employee to go to court, becoming involved in an often lengthy, expensive resolution process that the employee may not be able to afford either financially or emotionally. To an extent, when an employer refuses mediation, it "dares" the employee to continue the process. This dare, however, is not without risk: Litigation is time-consuming and expensive for the employer as well as the employee. It also can be disruptive to the employer's workplace during the investigatory process and may result in hard feelings toward the employer among other employees, who may sympathize with the charging employee. Essentially, the decision by an employer to accept or reject EEOC-assisted mediation may come down to a simple cost-benefit analysis. However, even though many of those costs and benefits can be estimated, their certainty of incurrence is unknown.

Executive Orders

In addition to federal laws that regulate the employment relationship, certain employers are required to comply with executive orders. Executive orders are issued by the president and apply to all federal agencies and organizations with federal contracts. Executive Orders 11246 and 11375, taken together, prohibit those organizations from discriminating against the same protected classes that Title VII does. Compliance with executive orders is overseen by the Office of Federal Contracts Compliance Programs (OFCCP), an agency of the U.S. Department of Labor, which performs similar investigatory functions as the EEOC. However, unlike the EEOC, the OFCCP actively monitors compliance with laws and executive orders instead of waiting for employees or job applicants to file complaints. The OFCCP also has enforcement power, unlike the EEOC, allowing it to levy fines and punishments, including revocation of the federal government contracts.

Affirmative Action

Executive orders also require organizations with 100 or more employees *and* $50,000 or more in federal contracts to develop, implement, and maintain a program of affirmative action. The concept of affirmative action addresses the fact that there has been significant past discrimination in employment and other aspects of life in the United States and attempts to remedy these injustices. Affirmative action requires organizations to make special efforts to ensure that their workforce is representative of the society where the business operates. Affirmative action rests on the assumption that we still have not progressed to the point, as a society, where we can treat all individuals equally and that the only way to rectify past injustices is to provide individuals from protected classes special consideration and treatment in employment opportunities.

Although the doctrine of equal employment opportunity (EEO) requires that organizations provide a discrimination-free workplace, it does not imply that organizations should attempt to go back and correct past injustices. EEO rests on the assumption that any initiatives to show preference to any member of a protected class would be, in and of themselves, illegal and just turn the tables by unfairly discriminating against the majority. Therefore, the only way to ensure a discrimination-free society and workplace is to wipe the slate clean. History cannot be rewritten, and past injustices cannot be corrected by discriminatory treatment in the present. In short, EEO argues that "two wrongs do not make things right."

Affirmative action plans, however, are usually meant to be temporary measures that require organizations to take corrective action to address "underutilization" of certain protected classes. Preferential treatment, in this regard, is a means of allowing the organization to ensure that its workplace is well-represented by various protected classes. Nonetheless, critics of affirmative action have called for dismantling affirmative action programs because of the problems of reverse discrimination that they create. Proponents of affirmative action argue that such programs are necessary because our society is not yet blind to personal characteristics that have nothing to do with the ability to perform a given job. Reading 7.1, "In Defense of Preference," illustrates that affirmative action is problematic in both concept and practice but argues that society without affirmative action is worse off than with it.

Affirmative action plans are filed with the Department of Labor and monitored by the OFCCP. They consist of four separate sections. The first section is a utilization analysis in which the employer identifies its employees by gender, race, ethnicity, religion, physical ability, and any other protected class. This is merely a counting and summation and is often performed for various levels of employment in the organizational hierarchy rather than being aggregated to ensure that representation of protected classes is not limited to low-level positions. The second portion is an availability analysis that examines the availability for employment of all protected classes in the immediate recruiting vicinity. The third portion is an identification of problem areas in which the employer notes over- and underutilization of certain groups in the employee mix. The final section is a narrative statement of a corrective action in which the organization details plans with timetables to rectify the discrepancies between utilization and availability.

Those who support and those who oppose affirmative action do agree on one thing: Our society has unfairly and unlawfully discriminated against a variety of protected classes for a long period of time. Where they disagree is the means of correcting such injustices. Those who argue that EEO laws are sufficient without affirmative action feel that affirmative action does nothing more than perpetuate the discrimination that federal law tries to prohibit by merely shifting the target of unfair treatment from the minorities to the majorities. This group argues that our society *can* treat all individuals equally. Proponents of affirmative action argue that discrimination is still rampant in our society, and the only way to remedy this is to force organizations to employ and promote individuals from all protected classes through government regulation because the organizations themselves are not capable of doing this on their own. Even proponents of affirmative action realize that it can be problematic: Individuals in protected classes often argue that they are never really sure whether they receive jobs or promotions because of their protected-class status or their own individual abilities, qualifications, and accomplishments.

Affirmative action does not require organizations to hire individuals who are not qualified to hold positions for which they apply. If the organization has a clear job description and qualifications that it can prove are specifically job-related—and can show that it has made a sincere effort to recruit individuals from underutilized populations—it may continue to show discrepancies between utilization and availability.

Sexual Harassment

In 1986, the Supreme Court ruled in *Meritor Savings Bank v. Vinson* that sexual harassment constituted a form of sex discrimination under Title VII. To date, the majority of sexual harassment cases have involved situations where a man sexually harasses a woman who holds a lower or equal position. In 1998, the high court further ruled in *Oncale v. Sundowner Offshore Services, Inc.*, that same-sex harassment was also actionable under Title VII. Every year, organizations pay workers millions of dollars in claims involving allegations of sexual harassment. In addition to the direct monetary costs of sexual harassment, there can also be significant costs in terms of negative public relations and damaged employee morale. Managing sexual harassment becomes even more complicated in light of the fact that sexual attraction and even interoffice romances between consenting adults do happen in the workplace. As a result, sexual harassment compliance remains one of the more challenging aspects of legal compliance for employers.

What Sexual Harassment Is

Courts have identified several key concepts that influence whether behavior constitutes sexual harassment. The first is that the advances are of an "unwelcome" nature. It is imperative in sexual harassment cases that the individual who is the target of the harassment make clear that the behavior is considered offensive and inappropriate. Two individuals may be privy to the same behavior; although one may find the behavior offensive, the other may find it perfectly acceptable. Sexual harassment, being subjective in nature, places the initial burden on the complainant to communicate the "unwelcomeness" to the alleged harasser.

The second key concept is the nature of the harassment. The courts have identified two kinds of harassment: quid pro quo and hostile environment. Quid pro quo, which translated from the Latin means "this for that," happens when certain benefits are promised to an individual in return for sexual favors or threats of punishment are made if sexual favors are withheld. Hostile environment constitutes the majority of sexual harassment claims and is much more subtle than quid pro quo. Hostile environment happens when an employee is subjected to an offensive working environment. However, the subjective nature of what constitutes an offensive or hostile working environment can make it difficult for employers to identify whether sexual harassment is taking place.

In an attempt to alleviate the uncertainty of defining a working environment as "offensive," the courts have utilized the standard of "reasonable woman." Realizing that in some cases that employee claims of harassment may be unwarranted, the courts have attempted to apply a neutral standard to determine whether the working environment is indeed offensive. This involves an assessment of how a reasonable woman (or reasonable person, if the complainant were male) would be expected to react to such working conditions.

Another key consideration in sexual harassment claims concerns whether a pattern of behavior was displayed. Isolated incidents of alleged harassment usually carry less weight with the courts than continued harassment of an individual or ongoing harassment of a number of individuals perpetrated by a single individual. The courts will also attempt to determine whether the organization took any action if and when it was made aware of earlier allegations of harassment in determining ultimate liability for the conduct and the full extent of such liability.

A final concern is that many incidents of harassment involve the words of one employee against those of another and can be difficult to prove. Allegations need to be provable and verifiable. Such evidence is often provided through witnesses and/or written or printed documentation that supports the allegations of harassment.

Cleaning Up Sexual Harassment at Dial

Sexual harassment can be very costly to an organization. In 2003, Dial Corporation agreed to pay $10 million in settlement of a federal lawsuit brought when women at its Aurora, Illinois, plant argued that the employer had ignored their sexual harassment complaints. The suit charged that 90 current and former female employees had been groped, shown pornography, and called names on the job. This settlement was eclipsed by one involving Mitsubishi Motors in 1998. Facing allegations that women working on an assembly line were groped and insulted and their complaints then met with indifference, Mitsubishi settled this case, which involved 486 plaintiffs, for $34 million.[6]

Problems in Managing Sexual Harassment

In managing sexual harassment, organizations have to deal with four specific problems. The first is that many workers and managers are not aware of what sexual harassment is and what constitutes harassment. Several key management challenges need to be addressed in remedying this: Employees have different perceptions and standards of what is offensive; sexual harassment can be difficult to identify; and the intention of the harassing party is irrelevant relative to how the receiving party interpreted the behavior or action.

These challenges can be dealt with effectively through training that centers on *discussion rather than merely knowledge or skills.* Awareness of and attitudes toward sexual behavior at work need to be addressed among both men and women. Perceptions need to be shared and clarified, and employees, particularly managers, need to be aware of different ways of understanding or framing action and behaviors that may be sexual in nature.

The second problem is that although an organization may have a policy that prohibits sexual harassment, many employees may be unaware of the policy or know that there is a policy but not know what it says. A challenge that management faces in addressing this problem is that although every allegation of sexual harassment is unique, any established policy needs consistency in application but flexibility in enforcement to suit the specific circumstances and their severity. This issue can be dealt with through training that focuses on procedures, policies, and processes. Employees need to understand exactly the organization's position on sexual harassment and how it will be enforced. This type of training is probably most effective when conducted in conjunction with training that deals with attitudes and awareness.

The third problem in managing sexual harassment is that employees often fear reporting any incidents of sexual harassment. For the average employee, reporting sexual harassment means challenging the power base of the organization and often confronting a direct supervisor. Employees need to know that their claims will be taken seriously. Although Title VII expressly prohibits retaliation against any employee who files a claim under the law, it is not difficult for a supervisor or an organization to "dance around the law" and make an employee's life miserable without running afoul of the law. Employees often feel that challenging the organization is a losing proposition in which the individual employee is pitted against a large, powerful, resource-abundant organization. This also has significant implications for those who investigate any such charges within the organization. This individual or these individuals need to be objective. If employees distrust the process or investigator, they are more likely to allow acts of harassment to continue. To encourage reporting of sexually offensive behavior, it is important to create a climate of trust within the organization. Employees need to be assured of some confidentiality and provided with some support in continuing in their jobs during the course of the investigation into the allegations. Investigations also need to be conducted by an impartial, preferably neutral, outside source to prevent bias.

The fourth problem is determining how best to investigate allegations of sexual harassment. The challenges to doing this effectively involve the fact that there are two sides to every story, and there are neither witnesses nor evidence to support the claims levied by one or both parties. To facilitate the investigation, those looking into claims of sexual harassment should seek out all others who may have knowledge about the effects of the harassment, particularly on the complainant, or of other incidents that might support or disclaim the allegations of harassment. Complaints should also be investigated immediately. This might help in curtailing any ongoing harassment or offensive behavior, and it is also generally looked upon favorably by the courts. In investigating claims of sexual harassment, if the charges cannot be proven, it can be useful to notify the accused party in writing that if the conduct did occur, it would constitute sexual harassment and be in violation of company policy. A notification using neutral language serves notice to the employee without accusing the employee of wrongdoing and setting up a potential defamation claim. Exhibit 7.3 summarizes how to overcome some of the problems inherent in addressing sexual harassment in organizations.

Sexual Harassment at W. R. Grace & Co.:

On June 1, 2000, the United States Equal Employment Opportunity Commission (EEOC) announced that a subsidiary of W.R. Grace & Co. and a company that subsequently operated one of its facilities had agreed to pay $1 million to the victims of widespread sexual harassment at one of its food-processing plants in Laurel, Maryland. The class-action lawsuit had been filed by the EEOC on behalf of 22 Hispanic females, all recent immigrants from Central America who spoke limited English, who

EXHIBIT 7.3 Problems and Challenges in Managing Sexual Harassment

Problems	Challenges	Strategies

• Workers/managers still not sure what it is	• Perceptions
	• Difficult to identify
	• Intention irrelevant, interpretation important
		• Training
		  • Centering on discussion between men and women
		  • Not skills; awareness and attitudes

• Workers unaware of policy or know there's a policy but not what it says	• Need consistency in application (to ensure fair and legal treatment of employees) but flexibility in enforcement (to suit special circumstances)	• Training • Centering on policy, processes, etc.
• Fear of reporting	• Retaliation • Biases of investigators	• Create climate of trust • Investigation by impartial, outside source • Confidentiality • Support those filing allegations
• How to investigate	• Two sides to every story • Often no outside witnesses	• Seek out others for any knowledge about effects, other incidents • Investigate immediately while issue is still "fresh"; also looks good with courts • If no resolution, notify accused in writing that if conduct did occur, it would constitute sexual harassment

had been routinely subjected to unwanted groping and explicit requests for sexual favors from male managers and coworkers over a period of several years.

The harassment directed at the workers took many forms. One woman was locked in a freezer by her supervisor upon turning down his request for a sexual favor. Two other women, who were pregnant at the time, were asked to perform sexual favors and subsequently demoted and fired following their refusal to comply with the requests. Many of the other women had their job duties reassigned to especially menial or difficult tasks when refusing requests for sexual favors from plant management.

EEOC Chairwoman Ida L. Castro noted that the EEOC would "remain vigilant to ensure that no worker endures this type of discrimination in order to earn a paycheck and support their family.[7]

Strategy for Managing Sexual Harassment

Exhibit 7.4 presents some general guidelines organizations can use to strategically manage sexual harassment in the workplace and minimize both legal liability and other adverse consequences of sexual harassment. First, the organization should investigate *all* allegations of harassment. Lack of knowledge or ignorance concerning the harassment would not be an acceptable defense in court. Second, a thorough and prompt investigation of all charges should be conducted. Determining potential liability is critical, as is dealing with the charges and curtailing any harassment in a timely manner. Third, the investigator that is appointed needs to be unbiased and objective. This is critical in avoiding company politics and preventing conflicts of interest. An improperly or poorly conducted investigation will not only be a waste of time and resources but may further damage employee trust and morale. Fourth, steps should be taken to ensure that no retaliation takes place against the complainant. As stated, such action is prohibited under Title VII, regardless of whether the allegations of harassment are ultimately proven. Even if no harassment has taken place, a Title VII violation may be found in how the complainant was subsequently treated. Unfounded claims do not remove the retaliation protection offered by Title VII. Fifth, the accused employee must be treated fairly. There are two sides to every story, and the accused's story should be heard in a nonjudgmental manner. Many unfairly accused employees have turned around and successfully sued their employers for wrongful discharge. Sixth, both parties should sign written statements that outline facts and completely disclose all pertinent information and clarify where they stand. This assists the investigator and prevents the parties from subsequently changing their stories. Seventh, in cases where harassment is found, employers need to take prompt action to rectify the situation and equate the consequences with the behavior. Any and all appropriate measures should be taken to ensure that the behavior never

EXHIBIT 7.4 Guidelines for Managing Sexual Harassment in the Workplace

- Investigate *all* allegations (lack of knowledge, ignorance not a defense)
- Conduct a thorough and prompt investigation (determining actual liability often easier at this point)
- Ensure that investigator is unbiased, objective (avoid company politics, conflicts of interest)
- Ensure that no retaliation takes place (could result in additional Title VII liability)
- Treat accused employee fairly (hear his or her side, avoid wrongful discharge)
- Have both parties sign written statements (prevents "facts" in stories from changing)
- Take prompt action and equate consequences with behavior (goal is to ensure that behavior never happens again)
- Have clear, defined process for investigation (apply consistently, document everything)

happens again. Finally, the organization needs to develop a clear, well-defined investigative process. This process should be applied consistently across cases and involve extensive written documentation of every step of the investigation. Information collected should be held in confidence due to its sensitive nature.

Complications Abroad

The increasing rate at which U.S. organizations set up operations abroad has some significant implications for how sexual harassment is handled. Although the Civil Rights Act of 1991 provides for extraterritorial enforcement of U.S. labor laws, many cultures do not acknowledge sexual harassment as a workplace or societal problem. Ethical dilemmas arise concerning how such behavior should be tolerated when it is not considered inappropriate in another culture.

In managing sexual harassment in the workplace, employers *always* have a chance to rectify wrongdoings if they have a policy in place. Although courts place a responsibility on complainants to inform harassers that advances or behaviors are "unwelcome," this does not relieve the employer of the burden of establishing, communicating, and implementing a clear policy on sexual harassment. Sexual harassment can and will happen in virtually any workplace. Clear measures can be taken to strategically manage this form of unlawful discrimination, ensuring that all employees have a workplace more conducive to high performance.

Trends in Employment Litigation

As can be seen from the previous discussion, the legal dimensions of the employment relationship are complex and require careful management. Within this arena, there are a number of trends taking place in employment-related litigation that are evolving and impacting the employment relationship. First among these is the trend away from blatant to subtle discrimination. As our society and workplaces have become more tolerant and accepting of individual differences, at least on the surface, and employers have been subjected to significant penalties for violating anti-discrimination statutes, the nature of discrimination has changed. The Equal Employment Opportunity Commission has noted that during the 20th century discrimination tended to be very blatant and pervasive. Today, however, it often takes more subtle forms, which can be just as unnerving to employees yet much more difficult to prove. Rather than taking the form or hate speech or physical violence, for example, discrimination today might involve shunning, non-inclusion, or marginalization of employees, sometimes referred to as micro-inequities. Such behaviors might involve negative and/or extreme facial expressions or tones of voice, leaving individuals off of distribution of team or group e-mails or other correspondence, not including an individual in meetings, mistaking an executive of color for a support or cleaning staff member, repeatedly mistaking individuals from a common ethnic or racial background for each other, repeatedly mispronouncing a coworker's name after having been corrected several times, mocking or copying accents or interrupting continuously when a minority group member is speaking, or continuously asking questions of such an individual in an attempt to discredit her/him.[8]

A second trend in employment litigation is the use of electronically produced and stored evidence. Most employees find e-mail the most simple, direct, and expeditious means of communicating with coworkers, customers, and supervisors, particularly in cases where individuals are located at different sites. E-mail is also advantageous for employees in that it can be conveniently archived and referenced as need be. However, there is also a potential problem with e-mail, as its informal nature often invites employees to make spontaneous, emotional comments to each other that once "sent" can usually not be rescinded. Such communications can later be used against the organization as evidence in legal proceedings. This same caveat is true for instant messaging that may be utilized at work. Employers need to establish formal policies regarding the content of electronic conversations and communication and train managers, in particular, to keep such communication fact-based, with more sensitive information communicated in person or by telephone. Employers have a legal obligation under amendments to the Federal Rules of Civil Procedure to preserve all electronically stored information relevant to current or reasonably foreseeable future litigation. Hence, employers need to set policy relative to how long electronic information not subject to litigation holds should be backed up and stored, balancing the potential benefits of retaining data for legal and operational benefits versus the potential costs of storage and loss associated with not retaining it.

A third trend is the increasing number of complaints by employees and former employees regarding employer retaliation for employee assertion of their employment rights. Title VII of the Civil Rights Act prohibits retaliation against employees or coworkers who have aided in the filing of Title VII or other claims. Despite this, the number of retaliation claims filed with the EEOC increased by 35 percent over the past decade. A recent Supreme Court ruling, *Burlington Northern & Santa Fe Railway Co. v. White*, made it easier for workers to file retaliation claims by allowing suits even when an employment action does not diminish pay or benefits or cause any kind of economic or monetary loss for the employee as well as ruling that anti-retaliation behavior extends to non-work-related employer conduct. Retaliation claims are often brought by employees who have a history of performance problems who use their complaint as a basis for arguing that future employer actions are being taken in retaliation.[9] One particularly challenging feature of the Title VII anti-retaliation provision is the fact that HR managers are exempt from its protection. This has created some complex ethical dilemmas for HR professionals, as outlined in Reading 7.2, "The Dual Loyalty Dilemma for HR Managers Under Title VII Compliance."

A fourth trend in employment litigation is the movement toward employer settlement of charges in an expeditious manner. Litigation has many economic and non-economic costs for both employers and employees, and while the EEOC has advocated the use of its mediation program, such a process can still be time-consuming. From the perspective of the employers, unless the organization is successful in having charges dismissed by a judge via summary judgment, settlement is often the best option for a speedy resolution. The questions surrounding settlement, however, are when and at what cost. One study found that in cases of gender, age, disability, or religious discrimination, employers generally initially denied claims but settled out-of-court within one year. In cases involving race, most employers sought quick settlement and promised to adopt policies to prevent future claims of race discrimination by employees. Sexual harassment claims usually involved denied charges, retaliation, and a refusal to settle.[10] Quicker settlements generally incur lower costs. One study found that cases that settled in two years cost employers double that of those that settled in one year, and cases that settled in three years cost two-and-a-half times those that settled in one year—in both attorney fees and settlement amounts.[11] Employers, however, often resist early settlements because of: 1) a sense that the organization did nothing wrong and that justice should prevent a dishonest employee from benefitting; 2) a need for vindication of the individuals involved; and 3) a fear of "opening the floodgates" for all kinds of frivolous employee litigation if the employer gains a reputation of settling quickly and easily and not defending charges.[12] Hence, employers need to consider these balancing act factors in deciding if and when to settle an employment discrimination claim.

A fifth trend is the use of employment practices liability insurance (EPLI) by employers to prevent having to pay large settlements in discrimination cases. EPLI has becoming increasingly popular, as large settlements are offered and judgments are rendered against employers. EPLI assumes some of the risk incurred by an employer's illegal or questionable employment practices. With employment law becoming an increasingly complicated dimension of the employment relationship, it is more likely that managers and supervisors unversed in the changing aspects of the law may commit violations. Premiums for EPLI are dependent on the size of the employer and the frequency of past serious claims. Much like various kinds of consumer insurance, EPLI assesses an employer based on risk. Insurers who offer EPLI look favorably on employers who provide ongoing training for managers and supervisors and have strong policies against sexual harassment—and all kinds of discrimination—as well as procedures that call for a quick, thorough, and impartial investigation of complaints.

A final trend in employment litigation is the use of various kinds of language rules in the workplace. Because national origin discrimination is expressly prohibited in Title VII of the Civil Rights Act of 1964, employers who adopt "speak-English-only" rules in their workplaces may be putting themselves at risk of Title VII violations. This is also true of English language proficiency for job applicants and employers. This challenge is heightened by the fact that by the year 2050, 19 percent of Americans will be immigrants. By that time, Hispanics are expected to grow to 29 percent of the U.S. population from the current 14 percent proportion. More so, certain populous border states, such as California, Texas, and Florida, have much higher percentages of immigrants and non-English-speaking residents. In 2009, Hispanics constituted 62 percent of the population in Miami-Dade County. In 2007, the EEOC received 9,396 complaints of national origin discrimination, many of which involved language restrictions and policies.[13] The EEOC has adopted a blanket rule that English-language only rules will automatically constitute national origin discrimination unless the employer can argue for its policy. This rule has been rejected by some courts but embraced by others. A key factor in determining whether such policies are justified is business necessity. English-at-all-times rules have been found burdensome to employees but acceptable, for example, when communicating with customers, coworkers, or supervisors who only speak English, in emergency situations to promote safety, and for cooperative/teamwork assignments. Clearly, this is an area of employment law and litigation that will evolve as different courts interpret the EEOC's position and our workplaces and society become more diverse.

Conclusion

Although employment law is a key strategic area for HR, it remains the single area in which managers throughout organizations are most uninformed and ill-prepared to manage. The laws regulating employment relationships are numerous, complex, and ambiguous. Although no manager can be expected to be a legal expert, the move toward decentralized operations and the establishment of autonomous subsidiaries and work groups requires line managers to increasingly have full responsibility for HR issues. However, of all the traditional HR functions, employment law is probably the most difficult to manage effectively. Not only are there myriad laws and technical details as to how the laws have been interpreted by the courts, but there is also ambiguity in most of the newer laws (and also many of the older laws) that requires informed strategic decision-making by managers at all levels in an organization.

Laws that regulate the employment relationship attempt, in part, to neutralize the power disparity between employers and employees, particularly in light of the prevalence of the employment-at-will doctrine in employee handbooks and court decisions. Employment laws set minimum standards for compliance relative to the fair and just treatment of employees. Organizational justice has been found to be a key factor that impacts employee motivation, performance, and commitment. However, justice goes far beyond simple legal compliance and extends to a variety of organizational activities and policies. Reading 7-3, "The Management of Organizational Justice," introduces the types and components of organizational justice and explains how concepts of fair and just treatment extend beyond employment laws to the design, implementation, and maintenance of a variety of HR systems, which are discussed in Part II of this book.

Critical Thinking

1. What is a protected class, and what laws exist that safeguard the rights of each protected class?
2. Explain the process under which an EEOC complaint is processed. To what extent is it more advantageous for an employee to file an EEOC complaint at the local or federal level?
3. How can an employer lawfully respond to an allegation of employment discrimination?

4. Why does illegal discrimination persist nearly 40 years after the passage of Title VII?
5. What constitutes sexual harassment? What rights and responsibilities does an alleged recipient of sexual harassment have?
6. To what extent do cultural norms influence how other societies and cultures deal with the issue of sexual harassment in the workplace?
7. What are the pros and cons of mediation for an employer? What factors might influence whether an employer agrees to the mediation of an employee charge? What can be done to make mediation more attractive to employers?

Reading 7.1

8. Why is affirmative action such a controversial issue? Is society better served with or without affirmative action? In small groups, take a position either in favor of or against affirmative action and then debate the issue within your group.

Reading 7.2

9. The reading outlines a problem with Title VII, which has backlogged the court system with cases. What are the pros and cons of providing the HR manager with anti-retaliation protection under Title VII? How can the problem addressed in this article be rectified?

Reading 7.3

10. Explain the different components of organizational justice and the outcomes of perceived organizational justice and injustice.

Exercises

1. In small groups, investigate any laws that prohibit employment discrimination in the European Union, Australia, Japan, or China. Note similarities and differences from American laws. What values or assumptions do the laws of these countries make about the employment relationship?
2. You are an HR manager for a medium-sized financial services institution. You overhear an employee, Pat, tell a coworker, Chris, that a third employee, Jamie, told Pat about being the recipient of harassing behavior from Chris. How would you handle this situation? Role-play this with several classmates, and have the remainder of the class critique the approach used.
3. Evaluate California law A.B. 2222. Does it go too far in protecting the rights of employees with disabilities? Break into two groups, with one arguing the need for the provision of the law and the other arguing against the law.
4. Visit the Equal Employment Opportunity Commission Web site at http://www.eeoc.gov. Identify current trends in complaints being filed with the EEOC and the processes by which claims are being resolved. Review the EEOC press releases posted on the site. What appear to be the agency's current priorities, and how appropriate do you feel these priorities are for the U.S. society?

Chapter References

1. Gurchiek, K. "Lockheed Martin Settlement Sends 'Powerful Message,' *Society for Human Resource Management*, article 024101, published at www.shrm.org/hrnews_/published/articles/CMS_024101.asp, January 4, 2008.
2. Schafer, S. "Coke to Pay $193 Million in Bias Suit," *Washington Post*, November 17, 2000, p. A1.
3. Wells, S. "Is the ADA Working?" *HR Magazine*, April 2001, pp. 38–46.
4. Equal Employment Opportunity Commission. Fiscal Year 2008 Performance and Accountability Report. (2009).
5. Barrier, M. "The Mediation Disconnect," *HR Magazine*, May 2003, pp. 54–58.
6. "Dial to Pay $10 Million to Settle Sexual Harassment Case," *Baltimore Sun*, April 30, 2003, p. 9C.
7. EEOC Press Release, "EEOC Obtains $1 Million for Low-Wage Workers Who Were Sexually Harassed at Food Processing Plant," June 1, 2000, available at http://www.eeoc.gov.
8. Hastings, R. "Little Slights Can Erode Employee Engagement," *Society for Human Resource Management*, article 023952, published at www.shrm.org/hrnews_/published/articles/CMS_023952.asp, December, 2007.
9. Janove, J. "Retaliation Nation," *HR Magazine*, 51, (10), October, 2006, pp. 63–67.
10. James, E. and Wooten, L. "Diversity Crises: How Firms Management Discrimination Lawsuits," *Academy of Management Journal*, 49, (3), December 2006, pp. 1103–1118.
11. Parauda, J. and Janove, J. "Settle for Less," *HR Magazine*, 49, (11), November 2004, pp. 135–139.
12. Ibid.
13. Jackson Lewis, "LLP English Language Rules in the Workplace Remain a Potential Liability," *The Florida Employers*, Spring 2009, pp. 1–2.

READING 7.1

In Defense of Preference

Nathan Glazer

Affirmative action is bad. Banning it is worse.

The battle over affirmative action today is a contest between a clear principle on the one hand and a clear reality on the other. The principle is that ability, qualifications, and merit, independent of race, national origin, or sex should prevail when one applies for a job or promotion, or for entry into selective institutions of higher education, or when one bids for contracts. The reality is that strict adherence to this principle would result in few African Americans getting jobs, admissions, and contracts. What makes the debate so confused is that the facts that make a compelling case for affirmative action are often obscured by the defenders of affirmative action themselves. They have resisted acknowledging how serious that gaps are between African Americans and others, how deep the preferences reach, how systematic they have become. Considerably more than a mild bent in the direction of diversity now exists, but it exists because painful facts make it necessary if blacks are to participate in more than token numbers in some key institutions of our society. The opponents of affirmative action can also be faulted: they have not fully confronted the consequences that must follow from the implementation of the principle that measured ability, qualification, merit, applied without regard to color, should be our only guide.

I argued for that principle in a 1975 book titled, provocatively, *Affirmative Discrimination*. It seemed obvious that that was what all of us, black and white, were aiming to achieve through the revolutionary civil rights legislation of the 1960s. That book dealt with affirmative action in employment, and with two other kinds of governmentally or judicially imposed "affirmative action," the equalization of the racial proportions in public schools and the integration of residential neighborhoods. I continued to argue and write regularly against governmentally required affirmative action, that is, racial preference, for the next two decades or more; it was against the spirit of the Constitution, the clear language of the civil rights acts, and the interests of all of us in the United States in achieving an integrated and just society.

It is not the unpopularity of this position in the world in which I live, liberal academia, that has led me to change my mind but, rather, developments that were unforeseen and unexpected in the wake of the successful civil rights movement. What was unforeseen and unexpected was that the gap between the educational performance of blacks and whites would persist and, in some respects, deepen despite the civil rights revolution and hugely expanded social and educational programs, that inner-city schools would continue to decline, and that the black family would unravel to a remarkable degree, contributing to social conditions for large numbers of black children far worse than those in the 1960s. In the presence of those conditions, an insistence on color-blindness means the effective exclusion today of African Americans from positions of influence, wealth, and power. It is not a prospect that any of us can contemplate with equanimity. We have to rethink affirmative action.

In a sense, it is a surprise that a fierce national debate over affirmative action has not only persisted but intensified during the Clinton years. After twelve years under two Republican presidents, Ronald Reagan and George Bush, who said they opposed affirmative action but did nothing to scale it back, the programs seemed secure. After all, affirmative action rests primarily on a presidential executive order dating back to the presidencies of Lyndon Johnson and Richard Nixon which requires "affirmative action" in employment practices from federal contractors—who include almost every large employer, university, and hospital. The legal basis for most of affirmative action could thus have been swept away, as so many noted at the time, with a "stroke of the pen" by the president. Yet two presidents who claimed to oppose affirmative action never wielded the pen.

Despite the popular majority that grumbles against affirmative action, there was (and is) no major elite constituency strongly opposed to it: neither business nor organized labor, religious leaders nor university presidents, local officials nor serious presidential candidates are to be found in opposition. Big business used to fear that affirmative action would undermine the principle of employment and promotion on the basis of qualifications. It has since become a supporter. Along with mayors and other local officials (and of course the civil rights movement), it played a key role in stopping the Reagan administration from moving against affirmative action. Most city administrations have also made their peace with affirmative action.

Two developments outside the arena of presidential politics galvanized both opponents and defenders of affirmative action. The Supreme Court changed glacially after successive Republican appointments—each of which, however, had been vetted by a Democratic Senate—and a number of circuit courts began to chip away at the edifice of affirmative action. But playing the largest role was the politically unsophisticated effort of two California professors to place on the California ballot a proposition that would insert in the California Constitution the simple and clear words, taken from the Civil Rights Act of 1964, which ban discrimination on the basis of race, national origin, or sex. The decision to launch a state constitutional proposition. Proposition 209, suddenly gave opponents the political instrument they needed to tap the majority sentiment that has always existed against preferences.

While supporters of affirmative action do not have public opinion on their side, they do have the still-powerful civil rights movement, the major elites in education, religion, philanthropy, government, and the mass media. And their position is bolstered by a key fact: how far behind African Americans are when judged by the tests and measures that have become the common coin of American meritocracy.

The reality of this enormous gap is clearest where the tests in use are the most objective, the most reliable, and the best validated, as in the case of the various tests used for admission to selective institutions of higher education, for entry into elite occupations such as law and medicine, or for civil service jobs. These tests have been developed over many years specifically for the purpose of eliminating biases in admissions and appointments. As defenders of affirmative action often point out, paper-and-pencil tests of information, reading comprehension, vocabulary, reasoning, and the like are not perfect indicators of individual ability. But they are the best measures we have for success in college and professional schools, which, after all, require just the skills the tests measure. And the test can clearly differentiate the literate teacher from the illiterate one or the policeman who can make out a coherent arrest report from one who cannot.

To concentrate on the most hotly contested area of affirmative action—admission to selective institutions of higher education—and on the group in the center of the storm—African Americans: If the Scholastic Assessment Test were used for selection in a color-blind fashion, African Americans, who today make up about six percent of the student bodies in selective colleges and universities, would drop to less than two percent, according to a 1994 study by the editor of the *Journal of Blacks in Higher Education.*

Why is this so? According to studies summarized in Stephan and Abigail Thernstrom's book, *America in Black and White*, the average combined SAT score for entering freshmen in the nation's top 25 institutions is about 1300. White applicants generally need to score a minimum of 600 on the verbal portion of the test—a score obtained by eight percent of the test-takers in 1995—and at least 650 on the mathematics section—a score obtained by seven percent of the test-takers in 1995. In contrast, only 1.7 percent of black students scored over 600 on the verbal section in 1995, and only two percent scored over 650 on the math. This represents considerable progress over the last 15 years, but black students still lag distressingly far behind their white counterparts.

There is no way of getting around this reality. Perhaps the tests are irrelevant to success in college? That cannot be sustained. They have been improved and revised over decades and predict achievement in college better than any alternative. Some of the revisions have been carried out in a near-desperate effort to exclude items which would discriminate against blacks. Some institutions have decided they will not use the tests, not because they are invalid per se, but because they pose a barrier to the increased admission of black students. Nor would emphasizing other admissions criteria, such as high school grades, make a radical difference. In any case, there is considerable value to a uniform national standard, given the enormous difference among high schools.

Do qualifications at the time of admission matter? Isn't the important thing what the institutions manage to do with those they admit? If they graduate, are they not qualified? Yes, but many do not graduate. Two or three times as many African American students as white students drop out before graduation. And the tests for admission to graduate schools show the same radical disparities between blacks and others. Are there not also preferences for athletes, children of alumni, students gifted in some particular respect? Yes, but except for athletes, the disparities in academic aptitude that result from such preferences are not nearly as substantial as those which must be elided in order to reach target figures for black students. Can we not substitute for the tests other factors—such as the poverty and other hardships students have overcome to reach the point of applying to college? This might keep up the number of African Americans, but not by much, if the studies are to be believed. A good number of white and Asian applicants would also benefit from such "class-based" affirmative action.

(I have focused on the effect of affirmative action—and its possible abolition—on African Americans. But, of course, there are other beneficiaries. Through bureaucratic mindlessness, Asian Americans and Hispanics were also given affirmative action. But Asian Americans scarcely need it. Major groups—not all—of Hispanic Americans trial behind whites but mostly for reasons we understand: problems with the English language and the effect on immigrant children of the poor educational and economic status of their parents. We expect these to improve in time as they always have with immigrants to the United States. And, when it comes to women, there is simply no issue today when it comes to qualifying in equal numbers for selective institutions of higher and professional education.)

How, then, should we respond to this undeniable reality? The opponents of affirmative action say, "Let standards prevail whatever the result." So what if black students are reduced to two percent of our selective and elite student bodies? Those who gain entry will know that they are properly qualified for entry, that they have been selected without discrimination, and their classmates will know it too. The result will actually be improved race relations and a continuance of the improvements we have seen in black performance in recent decades. Fifteen years from now, perhaps three or four percent of students in the top schools will be black. Until then, blacks can go to less competitive institutions of higher education, perhaps gaining greater advantage from their education in so doing. And, meanwhile, let us improve elementary and high school education—as we have been trying to do for the last 15 years.

Yet we cannot be quite so cavalier about the impact on public opinion—black and white—of a radical reduction in the number of black students at the Harvards, the Berkeleys, and the Amhersts. These institutions have become, for better or worse, the gateways to prominence, privilege, wealth, and power in American society. To admit blacks under affirmative action no doubt undermines the American meritocracy, but to exclude blacks from them by abolishing affirmative action would undermine the legitimacy of American democracy.

My argument is rooted in history. African Americans—and the struggle for their full and fair inclusion in U.S. society—have been a part of American history from the beginning. Our Constitution took special—but grossly unfair—account of their status, our greatest war was fought over their status, and our most important constitutional amendments were adopted because of the need to right past wrongs done to them. And, amid the civil rights revolution of the 1960s, affirmative action was instituted to compensate for the damage done to black achievement and life chances by almost 400 years of slavery, followed by state-sanctioned discrimination and massive prejudice.

Yet, today, a vast gulf of difference persists between the educational and occupational status of blacks and whites, a gulf that encompasses statistical measures of wealth, residential segregation, and social relationships with other Americans. Thirty years ago, with the passage of the great civil rights laws, one could have reasonably expected—as I did—that all would be set right by now. But today, even after taking account of substantial progress and change, it is borne upon us how continuous, rooted, and substantial the differences between African Americans and other Americans remain.

The judgment of the elites who support affirmative action—the college presidents and trustees, the religious leaders, the corporate executives—and the judgment even of many of those who oppose it but hesitate to act against it—the Republican leaders in Congress, for example—is that the banning of preference would be bad for the country. I agree. Not that everyone's motives are entirely admirable; many conservative congressmen, for example, are simply afraid of being portrayed as racists even if their opposition to affirmative action is based on a sincere desire to support meritocratic principle. The college presidents who support affirmative action, under the fashionable mantra of diversity, also undoubtedly fear the student demonstrations that would occur if they were to speak out against preferences.

But there are also good-faith motives in this stand, and there is something behind the argument for diversity. What kind of institutions of higher education would we have if blacks suddenly dropped from six or seven percent of enrollment to one or two percent? The presence of blacks, in classes in social studies and the humanities, immediately introduces another tone, another range of questions (often to the discomfort of black students who do not want this representation burden placed upon them). The tone may be one of embarrassment and hesitation and self-censorship among whites (students and faculty). But must we not all learn how to face these questions together with our fellow citizens? *We* should not be able to escape from this embarrassment by the reduction of black students to minuscule numbers.

The weakness in the "diversity" defense is that college presidents are not much worried about the diversity that white working-class kids, or students of Italian or Slavic background, have to offer. Still there is a reputable reason for that apparent discrepancy. It is that the varied ethnic and racial groups in the United States do not, to the same extent as African Americans, pose a test of the fairness of American institutions. These other groups have not been subjected to the same degree of persecution or exclusion. Their status is not, as the social status of African Americans is, the most enduring reproach to the egalitarian ideals of American society. And these other groups have made progress historically, and make progress today, at a rate that incorporates them into American society quickly compared to blacks.

This is the principal flaw in the critique of affirmative action. The critics are defending a vitally important principle, indeed, the one that should be the governing principle of institutions of higher education: academic competence as the sole test for distinguishing among applicants and students. This principle, which was fought for so energetically during the 1940s and 1950s through laws banning discrimination in admission on the basis of race, national origin, or religion, should not be put aside lightly. But, at present, it would mean the near exclusion from our best educational institutions of a group that makes up twelve percent of the population. In time, I am convinced, this preference will not be needed. Our laws and customs and our primary and secondary educational systems will fully incorporate black Americans into American society, as other disadvantaged groups have been incorporated. The positive trends of recent decades will continue. But we are still, though less than in the past, "two nations," and one of the nations cannot be excluded so throughly from institutions that confer access to the positions of greatest prestige and power.

On what basis can *we* justify violating the principle that measured criteria of merit should govern admission to selective institutions of higher education today? It is of some significance to begin with that we in the United States have always been looser in this respect than more examination-bound systems of higher education in, say, Western Europe: we have always left room for a large degree of freedom for institutions of higher education, public as well as private, to admit students based on nonacademic criteria. But I believe the main reasons we have to continue racial preferences for blacks are, first, because this country has a special obligation to blacks that has not been fully discharged, and second, because strict application of the principle of qualification would send a message of despair to many blacks, a message that the nation is indifferent to their difficulties and problems.

Many, including leading black advocates of eliminating preferences, say no: the message would be, "Work harder and you can do it." Well, now that affirmative action is becoming a thing of the past in the public colleges and universities of California and Texas, we will have a chance to find out. Yet I wonder whether the message of affirmative action to black students today really ever has been, "Don't work hard; it doesn't matter for you because you're black; you will make it into college anyway." Colleges are indeed looking for black students, but they are also looking for some minimal degree of academic effort and accomplishment, and it is a rare ambitious African American student seeking college entry who relaxes because he believes his grades won't matter *at all*.

One of the chief arguments against racial preference in college and professional school admissions is that more blacks will drop out, the quality of blacks who complete the courses of instruction will be inferior, and they will make poorer lawyers, doctors, or businessmen. Dropping out is common in American higher education and does not necessarily mean that one's attendance was a total loss. Still, the average lower degree of academic performance has, and will continue to have, effects even for the successful: fewer graduating black doctors will go into research; more will go into practice and administration. More blacks in business corporations will be in personnel. Fewer graduating black lawyers will go into corporate law firms; more will work for government.

And more will become judges, because of another and less disputed form of affirmative action, politics. Few protest at the high number of black magistrates in cities with large black populations—we do not appoint judges by examination. Nor do we find it odd or objectionable that Democratic presidents will appoint more black lawyers as judges, or that even a Republican president will be sure to appoint one black Supreme Court justice. What is at work here is the principle of participation. It is a more legitimate principle in politics and government than it is for admission to selective institutions of higher education. But these are also gateways to power, and the principle of participation cannot be flatly ruled out for them.

Whatever the case one may make in general for affirmative action, many difficult issues remain: What kind, to what extent, how long, imposed by whom, by what decision-making process? It is important to bear in mind that affirmative action in higher education admissions is, for the most part, a policy that has been chosen (albeit sometimes under political pressure) by the institutions themselves. There are racial goals and targets for employment and promotion for all government contractors, including colleges and universities, set by government fiat, but targets on student admissions are not imposed by government, except for a few traditionally black or white institutions in the South.

Let us preserve this institutional autonomy. Just as I would resist governmentally imposed requirements that these institutions meet quotas of black admissions, so would I also oppose a judicial or legislative *ban* on the use of race in making decisions on admission. Ballot measures like Proposition 209 are more understandable given the abuses so common in systems of racial preference. But it is revealing that so many other states appear to have had second thoughts and that the California vote is therefore not likely to be repeated. (A recent report in *The Chronicle of Higher Education* was headlined "LEGISLATURES SHOW LITTLE ENTHUSIASM FOR MEASURES TO END RACIAL PREFERENCES"; in this respect, the states are not unlike Congress.)

We should retain the freedom of institutions of higher and professional education to make these determinations for themselves. As we know, they would almost all make room for a larger percentage of black students than would otherwise qualify. This is what these institutions do today. They defend what they do with the argument that diversity is a good thing. I think what they really mean is that a large segment of the American population, significant not only demographically but historically and politically and morally, cannot be so thoroughly excluded. I agree with them.

I have discussed affirmative action only in the context of academic admissions policy. Other areas raise other questions, other problems. And, even in this one area of college and university admissions, affirmative action is not a simple and clear and uncomplicated solution. It can be implemented wisely or foolishly, and it is often done foolishly, as when college presidents make promises to protesting students that they cannot fulfill, or when institutions reach too far below their minimal standards with deleterious results for the academic success of the students they admit, for their grading practices, and for the legitimacy of the degrees they offer. No matter how affirmative action in admissions is dealt with, other issues remain or will emerge. More black students, for example, mean demands for more black faculty and administrators and for more black-oriented courses. Preference is no final answer (just as the elimination of preference is no final answer). It is rather what is necessary to respond to the reality that, for some years to come, yes, we are still two nations, and both nations must participate in the society to some reasonable degree.

Fortunately, those two nations, by and large, want to become more united. The United States is not Canada or Bosnia, Lebanon or Malaysia. But, for the foreseeable future, the strict use of certain generally reasonable tests as a benchmark criterion for admissions would mean the de facto exclusion of one of the two nations from a key institutional system of the society, higher education. Higher education's governing principle is qualification—merit. Should it make room for another and quite different principle, equal participation? The latter should never become dominant. Racial proportional representation would be a disaster. But basically the answer is yes—the principle of equal participation can and should be given some role. This decision has costs. But the alternative is too grim to contemplate.

Testing Texas

The University of Texas Law School is ground zero of the post–affirmative action world. In a 1996 case, *Hopwood v. Texas*, the Fifth Circuit Court of Appeals struck down the law school's affirmative action policy. To ensure that each entering class of 500 or so included about 75 black and Hispanic students, the law school had been operating, in effect, a "dual" admissions system under which minority and nonminority students were being admitted by separate criteria—a method that the Supreme Court had struck down in the 1978 Bakke case. This fall, at the beginning of the first semester since *Hopwood*, 26 Mexican-American students, and four blacks, enrolled in Texas's first-year class—only a few more than the law school had had during the late '60s. Back then, the lack of minority representation hadn't been a big issue at the law school. Now, it is seen as a political and marketing disaster. Qualified minority students, whom schools fight over like star quarterbacks, are proving reluctant to apply to Texas. And so are the kind of progressively minded, out-of-state white students who help make the law school a national, rather than local, institution. "There have been times at recruitment events when majority and minority students approach the table together and say 'What does the entering class look like?'" Shelli Soto, the law school's assistant dean of admissions, told me.

Since *Hopwood* the law school has labored mightily to thread the eye of a legal needle—to admit large numbers of minority students without applying explicitly racial or ethnic criteria. The law school's application now includes an optional "Statement on Economic, Social or Personal Disadvantage"—an effort to tease more minority applicants out of the pool. "'Qualified' really means a combination of your accomplishments and your experiences," Soto explains. But this effort to side-step such statistical criteria as LSAT results doesn't really work. Black students do not have more extracurricular activities than whites and do not have better grade-point averages relative to their LSAT scores. And, because so few black students from truly disadvantaged backgrounds do well enough academically to qualify even under affirmative action criteria, "class-based" affirmative action doesn't help either. It seems the only way to admit large numbers of blacks is to admit them *because* they are black.

When I posed this problem to William Cunningham, the chancellor of the U.T. system, he said that the University of Texas Medical School had already adjusted its admissions criteria. "They want to look at people's motivation," the chancellor said, "the human traits that have to do with their wanting to be doctors." Was this being done in the hope that it would have a "race-positive effect"? I asked. Cunningham paused for a long, careful moment. "I don't want to say 'race-positive,'" he said. It wasn't clear what he *could* say without violating *Hopwood*. "We want to have a diverse student body," he said, "and we want to look at broader criteria than we have in the past to insure that we have a diverse student body." I told Cunningham that some law school faculty members were concerned about diluting admissions standards. The chancellor said very carefully, "I do think this is a time for us to be thoughtful and flexible." Was it possible to be "flexible" without either violating the terms of *Hopwood* or lowering standards? "It is," Cunningham signed, "a difficult problem."

U.T.'s administrators are also looking over their shoulders at the Texas state legislature. A quarter of a century ago, it was virtually all white; now it has significant, and growing, black and Hispanic representation. As Russell Weintraub, a professor of contracts at the law school who was uneasy about affirmative action, says: "If the majority of people in this state are going to be Mexican-American and African American, and they are going to assume many of the leadership roles in the state, then it's going to be big trouble if the law school doesn't admit many minority students—it's going to be a bomb ready to explode."

Indeed, a few small bombs have detonated already. Soon after the *Hopwood* decision the state legislature passed a law that would require the University of Texas undergraduate college to accept the top ten percent of graduates from every high school in the state. This law, which would increase minority enrollment by automatically admitting the best students from heavily minority high schools, effectively reinstated a rule the college had abandoned three years ago in order to strengthen its standards.

The legislature then passed another law that requires public universities to apply the minimum grade-point average demanded of entering students to everyone—including athletes admitted on scholarship. The law, whose interpretation is now a matter of debate, would destroy the Texas Longhorn football team. Its sponsor, Ron Wilson, is a black State Assemblyman from Houston who attended both U.T. and U.T. Law. Wilson freely admits that the bill was designed to punish the university, which he saw as complicit in the Hopwood ruling. "If you're just a regular African American student with a two-point-five grade-point average, you can't get into the University of Texas," he told me. "But, if you can play the court jester out there on the football field and earn the university a million dollars, you can get it. As far as I'm concerned, that's hypocrisy. My bill says you can't have it both ways."

Wilson's real goal, of course, is not to exclude the athletes but to force the university to take everyone else. One solution, Wilson said, was "open admission." I asked if that wouldn't lead to a lowering of standards. Wilson said: "I don't look at academic standards as the Bible for academic excellence. There hasn't been enough input into those standards from African Americans and Hispanics to make them relevant to their community." And he added one more threat: if the university couldn't counteract the effect of *Hopwood*, he said, "We're going to move the money to follow the students to historically black colleges, if necessary."

The revenge of the legislature implies that the costs of doing away with affirmative action may turn out to be higher than the costs of keeping it. One of the most intriguing documents of the post-affirmative action era is an amicus brief which three professors at U.T. Law submitted to the Supreme Court in an affirmative action case last year. The three made the usual case in favor of affirmative action—but added a more novel, purely pragmatic argument: "A large public institution that serves the whole state cannot maintain its legitimacy if it is perceived to exclude minority students." The authors described the two bills that had passed the Texas legislature and noted that the University of California system is considering waiving its SAT requirement. If *Hopwood* becomes law for the country as a whole, the authors declared apocalyptically, "there will eventually be no great public universities—not for the nation and not for the white plaintiffs either."

In other words, affirmative action represents not a threat to academic standards but the surest means of preserving them. This argument sounds so perverse that it's hard to take seriously, but it's not without foundation. Douglas Laycock, one of the authors of the brief, said: "We're in the middle of a full-blown attack on every means we have to measure merit and on the very idea of merit, and it's mostly driven by the issue of race." What Laycock was suggesting is that, in a straightforward battle between the old meritocratic principle on which conservatives make their stand on the new ideals of diversity and inclusion, meritocracy is likely to lose. And, several weeks later, *The New York Times* inadvertently confirmed his point in a front-page story headlined, "COLLEGES LOOK FOR ANSWERS TO RACIAL GAPS IN TESTING." Donald M. Stewart, president of the College Board, lamented the "social cost" of relying on standardized tests on which minority students fare poorly. "America can't stand that," Stewart said.

Should we regret the political and marketplace dynamics that essentially *force* institutions like the University of Texas Law School to practice affirmative action? The original rationale for affirmative action was that it helped disadvantaged students overcome the effects of discrimination, both current and historical. No one questions that U.T. Law is guilty of past discrimination. The school was off-limits to black students as a matter of state law until a celebrated 1950 Supreme court decisions, *Sweatt v. Painter*. But most of the black students who attend the law school now come from other states, and they are scarcely more likely than the white students to come from a disadvantaged background.

What about "diversity"? The diversity argument has rapidly eclipsed the past-discrimination argument, because it is so much rosier and more consensual. It's hard to dispute the notion that institutions benefit from "diverse" points of view. But is that a large enough good to justify disadvantaging whites? And there's something arbitrary about the math. Randall Kennedy, a professor at Harvard Law School and another uneasy supporter of affirmative action, says: "I have my problems with the idea that we've got to have diversity because in the year 2000 the census says this and this about a jurisdiction. Does that mean that, if you're in Maine, you don't have to have more than one black student?"

The simple and painful truth is that affirmative action rests on a bedrock of failure. The reason why the University of Texas Law School needed affirmative action in the first place is that, according to a university deposition in *Hopwood*, only 88 black students in the entire country had a combination of grades and law boards in 1992 that reached the mean of admitted white students; only one of those black students came from Texas. One lesson of post-*Hopwood* Texas is that eliminating affirmative action would virtually wipe out the black presence in top schools. For conservatives, that's just the way the meritocratic cookie crumbles, but for most Americans, justly proud of the extent to which our leading institutions have been integrated over the last quarter century, that's likely to be an unacceptable outcome.

Affirmative action is, at bottom, a dodge. It allows us to put off the far harder work: ending the isolation of young black people and closing the academic gap that separates black students—even middle-class black students—from whites. When we commit ourselves to that, we can do without affirmative action, but not before.

James Traub

Source: The New Republic, 218 (14), 18–25 (1998).

READING 7.2

The Dual Loyalty Dilemma for HR Managers Under Title VII Compliance

Jeffrey A. Mello

Introduction

When Congress passed Title VII of the Civil Rights Act of 1964 (42 U.S.C. Sect. 2000e, *et. seq.*), it sought to eradicate employment discrimination based on race, color, national origin, sex, and religion. Under the Act the Equal Employment Opportunity Commission (EEOC) was created with an envisioned role of conciliating allegations of discrimination as opposed to functioning as a watchdog agency. Congress intended the main responsibility for compliance with Title VII to rest with employers, who were expected to establish their own internal voluntary Title VII compliance mechanisms.

To ensure that any employee allegations of unlawful discrimination were not met with any kind of employer retaliation, the Act expressly prohibits employers from engaging in any such behavior. A problem has arisen, however, because judicial interpretations of this retaliation provision have excluded managerial personnel, particularly human resource and equal employment opportunity (HR/EEO) managers, from its protection. By excluding these managers from protection, the courts have favored management prerogatives to terminate employees perceived to be disloyal to the employer over the rights provided to employees under Title VII. Consequently, the protection Congress intended to afford employees under Title VII has been severely undermined. This article discusses the purpose of Title VII, its anti-retaliation provision, the dual and conflicting roles of the HR manager relative to Title VII, and the need for a judicial interpretation of role of the HR/EEO manager that is more consistent with Congressional intent.

The Purpose of Title VII

When Congress enacted Title VII, it sought to create a largely self-regulating system by which employers would voluntarily abandon the discriminatory practices prohibited in the Act and do so with minimal outside intervention by government agencies. Congress sought to promote voluntary compliance due to its serious concerns that any governmental oversight and control efforts to eradicate employment discrimination would prohibitively interfere with individual business prerogatives. In fact, when Congress established the EEOC, it envisioned an agency that would respond to complaints rather than initiate them and would perform a mediation or conciliation function as opposed to an adjudication role (42 U.S.C. Sect. 2000e – 5(f) and (g)). This very point was noted by the Supreme Court in *Alexander v. Gardner-Denver Co.* (415 U.S. 36, 44, 94 S. Ct. 1011, 1017, 39 L.Ed. 147 (1974)), which also noted that the EEOC was not empowered by Congress with any direct authority to enforce Title VII. Such powers rested with the federal court system.

It has become apparent to even the Commissioner of the EEOC that Congress's intended voluntary compliance scheme is not working; EEOC Vice-Chairman Paul Igalaski recently commented that "our process is broken and needs substantial reform" (Lawyers Committee for Civil Rights Under Law, 1995). Each year, the volume of discrimination litigation continues to soar. In fiscal year 1994, the EEOC received 91,189 charges of discrimination compared to 63,898 in 1991, a 42.7% increase in three years (EEOC Annual Report; Fiscal Year 1994). As a result, there has been increased and unwelcome government intervention through judicial scrutiny of business affairs that Congress intended to remain as prerogatives of individual businesses through its voluntary compliance plan. Even though Congress designed Title VII to keep employment discrimination allegations out of court, dockets continue to be flooded with such cases.

At first glance the cause of this is not readily apparent. The means of enforcing Title VII are relatively sound, and the role of the EEOC is quite clear. The EEOC receives employee complaints for the purpose of conciliation as a prerequisite for obtaining relief through the courts. The EEOC conducts a preliminary investigation, and complaints without merit are dismissed, with the complainant presumably discouraged from litigating. EEOC investigations that find charges with merit provide an incentive for employers to rectify behavior and practices because the EEOC has the power to file suit on behalf of the aggrieved employee or employees. Hence, there is a strong incentive for employers, if they do unlawfully discriminate, to resolve matters in-house quickly and quietly.

Ideally the process outlined in Title VII should dispose of most claims without litigation. The voluntary compliance mechanism would allow an organization to keep its "dirty laundry" from the public domain and, in cases where the EEOC found discriminatory behavior on the part of employers and attempted conciliation, there was a clear incentive for organizations to cooperate, given the cost and time involved with litigation, not to mention having a mark on their records with the federal government and EEOC.

In 1991, Congress passed an amendment to Title VII which greatly altered employee/employer Title VII dynamics. In the years that had passed since the original passage of Title VII, a number of EEOC complaints had made their way to the courts, and it became painfully apparent that Title VII's remedies for aggrieved plaintiffs were far inferior to those found in other federal anti-discrimination laws. For example, the Age Discrimination In Employment Act of 1967 (29 U.S.C. Sect. 626(b)) allows punitive double liquidated damages and jury trials. In contrast, Title VII prior to the 1991 amendment, provided neither compensation or punitive damages nor jury trials.

As a result, Congress enacted the Civil Rights Act of 1991 (42 U.S.C. Sect. 1981 A(2)), which added compensatory and punitive damages as well as the opportunity for jury trials as remedies for Title VII violations. These new remedies gave grievants an additional incentive to file complaints and to litigate. The combination of these new remedies with the passage of the Americans With Disabilities Act of 1990 (42 U.S.C. Sect. 12101, *et. seq.*) caused EEOC litigation to skyrocket. Since 1992, the EEOC has averaged more than 85,000 charges per year (Shapiro, 1998). As employment discrimination complaints have overwhelmed the EEOC and litigation has swamped the courts, the EEOC has responded by instituting mandatory mediation programs as well as limiting EEOC investigations to selected cases (Bureau of National Affairs, 1996). In fact, the EEOC has attempted to slash its pending caseload by offering mediation-based alternative dispute resolution for nearly half the charges it finds valid (EEOC Annual Report: Fiscal Year 1997).

Unfortunately, the effect of such selective enforcement of laws does not prevent the type of employment discrimination Congress sought to eradicate when it passed Title VII. Certainly, employers who become aware that the EEOC selectively enforces Title VII, due to the hemorrhaging burdens on the agency, may be more likely to discriminate, given the lesser likelihood of incurring Title VII enforcement and penalties. The commission had more than 100,000 backlogged cases by 1995, which caused Vice Chairman Igasaki to state that "the enormous build-up of pending cases has resulted in a serious loss of public confidence and faith in the EEOC's ability to effectively carry out its responsibilities" (Lawyers Committee for Civil Rights Under Law, 1995).

While the source of this problem may largely rest with the fact that the EEOC has strayed from its role as originally envisioned by Congress, there is an additional issue contributing to the problem that relates to the failure of voluntary compliance mechanisms. Judicial interpretations of Title VII have essentially debilitated the key persons, human resource managers responsible for EEOC, who would be overseeing internal compliance systems from effectively performing this role. As a result, the system that attempts to resolve claims of discrimination under Title VII has been brought to the virtual standstill.

The Nature of the Role of the HR Manager

In many organizations the role of the HR manager is often somewhat ambiguous. Ideally, when chasms exist between employees and management, the role of the human resources function is to bridge these chasms and resolve conflict between employees and management in creating and maintaining a motivating work environment conducive to high performance. Whether the HR manager is principally more a representative of management to handle employee problems or an advocate of employee concerns to management is not always clear, and the dual expectations often placed on the HR manager can create an ambiguous and conflicting dual loyalty.

This has been especially true as the role of HR has evolved in modern organizations. While HR was once largely an administrative function, its role has changed to one that is centrally involved in top management arenas such as strategic planning and legal compliance. In managing workplace dynamics such as conflict resolution and change processes such as restructuring, HR is often called upon to bridge the needs of the organization and the rights and interests of workers, particularly in collective bargaining environments. The HR manager is expected to establish an atmosphere of trust and confidentiality with employees to facilitate in-house resolution of grievances.

In many instances, advocating for employees or employee groups does not conflict with the responsibility of loyalty to the employer, and the HR manager avoids any duality of responsibility. In many organizations, the HR manager is relied upon to be the voice of the employees in bringing up and resolving employee concerns. However, in certain instances, the role of employee advocacy can directly conflict with the employer's interests and goals for the organization and, therefore, creates a tension for the HR manager between loyalty to employer and responsibility to employees. In this regard, the HR manager's primary role is far less apparent.

The management literature is conspicuously silent concerning any examination or study of this potential conflict of interest. Even the Code of Ethics of the nation's largest professional HR organization, the Society of Human Resource Management, states that the HR manager is supposed "to make the fair and equitable treatment of all employees a primary concern" while simultaneously stating expectations "to maintain loyalty to the employer, even while upholding all laws and regulations relating to the employer's activities."

Because HR generally has principal responsibility for compliance with EEOC legislation, HR is usually the place where employees initially file complaints of behaviors that violate their Title VII rights. Ideally, HR tries to resolve any such complaints in-house. This process is not only in line with what Congress intended but is also clearly in the employer's best interest (in maintaining employee morale, minimizing the time and cost of possible litigation, and avoiding any public disclosure of claims) as well as the best interest of the employee (in securing a more timely resolution and avoiding the stressful EEOC investigation and possible litigation). Clearly, the appropriate posture for HR is not to simply advocate or, at worst, defend management's position nor to do anything to placate a disgruntled employee, but to ensure that the issues are resolved fairly in-house. This may involve attempting to persuade management that the employee's point of view is more valid than that of management from a practical, ethical, or most important, legal perspective.

The HR manager will only succeed to the extent that employees perceive that he or she is their advocate against allegedly unlawful management practices. If HR lacks credibility, employees are far more likely to seek redress outside of the organization. The role of the HR manager in developing and managing an internal grievance policy requires a delicate balancing act between the interest of employees and those of the employer. Given this tension, an HR manager in an organization in which senior management supports full compliance with Title VII will find it rarely necessary to advocate employee positions that may be at odds with those of management. Management's support of Title VII should prevent such adversarial dilemmas. However, in an organization where commitment to Title VII and EEO are absent or, at worst, where management knowingly or unknowingly continues to illegally discriminate against employees, the HR function may find itself in a precarious position.

The HR manager clearly needs to be able to promote a law-abiding workplace in which employee trust can be maintained without fear of reprisal by the employer in cases where HR must challenge management. This is in the best interest of the employer and is clearly consistent with Congressional intent. Even though this posture would strengthen the system that Congress sought to establish under Title VII, Congress itself has made this end unobtainable due to judicial interpretations of a provision in Title VII that pertains to anti-retaliation protection.

Anti-Retaliation Under Title VII

Title VII's anti-retaliation provision has been described as the broadest found in any federal law where rank-and-file employees are concerned (Walterscheid, 1988). A specific portion of Section 704(a) of the Civil Rights Act of 1964 prohibits employers from discriminating against any employee who has opposed any practice made unlawful by the Act, filed any charge under the Act, or testified, asserted or participated in any manner in an investigation, proceeding or hearing under the Act. It states, "It shall be an unlawful employment practice for an employer to discriminate... against any employee or applicant for employment... because [the employee or applicant] has opposed any practice made an unlawful employment practice by this title, or because [the employee or applicant] has made a charge, testified, assisted or participated in any manner in an investigation, proceeding or hearing under this title" (42 U.S.C. Sect. 2000e-3(a)). Even employees who participate in a process in which the employer's conduct is deemed lawful would receive protection under 704(a) as long as the opposition was done in good faith and based on an objectively reasonable belief that unlawful discrimination had in fact occurred (Bales, 1994). Acts of retaliation by employers are extensive. The EEOC reports that 22.5% of the complaints it receives pertain to employer retaliation (Shapiro, 1998).

While the language and framework that prohibit retaliation may seem cut and dried, a series of retaliation cases have revolved around the argument by the employer that when the employee was "punished," the action was not taken on account of his or her oppositional position or conduct but rather because the employee had been disruptive or disloyal to the employer in the course of opposing the allegedly discriminatory employment practice or had caused the employer excessive harm that infringed on the employer's right to run his business. The first federal appellate court to address this issue was the First Circuit Court of Appeals in *Hochstadt v. Worcester Foundation for Experimental Biology* (545 F.2d 222 (1st Cir. 1976)). In this case, a research scientist claimed illegal sex discrimination based on a perceived pay disparity and filed charges with the Massachusetts Commission Against Discrimination, the EEOC, the Department of Labor and the Department of Health, Education, and Welfare. In preparing her claim, Hochstadt conducted her legal business on company time and solicited information from coworkers, who, in turn, complained that she disrupted their work. Hochstadt alleged that her termination was in retaliation for her sex discrimination claim, while the employer said she was terminated for her performance and disruptive behavior.

As the court weighed the respective interests of the parties, it sought to determine whether the plaintiff's oppositional conduct was "excessive" in terms of its injury to the employer's interests. In attempting to find the appropriate balance between the rights of the employer (to "run his business") versus the rights of the employee (to "express her grievance and promote her own welfare"), the court reasoned that Section 704(a) did not afford employees unlimited license to complain at any and all times and places and that oppositional conduct should not be deliberately calculated to inflict needless economic hardship on the employer. It ruled that Hochstadt's poor work performance and disruptive behavior resulted in the discharge, and that while her complaint had some merit, her actions were so excessive as to be outside of the protection of section 704(a).

The Hochstadt case became a precedent for other courts who followed by denying anti-retaliation protection to employees who engaged in a variety of behaviors including disclosing confidential records, making loud threats of calling the "labor board" in the presence of others, participating in a disruptive, noise demonstration during working hours, making militant demands for paid time to prepare EEO complaints, and engaging in loud and insubordinate conduct in public working areas. The Ninth Circuit later questioned the logic behind the Hochstadt court's reasoning in *EEOC v. Crown Zellerbach Corporation* (720 F.2d 1008 (9th Cir. 1983)) when it ruled that under the Hochstadt decision every oppositional action by employees can be deemed disloyal or disruptive and, hence, virtually every opposition claim could easily be defeated by employers.

While the *Hochstadt* precedent has made it relatively easy for employers to defeat the retaliation charges levied by nonmanagerial employees, cases in which the plaintiffs were management-level employers have been even easier to defeat. In *Hicks v. ABT Associated, Inc.* (572 F.2d 960 (3d Cir. 1978)) and *Silas v. City Demonstration Agency* (588 F.2d 297 (9th Cir. 1978)), the courts found that anti-retaliation was not available when the employees' directly conflicted with their job duties. One court ruled, in *Notovny v. Great American Federal Savings & Loan Association* (539 F.Supp. 437 (W. D. Pa. 1982)), that the higher an employee is on the management ladder, the more circumspect that employee should be in expressing opposition to employment practices of which he disapproves. This argument essentially eradicates any protection managerial employees could expect to receive for any perceived opposition, given the fact that managers are essentially "agents" of their employers.

This raises the questions as to how the HR manager with EEO responsibility can be assertive concerning compliance with and violations of Title VII's express terms and policies when he or she is totally deprived of any protection from retaliation. The first court to address this problems was the Court of Appeals for the District of Columbia in *Pendleton v. Rumsfield* (628 F.2d 102 (9 D.C. Cir. 1980)). In this case, two individuals who were employed as EEO counselors attended an employee demonstration protesting employer policies relating to EEO and were fired for doing so and sued under the 704(a) anti-retaliation provision. The sharply divided court in this case noted the dual responsibilities of the counselors, particularly in light of the fact that the employer had provided the counselors with a very ambiguous job description. The majority of the court held that the counselors constantly needed to reaffirm their "undivided loyalty" to management in a way that did not tolerate oppositional conduct such as attending the protest. The dissent recognized that the counselors attending the protest were acting as true intermediaries in attempting to gain the confidence of employees and information necessary to settle the disputes.

This decision was followed by a redefining of the role of the HR/EEO manager in very narrow, one-dimensional terms, in which managers engaged in any conduct perceived by management as oppositional may be viewed as "ineffective" if management decide it can no longer place absolute trust in such employees. In *Smith v. Singer* (650 F.2d 214 (9th Cir. 1981)), an EEO counselor himself contacted and filed a charge with the EEOC on behalf of an employee after attempts to reconcile the complaint with management were futile. In upholding the counselor's dismissal based on disloyalty, the court ruled that "to grant protection to a manager engaged in oppositional conduct would force the company to keep in its ranks an adversary who would be forever immune from dismissal" and that once a manager becomes an adversary, he or she is "wholly disabled" from "representing the company before any agencies as well as working with executives in the voluntary development of nondiscriminatory hiring programs." This court took the express position that adversarial views within the management ranks threaten rather than foster voluntary tart' compliance. It reasoned that an interpretation of Section 704(a) to protect oppositional conduct by HR/EEO managers "would render wholly unworkable the program of voluntary compliance which [the manager] was employed to conduct."

Similarly, in *Jones v. Flagship* (793 F.2d 714 (5th Cir. 1986), cert. denied, 479 U.S. 1065 (1987)), the Fifth Circuit ruled and the Supreme Court affirmed that an EEO counselor's need to maintain the trust and confidence of management superseded any rights or goals that might be advanced by affording the manager anti-retaliation protection under Section 704(a). The court reasoned that in providing aid and comfort to an employee, Jones had undermined her role in "acting as the representative of the company before administrative agencies in cases filed against the company" and "critically harmed [the employer's] posture in the defense of discrimination suits brought against the company." Likewise in *Herrera v. Mobile Oil, Inc.* (53 Fair Empl. Prac. Cas. (BNA) 1406 (W. D. Tex. 1990)), the court found that when Herrera, an employee relations advisor, counseled and advised a disgruntled employee to file an EEOC charge, such action placed Herrera in a "squarely adversarial position" with his employer, leaving the employer "no option but to terminate him."

Lack of confidence was also upheld as a legitimate reason to usurp any protection an EEO manager might expect against retaliation in the Sixth Circuit case of *Holden v. Owen-Illinois* (793 F.2d 745 (6th Cir. 1986), cert. denied 479 U.S. 1008 (1986)). In this case the dismissal of a plaintiff who had been hired to design and implement an affirmative action program and subsequently developed a stronger program than her employer desired was upheld. The Eleventh Circuit also failed to provide Section 704(a) protection to an EEO officer in *Hamm v. Members of Board of Regents of State of Florida* (708 F.2d 647 (11th Cir. 1983)). When the officer released reports to newspapers and files to employees, the court found that such a breach of duty was outside of the protection of Section 704(a). The court also found that the plaintiff's duties required obedience to management prerogatives, as opposed to discretionary conduct.

Need for a New Interpretation

A call has been made for all opposition activity by rank-and-file employees to be afforded unconditional 704(a) protection to prevent judicial abandonment of employees' anti-retaliation rights and to ensure that Title VII's protection is not totally undermined (Bales, 1994). However, this argument for reform has also provided for retaining the lack of 704(a) protection to managerial employees involved with EEO enforcement due to the precarious nature of their roles.

Management staff, particularly HR managers, have been clearly distinguished from rank-and-file employees by the courts, who have denied protection against employer retaliation. Because HR managers are an increasingly integral part of their organization's management teams, they obviously should be expected to comply with and enforce their employer's policy decisions. No employer should be forced to tolerate disruption, disloyalty, or insubordination from key players of its management team.

However, a critical problem remains in that the courts have placed the HR manager's responsibility to employers on a direct collision course with the intentions of Congress in eradicating many types of discrimination in employment. An HR manager who values his or her job and career may be forced to make a difficult choice when these two responsibilities collide. In fact, when this paper was presented at the 1998 International Society for the Advancement of Management Conference in Washington, DC, one individual in the audience described how she had been faced with this very dilemma as a senior HR manager with EEO responsibility. When asked how she handled it, she replied, "I was in a no-win situation and did the only thing I could do—I resigned," to audible gasps in the room. She further noted that resignations of senior HR officials for that reason were common and accepted within her professional network.

In the public sector, the issue becomes even more complex. First Amendment rights can be raised in connection with the government's action as an employer seeking to discharge or discipline an HR manager or any other employee. Employees' rights to be free from government restriction on speech involving matters of public concern would also need to be balanced (along with Title VII protection against retaliation) with the government employer's right to set management policy. The public employee's ultimate loyalty should be to the public, which places further strain on efforts to promote loyalty and strict obedience to agency leadership (Rosenbloom, 1998).

Summary

Clearly there is a need to reexamine the roles, rights, and responsibilities of the HR manager relative to Title VII. If the HR manager is expected to be the catalyst to promoting voluntary compliance, her or she needs to be able to be more of an intermediary and not just a "management employee whose job is to make claims go away." The dual roles of HR in attending to the needs and upholding the legal rights of employees while simultaneously looking out for the interests and needs of management involves a precarious balancing act. This is particularly true when the issues involve Title VII compliance.

As it stands, Title VII's anti-retaliation provision effectively prohibits the HR manager from any employee advocacy whatsoever, assuming that the HR manager values and wishes to retain his/her job. As a result, the burden is essentially imposed on individual employees to challenge management and file their own claims, further burdening the EEOC and court system. If the HR manager had a reasonably good faith belief that management practices or behavior were in violation of Title VII, anti-retaliation protection should not be denied, as it is not denied to rank-and-file employees. Without 704(a) anti-retaliation protection, the HR manager has little choice than to advocate management's point of view and totally abandon the employee advocacy role intended by Congress to be played by someone internal to the organization. Absent this protection, the EEOC is forced to assume this advocacy role, unleashing the floodgates of litigation on an agency and court system that are already overburdened and unable to respond to complaints in a timely manner, if at all. The end result is that employers are afforded the opportunity to ignore Title VII, at least in the short run, and frustrated employees, feeling that the system is unresponsive to their needs, are forced to live with and accept the various forms of discrimination in employment that Congress sought to eradicate under the Title VII. Moreover, the human resources function will be able to gain the trust and confidence of employees, deepening any chasms that might exist between employee groups and management.

As long as any opposition whatsoever by managerial employees, particularly HR/EEO managers, continues to be seen by the courts as disloyal and indefensible and outside of Section 704(a) protection, the interests and goals of Title VII will be undermined. Absent an act of Congress to amend Title VII and provide anti-retaliation protection for HR managers, HR/EEO managers must be afforded some alternative interpretation of their job duties and responsibilities by the courts that will allow the internal compliance function to operate effectively. Until HR/EEO managers can persuade the courts to adopt a different rule of law, the internal compliance ideal of Congress will remain just that, an ideal, and the provisions of law of Title VII will continue to be undermined and circumvented in the workplace.

Source: Society for the Advancement of Management Advanced Management Journal, 65, (1), 10–15, 51 (2000).

REFERENCES

Bales, R. (1994). A New Standard for Title VII Opposition Cases: Fitting the Personnel Manager Double Standard Into A Cognizable Framework. 35 *South Texas Law Review*, 95.

Bureau of National Affairs. National Enforcement Plan of the Equal Employment Opportunity Commission in *Employment Discrimination Report*, 6, 18 February, 1996.

Equal Employment Commission. *EEOC Annual Report: Fiscal Year 1994.*

Equal Employment Commission. *EEOC Annual Report: Fiscal Year 1997.*

Lawyers Committee for Civil Rights Under Law, *Civil Rights Act and EEO News*, 19, May, 1995.

Rosenbloom, D. (1998). *Public Administration.* New York: McGraw-Hill.

Shapiro, L. (1998). EEOC Backlog Reduced: Race Bias Charges Most Common. *California Employer Advisor*, 7, (10), 8.

Waltersceid, E. C. (1988). A Question of Retaliation: Opposition Conduct As Protected Expression Under Title VII of the Civil Rights Act of 1964. *Boston College Law Review*, 29.

READING 7.3

The Management of Organizational Justice

Russell Cropanzano, David E. Bowen and Stephen W. Gilliland

Executive Overview

Organizational justice has the potential to create powerful benefits for organizations and employees alike. These include greater trust and commitment, improved job performance, more helpful citizenship behaviors, improved customer satisfaction, and diminished conflict. We demonstrate the management of organizational justice with some suggestions for building fairness into widely used managerial activities. These include hiring, performance appraisal, reward systems, conflict management, and downsizing.

Justice, Sir, is the greatest interest of man on earth
—Daniel Webster

Business organizations are generally understood to be economic institutions. Sometimes implicitly, other times explicitly, this "rational" perspective has shaped the relationship that many employers have with their workforce (Ashforth & Humphrey, 1995). Many organizations, for example, emphasize the quid pro quo exchange of monetary payment for the performance of concrete tasks (Barley & Kunda, 1992). These tasks are often rationally described via job analysis and formally appraised by a supervisor. Hierarchical authority of this type is legitimized based upon the manager's special knowledge or expertise (Miller & O'Leary, 1989). Employee motivation is viewed as a quest for personal economic gain, so individual merit pay is presumed to be effective. Using the rational model, one can make a case for downsizing workers who are not contributing adequately to the "bottom line." And the rational model is found at the heart of the short-term uptick in the stock price of firms that carry out aggressive cost-cutting measures (Pfeffer, 1998).

Businesses certainly are economic institutions, but they are not *only* economic institutions. Indeed, adherence to this paradigm without consideration of other possibilities can have problematic side effects. Merit pay is sometimes ineffective (Pfeffer & Sutton, 2006), downsizing often has pernicious long-term effects (Pfeffer, 1998), and bureaucratic management can straitjacket workers and reduce innovation. We should attend to economic matters, but also to the sense of duty that goes beyond narrowly defined quid pro quo exchanges. It includes the ethical obligations that one party has to the other. Members may want a lot of benefits, but they also want something more. Organizational justice—members' sense of the moral propriety of how they are treated—is the "glue" that allows people to work together effectively. Justice defines the very essence of individuals' relationship to employers. In contrast, *in*justice is like a corrosive solvent that can dissolve bonds within the community. Injustice is hurtful to individuals and harmful to organizations.

In this paper we will discuss organizational justice, with an emphasis on how it can be brought to the workplace. We first define justice, paying careful attention to its three core dimensions: distributive, procedural, and interactional. We then examine why justice is important; we will consider various criterion variables that justice favorably influences. Once we understand the nature of justice we will be in a better position to describe how it can be brought about. The lesson here is that organizational justice actually has to be managed. This paper will provide specific techniques and recommendations for doing so.

What Is Organizational Justice?

Prescription vs. Description

Philosophers and social commentators were writing about justice long before management scientists were. Among the ancient Greeks, for example, Herodotus' *History* and Plutarch's *Lives* described the achievements of the lawgiver Solon, who reformed Athenian government. These are the *prescriptive* approaches, since they seek to logically determine what sorts of actions *truly are just*. As such, they reside comfortably within the domain of business ethics.

While organizational justice borrows from these older traditions, it has its own distinctions. Unlike the work of philosophers and attorneys, managerial scientists are less concerned with what *is* just and more concerned with what people *believe* to be just. In other words, these researchers are pursuing a *descriptive* agenda. They seek to understand why people view certain events as just, as well as the consequences that follow from these evaluations. In this regard, justice is a subjective and descriptive concept in that it captures what individuals believe to be right, rather than an objective reality or a prescriptive moral code. As defined here, organizational justice is a personal evaluation about the ethical and moral standing of managerial conduct. It follows from this approach that producing justice requires management to take the perspective of an employee. That is, they need to understand what sorts of events engender this subjective feeling of organizational justice. On this important competency, many fall short.

Why Employees Care About Justice

Managers too often assume that justice, in the minds of employees, means only that they receive desirable outcomes. These managers are confusing outcome *favorability* with outcome *justice*. The former is a judgment of personal worth or value; the latter is a judgment of moral propriety. Evidence shows that outcome justice and outcome favorability are distinct (Skitka, Winquist, & Hutchinson, 2003) and correlated between .19 and .49, depending on where and how the variables are measured (Cohen-Charash & Spector, 2001). In so many words, it's important to get what you want, but other things matter as well. For this reason it is useful to consider three reasons justice matters to people (for details, see Cropanzano, Rupp, Mohler, & Schminke, 2001).

Long-Range Benefits People often "sign on" for the long haul. Consequently, they need to estimate *now* how they are likely to be treated *over time*. A just organization makes this prediction easy. According to the "control model," employees prefer justice because it allows them to predict and control the outcomes they are likely to receive from organizations. According to the control model of justice, appropriate personnel policies signal that things are likely to work out eventually. Most of us understand that every personnel decision cannot go our way, but justice provides us with more certainty regarding our future benefits.

For this reason the control model proposes that people are often motivated by economic and quasi-economic interests (cf. Tyler & Smith, 1998). People want fairness because fairness provides things they like. There is more than a little truth to this idea. For instance, when individuals are rewarded for successfully completing a task they report being happy (Weiss, Suckow, & Cropanzano, 1999) and having pride in their performance (Krehbiel & Cropanzano, 2000). This is so even when their success resulted from cheating. At the same time, these individuals also report feeling guilty for their unfair behavior, suggesting that individuals can recognize and react to injustice, even when it is personally beneficial.

There is sometimes a certain tension between getting what we want and playing by the rules. The two tend to go together, but less so than many believe. For example, pay satisfaction is only modestly correlated with perceptions of pay justice (Williams, McDaniel, & Nguyen, 2006). If "justice" were based exclusively on obtaining benefits, then one would expect a higher association. Later we shall discuss evidence suggesting that individuals can accept an unfortunate outcome as long as the process is fair and they are treated with interpersonal dignity (e.g., Goldman, 2003; Skarlicki & Folger, 1997).

Social Considerations People are social animals. We wish to be accepted and valued by important others while not being exploited or harmed by powerful decision-makers. In the "group-value model," just treatment tells us that we are respected and esteemed by the larger group. We are also at less risk for mistreatment. This sense of belonging is important to us even apart from the economic benefits it can bring (Tyler & Blader, 2000; Tyler & Smith, 1998). As you might expect, this can pose a potential problem for organizations. To the extent that justice signals our value to an employer, the more we care about the organization the more distressed we become when we are treated unfairly. Brockner, Tyler, and Cooper-Schneider (1992) assessed the commitment of a group of employees before a layoff occurred. After the downsizing those people who were initially the *most* committed responded the *most* negatively to the downsizing. When we treat workers unfairly, we may end up doing the most harm to those who are most loyal.

Ethical Considerations People also care about justice because they believe it is the morally appropriate way others should be treated (Folger, 2001). When individuals witness an event they believe is ethically inappropriate, they are likely to take considerable risks in the hopes of extracting retribution (Bies & Tripp, 2001, 2002). Such unfortunate (from the organization's point of view) reactions may occur even when an employee simply witnesses the harm and is not personally wronged (Ellard & Skarlicki, 2002; Spencer & Rupp, 2006). Consider, for example, a day-to-day problem faced by many service workers. When these employees see a customer treating one of their coworkers unfairly, the observing worker is apt to experience stress symptoms. Through this mechanism, injustice may spread ill will throughout a workgroup.

Three Components of Justice

Research has shown that employees appraise three families of workplace events. They examine the justice of outcomes (distributive justice), the justice of the formal allocation processes (procedural justice), and the justice of interpersonal transactions they encounter with others (interactional justice). These are shown in Table 1.

Distributive, procedural, and interactional justice tend to be correlated. They can be meaningfully treated as three components of overall fairness (Ambrose & Arnaud, 2005; Ambrose & Schminke, 2007), and the three components can work together. However, if one's goal is to promote workplace justice, it is useful to consider them separately and in detail. This is because each component is engendered in distinct ways, arising from different managerial actions.

Distributive Justice

Researchers call the first component of justice *distributive justice* because it has to do with the allocations or outcomes that some get and others do not. Distributive justice is concerned with the reality that not all workers are treated alike; the allocation of outcomes is differentiated in the workplace. Individuals are concerned with whether or not they

Table 1 Components of Organizational Justice

1. Distributive Justice: Appropriateness of outcomes.
• Equity: Rewarding employees based on their contributions.
• Equality: Providing each employee roughly the same compensation.
• Need: Providing a benefit based on one's personal requirements.
2. Procedural Justice: Appropriateness of the allocation process.
• Consistency: All employees are treated the same.
• Lack of Bias: No person or group is singled out for discrimination or ill-treatment.
• Accuracy: Decisions are based on accurate information.
• Representation of All Concerned: Appropriate stakeholders have input into a decision.
• Correction: There is an appeals process or other mechanism for fixing mistakes.
• Ethics: Norms of professional conduct are not violated.
3. Interactional Justice: Appropriateness of the treatment one receives from authority figures.
• Interpersonal Justice: Treating an employee with dignity, courtesy, and respect.
• Informational Justice: Sharing relevant information with employees.

received their "just share." Sometimes things are distributively just, as when the most qualified person gets promoted. Other times they are not, as when advancement goes to corporate "insiders" with a political relationship to upper management.

Equity Theory Perhaps the earliest theory of distributive justice can be attributed to Aristotle. In his *Nicomachean Ethics*, the philosopher maintained that just distribution involved "something proportionate," which he defined as "equality of ratios." Specification, and a bit of rearrangement, led Adams (1965) to represent his influential equity theory of distributive justice with the following equation:

$$\frac{O_1}{I_1} = \frac{O_2}{I_2}$$

According to equity theory, we are interested in how much we get (outcomes or O_1) relative to how much we contribute (inputs or I_1). Such a ratio is meaningless, however, unless anchored against some standard. To accomplish this, we examine the outcomes (O_2) and inputs (I_2) of some referent. Usually, though not necessarily, this is another person who is similar to us. Things are "equitable" when the ratios, not the individual terms, are in agreement. When the ratios are out of alignment, employees may feel uneasy. They are motivated to "balance" the equation by modifying the terms. For example, one who is underpaid might reduce inputs by a corresponding amount.

This simple equation leads to a number of predictions, some of which are not obvious. For example, an individual who earns less than another may still be satisfied, as long as he or she also contributes less. Likewise, a person who is paid equally to another may feel unjustly treated if he or she also contributes substantially more to the organization. These consequences often do not occur to managers, but they make good sense in light of equity theory. But by far the most famous prediction from equity theory is the "over-reward effect"—that is, what happens when the equation is unbalanced in one's own favor.

According to equity theory, when one is *overpaid* the two sides of the ratios are misaligned. Consequently, one must work harder (i.e., increase inputs) in order to be equitable. These effects seem to occur. Greenberg (1988) studied managers who were temporarily moved to higher- or lower-status offices than their position actually warranted. Those moved to higher-status offices boosted performance, whereas those moved to lower-status offices showed decrements. These gains and losses later disappeared when individuals were returned to status-appropriate office spaces. Apart from its impact on performance, inequity can also cause workplace sabotage (Ambrose, Seabright, & Schminke, 2002) and employee theft (Greenberg, 1993). It is personally painful for employees, as distributive injustice is associated with stress symptoms (Cropanzano, Goldman, & Benson, 2005).

Recent Advances in Distributive Justice As Table 1 makes clear, there is more to distributive justice than simple equity. These different standards can be in conflict with one another. Generally speaking, we can distinguish three allocation rules that can lead to distributive justice if they are applied appropriately: equality (to each the same), equity (to each in accordance with contributions), and need (to each in accordance with the most urgency). These rules map onto Aristotle's famous dictum that all men wish to be treated like all other people (equality), like some other people (equality), and like no other person (need). While it is no mean task to find the correct alchemistic combination among these three allocation rules, there are three basic suggestions that can be helpful.

First, it is useful to consider one's strategic goals (Colquitt, Greenberg, & Zapata-Phelan, 2005). Equity tends to provide individual rewards for high performance, whereas equality tends to build esprit de corps among teammates. If one desires to stimulate individual motivation, err toward equity. If one desires to build group cohesion, err toward equality. We shall return to this issue later when we discuss reward systems.

Second, organizations can balance these considerations by mixing equality and equity together. It need not be either-or. Experiments with work groups suggest that it is often best to provide team members with a basic minimum of benefit. This is analogous to equality. Above that minimum, however, it can be useful to reward based on performance. This is analogous to equity. This sort of hybrid approach has been adopted by many organizations. Their compensation systems contain a "fixed" base; everyone in a particular job class and with a particular tenure receives this base. Employees are also encouraged to go beyond this minimum, earning additional pay through the allocation of merit bonuses (Milkovich & Newman, 2005, see especially Chapters 9 and 10).

Third, different rewards should be provided in accordance with different rules. Equity works well for some things, such as money, but less well for others, such as status symbols. Among American managers, it is often seen as fair to allocate economic benefits in accordance with equity (i.e., those who perform better might earn more). On the other hand, social-emotional benefits, such as reserved parking places, are best allocated equally (Martin & Harder, 1994). Employees often see themselves and their peers as belonging to a group or, in the most beneficial case, a community. Allocating social-emotional rewards equally signals that everyone in the organization matters and is worthy of respect.

Procedural Justice

Procedural justice refers to the means by which outcomes are allocated, but not specifically to the outcomes themselves. Procedural justice establishes certain principles specifying and governing the roles of participants within the decision-making processes. In three papers, Leventhal and his colleagues (Leventhal, 1976, 1980; Leventhal, Karuza, & Fry, 1980) established some core attributes that make procedures just; these are displayed in Table 1. A just process is one that is applied consistently to all, free of bias, accurate, representative of relevant stakeholders, correctable, and consistent with ethical norms. Though surprising to some, research has shown that just procedures can mitigate the ill effects of unfavorable outcomes. Researchers have named this the "fair process effect."

To illustrate let us consider the case of strategic planning. Kim and Mauborgne (1991, 1993) reported that when managers believed that their headquarters used a fair planning process, they were more supportive of the plan, trusted their leaders more, and were more committed to their employers. In their well-known book, *Blue Ocean Strategy*, Kim and Mauborgne (2005) explain why. Fair processes lead to intellectual and emotional recognition. This, in turn, creates the trust and commitment that build voluntary cooperation in strategy execution. Procedural injustice, on the other hand, produces "intellectual and emotional indignation," resulting in "distrust and resentment" (p. 183). Ultimately, this reduces cooperation in strategy execution.

We can go further. Procedural justice seems to be essential to maintaining institutional legitimacy. When personnel decisions are made, individuals are likely to receive certain outcomes. For instance, one may or may not be promoted. According to Tyler and Blader (2000), outcome favorability tends to affect satisfaction with the particular decision. This is not surprising. What is more interesting is that procedural justice affects what workers believe about the organization as a whole. If the process is perceived as just, employees show greater loyalty and more willingness to behave in an organization's best interests. They are also less likely to betray the institution and its leaders.

Interactional Justice

In a sense, *interactional justice* may be the simplest of the three components. It refers to how one person treats another. A person is interactionally just if he or she appropriately shares information and avoids rude or cruel remarks. In other words, there are two aspects of interactional justice (Colquitt, Conlon, Wesson, Porter, & Ng, 2001). The first part, sometimes called *informational justice* refers to whether one is truthful and provides adequate justifications when things go badly. The second part, sometimes called *interpersonal justice,* refers to the respect and dignity with which one treats another. As shown in Table 1, both are important.

Because interactional justice emphasizes one-on-one transactions, employees often seek it from their supervisors. This presents an opportunity for organizations. In a quasi-experimental study, Skarlicki and Latham (1996) trained union leaders to behave more justly. Among other things, these leaders were taught to provide explanations and apologies (informational justice) and to treat their reports with courtesy and respect (interpersonal justice). When work groups were examined three months later, individuals who reported to trained leaders exhibited more helpful citizenship behaviors than individuals who reported to untrained leaders.

Working Together: The Three Components of Justice Interact

Maintaining the three components of justice simultaneously is a worthwhile task, but it may also seem daunting. Fortunately, there is good news. Evidence suggests that the three components of justice interact (Cropanzano, Slaughter, & Bachiochi, 2005; Skarlicki & Folger, 1997). Though this interaction can be described in different ways, the key point is this: The ill effects of injustice can be at least partially mitigated if at least one component of justice is maintained. For example, a distributive and a procedural injustice will have fewer negative effects if interactional justice is high.

To understand this phenomenon one can look at a study by Goldman (2003). Goldman studied the relationship between justice and filing legal claims for alleged workplace discrimination. He found that claimants were most likely to purse litigation when distributive, procedural, and interactional justice were all low. If just one component of justice was judged to be high, the likelihood of a legal claim dropped. This is good news, because it suggests that organizations have three bites at the apple. If they can get at least one component of justice right, some important benefits should result. We will consider the beneficial consequences of justice in our next section.

The Impact of Organizational Justice

Over the past few decades a considerable body of research has investigated the consequences of just and unjust treatment by work organizations. This literature has been summarized in three different meta-analytic reviews (Cohen-Charash & Spector, 2001; Colquitt et al., 2001; Viswesvaran & Ones, 2002). While these quantitative reviews differ in some specifics, they all underscore the propitious effects of workplace justice. We will look at each of the findings individually.

Justice Builds Trust and Commitment

Trust is a willingness to become vulnerable with respect to another party. As one might expect given our comments so far, Colquitt and his colleagues (2001) found that all three components of justice (distributive, procedural, and interactional) predict trust. These relationships can be quite strong. For example, the association between perceptions of just procedures and trust can be as high as .60. In a like fashion, justly treated employees are also more committed to their employers. Findings again vary somewhat with how justice is measured, but the correlation of perceived justice and affective commitment can range between .37 and .43 (Cohen-Charash & Spector, 2001).

Justice Improves Job Performance

As is true for other scholars, we use the term "job performance" to refer to formal job duties, assigned by organizational authorities and evaluated during performance appraisals (for a similar discussion, see Organ, 1988). Workplace justice predicts the effectiveness with which workers discharge their job duties (Colquitt et al., 2001), though more so in field settings and less so in the undergraduate laboratory (Cohen-Charash & Spector, 2001). As Lerner (2003) observed, justice effects are often strongest in real life. In part, this is because, over time, fairness leads to strong interpersonal relationships. In two studies, Cropanzano, Prehar, and Chen (2002) and Rupp and Cropanzano (2002) examined whether supervisors treated their reports with interactional justice. When they did, the leader and the subordinate had a higher-quality relationship. This strong relationship, in turn, motivated employees to higher job performance. Supervisors worried that just pay and process are expensive and time-consuming might take heart. These costs may be partially defrayed by higher productivity.

Justice Fosters Employee Organizational Citizenship Behaviors

Organizational citizenship behaviors (OCBs) are employee behaviors that go beyond the call of duty (Organ, 1988). Several studies have found that justly treated employees are more likely to comply with workplace policies, show extra conscientiousness, and behave altruistically toward others (Cohen-Charash & Spector, 2001). Indeed, workers tend to tailor their citizenship behaviors carefully, doling them out to those groups or individuals who have treated them justly and withholding them from those who have not.

To illustrate this point, consider the case of temporary employees. A contingent worker is likely to be associated with two different organizations—the temporary agency and the organization that contracts with it. In an interesting study, Liden, Wayne, Kraimer, and Sparrowe (2003) surveyed contingent workers who were assigned to a Fortune 500 manufacturing firm. Liden and his colleagues discovered that citizenship behaviors toward this manufacturing organization were influenced by the procedural fairness with which the manufacturing company treated the workers. Contingent employees who received just processes from the contracting organization (the manufacturing firm) performed more OCBs. However, the procedural justice these workers received from the employment agency did nothing to boost citizenship behaviors toward the manufacturing firm. In other words, individuals repaid procedural justice with hard work, but they reciprocated only to the organization that treated them justly in the first place. The manufacturing firm did not benefit from the temporary agency's efforts at procedural justice. If you want justice to work to your benefit, you have to do it yourself.

Justice Builds Customer Satisfaction and Loyalty

Justice-inspired employee OCBs, such as behaving altruistically toward others, sound much like employee customer service–oriented behaviors, such as helping others and listening carefully to their needs. Building on this, Bowen, Gilliland and Folger (1999) suggested that just treatment of employees would lead to OCBs that "spill over" to customers. This "just play" results in customers feeling appropriately treated, thereby yielding customer satisfaction and loyalty. These types of internal-external relationships have been empirically validated by such scholars as Masterson (2001) and Maxham and Netemyer (2003). For example, Masterson (2001) asked a large group of university instructors how they were being treated. When teachers felt that they received distributive and procedural justice they tended to report higher organizational commitment. This commitment, in turn, improved student responses toward the instructor. Since small gains in customer loyalty can translate into much larger gains in profitability (e.g., Heskett, Sasser, & Schlesinger, 1997; Smith, Bolton, & Wagner, 1999), these are very potent effects.

Thoughts Before Moving On

More broadly, we suggest that justice can be a core value that defines an organization's identity with its stakeholders, both internally and externally. When justice is espoused as a core value of an organization's management philosophy and enacted through a set of internally consistent management

Table 2 Building Justice Into Management Systems

1. Positive Job Candidates: The Justice Paradox in Selection Procedures.
2. Justly Balancing Multiple Goals: The Two-Factor Model in Just Reward Systems
3. You Don't Have to Win: How the Process by Outcome Interaction Helps Us Resolve Conflicts
4. Softening Hardship: The Fair Process Effect in Layoffs
5. Keeping Score Fairly: A Due Process Approach to Performance Appraisal.

practices, it can build a "culture of justice," a system-wide commitment that is valuable and unique in the eyes of employees and customers, and tough to copy in the minds of competitors. And that can translate into the makings of sustainable competitive advantage. In our next section, we will look at management practices that can help develop a culture of justice.

How to Create Perceptions of Justice

We will now turn to common and important workplace situations, discussing a variety of managerial and personnel functions. These are displayed in Table 2. In each case, we will provide a lesson for promoting justice, including some normative recommendations regarding how individuals should be treated. And in each case we will return to one or more of our conceptual observations, such as the fair process effect and the two-factor model, illustrating how these phenomena affect real-life organizations.

Selection Procedures: Positive Job Candidates

For most job candidates, the recruiting and selection process is their first introduction to an organization. How they are treated at this time can have ramifications later. Applicants who feel justly treated are more likely to form positive impressions of the organization (Bauer et al., 2001) and recommend it to their friends (Smither, Reilly, Millsap, Pearlman, & Stoffey, 1993). And the flip side is also true. When applicants feel unjustly treated they are more likely to consider litigation as a potential remedy (Bauer et al., 2001). This research suggests that it pays for organizations to put their best foot forward. By treating applicants justly in the hiring process, organizations are setting the foundation for a relationship of justice and trust when those applicants become employees.

The research on job candidates' reactions to recruiting and hiring processes suggests that it is about much more than whether or not someone gets the job. Further, because applicants don't often know why they didn't get the job or the qualifications of the person who did, distributive justice is less of a concern in selection. However, managers do need to be mindful of procedural and interactional justice. It is also important to realize that the selection process begins with recruiting and initial communication, and encompasses all contact with job candidates up to and including extending an offer and rejecting an individual for a job (Gilliland & Hale, 2005). In terms of procedural justice, research has identified two broad sets of concerns:

- *Appropriate questions and criteria* are critical for procedural justice. Job candidates expect interview questions and screening tests to be related to the job, or at least to appear to be related to the job (Gilliland, 1994; Ryan & Chan, 1999). Overly personal interview questions and some screening tests, such as honesty tests, are often seen as inappropriate and an invasion of candidates' privacy (Bies & Moag, 1986; Kravitz, Stinson, & Chavez, 1996).
- *Adequate opportunity to perform* during the selection process means giving job candidates the chances to make a case for themselves and allowing sufficient time in interviews (Truxillo, Bauer, & Sanchez, 2001). If standardized tests are used to screen applicants, justice can be enhanced by allowing candidates to retest if they feel they did not perform their best (Truxillo et al., 2001).

On the face, these two criteria seem reasonable and pretty straightforward. However, when compared with recommended hiring practices, managers are often faced with a "justice paradox" (Folger & Cropanzano, 1998). That is, many of the selection procedures with the highest predictive validity—those that are the best screening tools—are unfortunately those that fail to satisfy these justice concerns. Consider cognitive ability and personality tests. These screening methods have high demonstrated validity (Schmidt & Hunter, 1998), but both are seen by job applicants as not particularly fair (Steiner & Gilliland, 1996). Questions on these tests are often not related to the job, and applicants don't feel they have an opportunity to present their true abilities. The converse is also observed with the justice paradox. Traditional unstructured interviews have long demonstrated weak predictive validity, not much better than chance (Huffcutt & Arthur, 1994). However, job applicants perceive these interviews as having high procedural justice because they are able to demonstrate their qualifications (Latham & Finnegan, 1993). Adding structured situations and questions to the interview increases predictive validity, but decreases perceptions of procedural justice.

So how can this justice paradox be managed effectively? We have three suggestions. First, there are some screening tools that have both predictive validity and procedural justice. Work sample tests and performance-based simulations demonstrate reasonable predictive validity (Roth, Bobko, & McFarland, 2005) and are also seen as procedurally just (Steiner & Gilliland, 1996). A second solution is to modify existing screening tools to increase job applicants' perceived procedural justice. Smither and colleagues (1993) found that cognitive ability tests with concrete, rather than abstract, items tended to be viewed more positively by job applicants. Based on the observation that applicants perceive greater justice in unstructured interviews, Gilliland and Steiner (1999) suggest a combined interview that has both structured behavioral questions to maximize predictive validity and unstructured questions to allow applicants the "opportunity to perform."

The third suggestion is based on our earlier discussion of interactional justice. Recall that interactional justice can attenuate the negative effects of procedural injustice. Research has demonstrated that interactional justice is very important for job candidates (Bies & Moag, 1986; Gilliland, 1995). With attention to considerate interpersonal treatment, honest information, and timely feedback, organizations can create hiring processes that embody interactional justice. Research has demonstrated that the informational components are particularly important if there are unanticipated delays or unusual screening procedures involved in the process (Rynes, Bretz, & Gerhart, 1991).

Reward Systems: Justly Balancing Multiple Goals

At the most basic level, rewards systems need to accomplish two goals: They need to motivate individual performance, and they need to maintain group cohesion. While both goals are worthwhile, distributive justice research tells us that it is difficult to accomplish them simultaneously. Equity allocations, which reward for performance, can spur individual effort. But the resulting inequality that is likely to occur can be disruptive. In a study of academic faculty, Pfeffer and Langton (1993) examined wage dispersion in their home departments. When wage dispersion was high, faculty reported less satisfaction and less collaboration with colleagues. Overall research productivity dropped as well. This is not what merit pay is supposed to do.

Paying everyone the same thing, though, is not the answer either. Indeed, equality distributions can boost group harmony, but they bring troubles of their own. A key problem is one of external equity. High-performing employees, or those with rare skills, may be worth more in the external marketplace. If their salaries are "capped" to maintain internal equality, these workers may seek employment elsewhere. This is just another way of saying that no matter how people are paid, not everyone will be satisfied.

How then to position rewards? The research discussed earlier underscores an opportunity. To be sure, individuals who do not receive the compensation they desire will want more. However, they often remain loyal to their employer if the pay administration procedures are viewed as fair. Consequently, if an organization needs to maintain external equity, it can do so and risk internal inequality, but only as long as the allocation process is just. To illustrate, McFarlin and Sweeney (1992) surveyed more than 600 banking employees. As expected, when distributive justice was low, workers reported less pay satisfaction and less job satisfaction. This is bad news, but it is partially compensated for by the procedural justice results. When procedural justice was high, workers experienced higher organizational commitment and a positive reaction to their supervisors. This is the two-factor model in action. Individuals who were not necessarily satisfied with their pay were still unlikely to derogate the organization when the procedures were just.

In addition to procedural justice, interactional justice can be helpful in administering pay fairly. To illustrate this point, let us consider a situation that everyone dislikes: pay cuts. Greenberg (1993) found that differences in how pay cuts were managed at two manufacturing plants produced dramatically different outcomes. The key is interpersonal treatment. In one, an executive politely, but quickly in about 15 minutes, announced a 15% pay cut. In the other, an executive spent about an hour and a half speaking, taking questions, and expressing regrets about making an identical pay cut. During a subsequent 10-week period, employee theft was about 80% lower in the second case, and employees in that plant were 15 times less likely to resign. No one wanted to have his or her pay cut. But workers understood why it happened, appreciated the supportive interpersonal treatment, and did not vent their ire on the organization.

Conflict Management: You Don't Have to Win

Thomas and Schmidt (1976) tell us that managers may spend about 20% of their time settling disputes among employees, and they are not always successful (Schoorman & Champagne, 1994). Conflict resolution is likely to be most difficult when one or both parties is intransigent. At this point the manager may listen to both disputants, but will need to impose a settlement on them. This is called arbitration, and it is ultimately autocratic. As a result, arbitration may sound risky because it hazards a distributive injustice; the settlement is imposed and not approved in advance by other parties.

There is good news, however. If *any* component of justice is present during arbitration (distributive or procedural or interactional), the overall appraisal of the situation will be improved (Goldman, 2003). Because arbitration preserves procedural justice, an unfortunate outcome is less destructive than one might imagine. Or, we might say, managers can make hard choices, but they have to make them justly (for details see Folger & Cropanzano, 1998). This illustrates a simple yet powerful lesson from research on conflict resolution: If you can't give people the outcome they want, at least give them a fair process.

Layoffs: Softening Hardship

So far we have reviewed evidence pertaining to justice in the context of hiring, reward systems, and conflict resolution. These are everyday events in a large organization, and each will function more effectively if justice is taken into account. Even a reader willing to indulge our arguments so far might be wondering whether justice helps when something really bad happens.

Among common management situations that affect employees, downsizing is among the worst (Richman, 1993).

Layoffs have pernicious effects, harming the victims while undermining the morale of survivors who remain employed. Though downsizing is a widely used cost-cutting strategy, it is highly risky. The costs of workforce reductions often outweigh the benefits (Kammeyer-Mueller, Liao, & Arvey, 2001). In these circumstances people not only lose, they lose big. The event can be so negative that a sense of distributive injustice is virtually a given. Can the guidelines suggested in this paper do any good at all?

As a matter of fact, they can. When a layoff is handled with procedural and interactional justice, victims are less likely to derogate their former employers (Brockner et al., 1994, Study 1). Indeed, justice can have direct bottom-line effects. Lind, Greenberg, Scott, and Welchans (2000) interviewed a large number of layoff victims. Many of these individuals considered legal action following their downsizing, and almost a quarter of the victims went so far as to speak to an attorney. The single best predictor of willingness to take legal action was the justice of the treatment they received at the time of their discharge. Among those who felt unjustly treated, Lind and his colleagues found that a full 66% contemplated litigation. Among those who felt justly treated, this dropped to just 16%. These are impressive findings. Although managers are often coached by attorneys or HR representatives to avoid apologizing—an apology can be seen as an admission of guilt—these results suggest that an apology may help promote the feelings of interactional justice that actually reduce the risk of litigation. Justice, it would seem, provides a useful way to survive a crisis with one's business reputation intact.

While we have so far discussed the victims of layoffs, workforce reductions also affect survivors. Those left behind, though retaining their jobs, tend to suffer from "survivor guilt" (Brockner & Greenberg, 1990). However, if organizations provide a good explanation as to why the downsizing is necessary—an aspect of interactional justice—the remaining employees respond much less negatively (Brockner, DeWitt, Grover, & Reed, 1990). Providing unemployment benefits is also advantageous, as one might expect. However, if these benefits are lacking, an advance warning that a layoff is about to occur will blunt the negative reactions that might otherwise transpire (Brockner et al., 1994, Studies 2 and 3).

Performance Appraisals: Keeping Score Fairly

In order to assign rewards, identify candidates for promotion, and develop human capital, most large organizations conduct performance evaluations. While these appraisals are useful, concerns remain, and their implementation is often troubled. For example, scholars have observed a phenomenon called the "vanishing performance appraisal" (for a review, see Folger & Cropanzano, 1998). When surveyed, most managers reported having provided performance reviews, while many of their subordinates reported never receiving one. Other research suggests that evaluations are affected by political considerations (Longenecker, Gioia, & Sims, 1987), cognitive processing limitations of the rater (DeNisi & Williams, 1988), and the social context in which they are conducted (Levy & Williams, 2004). These concerns tell us that the performance appraisal process often contains a good deal of ambiguity as well as room for reasonable people to disagree.

For this reason, it is helpful to approach performance evaluations with an eye to their subjectivity. Historically, much of the advice academics provided to practitioners encouraged them to think of the performance review as a sort of test, whereby the central task is to assign a valid rating to a more-or-less objective quantity. For example, raters have been advised to "become expert at applying principles of test development" (Banks & Roberson, 1985, p. 129) and that "psychometric issues surrounding performance measurement [are] more relevant than ever" (DeVries, Morrison, Shullman, & Gerlach, 1981). This venerable, measurement-oriented understanding of performance appraisal has been termed the "test metaphor" (Folger, Konovsky, & Cropanzano, 1992).

More recent performance appraisal work has taken a broader perspective, emphasizing the social setting (Levy & Williams, 2004) and input from multiple sources (Smither, London, & Reilly, 2005). In this vein, Cawley, Keeping, and Levy (1998) meta-analyzed 27 field studies, each of which examined employee participation in performance appraisal. They found that when employees had a voice they were more satisfied, saw the process as more fair, and were more motivated to do better. This is interesting, but probably not terribly surprising. The really impressive finding was that these effects occurred even when participation could not affect the rating. Simply being able to speak one's mind (what Cawley and coauthors termed "value-expressive" participation) caused employees to be more favorable toward the performance appraisal system. Notice how these findings are consistent with the fair process effect mentioned earlier.

Research on organizational justice is providing a new paradigm for understanding performance review. Consistent with Folger, Konovsky, and Cropanzano (1992), we call this the due process approach to performance appraisal. Adopting a due process metaphor sensitizes one to the distinct interpretations, potential conflicts of interest, and legitimate disagreement about facts. The due process approach to performance review has three core elements: adequate notice, just hearing, and judgment based on evidence.

- *Adequate notice*, as one might expect, involves letting people know in advance when they will be appraised and on what criteria they will be appraised. However, from a justice point of view, it goes beyond this. It is also useful to have workers involved in devising performance standards and making these widely available. Of course, it follows that feedback should be provided regularly.
- *Just hearing* means limiting the feedback review to "admissible" evidence, such as worker performance rather than personal attacks. It also means providing workers

with a chance to provide their own interpretation of events, including disagreeing with the supervisor where this is appropriate.

- *Judgment based on evidence* means that the standards should be accurate, data should be gathered, and decisions should be based on this formal process. Steps should be taken to provide rater training, so as to improve accuracy and to keep the process free of political influence.

Taylor, Tracy, Renard, Harrison, and Carroll (1995) redesigned the performance appraisal system of a large state agency so that it included these principles of due process. They discovered that workers preferred the new system, finding it fairer and more effective. Managers liked it as well, believing that it allowed them to be honest and feeling that it was more effective for solving work problems. This occurred even though workers in the due process system received *lower* ratings than did workers under the older approach.

This is all to the good, but there are risks involved. Adequate notice, just hearing, and judgment based on evidence are complicated to administer. A key problem is that they may raise expectations while simultaneously providing employees with a set of tools for making their discontent felt. Consider the case of two companies studied over six years by Mesch and Dalton (1992). Each firm was in the same region, and workers in each were represented by the same union. In fact, grievances at both organizations were assigned to the same union local. After 36 months, one of the firms decided to improve its grievance process by adding a fact-finding intervention. Before the grievance process began, both the union and management provided a "fact finder" to determine the merits of the case, prevent concealment of information, and encourage negotiated settlements. This provided an additional stage of process protection. The result? The number of grievances filed skyrocketed at the firm with the new procedural safeguard, but stayed roughly constant at the other organization. After about two years, the fact-finding intervention was abandoned, and the grievance rate returned to normal. The new intervention seems to have raised expectations and thereby encouraged workers to complain about real and imagined ill-treatment. In the long run this was counterproductive. The implications of Mesch and Dalton's (1992) study need to be appreciated. If procedures are not designed appropriately, they could create more problems than they solve.

Concluding Thoughts

There are two sides to the justice coin. On the negative side, the absence of justice is likely to provide problems for organizations. There is strong evidence that injustice can provoke retaliation, lower performance, and harm morale (Cohen-Charash & Spector, 2001; Colquitt et al., 2001; Viswesvaran & Ones, 2002). On the positive side, justice can do more than forestall these unfortunate outcomes. Justice acts as a sort of buffer, allowing employees to maintain respect and trust for an organization even when things do not go as they would have liked (Brockner & Wiesenfeld, 1996). It is inevitable in life that things will not always go our way. However, the negative effects of an unfortunate event are less severe if an organization is able to maintain procedural and interactional justice (Goldman, 2003; Skarlicki & Folger, 1997).

Justice provides an excellent business opportunity, from reaping specific returns such as stronger employee commitment to gaining an overall tough-to-copy competitive edge that resides in a "culture of justice." In this paper we have examined justice from the perspective of five managerial tasks: hiring, reward systems, conflict management, layoffs, and performance appraisals. These tasks are diverse, but they all involve a degree of risk. Each has the potential to designate some as "winners" and others as "losers." After all, there will always be people who fail to get the job, receive a lower than expected performance appraisal, or are downsized in the face of business exigencies. As a result, organizations hazard the ill will of employees simply because they are making the sorts of decisions necessary to run their businesses. Organizational justice allows managers to make these tough decisions more smoothly. Just play certainly does not guarantee all parties what they want. However, it does hold out the possibility that power will be used in accordance with normative principles that respect the dignity of all involved. This is sound business advice. *It is also the right thing to do.*

Source: Academy of Management Perspectives, 21, (4), 34–48 (2007). Reprinted by permission of the Copyright Clearance Center.

REFERENCES

Adams, J. S. (1965). Inequity in social exchange. In L. Berkowitz (Ed.), *Advances in experimental social psychology* (Vol. 2, pp. 267–299). New York: Academic Press.

Ambrose, M. L., & Arnaud, A. (2005). Are procedural justice and distributive justice conceptually distinct? In J. A. Colquitt & J. Greenberg (Eds.), *Handbook of organizational justice* (pp. 85–112). Mahwah, NJ: Lawrence Erlbaum Associates.

Ambrose, M. L., & Schminke, M. (2007). Examining justice climate: Issues of fit, simplicity, and content. In F. Dansereau & F. J. Yammarino (Eds.), *Research in multilevel issues* (Vol. 6, pp. 397–413). Oxford, England: Elsevier.

Ambrose, M. L., Seabright, M. A., & Schminke, M. (2002). Sabotage in the workplace: The role of organizational injustice. *Organizational Behavior and Human Decision Processes*, *89*, 947–965.

Ashforth, B. E., & Humphrey, R. H. (1995). Emotion in the workplace: A reappraisal. *Human Relations*, *48*, 97–125.

Banks, C. G., & Roberson, L. (1985). Performance appraisers as test developers. *Academy of Management Review*, *10*, 128–142.

Barley, S. R., & Kunda, G. (1992). Design and devotion: Surges of rational and normative ideologies of control in managerial discourse. *Administrative Science Quarterly*, *37*, 363–399.

Bauer, T. N., Truxillo, D. M., Sanchez, R. J., Craig, J., Ferrara, P., & Campion, M. A. (2001). Applicant reactions to selection: Development of the selection procedural justice scale (SPJS). *Personnel Psychology*, *54*, 387–419.

Bies, R. J., & Moag, J. S. (1986). Interactional justice: Communication criteria for justice. In B. Sheppard (Ed.), *Research on negotiation in organizations* (Vol. 1, pp. 43–55). Greenwich, CT: JAI Press.

Bies, R. J., & Tripp, T. M. (2001). A passion for justice: The rationality and morality of revenge. In R. Cropanzano (Ed.), *Justice in the workplace* (pp. 197–208). Mahwah, NJ: Lawrence Erlbaum Associates.

Bies, R. J., & Tripp, T. M. (2002). "Hot flashes, open wounds": Injustice and the tyranny of its emotions. In S. W. Gilliland, D. D. Steiner, & D. P. Skarlicki (Eds.), *Emerging perspectives on managing organizational justice* (pp. 203–221). Greenwich, CT: Information Age Publishing.

Bowen, D. E., Gilliland, S. W., & Folger, R. (1999). HRM and service justice: How being just with employees spills over to customers. *Organizational Dynamics*, ***27***, 7–23.

Brockner, J., DeWitt, R. L., Grover, S., & Reed, T. (1990) When it is especially important to explain why: Factors affecting the relationship between managers' explanations of a layoff and survivors' reactions to the layoff. *Journal of Experimental Social Psychology*, ***26***, 389–407.

Brockner, J., & Greenberg, J. (1990) The impact of layoffs on survivors: An organizational justice perspective. In J. S. Carroll (Ed.), *Applied social psychology and organizational settings* (pp. 45–75). Hillsdale, NJ: Erlbaum.

Brockner, J., Konovsky, M., Cooper-Schneider, R., Folger, R., Martin, C., & Bies, R. J. (1994). Interactive effects of procedural justice and outcome negativity on victims and survivors of job loss. *Academy of Management Journal*, ***37***, 397–409.

Brockner, J., Tyler, T. R., & Cooper-Schneider, R. (1992). The influence of prior commitment to an institution on reactions to perceived unfairness: The higher they are, the harder they fall. *Administrative Science Quarterly*, ***37***, 241–261.

Brockner, J., & Wiesenfeld, B. M. (1996). An integrative framework for explaining attractiveness of decisions: The interactive effects of outcomes and processes. *Psychological Bulletin*, ***120***, 189–208.

Cawley, B. D., Keeping, L. M., & Levy, P. E. (1998). Participation in the performance appraisal process and employee reactions: A meta-analytic review of field investigations. *Journal of Applied Psychology*, ***83***, 615–633.

Cohen-Charash, Y., & Spector, P. E. (2001). The role of justice in organizations: A meta-analysis. *Organizational Behavior and Human Decision Processes*, 86, 278–321.

Colquitt, J. A., Conlon, D. E., Wesson, M. J., Porter, C. O. L. H., & Ng, K. Y. (2001). Justice at the millennium: A meta-analytic review of 25 years of organizational justice research. *Journal of Applied Psychology*, ***86***, 425–445.

Colquitt, J. A., Greenberg, J., & Zapata-Phelan, C. P. (2005). What is organizational justice? A historical overview. In J. Greenberg & J. A. Colquitt (Eds.), *Handbook of organizational justice* (pp. 3–56). Mahwah, NJ: Lawrence Erlbaum Associates.

Cropanzano, R., Goldman, B., & Benson, L., III. (2005). Organizational justice. In J. Barling, K. Kelloway, & M. Frone (Eds.), *Handbook of work stress* (pp. 63–87). Beverly Hills, CA: Sage.

Cropanzano, R., Prehar, C. A., & Chen, P. Y. (2002). Using social exchange theory to distinguish procedural from interactional justice. *Group and Organizational Management*, ***27***, 324–351.

Cropanzano, R., Rupp, D. E., Mohler, C. J., & Schminke, M. (2001). Three roads to organizational justice. In J. Ferris (Ed.), *Research in personnel and human resources management* (Vol. 20, pp. 1–113). Greenwich, CT: JAI Press.

Cropanzano, R., Slaughter, J. E., & Bachiochi, P. D. (2005). Organizational justice and black applicants' reactions to affirmative action. *Journal of Applied Psychology*, ***90***, 1168–1184.

DeNisi, A. S., & Williams, K. J. (1988). Cognitive research in performance appraisal. In K. Rowland & G. S. Ferris (Eds.), *Research in personnel and human resources management* (Vol. 6, pp. 109–156). Greenwich, CT: JAI Press.

DeVries, D. L., Morrison, A. M., Shullman, S. L., & Gerlach, M. L. (1981). *Performance appraisal on the line*. New York: Wiley.

Ellard, J. H., & Skarlicki, D. P. (2002). A third-party observer's reactions to employee mistreatment: Motivational and cognitive processes in deservingness assessments. In S. W. Gilliland, D. D. Steiner, & D. P. Skarlicki (Eds.), *Emerging perspectives on managing organizational justice* (pp. 133–158). Greenwich, CT: Information Age Publishing.

Folger, R. (2001). Justice as deonance. In S. W. Gilliland, D. D. Steiner, & D. P. Skarlicki (Eds.), *Research in social issues in management* (Vol. 1, pp. 3–33). New York: Information Age Publishing.

Folger, R., & Cropanzano, R. (1998). *Organizational justice and human resource management*. Beverly Hills, CA: Sage.

Folger, R., Konovsky, M. A., & Cropanzano, R. (1992). A due process metaphor for performance appraisal. In B. M. Staw & L. L. Cummings (Eds.), *Research in organizational behavior* (Vol. 14, pp. 129–177). Greenwich, CT: JAI Press.

Gilliland, S. W. (1994). Effects of procedural and distributive justice on reactions to a selection system. *Journal of Applied Psychology*, ***79***, 691–701.

Gilliland, S. W. (1995). Justice from the applicant's perspective: Reactions to employee selection procedures. *International Journal of Selection and Assessment*, ***3***, 11–19.

Gilliland, S. W., & Hale, J. (2005). How do theories of organizational justice inform just employee selection practices? In J. Greenberg & J. A. Colquitt (Eds.), *Handbook of organizational justice: Fundamental questions about justice in the workplace* (pp. 411–438). Mahwah, NJ: Erlbaum.

Gilliland, S. W., & Steiner, D. D. (1999). Applicant reactions to interviews: Procedural and interactional justice of recent interview technology. In R. W. Eder & M. M. Harris (Eds.), *The employment interview: Theory, research, and practice* (pp. 69–82). Thousand Oaks, CA: Sage.

Goldman, B. M. (2003). The application of reference cognitions theory to legal-claiming by terminated workers: The role of organizational justice and anger. *Journal of Management*, ***29***, 705–728.

Greenberg, J. (1988). Equity and workplace status: A field experiment. *Journal of Applied Psychology*, ***73***, 606–613.

Greenberg, J. (1993). Stealing in the name of justice: Informational and interpersonal moderators of theft reactions to underpayment inequity. *Organizational Behavior and Human Decision Processes*, 54, 81–103.

Heskett, J. L., Sasser, W. E., Jr., & Schlesinger, L. A. (1997). *The service profit chain: How leading companies link profit and growth to loyalty, satisfaction, and value*. New York: The Free Press.

Huffcutt, A. I., & Arthur, W. Jr. (1994). Hunter and Hunter (1984) revisited: Interview validity for entry-level jobs. *Journal of Applied Psychology*, ***79***, 184–190.

Kammeyer-Mueller, J., Liao, H., & Arvey, R. D. (2001). Downsizing and organizational performance: A review of the literature from a stakeholder perspective. In G. R. Ferris (Ed.), *Research in personnel and human resource management* (Vol. 20, pp. 269–230). Amsterdam: JAI Press.

Kim, W. C., & Mauborgne, R. A. (1991). Implementing global strategies: The role of procedural justice. *Strategic Management Journal*, ***12***, 125–143.

Kim, W. C., & Mauborgne, R. A. (1993). Procedural justice, attitudes, and subsidiary top management compliance with multinationals' corporate strategic decisions. *Academy of Management Journal*, ***36***, 502–526.

Kim, W. C., & Mauborgne, R. A. (2005). *Blue ocean strategy: How to create uncontested market space and make competition irrelevant*. Cambridge, MA: Harvard Business School Press.

Kravitz, D. A., Stinson, V., & Chavez, T. L. (1996). Evaluations of tests used for making selection and promotion decisions. *International Journal of Selection and Assessment*, ***4***, 24–34.

Krehbiel, P. J., & Cropanzano, R. (2000). Procedural justice, outcome favorability, and emotion. *Social Justice Research*, ***13***, 337–358.

Latham, G. P., & Finnegan, B. J. (1993). Perceived practicality of unstructured, patterned, and situational interviews. In H. Schuler, J. L. Farr, & M. Smith (Eds.), *Personnel selection and assessment: Individual and organizational perspectives* (pp. 41–55). Hillsdale, NJ: Erlbaum.

Lerner, M. J. (2003). The justice motive: Where social psychologists found it, how they lost it, and why they may not find it again. *Personality and Social Psychology Review*, *7*, 388–389.

Leventhal, G. S. (1976). Justice in social relationships. In J. W. Thibaut, J. T. Spence, & R. C. Carson (Eds.), *Contemporary topics in social psychology* (pp. 211–240). Morristown, NJ: General Learning Press.

Leventhal, G. S. (1980). What should be done with equity theory? New approaches to the study of justice in social relationships. In K. Gergen, M. Greenberg, and R. Willis (Eds.), *Social exchange: Advances in experimental and social psychology* (Vol. 9, pp. 91–131). New York: Plenum.

Leventhal, G. S., Karuza, J., & Fry, W. R. (1980). Beyond justice: A theory of allocation preferences. In G. Mikula (Ed.), *Justice and social interaction* (pp. 167–218). New York: Springer-Verlag.

Levy, P. E., & Williams, J. R. (2004). The social context of performance appraisal. *Journal of Management*, *30*, 881–905.

Liden, R. C., Wayne, S. J., Kraimer, M. L., & Sparrowe, R. T. (2003). The dual commitments of contingent workers: An examination of contingents' commitment to the agency and the organization. *Journal of Organizational Behavior*, *24*, 609–625.

Lind, E. A., Greenberg, J., Scott, K. S., & Welchans, T. D. (2000). The winding road from employee to complainant: Situational and psychological determinants of wrongful termination claims. *Administrative Science Quarterly*, *45*, 557–590.

Longenecker, C. O., Gioia, D. A., & Sims, H. P. (1987). Behind the mask: The politics of employee appraisal. *Academy of Management Executive*, *1*, 183–193.

Martin, J., & Harder, J. W. (1994). Bread and roses: Justice and the distribution of financial and socioemotional rewards in organizations. *Social Justice Research*, *7*, 241–264.

Masterson, S. (2001). A trickle-down model of organizational justice: Relating employees' and customers' perceptions of and reactions to justice. *Journal of Applied Psychology*, *86*, 594–604.

Maxham, J. G., & Netemeyer, R. G. (2003). Firms reap what they sow: The effects of shared values and perceived organizational justice on customers' evaluations of complaint handling. *Journal of Marketing*, *67*, 46–62.

McFarlin, D. B., & Sweeney, P. D. (1992). Distributive and procedural justice as predictors of satisfaction with personal and organizational outcomes. *Academy of Management Journal*, *35*, 626–637.

Mesch, D. J., & Dalton, D. R. (1992). Unexpected consequences of improving workplace justice: A six-year time series assessment. *Academy of Management Journal*, *5*, 1099–1114.

Milkovich, G. T., & Newman, J. M. (2005). *Compensation* (8th Ed.). Boston: McGraw-Hill.

Miller, P., & O'Leary, T. (1989). Hierarchies and American ideals: 1900–1940. *Administrative Science Quarterly*, *14*, 250–265.

Organ, D. W. (1988). *Organizational citizenship behavior: The good soldier syndrome*. Lexington, MA: Lexington Books.

Pfeffer, P. (1998). *The human equation: Building profits by putting people first*. Cambridge, MA: Harvard Business School Press.

Pfeffer, J., & Langton, N. (1993). The effect of wage dispersion on satisfaction, productivity, and working collaboratively: Evidence from college and university faculty. *Administrative Science Quarterly*, *38*, 382–407.

Pfeffer, J., & Sutton, R. I. (2006). *Hard facts, dangerous half-truths, and total nonsense: Profiting from evidence-based management*. Cambridge, MA: Harvard Business School Press.

Richman, L. S. (1993, September 20). When will the layoffs end? *Fortune*, pp. 54–56.

Roth, P. L., Bobko, P., & McFarland, L. A. (2005). A meta-analysis of work sample test validity: Updating and integrating some classic literature. *Personnel Psychology*, *58*, 1009–1037.

Rupp, D. E., & Cropanzano, R. (2002). The mediating effects of social exchange relationships in predicting workplace outcomes from multifoci organizational justice. *Organizational Behavior and Human Decision Processes*, *89*, 925–946.

Ryan, A. M., & Chan, D. (1999). Perceptions of the EPPP: How do licensure candidates view the process? *Professional Psychology*, *30*, 519–530.

Rynes, S. L., Bretz, R. D., & Gerhart, B. (1991). The importance of recruitment on job choice: A different way of looking. *Personnel Psychology*, *33*, 529–542.

Schmidt, F. L., & Hunter, J. E. (1998). The validity and utility of selection methods in personnel psychology: Practical and theoretical implications of 85 years of research findings. *Psychological Bulletin*, *124*, 262–274.

Schoorman, F. D., & Champagne, M. V. (1994). Managers as informal third parties: The impact of supervisor-subordinate relationships on interventions. *Employee Responsibilities and Rights Journal*, *7*, 73–84.

Skarlicki, D. P., & Folger, R. (1997). Retaliation in the workplace: The roles of distributive, procedural, and interactional justice. *Journal of Applied Psychology*, *82*, 434–443.

Skarlicki, D. P., & Latham, G. P. (1996). Increasing citizenship behavior within a labor union: A test of organizational justice theory. *Journal of Applied Psychology*, *81*, 161–169.

Skitka, L. J., Winquist, J., & Hutchinson, S. (2003). Are outcome justice and outcome favorability distinguishable psychological constructs? A meta-analytic review. *Social Justice Research*, *16*, 309–341.

Smith, A. K., Bolton, R. N., & Wagner, J. (1999). A model of customer satisfaction with service encounters involving failure and recovery. *Journal of Marketing Research*, *36*, 356–372.

Smither, J. W., London, M., & Reilly, R. R. (2005). Does performance improve following multisource feedback? A theoretical model, meta-analysis, and review of empirical findings. *Personnel Psychology*, *58*, 33–66.

Smither, J. W., Reilly, R. R., Millsap, R. E., Pearlman, K., & Stoffey, R. W. (1993). Applicant reactions to selection procedures. *Personnel Psychology*, *46*, 49–77.

Spencer, S., & Rupp, D. E. (2006, May). *Angry, guilty, and conflicted: Injustice toward coworkers heightens emotional labor*. Paper presented at the Annual Meeting of the Society for Industrial and Organizational Psychology, Dallas, TX.

Steiner, D., & Gilliland, S. W. (1996). Justice reactions to personnel selection techniques in France and the United States. *Journal of Applied Psychology*, *81*, 134–141.

Taylor, M. S., Tracy, K. B., Renard, M. K., Harrison, J. K., & Carroll, S. J. (1995). Due process in performance appraisal: A quasi-experiment in procedural justice. *Administrative Science Quarterly*, *40*, 495–523.

Thomas, K. W., & Schmidt, W. H. (1976). A survey of managerial interests with respect to conflict. *Academy of Management Journal*, *19*, 315–318.

Truxillo, D. M., Bauer, T. N., & Sanchez, R. J. (2001). Multiple dimensions of procedural justice: Longitudinal effects on selection system justice and test-taking self-efficacy. *International Journal of Selection and Assessment*, *9*, 330–349.

Tyler, T. R., & Blader, S. L. (2000). *Cooperation in groups: Procedural justice, social identity, and behavioral engagement*. Philadelphia: Psychology Press.

Tyler, T. R., & Smith, H. J. (1998). Social justice and social movements. In D. Gilbert, S. T. Fiske, & G. Lindzey (Eds.), *Handbook of social psychology* (Vol. 4, pp. 595–629). Boston: McGraw-Hill.

Viswesvaran, C., & Ones, D. S. (2002). Examining the construct of organizational justice: A meta-analytic evaluation of relations with work attitudes and behaviors. *Journal of Business Ethics*, *38*, 193–203.

Weiss, H. M., Suckow, K., & Cropanzano, R. (1999). Effects of justice conditions on discrete emotions. *Journal of Applied Psychology*, *84*, 786–794.

Williams, M. L., McDaniel, M. A., & Nguyen, N. T. (2006). A meta-analysis of the antecedents and consequences of pay level satisfaction. *Journal of Applied Psychology*, *91*, 392–413.

Implementation of Strategic Human Resource Management

part two

Staffing

8

Learning Objectives

- Understand the strategic issues associated with recruiting employees
- Develop an appreciation and the relative advantages of the various means of assessing job candidates
- Appreciate the benefits associated with behaviorally based interviews
- Gain an awareness of the legal, economic, social, and political ramifications of foreign workers
- Describe the processes of employment branding and candidate relationship management and the benefits they provide to employers

Strategic Staffing at Kroger Supermarkets

Kroger Co. is currently the nation's largest supermarket chain with over 1,400 supermarkets, 200,000 employees, 500 convenience stores, 40 manufacturing plants, and $27 billion in annual sales. Faced with a constant need to hire new employees and with problems concerning the quality of new hires, Kroger set out to improve its selection processes. Kroger's goal was to enhance the effectiveness of its ability to hire and retain outstanding customer service employees. Its traditional structured interview approach was very time-consuming. Numerous interviewers needed to be trained and certified, and each interview took an average of 45 minutes of management time. At the same time, Kroger faced pressures to develop a system that was efficient and cost-effective. The answer was a computer-based, self-administered employee selection system.

Kroger began by conducting a survey of its customers to gather information regarding customer perceptions of customer service. This information was then converted to scales that measured the knowledge, skills, and competencies that impact outstanding customer service. The end result—an employability index—was able to evaluate an applicant's thought process, management of job-related stress, self-control, and general job-related attitudes. The index was determined entirely by an online, interactive interview with applicants; a recommendation was then offered as to whether the individual should be offered a job. This innovative approach is designed to improve both effectiveness and efficiency by matching selection criteria with carefully chosen strategic objectives. Although the program has not been formally evaluated, Kroger has already determined the three criteria by which it will assess the program: customer service measures, turnover rate, and employee safety.[1]

Staffing, the process of recruiting applicants and selecting prospective employees, remains a key strategic area for human resource management. Given that an organization's performance is a direct result of the individuals it employs, the specific strategies used and decisions made in the staffing process will directly impact an organization's success or lack thereof.

Decisions made as part of the staffing process can have a significant impact on an organization's bottom line. One study found that 45 percent of companies calculated the cost of turnover at more than $10,000 per person, while 10 percent calculated it at more than $40,000 per person.[2] Turnover costs tend to rise as the level of the job and its complexity increase. In technology companies, the costs of turnover can be staggering. Agilent Technologies of Palo Alto, California, estimates an average turnover costs of $200,000 per departing employee and $250,000 per software engineer.[3]

The activities performed as part of recruiting and selection offer an organization numerous choices for finding and screening new employees. These options can have a significant impact on an organization's efficiency because some are much more extensive, costly, and time-consuming than others. Organizations have great latitude to select from a variety of staffing techniques, each of which offers various degrees of sophistication and selectivity; however, such benefits come at a price.

In addition to the time and financial costs involved with staffing, many changes are taking place concerning how work is performed. Trends such as broader job scope and responsibilities, the move toward leaner staffing and operating with fewer full-time permanent employees, smaller autonomous units, pay for company-wide performance, and flatter organization structures affect the types of individuals and skills that organizations seek and influence how organizations find and screen applicants. The staffing process must be more strategically focused: Newer challenges and considerations must be directly incorporated into an organization's staffing strategy.

Staffing takes on even greater importance in the service sector, which continues to create the largest number of jobs in our economy. However, a service-based economy requires different skills and has higher turnover costs than those associated with manufacturing. In addition, payroll typically assumes a higher percentage of overall costs in service organizations. Companies in this traditionally high-turnover sector need strategic staffing initiatives that allow them to attract and retain productive employees, thereby minimizing operating expenses.

Probably most important is ensuring that employees fit with the culture of the organization. Technical skills alone do not guarantee high performance, particularly as organizations move toward process- and project-oriented work teams.

Recruiting

Temporary Versus Permanent Employees

When an organization needs to increase its headcount, the first strategic choice is whether to hire temporary or permanent employees. To do this, the organization must accurately forecast how long it expects the employee shortage to last. Temporary employees obtained from an agency usually cost more per hour to employ than permanent worker; however, unlike permanent employees, temporary employees are not paid when there is no work for them to do, particularly if they are hired on a project basis. Temporary employees are not provided benefits; thus, unlike permanent employees, they cannot file claims for unemployment compensation when their employment ends. Temporary employees also provide flexibility for employers because payroll can be quickly and easily contracted during downturns without having to result to layoffs.

In addition to hiring temporary employees from an agency, an organization can subcontract work to an outside vendor; this is usually done on a project basis. Larger organizations can also move permanent employees from department to department as needs dictate. This promotes efficiency through lower costs and flexible utilization of employees. These in-house "temporary" employees have more permanent status, including benefits; are generally more committed to the organization; and know the inside workings of the organization. They can be extremely useful when regular employees take extended vacation or sick leaves. In-house temporary employees provide the organization with more flexibility and efficiency than it would garner from outside temps; also, employees have more variety in their work assignments.

The use of temporary employees has greatly increased in recent years and to the point where an entire industry has been created for the employment of temporary workers. The "contingent workforce" industry involves 5.7 million workers, or 4 percent of United States workforce.[4] Employees in almost every job category are now being considered and employed on a temporary-for-permanent basis without any promise or legal obligation for continued employment. Short-term temporary employment has also found its way into the executive ranks, including the CEO office.[5] Interim CEOs are typically retired or laid-off senior executives who wish to return to work for a limited time commitment to help a particular organization or contribute and build their résumés and professional networks while they seek more permanent employment. Similar to other levels of temporary employment, contingent executives can also allow a trial period of employment for consideration of permanent employment. Reading 8-1, "Temporary Help Agencies and the Making of a New Employment Practices," traces the rise of the temporary employment movement and explains its current uses and potential.

Internal Versus External Recruiting

If an organization decides to hire permanent employees, the first critical question it needs to address is whether to recruit internally or externally. Recruiting from the current employee pool can benefit the organization in a number of ways. First, the organization already has performance data on employees. Ample opportunity has been afforded to observe the applicant's work habits, skills and capabilities, ability to get along with others, and fit with the organization.

Second, promotion from within motivates employees. Employees feel that the organization is trying to provide them with promotional and developmental opportunities in reward for their performance and loyalty. Third, training and socialization time are reduced. Current employees know the organization, its procedures, politics, and customers and have already established relationships with coworkers. Consequently, they need far less formal or informal socialization time than those hired from the outside. Finally, internal recruiting is often much faster and far less expensive than going outside of the organization for applicants.

Although internal recruiting has advantages, this approach also has some disadvantages. First, internal recruiting can become very political and competitive, particularly when coworkers apply for the same position. Dysfunctional conflict may result, and collegiality and interpersonal relationships can be strained. Second, those employees not selected for the position can suffer from diminished morale and performance, particularly when they feel equally or better qualified than the candidate selected.

Third, the organization can become inbred through excessive internal recruitment. Continuing to promote from within can encourage maintaining the status quo. An organization that needs to improve organizational processes should usually recruit from the outside. Finally, excessive internal recruitment can cause inefficiency by creating multiple vacancies. For instance, if a senior-level manager leaves the organization and is replaced by a direct subordinate, that subordinate's job will then need to be filled. As this promotion chain continues down the hierarchy, an initial vacancy could spur promotions for a large number of people. Nearly all employees require a certain period of time to learn a new job. Even when an employee has worked in the organization for several years, a new position requires adjusting to new responsibilities and redefining interpersonal relationships with coworkers. Internal recruiting can exacerbate this effect by creating a large number of employees having new positions. Until these employees gain the level of competence that their predecessors had and sufficiently redefine their working relationships, inefficiency will result.

Internal recruiting has its advantages and disadvantages. It is probably best utilized when the organization pursues a strategy related to stability, faces few major threats from its external environment, and is concerned with maintaining the status quo relative to its operating systems. When time and/or money are limited, internal recruiting can also be beneficial.

External recruiting also has advantages and disadvantages. Not surprisingly, the advantages of external recruiting are consistent with the disadvantages of internal recruiting. External recruiting facilitates change and tends to be more useful for organizations with volatile external environments. External recruiting can allow an organization to expand its knowledge base beyond that of its existing employees and bring in new ideas and viewpoints; external recruits are not bound by existing ways of thinking or doing things. They can bring a fresh approach to problems that have plagued the organization. At the senior level, candidates are often recruited for their history of bringing about high-level change in other organizations.

External recruiting, however, can be expensive and time-consuming. Employees from outside the organization will often need a longer socialization period to know the organization, its products or services, coworkers, and customers. External recruits are also unknown entities in that the organization has no experience working with them. Although an applicant may have outstanding skills, training, or experience and may have had past success in another organization, those factors do not guarantee similar success with a new organization or an ability to fit with a new organization's culture. Finally, external recruiting can have detrimental effects on the morale of those employees who have applied for the job internally but have not been selected. Exhibit 8.1 summarizes the strategic issues surrounding internal versus external recruiting.

When recruiting employees from outside the organization, employers have a variety of applicant sources from which to choose. Proper sourcing can save not only time and money can also reduce the time it takes to have new employees actually on the job. A recent survey of recruiters found that the top five recruitment goals were: (1) generating high-quality employment applications; (2) generating the best possible return on investment; (3) stimulating a desire to work for the organization; (4) filling specific positions; and (5) generating diversity.[6]

EXHIBIT 8.1 Advantages and Disadvantages of Internal and External Recruiting

	Advantages	Disadvantages	When Useful
Internal	Have performance data available	Possible politics	Stability strategy
	Motivation	"Loser" effects	Stable external environment
	Less training/socialization time	Inbreeding	Limited time and money
	Faster	Promotion chains	
	Less Expensive		
	Advantages	**Disadvantages**	**When Useful**
External	Fresh ideas and viewpoints	Unknown entities	Need for change
	Expand knowledge base	Detrimental to internal applicants	Volatile external environment
		Training and socialization time	
		Time-consuming	
		Can be expensive	

When and How Extensively to Recruit

Regardless of whether recruiting is done internally or externally, effective planning and strategizing are essential to the success of the process. An organization needs to know that it has the right employees with the right skills in the right places at the right time. This involves determining (1) how large an applicant pool is needed and (2) when recruiting efforts should begin. Both of these questions can be answered by reviewing data from past recruiting efforts. A recruiting pyramid can be constructed by using yield ratios that show, traditionally, how many employees pass from one stage of the recruiting process to the next. This can help the organization determine how large an applicant pool to seek. An example of a recruiting pyramid is presented in Exhibit 8.2. In this case, the organization could use historic yield ratios to determine how extensively to recruit. For example, if the organization is seeking 20 new employees, it should obtain 240 résumés.

An organization must determine when to begin its recruiting efforts to ensure that trained employees will be ready when the organization needs them. Timelines of past recruiting efforts can help the organization determine when to time its recruiting efforts. Here, an organization works backward from the time employees will be needed to determine when to begin recruiting. An example of a recruiting timeline is presented in Exhibit 8.3. In this case, the organization should begin recruiting 14 weeks before the intended start date.

One caveat must be issued concerning the use of recruiting pyramids and timelines. Because they are based on past recruiting data, they may need to be adjusted if labor market conditions have changed dramatically. Higher or lower unemployment, changes in the competitiveness of the industry, and/or the attractiveness of the employer vis-à-vis competitors might make the staffing process easier or more difficult than it had been in the past. Managers should assess how any changed conditions might impact the size of the applicant pool, the ratios, and the timeline.

Methods of Recruiting

Small organizations often do their recruiting very informally. Job openings or new positions may be communicated by word of mouth or by allowing the direct supervisor to

EXHIBIT 8.2 Recruiting Pyramid

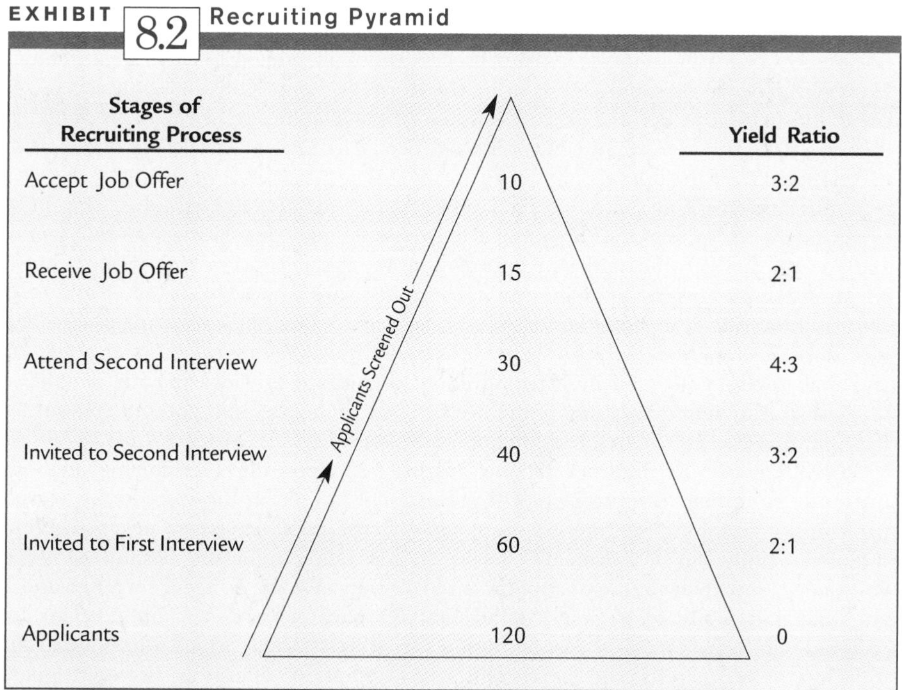

EXHIBIT 8.3 Recruiting Timeline

Stages of Recruiting Process	Normal Time Taken to Complete
Candidate begins work	2 weeks
Acceptance of offer by candidate	1 week
Making an offer to candidate	1 week
Second interview cycle	1 week
Arranging second interviews	2 weeks
First interview cycle	1 week
Arranging first interviews	2 weeks
Screening résumés	2 weeks
Recruiting for position	3 weeks

find someone of his or her own choosing. Most larger organizations do their internal recruiting through some means of formal job posting. This process involves posting the available position where all employees have access, such as a physical or online bulletin board. Employees then decide whether they want to apply for any position.

When such a system is used and several people apply for the job, the detrimental effects of nonselection on employee morale can be minimized by providing nonselected employees with specific, objective feedback concerning the screening process. These employees should also be counseled regarding how they might enhance their skills and experience if they plan to apply for future job openings. However, no guarantee or promise of appointment or promotion should be made.

If the organization maintains employee information in a computerized database, the skills inventory component of the human resource information system can be used to assist in internal recruiting. The employee database can be searched for employees having skills, experiences, and personal qualities that are required for a job. This can save the organization a great deal of time in identifying strong internal candidates for a job. These candidates can then be contacted to determine their interest in a position.

External recruiting may also be done informally through contact with friends and acquaintances of existing employees; this process is usually limited to small organizations. However, informal recruiting tends to be the norm at the executive level. A recent survey found that 64 percent of executives found their jobs through peer networking.[7] In the year 2000, the number of CEOs who had been hired from outside the organization had doubled from 1990 levels.[8]

A primary source of recruiting for larger organizations is targeted advertising in selected media. In writing and designing a help wanted ad, it is important to be accurate and specific and provide sufficient information about the position and organization to encourage applicants to apply. Interestingly, studies have shown that fewer than 20 percent of those who read help wanted ads are actively looking for employment. Competitors, current employees, investors, stockbrokers and analysts, recruiters, and regulators also read such ads to gain information about organizations. Consequently, employers who use recruitment advertising need to take these audiences into account without losing sight of the need to attract strong applicants.

Recruiting on the Internet is one of the fastest-growing recruitment methods. Currently more than 70 percent of HR professionals are using the Internet for recruiting.[9] Most found using the Internet more cost-effective than newspaper advertising.[10] Internet recruiting can be extremely effective in generating applicants because of its low cost, speed, and ability to target applicants with technical skills. A recent survey of undergraduate and graduate students found that 75 percent used the Internet for job searches.[11] Information on the organization is readily available, which allows applicants to assess their interests and needs with the employer's offerings. However, poorly designed or user-unfriendly Web sites can damage an organization's reputation and its ability to attract applicants. The same survey found that 25 percent of job candidates rejected a potential employer on account of its Web site.[12]

Because Internet recruiting is worldwide, it gives an employer global exposure to potential applicants, which can be critical if particular language skills or cultural backgrounds are needed. Technology-based employers have found the Internet to be a fertile recruiting ground for applicants who are technologically savvy. For example, Cisco Systems receives more than 80 percent of its résumés electronically.[13]

Interestingly, the strategies used by recruiters often do not fit the job search strategies being used by applicants. Networking, or the use of personal and professional contacts to obtain employment, is the strategy of choice for the majority of job seekers: Seventy-eight percent use this approach.[14] Sixty-seven percent of recruiters, however, find that the Internet is their top source for attracting new employees.[15] This is not to say that job seekers do not use the Internet, as they have been shown to utilize more search tactics than recruiters,[16] but, rather, implies that HR professionals need to think carefully about their recruiting sources and think strategically about how best to achieve the recruitment goals they have set.

Internet recruiting has become increasingly popular with employers and can cut the search process time by as much as 75 percent.[17] Sophisticated technology allows employers to quickly process large numbers of applications through the use of spiders, which are programs that search résumés for specific characteristics or words. Many employers attempt to attract applicants by developing Web sites that provide information about the organization that can allow applicants to determine if there might be an optimal "fit" between their career goals and the goals of the organization, guide candidates through the application process, and even allow prospective applicants to take a virtual tour of the organization. While Internet recruiting can speed up the employment process, it is also fraught with some potential challenges that must be weighed by an organization considering Internet recruiting.[18]

The first of these challenges is ensuring security. Online recruiting means that the employer will be receiving electronic inquiries from unknown sources. Many of these communications will include attached files, making viruses a security concern; another consideration is ensuring that those visiting the Web site do not obtain access to unauthorized areas of the site. A second challenge is that overreliance on Internet recruiting can result in a disparate impact against certain protected classes of applicants. Studies have shown that members of certain ethnic minority groups, women, and older individuals either may not have access to or be less likely to use the Internet.[19] Individuals with disabilities may also have conditions that limit or prevent their ability to easily access the Internet as well. Consequently, employers may unintentionally screen out large groups of potential applicants who are members of protected classes in the interest of the efficiency afforded by Internet recruiting. Finally, Internet recruiting can complicate reporting of data related to compliance with federal and state laws. A difficult question arises as to whether an individual who sends an unsolicited résumé via the Internet needs to be "counted" and considered an "applicant" for the purpose of federal reporting. The EEOC and OFCCP have continuously wrestled with the definition of "job applicant" for reporting purposes; combining this with the greatly increased number of job applicants that result from Internet recruiting creates a challenging situation for employers.

E-cruiting at Air Products and Chemicals, Inc.

One organization that has developed a satisfactory strategy for reporting its Internet recruiting activities to federal agencies is Air Products and Chemicals, Inc. (APC). Based in Allentown, Pennsylvania, APC supplies gases and chemicals to various industries as well as to the federal government. With 16,000 employees worldwide, including 9,000 in the United States, APC falls under the purview of the Office of Federal Contracts Compliance Programs as a government contractor. As APC began to use the Internet for recruiting with greater frequency, a conflict arose relative to its reporting with the OFCCP. The OFCCP considered résumés submitted electronically as an expression of interest in employment, and APC's reading of that résumé constituted acceptance of it, making the submitting party an "applicant" for reporting purposes. Because the organization could not control who submitted unsolicited résumés, it found itself at a disadvantage relative to its affirmative action goals. APC eventually solved the dilemma. Each unsolicited résumé received an automatic e-mail reply, instructing the individual to apply for a specific open position listed on the company Web site. Only when a position was chosen would the individual be considered an "applicant." In addition, applicants were required to submit information identifying their race and gender. This system met with the OFCCP's enthusiastic approval and has allowed APC to reap the benefits of Internet recruiting while satisfying the OFCCP's reporting requirements for federal contractors.[20]

An organization's existing employees can often be a very valuable source for recruiting new employees. Consumer products manufacturer Johnson & Johnson relies extensively on its employee referral program to recruit new hires. J&J offers up to $1,500 for each employee recruit, paid in full two weeks after the new employee's start date.[21] Hartford-based Lincoln Financial's referral program results in 55 percent of all external hires and saves the organization more than 97 percent of the costs it would incur by using an executive search firm.[22] One innovative approach to staffing has existing employees recruit themselves, as illustrated below.

Staffing at St. Peter's Health Care

St. Peter's Health Care is an Albany, New York–based hospital that, like many healthcare institutions, suffered from a severe shortage of qualified nurses. Nurses hired from outside agencies to assume unstaffed shifts not only commanded a premium price but were also unfamiliar with operations and procedures at St. Peter's. To alleviate this problem, St. Peter's launched an online bidding system by which any nurse could bid for an open shift. Nurses must be existing employees or approved to work for the hospital and bid on shifts for a certain pay rate per hour. Nurse managers have the authority to accept or reject any bid, and applicants whose bids have been rejected are free to rebid at a lower pay rate. Because the hospital cannot mandate overtime for workers, this system allows maximum flexibility for both St. Peter's and nurse-employees. In 2002, St. Peter's filled 43,400 available hours under the bidding system at an average pay rate of $37 per hour. Two thirds of those hours were filled by existing employees. Outside agency nurses would have cost the hospital $54 per hour. In addition to the cost savings, turnover among nurses has decreased from 11 percent to below 5 percent annually, and both patient and employee satisfaction have increased.[23]

Organizations can also address their staffing needs by turning to other organizations and outsourcing all or part of their staffing. Employment agencies, more commonly called staffing agencies or staffing services, can locate and prescreen applicants for an employer. Because locating and prescreening applicants are often the most time-consuming, expensive, and laborious processes for managers, many organizations are quite willing to use staffing agencies to perform these functions. In addition, the risk of running afoul of the law and having initial screening influenced by the biases of current employees is minimized because the staffing service is often able to bring a more objective perspective to the process.

In addition to traditional staffing agencies, there are several other kinds of organizations that may help an employer with external recruiting. The first of these are state job service agencies. State job service agencies are public funded by the federal government but are operated by individual states. All citizens who file unemployment compensation claims are required to register with the state job service agency and remain actively looking for work as a condition of receiving ongoing unemployment compensation. Employers can call and list positions with their state job service agency for no fee and, at the same time, assist those who have lost their jobs.

Another source of prospective employees is the Private Industry Council (PIC), a local agency that administers federal funds to assist individuals who are hard to employ in finding jobs. These individuals are generally those who depend on public welfare assistance but have either limited or no marketable job skills or lack the means to obtain appropriate training. Employers who are willing to train individuals for entry-level jobs can obtain assistance in locating such applicants from the local PIC. If the organization provides training and then subsequently hires the individual referred from the PIC for a permanent position, then the employer can seek partial reimbursement for the wages paid during the training period from the PIC. The Private Industry Council receives federal money for such reimbursement under the Job Training Partnership Act.

Executive search firms are a specialized type of staffing agency that assist organizations in filling skilled technical and senior- and executive-level management positions. Executive search firms usually charge significant fees for their services; these fees are paid by the employer. Searches are usually conducted for a contracted period of time and for a set fee, which is paid regardless of whether the search is successful. Estimates are that fewer than 50 percent of searches are successful during the contracted time period.[24]

Despite their relatively low rates of success, the services of executive search firms continue to be in demand because search firms provide employers with several benefits. First, search firms are usually better and faster than the organization's in-house recruiters in locating talent. The majority of search firms focus on specific industries, and they have extensive networks and numerous contacts. Consequently, they can locate and attract candidates who are not actively looking for new jobs. Although most employers would not directly call someone who works for a competitor to recruit that individual, an executive search firm can and does. The executive search firm can also keep the organization's identity confidential during the recruiting and prescreening process. Some organizations have hired executive search firms to contact their own employees in efforts to determine whether the employees might have any interest in leaving the organization. Although this kind of behavior may be unethical, it shows that executive search firms can offer an organization a means of secretly recruiting candidates. Finally, executive search firms will often, upon request, provide their client organizations with a written and signed "anti-raiding" agreement, whereby the search firm promises not to contact or recruit any of the organization's employees for a given time period in searches being conducted for other client organizations.

Outsourced Recruiting at Kellogg

Michigan-based cereal manufacturer Kellogg recently revamped its recruiting function for all its non-hourly employees. With more than 14,000 employees worldwide, coordination of the recruiting function had become cumbersome, prompting Kellogg to outsource its entire exempt recruiting operation. Because the industry is highly cyclical, Kellogg did not want to have to continuously hire and lay off recruiting staff and sought a system that was more flexible and better aligned with its business needs and strategy. When Kellogg needed to hire 200 new salespeople in a short time, the vendor was able to fill the positions much more quickly and efficiently than Kellogg would have been using its own staff and an outside search firm. The vendor's performance is overseen by a project manager at Kellogg and evaluated according to a variety of metrics, including cost, timeliness, quality of applicants, service to managers, and diversity. During the first year of implementation, the outsourced recruiting program saved Kellogg more than $1.3 million and reduced average cost per hire by more than 35 percent.[25]

Many organizations use college and university on-campus recruiting as a means of attracting a relatively large number of qualified applicants. Campus recruiting can generate a large applicant pool in a short time period at a minimal cost and, therefore, create efficiency in the recruiting process. However, this can also create inefficiencies because of having to screen an excessively large number of applicants. Campus recruiting can often result in motivated, highly skilled, energetic applicants, but these applicants are usually available only at certain times of the year; they may also have very limited prior work experience. Success in the classroom does not necessarily translate to success in the workplace. Campus recruiting involves higher risk, given the practical inexperience of most applicants; however, there is a potential for higher return, given the intelligence, level of training, energy, and ambition that many applicants possess.

To alleviate some of the difficulties associated with campus recruiting, an increasing number of employers are offering co-op and/or internship programs. Such programs allow both the employer and student a trial period with no obligation. Employers have an advantage in recruiting interns for permanent positions; students gain marketable experience for their résumés.

College Recruiting via Internships at Microsoft

Redmond, Washington–based Microsoft is one of the most sought-after employers in the world. The software giant receives upwards of 50,000 résumés a month and is clearly an "employer of choice" for many applicants. One way to heighten one's chances of obtaining employment with Microsoft is through interning at the organization. While the internship program itself is highly competitive, it provides Microsoft and interns with an opportunity to try each other out for a limited time period. Microsoft provides paid internships to approximately 800 college students each summer. After a rigorous screening process, fewer than 10 percent of applicants eventually end up with Microsoft for the summer. Those who are selected receive "competitive salaries," company-subsidized housing, training, and full benefits. Microsoft, with employee turnover at less than 6 percent, hires as much as 45 percent of its interns for permanent positions. Microsoft expects that after the 12-week internship concludes, each intern will be ready for permanent full-time employment.[26]

Selection

Once a sufficient pool of applicants has been recruited, critical decisions need to be made regarding applicant screening. Selection decisions can and do have significant economic and strategic consequences for organizations, and these decisions need to be made with great care. Before the application of any selection tools or criteria, the organization needs to determine if the methods being employed are both reliable and valid.

Reliability refers to the consistency of the measurement being taken. Ideally, the application of any screening criteria should elicit the same results in repeat trials. For example, if an applicant is asked to take a pre-employment test, the test should have consistent results each time it is administered to an applicant. Similarly, when different interviewers evaluate an applicant's ability to make spontaneous decisions, they should assess the applicant's skill level similarly. Consequently, in planning a screening process, the organization needs to ensure that there is reliability on two levels: across time and across evaluators.

Because many factors can impact assessment, 100 percent reliability is rarely, if ever, achieved. An individual might score poorly on a test on a given day because of a preoccupation with personal matters. Interrater reliability, which is the correlation among different judges who interview an applicant, is often low because these evaluators may bring different perceptions and biases to the process. However, low interrater reliability is not always bad. A supervisor might evaluate an applicant by using different criteria from those a subordinate might use. Such differences in perception are important in getting a holistic assessment of a potential employee.

Low reliability is often the result of one of two types of errors in assessment. The first of these is deficiency error. Much as the name implies, deficiency error occurs when one important criterion for assessment is not included in the measure. For example, if the test for an applicant for an editor's position did not attempt to measure the applicant's writing ability, deficiency error would be present.

The second type of error is contamination error. Contamination error is caused by unwanted influences that affect the assessment. If an interviewer is under intense time pressure to complete other tasks and rushes the interview process so that it is impossible to gather sufficient information on a candidate, contamination error would result. Similarly, if a test measures knowledge, skills, or abilities that are not essential for the job and the evaluation of these noncritical factors impacts the ratings for the more important dimension, contamination error would result.

Reliability is a prerequisite for validity. A test cannot be valid without first being reliable. Validity refers to whether what is being assessed relates or corresponds to actual performance on the job. It examines whether the skills, abilities, and knowledge being measured make a difference in performance. Validity is critical not only to ensure proper selection, but it also becomes the chief measure by which employers defend discrimination allegations in court. Although no laws specifically require employers to assess the validity of their screening devices, illustrating that specific criteria are valid selection measures and are, therefore, job-related is the major way for employers to respond to such claims.

There are two types of validity that support selection criteria. The first is content validity. Content validity illustrates that the measure or criterion is representative of the actual job content and/or the desired knowledge that the employee should have to perform the job. Content validity is determined through the process of job analysis, which is discussed in Chapter 6. For example, in order to receive a real estate license and work as a licensed salesperson or broker, an individual must pass an exam that tests knowledge of job-related concepts, activities, and processes. Content validity, in and of itself, does not guarantee successful performance on the job, much as completing a prerequisite course in a degree program does not guarantee successful completion of a later course.

The second validity measure is empirical, or criterion-related, validity. This measure demonstrates the relationship between certain screening criteria and job performance. If individuals who obtain higher scores or evaluations on these screening criteria also turn out to be high performers on the job, then this type of validity is established.

It is important to realize that reliability alone is not sufficient for determining the appropriate screening criteria. These criteria must also be valid. Validity not only ensures the best possible strategic fit between applicant and job, but it also ensures that the organization will have a readily accepted means of defending discrimination charges at hand. Criteria cannot be valid that are not already reliable. Conversely, criteria can be reliable without being valid. It is critical for decision-makers to understand this difference and develop their screening criteria accordingly.

Interviewing

The first set of critical decisions in the selection process involves the interviewing process. Employers first need to determine who should be involved in interviewing applicants. A number of different constituents can provide input.

Prospective immediate supervisors, peers, and/or subordinates might be asked to participate in interviewing candidates. Coworker input can be critical in organizations that emphasize teams and project groups. The input of customers might also be sought, particularly for employers in service industries. Those involved in selecting appropriate interviewers must consider the different perspectives that different individuals or groups offer and the relevance of these perspectives for selecting the best applicant. Interviewers should be chosen from diverse racial, ethnic, age, and gender backgrounds. Another decision must be made as to whether interviews will be conducted in an individual or group format. Group interviews can save time for both the organization and applicant, but they often involve creating a less personal atmosphere for applicants. Group interviews may make it more difficult for interviewers to get a sense of the applicant's interpersonal style.

Interviewing applicants involves making subjective assessments of each applicant's qualifications for a job. However, interviewers commonly make interpretation errors that should be avoided in an effective interviewing process. Among these are similarity error, in which the interviewer has a positive disposition toward an applicant considered to be similar to the interviewer in some way; contrast error, in which the candidates are compared to each other during the interview process instead of the absolute standards and requirements of the job; first impression error, in which the interviewer immediately makes a positive or negative assessment of the candidate and uses the remaining interview time to seek information to support that contention; halo error, in which a single characteristic, positive or negative, outweighs all other dimensions; and biases that are based on the interviewee's race, gender, religion, age, ethnicity, sexual orientation, or physical condition rather than factors that relate to job performance.

One recent study examined the effects of interviewee behavior on the assessments made by those conducting interviews.[27] Two different interviewee behaviors, ingratiation and self-promotion, were examined related to interview outcomes. Ingratiation involves displaying behavior that is perceived to conform to the desires of the interviewer, while self-promotion involves the assertion of the interviewee's own strengths and competencies. The study found that ingratiation played a bigger role in interview outcomes than any other factor, including objective credentials. This added potential bias on the part of interviewers needs to be controlled to ensure the efficacy of the interview process.

Group interviewing allows different interviewers to compare and contrast their interpretations of the same interview information. Consequently, this often helps overcome many of the errors that individual interviewers might make.

One interviewing technique that has become increasingly popular in recent years is behavioral interviewing, which involves determining whether an applicant's anticipated behavior in a variety of situations and scenarios posed in interview questions would be appropriate for the employer. Behavioral interviewing can be used with experienced applicants as well as with those who have little or no professional work experience because it asks about situations the candidate might likely find him or herself facing on the job. Behavioral interviewing with candidates who have professional experience can also involve candidates presenting real-life situations in which they were involved and how they handled them.

To use behavioral interviewing, the first step is to determine the most important behavioral characteristics required for a given job or to work in a certain unit. These can be identified by examining the key traits displayed by high-performing incumbents. Behavioral interviewing assumes that candidates have already been screened for technical skills and focuses more on the human interaction traits and people skills an applicant would bring to a job. Questions might be what an applicant did in a certain past situation or might do in a given situation as well as things he or she most enjoyed, least enjoyed, and would opt to change about a given situation. Behavioral interviewing is used extensively by Dell Computer, AT&T, and Clean Harbors Environmental Services.[28] Dell collects data from 300 of its executives to determine the qualities most needed for success within the organization. AT&T has developed a series of behavioral questions that address the core competencies of organization, interpersonal communication style, decision making, and problem analysis. Clean Harbors, which specializes in cleanups of hazardous materials in the environment, looks for problem-solving ability, openness to new ideas, and enthusiasm.[29]

Behavioral interviewing generally reduces potential employer liability because of its focus on specific behaviors that are considered critical for effective performance. Typically, in asking interviewees to provide examples of behavior, job candidates might be asked to describe situations, explain actions taken and the reasons for such actions, and explain outcomes. Proper behavioral interviewing will involve all three dimensions of questioning: situations, actions, and outcomes. Exhibit 8.4 provides some examples of behaviorally based questions.

Regardless of who conducts the interviews and whether they are administered in a group or individual format, a decision needs to be made as to whether the actual format or process of the interviews should be structured or unstructured. Structured interviews follow a set protocol: All interviewees are asked the same questions and are given the same opportunity to respond. There is standardization in that it becomes easier to compare applicant responses to identical questions, and legal liability can be minimized because all applicants are treated the same. However, structured interviewing provides

EXHIBIT 8.4 Sample Behavioral Interview Questions

Describe a situation in which you experienced conflict with a coworker (or supervisor).

Provide an example of your seeing a project from conceptualization to implementation and the challenges encountered.

Provide an example of a problem that you failed to anticipate.

Provide an example of a decision you made that you would make differently if given the opportunity again.

Describe a situation in which you had to manage a problem employee or confront a performance problem.

limited opportunity to adapt the interview process to any unique circumstances surrounding any applicant.

An unstructured interview is totally spontaneous and one in which questions are not planned in advance. The topics of discussion can vary dramatically from one candidate to another. Such a process allows interviewers to gain a greater sense of the applicant as an individual, but it often makes comparison among different candidates difficult. A semistructured interview would fall somewhere between these two extremes. With a semistructured interview, the interviewer asks each candidate a set of standard questions. However, the interviewer can determine exactly which questions each candidate is asked and can be flexible and probe for specifics when answers are provided. Although structured interviews provide the greatest consistency, unstructured interviews provide the greatest flexibility. The organization must determine which is more important strategically. For example, in interviewing for jobs that require a great degree of creativity, the interviewer may wish to use a less-structured approach to determine how the applicant handles an unstructured situation. If it is critical to compare candidates closely across several criteria, a more structured approach might be more advantageous.

Regardless of interview structure, the selection process is aided when the interviewer asks specific, pointed questions. Asking candidates to describe behaviors they have engaged in or actions they have taken in specific situations is far more meaningful for assessment purposes than closed-ended "yes or no" questions. This strategy of behavioral interviewing has become increasingly popular in organizations. Candidates can and should be presented with scenarios they might expect to encounter on the job for which they are interviewing and be asked how they had handle the situation. This can assist the organization in determining the fit between the applicant and organizational culture and processes. Interviewing by itself generally has relatively low reliability and validity. Consequently, it is critical to employ other criteria in the screening process to increase the likelihood of selection of the best applicants.

Testing

Another critical decision in the selection process involves applicant testing and the kinds of tests to use. The needs of the organization and job structure (specific responsibilities, interpersonal relationships with others, and so forth) will determine whether any or all of the following should be assessed: technical skills, interpersonal skills, personality traits, problem-solving abilities, or any other job-related performance indicators. The key variable that should influence testing is job requirements. Any testing that is not specifically job-related could be legally challenged, particularly if adverse impact can be shown.

The timing of testing can vary from organization to organization. Traditionally, testing has been conducted after the interviewing and screening process because of the expense of testing and time required to score and evaluate test results. However, some organizations are now testing earlier in the selection process because costs involved with interviewing often exceed the costs of testing. Clearly, it makes sense for an employer to use more cost-effective screening techniques earlier in the selection process.

Perhaps the most useful types of tests are work sample and trainability tests. Work sample tests simply involve giving the applicant a representative sample of work that would be part of the job and asking the individual to complete it. These tests are useful when the employer needs employees who will be able to perform job responsibilities from the first day of employment. Trainability tests measure an applicant's aptitude and ability to understand critical components of the job that the company may be willing to teach once the employee is hired. They are useful when the employer needs some familiarity with the nature of the work but seeks to train the new employee in the organization's way of doing things.

Both work sample and trainability tests can provide candidates with realistic job previews. Traditionally, organizations emphasized only the positive aspects of jobs during the recruiting process. This approach kept the applicant pool large and allowed the organization to reject the applicant, instead of vice versa. However, by hiding negative aspects of jobs, employers often hired individuals who became disillusioned once employed and left the organization shortly after hire. This results in a waste of both time and money and a loss of efficiency. The idea behind realistic job previews is to make applicants aware of both positive and negative aspects of the job. If the applicant is hired, the new employee has realistic expectations and is less likely to become dissatisfied with the job and quit. Realistic job previews also increase the likelihood of a candidate's self-selecting out of a position; however, this is in both the applicant's and employee's best interests. The predictive power of work sample and trainability tests for an appropriate fit between an applicant and job/organization has been found to be quite high.

Applicants might also be asked to provide samples of their previous work. A means of assessing the validity of collected information (such as samples of work and past work projects) also needs to be determined. Such work may be falsified. Its integrity can be verified by asking candidates detailed questions about its content or the process by which it was completed.

Other types of testing need to be administered very carefully. Personality testing often centers around what have been called the "Big Five" personality dimensions.[30] Those traits considered most relevant to performance in any kind of work environment. As illustrated in Exhibit 8.5, they are sociability, agreeableness, conscientiousness, emotional stability, and intellectual openness. Personality testing can be useful to anticipate how employees might behave, particularly on an interpersonal level, but personality tests can be problematic on two levels. First, personality testing has been successfully challenged in many courts because of the impact of certain questions on members of protected classes. Second, few, if any, jobs require one specific type of personality to ensure success. No employer has ever been able to argue successfully in court that a specific personality type or dimension was necessary for effective job performance.

Personality testing is easier to defend, however, when certain personality traits can be direct attributed to superior job performance and an absence of such traits attributed to poorer performance. Yankee Candle, based in South Deerfield, Massachusetts, asks each of its managers to complete a standard personality assessment and then compares the

EXHIBIT 8.5 The Big Five Personality Dimensions

Personality Dimension	Characteristics of a Person Scoring Positively on the Dimension
1) Sociability	Gregarious, energetic, talkative, assertive
2) Agreeableness	Trusting, considerate, cooperative, tactful
3) Conscientiousness	Dependable, responsible, achievement-oriented, persistent
4) Emotional stability	Stable, secure, unworried, confident
5) Intellectual openness	Intellectual, imaginative, curious, original

results to individual store performance. This has allowed the organization to develop a behavioral profile of high-performing managers, which considers traits such as sense of urgency, independence, motivation, communication style and attention to detail, and becomes the basis for assessing applicants for future employment.[31]

Under the Americans with Disabilities Act, physical testing can be done only after a job offer has been made unless an employer can show that there are specific, critical physical requirements for job performance. The use of honesty testing has been declining since Congress passed the Employee Polygraph Protection Act in 1988. This act, which prohibits such tests, is problematic and generally unreliable. Research has shown that employee theft is usually influenced more by factors external to the individual (pay inequity, working conditions, or abusive treatment from superiors) than internal factors, such as inherent dishonesty. Drug testing has been challenged in the courts under the legal doctrine of invasion of privacy; however, no federal right-to-privacy statutes prohibit testing of either on- or off-the-job drug use by employees. Drug testing is, however, coming under increased scrutiny by the courts, and rulings favoring employers versus employees/applicants have been inconsistent. If any drug testing is conducted, those who sanction and administer the tests need to ensure that they do not unduly target members of protected classes.

Call-Center Staffing at Capital One

Capital One is one of the largest suppliers of consumer MasterCard and Visa credit cards in the world, with more than 44 million cardholders and more than 20,000 employees. More than 75 percent of its employees are call-center customer service associates, and 3,000 new call-center employees are hired annually. The tremendous growth of the organization required that it develop a strategy for staffing its call centers that would recruit and retain the best individuals, reduce turnover and associated costs, and increase sales volume. After a three-year planning period, Capital One rolled out its company information-based strategy (IBS). A major component of IBS is the proprietary database software that allows Capital One to achieve its staffing goals. Applicants for call-center associate jobs can either call a toll-free telephone number and proceed through a battery of screening questions or answer the same questions online. These questions relate to the job characteristics deemed to be most critical to success as a call-center associate at Capital One. Those who receive acceptable scores are invited to a regional assessment center, where they undergo an average of five hours of additional computer-based tests and assessments spread over a two-day period. The IBS uses multiple technologies, including real-time automated decision-making, simulations, and online videos. The IBS has decreased time-to-hire by 52 percent, increasing the rate at which Capital One can hire by 71 percent. Moreover, the system has resulted in a 12 percent increase in the number of calls handled per hour, a 36 percent increase in the rate of closing sales, an 18 percent decrease in unproductive downtime, and a 75 percent decrease in involuntary attrition during the first six months on the job.[32]

The most important criterion for determining whether testing will be effective and withstand any potential legal challenges is whether the testing is specifically related to the job for which an applicant has applied. Job-relatedness is most commonly shown through validation of a specific test. There are three types of validation: content validity, criterion-related validity, and construct validity. Content validity involves the use of specific job requirements as a means of testing, where the applicant is tested on skills that will be used on the job. For example, an applicant for a bookkeeping or accounting position might be asked to post ledger entries or prepare a financial statement accurately. Criterion-related validity involves the testing of attributes that have been shown to correspond to successful performance on the job. For example, an applicant could be asked to complete a simulation based on actual experiences incumbents in the position have encountered. Construct validity is similar to criterion-related validity but focuses on traits, such as honesty and integrity, rather than on specific skills.

Simulation Testing at Toyota

In 2005, Toyota Motors needed to fill 2,000 jobs from tens of thousands of applicants for its new $800 million assembly plant in San Antonio. Applicants for these positions began their application process not via an application form or interview but, rather, at a computer screen, performing a job simulation. Skills such as the reading of dials and gauges, identification of safety issues, and assemblage components and processes were measured as well as candidates' abilities to assess and solve problems and learn. Applicants were also provided with video links where they could actually see and hear about the jobs for which they were applying from current employees. Those who successfully completed the simulation were invited to return for a hands-on opportunity to demonstrate their skills. Online simulations such as these allow employers to make better hiring decision, allow prospective employees a better sense of the reality of their jobs, and reduce both recruiting costs and employee turnover. Toyota estimates that the use of this screening process saved the organization $2.6 million associated with the opening of the San Antonio plant. The assembler testing process has been cited as a "best practice" at Toyota and is being used to assist with the opening of new plants in Canada and Europe. The simulation process is also being expanded for administrative jobs.[33]

As the economy and workforces have become more diverse and global, organizations have developed a much heightened interest in assessing how well an individual might function in an increasingly global and multicultural work environment. Consequently, a large number of assessment tools have been developed that attempt to measure an individual's adaptability, cultural sensitivity, and values. These instruments are useful not only for employees who are being considered for international assignments but also for domestic employees in organizations that have global customer and/or employee bases and/or value an understanding of and appreciation for cross-cultural sensitivity. Reading 8-2, "Assessment Instruments for the Global Workforce," identifies and explains 18 different tools for measuring these traits and qualities in individuals.

References

Reference-checking is usually part of the selection process; however, most prospective employers do little more than waste valuable time during this process. Generally, employers contact individuals whose names have been provided by the applicant, despite the fact that common sense dictates that an applicant would not submit a reference who would provide a negative recommendation. However, few employers bother to investigate the applicant's background any further. Employers can and should call individuals other than those named by the applicant. When contacting references the applicant has provided, requests can be made for additional contacts within or outside of the organization. Once an individual has worked within a given industry in a given geographical location for a few years, he or she becomes well-networked within the local industry. These contacts can and should be used for checking references. There are often far fewer degrees of separation between an applicant and an employer than the employer might imagine.

Much like testing, reference-checking was often done after the interviewing process and usually as the final step in the selection decision. More recently, however, many organizations have begun checking references prior to interviewing to allow them to eliminate candidates and gather information to be used later in the interviewing process.

One potential limitation with reference-checking is that many past employers will not provide any information at all; they may do nothing more than verify the dates of employment, position held, and/or salary level. Increasing liability for libel, slander, and defamation of past employees has caused more organizations to adopt a policy of not commenting on past employees' employment history. This can be overcome at times through a well-established professional network, whereby individuals will confidentially tell those in other organizations whom they know and trust about a problem former employee.

Reference-checking has become more critical for organizations because courts have been holding employers responsible for an employee's acts if the employer did not conduct a reasonable investigation into the employee's background. The doctrine of negligent hiring requires employers to balance an applicant's right to privacy with the responsibility for providing a safe workplace for employees and customers. At the very least, the employer should verify all dates of employment and education and investigate any time gaps on an applicant's résumé.

In attempting to balance the need to avoid defamation suits brought by former employees with the need to avoid possible negligent referral charges for failure to warn another employer about a past employee's suspected potential to cause harm, employers are faced with a catch-22: Giving either too much or too little information can expose them to a lawsuit. As a public policy issue, many states have adopted laws that provide qualified immunity to an employer who provides reference information in good faith. Employers who knowingly provide false or misleading information are not immune from liability. To date, 35 states have enacted such legislation, which has been supported by the Society for Human Resource Management.[34]

International Assignments

One final challenge that organizations face in staffing selecting among current employees for overseas assignments. Traditionally, such assignments have been made based on past proven successes within the organization and the employee's work-related technical skills. Although technical ability is certainly a valid selection criterion, the main reason employees fail on international assignments has less to do with technical skills than with interpersonal and acculturation abilities. Lack of adaptation of not just the employee but the employee's family has caused problems for numerous organizations in their international operations as well as with relations with foreign officials, customers, and business partners.

Organizations are now realizing that assessing the technical backgrounds of such employees is merely an initial screening criterion. To ensure the success of overseas assignments, employers are increasingly testing employees' adaptability, open-mindedness, ability to tolerate uncertainty and ambiguity, and independence. Similarly, many are also interviewing and screening family members who would be accompanying the employee on the assignment. In certain cases, the employee is able to adapt, but problems with family members adapting either require the employee to return home before the end of the assignment or have a negative impact on the employee's performance. Screening employees as part of staffing international operations has consequently become much more elaborate and strategic to ensure the success of the assignment.

One significant challenge with international staffing involves the sourcing and acquisition of talent in emerging economies. The tremendous potential for growth in the economies of countries such as Brazil, Russia, India, and China has set off a near-frenzy of organizational entry into these markets. However, in many cases, the demand for workers with certain skills exceeds the supply available locally. Reading 8.3, "Winning the Race for Talent in Emerging Markets," discusses strategies for attracting and retaining talent in developing countries.

Documentation of Employment Eligibility

One of the chief challenges employers face in the hiring of low-skilled employees is ensuring that applicants have the legal right to work in the United States. Because there is no widespread, reliable system for verification of the legitimacy of documentation an applicant might provide, employers have to utilize extra caution in hiring. If documentation is suspect but later found to be valid, an employer can face unlawful discrimination charges. On the other hand, in spite of stiffer penalties and increased enforcement of worker eligibility, some employers feel that they have no choice but to hire illegal immigrants because of the unduly slow process associated with obtaining work visas vis-à-vis the employer's need for employees. This is particularly true in industries such as agriculture and hospitality and seasonal businesses that rely on large numbers of foreign employees.

Employers who wish to hire foreign workers who have not obtained citizenship first need to prove that there are no domestic workers with the skills and availability to perform the responsibilities of a given job and that the employment of foreign workers will have no adverse impact on wages and working conditions. Even once an employer decides to hire a foreign employee whose documentation appears to be valid, verification of the authenticity of the documentation by the Social Security Administration can take months.

It is estimated that there are more than 11 million foreign individuals working illegally in the United States and that these individuals account for nearly 5 percent of the U.S. labor force.[35] In many instances, these individuals work in low-skilled jobs that are being shunned by an increasingly educated U.S. citizenry. In 1960, 50 percent of employees in the United States had not completed high school; currently, that figure is less than 10 percent.[36] Simply deporting such workers, even if were logistically possible, would decimate certain sectors of our economy. The economic arguments both in favor of and against the employment of illegal workers are compelling. These individuals tend to pay less in taxes than the financial burdens they impose on services such as medical care and education. However, they also contribute billions of dollars annually into the Social Security system, for whose benefits they are ineligible. They also pay state and local sales and property taxes in the communities in which they reside.

While the political and economic debates concerning foreign workers will continue, this area of employment provides both tremendous opportunities for employers to fill their ranks with low-skilled workers for whom there is a demand, but at the same time, ensuring the legality of such individuals' employment status is fraught with delays, possible penalties, and ambiguity. Employers need to carefully and strategically monitor employment of foreign workers as well as maintain their currency in the relevant and evolving laws and regulations in this area.

New Trends in Staffing

Two notable trends are taking place in organizations related to their staffing programs. The first of these is employment branding. Employment branding involves the creation of an image of the organization as an employer, much like an organization may attempt to create a brand around its products and services. An employer's employment brand involves the dissemination of information that allows current and prospective employees as well as the business community to perceive the organization in a certain way. Numerous "best" lists are published each year, which employers strive to be a part of, including best employers for women, older workers, workers with disabilities, gay and lesbian employees, working mothers, and so on. Organizations may brand themselves through their advancement opportunities, higher-than-market compensation, flexible work arrangements, prestige of the employer's reputation, or the organization's social consciousness. Branding initiatives generally involve an attempt to make an employer the "employer of choice" for at least a certain segment of the workforce.

Employers create an employment brand by first making a candid assessment of their strengths as an employer. Employee satisfaction and attitude surveys can provide data as to what aspects of their employment current employees most value. Applicant cover letters can also contain information regarding why applicants seek employment with a given organization. Once these factors have been identified, employers need to consider if they are currently attracting the applicant pool they seek to employ. If not, surveys can be conducted to determine why desired applicants are not seeking employment with the organization.

Once this information has been collected, an employer can then develop its message for prospective employees regarding what the organization is and what it aspires to be. Follow-through requires careful oversight and management of the organization's culture, mission, and employment policies and practices. A critical part of an organization's employment branding is its culture, particularly relative to relationships, authority, and accountability.[37] Meetings and interviews with prospective employees should communicate the organization's culture as part of the employment brand. Ideally, strong employment branding combined with effective recruitment and selection processes should result in higher retention rates, lower overall recruitment costs, and improved company image.

The second trend in staffing is candidate relationship management (CRM). CRM involves building a relationship with job applicants that transcends the current hiring cycle and process. Similar to employment branding, CRM is designed to engage candidates in an ongoing manner and heighten the image of the organization as a desirable place to work. It may be the case that a position is not available for a strong candidate at the time of candidate inquiry, there may be more desirable candidates than there are current openings, or a candidate may have personal circumstances that prevent acceptance of an offer of employment at a particular point in time. CRM involves the creation of an ongoing relationship with potential employees that can be capitalized on when a position becomes available within the organization and/or the candidate becomes available. The end result of this activity is the creation of a pipeline of talent that remains interested in and available for employment with an organization over time.

CRM activities usually center on the creation and maintenance of a database of possible candidates for employment as well as regular communication with these individuals to keep them engaged and their interest level elevated. Many CRM activities parallel those that organizations have developed with key customers to maintain and nurture the client relationship. Prospective employees can be sent e-mails, newsletters, links to blogs, birthday cards, and other correspondence to keep the organization in the forefront of their minds. Such activities tend to be extremely cost-effective relative to later savings realized relative to both time and direct out-of-pocket recruiting expenses.[38]

CRM at Whirlpool

Whirlpool Corporation is a global manufacturer of major home appliances under brand names that include Maytag, Amana, KitchenAid, and Jenn-Air. Candidate recruiting at Whirlpool is treated as an opportunity to market both the organization and its product lines. Every job candidate is an existing or potential customer, so Whirlpool's Exceptional Candidate Experience (ECE) program was designed to develop both the employer brand and customer loyalty.

The ECE involves a three-stage process—initial candidate touch points, candidate engagement, and candidate closings—with the goal of providing an exceptional experience to ensure that the candidate leaves with a positive impression of the organization, regardless of whether an offer of employment is made. The first stage—initial candidate touch points—focuses on consistent, positively branded messages about the organization and its products, which are designed to create an inviting image. Candidate engagement ensures that every candidate is treated warmly and engaged during the interview process. This includes gifts of Whirlpool products in appreciation for the time candidates spend during the interview process. The final stage—candidate closings—attempts to ensure that all job candidates remain customers for life, regardless of the outcome of the interview.

Whirlpool realizes that prospective and existing employees have many choices for employment and that top performers have near-limitless choices. The ECE is designed to ensure that Whirlpool is not only successful in recruiting the best available talent but that the process also creates ambassadors of the company and its products.[39]

Candidate relationship management activities go beyond simply engaging current and prospective applicants in seeking to attract applicants from unconventional places. Two commonly overlooked sources of employees are customers and former employees. Recruiting employees from an organization's customer base can be convenient, cost-effective, and result in highly qualified, enthusiastic employees who already believe in the organization and its products or services. Targeting customers who may not currently be on the job market can increase both the quantity and quality of the employer's applicant pool. Existing customers have experience with the organization's products and services and can provide additional insights into the development and marketing of the organization's offerings. A perennial favorite on Fortune magazine's "100 Best Companies for Work For" list is The Container Store, which recruits employees almost exclusively from its customer base.[40]

A number of organizations are increasingly utilizing former employees as a target applicant pool. This activity has been prompted by a fundamental shift in the employment relationship from the traditional, long-term "loyalty" paradigm to one that is more short-term and transactional in nature.[41] Former employees can be a valuable resource to an employer, given that they know the organization's products/services, culture, market, and customers. Many employers are also creating alumni networks for former employees, keeping these individuals in touch via social events and written and electronic communications. Former employees can be similar to internal hires in that they result in lower recruiting costs and a shortened time-to-hire cycle, given that they are known entities within the organization. Former employees can also bring a heightened sense of the marketplace, depending on their interim employment. Former employees also tend to be more productive because of the loyalty and goodwill created by the employer as part of the re-employment decision.[42] Returning employees have higher retention rates than other employees, and re-employment also allows employers to recoup some of the training and development costs of these former employees as well as benefit from any additional training and skill development that the employee has obtained since leaving the organization.[43]

Conclusion

An organization can only be successful and reach its strategic objectives by employing individuals who have the capacity and desire to contribute to its mission. The staffing function, therefore, plays an important role in facilitating an organization's success. When unemployment is low, organizations face even greater challenges in staffing because the forces of supply and demand drive wages up and provide greater career opportunities with other organizations.

An effective staffing strategy requires in-depth planning for the recruiting process to ensure efficiency and generation of a qualified applicant pool. How selection will proceed relative to process and the kinds of applicant information needed must also be determined. The strategic decisions organizations need to make relative to staffing are summarized in Exhibit 8.6. Staffing is the key or core component that forms the backbone of an integrated, strategic system of human resource management by ensuring that there is an optimal fit between employees and the strategic needs of the organization. If an organization's staffing is deficient, the effectiveness of its HR programs and policies will be impaired. As one HR professional commented, "Good training will not fix bad selection."

EXHIBIT 8.6 Strategic Issues in Staffing

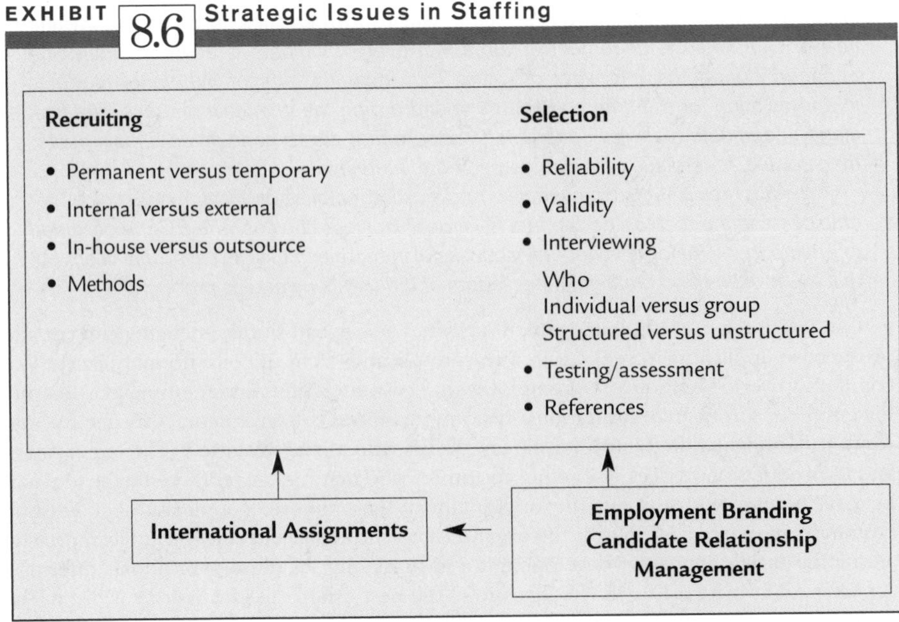

Critical Thinking

1. How does an organization's investment in staffing benefit the organization after an applicant becomes an employee?
2. What problems can result from cutting corners to save time or money in the staffing process?
3. What are the major strategic choices an organization faces concerning staffing? What are the advantages and disadvantages of each alternative?
4. Devise a staffing strategy for the following organizations:
   - A church-based soup kitchen staffed with volunteers
   - A professional baseball team
   - A small Internet startup
   - A publisher of a large daily newspaper in a major city
   - A police department
   - A 400-room luxury hotel
5. Develop a set of behaviorally based interview questions for the following jobs:
   - High school principal
   - Nursing supervisor
   - Factory foreman
   - Chief medical resident
   - Police chief
6. Discuss the challenges organizations face associated with the employment of foreign workers.
7. How might an employer create an employment branding strategy?
8. What are the pros and cons of establishing a candidate relationship management program?

Reading 8.1

9. Evaluate the future potential and possibilities for the contingent employment market and industry.

Reading 8.2

10. What types of positions in what types of industries might each of the eighteen inventories be used to assess?

Reading 8.3

11. What commonalities and differences do employers face when trying to recruit and retain talent in Brazil, Russia, India, and China?

Exercises

1. Visit a major employer's Web site (such as those provided here or any others). Apply for a specific job with the same company both via online means and through submitting a résumé by postal mail. Compare and contrast the processes. As an applicant, which did you find preferable and why?

Cisco Systems	http://www.cisco.com
GE Energy	http://www.gepower-careers.com
Advanced Micro Devices	http://www.amd.com
Booz Allen Hamilton	http://www.bah.com
Bank of America	http://www.bankofamerica.com
Compaq Computer	http://www.compaq.com
Eastman Kodak	http://www.kodak.com
Specialized Bicycles	http://www.specialized.com

2. In small groups, discuss your experiences with and determine the pros and cons of online recruiting from the employer's perspective.
3. Develop a behavioral interviewing protocol for your current or most recent job.
4. Visit the Web sites for the following employment services:

   http://www.monster.com

   http://www.hotjobs.com

   http://www.careerbuilder.com

   Compare and contrast the features and attractiveness of each site.

Chapter References

1. Murphy, T. E. and Zandvakili, S. "Data- and Metrics-Driven Approach to Human Resource Practices: Using Customers, Employees and Financial Metrics," Human Resource Management, Vol. 39, No. 1, pp. 93–105.
2. Joinson, C. "Capturing Turnover Costs," *HR Magazine*, July 2000, pp. 107–119.
3. Ibid. p. 118.

4. Tyler, K. "Treat Contingent Workers With Care," *HR Magazine*, 53, (3), March 2008, pp. 75–79.
5. Frase-Blunt, M. "Short-term Executives," *HR Magazine*, 49, (6), June 2004, pp. 110–114.
6. McConnell, B. "Recruiting How-tos as Important as Who-tos, SHRM Survey Reveals," *HR News*, December 2002, pp. 2, 5.
7. Miraz, P. "Networking: An Executive Recruiter's Best Friend," *HR Magazine*, September 2000, p. 22.
8. Miraz, P. "Where Are All the Home-Grown CEOs?," *HR Magazine*, September 2000, p. 22.
9. Leonard, B. "Online and Overwhelmed," *HR Magazine*, August 2000, pp. 37–39.
10. Ibid.
11. Leonard, B. "Job Candidates Judge Employers by Their Web Sites," *HR Magazine*, July 2000, pp. 30–31.
12. Ibid.
13. Martinez, M. N. "Get Job Seekers to Come to You," *HR Magazine*, August 2000, pp. 45–52.
14. "Networking Rules, Say Job Seekers and Employers," *HR News*, 20, (5), May 2001, p. 2.
15. Leonard, B. "Job-Hunting Professionals Rank Networking over Internet," *HR Magazine*, May 2002, pp. 25–26.
16. "Networking Rules, Say Job Seekers and Employers," *HR News*, 20, (5), May 2001, p. 2.
17. McConnell, B. "Recruiting How-tos as Important as Who-tos, SHRM Survey Reveals," *HR News*, December 2002, pp. 2, 5.
18. Grensing-Pophal, L. "The Perils of Internet Recruiting," www.shrm.org.hrresources.whitepapers_published/CMS_000408.asp.
19. Ibid.
20. Roberts, B. "System Addresses 'Applicant' Dilemma," *HR Magazine*, September 2002, pp. 111–119.
21. Martinez, M. N. "The Headhunter Within," *HR Magazine*, August 2001, pp. 48–55.
22. Ibid.
23. Robinson, K. "Online Bidding Fills Nursing Jobs," *HR Magazine*, December 2003, p. 44.
24. Fisher, C. D., Schoenfeldt, L. F. and Shaw, J. B. *Human Resource Management*, 4th ed. Boston: Houghton Mifflin Co., 1999, p. 274.
25. Martinez, M. N. "Recruiting Here and There," *HR Magazine*, September 2002, pp. 95–100.
26. Hirsh, S. "Software King Builds Young Careers, Too," *Baltimore Sun*, March 9, 2003, p. 1D.
27. Higgins, C. and Judge, T. "The Effect of Applicant Influence Tactics on Recruiter Perceptions of Fit and Hiring Recommendations: A Field Study," *Journal of Applied Psychology*, 89(4), pp. 622–632.
28. Poe, A. C. "Graduate Work," *HR Magazine*, October 2003, pp. 95–100.
29. Ibid.
30. Goldberg, L. R. "An Alternative 'Description of Personality': The Big-Five Structure," *Journal of Personality and Social Psychology*, 59, (6), December 1990, pp. 1216–1229.
31. Krell, E. "Personality Counts," *HR Magazine*, 50, (11), November, 2005, pp. 47–52.
32. Romeo, J. "Answering the Call," *HR Magazine*, October 2003, pp. 81–84.
33. Winkler, C. "Job Tryouts Go Virtual," *HR Magazine*, 51, (9), September 2006, 131–134.
34. "SHRM Board Oks Investment Advice, Safety, Reference Positions," *HR News*, May 2002, p. 11.
35. Ladika, S. "Trouble on the Hiring Front," *HR Magazine*, 51, (10), October 2006, pp. 56–61.
36. Ibid.
37. Brandon, C. "Truth in Recruitment Branding," *HR Magazine*, 50, (11), November 2005, pp. 89–96.
38. Frase, M. "Stocking Your Talent Pool," *HR Magazine*, 52, (4), April 2007, pp. 67–74.
39. Weirick, K. "The Perfect Interview," *HR Magazine*, 53, (4), April 2008, pp. 85–88.
40. Arnold, J. "Customers as Employees," *HR Magazine*, 52, (4), April 2007, pp. 77–82
41. Pulley, J. "When the Grass Wasn't Greener," *Staffing Management*, 2, (3), September 2006.
42. Weaver, P. "Tap Ex-Employees' Recruitment Potential," *HR Magazine*, 51, (7), July 2006, pp. 89–91.
43. Pulley, J. "When the Grass Wasn't Greener," *Staffing Management*, 2, (3), September 2006.

READING 8.1

Temporary Help Agencies and the Making of a New Employment Practice

Vicki Smith and Esther B. Neuwirth

Executive Overview

Over the past 50 years in America, we have gone from a system of work characterized by lifetime employment at a single employer to a patchwork system characterized by low security and high volatility. A major player in our new world of work is the temporary help agency, which serves as the intermediary between workers and companies. Traditionally, temporary help agencies have been regarded, at best, as a necessary evil, and, at worst, as machines that eat up and spit out workers. In fact, the reality is far more nuanced. When job seekers' options are unemployment or degraded employment, working with the staff of an agency that has an investment in promoting its profit-making commodity—good temporary workers—gives them a distinct advantage. Agency staff help applicants and valued workers improve résumés and refine their job expectations in productive ways, and often advocate for better wages, higher-level positions, and more humane, safer working conditions for their temps. Temporary employment today is thus a double-edged sword. While, on average, agency temps receive lower wages, rarely can purchase health insurance, and have virtually no employment security, they can also be buffered from the worst aspects of new employment relations by labor market intermediaries such as temporary placement agencies.

Fifty years ago, temporary employment was such a marginal labor practice that the Bureau of Labor Statistics did not track the size or composition of the temporary workforce, nor did it collect systematic data about employers' use of such workers (Watson, personal communication, 2007). This occupational ghetto appears to have been staffed almost exclusively by married women who lacked viable employment alternatives (Goldin, 1990) and often had weak labor market attachments (Moore, 1965). Employers and managers used temps, mostly in office positions, on a short-term, stopgap basis, bringing them in to cover for permanent employees. In post-World War II offices, the jobs were permanent; it was the workers who were temps.

This model of temporary employment has experienced a sea change since the mid-20th century. Far from being a marginal labor practice, temporary employment today is widespread and normalized. Employers hire temporary workers—almost three million each day (Berchem, 2008, Fig. 3)—as a routine staffing strategy rather than simply to fill in for permanent workers on a stopgap basis. Many companies today have limited budgets for hiring permanent workers but ample resources—and top management approval—for hiring temps.[1] Companies that are reluctant to add to their permanent workforces instead create short- and long-term temporary positions, the latter evidenced by the steady growth of "permatemps."[2] In 2005, for example, 35% of temporary agency workers held a single temp job for more than a year, compared to 24% in 1995 (Mishel, Bernstein, & Allegretto, 2007, p. 241, Table 4.8). In contrast to the post-World War II era, now, both the jobs and the workers are temporary.

Temps today are about as likely to be adult men as adult women, with women comprising 52.8% and men comprising 47.2% of temporary agency workers (Mishel, Bernstein, & Allegretto, 2007, p. 242, Table 9). They can be found in low (those we refer to as temporary agency workers) and high (contract workers) ranks of the occupational and professional structure, in blue- and white-collar jobs, in services and manufacturing.

The temporary help service (THS) industry has grown exponentially. The number of THS offices surged from about 800 in the early 1960s to 5,000 by 1981 to nearly 40,000 today. Temporary help service revenue has likewise exploded over the years; annual earnings expanded from about $250 million in the early 1960s to $73.5 billion in 2007. Growth in industry earnings was paralleled by growth in the size of the temporary workforce, which was a little over 11 million in 2007 (Berchem, 2008; Mangum, Mayall, & Nelson, 1985; Moore, 1965). The growth of temporary employment has mixed effects for workers, which has been confirmed in numerous studies by labor economists, sociologists, and organizational scholars. On the one hand, the majority of those who work in temp jobs prefer permanent work (they are involuntary temps), they experience high levels of job insecurity, and they lack health benefits and mobility opportunities. On the other hand, temporary jobs provide opportunities to earn income when job seekers can't get hired into a permanent or regular job; they have become a valuable source of employment, often on a longterm, albeit destabilized, basis.

How did temporary employment evolve from a small, peripheral practice to one that is large and central to contemporary hiring practices? Much is known about the historic rise of the temporary help services industry, which actively worked to enlarge and legitimate this previously marginal employment relationship. In the 1970s and '80s representatives of the industry directly marketed their product—temporary laborers—to hiring managers, overcoming their resistance to using nonpermanent workers (Ofstead, 1999). Convincing hiring managers to transition from the stopgap to the staffing model of using temps required work and persuasion. Temporary staffing agencies had to appease hiring managers' anxieties about the logistical complexities of bringing in temps, and overcome their reluctance to change long-standing employment practices of hiring permanent workers. Industry representatives worked to convince hiring managers that using temps would not compromise trade secrets, that the costs associated with training and retraining workers would not be prohibitive, and that temps could be loyal to the companies that employed them (Vosko, 2000, p. 149).

The THS industry also fought its case in the courts and reshaped labor law, striving to generate new demand for its product and improve the competitive conditions under which it operated (Gonos, 1997). The industry lobbied and worked through state and federal courts to become legal employers of temporary workers. This accomplishment had two profound implications: First, it meant that the temporary agency, rather than the hiring company, became the employer of record and that firms rid themselves of legal obligations to a subset of their workers. Second, given that managers in hiring firms did not actually have to fire and hire temps themselves—given that they could simply inform agencies if they didn't want a particular temp to return or if they needed a fresh supply of temps—the corporate world gained great latitude in its use of labor.

On top of these institutional and legal changes, THS industry leaders cultivated a new, positive image of temporary workers in the popular media, paving the way for greater acceptance of temps and greater skepticism about permanent workers' productivity and work ethic (Smith & Neuwirth, 2008). Writing articles in personnel and business magazines, many THS leaders highlighted the value of their new product, emphasizing the hidden costs of permanent labor; discussing groups of people (besides married women) who had the capacity to be good temporary workers; and identifying new occupations, industries, and task niches where temporary workers could be used. Through these combined measures, the industry engaged extensively in market-making activities.

But what few understand is the active work undertaken by temporary help placement agencies to create a high-quality, marketable product: good temporary workers and workforces. Since the late 1990s we have interviewed and observed temporary workers, interviewed production and hiring managers, and worked in the office of a temporary help service agency in Silicon Valley (an agency we call Select Labor).[3] Our focus during this time has been on the labor market segment that includes office, assembly, warehouse, and other types of entry-level temporary agency workers and the agencies that employ them. Although there are other types of temporary workers, such as high-level contractors (Barley & Kunda, 2006), day laborers (Bartley & Roberts, 2006), and contract company employees, temporary agency workers constitute the largest proportion of the temporary workforce (Dey, Houseman, & Polivka, 2007). We found that both temporary help service agencies and the industry at large have a significant interest in constructing a labor force of good temporary employees, creating temporary jobs, and reshaping managerial practices to optimize outcomes for both temps and hiring firms.

Our findings help correct an outdated image of temporary employment and temporary workers. Contrary to the perception of temporary help agencies as machines that eat and spit out workers, treating them as if they were disposable, even interchangeable commodities, temporary help agencies have created a set of practices that buffer their workers from the most insecure and exploitative aspects of temporary employment. Indeed, some of their screening, selection, and retention practices closely resemble those used when companies hire workers on a standard basis. Temporary workers, frequently assumed to be disposable, are in contrast often valued workers whom companies and agencies seek to use on a steady, long-term basis.

The paper unfolds as follows: First, we look at the economics of temporary help agencies as a way of understanding their unique position of serving two "masters": their temporary workers (their products) and the companies who employ their workers (their clients). In the second and third sections of the paper, we look at Select Labor, a temporary help agency that we studied over several years, and use the case to show how temporary agencies work to get the best possible employees and also how they must negotiate and work with client companies to ensure a good "fit" for the temporary workers they place there.

The Economics of Temporary Help Agencies

To understand the rise of temporary agencies, it is first important to look at the economics of THS agencies. These agencies compete with one another and earn their profits in a variety of ways. Most fundamentally, they sell services: expertise and ability to assist with recruitment, screening, hiring, placing, monitoring, and firing temporary workers and managing payroll (temps are on the agencies' payroll, not the payroll of the hiring companies) (Pfeffer & Baron, 1988). They also help companies develop and manage temp-to-perm programs, set up on-site offices ("vendor on premises"), and sometimes transport temps to their work sites (Vosko, 2000).

Agencies can compete for new clients (the hiring companies that need temps) by offering smaller markups than their competitors do. An agency profits from every hour its temps are employed because of the markup, a standard practice whereby a client firm pays an hourly wage for each temp plus a negotiated additional amount that goes directly to the agency and constitutes the agency's profits (Gonos, 2000/01). Hourly wages for temporary workers are often benchmarked to prevailing regional wages for entry-level jobs, although agency representatives often play a role in negotiating higher wages for their temps (Smith & Neuwirth, 2008).

Beyond being economically competitive, agencies can also compete with one another by selling quality temporary workers. Temporary workers are the grist for the THS mill, and agencies work in a field that is dense with other agencies striving to place their product first.[4] The increased emphasis on providing quality temps parallels the larger preoccupation with "quality service" that has swept through American business over the past few decades. As companies compete to survive, they strive to distinguish themselves by the high quality of the goods and services they provide to consumers (Martin, 1994). Client firms play their own role in pressuring agencies to produce a pool of good temps: They threaten to use the temps of other agencies if they are not satisfied with one agency's workers (Peck & Theodore, 1998). Companies may demand "good" quality temps because they are concerned with productivity, skills, effort, and motivation (Nollen & Axel, 1998, p. 138).

Promoting an image of temporary workers as good workers and actually creating temporary workers who can live up to that image leads THS agencies to adopt a unique set of practices. A good temp, we argue, is a specific type of worker but also an image, a sales pitch, and a source of competitiveness for the THS industry. Sometimes temporary workers measure up to this ideal; sometimes they don't. Sometimes people want to be good temps; sometimes they don't. What is important is that promising then constructing good temporary workers is at the heart of the mainstream temporary placement industry.

Characteristics of a Good Temporary Employee

There are multiple dimensions that can come into play in selecting and making an employee not simply a good worker but a good temporary worker, and ensuring that an agency is not simply a purveyor of generic labor but of a reliable, on-call workforce of temps. In theory, a good temp has specific characteristics. The first concerns attitude. Agencies look for job applicants with attitudes and dispositions appropriate for temporary work (Cappelli, 1995). Successful temporary workers must understand and accept the unique terms of temporary employment. When people are new to temporary employment it is imperative that they are or become familiar with the concept of "at will" employment and the fact that there is no employment guarantee; that a job might last just a few days but that it might last several months or more with no guarantee of a permanent position; that the agency will receive a portion of every hour's wages paid by the client firm as a result of the markup; that their hourly wage almost certainly will be lower than the hourly wage of their permanent counterparts, even though they may work side by side doing exactly the same tasks[5]; and that the agency, not the client firm, is their boss.

These conditions can signal to applicants that they are second-class citizens, posing a challenge to the companies that hire them. For example, these terms may be troubling to an individual who is determined to land a permanent, secure job—and as American Staffing Association data show, the majority of people who take a temporary job do so with the hope that it will lead them to permanent employment (Berchem, 2006, Figure 6). An individual with predictable resentment, anxiety, and possible confusion about having to accept temporary employment would likely be a difficult person to place and keep on the job.

Even a person who prefers a temp job because it allows him to attend school or raise a family can find it impossible to succeed in these pursuits given the inherent unpredictability of a "no guarantee" job. This person may not want a permanent job but still may desire something relatively stable. For these reasons, a desirable attitude might consist of a demonstrable level of mental flexibility and a willingness to work on an open-ended basis. We expect such characteristics of good employees, but the idea that good attitude would be expected of temporary workers runs counter to traditional notions of temps as disposable labor. It is incumbent on agencies to select or create workers with reasonable attitudes, as illustrated by our data.

The second characteristic of a good temp has to do with a minimum level of competence, responsibility, and adaptability. Even jobs that appear to be unskilled nearly always require some ability and judgment. An ideal temp would be able to walk into a variety of situations and get to work. A materials handler position, for example—where someone delivers materials and supplies to various production units in a workplace—might be thought of as a position requiring primarily physical strength and endurance, but it can entail greater complexity (such as social-relational competencies). Language competencies might be essential in such jobs, as might the capacity for teamwork. Individuals with previous experience in an environment characterized by authoritarian management might be ill equipped to survive in a production setting that stresses participation and initiative. Someone who has worked in a professional position in a law office may feel qualified for a white-collar work environment and be frustrated and resentful if sent to a comparatively deskilled white-collar job, repetitively entering data. For these reasons, we might say that a good temp will be adaptable and able to learn, and that agencies must engage in selection methods more extensively than might be anticipated (Wilk & Cappelli, 2003).

Additional Challenges Affecting Temporary Help Agencies

A good temporary *workforce* is something above and beyond a good temporary worker. Temp placement agencies need to be able to guarantee that if a hiring company places an order for a batch of temps, the agency will be able to quickly produce decent temporary workers in volume, a strong motivation for having a just-in-time pool of good temporary workers.

Inherent in the promise of producing a batch of temps on demand is the promise of a steady stream of temps who can be sent and will stay for the duration of a project, whether it is fulfilling a one-time order that requires assembling 1,000 servers or, testing circuit boards in a company that has a freeze on hiring permanent workers but has authorization to hire temporary workers—all in positions that are defined as temporary, may last months, and will ultimately disappear. For this reason, agencies can be committed to retention and minimizing turnover of good temps (Autor, 2001). In the era of widespread and long-term use of temporary workers, agencies lose if turnover is too high. As when companies hire permanent workers, invest in their training, and pay a cost if they quit prematurely, temporary placement agencies invest in their temps and pay a cost if temps walk off the job without completing the job assignment or refuse to return to an assignment. Having to continually create new temps becomes a burden to the agency.

This cost has been underestimated in previous studies, which insinuate that, from the perspective of the agency, entry-level temporary workers are interchangeable, almost disposable. On the contrary, THS agencies incur fixed costs that they strive to minimize. Every new job applicant must be administratively processed: tested, screened, and interviewed for a job. Agency staff must nurture their social relationships with temps, particularly good temps who are valued members of a temporary pool and will work diligently for long periods of time in one temporary position. Since the agency profits from every hour a temp is employed, it is ideal that any given temp work as long as possible in one position, without disruption or the need to find a replacement. These relations build momentum and endure, and losing them means the agency has to begin all over again with new "raw material."

Hiring companies (the clients of the temp agencies), too, must train and retrain new temps, leading shop-floor managers to try to avoid turnover of long-term temps (Smith, 2001). Having to deal with a hiring company where bad management practices lead temps to quit their assignments poses a distinct challenge for a placement firm that wishes to maintain a steady and reliable supply of temporary workers. In the following pages we use case study data to detail how an agency manages these contradictory issues. These strategies, we argue, are at the center of the growth, the normalization, and the continuation of temporary employment in the United States.

How an Agency Constructs Good Temporary Workers and Workforces

For Select Labor, a pseudonym for the agency we studied, attracting, developing, keeping, and controlling good temps was by no means automatic or straightforward. Just as the THS industry has had to work over decades to achieve legitimacy for a new type of employment relationship, so too did Select Labor have to repeatedly build and control its temp workforce. We cannot take this process for granted. Agencies have to construct good, qualified temps to cultivate and maintain marketable workforces. What sells in the world of temporary employment is not simply warm bodies; it is good workers who are willing to work on a temporary basis.

According to Select Labor's marketing brochures, the agency promised temps who were "productive," "committed to quality performance," and "reliable," and who "would make significant contributions to [hiring company] products." Agency staff had many reasons to guard against hiring people they suspected wouldn't succeed as temps, whether because they would not be productive, wouldn't cooperate with supervisors and managers, or in other ways didn't show potential for positive work performance. Having a reliable stream of quality temporary workers supported the agency's reputation, attracted additional client firms, and added to the bottom line. Sending temporary workers who wouldn't last on a job was directly counterproductive to these goals. We found that these interwoven imperatives led Select Labor to adopt a variety of strategies to improve the quality of its temporary labor and the quality of its services (for a fuller analysis see Smith & Neuwirth, 2008).

Selective Recruitment

Like virtually every business in America, Select Labor (SL) advertised its services in customary places and ways. Anybody wishing to find employment—whether as a temporary worker or as a temporary who could convert to a permanent worker—could find out about SL on its Web site, in the yellow pages of the local telephone directory, in a regional *Employment Guide and Career Source* magazine, and at community colleges and training centers. In addition to these impersonal methods of advertising, SL staff widely and selectively recruited people who could help secure the firm's claim to sell a high-quality temporary workforce.

For one thing, SL staff attended local job fairs when possible. Job fairs are fascinating terrain for anyone studying contemporary employment practices. Visitors can find dozens if not hundreds of employers hawking their products, services, and reputations to potential employees. Fairs, particularly large urban fairs, attract thousands of the job-seeking unemployed as well as employed people just curious about what the labor market has to offer. Job fairs encompass a surprising number of employers and industries (including government agencies, goods and service providers, Internet companies and high-tech firms, and temp/staffing agencies). When Select Labor staff sponsored tables at a fair, they could keep their eyes open for job seekers who were looking for permanent work but were receptive to learning about the advantages and disadvantages of temporary jobs. At the same time, the staff used this opportunity to discourage those job seekers for whom temporary employment would be an unacceptable alternative to permanent jobs: In other words, agency staff engaged in nurturing some potential applicants and weeding out others before they even came to the agency office.

Reeling in job fair attendees by offering promotional items such as chocolates, pens, calendars, and notepads, agency reps collected résumés from attendees (as do virtually all those who staff the tables at job fairs). They conducted impromptu interviews, speaking with and taking notes on potential job candidates about their preferred hours of work and wages. Conversations at these fairs gave SL reps an opening to educate job seekers about temporary work and collect information for their database of potential recruits to the industry.

Staffing specialists tried to recruit competitive, good temporary workers through networks with job development specialists in the region. These job development specialists worked for state agencies (both training and placement); they worked with community colleges, and they worked for for-profit training schools and colleges. One staff member in the SL office, for example, sent off job announcements each week to a group of job specialists in the region with whom he had developed close relations throughout his career in the staffing industry, trusting that they would direct these announcements to appropriate individuals. Alex, an energetic recruiter at Select Labor, said of his systematic approach:

> *Many of these people don't make money by placing people—they either work for the county, the city, or the state, and it's their job to help people find work. So if I have a job opening, I'll go down my list and start calling these folks and say, "Hey, I need this type of candidate with these skills" and so on. I'll ask if they have anyone they can send my way. And every Monday morning I try and type out a spreadsheet with all my job openings. Then I fax this list to over 33 agencies, schools, and places like that. I'll follow that up with a phone call or even a visit if I have time. Sometimes I'll go ahead and visit the place and post a flyer with my open job orders, and I'll attach an envelope to the flyer with my business cards.*

Other staff routinely telephoned their contacts at agencies and schools to find out about new graduates who might be good "material" for temporary positions.

Trust is an important ingredient in hiring new workers, and as sociologists and labor economists well know, relying on established networks is a common way for employers to recruit good workers they can trust (Granovetter, 1995; Smith, 2005). Select Labor recruited reliable temps by tapping the networks of the temps already on its payroll. SL had a formal program that offered modest bonuses to temporary workers who recommended friends or family members for jobs with SL. (The parent company estimated that approximately 50% of SL's recruits were friends and family members of current employees.) To maximize the quality of those who were referred, SL gave temps the bonus only if the recommended person was able to work in good standing for several weeks of full-time temporary employment. On occasion, SL staff declined to hire someone recommended by one of their regular temps, a person who was good enough to be sent out to some jobs but just questionable enough to make Select Labor staff wary of his recommendations. In other words, agency staff did not leave the quality of their temporary labor pool to chance, or passively wait for the right kind of temps: They sought job applicants who might be reasonably compatible with temporary positions.

Screening for Good and Weeding Out Undesirable Applicants

Selective recruitment doesn't guarantee that a temp will succeed on the job. Once the agency succeeded in persuading people to visit the office, follow-up measures were critical. SL staff used a rigorous intake process as a filter to separate questionable from promising temps. What is surprising is the high level of quality control agency representatives used to select the members of their temporary employment pool. While we would expect that a company hiring a permanent worker for a complex or demanding job might use rigorous selection measures (Wilk & Cappelli, 2003), we would not have the same expectation for those who hire workers who are commonly thought of as "disposable."

The primary objective of the intake process was the inextricably entwined work of weeding out unacceptable candidates and identifying acceptable ones. First, minimal skills tests were administered in the office: SL had one room in the facility dedicated to testing the computer skills (word processing, graphics, and database management) of candidates for office positions, and the soldering skills of applicants for positions with integrated circuit producers who needed expert solderers. Beyond their technical skills, job applicants were assessed on their understanding of the parameters of temporary employment. SL placement specialists were trained to carefully follow a scripted interview protocol when new temps came in seeking work. SL staff gave job seekers a pamphlet outlining the features of temporary employment, including minimum standards of job participation (arriving on time for an assignment, observing all client rules, volunteering for more tasks once on the job), the importance of maintaining confidentiality about the client's business, and covering how payroll was handled.

Staff were instructed to use the interview to find out how much the candidate knew about temping. Training literature exhorted them to consider: "What does the candidate hope we can do for him/her? How flexible is he/she regarding assignments and pay? How realistic is the candidate? Do they understand the meaning of 'at will' employment?" The brochure went on to implore recruitment specialists to "set forth Select Labor's expectations, policies regarding communication and commitment, business dress and attendance. Gauge what you emphasize by the strengths/weaknesses/problems you suspect."[6] If a recruitment specialist suspected that an applicant's expectations were way out of line, or that an applicant misrepresented his skills or wasn't really serious about taking a temporary position, the specialist would attempt to discourage him and, more notably, "encourage poor candidates to register at other services."

Agency staff were primed to detect behaviors believed to predict an applicant's potential for good and bad work performance. Promising applicants were said to have some combination of these good traits: positive attitude, responsibility, reliability, loyalty, energy, intelligence, honesty, and trustworthiness; these traits, in turn, were associated with close to 100 examples of "good" behavior. Questionable applicants were said to have a set of traits that were the polar opposites of those typical of the promising applicants and were similarly associated with close to 100 behavioral propensities, all "bad."

Placement specialists were asked to check off other traits during the interview, using categories for grooming, verbal facility, awareness, and behavior. Each category contained a list of characteristics ranging from very desirable to unacceptable. Under "grooming," for example, job seekers were ranked as to whether they appeared to be management and professional or "casual" material, fit for light industrial or clerical work, unkempt or unhygienic, "counselable," or unacceptable. Under "awareness," a job seeker could be interpreted as excellent, with strong understanding of expectations, all the way down to unsatisfactory, "shows total lack of understanding of expectations." And under "behavior" someone seeking temporary employment could be interpreted as extremely good with a positive attitude, all the way down to "unacceptable, exhibits poor attitude."

SL staff engaged in quality control of temps after they were placed in jobs by collecting and studying data on worker performance, monitoring temps at job sites, and rewarding good temps while sanctioning problematic temps. For example, agency staff sent a survey to the managers at client companies asking managers to evaluate individual temps. The short survey created a track record about general aptitudes and behaviors rather than specific skill sets: "production" and "skill level" (both undefined), attendance, judgment, cooperation, dress/grooming, and accuracy—with a telling question, "Would you accept his/her return?" concluding the survey.

Quality control was exercised in other ways as well. Agency staff were required to conduct a "quality check" by calling hiring managers within 30 minutes of the arrival of a new temp or batch of temps to make sure their transition into the workplace had been successful. Had the temp or temps arrived on time? Had they been able to understand and follow directions? SL staff always hoped that the new temps would blend into the client company in a relatively seamless way. As further follow-up, agency staff would conduct unannounced "spot checks," visiting different work sites to check in with managers, touch base with the temps they had hired, and observe the work site to make sure that everything was in place. At companies where they had on-site offices—vendor-on-premise arrangements—staff were easily able to monitor temps on the job for evidence of satisfactory behavior and attitude. All these methods allowed agency staff to identify the good performers and gather ammunition for weeding out the bad.

SL staff used incentives to reward and reinforce good temp behaviors. By using an employee reward system that set a bar for quality work performance, they communicated what they expected of all their temporary workers, simultaneously acting to retain good temps. The employee recognition program awarded bonuses to temps who were deemed of the highest quality, with good temps receiving cash, paid days off, and gift cards. SL staff encouraged client firms to have employee-of-the-month award programs for temporary workers as well.

On the other hand, agency staff could refuse to rehire or replace temps who, for various reasons, didn't succeed on the job. Agencies are not legally bound to place or replace applicants once they have hired them. And on the other side of the employment relationship, hiring firms can easily request that a temp not be sent back to them. Select Labor staff could cast off substandard or "suboptimal" (Peck & Theodore, 1998, p. 670) temps, noting who was unsatisfactory, who was making managers at client firms unhappy, and who was unlikely to make it as a temp in the long run. Agency staff occasionally sent a temporary worker off to interview for a position at a company, only to hear later that the individual never arrived. When and if the job candidate called the agency begging for a second chance, Select Labor's staff had the option of deactivating his job application. SL staff generally gave temps with problems a second chance but usually stopped before giving them a third. Occasionally, the placement staff at SL would tell job seekers after an infraction (such as not showing up for an interview or a job, or failing to meet the minimum standards for job performance) that they weren't able to find another position for them, a passive antiretention strategy. The agency's guarantee that Select Labor would not charge a client firm for the final eight hours of a "failed" temp's work subtly reminded staff about the financial cost of keeping a bad temp.

Maximizing Fit, Modifying Workers' Aspirations

Successful sales in the staffing industry come from knowing how to place the right worker in the right job. Select Labor management continually stressed that the work of agency representatives was not primarily to help workers who wanted excellent employment opportunities. Rather, their primary goal was to give employers what they wanted. And part and parcel of that goal was to know how to avoid setting up temps for failure, which would of course redound on SL's reputation. Time and again, SL staff would refrain from sending a job applicant out to a job the individual was particularly interested in but was not qualified for. Staff also worked to modify job applicants' aspirations, encouraging them to postpone immediate goals that were unrealistic and adjust their expectations to the realities of existing opportunities. In both cases, Select Labor's goal was to eliminate or at least narrow the mismatch between temporary worker and temporary job, and increase the success of the former on the latter. A successful placement, with a maximum of fit between job seeker and job, was one where a temp could fulfill the terms of the contract, and doing so was an integral element of good temporary performance.

For example, Rowena, a Filipina-American in her late 30s, came to SL to find a job as an assembler, explaining that she had previously worked for a photocopy company that was subcontracted through a legal firm. She worked for the photocopy firm for several years and had experienced some upward mobility, but had tired of the job and desired change. Her goal was to work as a circuit board assembler, and eventually rise to the ranks of management. However, Lisa, SL's branch manager, cognizant of the lack of bridge jobs between assembly and management positions (not to mention between most temporary positions and the ranks of management), advised Rowena to rethink her strategy for achieving upward mobility. Lisa, who had several years of experience placing people in circuit board assembly and manufacturing jobs, explained to Rowena during an interview:

> *From what I've seen in all the years I've been placing people in circuit board assembly line jobs, it is not easy to rise to a managerial position. At these places, they typically use people up and spit them out. These jobs are draining, and they work people very hard and replace them often. Surely people become managers and rise in the ranks, but I've rarely seen that in the whole time I've been placing people.*

Lisa advised Rowena to give her résumé to the SL clerical and administrative recruiters, who might be able to place her in a position that was more appropriate to her skills and experience. Rowena had strong word processing skills, she was an excellent communicator, and she was fluent in Tagalog. Lisa could easily have placed Rowena in an assembler position; SL had many such job orders, and Rowena would easily have qualified for these jobs. Lisa, however, believed that Rowena would quickly become frustrated with that type of work and quit (an indicator of an unsuccessful placement), so she tried to help place Rowena in a job that she thought better suited her skills and background and that provided a more realistic path to management, possibly to the supervision of other white-collar, entry-level workers. Eventually Select Labor was able to place Rowena in a position that seemed to have the potential to become a permanent position: as a customer service representative in a company that was looking for a bilingual English-Tagalog speaker, a job that paid more than assembly line work and had opportunities for upward mobility.

Some workers came to the agency with recently acquired skills but little or no job experience in their new skill area. Silicon Valley was and continues to be a land of dream making and dream breaking, and many people hoped to capitalize on the prosperity of the high-tech industry. Some SL job applicants had paid significant amounts of money for training in various areas of the hightech industry only to learn that getting a job in their field was extremely difficult without experience and connections.

Job applicants often invested in training programs with little real understanding of how they would deploy their newfound skills or whether their training programs would link them to actual jobs. SL reps recognized the potential of these applicants but were aware that they were not going to be able to place them until they had gotten a foot in the door of a desirable company, possibly in an entry-level temporary job that had little to do with their newly acquired area of expertise. Entering a company or a field this way could help the job applicant connect to helpful networks for landing jobs. SL advisers worked with these applicants to modify their goals, to gradually adjust and maneuver their way into new fields, and to maximize their fit to particular job assignments.

Mark, for example, was working on getting an MCSE (Microsoft Certified Systems Engineer) certificate and wanted to know what SL might have for him. Mark was employed as a tester (a fairly low-level position in high tech) inspecting hard drives, printers, and hardware, but he wanted to get into the software industry. He had decided to take the MCSE course because he was persuaded by Microsoft's claim that people possessing this certificate would be very marketable. He wanted a high-paying, better job but was not sure how to find one, so he had decided to learn UNIX because he believed that companies were looking for people proficient with that operating system. SL staff convinced him that starting with a temporary job as a PC technician at one of the local computer manufacturing firms would be a good bridge job for him, increasing the chances that he would eventually obtain the position he hoped for.

Often, when one of the agency's good temporary workers was seeking a temp job but didn't possess the requisite skills for an advertised position, SL placement staff would go out of their way to talk to the manager at the client firm to discern whether there might be other opportunities for the individual. Good temps were something to retain, and SL went to lengths to do so. In one instance, SL sent Navit, a long-term temp, to interview at a company for a technician position. In the course of the interview, the manager determined that Navit was not qualified for the position and communicated this to the Select Labor placement specialist. The latter, however, was impressed by Navit's previous record and felt that he would be a good fit with this particular company, a firm that assembled computer components. She spent a fair amount of time telephoning other contacts she had in the company to see if anyone had a need for a trustworthy, hardworking temporary worker. Navit's case and others like it highlight how temporary workers can receive better career advice and be the recipients of advocacy efforts in ways superior to what regular employees might experience.

Agency staff used other seemingly small but important measures to retain valued temps. A branch manager at SL, for example, personally gave a cash advance from her own pocket to a regular temp whose paycheck had not come through. When one valued temp, a woman who had contracted for several jobs through Select Labor and had been working in a clerical position for more than nine months, asked for an additional day off over a long weekend so that she could spend it with her young child, the agency staff found a temp to fill her place for that short time—a temp filling in for a temp. On the whole, the agency attempted to pursue and optimize its chances for building and retaining the best temporary workforce possible. This workforce was the agency's cutting edge, its competitive commodity, and staff devoted an enormous amount of time to its manufacture.

Reshaping Managerial Practices and Creating Good Enough Temporary Jobs

Shaping labor supple—doing what they could to improve the quality of their temporary workers, increase the likelihood that their temps would succeed on the job, and hold turnover rates to a minimum—constituted one part of agency staff's work. They also worked to shape the demand side of temporary employment. Specifically, agency staff brokered relations between the temporary workforce and the supervisors and managers in hiring companies. They had to be attentive to the practices of the hiring companies and the ways in which those practices potentially could compromise the quality and output of temporary workers. Agency staff had to interpret hiring companies' distinct cultures and markets and learn how to work with and around them. They had to teach managers in client firms how to effectively use temps and gain their compliance. If agency staff placed temps at companies with bad work conditions—work sites that were unsafe or were managed by supervisors who resented the addition of temps to their units or acted "rough and tough," as one agency staff member put it—they had to deal with an increasing volume of complaints and labor turnover.

Recalibrating Abusive Managers

Caricatures of hiring company supervisors and managers and the way they deal with temporary employees abound. Researchers have blamed onsite managers for degrading temporary employees' work, for subjecting temps to toxic and hazardous work conditions (McAllister, 1998; Parker, 1994), and for sexual harassment (Rogers & Henson, 1997) and homophobia (Henson, 1996). This portrayal of managers, although partial (Smith, 2001), contains a kernel of truth: One of the major factors shaping the work experiences of Select Labor's temps was the attitude, interpersonal style, and management philosophy of the person for whom the temp worked. Whether the temp was integrated into a workforce of regular employees or worked in an enclave of other temporary workers, on-site supervisors and managers gave directions, kept an eye on the pace at which temps worked, commented on the products temps turned out, and reprimanded or praised temps for the quality of their work. Moreover, some supervisors and managers held implicit and explicit biases toward temps qua temps.

Select Labor staff had to moderate and rationalize—recalibrate—the behavior of on-site managers who were abusive, despotic, or confused when carrying out their normal oversight functions. In some cases, managers and supervisors on the shop floor were engaged in statistical discrimination, assuming temporary workers on the whole were untrustworthy and ignoring the laudable qualities or attributes of any individual temp. Occasionally managers baldly revealed their contempt for temps and attacked their vulnerable status. The comments of a disgruntled temp who had been sent for an interview revealed the humiliation that at least some managers were willing to heap upon "the temp." The temp, upon returning from the interview, reported the interaction in this way:

> *I told Steve [the hiring manager] that I hoped to earn $10 an hour. Steve laughed at me and said, "With your lack of skills and knowledge of computers, you should just be happy with the salary I'm offering and just be happy to have the job."*

In other cases, managers were disrespectful and injurious to all subordinates, permanent and temporary workers alike. Morale at firms could be severely affected when there was a sense of unfair or capricious treatment or when workers perceived that management did not care about their complaints. Demoralization registered strongly in the agency when temps' complaints about a particular boss added up. As study after study of work has shown, despotic or coercive managers can create significant organizational costs (to productivity, efficiency, and quality) and can lead to high turnover, resistance, and even sabotage (Hodson, 2001; Jacoby, 1985). Supervisors of temporary workers are no exception to this rule: They can incur obvious and concealed costs when they act out their contempt for temps.

One day the senior human resources manager at Computers R Us (CRU) invited Lisa, SL's branch manager, to sit in on a special staff meeting convened to review Rina's performance. Rina, a production supervisor, oversaw both temporary and permanent workers. Lisa was already well aware that Rina was causing problems for workers. Temporary workers assigned to CRU had complained to SL placement specialists about the routine humiliation Rina handed out: She was rude to them on the shop floor, snapped at them on a regular basis, and had even yelled at them. Some refused to return to CRU for their assignments.

Lisa expressed concern for her two equally pressing constituencies: "her workers"—Select Labor's temps—and the client firm. The human resource manager at CRU told Lisa that she needed her help, that she wanted her to give Rina direct feedback from temporary workers. After a meeting between Lisa and Rina, Rina's behavior appeared to improve. In the weeks that followed SL had far fewer complaints from the workers Rina supervised. Rina's actions had had a destabilizing effect on CRU's ability to hold on to its much-needed temporary workers, and SL willingly stepped in to help ameliorate the problem. In so doing, SL took on aspects of the traditional HR function, participating in performance appraisal, representing employees' grievances, and helping to manage tensions between the temporary and permanent workforce.

SL was asked on another occasion to help manage another problematic supervisor at CRU, to again assist HR in communicating employee grievances to him. Alex, a Select Labor placement specialist, was brought in to deal with Steve, the facilities management supervisor at CRU. Steve, like Rina, evoked many complaints from temporary workers. The HR person in charge of temporary workers at CRU had not wanted to approach

Steve about his attitude but finally felt there was no alternative but to confront him: Steve's actions were negatively affecting morale and retention of temporary workers. Alex explained:

> *Steve's a rough and tough guy. I haven't met him but I've placed a few janitors with him, and he takes a lot of workers. But he gets people and spits them out. Like, he waits to sign timecards and then sends them in after they are due. He also talks rough with his workers—so people don't want to stay working for him for 10 bucks an hour and get that kind of treatment. Laura [a human resources manager at Computers R Us] wants me to talk with Steve about these issues—she wants me to handle these things and keep her out of having these kinds of talks with managers. She's relying on me to have these talks. I'm not sure what to do, but I'll have a talk with him. Maybe I'll take him out to lunch.*

Alex's solution was to address Steve outside the workplace and to "socialize" him about some of the distinct issues facing temporary workers, and to educate Steve about the fact that the SL temps were usually very willing to work hard and comply with orders if they were treated respectfully. A significant goal of these one-on-one interventions was to eliminate capriciousness in the handling of temps.

In yet another company, Lisa had a series of conversations with a line manager at a client firm, criticizing his harsh attitude and actions toward Select Labor temps. Lisa had heard from a number of temporary workers, as well as from SL office staff, that this particular manager was intimidating temps when he interviewed them. And once they started the job, the manager often required the temps to work very long shifts on short notice. Lisa perceived this manager as being unresponsive to her concerns and decided to go over his head to the manager of the company's HR department. After his conversation with Lisa, this senior-level HR manager reprimanded the abusive line managers, leading Lisa to feel that she had succeeded in communicating to both of them that rude and thuggish behavior toward temporary workers would not be tolerated.

Agency staff did not always succeed in improving bad workplaces. The financial power of a client could limit the agency's ability to battle that client's damaging management practices. With a client that was a significant source of revenue, the agency could only try to contain the disgruntlement and turmoil. For example, SL staff had placed a number of workers in a firm, packaging computers. Although SL staff had visited the job site and determined that the quality of the worksite and the health and safety standards were acceptable, over time it emerged that some African American male and female temps felt that the line manager was discriminating against them. SL staff had wondered why many of their workers came back to Select Labor requesting new placements and tried to determine the source of the problem. A handful had walked off the job and returned to SL with complaints that were so vague that SL staff had trouble pinning down the precise problem. It took several weeks of inquiry for SL staff to get a handle on this particular manager's racism. The line manager, SL staff discovered, had publicly stated that he favored male Vietnamese workers and was perceived as treating all the female workers and men of a different racial or ethnic background unfairly.

Workers of the "wrong" gender or ethnicity told Rosa (a specialist at SL) that the foreman yelled at them, pressured them to work harder, and gave them tasks they claimed were "dirty" or "demeaning." Select Labor staff met with upper management at the firm and complained about the line manager's actions. However, the line manager remained in the position and SL continued to place workers at this job site: The hiring firm was taking on so many of its temps that SL feared the loss of the considerable revenue. SL's goal to create decent work conditions could not be perfectly achieved all the time, but the issue was of ongoing concern nevertheless.

Socializing Managers

Agency staff did not limit themselves to trying to recalibrate "bad" managers. Their larger goal was to socialize managers across the board, to familiarize everyone with the administrative logistics of temporary employment. Staffing agency placement specialists would teach hiring managers how to use temporary workers and how to use staffing services in general. Partly this entailed building an infrastructure in which agency staff could support line managers on the shop floor. Many managers lacked experience working on a regular basis with this different set of employment arrangements. While acquainting managers about the unique aspects and virtues of working with temps, SL staff were trying to rationalize and standardize the way the latter were deployed.

The experience of one Select Labor staff member, Jill, who managed a vendor-on-premises (VOP) unit at Technology Pathways (TP or Tech Path), highlights this process. Jill's desk was situated among the desks of other administrative staff. To anyone who was not in the know, Jill was indistinguishable from other permanent company employees. When not attending to daily paperwork and administrative tasks at her desk, Jill walked around the TP "campus" visiting with managers, informally instructing them on how to use SL's services. Jill mused that:

> *When people come off the street to Technology Pathways to apply for temporary jobs, they go on our payroll if they are to start as a temp, but Tech Path doesn't yet understand that they can send the person directly to me and I'll handle that paperwork. Now they are putting the person into their system and making a lot of work for themselves. I'll have to teach them and explain the options and possibilities for me to help them out. We can handle all that and save them time: I'm not sure why they are doing all that themselves.*

In her first few weeks, Jill spent a great deal of time with managers, getting to know them and learning about their hiring needs, advising them on how SL could save them time by searching for and interviewing potential employees. Working on-site, Jill also attended regular HR meetings to gain insight into and shape personnel practices at the company. SL had a vested economic interest in successfully teaching managers how to use temps, at TP and at all client work sites. The following example explains this interest.

When SL first started its VOP program at Technology Pathways, there were approximately six temporary workers at the company. Three months later there were a total of 76 temps working at TP (35 of whom were recruited by Select Labor). Jill explained:

> *Even though some of these temps were not recruited by us, we make money on all of them because we have a primary vendor contract with Technology Pathways, so we have a subcontracting relationship with the other agencies—they are subcontracting with us to have temps at Technology Pathways.*

These multiple layers of subcontracting were common with VOP arrangements, and Jill's presence on-site at TP facilitated both the growth of Technology Pathway's contingent workforce and Select Labor's share of this growth. Simply put, the larger the workforce of temps at Technology Pathways, the larger the flow of revenue to Select Labor.

At various sites, Jill advised managers on how to enlist SL's help in getting the kinds of workers they needed quickly and efficiently. She wrote and designed job descriptions after discussions with managers about their labor force needs. Jill conducted the orientation for temporary employees, helping them with necessary paperwork, giving them a tour of the facility, and training them in matters related to safety and the grievance process. She oversaw performance appraisals for temporary workers, conducted ergonomic evaluations of workstations, and made recommendations to managers for improvements. She had regular access to managers through meetings and informal encounters, and often these interactions afforded Jill a significant impact on the direction of HR management at the firm. She even negotiated on behalf of temporary Workers for higher wages when hiring managers offered pay rates that she thought were too low given prevailing market wages for temps. As Jill explained about another company where SL had a VOP account:

> *I'm shocked at how low the pay rates are [at Company X]. They don't realize the current pay rates in the Valley now and how competitive things are and how much more people are making these days.... I'll try and negotiate with them, and I know I'll have to advocate for some candidates.*

Negotiating higher pay for temps was not uncommon for SL staff. Elsewhere, Select Labor staff had been cultivating an account with Building Blocks (BB), working as consultants with BB management when the company relocated from the west side to the east side of the San Francisco Bay. Managers at BB initially insisted to SL staff that they intended to pay temporary workers the minimum wage. The SL salesperson told them there would be trouble if they paid minimum wage: She stated bluntly that no one competent or reliable would come work for them. After lengthy negotiations the BB managers agreed to start temps at two dollars above minimum wage, a low wage to be sure, but high enough to increase the chance of filling positions and minimizing turnover.

As Jill's experiences at Technology Pathways highlight, agency staff could be called upon to assess unanticipated work orders, predict employers' needs, and then prepare job descriptions for hiring companies. One manager from Computer Driven called SL to place a job order. She needed some temporary workers who could work as testers but had not prepared a description for the position. She requested that Alex (the SL recruiter mentioned earlier) write up a job description and let her review it, after which she planned to authorize SL to recruit people for the position. In addition to specifying the production schedule and the length of the job, the tasks it entailed, and the minimal skills required, the Computer Driven manager wanted Alex to benchmark this position by comparing it to prevailing wages for testers that CD would consider and possibly use. Alex used job descriptions that were on file in the agency as a template for CD's positions. In this way, Computer Driven relied on the signaling from Select Labor about what constituted a reasonable job, reasonable job expectations, and prevailing wages. In turn, Alex was able to transmit to CD a normative model for a temporary placement.

For all intents and purposes, agency staff were production engineers and organizational consultants, trained to size up jobs, workforce head counts, labor processes, and production procedures and figure out what was necessary to achieve outcomes in optimally efficient ways. If managers did not request the right types or numbers of temps, the ensuing mismatch between worker and position could undermine the likelihood for a successful temporary placement, and SL staff had a strong commitment to avoiding failure on this score.

Assessing Workplace Safety

Occasionally temps found themselves working at sites where they faced genuine risks to their bodily well-being. Being denied appropriate tools or laboring in workplaces where physical arrangements were dangerously configured had the potential to inflict meaningful damage on workers. Temps complained of dangerous work settings, and some refused to return to these jobs. These combined factors led agency staff to go to lengths to ensure that risk was minimized and safety maximized.

Agency staff were advised to "hire safe workers," "give all temps safety training," and "make sure clients have safe workplaces and good supervision." On top of this, agency staff were instructed to ask themselves: Were they providing appropriate safety training? What office procedures did they have in place for responding to accidents? Did they know for sure that the work sites where they were sending temps were safe? Were they "sending temps with proper experience, skill, strength, and attitude"? On several occasions agency staff refused to open accounts with companies that were reputedly negligent about work conditions and let go of accounts with companies that didn't comply with Select Labor's requests for improvement. Temps repeatedly told agency staff that one client firm, McTech, was a "bad" place to work, claiming that supervisors were abrasive and forced the temps to do the most dirty, heavy-lifting tasks. SL began the process of managing out the account, slowly shrinking the number of placements there. Similarly, agency staff were in the process of phasing out another company that routinely ignored requests to improve the safety conditions where temps worked. Select Labor staff also simply dropped a client firm that refused to correct a situation where heavy boxes kept falling on top of the temporary workers.

Select Labor staff believed that the best way they could keep tabs on what their temps were walking into was to conduct a thorough evaluation of different work sites. When possible, recruitment specialists would inspect the work sites when they set up new accounts with hiring companies. They might make recommendations for improving a work site. They made routine spot checks, visiting a client's site unannounced to monitor work conditions, and when they worked in VOP setups they scoped out potential risks to their temps. At a corporate training session an SL vice president warned participants from the agency office:

> *You have to make sure that you are eyeballing the job sites where you are sending people. Think to yourself, would I want to work here? Don't just send people to a site you know nothing about. It helps to do on-site visits when possible and see as many places as you can. Yes, we are the legal employer of temps, but we have dual—joint—employment so companies can't totally clean their hands of bad practices. As placement specialists, you should be getting detailed job descriptions when possible and remind the client about their joint employment responsibilities. Do as much quality control as possible. Visit clients when possible and develop a rapport with them.*

Conclusion

This study of the active work that goes into sustaining good temps and good temp workforces helps us understand how a trivial labor practice became a significant one and how temporary employment has become so entrenched in today's economy. Regularizing a system of temporary employment, building it from the ground up, as agency staff do, contributes enormously to the normalization of temporary work. For temporary workers themselves there are unexpectedly positive consequences. Applicants seeking temporary positions and individuals who work as temps on an ongoing basis receive advice and mentoring not otherwise available to them as job seekers on the open labor market. Agency staff help applicants and valued workers improve résumés and refine their job expectations in productive ways; they help workers anticipate what can be expected of them in various production settings (which can help the worker succeed on the job); agency staff often advocate for better wages, higher-level positions, and more humane, safer working conditions for their temps.

In general, agency staff, in striving to construct good temps and maintain a pool of decent and available temporary workers, engage in practices that benefit a segment of the labor force that might otherwise be stranded high and dry by the shifting currents of labor market practices in today's economy. When job seekers' options are unemployment or degraded employment, working with the staff of an agency that has an investment in promoting its profit-making commodity—good temporary workers—gives them a distinct advantage.

Temporary employment today is thus a double-edged sword. While, on average, agency temps receive lower wages, rarely can purchase health insurance, and have virtually no employment security, they can also be buffered from the worst aspects of new employment relations by virtue of the practices of labor market intermediaries such as temporary placement agencies. Researchers have identified additional benefits that can accrue to some workers because of access to temporary employment: Working at temporary jobs allows individuals who otherwise can't find permanent work to stay in the labor market (Farber, 1999); some workers segue from temporary jobs to permanent jobs (Autor, 2003); people who would be considered high-risk hires can gain work experience through temporary positions (Houseman & Erickcek, 2002); and disadvantaged job seekers can improve the extent and quality of their social networks that can be so vital to finding a good job (Benner, Leete, & Pastor, 2007). In general, temporary employment represents a path of mobility for diverse groups of workers.

Ironically, in an era when more workers are shouldering the risks of employment and when fewer workers are protected by unions, temporary help placement agencies in the United States can play a vital role insulating job seekers from the more precarious aspects of the labor market. Moreover, given the kinds of services that agencies such as Select Labor extend to their temporary workers, workers may feel greater loyalty and commitment to agencies—where they work on a regularly destabilized basis—than they do to "regular" employers, a sad comment on the state of employment relations today.

However, our analysis should not be construed as an endorsement of profit-making temporary help service agencies or the industry as a whole. The fact that the practices we've discussed take the edge off of temporary employment, in our view, is a by-product of the explicit profit-seeking strategies of private-sector business, profits that are earned from the labor of temporary workers. Nevertheless, as temporary employment has become widespread, normalized, and arguably permanent, the infrastructure of the temporary help industry may provide unusual forms of assistance and protections for workers who lack options for better jobs.

Source: Academy of Management Perspectives, 23, (1), 56–72 (2009). Reprinted by permission of the CCC.

REFERENCES

Autor, D. (2001). Why do temporary help firms provide free general skills training? *Quarterly Journal of Economics, 116*(4), 1409–1448.

Autor, D. (2003). Outsourcing at will: The contribution of unjust dismissal doctrine and the growth of employment outsourcing. *Journal of Labor Economics, 21*(1), 1042.

Barley, S., & Kunda, G. (2006). Contracting: A new form of professional practice. *Academy of Management Perspectives, 20*(1), 45–66.

Bartley, T., & Roberts, W. (2006). Regional exploitation: The informal organization of day labor agencies. *Working USA: The Journal of Labor and Society, 9*(4), 41–58.

Benner, C., Leete, L., & Pastor, M. (2007). *Staircases or treadmills: Labor market intermediaries and economic opportunity in a changing economy.* New York: Russell Sage Foundation.

Berchem, S. (2006). *A profile of temporary and contract employees.* American Staffing Association. Available at http://www.americanstaffing.net/statistics/pdf/Staffing_Employee_Survey_Executive_Summary.pdf.

Berchem, S. (2008). *Uncharted territory: Annual economic analysis puzzles through the data and explains the trends.* American Staffing Association. Available at http: www.americanstaffing.net/statistics/pdf/American_Staffing_2008.pdf.

Bureau of Labor Statistics. (2005). Employment services outlook: Employment services. Accessed January 13, 2009, from www.bls.gov/oco/cg/cgs039.htm.

Cappelli, P. (1995). Is the skills gap really about attitudes? *California Management Review, 37*(4), 108–124.

Dey, M., Houseman, S., &. Polivka, A. (2007). Outsourcing to staffing services: How manufacturers' use of staffing agencies affects employment and productivity measurement. *Employment Research, 14*(1), 4–6.

DuRivage, V. (2001). CWA's organizing strategies: Transforming contract work into union jobs. In F. Carre, M. Ferber, L. Golden, &. S. Herzenberg (Eds.), *Nonstandard work: The nature and challenges of changing employment relations* (pp. 377–392). Champaign, IL: Industrial Relations and Research Associates and University of Illinois Press.

Farber, H. (1999). Alternative and part-time employment relationships as a response to job loss. *Journal of Labor Economic, 17*(4, pt. 2), S142–169.

Goldin, C. (1990). *Understanding the gender gap.* New York: Oxford University Press.

Gonos, G. (1997). The contest over "employer" status in the postwar United States: The case of temporary help firms. *Law & Society Review, 31*(1), 81–110.

Gonos, G. (2000/2001). Never a fee! The miracle of the postmodern temporary help and staffing agency. *Working USA, 4*(3), 9–36.

Granovetter, M. (1995). *Getting a job: A study of contacts and careers.* Chicago: University of Chicago Press.

Henson, K. (1996). *Just a temp.* Philadelphia: Temple University Press.

Hodson, R. (2001). *Dignity at work.* Cambridge, England: Cambridge University Press.

Houseman, S., & Erickcek, G. (2002). Temporary services and contracting out: Effects on low-skilled workers. *Employment Research, 9*(3), 1–3.

Houseman, S., Kalleberg, A., & Erickcek, G. (2003). The role of temporary agency employment in tight labor markets. *Industrial and Labor Relations Review, 57*(1), 105–127.

Jacoby, S. (1985). *Employing bureaucracy: Managers, unions, and the transformation of work in American industry, 1900–1945.* New York: Columbia University Press.

Mangum, G., Mayall, D., & Nelson, K. (1985). The temporary help industry. *Industrial and Labor Relations Review, 38*(4), 599–611.

Martin, J. (1994). *Command performance: The art of delivering quality service.* Boston, MA: Harvard Business School Press.

McAllister, J. (1998). Sisyphus at work in the warehouse: Temporary employment in Greenville, South Carolina. In K. Barker & K. Christensen (Eds.), *Contingent work: American employment relations in transition* (pp. 221–242). Ithaca: Cornell/ILR Press.

Mishel, L., Bernstein, J., &. Allegretto, S. (2007). *The state of working America: 2006/2007.* Economic Policy Institute and Ithaca, NY: Cornell University/ILR Press.

Moore, M. (1965). The temporary help service industry: Historical development, operation, and scope. *Industrial and Labor Relations Review, 18*(4), 554–569.

Nollen, S., & Axel, H. (1998). Benefits and costs to employers. In K. Barker & K. Christensen (Eds.), *Contingent work: American employment relations in transition* (pp. 126–143). Ithaca, NY: Cornell/ILR Press.

Ofstead, C. (1999). Temporary help firms as entrepreneurial actors. *Sociological Forum, 14*(2), 273–294.

Parker, R. (1994). *Flesh peddlers and warm bodies: The temporary help industry and its workers.* New Brunswick, NJ: Rutgers University Press.

Peck, J., & Theodore, N. (1998). The business of contingent work: Growth and restructuring in Chicago's temporary employment industry. *Work, Employment, and Society, 12*(4), 655–674.

Pfeffer, J., & Baron, J. (1988). Taking the workers back out: Recent trends in the structuring of employment. *Research in Organizational Behavior, 10,* 257–303.

Rogers, J. K., & Henson, K. (1997). Hey, why don't you wear a shorter skirt? Structural vulnerability and the organization of sexual harassment in temporary clerical employment. *Gender and Society, 11*(2), 215–237.

Smith, S. (2005). "Don't put my name on it": (Dis) trust and job-finding assistance among the black urban poor. *American Journal of Sociology, 111*(1), 1–57.

Smith, V. (2001). Teamwork vs. tempwork: Managers and the dualisms of workplace restructuring. In D. Cornfield, K. Campbell, & H. McCammon (Eds.), *Working in restructured workplaces: Challenges and new directions for the sociology of work* (pp. 7–28). Thousand Oaks, CA: Sage Publications.

Smith, V., &. Neuwirth, E. B. (2008). *The good temp.* Ithaca, NY: Cornell University/ILR Press.

Vosko, L. (2000). *Temporary work: The gendered rise of a precarious employment relationship.* Toronto: University of Toronto Press.

Wilk, S., & Cappelli, P. (2003). Understanding the determinants of employer use of selection methods. *Personnel Psychology, 56*(1), 103–124.

ENDNOTES

1. This issue is explored in Smith (2001), Hiring temporary instead or permanent workers allows companies to avoid paying federal insurance contributions, unemployment, taxes, Social security taxes, health care, sick leave, and vacation and holiday pay. When budgets for fixed labor decrease while funds for variable labor increase, managers can be forced to hire temps even when they may prefer permanent workers.
2. The term permatemps seems to have first been used to characterize a class of high-technology contractors who worked at Microsoft in the 1990s for extremely long periods of time. These contractors sued Microsoft on the grounds that they worked side by side with permanent Microsoft workers and performed the same type of work, yet they were denied access to Microsoft's benefits and the company's lucrative stock option plan because they lacked employee status. The Ninth Circuit. Court of Appeals ruled that these permatemps were "common law" employees of Microsoft and therefore eligible for the same benefits and rights as permanently employed workers (DuRivage, 2001, p. 386).
3. The insider's view of these processes was acquired on the job. Neuwirth was employed full time for four months as a placement specialist at Select Labor, a pseudonym for a staffing firm in Silicon Valley. As a participant observer at Select Labor (SL). Neuwirth was trained directly by SL's branch manager. In her job, she interviewed and placed applicants in temporary jobs, conducted skills training tests, worked with managers and human resources

specialists in hiring companies, went through SL corporate training seminars, attended industry-relevant workshops and job fairs, and, in general, engaged in all aspects of agency life. She visited the sites of client firms, interacting with line and human resource managers and observing temps on the job. In all, Neuwirth logged approximately 1,400 hours of participant observation and collected massive amounts of industry data for the study of temporary help staffing firms. Neuwirth worked at Select Labor in 2000, a time when the high-tech economy of the Valley was hot: robust and with a considerable amount of churning in the labor market for temporary workers. For understanding the dynamics of temporary employment, the timing was perfect, as it meant that the full range of agency practices and agency/firm relationships was in play and observable. However, because the labor market in Silicon Valley was tight, hiring companies' dependence on the agency may have been greater than normal, giving the latter greater leverage over the former (Houseman, Kalleberg, &. Erickcek, 2003). Further, a tight labor market may have forced agency representatives to craft more beneficial policies for temps in order to attract them. However, based on Neuwirth's extensive fieldwork in the Valley and our reading of the now-voluminous literature on temporary employment (including Benner, Leete, and Pastor's excellent comparative study of agencies in Silicon Valley and Milwaukee [2007]), we have a fair degree of confidence that the practices of Select Labor were extremely similar to those of other moderately sized agencies.

4. Approximately 37,000 of the 64,000 firms in the employment services industry are temporary help placement, firms, making this a densely populated business field (Bureau of Labor Statistics 2005).
5. Virtually all studies find that temporary agency workers earn lower wages than do their permanent co-workers, even when they do the same work.
6. Quotes come from Select Labor training literature on how to interview and select workers.

READING 8.2

Assessment Instruments for the Global Workforce

Douglas Stuart

Spurred by the demands of globalization, international relocation and the increasingly multicultural workplace, intercultural assessment instruments have proliferated in the last decade. The growing supply of instruments reflects the increasing importance of selecting appropriate people for international assignments or positions in multicultural work environments and preparing them for these unfamiliar circumstances. Because such positions often require competencies beyond the standard set of professional knowledge and skills needed for familiar first-culture work environments, international human resource professionals responsible for selection and development seek tools to assess and enhance aptitude, awareness and skills.

There are dozens of commercially available and increasingly sophisticated instruments purporting or measure various aspects of intercultural adaptability or suitability; intercultural sensitivity, development or competence; or work style and/or cultural values orientation. It has become increasingly difficult to keep up with what tools are available in the market, what they measure and whether they are appropriate for particular needs.

This paper summarizes various aspects of competence required for successful performance in the global environment, organizes commercially available instruments that attempt to measure some aspects of that competence according to their appropriate application—selection or development—and describes several appropriate instruments in each category with respect to purpose and design, supporting research, presentation languages, source and other pertinent or unique attributes. Part 1 focuses on instruments particularly applicable to the selection process. Part 2 focuses on instruments primarily designed for the development process.

In total 18 tools are included, originating in the United States (10), United Kingdom (3), Netherlands (3), Canada (1) and the United Arab Emirates (1). For quick reference, all instruments discussed are summarized in a table at the end of this paper.

Global Intercultural Competence: A Cluster of Traits, Attitudes, Knowledge and Skills

Although a lot of research has examined the traits and skills associated with success in international assignments and, more recently, success in the multicultural workplace domestically or abroad, the selection and development process is still more of an art than a science. With respect to international assignments, there are so many variables affecting the outcome that it is difficult to predict success or failure. One must look at the personal situation of the candidate—single or married, with or without children, of what ages, separation issues with respect to extended family or support group, point in career path, etc. Variables in the assignment itself include location (developed or undeveloped economy, urban versus rural setting, remoteness, degree of cultural difference and language challenge, climate, number of other expatriates at the workplace and in the community, experience of the local workforce with foreigners, etc.) and the nature of the work (a technical versus a management focus, the relative importance of external relationship-building with client, customer, local government and community versus internal management, and more).

There are many variables affecting the nature and the degree of challenge of an assignment. The fundamental question is: what factors, beyond technical competence, predict success in the global business environment? *In general, the global workplace requires the ability to operate comfortably and effectively within a broad spectrum of difference—human, cultural and environmental*, all of which overlap naturally. While research has identified numerous attitudes, traits and skills that make up this broad ability or competence, here is a short and reasonably comprehensive list:

1. Action orientation (conscientiousness).
2. Flexibility.
3. Emotional stability.
4. Openness (open-mindedness).
5. Sociability (extraversion, agreeableness).
6. Cultural empathy (cultural sensitivity, cultural intelligence).

Taken as universal across cultures, the first "big five" attributes listed above are transparent and make common sense with respect to fostering comfort and competence in unfamiliar and diverse situations. Such traits are generally not learned but rather part of one's personality, their presence or absence appearing early in life. Although traits are generally considered stable rather than trainable competencies, the latter, more social dimensions, have been shown to increase as a result of training or living abroad. For convenience, let us associate the "big five" cluster with *adaptability*.

Cultural empathy, however, differs from the others. As noted by Milton Bennett, empathy requires a shift in frame of reference, an experiencing of a situation from another person's perspective.[1] Research in social neuroscience, as reviewed recently by Daniel Goleman, confirms ever more strongly that empathy, the major component of cultural sensitivity, is learned and that cultural sensitivity plays a primary role in intercultural competence.[2] We will associate this factor with *competence*.

The successful global manager, whether expatriating, simply working In a multicultural environment or supporting a multicultural workforce, exhibits a complex *global competence* that comprises the following:

1. Knowledge of one's own and other pertinent cultures.
2. Recognition of specific differences between cultures.
3. Understanding of how culture influences behavior in the workplace.
4. Ability to empathize with, adapt to and/or manage differences, as expressed in business structures, systems and priorities, within multicultural work environments.

Together with the factors discussed above, this emotional, cognitive and behavioral set provides the foundation for successful participation in global business.

Tools for Building the Global Workforce

Whether the task is selecting employees to fill sensitive positions or development planning for managers, there are sophisticated and well-researched tools for measuring and developing various aspects of intercultural competence. It is crucial to understand the attitudes, knowledge and skills needed for management of the global workplace and to be able to measure and develop these. The instruments discussed below present a strong and consistent basis for these processes.

The somewhat artificial separation of *adaptability* and *competence* above allows us to group the nine instruments of Part 1 into two sections.

Part 1

Tools for the Selection Process: Adaptability

When selecting candidates for international or multicultural assignments from a pool of personnel of roughly equal technical qualifications, it is useful to assess both intercultural adaptability and intercultural competence. Ideally, candidates are offered the confidential opportunity to complete instruments relating to both categories in order to self-select into or out of consideration for a specific assignment. There are numerous instruments designed to assess adaptability or intercultural competence or some combination of both. We will first look at adaptability instruments.

Adaptability instruments were the first assessment tools developed in response to the globalization of business and the increase of international assignments. Some have been available for more than 30 years, and new ones continue to be developed. Most of these instruments are based primarily on a self-assessment of a set of personality traits (listed above under Global Competencies for Global Work) associated with adaptability to new situations.

Note that HR personnel often elect to review the individual profiles resulting from these instruments. This can compromise the results because, in many cases, the questions are quite transparent in terms of what the desirable answers might be. Thus, if a candidate suspects that his or her profile, as revealed by the instrument, might be a factor in an employment decision, he or she may not answer the questions candidly.

Questions focusing on adaptability traits generally employ five- or six-point Likert scales expressing degrees of agreement or disagreement. Typical questions, taken from several of the instruments described below, include:

- I can think of very few people who dislike me.
- I try to understand people's thoughts and feelings when I talk to them.
- My closest friends are similar to me in terms of their religious affiliations.
- I like to get the opinions of others when making decisions at work.
- I could live anywhere and enjoy life.
- I generally eat my meals at the same time each day.
- When I meet people who are different from me, I tend to feel judgmental about their differences.
- I can laugh at myself and not take myself too seriously.
- Most of what I do is governed by the demands of others.

Recognizing the transparency of such questions, it is advisable to use these tools for self-selection prior to offering international assignments.

Note also that use of such instruments in employment decisions can entail legal liability, since the tools are generally not job-specific. That is, if the candidate's profile from an instrument influences the hiring decision and the candidate is unhappy with the decision, he or she may have legal recourse in protesting that the instrument was irrelevant to the job and thus used inappropriately. This can work both ways, in rejecting an employee for a desired position or in selecting an employee for an assignment that results in failure. Instruments designed to assist the management decision process are so noted.

Here are six quite different instruments that assess variations of these traits or these plus other competencies. Four of these tools below were developed in the United States, one in Canada and one in the Netherlands. Tools developed outside of the United States are marked. Throughout the paper, instruments are ordered alphabetically by acronym to avoid any implication of ranking:

- Cross-Cultural Adaptability Inventory (CCAI).
- International Assignment Profile (IAP).
- International Personnel Assessment tool (iPASS) *Canada.*
- Overseas Assignment Inventory (OAI).
- Multicultural Personality Questionnaire (MPQ) *Netherlands.*
- Self-Assessment for Global Endeavors (SAGE).

Cross-Cultural Adaptability Inventory (CCAI) The CCAI, developed by Colleen Kelley, Ph.D. and Judith Meyers, PsyD, was copyrighted in 1987. It is designed to provide information to an individual about his or her potential for cross-cultural effectiveness. Both versions consist of 50 questions that assess four components of cross-cultural adaptability. Initial statistical studies indicated that the CCAI had sufficient reliability and validity for a training instrument. While some recent research has questioned the validity of the four-factor structure, other research has correlated it with emotional intelligence. The CCAI remains a convenient tool for the self-selection process because of its simplicity and low cost. The instrument can be purchased in any quantity and does not require certified administrators. It can be used as a stand-alone instrument for self-selection for international assignments, as part of a larger selection battery, for pre- and post-testing or as part of a cross-cultural training. There is a follow-up training tool, called the CCAI Action-Planning Guide, that suggests actions to address factors assessed as weak, and there is also a Facilitator's Guide and Cultural Passport to Anywhere for use in group debriefs. The Multi-Rater Kit provides 360-degree feedback with three observers. The CCAI is available in two versions, a self-scoring paper-and-pencil instrument that provides immediate turnaround and an online version that provides the scoring and a printed feedback report, from Pearson Performance Solutions at 1-800-922-7343 or www.pearsonps.com under Solutions/ Performance Management/Organization Surveys/CCAI.

International Assignment Profile (IAP) It is common knowledge that family adjustment is the most significant threat to the success of an international assignment. The IAP, from International Assignment Profile Systems, is a unique and technologically sophisticated tool designed primarily as a preparation instrument to assist those selected for international assignment to prepare well for their destination. Its goal is to make a good match between the employee, the family and the particular destination. However, the tool has selection implications; if the IAP report indicates that the required support is too onerous or extensive, then manager and employee may want to reconsider the timing or destination. The IAP is a multi-faceted process that gathers and organizes extensive information about a family anticipating international assignment and integrates it with information about the destination to which they are being sent. It also provides the means of archiving this information for learning and future research. The IAP recognizes the client company and can be customized to convey specific information; it can be modified, customized or "branded" to fit a client's or vendor's specific requirements.

The IAP report summarizes family information in a comprehensive, easily understood format identifying core issues that need to be addressed prior to departure:

- Critical planning issues and adjustments that must occur to ensure assignment success.
- A list of "sleeper" issues that could emerge post-arrival to compromise the assignment.
- Information on "back home" issues that may affect the assignment.
- "Pleasant surprises"—essential or important things to the family that will meet or exceed expectations in the destination.
- Destination information on spousal employment and spousal impact.
- Traits and behaviors that may hinder or enhance cultural adjustment.

The two-part questionnaire can be completed in approximately 35 minutes per section for employee and spouse. The survey is secure and does not have to be completed in one sitting. The report is typically generated within 24 hours but can be received more quickly if necessary. While information on how to use and interpret the IAP is available from IAP Systems, the IAP requires no special training. (No information on research support was offered.) More information is available from www.iapsystems.com.

International Personnel Assessment tool (iPASS) With Part 2 still under development, iPASS is already a comprehensive, behaviorally based tool to assess intercultural effectiveness and readiness for undertaking an international assignment. Designed for HR and recruiting specialists in the international field, iPASS is being developed by the Centre for Intercultural Learning, Foreign Affairs department, Canada. *In contrast to most intercultural assessment instruments, iPASS is intended to provide a strong, reliable basis for HR and management in employment decisions.* Part 1, available now in French and English, is the Behavioral-Based Interview Kit, providing a reliable intercultural competency interview. Based on 35+ years of research, the interview kit employs seven competencies for intercultural effectiveness: cultural adaptation, knowledge of the host country, sensitivity and respect, network and relationship building, intercultural communication, intercultural leadership, and personal and professional commitment. Each competency has four levels of mastery. A client chooses three competencies necessary for success in the intended assignment as well as the level of each competency required for adequate functioning. Based on this, a customized interview kit is then prepared for the iPASS-certified HR/recruiter specialist with a set of comprehensive questions appropriate to the selected competencies and levels, including questions on motivation, interest and attitude toward cultural difference as well. These questions are then addressed during a two-hour interview.

Part 2, a 40-question Situational Judgment test based on actual intercultural conflict situations, will provide an additional screening tool when completed. Qualification for use of the Behavioral-Based Interview Kit is obtained through a three-day training delivered for 8-12 people wherever required. For further information, go to http://www.dfait-maeci.gc.ca/cfsi-icse/cil-cai/iPAss-en.asp?lvl=6 or contact the project leader, Nicole Paulun, at nicole.paulun@international.gc.ca (access from www.intercultures.gc.ca).

Multicultural Personality Questionnaire (MPQ) Karen I. Van der Zee, Ph.D., and Jan Pieter Van Oudenhoven, Ph.D., University of Groningen, the Netherlands developed the Multicultural Personality Questionnaire of 91 items as a multidimensional instrument to measure intercultural effectiveness. Developed in 1998 and revised in 2000, the MPQ measures five traits: cultural empathy, open-mindedness, social initiative, emotional stability and flexibility. Designed primarily for self-assessment, it can be used as well for risk assessment as part of the selection process. More information on the MPQ can be found at www.interculturalcontact.org or www.intercultureelcontact.nl/en/. The Questionnaire is available through Van der Maesen Personnel Management in Dutch, English, German, Italian (all research-supported) and French online at www.psychecommerce.nl; a report is generated and available immediately for download.

Overseas Assignment Inventory (OAI) Developed by Michael Tucker, Tucker International, the OAI was the first major instrument assessing suitability for an international assignment. Available since the early 1970s and first designed for the U.S. Navy, the self-awareness questionnaire examines six factors of acceptance, knowledge, affect, lifestyle, interaction and communication found crucial for successful adaptation to another culture. The factors include 14 specific motivations, expectations, attributes and attitudes, including motivations for accepting or wanting an international assignment. Studies of validity and reliability have been conducted at intervals on various populations since its implementation, and the OAI has undergone significant redevelopment. It continues to be well-known and respected in the relocation industry.

The questionnaire is available in booklet form or online, although the reports, in two versions—one to the candidate and another to HR or management—are furnished in hard copy only and may take several weeks for delivery.[3] Reports are self-explanatory and do not require certified administrators. However, for the corporate selection process, the OAI can be combined with a behavioral interview; in this case, HR must be certified in the interview technique incorporating the OAI report. The OAI report can be integrated into intercultural training as well. Use of the OAI can be arranged through Tucker International www.tuckerintl.com in English, French and German. Tucker International also offers several other assessment instruments. The OAI is appropriate for self-selection and may be helpful for HR in its decision process. The OAI provides a limited basis for professional development in preparation for an international assignment, and its debrief can become a major component of cultural training.

Self-Assessment for Global Endeavors (The SAGE)
The SAGE was developed by Paula Caligiuri, Ph.D., Director of the Center for Human Resource Strategy at Rutgers University, at the time of writing. Available since 1997, the instrument was designed to assist individuals and families as a confidential tool in their decision process of whether to accept an international assignment. The tool's three sections address issues of personality (six factors), motivation and family situation. Validity and reliability is supported by considerable research. The SAGE is available in two versions—one for the employee and a second for the accompanying partner—online in English with the report immediately available for reading online or printing. Paper-based versions are also available in French, Japanese, Mandarin and Taiwanese. These versions are not merely translation/back translations but recreations of the instrument using cultural resources to assure the appropriateness of the questions. The first two sections, on traits and motivation, are scored with ranges marked in green, yellow or red as indications of one's suitability and readiness for assignment. The third section, on family, is not scored but is designed to facilitate the family conversation necessary for an informed decision about seeking and accepting an assignment. While designed to support the self-selection process, the SAGE report can also be within a pre-departure or post-arrival cultural training program. Information on The SAGE is available at www.caligiuri.com; the tool can be purchased from RW^3 LLC, 212-691-8900 or www.rw-3llc.com.

Tools for the Selection Process: Competence
While the dividing line between adaptability and competency instruments is blurry because many—such as the OAI and iPASS above—incorporate aspects of both, there are a number of tools designed more for the assessment of competencies than for adaptability. The next three disparate instruments focus more on the complex skills essential for effective functioning in international assignments. Proprietary considerations prevent the presentation of sample questions, and in any case, because of the complexity of these tools, the presentation of a few sample questions would not be illustrative and might be misleading.

- Global Candidate Assessment (GCA 360°)
- Intercultural Development Inventory (IDI)
- Survey on Intercultural (Relocation) Adaptability (SIA, SIRA)

Global Candidate Assessment℠ (GCA 360°) The Global Candidate Assessment is an elaborate 3-step online assessment process, developed by Aperian Global, that involves self-assessment and assessment by up to 10 colleagues, supervisors and subordinates on the same items (not identified in the available description), including written commentary on selected questions about the candidate's attitudes and abilities. While the assessment examines workplace behaviors and adaptability, the instrument does not focus specifically on intercultural competencies as defined above. Once the surveys are completed, the tool generates an instant compilation, the Candidate Summary Report, which is viewable by the client assessment administrator. This includes overall scores, a combined visual display, a gap analysis indicating difference between the candidate's and others' scores, and a compilation of written comments. Administrative functions can be performed by Aperian or by a client HR person. Step Two is a three-hour interview with the candidate conducted by an Aperian consultant. This may include the spouse or partner as well and covers motivation, challenges, relocation issues, career impact, personal strengths/weaknesses and self-rating of adaptability, all resulting in a verbal summary report to client HR. Step Three is a candidate meeting with client HR to debrief the process and indicate current level of commitment to an international assignment. As an optional Step 4 after the candidate has been accepted, the candidate and key colleagues in the new position can take the GlobeSmart Assessment Profile (GAP), which compares a profile of the candidate with that of the selected colleagues and generates a report to each suggesting various behavior modifications to enhance collaboration. *Clearly the GCA 360° is designed to support employment decisions.* (No information on research support was offered.) More information on the Global Candidate Assessment is available from www.aperianglobal.com, which also offers a number of other Web-based tools.

Intercultural Development Inventory™ (IDI) The IDI is a theory-based instrument, developed by Mitchell Hammer, Ph.D., and Milton Bennett, Ph.D., that measures intercultural sensitivity as conceptualized in Bennett's Development Model of Intercultural Sensitivity (DMIS—1986, 1993). First introduced in 1997 and revised in 2002, the 50-item instrument measures people's reaction to cultural difference along a developmental six-stage scale of cognitive structures or "worldviews" reflecting increasing intercultural sensitivity or competence. These worldviews range from denial and defense through minimization to acceptance, adaptation and integration, with the first three labeled as ethnocentric and the last three—ethnorelative. Intercultural competence minimally requires development into the acceptance/ adaptation stage of intercultural sensitivity. The IDI is supported by impressive reliability and validity studies, available from www.intercultural.org, and *can be used with confidence in both the selection process and developmental planning*, where it predicts the kind of intervention most effective for development according to the revealed stage of intercultural sensitivity. It is equally applicable for measuring the intercultural competence of work or leadership teams (as an average) and for planning further competence development.

The IDI is available as a paper-and-pencil instrument or online in 12 languages: Bahasa Indonesia/Malay, Chinese, English, French, German, Italian, Japanese, Korean, Norwegian, Portuguese, Russian and Spanish. While inexpensive to purchase, it must be purchased and debriefed by a certified interpreter. Further information is available at www.intercultural.org.

Survey on Intercultural (Relocation) Adaptability (SIA & SIRA) From Grovewell LLC, SIA and SIRA are online 360° assessment instruments for global leadership or relocation candidates. For global leadership candidates, the SIA assesses seven skills/qualities that facilitate successful adaptation to global realities: flexibility, non-judgmentalness, interest in different views and values, awareness of others' feelings, attention to relationships, responding well in unclear situations and self-confidence. The 360° process (up to 12 raters) also assesses 20 behaviors that undermine relationships with diverse counterparts. For global relocation candidates, the SIRA adds a self-assessment (not 360°) for candidate and separately for the spouse or partner of motivations, concerns and expectations around long-term living and working in an unfamiliar environment. The Feedback Report of these instruments is provided directly and solely to the user, who is advised to share results with HR or management. While no certification is required for the administration of these instruments, a separate manual plus phone consultation is provided to HR and EAP professionals in contracting firms. Usage prices are available on the Web site at www.grovewell.com/expat-360-assessment.html.

Conclusion: Part 1

Part 1 described nine varied instruments in support of the selection process for international assignments or entry into the multicultural workplace, with respect to both adaptability and intercultural competence. These were selected from a larger pool for various reasons, including design, research support, commercial availability and application to varied needs. As a final comment, users of selection instruments are often concerned about their reliability and validity, often because of a desire to use the tool to predict performance success and thus tie it to employment decisions. It is important to understand that although many of these instruments are well supported by significant research, the linking of their results to the probability of assignment success is problematic since such instruments (with the exception of iPASS and GCA 360°) are not job-specific in their design. That is, the need for adaptability and intercultural competence varies greatly with the job and the work and living environments. Therefore, results of these instruments (again, with the exception of iPASS, GCA 360° and, to some extent, the IDI) should not be used as the sole or even the primary basis of employment decisions.

Part 2 below describes another set of instruments primarily suited for the development of intercultural competence.

Part 2

Tools for the Development Process: Intercultural Awareness

Intercultural research by authors ranging from Florence Kluckhohn and Fred Strodbeck in the 1950s through Edward Hall in the 1960s and 1970s and Geert Hofstede and Fons Trompenaars (with Charles Hampden-Turner) in the 1980s and 1990s, plus the large value surveys such as the World Values Survey, Shalom Schwartz's work in Europe and most recently the seminal publication of *Culture, Leadership, and Organizations: The GLOBE Study of 62 Societies*,[4] the contrast of cultures through the lens of value dimensions has provided a research-supported, practical means of comparison in which values can be predictably linked to patterns of behavior in a variety of situations. Such information forms the basis of the knowledge component of intercultural competence and can be invaluable in the preparation for an international assignment, working in a multicultural environment or leading a global team. It is no surprise, then, that a number of assessment instruments have been developed to enable people to understand their own cultural value preferences and compare these with core values of other cultures in order to understand the challenges these differences might present in the work environment.

Since each of the following instruments focuses on value preferences, a list of sample questions will provide an idea of how these tools are designed (because of their proprietary nature, the tools from which the questions are drawn are not identified):

- You take more pride in...
  - Your contributions to your company.
  - The accomplishments of your company.
- Outperforming co-workers is a motivator for you.
  - Yes.
  - No.
- It is more important that business decisions be made in accordance with...
  - General principles and theories.
  - The particular circumstances.
- Most organizations would be better off if conflict could be eliminated forever. (Five-point Likert scale of disagreement/agreement)
- In order to have efficient work relationships, it is often necessary to bypass the hierarchical lines. (Five-point Likert scale)
- Gaining consensus is more important than decisive action. (Five-point Likert scale)

Below are descriptions of six instruments (three from the United States and one each from the United Kingdom, the United Arab Emirates and the Netherlands) with a focus on cultural values and their impact on how we work. These tools are not evaluative and are not designed to support employment decisions by candidates or management.

- Argonaut Assessment (AA) U.K.
- Cultural Mapping and Navigation© Assessment Tool (CMNAT) U.A.E.
- Cultural Orientation Indicator (COI)
- Culture in the Workplace Questionnaire (CWQ)
- Intercultural Awareness Profiler (IAP) Netherlands
- Peterson Cultural Style Indicator (PCSI)

Argonaut™ Developed by Coghill & Beery International in the United Kingdom, ArgonautOnline™ is a suite of cross-cultural e-learning tools that includes an assessment instrument. The Argonaut Assessment (AA) instrument, available in English only, employs a 20-minute questionnaire involving 12 dimensions (communication, conflict, problem solving, space, use of time, time spans, fate, rules, power, responsibility, group membership, tasks) to produce a graphical map allowing comparison of the learner's self-perception, home culture and target cultures from a list of 50+ countries. This contrastive mapping provides a basis for the formation of "personal strategies for international success." Results from the AA instrument can be combined with other online learning tools, including personalized feedback and interactive tutorials. Access to the AA is gained through accreditation as a trainer or coach to use the ArgonautOnline tool suite. For more information, visit www.argonautonline.com.

Cultural Mapping and Navigation© Assessment Tool (CMNAT) Created by Knowledgeworkx in the United Arab Emirates, this tool employs a 72-question online inventory to produce a personal profile that details preferences on 12 bipolar cultural dimensions affecting workplace behaviors: growth (people vs. material), relationship (universal vs. situational), outlook (tradition vs. Innovation), destiny (directed vs. directive), context (informal vs. formal), connecting (exclusive vs. inclusive), expression (reveal vs. conceal), decision making (relationship vs. rules), planning (people vs. time), communication (direct vs. indirect), accountability (community vs. individual) and status (ascribed vs. achieved). The CMNAT profile is incorporated in the second level of a four-level program (three days of training for Levels 1–3 and ongoing coaching toward intercultural excellence in Level 4). The goal is the growth and application of intercultural intelligence to achieve intercultural excellence within multicultural teams. The Assessment Tool is also integrated with other (noncultural) assessment instruments (the Diamond Profiling Process) as part of intercultural leadership consultation. There is a five-day intensive program for certification in the delivery of Levels 1–3 of the Cultural Mapping & Navigation Program© suite of products. More information in available at www.KnowledgeWorkx.com.

Cultural Orientations Indicator® (COI) Developed by Training Management Corporation (TCM), the COI is a

Web-based self-reporting instrument that assesses individual preference within 10 cultural dimensions (environment, time, action, communication, space, power, individualism, competitiveness, structure, thinking) drawn from the social science research mentioned at the beginning of Part 2, plus other contributors, such as Edward Stuart, Milton Bennett and Stephen Rhinesmith. The 108-question inventory yields a profile of preferences along a series of continua–17 in all, as several of the 10 dimensions have sub-continua. The profile of preferences (restricted to work-related behaviors and situations) enables comparison to other team members and national norms, allowing "gap analysis" and the coaching of strategies for bridging differences. Group or team aggregate reports are also available. The COI is also integrated into the Cultural Navigator™, an online learning portal, and other programs offered by TMC. Test construction has been psychometrically validated (but not all the 10 dimensions have been validated globally). The COI is available in Chinese, English, French, German, Italian, Japanese and Spanish. The COI is supported by the *Cultural Orientations Guide* (4th edition), which supplies a context for understanding the instrument and its applications. Further information is available at www.tmcorp.com.

Culture in the Workplace Questionnaire™ (CWQ) Based on the research and developed with the support of Geert Hofstede,[5] the CWQ, recently revised and Web-enabled, provides individual cultural profiles incorporating five cultural dimensions validated by extensive research: individualism, power distance, certainty (uncertainty avoidance), achievement (masculinity) and time orientation (long-term orientation). The instrument is available through ITAP International, which licenses the Culture in the Workplace Questionnaire™ from Professor Hofstede. Profiles can be compared to average national values (established through the research of Hofstede and others) of 60 countries.

The 60-question inventory is completed online, resulting in a seven-page personal report, which can be downloaded and printed by the user or saved for later distribution by a facilitator. The individual profile illustrates the user's score on each dimension in comparison with national averages of up to 15 selected countries. The report explains each dimension, lists the impact on work style of values at either end of the dimension, such as individual vs. group orientation, and illustrates in a scenario the misunderstanding and conflict typical of interaction between individuals holding different orientations. It also provides specific analyses on the user's score on each dimension and the implications of the differences between the user scores and the comparison country averages and adaptive recommendations.

The CWQ can be used with individuals or groups and also provides team reports for printing or download. Group averages can be compared in PowerPoint slides to numerous countries' average values, and the scores of individual members of the group can be confidentially compared with respect to each dimension, which is very useful for global teams. The CW Questionnaire is currently available in a simple world business English; by the end of 2007 it will be available in multiple languages. Clients can also add special demographic fields so that, for example, data can be analyzed by location of multiple users.

CWQ profiles must be requested and debriefed by trainers or consultants certified in CW profile interpretation. More information on the CWQ is available from www.itapintl.com

Intercultural Awareness Profiler (IAP) Created by Fons Trompenaars, the IAP employs Trompenaars' seven cultural dimensions or polarities, a list drawn from sociological theories of the 1950s and 1960s: universalism vs. particularism, individualism vs. communitarianism, specific vs. diffuse cultures, affective vs. neutral, achievement vs. ascription, sequential vs. synchronic, internal vs. external control. A diagnostic questionnaire, available online, is used to produce a personal cross-cultural orientation against a reference model. Further questions provide sub-group identifications of organizational culture, functional areas and other variables. The analysis is cross-referenced against the Trompenaars' cross-cultural database, including the data of 55,000 + managers in many countries gathered over a 10-year period. The personal report offers advice for doing business and managing in and with other cultures. For information on using the IAP, contact Trompenaars Hampden-Turner (THT) Consulting at www.thtconsulting.com.

Peterson Cultural Style Indicator™ The PCSI, designed by Brooks Peterson of Across Cultures, Inc., consists of a 20-question online inventory that generates a five-dimensional profile. The five bipolar dimensions are hierarchy/equality, direct/indirect, individuality/group, task/relationship and risk/caution. One's profile is comparable to 70 country "norms" (chosen scores based on comparing various studies and updated in 2004), with strategic recommendations for increasing business success. Research supporting the instrument is discussed on the Web site, which includes a list of corporate clients. The PCSI, designed as a stand-alone instrument, can be accessed immediately online for $50 per use, including the comparison of your profile with other countries and suggestions for bridging gaps based on your score. For more information, go to www.acrosscultures.com.

Tools for the Development Process: Intercultural Coaching

One of the tools introduced in Part 1 of this paper, Tools for the Selection Process: Competence, the *Intercultural Development Inventory*, is equally suitable for the development process, particularly in a coaching environment. The explanatory material provided in an IDI profile contains descriptions for each of its scales, including behaviors or attitudes associated with particular scores, the strengths associated with these and the developmental tasks. With the help of an intercultural coach, a user can create and implement a developmental plan.

Here are three more instruments, two developed in the United Kingdom and one in the Netherlands, all intended to be used developmentally. The first of these instruments focuses on competencies, the second incorporates cultural values and an overlay of workplace behaviors, while the third focuses on adaptability and workplace behaviors. Again, proprietary considerations prevent the presentation of sample questions, and because of the complexity of these tools, a few sample questions would not be illustrative and might be misleading.

- Intercultural Readiness Check (IRC) Netherlands
- The Spony Profiling Model (SPM) U.K.
- The International Profiler (TIP) U.K.

Intercultural Readiness Check (IRC) The intercultural readiness check was developed in 2002 by Ursula Brinkman, Ph.D., of Intercultural Business Improvement in the Netherlands. Focused entirely on learnable complex skills crucial to effective intercultural interaction, the IRC examines the following four competencies: intercultural sensitivity, intercultural communication, building commitment and preference for certainty (defined as "ability to manage the greater uncertainty of intercultural situations"). The tool can be used before entering a multicultural environment or during and international assignment. In the debrief of the personal profile, a participant is advised of potential pitfalls and provided practical suggestions for development. In collaboration with an intercultural trainer or coach, the participant can then create a plan for applying strengths and developing weak points, which can be carried out with or without continued coaching. Reliability and validity research was conducted on an international business population of Europeans, U.S. Americans and others. Studies show high reliability (reconfirmed based on a population of more than 2,600 individuals) and sufficient validity to make the IRC a useful instrument for specific developmental training on any of the four competencies. Research continues on the instrument, and scores can be compared to a large data bank of more than 7,000 respondents. The questionnaire can be accessed online, but results must be presented by a licensed intercultural consultant. Information concerning use of the IRC and certification is available from www.ibinet.nl and www.irc-center.com.

The Spony Profiling Model (SPM) Offered by FutureToBe in the United Kingdom, the SPM is a unique integrated online instrument that combines aspects of cultural values and work style instruments with 360° reporting on communication style (three work colleagues). It can be used to produce individual, team and organizational culture profiles using the same concepts and frameworks, thereby providing consistency, rigor and integration between the development of individuals, the building of teams and the strategic alignment of organizations. Developed over eight years of research and testing in Britain and France by Dr. Gilles Spony at the Cranfield School of Management, the SPM incorporates the work of cross-cultural psychologist Shalom Schwartz as well as the research of Geert Hofstede to produce profiles of work style preferences. These are graphically displayed on a values framework of two perpendicular Universal axes, the vertical RELATIONSHIP axis of Self-Enhancement vs. Consideration for Others and the horizontal TASK ORIENTATION axis of Group Dynamics vs. Individual Dynamics. This results in a profile of 12 attitudinal orientations that yield 12 operational styles with a total of 36 subdivisions. The individual profile is then overlaid on a cultural values map in order to understand how work style may fit into or clash with various national cultures. The 230 questions of the work style questionnaire require about 45 minutes, while the communication style questionnaire for colleagues takes about 15 minutes. Because of the SPM's sophistication and complexity, accreditation in its use requires a three-day training plus one day of assessment in order to use the instrument to a professional standard with respect to individuals, teams and organizations. Candidates for accreditation are preferred to be holders of a Certificate of Competence in Occupational Testing (Level A) from the British Psychological Society and/or to have experience with other management models. More information on the SPM is available at www.futuretobe.net/.

The International Profiler (TIP) TIP, developed by WorldWork Ltd. in the United Kingdom, is a Web-based questionnaire and feedback process, available in English, German, French and Italian, to assess the development needs of managers and other professions for international work. It is based on a set of 10 competencies with 22 associated skills, attitudes and areas of knowledge derived from intercultural research and the practical experience of international professionals. The competencies are openness, flexibility, personal autonomy, emotional strength, perceptiveness, listening orientation, transparency, cultural knowledge, influencing and synergy. TIP is an online psychometric inventory of 80 questions requiring about 45 minutes and generating a scored report within a hefty Feedback Book for the certified consultant and client that provides structured feedback in terms of the energy, emphasis and attention the user typically brings to a competency set. The feedback session, face-to-face or by telephone, consists of a structured discussion of the report with respect to the user's present or future international challenges. The intent is to identify three or four qualities requiring greater energy in the future. This results in a completion of a Personal Development Plan by the user entailing developmental areas, expected benefits from the development and an action plan. The licensing process, required in order to employ TIP, provides a Coaching Manual.

WorldWork Ltd. also offers **Global View 360°**, a panoramic version of the TIP providing feedback from 6–10 international colleagues, clients, friends, etc. who have observed the user in international contexts. It employs a reduced questionnaire (55 questions) focusing solely on the 10 key competencies and provides a gap analysis in the feedback report of the difference between the level of importance given to selected behaviors as compared with the perceived level of performance. Two free fields allow for open-ended commentary. The Global View 360° can be administered in its entirety by its subject. For more information on both instruments, email **info@worldwork.biz** or go to **www.worldwork.biz**.

Conclusion: PART 2

The six value orientation tools described in section titled "Tools for the Development Process: Intercultural Awareness" incorporate the concept of differing behaviors (generally in a business context) rather predictably according to deeply held cultural preferences on values spectra that have undergone extensive global research over the last 50+ years. The instruments differ with respect to the value dimensions they employ, but they all produce personal profiles for comparison with other individuals and group or national averages. Such instruments can be powerful teaching tools for the knowledge component of intercultural competence, both before and during an assignment or while in a multicultural team; they provide a structured comparative bases for intercultural training and can also be used for coaching.

Two of the instruments described in the section "Tools for the Development Process: Intercultural Coaching" look at workplace behaviors—one from an adaptability and the other from a cultural values perspective. The third tool examines complex skills in the work environment. All these tools are more appropriate to a coaching than a training process.

The increasing demands of globalization raise the stakes of cultural due diligence, both in the selection of appropriate personnel for sensitive positions in the multicultural workforce at home and abroad and in the preparation of employees for the intercultural demands of these assignments.

In making employment decisions with intercultural implications, no assessment instrument by itself can replace a thorough and systematic selection process that includes job-specific performance evaluation and interviews with candidates, colleagues, superiors, direct reports and family (in the case of international assignments). On the other hand, with the availability of the instruments described above, it is equally inexcusable to make such decisions without the support of an appropriate intercultural assessment tool.

Whether you intend to help an employee or family decide whether to accept an international assignment; gather significant information for HR and management to assist in a culturally sensitive employment decision; choose the most culturally competent manager from a pool of candidates to lead a virtual multicultural team; determine the intercultural competence of a work group or leadership team; prepare a manager for an international assignment or a multicultural leadership position; prepare an individual or team for work with a specific cultural group; coach an international transferee or the leader of a multicultural team; provide developmental input to a multicultural team; or affect any other situation involving a need to select for or further develop intercultural competence, there are competitive choices among the sophisticated and powerful assessment tools described in this paper to assist you in that task.

Assessment Instruments for the Global Workforce I: Tools for the Selection Process: Intercultural Adaptability and Intercultural Competence.

Source: Society for Human Resource Management White Paper 022010. June, 2007. Reprinted by permission of the CCC.

ENDNOTES

1. Bennett, M. J. (1993). Towards ethnorelativism: A developmental model of intercultural sensitivity. In R. Michael Paige (Ed.), *Education for the intercultural experience.* Intercultural Press, pp. 53–54.
2. Goleman, D. (2006). *Social intelligence: The new science of human relationships.* United States: Random House.
3. Information concerning commercially available instruments is based on what was readily available publicly at the time of writing. Because all these instruments are proprietary, full information on availability and cost may be provided solely to potential purchasers.
4. House, Hanges, Javidan, Dorfman, & Gupta (Eds.). (2004). *Culture, leadership, and organizations: The GLOBE Study of 62 Societies.* Sage Publications.
5. Dr. Hofstede is Professor Emeritus, the University of Limburg at Maastricht, Director (Emeritus) of the Institute for Research on Intercultural Cooperation (IRIC), the Netherlands, and author of *Culture and Organizations: Software of the Mind* (McGraw Hill, 1991) and *Culture's Consequences: Comparing Values, Behaviors, Institutions, and Organizations across Nations,* which presents the research basis for the CWQ.

READING 8.3

Winning the Race for Talent in Emerging Markets

Douglas A. Ready, Linda A. Hill, and Jay A. Conger

With economic activity in emerging markets growing at compounded rates of around 40% – as compared with 2% to 5% in the West and Japan – it's little wonder that many companies are pegging their prospects for growth to Brazil, Russia, India, and China (BRIC) and, increasingly, other developing nations. Businesses based all over the globe are feverishly competing for people who, often for the first time in their lives, have numerous options and high expectations. Not even companies with established global experience can coast on past success in meeting their staffing needs.

One might assume, for instance, that Standard Chartered Bank, whose heritage dates back to the 1850s in India, Hong Kong, and Singapore, could easily maintain a lead in the race for Asian talent. But just a couple of years ago SCB's China division was unable to find seasoned managers to lead the bank's retail and commercial banking operations. In the words of Hemant Mishr, the head of corporate global sales, "These people and the generations that preceded them have known nothing but poverty and the lack of opportunity. Yet we expect them to be patient, loyal soldiers, and to advance at an orderly pace. It is time to get real. It is their time now."

Idea in Brief

- Emerging markets are growing by compounded rates of as much as 40%, and finding talent to keep up with that growth is extraordinarily challenging.
- Companies in the developed world often try to export the talent strategies they use at home – with abysmal results.
- SCB, Lenovo, and others win over employees by promising – and delivering – accelerated careers, a chance to contribute meaningfully, and a meritocratic culture.

All three of us have spent decades studying talent management and leadership development, but this war for talent is like nothing we've ever seen before. We recently completed an eight-month research project that involved interviewing dozens of executives and collecting data from more than 20 global companies. Our goal was to identify the factors that differentiate the successful from the less so in emerging markets, and our first analysis revealed four: brand, opportunity, purpose, and culture. These may sound somewhat generic – and logical in any talent market – but they play out in developing nations in particular ways.

Employees in the developing world aren't used to thinking about the future in expansive terms. Now they can look beyond simply making a living. They are particularly attuned to *brand*, for instance, because a desirable affiliation may lead to personal advancement – especially when the brand is associated with inspirational leadership, the kind that challenges employees to develop themselves as leaders and to help build a great company that plays on a global stage.

Not surprisingly, *opportunity* means much the same in the developed and developing worlds: challenging work, stretch assignments, continual training and development, and competitive pay. In emerging markets, however, opportunity must imply an accelerated career track to senior positions. High-potential employees don't focus exclusively on climbing the ladder, however, they are willing to make lateral moves as long as their skills and experience accrue at a pace that matches the growth in their markets.

As for *purpose*, emerging-market job candidates prize a company with a game-changing business model, where they can be part of redefining their nation and the world economy. They are also attracted by a mission that focuses on helping the unfortunate – many have experienced poverty firsthand – and expresses the value of global citizenship.

A company's *culture* matters in several distinct ways in emerging markets. First, its "story," or brand promise, has to feel authentic. Second, employees must be rewarded for reasons of merit; a high potential from Brazil or Dubai must believe that the executive suite in China or the United Kingdom is within reach. Third, although employees want to be recognized for individual achievements, they also want to feel a connection with their teams. Finally, the culture has to be truly "talent-centric," so that people know they're critical to the company's success.

A closer look at our interviews gave us new insights into how these four factors work in concert. We found that they could be united under two guiding principles: *promises made* (the combination of brand, opportunity, and purpose) and *promises kept* (most significantly, employees' day-to-day experiences within an organization's culture). All four factors play a role in all aspects of the talent management process, but each influences recruitment and retention in different ways. (See the Exhibit "A Framework for Attracting and Retaining Talent.") Promises made and kept affect any quest for talent, but the intensity of competition in the fast-growing BRIC and other economies makes strong differentiation urgent. Most companies continue to believe that a big salary and a name brand will suffice to meet their needs, but a local company that creates genuine opportunities and exhibits desirable cultural conditions will often win out over a Western multinational that offers higher pay.

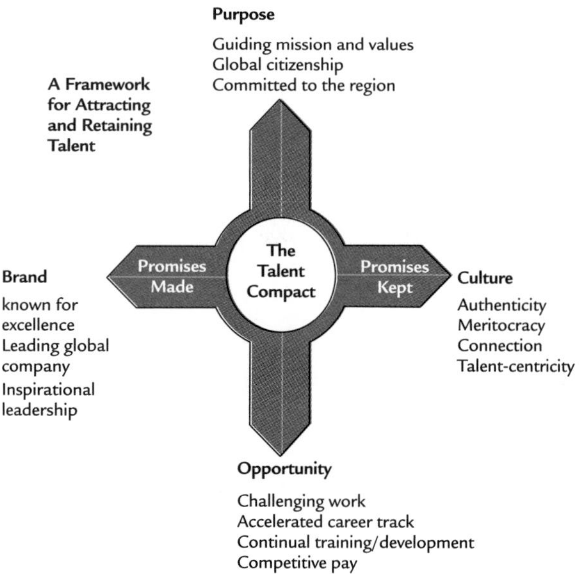

Idea in Practice

To find and keep employees in China, Brazil, and other developing nations, recruiters have to offer a whole lot more than a fat paycheck and a standard career path. These young managers have a tremendous sense of opportunity – in many cases, for the first time in their lives. Companies that succeed at recruitment and retention in emerging markets focus on four key distinctions: brand, purpose, opportunity, and culture.

Factor	What Matters	Example
Brand	A reputation for excellence; a ticket to future success; inspirational leadership	TCS Iberoamerica, which provides software and technology services in Latin America, Spain, and Portugal, stands for technical excellence. When expanding into Brazil and Uruguay, the company first hired engineers – not salespeople – and sent them to India to observe TCS's core strengths and standards firsthand. They returned energized and eager to recruit their compatriots.
Purpose	Opportunity to be part of a game-changing business model; a chance to participate in cultural transformation	The acquisition of IBM's personal computer operations helped Lenovo become a leader in the global PC market. Its founder's vision, to be a "great company," attracted employees who wanted not a job but a career – at a time when China had very few "great" companies. And workers felt pride that their country had bought part of an American icon.
Opportunity	Accelerated career path from day one; seemingly unlimited prospects for growth	Lenovo has methodically developed career maps and talent pipelines for everyone in its pool of high potentials, including the CEO. Career maps link directly to key slots across the globe; accountability for the entire process rests with line leadership, not with HR.
Culture	Meritocracy and transparency; follow-through on promises	The CEO of HCL Technologies, a global IT company headquartered in India, posted his own 360-degree feedback on the company intranet; 2,000 managers now publicly post theirs. The intranet also invites employees to approach the CEO with any question at all; he personally answers as many as 100 inquiries a week.

We're not proposing a simple solution to a complex problem. Company needs vary by market (see the exhibit "The Talent Market in BRIC"). Prospective employees don't necessarily value the same things: Among certain demographic groups opportunity may matter more than purpose, for instance, and individual preferences vary widely as well. But regardless of any company's strategy for a given market, the same overarching principles apply.

Attracting Talent: Promises Made

Lenovo is a good illustration of the strong lure of brand, opportunity, and purpose. Its acquisition of IBM's personal computer operations, in 2005, made it the third-largest personal computer company in the world. In 1994 the founder of Legend (as Lenovo was then known), Liu Chuanzhi, forecast that it would be a great company – an astonishing leap of faith in the early 1990s. "At the time, there were very few great Chinese companies, so Chuanzhi's vision stood out," Chen Shaopeng, president of Lenovo Greater China and senior vice president of Lenovo Group, told us. "In China, the biggest draw is Lenovo's ambition and vision." The IBM acquisition produced something of a halo effect for Lenovo, and Chinese workers felt pride that China had been able to buy part of an American business icon. Lenovo's brand was and is attractive to ambitious young workers with dreams of their own – people who are building careers and not simply looking for jobs. Lenovo was an early standout for these rising stars.

Lenovo also built a global perspective into its brand promise; to become a great company it would have to expand beyond its home market. That meant opportunity. President and CEO Bill Amelio describes his company as a "stage without a ceiling for every employee" – worldwide. In a truly global spirit, Lenovo's top-team meetings rotate among Beijing, Hong Kong, Singapore, Paris, and Raleigh, North Carolina. "Instead of having everyone travel to me, I travel to them," Amelio says. Lenovo's brand promise credibly communicates that nationality doesn't matter; if an employee demonstrates capability and vision, there are no limits. The playing field is level.

TCS Iberoamerica, a $160 million unit of Tata Consultancy Services (itself a division of the $28.5 billion Tata Group), provides software and technology services to clients in Latin America, Spain, and Portugal, while also contributing to other TCS endeavors worldwide. It's easy to understand why an Indian would want to work for Tata Group in India. But what motivates a Uruguayan software engineer to work for an Indian company in Brazil? The combination of a strong brand and opportunity. TCS Iberoamerica's president, Gabriel Rozman, told us, "When people in our region read about Tata buying Jaguar or making a $2,000 car that will change the industry ... they get excited."

The Tata brand stands for technical excellence, so when expanding into Brazil and Uruguay, Rozman started by hiring engineers – not salespeople – and sent them to India to observe firsthand the company's core strengths and standards. They returned energized and eager to recruit their compatriots. One Uruguayan engineer saw working at Tata as an opportunity to help his country make its mark; he said, "I wanted to work at TCS because I wanted to show the world what Uruguay was all about. Even though we're a tiny country, we have value to add." Rozman also emphasized the appeal of having local Brazilian and Uruguayan leaders who are well connected and admired in the community heading up operations, rather than expatriates.

The Talent Market in BRIC

ALTHOUGH THE TALENT GAP between supply and demand is pervasive in the developing world, the particulars vary by country. The charts below show where deficits and surpluses exist in Brazil, Russia, India, and China at four levels: entry, middle management, country leadership, and regional leadership. The shaded areas represent the talent pool; the white areas show deficits or surpluses of talent. The charts illustrate averages for these countries; further analysis reveals variations across business sectors. A few highlights are boxed below.

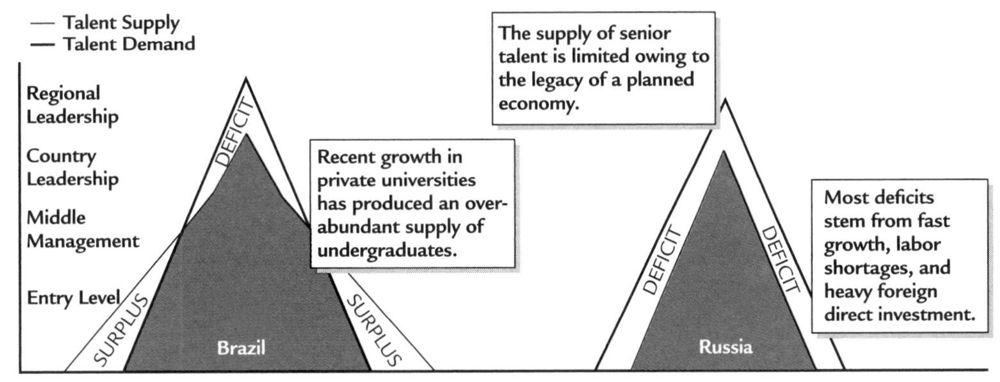

Many other managers spoke of the pride they felt in working for companies with strong brands that were also contributing to their countries' economic development. Novartis's sense of purpose, for instance, is a major draw for talent. Its Project Arogya, one of Novartis's socially conscious business operations, provides services to some 10 million villagers in 24 territories of India. Arogya's leader, Olivier Jarry, joined because of the brand promise to make lives better around the world. "We improve the health and health education of the villagers," he says. "We provide a source of revenue for local talent working with us on the ground. We are helping local doctors and pharmacists. This is a tremendously exciting mission."

How do brand, opportunity, and purpose come together as a promise made at Standard Chartered Bank? The company's CEO, Peter Sands, explains, "We are serious about being a force for good in the world. It's not an add-on for us. We are leaders in microfinance, supporting fledgling entrepreneurs in some of the world's poorest regions. We seek out, as a part of our strategic intent, opportunities to support renewable-energy businesses. By design we are among the world's most diverse organizations, so top talents from all walks of life are attracted to us because they know they will be embraced as central to our mission, not peripheral."

Retaining Talent: Promises Kept

Brand, opportunity, and purpose can create compelling promises, but in such a competitive market the temptation is to overpromise just to get people in the door. Failure to deliver will sour current employees on the company and ultimately hurt its appeal for potential employees. That is why keeping promises – important in any market – takes on particular urgency in emerging markets, where employees can quickly and easily move to global competitors or local companies that appear to offer greater overall rewards. Many companies we've studied have experienced extraordinarily high attrition rates.

Culture, however, can play a central role in employee retention. Hemant Mishr's team at SCB sells into several of the most economically depressed areas in the world; Mishr joined SCB largely because of its brand and its purpose, which includes a commitment to supporting local communities. He stays, he says, because of the culture: SCB is a meritocracy that carefully nurtures his career, and it lives up to the values that attracted him in the first place. "It's not about pay," he says. "I could go elsewhere and earn more – lots more."

Like Mishr, many of the people we interviewed were seeking a culture that would support the promise of an accelerated career path with growth opportunities for everyone, a commitment to meritocracy, and custom career planning. HCL Technologies has such a culture. A global IT company headquartered in India, HCL employs about 55,000 people in 18 countries. When Vineet Nayar became its president, in 2005, he knew he had to do something drastic to turn around the company, formerly one of India's most innovative, which in 1999 had been first in the country in terms of revenues but by 2005 was fifth.

Nayar started with culture. He told us, "I wanted to create an environment where employee development and empowerment was the most important thing, because ultimately I wanted value-focused employees who were willing and able to drive an innovative, sophisticated experience for customers." Nayar quickly assembled a 20-person team of "young sparks" an energetic group from among HCL's top employees; they coined the slogan that became HCL's strategy for the next two years: "Employee first, customer second." The notion is simple – the best way to bring value to customers is to empower employees.

Throughout 2005 Nayar and the young sparks unveiled initiatives designed to remove barriers to employees' doing their best work. They started by revamping the company's intranet. Using a software application, employees can "raise

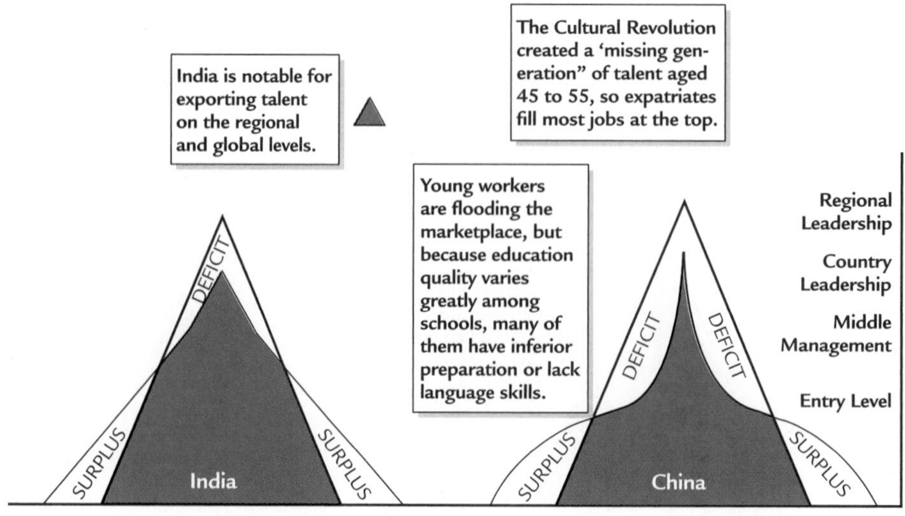

tickets" to report problems with HCL services and processes. In real time they can watch the actions taken to correct a problem, and a ticket can be closed only by the employee who raised it. By 2006, employees were raising 30,000 tickets a month. The site also created transparency: An employee can pose any question at all to Nayar, who personally answers up to 100 inquiries a week. Shortly after its revitalization the intranet was being visited by close to 25,000 employees every week.

In addition, after a few months in office Nayar posted his own 360-degree feedback on the intranet and encouraged his senior managers to do the same; today more than 2,000 managers publicly post their feedback. Indian companies traditionally control information at the top, so the move to public 360s truly distinguished HCL. In interview after interview employees told us of the tremendous impact such transparency has on their career choices.

In another differentiating move, HCL instituted "trust pay." Many IT companies in India offer employees a combination of 70% fixed pay and 30% variable pay. In practice, high internal targets make it difficult to earn that 30%. HCL decided to offer 85% of its employees (mostly junior engineers) a fixed compensation rate, to be set at the beginning of each annual cycle. Some new hires actually thought a mistake had been made in their offer letters, because they'd never known another company to offer trust pay. This is very appealing to recruits from the developing world, because often their whole families are invested in their success. Parents, siblings, and other relatives have worked hard to send them to school, and once they know they can support their loved ones, they can focus on their work.

Because HCL has stayed true to its promises, its employees are dedicated and its customers are taking note. The company's reputation for customer service has consistently improved over the past four years, resulting in major new contracts. Nayar, who is now the CEO, says, "Putting employees first isn't about launching a few initiatives that make them feel good. It's about offering a workplace where employees, no matter their level, can have an impact, can be a part of something exciting, and can grow professionally and personally."

Leadership development is another cultural element that strongly influences retention. Careers must be carefully nurtured, and finding the time to do that may seem like a luxury when the pressure to grow is so great. But companies can't set such concerns aside, lest they lose high-potential talent as fast as they bring it in.

Lenovo very methodically provides accelerated development opportunities for its employees. Mary Eckenrod, the head of talent management, has conducted extensive research into how leaders learn and the potential career stages at technology-based organizations in emerging markets. She has worked with Lenovo's top team to construct career maps and pipelines for every member of the company's pool of high potentials, including the CEO. All employees are asked to reflect on their career aspirations, the experiences and education that have led to their current roles in the organization, and the development they need to reach their goals.

What makes Lenovo's talent-tracking process work, however, is that the career maps are linked to key slots across the globe and accountability for the entire process rests squarely with line leadership, not with HR. Its employees are ambitious, and Lenovo needs to demonstrate that it is serious about developing their careers.

Do SCB, HCL, and Lenovo have a choice about how they approach development? Absolutely. They could focus on attracting the small handful of people with proven experience, as many companies do, but instead they hire largely on the basis of potential. They could enroll in the "cream rises to the top" school of leadership development, believing that the best talent will emerge even if the company fails to provide development opportunities. But the companies that are winning the talent race in emerging markets are not only using brand, opportunity, and purpose to attract the best people; they are investing heavily in career planning and professional development even at the lowest levels, because the workforce is so young. These companies' cultures send a powerful message to employees: Your potential is limited only by your dedication, effort, and ability to produce results.

The Talent Compact at Standard Chartered Bank

As China's economy continues to grow at a breakneck pace, thousands of new businesses are starting up, discretionary income is growing rapidly with the emergence of a new middle class, and wealth is being created as never before. Trying to recruit and retain high-caliber talent in the financial services field, the engine of much of the economy's growth, can be daunting – especially since April 2007, when the Chinese government loosened restrictions on foreign ownership of local banks. Multinational financial services firms have since flooded China.

The gap between employee supply and demand is especially wide when it comes to candidates capable of moving into senior leadership roles. Many recruits fresh out of universities lack the language and other skills to take on even entry-level positions in global companies. Nevertheless, salaries in China have risen out of proportion to the expertise of the talent pool, creating unrealistic expectations among potential employees.

Moreover, China's one-child policy has created a unique problem. As one manager put it, "Consider that millions of young Chinese have no siblings and no cousins. It's not too difficult to see how the child can become the center of attention for the entire family. It's not easy giving critical feedback to someone who is not used to it and who has lots of employment options elsewhere."

Recall SCB's former difficulty in recruiting leaders for its banking operations in China. The company's strategy illustrates our framework in particularly illuminating ways.

Katherine Tsang, the CEO of SCB China since 2005, says, "These challenges forced us to tell the SCB story with passion, but to make sure that our culture and management practices matched that story in an honest way. We tell lots of stories here about our mission, our sense of purpose, and our brand, and the many opportunities that young people will get when they come to work for us. But we need to keep those promises." Together with Geraldine Haley, SCB's group head of talent management, Tsang created what the company calls the "raw talent superhighway" for SCB China, which is designed to attract and retain good people. The bank emphasizes acquiring specialized skills, followed by broad managerial training and development, followed by global networks and leadership development. Several components went into the highway's construction.

Selection Tsang's and Haley's teams conducted extensive analyses of the skills and talents required by both retail and commercial bankers in China. Then they investigated non-banking industries, such as travel and tourism, that had developed similar expertise, especially in customer relations. SCB China set out to aggressively recruit promising employees from these other industries; it was able to offer higher pay and significantly greater opportunities for career advancement.

Induction and Orientation SCB runs a standard induction program, but it offers an intensive version for its raw-talent hires – employees who demonstrate the desired behaviors and values but have no skills in financial services. This program introduces recruits to the company's culture and values and teaches them the ethical management of financial services, including money-laundering prevention and codes of conduct.

Technical Training SCB's retail division offers extensive training, and relationship managers in its wholesale business must complete a rigorous five-day "boot camp." All trainees must pass a strict examination before they are exposed to the bank's customers and clients. Skilled and seasoned managers conduct most of these sessions.

Professional and Management Development SCB's raw recruits also get intensive training in the English language, communication and listening skills, and business etiquette, and they have a variety of ongoing educational opportunities. They receive career guidance and access to networking sessions, enabling them to explore different paths at the bank. In addition, SCB offers the Great Manager Program, which has won best-practice awards in China and elsewhere in Asia for its creativity and effectiveness in management development. The company has regional learning centers throughout China and e-learning platforms, so development is accessible to all. SCB is forming strategic partnerships with Chinese universities, both to strengthen relationships for recruitment and to offer those who join the company ongoing professional development at those schools.

Stretch Assignments and Deployment One SCB message to recruits is captured in "Go places...," which has a double meaning: It tells people that if they join the bank and do well they will move ahead in their careers, and it reminds them that SCB is a global company with opportunities around the world. Chinese talent is often moved elsewhere, including to the group head office in London.

Personal Development and Performance Management SCB employees explore their passions and strengths, with coaching and guidance, to find a starting point for their careers. Although the SCB environment is nurturing, Tsang and other leaders don't hesitate to give regular and often tough feedback. "We deal with problems openly and honestly, and that has led to the creation of an authentic and trust-based culture. People know we are a straight meritocracy, and that motivates them."

CEO Peter Sands says, "We have an exciting growth story, but more important, people can translate that story into growth opportunities for themselves. We have 25-year-olds looking at 32-year-olds doing big jobs. These young people see who they can become, and that they don't have to wait 30 years to do it." Through these efforts the bank was able to decrease attrition by 3% from 2007 to 2008. That may not sound like much, but consider that SCB is bringing thousands of people on board every year. What's more, most companies in these markets are experiencing a dramatic increase in attrition.

Thoughtful Execution

We have described principles that any company, in any market, would probably do well to heed. But emerging markets pose some special challenges worth noting. First, beware of exporting your domestic talent strategy to emerging markets. Even if that strategy is highly successful at home, it will probably need extensive tailoring to succeed in the developing world. Second, it's critical to establish a core of local talent (or of outsiders with a long history in emerging markets) that can guide you in understanding the region. Sending in a talent officer from the corporate center is unlikely to do the trick; despite the pressure to bring people on board quickly, investments in talent take root only with patience. Third, keep in mind that an overreliance on English as the "official language" of the business may prove an impediment to spotting talent. Some of your most promising people may not speak English fluently.

Finally, it's not easy to embrace and leverage diversity; companies struggle with this in the developed world, too, and very few demonstrate much diversity at the top. In emerging economies, companies have no choice but to nurture local talent, because that's the pool available and because those bright young recruits want to see others like them in positions of power. A truly merit-based company will stand out to them – particularly in hierarchical societies where getting ahead has often relied on family connections and other relationships, social status, age, or length of tenure.

People in different cultures want and expect different things from their work. Gabriel Rozman, of TCS Iberoamerica, reminded us that leading a team in India is not the same as leading a team in Brazil or Uruguay. He recognizes that his company must develop people who can lead diverse teams in various settings. Of course, this makes a commitment to keeping promises made all the more daunting, because companies can't implement one-size-fits-all processes. First figuring out which aspects of the strategy can be standardized and executed at scale and which must be sharply tuned to local needs and then coordinating implementation takes some effort–but it delivers payback. Over time, global companies may even be able to bring home some lessons about meritocracy and diversity.

As global companies are well aware, winning the race for talent in emerging markets is hard work. It requires both the explosiveness of the sprinter and the determination of the marathon runner. The framework we have outlined here should help companies assemble the workforce they need to compete on a world-class level.

Source: Harvard Business Review, November, 2008, 63–70. Reprinted by permission of Harvard Business Publishing.

Training and Development 9

Learning Objectives

- Understand how training and development activities can contribute to an organization's strategic objectives
- Describe how to conduct a needs assessment as part of a training program
- Explain the different modes of delivery of training and how to maximize transfer of training
- Gain an appreciation for the various levels of evaluation of training and the benefits and limitations of each
- Describe the role of organizational development in promoting change with an organization
- Understand the critical link between training, performance management, and compensation in ensuring the success of training

Leadership Development at Virgin Atlantic Airlines

With 37 aircraft, more than 9,000 employees and more than 4.5 million annual passengers, Virgin Atlantic is Britain's second-largest airline. Established in 1985, the organization has been successful in building a brand and image that resonates with consumers. However, the rapid demand for its services created a challenge for staffing the organization's executive ranks. Given Virgin's strong corporate culture and desire to maintain this culture by promoting from within, Virgin realized that it quickly needed to develop its young and inexperienced but enthusiastic management team.

To accomplish this, Virgin developed its own leadership development program. Centered on strategic business objectives, Virgin's executive team started by identifying those traits if felt had contributed most to Virgin's success. It then followed this with a comprehensive assessment of the strengths and weaknesses of Virgin's management team. All the organization's 120 managers were sent to external personal development workshops, which consisted of personality testing and reviews of performance feedback from within the organization. The results were individual assessments, coaching sessions, and personal development plans. Ongoing efforts consist of activities that instill Virgin's culture and values into leadership development cohorts of six managers who met regularly to monitor and discuss their own progress and share ideas. The program has increased both motivation and retention and increased the ratio of management positions filled internally by 20 percent.[1]

If an organization considers its employees to be human assets, training and development represents an ongoing investment in these assets and one of the most significant investments an organization can make. Training involves employees acquiring knowledge and learning skills that they will be able to use immediately; employee development involves learning that will aid the organization and employee later in the employee's career. Many organizations use the term *learning* rather than *training* to emphasize the point that the activities engaged in as part of this developmental process are broad-based and involve much more than straightforward acquisition of manual or technical skills.

Learning implies ongoing development and continuously adding to employees' skills and knowledge to meet the challenges the organization faces from its external environment. A focus on learning, as opposed to training, emphasizes results rather than process, making such an approach more palatable to senior executives. Any kind of employee learning that is not reinforced by the organization's reward system has little chance of impacting employee behavior and performance.

Employee training and development is increasingly becoming a major strategic issue for organizations for several reasons. First, rapid changes in technology continue to cause increasing rates of skill obsolescence. In order to remain competitive, organizations need to continue training their employees to use the best and latest technologies available. Managing in such a turbulent environment has created the need for continuous learning among managers.[2] Second, the redesign of work into jobs having broader responsibilities (that are often part of self-managed teams) requires employees to assume more responsibility, take initiative, and further develop interpersonal skills to ensure their performance and success. Employees need to acquire a broader skill base and be provided with development opportunities to assist with teamwork, collaboration, and conflict management. Third, mergers and acquisitions have greatly increased. These activities require integrating employees of one organization into another having a vastly different culture. When financial and performance results of merger and acquisition activity fall short of plans, the reason usually rests with people management systems rather than operational or financial management systems. Fourth, employees are moving from one employer to another with far more frequency than they did in the past. With less loyalty to a particular employer and more to the employees' own careers, more time must be spent on integrating new hires into the workplace. Finally, the globalization of business operations requires managers to acquire knowledge and skills related to language and cultural differences.

These strategic challenges for training exist alongside standard types of training that are done for new organizational hires (orientation and socialization) and for those employees assuming new job responsibilities. In organizations that emphasize both promotion from within and the career development of existing employees, continual training and development opportunities are critical. Employees must be updated in industry best practices and changing technology. For an employer who hires a significant number of skilled workers from outside the organization, new employees need to understand rules, policies, and procedures and be socialized into company operations and employee networks.

New employee orientation can be a daunting challenge for employers. New hires are often inundated with forms, procedures, and people but lack a strong sense of the business and operations in which they have begun to work. While new-hire orientation programs can attempt to assist new employees in their transition into the workplace, if the programs were not developed in tandem with any strategic objectives or in concert with other HR programs and/or critical operational areas of the organization, they often do not have a significant impact on the new hire's ability to fully understand the entire organization and their place in it. Ideally, new employee orientation programs will teach employees not only about their jobs and the organization's culture and strategy but also how their individual jobs are critical to the organization's success. Orientation training, sometimes called "onboarding," should allow employees the opportunity to ask questions and interact with those providing information as well as facilitate the development of a network of work relationships for employees. Coworkers can be critical catalysts in helping new employees obtain information they need to be productive.[3] Exemplary new employee orientation/training programs have been developed at Black and Decker and MicroStrategy.

New Employee Training at Black and Decker

Towson, Maryland–based tool manufacturer Black and Decker (B&D) has developed a new employee training program that literally puts employees to work. College grads who gain entry-level professional employment in sales with B&D traditionally received their training via a three-ring binder that provided information about B&D products. New employees would study and learn the material to assist them with their selling. Establishing credibility was not part of the training equation, and many trainees never even touched the products they were selling, let alone used them. Black and Decker has recently revamped its sales training for new hires to combine classroom training, online courses, and, most important, a training floor where new hires engage in hands-on learning about construction and tool use. This program, a component of Black and Decker University, enrolls 100 to 200 new sales and marketing employees annually. B&D University has a staff of 15 employees and an annual budget of $3 million. As part of their training, sales and marketing trainees take an online course that explains the four basic applications of tools: cutting, removing, fastening, and making holes. They then go to work in a product training area, where they must use the tools to build things, such as roofs, moldings, and stairs. Such experience allows them to go to retailers and fully explain product features and benefits. As a result of its program, Black & Decker has drastically reduced turnover, sent out more credible sales staff, enhanced the Black & Decker name, and reported higher employee satisfaction and loyalty.[4]

Boot Camp at MicroStrategy

MicroStrategy is a Vienna, Virginia–based organization that provides data mining services and has long held a spot on Fortune's *best employers' list. With a strong corporate culture, based on the convictions and beliefs of its founder, Michael Saylor, MicroStrategy has developed a new-hire orientation program that attempts to infuse elements of its culture into employees from the first day of work. The program, known as "boot camp," goes beyond mere orientation and is a written requirement in every employment contract for MicroStrategy employees, who work in 18 states and 35 countries. It is an intensive immersion into MicroStrategy culture to which Saylor wants each employee exposed and committed. There are three different variations of boot camp, each targeted to a different group of employees. The first is a three-day general boot camp that concludes with a 20- to 25-question exam that covers information such as MicroStrategy's products and company structure. The second is a two-week sales boot camp that culminates in a mock marketing presentation. The third is a five-week technical boot camp that features continuous testing. Despite its intensity, employee feedback on boot camp has been very positive and the only complaint heard is that it is too short.*[5]

Another approach to new-employee training is rotation. Discussed in Chapter 6, rotational programs can have an added benefit for new employees, particularly those who have limited full-time professional work experience. Rotations allow new hires to sample different kinds of work within the organization and determine an optimal fit between their needs and interests and those of the organization. Rotation programs can be expensive in the short run, but they represent a longer-term investment in employees that can provide significant benefits to an organization. Employers benefit in that rotation programs allow more flexibility in work assignments. Employees who have been cross-trained not only better understand how their individual jobs contribute to the whole but can also be reassigned as business and organization conditions change. Rotational programs also have the benefit of minimizing the chance that specialized knowledge will be vested in only one individual in the organization, causing disruptions when such an individual resigns, retires, or otherwise leaves the organization. In addition to helping develop a knowledgeable and flexible workforce, rotation programs can enhance retention because the versatility they offer allows employees to pursue more opportunities within the organization.[6]

Organizations that wish to remain competitive must consider the types of employees they should hire and the skills and knowledge these employees will need to ensure optimal performance over time. Ironically, however, training budgets and programs are usually some of the first expenses organizations cut in response to economic downturns. Many key decision-makers consider these to be luxury expenditures for prosperous times instead of the necessary investments in the organization's future that they are.

Training and development activities are equally important to both employees and employers. One recent survey found that 96percent of job applicants reported that the opportunity to learn new skills was very important when evaluating a prospective employer.[7] Employers also see a bottom-line benefit from strategically designed training activities. One study found that employers who were in the top quartile of their peers relative to the average training expenditure per employee experienced 24 percent higher-gross profit margins, 218 percent higher income generation per employee, and a 26 percent higher price-to-book value of company stock price relative to those employers in the bottom quartile.[8] Investment in training and development, however, remains a catch-22 for employers. While additional training can improve bottom-line operating results, that same training can make employees much more attractive targets of competitors' recruiting efforts. This is particularly true for technical employees, a majority of whom view training primarily as an opportunity to obtain another job.[9]

Benefits of Training and Development

Training involves some kind of change for employees: changes in how they do their jobs, how they relate to others, the conditions under which they perform, or changes in their job responsibilities. Although some employees may find any kind of change threatening, change that results from employee training and development has nothing short of win-win outcomes for both employees and employers. Strategically targeted training in critical skills and knowledge bases adds to employee marketability and employability security that is critical in the current environment of rapidly developing technology and changing jobs and work processes. Organizations continue to seek out and employ knowledge workers rather than workers with narrowly defined technical skills.

Organizations can benefit from training, beyond bottom-line and general efficiency and profitability measures, when they create more flexible workers who can assume varied responsibilities and have a more holistic understanding of what the organization does and the role they play in the organization's success. Providing employees with broader knowledge and skills and emphasizing and supporting ongoing employee development also help organizations reduce layers of management and make employees more accountable for results. Everyone (employees, employers, and customers) benefits from effective training and development programs. The key strategic issue then becomes how to make training effective.

In order for organizations to provide effective employee training and development, key decision-makers must consider employees from the investment perspective described earlier in this book. Training and development quite frequently involve short-term costs (for design and delivery of the learning activities) and long-term benefits. Particularly with issues of employee development, there may be no return on investment for the immediate time period. Organizations that are bound by short-term financial performance indicators are less likely to value training and less likely to create and support a culture that fosters employee development.

One critical decision that can impact the benefits and outcomes achieved by training is whether training activities will be centralized or decentralized within the organization.

Centralized training provides economies of scale and can allow the organization tighter control over all training initiatives. This can ensure that all training programs are consistent with the organization's strategy and each other as well as ensure that there is little to no duplication of effort. Decentralized training moves training into each individual business unit and can facilitate stronger alignment between division needs and training. This is particularly true when considering that different divisions within an organization may have drastically different responsibilities and make significantly different contributions to the organization's strategy.

Organizations that take a strategic approach to human resources can find that employee training can be much more efficacious as part of an integrated approach to HR. For example, training and development are greatly assisted by having appropriate and well-thought-out staffing strategies. Judicious recruitment and selection of new employees will not only allow more targeted training that addresses specific needs but also minimize the need to conduct any extensive or remedial training among new employees.

Planning and Strategizing Training

There are two keys to developing successful training programs in organizations. The first is planning and strategizing the training. This involves four distinct steps: needs assessment, the establishment of objectives and measures, delivery of the training, and evaluation. A model for planning and strategizing training is presented and explained in Exhibit 9.1.

Needs Assessment

The first step—needs assessment—involves determining why specific training activities are required and placing the training within an appropriate organizational context. Needs assessment involves three levels of analysis: organizational, task, and individual. At the organizational level, the training is considered within the context of the organization's culture, politics, structure, and strategy. This analysis considers how the training will assist the organization or unit in meeting its objectives and how the training may affect day-to-day workplace dynamics between and among different units. It also considers the cost of training relative to the benefits that may be expected and considers the opportunity costs of foregoing the training.

Task-level assessment involves looking at specific duties and responsibilities assigned to different jobs and the types of skills and knowledge needed to perform each task. This level also considers whether the learning can or should take place on or away from the job, the implications of mistakes, and how the job can be designed to provide the employee with direct feedback on his or her performance. This level also involves determining whether the training needs of certain jobs are similar to or different from the training needs of other jobs in the organization.

The individual level of assessment considers the people to be trained. It requires an analysis of their existing levels of knowledge and skills as well as factors relating to their preferred learning styles, personality, interpersonal styles in interacting with others, and

EXHIBIT 9.1 Strategizing Training

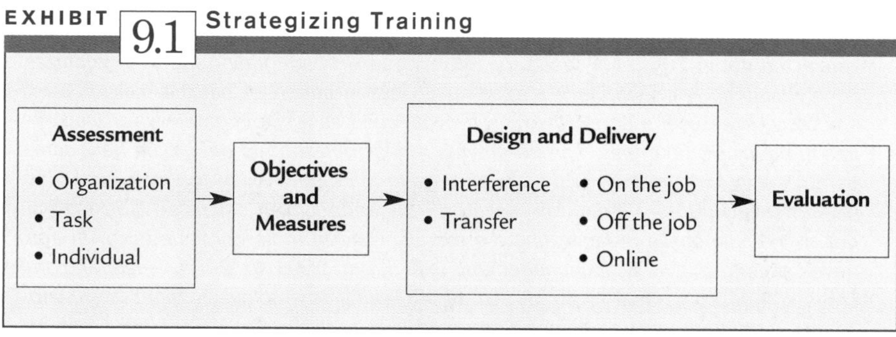

EXHIBIT 9.2 Levels of Needs Assessment

Organizational Level

- How does the training relate to organizational objectives?
- How does the training impact day-to-day workplace dynamics?
- What are the costs and expected benefits of the training?

Task Level

- What responsibilities are assigned to the job?
- What skills or knowledge are needed for successful performance?
- Should the learning setting be the actual job setting?
- What are the implications of mistakes?
- How can the job provide the employee with direct feedback?
- How similar to or different from the training needs of other jobs are the needs of this job?

Individual Level

- What knowledge, skills, and abilities do trainees already have?
- What are the trainees' learning styles?
- What special needs do the trainees have?

any special needs individual employees might have, such as any physical or mental condition that might need to be addressed in the design and delivery of the training. The three levels of needs analysis are summarized in Exhibit 9.2.

Objectives

After training needs have been assessed, objectives for the training activities must be developed. These objectives should follow directly from the assessed needs and be described in specific, measurable terms. Measures should be stated in terms of both desired employee behaviors as well as the results that are expected to follow such behavior. A common problem at this stage is that an organization's objectives may be so vague that success in achieving them cannot be accurately measured or evaluated. On the other hand, an organization may have no plan for measuring these objectives. Training programs that cannot be evaluated are of little value to the organization in the long run.

One important source of information in setting objectives can be the data contained in the organization's performance management system, which is discussed in detail in Chapter 10. Specific training objectives can be derived from the performance deficiencies noted in the performance feedback process. Both individual and group training can be developed around these measures

Using Training to Facilitate a Merger at Hewlett-Packard

When computer giants Hewlett-Packard (HP) and Compaq completed their controversial merger in 2002, HP faced the daunting task of integrating the two organizations. Training via e-learning played a major role in ensuring that the merger went smoothly. The existing portal, Learn@HP, was used as a single gateway for employees in nearly 60 countries. The portal was redesigned to help define the new company identity and structure and to communicate HP's new vision to employees. This helped speed up the merger and saved the organization an estimated $50 million. Learn@HP's success in facilitating the merger has led to its continued growth and development as a critical management tool. From 2003 to 2004, e-learning increased from 25 percent to 40 percent of the total time employees spent in training. A new agreement with Microsoft required the retraining of 3,000 HP/Compaq *employees. E-learning not only reduced the training time for certification from eight weeks to three weeks, but it also saved the organization an estimated $10 million.*[10]

Design and Delivery

After objectives and measures have been set, the next step is the design and delivery of the training itself. Two critical issues must be considered in the design of the training prior to its delivery. The first is interference. Interference occurs when prior training, learning, or established habits act as a block or obstacle in the learning process. Anyone who learned to drive an automobile having an automatic transmission and later attempted to drive a manual or standard transmission probably experienced interference in their learning. The more experience someone has in behaving in a certain way, the more difficult it may be to modify the response he or she displays. When individuals are stressed, they tend to revert to conditioned behavior.

The second critical issue that must be addressed in design is transfer. Transfer refers to whether the trainee or learner can actually perform the new skills or use the new knowledge on the job. In other words, transfer is the extent to which the trainee or learner is able to "transfer" the learning to the actual job setting. Many training programs that are conducted away from the worksite have been criticized for their lack of transfer because the conditions under which employees have been trained are vastly different from those in which they actually work. Obviously, it is inefficient to conduct training and receive no benefit from it in terms of employee job performance; those responsible for training need to ensure that it provides maximum transfer.

The delivery of the training should anticipate any interference that might be present, and a strategy should be planned to overcome it and ensure transfer. Interference is not caused only by conditioned or learned behavior. The attitudes of supervisors or peers may also produce interference. Coworkers who publicly express negative concerns about the training may cause learners to be predisposed against the training. When trainers examine the potential sources of interference, they need to look beyond the backgrounds, skills, and habits of the trainees themselves to the broader organizational context, which includes culture, politics, and organization structure. Training and development will not be effective unless it is conducted within a larger supportive organizational environment. Having the CEO or other senior executives attend training sessions communicates strong organizational support for training.

Transfer can be facilitated by delivering the training in an environment that simulates the actual job conditions as much as possible. In some cases, it may be feasible to provide direct on-the-job training where the employee is trained under the exact working conditions in which he or she will be expected to perform. However, in other cases, on-the-job training may not be feasible, and the delivery of the training should then replicate exact working conditions as much as possible. Airline pilots do not learn to fly by going up in an airplane and being told what to do. Their training involves extensive exposure to simulated flight conditions on the ground, which tests their learning and ability to react to a variety of situations, including crisis situations.

On-the-job training may help to maximize transfer, but it is obviously not feasible for all jobs. In addition, off-the-job training allows learners to focus on their learning by minimizing interruptions or distractions that might take place in the actual work environment. An increasing amount of training is being conducted away from the workplace. This sort of training utilizes techniques that attempt to simulate what happens on the job. Instructional techniques that facilitate such simulation involve the use of case studies, role-plays, and interactive and experiential methods of learning. Individuals being trained are asked to assume a role and the responsibilities that they might have on the job and then perform accordingly.

An increasing amount of organizational training is being conducted online. Many organizations have entire training libraries that consist of skills-related training and information/knowledge-based learning that have been packaged into computer-based instruction modules or programs. Colleges and universities are offering an increasing number of courses and even entire degree programs online.

Computer-Based Training at QUALCOMM

San Diego–based QUALCOMM is unquestionably one of the leaders in computer-based training for its employees. The 6,000-plus employee organization, which invented the multiple access technology used in digital wireless communication worldwide, offers more than 250 custom-designed courses online. These courses include offerings in both technical and professional/management development areas and were initially designed for delivery to fit different learning schedules and different learning styles. Online courses are offered 24 hours a day, 7 days a week, but certain courses are still available in a traditional classroom delivery setting for those who prefer this type of learning environment.

Probably most critical is the fact that the training is strategically focused. All instruction is developed in concert with QUALCOMM's culture and business needs. Learning specialists are assigned to track the needs of various business units by attending staff meetings, meeting regularly with senior management, and conducting group needs assessments. They are then charged with identifying training needs and working with vendors and management to define the course and create appropriate and unique content geared to the needs of the business unit and QUALCOMM.

Training at QUALCOMM is tightly integrated with the organization's competency management initiative, MySource. MySource is an intranet-based employee development tool that allows employees to access their employment records and view their skills and accomplishments. Individuals can map out career options and then enroll in the appropriate learning modules to facilitate promotion and skill development.

In moving to computer-based training, QUALCOMM has saved millions of dollars from the cost of ineffective centralized training. More important, its system successfully unleashes the full potential of its employees through training and skill development, career planning, and competency management.[11]

Online computer-based instruction provides a number of benefits. It is self-paced, allowing different individuals to learn and absorb material at their own level of comfort and understanding. It is adaptive to different needs and can be customized for different employees. It is also easy to deliver: All an employee has to do is turn on a computer at a workstation or at home. There is no need to leave one's desk or coordinate schedules with trainers or trainees nor a need to have trainers and trainees in the same physical space. Computer-based training is also usually less expensive to administer when different units in the organization are geographically dispersed. Finally, training can be conducted whenever it is convenient for the employee. An employee who has finished assigned work early no longer needs to look busy or find a way to kill time. The training can be undertaken without any advance scheduling.

The popularity of online training cannot be underestimated. A recent survey of 100 companies with an average of 15,000 employees found that 42 percent currently used online learning applications. More importantly, however, 92 percent of the respondents planned to introduce or accelerate the volume of online training within 12 months.[12]

Despite its popularity, there are some drawbacks to computer-based instruction. First, learners must be self-motivated and take both initiative and responsibility for their learning. Second, the cost of producing online, interactive materials can be quite high. The content of the learning can become outdated quickly and require revision and possible redesign of the entire online learning environment. Finally, the lack of both interaction with others and two-way communication may work against the needs and preferred learning styles of many employees, particularly adult learners. Consequently, computer-based training can either be advantageous for an employer or a waste of time, resources, and money. Clearly, it needs to be considered within the larger context of the training objectives and the assessed organizational, task, and individual considerations discussed previously.

E-Learning at EMC Corporation

EMC is a Hopkinton, Massachusetts–based supplier of software, networks, and services for data and information storage. Dramatic improvements in technology related to data storage and retrieval have made product life cycles at EMC increasingly short. This has prompted a need for continuous new product development and, consequently, training. The use of traditional classrooms to meet these accelerated training needs would have involved great expense, as it required the building or leasing of physical space as well as the cost of moving employees out of the field to the training site. As EMC expanded globally, there was also a need to deliver more standardized training to prevent inconsistencies that were taking place in different locations relative to content and approach. In response to these challenges, EMC installed a single learning management system that moved training from a traditional instructor-led process to an integrated e-learning process. This move has allowed new employees to complete product training in five months rather than the nine months previously required, and the sales staff is now able to meet quotas in four months rather than nine to twelve months. Perhaps the biggest benefit has been realized with new product launches. Updated courses are available to coincide with a new product's release, resulting in increased customers' willingness to become early adapters. Customers also are now more prone to buy multiple products, knowing that online support is readily available for them. While EMC initially developed its e-learning program with an eye on costs, the longer-term investments in this area are also yielding significant productivity and revenue gains.[13]

Evaluation

After the training has been delivered, it needs to be evaluated. This evaluation should be an integral part of the overall training program. The organization needs to receive feedback on the training and decide whether the training should be continued in its current form, modified, or eliminated altogether. The ultimate evaluation criteria should also be assessed prior to training delivery to provide a comparison basis for post-training assessment. Evaluation techniques that are not developed when objectives are set will usually have little value to the organization. The decision of how to evaluate training should be made at the same time the training objectives are set.

A highly regarded model has been developed for training evaluation that suggests that evaluation can take place on four levels and that these levels form a hierarchy, meaning that lower levels are prerequisites for higher levels.[12] In other words, if one of the lower-level measures is not affected, then those measures that follow it will automatically not be affected. These levels are reaction, learning, behavior, and results and are illustrated in Exhibit 9.3.

Reaction measures whether the employees liked the training, the trainer, and the facilities; it is usually measured by a questionnaire. If employees have less-than-favorable reactions to the program, it is unlikely that other employees will have an interest in the training or that employees attending the training received anything of value from it. A favorable reaction, in and of itself, does not ensure that the training was effective.

Learning measures whether the employees know more than they did prior to undertaking the training. Knowledge-based training can be measured by tests; skills-based training can be measured through demonstrations or simulations. If employees did not learn anything, then obviously we can expect no change in their behavior on the job. For any change to occur as a result of training, the trainees must have learned something.

Behavior measures what employees do on the job after the training. This measure allows organizations to assess not only whether transfer has taken place but also whether the employees are able to do anything differently (skills-based training) or think or solve problems in different ways (knowledge-based training). Behavioral impact is usually measured through performance appraisal, which is done by those who are able to witness and observe the employee. If there is no change in behavior, we cannot expect employees' performance to have been enhanced.

EXHIBIT 9.3 Four Levels of Training Evaluation

Level	Questions Being Asked	Measures
Results	Is the organization or unit better because of the training?	Accidents Quality Productivity Turnover Morale Costs Profits
Behavior	Are trainees behaving differently on the job after training? Are they using the skills and knowledge they learned in training?	Performance appraisal by superior, peer, client, subordinate
Learning	To what extent do trainees have greater knowledge or skill after the training program than they did before?	Written Tests Performance Tests Graded Simulations
Reaction	Did the trainees like the program, the trainers, the facilities? Do they think the course was useful? What improvements can they suggest?	Questionnaires

Evaluation of results looks at the overall outcomes of the training and the impact that the training has had on productivity, efficiency, quality, customer service, or any other means the organization uses to measure contributions and performance of employees. This can be assessed by budget and cost reports, sales figures, production, customer surveys, or any other means that correspond to the organization's performance measures. However, results of training programs are often not immediate. Training programs may be ongoing or involve employees' developing a level of proficiency, which takes time to achieve and master. Although results-based measures of training are usually the most meaningful and economically significant for an organization, undue reliance on them may cause key decision-makers to abandon training programs that do not produce immediate short-term results. In addition, there are those who question whether results-based approaches are always the most appropriate measures for training evaluation. Reading 9.1, "Learning Versus Performance Goals: When Should Each Be Used?" presents a compelling argument concerning the problems often associated with the insistence of results-based measures of learning. Given the author's arguments in tandem with some of the mentioned limitations of each of the four levels of training evaluation, it is advisable to consider all four levels of training evaluation, either in part or in total, contingent on the organization's strategy when making a determination of how training will be evaluated.

Organizational Development

The majority of training programs and initiatives are designed to address the training needs of individual employees or small groups of employees. Largely focused on skill acquisition and development, these programs attempt to provide employees with the knowledge and skills that will result in improved productivity as well as a workforce that is more able to achieve the organization's strategic objectives. However, in order to continue to survive and prosper in a rapidly changing global environment, organizations need to respond to changes in their external environments by undertaking large-scale organization-wide changes. These activities constitute organizational development (OD), which focuses on the entire organization rather than individual employees or employees groups. OD initiatives attempt to improve an organization's overall effectiveness through planned interventions that are undertaken in response to the organization's strategy. While training and development focuses on the micro aspects of organizational needs and responsiveness, OD focuses on the macro or organization-wide perspective of performance and responsiveness.

OD initiatives generally involve organizational processes as well as organization's culture. Typical OD interventions might include culture change, facilitating mergers and acquisitions, organizational learning, knowledge management, process improvement, and organization design and structure.[14] In addition to considering issues related to performance, efficiency, and profitability, OD interventions also consider the organization's people. Initiatives are driven by humanistic values, such as respect, inclusion, authenticity and collaboration, with desired outcomes of values, norms, attitudes, and management practices that result in a positive organizational climate that engages employees and acknowledges and rewards their efforts.[15]

Such changes require a clear understanding of organization-wide issues and consideration of the organization as an open system of interrelated functions and processes. The open systems model of organizations acknowledges the importance of examining the organization within the broader context of external influences on the organization. It also considers the fact that organizations consists of a variety of different functions and processes that influence each other, resulting in the need for a holistic analysis of any planned intervention of change initiative. Those involved must consider not only the organization's relationship with external constituents but also how changes undertaken in one part of the organizations might impact other parts of the organization.

Organizations can undertake a variety of interventions as part of organizations development. A variety of tools are available to assist the organization with such initiatives. These include individual self-assessment tools, such as personality inventories, coaching and mentoring, performance feedback, and career planning and progress charting. At the organizational level, team-building initiatives, brainstorming, knowledge transfer and retention programs, conflict resolution sessions, and process feedback consultation aid in organizational development.

Knowledge Transfer and Retention at Hewlett-Packard

Palo Alto, California–based Hewlett-Packard (HP) is the world's largest seller of personal computers and the world's largest technology organization. HP has recognized the need for knowledge retention as its workforce has become more transient and key individuals have approached retirement. To assist with knowledge retention, the organization has developed a program called "Knowledge Briefs" (KB), which facilitates knowledge transfer and retention through a documentation process and incentive scheme. The program is based on the premise that employee turnover can be unpredictable and that resultant knowledge transfer needs to happen on a regular, continuous basis and is best accomplished within the context of an employee's everyday work and without time pressures.

The KB program asks key technical employees to document in writing their main technical responsibilities as well as "best practices" they have observed in their work. Given that so much of the work at HP involves knowledge and process generation, such documentation allows employees to communicate their individual experiences, perspectives, and successes to others. These technical reports, or knowledge briefs, can be no more than ten pages long and can be prepared by any employee at HP. They must address a technical topic of the employee's choice in a precise and succinct manner and be prepared by using specific written guidelines and template format. Once written, KBs are subject to a strict internal review process to ensure quality and uniformity and provide authors with feedback from those unfamiliar with the content of the brief. Incentives and awards, which include monetary bonuses *and publication in an in-house technical journal, are provided to employees who produce accepted KBs. The program now has more than 4,000 KBs available to HP employees, with approximately 600 new KBs published annually. HP has attempted to measure the value of the KB program relative to cost savings associated with the transfer of knowledge. To date, the program has incurred just under $13 million in costs and has produced $75 million in value relative to knowledge retention.*[16]

In taking a more macro perspective on the organization and its need to change and evolve, key attention must be paid to the development of appropriate international relationships. This is particularly true relative to the development of leaders and the management of groups and group processes. Leadership development has been positively correlated to an organization's financial performance. Organizations with strong leadership development programs frequently display strong financial performance, particularly relative to organizations that do not focus on developing leaders.[17] Ongoing development of leaders is discussed in part in Chapter 5 in the discussion of succession planning. However, the specific means and strategies for leadership development need to be addressed. Reading 9.2, "The Imperative of Development Global Leaders," provides some recommendation for the development of global leaders in government, which can also serve as a blueprint for the development of global leaders in the private sector.

The increasing use of work groups and teams is addressed in Chapter 6. Teams and groups can be temporary or permanent, live or virtual, within functions or cross-functional, and domestic or global. However, all teams and groups present different learning and training challenges than do individuals. Successful organizational development initiatives need to consider how groups evolve and learn and incorporate these theories and concepts into the design and delivery of any intervention initiatives. Reading 9.3, "How Groups Learning Continuously," discusses strategies on how to create and maintain the most effective learning environment for groups.

One significant OD-related practice that many organizations are undertaking is the establishment of corporate universities (CUs). The activities of corporate universities usually involve both training and organizational development activities. A CU is an in-house operation that attempts to develop both individuals and the organization toward the organization's strategic objectives and facilitate and manage any planned change initiatives. It is estimated that there are currently more than 2,000 existing corporate universities, which exist either physically or virtually.[18] CUs tend to evolve through several stages prior to becoming full-fledged corporate universities.

Activities of CUs may be developed in-house or in full or partial consultation with consultants and/or traditional universities. In some cases, programs and activities of a CU may be custom-designed or consist of standard assessments, programs, and activities. Successful corporate universities need to have the support of top management, including financial support, a well-defined mission and business plan, high-quality instruction and corresponding student satisfaction, strong internal marketing, a high level of online

EXHIBIT 9.4 Stages of Corporate University (CU) Development[19]

Stage	Operational	Tactical	Strategic
Focus	Consolidation of existing training activities	Development of targeted programs to address specific needs	Knowledge management, development, and retention
Goal	Efficiency	Alignment with organization needs	Competitive advantage
Strategic perspective	Random and reactive	Targeted and reactive	Targeted and proactive
Man activity	Centralizing training functions and activities	Matching activities to organizational strategy	Strategic partnership

instruction, and the ability to document the impact of CU activities on the organization's outcomes, particularly financial outcomes.[20] Effective corporate universities can contribute to an organization's leadership development, employee engagement, talent management, organizational change initiatives, and innovation, each of which can be significant sources of competitive advantage.[21]

Liverpool Virtual University

With 63 stores and more than 33,000 employees, Mexico City–based Liverpool is the largest department store chain in Mexico. Several years ago, the organization began creating what would evolve into Liverpool Virtual University. With an initial $2 million investment, Liverpool created a corporate television network, which provided employees access to two different learning management systems. Today, Liverpool Virtual University (LVU) offers 22 separate programs. Ten of these are academic programs, ranging from a high school degree to master degree programs in leadership and finance, while 12 are corporate programs focused on various aspects of management and leadership. Liverpool directly attributes increased employee retention and improved productivity to the activities and programs offered by LVU.

The organization has already recouped its $2 million investment through the elimination of costs associated with external trainer fees, rental and maintenance of training facilities, and employee transportation costs associated with attending in-person training. Liverpool is preparing to turn LVU into a profit center by enrolling employees of other organizations on a contract basis. In addition, LVU is supporting Liverpool's commitment to social responsibility by signing a partnership agreement with the National Institute for Adult Education (NIAE) of Mexico, under which LVU will provide NIAE employees and their children opportunities to finish their secondary school studies.[22]

Organizational development interventions can be used as a key catalyst to facilitate global initiatives an organization may be undertaking. Such activities might include cross-cultural communication, understanding and team building, training and placement for employees abroad, and integration of domestic and foreign operations. However, because OD interventions are built on a foundation of humanistic approaches to work and organization, care must be exercised when attempting to implement OD initiatives abroad. The United States' social values of democracy, participation, and human dignity are not globally accepted, so OD initiatives undertaken abroad must be developed with an appreciation for and empathy toward cultural differences. These issues are discussed in greater depth in Chapter 14.

Integrating Training with Performance Management Systems and Compensation

The second key factor in strategizing training programs is to ensure that desired results of training are reinforced when employees achieve or accomplish them. In larger organizations, it is not uncommon to see an entire department devoted solely to employee training and development. This unit may be separate and autonomous from other human resource functions, such as performance measurement (appraisal) and compensation and benefits administration. When employees expend the effort to learn new skills and knowledge and are expected to implement such learning in their jobs, there should be some incentive to do so and some acknowledgment and reinforcement of that performance once it is achieved. However, when training, performance measurement, and compensation are administered separately and not integrated within a larger, integrative HR strategy, there is less chance of that appropriate and necessary reinforcement.

When employees are asked to learn critical new skills and/or absorb important new knowledge and apply this in their jobs, the means by which their performance is assessed

EXHIBIT 9.5 The Link between Training and Performance Management and Compensation

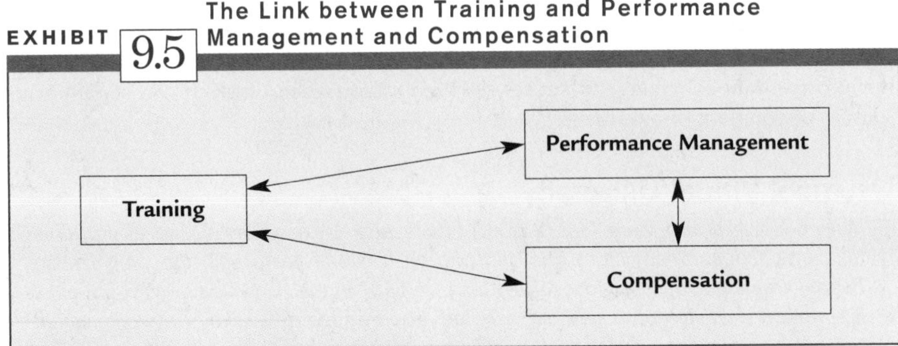

must reflect these changes. The more critical the skills and knowledge are to the organization's strategy, the greater the emphasis that should be placed on assessing them in the organization's performance management system. Similarly, compensation should reflect the results of training. If employees have learned new skills and knowledge and successfully implemented this learning to enhance the performance of the organization, they should be compensated accordingly in a way that is significant to them. A training program that is not linked to the organization's performance management and compensation systems, as indicated in Exhibit 9.5, has far less chance of success than one that does. Training should be conceptualized, designed, and delivered within a larger strategic context and receive an organization-wide commitment to ensure its success.

Strategizing Training and Performance Management at Anheuser-Busch

The past decade has seen a tremendous boom in the use of online training programs. One of the most comprehensive was developed by St. Louis–based beer brewer Anheuser-Busch. Anheuser-Busch has developed its Wholesaler Integrated Learning (WIL) program for its 13 company-owned branch operations, 12 breweries, and 700 independent distributors. The WIL took more than a year to develop, starting with data collection related to employee skills, knowledge, and attributes that was used to create a competency database, which in turn was used to create unique job descriptions based on almost 400 different competencies. The WIL allows employees to access the company Web site from virtually anywhere to take advantage of e-learning opportunities and measure proficiencies deemed critical for a given job description. Immediate feedback is offered and a gap analysis prepared that shows employee skill levels relative to those needed for a position, along with specific suggestions that might include classroom training, online training, reference materials, apprenticeships, coaching, and on-the-job training for bridging any gap. The WIL is far from being a simple testing and assessment program though; the program also ties a comprehensive performance management system into its training components. The WIL analyzes employee performance relative to individual jobs and increases manager accountability by tracking when managers evaluate their employees, whether the manager has produced a development plan for each employee, and how the employee acts on that plan throughout the year.[23]

Conclusion

Training and development of employees is a key strategic issue for organizations: It is the means by which organizations determine the extent to which their human assets are viable investments. Because much of the return on investment in training and development may be difficult to quantify, particularly in the short run, organizations should take a holistic view of training and development, particularly with regard to the kinds of employees and the skills and knowledge bases necessary to achieve strategic objectives. Changes in how work is performed and the organizational contexts in which work is conducted mandate that organizations conduct specific, targeted, strategic training and development initiatives as a prerequisite for continued success.

Critical Thinking

1. Why is training such a critical strategic issue for organizations?
2. What is transfer, and how can it best be facilitated?
3. What are the advantages and disadvantages of on-the-job, off-the-job, and online training? For what types of training is each approach most appropriate?
4. How is training likely to change in the future?
5. Using Exhibit 9.1, develop a training module to teach your classmates about your company and job responsibilities.
6. Explain the relationship between training and organizational development. How might each contribute to strategic human resource management?

Reading 9.1

7. What are the relative advantages and disadvantages of using learning versus performance goals to measure training? In which contexts might the use of each be more appropriate?

Reading 9.2

8. What are the competencies needed for global leaders in government? What similarities and differences exist from those needed in private industry? To what can these similarities and differences be attributed?

Reading 9.3

9. What factors most facilitate group learning, and what implications do these factors have for the design and delivery of group-based learning?

Exercises

1. In small groups, develop a tool to evaluate the learning/training taking place in the course in which you are enrolled. Be sure to consider the needs of the organization, task, and individuals; specific objectives; and design and delivery issues.
2. Trace the growth and evolution of the corporate university of your choice. Share your findings with classmates, and determine specifically how each CU contributes to its organization's strategy.
3. Visit the Web site for Virtual Learn, Inc. (http://www.virtuallearn.com). This site offers thousands of products from nearly 100 well-known vendors and publishers. Select a subject module and evaluate the opportunities for training with the following media:
   - Web
   - Book
   - Live
   - Video
   - Audio
   - CD-ROM

   What modes of delivery appear to be most popular for various subject areas? To what do you attribute this?

Chapter References

1. Martindale, N. "Virgin Atlantic's HR in Practice: High-flying Management," *Personnel Today*, August 20, 2007, article 41937.
2. Alutto, J. A. "Just-in-time Management Education for the 21st Century," *HR Magazine*, July 2000, p. 57.
3. Rollag, K., Parise, S., and Cross, R. "Getting New Hires up to Speed Quickly," *MIT Sloan Management Review*, 46, (2), Winter 2005, pp. 35–41.
4. Henry, K. "Local Grad School Teaches Power Tools," *Baltimore Sun*, October 13, 2002, pp. 1C, 8C.
5. Garvey, C. "The Whirlwind of a New Job," *HR Magazine*, June 2001, pp. 111–118.
6. Frase-Blunt, M. "Ready, Set, Rotate," *HR Magazine*, October 2001, pp. 46–53.
7. Leonard, B. "Training Can Be a Valuable Job Perk," *HR Magazine*, February 2001, p. 37.
8. Wells, S. "Stepping Carefully," *HR Magazine*, January 2001, 461. pp. 44–49.

9. Leonard, B. "Training Can Be a Valuable Job Perk," *HR Magazine*, February 2001, p. 37.
10. Overman, S. "Dow, Hewlett-Packard Put E-Learning to Work to Save Time and Money," *HR Magazine*, February 2004, p. 32.
11. Greengard, S. "Keyboarding Courses at Work or Home," *Workforce*, March 2000, pp. 88–92.
12. Anonymous. "Growing Number of Employers Jump on E-Learning Bandwagon," *HR Magazine*, September 2000, p. 34.
13. Silberman, R. "E-Learning Is Strategic Corporate Move, Not Just Cost-Saver," *HR News*, May 2002, p. 15.
14. Yaeger, T. and Sorenson, P. "Strategic Organization Development: Past to Present," *Organization Development Journal*, 24, (4), Winter 2006, pp. 10–17.
15. McLean, G. and McLean, D. "If We Can't Define HRD in One Country, How Can We Define It in an International Context?," *Human Resource International*, 4, (3), 2001, pp. 313–326.
16. Gotthart, B. and Haghi, G. "How Hewlett-Packard Minimises Knowledge Loss," *International Journal of Human Resources Development and Management*, 9, (2/3), 2009, pp. 305–311.
17. Pollitt, D. "Leadership Success Planning Affects Commercial Success," *Human Resource Management International Digest*, 13, (91), 2005, pp. 36–39.
18. Knight, R. "Move to a Collaborative Effort," *Financial Times*, 19 March, 2007, 2.
19. Adapted from Jansink, F. "The Knowledge-Productive Corporate University," *Journal of European Industrial Learning*, 29, (1), 2005, pp. 40–57.
20. Graebner, R. and Lockwood, N. "Corporate Universities," Society for Human Resource Management research brief, October 2007.
21. Ibid.
22. Moss, D. "A Lesson in Learning," *HR Magazine*, 52, (11), November 2007, pp. 51–52.
23. Tyler, K. "Take E-Learning to the Next Step," *HR Magazine*, February 2002, pp. 56–61.

READING 9.1

Learning versus Performance Goals: When Should Each Be Used?

Gerard H. Seijts and Gary P. Latham

Executive Overview

Contrary to the extant thinking on motivation in the workplace, we argue that performance or outcome goals can have a deleterious effect on one's performance. We demonstrate that in situations where primarily the acquisition of knowledge and skills rather than an increase in effort and persistence is required, a specific challenging learning rather than an outcome goal should be set. A learning goal draws attention away from the end result. The focus instead is on the discovery of effective strategies or processes to attain desired results. The practical implications of learning goals for leadership, performance appraisal, and professional development are explained.

Nearly all executives understand the importance of goal setting. And yet, most organizations have no idea as to how to manage specific challenging goals, or what are sometimes labelled "stretch goals."[1] Some organizations may ask employees to double sales or reduce product-development time from years to months, but fail to provide them the knowledge to meet these challenging goals. The assignment of ambitious goals without any guidance on ways to attain them often leads to stress, pressures on personal time, burnout, and in some instances unethical behavior. It is both foolish and immoral for organizations to assign "stretch goals," and then fail to give employees the means to succeed, yet punish them when they fail to attain the goals.

The Lucent scandal is a compelling example of what can happen when people feel undue pressure to "make the numbers." Richard McGinn, former CEO of Lucent, prided himself on imposing "audacious" goals on his managers, believing that the push for performance would produce "dream" results. In 2000, McGinn pushed his managers for results they could not deliver—not, apparently, without some crossing a legal line.[2] The pressures that McGinn applied were described in a complaint that a former Lucent employee filed, which charged that McGinn and the company had set unreachable goals that caused them to mislead the public. Empirical research provides support for this assertion. High performance outcome goals sometimes cause people to distort the truth regarding goal attainment.[3]

These findings point to a fault in the type of goal that was set. In the above examples, a *performance outcome* goal was set. Setting a specific challenging *learning goal*, on the other hand, is likely to be far more effective for discovering radical, out-of-the-box ideas or action plans that will enable organizations to regain a competitive edge. For example, consider what Arthur Martinez, a former CEO of Sears, Roebuck and Company, wrote in *The Hard Road to the Softer Side*:[4]

> *Sears was in love with its past and entrapped by it at the same time...these kinds of things happen to institutions all the time. They keep playing yesterday's agenda without recognizing that the world has changed and that it continues to change every minute of the day. They ride their old horses onto a modern battlefield, then puzzle about why they are losing a war to an enemy who has tanks and machine guns.*

Martinez concluded that had Sears realized that the competitive landscape was changing, had Sears placed a stronger emphasis on learning what was changing and how to respond to these changes, had Sears examined information that was critical to the decisions that needed to be made prior to the emergence of the crisis, and had Sears sought feedback on their strategic responses, then Sears might not have found itself in a "near-death" situation.

This paper explains when to set performance versus learning goals to increase the productivity of the workforce. With a performance goal, the goal is framed so that the focus is on performance (e.g., decrease costs by 10 percent this quarter). In contrast, the instructions regarding a learning goal are framed to focus attention on knowledge or skill acquisition (e.g., find ten ways of developing a relationship with end-users of our products).

Performance Goals: Examples of Success

The American Pulpwood Association found that goal setting was an effective way to increase the productivity of loggers.[5] Pulpwood crews were matched and assigned to either an experimental goal-setting group or a control group. The saw hands were given a tally meter to keep track of the number of trees they cut down. The crews with a specific challenging goal immediately out-performed those in the control group. The assignment of goals resulted in these workers seeing their work as challenging and meaningful. Hence, job attendance sky-rocketed as the employees began to take pride in comparing their performance relative to the goal. They left work each day with a sense of accomplishment and a sense of personal effectiveness as a result of goal attainment.

The Weyerhaeuser Company found that setting specific high goals leads to high performance of employees in highly complex jobs.[6] Those engineers and scientists in the R & D division who received praise, public recognition, or a monetary incentive, but who did not set goals, performed no better than those who were in a control group. Those who participated in setting a specific high-performance goal regarding their performance appraisal increased their performance significantly. In fact, they set significantly higher goals than was the case where the boss assigned them unilaterally. The higher the goal, the higher one's performance.

The positive effects of setting specific challenging performance goals, in addition to organizational settings, have also been shown in sports and in health care. For example, Swimmer John Naber, winner of four gold medals and one silver medal at the 1976 Olympics, attributed his success, in part, to the performance goals he set. His distal goal was to win a gold medal. He then set proximal or sub-goals for each training session—to gain a few hundredths of a second each day, week, month, and year over a time span of several years in preparation for the Olympics. In the self-management of one's health, individuals who set specific challenging goals in a weight loss or smoking cessation program lose more weight or smoke less than individuals who strive to "do their best" to do so.[7] When goals are set, the dieters and smokers are able to evaluate their on-going goal-directed behavior accurately. Remedial action is taken when there is a discrepancy between the goal that is set and one's actual performance. In contrast, an abstract goal to "do one's best" does not provide a clear marker of progress.

Goal Mechanisms

Why does goal setting increase an employee's effectiveness? First, specific challenging performance goals affect an employee's choice as to what to focus on, as well as effort and persistence in doing so. A goal directs an employee's attention toward actions which are goal relevant at the expense of actions that are not relevant. Second, employees adjust their effort to the difficulty level of the goal. Third, they persist in their effort until the goal is reached.[8] These three motivational mechanisms alone, however, are not always sufficient to attain a goal.

A fourth benefit of goal setting is cognitive rather than motivational. On those tasks that are complex for the individual, goal setting stimulates the development of task strategies, based on one's knowledge, to attain it. For example, the Weyerhaeuser Company discovered that unionized truck drivers who had been assigned a specific high-performance goal in terms of the number of trips per day from the logging site to the mill started to work "smarter rather than harder."[9] Upon receiving the goal, truck drivers developed strategies to attain it. This included using radios to coordinate their efforts so that there would always be a truck at the logging site when logs were available to be loaded. Performance increased because of productive reasoning on their part regarding the strategies necessary to attain the goal. In short, these people were drawing upon their existing knowledge to attain their goal. All of them already knew how to use a radio for communication purposes. Because they purposefully chose to apply this knowledge, productivity increased.

Motivation versus Knowledge Acquisition

Goal setting is viewed by most executives and behavioral scientists as a motivational technique. The tasks that have been studied by behavioral scientists have generally been straightforward for the individual so that the effect of a goal on an employee's choice, effort, and persistence could be easily assessed. But when the task is not straight-forward for people, are there still motivational benefits from setting a specific challenging performance goal? What happens when learning in addition to effort and persistence is critical to one's success? What happens when people lack the requisite knowledge to master a task? Both anecdotal evidence and empirical research provides a thought-provoking answer.

The ordeals of Wagner Dodge and the 15 fire-fighters under his command are a compelling illustration of the difference between working hard ("motivation") and working smart ("knowledge acquisition"). A hellish, fast-moving forest-and-grass fire caused them to run for their lives. With less than a minute remaining until the fire would swallow the group. Dodge discovered a way to attain their goal for survival. He started an "escape fire" that cleared a small area of flammable prairie grass and bushes. As Michael Useem explained in his book, *The Leadership Moment*, Dodge survived because "he had literally burned a hole in the raging fire."[10] Dodge's crew ignored his order to jump inside the expanding ring of fire. Instead they tried in vain to outrun the blaze. Despite their high motivation to survive, they died. Working smart, that is, knowledge acquisition, led to a far better result for Dodge than "working hard."

In the context of running a successful business, Michael Dell, CEO of Dell Computer Corporation, emphasizes the importance of information and knowledge acquisition:[11]

> *It's all about knowledge and execution. Traditionally, it was thought that lack of capital was the barrier to entry into a new competitive market. Take a look around, and you'll see that's just not true anymore. Information will increasingly become both a tool to help businesses hone their competitive edge and a weapon to protect them against the competition. Besides Dell, there are countless successful companies that are thriving now despite the fact that they started with little more than passion and a good idea. There are also*

many that failed, for the very some reason. The difference is that the thriving companies gathered the knowledge that gave them a substantial edge over their competition, which they then used to improve their execution, whatever their product or service. Those that didn't simply didn't make it.

In sum, a person's quest to be effective is influenced by one's ability as well as one's motivation. Performance is a function of creative imagination or learning, in addition to sheer effort and persistence. This is particularly true on tasks where the person lacks the requisite knowledge or skill to master it. Thus the answer to the three previous questions is that there can be a downside to setting a performance goal.

Downside to Performance Outcome Goals

Knowledge acquisition before a performance outcome goal is set can be critically important. Setting a specific challenging performance goal has a detrimental effect on a person's effectiveness in the early stages of learning.[12] This is because in the early stage of learning, before effective performance routines have been identified and have become automatic, a person's attention needs to be focused on discovering and mastering the processes required to perform well, rather than on the attainment of a specific level of performance. The attentional demands that can be imposed on people are limited. Trying to attain a specific challenging performance goal places additional demands on people, so much so that they are unable to devote the necessary cognitive resources to mastering the task. A performance outcome goal often distracts attention from the discovery of task-relevant strategies. For example, focusing on a golf score of 95 by novices may prevent them from focusing on the mastery of the swing and weight transfer and using the proper clubs necessary for attaining that score.

In sum, interventions designed to engage motivational processes may impede task learning when presented prior to an understanding of what the task is about. In these instances, cognitive resources necessary for task understanding are diverted toward self-regulatory activities. Because people have few spare resources at this phase of skill acquisition, these self-regulatory activities can provide little benefit for learning.[13]

In addition, the assignment of a specific challenging performance goal makes some people so anxious to perform at a high level that they scramble to discover the task-relevant strategies in an unsystematic way. In doing so, they fail to learn in a timely fashion the most efficient ways to accelerate their effectiveness.[14] For example, a novice golfer might start switching from one iron to another with the vain hope of attaining the desired score.

Learning versus Performance Outcome Goals

That setting specific challenging performance goals can sometimes lead to worse performance than urging individuals to do their best is at first glance astonishing in that this conclusion is contrary to the weight of over a quarter of a century of accumulated findings in the behavioral sciences. For at least three decades, research in domains ranging from health to organizational settings has shown that goal setting is a powerful motivational technique that truly works. As noted earlier, what is common to these findings is that an employee's ability to attain the goal was seldom if ever an issue. Setting high performance goals affected the person's desire to draw upon extant knowledge and skills to become a high performer. Hence, these studies show again and again that a performance goal influences choice, effort, and persistence to attain it—the three cornerstones of motivation.[15] However, what is often forgotten is that high performance is a function of one's ability as well as one's motivation. Consequently, we speculated that tasks for which minimal prior learning or performance routines exist, or tasks where strategies that were once effective suddenly cease to be so, relocate the purpose or benefit of goal setting from one of primarily motivation to that of knowledge acquisition, environmental scanning, and seeking feedback. In situations where primarily learning rather than an increase in motivation (e.g., effort or persistence) is required for an employee to be effective, setting a specific challenging goal in terms of a performance level to be attained is not likely to be prudent. Perhaps a specific high-learning goal should be set instead. For example, a novice golfer should consider setting a high learning goal rather than a high performance outcome goal in terms of learning how to hold a club, when to use a specific iron, when to use an iron versus a wood, when to hit the ball a short distance rather than a long one, etc. In short, the novice golfer must learn how to play the game before becoming concerned with attaining a challenging performance outcome (e.g., score equals 95).

To test our idea, we examined the effects of learning versus performance outcome goals using a complex business simulation, namely, the Cellular Industry Business Game (CIBG), where people were randomly assigned to conditions. Among the advantages of using a business simulation is that the results of a person's reasoning occur much faster than in a day-to-day organizational setting.

The CIBG is an interactive, computer-based simulation that is based on the events that occurred in the U.S. cellular telephone industry.[16] The simulation uses a complex set of formulas to link the various strategic choices to performance outcomes. Formulas vary over time to reflect the changes that occurred in the industry. The CIBG consists of 13 rounds of decision making, each corresponding to a year of activity. Participants were asked to make decisions concerning ten areas of activity during each round. Examples of the strategic options are pricing, advertising, sales-force, cost containment, finance, geographic scope, and alliances with other companies. Each area of activity allowed numerous choices. For example, in the finance area, participants could raise funds by issuing bonds, issuing public shares, or borrowing from the bank; pay down debt on any one of the three fund-raising methods; or issue dividend payments.[17]

The evolution of the cellular telephone industry was predetermined in the simulation. For example, during the first eight decision periods (simulating the industry's first eight years) competition was restricted on a regional basis. Following year eight, however, the telecommunications industry experienced a radical environmental change in the form of deregulation. Hence, participants in the simulation were given several messages warning that deregulation was likely to occur. The strategic options that were successful before the deregulation ceased to be as effective. Thus, to maintain or increase market share, participants needed to discover a new set of effective strategies following round eight. This aspect of the CIBG simulation reflects a business environment, where past success strategies are by no means a guarantee for future success.

The participants assigned a specific high-learning goal were told to identify and implement six or more strategies to increase market share. The results of using this CIBG simulation revealed that:[18]

1. Performance was highest for individuals with a specific high learning goal. The market share achieved by those with a learning goal was almost twice as high as those with a performance outcome goal. There was no significant difference in performance between individuals with a performance goal, set in terms of total market share (21 percent) to be attained, or those who were simply urged to do their best.
2. Individuals who had a learning goal took the time necessary to acquire the knowledge to perform the task effectively. They took the time to analyze the task-relevant information that was available to them.
3. Those with a learning goal were convinced that they were capable of mastering the task. This suggests that the increase in self-efficacy resulting from a learning goal occurs as a result of the discovery of appropriate strategies for task mastery, whereas a performance goal, as noted previously, can lead to a "mad scramble" for solutions.[19]
4. Hence, not surprisingly, those with a learning goal had higher commitment to their goal than did those with a performance goal. The correlation between goal commitment and performance was also significant.

These research findings are consistent with the observations of Arthur Martinez, Wagner Dodge, Michael Dell, Michael Eisner, and Howard Schultz cited throughout the paper.

Why Learning Goals?

How does a learning goal differ from a performance-outcome goal? What explains the superiority of a learning goal over a performance goal on a task that is complex for an individual? How can specific challenging learning goals be applied in business settings?

The primary distinction between a performance and a learning goal is the framing of the instructions given to employees. Hence, the difference between these two types of goals is first and foremost a "mindset." The respective instructions focus attention on two different domains—motivation versus ability. A performance goal, as the name implies, frames the instructions so that an employee's focus is on task performance (e.g., attain 20 percent market share by the end of the next fiscal year). The search for information to attain the goal is neither mentioned nor implied because knowledge and skills are considered a given on tasks that require primarily choice, effort, or persistence on the part of the people who have been assigned the goal. Similarly, a learning goal, as the name implies, frames the instructions in terms of knowledge or skill acquisition (e.g., discover three effective strategies to increase market share). A learning goal draws attention away from the end result. The focus is on the discovery of effective task processes. Once an employee has the knowledge and skills necessary to effectively perform the task, a specific challenging performance goal should be set to direct attention to the exertion of effort and persistence required to achieve it. The performance goal cues individuals to use strategies or performance routines that the person has learned previously are effective. Setting a learning goal on a task that is relatively straightforward for an individual wastes time, and is ineffective in that the person has already mastered the requisite performance routines and is aware of the requisite job behaviors.[20] In short, learning goals help people progress to the point where performance outcome goals become beneficial for increasing one's effectiveness. The focus of a learning goal is to increase one's knowledge (ability); the focus of a performance goal is to increase one's motivation to implement that knowledge. Therefore, both learning and performance goals are needed to be successful. But, as noted earlier, our research shows that a performance goal should not be set until an employee has the knowledge to attain it.

Practical Applications

Based on our findings, as well as the experiences of the CEOs whom we have cited, there are at least three interrelated areas where the application of learning goals should prove particularly helpful in improving performance.

Leadership

Jack Welch stated that, "An organization's ability to learn and translate that learning into action is the ultimate competitive advantage ... I wish we'd understood all along how much leverage you can get from the flow of ideas among all business units ... the enormous advantage we have today is that we can run GE as a laboratory for ideas."[21]

Three examples suggest the benefits of a leader focusing employee attention on the attainment of learning goals. First, when Andy Grove was CEO at Intel Corporation, he was obsessed with learning as much as possible about the changing environment. In Grove's own words, "I attribute Intel's ability to sustain success to being constantly on the alert for threats, either technological or competitive in nature."[22] Second, Sam Walton continued to refine his business strategies and discover ways that he could improve his stores. He never stopped learning from competitors, customers, and his own employees. He believed that there was at least one good idea he could learn, even from his worst competitor. Walton passed on this philosophy to his employees. As Kurt Bernard, a retailing consultant, noted:[23]

> *When he meets you ... he proceeds to extract every piece of information in your possession. He always makes little notes. And he pushes on and on. After two and a half hours, he left, and I was totally drained. I wasn't sure what I had just met, but I was sure we would hear more from him.*

Leaders such as Welch, Grove, and Walton would increase the effectiveness of their workforce if they systematically set specific high learning goals to be attained regarding the sharing of ideas among divisions, identifying potential threats in the environment, or extracting ideas from competitors, customers and employees.

Third, the primary use of learning goals at Goldman Sachs, as described by Steve Kerr, is to develop present and future leaders.[24] For example, a sales manager might be asked to join or even lead a taskforce whose goal is to discover a new process for product development. People are developed through the use of assigned specific learning goals that require them to go outside their comfort zone.

Performance Management

Coca Cola Foods and PricewaterhouseCoopers (PWC) are among the many companies that have incorporated goal setting into their coaching and mentoring practices. The goals are typically performance outcomes to be attained (e.g., increase client revenue by 18 percent) or they are behavioral goals that are within the employees' repertory of knowledge and abilities to increase in frequency (e.g., communicate the objectives of the program to the people with whom you work, or hold people accountable for their technical levels of performance). Recognizing that this approach is not effective for every employee, learning goals are also set at PWC. For example, many organizations, including PWC, hire job applicants for their aptitude rather than their existing skills. New employees, therefore, benefit from mentors who actively help them discover ways to develop their competencies within the firm, and who assign them specific high learning rather than performance goals. Employees who are assigned specific challenging learning goals in the early stages of discovering how to execute the various aspects of their job, typically outperform those who are immediately given specific high-performance targets to attain.

Learning goals are also appropriate for seasoned managers. For example, those who operate in globally diverse organizations find it fruitful to focus on ways to effectively manage myriad social identity groups so as to minimize rigidity, insensitivity, and intolerance within a multicultural workforce.[25] Newly formed work teams, especially culturally diverse teams, need time to gel. Ilya Adler observed that managers view, "the cultural issue as an additional burden to the already difficult task of making a team function effectively."[26] Focusing on the end result before difficulties in team dynamics have been ironed out can be detrimental to the team's performance. Thus, a team-leader may be well advised to focus on the discovery of 3–5 strategies, processes, or procedures for accelerating effective interaction and teamwork, particularly ways to foster understanding of local customs and values, develop mutual understanding and trust, and decide how team members are going to work together on sundry tasks.[27] In contrast, assigning a culturally diverse work team a specific challenging performance goal to attain before the team's rules of conduct have become accepted is likely to lead to prolonged "storming" and "norming." Indeed, it is not uncommon to see culturally diverse teams spend more time working out their differences than doing the actual work.

Professional Development

Jack Welch often moved his top executives from one functional business area to another.[28] Similar to the mentoring practice at PWC, he did this with the purpose of broadening their knowledge base. When this is done, employees should be asked to discover a specific number of ideas that would help them improve the performance of their respective businesses. Jack Welch also introduced Work-Out, a forum that was intended to share knowledge between management and employees. Facilitators of these types of sessions should be asked to set a goal of discovering a specific number of ideas or strategies that will improve organizational effectiveness. Other executives also ensure the on-going professional development of their senior executives through job rotation. The purpose of the rotation is to "shake the executives up," provide them with opportunities to learn new perspectives, get them out of their comfort zones, and develop greater creativity. To ensure that this occurs, specific learning goals should be set to ensure that the broad perspective to which the executives are exposed actually helps the company to make decisions in a coherent fashion.[29]

Taking the Time to Learn

Today's workforce continues to be under intense pressure to produce tangible results. They are in a "performance mode."[30] This is a plus when known performance routines continue to be effective, and when the issue is fostering the conditions for a highly motivated workforce. In such instances, countless studies in the behavioral sciences support the significant motivational benefits of setting specific challenging performance goals. However, a high performing workforce is a function of both high ability and high motivation. This is particularly true in today's business environment in which organizations face rapidly changing technologies, information overload, escalating competitive pressures, and a host of other challenges. Hence the importance of knowing that learning and performance goals differ in their purposes. They differ in the resulting behavior/actions required to attain them. They differ in their appropriateness for increasing an organization's effectiveness. The purpose of a learning goal is to stimulate one's imagination, to engage in discovery, and to "think outside the box," whereas the purpose of a performance goal is to choose to exert effort, and to persist in the attainment of a desired objective or outcome using the knowledge one already possesses. Thus the behavior of a person with a learning goal is to systematically search for new ideas, actively seek feedback, be reflective, and execute a specific number of ideas in order to test newly formed hypotheses. The resulting behavior of a person with a performance goal is to focus on known ways to quickly implement knowledge and skills that have already been mastered. When the strategy for an organization is already known, and the ways to attain it have been deciphered, setting performance goals for an individual or team is appropriate. When an effective strategy requires innovation that has yet to emerge, specific high learning goals should be set.

Acknowledgement

The authors acknowledge the suggestions of Paul Beamish and Ed Locke in preparing this paper.

Source: Academy of Management Executive, 19, (1), 124–131 (2005). Reprinted by permission of the CCC.

ENDNOTES

1. Sherman, S. Stretch goals: The dark side of asking for miracles. *Fortune*, 13 November, 1995, 231–232; Kerr, S., & Landauer, S. 2004. Using stretch goals to promote organizational effectiveness and personal growth. *Academy of management Executive*, 18(4). 134–39. Steve Kerr is an organizational psychologist formerly at the General Electric Company (GE) and now Chief Learning Officer and a Managing Director at Goldman Sachs.
2. Loomis, C. The whistleblower and the CEO. *Fortune*, 7 July, 2003, 88–96.
3. Research reported in the Academy of Management Journal supports Loomis' interpretation of the culture in Lucent. Schweitzer, M.E., Ordonez, L., & Douma, B. 2004. Goal setting as a motivator of unethical behavior. *Academy of Management Journal*, 47: 422–432.
4. Martinez, A.C., & Madigan, C. 2001. *The hard road to the softer side. Lessons from the transformation of Sears.* New York, NY: Crown Business.
5. Latham, G.P., & Kinne, S.B. 1974. Improving job performance through training in goal setting. *Journal of Applied Psychology*, 59: 187–191. For reviews of goal setting theory, see Locke, E.A., & Latham, G.P. 1990. *A theory of goal setting and task performance.* Englewood Cliffs, NJ: Prentice-Hall: Locke, E.A., & Latham, G.P. 2002. Building a practically useful theory of goal setting and task motivation: A 35-year odyssey. *American Psychologist*, 57: 705–717; Mitchell, T.R., & Daniels, D. 2003. Motivation. In W.C. Borman, D.R. Ilgen, and R.J. Klimoski (Eds.), *Handbook of psychology, 12: Industrial organizational psychology.* New York: Wiley & Sons, Inc. Goal setting theory is derived from more than 500 laboratory and field experiments. In short, the theory states that (a) people with specific challenging goals have higher performance than those who do not set goals, as well as those who embrace abstract goals such as "to do my best." (b) In addition, given goal commitment, there is a positive, linear relationship between goal difficulty and the level of performance. This linear relationship levels off only when people reach the limits of their cognitive and motor abilities. (c) Praise, feedback, and participation in decision making only increase a person's effectiveness to the extent that they lead to the setting of and commitment to a specific high goal. But, the theory yields no clues as to when to set performance versus learning goals.
6. Latham, G.P., Mitchell, T.R., & Dossett, D.L. 1978. Importance of participative goal setting and anticipated rewards on goal difficulty and job performance. *Journal of Applied Psychology*, 63: 163–171.
7. Bandura, A., & Simon, K.M. 1977. The role of proximal intentions in self-regulation of refractory behavior. *Cognitive Therapy and Research*, 1: 177–193; Strecher, V.J., Seijts, G.H., Kok, G., Latham, G.P., Glasgow, R., DeVellis, B., Meertens, R.M., & Bulger, D.W. 1995. Goal setting as a strategy for health behavior change. *Health Education Quarterly*, 22: 190–200.
8. Locke & Latham, 1990, op. cit.
9. Latham, G.P., & Saari, L. 1982. The importance of union acceptance for productivity improvement through goal setting. *Personnel Psychology, 35*: 781–787.
10. Useem, M. 1998. *The leadership moment. Nine true stories of triumph and disaster and their lessons for us all.* New York, NY: Three Rivers Press. Also consult the following sources: Weick, K. 1996. Prepare your organization to fight fires. *Harvard Business Review*, 74(3): 143–148; Maclean, N. 1992. *Young men and fire.* Chicago, IL: The University of Chicago Press.
11. Dell, M., & Fredman, K. 1999. *Direct from Dell. Strategies that revolutionized an industry.* New York, NY: Harper Business.
12. Kanfer, R., & Ackerman, P.L. 1989. Motivation and cognitive abilities: An integrative/aptitude-treatment interaction approach to skill acquisition. *Journal of Applied Psychology*, 74: 657–690. Kanfer and Ackerman examined the performance of US Air Force enlisted personnel who were undergoing basic training on an Air Traffic Control (ATC) task. The ATC task is a rule-based, real-time, computer-driven task that simulates activities performed by air traffic controllers. Trainees have to attend to numerous information cues (e.g., airport weather conditions; and hold pattern from the cue), and learn various rules (e.g., planes with less than three minutes fuel left must be landed immediately; and ground conditions and wind speed determine the runway length required by different plane types) to land planes in a safe and efficient manner. Giving the Air Force enlisted personnel a specific challenging performance goal with regard to the number of planes to be landed decreased rather than increased their effectiveness.
13. Kanfer & Ackerman, op. cit.
14. Locke & Latham, 1990, op. cit.
15. Locke & Latham, 2002, op. cit.
16. The task was developed by Pino Audia. See, for example, Audia, P.G., Locke, E.A., & Smith, K.G. 2000. The paradox of success: An archival and a laboratory study of strategic persistence following radical environmental change. *Academy of Management Journal*, 43: 837–853. This simulation was chosen as a result of Lucent's failed attempt, described earlier, to increase market share, as well as comments by Michael Eisner, CEO of the Walt Disney Company, who once observed that, "Today's hottest company is tomorrow's struggling, helpless giant." Likewise, Howard Schultz, the man who built Starbucks, and now the chair and chief strategist, argued that, "We are in the second inning of a nine inning game ... We are just beginning to tap into all sorts of new markets, new customers, and new products." Similar to Martinez's comments cited earlier, he argued further that there is a strong likelihood that strategies that have worked in the past may not work in the future as a result of on-going changes in the market-place. The CIBG provides an ideal way to test the validity of these assertions.

17. After each round of decision making, participants obtained feedback regarding market share, number of cell phone subscribers, and operating profit. An optional screen provided longitudinal results on 12 other business-related indicators (e.g., advertising expenses and total debt). Performance was the direct result of the strategic decisions that each individual made. Participants were given extensive feedback because feedback is often present in the business environment; individuals either search for information on the outcomes of their decisions or feedback is provided in real-time (e.g., units sold, the stock price, or dollar amount of tips received). The set-up of the simulation allowed the participants to request industry-specific information (e.g., new technologies developed) as well as information on customers (e.g., hours spent on using particular services) to help them make informed decisions. Each of these information sources could be obtained at a cost of $25,000 per decision period. The information available in the simulation was the same for each participant and, over time, reflected the different stages of the telecommunications industry. Seeking task-specific information helped participants to make strategic decisions that would enable them to improve their performance. In business settings, too, those executives with an active mind ask questions and question assumptions in order to achieve high levels of performance. In contrast, those that are reluctant to dig beneath appearances and uncover the true state of their business often fail to run a successful business.
18. Seijts, G.H., Latham, G.P., Tasa, K., & Latham, B.W. 2004. Goal setting and goal orientation: An integration of two different yet related literatures. *Academy of Management Journal*, 47: 227–239.
19. See also, Seijts, G.H., & Latham, G.P. 2001. The effect of distal learning, outcome, and proximal goals on a moderately complex task. *Journal of Organizational Behavior*, 22: 291–302.
20. Brown, T.C., & Latham, G.P. 2002. The effects of behavioral outcome goals, learning goals, and urging people to do their best on an individual's teamwork behavior in a group problem-solving task. *Canadian Journal of Behavioral Science, 34*: 276–285; Winters, D., & Latham, G.P. 1996. The effect of learning versus outcome goals on a simple versus a complex task. *Group and Organization Management*, 21: 235–250.
21. Tichy, N., & Sherman, S. 1993. *Control your own destiny or someone else will. Lessons in mastering change—from the principles Jack Welch is using to revolutionalize GE.* New York, NY: HarperCollins Publishers.
22. Krames, J.A. 2003. *What the best CEOs know. Seven exceptional leaders and their lessons for transforming any business.* New York, NY: McGraw-Hill.
23. Walton, S., & Huey, J. 1992. *Made in America.* New York, NY: Doubleday.
24. Kerr & Landauer, op. cit. Kerr referred to learning goals as horizontal stretch goals. Challenging performance outcome goals he referred to as vertical stretch goals.
25. Latham, G.P., & McCauley, C.D. forthcoming. Leadership in the private sector: Yesterday versus tomorrow. In C. Cooper (Ed.), *The twenty-first century manager.* Oxford, England: Oxford University Press.
26. Adler, I. 2001. Culture shock. *Business Mexico*, 11(5): 21.
27. Steers, R.M., & Sanchez-Runde, C.J. 2002. Culture, motivation, and work behavior. In M.J. Gannon, and K.L. Newman (Eds.), *The Blackwell handbook of principles of cross-cultural management.* Bodmin, Cornwall: MPG Books.
28. Locke, E.A. 2004. The leader as integrator: The case of Jack Welch at General Electric. In L. Neider, and C. Schriesheim (Eds.), *Research in Management for Information Age Publishing*, 2.
29. Pringle, D. Nokia CEO: Long tenure, big challenge. *Wall Street Journal*, 23 January, 2002, B7E.
30. Katz, N. 2001. Sports teams as a model for workplace teams: Lessons and liabilities. *Academy of Management Executive*, 15(3): 56–69.

READING 9.2

The Imperative of Developing Global Leaders

Dana Brower, Terry Newell, and Peter Ronayne

Introduction

Throughout U.S. history, the domestic and foreign policy arenas have been viewed as mostly separate and distinct spheres of action. Government executives who worked in domestic agencies felt they needed to know little about other countries and seldom interacted with them, if at all. In recent years, this view has begun to change. The combined and accelerating forces of globalization and technology have forged an interconnected world in which change—and the need to anticipate and respond to it—is both faster and more complex and where the international and the domestic are inextricably linked. The United States' economic, military, and cultural power and influence make it a global actor by default, and therefore federal organizations and the people who lead them find themselves increasingly thrust into the global context.

As countless observers have noted and as individual experience tells us, with each passing day the public policy agenda is increasingly both international and domestic, or "intermestic." Indeed, "global" is the word of the new century, filling newspapers, journals, and books on current events. The new century brings with it accelerated globalization, complete with a proliferation of international agreements, institutions, and mechanisms for consultation and partnership. The events of September 11th, 2001, further these developments and remind us of the United States' role in and connection to the world.

With these thoughts in mind, the U.S. Office of Personnel Management (OPM) Federal Executive Institute (FEI), a residential executive education center for senior career government leaders, hosted a colloquium in November 2001. The colloquium, attended by over 40 leaders from the United States and other nations' governments, the private sector, academe, and the nonprofit sector, focused on the evolving global leadership role of government executives and the competencies needed to succeed in international work. This article reports on the colloquium and the implications of its findings for developing global leaders.

Whether due to the importance of building bilateral relationships or international coalitions, the heightened priority of improving homeland defense, or the simple realization that the domestic and international arenas are intricately connected, colloquium participants concluded that it is imperative that government executives lead in a global context. "So many of the issues that we deal with now, such as organized crime, are transnational in nature. We need to continually build coalitions and dialogue with leaders of all countries to address these matters in a global manner," said Jean M. Christensen, district director for the Immigration and Naturalization Service's Asia District, a colloquium participant. "We must develop leaders to work globally who fully understand the issues, possess diplomatic skills and cultural sensitivity, and can speak on behalf of the U.S. government in a multinational environment."

Like their private-sector counterparts, a considerable and growing number of federal agencies are involved in international work in this networked world. The Social Security Administration, for example, has bilateral agreements with 18 nations. The Environmental Protection Agency works with foreign counterparts to implement the Montreal Protocol, designed to protect the ozone layer from chlorofluorocarbons. The promise of agricultural biotechnology depends in large part on the U.S. Department of Agriculture and its work to ensure that biotech products can access markets abroad. The U.S. Customs Service works to combat money laundering, a transnational threat estimated at a minimum of $600 million annually. The U.S. Geological Survey faces international challenges ranging from protecting diverse biological resources to identifying the world's remaining energy resources.

The imperative of global leadership is felt particularly at the National Aeronautics and Space Administration (NASA), which has more than 3,000 international agreements with over 130 countries. NASA's approach to leadership development includes emphasis on several international competencies (Figure 1). "Global competencies are critical in today's ever changing world, from an understanding of the political, social, and economic environment to cross-cultural relationships and international partnerships and alliances," explains Jan Moore, program manager for NASA's Leadership and Management Development. "At NASA," explains Moore, "international cooperation and an understanding of working in a global environment are critical to organizational success. Understanding and cooperation create access to unique capabilities and expertise, provide access to locations outside the United States, and open new avenues for discovery."

FIGURE 1 NASA Leadership Model

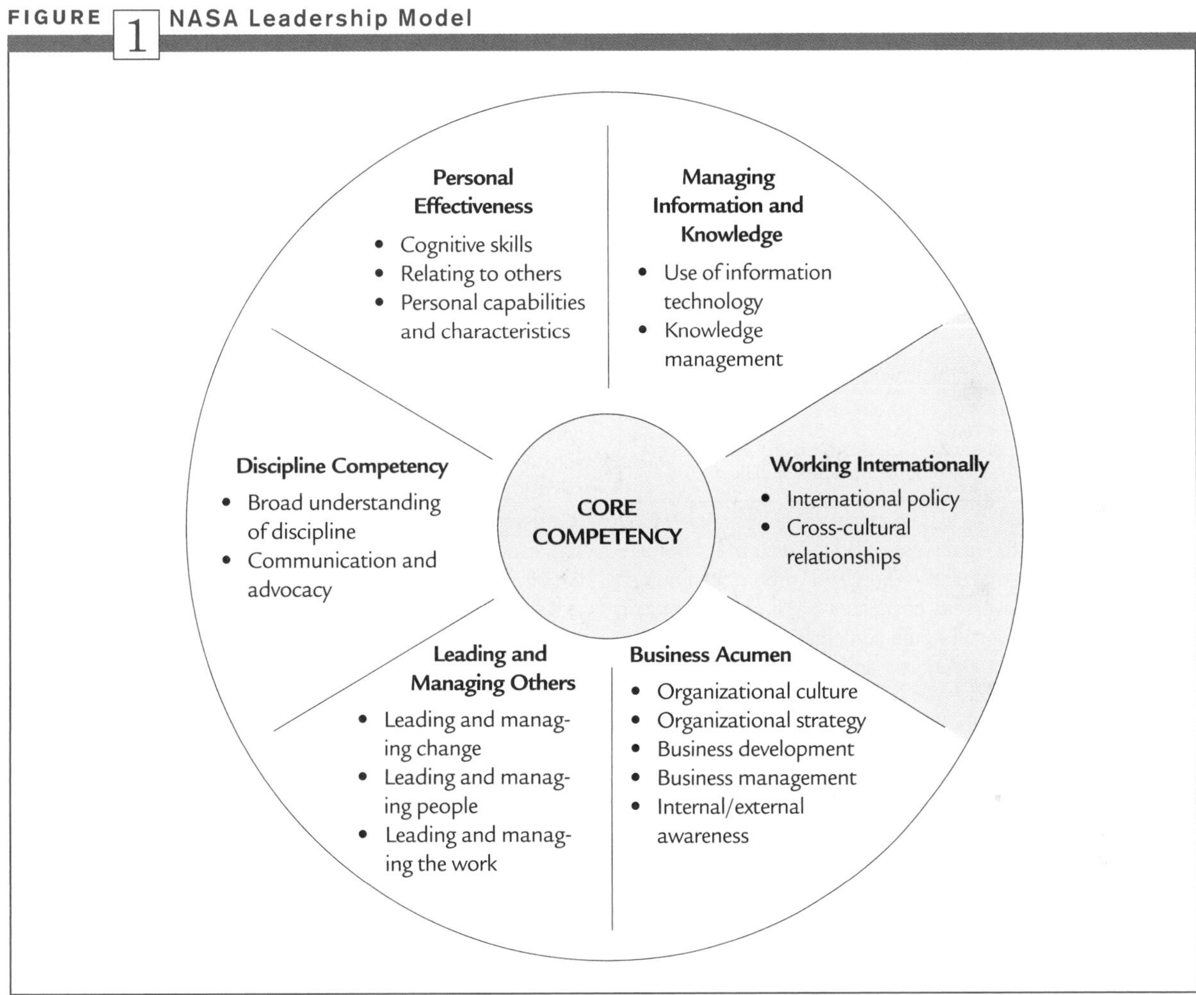

A 2001 State Department working paper observed, "Currently, there are approximately 42 different U.S. federal agencies in more than 160 countries performing a variety of functions that serve the national interest and help assure national security. These functions have significant impact on our domestic economy as well as on U.S. world relations. U.S. government personnel, regardless of agency, performing these core functions at home and abroad face significant challenges as they struggle to keep pace with world events and represent the U.S. from an informed position." Similarly, in a report on the future of human capital in the federal workforce, the General Accounting Office emphasized that "government organizations must undergo a cultural transformation allowing them to work better with other governmental organizations, non-governmental organizations, and the private sector, *both domestically and internationally* [emphasis added], to achieve results."

Mirroring federal agency trends, a significant number of federal executives are involved in international work. Overall, the federal government has more than 50,000 employees stationed overseas. It is important to keep in mind, however, that global leadership does not require travel abroad. Many federal executives act and lead in a global context from the confines of their offices in the United States.

Recent surveys by the FEI help illustrate the extensive international roles filled by today's executives. Although only about 3 percent of the career federal executives (GS-15s and Senior Executive Service) who attend FEI are actually stationed abroad, a much higher percentage is involved in international work. For example, 37 percent report collaborating with other agencies or organizations on international projects, 37 percent report traveling abroad for work, and 20 percent report managing programs that provide goods or services to other nations. (See Table 1.)

"Going Global" Requires Globally Competent Leaders

Although executives' roles overseas are expanding, their preparation for success in international work may not be keeping pace. The State Department's Overseas Presence Advisory Panel (OPAP), established in the wake of the 1998 terrorist bombings of U.S. embassies in Nairobi and Dar es

Table 1 Types of International Work Reported by Federal Executives

- Collaborating with other agencies/organizations on international projects (37%)
- Travel abroad (37%)
- Managing programs that provide goods/services to other nations (20%)
- International negotiations (16%)
- International policy development (14%)
- Managing programs that receive/inspect people, goods, and services from other nations (10%)
- Supervising government workers/contractors abroad (8%)
- Living abroad (3%)

Source: 2001–2002 Survey by Federal Executive Institute

Salaam, looked at the readiness of State Department personnel to succeed internationally. The OPAP report cited human resource issues in overseas posts as a major concern, stating that "there was universal agreement that more training was needed in languages, leadership and management, and new issues." The report also estimated that "up to one-half of Department personnel who took assignments abroad last year did so without appropriate training. In addition, the training available was truncated or ignored." Finally, the OPAP report recommended "that the Department and other agencies mandate that all employees undergo security training and area studies before going overseas."

If the State Department recognizes a need to augment its training programs for employees assigned overseas, it seems logical that other domestic agencies might also have work to do in training their employees for international work. A series of leadership development surveys conducted by FEI in 2001–2002 bear this out. The surveys found that 57 percent of executives reported that their responsibilities included some type of international work. Yet among those executives involved in international work, almost 60 percent received no formal preparation for their assignments. Over two-thirds (68 percent) of federal executives surveyed reported that they spoke no language other than English, and executives rated their own proficiency for international work below the midpoint of a five-point scale on six of eight key topics. (See Figure 2.)

The President's Management Agenda (PMA) calls for establishing a "right-sized" U.S. overseas presence, which

FIGURE 2 Executives Perceived Proficiency in Working Internationally where 1 = Poor and 5 = Excellent

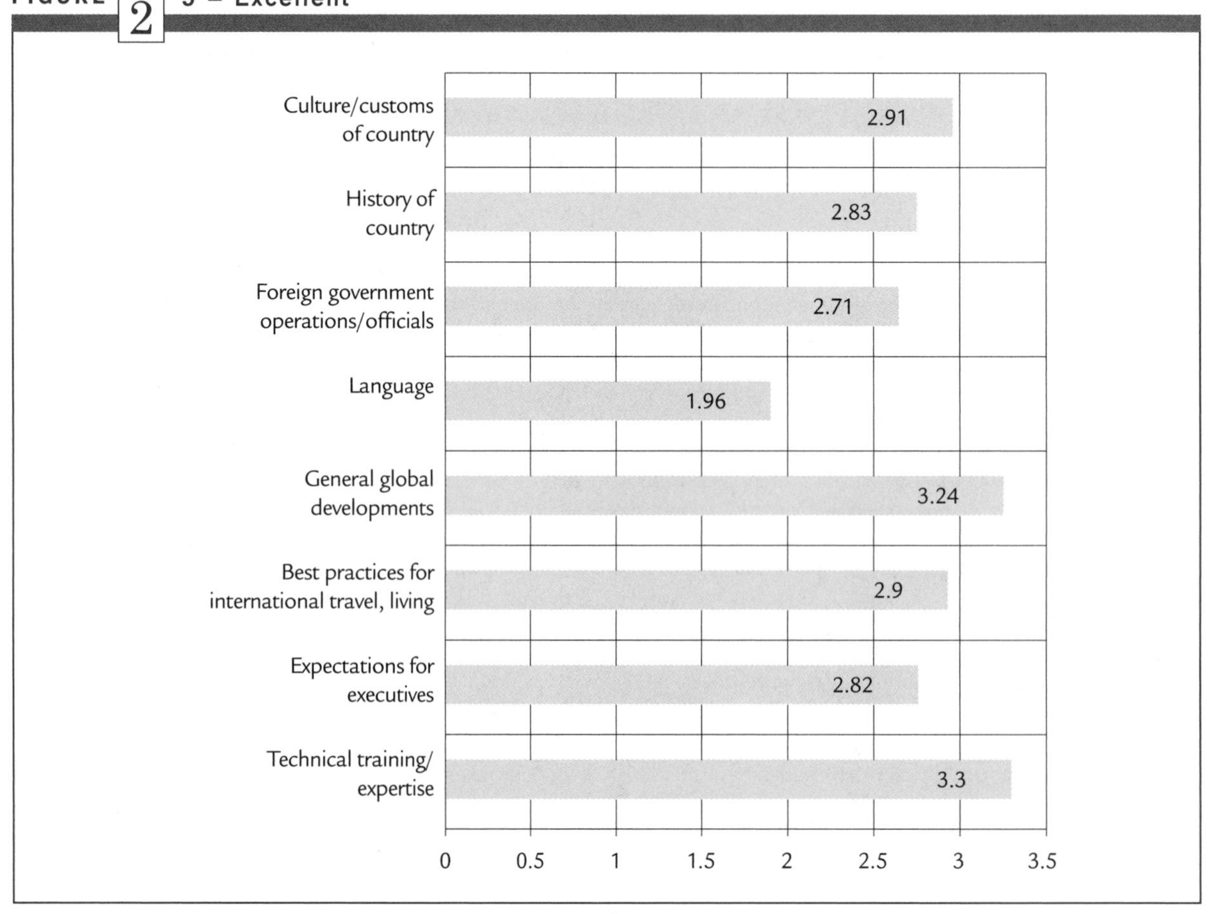

includes better coordination among federal agencies to ensure that the right number of people with the right talents are deployed internationally. President Bush's call for better strategic management of human capital also supports the notion that all personnel involved in international work should be recruited, selected, trained, and managed effectively. Without sufficient attention to developing the global leadership competence of U.S. government executives, it will be difficult to achieve these PMA goals and effectively serve the interests of the United States in an age of globalization. Patricia McGinnis, president and CEO of the Council for Excellence in Government, underscores this point: "The Council believes that career federal executives must be able to lead for results in all aspects of their work. Today, an increasing number of career public servants outside the federal government's traditional foreign affairs community have responsibilities with an international dimension. Improving their ability as leaders in a global context has therefore become a very important goal."

The World of Global Competencies

Although no concrete consensus or definitive work exists on exactly what skills and attitudes federal executives need to succeed as global leaders, experts echo common themes and elements. Lists of critical global competencies invariably include emphasis on the need for effective intercultural communication skills and broader knowledge of world affairs and trends, combined with the ability to represent U.S. interests effectively.

The Centre for Intercultural Learning of the Canadian Foreign Service Institute recently conducted a major research project on intercultural effectiveness. Their Year 2000 report identified nine critical competencies, including understanding the concept of culture, intercultural communication, and an attitude of modesty and respect. All nine competencies are outlined in Table 2.

In his research on global leadership effectiveness in the private sector, Dr. Robert Rosen of Healthy Companies International found four broad areas of competence critical to global leadership success. In his book *Global Literacies*, he labels these as personal literacy (understanding and valuing yourself), social literacy (engaging and challenging others), business literacy (focusing and mobilizing your organization), and cultural literacy (valuing and leveraging cultural differences).

Explains Rosen: "To thrive, all companies must adopt a global-centric approach to business. They must develop a multi-cultural perspective, an international knowledge base, and a global imagination—in other words, a cultural literacy." While Rosen's work focused on the private sector, he finds the lessons equally applicable, indeed perhaps even more essential, for the public sector. "The public sector faces the same trends—namely the new context of interconnectedness and globalization—that are influencing the private sector. These trends are likewise transforming the roles of federal, state, and local government in a global society." And, adds Rosen, "America's role as the sole superpower requires that government executives be prepared for global responsibility."

The frameworks offered by Rosen and the Canadian Foreign Service Institute have much in common, including the strong emphasis on learning other languages—not only to be able to communicate but also to appreciate another's culture. Those gathered at FEI's global leadership colloquium validated and stressed these frameworks. Given the unique role of U.S. government executives in representing not only their agencies and their missions but also the United States

Table 2 The Interculturally Effective Person

In 1995, the Centre for Intercultural Learning at the Canadian Foreign Service Institute began a project to more fully understand executive effectiveness in a global context. According to the Centre's findings, globally effective executives possess the following nine competencies:

1. Adaptation skills—the ability to cope personally, professionally, and in one's family context with the conditions and challenges of living and working in another culture.
2. An Attitude of Modesty and Respect—demonstrating modesty about one's own culture's answers to problems, a respect for the ways of the local culture, a willingness to learn from and consult with locals before coming to conclusions.
3. An Understanding of the Concept of Culture—and the pervasive influence it will have on life and work abroad.
4. Knowledge of the Host Country and Culture—and trying constantly to expand that knowledge.
5. Relationship-Building Skills—both social/personal and professional.
6. Self-Knowledge—one's own background, motivations, strengths, and weaknesses.
7. Intercultural Communication—the ability to convey thoughts and expectations in ways that are understandable and culturally sensitive, without fear of participating in the local culture and language, and that empathize with how locals see the world.
8. Organizational Skills—improving organizational structures, processes, and morale in ways that balance one's own and the host culture's values.
9. Personal and Professional Commitment—to the intercultural assignment and the life experience in another culture.

and its Constitution, additional global leadership competencies were identified:

- Understanding the history of U.S. foreign relations, its constitutional history, and how both are understood and examined by the rest of the world.
- Understanding U.S. business, global economics, and key U.S. government domestic and international goals and policies and how they interact with each other—sometimes in consistent and reinforcing ways and sometimes in ways that make the nation's international agenda more challenging to implement.
- Understanding the evolving structure of international relationships, including regional and international organizations and alliances and how these influence U.S. policies and agencies.
- Strong negotiation skills.
- Security consciousness.

These competencies are critical for government executive leadership in international work *whether or not* an executive actually travels or works overseas. It is a potentially costly myth that a government executive sitting in an office in the United States can succeed internationally by relying solely on technical competence.

A Food and Drug Administration Experience

Of course, models and lists of competencies only go so far in communicating what executives must know and be able to do in their international work. The presentation by one of the colloquium participants, Naomi Kawin, put the competencies in context. As the associate director for International Agreements of the Office of International Programs of the Food and Drug Administration (FDA), Kawin's job involves no less than helping ensure the safety of foods and medical products coming to the United States from abroad. Although she travels overseas only occasionally in her work, she interacts extensively with other nations. To succeed, she and her FDA colleagues must wear at least three hats: regulator, diplomat, and leader. Reflecting on her work, Kawin offered a set of competencies for federal executives drawn from her experience.

Kawin's comments and suggestions bear a striking resemblance to the global literacies identified by Rosen and the critical skills identified by the Canadian government. The benefit and importance of global leadership competencies have strong domestic connections as well. Many of the skills essential for leadership in a global context, especially those related to understanding and working with people from other cultures, are increasingly important to government executive effectiveness *within* U.S. society. U.S. Census Bureau data and projections demonstrate that our society is already very culturally diverse and will become more so. California, for example, no longer has an ethnic group that constitutes more than half of the population. Successful domestic programs thus demand leadership from executives knowledgeable about and comfortable working across the cultures that define not only the world but also U.S. society in the 21st century.

Lessons from the Food and Drug Administration

International work takes several forms in the FDA. Inspectors travel to other countries to examine industry and government practices, Scientists work on international issues, including the development of international standards. And FDA staff work on negotiating international agreements and other collaborative international ventures.

Whether or not they travel overseas, all these staff need an awareness of cultural differences including how another's culture can affect regulation and product safety. In light of the September 11th attacks, personal security awareness is critical. Another set of skills—"International Survival 101"—includes protocol, diplomatic sensibilities, how to work with American embassies and interpreters, and being cognizant of ethical issues. In terms of effective leadership in a global context, federal executives across government need to possess a fuller understanding of international organizations, trade agreements and regional blocs, prominent global trends, and the influence of all of these on the United States. Also needed is openness both to collaboration and to new ways of doing business, supported in turn by knowledge of negotiation skills—even for seemingly non-negotiating contexts.

Developing Global Leaders

Although we may know what competencies government leaders need for effective global leadership, we do not excel at providing them. A few agencies, including the State Department and OPM, have programs to address some of the essential skills and attitudes.

Agencies are clearly at various stages in implementing development programs focused on global leadership. At OPM's FEI, the four-week long *Leadership for a Democratic Society* experience includes a central "global perspectives" theme as part of FEI's ongoing work to prepare senior civil servants for leadership in a global context. The sessions and courses on this curriculum theme provide an opportunity for executives to examine critical global developments and their implications for U.S. society and government. In addition, FEI works to foster global perspectives by periodically hosting international executives as participants in the program.

The State Department has long stood at the forefront of international and multi-cultural development in the federal sector. The Foreign Service Institute (FSI) is the U.S. government's primary training institution for officers and support personnel of the U.S. foreign affairs community, preparing U.S. diplomats and other professionals to advance U.S. foreign affairs interests overseas and in Washington, D.C. At the National Foreign Affairs Training Center, the FSI provides more than 400 courses, including some 60 foreign languages, to more than 30,000 enrollees a year from the State Department and to more than 40 other government agencies and the military service branches.

More recently, the State Department has placed renewed focus on leadership issues and competency development with the establishment of FSI's School of Leadership and Management. Inaugurated in June 2000, the School of Leadership and Management offers a competency-based curriculum with classes that emphasize valuing diversity, creativity, flexibility, ethical behavior, strategic thinking, transparency, and effective communication. The School's first dean, Ambassador Aurelia E. Brazeal, stressed the importance of its mission: "Clearly, the challenges to American global leadership are unprecedented. FSI's School of Leadership and Management is committed to bringing innovative, world-class leadership development programs to professionals in our foreign affairs community. Our curriculum is designed to foster leadership qualities that are, in my view, essential to effectiveness in our rapidly changing world." These and similar programs play an important role in fostering global leadership competencies in the federal executive corps. However, the U.S. government has no comprehensive approach or system in place to deliberately and carefully develop public-sector leaders for success in their critical "intermestic" work. An unwavering federal commitment to *this type* of global leadership training needed by government executives will be a requisite first step in developing such a system of executive development.

Participants in the November colloquium called for just this type of comprehensive, systemic approach in which training would play a key role but by no means the only role in developing government leaders to succeed in their international assignments.

The colloquium identified seven specific recommendations aimed toward building this comprehensive development system for our nation's global leaders.

Recommendation 1: Build the business case for global leadership competence. Without a shared understanding of how and where effective global leadership matters to government agencies, it will be hard to enlist support for developing global leaders. The consensus at the colloquium was that there is a need but that need has not been well documented in business terms.

Recommendation 2: Build support for developing global leaders in government among government agencies and in the broader society. Although a documented business case may serve the needs of policy makers, more broad-based support is needed within agencies and from the public. Public events, speeches, and other means are needed to demonstrate that effective global leadership is as important in building a healthy food supply as it is in building foreign policy.

Recommendation 3: Develop a model of global leadership competence. The colloquium participants urged that specific competencies be identified and communicated to illustrate what effective global leaders do. What skills, knowledge, and attitudes do they need to be competent internationally? The colloquium concluded that the competencies government executives need, for example, can be thought of as falling into three broad groups:

- **Broad-based leadership knowledge**—for example, U.S. and foreign government operations, U.S. foreign and domestic policies, and global economics.
- **Generic leadership skills**—for example, self-knowledge, communication, cultural sensitivity, security consciousness, and negotiation skills.
- **Agency-, sector-, or country-specific knowledge and skills**—for example, international trading blocs, intellectual property protection, international labor agreements, global environmental issues, and Chinese history and politics.

The third group is important for executives working in specific areas or countries. The first and second skill areas can reasonably be delivered to a more diverse government audience.

Recommendation 4: Integrate global competencies into leadership selection and development programs. Identifying needed competencies is necessary but not sufficient for leadership development. The colloquium urged that these competencies be integrated into OPM's Executive Core Qualifications and that they be used to help select, develop, and appraise leaders with significant international responsibilities.

Recommendation 5: Strengthen interagency and public/private partnerships to provide for global leadership development. Global leadership in government depends on a collaborative partnership among the public, private, and non-profit sectors. So too should the *development* of global leaders in government. There was consensus at the colloquium that the three sectors working collaboratively could produce more innovative and effective models of developing leaders for the "intermestic" world than just relying on government to do it alone.

Recommendation 6: Create certification programs for developing global leaders in government. Such programs would draw attention to this important area and ensure the sufficient depth and breadth of coverage needed to go beyond "awareness" to skill mastery.

Recommendation 7: Develop a center of excellence—a place or consortium that could gather, offer, and spread the best programs, tools, and resources for developing global leaders in government. The colloquium recognized that many innovative training and development resources already exist within and outside the United States, while others need to be created. But it is nearly impossible for a busy government worker to find and access what is available, much less what needs to be created. Until such resources become easy to access, global leadership development remains a promise, not a program.

The development of public-sector leaders prepared for success in a dynamic global context is a long-term journey that members of the federal community must travel together. U.S. leadership on the world stage requires individual leaders prepared for the international context in which they operate. Overall, a commitment to a globally savvy leadership corps represents a farsighted vision of leadership development: one that provides government executives with a greater perspective with which to lead organizations and design public policy in the global context of the 21st century.

Source: In Lawrence, P. (ed.), The Business of Government, IBM Business Consulting Services, 18–24 (2002).

READING 9.3

How Groups Learn, Continuously

Manuel London and Valerie I. Sessa

This article examines how groups learn, conditions that affect learning, and interventions to improve the learning process. Adaptive group learning is reacting almost automatically to stimuli to make minor changes in process and outcome. Generative group learning is proactive learning for mastery. Transformative group learning is reconstructing meaning and fundamentally changing the way the group operates. Pressures and opportunities in the environment and group readiness stimulate and support these different types of learning. Group leaders, members, and human resource professionals who facilitate, coach, and provide resources for development can apply this knowledge to diagnose group conditions and encourage continuous learning.

Understanding group process is an important part of human resource management because so much of work in organizations gets done in groups. Groups bring together individuals with different knowledge, expertise, and functions to discuss issues, produce outcomes (e.g., new products), and make decisions. Human resource managers often have a role in advising or organizing these groups, possibly selecting members, setting agendas, coaching the group leader, facilitating group process, and designing learning interventions, when needed. Groups learn as they do their work (Jaques, 2002; Sessa & London, 2006). A group's ability to learn allows the group to (a) handle unpredictable work situations, (b) cope with emergencies or crises, (c) manage interactions across group boundaries, (d) reduce or avoid work stress, (e) solve problems creatively, and (f) perform new tasks, technologies, and procedures (Pulakos, Dorsey, & Mueller-Hanson, 2005). As they work, some groups learn high-performing strategies. Other groups learn structures of interaction patterns that lead to burnout. Still others learn how to perform the minimal amount of work necessary to avoid attracting attention from the larger organization.

This article considers how group leaders, facilitators, and group members can help groups learn in ways that are effective for the group itself, for the individual members within the group, and for the larger organization.

The article makes several contributions to the research literature. By extending existing learning theories, we distinguish between adaptive, generative, and transformative learning. This distinction provides a language for describing group learning and for comparing learning processes across different groups and between individual, group, and organizational levels of analysis. This article also provides a framework for understanding the evolution of group learning over time. Finally, we present diagnostic methods and interventions that human resource professionals, trainers, group facilitators, and group leaders can use to promote group learning in relation to pressures and opportunities in the environment and the group's readiness to learn.

The Group Learning Process

Group learning has been defined in several ways. For instance, it has been viewed as an *aggregate of individual learning* (Druskat & Kayes, 2000; Ellis et al., 2003). According to this view, group learning occurs when individual group members create, acquire, and share unique knowledge and information. Group learning has been viewed as a *process* for effecting change in interactions as members acquire, share, and combine knowledge; test assumptions; discuss differences openly; form new routines; and adjust strategies in response to errors (Edmondson, 1999; Edmondson, Bohmer, & Pisano, 2001). Another view uses the idea of the *group as a system* (Arrow, McGrath, & Berdahl, 2000; Sessa & London, 2006). This perspective portrays group learning as a dynamic system in which learning processes, the conditions that support them, the individuals in the group, and the group "behaviors" change as the group learns (Argote, Gruenfeld, & Naquin, 2001; Kasl, Marsick, & Dechant, 1997; Sessa & London, 2006). In this vein, Kasl and colleagues (1997) suggested that groups progress from fragmented, individualistic behaviors to synergistic, group-as-a-whole interactions that foster continuous learning. Similarly, group learning has been viewed as a cycle of activities, including reflective communication, experimentation, and knowledge codification (Gibson & Vermeulen, 2003). The consequence of group learning may be a change in group process and performance in response to salient stimuli (Burke, Stagl, Salas, Pierce, & Kendall, 2006). This change may be manifest in the innovation of new or modification of existing group interaction patterns, capabilities, and goal-directed activities (Burke et al., 2006).[1]

In line with a process and systems view, we define group continuous learning as a deepening and broadening of the group's capabilities in (a) (re)structuring to meet changing conditions; (b) adding and using new skills, knowledge, and behaviors; and (c) becoming an increasingly sophisticated system through reflection of its own actions and consequences. Continuous learning in groups and organizations is an ongoing cycle that includes recognition of the need to learn, motivation to learn, learning experiences, and applications (Tannenbaum, 1997).

Figure 1 and Table 1 describe the elements of group learning and their relationships. Antecedents are learning stimuli (pressures, challenges, and opportunities) and readiness to learn. Readiness to learn determines what stimuli are noticed and what responses to stimuli occur. In this table, we describe three interaction patterns or "forms of learning": adaptive, generative, and transformative. In adaptive learning, the group automatically reacts to changes in the environment so that the group is able to adapt. Generative group learning refers to situations where the group purposefully is proactive and generates and uses new knowledge, skills, and behaviors. However, the purpose and form of the group remains the same. Transformative group learning refers to the transformation of the group into a new entity. In the process, the group learns adaptive, generative, and/or transformative patterns of interaction. If the group is successful, it will continue to use adaptive, generative, and transformative interaction patterns when they are needed in the future.

These learning patterns may be actively managed by a group's leader and/or facilitator (Edmondson et al., 2001; Van de Ven, 1992). The leader, facilitator, or even group members can diagnose learning stimuli and readiness to learn, and design interventions to support group learning. These interventions may direct the group's attention to certain stimuli, help the group become ready to learn (e.g., by discussing new ideas), and provide the group with the necessary resources and support during the learning process. Outcomes are the learned patterns of adaptive, generative, and transformative learning that are codified, become part of the group's mental model, and then may be transmitted to other groups through observation and communication. These learned patterns of interaction may strengthen (or weaken) the group's readiness to learn in the future.

Next, we consider the elements of the model—the stimuli for learning, the group's and individual members' readiness to learn, and adaptive, generative, and transformative learning. We then introduce a case example.

Stimuli for Learning

As groups work, they act within a complex environment that bombards them with continuous information. Groups need to pick and choose what they notice out of this continuous flow, or they may become overloaded with information (Starbuck & Milliken, 1988). Learning stimuli (or triggers) are pressures, demands, challenges, and opportunities that arise internally from group leaders or members or externally from the environment. These stimuli affect the group's work such that the group cannot continue to work in the same way and be successful (Sessa & London, 2006). For example, problems or obstacles may be production breakdowns, miscommunications, or resource constraints. New competitors and suppliers may pose challenges. New technologies for products or task production may be opportunities. Individuals in the group may see opportunities, or create them, and encourage the group to respond. These events may occur even without external pressures.

Learning stimuli vary in strength as well as source. For instance, group members may be forceful in expressing their ideas and implementing new initiatives that cause the group

FIGURE 1 A Model of Group Continuous Learning

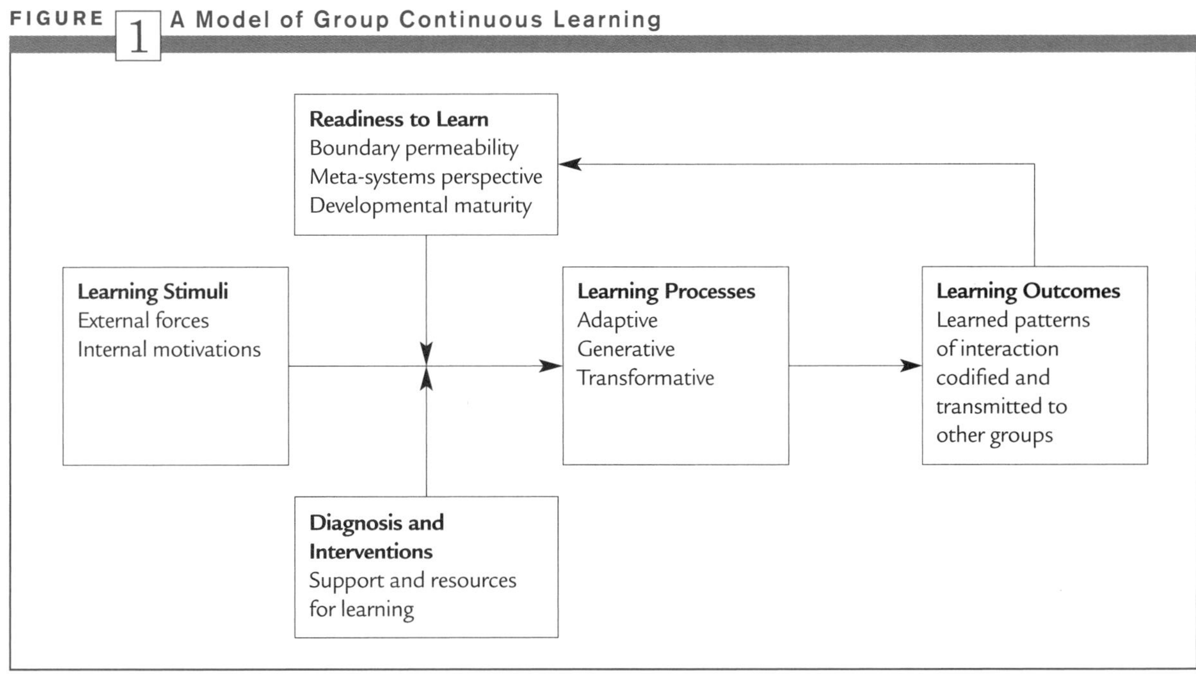

Table 1 Learning Processes and Outcomes

Continuous Learning	Learning Processes	Learning Outcomes
Adaptive	Reactive/coping • Reactive to outside pressures and challenges • Automatic (unplanned, possibly imperceptible, and unconscious) • Trial and error • Building from current capabilities, skills, and knowledge • Incremental changes and improvements • Making adjustments to work routines and interactions	• Reducing/eliminating external pressures • Maintaining homeostasis and constancy within a changing environment • Instituting changes in group operations, structure, etc., in response to changes in the environment or to feedback
Generative	Purposefully proactive • Proactive initiatives stimulated within the group • Learning new skills, knowledge, and behaviors and trying them out in the group • Trying new behaviors and interaction patterns and evaluating the effects of these changes • Exploring alternative methods • Observing competitors • Identifying, modifying, and adopting best practices	• Instituting new procedures to meet current and future contingencies • Incorporating new skills, behaviors, and knowledge into group practice
Transformative	Radically re-creative • Giving up old behaviors and interaction patterns • Creating radically new modes of operation • Dialogue, appreciative inquiry, reflection • Evaluating ideas by experimentation • Choosing new modes of operation based on results	• Introducing wholly new behaviors and outcomes • Adopting new goals • Creating new products or services • Going after new markets • Forming new alliances

to learn and change. Other times, group members may suggest ideas or new directions with little conviction or effort to convince the group to change. An executive who oversees a group may impose a tight deadline or difficult goal with stiff consequences for not meeting it. Alternatively, the executive may make a suggestion that the group can take or leave with few repercussions.

Forceful pressures, demands, challenges, or opportunities disturb the group's status quo and thereby stimulate learning. In some cases, the group can respond by making a fairly minor change in its operations and interactions. That is, it adapts. In other cases, the group needs to learn different modes of operation, first acquiring new skills and knowledge, and then using them in different and creative ways. Such a group engages in generative learning by seeking new skills and information and then working to generate new ways of interacting. In some cases, a group may be pressured to shift goals, roles, and/or interactions in ways that transform the group into a very different entity.

Readiness to Learn

Readiness to learn is how a group comes to recognize that stimuli for learning are occurring and that the group needs to change, learn something in order to accomplish its work, and to actually make a decision to take action (Sessa & London, 2006). Groups are more likely to be ready to learn when they have appropriate boundary permeability and when they are sensitive to the demands and concerns of other individuals, other groups, and the organization as a whole (meta-systems perspective), and as they grow in maturity (Sessa & London, 2006). Boundary permeability is the ease with which people and resources move into and out of the group (Arrow et al., 2000). Group boundaries need to be sufficiently permeable so that groups can access the resources they need but not so permeable that outside input overwhelms the group or that group resources are drained from the group (Alderfer, 1980). As groups mature, they appreciate teamwork, welcome individual expression, and engage in experimentation and collaboration (Kasl et al., 1997).

Group maturity is evident in its members' confidence, focus under stress, and strong group identity and commitment to group goals (Bergami & Bagozzi, 2000; Earley & Mosakowski, 2000; Pulakos et al., 2005).

Adaptive Learning

Adaptive learning is reacting almost automatically to stimuli to make changes in process and outcome as a coping mechanism (Berry & Dienes, 1993; Reber, 1993; Senge, 1990). At the simplest level, a group can change in reaction to a stimulus in the external environment or to feedback. This type of learning stems from the behaviorist tradition of learning theorists (Guthrie, 1952; Thorndike, 1932; Tolman, 1932; Watson, 1924). Adaptive learning is Senge's (1990) term. Vera and Crossan (2003) referred to "exploitive learning," while Argyris (1999; Argyris & Schön, 1996) used the phrase "single-loop learning." It is making existing processes more efficient. Groups in organizations respond to stimuli from their organizational surroundings—clues about changes in the organization's climate, culture, norms, policies, procedures, and rules that inform them about the new way to negotiate and get their work done and thus change the group's behavior accordingly. They engage in an iterative, incremental change process as they adjust their typical behaviors and clarify their interdependencies (Pulakos, Arad, Donovan, & Plamondon, 2000).

How well groups adapt to stimuli will determine their sustainability and success. Some groups are better at adapting than others, and group leaders and facilitators need to support adaptive learning. Adaptation reduces or eliminates the pressures and challenges that stimulated the need to learn. These changes may be in line with what the organization needed. For example, due to unexpected pressure to finish, the group may be forced to quickly alter its structure in a minor way (e.g., divide responsibilities), form a subcommittee to address critical issues, save money by eliminating food at meetings, and so on. The adaptation may lead to better performance, and these changes may generate positive messages (reinforcement) from stakeholders that the group is headed in the right direction. However, the possibility remains that these changes will *not* be in line with what the organization expected. For example, an adaptation may lead the group to rely heavily on a single member, collapsing members' interdependencies in such a way that the group members can no longer work together on another project.

A group learns to be adaptive by reacting to events, pressures, and demands and receiving feedback that the adaptation "worked." When the adaptation is in line with group and organization goals, members can gain a stronger sense of their potential to be effective (group self-efficacy) and an increased feeling of being part of the group, even though they may not be entirely sure what they are doing right. Group cohesiveness increases, and members feel a stronger identification with the group. Work relationships become tighter—more in synch—and the adaptation becomes part of a shared mental model of how the group operates. These changes may improve group member satisfaction and make them feel more positive about change. As a result, these groups are in a better position to adapt in the future to unexpected pressures and challenges.

Unfortunately, the opposite can occur as well. Group members can come to believe that they are unable to perform, perhaps because the organization's climate is detrimental to group work. The group can feel fragmented, overwhelmed, and underprepared to deal with changes. Continuous adaptation in this case can include learning to hunker down and "fly under the radar," hoping that no one notices the group and its poor performance. This can happen when people misjudge others' likely reactions to decisions, do not realize the consequences of their actions, and/or avoid confronting unpleasant situations. These problems can be avoided by discussing issues and possible reactions before taking action to ensure the group is mindful and aware, expressing ideas to test reactions, asking for feedback, and tracking indicators to evaluate the effects of small adjustments. These interventions may increase adaptiveness and set the stage for generative behavior.

Generative Learning

Generative learning is proactively learning and applying new skills, knowledge, behaviors, and interaction patterns to improve the group's performance. It is proactive learning for mastery (Senge, 1990). Generative learning stems from cognitive learning theories (Ausubel, 1968; Bruner, 1960; Gagné, 1978). Vera and Crossan (2003) call this explorative learning. It parallels Argyris's (1999; Argyris & Schön, 1996) concept of double-loop learning. Generative learning entails (a) a mastery learning orientation (Bunderson & Sutcliffe, 2003; Dweck, 1986; Vande Walle, 1997); (b) self-efficacy derived from learning from others (Bandura, 1997); and (c) andragogy (adults who are ready to learn and are responsible for their own learning; Knowles, 1975). Group members explore alternative methods, ask questions, challenge assumptions, seek different perspectives, evaluate alternatives, and reflect on their actions (Van der Vegt & Bunderson, 2005). As members work with each other, they clarify their expertise and demonstrate capabilities they haven't demonstrated before (the process of identity negotiation; Polzer, Milton, & Swann, 2002). As the group experiments with new behavior patterns, individual members learn new skills and the group discovers new, constructive interaction patterns (Kasl et al., 1997).

Generative learning is about creating—continuously exploring new opportunities that create potential for new sources of growth (Senge, 1990). When generative learning works well, changes in performance are measured and tracked. Improvements are confirmed and made part of standard operating procedures or practiced for future use. The group receives positive responses from others as signs that changes were appropriate and worth the effort. The group is likely to adopt higher performance standards for the future and more challenging goals.

An outcome of purposefully proactive learning processes and being generative is that the group learns better how to be generative in the future. They become more open to new ideas and more confident in the ability of the group to face an uncertain future and handle emergencies that may arise. Seeking continuous improvement becomes a group habit. Members are increasingly willing to create and implement new ways of operating in the future. They become more entrepreneurial, and a culture of experimentation emerges in the group.

A potential downside of a group becoming successful at generative learning is that the group continues to engage in generative learning even when it is not needed or negatively impacts performance (Bunderson & Sutcliffe, 2003). When generative learning doesn't work well, the group may try other new behaviors, skills, and knowledge until they do work. Or the group may go back to its original way of coping and learn not to engage in generative learning, at least for awhile. Dysfunctional outcomes of generative learning may occur because of unexpected reactions to major changes, being too cautious, not running experiments or trials to test opinions, or, once changes are made, institutionalizing the changes so the group reverts to conformity or adaptiveness to cope with environmental pressures (Henderson, 2002). Adaptive learning becomes the default condition.

Transformative Learning

Transformative learning is re-creating or altering the group's purpose, goals, and/or structure or in other ways changing the core nature of the group. Unlike generative learning, which builds on prior perspectives, transformative learning requires experiencing disorientation and then reorientation as a new direction for growth. This reorientation produces a new group structure, strategy, goals, and identity. Transformational change alters the way people in the group perceive their roles, responsibilities, and relationships (Anderson, 1997; Boyd & Myers, 1988; Gergen, 1991; Grabov, 1997; Henderson, 2002; Wenger, 1999). A new, higher order of consciousness emerges, to borrow Kegan's (2000) concept of developing consciousness. Transformative learning stems from constructivist theories of learning that hold that people (re)construct meaning and reality from experience (Dewey, 1933/1986; Glaserfeld, 1996; Rogoff, 1990; Vygotsky, 1978; see also Mezirow, 1991, 1994). Group members engage in critical reflection on their experiences to focus on and alter their specific beliefs, attitudes, and emotional reaction. Just as increasing adaptive learning contributes to generativity, increasing generative learning contributes to transformative learning.

Groups that learn transformatively engage in re-creative learning processes. These learning processes include giving up old behaviors and interaction patterns (unfreezing), generating new ideas, evaluating them, and making choices. It is the process of inventing and experimenting with new modes of operations. It is trying and practicing new routines and evaluating what works and what doesn't. Sometimes, groups are forced into transformational change for their survival. The group can also recognize the need and take the initiative to embark on a process of critical reflection and experience (Langer, 2000). When the group successfully transforms itself, it becomes a different (or indeed a "new") group, not a group that has adapted and not a group that has added new behaviors, skills, and knowledge, but a group that now interacts with its environment in a fundamentally new manner.

Groups that attempt a transformation and fail may either "die" or disband or have great difficulty working as a unit in the future. Transformative learning is essentially breaking new ground, so failure is possible and maybe even likely. Group leaders can avoid or at least minimize failure by encouraging critical, mindful thinking as changes are developed and implemented. They can enhance learning by helping group members discuss and understand the results of their transformations.

Case Example

We use a case to illustrate our conceptualization of how groups learn, including the conditions that affect, and the interventions that facilitate, learning processes.

The Cardiac Surgery Quality Improvement Group A group of two surgeons, one anesthesiologist, one physician assistant, two nurses, and one operating room technician worked to shift the group's operations from open heart bypass surgery to catheter-inserted stint and balloon placement and minimally invasive, laparoscopic bypasses.[2] The group members represented a renowned heart surgery unit in a large, suburban tertiary care teaching hospital. With the change in technology and the ability to treat patients with less invasive methods (the stimulus for learning), the unit needed to learn new technology and gain more experience with the new methods. The group's task was to develop new protocols, train the other employees in the unit, hold practice sessions, set goals for efficiency and effectiveness, and monitor improvements. The two surgeons led the group jointly, and a facilitator from the hospital's organization development department was assigned to work with the group.

This group needed to engage in all three types of learning patterns to remain successful. First, in terms of adaptive learning, the cardiac surgery group members needed to sustain their expertise in open heart surgery while they simultaneously prepared for more substantial changes. Similar to their work in the past, they had to continue to keep up with medical technology, surgical methods, and care protocols. Constantly attuned to patient outcomes, they knew they needed to be at the forefront of their field and responsive to hospital and community expectations. In addition to adapting to changing methods, the members needed to be generative learners. They proactively sought new skills and knowledge and formulated new applications to bring about continuous improvement. So they seemed to be ready to learn. However, learning and implementing the less invasive method required a transformation for which they were not prepared. The group struggled with interpersonal interactions. One of the surgeons was autocratic, demanding, and failed to show respect for other group members. The group members could adapt and be generative in the old way because they worked largely independently during surgery, doing their own tasks and not communicating unless necessary. The minimally invasive procedures required group members to work far more interdependently with constant communication.

Something very different was needed for the group in terms of their interpersonal interactions. The surgical group needed to become like a musical ensemble, always in synch. This could not be learned simply by following a cookbook procedure. Rather, it required new ways of relating to fellow group members, new roles and coordination mechanisms, and continuous practice and feedback.

Case Summary

Group continuous learning is a function of stimuli and readiness to learn. Adaptive learning is reactively coping with changes in the environment. Generative learning is proactively learning and applying new skills, knowledge, behaviors, and interactions. Transformative learning is re-creating the group in fundamental ways. The cardiac surgical group provided examples of adaptive, generative, and transformative learning. We return to the case later to demonstrate interventions to support learning.

Implications for Practice

Our model suggests ways to diagnose a group's learning potential, which in turn can be used to formulate learning interventions. A group leader or facilitator can use the questions in Table 2 to diagnose a group's potential and need for learning. The questions ask about pressures and opportunities for learning, perceived need for change, readiness to learn, past experience learning, time available for generative learning, the results of prior learning interventions, and the group's capacity for adaptive, generative, and/or transformational learning in the future.

Our model also suggests interventions that group leaders, facilitators, and human resource professionals can use to support group learning and diagnose conditions and needs for group learning. Outsiders to a group cannot learn for the group; they can only stimulate the group, provide resources to it, and support it. Managers and human resource professionals, including consultants and group facilitators, can impose stimuli, help groups be ready to learn, give feedback, and encourage learning in the direction the organization needs. However, they are not able to make learning occur, know for certain what will be learned (if anything), or even make the group use what it learns. The group must be ready to learn before it will accept an intervention (Hackman & Wageman, 2005).

Groups perform better when members have a sense from the start that the group has the inner resources to be effective (Ericksen & Dyer, 2004). In addition, knowing that support is available may stimulate group members to engage in learning behavior. Support may come from the environment in the form of resources, time, structure, and direction from leaders. Alternatively, or in addition, it may come from the group leader, the facilitator, and/or the members themselves. Early interventions that create high-performing groups include being sure members have essential task-related competencies, sufficient time to complete the task, and the time to develop complete performance strategies.

A number of environmental conditions are likely to promote group continuous generative learning. These include group members supporting each other's acquiring and sharing ideas and leaders who are open to new ideas and provide learning opportunities, tolerate mistakes, and hold members accountable for learning (Eddy, Tannenbaum, Lorenzet, & Smith-Jentsch, 2005; Edmondson, 2003; Tannenbaum, 1997).

Table 2 Suggested Questions for Diagnosing Learning Needs and Potential

- What are the pressures and opportunities for learning? How strong are they? Are these learning triggers clear and consistent or unclear and at cross purposes with each other? Do they come from inside the group or outside the group?
- Does the leader, and do the group members, perceive a need for learning?
- Are group members ready to learn? Are their boundaries sufficiently open to allow stimuli in? What development or life stage is the group in? Does the group know where and how it "fits" in the organization?
- What are the possible barriers to learning (e.g., members don't perceive external forces for change; some members see opportunities, but others don't)?
- Does the group have experience learning beyond adaptation? Do members need resources and support so that they can learn to learn? Do groups have time to learn beyond adaptation?
- Has the group experienced learning interventions in the past? What learning resulted from one or more learning interventions? Is the group better prepared for future adaptation? On-going generative learning? Possible transformation?
- How has learning capacity changed over time? Has the group made adaptations, and does it feel good about the changes? Has this opened the door for generative and transformational learning?

Interventions for helping groups learn include didactic classroom instruction, structured on-the-job training, simulations, field exercises, and self-development activities such as keeping journals and compiling portfolios (Pulakos et al., 2000; White, Dorsey, & Pulakos, 2003).

Consider coaching interventions as an example. Group coaching is helping group members coordinate and appropriately use their collective resources to accomplish a group's work (Hackman & Wageman, 2005). Leaders, facilitators, or fellow group members must focus their coaching on factors important to the group's task. Helping to coordinate activities and reinforcing constructive behaviors (adaptive learning) can be valuable anytime. However, coaching works best when it addresses issues that are salient to the group at the time. That is, coaching works best when it is in line with the stimuli the group has recognized and identified as important. Coaching will be counterproductive when it is not needed.

Coaching effectiveness depends on group readiness, and one component of readiness is the stage in the group's life cycle. Consider the following conditions (Hackman & Wageman, 2005): (a) Coaching that focuses on motivating effort is important at the outset of the group process. (b) Coaching that focuses on performance strategy consultation is required midway into the group process to deal with uncertainties mindfully and make the most of environments that foster innovation. (c) Coaching that focuses on conceptualizing the knowledge and skills learned is most useful after the task is completed and the members have the time and emotional stamina to reflect on their accomplishments. Coaching that does not match readiness may be counterproductive—a waste of time or possibly destructive in preventing a group from concentrating on what it needs to do.

Coaching results in a foundation of trust, a constructive resolution of conflicts, greater commitment, and increased accountability (Kets de Vries, 2005). This foundation sets the stage for generative and transformative learning. Group leaders and facilitators increase learning through the use of authority structures and the promotion of psychological safety and group stability (Edmondson et al., 2001). For instance, they engage in many of the following behaviors: they select group members carefully; add new members (talent) when necessary; help group members understand each other's roles and how to coordinate activities; encourage the group to practice new skills and routines; prompt members to give each other feedback while the group tries new interaction patterns; assure members that it is okay to seek help from others within and outside the group; help the group learn how to exchange and combine information and resources; encourage the members to discuss problems and conflicts openly as they support and encourage each other; create an environment in which people can learn from their mistakes; and give the group time to reflect collectively on how the trials are going and making changes depending on results (Leonard-Barton, 1988; Levine & Moreland, 1999; Milton & Westphal, 2005; Moreland & Myaskovsky, 2000; Orlikowski & Hofman, 1997; Polzer, Swann, & Milton, 2003; Swann, Milton, & Polzer, 2000; Thomke, 1998; Tjosvold, 1998).

Below, we consider possible ways to facilitate adaptive, generative, and transformative learning and avoid dysfunctional learning. We discuss these ideas separately, although we recognize that they may be combined in any interventions. These methods are summarized in Table 3.

Facilitating Adaptive Learning

To encourage adaptive learning, group leaders or facilitators need to focus on stimuli, encourage group identification, provide resources, and give feedback. To be specific, first, they must provide or direct attention toward strong stimuli for change. Similar and clear messages through multiple channels can stimulate the group to learn. For example, if a company implements a new client services system that requires regular input from various groups across the organization, the company may begin preparing affected groups by holding information, question-and-answer, and training sessions; improving support services, such as technical support; and establishing new measurement systems. Affected groups will soon adapt their work to be in line with the new organizational need.

Second, since adaptive learning does not require a particularly high readiness to learn compared to the other types of learning, the leader can encourage the members to identify with the group; for example, by holding a kickoff event, publishing an article in the company bulletin or Web site, or posting symbols of pride such as pins or banners.

Third, the leader must provide support and resources to make necessary changes. For example, the leader can create a climate in which members know that they can learn from their mistakes without being punished. The leader can facilitate learning by assigning and clarifying roles and providing support to maintain existing processes while trying to improve. The leader can outline steps for changing procedures.

Fourth, the leader needs to provide regular feedback to the group on task processes and outcomes. The leader or facilitator can help the group members assess and understand the need for change and evaluate the group's capabilities. Adaptive learning can be captured by codifying the alterations to standard processes. The leader can add to or revise the documentation of standard operating procedures and teach members tools for assessing group process and outcomes.

Our case example elucidates how to facilitate adaptive learning. Members of the cardiac surgery group met early each day in grand rounds style to review surgical cases. The group needed to adapt routinely to the specific conditions posed by the different patients, the introduction of new equipment and methods, and minor changes in hospital regulations and standards of practice. These daily reviews sometimes resulted in ideas for adaptive changes in open heart procedures. These adaptations would quickly become routine.

Table 3 Ways Group Leaders Can Facilitate Group Learning

Learning Processes	Stimuli for Learning	Readiness for Learning	Support and Resources for Learning	Capturing the Learning
Adaptive	• Provide strong, clear, and consistent stimuli for learning across multiple channels	• Assess capabilities • Assess stage of group development • Support group identity • Overcome resistance to change	• Assign roles • Encourage trying new behaviors • Try new methods while perfecting old methods • Outline steps for changes in procedures • Create a climate that supports calculated risks	• Document changes • Teach members assessment methods
Generative	• Invite group to stimulate own learning • Hold group strategy sessions • Have group members use their own products or services to do their work	• Help the group to use boundary spanners, scouts, and ambassadors • Help the group self-analyze • Help group see its role in the organization	• Help locate resources and best practices • Survey competition • Provide training • Encourage members to express new ideas and try them • Be a role model for learning • Teach continuous quality improvement methods • Shift roles to give fresh perspectives • Create a climate where failure is a learning experience • Allow groups time to practice	• Provide ways to evaluate change • Codify new business practices • Evaluate outcomes and methods • Inculcate continuous quality improvement methods • Make generative learning methods a habit • Help groups determine when generative learning is necessary and when it is not.
Transformative	• Communicate compelling vision of outcome and process • Invite group to stimulate own learning • Elicit expressions of support and commitment	• Help group to use boundary spanners, scouts, and ambassadors • Help members analyze the group's development and how the group fits in the organization • Bring in new members • Evaluate and support member identification with the group's openness and maturity	• Provide mechanisms for transformation including dialogue, appreciative inquiry, and reflection • Experiment; compare old and new • Practice new routines, evaluate, and improve • Be a role model for new behavior • Demonstrate the value of what is learned • Schedule practice • Change membership (unfreeze and get needed talents, attitudes, and perspectives)	• Assess learning outcomes • Describe/share common vision for the future • Routinize and document • Spread the learning to new members and other groups • Discuss feelings of uncertainty

Facilitating Generative Learning

Leaders and facilitators can stimulate generative learning by leading the group through a mission- and strategy-setting process similar to that undertaken by top management groups. For example, groups may strategize, analyze competitors' best practices, or try new work methods to incite dissatisfaction with the status quo, even when the organization they are part of perceives no need for change.

These learning sessions can be used to help groups open their boundaries, understand their developmental stage, and enhance their meta-systems perspective. Further, group leaders and facilitators can help groups open their boundaries by using such mechanisms as boundary spanners, scouts, and ambassadors who regularly bring in new information. Groups can analyze their developmental stage by reviewing their task progress, discussing conflicts and uncertainties, and examining their strengths and weaknesses. Finally, groups may develop a meta-systems perspective by asking and discussing questions such as: How does the group define itself in reference to its members or the organization? What are the needs, expectations, and tensions of other groups or the organization as a whole? Do group members understand each others' roles, responsibilities, and capabilities? Are they in agreement on the group's work?

Groups need support and resources to help them with proactive learning processes. These learning processes are purposeful and do not immediately affect the group's work. They may be antithetical to doing work in an efficient and timely manner, initially at least. They require time, space, and some encouragement that the group is not "wasting time." Processes for supporting generative learning include helping members locate resources, identify best practices, and survey the competition. Leaders and facilitators can provide the group with training in new methods and the chance to try new approaches even if it means that performance is lowered or efficiency is reduced for a short time. They can encourage members to express and try new ideas. They can be a role model for learning and educating group members. Facilitators can explain continuous quality improvement methods, such as analysis of root causes of problems or barriers to being effective. Leaders can shift members' roles to provide fresh perspectives. Moreover, leaders can request input from members with diverse backgrounds and expertise.

Capturing generative learning includes helping members reflect on the learning process. This reflection may involve providing ways to evaluate change, codify changed business practices, and assess efficiency of group operations. Groups need to know when to engage in generative learning and when it is not appropriate. They do not need to be generative all the time. A period of stability may be required to routinize new patterns of interaction.

Turning to our case, the two leaders of the cardiac surgery team ultimately learned how to provide resources to make generative learning a way of keeping the unit up to date and competitive. Together with the facilitator, they encouraged individual group members to engage in learning on their own and then share the learning. Group members learned from each other as they occasionally shifted roles and regularly discussed their newly acquired observations and knowledge. They developed the habit of generating new, more effective ways of working together.

Facilitating Transformative Learning

Transformative learning methods include holding practice sessions, designing experiments, and comparing the outcomes of old and new practices. Leaders can give the group time to practice new routines, be a role model for new behaviors, evaluate their effectiveness, and improve. Another strategy is to change membership to unfreeze the group and bring in needed talents, positive attitudes, and fresh perspectives. Leaders and facilitators of transformative learning can help members be mindful of what they learned. Group leaders can encourage transformative learning by (a) defining change initiatives as transformational, (b) encouraging critical reflection, (c) helping to assess the current group culture and determine what elements must change to align with a new strategic direction, and (d) encouraging discussion about what it means to respect and value a diversity of disciplines and perspectives (Henderson, 2002).

Holding the gains of transformative learning requires assessing learning outcomes, articulating the common/shared vision, and routinizing the learning, perhaps by creating documents that describe methods and procedures. It also includes teaching others to emphasize how change should be handled. Facilitators can lead discussions about members' feelings of dealing with uncertainty.

Returning to our case, before the cardiac surgery group formed to learn the new surgical procedures, the two lead surgeons had been at each other's throats. One was new to the hospital and, perhaps in an effort to exert his authority, alienated the medical staff with his autocratic, demanding style. He didn't seem to respect anyone in the group, including fellow physicians.

When the group was formed and charged with introducing the new medical procedures into the cardiac unit, the group began by holding an off-site, three-day retreat led by the facilitator and an organization change consultant funded by a grant from an outside agency. The consultant led the group through a process of self-awareness. Members shared their feelings and backgrounds with each other. They discussed their perceptions of how they were working together. A 360-degree feedback survey was conducted prior to leaving for the retreat, which required members to rate themselves and each other.

The feedback results were presented at the retreat, providing stimuli for discussions about how members viewed each other. The surgeon, who was a relative newcomer to the hospital, was stunned by how he was perceived by the group, and his expressions of intent and commitment to the unit helped the members understand him better. After considerable discussion, they all realized that they were in agreement—they cared about the hospital, were proud of their accomplishments, and were excited by the challenge of implementing new methods at the forefront of medical technology. Back home, this retreat set the stage for more open communication and a habit of regular, honest feedback as the group learned, practiced, fine-tuned the new methods, and made innovations that advanced their effectiveness and contributed to the field.

The retreat was repeated two more times during the nine-month duration of the group project. It increased members' readiness to learn by providing time for group members to reflect on what the group learned about both the methods and how they worked with each other. Moreover, it made the members mindful about what they learned so they could continue to build on their accomplishments and support their transformative learning. During the retreats and their daily group meetings and practice sessions, the group worked through numerous disagreements. Heated discussions were common. Twice, new members joined the group and others left. These transitions introduced the challenge of bringing new members up to speed. During these transitions, momentum was lost and the commitment of some members waned with the strain. Still, the group persisted, perhaps because the members recognized the tremendous value of the new medical advances and realized that there was really no choice but to transform the unit and to be successful.

The last stage of the process was to introduce the new methods to the rest of the staff. These methods required members of the original group to educate others through lectures, demonstrations, painstaking practice sessions, and, eventually, actual surgery—a model of communicating and spreading the generative and transformative learning experiences. The goal was to make feedback and continuous improvement a hallmark of the unit as transformative learning gave way to ongoing adaptive and generative learning.

Discussion

Adaptive, generative, and transformative learning outcomes are not mutually exclusive. Rather, they may blend into each other and occur together. A group can be automatically reactive (adaptive) in meeting immediate needs; purposefully proactive (generative) in adding new behaviors, skills, and knowledge; and re-creative (transformative) as it identifies and tries new interaction patterns that go beyond what is required by existing pressures for adaptation.

Tushman and O'Reilly (1996) and Taylor and Greve (2006) indicated the importance of an organization being ambidextrous in striking a balance between exploitative (adaptive) and explorative (generative) learning. To Senge (1990), adaptive learning is about coping with environmental contingencies. As the group increases its adaptiveness, it moves toward generativity. Generative and transformational learners focus less on the end result than on effective strategies or processes that lead to goal accomplishment (Seijts & Latham, 2005). A mature learning culture emerges as the group engages in generative and transformative learning. The group becomes adept at such behaviors as sharing ideas, identifying potential threats in the environment, and using ideas from competitors, customers, and employees.

At any one time in a group's history, one learning process may be dominant depending on the work the group is doing. This dominant learning process may change over time. We suggest that adaptive, generative, and transformative learning form a hierarchy: generative learning requires the ability to adapt to the environment, and transformative learning requires the openness and forward/mindful thinking of generative learning as well as the ability to adapt. Adaptive learning can set the stage for generative learning, which in turn provides fertile ground for transformative learning. However, sometimes adaptive learning prevents generative learning and transformative learning from occurring because the adaptation is a sufficient response to pressures or opportunities. Or a failure at generative learning may set the stage for learning that anything beyond adaptation is futile.

Stimuli for learning and readiness are likely to interact to affect the learning process (London & Sessa, 2006). Research is needed to examine the effects of different combinations of readiness and stimuli on types of learning. We propose that if external stimuli are strong but members are not ready to change, adaptive learning may occur, but probably not generative or transformative learning. If readiness is strong but external stimuli are not, the group may engage in generative learning, but the motivation may not be strong and the learning may not produce meaningful change. However, meaningful change might result, for example, when a group's learning creates innovations that generate exciting new production methods, products, or markets. If both stimuli and readiness are strong, generative and, if needed, transformative learning are likely to occur.

Different learning processes may lead to negative or positive outcomes. To apply our model of group learning, dysfunctional outcomes may occur if the group's responses (i.e., learning interaction patterns) do not match the strength of the stimuli and the group's readiness to learn. This mismatch could happen if the group fails to recognize or respond to pressure or opportunities and is stuck in familiar and comfortable ways of responding (Edmondson et al., 2001). It may also happen if the group is not ready to learn in response to internal or external stimuli. Moreover, it can happen if the resources, encouragement, and other forms of support (e.g., coaching) are not available. For example, adaptive learning patterns may occur though the stimuli warrant a generative (e.g., innovative) or transformative response. Alternatively, if the group is ready to learn (e.g., members are open to experimenting with new ideas) but there are few pressures or opportunities for change, generative behaviors may result in responses that the environment is not ready to accept.

Conclusion

Groups learn continuously. Groups learn as they work, encounter obstacles to doing their work, and see opportunities that will aid their work. They learn how to work more effectively as a unit, how to do things, and how to do things better. They also learn about new things—ideas, concepts, and the like. Here, we outlined three ways groups can learn, and thus learn to *learn continuously*. Most often, groups learn adaptively, but they can learn generatively and transformatively depending on the stimuli for learning, the group's readiness to learn, and the learning processes they engage in. We proposed that adaptive learning is likely to occur when the stimuli (pressures and opportunities) are present but the group is not ready to learn, such as when members are not yet open to new ideas and/or are not sensitive to outside pressures. When readiness is high and stimuli are strong, generative and/or transformative learning are likely to produce positive outcomes.

However, a mismatch may exist between the group's learning response, stimuli for learning, and readiness to learn, perhaps because of lack of resources, misperceptions of the environment, or inadequate support, encouragement, or coaching. Group leaders, facilitators, and human resource professionals should implement interventions that provide stimuli for learning, help groups become ready to learn, and provide resources and support during the learning process. We suggested different ways to promote adaptive, generative, and transformative learning by clarifying stimuli, promoting learning readiness, providing resources, and capturing the learning. Understanding these processes may help group members, leaders, and human resource professionals who serve as group facilitators, coaches, and consultants to diagnose group processes and foster a group culture of continuous learning.

Finally, we should note that just as our formulation of group learning processes has its foundation in learning theories, it also can contribute to theory and research. We need to understand how adaptive, generative, and transformative learning are related to components of group learning, such as experimentation, reflective communication, and codification of what is learned (Gibson & Vermeulen, 2003). We also need to understand how adaptive, generative, and transformative learning unfold as cycles of recognizing and reacting to stimuli, planning, taking action, and the emergence of repeatable patterns of interaction (Burke et al., 2006). We need to explore the interrelationships between adaptive, generative, and transformative learning as they occur together or contribute to each other over time and as they result from, and contribute to, learning readiness and stimuli. Moreover, we need to determine how diagnosing conditions and designing interventions can facilitate continuous group learning (Eddy et al., 2005; Tannenbaum, 1997).

Source: Human Resource Management, 46, (4), 651–669 (Winter 2007). Reprinted by permission of John Wiley & Sons, Inc.

ENDNOTES

1. Burke et al. (2006) refer to the change in team performance as team adaptation. We use the term *adaptive learning* more specifically to refer to the way groups learn and the degree of change that results.
2. This group was studied as part of a larger study of hospital quality improvement teams (Wilkens & London, 2006).

REFERENCES

Alderfer, C. P. (1980). Consulting to underbounded systems. In C. P. Alderfer & C. L. Cooper (Eds.), Advances in experiential social processes (pp. 267–295). New York: Wiley.

Anderson, W. T. (1997). The future of self: Inventing the postmodern person. New York: Putnam.

Argote, L., Gruenfeld, D., & Naquin, C. (2001). Group learning in organizations. In M. E. Turner (Ed.), Groups at work: Theory and research (pp. 369–412). Mahwah, NJ: Lawrence Erlbaum Associates.

Argyris, C. (1999). On organizational learning (2nd ed.). Malden, MA: Blackwell.

Argyris, C., & Schön, D. A. (1996). Organization learning 2: Theory, method, and practice. Reading, MA: Addison-Wesley.

Arrow, H., McGrath, J. E., & Berdahl, J. L. (2000). Small groups as complex systems: Formation, coordination, development, and adaptation. Thousand Oaks, CA: Sage.

Ausubel, D. P. (1968). Educational psychology: A cognitive view. New York: Holt, Rinehart & Winston.

Bandura, A. (1997). Self-efficacy: The exercise of control. New York: W. H. Freeman.

Bergami, M., & Bagozzi, R. P. (2000). Self-categorization, affective commitment, and group self-esteem as distinct aspects of social identity in the organization. British Journal of Social Psychology, 39, 555–577.

Berry, D. C., & Dienes, Z. (1993). Implicit learning: Theoretical and empirical issues. Hove, UK: Erlbaum.

Boyd, R. D., & Myers, J. G. (1988). Transformative education. International Journal of Lifelong Education, 7, 261–284.

Bruner, J. S. (1960). The process of education. New York: Vintage.

Bunderson, J. S., & Sutcliffe, K. M. (2003). Management team learning orientation and business unit performance. Journal of Applied Psychology, 883, 552–560.

Burke, C. S., Stagl, K. C., Salas, E., Pierce, L., & Kendall, D. (2006). Understanding team adaptation: A conceptual analysis and model. Journal of Applied Psychology, 91, 1189–1207.

Dewey, J. (1986). How we think: A restatement of the relation of reflective thinking to the educative process. Boston: D. C. Heath and Company. (Original work published 1933).

Druskat, V. U., & Kayes, D. C. (2000). Learning versus performance in short-term project teams. Small Group Research, 31, 328–353.

Dweck, C. S. (1986). Motivational processes affecting learning. American Psychologist, 41, 1040–1048.

Earley, P. C., & Mosakowski, E. (2000). Creating hybrid team cultures: An empirical test of transnational team functioning. Academy of Management Journal, 43, 26–49.

Eddy, E. R., Tannenbaum, S. I., Lorenzet, S. J., & Smith-Jentsch, K. A. (2005). The influence of a continuous learning environment on peer mentoring behaviors. Journal of Managerial Issues, 17, 383–395.

Edmondson, A. (1999). Psychological safety and learning behavior in work teams. Administrative Science Quarterly, 44, 350–383.

Edmondson, A. (2003). Speaking up in the operating room: How team leaders promote learning in interdisciplinary action teams. Journal of Management Studies, 40, 1419–1452.

Edmondson, A. C., Bohmer, R. M., & Pisano, G. P. (2001). Disrupted routines: Team learning and new technology implementation in hospitals. Administrative Science Quarterly, 46, 685–716.

Ellis, A. P. J., Hollenbeck, J. R., Ilgen, D. R., Porter, C. O. L. H., West, B. J., & Moon, H. (2003). Team learning: Collectively connecting the dots. Journal of Applied Psychology, 85(5), 821–835.

Ericksen, J., & Dyer, L. (2004). Right from the start: Exploring the effects of early team events on subsequent project team development and performance. Administrative Science Quarterly, 49, 438–471.

Gagné, N. L. (1978). The scientific basis of the art of teaching. New York: Teachers College Press.

Gergen, J. J. (1991). The saturated self: Dilemmas of identity in contemporary life. New York: Basic Books.

Gibson, C., & Vermeulen, F. (2003). A healthy divide: Subgroups as a stimulus for team learning behavior. Administrative Science Quarterly, 48, 202–239.

Glaserfeld, E. (1996). Introduction: Aspects of constructivism. In C. T. Fosnot (Ed.), Constructivism: Theory, perspectives, and practice (pp. 3–7). New York: Teachers College Press.

Grabov, V. (1997). The many facets of transformative learning theory and practice. In P. Cranton (Ed.), Transformative learning in action: Insights from practice (pp. 89–96). New Directions for Adult and Continuing Education No. 74. San Francisco, CA: Jossey-Bass.

Guthrie, E. R. (1952). The psychology of learning. New York: Harper & Brothers.

Hackman, J. R., & Wageman, R. (2005). A theory of team coaching. Academy of Management Review, 302, 269–288.

Henderson, G. M. (2002). Transformative learning as a condition for transformational change in organizations. Human Resource Development Review, 1, 186–214.

Jaques, E. (2002). The life and behavior of living organisms: A general theory. Westport, CT: Praeger.

Kasl, E., Marsick, V. J., & Dechant, K. (1997). Team as learners: A research-based model of team learning. Journal of Applied Behavioral Science, 33, 227–246.

Kegan, R. (2000). A constructive-developmental approach to transformative learning. In J. Mezirow & Associates (Eds.), Learning as transformation (pp. 35–69). San Francisco, CA: Jossey-Bass.

Kets de Vries, M. F. R. (2005). Leadership group coaching in action: The zen of creating high performance teams. Academy of Management Executive, 19, 61–76.

Knowles, M. S. (1975). Self-directed learning. River Grove, IL: Follett.

Langer, E. J. (2000). Mindful learning. Current Directions in Psychological Science, 9, 220–223.

Leonard-Barton, D. A. (1988). Implementation as mutual adaptation of technology and organization. Research Policy, 17, 251–267.

Levine, J. L., & Moreland, R. L. (1999). Knowledge transmission in work groups: Helping newcomers to succeed. In L. L. Thompson, J. M. Levine, & D. M. Messick (Eds.), Shared cognition in organizations: The management of knowledge (pp. 267–296). Mahwah, NJ: Lawrence Erlbaum Associates.

London, M., & Sessa, V. I. (2006). Continuous learning in organizations: A living systems analysis of individual, group, and organization learning. Research in Multi-Level Issues, 5, 123–172.

Mezirow, J. (1991). Tranformative dimensions of adult learning. San Francisco, CA: Jossey-Bass.

Mezirow, J. (1994). Understanding transformation theory. Adult Education Quarterly, 444, 222–232.

Milton, L. P., & Westphal, J. D. (2005). Identity confirmation networks and cooperation in work groups. Academy of Management Journal, 48, 191–212.

Moreland, R. L., & Myaskovsky, L. L. (2000). Exploring the performance benefits of group training: Transactive memory or improved communication? Organizational Behavior and Human Decision Processes, 82, 117–133.

Orlikowski, W. J., & Hofman, J. D. (1997, Winter). An improvisational model for change management: The case of groupware technologies. Sloan Management Review, pp. 11–21.

Polzer, J. T., Milton, L. P., & Swann, W. B., Jr. (2002). Capitalizing on diversity: Interpersonal congruence in small work groups. Administrative Science Quarterly, 47, 296–324.

Polzer, J., Swann, W., & Milton, L. (2003). The benefits of verifying diverse identities for group performance. In M. Neale, E. Mannix, & J. Polzer (Eds.), Research on managing groups and teams: Identity issues in groups (Vol. 5, pp. 91–112). Stamford, CT: JAI Press.

Pulakos, E. D., Arad, S., Donovan, M. A., & Plamondon, K. E. (2000). Adaptability in the work place: Development of a taxonomy of adaptive performance. Journal of Applied Psychology, 85, 612–624.

Pulakos, E. D., Dorsey, D. W., & Mueller-Hanson, R. A. (2005). PDRI's adaptability research program. The Industrial-Organizational Psychologist, 431, 25–32.

Reber, A. S. (1993). Implicit learning and tacit knowledge. Oxford, UK: Oxford University Press.

Rogoff, B. (1990). Apprenticeship in thinking: Cognitive development in the social context. New York: Oxford University Press.

Seijts, G. H., & Latham, G. P. (2005). Learning versus performance goals: When should each be used? Academy of Management Executive, 19, 124–131.

Senge, P. M. (1990). The fifth discipline: The art and practice of the learning organization. New York: Doubleday.

Sessa, V. I., & London, M. (2006). Continuous learning: Individual, group, and organizational perspectives. Mahwah, NJ: Lawrence Erlbaum Associates.

Starbuck, W. H., & Milliken, F. J., (1988). Executives' perceptual filters: what they notice and they make sense. In D. C. Hamerick (Ed.): The executive effect: Concepts and methods for studying top executives (pp. 35–65), Greenwich, CT: JAI.

Swann, W. B., Jr., Milton, L. P., & Polzer, J. T. (2000). Should we create a niche or fall in line? Journal of Personality and Social Psychology, 792, 238–250.

Tannenbaum, S. I. (1997). Enhancing continuous learning: Diagnostic findings from multiple companies. Human Resource Management, 36, 437–452.

Taylor, A., & Greve, H. R. (2006). Superman or the fantastic four? Knowledge combination and experience in innovative teams. Academy of Management Journal, 49, 723–740.

Thomke, S. (1998). Managing experimentation in the design of new products. Management Science, 44, 743–762.

Thorndike, E. L. (1932). The fundamentals of learning. New York: Teachers College Press.

Tjosvold, D. (1998). Cooperation and competitive dynamics within and between organizational units. Human Relations, 39, 517–554.

Tolman, E. C. (1932). Purposive behavior in animals and men. New York: Appleton-Century-Crofts.

Tushman, M. L., & O'Reilly, C. (1996). Ambidextrous organizations: Managing evolutionary and revolutionary change. California Management Review, 38, 8–30.

Van de Ven, A. (1992). Suggestions for studying strategy process: A research note. Strategic Management Journal, 13, 169–191.

Van der Vegt, G. S., & Bunderson, J. S. (2005). Learning and performance in multidisciplinary teams: The importance of collective team identification. Academy of Management Journal, 48, 532–547.

VandeWalle, D. (1997). Development and validation of a work domain goal orientation instrument. Educational and Psychological Measurement, 57, 995–1015.

Vera, D., & Crossan, M. (2003). Organizational learning and knowledge management: Toward an integrative framework. In M. Easterby-Smith & M. A. Lyles (Eds.), The Blackwell handbook of organizational learning and knowledge management (pp. 122–141). Malden, MA: Blackwell.

Vygotsky, L. (1978). Mind in society: The development of higher psychological process. Cambridge, MA: Harvard University Press.

Watson, J. B. (1924). Behaviorism. New York: Norton.

Wenger, E. (1999). Communities of practice: Learning, meaning, and identity. Cambridge, UK: Cambridge University Press.

White, S. S., Dorsey, D. W., & Pulakos, E. D. (2003). A proposed model of team adaptive performance. Washington, DC: Personnel Decisions Research Institutes.

Wilkens, R., & London, M. (2006). Relationships between climate, process, and performance in continuous quality improvement groups. Journal of Vocational Behavior, 69, 520–523.

Performance Management and Feedback

10

Learning Objectives

- Understand the process of performance management and the role performance feedback plays in performance management
- Examine the strategic choices an organization faces in establishing a performance management system
- Evaluate the associated pros and cons of decisions related to the use of the performance management system as well as who evaluates, what is evaluated, how performance is evaluated, and the methods of evaluation
- Gain an awareness of why performance management systems may fail
- Understand the strategies by which performance management systems may be improved

Performance Management at Otis Elevator

Farmington, Connecticut–based Otis Elevator is the world's largest manufacturer, installer, and servicer of elevators, escalators, moving walkways, and other vertical and horizontal passenger transportation systems. Otis products are offered in more than 200 countries worldwide, and the company employs more than 63,000 people. Among its many installations are the human transport systems of the Eiffel Tower, Sydney Opera House, Vatican, CN Tower (Toronto), and Hong Kong Convention Center.

For years, the company had an ineffective performance management system that was excessively time-consuming and inspired little confidence among employees or managers. In revamping its performance management, Otis moved toward a system that provided performance feedback based on critical strategic competencies related to the company's new focus on project teams. For this realignment into project teams to be successful, managers were required to demonstrate specific competencies in both team leadership and project management as well as remain accountable for the financial and operating results of projects.

Realizing that critical feedback in these areas could not come exclusively from immediate supervisors, Otis had a custom-designed 360-degree feedback system developed that provided managers with feedback from those most directly affected by their performance: their subordinates, peers, and customers. The system provides ratings on several critical core competencies and is administered entirely online via the company intranet. The online system is easy to use, employs encryption technology to secure all data, and allows a performance review to be completed in 20 minutes. The system allows Otis to provide performance feedback in tandem with the organization's strategic objectives; is far more efficient than the previous paper-driven system; and, perhaps most importantly, has restored employee faith in the company's performance feedback system.[1]

An organization's long-term success in meeting its strategic objectives rests with its ability to manage employee performance and ensure that performance measures are consistent with the organization's needs. Consequently, performance management—also called *performance evaluation, performance appraisal,* or *performance measurement*—is becoming more of a strategic issue for organizations than in the past. The term *performance feedback* will be used frequently in this chapter to stress that the performance management system needs to be understood and accepted by the organization's employees and must provide them with meaningful information if it is to be effective. Effective performance management systems require employees and supervisors to work together to set performance expectations, review results, assess organizational and individual needs, and plan for the future. On the other hand, the terms *performance appraisal* and *performance evaluation* imply a one-sided judgmental approach to performance management, where employees have little involvement in the process.

Traditional performance appraisal simply involves evaluative supervisory comments on past performance. Such a process does not involve any kind of management, per se, as the only performance that can be managed is present and future performance. Performance appraisal involves hierarchical, downward communication from supervisor to subordinate concerning the value the supervisor places on the subordinate's performance. Feedback involves a mutual exchange of information that both parties share, discuss, and jointly assess in planning future work activities. Appraisals often put employees in a defensive position, whereas feedback is usually perceived as more neutral and a process over which employees have some control and influence. Exhibit 10.1 summarizes the key differences between performance feedback and performance appraisal.

Performance management systems need not be formal in order to be effective. The most important concern in designing a performance management system is its fit with the organization's strategic objectives, and the most important concern in providing performance-related feedback is its fit with the organization's culture. SAS, an international, 8,000-employee software company headquartered in Cary, North Carolina, decided to do away with formal performance feedback entirely. Instead, SAS opted for a system that provides continuous dialogue on performance-related matters. Executives report that the system works well because it is built on the values of open communication, trust, and self-motivation of employees to do their best. Moreover, any performance-related issues are dealt with in a timely manner because the lack of formality in the process allows feedback to be provided on an ongoing basis.[2]

EXHIBIT 10.1 Performance Feedback versus Performance Appraisal

	Performance Feedback	Performance Appraisal
Time period	Past, present, and future	Past
Focus	Link employee work activities to specific business objectives and strategy	Create records; document performance problems
Nature of communication	Two-way	One-sided, downward, directive; "rebuttal" sometimes allowed
Employee role	Active participant	Passive
Formality	Informal, verbal	High formality, written forms with signatures
Timing	Spontaneous, ad hoc needed	As prescribed (usually annual)
Basis of relationship	Collegiality	Power
Role of supervisor	Coach, motivator, partner	Authority figure
Outcomes	Participation; enhanced, targeted performance; improved relationships	Compensation decision; task directives

The trends toward more streamlined organizations and hierarchies with fewer employees having broader job assignments have resulted in performance feedback taking on a more critical role than it has assumed in the past. Organizations today cannot afford to have weak links or unproductive employees. More than ever, organizations need broader measures of employee performance to ensure that (1) performance deficiencies are addressed in a timely manner through employee development programs that meet the changing needs of the organization and its markets; (2) employee behaviors are being channeled in the appropriate direction toward performance of specific objectives that are consistent with the work unit and organization's strategy; and (3) employees are provided with appropriate and specific feedback to assist with their career development.

An effective performance management process can be conceptualized as one that connects three time periods, as illustrated in Exhibit 10.2. It utilizes data about past performance to set goals, plans, and objectives for the present that should result in high levels of performance in the future. However, a number of critical strategic issues must be addressed to establish an effective performance management system, as will be discussed below.

EXHIBIT 10.2 Performance Management Timeline

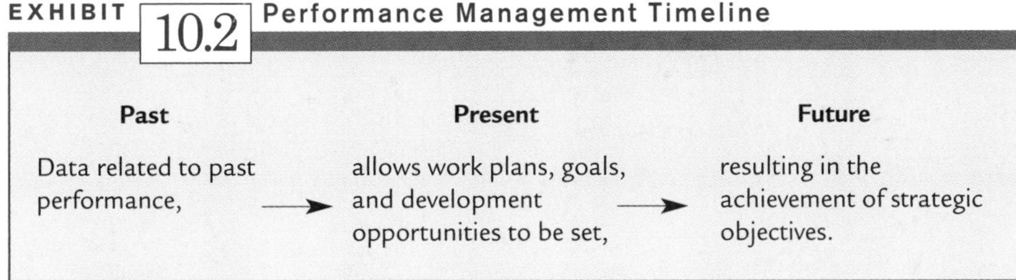

Use of the System

An organization faces five strategic decisions in establishing its performance management system, as illustrated in Exhibit 10.3. The first is a determination of the purpose of the system and how it will be used. A performance management system can serve multiple purposes, and it is important for the organization to strategize why the system is being used before further design decisions can be made. The organization also needs to ensure that if the system is developed to serve several purposes that these purposes not be at odds with each other and that any purpose not undermine data collection for the other(s).

One purpose of performance management systems is to facilitate employee development. By assessing deficiencies in performance levels and skills, an organization can determine specific training and development needs. In fact, the performance feedback process can be designed to provide information to fuel the organization's training and development programs. Assessing individual and team strengths and weaknesses can allow employee and team development plans to be established. A reciprocal relationship exists between the two, as the desired outcomes of training and development initiatives must be incorporated into the performance management system, as discussed in Chapter 9. At the same time, the performance management system provides data that impacts the needs assessment of training and development, as displayed in Exhibit 10.4.

A second purpose of performance management systems is to determine appropriate rewards and compensation. Salary, promotion, retention, and bonus decisions are frequently based on data collected as part of performance measurement. Therefore, employees must understand and accept the performance feedback system as a prerequisite for accepting decisions made relative to rewards and compensation. Any perceived unfairness of the performance feedback system on the part of employees will result in a perceived unfairness of the compensation system.

A third purpose of managing performance is to enhance employee motivation. A formal process that allows for employee acknowledgment and praise can reinforce the behaviors and outcomes that are beneficial to the unit or organization. Employees can be told specifically what the organization's expectations for them are, and employees can inform their employers of the types of job assignments and responsibilities they desire.

EXHIBIT 10.3 Strategic Choices in Performance Management Systems

How System Will Be Used
• Employee development
• Determine rewards and compensation
• Enhance motivation
• Facilitate legal compliance
• Facilitate human resource planning
Who Evaluates
• Supervisor
• Peers
• Subordinates
• Customers
• Self
What to Evaluate
• Traits
• Behaviors
• Results
How to Evaluate
• Absolute
• Relative
Means of Evaluation
• Graphic rating scale
• Weighted checklist
• BARS
• BOS
• Critical incident
• Objectives-based
Link with Training
Link with Compensation
Flexible/ Standardized
Individual/ Team
Time Periods

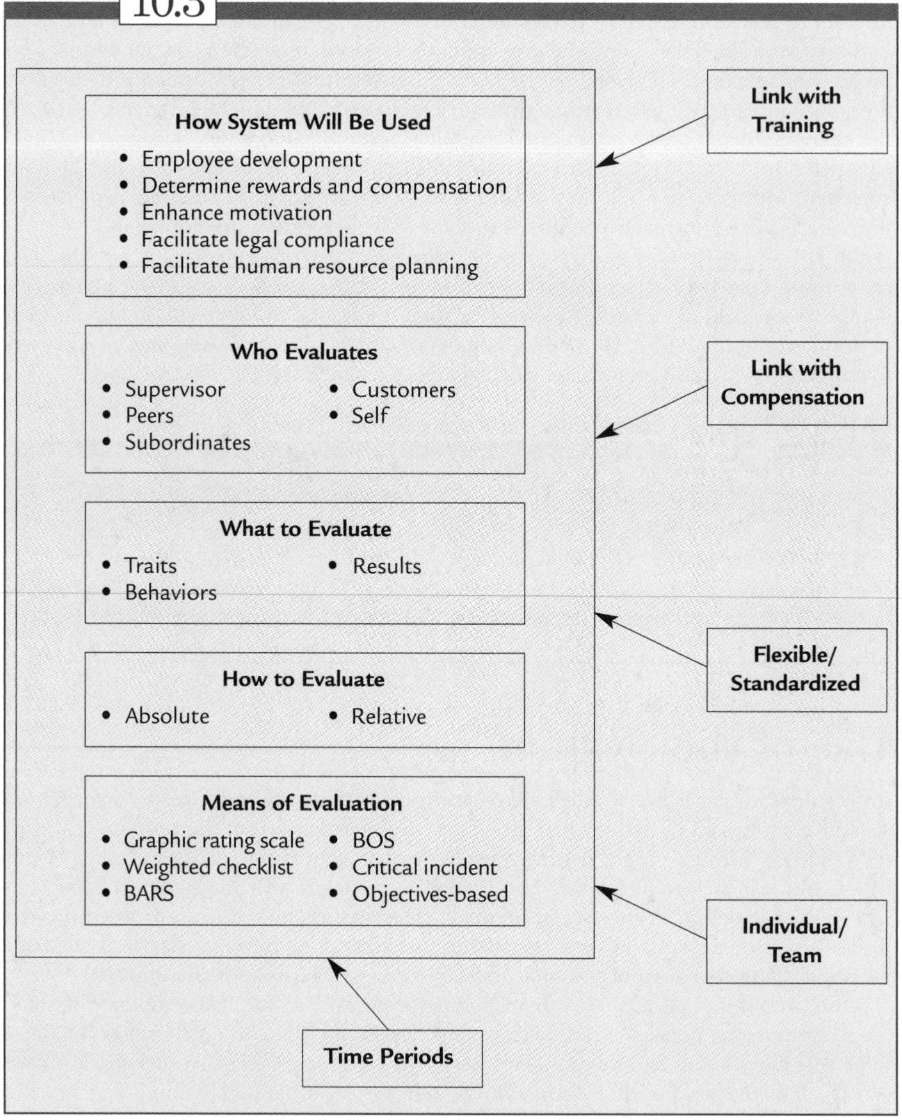

EXHIBIT 10.4 Reciprocal Relationship between Training and Development and Performance Management

Training and Development
outcomes
needs assessment data
Performance Management System

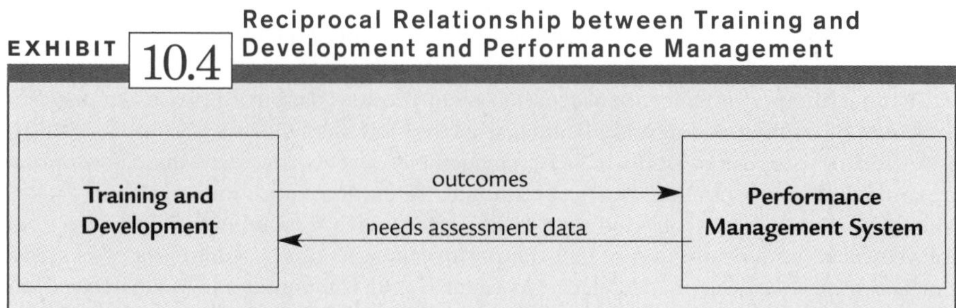

A fourth purpose of performance management systems is to facilitate legal compliance. Claims of unfair dismissal and/or Title VII violations are best supported when the organization has documentation of performance deficiencies. Such information is often admitted into court to prove nondiscriminatory means of taking remedial action against employees and for termination of employment. Data showing unacceptable performance, particularly over a period of time, is a strong defense against such charges of unlawful bias.

Finally, performance management systems facilitate the human resource planning process. Performance data can alert the organization to deficiencies in the overall level and focus of employee skills and can be used in critically planning for future staffing needs relative to the skills and abilities of current employees. Because performance feedback can perform multiple functions in any organization, the organization must determine how it will be used prior to developing the system. This will keep the system focused—rather than random—and allow the organization to determine the specifications of its design.

Who Evaluates

The second strategic decision that must be made relative to the development of the performance management system concerns who provides performance data. Traditionally, performance evaluation was performed by the employee's immediate supervisor, who communicated to the employee the supervisory assessment of performance. This system offered very little opportunity for input or feedback from the employee. This approach, by itself, can be problematic for a number of reasons. Immediate supervisors often do not have the appropriate information to provide informed feedback and do not observe the employee's day-to-day work enough to assess performance accurately. It is also common in today's organizations for supervisors not to be current on the technical dimensions of a subordinate's work, which may be best evaluated by peers, customers, or other external constituencies. Technical line managers often have no training in or appreciation for the process and can see it as nothing more than an administrative burden. Finally, performance assessment is an inherently subjective process that is prone to a variety of perceptual errors by supervisors.

These errors include the halo effect, in which the rater allows one positive or negative trait, outcome, or consideration to influence other measures (for example, if an employee is often late for work, that fact may impact ratings having nothing to do with tardiness); stereotyping or personal bias, in which the rater makes performance judgments based on characteristics of the employee rather than on employee performance (for example, a bias that older workers are more resistant to change, less mentally agile, and less capable than younger workers of working longer hours); contrast error, in which the employee's assessment is based on those being given to other employees; recency error, in which the evaluation is biased toward events and behaviors that happened immediately prior to the time the evaluation is completed, with little or no consideration given to events occurring earlier in the evaluation period; central tendency error, in which the evaluator avoids the higher and lower ends of performance assessment ratings in favor of placing all employees at or near the middle of the scales; and leniency or strictness error, in which employees are generally all rated well above the standards (making the supervisor look effective and/or attempting to appease employees) or well below the standards (making the supervisor look demanding). Personal biases and organizational politics may have a significant impact on the ratings employees receive from their supervisors.

There may also be a number of reasons why supervisors might intentionally inflate or deflate employee ratings. For example, an empathetic supervisor might inflate the rating given to an employee having difficulties with personal matters. Conversely, a supervisor who sees a subordinate as a threat to the supervisor's job might intentionally deflate performance ratings. The performance management process can be inherently political in many organizations. In most instances, when supervisors conduct performance evaluations, they personally have job and career issues at stake in the ratings they give to their employees.

In addition to these errors, supervisors and subordinates may agree on levels of performance but disagree on the causes for such performance. Research has shown that supervisors are much more likely to place the responsibility for poor performance with the employee, whereas the employee is likely to cite organizational factors outside his or her control for performance deficiencies.[3] Employees are much more likely to attribute their own job success to their own behaviors rather than to external factors, such as easy job assignments or assistance from others.

For these reasons, organizations have been moving away from traditional means of performance feedback where only one assessment of an employee's performance is conducted and completed by the immediate supervisor. In addition to supervisory input, performance feedback can also be sought from peers, subordinates, customers, and/or the employee. Feedback from peers can be useful for developmental purposes, but peer feedback systems must be administered with care. They can be very political and self-serving in organizations where employees compete with each other either formally or informally. When a peer has personal gain or loss at stake in the assessment of a colleague, he or she can hardly be expected to exercise objectivity. Competitive organizational cultures could cause a peer evaluation system to raise havoc throughout the organization by escalating conflict. This could have detrimental effects on morale and teamwork. Peer feedback systems can only be effective when political considerations and consequences are minimized (meaning that peers have nothing at stake in their assessments of colleagues) and employees have a sense of trust in the organization and its performance measurement system.

Performance feedback from subordinates can provide insights into the interpersonal and managerial styles of employees and can assist the organization in addressing employee developmental needs, particularly for high-potential employees. Subordinate evaluations are also excellent measures of an individual's leadership capabilities. However, subordinate evaluations can suffer from the same political problems as peer evaluations. They can also be used by either the supervisor or subordinates to retaliate against each other. However, in assessing an employee's ability to manage others, valuable performance data pertaining to behavior and skills can be uniquely provided from subordinates.

Because our economy is becoming increasingly service-oriented and because many organizations emphasize customer service as a key competitive and strategic issue, customers are increasingly being sought for feedback on employee performance. In most instances, customers can provide the feedback that is most free from bias: They usually have little or nothing at stake in their assessment of employees. Feedback from customers can be critical for facilitating employee development and determining appropriate rewards because it is most clearly related to the organization's bottom line.

Self-evaluations allow employees to provide their own assessments and measures of their own performance. Although it should be obvious that self-evaluation can be self-serving, allowing employees to evaluate their own performance has at least two important benefits for organizations. First, it can be motivating because it allows the employee to participate in a critical decision that impacts his or her employment and career. Second, the employee can provide insights, examples, and a more holistic assessment of performance than that provided by supervisors or peers, who generally spend a limited time observing and interacting with each employee. Individual employees are far more likely to remember significant examples of effective performance than their supervisors, and they can often provide specific examples of behaviors and outcomes rather than the generalities often cited by supervisors. Individual employees may also be able to provide performance information of which others may be unaware.

Performance management systems that solicit the input and advice of others besides the immediate supervisor are referred to as multirater systems or 360-degree feedback systems. These systems can be beneficial because the organization and employee gain multiple perspectives and insights into the employee's performance. Each of these sources of performance feedback can balance each other relative to any inherent organizational politics that may be at play in the process. However, there is a cost to such systems: They can be very time-consuming and laborious to administer. Data from numerous sources need to be analyzed, synthesized, and, occasionally, reconciled. There is inherently a cost-benefit aspect to any type of multirater performance feedback system.

The more performance data collected, the greater the overall facilitation of the assessment and development of the employee. At the same time, larger volumes of data are costly to collect and process. At some point, the collection of additional data will undoubtedly provide diminishing returns.

The popularity and use of 360-degree feedback programs have increased dramatically in recent years: More than 65 percent of organizations now use some form of multirater feedback, despite the fact that 360-degree feedback programs have been associated with a 10.6 percent decline in shareholder value.[4] The reason appears to be that many organizations have jumped on the 360-degree bandwagon without careful planning and strategizing about why and how the program is being used within the organization. Unless each rater has a consistent view of effective performance relative to the organization's strategy, disagreements can cause unexpected conflicts and problems and result in communication breakdowns that require time to resolve. Despite their popularity, 360-degree feedback programs can create severe problems if not designed, implemented, and managed carefully. The organization's strategy and culture must support such a system. Otherwise, the organization runs the risk of performance problems that will inevitably impact bottom-line profitability and value.

Despite the advantages of multirater systems, collecting additional performance data results in a greater economic cost (relative to opportunity cost of the time of those involved in the process) and a more complex process in attempting to process and analyze the data to provide meaningful feedback to employees. If not designed and implemented carefully, 360-degree feedback systems can result in the collection and processing of excessive amounts of information that provide no benefit to either the organization or the employee. Such data overload can cause the most relevant, critical performance data to be lost or obscured in the process.

The question then becomes how to gain the unique benefits associated with 360-degree feedback while overcoming some of the potential problems associated with the practice. Reading 10.1, "Multisource Feedback: Lessons Learned and Implications for Practice," examines a variety of factors that can impact the outcomes associated with such feedback and illustrates lessons learned in two different organizations that implemented the process.

What to Evaluate

The next strategic question that needs to be addressed involves determining what is to be evaluated. Essentially, employee evaluations can be based on their traits, their behaviors, or the results or outcomes they achieve. Traits-based measures focus on the general abilities and characteristics of the employee. They might include dimensions such as loyalty to the organization, industriousness, and gregariousness. Although assessment of traits can often allow the organization to determine how the employee fits with the organization's culture, such measures ignore what the employee actually *does.* Traits-based measures, therefore, are of limited use or value; the subjective nature of such nonperformance-related criteria would probably not hold up well in court in a discrimination complaint.

Behavior-based measures focus on what an employee does by examining specific behaviors of the employee. Factors assessed here might include the employee's ability to get along with others, punctuality, willingness to take initiative, and ability to meet deadlines. Behavioral measures are very useful for feedback purposes because they specify exactly what the employee is doing correctly and what the employee should do differently. This is critical; work-related behaviors are generally within the control of most employees. However, it is possible for employees to engage in appropriate behaviors but not achieve results for the organization. Although employees may do the right things, their performance may not make a difference for the organization in terms of performance that relates to strategic objectives.

The third basis for performance feedback is to assess outcomes or results. Results-based measures focus on specific accomplishments or direct outcomes of an employee's work. These might include measures of number of units sold, divisional profitability, cost reduction, efficiency, or quality. Unlike traits and behaviors, results-based measures are often criteria than can be measured objectively. More important, results are generally more meaningful to the organization due to their more direct correlation with performance relating to the divisional or organizational strategy.

Although results may be a more significant measure of performance than traits or behaviors, there are some limitations to the utilization of results-based feedback measures. First, it may be difficult to obtain results for certain job responsibilities. Any tasks that involve dealing with the future (i.e., forecasting and planning relative to competition or assessing other dimensions of the external environment) will not show immediate results nor will the quality or accuracy of the work be assessable until sometime in the future. Second, results are sometimes beyond an individual employee's control. Budget cuts and resource availability may be at the discretion of others, but they may impact the employee's ability to generate specific performance objectives. Third, results—taken by themselves—focus on the ends or outcomes while ignoring the means or processes by which the results were obtained. An employee might achieve targeted goals but do so in an unproductive way by incurring excessive costs, alienating coworkers, or damaging customer relations. Finally, results are limiting in that they fail to tap into some critical areas—such as teamwork, initiative, and openness to change—of performance for modern organizations. The need for organizations to remain flexible and responsive to change in their environments requires them to have internal processes to facilitate internal change. Results-based measures would ignore these processes.

As can be seen, all three types of performance measures have some limitations. However, the strengths of one approach can offset the limitations of the others. Nothing prevents an organization from utilizing any combination of traits, behaviors, and results-based measures in attempting to develop a performance feedback system that is in sync with the organization's strategic objectives. In short, the decision of what to evaluate is contingent upon what the organization seeks to achieve.

Strategic Performance Management at Continental Airlines

When Gordon Bethune became CEO of Continental Airlines in the mid-1990s, he faced a daunting challenge. Years of cost-cutting measures had resulted in a consumer image of the airline as unreliable and unpredictable, employees were deeply unhappy and distrustful of management, late and canceled flights were costing Continental $6 million each month, and Continental was dead-last in the Department of Transportation's monthly performance rankings. Bethune decided to implement one overriding measure of performance in this complex work environment and industry to help turn the struggling airline around. He proposed that if Continental were to attain a top-three on-time ranking in the Department of Transportation's monthly rankings, half the cost savings incurred would be split with every nonmanagement employee. No other performance measures were to be considered. This risky strategy paid off well. By the second month of the offer, Continental had moved from last to first in the rankings and each employee enjoyed a $65 bonus. However, as on-time performance improved, the number of lost customer baggage increased. As a result, the program was modified to include baggage handling, with Continental immediately moving into the top three in the rankings for this measure. By 2000, Continental was consistently ranked number one in on-time arrivals among all U.S. airlines and named number one in customer satisfaction in industry surveys. In that year, bonuses of $785 were paid to employees. Continental's program was a resounding success because of the importance of the performance measure to the organization (and industry) and the means by which it was communicated, implemented, and rewarded.[5]

EXHIBIT 10.5 Multilevel Corporate Competency Model

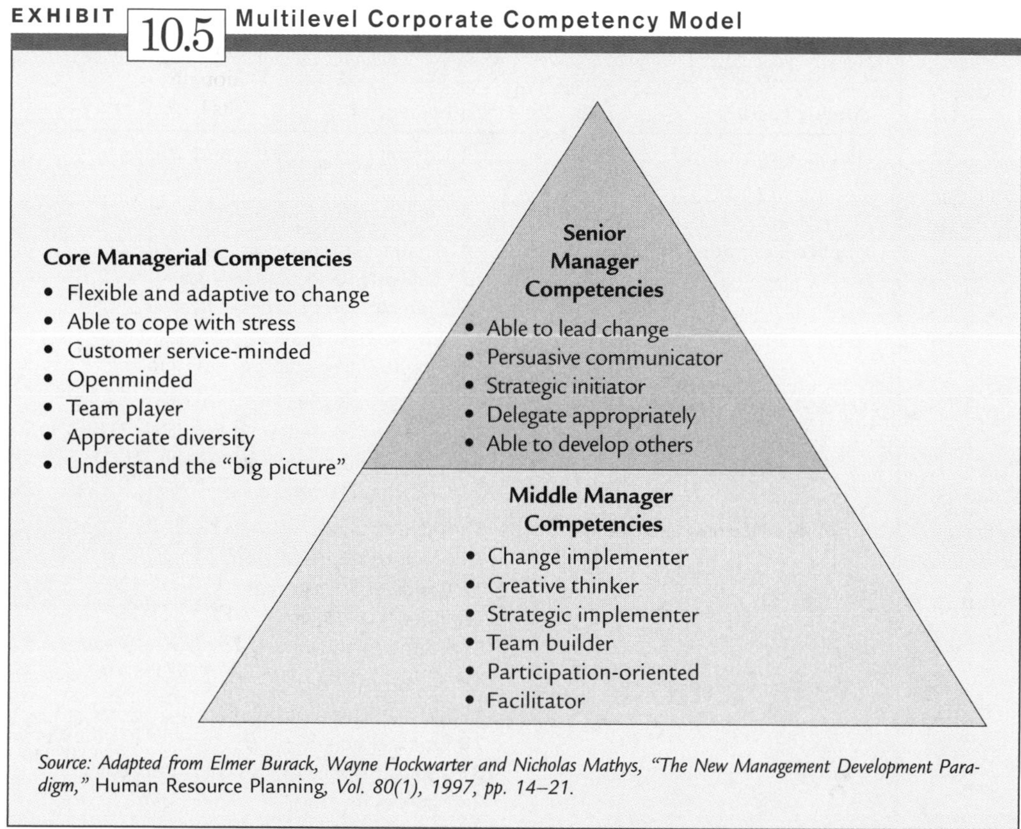

Source: Adapted from Elmer Burack, Wayne Hockwarter and Nicholas Mathys, "The New Management Development Paradigm," Human Resource Planning, *Vol. 80(1), 1997, pp. 14–21.*

In addition to traits, behaviors, and outcomes, one area that employers are beginning to measure is the job performance competencies the employee displays. Competencies can often be closely tied to an organization's strategic objectives and therefore provide a more critical measure of performance—as well as more valuable feedback for employees in their careers. A competency-based performance management program can take a tremendous amount of time to establish, must be communicated clearly to employees, and should also tie in with the organization's reward structure. Core competencies should be limited in number to those most central to the organization's success, and corresponding opportunities should be established by which employees can obtain and build on these competencies. Exhibit 10.5 presents a sample competency model for managers that cuts across organization size and industry.

Competency-Based Performance and Development at Capital One

Capital One is one of the world's fastest-growing consumer credit companies. In 2002, Capital One developed a competency-based performance management system, known as the Success Profile, which is designed to support the organization's strategy and long-term growth objectives. The Success Profile is designed to provide specific measurable performance feedback as well as to allow employees to plan their own professional development activities. The Success Profile contains 23 competencies that are seen as critical to the mission and objectives of Capital One. These competencies are grouped together into five access factors, as illustrated in Exhibit 10.6. Each competency is measured on a behavioral-based rating scale containing up to four stages. Employees receive detailed performance feedback and work with their managers to develop a personal development plan for the future.

EXHIBIT 10.6 Capital One Competencies

Success Factors	Competencies
Builds relationships	1 Communicates clearly and openly 2 Treats others with respect 3 Collaborates with others
Applies integrative thinking	4 Analyzes information 5 Generates and pursues ideas 6 Develops and shapes strategies 7 Identifies and solves problems 8 Applies integrated decision-making
Drives toward results	9 Focuses on strategic priorities 10 Organizes and manages multiple tasks 11 Directs and coordinates work 12 Gets the job done
Leads in a learning environment	13 Recruits talent 14 Motivates and develops 15 Builds and leads teams 16 Influences others 17 Promotes the culture
Takes personal ownership	18 Takes responsibility 19 Learns continuously 20 Embraces change 21 Initiates opportunities for improvement 22 Shows integrity 23 Maintains perspective

How to Evaluate

The next strategic decision that must be addressed in designing the performance management system is how to assess employees. Performance feedback can be performed on an absolute or relative basis. Absolute measures evaluate employees strictly according to the performance requirements or standards of the job; relative measures evaluate employees in comparison to coworkers. Relative measures may further involve slotting employees into categories, such as the top 10 percent of the employees in the work unit receiving an overall outstanding evaluation, similar to what is known in education as grading on a curve.

Relative assessment of employees can be useful in allowing the organization to identify overall top performers, much as high schools provide class rank to their students to facilitate college and university assessments for admission. However, if performance is not normally distributed, skewed results can provide misleading data: If all employees are outstanding performers, some will still be ranked poorly. Conversely, if all employees are deficient in performance, some will still be ranked as outstánding. For example, in a classroom setting, assume that there are 30 students in a class and that on a midterm exam, all 30 students score 90 or above. If performance was ranked on a relative basis, a student who scored 90 would be ranked 30th out of 30, despite the fact that the student did "A" work in absolute means. Similarly, if on the final exam, the highest grade was a 55, that student would be ranked 1st out of 30, despite the fact that, on an absolute basis, the student failed the exam. Relative measures can easily facilitate distorted perceptions of performance when all employees are superior or deficient. Although they are useful in identifying the best employees, they should not be used without some supplementary absolute assessment and ratings that are specifically related to strategic objectives.

One popular—although controversial—means of relative assessment is forced ranking. Forced ranking, or forced distribution, involves placing employees into clusters or groupings based on a distribution schema. Forced ranking is premised on a social science theory that finds that human phenomena tend to distribute normally along a bell-shaped curve when measured by using sufficiently large samples.[6] Forced rankings ideally can help build a high-performance organization by ensuring that managers clearly distinguish among employee performance levels.

Forced ranking systems were pioneered by General Electric (GE) under former CEO Jack Welch. At GE, employees are sorted into three groups: the top 20 percent on whom rewards, promotions, and stock options are showered; the "high performing" middle 70 percent with promising futures; and the bottom 10 percent, whose employment is terminated, either voluntarily or involuntarily.[7] Other large employers who use forced ranking systems include Cisco Systems, Hewlett-Packard, Microsoft, Sun Microsystems, and Pepsico.[8]

Those who favor forced ranking argue that it is the best way to identify both the highest-performing employees, who should receive generous incentives, and bottom performers, who should be helped up or out. It also provides data-driven bases for compensation decisions and forces managers to make and justify sometimes tough decisions and will not allow them to avoid giving employees needed feedback. Critics, however, argue that forced ranking can be arbitrary, unfair, and expose an organization to lawsuits.[9] Ford Motor Company abandoned its practice of forced rankings in 2001 when it settled two class-action lawsuits for $10.5 million.[10] To avoid some of the inherent subjectivity that might come with the final rankings, some employers outsource the final distributions to outside consultants who are able to analyze trends and correct biases in final ratings.[11]

Forced rankings can also help to overcome some problems associated with inflated reviews as well as remedy the dilemma presented when a supervisor rates everyone on a "satisfactory" basis. Most performance management systems leave top performers feeling unrecognized and other employees upset that poor performers are not handled appropriately.[12] Forced ranking prevents these problems, particularly if the system involves measures to terminate consistently low-ranked employees.

While forced rankings may be controversial, they tend to be more effective in organizations with a high-pressure, results-driven culture.[13] Forced rankings are certainly not appropriate for every organization, but in concept, forced rankings are consistent with a strategic approach toward human resource management because they emphasize differentiating employees by performance level and investing more resources in those human assets that have displayed the highest returns.

Measures of Evaluation

Another strategic decision that needs to be made in the design of the performance management system is the means of evaluation. There are a variety of tools or formats to use in measuring performance. These include graphic rating scales, weighted checklists, behaviorally anchored rating scales, behavioral observation scales, critical incident measures, and objectives-based measures.

Graphic rating scales are one of the most widely used assessment and feedback devices. Relatively easy to design, use, and update as job requirements change, they involve a scale that gives the evaluator the performance measures for traits, behaviors, or results. Some examples of graphic rating scales are illustrated in Exhibit 10.7.

Weighted checklists provide the evaluator with specific criteria on which performance is to be assessed and ask the evaluator to check those criteria that apply to the employee. The different dimensions are weighted based on their importance to the organization; weights are unknown to the evaluator as the checklist is being completed. A sample weighted checklist is presented in Exhibit 10.8.

EXHIBIT 10.7 Examples of Graphic Rating Scales

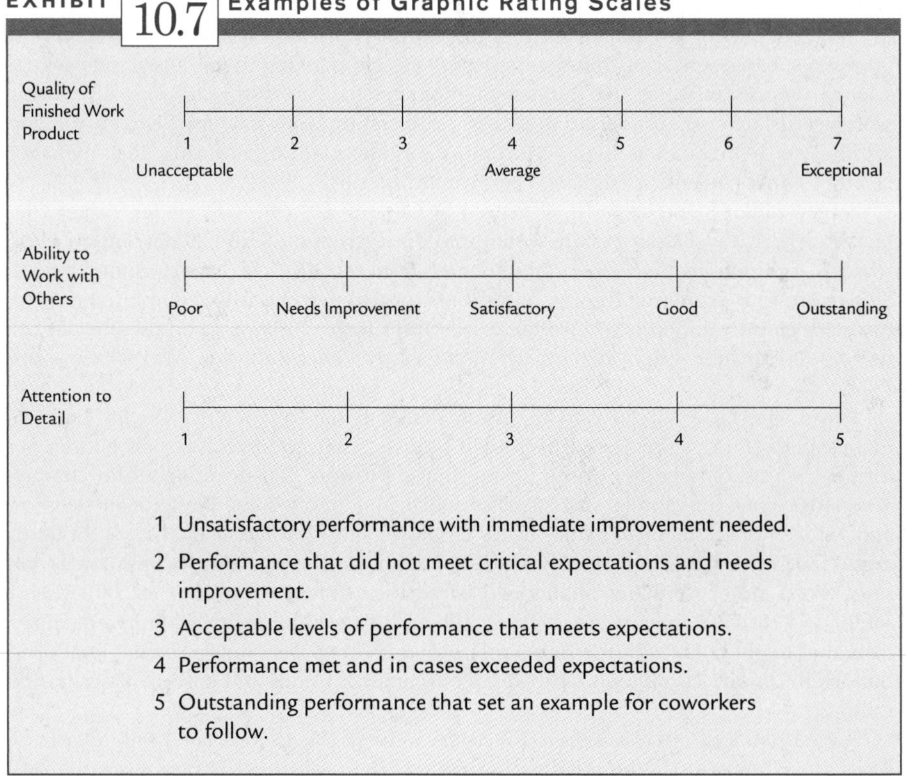

EXHIBIT 10.8 Example of a Weighted Checklist

Instructions: Check all those qualities that are accurate assessments of the employee's performance.

		Weight
____	Is able to address routine day-to-day problems effectively.	4.2
____	Maintains cordial and productive relationships with coworkers.	3.7
____	Displays the ability to delegate effectively and develop subordinates.	4.1
____	Works well without direct supervision.	5.1
____	Is able to meet deadlines and follow through on commitments.	4.8
____	Engages in appropriate activity to further individual career development.	2.9
____	Adheres to rules, procedures, and standard operating protocols.	3.4

Note: The weights are not included on the actual rating form that the evaluator completes. Higher values indicate more critical requirements for the job.

EXHIBIT 10.9 Example of A Behaviorally Anchored Rating Scale

Position: ____________________

Job Dimension: ____________________

Plans work and organizes time carefully in order to maximize resources and meet commitments.	9	
	8	Even though this associate has a report due on another project, he or she would be well-prepared for the assigned discussion on your project.
	7	This associate would keep a calendar or schedule on which deadlines and activities are carefully noted and which would be consulted before making new commitments.
	6	As program chief, this associate would manage arrangements for enlisting resources for a special project reasonably well but would probably omit one or two details that would have to be handled by improvisation.
Plans and organizes time and effort primarily for large segments of a task. Usually meets commitments but may overlook what are considered secondary details.	5	This associate would meet a deadline in handing in a report, but the report might be below the usual standard if other deadlines occur on the same day the report is due.
	4	This associate's evaluations are likely not to reflect abilities because of overcommitments in other activities.
	3	This associate would plan more by enthusiasm than by timetable and frequently have to work late the night before an assignment is due, although it would be completed on time.
	2	This associate would often be late for meetings, although others in similar circumstances do not seem to find it difficult to be on time.
Appears to do little planning. May perform effectively, despite what seems to be a disorganized approach, although deadlines may be missed.	1	This associate never makes a deadline, even with sufficient notice.

Source: Anthony, W. P. et al. Human Resource Management, *3 ed., Dryden, 1999, p. 389.*

A behaviorally anchored rating scale (BARS) is a more specific type of graphic rating scale. The evaluator is given specific descriptions of behaviors along a numerically rated scale and is asked to select the behavior that most corresponds to the employee's performance for the time period being evaluated. A BARS can be difficult and time-consuming to develop, but it can help to overcome some of the subjectivity and biases that may result when evaluators are given no set descriptions for performance measures. A sample BARS is presented in Exhibit 10.9.

A potential problem with a BARS may be that an employee's behavior is inconsistent. Sometimes, the employee might merit a 6 on a scale of 1 to 7; at other times, performance would be closer to 2. A behavioral observation scale (BOS) addresses the problem of inconsistent employee performance by measuring frequencies along the scale. Instead of providing examples of different behaviors as would be presented in a BARS, a BOS determines which behavior of a BARS is optimal and asks for an assessment of the frequency with which the employee displays it. A sample BOS is presented in Exhibit 10.10.

EXHIBIT 10.10 Example of a Behavioral Observation Scale

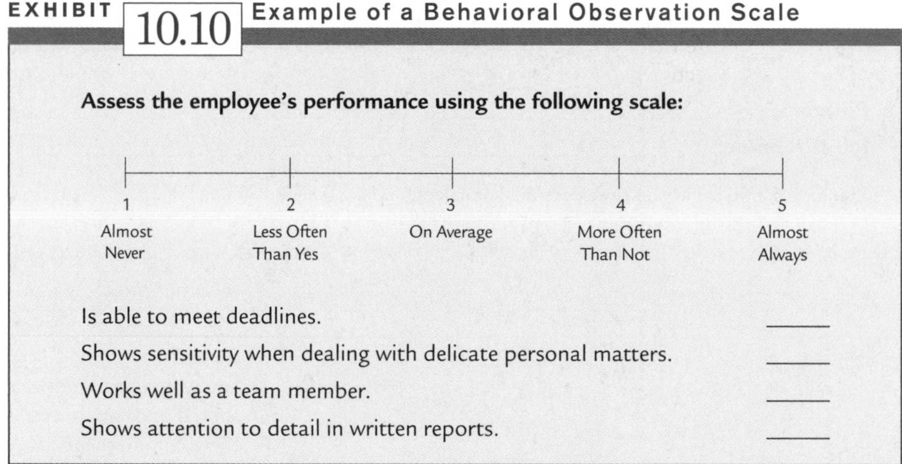

Critical incident measures do not generally utilize a scale. The evaluator provides specific examples of the employee's critical behaviors or results—either outstanding or problematic—during the performance period. The evaluator must maintain a log or diary for each employee and make periodic notation of noteworthy behaviors or results that were particularly effective or ineffective. This process can be very time-consuming, but it allows the feedback to cite specific examples of performance measures instead of general impressions. Feedback that is specific and directed is not only more meaningful to the employee, but it can also be targeted to specific objectives of the work unit or organization. The critical incident technique can be utilized by itself or incorporated into a rating scale where space is provided for open-ended comments by the evaluator.

A final way to assess performance is to base feedback on predetermined, negotiated work objectives. Traditionally called *management by objectives (MBO)*, this process involves having the employee meet with his or her immediate supervisor prior to the time period for which performance is to be assessed. The two parties jointly agree on the employee's work objectives for the forthcoming time period. The process of negotiation is important here. Ideally, this process involves setting objectives that are simultaneously consistent with the organization's strategy and satisfy job requirements and also provide challenging work assignments that are consistent with the employee's developmental needs and career aspirations.

Objectives-based performance management systems are based on a goal-setting theory, which was pioneered by Edwin Locke.[14] Goal-setting theory assumes that motivation is enhanced when individuals work toward a specific, targeted goal or goals and also receive feedback as to their progress toward reaching their goals.[15] Even though objectives are determined for a set time period, commonly six months or one year, this does not mean that performance feedback should be withheld until the end of the time period. Informal, regular feedback is more effective; particularly when it is provided immediately following some outcome or behavior, it has a far stronger and more constant impact on motivation than feedback that is only provided annually in a more formal manner.

Objectives-based performance measurement systems often result in enhanced employee motivation because employees are allowed to provide input in determining their job responsibilities and in discussing critical organizational goals to which they can contribute.[16] Employee commitment is also usually enhanced; employees can be expected to be far more committed to reaching performance objectives that they have agreed to and negotiated for themselves rather than having objectives determined for them by the organization.[17] When an employee participates in this process, the employee's trust and dependability are placed on the line. Nonperformance cannot be as readily dismissed through claims that the supervisor does not understand the job or the pressures inherently involved with it or that the objectives set were therefore unrealistic.

Three common oversights can inhibit the effectiveness of any objectives-based feedback system. These oversights are: (1) setting objectives that are too vague; (2) setting objectives that are unrealistically difficult; and (3) not clarifying how performance will be measured, particularly when the objective itself is not quantifiable and requires some subjectivity in evaluation. Any objectives set as part of such a process must be specific, measurable, and within the employee's control if the feedback system is to be beneficial to the organization and to the employee. Objectives also need to be challenging yet obtainable. Unrealistic goals may hamper motivation; supervisors need to have faith in their employees' abilities yet realize where to draw the line. When the objectives are set, the parties must also reach agreement as to how the performance criteria will be measured and assessed. This is particularly important when there are no objective measures available for assessing performance.

The objectives selected must also be valid. Much as selection measures need to be valid, objective performance measures must be also valid. Occasionally, inappropriate objective measures may be selected. These measures may be easily quantifiable and accurately measurable but not directly related to performance. For example, a teacher could be evaluated on the test scores of students. Although this is an objective measure, it might encourage the teacher to teach students to maximize test scores rather than learn. A salesperson could similarly be evaluated on sales volume, which is easily measurable, but not get evaluated on expenses incurred, customer service, returns, or professional demeanor. Most employees will focus on the behavior or outcome that is evaluated and rewarded at the expense of other elements of the job.[18]

These various means of measuring performance are not mutually exclusive. Nothing prevents an organization from using some combination of methods. However, it should be remembered that much like the decision of who should provide performance feedback, more is not necessarily better. Organizations need to ensure that the methods employed in measuring performance are not cumbersome, contradictory, or excessively laborious. The methods of providing performance data must be consistent with the uses of the system and the organization's strategic objectives.

Other Considerations

In addition to the five strategic design decisions previously outlined, several other critical factors must be considered when developing an effective performance management system. First, the organization needs to ensure the link between the performance management system and the training and development and compensation systems. This link was explained in Chapter 9, but it bears reiteration here. Training and development goals and objectives must be reflected in performance feedback systems. Subsequently, the criteria by which performance is evaluated must be incorporated into the compensation or reward system. If either of these two links is not established and maintained, the performance management system will be of limited value. The performance management system lies within the much larger framework of human resource management systems and must be conceptualized and designed with this strategic perspective in mind.

Traditional performance evaluation systems stress the most recent, immediate time period and evaluate individual employee performance. However, many organizations have strategic initiatives that involve long-range planning and growth, requiring the use of criteria that cannot be measured based on performance during the immediate past time period. In addition, many organizations are moving toward more flexible job assignments and responsibilities. Organizations having self-managed work teams place more responsibility for performance on the group rather than at the individual level. Traditional means of performance evaluation may need to be significantly recast in the light of changes taking place in contemporary organizations. There are few, if any, models of evaluation systems that can assess work responsibilities associated with longer-range objectives or team-based evaluation. Reading 10.2, "Managing the Life Cycle of Virtual Teams," provides some insights as to how teams—specifically increasingly popular virtual teams—function and the implications that team life cycle stages have for the management of team performance.

A final consideration is the degree of standardization or flexibility of the performance management system. Standardization is important to prevent job bias or allegations of discriminatory treatment. Flexibility in the system is important because jobs have different levels of responsibility and accountability and require different types and mixes of skills (technical, interpersonal, or administrative). Organizations need to strike a balance between having some consistency (standardization) and some variance (flexibility) in their performance feedback systems. The single-most important criterion in addressing this issue is the nature of the job responsibilities assigned to the employee. Specific job-related criteria are not only most meaningful for feedback and developmental purposes but are also most defendable under the law. This does not imply that each individual job should have a unique means and method for measuring performance. That is clearly impractical and unrealistic. It does mean, however, that there is no one appropriate way to develop a performance management system in any organization; the system must be tailored to the objectives of the organization.

Why Performance Management Systems Often Fail

Despite the importance of performance management systems, many managers and executives are not committed to providing performance feedback. The process is often seen as time-consuming and cumbersome and can make managers uncomfortable. This dissatisfaction is also seen in the HR suite. One survey of HR directors and executives found that 90 percent felt that their performance management system needed reform.[19] Exhibit 10.11 outlines some of the reasons managers may resist—or totally ignore—performance management processes.

First, many managers are disheartened by the complexity of the process. Performance data may be subject to multiple levels of review and/or require the collection of large amounts of data that must be analyzed and condensed. A system that requires the collection of data from multiple individuals may further require that contradictory and/or inconsistent feedback be reconciled. Second, unless the performance management process involves some planning by which managers and subordinates use the performance data to set clear goals for future performance, there may be little, if any, impact on subsequent job performance. An ideal performance management system connects data about recent past performance to future plans that incorporate the employee's career goals and the strategic goals of the organization and/or unit. Third, when salary, promotion, and retention decisions are made based on performance management data, claims of unlawful discrimination may be made by employees who did not feel appropriately rewarded. The inherently subjective nature of performance management data fuels this possibility and, as a result, may cause organizations to limit the performance feedback given and/or how such feedback is used. Fourth, many managers feel that they have little control over the process by which they manage their subordinates' performance. When standards related to expectations of the end results are set by senior management, managers may feel that the process is less than legitimate. Fifth, employees and managers alike lament the fact that many performance management systems are totally divorced from the organization's reward system. If there are no consequences, results, or outcomes from the performance management process, it most likely will be shortchanged and not taken seriously by those at all levels in the organization. Finally, the

EXHIBIT 10.11 Reasons Managers Resist or Ignore Performance Managment

- Process is too complicated
- No impact on job performance
- Possible legal challenges
- Lack of control over process
- No connection with rewards
- Complexity and length of forms

Source: Adapted from Grensing-Pophal, L. "Motivate Managers to Review Performance," HR Magazine, *March 2001, pp. 45–48.*

EXHIBIT 10.12 Strategies for Improving the Performance Management System

- Involve managers in the design of the system
- Hold managers accountable for the performance and development of their subordinates
- Set clear expectations for performance
- Set specific objectives for the system
- Tie performance measures to rewards
- Gain commitment from senior management

forms and paperwork that often accompany the performance management system can be lengthy and complex. A process that takes managers away from their day-to-day responsibilities for an unduly long time may result in them looking for shortcuts that compromise the efficacy and integrity of the overall process.

Addressing the Shortcomings of Performance Management Systems

The challenge then becomes how to get buy-in from managers to improve the performance management system. Exhibit 10.12 highlights some strategies for addressing some of the managerial reluctance or resistance to fully commit to performance management. First, managers should be involved in the design of the system. Because they are its true users, their input as "consumers" should be sought to facilitate the design of a system that works both for them and the organization. Second, managers should be held accountable for the performance of their subordinates as well as for the development of their direct reports. By tying managers' performance in meeting organization and divisional goals to their effective use of the performance management system, managers are more likely to take the system seriously. Third, clear expectations should be set for individual performance at all levels of performance review to facilitate a timely review of recent performance data and allow more specific feedback to be provided to employees. Fourth, the organization should identify the specific purpose and goals of its performance management system. Clarification of the relationship of the system to the organization's strategy makes the system more salient and relevant to organizational participants and further legitimizes the entire process. Fifth, performance measures should be clearly linked to rewards, solidifying the legitimacy of the system. Finally, absolute commitment to the performance management system needs to be gained from top management. One recent survey found that at the executive level, 42 percent of executives do not even review the performance management system at all.[20] When senior managers publicly support and personally use the performance management system, a strong message is sent regarding its importance to all employees.

Commitment of top management to the process of performance management as well as to the specific process used by the organization sends a strong message to employees and influences a performance-based culture. Reading 10.3, "Performance Leadership: 11 Better Practices That Can Ratchet Up Performance," provides a unique perspective on performance management by considering the role of leadership and associated activities or practices that can spur improvements in and commitment to performance. While the reading focuses on public sector management, the practices cited can be applied to all organizations.

Conclusion

Performance management systems can significantly impact organizational performance and processes. However, there is single one optimal way to develop and design an effective performance management system. Organizations face a number of strategic choices as to how they measure performance and provide employees feedback on the process.

Although effective performance management systems need to be developed within the context of specific organizational contingencies, five critical guidelines should be followed in any performance management system: (1) Any feedback provided to employees should be specific rather than general; (2) feedback should only be provided from credible, trustworthy sources that have ample opportunity and background to make an assessment of performance; (3) feedback should be provided as soon as possible after events, behaviors, or outcomes take place to be of maximum benefit; (4) performance measures should be based on clear, measurable goals; and (5) the process should involve a dialogue between the employee and the manager that addresses the most recent period and also plans for the future.

Critical Thinking

1. Identify the major strategic issues an employer faces in designing a performance management system.
2. What are the major purposes of a performance management system? To what extent can all the purposes be realized simultaneously?
3. What are the advantages and disadvantages of 360-degree feedback systems? How should an organization decide whose feedback to seek?
4. Describe the strengths and weaknesses of traits, behaviors, and outcomes-based measurements. For what kinds of positions is each appropriate?
5. Do performance management systems usually measure the right things? How can performance management systems encourage performance that is more consistent with long-range rather than short-term issues?
6. Devise an appropriate performance management system for your current position.
7. Debate the pros and cons of forced rankings. What kinds of organizations would most benefit from forced ranking systems?
8. How does performance appraisal differ from performance feedback?

Reading 10.1

9. What recommendation can be provided to an organization considering the implementation of a 360-degree feedback system? What limitations exist to the success of these programs?

Reading 10.2

10. What are the stages of a virtual team's life cycle, and what performance issues arise during the life cycle stages?

Reading 10.3

11. How can leaders influence the creation of a performance-based culture in an organization?

Exercises

1. Individually or in small groups, select one occupation from the following list and then design a performance management system for this position.
   - University professor
   - Convenience store clerk
   - Attorney
   - Marriage counselor
   - Software engineer
   - Clergy member
2. Develop a competency-based performance management system for a student in the degree program in which you are enrolled. How would you go about determining and measuring important competencies? What benefits might such a system provide?
3. In an organization of your choosing, briefly interview three managers who work in different divisions/departments/units and are at different levels of managerial responsibility. How does each feel about performance management in the organization?
4. This chapter begins with a description of a 360-degree performance management system that is administered on an intranet. What are the pros and cons of an intranet-based performance management system compared to a paper-based system? Investigate the costs of moving a traditional, paper-based performance management system to an online system in economic terms, technical terms, and human terms.

Chapter References

1. Grote, D. *Forced Ranking*, Harvard Business School Press, 2005.
2. Johnson, C. "Making Sure Employees Measure Up," *HR Magazine*, March 2001, pp. 36–41.
3. Carson, K. P., Cardy, R. L. and Dobbins, G. H. "Performance Appraisal as Effective Management or Deadly Management Disease: Two Empirical Investigations," *Group and Organization Studies*, 16, 1991, pp. 143–159.
4. Pfau, B. and Kay, I. "Does 360-Degree Feedback Negatively Affect Company Performance" *HR Magazine*, June 2002, pp. 55–59.
5. Morgan, I. and Rao, J. "Aligning Service Strategy through Super-Measure Management," *Academy of Management Executive*, 16, (4), 2002, pp. 121–135.
6. Guralnik, O. and Wardi, L. "Forced Distribution: A Controversy," www.shrm.org/research/articles/articles/pages/CMS_005247.aspx.
7. Grote, D. "Are Most Layoffs Carried Out Fairly? Yes," www.mbadepot.com/content/2756.
8. Ibid.
9. Guralnik, O. and Wardi, L. "Forced Distribution: A Controversy," www.shrm.org/research/articles/articles/pages/CMS_005247.aspx.
10. Bates, S. "Forced Ranking," *HR Magazine*, July 2003, pp. 63–68.
11. Guralink, O. and Wardi, L. "Forced Distribution: A Controversy," www.shrm.org/research/articles/articles/pages/CMS_005247.aspx.
12. Grote, D. *Forced Ranking*, Harvard Business School Press, 2005.
13. Bates, S. "Forced Ranking," *HR Magazine*, July 2003, pp. 63–68.
14. Locke, E. "Toward a Theory of Task Moves and Incentives," *Organizational Behavior and Human Performance*, 3, 1968, pp. 157–189.
15. Pinder, C. *Work Motivation*, Glenview, IL: Scott Foresman, 1984.
16. Ibid.
17. Ibid.
18. Kerr. S. "On the Folly of Rewarding A, While Hoping for B," *Academy of Management Journal*, 18, 1975, pp. 766–783.
19. Grensing-Pophal, L. "Motivate Managers to Review Performance," *HR Magazine*, May 2001, pp. 45–48.
20. "Performance Management Gaps Need Filled, Survey Says" *HR News*, November 2000, pp. 14, 21.

READING 10.1

Multisource Feedback: Lessons Learned and Implications for Practice

Leanne E. Atwater, Joan F. Brett, and Atira Cherise Charles

Organizations around the world are using multisource, or 360-degree, feedback. Although many HR practitioners embrace it as an important mechanism for leadership development, organizations must attend to and address several issues in order to maximize the utility of multisource feedback (MSF). We discuss current research findings and highlight issues for managers to consider both before starting a multisource feedback process and after the feedback is given, plus we review potential outcomes of the process. We also describe lessons learned from an intensive three-year investigation of an MSF implementation in two organizations.

Introduction

Multisource feedback (MSF), also known as 360-degree feedback, is a process in which a leader receives anonymous feedback from subordinates, peers, bosses, and customers. MSF is pervasive throughout U.S. organizations and is spreading to other parts of the world. Estimates indicate that as many as 29% of U.S. organizations (Church, 2000) are using this process. Many organizations embrace the 360-degree feedback process as part of their overall leadership development programs. However, recent research suggests that results may be modest. Smither, London, and Reilly (2005) analyzed the results of 24 longitudinal studies on MSF and concluded, "Practitioners should not expect large, widespread performance improvements after employees receive multi-source feedback" (p. 33). While their results found modest, yet positive improvements in employee behaviors and attitudes, practitioners that seek ways to increase the effectiveness of their firm's MSF interventions can look to the existing and current research on MSF processes.

The purpose of this article is to outline recent studies on MSF in order to inform practice and increase the likelihood that more leaders and organizations will benefit from this developmental process. Our intentions are threefold. First, we highlight research knowledge in the area of MSF. Second, we describe all we have learned from an intensive three-year investigation of an MSF implementation in two organizations. Third, we discuss the implications of MSF research for leaders and human resource professionals in the field. Where appropriate, we indicate where MSF research has relevance to performance appraisal (PA), since both processes involve feedback.

Figure 1 presents a framework for presenting recent research on MSF. The framework includes factors that HR practitioners should consider prior to implementation, factors to consider about the actual MSF process, factors to consider after leaders receive feedback, and outcomes that organizations can anticipate. For each of these topic areas, a table summarizes the MSF findings and applications for practice. The issues noted in italics in Figure 1 and the tables indicate results from our three-year study.

We also highlight those areas in which findings from the literature on performance appraisal (PA) and MSF are similar. While this article is not intended to summarize the vast literature on PA, there are areas in which practitioners interested in MSF can learn from the PA literature. However, for the most part, MSF has been designed and implemented as a developmental rather than evaluative process. Unlike MSF, PAs are often linked to administrative purposes and have consequences for merit increases and promotion and layoff decisions. In addition, PA traditionally relies upon a supervisor evaluation, whereas MSF relies on multiple, often anonymous sources. Because of these differences, many of the findings pertinent to MSF are not particularly relevant to PA (e.g., anonymity, confidentiality, time involved in the process, method of feedback distribution). In addition, one of the purposes of this article is to highlight findings from a three-year study of MSF that has limited relevance to PA. Throughout the article, however, we will indicate findings that should have relevance for both MSF and PA.

Factors to Consider Before Feedback

Organizational Context

MSF can be initiated by an individual leader as a means of self-development. More commonly, an organization or unit embarks on an MSF process because of pressing needs for its leaders to engage in different behaviors to respond to organizational challenges. Often, an MSF process becomes one of several approaches to resolving organizational issues. Under

FIGURE 1 Issues to Consider in a Multisource Feedback Process

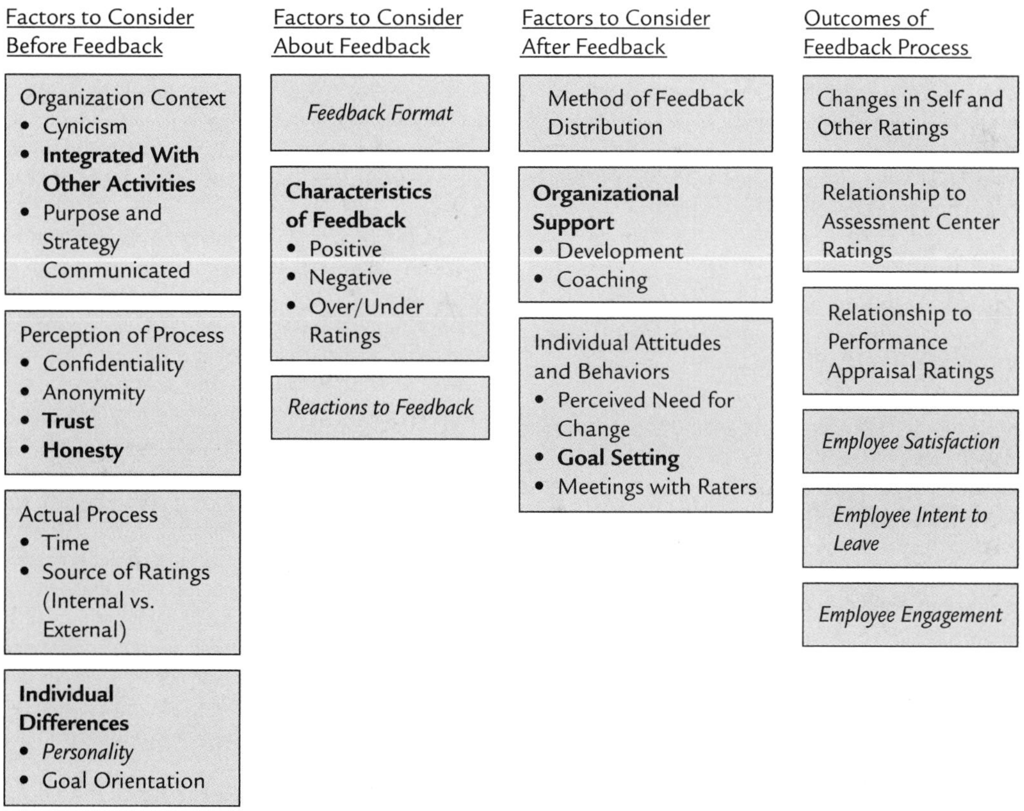

Factors to Consider Before Feedback

Organization Context
- Cynicism
- **Integrated With Other Activities**
- Purpose and Strategy Communicated

Perception of Process
- Confidentiality
- Anonymity
- **Trust**
- **Honesty**

Actual Process
- Time
- Source of Ratings (Internal vs. External)

Individual Differences
- *Personality*
- Goal Orientation

Factors to Consider About Feedback

Feedback Format

Characteristics of Feedback
- Positive
- Negative
- Over/Under Ratings

Reactions to Feedback

Factors to Consider After Feedback

Method of Feedback Distribution

Organizational Support
- Development
- Coaching

Individual Attitudes and Behaviors
- Perceived Need for Change
- **Goal Setting**
- Meetings with Raters

Outcomes of Feedback Process

Changes in Self and Other Ratings

Relationship to Assessment Center Ratings

Relationship to Performance Appraisal Ratings

Employee Satisfaction

Employee Intent to Leave

Employee Engagement

Note: **Bold** indicates findings that apply to PA and MSF, *Italics* indicate findings that were part of the three-year study described in this article.

these circumstances, developmental feedback may reinforce positive leadership change or may garner resistance. How well the feedback process works depends, in part, on the organizational context surrounding its implementation. For example, organizations considering serious restructuring or downsizing are not in a good position to begin implementing MSF, because they will have difficulty garnering the trust needed from participants in the midst of serious organizational change. Additionally, organizational cynicism (e.g., employees believe efforts to change are not worth it, or positive change is not possible) can interfere with the success of the MSF intervention. Atwater, Waldman, Atwater, and Cartier (2000) found that MSF participants who were cynical were less likely to improve following MSF ($r = -.25, p < .10$).

In a study of MSF practices in more than 100 organizations (Brutus & Derayeh, 2002), 19% of the companies indicated that the absence of integration of the MSF process with other human resources systems (i.e., development, performance appraisal, training support) created resistance to the MSF process. HR practitioners must do more than obtain organizational commitment to the MSF process; they also need to assist all MSF participants in understanding how the feedback intervention fits with the organizations' initiatives and goals and how the process aligns with other HR activities. This finding holds for performance appraisal as well. In a review of the PA literature, Bretz Jr., Milkovich, and Read (1992) concluded that we need a better understanding of how organizational context affects performance appraisal issues. Employees need to see how the results of their PA fit with rewards and development opportunities offered in the organization (Heneman & Gresham, 1998).

Research also suggests the importance of clear and careful implementation strategies (e.g., meetings with leaders and their raters to discuss the process, its purpose, and implementation) (Waldman & Atwater, 1998). In these meetings, leaders and raters can ask questions and should have their anxieties relieved about anonymity, confidentiality, and the developmental purpose of the process.

London (2001) addresses the lively debate surrounding the decision to use MSF for development or administrative decisions. He concludes that "feedback can be used for both developmental and administrative purposes, but this takes time" (p. 383). MSF works best when used (at least initially, e.g., for 2–4 rounds) for developmental purposes rather than evaluative purposes. That is, organizations should not require feedback recipients to share their feedback results with bosses, nor should they use their ratings for decision purposes such as raises or other outcomes. Once managers and employees are able to trust the process, it can be carefully (e.g., used in addition to other indicators) incorporated into personnel decision making. Managers tend to want to rush into using MSF for evaluation, as they often believe that without accountability managers will be less likely to change. Patience is encouraged.

Perceptions of the Process

Consistent research findings indicate that acceptance and trust in appraisal and feedback processes are critical for those involved in a feedback process (cf., Longnecker, Sims, & Gioia, 1987). Several factors influence acceptance and resistance to the process.

Rater anonymity among peer and subordinate raters has been shown to be important to promote honest responding (Brutus & Derayeh, 2002). Subordinate raters are often wary that the leader will somehow trace their responses back to them. If their ratings are low or unfavorable, raters may fear retaliation. Thus, if raters do not trust that ratings will be anonymous, they may choose not to rate the leader, or may inflate their ratings to avoid confrontation or reprisals. Antonioni (1994) found that employees who believe their ratings are anonymous are likely to give more honest feedback than are employees who think their responses will be associated with them. To increase raters' perceptions of anonymity, HR practitioners may want to ensure that only leaders with feedback from three or more subordinates participate in the MSF process. Facilitators working with feedback recipients should emphasize to them that it is problematic if they try to attribute ratings or comments to one of their subordinates, as they are very often wrong.

Recipients must believe in the confidentiality of the feedback and that they are the only ones who will see it if they are to trust the process. If they believe that the feedback will be shared without their knowledge, it will create distrust and problems for accurate rating and effective responses to the feedback.

Individual Differences and Responses to Feedback

Characteristics of the leader may influence how he/she responds to and uses the feedback. Funderburg and Levy (1997) reported that individuals with high self-esteem reported more favorable attitudes toward the MSF system than those with low self-esteem ($r = .27$, $p < .05$). Feedback recipients that rate themselves higher on receptivity and the desire to make a good first impression were perceived by feedback providers as having more positive reactions to their feedback (Ryan, Brutus, Greguras, & Hakel, 2000).

Smither, London, and Richmond (2005) examined the influence of leaders' personality traits on their reactions to MSF. Extroverted leaders who were open to experience were more likely to perceive and view negative feedback as valuable. Additionally, they were most likely to seek further information about their feedback. Leaders with an internal locus of control (i.e., those who believe they have some control over what happens to them) also reacted to peer and subordinate feedback more favorably and intended to improve their skills (Funderburg & Levy, 1997; Maurer & Palmer, 1999). Colquitt, LePine, and Noe (2000) found that people were more motivated to use PA feedback for development when they were conscientious and when they had high self-efficacy, an internal locus of control, and low anxiety.

Dispositional goal orientation also may influence whether an individual views feedback as a development opportunity or a challenge to his or her self-perception. Individuals with a learning goal orientation tend to hold a view of ability as modifiable and believe they are capable of improving their level of abilities. Individuals with a performance goal orientation view ability as fixed and uncontrollable (Dweck, 1986). These goal orientations are associated with different responses to feedback (Dweck & Leggett, 1988). Brett and Atwater (2001) reported that goal orientation was not related to immediate reactions to MSF. However, several weeks later, those with a learning goal orientation believed the feedback was more useful than those with a performance goal orientation. Heslin and Latham (2004) found that leaders with higher learning goal orientation showed higher ratings than those with lower learning goal orientation. However, six months later, learning goal orientation did not moderate change in behavior between their initial and subsequent ratings.

Self-efficacy is an individual's belief in his or her capability to engage in actions required to achieve successful performance levels (Bandura, 1997). Individuals with high self-efficacy focus attention on analyzing solutions to problems, whereas those low in self-efficacy have evaluative concerns and dwell on their personal failures. Individuals with high self-efficacy are more likely to cope and engage in activities in response to the challenges and adjustments at work (Raghuram, Wiesenfeld, & Garud, 2003). Maurer, Mitchell, and Barbeite (2002) found that those with higher self-efficacy held more positive attitudes toward MSF ($r = .32$, $p < .001$) and participated more in developmental activities off the job ($r = .19$, $p < .05$) than those with lower self-efficacy. Heslin and Latham (2004) found that after controlling for initial feedback those with higher self-efficacy showed more improvement after six months.

The research on individual differences and responses to MSF and PA feedback suggests that individuals will differ in their reactions and responses to developmental feedback. Individuals who conduct feedback sessions and deliver feedback should be sensitive to individual differences. Some individuals are proactive in their response to feedback, while others will need assistance in using the feedback for development. Facilitators will need to spend more time with some leaders to assist them in overcoming their initial reactions to the feedback. They should discuss strategies for overcoming any initial negative reactions and motivate leaders to focus on the developmental aspects of the feedback and the actions they could take in response to the feedback.

Actual Process

Time and effort associated with MSF may deter continued use, particularly due to the overloading of the bosses of the leader participants. Bosses may have 10 or more individuals reporting to them. A boss that rates each employee would incur a substantial burden of time and effort. One practical solution is to have the boss rate only half of the supervisors each year. This tactic works quite well when the MSF process has been in place for some time (Brutus & Derayeh, 2002).

Some researchers suggest that in addition to internal stakeholders, external stakeholders should be a part of the MSF process. Testa (2002) suggests that along with employees, an MSF leadership assessment should include customers, suppliers, and business partners. Testa (2002) contends that MSF will identify misalignment between internal and external stakeholders, which in turn can help develop relationships between them. However, HR practitioners should evaluate whether the costs of gathering external data justify the benefits.

Many companies seeking to minimize the time and costs associated with paper feedback surveys have turned to electronic means of data collection. Companies, such as Otis Elevator Co., that use the Internet as the primary response mode believe that it adds security and confidentiality to the MSF process, while offering a more speedy and convenient method (Huet-Cox, Nielsen, & Sundstrom, 1999). Smither, Walker, and Yap (2004) found no differences in ratees' feedback scores as a function of how the data were collected (e.g., electronically versus paper and pencil). Although electronic data collection has merits, we caution against using this as the sole means of feedback distribution.

Factors to Consider About Feedback

Characteristics of Feedback and Recipient Reactions

The MSF process is a very different experience for leaders who receive positive feedback compared to those who receive negative feedback. Feedback recipients view positive ratings as more accurate and useful than negative ratings (Brett & Atwater, 2001; Facteau, Facteau, Shoel, Russell, & Poteet, 1998). Reactions to positive and negative performance appraisal feedback also vary widely (Taylor, Fisher, & Ilgen, 1984). In a review of the performance evaluation and pay-for-performance literature, Rynes, Gerhart, and Parks (2005) state that stronger performance gains may result after negative feedback, but this finding does not hold when an individual focuses on the self and not the task or task learning.

Negative reactions to less-than-positive feedback may reflect transitory mood states or may have serious ramifications for how feedback recipients will use their feedback. Smither, London, and Richmond (2005) found that leaders who received unfavorable feedback initially had negative reactions, but six months later they had set more improvement goals than other leaders. They suggested "negative feedback may take awhile to sink in or recipients may need some time to reflect and absorb the feedback" (p. 203) after the initial emotions have sub-sided. Brett and Atwater (2001) found that individuals who received negative feedback from bosses and peers were discouraged and angry (r = −38, −.25 respectively, $p < .01$). These same individuals also perceived the feedback as less accurate or useful. However, the impact of initial reactions dissipated after several weeks, and feedback sign was not related to perceived feedback usefulness. These research findings suggest the special challenges HR practitioners face in getting recipients to respond constructively to negative feedback (whether PA or MSF) and highlight the importance of planned interventions to assist feedback recipients in working with their feedback.

Managers' reactions to feedback may relate not only to the positive and negative nature of the feedback, but also to the extent to which the feedback is discrepant from the manager's self-view. Several theories, such as control theory (Carver & Scheier, 1990) and feedback intervention theory (Kluger & DeNisi, 1996), suggest that when individuals detect a discrepancy between behavior and a personal standard, they are motivated to reduce the discrepancy. Taylor et al. (1984) proposed that when self-ratings and other ratings are discrepant, individuals may make changes in order to align their evaluations from others with their self-view, or they may rationalize or discount the ratings from others. Brett and Atwater (2001) found that overratings on a 360-degree instrument (self-ratings were higher than those from others) were related to negative reactions ($r = .26$, $p < .001$) as well as to perceptions that the feedback was not accurate ($r = .16$, $p < .05$). Individuals who gave themselves lower ratings than those received from others reported fewer negative reactions. With respect to PA, Klimoski and Jones (1989) found that when self-rating is substantially higher than supervisor ratings, it may strengthen the ratees' confidence in his or her own ratings and decrease acceptance of the supervisor's rating.

Factors to Consider After Feedback

Method of Feedback Distribution

Two themes emerged from the limited literature on the methods of MSF distribution—ease of process and inducement of trust. Operations and management science scholars have investigated online feedback distribution in the context of online transactions. They found that online feedback mechanisms promote anonymity, which in turn increases the amount of trust among the users (Bolton, Katok, & Ockenfels, 2004; Dellarocas, 2003). Online MSF delivery may increase employees' perceptions of trust in the authenticity of their feedback.

Kamen (2003) discusses several benefits to online MSF distribution. In a case study and in interviews with MSF users and consultants, he suggests that online distribution facilitates the ability to integrate with HR software and technology, to invite and facilitate participation, to submit feedback data online, and to have speedy data analysis and distribution. Kamen further suggests that off-site processing and the integrity and respectability of the in-house contact person (receiver and distributor) increases the confidence and trust of those receiving the feedback. This may be an effective distribution method; however, we do not recommend online feedback delivery without facilitation and support in processing the feedback.

Organizational Support

Many organizations spend considerable time and money in the data collection phase of an MSF process, involving employees throughout all levels of the organization, yet pay little attention to encouraging or requiring feedback recipients to participate in any developmental activities or discussions using the feedback they received. The same is often true of performance appraisal feedback (Levy & Williams, 2004; London, 2003). Healy, Walsh, and Rose (2003) conducted a survey of 53 companies using MSF and found that the majority did not require follow-up activities, and as few as 20% required feedback recipients to discuss their results with a supervisor. However, according to their survey, many organizations provide voluntary opportunities for feedback recipients to receive coaching (55%) or attend developmental workshops (70%). In a survey on MSF practices, Brutus and Derayeh (2002) found that the majority of MSF programs (70%) had some tie to development activities. While many companies rely on voluntary participation in follow-up and developmental activities, our experience is that they are rarely used. The following research suggests that follow-up activities after feedback are critical.

Feedback recipients who perceived support from coworkers and supervisors for development-related activities reported more positive attitudes toward the feedback system and were involved in more on- and off-the-job development activities after the receipt of MSF (Maurer et al., 2002). Mabey (2001) studied participants in an MSF program compared to nonparticipants in terms of their perceptions of the training and development offered by the organization. Participants in the MSF process believed that they received more regular feedback on performance, received more recognition for developing skills, and had more opportunities for training than nonparticipants. Participants also were more satisfied with their training and their employer than were nonparticipants. This suggests that the MSF process can have benefits that extend beyond individual awareness and development.

Reinforcing MSF with training or coaching has been found to enhance the benefits of the feedback process. Seifert, Yukl, and McDonald (2003) examined the effects of MSF and a training workshop on managerial influence tactics. They compared managers in three conditions (no MSF and no training, MSF and no training, and MSF and training) and found that managers who received MSF and training on influence tactics increased their use of influence tactics with direct reports. Managers who worked with an executive coach to understand their feedback set more specific rather than vague goals, solicited more ideas for improvement from others, and improved more in terms of subsequent subordinate and supervisor ratings (Smither, London, Flautt, Vargas, & Kucine, 2003). Luthans and Peterson (2003) reinforced this finding and found that an MSF coaching session that analyzed self-other rating discrepancies in detail encouraged managers to analyze discrepancies and set goals based on what they learned about themselves. Those who received coaching saw significant improvements in their own job attitudes (i.e., satisfaction, commitment, and reduced intent to leave), as well as in the attitudes of their employees (Luthans & Peterson, 2003).

Managers who take action, whether this involves participation in a training program or developmental activities (such as receiving coaching or reviewing progress), were more likely to improve than those who did not (Hazucha, Hezlett, & Schneider, 1993). In a study of over 100 companies (Brutus & Derayeh, 2002), every organization that failed to meet the objectives of the MSF process also failed to facilitate the feedback process. That is, recipients received reports in the mail without individual or group discussion with a trained facilitator. Those organizations that were successful in meeting their objectives for the program (63%) facilitated the feedback process. Facilitation sessions are critical to help the individual identify goals and strategies for needed behavior change indicated by the feedback.

Individual Attitudes and Behaviors

Perceived Need for Change In order for an individual to make the recommended changes as indicated by their feedback results, they must perceive that there is an actual need for change. Smither, London, and Reilly (2005) suggested that improvement is more likely to occur when organizational members perceive a need for behavioral change. They proposed that the organization can play a role in the way that organizational members perceive a need for change, by providing feedback in a nonthreatening manner and by rewarding participation in activities that promote learning and self-development.

Other studies have also addressed the importance of one's perceived need for change. London and Smither (2002) argue that discrepancies between self-ratings and other feedback ratings catalyze the employee's perceived need for change. Several studies indicate that leaders who receive feedback that is lower than their self-ratings may improve more than others (Atwater, Roush, & Fischthal, 1995; Johnson & Ferstl, 1999).

Goal Setting Goals have an effect on employee behaviors, efforts, and levels of task persistence (Locke & Latham, 1990). While many studies have addressed the value of goal setting in the contexts of employee performance appraisal (Roberts, 2002) and group-based feedback (Mesch, Farh, & Podsakoff, 1994), there is limited research on MSF and goal setting. Mesch et al. (1994) found that leaders who received negative feedback set higher goals. Similarly, Smither et al. (2003) found those who received negative feedback set more improvement goals than individuals who received positive feedback.

Meetings with Raters Many facilitators provide leaders with guidance and assistance in how to discuss their feedback ratings and follow up with the individuals who rated them. Walker and Smither (1999) conducted a five-year study of an MSF program and found that leaders who met with direct reports to share their feedback improved more than those leaders who did not. In addition, leaders improved more in the years when they met with direct reports to discuss the prior year's feedback than in years when they did not do so. Goldsmith and Underhill (2001) reported that when raters were asked about their leader's improvement 3–6 months after feedback, 84% of leaders who followed up with raters reportedly improved, whereas only 67% of leaders who did not follow up improved. Follow-up consisted of sharing with followers what the leader learned from their leadership feedback. Further, managers that shared their feedback with raters and asked for input were more likely to improve over time (Smither, London, Reilly, Flautt, Vargas, & Kucine, 2004).

Outcomes of the Feedback Process

Organizations embark on MSF processes as a means to increase self-awareness of critical leadership performance dimensions in a developmental context. Recent research suggests that the MSF is related to a variety of other types of evaluations. These findings highlight the validity of MSF.

Change in Ratings of Leaders

Generally, studies suggest that with multiple MSF administrations, leaders will improve performance (cf. Luthans & Peterson, 2003; Smither, London, & Reilly, 2005). However, not all leaders improve. Atwater et al. (2000) found that only half of leaders receiving feedback improved significantly after one year and one feedback session. Results vary some from study to study, but the general conclusion is that, over time, MSF results in improved leader ratings from other sources and more accurate self-ratings (in greater agreement with others). The results from studies of PA and improvement are less optimistic. Kluger and DeNisi's (1996) review found improvement in only one-third of the cases, and in another one-third, performance actually declined following feedback.

Assessment Center/Performance Appraisal Ratings

MSF ratings by peers, supervisors, and subordinates predicted assessment center ratings of the manager's competence that were generated by trained assessors not involved in the MSF process ($r = .29$, $p < .05$; Atkins & Wood, 2002). Self-ratings collected as part of the MSF process were nonlinearly related to assessment center ratings. That is, managers giving themselves the highest ratings scored the lowest on the assessment center ratings of competence. Those who rated themselves in the midrange were more likely to be high performers than those who rated themselves at the top or bottom of the scale.

In a study with more than 2,000 insurance employees, MSF boss and peer ratings were compared to three- and four-year-old performance appraisal ratings (Beehr, Ivanitskaya, Hansen, Erofeev, & Gudanowski, 2001). As expected, MSF ratings from bosses and peers were moderately correlated with the performance appraisal ratings. Self-ratings were not correlated with performance appraisals, even though the employees had knowledge of their past performance appraisals. However, Bailey and Fletcher (2002) reported the value of MSF in raising leaders' awareness regarding critical performance appraisal criteria. They found that participation in an MSF process strengthened the relationship between leaders' self-ratings and their formal performance appraisal ratings. At Time 1, leaders' self-ratings were not related to performance appraisal ratings; however, at Time 2 a significant positive relationship was observed for self-ratings and formal appraisal ratings. Thus, MSF helped managers become more aware of the behaviors that the organization valued and rewarded (Bailey & Fletcher, 2002).

The implication of these studies is that leaders are not good assessors of their own leadership behaviors and others are better judges of the leader's managerial competence. These results suggest that MSF may be a better approach to identifying a leader's development needs than relying on a leader's self-assessments of his or her competencies. Additionally, self-ratings may become more in line with other's ratings when the leader receives MSF.

Results from a Three-Year Intensive Field Study in Two Organizations

We have learned a great deal about the MSF process and its outcomes as part of a three-year investigation. We were interested in factors that influenced reactions to the feedback as well as outcomes for the individual leaders and the organization. We embarked on an intensive study of an MSF process in two separate organizations that had no prior experience with MSF. One was a retail organization headquartered in the southwest and a second was an elementary school district, also in the southwest. One hundred forty-five leaders participated in the process at two periods approximately one year apart. Leaders were rated by their peers, subordinates, and managers and also provided self-ratings on 47 leadership items that measured aspects of consideration, performance orientation, and employee development. In each organization, all leaders with three or more direct reports were asked to participate in the process. HR personnel in each organization prepared a master list of leaders, their manager, peers (ranging from 6–9 peers) and all direct reports. Top managers in each organization sent a letter that explained the 360-degree process to all followers, and leaders were briefed in meetings. Approximately 70% of the leaders were male.

Administration of Surveys

The researchers prepared the survey packages for each leader and his/her raters. Raters received the surveys via internal mail. Participants mailed the surveys directly to the researchers in prestamped and addressed envelopes. All subordinate and peer surveys were anonymous. Return rates at Time 1 were self = 100%, managers = 98%, peers = 83%, and subordinates = 68%. Corresponding return rates at Time 2 were self = 92%, managers = 95%, peers = 75%, and subordinates = 58%.

Feedback Delivery

Researchers delivered the feedback reports to leaders in groups ranging in size from 6 to 15. All leaders were guaranteed confidentiality of the data in their feedback reports. The data in their reports were explained, and efforts were made to help leaders react constructively to the feedback. After a discussion of how to interpret and use the feedback, the recipients completed a survey describing their reactions to the feedback. Recipients indicated the extent to which they were experiencing 24 emotions. Three categories were created from these data: "positive reactions" (e.g., pleased, proud, happy, encouraged, grateful), "negative reactions" (e.g., angry, frustrated, disappointed, unhappy), and "motivated" (e.g., motivated, aware, enlightened, inspired).

In addition to leader behavior measures, we also collected personality and attitude data (e.g., self-efficacy, usefulness of feedback) from the leaders during the first feedback session before leaders received feedback. Outcome data were also collected from subordinate raters (intent to leave, employee engagement, and job satisfaction) as part of the leadership feedback surveys.

We highlight the major findings from this study and their implications for managers. Incidentally, the major findings of the study were consistent across both organizations. The areas highlighted in italics in Figure 1 and Tables 1–4 show the contributions to new knowledge gained from this intensive field study.

Table 1 Factors to Consider Before Beginning MSF Process

Source	Findings	Our Recommendations
	Organizational Context	
Atwater, Waldman, Atwater, and Cartier (2000)	Participants who are cynical about the organization or who are unclear about how MSF fits into organizational goals are less likely to improve with MSF and may resist the process.	Implementation of MSF interventions when the organization is undergoing restructuring and downsizing is not advised.
Waldman and Atwater (1998)		Integrate MSF with HR processes.
Brutus and Derayeh (2002)	It's important to have clear and careful implementation strategies with MSF.	Establish a clear purpose for MSF and adequately communicate to employees how it fits into organizational goals.
London (2001)	Multisource feedback can be used for both developmental and administrative purposes, but it takes time.	Use MSF for developmental purposes first before implementing MSF for evaluative and administrative purposes.
	Perceptions of the Process	
Antonioni (1994)	Rater anonymity is needed for honest responses.	Consider if data-collection process ensures anonymity.
Brutus and Derayeh (2002)		Inform employees about the process to assure anonymity and confidentiality.
	Individual Differences	
Funderburg and Levy (1997)	High self-esteem individuals reported more favorable attitudes to MSF.	Be aware of individual differences when considering potential reactions and responses to MSF.
Smither, London, and Richmond (2005)	Extroverted leaders who were open to experience were more likely than other leaders to react to negative feedback as valuable and to seek more information about their feedback.	Spend time with leaders to discuss strategies for overcoming the initial reactions and to motivate leaders to focus on the developmental aspects of the feedback and the actions they could take in response to the feedback.

	Individual Differences *(continued)*	
Funderburg and Levy (1997)	High internal locus of control leaders reported more favorable attitudes toward the 360-degree feedback system.	Facilitators delivering the feedback should be sensitive to individual differences.
Maurer and Palmer (1999)	Leaders with an internal locus of control reacted to peer and subordinate feedback more favorably and intended to improve their skills.	
Brett and Atwater (2001)	Individuals with a learning goal orientation perceived feedback as more useful several weeks after feedback than those with a performance goal orientation.	Consider focusing on the developmental aspects of the feedback process, particularly those with a performance goal orientation.
Maurer, Mitchell, and Barbeite (2002)	Self-efficacy was related to positive or negative evaluative feelings toward MSF and to off-the-job development activities.	Consider interventions to enhance individual self-efficacy to assist low self-efficacy leaders in using the feedback for developmental purposes.
Heslin and Latham (2004)	Self-efficacy moderated the relationship between ratings and improvement in ratings six months later. Those with high self-efficacy showed a greater increase in performance.	
Atwater and Brett (2005)	*Those with higher self-efficacy more likely to report follow-up activities.* *No relationship found between personality characteristics and reactions to feedback.*	
	Actual Process	
Brutus and Derayeh (2002)	The time required to rate several staff burdens managers.	Consider having the manager only rate a subset of the leaders each year.
Testa (2002)	External raters can provide valuable insight on the manager.	Weigh the value of feedback from external raters against the time and cost.
Huet-Cox, Nielsen, and Sundstrom (1999)	Some organizations use the Internet to increase confidentiality, timeliness, and convenience of the process.	Electronic methods can be used to collect ratings for convenience and to increase confidentiality and perceived trustworthiness.
Smither, Walker, and Yap(2004)	The data-collection method did not influence ratees' feedback scores.	We caution using electronic means to return feedback results without facilitation assistance.

Note: Italics indicate findings that were part of the three-year study described in this article.

Table 2 Factors to Consider About Feedback

Source	Findings	Our Recommendations
	Feedback Format	
Atwater and Brett (in press)	*Text feedback was reacted significantly less favorably than numeric feedback.*	*Provide numeric feedback that is specific, easy to read, and clarifies strengths and weaknesses.*
	Characteristics of Feedback and Reactions	
Brett and Atwater (2001)	Feedback recipients with positive ratings viewed the process as more accurate and useful than those with negative ratings and reactions.	Consider how managers may respond to feedback before sharing it so that feedback validity does not come into question.
Atwater and Brett (2005)	*Leaders with more positive attitudes toward the process were more motivated and positive following feedback.*	
Facteau, Facteau, Shoel, Russell, and Poteet (1998)	Feedback recipients with fewer negative emotions used the feedback more constructively.	Recognize that some managers may react negatively to feedback. Consider strategies to assist managers in overcoming these reactions.
Smither, London, Flautt, Vargas, and Kucine (2003)	Managers receiving negative feedback had negative initial reactions but set more goals six months later than other managers.	Consider strategies to assist managers in overcoming reactions to feedback and to set development goals.
Brett and Atwater (2001)	Overraters reported more negative reactions and viewed the feedback as less accurate.	
Atwater and Brett (2005)	*Leaders' reactions to feedback were more strongly related to direct reports' ratings of leadership than to ratings from peers and managers.*	*Understand that leaders may react When they receive negative ratings from their direct reports.*
	Immediate reactions do matter and they likely influence how the leader responds to the feedback.	*Provide support to leaders to overcome initial negative reactions.*
Atwater and Brett (2005)	*Leaders who received low ratings and overrated themselves were more motivated than leaders who received low ratings and gave themselves low ratings.*	*Facilitation and coaching may be important to reduce negative reactions by overraters.*
	These overraters were more disappointed and angry than those who did not overrate.	*Provide individuals with leadership weaknesses encouragement and support to engage in developmental activities.*
Atwater and Brett (2005)	*Leaders who overrated relative to their managers' or direct report ratings were more motivated than underraters.*	*The discrepancy between self and other, when other ratings are low, appears to be motivational.*

Note: Italics indicate findings that were part of the three-year study described in this article.

Table 3 Factors to Consider After Feedback

Source	Findings	Our Recommendations
	Method of Distribution	
Kamen (2003)	Proposes that online rating will improve the feedback process.	Consider online MSF rating.
	Organizational Support	
Brutus and Derayeh (2002) Healy, Walsh, and Rose (2003)	Many MSF programs have some tie to developmental activities, but do not require follow-up or developmental activities.	If organizations want to recoup their investment in MSF, they should *do more than suggest* that leaders hold follow-up conversations with their employees and their supervisors or engage in developmental activities and coaching.
Maurer, Mitchell, and Barbeite (2002)	Managers who perceived support from coworkers and supervisors for development-related activities reported more positive attitudes toward the feedback system and were involved in more on- and off-the-job development activities.	Provide support for development activities following feedback.
Mabey (2001)	MSF participants, compared to nonparticipants, believed that they received more regular feedback on performance, more recognition, had more opportunities for training, and were more satisfied with training and the employer.	Be aware of the positive impact of MSF on participants and organization beyond individual awareness and development.
Seifert, Yukl, and McDonald (2003)	Managers who received MSF and training on influence tactics increased use of influence tactics.	Using MSF along with training or coach may lead to more positive impact on the leader and organization.
Smither, London, Flautt, Vargas, and Kucine (2003)	Managers who worked with a coach were more likely to set specific goals, share feedback and solicit ideas for improvement from a supervisor and improve in direct reports' and supervisor's ratings.	
Luthans and Peterson (2003)	Managers who worked with a coach were more likely to improve in self-awareness, employee satisfaction, commitment and intention to quit.	
Brutus and Derayeh (2002)	Every company studied who failed to meet the objectives of MSF did not facilitate the feedback process.	If organizations want to maximize improvements, it is advised that they facilitate the feedback process.
	Individual Attitudes and Behaviors	
London and Smither (2002) Smither, London, and Reilly (2005)	Improvement is more likely when managers perceive a need for change.	Assist recipients to recognize the need for behavioral change.
Mesch, Farh, and Podsakoff (1994)	Leaders who received negative feedback set more improvement goals than those who received positive feedback.	Negative feedback can promote goal setting; managers should help leaders achieve newly set goals.
Walker and Smither (1999) Goldsmith and Underhill (2001)	Leaders who follow up and meet with raters as a group after receiving feedback are more likely to realize improvements.	Encourage leaders to meet with those who rated them to discuss further actions based on the ratings.

Note: Italics indicate findings that were part of the three-year study described in this article.

Table 4 Factors to Consider After Feedback

Source	Findings	Our Recommendations
	Change in Ratings of Leaders	
Walker and Smither (1999) Atwater, Waldman, Atwater, and Cartier (2000)	Though small changes may be made after multisource feedback, significant results may not be seen for a year or two.	Expect only modest positive improvement with MSF. MSF is not a quick fix, but a process that, over time, can have a significant impact on organizations.
	Comparison to Other Ratings	
Atkins and Wood (2002)	MSF ratings predict assessment center ratings of the manager's competence. Self-ratings were unrelated to assessment center ratings.	Supports validity of MSF ratings. Be aware of using assessment of development needs or development activities that rely only on self-ratings.
Beehr, Ivanitskaya, Hansen, Erobeev and Gudanowski (2001)	Self-ratings were not correlated with past performance appraisals. MSF ratings from bosses and peers were moderately correlated with the performance appraisal ratings.	MSF may be a better approach to identifying a leader's development needs than relying on self-assessments of one's competencies.
Bailey and Fletcher (2002)	Self-ratings and formal appraisal ratings become more closely in line with one another after MSF.	MSF may help managers become more aware of valued and rewarded organizational behaviors.
Goldsmith and Underhill (2001)	Subordinate ratings of leaders did not improve significantly, but subordinates perceived some positive changes in most managers' performance.	Although ratings may not significantly improve, subordinates may perceive positive results from the process.
	Employee Attitudes	
Atwater and Brett (2006)	*Changes in leader behaviors made a difference in employee attitudes.* *Intent to leave is most highly related to employee development behaviors.* *Leaders who became more encouraging of staff to learn and grow and gave them recognition and feedback had employees who were reportedly less likely to leave the organization.* *Leaders who improved on consideration had more satisfied employees.* *Leaders who improved on performance-oriented, task-related behaviors (decision making, communication) had employees more engaged in their work.*	*By providing the resources to facilitate MSF, the organization may benefit from the positive impact on leaders, as well as subordinates' satisfaction, intent to leave, and engagement.*

Note: Italics indicate findings that were part of the three-year study described in this article.

Will Individual Differences in Emotional Stability, Trust, Openness to New Experiences, and Self-Efficacy Influence Reactions to Feedback?

Based on the research on individual differences, we expected differences in how individuals would react to MSF depending on their levels of emotional stability, trust, openness to new experiences, and self-efficacy. We found individual differences generally unrelated to reactions to feedback; however, those with higher self-efficacy were more likely to engage in follow-up activities (e.g., meet with rater groups, set goals, discuss feedback with supervisors). Individuals with higher self-efficacy took more positive steps toward change. Most likely, they felt more confident that they could realize positive changes in their leader behavior and thus were more likely to take steps in that direction. It would be worthwhile to increase self-efficacy by letting recipients know that there are resources available to help them achieve their development goals.

Will Feedback Format Influence Reactions to Feedback?

Positive behavior change and self-awareness often result from feedback; however, a number of studies have cautioned that reduced motivation and performance can result when individuals receive negative feedback or feedback that is more negative than expected (cf. Kluger & DeNisi, 1996). The format of the feedback is one of the factors that may influence how individuals react to the feedback. Earlier work tentatively suggests that not only is the amount of negative feedback relevant (more negative feedback being reacted to more negatively), but a scoring format, which is typically used in MSF, also may contribute to more negative reactions (Kluger & DeNisi, 1996). This scoring format may be particularly problematic when it is combined with comparative information where the recipient is given data to compare his or her ratings with the ways his or her peers were rated on the same dimensions. Scores draw the recipients' attention to themselves and their evaluation rather than to the behavioral statements and what these might suggest about needed changes.

In our study, we created two different formats for providing MSF. Recipients were randomly assigned to receive either text or numeric feedback. In the numeric format, MSF ratings (averaged subordinate and peer ratings, self-ratings, and the manager's rating of the recipient) were provided in numeric averages. The recipient also saw the normative data (averages) for the entire group of leaders who had participated in the process. Thus, leaders could compare their self-ratings to the ratings they received from their boss, peers, or subordinates, and they could compare the ratings they received from each rating source with the ratings other managers received. This format is the one typically used for providing MSF to leaders. Scores were color-coded such that high ratings were highlighted in light green, very high ratings were highlighted in dark green, development needs were highlighted in red, and serious development needs were highlighted in purple. We used average scores and standard deviations to set cutoff scores to determine strengths and development needs.

The alternative text format included words rather than numbers. In place of the averages, the recipient saw words that indicated whether his or her score from the rater group was a "high strength," "strength," "neither strength nor development need," "development need," or "serious development need." The same cutoff scores were used to determine what color the words would represent. We hypothesized that feedback presented in words rather than numbers and without normative comparisons would be perceived as less evaluative and less threatening, and thus would be reacted to more positively or less negatively if scores were low. Based on earlier research (Brett & Atwater, 2001), we reasoned that if the recipient reacted to the feedback with fewer negative emotions, he or she would use the feedback more constructively.

The results indicated that *contrary to our hypothesis*, text feedback was reacted to significantly less favorably than numeric feedback. When leaders received text feedback that showed that they had a high number of development needs as perceived by their subordinates, their negative reactions were particularly severe, more severe than when either peers or managers suggested the leader had numerous development needs. In addition to more negative reactions, individuals receiving text feedback also had fewer positive reactions and were less motivated following feedback.

A year later, when the recipients received a second round of feedback, those who had originally received text feedback were presented with both text and numeric feedback and asked to comment on the two feedback formats. Essentially, their comments indicated that the text format was seen as vague and not concise. They preferred the numeric feedback because it was more specific, easy to read, and clarified strengths and weaknesses. In a society where many aspects of daily life are measured in numbers (e.g., blood pressure, IQ), we may now expect and be more comfortable with numbers. We recommend that MSF providers should provide specific, numeric feedback rather than text reports. This does not mean narrative comments by raters should be avoided, but rather used in addition to quantitative ratings.

Interestingly, however, when we assessed whether leaders in the text or numeric format groups changed more at the second administration of feedback (that is, did the text or numeric group get higher ratings at Time 2), the answer was that format per se didn't matter. However, initial reactions did matter. Those who reacted most negatively (e.g., angry, defensive) after receiving their first round of feedback had *more* development needs reported at Time 2, even after controlling for the number of needs reported at Time 1. In other words, they got worse. Similarly those who had the most positive reactions at Time 1 showed a decline in development needs at Time 2; they actually improved. Those who receive negative feedback and react negatively are least likely to demonstrate positive changes in ratings a year later, and in fact, they may get worse. Those who react positively to the feedback and feel motivated are most likely to see positive changes in ratings a year later. This finding suggests that HR practitioners carefully plan how to help leaders to minimize any negative reactions, perhaps by using a facilitator or coach.

What Factors Influence Negative Reactions to MSF?

We were interested to see what factors other than the format or sign of the feedback (positive or negative) would contribute to recipients' reactions to feedback. For example, if leaders overrate themselves, does this affect their reactions to the feedback they receive? Are low ratings reacted to more negatively when the recipient rated himself or herself high? In what ways might the attitudes individuals hold about the feedback process influence their reactions to the feedback?

We learned that leaders who received low ratings and over-rated themselves were more motivated than leaders who received low ratings and gave themselves low ratings. The discrepancy between self-ratings and other ratings can be motivational. However, these overraters also had more disappointed and angry) than those who did not overrate. This findings suggests that interventions (such as MSF) designed to create more self-awareness may help in the long term as leaders gain awareness of how they are perceived by others, and try to reduce the discrepancies between self and other ratings. However, we would advise HR practitioners to help overraters overcome any negative reactions that occur because of this new self-awareness.

Leaders completed attitude measures during the first feedback session, prior to receiving their feedback reports. Not surprisingly, those who held more positive attitudes toward using feedback also were more motivated and had more positive emotions following feedback, regardless of the type of feedback they received. We recommend that HR practitioners consider the importance of taking time to introduce the MSF process into the organization in a careful and thoughtful way so both raters and leaders feel comfortable with how the data will be collected and used, its confidentiality, rater anonymity, and so on. If leaders enter the process with bad attitudes about the feedback process, its validity, or its usefulness, they will not reap the most from the process. All efforts should be made to help reduce negative reactions to feedback. Coaching, counseling, and follow-up with recipients are advisable or the feedback may have negative rather than positive effects on those who react negatively.

What Are the Outcomes Beyond Changes in Leader Behavior?

The most common method used to assess the success of an MSF intervention is to compare the leaders' ratings before and after he/she receives feedback. Generally, the literature shows modest positive improvement in ratings (Smither, London, & Reilly, 2005). In our study, when we compared Time 1 and Time 2 ratings provided by peers, subordinates, and managers across all leadership items, we only found significant improvement in bosses' ratings of the feedback recipients (perhaps due to the fact that the bosses' ratings were not anonymous). There are a number of possible explanations for this result. First, it may be that because we assessed so many items, even positive changes were washed out when overall averages were compared. Given that this is the first time MSF had been used, changes may be in the right direction, but it may take another year or two for the changes to be statistically significant, as per Walker and Smither (1999).

We also were interested in how changes in leaders' behavior might influence outcomes other than their behavior or ratings of their behavior. While MSF has become very popular, little attention has been given to evaluating the effects of the MSF process on outcomes other than subsequent ratings. We reasoned that because there is a great deal of literature attesting to the relevance of supervisory behavior to employee attitudes, if leader behavior improves, we should expect employee attitudes to improve as well. The question arises, if MSF can improve leadership, will those changes translate into changes in employee attitudes?

We assessed employee attitudes as part of the MSF survey. Therefore, in addition to rating their supervisor's leadership, subordinates rated their own satisfaction, intent to leave, and engagement at both Times 1 and 2. Our primary question was if the leader's behaviors improve, do employee attitudes also improve? We adjusted the Time 2 attitude and leadership scores for their Time 1 values so we could explain change in attitudes with change in leader behavior. We learned that positive changes in the leader's consideration behavior (e.g., listens, is tactful and sensitive, accepts feedback) were related to positive changes on each of the three attitude measures. The biggest impact for changes in consideration was seen in improved employee satisfaction as compared to engagement or intent to leave. Positive changes in the leader's employee development behavior (talks to direct reports about progress; encourages direct reports development) also were related to positive changes on each of the attitude measures, with the strongest effect for intent to leave.

Positive changes in leaders' performance orientation (e.g., sets goals, follows up, makes tough decisions) were related to positive changes in employee engagement (e.g., know what is expected; receive recognition or praise, and have necessary materials and equipment to do the job). MSF can be a useful method for improving leader behavior and ultimately influencing employee attitudes in a positive way. If leader behaviors improve, we can expect employee attitudes (job satisfaction, engagement, and intent to leave) to improve.

Summary and Conclusions

In sum, our study reinforces the implications of prior research on MSF practices and adds new insights. First, the positive relationship between attitudes toward using the feedback and reactions emphasizes that human resource professionals should understand the importance of paying attention to how they introduce and implement the MSF process in their organizations. Second, reactions to negative feedback were not transitory mood states with minimal implications for leadership development, but rather influenced subsequent behavior. These findings reinforce the need for organizations to consider how they facilitate feedback distribution and how they encourage developmental activities following feedback.

Our findings show that those leaders who improved were more likely to see subsequent changes in employee attitudes. This result indicates that with regard to organizational outcomes, MSF can do more than just develop leaders. It can have a positive ripple effect upon others in the organization. Understanding and implementing the practical findings from the research summarized and presented in this article should assist organizations in reaping the rewards of their investment in a MSF process.

However, clearly the costs and benefits of implementing MSF should be considered. For example, Bettenhausen and Fedor (1997) suggest a number of potential benefits of MSF such as higher-quality feedback, input for employee development recommendations, and uses in performance coaching. However, they also highlight some possible downsides, including fostering defensiveness and creating situations where leaders become overly concerned about pleasing employees. In all cases, the goals of implementing MSF should be clear and should align with the organization's goals and personnel practices.

Research can inform and enhance the benefits organizations derive from their investment in MSF. However, many questions remain regarding the MSF process that could provide additional insight to practitioners. Rynes et al. (2005) suggest that future MSF research focus on better understanding the individual or program characteristics that are most likely to improve the returns from this process. Likewise, Smither, London, and Reilly (2005) suggest that we move from asking "Does MSF work?" to asking "Under what conditions and for whom does MSF work?"

As indicated from our summary, the role of organizational context is critical to the success of MSF. However, we need a better understanding of what organizations can do to create an environment and culture that supports feedback, whether it is performance appraisal or multisource feedback (Levy & Williams, 2004; London & Smither, 2002; Rynes et al., 2005). We need research to illuminate how the feedback culture in organizations influences "how feedback is sought, perceived, processed, accepted, used and reacted to" (Levy & Williams, 2004, p. 895). For example: How do perceptions of the motivation for the MSF process (i.e., individual initiative, new boss, organizational change, or decline in organizational performance) influence acceptance and commitment to the process? How do perceptions of others in the social context influence the process (i.e., is the boss supportive or negative toward the process or is the process companywide)?

Some individuals benefit from the MSF process and others do not. We need a better understanding of why some individuals use feedback and take actions and others do not. Recent work on feedback orientation (i.e., responsiveness to feedback and evaluation) may provide answers to these questions (London & Smither, 2002). In addition, research is needed that examines the combined effects of individual differences and organizational support for development on the reactions to and use of feedback (Smither, London, & Richmond, 2005).

Performance appraisal and MSF research indicates that when individuals focus attention on the self and not the task, negative feedback is debilitating. We need a better understanding of how the 360-degree process creates a self-awareness that is motivating versus creating a self-focus that is debilitating. For example: Are we overwhelming managers with too much information when they receive self, other, and normative feedback? What role does each of these feedback components play in improving performance versus overwhelming those who receive negative information?

It is clear from research that MSF alone may not be enough to motivate changes in a leader's behavior. How do interventions such as coaching, goal setting, and training complement and reinforce leadership change? Do coaching, goal setting, and training enhance MSF because it helps managers move from a self-focus to a task focus? If the ultimate goal of an MSF process is leadership development, the questions may not be limited to how coaching and training facilitate the value of MSF, but how the MSF process can facilitate training, executive coaching, and other leadership development interventions to be more effective in developing and changing leadership behavior. Finally, we need more research that demonstrates the cost-effectiveness of MSF. What are the organizational and bottom-line costs and benefits to organizations undertaking an MSF process?

While we wait for researchers to address these issues, we encourage practitioners to consider how the research discussed in this article can improve the MSF process in their organizations and, ultimately, the effectiveness of leaders and organizations.

Source: Human Resource Management, 46, (2), 285–207 (2007). Reprinted by permission of John Wiley & Sons, Inc.

REFERENCES

Antonioni, D. (1994). The effects of feedback accountability on upward appraisal ratings. Personnel Psychology, 47, 349–356.

Atkins, P., & Wood, R. E. (2002). Self-versus others' ratings as predictors of assessment center ratings: Validation evidence for 360-degree feedback programs. Personnel Psychology, 55, 871–904.

Atwater, L., & Brett, J. (in press). Feedback format: Does it influence managers' reactions to feedback. Journal of Occupational and Organizational Psychology.

Atwater, L., & Brett, J. (2005). Antecedents and consequences of reactions to developmental 360 degree feedback. Journal of Vocational Behavior, 66, 532–548.

Atwater, L., & Brett, J. (2006). 360 degree feedback to managers: Does it result in changes in employee attitudes? Group & Organization Management, 31, 578–600.

Atwater, L., Roush, P., & Fischthal, A. (1995). The influence of upward feedback on self- and follower ratings of leadership. Personnel Psychology, 48, 35–59.

Atwater, L., Waldman, D., Atwater, D., & Cartier, T. (2000). An upward feedback field experiment. Supervisors' cynicism, follow-up and commitment to subordinates. Personnel Psychology, 53, 275–297.

Bailey, C., & Fletcher, C. (2002). The impact of multiple source feedback on management development: Findings from a longitudinal study. Journal of Organizational Behavior, 23, 853–867.

Bandura, A. (1997). Self-efficacy: The exercise of control. New York: W. H. Freeman.

Beehr, T., Ivanitskaya, L., Hansen, C., Erofeev, D., & Gudanowski, D. (2001). Evaluation of 360 degree feedback ratings: Relationships with each other and with performance and selection predictors. *Journal of Organizational Behavior*, 22, 775–788.

Bettenhausen, K. L., & Fedor, D. B. (1997). Peer and upward appraisals: A comparison of their benefits and problems. Group & Organization Management, 22, 236–263.

Bolton, G. E., Katok, E., & Ockenfels, A. (2004). How effective are electronic reputation mechanisms? An experimental investigation. Management Science, 50, 1587–1602.

Brett, J., & Atwater, L. (2001). 360-degree feedback: Accuracy, reactions and perceptions of usefulness. Journal of Applied Psychology, 86, 930–942.

Bretz, R. D., Jr., Milkovich, G. T., & Read, W. (1992). The current state of performance appraisal research and practice: Concerns, directions and implications. Journal of Management, 18, 321–352.

Brutus, S., & Derayeh, M. (2002). Multi-source assessment programs in organizations: An insider's perspective. Human Resource Development Quarterly, 13, 187–201.

Carver, C. S., & Scheier, M. F. (1990). Origins and functions of positive and negative effect. A control-process view. Psychological Review, 97, 19–35.

Church, A. H. (2000). Do higher performing managers actually receive better ratings? A validation of multirater assessment methodology. Consulting Psychology Journal: Practice and Research, 52, 99–116.

Colquitt, J., LePine, J., & Noe, R. (2000). Toward an integrative theory of training motivation: A meta-analytic path analysis of 20 years of research. Journal of Applied Psychology, 85, 678–707.

Dellarocas, C. (2003). The digitization of word of mouth: Promise and challenges of online feedback mechanisms. Management Science, 49, 1407–1424.

Dweck, C. S. (1986). Motivational processes affecting learning. American Psychologist, 41, 1040–1048.

Dweck, C. S., & Leggett, E. L. (1988). A social-cognitive approach to motivation and personality, Psychological Review, 95, 256–273.

Facteau, C. L., Facteau, J. D., Shoel, L. C., Russell, J. A., & Poteet, M. (1998). Reactions of leaders to 360-degree feedback from subordinates and peers. Leadership Quarterly, 9, 427–448.

Funderburg, S. A., & Levy, P. E. (1997). The influence of individual and contextual variables and 360-degree feedback system attitudes. Group and Organizational Studies, 22, 210–230.

Goldsmith, M., & Underhill, B. (2001). Multi-source feedback for executive development. In D. Bracken, C. Timmreck, & A. Church (Eds.). The handbook of multi-source feedback (pp. 275–288). San Francisco, CA: Jossey-Bass.

Hazucha, J. F., Hezlett, S. A., & Schneider, R. J. (1993). The impact of 360-degree feedback on management skills development. Human Resource Management, 32, 325–351.

Healy, M. C., Walsh, A. B., & Rose, D. S. (2003). A benchmarking study of North American 360 degree feed back practices. Poster presented at the 18th Annual Conference of the Society for Industrial and Organizational Psychology, Orlando, FL.

Heneman, R., & Gresham, M. (1998). Performance-based pay plans. In J. Smither (Ed.), Performance appraisal: State of the art in practice (pp. 496–536). San Francisco, CA: Jossey-Bass.

Heslin, P. A., & Latham, G. P. (2004). The effect of upward feedback on managerial behavior. Applied Psychology: An International Review, 53, 23–37.

Huet-Cox, G. D., Nielsen, T. M., & Sundstrom, E. (1999). Get the most from 360-degree feedback: Put it on the Internet. HR Magazine, 44, 92–99.

Johnson, J. W., & Ferstl, K. L. (1999). The effects of interrater and self-other agreement on performance improvement following upward feedback. Personnel Psychology, 52, 271–303.

Kamen, P. (2003). The way you use it. CMA Management, 77, 10.

Klimoski, R., & Jones, R. (1989, August). Acceptance of feedback as a function of self-appraisal. Paper presented at the National Meeting of the Academy of Management, Washington, DC.

Kluger, A. N., & DeNisi, A. (1996). The effects of feedback intervention on performance: A historical review, a meta-analysis, and a preliminary feedback intervention theory. Psychological Bulletin, 119, 254–284.

Levy, P. W., & Williams, J. R. (2004). The social context of performance appraisal: A review and framework for the future. Journal of Management, 30, 881–905.

Locke, E. A., & Latham, G. P. (1990). A theory of goal setting and task performance. Englewood Cliffs, NJ: Prentice Hall.

London, M. (2001). The great debate: Should multi-source feedback be used for administration or development only? In D. Bracken, C. Timmreck, & A. Church (Eds.), The handbook of multi-source feedback (pp. 368–387). San Francisco, CA: Jossey-Bass.

London, M. (2003). Job feedback. Mahwah, NJ: LEA.

London, M., & Smither, J. W. (2002). Feedback orientation, feedback culture, and the longitudinal performance management process. Human Resource Management Review, 12, 81–100.

Longnecker, C., Sims, H., & Gioia, D. (1987). Behind the mask: The politics of employee appraisal. Academy of Management Executive, 1(3), 183–193.

Luthans, F., & Peterson, S. J. (2003). 360-degree feedback with systematic coaching: Empirical analysis suggests a winning combination. Human Resource Management, 42, 243–256.

Mabey, C. (2001). Closing the circle: Participant views of a 360 degree feedback programme. Human Resource Management Journal, 11, 41–54.

Maurer, T. J., Mitchell, D., & Barbeite, F. G. (2002). Predictors of attitudes toward a 360-degree feedback system and involvement in post-feedback management development activity. Journal of Occupational and Organizational Psychology, 75, 87–107.

Maurer. T. J., & Palmer, J. K. (1999). Management development intentions following feedback: Role of perceived outcomes, social pressures, and control. Journal of Management Development, 18, 733–751.

Mesch, D. J., Farh, J., & Podsakoff, P. M. (1994). Effects of feedback sign on group goal setting, strategies, and performance. Group & Organization Management, 19, 309–333.

Raghuram, S., Wiesenfeld, B., & Garud, R. (2003). Technology enabled work: The role of self-efficacy in determining telecommuter adjustment and structuring behavior. Journal of Vocational Behavior, 63,180–198.

Roberts, G. E. (2002). Employee performance appraisal system participation: A technique that works. Public Personnel Management, 31, 333–342.

Ryan, A. M., Brutus, S., Greguras, G., & Hakel, M. D. (2000). Receptivity to assessment-based feedback for management development: Extending our understanding of reactions to feedback. Journal of Management Development, 19, 252–276.

Rynes, S. L., Gerhart, B., & Parks, L. (2005). Personnel psychology: Performance evaluation and pay for performance. Annual Review of Psychology, 56, 571–600.

Seifert, C. F., Yukl, G., & McDonald, R. A. (2003). Effects of multisource feedback and a feedback facilitator on the influence behavior of managers towards subordinates. Journal of Applied Psychology, 88, 561–569.

Smither, J. W., London, M., Flautt, R., Vargas, Y., & Kucine, I. (2003). Can executive coaches enhance the impact of multi-source feedback on behavior change? A quasi-experimental field study. Personnel Psychology, 56, 23–44.

Smither, J. W., London, M., & Reilly, R. R. (2005). Does performance improve following multi-source feedback? A theoretical model, meta-analysis, and review of empirical findings. Personnel Psychology, 58, 33–66.

Smither, J. W., London, M., Reilly, R. R., Flautt, R., Vargas, Y., & Kucine, T. (2004). Discussing multisource feedback with raters and performance improvement. Journal of Management Development, 23, 456–468.

Smither, J. W., London, M., & Richmond, K. R. (2005). The relationship between leaders' personality and their reactions to and use of multisource feedback: A longitudinal study. Group & Organization Management, 30, 181–211.

Smither, J. W., Walker, A. G., & Yap, M. (2004). An examination of the equivalence of web-based versus paper-and-pencil upward feedback ratings: Rater-and-ratee-level analyses. Education and Psychological Measurement, 64, 40–61

Taylor, M., Fisher, C., & Ilgen, D. (1984). Individuals' reactions to performance feedback in organizations: A control theory perspective. Research in Personnel and Human Resources Management, 2, 81–124.

Testa, M. R. (2002). A model for organizational-based 360 degree leadership assessment. Leadership & Organization Development Journal, 23, 260–269.

Waldman, D., & Atwater, L. (1998). The power of 360 degree feedback. Houston, TX: Gulf.

Walker, A. G., & Smither, J. W. (1999). A five-year study of upward feedback: What managers do with their results matters. Personnel Psychology, 52, 393–423.

READING 10.2

Managing the Life Cycle of Virtual Teams

Stacie A. Furst, Martha Reeves, Benson Rosen, and Richard S. Blackburn

Executive Overview

In the fast-paced, technology-driven 21st century, virtual project teams represent a growing response to the need for high-quality, low-cost, rapid solutions to complex organizational problems. Virtual project teams enable organizations to pool the talents and expertise of employees (and non-employees) by eliminating time and space barriers. Yet, there is growing evidence that virtual teams fail more often than they succeed. To understand the factors that contribute to virtual team effectiveness, we tracked six virtual project teams from a large food distribution company from inception to project delivery. We identified factors at each stage of the virtual-team life cycle that affected team performance. These results provide specific examples of what managers can do, at various points in time, to increase a virtual team's chances to fully develop and contribute to firm performance.

FOODCO* has grown dramatically over the last several years as the result of numerous acquisitions. One of the nation's largest food distributors, FOODCO has more than 20 operating companies located throughout the United States. To maximize long-term performance, FOODCO executives wanted to tap into the knowledge and expertise of employees located throughout the newly expanded company. In particular, executives wanted to encourage the sharing of best practices across operating companies, streamline work processes, prepare managers for promotion, and develop a unified culture. To address these issues intelligently, quickly, and effectively, FOODCO created virtual project teams.

Virtual project teams represent a recent response to the demand for high-quality, rapid solutions to complex issues such as those faced by FOODCO. Virtual project teams include individuals who are geographically dispersed and interact primarily through telecommunications and information technologies to accomplish specific objectives within specified timeframes.[1] Assignments for these teams might include designing new products, developing strategies, and revising operating procedures. Virtual project teams allow organizations to pool the talents and expertise of employees regardless of employee location, overcoming time and distance barriers to accomplish critical tasks quickly and effectively.

But simply establishing virtual project teams does not guarantee success. In fact, virtual teams are often less effective than face-to-face teams on many outcome measures.[2] Virtual project teams can experience difficulties at every stage of their development. Improved understanding of how virtual project teams develop and mature will provide managers with important insights that might increase a team's contributions to firm performance.

The authors were able to follow six virtual project teams at FOODCO from inception through project delivery to assess how teams developed and to determine what factors contributed to performance at each stage of the project-team life cycle. We surveyed and interviewed team members throughout an eight-month project period and gathered information on how top executives at FOODCO and outside experts evaluated each team's deliverables. Our data provide useful insights about virtual project team development, the challenges encountered at various points in team life cycles, and suggestions for overcoming these challenges. We discuss the implications of our findings for organizations planning to adopt or currently using virtual project teams. We also offer specific recommendations for coaching virtual teams at each stage of their life cycle.

The Emergence of Virtual Teams

Globalization and technological advancements have led to an increase in virtual team use over the last decade. Estimates suggest that in the US alone, as many as 8.4 million employees are members of one or more virtual teams or groups.[3] Numerous studies of virtual teams document how they operate and how they compare to traditional, face-to-face teams. For example, *The Executive* has published several articles discussing the birth of virtual teams as an alternative work form, the advantages and disadvantages of virtual work, and the specific challenges confronting virtual teams.[4]

* FOODCO is a pseudonym being used to protect the anonymity of the company.

Virtual teams afford many advantages to organizations, including increased knowledge sharing and employee job satisfaction and commitment, as well as improved organizational performance.[5] However, virtual teams can also face a number of unique challenges that often prevent them from obtaining successful outcomes. Broadly, these challenges include (1) logistical problems, such as communicating and coordinating work across time and space, (2) interpersonal concerns, such as establishing effective working relationships with team members in the absence of frequent face-to-face communication, and (3) technology issues, such as identifying, learning, and using technologies most appropriate for certain tasks.[6]

There is an abundance of advice to managers on how to motivate virtual teams to high levels of performance. Some authors encourage managers to help virtual teams draft mission statements, set goals, and coordinate their work. Others emphasize the importance of teambuilding exercises to create a team identity and strengthen interpersonal relationships. Much of this advice is based on single observations or laboratory studies with student virtual teams. Our goal is to understand how virtual teams of real employees develop through every phase of a team life cycle from team formation through product delivery. Our focus is on helping managers understand the special challenges that virtual project teams confront at each stage of development and how to time intervention strategies so that teams can make smooth transitions.

The Life Cycle of Virtual Project Teams

Teams are more effective when members can combine their individual talents, skills, and experiences via appropriate working relationships and processes.[7] Two models that describe how teams evolve through this process have been proposed by Tuckman (1965) and Gersick (1988).[8]

Tuckman's Stage Model of Development

Based on an extensive analysis of groups located in one place, Tuckman identified four distinct stages of team development: forming, storming, norming, and performing. During the forming stage, team members share information about themselves and their task explicitly through discussions or implicitly through non-verbal cues, such as status symbols or physical traits. Ideally, team members also establish trust, clarify group goals, and develop shared expectation's in this stage. Efforts to resolve these issues often surface differences of opinions, and in the storming stage, conflicts emerge as team members work to identify appropriate roles and responsibilities. Groups able to resolve conflicts move to the norming stage. In this stage, teams recognize and agree on ways of working together, strengthen relationships, and solidify understanding of member obligations, all of which increase levels of trust, mission clarity, and coordination. Finally, teams reach the performing stage during which team members work toward project completion, actively helping and encouraging each other.

Gersick's Punctuated Equilibrium Model

Gersick examined the impact of deadline pressures on the development processes of work teams. She described a "punctuated equilibrium" model of development in which a team's evolution is marked by two periods of stability—Phase I and Phase II—punctuated by abrupt changes at the project midpoint that occurs halfway to the deadline.[9] Phase I begins with the first team meeting and continues until the team is halfway to a project's deadline. During Phase I, teams try to establish a working agenda and to develop norms that guide early project efforts. These activities parallel Tuckman's forming, storming, and norming stages. At the project midpoint, a transition occurs as teams assess the norms and assumptions set during Phase I. Teams dissatisfied with their progress may seek advice from an outside leader or facilitator in order to develop more effective norms. Teams satisfied with their performance maintain the status quo. With a successful transition, team members focus on their performance for the duration of the project (Phase II). This transition is usually followed by a burst of activity to insure that the team meets the deadline with an acceptable outcome.

Some evidence shows that virtual teams evolve through processes similar to those described by Tuckman and Gersick, although differences in the speed and pattern of development appear to exist.[10] These findings provide some clues that the evolution of virtual project teams may be more complex and challenging than for co-located teams. For instance, reliance on electronic communication may slow the establishment of trust, limit conflict resolution, promote free riding, and inhibit team synergy and performance. Similarly, it may be more difficult for virtual project teams to (re)assess their progress, reflect on collective work ethics, and recommit to task completion within designated time frames, as described by the punctuated equilibrium model. These issues, which we detail in the next section, are summarized in Table 1.

The Challenges Associated with Virtual Team Development

Forming

In co-located teams, face-to-face interactions during the early stages of a project provide opportunities for building relationships based on common interests and permit individuals to analyze their colleagues' trustworthiness based on observation and conversation. Developing high-quality relationships is more difficult and takes longer when team members are geographically dispersed because reliance on electronic communications often diminishes communication frequency.[11] Proximity enables team members to engage in informal work and non-work related conversations that can occur over coffee, at the water cooler, or during lunch.[12] More frequent interaction increases opportunities to break the ice, establish lines of communication, and identify points of similarity, all of which are critical for successful team formation.

Table 1 Stages of Virtual Project Team Development

Model				
Tuckman: **Gersick:**	**Forming**	**Storming** **Phase I**	**Norming** **Midpoint** **Transition**	**Performing** **Phase II**
Description of Team Behavior During Each Stage	Team members get to know each other, exchange information about themselves and the task at hand, establish trust among group members, and clarify group goals and expectations	Similarities and differences are revealed and conflicts surface as the group attempts to identify appropriate roles and responsibilities among the members	Team members recognize and agree on ways of sharing information and working together; relationships are strengthened, and team members agree on member obligations and team strategy	Team members work toward project completion, actively helping and encouraging each other
Challenges to Virtual Teams	Fewer opportunities for informal work- and non-work-related conversations; risk of making erroneous stereotypes in the absence of complete information; trust slower and more difficult to develop	Reliance on less rich communication channels may exacerbate conflicts by provoking misunderstandings; ease of withdrawing behaviors; diversity of work contexts; reliance on an emergent or assigned team leader	Difficulty in developing norms around modes of communication, speed, and frequency of responding, and commitment to use special software	Vulnerability to competing pressures from local assignments, frustrations over free-riding or non-committed teammates, and communication discontinuities due to asynchronous communication

Reliance on electronic communications also increases the potential for faulty first impressions and erroneous stereotypes.[13] In the absence of visual or audio cues provided by some technologies, team members may develop incorrect stereotypes based on geographic and cultural differences, or differences in functional expertise. These mistaken stereotypes or presumed differences between team members can undermine relationship-building efforts.[14] In particular, teams may struggle to form a collective identity that promotes a shared commitment to a common goal.[15]

Successful navigation through the forming stage requires that team members establish a sense of trust.[16] In face-to-face teams, trust develops based on social and emotional attachments. In virtual teams, trust develops based on more identifiable actions as timely information sharing, appropriate responses to electronic communications, and keeping commitments to virtual teammates.[17] These actions signal that team members are competent and want to help the team, but they take time to occur in the virtual environment.

Storming

As Table 1 notes, past research on co-located teams suggests that disagreement and conflict characterize the storming stage of team development. In the virtual environment, the use of communication technologies may prolong these conflicts. Without the benefit of the subtle social cues associated with face-to-face communications (body language, tone of voice, and facial expressions), misunderstandings can occur more readily.[18] Electronic communication can exacerbate conflict when team members simply refuse to respond to electronic messages. This explains why virtual teams, particularly those working on complex, non-technical issues, take longer to reach consensus on team process issues than do co-located teams.[19]

The presumed diversity of work settings can also inhibit conflict resolution for virtual teams. For example, in some work settings, technology and support staff are available to support virtual teams. In less advanced settings, even minor technical problems can be disruptive for teams and team members. Similarly, in some settings, managers or team members may view virtual team participation as a high priority, while others may view it as a distraction from more immediate concerns. Team members in different work settings can form different expectations regarding how to coordinate work and accomplish team objectives.[20]

In the storming stage, virtual project team sponsors can appoint team leaders to help minimize conflicts that can occur over role assignments. When leadership selection is based on the skills critical for virtual team success, including conflict management, virtual teams are more likely to survive the storming stage.[21] However, self-managed virtual project teams are created without a formal leader, and other teams are formed with a misplaced emphasis on a leader's technical as opposed to interpersonal skills. In such cases, the emergence of an informal or social leader may be an agonizingly slow process. And, if virtual teams are low in trust, the absence of an emergent or formal leader can have serious consequences for later team performance.[22]

Norming

Table 1 shows that in the norming stage of development, virtual teams work to strengthen relationships, solidify norms around team processes, and reach consensus regarding obligations, timetables, and deadlines. These efforts mirror the activities that teams may engage in at Gersick's "midpoint transition." At this point, teams assess whether their work processes have been effective or if they need to be revised. Special challenges confronting virtual teams in the norming stage include coordinating work, developing a shared understanding around modes of communication, and the speed and frequency of responding.

Virtual teams must establish norms governing both work processes and communication content. Agreements on timetables and individual areas of responsibility are essential for virtual team effectiveness.[23] Structured schedules and timelines enable virtual team members to coordinate work across time zones and to manage variations in team members' "local" work schedules and demands. Working virtually also requires keeping all members informed. Unfortunately, some members may initially lack the discipline to follow virtual team agreements with respect to information sharing. For example, phone calls and emails between a subset of team members may feel comfortable and appear efficient but could prove to be self-defeating when other members are deprived of critical information or made to feel like second-class team members.[24] Creating new habits around the use of shareware and other technology platforms which allow members to archive documents and use message boards are among the challenges facing virtual teams during the norming stage.

Norms must also address the quality and candidness of communication. In any team, members may be reluctant to share creative but potentially divisive ideas with their teammates. In the virtual context, it is not easy to test the waters, gauge potential reactions, and/or modify ideas based on the subtle feedback often available in co-located teams. Virtual team members may also withhold message postings critical of teammate suggestions to spare others from embarrassment. Thus, norms that require complete information sharing have the paradoxical effect of making virtual team members more cautious when it comes to publicly sharing untested ideas or offering criticisms of others.[25] Clearly, establishing trust in earlier stages of team development is a necessary condition for solidifying these kinds of norms at this stage.

Performing

The performing stage of development requires that teams effectively collect and share information, integrate members' inputs, look for creative solutions to problems, and prepare deliverables for outside sponsors. At this stage, virtual team members are able to collaborate and sustain a task focus across multiple assignments.[26] This is "crunch time" as teams become aware of impending deadlines and increase their activity to ensure that the deadline is met.

Maintaining team performance and synergy during this stage is particularly challenging for virtual project teams. Virtual team members can face competing pressures from local assignments, frustrations over free-riding teammates, and communication problems associated with asynchronous communication. Without a formal leader of maintain team morale and motivation, virtual team members may lose focus. Failure to meet deadlines, poorly written reports, and ill-conceived recommendations may have serious career consequences for all concerned. Hence, the performing stage of team development can be a period of great satisfaction and/or stress.

The experiences of virtual project teams throughout their life cycles are more complex and challenging when compared to face-to-face project teams. For managers charged with supporting virtual project teams, additional insights may be gained from studying multiple "real life" virtual teams as they move through their life cycles. Of specific interest are the factors associated with performance effectiveness at each stage of team development.

FOODCO: A Longitudinal Study of Virtual Project Teams

To learn more about how virtual project teams develop, we followed six virtual project teams from FOODCO, one of the nation's leading food service distributors. The six project teams were formed as part of an Executive Leadership Institute (ELI) commissioned by FOODCO's top executives at a major southeastern university in the US. FOODCO executives requested that a key component of the ELI be projects requiring participants to work in cross-disciplinary virtual project teams addressing business issues that executives deemed "critical" to company performance. ELI administrators assigned four to five participants to each project team, ensuring that each team had cross-functional representation and included at least one participant with expertise relevant to the issue under investigation. Team assignments, listed in Table 2, required the collection of archival data, interviews with key employees in the company, analysis and synthesis of this information, and the development of recommendations and presentations for these projects. A complete description of the ELI goals and objectives, the virtual team

Table 2 Project Team Assignments

Team	Name	Project Objective
1	ACQUIRE	To develop an integration strategy for acquisitions
2	ITECH	To determine how to efficiently transfer information technology from one subsidiary company to other parts of the firm
3	TRANSFER	To determine how to transfer best practices from one division of the company to another
4	AP	To streamline the accounts payable process
5	COMM	To conduct a corporate communications audit
6	CAREER	To develop career paths of specific jobs

assignments, and the methodology used to assess the evolution of virtual teams is provided in the Appendix.

The project design allowed team members to work briefly face-to-face during each of three residency periods prior to the project presentations. However, the majority of their work was necessarily completed while team members worked in their home offices. Technology available to the teams included phone, email, fax, conference calling, and other resources necessary to work collaboratively. FOODCO assigned a senior sponsor to each virtual team to assist in the project. Sponsors were company executives who had a vested interest in seeing the team succeed and were willing to help obtain needed resources, overcome organizational barriers, and provide guidance on how to approach and complete the team's work.[27] Teams were instructed to initiate contact with their senior sponsors, as needed, throughout the eight-month project period. Sponsors would not do a team's work nor be responsible for the quality of the team's deliverables.

Next, we summarize our survey and interview findings for each time period.

The Virtual Team Life Cycle

Time 1: Forming—Unbridled Optimism

During the first residency period, team members' perceptions of the likelihood of team success reflected a sense of unbridled optimism, which is also characteristic of most non-virtual work teams. Team members were able to meet briefly with their project teammates, and survey results following these early meetings suggested that teams started on an equal footing. There were no differences in team members' initial assessments of their time available to work on the project, their comfort with technology, and their confidence in working virtually. Perceptions regarding the meaningfulness of their assignment, the support for the project in their local offices, and the availability of resources to carry out the project also did not differ.

Team members felt confident that they could meet the desired performance goals despite the nature of the virtual task. Responses to open-ended questions illustrated invariably high levels of optimism regarding how easily team members expected to complete their projects and how well they would work together. Some representative comments included:

> *"I believe we have a great team and will work well together. We all understand the importance of the project and intend to take it seriously." (ACQUIRE team member)*
>
> *"I feel the team will work well together, and I expect us to be very effective." (COMM team member)*
>
> *"I think the team will work very well together. We all agree on the substance and the goal." (CAREER team member)*

Time 2: Storming—Reality Shock

A second survey was administered early in the second residency, approximately two months later. At this time, several teams reported having spent little, if any time working on their virtual team projects since their initial meeting. Other teams reported spending several hours a week on their projects. Asked to describe which stage of development best characterized their team at Time 2, one team reported that they had already reached the performing stage ("Team members are clear about their responsibilities, and we are making excellent progress"). Other teams felt they were still in the forming stage ("We're just getting started").

At Time 2, we noted several differences between team members' perceptions of mission clarity, team trust and support, involvement of senior sponsors, and productivity. Most teams had not yet identified a leader by this point in the program. Some teams neglected boundary management issues—failing to keep sponsors informed of problems or developing strategies for using sponsors to assist with resource acquisition, for instance. One team member, indicating that his team had been delayed by the absence of senior sponsor input, remarked, "Due to other business problems, our senior sponsor has been unavailable. This has made it difficult for us to get a clear focus on the project."

More than half of the program participants indicated that their teams had encountered some difficulties working on their project in the virtual environment between Times 1 and 2. Lack of commitment from some team members became evident at this point as several teams reported occurrences of "free riding." While it is not uncommon for members of co-located teams to express concern over some team members not doing "their fair share," the frustrations that our virtual team members expressed with nonperformers appeared amplified because team members could not directly observe or influence one another's behavior. Specific comments reflected four primary issues with which some groups had struggled: establishing leadership roles, setting direction, coordinating work, and building commitment to the task. Comments in these areas included,

> *"No one has taken a leadership role. We have not made the project the priority that it deserves." (ITECH team member)*
>
> *"Team members' day-to-day tasks are being used as an excuse to avoid doing the project." (ITECH team member)*
>
> *"It has been difficult to get all members to attend each conference call. Out of 5 calls there has not been perfect attendance yet." (AP team member)*

These comments reflect a variety of issues impeding trust-building and commitment. To their credit, many teams began to address these issues during the second ELI residence period. The opportunity for face-to-face interaction allowed some teams to "clear the air" and deal with passive and destructive individual and team behaviors. Resolution of team issues provided a basis for the establishment of team norms, reflecting an example of "punctuation" where some teams discussed and changed their work processes.

Time 3: Norming—Refocus and Recommit

By Time 3 (during the third residency period, approximately mid-way through the project life cycle), most teams recognized the need for reaching agreement on how they would operate going forward. Teams had revisited (and reinforced) existing norms or had established new norms regarding information collection, document sharing, task responsibilities, acceptable attendance at conference calls, and team commitment. Teams discussed ways in which members could be held more accountable for timely delivery of project assignments and openly confronted problems that might interfere with the completion of their projects. Teams also expressed some regret about their initial passivity, lack of initiative, and delays in collecting information.

Our survey and interview data at this point suggested that teams now differed with respect to perceived levels of team trust, sponsor support, and team performance (the percentage of work completed to date). For example, several teams reported high levels of trust in their teammates, while others reported minimal intra-team trust. At Time 3, the ACQUIRE and AP teams reported making the most progress, indicating that they had completed more than half of their projects. ITECH members reported making the least amount of progress on their assignment, having completed only a quarter of their planned work.

We used team-member perceptions of progress toward project completion as a proxy for team performance and examined what factors measured at Time 2 predicted team performance at Time 3. Results indicated that progress at Time 3 was associated with greater levels of communication, knowledge sharing, and confidence in performing the task at Time 2. Participant comments indicated that several teams struggled with issues of commitment and accountability during the norming stage that likely inhibited their progress. Developing norms required each team member to fulfill his/her assigned role, share important information, and meet deadlines. A majority of comments reflected the desire for greater commitment to the project, more discipline in working on the project, and better time management, communication, and coordination. Below are several illustrative comments:

> *"Virtual teaming is something that requires discipline." (ACQUIRE team member)*
>
> *"We need to develop a sense of urgency." (ITECH team member)*
>
> *"It is difficult to get people to do what they say." (TRANSFER team member)*
>
> *"You must make firm commitments to specific time schedules." (CAREER team member)*

These observations prompted some team members to increase their commitment levels and their communications with one another. When asked "What additional changes, if any, do you need to make to deliver an outstanding project?" many participants reported the need to develop a greater sense of urgency about the project, to speed up their work, and to communicate responsibilities more explicitly. Representative comments included:

> *"We may need to buckle down to get to work. Devoting the necessary time to the project has it challenges." (CAREER team member)*
>
> *"We really need to communicate each team member's responsibilities" (ACQUIRE team member)*
>
> *"We need to refocus our energy on moving forward." (COMM team member)*

Time 4: Performing—A (Sometimes Mad) Dash to the Finish

At Time 4, differences among teams emerged with respect to levels of team commitment, sponsor involvement, coordination, intra-team trust, and member "loafing." During the final week of the ELI, the teams presented their project findings and recommendations to the other ELI participants, seven senior FOODCO executives, including the CEO, CFO, and president, and five faculty members. These twelve non-participants evaluated each project for content, quality, and anticipated effectiveness. Aggregated team scores from these observations provided the performance data used to assess how a variety of factors affected team effectiveness.

Project team effectiveness as measured above was found to be a function of team members' perceptions of the availability of resources at Time 1. Teams that perceived greater amounts of resource availability at the onset of their projects performed better at the end of the project. At Time 2, teams with greater mission clarity, more time to examine work process effectiveness, and higher perceived levels of sponsor support were more effective at Time 4. At Time 3, none of the variables we examined predicted team performance at Time 4.

At Time 4, we also asked participants to reflect on their experiences and to consider what they had learned from their virtual projects. Responses suggest that the teams clearly underestimated the challenges associated with working virtually. During the "honeymoon period" (Time 1), they had anticipated minimal conflict, strong individual contributions from team members, and few obstacles to project completion. By the end of the project, participants uniformly remarked that virtual interactions were far more difficult than they had expected. Participants' responses to the question "If you could turn back the clock and start over, what would you do differently?" included,

> *"Better define what the project was. We had a lot of problems at the beginning not knowing about what we were to work on." (AP team member)*
>
> *"We could have included our mentor (sponsor) more in the planning phase of the project; this would have helped eliminate any wrong paths." (CAREER team member)*
>
> *"More discipline in hitting timeline." (TRANSFER team member)*

Additionally, when asked "What advice would you give future virtual teams?" nearly three quarters of the participants replied "Start earlier!" stressing the importance of establishing a clear mission and structured work processes from the outset. Representative comments included:

> *"Start early, meet often, and hold each other accountable to timelines and workloads." (TRANSFER team member)*
>
> *"Communicate a lot in the early stages. Find out what each person's strengths are, and get everyone involved. Hold members accountable." (AP team member)*
>
> *"Start early and talk at least every other week. Set firm deadlines." (CAREER team member)*

Comparing the Most and Least Effective Teams

A profile of the "best" team shows that at each step of the life cycle this team was proactive, focused, resourceful, and unafraid to seek support and guidance as needed. Specifically, evaluations of team effectiveness demonstrated that among the six virtual teams, CAREER was the most effective while AP was the least effective. A comparison of these teams at each data collection period reveals the significant issues that successful virtual teams resolve at various stages of their development. At Time 2, CAREER had developed much stronger consensus regarding team mission compared to the AP team. CAREER also reported greater levels of sponsor support and more frequent assessments of team processes than the AP team. These differences likely reflect the amount of time that the CAREER team committed to their project at the beginning of the assignment compared to their colleagues on the AP team.

Results at Time 3 revealed other differences between the CAREER and AP teams. For instance, the CAREER team recognized that they had developed effective working procedures but were not fully clear about responsibilities. Team members realized that their work processes might need to be revised to meet their deadline and perform well. The AP team, in contrast, struggled with how they could best accomplish their work. CAREER was also more confident than AP that they could deliver an outstanding product and that their recommendations would be acted upon by the firm.

At Time 4, differences between the two teams were even more apparent. In particular, CAREER reported maintaining higher levels of mission clarity, communication, commitment, and trust among team members. These differences suggest that between Times 3 and 4 the CAREER team recognized what changes needed to be made and successfully adapted their work processes to deliver an outstanding final product.

Guiding Virtual Teams Through the Life Cycle: Guidelines for Managers

This study represents one of the few research efforts that follow virtual project teams from project inception to completion. We were fortunate to have access to six virtual teams situated in an organization, dealing with real issues that required a tangible outcome for top management. Our findings thus provide a rare glimpse into the dynamics of "real life" virtual teams. Our data enabled us to explore which factors at each stage of development contribute to team performance and to identify the special challenges confronting virtual project teams as they develop. Importantly, however, our results should be interpreted with some caution as the experiences of our 29 participants and the six teams they formed as part of the ELI may not have been captured fully in our data nor may their experiences be applicable to all virtual project teams. For example, we do not know the extent to which the teams were evenly distributed in talent and capabilities or the extent to which team sponsors or local managers encouraged team members to take the endeavor seriously. These limitations notwithstanding, we offer our insights into how managers can guide virtual project teams through the project life cycle.

Not surprisingly, we found that working virtually delayed team progress through the forming stage by diminishing opportunities to communicate. Indeed, many of the virtual project teams communicated infrequently (if at all) during the early, forming stages of their projects. The lack of communication among team members reduced mission clarity and productivity at the project's onset, stifling early momentum and sending these teams into a spiral of failure. Contrary to our expectations and past research on virtual student teams, trust was not particularly difficult to establish at the beginning of the teams' projects. In fact, for almost all of the teams, perceptions of trust peaked at Time 2 and declined thereafter. Perhaps team members recognized that participation in the ELI was highly selective and inferred that teammates should be competent, hard working, and trustworthy. As the projects progressed and some team members failed to demonstrate competence and commitment to the team during the storming and norming stages, disillusionment set in, and perceptions of trust eroded.

Our findings underscore the critical role that senior sponsors can play in assisting virtual project teams through the early stages of development. The most successful teams we observed actively sought and initiated senior sponsor involvement at the early and middle stages of team life cycles. Sponsors helped these teams define their mission, set guidelines and accountabilities, and build confidence, facilitating team formation and reducing the length of the storming stage. In contrast, teams without early sponsor involvement lacked direction and momentum during this formative period. The lack of support prevented these teams from successfully navigating through the storming stage, often undermining team members' confidence and motivation to learn through the remainder of the projects. Indeed, our observations of the ELI teams are consistent with prior research in the project management literature which suggests the importance of early, pre-project planning and leadership support. This literature concludes that successful project teams invest time upfront with project managers to deal with the "fuzzy front end" of their projects which are often characterized by an ill-defined purpose, ambiguity regarding roles and responsibilities, and the uncertainty of acquiring resources and support. Hackman has recently offered the same insights in his discussion of the role of leaders in managing successful teams.[28]

As the ELI teams entered the norming stage of development and attempted to more clearly define work processes, many struggled with coordination and commitment issues. Team members expressed doubts about one another's commitment to the projects and raised concerns of possible "free riding" by some members, reflected in missed meetings, scheduling conflicts, and unreturned emails and phone calls. These behaviors may have been due to more pressing local work demands or technological breakdowns. However, without the benefit of direct observation and a full understanding of team members' local work contexts, both of which are typically afforded to co-located teams, virtual team members attributed the lack of participation and communication to a lack of commitment. Managers should encourage communication between team members to clarify whether lapses in participation are due to a lack of commitment or competing demands.

Consistent with prior research on virtual teams, we found that periodic face-to-face meetings marked periods of "punctuation" and provided teams with an opportunity to (re)assess their progress. For some teams, a pattern emerged in which energy devoted to working on the projects peaked shortly before each residency and quickly dissipated when team members dispersed. However, our best performing teams took advantage of the time between residencies to maintain momentum and developed a learning orientation by continuously sharing information and knowledge with one another. This disciplined approach to managing their "virtual" activities enabled teams to be more confident of their ability to deliver an outstanding project and more confident that their recommendations would be implemented.

Our observations and analyses suggest important implications for organizations considering the use of virtual project teams. Based on prior research regarding on-site team development and supported by findings derived from our longitudinal observations of the six ELI virtual teams, we offer suggestions for possible interventions appropriate to each stage in the virtual team life cycle. These interventions, described below, are summarized in Table 3.

Interventions at the Forming Stage

Our findings highlight a degree of unbounded but perhaps unrealistic optimism about potential virtual team success during the forming stage. This was often followed by the shock of slow progress, concern about teammates' commitment levels, problems with sponsor support, and anxiety over pending deadlines during later stages of team development. All six of our teams reported that their first experience working virtually was surprisingly difficult, and many commented that the opportunity provided valuable lessons that would help them in any future virtual team assignments. Frustrations stemming from unrealistically high expectations are not uncommon to project teams.[29] However, we believe that managerial prescriptions for helping virtual teams establish reasonable expectations must be sensitive to the unique challenges of virtual work.

Providing virtual project team members with insights from those who have served in similar situations is one way we suggest to improve team formation, as it should alert new teams to potential problems and pitfalls.[30] For example, Sabre uses realistic previews to focus virtual team members' attention on the importance of getting off to a fast start, contacting sponsors early, and scheduling opportunities for synchronous communication well in advance. Previews might

Table 3 Managerial Interventions During the Virtual Project Team Life Cycle

Formation	Storming	Norming	Performing
• Realistic virtual project team previews	• Face-to-face team building sessions	• Create customized templates or team charters specifying task requirements	• Ensure departmental and company culture supports virtual team work
• Coaching from experienced team members	• Training on conflict resolution	• Set individual accountabilities, completion dates, and schedules	• Provide sponsor support and resources for team to perform
• Develop a shared understanding and sense of team identity	• Encourage conflicting employees to work together to find common ground	• Establish procedures for information sharing	
• Develop a clear mission	• Shuttle diplomacy and mediation to create compromise solutions	• Distinguish task, social, and contextual information; design procedures appropriate for each	
• Acquire senior manager support		• Assign a team coach with skills for managing virtually	

also include other specific insights gained from previous virtual project team experience or might profile the characteristics of successful virtual teams as a benchmark against which new teams can chart their progress.

At the forming stage, care should be taken to help the virtual project team establish a shared team identity to prevent team members from abandoning the virtual project when they return to their home offices. Initial communications, whether face-to-face, teleconference, videoconference, or on-line, should encourage the exchange of personal information about backgrounds, skills, and experiences designed to help team members get to know one another and identify common ground. To help the team create a unique identity, teams might develop their own language or jargon to engage members or develop logos/symbols to serve as a constant visual reminder of the team and its mission.[31]

Our findings complement prior research on work teams by highlighting the importance of involving a senior sponsor early in the team's life cycle and gaining "unequivocal support from the top of the organization."[32] Indeed, the least effective sponsors we observed proceeded with their roles in a laissez-faire manner, did not proactively contact the teams, and did not attend their final presentations. Moreover, these sponsors failed to clarify their teams' missions until the teams had completed a considerable amount of work. This created enormous frustration when midway through the projects the sponsors expressed concern that the teams were not meeting expectations.

Effective senior sponsors can help virtual project teams clarify their mission and ensure that team members have the resources needed to accomplish their tasks, such as funding travel costs for intermittent face-to-face meetings.[33] Senior sponsors can also be used to provide pertinent information and an "expert opinion" on the teams' task. For example, in the virtual teams that Lipnack and Stamps observed from Eastman Chemical Co. and Sun Microsystems, senior sponsors advised teams on their task, were invited to key meetings, and were included in email correspondence between team members.[34] Finally, sponsors can help teams create "small wins" upfront that provide a springboard for future performance. For example, one of the more successful virtual teams we followed used their sponsor to help develop and administer a survey shortly after the initial meeting. The launch of the survey energized team members and provided a confidence boost for their efforts going forward. This practice has been used successfully at IBM where virtual team sponsors assist teams in creating an important 30-day goal upfront that requires full team participation. Similar to the team we observed, teams at IBM use these 30-day projects as vehicles to come together and build early momentum.[35] An important intervention at the forming stage requires managers to foster a collaborative partnership between sponsors and their virtual teams.

Interventions at the Storming Stage

Much has been written about the self-fueling spiral of success or failure experienced by many types of teams.[36] In particular, teams that experience early success gain confidence and motivation, which fuels future efforts and continued success. Conversely, teams that struggle initially lose confidence and momentum, stifling motivation and sending these teams into a spiral of failure. The importance of teams getting off to a fast start and building on early successes to generate momentum cannot be overemphasized. The virtual project team members we followed consistently pointed to the need for teams to build consensus around the team mission, work out role assignments, commit to goals, and confront conflicts. The most effective virtual teams reported the eventual development of greater mission clarity and higher levels of coordination and agreement around monthly goals, all of which reflected the time that these teams invested up front on their projects and the active, early involvement of the senior sponsor. Less successful teams reported early ambiguity around the project's purpose, unresolved coordination problems, and conflict over some members' lack of commitment, all symptoms of the self-fueling spiral of failure.

Though sometimes costly and inconvenient, a face-to-face team-building session for virtual teams is highly recommended early in the team development process to reduce the impact of an unsuccessful storming stage on team development. The senior sponsor could assign an experienced team facilitator or "coach" to help virtual team members focus on building consensus around a team's mission, differentiating roles, clarifying assignments, and resolving conflicts. Meeting face-to-face provides the richest possible communication context, often proving critical for overcoming problems encountered early in a virtual team's development.[37]

In situations where early face-to-face meetings are not possible, alternatives such as video or teleconferencing meetings can still provide a relatively rich opportunity for exchanges and can offer many, but not all, of the advantages of face-to-face meetings. If conflict cannot be resolved at such meetings, teams may employ more overt techniques aimed at addressing specific points of conflict.[38] For instance, a team leader or facilitator may ask conflicting team members to work together to resolve a problem and to foster greater understanding and appreciation of each other's perspective. In rare cases where a consensus regarding protocol or other coordination issues cannot be reached, teams may consider using "shuttle diplomacy" or mediation.[39] Specifically, a facilitator will communicate with team members individually to hear issues, concerns, or ideas, and then consolidate these viewpoints to come up with a compromise solution.

Interventions at the Norming Stage

Our teams reported that problems with information gathering, commitment from some team members, and free riding by others became more apparent at the norming stage of development. Teams acknowledged that their current work pace would make it nearly impossible to meet deadlines. The seriousness of these shortcomings led many teams to markedly increase their work efforts. For the best teams, a renewed commitment proved critical for project completion. For those teams hopelessly behind, norms governing commitment and productivity developed too late, the teams became stressed, and the final results were relatively disappointing.

We believe that early managerial intervention will increase the likelihood that teams develop norms governing commitment, accountability, and productivity, as our successful teams did. Managers who observe teams struggling with scheduling and coordination conflicts, miscommunications between distal team members, and gaining team members' commitment to the task can provide virtual teams with templates that identify strategies for improved team coordination.[40] Teams can then customize a template to include specific task requirements, individual accountabilities, expected completion dates, and mechanisms for collecting, collating, and sharing information. Managers can also help virtual teams identify norms regarding communication content, including how to share contextual information. For example, managers at Intel encourage virtual team members to send a "face" depicting their mood on any given day so that team members can better understand how to interpret and respond to team member communications.[41]

Some virtual teams may benefit from using electronic decision support systems to stimulate brain-storming and group decision-making.[42] Managers should provide training to ensure that team members know how to use these technologies and use them appropriately, as needed. Virtual team leaders at Novartis recommend that training team members in the use of more complex collaborative technologies should be incremental, allowing team members to become comfortable with various features of a given technology over time.[43]

In addition to the impact of a supportive senior sponsor, another possible intervention is to assign project teams "coaches" skilled in virtual management to nurture virtual project teams through the early development stages. Senior sponsors may not have had experience managing virtual teams and/or may not be sufficiently accessible to team members to provide the type of personal suggestions a "coach" could provide. In addition to providing team members with a realistic preview of the virtual team experience, coaches could counsel team members on- or off-line, model the appropriate use of communication and collaboration technologies, and reinforce the value of managing boundary relationships.[44] Indeed, our most successful teams were particularly proactive, seeking out informal sources of coaching and support. Once team members experience success working virtually, they should become well situated to coaching new virtual project members and teams.

Interventions at the Performing Stage

As these results suggest, many factors contribute to virtual project team effectiveness. We have emphasized how team processes can contribute to or detract from team performance. However, it is equally important to recognize that virtual team members do not function in isolation. Corporate and sub-unit cultures may also influence virtual team effectiveness.

Virtual project team sponsors may need to intervene to shape a more supportive corporate and sub-unit context within which virtual teams can flourish. In most instances, serving on a virtual project team is a part-time assignment. Team members must balance competing local demands for their time with commitments made to their virtual project teams. Virtual team sponsors must be sensitive to these dual demands and, as needed, be willing to negotiate with local executives the relative importance and time commitment required for successful virtual project team participation.

One of our least successful teams reported minimal support for their project activities among executives in the divisions represented on this team. Team members also believed that their performance evaluation and compensation for their "real (non-virtual) job" were at risk if they made more than a token commitment to the virtual project team. In contrast, our most successful virtual team reported complete support for their virtual project efforts by senior managers in all of the divisions represented by the team. By providing team members with the necessary time and resources to work on both their local and virtual projects, senior management signaled that outcomes of the virtual project team were valued. The lesson seems obvious: To thrive, virtual project teams must be embedded in supportive corporate cultures.

In addition to providing sufficient resources, managers can use other strategies to create a supportive culture. For example, virtual team leaders at ARCO reported that to support their virtual team's efforts, team leaders "buffer" interference from on-site work demands.[45] When virtual team members are relieved from some of their typical local demands, they may focus more energy on the virtual team assignment without fear of reprisal from their local managers.

The creation of virtual teams will likely require that managers realign recognition and reward systems to better assess and reward virtual team performance.[46] For example, Sabre uses a balanced scorecard approach for tracking virtual team performance that provides quantitative and qualitative information including growth, profitability, process improvement, and customer satisfaction.[47] Teams may wish to complement this objective performance data with 360 degree evaluation procedures to capture unique individual contributions. By realigning recognition and reward systems, managers help their virtual teams discover how various stakeholders, including customers, other team members, and outsiders perceive the quality of their work.[48]

Conclusion: Timing the Interventions

To mobilize virtual project teams, managers need insights into the challenges associated with each stage of the virtual team life cycle. Based on our comparison of flourishing and floundering virtual teams, it appears that managers who can recognize the signs of steady progress as well as the signs of distress associated with virtual team development will be in stronger positions to keep their teams on track. Similar to the concept of a "teachable moment" for introducing skills training at the point where these skills are most salient, managers must learn to time the introduction of interventions to virtual team life cycle challenges.[49] To conclude, we suggest a number of stage-appropriate interventions.

In the formation stage, realistic previews, exercises surrounding the creation of mission statements, and assistance in building team identity are all potentially useful strategies for helping virtual project teams get off to a fast start. The active involvement of a senior sponsor to clarify the team's mission and to ensure that the team has the resources it needs to perform can also boost early success. Because teams typically experience frustration and conflict in the storming stage, most teams should benefit from managerial interventions to help select appropriate procedures for working through conflicts, pushing teams more quickly to the norming stage of team development. Encouraging teams to establish a strong work ethic and to create mechanisms for holding members accountable for meeting deadlines are interventions particularly important at the norming stage.

At the performing stage, managerial interventions to facilitate brainstorming, decision making, and monitoring of progress against objectives and timelines will enhance team performance. Finally, and perhaps most important, are ongoing managerial efforts to embed virtual teams in supportive work contexts. Similar to other virtual team experiences chronicled in the literature, our six teams struggled to balance their virtual team demands with home office priorities.[50] To combat these competing demands, managerial interventions could take the form of negotiating work priorities with on-site supervisors and aligning reward systems to recognize virtual team contributions.

Certainly, sponsors, coaches, managers, and virtual team leaders and members have many intervention options to assist struggling virtual teams. But, as with so many organizational activities, timing is everything. Introducing interventions at the appropriate stage of development represents an important tool for leveraging virtual team performance. Having the tools in the toolkit is only the beginning. Knowing which tool to use when is the sign of the true master craftsman.

Appendix

Descriptive Information Regarding the Six Virtual Project Team Participants

The members of the six virtual project teams that we followed were employed by FOODCO. This company distributes food products to schools, hospitals, fast-food chains, and individually owned and operated restaurants, and manufactures a limited number of its own products. Executives at FOODCO commissioned a large university located in the southeastern US to create an Executive Leadership Institute (ELI) that would (1) align organizational learning with strategic business needs, (2) establish cross-organizational networks to encourage the sharing of best practices, (3) prepare managers for expanded organizational roles, (4) integrate new managers from FOODCO's recent acquisitions, and (5) develop a unified company culture across its multiple operating companies.

The 29 participants in the ELI program held positions of substantial responsibility in human resources, finance, marketing, sales, and operations areas. Superiors nominated participants for the program based on their potential to contribute to the company beyond their current levels of responsibility. Fourteen participants were from the executive ranks, while the remaining participants held middle-management positions.

Summary of Methodology Used to Study Virtual Project Teams at FOODCO

To assess the factors that contributed to virtual project team performance at various stages of the teams' life cycles, we collected survey and interview data throughout the eight-month project period. Specifically, during each of the four residence sessions, ELI participants completed surveys and participated in interviews designed to assess their attitudes and behaviors during the virtual project team assignment.

Participant surveys included both quantitative and qualitative questions. The quantitative data we collected at each time period varied slightly to reflect anticipated differences in development issues. During the first residency, participants were asked about the meaning of their project, its usefulness to the firm, the impact that the project would have on the company, how competent they felt to complete the project, and the anticipated climate for teamwork. During subsequent residence periods, survey questions focused on team process variables, such as perceptions of mission clarity, trust levels among team members, learning capacity, extent of sponsor support, and specific performance outcomes, including percentage of project completed, perceptions of team productivity, and perceived efficacy of completing an outstanding project.

Surveys also included several open-ended questions allowing participants to describe their views of the project, the challenges associated with virtual work, and their teams' responses to these challenges. For instance, during the first residency, we asked participants to "Describe your expectations for how you think your team will work together." Questions at the third residency focused on what individuals had learned about working virtually and what they would do differently had they been able to start over. During the final residency, we asked participants to reflect on their experience, to discuss what they learned about team processes that they could carry over to their current jobs, and to consider what advice they might give future virtual teams.

At the end of the fourth residency, teams presented their analysis and recommendations to a group of FOODCO's top executives and ELI administrators. This group rated the quality and content of each team's analysis of the critical business issue they researched and the quality of the recommendations they provided. They also rated the quality of the presentation delivered by each team. Each observer calculated an overall score for each team based on these three dimensions. We aggregated and averaged ratings for each team and used the result as the measure of team performance in further analyses.

Source: Academy of Management Executive, 18, (2), 6–20 (2004). Reprinted by permission of the CCC.

ENDNOTES

1. Townsend, A. M., DeMarie, S. M., & Hendrickson, A. R. 1998. Virtual teams: Technology and the workplace of the future. *The Academy of Management Executive*, 12(3): 17–29.
2. Potter, R. E., & Balthazard, P. A. 2002. Understanding human interaction and performance in the virtual team. *Journal of Information Technology Theory and Application*, 4: 1–23; Baker, G. 2002. The effects of synchronous collaborative technologies on decision making: A study of virtual teams. *Information Resources Management Journal*, 15(4): 79–93.
3. Ahuja, M. K., & Galvin, J. E. 2001. Socialization in virtual groups. *Journal of Management*, 29: 1–25.
4. Townsend, et al., 1998, op. cit.; Cascio, W. F. 2000. Managing a virtual workplace. *The Academy of Management Executive*, 14(3): 81–90; Kirkman, B. L., et al. 2002. Five challenges to virtual team success: Lessons from Sabre, Inc. *The Academy of Management Executive*, 16(3): 67–79.
5. See, for example, Banker, Lee, Potter, & Srinivasan, 1996; Wellins, Byham, & Dixon, 1994; Cohen & Ledford, 1994; and Cordery, Mueller, & Smith, 1991.
6. For studies that investigate coordination, communication interpersonal dynamics, and technology issues in virtual or computer-mediated teams, see Straus, S. G. 1996. Getting a clue: The effects of communication media and information distribution on participation and performance in computer-mediated and face-to-face groups. *Small Group Research*, 27: 115–42; Lipnack. J., & Stamps, J. 2000. *Virtual teams: People working across boundaries with technology.* 2nd ed. New York: Wiley; Daft, R. T., & Lengel, R. H. 1986. Organizational information requirements, media richness, and structural design. *Management Science*, 32: 554–571; and Straus, S. G., & McGrath, L. E. 1994. Does medium matter? The interaction of task type and technology on group performance and member reactions. *Journal of Applied Psychology*, 79(1): 87–97.
7. Hackman, J. R. 1990. *Groups that work (and those that don't): Creating conditions for effective teamwork.* San Francisco: Jossey-Bass.
8. Tuckman, B. W. 1965. Development sequence in small groups. *Psychological Bulletin*, 63: 384–399; Gersick, C. J. G. 1988. Time and transition in work teams: Toward a new model of group development. *Academy of Management Journal*, 31: 9–41.
9. Gersick, C. J. G. 1994. Pacing strategic change: The case of a new venture. *Academy of Management Journal*, 37: 9–45.
10. See, for example, in Bordia, P., DiFonzo, N., & Chang, A. 1999. Rumor as group problem solving: Development patterns in informal computer-mediated teams. *Small Group Research*, 30: 8–28. For further evidence of pacing differences, see Gluesing, J. C., et al. 2002. The development of global virtual teams. In C. B. Gibson & S. G. Cohen (Eds.), *Virtual teams that work: Creating conditions for virtual team effectiveness:* 353–380. San Francisco: Jossey-Bass. For evidence of the punctuated equilibrium model in virtual teams, see Maznevski & Chudoba, 2000, op. cit.
11. Caproni, P. J. 2001. *The practical coach: Management skills for everyday life.* Upper Saddle River, NJ: Prentice-Hall (see specifically Chapter 8, entitled, "Diverse teams and virtual teams: Managing differences and distances," 247–287).
12. Cramton, C. D. 2001. The mutual knowledge problem and its consequences for dispersed collaboration. *Organization Science*, 12: 346–371.
13. Tsui, A. S., Egan, T. D., & O'Reilly III, C. A. 1992. Being different: Relational demography and organizational attachment. *Administrative Science Quarterly*, 37: 549–579.

14. Cramton, C. D. 2002. Finding common ground in dispersed collaboration. *Organizational Dynamics*, 30: 356–367.

15. Shapiro, D. L., et al. 2002. Transnational teams in the electronic age: Are team identity and high performance at risk? *Journal of Organizational Behavior*, 23: 455–467.

16. Handy, C. 1995. Trust and the virtual organization. *Harvard Business Review*, 73(9): 40–48.

17. Jarvenpaa, S. L., Knoll, K., & Leidner, D. E. 1998. Is anybody out there? Antecedents of trust in global virtual teams. *Journal of Management Information Systems*. 14; 29–64.

18. Cramton, 2002, op. cit.

19. Hollingshead, A. B., & McGrath, J. E. 1995. Computer assisted groups: A critical review of the empirical research. In Guzzo, R., & Salas, E. (Eds.), *Team effectiveness and decision making in organizations*, San Francisco: Jossey-Bass: 46–78.

20. Hinds, P. J., & Weisband, S. P. 2002. Knowledge sharing and shared understanding in virtual teams. In C. B. Gibson & S. G. Cohen (Eds.), *Virtual teams that work: Creating conditions for virtual team effectiveness:* 221–36. San Francisco: Jossey-Bass.

21. Blackburn, R. S., Furst, S. A., & Rosen, B. 2002. Building a winning team: KSAs, selection, training, and evaluation. In C. B. Gibson & S. G. Cohen (Eds.), *Virtual teams that work: Creating conditions for virtual team effectiveness:* 95–120. San Francisco: Jossey-Bass.

22. Tyran, K. L., Tyran, C. K., & Shepard, M. 2002. Exploring emerging leadership in virtual teams. In C. B. Gibson & S. G. Cohen (Eds.), *Virtual teams that work: Creating conditions for virtual team effectiveness:* 183–195. San Francisco: Jossey-Bass.

23. Furst, S. A., Blackburn, R. S., & Rosen, B. 1999. Virtual team effectiveness: A proposed research agenda. *Information Systems Journal*, 9: 249–269.

24. Kirkman, et al., 2002, op. cit.

25. Jarvenpaa, et al., 1998, op. cit.; Cascio, 2000, op. cit.

26. Gluesing, et al., 2002, op. cit.

27. Kossler, M., & Prestridge, S. 2004. *Leading dispersed teams: Ideas into action guidebook*. Greensboro, NC: Center for Creative Leadership.

28. Hackman, J. R. 2002. *Leading teams: Setting the stage for great performances:* 199–232. Boston: Harvard Business School; Jiang, J. J., Klein, G., & Discenza, R. 2002. Pre-project partnering impact on an information system project, project team and project manager. *European Journal of Information Systems*, 11: 86–97; Zhang, Q., & Doll, W. J. 2001. The fuzzy front end and success of new product development: A causal model. *European Journal of Innovation Management*, 4(2): 95–112.

29. Wetlaufer, S., et al. 1994. The team that wasn't. *Harvard Business Review*, 72(6): 22–38.

30. Kirkman, et al., 2002, op. cit.

31. Malhotra, A., et al. 2001. Radical innovation without collocation: A case study at Boeing-Rocketdyne. *MIS Quarterly*, 25: 229–249.

32. Kossler & Prestridge, 2004, op. cit.

33. Ibid.

34. Lipnack, J., & Stamps, J. 2000, op. cit.

35. Rosen, B., et al. 2001. Is virtual the same as being there?: Not really! Paper presented at the National Academy of Management Meetings, Toronto.

36. Hackman, J. R. 1990. *Groups that work (and those that don't)*. San Francisco: Jossey-Bass.

37. Joinson, C. 2002. Managing virtual teams. *HR Magazine*, 47(6): 69–73.

38. Gluesing, et al., 2002, op. cit.

39. Ibid.

40. Montoya-Weiss, M. M., Massey. A. P., & Song, M. 2001. Getting it together: Temporal coordination and conflict management in global virtual teams. *Academy of Management Journal*, 44: 1251–1262.

41. Rosen, et al., 2001, op. cit.

42. Lam, S. S. K., & Shaubroeck, J. 2000. Improving group decisions by better pooling information: A comparative advantage of group decision support systems. *Journal of Applied Psychology*, 85(4): 565–573.

43. Rosen, et al., 2001, op. cit.

44. Jarvenpaa, S., & Leidner, D. 1998. Communication and trust in global virtual teams. *Organization Science*, 10(6): 791–815.

45. Ibid.

46. Lawler, E. E. 2002. Pay systems for virtual teams. In C. B. Gibson & S. G. Cohen (Eds.), *Virtual teams that work: Creating conditions for virtual team effectiveness:* 121–144. San Francisco: Jossey-Bass.

47. Kirkman, et al., 2002, op. cit.

48. Blackburn, et al., 2002, op. cit.

49. Ibid.

50. Reeves, M. & Furst, S. 2004. Virtual teams in an executive education training program. In S. H. Godar, & S. P. Ferris (Eds.), *Virtual and collaborative teams: Process, technologies, and practice:* 232–252. Hershey, PA: Idea Publishing Group; Gluesing, et al., 2002, op. cit.: Hackman, et al., 2002, op. cit.

READING 10.3

Performance Leadership: 11 Better Practices That Can Ratchet Up Performance

Robert D. Behn

Helping the Managers Manage

How can the leaders of a public agency improve its performance? What can the leaders of a governmental organization possibly do that might have a positive effect on the results that their agency produces? This is an important question. This is a leadership question.

The Futile Search for a Performance System

This *leadership question* is not, however, the question about government performance that is usually asked. Traditionally, we have asked the *systems question*. Rather than develop public managers with the leadership capacity to improve the performance of their agencies, we have sought to create performance systems that will impose such improvements. We have sought to create government-wide schemes that will somehow require performance from all departments, agencies, and bureaus. Thus, we have tended (if only implicitly) to ignore the leadership question and, instead, have focused on the systems question: How can we compel, command, or coerce public agencies into improving their performance?

This systems approach is unlikely to prove very effective. Yes, it is possible for a legislature, a budget office, or a central administrative agency to force public agencies to do things that—if done with genuine enthusiasm and subtle intelligence—could contribute to improved performance. Those upon whom such requirements are imposed, however, are not likely to view them as helpful. They will see these requirements as another complex confusion of administrative regulations with which they must dutifully comply—not as a coherent collection of supportive principles that, if deployed discernably and employed adaptively, might actually help. Administrative requirements (for performance or anything else) are not designed to elicit discernment and adaptation. They are created to impose obedience and conformity.

Moreover, the senior managers upon whom such compliance is imposed have seen all this before. They have learned how to cope. Indeed, they became senior managers precisely because they learned how to cope. They learned that administrative requirements are hoops through which they must jump. And, as they moved up the organizational hierarchy, they learned to become very good hoop jumpers. They can now jump nimbly through big hoops and small hoops, red hoops and green hoops; they can even jump through flaming hoops without getting the least bit singed.

The following approach to performance leadership makes no claim to be a *best practice*. It might be, however, in Eugene Bardach's phrase, a "smart practice" (Bardach, 1998, 35–41). If employed with thoughtful discernment of the underlying principles and deployed with intelligent adaptation to the characteristics and needs of the particular organization and its environment, this approach might help some public managers improve their agency's performance, marginally or even significantly.

After all, to ratchet up performance a notch or two, most public managers do not require a best practice. All they need is a *better practice*—a set of operational principles, or just one good idea, that is an improvement over what they are currently doing.

I make no claim that employing all 11 practices is necessary to improve a public agency's performance. Still, each practice is, if the agency manager is not already using it, a *better* practice. Moreover, the 11 do reinforce each other. (Several of these practices are based on the same underlying principles, so that employing one practice without another is often difficult.) Consequently, public managers who employ several of them will have a better opportunity to exploit their reinforcing benefits. These 11 practices offer *one approach* to performance leadership.

Creating the Performance Framework

Practice 1: Articulate the Organization's Mission

This first practice is hardly profound. It is advocated by numerous management gurus and followed by many practicing managers. Everyone in the organization needs to understand the big picture. Thus, the leaders of the organization need to proclaim, clearly and frequently, what the organization is trying to accomplish.

When you walk into the main lobby of many business firms, government agencies, and nonprofit organizations, you will find the mission statement displayed on the wall. Yet, how many people know what these words say? How many appreciate the values that these words are designed to represent? How many act daily (or even occasionally) to further the basic purposes that are proclaimed in the mission statement and that thus constitute the rationale for the organization's existence? How many public employees go about their assigned tasks completely oblivious to how these tasks contribute (or not) to their agency's mission?

For any organization, particularly for a public agency, it is not enough to form a committee or engage a consultant to write or update the mission statement. After all, in the words of Scott Adams, a mission statement is nothing more than "a long awkward sentence that demonstrates management's inability to think clearly" (Adams, 1996, 36). Even if a public agency's mission statement is neither long, nor awkward, nor convoluted, posting the statement on the wall is not enough. If the agency's leaders want everyone in the organization to take the mission seriously, they need to reiterate its fundamental points at every opportunity.

Practice 2: Identify the Organization's Most Consequential Performance Deficit

The mission of any organization—public, private, or non-profit—is necessarily vague. It may be inspirational; nevertheless, it lacks specificity. It fails to provide any useful guidance about what to do next: What specific problem does the organization need to attack now to significantly improve its performance? The words in the mission statement do not answer this operational question. Thus, the organization needs to determine what key failure is keeping it from achieving its mission: "What is our most consequential performance deficit?"

Naturally, the organization will have a variety of failures and performance deficits. Just as naturally, it cannot attack all of them at once. It must choose. This is the first challenge to the organization's leadership—to figure out, from the variety of problems inhibiting its ability to produce results, that one performance deficit (or, at most, a very few) on which the organization should now focus its intelligence and energies.

Identifying the organization's performance deficit is clearly a subjective judgment. Every organization—no matter whether public or private; no matter how well it is performing—has multiple performance deficits. It has a variety of things that, if it did them better, would enhance its outputs, and thus the outcomes to which it contributes. Someone has to choose. This is a leadership requirement. If the individuals at the top of the organizational hierarchy fail to select the performance deficits on which their organization should focus, they have no claim to the title of leader.

The leaders of the organization can make this selection brilliantly or haphazardly. They can put some serious thought into the question, "On which performance deficit should our organization focus?" They can deliberately choose a big deficit that, when eliminated, will have a major impact on the organization's performance. Or they can just as deliberately select a small deficit that, when eliminated, will demonstrate to those working in the organization (and perhaps to multiple stakeholders) that they can accomplish even more. Of course, even if they choose deliberately, the organization's leaders can choose badly.

Still, the biggest mistake is not to choose at all—to avoid the responsibility for determining what the organization should fix next.

Practice 3: Establish a Specific Performance Target

Having made the admittedly subjective judgment about the aspect of the organization's performance deficit on which it will focus, the leaders need to make a second judgment. They need to create an explicit performance target for closing that deficit. That is, the leaders of the organization need to specify what new level of success the organization should attempt to achieve next and by when.

Practice 4: Clarify Your Theoretical Link between Target and Mission

Unfortunately, no performance target is precisely the same as the organization's mission. By achieving the target, the organization should further its mission. Otherwise the leadership team would not have chosen to focus on the related performance deficit or have selected this as its next target. Still, the leaders need to make this connection very clear. They need to define (for themselves individually, at least, and perhaps collectively) a mental model that explains how meeting the target will help accomplish the mission.

In some circumstances, the causal connection will be obvious. If a health department delivers the proper measles immunization to a child, that child's probability of actually being immune to measles, and thus healthier, is greater than 99 percent (Atkinson et al., 2002, 104). The output of immunization is directly connected to the outcome of a healthier child. Moreover, the immunization process is relatively simple and, if followed by certified personnel, does not have a lot of defects; if a certified nurse follows the standard operating procedures for measles immunization, the immunization will take. The theoretical linkage between achieving the performance target and furthering the agency's mission is not theoretical at all. It has been well established, very empirically.

Unfortunately, most actions taken by most public agencies are not connected this closely to their mission. The causal link between the actions taken by the agency to close its performance deficit and the achievement of its mission may be indirect, vague, poorly understood, or nonexistent. Consequently, the leaders of public agencies cannot merely define a performance deficit, select a performance target, and mobilize their organization to achieve this target—all under the (implicit) assumption that this will further its mission. These leaders need first to clarify explicitly the nature of their theory that connects reaching the target and furthering the mission. Then, once they have reached the target, they need to check to see whether this effort has, indeed, produced some real improvement.

11 Better Practices That Can Ratchet Up Performance

Creating the Performance Framework

Practice 1: Articulate the organization's mission.

Practice 2: Identify the organization's most consequential performance deficit.

Practice 3: Establish a specific performance target.

Practice 4: Clarify your theoretical link between target and mission.

Driving Performance Improvement

Practice 5: Monitor and report progress frequently, personally, and publicly.

Practice 6: Build operational capacity.

Practice 7: Take advantage of small wins to reward success.

Practice 8: Create "esteem opportunities."

Learning to Enhance Performance

Practice 9: Check for distortions and mission accomplishment.

Practice 10: Analyze a larger number and a wide variety of indicators.

Practice 11: Adjust mission, target, theory, monitoring and reporting, operational capacity, rewards, esteem opportunities, and/or analysis.

Driving Performance Improvement

Practice 5: Monitor and Report Progress Frequently, Personally, and Publicly

Again, this better practice is hardly mysterious. The leaders of the organization have to track and publish the performance data so that every team knows that the leadership knows (and that everyone else knows) how well every team is doing.

This is the first step in motivating teams (and the individuals on these teams) to achieve their performance targets. The mechanism chosen to monitor and report progress depends on both the culture of the organization and the nature of the performance targets. Still, whatever mechanism the leaders choose, they need to ensure that it provides several kinds of information.

First, this practice of monitoring and reporting needs to dramatize that the organization's leaders are paying attention to its progress. The people in any organization have an easy instrument for determining what their leaders care about; they measure how much time the leaders spend on their various initiatives. If the leaders do not spend time monitoring progress toward their performance targets, the entire organization quickly realizes that the leaders do not really care.

After all, the leaders' most valuable resource is their own time. They can invent clever ways to get around budgetary limits and regulatory constraints. But they face one eternal, immutable constraint; like all other humans, they have only 168 hours in any week. They cannot squeeze 169 hours out of any week, save an hour from one week to the next, or borrow an hour from a colleague or friend. Thus, the metaphor about "spending time" is not a metaphor at all. It is reality. People "spend" time just as they spend money. Both are extremely valuable resources—and time is scarcer than money.

Performance measurement is not performance leadership. Performance measurement is a passive activity easily delegated to a few wonks in a back office. Performance leadership, however, requires the ceaseless, active engagement of the organization's leaders.

If these leaders do not spend time monitoring the organization's performance targets, everyone soon figures out that they are really not interested. If, however, these leaders do spend the time necessary to dramatize that they are carefully following progress, many in the organization will begin to take the performance targets—and their part in achieving them—seriously.

Second, this practice of monitoring and reporting needs to dramatize how well different teams or individuals are contributing to the overall target.

In many circumstances, effective reporting can be done on a single piece of paper. If the responsibility for achieving the performance target is allocated among various teams within the agency, the single piece of paper need contain only two columns: Column A lists all the teams that made their target for the last month, last quarter, or last year; Column B lists all the teams that did not make their target. I call this "The List" (Behn, 2003).

Practice 6: Build Operational Capacity

Of course, no team can win unless the organization's leaders provide their teams with whatever they need to achieve their targets. W. Edwards Deming did not like goals or, as he often called them, "quotas." One of his reasons was that he believed most organizations set goals for individuals or teams but failed to provide them with the operational capacity to achieve the goals. "I have yet to see a quota that includes any trace of a system by which to help anyone to do a better job," wrote Deming. Personal "goals are necessary" and people should set them for themselves, he argued; "but numerical goals set for other people, without a road map to reach the goal, have effects opposite to the effects sought." (Deming, 1982, 1986; 69, 71).

Deming was, admittedly, talking about "numerical quotas for hourly workers," the classical "work standards" of scientific management (Deming, 1982, 1986; 70). Nevertheless, Deming's general point still applies. If the leaders of an organization wish to improve performance, they cannot just assign targets to individuals or teams. They have to provide everyone in the organization with the "system," the "road map"—whatever it takes to create the operational capacity necessary to achieve the targets.

This operational capacity might include money and other resources, people and training, technology and production systems, the cooperation of essential partners, and a road map of tactics and strategies that help teams achieve their targets. Leaders cannot simply demand improved performance. They cannot simply set new, demanding performance targets. The organization's leadership has to give teams the capabilities necessary for achieving these targets.

Practice 7: Take Advantage of Small Wins to Reward Success

Having established a performance target, the agency's leaders need to dramatize that they recognize and appreciate what teams (and the individuals on those teams) have accomplished. And although moving a team from Column B to Column A on a widely distributed piece of paper (or the home page on the agency's intranet) is itself a reward, the leaders can do more. When a team achieves its annual target—or even makes significant quarterly progress toward it—effective leaders understand how to celebrate the success. Some accomplishments warrant the simple recognition of a sincere thank you. Other triumphs require the leaders to kill the fatted calf. The magnitude of the ceremony should match the significance of the victory.

In public agencies, celebrating successes is undervalued. So is saying "thank you." There can be a danger in over-celebrating a minor achievement. In most organizations, however, the more common mistake is to under-acknowledge achievements of all sizes. Most public executives do not say thank you enough. As William James once wrote: "I now perceive one immense omission in my Psychology,—the deepest principle of Human Nature is the *craving to be appreciated*, and I left it out altogether from the book, because I never had it gratified till now" (James, 1920, 33).

To foster an environment in which successes will be celebrated more frequently, an agency's leaders can create more milestones. Do not just create a performance target for the year. Break that target down into quarterly and monthly targets. And when a team has an important breakthrough, the agency's leaders need to find a way to signal, both to this team and to everyone else throughout the agency, that this group of individuals has done something truly worthwhile.

This addiction strategy is really quite simple. Create performance targets that people can hit. Get them hooked on success. Give them an opportunity to earn the adrenaline rush that comes from accomplishing something worthwhile, and then give them the challenge of accomplishing even more.

This is why I describe this leadership approach as a way to *ratchet up* performance. Each small win creates not just a sense of accomplishment but also a new and higher plateau—a new baseline from which future performance must be compared.

Practice 8: Create "Esteem Opportunities"

Rewarding success is one way to ensure that the members of high-performing teams can earn a sense of accomplishment and thus gain both self-esteem and the esteem of their peers. And the opportunity to earn such esteem can be an important motivational strategy for any organization's leaders.

The leaders of a public agency can contribute to the esteem needs of their organization's employees and collaborators. The leaders can give people an opportunity to take pride in a real achievement. They can give people an opportunity to gain a reputation for real achievement. Moreover, in doing so, the agency's leaders can contribute to their organization's ability to do even more. For, writes Abraham Maslow, "satisfaction of the self-esteem need leads to feelings of self-confidence, worth, strength, capability and adequacy of being useful and necessary in the world" (Maslow, 1943, 382).

One practice (that I have seen employed in a variety of public organizations) is to ask the head of a particularly successful team: "Would you please come back to next month's meeting and tell us how you did it?" In doing so, the organization's leaders thereby reward the team's head by giving him or her an esteem opportunity. At the same time, they have rewarded this individual by giving him or her more work. For now, this team leader must (1) keep up team performance during the coming month so as not to be embarrassed by having to explain why the team regressed, and (2) devote additional time to preparing a coherent presentation to somehow explain the team's success. Still, the message will be clear. Everyone will get it. This team has been asked to report on its strategy, tactics, and processes precisely because it is a high-performing team.

This esteem opportunity need not be limited to the head of the team. The agency's leaders could also ask: "Would you please bring your team to next month's meeting and tell us how you all did it?" Like saying thank you, esteem opportunities are not a scare resource that can be awarded to just a few elites. They can be created for multiple individuals and teams throughout the organization.

Moreover, this kind of esteem opportunity provides for technology transfer, and thus helps to build operational capacity. It gives those on the less successful teams—and often those on the more successful teams, too—the chance to learn new strategies, tactics, and processes. Although the explanations offered by some team members may not be as articulate or clear as ones that the agency's leaders might produce, such imperfect explanations come with one added advantage. Those listening to a convoluted explanation of what everyone accepts to be a significant success can easily conclude: "They aren't so smart. If they can do it, we certainly can do it, too."

Learning to Enhance Performance

Practice 9: Check for Distortions and Mission Accomplishment

Unfortunately, achieving the performance target does not guarantee that the organization achieves its mission. Achieving the target does not even guarantee that the organization has helped to accomplish its mission. Thus, the leaders of the organization need to verify that people are pursuing their targets in ways that do, indeed, further the mission (not in ways that either fail to help or even undermine the effort). They need to check for a variety of distortions in which achieving the target may not have contributed significantly to accomplishing the mission.

After all, the leader's theoretical link between target and mission may not be perfect. Indeed, this link may not even exist. It is always difficult, in any organization, to predict cause-and-effect relationships—to understand the complex interactions that are going on inside the organizational black box. The organization's leaders can take specific actions based on the perfectly reasonable prediction (derived from established theory or personal experience) that it will create behavior that will then produce the results they desire—or, at least, something close to these results—only to discover that actual consequences of these actions are quite different. They have no guarantee that the mental model they used to create their theoretical link between target and mission is correct, or even close to correct.

The leaders need to check carefully to be sure that the agency has, by achieving its performance target, indeed helped further its true purpose. Did their organizational black box respond as they predicted? If their theoretical link does not appear to work as they predicted, they have to figure out why.

Practice 10: Analyze a Large Number and a Wide Variety of Indicators

The leaders of the organization need to learn not only whether they have created any distortions, whether their agency has engaged in any cheating, and whether their agency is making progress toward achieving its mission. Regardless of how well the agency has done, they also need to learn how to improve. For all of these purposes, the leaders need to examine many forms of data—both quantitative and qualitative.

Some of this learning will be quantitatively sophisticated. After all, doing a conscientious evaluation of a public agency's impact is a complex undertaking. It requires a sophisticated analysis of a multitude of potential influences as well as some subtle judgments about how to measure progress toward the mission. It also requires a lot of very clean, quantitative data.

Some of this learning, however, will rely on data that are significantly less quantitative and significantly less verifiable. It will come in the form of anecdotes and casual observations that may, however, be no less helpful. Particularly when the challenge is to uncover distortions and to develop ways to improve for next year, the organization's leaders may find that examining such qualitative data analytically (though not mathematically) can be of significant help.

The leaders can employ quantitative analysis to determine whether their agency is accomplishing its mission. But what they really want to know is whether they are moving their organization in the proper direction. A public agency's leaders need not seek to determine whether they have *achieved* their mission, for they never will. Instead, they need to learn whether or not they have done a better job recently. They need to learn whether or not their performance strategy is truly *furthering* their mission.

Once they are convinced that they are making progress, the leaders have to determine why: What are the things that they have done that have contributed significantly to their progress? It would be nice to be able to use quantitative analysis to answer this question—to determine precisely what actions contributed *most* to their progress. Their organization's data set, unfortunately, will rarely be robust enough to answer this question. But, then, the leaders do not need to determine *the best practice*. They need to uncover only *a better practice*—or two. Then they can employ these better practices in a way that ratchets up performance some more.

Thus, the analytical task of determining what has worked, what has not worked, and what needs to be done to improve performance requires examining a diversity of indicators. Some indicators will be found in formal data sets collected by the agency or by other organizations. Additional indicators will be found in careful, if serendipitous, observations in the reports from the heads of successful teams about how (they think) they achieved their targets, and in the complaints about inadequate resources, perverse incentives, or distortions.

Practice 11: Adjust Mission, Target, Theory, Monitoring and Reporting, Operational Capacity, Rewards, Esteem Opportunities, and/or Analysis

The learning that results from checking for distortions, from evaluating mission accomplishment, and from analyzing numerous indicators, itself, accomplishes very little. The leaders of the agency need to act on this learning, making the modifications necessary to ratchet performance up another notch.

The leaders may change any of the key components of their performance strategy—creating a new performance target, modifying how they monitor and report performance, reallocating resources, creating new operational capacity, revising rewards, inventing new esteem opportunities, or adjusting now they conduct their analyses. They might even decide to modify their mission. If they have significantly improved their operational capacity, they might extend their agency's operating mandate to include other authorized (but under-emphasized) purposes. Or, on discovering that they lack some key capability—be that essential funding or cooperative collaborators—they might contract their ambitions.

The Performance Treadmill

Thus, the cycle begins all over again. But I do not think of this as a neatly drawn, annual circle, containing 11 boxes with 11 (unidirectional) arrows connecting Box N to Box N+1 (and, at the end, Box 11 to Box 1). Rather, my operational diagram is quite messy. After all, if the leaders of a public agency learn something in month three, rather than waiting until the end of the year to make the implied change, they will make the change immediately. Indeed, if they are truly trying to ratchet up performance, they are constantly making changes.

Thus, this approach to performance leadership is a treadmill—a treadmill for the organization's leaders, for its employees, and for its collaborators. And once they jump on the treadmill, they cannot get off. They have to keep running—with the success on one lap requiring even more success on the next.

Business executives are accustomed to this treadmill. Shareholders do not say, "Because you did such a good job this year, you can take next year off." Instead, this year's performance becomes the baseline for measuring next year's accomplishments. In business, the expectations of the investors create the performance treadmill. Every year, the investors demand that a firm ratchet up its performance.

Although these 11 better practices reflect observations of public-sector organizations and are designed specifically for them, they can help any organization—public, private, or nonprofit—ratchet up performance. The leaders of a public-sector organization are not, however, required to jump on the performance treadmill. After all, they have a lot of other responsibilities. Citizens are not single-minded in demanding that this year's performance become the baseline for next year's improvements. They are at least as focused on demanding that the leaders of public agencies deploy their financial assets precisely as prescribed by legislation and that they treat citizens, employees and applicants, vendors and bidders very, very fairly. These demands are enough to keep any self-respecting public manager quite busy. Why not focus on meeting the accountability demands for finances and fairness, and leave the demands for improving performance to a successor?

If, however, the leaders of a public agency do wish to ratchet up performance—if they choose to jump on the performance treadmill—these 11 better practices offer one approach that they can employ to exercise performance leadership.

Source: Washington, DC: IBM Center for the Business of Government (2004).

REFERENCES

Adams, Scott (1996). *The Dilbert Principle: A Cubicle's-Eye View of Bosses, Meetings, Management Fads & Other Workplace Afflictions.* New York: HarperBusiness.

Atkinson, William L., Charles Wolfe, Sharon G. Humiston, Rick Nelson (eds.) (2002). *Epidemiology and Prevention of Vaccine-Preventable Diseases*, 7th edition. Atlanta, Ga.: The Centers for Disease Control and Prevention.

Bardach, Eugene (1998). *Getting Agencies to Work Together: The Practice and Theory of Managerial Craftsmanship.* Washington, D.C.: The Brookings Institution.

Behn, Robert D. (2003). "On the motivational impact of: The List," *Bob Behn's Public Management Report*, Vol. 1, No. 2 (October): http://www.ksg.harvard.edu/TheBehnReport/October2003.pdf.

Deming, W. Edwards (1982, 1986). *Out of the Crisis.* Cambridge, Mass.: Center for Advanced Engineering Study, Massachusetts Institute of Technology.

James, William (1920). *The Letters of William James*, Henry James (ed.). Boston: The Atlantic Monthly Press.

Maslow, A. H. (1943). "A Theory of Human Motivation," *Psychological Review*, Vol. 50, No. 4 (July), pp. 381–382.

Compensation 11

Learning Objectives

- Gain an awareness of the multifaceted nature of compensation
- Understand the different types of equity and their resultant effects on employee behavior
- Explain the nature of salary compression and the challenges it presents to employers
- Develop an awareness of the advantages and disadvantages of pay for performance/incentive pay and the conditions under which it might be most successful
- Describe the legal issues that influence compensation
- Appreciate the challenges inherent in setting executive compensation levels

Strategic Compensation at Jamba Juice

Founded in 1990, San Francisco–based Jamba Juice has expanded to 300 stores that employ more than 4,000 workers in 15 states. Jamba is a leading retailer of blended-to-order fruit smoothies, fresh-squeezed juices, and healthful soups and breads. Since its inception, one of Jamba's chief challenges has been finding and retaining qualified managers. In a high-growth company that has intense competition within the industry, Jamba is additionally challenged by its location in the San Francisco Bay area, which provides many other career opportunities to the younger employees Jamba recruits. A large number of these employers are technology-based and offer more generous financial incentives than the typical food retailer.

In order to expand, Jamba must attract and retain these younger workers. To assist them in this objective, Jamba has developed an innovative compensation policy that allows it to compete not only within the growing juice industry but also with the technology-based employers who attract the same young employees. Jamba's "J.U.I.C.E. Plan" allows general managers to receive a percentage of the store's cash flow, predicated on the financial performance of their business. To keep good managers on board, Jamba provides opportunities for general managers to share in store profits over a three-year period. When general managers increase year-to-year sales in their operation, money accrues in a retention account, which is payable only in three-year cycles. Much like stock options that vest over three or five years in technology companies, Jamba's retention account not only provides short-term performance incentives, but it also provides incentives to stay with Jamba. On top of this, Jamba also provides all employees at the managerial level with traditional stock options. When assistant managers are promoted, their general managers also receive a cash bonus of $1,000 for their development efforts.

In a fiercely competitive industry characterized by high turnover, Jamba was able to reduce turnover among managers during the first year of operating its J.U.I.C.E. Plan. Jamba has also received inquiries from Australia and Europe from prospective employees, managers, and franchisees. Ironically, the company's strategically designed compensation program has also provided the unintended benefit of fueling its growth.[1]

Compensation—a key strategic area for organizations—impacts an employer's ability to attract applicants, retain employees, and ensure optimal levels of performance from employees in meeting the organization's strategic objectives. Compensation is also a key economic issue: Compensation programs continue to assume an increasingly larger share of an organization's operating expenses. This is particularly true in service industries, which are highly labor-intensive. A critical balancing act must occur to ensure that compensation attracts, motivates, and retains employees; at the same time, compensation should allow the organization to maintain a cost structure that enables it to compete effectively and efficiently in its markets. Reading 11.1, "Key Trends of the Total Reward System in the 21st Century," examines the evolution of organizational reward systems relative to the changing needs of organizations and employees.

An organization's compensation system usually consists of three separate components, as illustrated in Exhibit 11.1. The first and largest component is the base compensation, or salary system. The second is the incentive system, where employees receive additional compensation based on individual, divisional, and/or organization-wide performance. Third is the indirect compensation system, where employees are provided

EXHIBIT 11.1 Compensation System

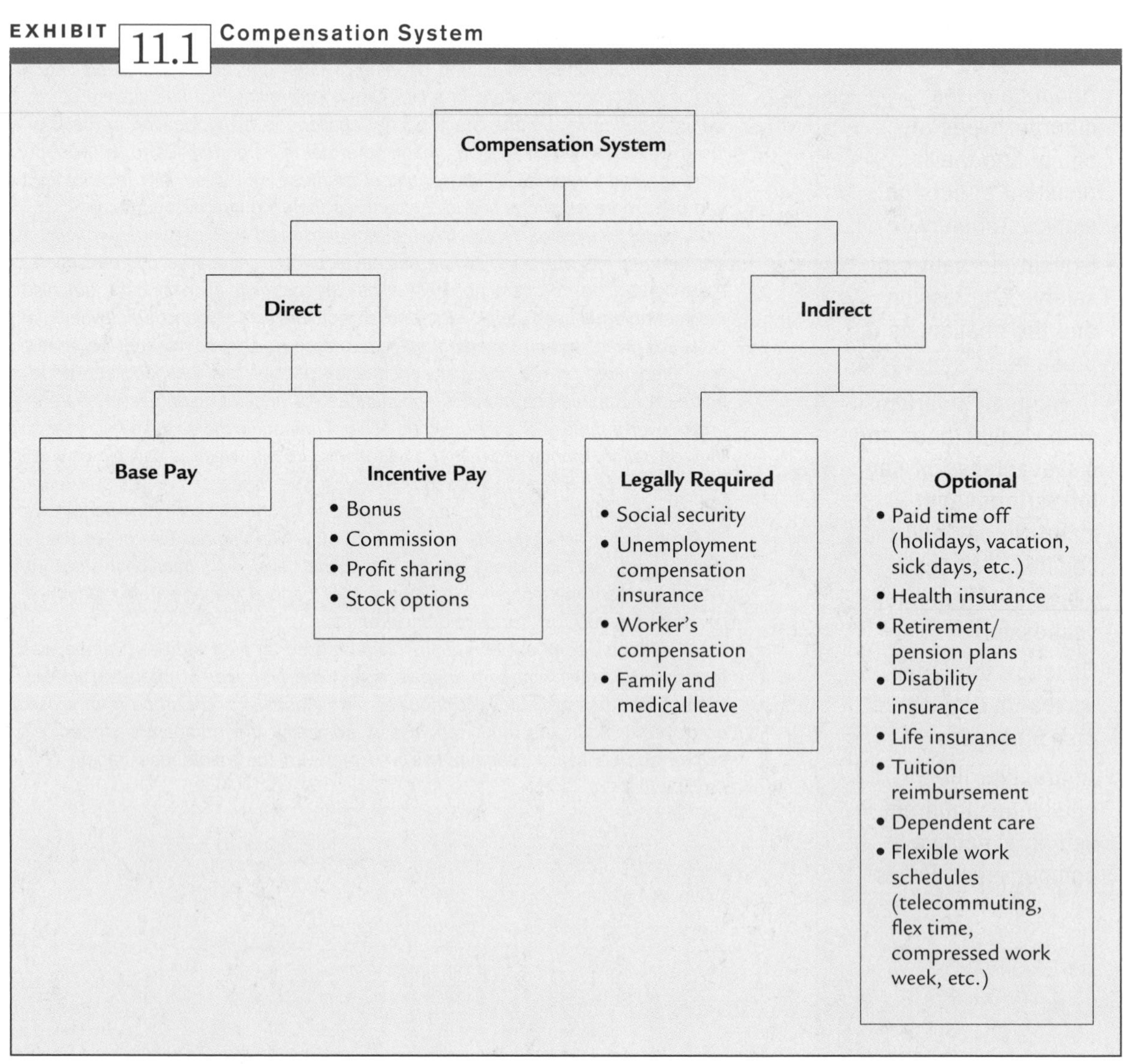

with certain benefits, some of which are legally required and others are provided at the discretion of the employer. This chapter focuses on the strategic and policy issues associated with compensation, as opposed to presenting details concerning many of the components of indirect compensation.

Equity

In designing the overall compensation system, an organization needs to be concerned with the perceived equity or fairness of the system for employees. All employees should feel that they are being compensated fairly relative to their coworkers and to individuals who hold comparable jobs in other organizations. The equity theory of motivation holds that workers assess their perceived inputs to their work and their outcomes to those of others, as depicted in Exhibit 11.2.[2]

When individuals perceive that they are being treated inequitably relative to their peers, they usually try to establish equity by increasing their outcomes or decreasing their inputs. Increasing outcomes might involve asking for additional compensation or pilfering from the organization. In the latter case, the individual might use the inequity to justify the theft. Decreasing inputs might involve not working as hard, taking longer breaks, coming in late, leaving early, or resigning.

EXHIBIT 11.2 Equity Theory

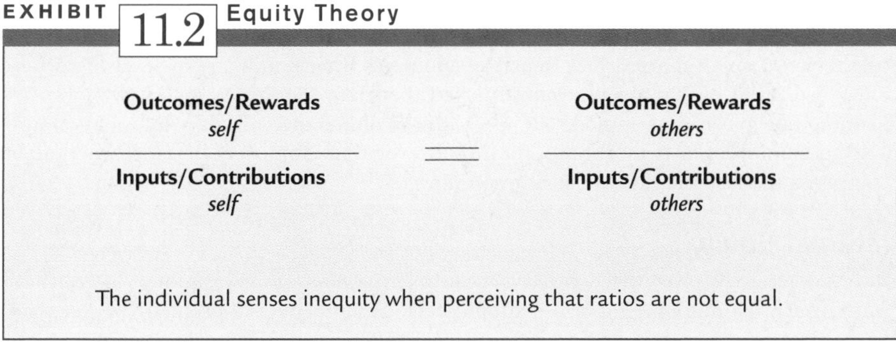

The design of an equitable compensation system must incorporate three types of equity: internal, external, and individual. These perceptions of equity directly impact motivation, commitment, and performance on the job, as illustrated in Exhibit 11.3. It is important to remember that employee assessments of equity are, in fact, perceptions. They may be based, in part, on incomplete or inaccurate information. Few employees really know the extent of their coworkers' inputs unless they are together throughout the workday.

EXHIBIT 11.3 Equity and Work-Related Outcomes

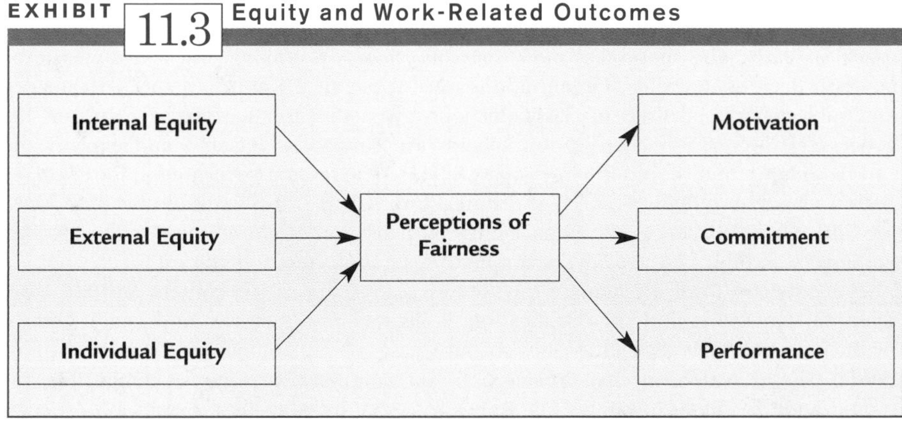

One critical policy decision employers must make is the extent to which compensation levels will be made public or kept private. Public employers usually have no choice in this matter, as relevant state laws may require full disclosure and reporting of and public access to such information. However, privately held and publically traded organizations have the option of disclosing the compensation of individuals and/or the compensation ranges associated with specific positions. Even if that information is not disclosed, employers frequently have policies that forbid employees from disclosing their compensation to others. Reading 11.2, "Exposing Pay Secrecy," explores the reasons for such policies as well as the advantages and disadvantages of such a practice.

The confidentiality of many compensation programs can also make it difficult for employees to obtain accurate information on coworker compensation. Nonetheless, these perceptions impact motivation, commitment, and performance and must be effectively managed. Although compensation is not the only work-related outcome employees receive, it is often the basis by which employees conclude that they are being treated appropriately.

The Internet can provide a wealth of information to employees about comparable salary data. A recent Google search turned up more than 28,000 hits for the search "salary comparison" sites. The most popular of these sites, www.salary.com, averages more than 26 million hits annually and hosts 1.7 million different visitors monthly. The *Wall Street Journal* even offers its own site, www.careerjournal.com.[3] Much of the salary information found by employees may be inaccurate, dated, or based on samples that are irrelevant to the individual employee's job. Employers, however, add to the confusion by failing to communicate compensation policy with employees. Although 60 percent of workers in one recent survey reported that their pay compares unfavorably to pay levels elsewhere, only 43 percent of that same group reported that their employers do a good job of explaining how pay is determined.[4] Hence, with the abundance of salary information available to employees, it is more important than ever that employers develop an equitable compensation system and explain it to employees.

Internal Equity

Internal equity involves the perceived fairness of pay differentials among different jobs within an organization. Employees should feel that the pay differentials between jobs are fair, given the corresponding differences in job responsibilities. In attempting to establish internal equity, employers can evaluate jobs by using four techniques: job ranking, job classification, point systems, and factor comparison.

Job ranking is a relatively simple, nonquantitative means of determining equity in compensation in smaller, less complex organizations. Senior management makes judgments as to which jobs are most challenging and ensures that the more challenging jobs receive higher compensation. This method, which is somewhat random and nonscientific, is more concerned with the hierarchical position of jobs rather than with the differential amounts of compensation. Because it is random, job ranking is used infrequently and usually only in small, informal organizations.

Job classification systems group jobs requiring similar effort, ability, training, and responsibility into predetermined grades or classes and compensates each job within a grade similarly. This method is more scientific than job ranking, but it has been criticized for lack of flexibility. Organizations must force each job into a specific category, and subjectivity is involved in classifying jobs, given the nonquantitative nature of the process.[5] However, job classification systems are easy to understand and explain and can be widely administered in large organizations. The federal government, for example, has an elaborate system of 18 job classes, each of which is distinguished by 10 levels of job difficulty or challenge; this impacts the compensation of more than 3 million federal employees. Exhibit 11.4 provides a sample of several of these job grades.

Point systems involve making a quantitative assessment of job content and are more scientific than job ranking or classification. Point systems are easy to understand and explain and—although difficult to design—are easy to implement once they are operational. The organization first creates a list of compensable factors—things that the organization is willing to pay its employees for, such as education, experience, specific

EXHIBIT 11.4 Grade Description and Representative Job Titles from the Classification System used by the Federal Government

Grade Level	Grade Description	Jobs Included in Grade
GS 1	Includes those classes of position the duties of which are to perform, under immediate supervision, with little or no latitude for the exercise of independent judgment: • The simplest routine work in office, business, of fiscal operations; or • Elementary work of a subordinate technical character in a professional, scientific, or technical field.	Typist, Messenger
GS 2	Includes those classes of position the duties which are: • to perform, under immediate supervision, with limited latitude for the exercise of independent judgment, routine work in office, business, or fiscal operations, of comparable subordinate technical work of limited scope in a professional, scientific, of technical field, requiring some training or experience; or • to perform other work of equal importance, difficulty, and responsibility, and requiring comparable qualifications.	Engineering aide
GS 5	Includes those classes of positions the duties which are: • to perform, under general supervision, difficult and responsible work in office, business, or fiscal administration, or comparable subordinate technical work in a professional, scientific, or technical field, requiring in either case; • considerable training and supervisory or other experience; • broad working knowledge of a special subject matter or of office, laboratory, engineering, scientific, or other procedure and practice; and • the exercise of independent judgment in a limited field; • to perform other work of equal importance, difficulty, and responsibility, and requiring comparable qualifications.	Chemist, Accountant, Engineer (civil), Statistical clerk

Source: From The Management of Compensation *by Alan, N. Nash and Stephen J. Carroll. Copyright © 1976 by Wadsworth, Inc.*

skills, working conditions, and responsibility. Each of these compensable factors is then assigned a factor scale, which describes progressive levels of mastery or accomplishment of each factor. Points are assigned to each level of each scale, and compensation is determined by the overall number of points that correspond to the job. A sample point system is presented in Exhibit 11.5. Note that some compensable factors receive higher points than others. For example, level one in technical skills receives 30 points; level one in working conditions receives only 5 points. Employers can determine the relative worth of each compensable factor by assessing its criticality for the organization's strategic objectives. The more a compensable factor relates to goals and objectives, the higher the values that should be present in the factor scales.

A special type of point system is often used for administrative and managerial positions. Developed by the consulting group Hay Associates, this system is known as the "Hay Plan" and is used by most of the Fortune 500 companies as well as over 5,000 organizations in more than 30 countries. The Hay Plan utilizes three factors, called

EXHIBIT 11.5 Sample Point System

	Level				
Factors	**1**	**2**	**3**	**4**	**5**
Education	15	30	45	60	75
Experience	20	40	60	80	100
Technical Skills	30	60	90	120	150
Working Conditions	5	10	15	20	25
Responsibility	25	50	75	100	125

The compensable factor "technical skills" might have its five levels defined as follows:

Knowledge

This factor measures the knowledge or equivalent training required to perform the job duties.

1st Degree

Use of reading and writing, adding and subtracting of whole numbers; following of instructions; use of fixed gauges, direct reading of instrument, and similar devices; where interpretation is not required.

2nd Degree

Use of addition, subtraction, multiplication, and division of numbers, including decimals and fractions; simple use of formulas, charts, tables, drawings, specifications, schedules, wiring diagrams; use of adjustable measuring instrument; checking of reports, forms, records, and comparable data; where interpretation is required.

3rd Degree

Use of mathematics with the use of complicated drawings, specifications, charts, tables; various types of precision measuring instruments. Equivalent to one to three years' applied traders training in a particular or specialized occupation.

4th Degree

Use of advanced trades mathematics, together with the use of complicated drawings, specifications, charts, tables, handbook formulas; all varieties of precision measuring instruments. Equivalent to complete accredited apprenticeship in a recognized trade, craft or occupation; or equivalent to a two-year technical college education.

5th Degree

Use of higher mathematics involved in the applications of engineering principles and the performance of related practical operations, together with a comprehensive knowledge of the theories and practices of mechanical, electrical, chemical, civil, or like engineering field. Equivalent to complete four years of technical college or university education.

Source: Adapted from Compensation, *3/c by George T. Milkovich and Jerry M. Newman. Copyright © 1990 by Richard D. Irwin.*

universal factors, which are common to all managerial and administrative jobs: know-how, problem-solving, and accountability. Know-how pertains to the technical knowledge required to do the job. Problem-solving assesses the amount of independent thinking and decision-making required in the job. Accountability considers the direct responsibility for people, resources, and results. A brief summary of the Hay Plan is presented in Exhibit 11.6.

Factor comparison is somewhat similar in concept to the point system. However, instead of assessing jobs independently of each other relative to compensable factors, factor comparison utilizes five standard factors in evaluating all jobs: responsibility, skills required, mental effort, physical effort, and working conditions. Jobs are evaluated relative to each other on each of these five dimensions to determine appropriate compensation. For example, an employer would try to determine whether the job of a paralegal

EXHIBIT 11.6 Hay Compensable Factors

Know-How

Know-how is the sum total of every kind of skill, however acquired, necessary for acceptable job performance. This sum total, which comprises the necessary overall "fund of knowledge" an employee needs, has three dimensions:

- Knowledge of practical procedures, specialized techniques, and learned disciplines.
- The ability to integrate and harmonize the diversified functions involved in managerial situations (operating, supporting, and administrative). This know-how may be exercised consultatively as well as executively and involves in some combination the areas of organizing, planning, executing, controlling, and evaluating.
- Active, practicing skills in the area of human relationships.

Problem-Solving

Problem-solving is the original "self-starting" thinking required by the job for analyzing, evaluating, creating, reasoning, and arriving at conclusions. To the extent that thinking is circumscribed by standards, covered by precedents, or referred to others, problem-solving is diminished and the emphasis correspondingly is on know-how.

Problem-solving has two dimensions:

- The environment in which the thinking takes place.
- The challenge presented by the thinking to be done.

Accountability

Accountability is the answerability for an action and for the consequences thereof. It is the measured effect of the job on end results. It has three dimensions:

- Freedom to act—the degree of personal or procedural control and guidance.
- Job impact on end results.
- Magnitude—indicated by the general dollar size of the areas(s) most clearly or primarily affected by the job (on an annual basis).

Source: Courtesy of the Hay Group, Boston, MA.

required more or less responsibility, skill, mental effort, physical effort, or unusual working conditions relative to the job of an accounting clerk to determine appropriate compensation for each job. Factor comparison can be difficult to administer in organizations where job content and responsibilities change frequently. It has also been criticized for its assumption that the five factors are universal to and equally important in all jobs. Factor comparison is best utilized in organizations where there is limited change and job responsibilities and content remain somewhat stable.

The consequences of having a compensation system that employees perceive to be inequitable can be severe. Employers have a choice of four systems for developing an internally equitable compensation system based on whether they wish to consider complete or specified job factors as well as whether they wish to compare jobs to each other or to some standard. Exhibit 11.7 compares the four techniques, noting the relative strengths and weaknesses of each technique. Regardless of the method chosen, employees must understand and accept the system to ensure optimal motivation, commitment, and performance.

A more recent issue that has arisen relative to the management of internal equity is salary compression. Salary compression happens when new hires earn higher salaries than employees who have more experience and/or tenure within the organization. It is the result of rising starting salaries in fields for which demand for employees exceeds supply. Salary compression has become a common and particularly problematic issue for faculty in colleges and universities.

Salary compression can be exacerbated in organizations in which individual salaries are made public. It can lead to severe morale problems due to the sense of inequity felt by long-term employees who may have shown tremendous loyalty to their employers. It can

EXHIBIT 11.7 Comparison of Job Evaluation Methods

	Unit of Analysis	
	Whole Job	**Selectors Factors of Job**
Basis of Comparison	**Job Ranking**	**Factor Comparisons**
Job vs. Job	• Identify jobs based on "worth" to organization relative to other jobs ▲ Simple, inexpensive, easy to understand ▼ Random, subjective, not useful in large organizations	• Define compensable factors and evaluate jobs on these factors relative to other jobs ▲ Ease of employee comprehension ▼ Cumbersome and requires constant updating; universal importance of factors in all jobs questionable
	Job Classification	**Point Method**
Job vs. Standard	• Prepare job grades/classification and assign job to appropriate class ▲ Apply to large number of varied jobs; easy to understand; flexible ▼ Detailed and time-consuming to develop; lack of flexibility	• Define compensable factors and levels of accomplishment and determine levels for each job ▲ Simple to understand and administer; easy for employees to aspire to high levels ▼ Extremely time-consuming to develop; lack of universal applicability of compensable factors

be difficult to remedy, as its effects are often far-reaching throughout the organization. Simply adjusting salaries to address salary compression can create additional problems relative to the basis for such adjustments as well as the availability of resources to support such adjustments. Frequently, the only solution for those employees who are on the short end of salary compression is to leave their organization and seek employment elsewhere on the open market at the going salary rates. When an organization realizes that its compensation system suffers from salary compression, there is no simple answer as to how to best remedy the situation, but action is necessary to retain top-performing employees. Chapter 13 provides some recommendations as to how to retain such individuals.

External Equity

External equity involves employee perception of the fairness of their compensation relative to those outside the organization. Obviously, employees would not be thrilled to discover that those who do similar work in other organizations receive greater compensation. Employers need to be aware of salary structures of competitors and understand that this can impact motivation, commitment, and productivity.

Assessing external equity is relatively a straightforward process. Organizations should first collect wage and salary information to determine market wage rates. This information, which can be collected in-house or through sources external to the organization, is usually readily available relative to the industry and geographic area through professional associations, HR consulting firms, or through the organization's own primary research. When making assessments of external equity, it is important to consider not only salaries but also other forms of compensation, such as bonus and incentive plans and benefits packages. Information pertaining to these additional forms of compensation may be more difficult to obtain, but it must be incorporated into the analysis, especially for higher-level managerial and executive positions that may have a significant portion of the overall compensation based on incentive pay.

After an investigation of the market has been completed, the organization then determines its own pay strategy relative to the market. The three strategies an employer can choose are a lead, lag, or market policy. A lead policy involves paying higher wages than competitors to ensure that the organization becomes the employer of choice. In other words, this strategy assumes that pay is a critical factor in an applicant's decision in choosing an employer and attempts to attract and help retain the highest-quality employees. In short, the employer desires to be the first-choice employer; that is, the organization wants first selection from available talent. However, any organization that offers higher compensation than its competitors needs to ensure that it has a means of remaining competitive relative to its cost structure and market prices. This requires the organization to have operational efficiencies that its competitors lack, a higher rate of employee productivity than its competitors, and/or a product or service for which consumers are willing to pay a premium price.

With a lag policy, the organization compensates employees below the rates of competitors. An organization employing this strategy attempts to compensate employees through some other means, such as opportunity for advancement, incentive plans, good location, good working conditions, or employment security. The organization believes that work-related outcomes are multifaceted and, more important, that employees consider more than just salary in weighing their employment options. An organization employing a lag policy needs strong insights into the personal and lifestyle choices of the employees it recruits to allow it to tailor compensation options for these individuals that will allow them to accept a lower base salary than that offered by the competition.

With a market policy, the organization sets its salary levels equal to those of competitors. An employer following this strategy attempts to neutralize pay as a factor in applicant decisions, assuming that it can compete in the labor market in attracting employees by other means such as those listed in the discussion of lag policy. It should come as no surprise that the majority of employers set their salary levels at or very near market levels. Such a strategy assumes that employees are less likely to leave if their salaries would remain the same with a new employer.

Individual Equity

Individual equity considers employee perceptions of pay differentials among individuals who hold identical jobs in the same organization. Determining individual salary levels and pay differentials among employees in identical jobs can be done in a number of ways. The most basic is basing pay on seniority. Seniority-based systems determine compensation according to the length of time on the job or length of time with the employer. Although this rewards a stable and experienced workforce, it has no direct relationship to performance on the job. Seniority systems are very common in union settings. They are also usually looked upon favorably by the court system because they are objective in nature. However, they provide little incentive to be more productive, and they encourage workers who may be mediocre or substandard performers to remain with the organization.

Merit pay systems compensate individuals for their proven performance on the job. Ideally, they provide an incentive for employees to work harder and accomplish more. Merit pay is generally permanently added to an employee's base pay. However, in practice, merit pay can be quite problematic. Because merit-based pay systems are anchored by the organization's performance feedback system, they can extend the subjectivity that is inherent in the feedback system. If an employee believes that the performance feedback process is biased or unfair, a compensation system that is based on this process can further add to the employee's perceptions of unfairness. Any merit-based pay plan must ensure that the performance feedback upon which it is built is understood and accepted by employees.

An increasing number of organizations are using incentive pay to compensate their employees. Incentive plans allow the employee to receive a portion of his or her compensation in direct relation to financial performance of the individual, unit, or entire organization. Incentive pay is provided for a given time period and is not added to the base salary. Consequently, it must be re-earned in subsequent time periods and can have a greater motivational impact than merit pay.

The philosophy behind this compensation system is to reward higher levels of performance by returning financial rewards to the employees who have been responsible for creating them. Incentive pay programs also allow organizations to adjust their compensation expenses based on organizational performance. These plans can take a variety of forms, such as commission sales plans, profit-sharing plans, gainsharing plans (in which cost savings are partially distributed to those responsible for them), and stock ownership, distribution, or option plans. Incentive plans also differ from merit pay plans in that the former are based on objective, measurable financial performance; the latter are based on subjective, generally nonfinancial performance-related criteria. A well-designed incentive pay plan can be the deciding factor in an applicant's decision to accept or reject a job offer when base compensation is set at market level and nondistinguishable from that of competitors.[6]

Performance-based pay that is variably tied into an employee's, work unit's, or organization's results is popular with both employers and employees. Performance-based pay—which was until recently offered to senior executives only—is now extended to many other employees, as organizations realize how variable compensation programs can impact individual employees' behavior and performance. Approximately two thirds of U.S. companies offer some form of variable performance-based pay, and about 10 percent of all compensation paid in the United States is variable.[7] More important, one survey found that employers who provide variable performance-based pay to their top employees are 68 percent more likely than those who do not to report outstanding bottom-line financial performance.[8]

One important consideration in the shift from straight salary to incentive compensation is the fact that incentive compensation will usually lower the base salary an individual receives in exchange for incentives that could significantly raise overall compensation. Not all employees, however, will find such a trade-off attractive, as illustrated below.

Joe Torre and the New York Yankees

In October 2007, the sporting world was stunned when Joe Torre parted ways with the New York Yankees baseball franchise. Torre had managed the Yankees for 12 seasons and in each of those seasons had led the Yankees to the postseason, including four World Series championships. However, the 2007 season ended for the Yankees with elimination during the first round of the playoffs for the third consecutive year. At the time, Torre was the highest-paid manager in baseball, having earned $7.5 million for the 2007 season.

Team owner George Steinbrenner, hungry for another World Series championship, decided to offer Torre an incentive compensation package. Torre's base salary for 2008 would be reduced to $5 million but with incentives of an additional $3 million possible, with $1 million being awarded for each successive level of Yankee postseason success. The incentive-laden short-term contract with a 33 percent decreased in base salary caused Torre to leave the Yankees and sign a $13 million, 3-year contract with the Los Angeles Dodgers two weeks later.

Incentive pay is popular with employers, in part because it is self-funded. Because it is tied to specific financial performance of a division or the entire organization and is not paid unless specific measurable financial metrics are achieved, it can and should appeal to even the most fiscally conservative organizations. The flexibility of variable compensation programs allows them to be tailored to organization-wide, divisional, team, or individual performance—or some combination thereof—depending on the interdependence present in jobs as well as organizational strategy. Perhaps their greatest value is that variable compensation programs, if well-communicated and implemented, allow employees to fully understand the organization's goals and objectives as well as how their individual jobs impact organizational performance. As discussed in Chapter 10, Continental Airlines used a performance-based variable compensation program to turn around poor performance. The result? Continental won more awards for customer satisfaction than any other U.S. airline and was named one of the "100 Best Companies to Work for in America" by *Fortune* for four consecutive years.[9]

Pay-for-performance plans have been identified as a means of aligning the interests of employers and owners. One study compared pay-for-performance plans with a fixed salary compensation program and found that the former resulted in significantly higher productivity and overall financial performance.[10] This is because of the fact that pay for performance generally attracts higher-quality applicants, which has a net effect of lowering unit cost of production or service delivery. Not surprisingly, higher performing employees show a marked preference for pay-for-performance compensation programs over salaried compensation without incentives. However, employers need to monitor such program to ensure that employees do not focus excessively on incentive-producing tasks and behaviors that result in individual financial rewards at the expense of other important tasks or goals.

Team-Based Incentive Pay at Children's Hospital Boston

The accounts receivable department at Children's Hospital Boston was suffering from low morale and inefficiencies after an unsuccessful change to a new billing system. With an average of more than 100 days from billing to payment, the organization was facing serious cash flow concerns in its fiscal operations. To alleviate this, management developed a team-based incentive plan that would allow employees to see the relationship between quarterly cash flow and the number of days a bill spent uncollected in accounts receivable. Employee-centered, the program allowed team members to set three possible goal levels—threshold, target, and optimal—with corresponding rewards of $500, $1,000, and $1,500 for the attainment of each. Meetings were set up with employees to explain the program and obtain employee input and support. Employees suddenly began to feel important, empowered, and energized: Weekly progress reports allow employees to self-monitor their progress. During the first year, the average number of days a bill spent in accounts receivable was reduced from more than 100 days to 76, and during the second year, the average was reduced to the mid-60s—and the satisfaction with the program has reduced employee turnover in the department.[11]

While performance-based rewards can be tremendous motivators and allow employees to see a stronger connection between their performance and organizational performance, they are clearly not for every organization. Cultural barriers, both institutional and national, can act as impediments to the successful implementation of a performance-based pay plan. Japanese conglomerate Fujitsu was the first Japanese organization to implement such a compensation plan. Hailed as a breakthrough and revolutionary when first introduced, the program ignited a trend in Japanese organizations to abandon archaic pay systems based almost entirely on seniority in favor of performance-based plans. After eight years, however, Fujitsu abandoned the program, calling it "flawed" and a poor fit with Japanese culture that respects and rewards loyalty and seniority. In addition, to maintain a positive self-image, employees fought to keep the performance standards under the plan as low as possible for fear of falling short and being embarrassed. Innovation was stifled, as employees resisted change, fearing that results might not accompany the change.[12]

Skill-based pay systems have been increasing in popularity in recent years because of the ease of measurement of many specific skills and because skills relating to the organization's strategy can be readily identified. Skill-based pay involves basing the employee's compensation on the acquisition and mastery of skills used on the job. Skill-based pay programs not only give employees incentives to learn new skills or upgrade existing ones, but they also promote flexibility for the organization. They can easily be linked with training programs and the strategic needs of the organization. During the strategic planning process, the organization must determine which kinds of employee skills are most critical to its objectives and future success. Then, the organization must either hire employees with these skills or with the capacity to learn these skills.

Despite their popularity, skill-based pay systems are not without problems. Employers should remember that the acquisition of skills and improved performance are two different things. Skill-based pay systems are often based on the acquisition of skills, without regard to whether the employee has successfully transferred the training to the work setting or achieved any results from the skill-based training. In a rapidly changing work environment, skill obsolescence may result in a pay system that compensates employees for previously learned skills that have become outdated and are no longer of value to the employer. Most employees would find it unfair for the organization to reduce compensation because it no longer values certain employee skills, particularly if the organization has not provided opportunities for employees to upgrade their skills. Employers need to implement skill-based pay plans very carefully and with a clear sense of what the future might hold for how work is performed.

Team-based pay plans are also becoming more prevalent in many organizations. With more work and responsibility being centered around self-managed teams, such compensation plans provide incentives to cooperate and be more flexible in working with others in achieving group and organizational objectives. Administering team-based pay systems can be less time-consuming than administering individual reward systems. However, team-based pay plans may impact group dynamics and can adversely impact and intensify conflict within a unit, particularly if team members feel that certain teammates are not doing their share of the work and living up to their responsibility to the team. Such free-riders can also greatly damage morale and enthusiasm for the plan.[13] Team-based pay plans present a key strategic issue for organizations in determining the percentage of overall employee compensation that should be based on team rather than individual performance. Consequently, team-based pay plans may require the oversight and attention of supervisors, particularly in their early stages of implementation.[14]

Team-based pay systems need a decentralized decision-making system that gives the team some autonomy and responsibility in order to be successful; they also need to be tied into specific measures of accountability and results. To the extent that they foster unhealthy competition and conflict among different teams within an organization, they can have adverse effects on overall performance. Although team-based pay plans may make sense given the changing nature of work and the emphasis on project teams and groups, their potential impact on both individual teams and intrateam relations and performance needs to be assessed before the plan is implemented. Despite the changing nature of job design, technology, and work relationships, certain organizations may find that their culture does not support the team-based pay concept. Team-based pay plans must be implemented within the context of an organizational culture that values sharing and collaboration, cooperation, and open communication.

While many employers realize the critical role that effective teams play in the success of their organization, few have been able to implement compensation systems that encourage and reward team effort. The few that have done so find that three criteria influence the success of such a plan. First, there has to be a high level of communication with employees regarding the details of the plan. Second, employees should have a voice and provide input into the design and implementation of the plan. Third, team members need to feel that the system is fair and equitable.[15]

Team-Based Pay at Phelps Dodge

Phoenix-based Phelps Dodge has a copper-mining operation that employs more than 4,200 individuals at six North American locations. When the employees decided to de-certify their existing labor union, management saw a golden opportunity to create a more incentive-based compensation system. The new plan involves a base salary, with bonuses awarded for meeting team-based goals set for a specific location or mine. Goals are set by team members, and the compensation is constantly being evaluated through the feedback provided by employees.[16]

Legal Issues in Compensation

Those designing compensation systems must also bear in mind that compensation is a condition of employment covered under Title VII of the Civil Rights Act of 1964. The design of any compensation system that intentionally or unintentionally discriminates against any protected class can subject the organization to legal action. The Equal Pay Act of 1963 also partially regulates compensation and must be considered when designing and administering compensation programs. These laws were discussed in Chapter 7.

Critics of the Equal Pay Act have noted that it has been of limited value because men and women are often not employed in the same jobs, and the act only requires equal pay for equal work. To combat this limitation, the concept of comparable worth has been advanced. Comparable worth argues that the standards of equal pay for equal work should be replaced with the doctrine of equal pay for equal value. Because many occupations, although becoming more gender-integrated, are still somewhat gender-segregated, women and men generally do not hold the same jobs or do the same work in our economy, so the Equal Pay Act does nothing to relieve the lower wages that women receive relative to men. For example, in a warehouse, men might be working on the loading dock, and women might be working in the office. Men will invariably be paid more, but the Equal Pay Act cannot address this because the jobs being performed by men and women are not the same. Comparable worth would argue that the work being done in the office (bookkeeping, clerical, and switchboard) has as much value as and is as important to the organization as that being done on the loading dock and should be compensated similarly.

Comparable worth of two different jobs, however, remains very difficult to prove because of the lack of objective, measurable data that would support an assessment of job value. Gender stereotyping of certain jobs creates an additional obstacle in this regard. For example, the majority of schoolteachers (particularly in elementary schools), secretaries, nurses, and flight attendants are female. Although the courts have been sympathetic to arguments for comparable worth, they have been extremely reluctant to take action because the doctrine falls outside existing federal law. In addition, the value of a particular job is very difficult to objectively determine and prove in a legal arena. Comparable worth may be our society's best hope for narrowing the gender gap in wages, in which women consistently have been found to earn 70 to 75 cents on the dollar of what men earn.[17] This is particularly true given that the Equal Pay Act does have exclusions that allow gender-based pay differentials to exist. Comparable worth, however, will most likely remain an unenforceable ideal until laws are passed that specifically address it. Equal pay for equal work is still the standard; the courts have refused to manufacture standards and policies that have not been legislated.

One additional law that impacts compensation is the Fair Labor Standards Act of 1938 (FLSA), which regulates the federal minimum wage, overtime policies, and the use of child labor. It exempts from minimum wage and overtime requirements certain groups of employees (managers, administrators, outside salespeople, and professionals) who exercise independent judgment in carrying out their job duties. However, there has been significant controversy concerning whether certain types of sales positions, temporary employees, and independent contractors are legally considered employees and/or covered under the FLSA. As nontraditional employment relationships continue to develop, this act will require the courts to increase scrutiny of the legal status of such nontraditional employees. In the interim, companies that employ these workers will have to exercise caution when designing compensation programs to ensure that they follow the law.

The FLSA has caused numerous problems for employers in recent years. Because it was written and passed long before our economy became based on services, knowledge, and information technology, Congress was unable to anticipate many of the changes that would take place relative to the nature of jobs, work, and organizational life. Problems have arisen because of the ambiguity of the law regarding specifically who is covered under the act and is therefore eligible for overtime pay. In response, there have been a number of high-profile class action lawsuits that have resulted in major payouts by employers. In 2002, RadioShack settled a class action lawsuit for $30 million that was filed by managers who claimed that they were classified improperly under the act in an attempt to avoid paying them overtime.[18] Similar settlements were offered in the same year by Starbucks ($18 million), Rite Aid ($25 million), and Pacific Bell (two separate cases settled for $35 million and $27 million).[19] While the U.S. Department of Labor offers employers a comprehensive FLSA compliance assistance program, much confusion still exists and lawsuits continue to be filed.

In 2006, Congress amended the FLSA to provide some additional clarification as to which employees are exempt from its provisions. Under the revised FLSA standards, an employee is exempt from FLSA coverage if he or she is paid a minimum salary of $455 per week, has primary duties that involve "management," customarily oversees at least two employees, and has the authority to hire and fire or provide recommendations for hiring and firing. This standard of hiring/firing decision-making or participation has become critical in determining FLSA exempt status.

Executive Compensation

One important and controversial area of compensation concerns the pay received by executives. There is no real average or standard for executive compensation, largely because of differences between industries as well as between organizations within a given industry. The demand for talented CEOs and other chief officers who can generate results for shareholders often results in significant compensation packages. Typically, a senior executive receives no more than 20 percent of annual compensation in the form of salary, with the remainder usually divided between annual (30 percent) and long-term (50 percent) incentives.[20]

Executive compensation has been criticized for its excessiveness as well as for the fact that it is often unrelated to actual performance. In 1980, the average CEO made 42 times the average hourly worker's pay; by the year 2000, average CEO pay had grown to 531 times the average hourly worker's pay.[21] Recent corporate accounting scandals in which executives reaped millions of dollars in compensation while their organizations were going bankrupt has drawn even more attention to executive compensation. The lesson learned from the Enron scandal is that heavy reliance on stock options as part of executive compensation can create a culture obsessed with improving stock performance at the expense of all other concerns. Nonetheless, stock options remain a key component of executive compensation packages.

Stock options provide employees with the opportunity to purchase shares at some future date, at a price that is determined at the time the options are awarded. They are designed to focus employee attention on creating shareholder value, and in doing so, employees are also able to reap the benefits of the organization's financial performance. However, stock options can prompt executives to engage in creative accounting practices in which revenues and profitability are artificially inflated, driving up the value of the stock and the options. In addition, stock options are deductible on corporate income taxes despite the fact that they do not have to be reported as expenses in the organization's financial reports.[22]

Several large organizations, including Coca-Cola and Bank One Corp., however, have voluntarily decided to expense stock options offered to employees. Designed to ease concerns in the investment community in light of the recent accounting scandals, this move will make earnings appear lower. Ideally, this may reduce the use of stock options, particularly among rank-and-file employees, as stock options and cash will cost the organization an identical amount. With stock options requiring more time and recordkeeping for the organization and oversight by employees, both employers and employees might find simple equivalent cash compensation more efficient than stock options. Regardless of the decisions that individual organizations make regarding the future of stock options, those organizations that continue to offer stock options to executives as well as other employees will now find their compensation practices more carefully scrutinized by those outside the organization.

A number of employers have been moving away from stock options and instead compensating employees, particularly executives, with stock grants.[23] Stock grants require that the organization meet specific financial goals, such as a given return on capital or return on assets, as a condition of their issuance. At the same time that organizations have been moving away from stock options, there has been a marked trend in privately held organizations offering equity stakes as part of executive compensation packages. Designed largely to allow these privately held organizations to compete with publically held organizations for executive talent, such plans are now offered by 43 percent of private employers. A recent study from PricewaterhouseCoopers found that the typical compensation package for executives at the fastest-growing privately held organizations generally consists of 74 percent base salary, 16 percent annual performance incentives and 5 percent each of long-term cash and equity-based incentives. The survey further found a trend toward privately held employers basing an increasing percentage of executive compensation on performance and longer-term measures.[24]

The "pay for performance" trend among executives has also made its way into the boardroom. In 2006, Coca-Cola announced a radically new plan for director compensation. Typical director compensation includes cash and/or stock options. In Coke's case, this amounted to $50,000 cash and $75,000 in options annually. However, under the new plan, all director compensation was to be performance-based. Directors would receive annual $175,000 option packages only if the organization posted annual compound growth in earnings per share of 8 percent. Coke saw this as a necessary step in light of the fact that the organization had been struggling financially for a number of years, as sales of its flagship products slipped and its expansion into noncarbonated drinks produced mixed results.[25]

Executive compensation decisions are among some of the most important policy decisions made today. Because the demand for seasoned, talented executives greatly exceeds the supply of such and with increasing rates of turnover in CEO positions, organizations need to carefully strategize their executive compensation packages. Reading 11.3, "Navigating Shareholder Influence: Compensation Plans and the Shareholder Approval Process," examines how management attempts to work in tandem with shareholders of publically held organizations to develop competitive and efficacious compensation plans.

Conclusion

Organizations face a number of key strategic issues in setting their compensation policies and programs. These include compensation relative to the market, the balance between fixed and variable compensation, utilization of individual versus team-based pay, the appropriate mix of financial and nonfinancial compensation, and developing an overall cost-effective program that results in high performance.

In addition to these strategic issues, the fast pace of change in our society and the corresponding need for organizations to respond in order to remain competitive create challenges for all HR programs but particularly for compensation. Probably more now than at any time in the past, organizations need to re-evaluate their compensation programs within the context of their corporate strategy and specific HR strategy to ensure that they are consistent with the necessary performance measures required by the organization. Overly rigid compensation systems inhibit the flexibility needed by most contemporary organization's competitive strategies, so it is no surprise to see such flexibility being incorporated into compensation systems.

At the same time, organizations wishing to be more innovative may need to alter their compensation systems to promote more intrapreneurial behavior that encourages employees to act as risk-taking entrepreneurs. Similarly, smaller entrepreneurial organizations will usually need different compensation systems than their larger counterparts. Organizations taking a strategic approach to compensation realize the need for creativity to meet strategic objectives. Also, within a given organization, different compensation programs may be needed for different divisions, departments, or groups of employees. Compensation systems must grow and evolve in the same manner as the organization to ensure that what is actually being rewarded is consistent with the organization's strategic objectives. This link between strategy and compensation is essential for ensuring optimal performance.

Critical Thinking

1. Does money motivate employees? Why or why not?
2. Why should compensation systems be equitable? How can an organization design an equitable compensation system?
3. Compare and contrast the four job evaluation methods. Give an example of an organization in which each of the four methods might provide an optimal strategic fit.
4. Discuss the pros and cons of employee pay being fixed versus variable and dependent on performance. How might such decisions impact recruiting, motivation, and retention?
5. Analyze your current job responsibilities. Determine whether the method by which you are compensated is appropriate.
6. Is performance-based pay effective? Why or why not? How can performance-based pay systems be better designed to ensure optimal results?

Reading 11.1

7. How have reward systems evolved in organizations relative to the six trends presented in the reading? Do these trends make sense for organizations pursuing every kind of strategy?

Reading 11.2

8. What are the advantages and disadvantages of organizational policies that mandate pay secrecy? Consider this question from the perspective of managers, employees, and owners. Is pay secrecy a good practice?

Reading 11.3

9. What strategies can executives use to influence owners on compensation policies and practices? What kinds of information should shareholders seek when considering a proposed compensation package for executives?

Exercises

1. Briefly interview an employee in his or her 20s, 30s, 40s, 50s, 60s, and 70s. Determine what motivates workers from different generations and design compensation plans for each generation that would result in high performance.
2. Is salary compression an issue at your college or university? If so, what are its effects, and how is it being handled? Interview administrators and individual faculty to gain a sense of the extent of the problem, how serious it is perceived as being, and how it is being managed.
3. Visit the Web site http://www.salary.com. Click on "salary trends" and then prepare a brief report on the latest developments in compensation practice.
4. At the same Web site, click on "salary wizard." Select a job category and then determine the median compensation figures for this position in eight different locations within the United States. Should an organization that operates in these different locations pay different salaries for identical work? Is cost of living a sufficient explanation for an employee who senses inequity?

Chapter References

1. Sunoo, B. P. "Blending a Successful Workforce," *Workforce*, March 2000, pp. 44–48.
2. Adams, J. S. "Toward an Understanding of Inequity," *Journal of Abnormal and Social Psychology*, October 1963, pp. 422–436.
3. Wellner, A. S. "Salaries in Site," *HR Magazine*, May 2001, pp. 89–96.
4. Shea, T. F. "Send Employees a Message—About Their Pay," *HR Magazine*, December 2002, p. 29.
5. Fisher, C. D., Schoenfeldt, L. F. and Shaw, J. B. *Human Resource Management*, 4th ed., Boston: Houghton Mifflin Co., 1999, p. 560.
6. Williams, V. L. and Grimaldi, S. E. "A Quick Breakdown of Strategic Pay," *Workforce*, *78*, (12), December 1999, pp. 72–75.
7. Bates, S. "Pay for Performance," *HR Magazine*, January 2003, pp. 31–38.
8. Ibid.
9. Minton-Eversole, T. "Bethune Flies High with Continental," *HR News*, August 2002, pp. 1, 7.
10. Cadsby, C., Song, F. and Tapon, F. "Sorting and Incentive Effects of Pay for Performance: An Experimental Investigation," *Academy of Management Journal*, *50*, (2), 2007, pp. 387–405.
11. Cadrain, D. "Put Success in Sight," *HR Magazine*, May 2003, pp. 85–92.
12. Tanikawa, M. "Fujitsu Decides to Backtrack on Performance-Based Pay," *New York Times*, March 21, 2001, p. W1.
13. Heneman, F. and Von Hippel, C. Interview in the *Wall Street Journal*, November 28, 1995, p. A1.
14. Albanese, R. and VanFleet, D. D. "Rational Behavior in Groups: The Free-Riding Tendency," *Academy of Management Review*, *10*, 1985, pp. 244–255.

15. McClurg, L. N. "Team Rewards: How Far Have We Come?" *Human Resource Management*, *40*, (1), pp. 73–86.
16. Garvey, C. "Steer Teams with the Right Pay," *HR Magazine*, May 2002, pp. 71–78.
17. U.S. Bureau of the Census. *Current Population Reports*, No. P60–197, Washington, DC: U.S. Government Printing Office, 1997.
18. "RadioShack Agrees to Pay $30 Million to Settle Suit," *Baltimore Sun*, July 17, 2002.
19. Clark, M. M. "FLSA: Will Ya Still Need Me When I'm 64?" *HR News*, October 2002, p. 3.
20. Overman, S. "Executive Compensation to Undergo Intense Scrutiny," *HR News*, May 2002, p. 1.
21. Patel, D. "The Evolution of Compensation," *Work Visions*, *No. 3*, 2002.
22. Bates, S. "More Firms Take High Road by Expensing Stock Options," *HR Magazine*, August 2002, p. 10.
23. Gerena-Morales, R. "Balancing Pay and Performance," *South Florida Sun-Sentinel*, May 23, 2003, p. 1E.
24. Public, "Private Exec Comp Programs Increasingly Similar," *HR Magazine*, *53*, (1), January 2008, p. 12.
25. Terhune, C. and Lubin, J. "In Unusual Move, Coke Ties All Pay for Directors to Earnings Targets," *Wall Street Journal*, April 6, 2006, pp. A1, A11.

READING 11.1

Key Trends of the Total Reward System in the 21st Century

Hai-Ming Chen and Yi-Hua Hsieh

Today's organizations operate in an intensely competitive landscape. During the past 20 years, enormous changes have caused many companies to think about better ways of doing business. These changes include increasing globalization, reducing costs, becoming more competitive, monitoring the volatility of currency movements, adjusting to the diffusion of information and new technologies, and a widespread emphasis on quality improvements and attentiveness to added value.

These factors have combined to intensify competition and increase the pressure for a major transformation in organizations and management. This article describes the transition in the global environment and human resource management. It looks at the traditional reward systems of the past and examines the recent innovations in rewarding employees arising from the changing needs of organizations in a competitive environment. It then describes the basic trends and evolution of the modern systems from the dimensions of basis, method, function, frequency, object, and design.

Viewpoint of Strategic HR Management

Competition, globalization and continuous changes in markets and technology are the principal reasons for the transformation of human resource management. Based on the conditions of competitive global markets, the new strategic roles for human resource management have been defined. In a marketplace that is characterized by the "war for talent," companies in every industry are facing a difficult time in attracting and retaining people.[1] To live in the changing environment, the notion of strategic human resource management has emerged.

Strategic human resource management focuses on the overall direction of the organization in pursuit of its stated goals and objectives. Increasing the core competencies of the firm, in particular human resources, is one of the key elements in the success of the firm. The idea that people management can be a key source of sustained competitive advantage calls for the integration of human resource management and business strategy.

Strategic human resource management encompasses decisions and actions concerning the management of employees at all levels in the business that are directed toward creating and sustaining competitive advantage. Strategic human resources management includes dramatically different views about the nature of rewards. Viewing employees as performance drivers means thinking differently about what it would take to attract, keep and engage them in giving discretionary effort on the job.

As business strategy and operations undergo a generational shift, reward systems and the philosophy of pay management must change to attract new talent and retain top performers. A reward system must motivate employees to perform in ways that contribute to a company's successful execution of its strategy. In addition, it must also be effective in attracting talent to the company and retaining employees who can effectively use their talent to deliver results. A reward system that is poorly suited to the organization, outdated or improperly designed has a number of negative organizational effects. Understanding the trends in total reward systems and implementing them properly is crucial to attracting and keeping talented employees and successfully executing organization strategy (see Exhibit 1).

EXHIBIT 1 Factors Influencing the Total Reward System

Key Trends in Total Reward Systems

Today organizations are facing changes generated by increased competition, mergers and acquisitions, shifting markets and changing employee demographics. In recent years, because of these changes and shifts in organizational strategy and the philosophy of human resource management, hundreds of organizations—from manufacturing concerns and services to government agencies—have developed and adopted new, nontraditional reward systems. We categorize reward systems trends in six dimensions: basis, method, function, frequency, object and design.

Trend 1: Seniority-Contribution

The traditional reward system is mainly based on seniority or length of service. Jobs have been defined in terms of tasks. That is, employees have to perform narrowly defined functions. They need narrowly defined skills. This kind of reward system has come to be viewed as an entitlement and thus is not capable of truly motivating or reinforcing employee behavior.[2]

To compete in today's marketplace, growing numbers of corporations are seeking new strategies to improve employee performance and development. The new trend in reward systems is based on employees' contributions, which includes competency and performance. A competency is a set of attributes including skills, knowledge, abilities and behaviors. Competencies are those attributes embedded in employees that constitute the potential of creating value. If properly motivated, they may be transformed into high performance.[3] Rewarding for competencies means that pay is strongly influenced by the competencies required to both perform a role and run a company. Performance is productivity and accomplishment. Rewarding for performance helps to hold workers accountable for specific objectives and provides an incentive for exceeding the objectives.

Today, strategic human resource management ideas emphasize the total contribution to the firm. In addition, enterprise information technology platforms have led to upgraded skills required in jobs throughout organizations. Because these advantages come from human capital, they cannot be replicated by other organizations. As a result, a company's human or intellectual capital is indeed its only true source of sustainable competitive advantage. Technological, financial, sales, manufacturing and distribution capabilities can all be copied, but human capital cannot.

In organizations where speed, flexibility and productivity are important, reward systems should not be solely based on tasks but also geared toward rewarding the development of an employee's skills and knowledge. An employee who becomes more skilled becomes more flexible. And if the employee becomes more knowledgeable, there is a better understanding of his or her role in contributing to the organization. Rapidly changing business environments mandate that employees continually upgrade their skill base. By explicitly linking pay to growth in skills and knowledge, organizations aim to modernize their human assets much as they upgrade their physical assets.

Most organizations view competencies, capabilities, skills or strategic assets as a source of sustainable competitive advantage for the firm. For organizations that experience rapid technological change, competent employees will adapt to these changes. Therefore, employees must continually learn new skills, knowledge, methods and techniques to keep up the changing environment. Skill-based pay is the motivator to keep employees learning. Skill-based pay rewards employees for keeping pace with the changing environment in which the company is operating.

Organizations that use a pay-for-competency setup typically find that it helps them to focus better on the core business strategy. It also helps to recognize the link between achieving this strategy and the top performance of employees. Therefore, one of the key trends of the total reward system in the 21st century is that the basis of the reward system has gradually shifted from employees' seniority to contribution.

Trend 2: Simplex-Multiplex

The traditional reward method just paid money. However, people work for more than just pay. A pay raise alone does not have sufficient power to motivate with time. The modern reward system embraces everything that is valued by employees in the employment relationship.

Successful companies use a portfolio approach to reward and do not rely on just one or two methods. Each method has a distinct purpose and structure to encourage a set of actions or attitudes. There is no single method that works in the long run. Successful companies have achieved an alignment between what the company needs to attain with its strategy and what it needs to reinforce in its core values.

Rewards are everything employees perceive to be of value resulting from the employment relationship. They primarily include cash compensation, benefits, and other noncash forms and the work experience.[4] Strategic reward plans go beyond cash to include training and educational opportunities, job redesign, flexible work schedules, stock options and recognition awards such as merchandise and travel. Noncash rewards, such as on-site day care, fitness centers, dry-cleaning services and automatic teller machines, add convenience to employees' daily lives and engender higher loyalty. Work-at-home and job-sharing arrangements enable employees to better balance work and family responsibilities and afford employers the necessary flexibility to respond to business needs. The total reward system is defined here to include base salary, variable pay, direct compensation, perquisites, benefits, performance management, training, career development, coaching and other employee-related policies.

Combinations of variable pay, recognition and celebration and benefits are essential to providing a total reward package. The reward tools found to be highly effective for attracting and retaining critical-skill employees include training and development opportunities, flexible schedules and recognition vehicles that send a more caring message to employees (see Exhibit 2).

EXHIBIT 2 Components of Total Reward System

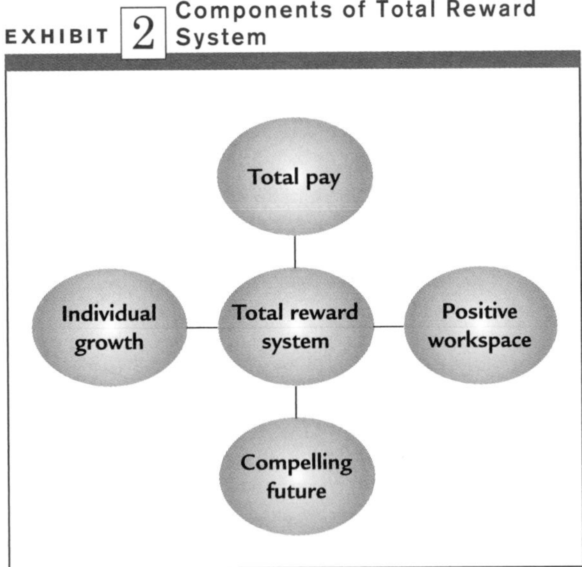

The concept of the contemporary reward system is composed of four components: total pay, attractive variable pay, benefits and recognition and celebration.

1. Individual growth: providing the training for workers to grow and learn during their whole career.
2. Positive workplace: branding your organization so that people are excited about coming to work.
3. Compelling future: making your company uniquely attractive to the people you need.

Different reward methods are likely to have different effects on organizational outcomes. Adopting appropriate methods will enable employers to deliver attractive and relevant rewards at a sustainable cost and help ensure that employees perceive they are receiving appropriate value from the company in exchange for their contributions to its success. A more multiplex rewarding method is another trend.

Trend 3: Extrinsic-Intrinsic

In the mid-1950s, the total-reward system was a concept on the far horizon, but it now forms the basis of the company mission for the 21st century. Nowadays, the function of the total-reward system has both extrinsic and intrinsic value because of the various reward methods. A traditional rewards system most likely applies financial payment and emphasizes the extrinsic function. However, the new trend of the total reward system has gradually turned to an intrinsic focus on incentive and motivation.

Reward practices play an important role in motivating employees to perform. Most researchers agree that reward practices logically serve as motivators in shaping the behavior of employees and motivating them to perform at higher levels, and the use of proper rewards can culminate in improved firm performance at the organizational level.[5] For behaviorists, learning only takes place through external positive and negative reinforcement. The right behavior could be encouraged through the use of rewards and praise.[6] An effective rewards system helps guide and inspire the workforce and provide a specific motivating direction. It can also play a major role in stimulating future performance.

Organizations and managers consistently acknowledge rewards and recognition as an important element in motivating individual employees.[7] It helps to motivate employees to achieve the vision and goals and reinforce the key roles and behaviors that are needed for a successful organization. An integrated reward system results in the attraction and retention of critical talent. It increases organizational commitment, encourages employees to increase capabilities and motivates behaviors that drive the high performance.

An effective reward system is not only a reward but also incentive and motivation. Therefore, we can conclude that the trend of the total-reward system, in function, has reached beyond extrinsic to intrinsic factors.

Trend 4: Periodic-Instantaneous

Most of the traditional reward takes place at the end of the year or twice a year. However, these days, rewards occur instantaneously because of the continuously changing environment and various reward methods.

A reward system can be a powerful motivational tool for employees, but only if it is implemented correctly and in a timely fashion. A reward system is most effective when employees can see how they contribute to bottom-line results and how their contributions will be recognized and rewarded immediately. A long-deferred reward loses most of its power.

Instead of the traditional reward being a fixed amount each month or year, a growing proportion should become contingent on performance. The total-reward system that offers frequent opportunities for awards, such as weekly, monthly or quarterly, creates frequent opportunities to talk with employees about their performance and celebrate their results. Employees can see more immediately how their efforts influence results. It actually delivers strong value to employees through several reward tools instantaneously.

Today's business environment demands reward strategies that point out employee value and contribution at the right moment. For human resource management practitioners, therefore, it becomes essential to look at the overall business needs and to identify how often the reward can assist in guiding and changing employee behaviors that will lead to long-term performance. In any case, periodic rewarding is not able to satisfy both employees' and employers' needs. Rewards offered instantaneously can bring the maximum result and function for organizations.

Trend 5: Unitary-Differential

Traditional reward systems have only one kind of program that is applied to all employees in the organization. In other words, the practice object of the reward system is unitary.

However, in today's competitive environment, many organizations are beginning to appropriately view employee rewards as an important investment rather than one of their largest expenses. Organizations clearly understand that they must attract, reward and retain different kinds of employees. They must also balance the need for different talent with their company's need to remain competitiveness. That is, reward systems must meet the needs of the organization and the needs of the employee. Therefore, the practice object should be different for different reward tools.

Every institution is unique, and one approach to rewarding and motivating employees does not fit all organizations. In certain situations, alternatives will prove to be in a company's best interests, and in other scenarios, they could be a poor choice. Also, each employee has different characteristic, needs and abilities that can best be met with different types of rewards. It is important to try to customize the options to suit the personality and interests of each performer to make the rewards more meaningful. Organizations should give employees several options from which to choose to ensure the reward is valued.[8]

The organization is responsible for providing every reasonable opportunity and all the tools necessary for employees to perform well. Superior companies use a variety of techniques to motivate employees and achieve their organizational goals. In brief, it is essential that reward systems take into account all of the employees' goals and motivations. The practice object of the modern reward system is differential, meaning that organizational reward plans will vary depending on types of positions and individual employee's special characteristics. The whole reward system also gives employers the flexibility to craft different combinations of rewards to meet individual employee needs.

Trend 6: Independent-Coordinate

In the past, reward systems had no strong linkage with organizational goals and conditions. In the increasing competitive marketplace, dramatically different views have developed about the nature of human resource management. The new notion, that people management can be a key source of sustained competitive advantage, calls for the integration of human resource management and business strategy. Therefore, total-reward systems are no longer independent in designing and implementing the broader strategy. On the contrary, they must be coordinated with the organizational mission, vision, values, goals and competitive atmosphere.

Revisiting total reward programs and assessing the effectiveness of the total-reward strategy and structure in meeting business needs is critical. The total-reward strategy should ensure that the reward framework matches the strategic needs of the business and that the mechanics of the total reward structure reinforce the desired corporate culture and management style. This begins with an articulation of the company's values and business strategies. The total reward strategy must be clear about where, when and how the links between business goals and rewards should and should not be made.

It is important for any manager who is reviewing the organization's current reward system first to consider the key results and behaviors that the organization needs to be successful. A through rethinking and restructuring of reward and recognition practices that are aligned with new organizational goals and culture will give companies the focused energy they need to succeed in challenging times. One critical element in designing and implementing a unique reward system is to carefully tailor it to the business strategy, structure and culture of the organization. The effectiveness of creating an alignment between these organizational systems has been clearly established in the practitioner and academic literature.

A typical way to approach strategic human resource management is to define it as bridging the concept of business strategy and human resource management. There must be a link between a firm's strategy and the use of its human resources. People management can be a key source of sustained competitive advantage, and total reward systems are one critical part of the human-resource management. Therefore, organizational needs and strategies should be included in designing and implementing the reward system. Strategically linking and coordinating the vision, mission, and goals of the organization while managing reward system is essential in contemporary circumstances.

Significance of the Strategic Total-Reward System

Recent developments have made it more important than ever for companies to make sure they have a strategic, holistic and integrated approach to compensation. To compete in a tough arena, organizations now more than ever need the support of an informed, involved and motivated workforce. The organization's primary objective in using strategic rewards is workforce effectiveness and not simply to stop people from leaving but to have them become engaged members of a productive and energized workforce.

Rapid change creates the chance for some new directions. Some companies will take advantage of this opportunity, and some will miss the chance and freeze where they are or even take some backward steps. But it is a chance for reward designers to shine. A well-designed reward system must motivate, direct and educate. It must keep people focused on current objectives while preparing them for future challenges. Most of all, it must effectively align the interests of key stakeholder groups: customers, owners and employees. When the system is well designed and implemented, it creates excellent outcomes for all stakeholders. Human-resource managers need to ensure that their reward system is designed to support the achievement of key business success factors, that the system delivers shareholder value and that they deliver increased value to employees.

In the 21st century, technological, political, regulatory, demographic and economic forces unleashed in the past will continue to exert pressures on organizations to change to ensure their survival and success. Initiating and sustaining successful change require considerable thought and action on related supportive structures and systems. Organizations and their subsystems, including critical human-resource management systems, have to become increasingly strategic to succeed in an environment that is in constant flux. That is, functional and unit strategies must be aligned with overall firm strategy to enhance organizational effectiveness. Strategic reward systems—an integral aspect of human resource management—are vital in ensuring desired employee behaviors and enhanced firm performance.

Marketing is the art and science of linking the product producers or service providers with existing and potential customers. Through positioning, marketers create an image for a particular brand or specific product and that image is designed to resonate with the predetermined target market. The concept of total rewards is about the positioning an organization assumes for employee attraction, retention and motivation. As marketers of a company's total-reward strategy, human-resource professionals are attempting to create an image of value that will retain and engage existing and potential employees.

Traditional reward systems are a thing of the past. Total-reward systems in today's world must be adjusted so that they are closely aligned with an organization's changing strategies and designed to reward exemplary performance. Understanding the trends explained here will help managers to design and implement a reward-system strategy that will satisfy employees, management and shareholders and strengthen organization's future.

EXHIBIT 3 Key Trends of the Total Reward System in the 21st Century

Dimension	From	To
Basis	Seniority	Contribution
Method	Simplex	Multiplex
Function	Extrinsic	Intrinsic
Frequency	Periodic	Instantaneous
Object	Unitary	Differential
Design	Independent	Coordinate

Conclusion

Many companies realize that the best people with the most important skills work for more than just pay. The best people work for companies with a compelling future to offer, plus the chance to grow as individuals, a place that offers a positive work experience and total pay including base pay, benefits, incentives and recognition. To create an effective reward system, companies need to understand where their reward dollars are being allocated. The companies that do the best job of linking rewards to business results and employee performance to attract and retain the best workers will be the ones best positioned for future success.

This article views the total-reward system from six dimensions: basis, method, function, frequency, object and design. Each dimension has obvious trends and transitions because of the rapidly changing environment. Exhibit 3 summarizes the conclusions of this article.

According to Miles and Snow[9], organizations differ from one another by the business strategies they pursue. Organizations may be prospectors or defenders depending on their business strategies. For organizations to perform successfully, the business strategy, organizational structure and reward system must align with one another. Organizations are looking for ways to achieve more than their competitors in terms of the value they retrieve from pay and reward dollars. The best executives are not merely copying the practices of others. Rather, they are looking at practices at other companies and determining how effective or ineffective those practices would be. For human-resource managers, developing and executing a practical total-reward system that adds value to the business is a critical issue.

Source: Compensation and Benefits Review, 38, (6), Nov–Dec 2006, 64–70. Reprinted by permission of the CCC.

ENDNOTES

1. Wilson, T. B. (2001). What's hot and what's not: Key trends in total compensation. *Compensation and Benefits Management, 17*(2), 45–50.
2. Hale, J. (1998). Strategic rewards: Keeping your best talent from walking out the door. *Compensation and Benefits Management, 14*(3), 39–50.
3. Chen, H. M., & Kuo, T. S. (2004). Performance appraisal across organizational life cycle. *Human System Management, 23*, 227–33.
4. Bush, T. J. (2003). Leverage employee rewards to drive performance. *Hoosier Banker, 87*(4), 26–29.
5. Allen, R. S., Helms, M. M., Takeda, M. B., White, C. S. (2004). Rewards and organizational performance in Japan and the United States: A comparison. *Compensation and Benefits Review, 36*{l), 7–14.
6. Cacioppe, R. (1999). Using team-individual reward and recognition strategies to drive organizational success. *Leadership and Organization Development Journal, 20*(6), 322–31.
7. Messmer, M. (2004). Creating an effective recognition program. *Strategic Finance, 85*(7), 13–14.
8. Scharff, R. L. (2001). Viewpoint: Companies need holistic strategies and incentives to attract and retain key executives. *Compensation and Benefits Management, 17*(4), 58–60.
9. Miles, R. E., & Snow, C. C. (1984). Designing strategic human resource systems. *Organization Dynamics, 13*, 36–52.

READING 11.2

Exposing Pay Secrecy

Adrienne Colella, Ramona L. Paetzold, Asghar Zardkoohi and Michael J. Wesson

Pay secrecy is a contentious issue in many organizations and a controversial one in our society. However, there has been little scholarly research on this topic. We hope to address this void by exposing the complexity of pay secrecy as a construct. What are its costs and benefits? What factors affect the link between pay secrecy and the extent to which it is a cost or benefit? This article reveals the complexity of pay secrecy and, we hope, generates ideas for much new research in the broad management field.

Pay secrecy in organizations is a contentious issue and has been for a long time. Take, for example, the following memoranda that were exchanged in October of 1919:

POLICY MEMORANDUM (October 14, 1919) Forbidding Discussion among Employees of Salary Received

It has been the policy of the organization to base salaries on the value of services rendered. We have, therefore, a long established rule that the salary question is a confidential matter between the organization and the individual.

It is obviously important that employees live up to this rule in order to avoid invidious comparison and dissatisfaction. Recently several cases have come to the notice of management where employees have discussed the salary question among themselves.

This memorandum should serve as a warning that anyone who breaks this rule in the future will be instantly discharged.

POLICY MEMORANDUM (October 15, 1919) Concerning the Forbidding of Discussion among Employees

We emphatically resent both the policy and working of your policy memorandum of October 14. We resent being told what we may and what we may not discuss, and we protest against the spirit of petty regulation which has made possible the sending out of such an edict (Robert Benchley, cited in Steele, 1975: 102–103).

The authors of the second memorandum then walked around the office with signs stating their salaries hanging from their necks, leading the organization to give up its pay secrecy policy. This anecdote describes the managerial viewpoint toward pay at a magazine where humorist Robert Benchley worked in 1919. Although Benchley and his coworkers chose a witty manner in which to voice their discontent with the magazine's pay secrecy policy, one perhaps different from how you or we would have chosen to respond, pay secrecy itself remains a serious, contentious issue in organizations today.

For example, Mary Craig, an assistant cook for an Ohio nursing home, was fired in 1997 after discussing her pay with her coworkers. Although the nursing home had told her never to discuss pay so as to avoid "hard feelings" among employees, she violated the mandate after listening to other workers' complaints of being shortchanged on overtime or not receiving a promised raise. A federal appellate court affirmed the National Labor Relations Board's (NLRB) determination that the nursing home had to reinstate her with back wages (*NLRB v. Main Street Terrace Center*, 2000).

Intuition tells us that there must be detriments flowing from pay secrecy. What is the big deal about how pay is distributed if we are not supposed to know about it? Why is our organization treating us as though we cannot handle knowledge of others' pay? What if our pay reflects illegal discrimination? And, if we cannot determine what pay levels are possible, wouldn't pay secrecy actually demotivate us so that our performance levels would be expected to drop?

In fact, the limited empirical research has shown that pay secrecy leads to employee dissatisfaction and low motivation (e.g., Burroughs, 1982; Futrell & Jenkins, 1978). In the scanty compensation literature addressing pay secrecy, researchers argue, in general, that pay secrecy is bad for organizations, also demonstrating lowered motivation (Bartol & Martin, 1988; Lawler, 1965a,b, 1967; Leventhal, Karuza, & Fry, 1980; Milkovich & Anderson, 1972). Thus, the state of empirical knowledge continues to suggest that pay secrecy is negative for both individuals and organizations. Further, evidence of the negative effects of pay secrecy include its being viewed as a way for organizations to hide pay discrimination. In fact, England recently passed legislation permitting employees who suspect pay discrimination to request detailed pay information from their supervisors (BBC News, 2004), suggesting a growing awareness that pay secrecy may be costly to society by covering discriminatory practices.

However, current attitudes and practices suggest that there may be beneficial aspects to pay secrecy. First, surveys asking how people feel about pay secrecy indicate that the majority of U.S. workers are in favor of it (*Hrnext.com Survey*, 2001; Walsh, 2000). Furthermore, many organizations seem to employ some form of pay secrecy. Employer surveys (Balkin & Gomez-Mejia, 1985; *Hrnext.com Survey*, 2001) and anecdotal data (e.g., Pappu, 2001; Walsh, 2000) indicate that some form of pay secrecy is prevalent in many organizations, despite its potential illegality (e.g., Fredricksburg Glass and Mirror, 1997; *NLRB v. Main Terrace Center*, 2000). This evidence seems to suggest that individual employees and many organizations find pay secrecy useful and desirable.

Thus, although the academic research of the 1960s and 1970s (e.g., Futrell & Jenkins, 1978; Lawler, 1965a,b, 1967; Milkovich & Anderson, 1972) seems to leave us with one view of pay secrecy—that it presents costs to organizations because, among other things, individual employees should not want it—there has been no scholarly investigation that we are aware of since then to determine whether there may also be benefits to organizations. No organizational scholars have investigated how individual demands and organizational practices can continue to be at such odds with this dated academic knowledge.

In this article we discuss the apparently contradictory positions about pay secrecy and argue that there is no simple answer to the question of whether pay secrecy is beneficial or detrimental to individuals and organizations. Instead, we posit that the effects of pay secrecy depend on a variety of factors that render it sometimes valuable or of benefit to employers and employees and other times costly. Throughout the course of our discussion, we examine arguments based on management, economics, psychology, and cultural perspectives to look at the role of pay secrecy in our lives and to suggest avenues for further study. Our ultimate goal is to reopen the discussion of pay secrecy in organizations so that new empirical work in this area can be generated. We first turn to a definition of pay secrecy.

What Is Pay Secrecy?

Although there is no one definition of pay secrecy, it can simply be viewed as a restriction of the amount of information employees are provided about what others are paid. In practice, however, pay secrecy can become quite complex. First, there is the issue of availability of information. An employer may keep pay information secret by never providing for its publication or release. Second, the employer may restrict the type of pay information made available. For example, it may choose to provide certain aggregate information about pay, such as pay ranges and/or average pay raises, but fail to give precise individual-level information about employees. Third, the employer may restrict the manner in which pay information is disseminated. For example, the employer may encourage strong norms against discussing pay, even if pay information is technically publicly available. In this case the employer may actually threaten to impose heavy sanctions against employees who disclose pay or engage in discussions about it.

The traditional venue for discussions of pay—the compensation literature—identifies several dimensions of pay: pay level, pay structure, the basis for pay, and the form of pay (see Gerhart & Rynes, 2003). Although pay secrecy can range across these various dimensions, the traditional focus has been on pay level itself (i.e., the average pay across jobs; Gerhart & Rynes, 2003). Because we are interested in advancing the discussion about pay secrecy as a general construct, and because we also do not want to limit ourselves to a micro human resource (HR) focus but intend, rather, to write for a much broader audience, we focus on pay-level discussions and avoid the complexities of compensation systems. In other words, when we speak of pay secrecy, we are talking about the lack of information that employees have about the level of other employees' pay in the organization.

Although much prior research has conceptualized pay secrecy as all-or-nothing, we argue that it is best understood along a continuum. Thus, for us, pay secrecy is conceptualized as representing the amount of information about pay available to employees. Burroughs (1982) was the first to hint at such a continuum when he referred to examples of how different organizations could have varying levels of pay secrecy, with the most secret anchor being represented by organizations in which no information is provided to employees other than their own pay and salary increase. The least secret (or most open) anchor reflects organizations where information about specific pay levels and increases for individuals is made available to all employees. We base our view on Burroughs'. In addition, we assume that any costs and benefits of pay secrecy become more extreme as pay becomes more secret.

Finally, we assume throughout that organizations are making good faith efforts to provide equitable compensation and that compensation accurately reflects an individual's contribution to the organization, however that is determined. Because equity is ultimately in the eye of the beholder, we recognize that employees' views on whether they receive pay that is fair may deviate from those of the organization. Thus, our discussion of pay secrecy will rely heavily on the perceptions it creates in the minds of employees.

Why Is Pay Secrecy Interesting?

Based on earlier discussion, we find pay secrecy interesting because it obviously has the potential to apply to many people across jobs, organizations, and industries (Balkin & Gomez-Mejia, 1985; *Hrnext.com Survey*, 2001). Since pay secrecy reflects a lack of information, one way of conceptualizing pay secrecy is in terms of pay uncertainty. Humans are generally motivated to reduce uncertainty or the discomfort that arises from it (Lind & van den Bos, 2002) and, thus, can be expected to engage in a variety of behaviors as a means of eliminating, reducing, or otherwise coping with pay uncertainty. In particular, a host of cognitive biases in information processing are known to result when judgments must be made under uncertainty (Kahneman & Tversky, 1973). Thus, the possible breadth of application of pay secrecy policies immediately raises controversial issues about the extent to which U.S. employees are making less than optimal decisions about jobs and career choices and what the impact might be on American society. Although the answer to such a question is beyond the scope of this article, the very nature of this consideration enhances our interest in thinking about pay secrecy.

Additionally, part of the fascinating character of this topic stems from the fact that it is not a new concern but, rather, one of continuing debate without many insights over the years. For example, pay secrecy was a major difficulty around the time of the passage of the National Labor Relations Act ([NLRA], 1935), because it was determined to interfere with the attempts of employees to unionize. Because information about pay is so critical to employee behaviors and decision making, the NLRA continues to make enforced pay secrecy illegal in order to promote maximal employee information about their job circumstances and workplace fairness (Bierman & Gely, 2004; Gely & Bierman, 2003). Given this historical background, we would have expected two things. First, its sheer illegality should have deterred employers from using pay secrecy over the period since the initial enforcement of the NLRA. Quite to the contrary, many employers willingly announce and promote their pay secrecy policies. For example, a survey of U.S. employers found that 36 percent of respondents indicated their companies prohibited discussion of pay (*Hrnext.com Survey*, 2001). Second, the controversial nature of this topic should have promoted extensive research in this area to build a nomological network of understanding about the costs and benefits of pay secrecy for individuals, organizations, and even society. No such comprehensive course of study exists.

Pay secrecy also seems to reflect current social or cultural values that are expressed or facilitated through its practice. One key value is that of privacy. Today, privacy concerns are reawakening, as evidenced by relatively new legislation or new awareness of older legislation (such as the Family Educational Rights and Privacy Act [FERPA], 1974, and the Health Insurance Portability and Accountability Act [HIPAA], 1996), as well as public outrage about technologically possible behaviors, such as identity theft. Pay secrecy promotes the notion that our own pay should be kept private—that *we, not the employer*, should have the right to determine whether to disclose our pay and to whom. Thus, its social and personal salience appears to be grounded in the general resurgence of privacy concerns that are part of our evolving world.

One final, but not less important, aspect of pay secrecy that renders it interesting to us is the fact that it might well be a culturally bound construct. Investigations of collectivist and individualist societies (Triandis, 1989) have indicated that Western cultures and economies reflect autonomous, individualistic goals and values, whereas Eastern cultures and economies tend to reflect collectivistic, group-based goals and values. Thus, pay secrecy may not be as controversial an issue in an Eastern culture. There, the tendency would be toward values that favor the collective (Triandis, 1989, 1994). Moreover, members of the collective typically are not truly recognized as "others" completely distinct from the self, causing the very notion of "others' pay" and "referent others for comparison" to be ill-defined. In addition, the collectivist's sense of trust in the group or organization might be expected to accompany lack of concern for what people other than oneself are making in the workplace. The interdependence that accompanies collectivism further suggests that a view of "what is good for one of us is good for all of us" would also tend to dominate and render pay secrecy less controversial (Markus & Kitayama, 1991). Finally, individuals in collectivist cultures typically do not want to stand out from the group or compete with others in the group; pay secrecy would allow this to flourish. Thus, pay secrecy may always be positive in an Eastern culture.

In contrast, in Western cultures, individuals engage in self-construal that tends not to include general "other in self" enhancements (at least outside of close partners and friends; Mashek, Aron, & Boncimino, 2003). Thus, each individual in the workplace is seen as fairly autonomous and a competitor for resources. Independence instead of interdependence is associated with individualistic societies, implying that each person's welfare depends on his or her own efforts and rewards. Pay secrecy reflects values emanating from this type of culture, and it is both supported and promoted by more capitalistic societies that promote individual competitiveness (Markus & Kityama, 1991). It may only be within Western culture that pay secrecy can produce the costs that are associated with it.

What Are the Costs and Benefits of Pay Secrecy?

Before turning to the focus of our article—that the costs and benefits of pay secrecy depend on a variety of previously undiscussed factors—it is essential to first lay out the costs and benefits themselves. In this section we first review the apparent costs of pay secrecy before turning to a discussion of the benefits. Perhaps surprisingly, some aspects of pay secrecy can turn out to be both costs and benefits, as we will show. Further, factors adding an even greater level of complexity will be addressed in the next section of the paper. For now, we try to elucidate the major costs and benefits as seen by researchers and practitioners.

Costs

There are at least three major costs to pay secrecy, according to research scholars (who continue to challenge the use of pay secrecy by organizations). First, employee judgments about fairness and their perceptions of trust may be sacrificed. Second, employee performance motivation can be expected to decrease. Third, from an economics perspective, the labor market may be less efficient because employees will not move to their highest valued use. This would mean that organizations are not obtaining the best employees for the jobs. Why, and from where, would these costs occur?

Pay secrecy is about lack of information, thus producing uncertainty for employees and an asymmetrical information status between employees and the organization. Based on this lack of information, employees may *infer* that pay outcomes and procedures for distributions are unfair, even when the organization is making a good faith effort to provide equitable compensation based on individual contributions. (Recall that this was an underlying assumption we made earlier.)

One reason this might occur is because the uncertainty of not knowing where employees stand with respect to others and the extent to which their contributions are valid may lead to general anxiety about workplace worth. According to recent work in the organizational justice literature on uncertainty management theory (Lind & van den Bos, 2002), increased uncertainty enhances the degree to which people care about fairness, because apparent fairness is one way of coping with the anxiety generated by uncertainty. When the environment is uncertain, people are able to gain some degree of predictability of their future treatment by looking at how fairly they recently have been or now are being treated. When treated fairly, people can develop trust and reduce their fears of being exploited in the future. When treated unfairly, however, they may take a defensive stance in an attempt to avoid exploitation. Thus, ceteris paribus, employees who are faced with pay secrecy should be more concerned about whether their pay is fair than employees who are in positions where pay information is open. As a result, they may be more vigilant about the extent to which pay and pay determination processes are fair, and this becomes a cost when fairness judgments are negative.

Unfortunately, under high levels of pay secrecy, judgments can be expected to be negative for all three general types of fairness judgments: informational, procedural, and distributive (Bies & Moag, 1986; Colquitt, Conlon, Wesson, Porter, & Ng, 2001; Leventhal, 1976; Thibaut & Walker, 1975). Obviously, judgments about informational fairness can be expected to be negative because information is being withheld. Judgments about procedural fairness can be expected to be negative because, for example, the lack of information restricts employee voice, permits inferences of bias, and suggests that decision making about pay may be done without accurate information. These deficits violate the known requirements for procedural justice to be perceived (Leventhal et al., 1980; Thibaut & Walker, 1975).

Distributive fairness judgments can be expected to be negative for two major reasons. First, inaccurate estimates about what referent others (Dornstein, 1989) are being paid can be expected owing to the lack of information about pay. Lawler's seminal research (1965a,b) indicated that, in the absence of individual pay information, managers overestimated the salaries of other managers at their own and lower levels and underestimated the salaries of managers at higher organizational levels. (In other words, they tended to compress the pay range.) The fact that those at lower levels of the organization were perceived as having higher pay than was actually the case would lead to judgments of distributive unfairness, because they would arguably be making lesser contributions to the organization than was commensurate with their perceived pay.

Second, fairness heuristic theory (Lind, 2001) states that people are likely to base specific fairness judgments on their general impression of organizational fairness in the absence of other information. Thus, in the absence of information about pay, distributive fairness concerning pay level cannot be known, and judgments about it will be inferred based on judgments about other aspects of fairness. If procedural and informational fairness judgments are negative, as indicated above, then distributive fairness judgments should be negative as well (van den Bos, Lind, Vermunt, & Wilke, 1997). This reliance on other fairness judgments generally may be viewed as akin to use of the availability heuristic in prospect theory (Kahneman & Tversky, 1973). In the absence of specific pay information, employees would be expected to rely on recent or vivid information that was readily available or accessible in memory. This information might well be other judgments about fairness regarding aspects of the organization—that is, even fairness judgments beyond those regarding pay could become relevant under pay secrecy.

Related to unfairness judgments resulting from pay secrecy is the notion of distrust in the organization. We follow Mayer, Davis, and Schoorman's definition of trust as "the willingness of a party to be vulnerable to the actions of another party based on the expectation that the other will perform a particular action important to the trustor, irrespective of the ability to monitor or control that other party" (1995: 712). Pay secrecy should generally be expected to lower employees' organizational trust. Research on organizational trust all points to the importance of managers' openness with both themselves and others (Butler, 1991), since this behavior suggests that management has both integrity and benevolence. Such openness has been shown to be a primary driver of trust (Mayer et al., 1995; Mishra, 1996).

Two other key factors strongly suggest that organizational trust should be affected by pay secrecy and its ensuing judgments of unfairness. First, media attention to young, self-made millionaires during the technology boom of the 1990s, astronomical executive pay levels, and corporate scandals have highlighted the wide discrepancy in pay in American society, tending to enhance perceptions that pay may be unfair. Pay secrecy in this environment enhances views of this unfairness and corruption, suggesting that organizations cannot be trusted. Second, pay secrecy signals that the organization does not trust its employees.

Pay secrecy should also reduce work motivation. Because a pay-performance linkage underlies many theories of motivation, one can argue that pay secrecy will reduce motivation by breaking that linkage. The only study we are aware of that examines this connection was conducted by Futrell and Jenkins (1978), who found that moving from pay secrecy to pay openness resulted in increased performance on the part of their sample of salespeople, suggesting that motivation was hampered by pay secrecy. This result appeared to stem from an equity theory explanation: since managers acting under pay secrecy compressed the managerial pay scale in their estimates, as mentioned earlier, the link between pay and performance was weakened, and there was less motivation to perform.

Other theories of work motivation also depend on linking pay to performance; without perceptions of this link, employees lack an essential driver of motivation. For example, expectancy theorists (Naylor, Pritchard, & Ilgen, 1980; Vroom, 1964) argue that the motivation to perform is a direct function of the subjective probability that engaging in a certain level of performance will result in given outcomes (i.e., instrumentality). Goal theorists suggest that performance goals employees are committed to drive motivation (Locke & Latham, 1990), and goal commitment is partially determined by the valence of outcomes associated with achieving a goal (Klein, Wesson, Hollenbeck, & Alge, 1999). Thus, if employees do not know the relative worth of their outcomes, they may be less likely to be committed to goals that assure the achievement of the desired outcomes. They may make poor estimates of their subjective probabilities or the valence of their outcomes.

Pay secrecy can also have an important and deleterious effect on the labor market, thereby imposing a cost on some businesses and society. Economic theory is based on the assumption of perfect information in order to have perfect markets so that resources can migrate to their most valued use (i.e., market efficiency). Labor markets would be one type of market to which this argument should apply (Brickley, Smith, & Zimmerman, 2000). Pay secrecy, by hindering information to employees, generates information *asymmetry* between workers and organizations, thus preventing workers from moving to better-fitting jobs. In other words, if a top-quality engineer is not aware of a higher-paying job that he or she could perform in his or her current company or in another company with a pay secrecy policy, then that engineer may stay in the "wrong" job and be underemployed. Employers cannot "lure" or "pull" good employees away from other employers if they maintain pay secrecy, because they cannot advertise current wage or salary levels. Thus, pay secrecy is one factor that prevents labor markets from clearing in an efficient manner. This represents a cost to employees who could hold better jobs, as well as to organizations that would prefer to hire these employees. Economists would argue that there are social costs imposed because of the inefficient use of human capital in society (Williamson, 1985).

Benefits

Although pay secrecy may have the foregoing costs, it is clear that it must also have benefits attached to it since it continues to be relatively pervasive in organizational practice. Here we identify three major benefits—organizational control, protection of privacy, and decreased labor mobility—which we now discuss in detail.

One benefit of pay secrecy would be that it appears to enhance efforts at organizational control. One major way in which organizations prefer to control employees is by maintaining a civil, peaceful workplace, free from conflicts. In fact, avoiding conflicts is one of the main reasons managers give for enforcing pay secrecy (Gomez-Mejia & Balkin, 1992; Steele, 1975). There are many reasons to believe that pay secrecy is a major source of avoiding or reducing conflict in the workplace.

First, for example, differentials in pay are hidden under pay secrecy, thus preventing problems in corps désprit and levels of satisfaction among workers. As Sally J. Scott, a partner in a Chicago law firm stated, "[Pay secrecy] would create morale problems if one person were allowed to boast about their huge merit bonus" (Walsh, 2000). Second, social psychologists (e.g., Leventhal et al., 1980; Leventhal, Michaels, & Sanford, 1972) have argued that people who allocate resources have a motivation not only to maintain equity but also to avoid conflict. If pay were open, managers might feel that they would have to keep the pay distribution artificially narrow in order to avoid conflict (Leventhal et al., 1980; Major & Adams, 1983). Pay secrecy, however, allows them to provide maximal separation in reward for performance (Bartol & Martin, 1988), while at the same time avoiding negative reactions by those who end up at the lower end of the distribution (Gomez-Mejia & Balkin, 1992; Leventhal et al., 1972). Finally, economists (Brickley et al., 2000) have argued that employers engage in pay secrecy because the cost of the political behavior (such as influence activities) and conflict resulting from pay openness policies makes pay openness inefficient.

In addition, pay secrecy allows organizations to correct pay inequities that arise (even despite good faith efforts to avoid them) without having to face employees' negative reactions to those inequities (Gomez-Mejia & Balkin, 1992). (Ironically, although pay secrecy may generate inferences of pay discrimination, as alluded to earlier, it may also prevent employee awareness of an unintentional pay inequity, thus precluding moderate reactance to or even charges of pay discrimination.) Pay secrecy can therefore be beneficial, because it can actually avoid perceptions of unfairness when pay inequities do exist and can minimize claims of discrimination or other organizational wrongdoing.

Furthermore, if we think of cooperation as the opposite of conflict, it seems clear that organizations, although major players in our capitalistic economic system, prefer some level of cooperation among employees and like to maintain competition in the workplace at a "healthy" or otherwise nondeleterious level. We can think of employers in North America as operating within an individualistic culture but seeking to transcend it by encouraging more of a tempered collectivistic culture within the workplace. For example, organizations may prefer that employees form identities that include the organization (Ashforth & Mael, 1989). The recent emphasis on teamwork in organizations means that organizations want to encourage employees, under many circumstances, to be good team players instead of striving for "superstardom" at the expense of the team. Pay secrecy should give employers operating in individualistic societies the opportunity to introduce a more interdependent approach to culture and values in the workplace.

Another way in which pay secrecy can serve as a form of organizational control is by being a form of organizational paternalism—a way of treating employees as children and limiting their autonomy, supposedly for their own benefit (cf. Colella & Garcia, 2004). Organizational sociologists and economists (e.g., Jackman, 1994; Padavic & Earnest, 1994) have often discussed how organizations use paternalism to control their employees. Pay secrecy can be viewed as a paternalistic policy when managers argue that pay should be kept secret for the benefit of their employees, because (1) employees really want pay kept secret, (2) it will upset them to know what others are making, or (3) they may make "irrational" decisions (such as leaving) if they know what others are being paid. In each case, managers are assuming that they know what is in employees' best interests while limiting their autonomy by failing to provide them with full pay information.

From the organization's point of view, using pay secrecy as a form of paternalistic control would be a benefit of pay secrecy. It would allow the organization to control its employees, but at the same time would let the employers feel good about it, since they were supposedly acting in the best interest of their employees (Abercrombie & Hill, 1976). It is unclear whether this would be a benefit from the employees' perspective. Some argue that paternalism always causes harm to its targets (Jackman, 1994), but targets often welcome paternalistic behavior (Jost & Banaji, 1994). An employee may reason, for example, that an organization really cares about her because, by enforcing pay secrecy, it protects her privacy rights. Regardless of the impact on targets, paternalism is generally seen as an organizational benefit.

A second benefit of pay secrecy would be expected to be the enhanced privacy that comes from having one's own pay kept secret from others. Stone and Stone (1990), in a review of the organizational privacy literature, found that employees' perceptions of privacy led to many positive organizational outcomes, such as performance (Klopfer & Rubenstein, 1977; Sundstrom, Burt, & Kamp, 1980), satisfaction and commitment (Klopfer & Rubenstein, 1977; Sundstrom et al., 1980), and retention (Sundstrom, 1978).

In today's society, in general, as previously mentioned, privacy has become a major concern. Living in an age of technology, we have all become more sensitized to the troublesome ease with which information about us is available and how it can be used to our disadvantage. Much information about us is requested by, and potentially available from, our employers (e.g., in order to work, we must present an official form of ID and a social security number; employers perform credit and sometimes criminal background checks). Given this, it is perhaps not at all surprising that surveys of employees often find that the majority of employees are in favor of pay secrecy policies (Markels & Berton, 1996). In addition, in North American culture there continues to be a strong norm against discussing one's pay (Steele, 1975). Many people prefer not to have their pay discussed by coworkers (Pappu, 2001; Sim, 2001). Most people would be more comfortable answering questions about personal family matters such as religion—or even perhaps sex—than about their salary (BBC News, 2004; Bierman & Gely, 2004). In addition, the discomfort of discussing pay may result from another's revealing too much information about himself or herself (Paetzold, Boswell, & Belsito, 2004).

Of course, some of us might be curious about the pay of others and, thus, be willing to trade off some secrecy about our own pay in order to learn something about how much referent others are making. To date, there is no empirical research that tests this notion. Based on employee surveys, we conclude that the desire for privacy about oneself and one's own pay dominates and overrides the desire to know pay information about others.

Finally, pay secrecy can actually benefit organizations with respect to labor market immobility. Although the labor market inefficiency resulting from pay secrecy may be a cost to society as a whole and some employers in particular, as mentioned above, other employers can profit from this inefficiency by reducing the mobility of their productive workers. For example, Danzinger and Katz (1997) argue that a policy of pay secrecy prevents employees from comparing their wages with others inside the firm, as well as wages of the firm with those in the job market. Such comparisons are needed for employees to switch jobs when it is to their advantage to do so. Thus, pay secrecy reduces this source of information and prevents employees from recognizing other good employment opportunities. A net benefit can accrue to the organization requiring pay secrecy, not only because the pay secrecy facilitates the organization's ability to keep productive employees but also because the organization can avoid costs associated with labor transitions—for example, recruiting and training. Thus, it is clear that pay secrecy can be advantageous for some employers, presumably those who continue to use it.

A related construct in the organizations literature is that of continuance commitment, which reflects an employee's commitment to an organization because of a need to remain with the organization (Meyer, Allen, & Gellatly, 1990). It is not necessary that the employee have positive feelings about the organization; instead, continuance commitment is a function of the opportunities that an employee perceives he or she has. As indicated above, pay secrecy operates by reducing the perceived number of alternative job possibilities, because pay information about other jobs is lacking and appropriate pay comparisons cannot be made. Hence, continuance commitment is increased. At the same time, pay secrecy also prevents "poaching" from other companies, because it keeps competitors from knowing what they must offer to lure good employees away (Sim, 2001). (Notice that we mentioned this earlier as a social cost and a cost to some organizations. Here, it is an organizational benefit.)

Trading off Costs and Benefits

As indicated so far in our discussion, there are both costs and benefits to pay secrecy, but it should also be clear that not all organizations will experience the costs and benefits to the same degree. This would appear to depend, in part, on the quality of employees, their individual needs and perceptions, and the history of those employees with the employer. Employers can therefore be "profiled" based on their employees in order to predict which of them should choose pay secrecy policies. For example, an organization that has many high-quality employees whom it would like to retain and also has high recruiting and training costs, all else being constant, should be more likely to use pay secrecy than an organization that does not.

Once we remove the constraint that all else is being held constant, pay secrecy can look even better for this organization. Consider that work motivation may not be as much of a concern if the "good" employees are intrinsically motivated (so that pay secrecy will not work to reduce their level of work motivation) and tend to have a lot of accumulated trust in the organization stemming from other aspects of the work relationship. Such an employer (who uses pay secrecy) may enjoy, therefore, the benefit of lack of labor mobility (continuance commitment), in addition to not suffering the costs associated with reduced work motivation and lack of trust in the organization.

Other employers with different cost/benefit trade-offs should be expected not to employ pay secrecy. An organization with employees having a low need for privacy, but with a history of organizational unfairness and distrust, should *not* use a pay secrecy policy. For this organization, pay openness could help with perceptions of fairness and trust, as well as potentially improve work motivation and performance. In addition, this organization may prefer to enhance the mobility of its dissatisfied employees and, thus, should prefer pay openness as a way of making outside opportunities more appealing. For example, as discussed above, the pay distribution under pay openness would tend to be narrower than under pay secrecy so that opportunities for pay raises would appear to be small. Although we mentioned that this has the benefit of reducing conflict, we must also note that it will tend to encourage employees to move to other positions, where they can be put to their "most valued use."

Thus, separate consideration of costs and benefits does not reveal the whole picture of pay secrecy; their joint consideration is relevant. In joint consideration, these costs and benefits can help us to identify why some employers may prefer pay secrecy while others do not; characteristics of individual employees, for example, suggest that some employers should prefer pay secrecy while others should not.

But individual characteristics cannot tell us the whole picture either. In fact, the *context* or *contextual factors* employers face may be the most important determinant of why some employers engage in pay secrecy policies while others do not. The relationships between pay secrecy and its costs or benefits are not fixed but depend on these contextual factors. Organizations and their environments are complex, and there are a number of contextual factors that are likely to accentuate or minimize the costs and benefits mentioned above. For example, which employees should respond more positively to pay secrecy—those who hold knowledge and skills specific to the organizations or those who do not? The answer to this and similar questions suggests that context, or a variety of contextual factors, helps to determine whether pay secrecy is costly or beneficial for organizations. This consideration has never been addressed in the academic literature, and our presentation of it follows.

When Do Costs and Benefits of Pay Secrecy Occur?

In addition to identifying that there are legitimate benefits to pay secrecy, despite its costs, we also view the thrust of our work as identifying a set of contextual factors that make pay secrecy more likely to be either a benefit or a cost—that is, they make it more likely for organizations to incur the costs or reap the benefits of pay secrecy. Because many organizations seem to prefer pay secrecy today, and because we have presented our discussion from the perspective of highlighting reasons why such a policy may be beneficial, we now assume that pay secrecy is operating throughout the discussion that follows. We identify contextual factors that exist at different levels of the organization and write from the perspective of how they mitigate the costs and help to make the benefits realizable for those organizations employing pay secrecy. We discuss, in order, the nature of human capital, the criteria used for pay allocation, and the gauging of employees' relative pay status.

We do not claim that these are the only contextual factors that can affect how organizations experience pay secrecy, but we view them as three major contexts that share commonality of importance for many organizations.

Contextual Factor 1: Nature of Human Capital

Consider the following scenario. Heather has worked at AAB (Anti-Ad-Bot) for just a few years, but she has reached a high rung on the internal employment ladder—operations manager. To accomplish this, she has held a variety of positions, beginning as a programmer and working her way up, one job after the other. She has received training and experience along the way that has enabled her to perform all jobs below her current position, and that training has also been essential to her knowledge of the unique culture at AAB. Eric started working at AAB at the same time as Heather, but he remains a programmer. He has never undergone specialized training, remaining in a "dead-end" position within AAB. Between Eric and Heather, who should react to AAB's pay secrecy policy more positively?

We would posit that Eric should. Because Eric has only lower-level skills and no firm-specific training about particular jobs within AAB, Eric also has no special, firm-specific value to AAB beyond what he would have to similar firms. Thus, Eric should be able to go outside the organization in the labor market that is pertinent to programmer jobs for pay information (Milgrom & Roberts, 1992). Heather, however, has such firm-specific skills that she probably cannot find another firm where her talents could be as valuable as they are to AAB. The market for her skills—the one inside AAB—does not allow her to find pay information because it maintains a policy of pay secrecy.

Firm-specific human capital refers to the skills, abilities, knowledge, and/or interpersonal relationships that positively affect employees' performance in their current employment but that are relatively useless if the employee moves to another organization (Williamson, 1985). Therefore, when employees hold primarily firm-specific human capital, external labor market information is less useful to them. In contrast, general human capital refers to human capital with value that remains the same across various organizations. For example, mathematics teachers are likely to provide the same value across various schools. Similarly, carpenters may move across sites to build homes without much change in their duties across those various sites. In both cases, employees can be replaced, requiring little, if any, additional training, and pay is relatively difficult to hide from employees having general human capital.

This means that although there is a relationship between pay secrecy and labor immobility (continuance commitment), the nature of the relationship is highly dependent on the type of human capital workers possess. Looking inside the firm for pay information, employees with firm-specific human capital will find their efforts to learn about pay levels thwarted. Employees with general human capital, however, can look to the external labor market and find little hindrance to obtaining pay information.

Similarly, because of the availability of external information, privacy should be less of a concern to employees with general human capital. These employees cannot keep their pay completely secret if an industry compensation norm exists. They may also be less likely to make incorrect fairness judgments, because they can use external comparison others. If the firm is paying market rates, then employees with general human capital should perceive that their pay is fair. (Those with firm-specific human capital lack external comparison others and may be more likely to make incorrect comparisons.) Also, pay secrecy should have less of an effect on motivation when employees have general human capital, because the employees should want to maintain high enough performance levels to make them attractive to other firms.

Thus, having general human capital should mitigate the costs of pay secrecy and enhance any benefits, at least marginally (assuming that an asymptotic level of benefits has not been reached). In our scenario, Heather cannot easily benefit from any outside pay information, but Eric perhaps can. The benefits of having no firm-specific skills accrue to him when pay secrecy is operating. The organization does not suffer costs from pay secrecy with regard to its general human capital employees—and is free to enjoy all the benefits—even though it may incur costs associated with its firm-specific human capital employees.

Contextual Factor 2: Criteria for Pay Allocation

The criteria for pay allocation are those elements or aspects of effort or performance used to determine pay levels. Pay criteria may be measured either *objectively* or *subjectively*, and we suggest that the nature of measurement helps to determine whether costs or benefits will be experienced during pay secrecy. Using objective criteria for pay allocation should mitigate the costs of pay secrecy.

Consider, for example, Ryan and Natasha, supervisors of two different sales teams at a retail outlet. Ryan's manager stresses "management by objectives" and has specific sales goals that Ryan's sales team must reach in order for Ryan to be evaluated highly. Natasha's manager uses more subjective criteria for evaluating her performance, including her communication skills, leadership abilities, and commitment to diversity. Assume that the retailer maintains pay secrecy policies for its employees. For which supervisor will the retailer be more likely to incur the benefits of pay secrecy?

We posit that it should be for Ryan. Recall that one major cost of pay secrecy is that any pay differentials that may exist—here, between Ryan and Natasha—will lose their power to motivate because they are unknown. In order to counter this difficulty, organizations can provide a clear linkage between pay and performance in order to create work incentives for employees (Thompson & Pronsky, 1975). One factor that would enable the pay-for-performance linkage to be clear would be the use of objective performance criteria. Here, Ryan's raises could be justified to him clearly, whereas Natasha's could not. Thus, if Natasha believes she is underpaid, her manager cannot point to objective performance criteria to justify her pay and attempt to convince her that her pay is commensurate with the goals that he or she has specified for Natasha. It would be difficult to discuss "how much" leadership or "how many" skills were necessary for Natasha to satisfy her supervisor's requirement. Ryan's manager would be in just such a position to get that specific, however. And when employees perceive a specific pay-performance linkage, they are more likely to be satisfied with their pay (Huber, Seybolt, & Venemon, 1992).

Second, the performance appraisal literature (DeNisi, 1996; Murphy & Cleveland, 1995) states that when there is objective information on which to base appraisals, managers are less likely to engage in biases when evaluating employees, and employees are more likely to perceive the appraisal as fair. Such perceptions of fairness will attenuate the general unfairness in justice perceptions that accompany pay secrecy, making the costs of pay secrecy less likely to be incurred and providing for greater organizational trust. This would be true regardless of the strength of the pay-for-performance link, but the two together provide a strong basis for arguing that the costs of pay secrecy will not be incurred.

Third, privacy, a benefit of pay secrecy, is not automatically threatened by having objective performance criteria. Just because performance may be measured more objectively, and hence may be more visible to others, this does not guarantee that pay will be. Privacy issues, however, may be of less concern to employees in this situation, because when objective performance criteria are clearly linked to pay, there is a somewhat natural transparency concerning what people are paid.

Thus, although pay secrecy is operating, an organization that uses objective performance criteria is more likely to experience benefits than one using subjective performance criteria. In addition, however, beyond the question of whether pay criteria are measured objectively or subjectively, is the question of whether pay criteria are *known and not secret.* We suggest also that when the criteria for pay—what we call the basis for one's pay—are known, then the costs of pay secrecy are less likely to be incurred, and the benefits are more likely to be reaped.

When the basis of pay is secret, individuals do not know why they receive the pay they get. The negative effects of pay secrecy (which, recall, has been pay-*level* secrecy by assumption) should be amplified, and the positive effects with respect to cooperation will be mitigated. Why? Go back to Ryan and Natasha, who, under pay basis secrecy, do not know whether their pay is based on leadership, diversity initiatives, communication skills, sales performance, or some other criteria. The level of uncertainty is even higher than under ordinary pay secrecy such that uncertainty management theory (Lind & van den Bos, 2002) suggests even more negative assessments than before, but for all of the same reasons.

Employees cannot predict their pay into the future. For all they know, chance factors, mistakes, and bias play a role in determining their pay. Fairness assessments will be highly negative and lead to a lack of trust. As employees seek out information about pay (which they are more predisposed to do under uncertainty management theory), they will be able to learn even less than before, thereby creating the possibility of greater conflict. The organization may have passed the point at which individuals are willing to keep their own pay information secret, because a need for uncertainty reduction may lead to an enhanced desire to know *others*' pay as a way of judging one's own.

Clearly, therefore, organizations that provide for pay secrecy should also provide *known* bases for pay if they want to highlight the benefits of the pay secrecy policy and incur fewer costs. In other words, it is not only the issue of measurement of pay criteria that determines whether costs or benefits will be experienced but also knowledge of those very criteria themselves.

Contextual Factor 3: Gauging of Relative Pay Status

Our last factor is at the most micro of the levels we consider, but it is nonetheless important. Employees may always attempt to "guess" where they stand or rank against the pay distribution, even though the distribution itself is unknown. In other words, even under pay secrecy, employees will believe that they are better or worse employees and, thus, closer to the top or bottom of the pay scale. We argue that this affects the organization's consequences of using pay secrecy.

For example, assume that LaToya has always been successful in her work as a loan officer and therefore believes that she probably falls near the top of the pay distribution for bank loan officers at Fifth National Bank. Jonathan, however, doesn't have as much confidence in his work, notices that a lot of the loan officers seem to be more successful than he is, and decides that he is probably closer to the bottom of the pay distribution for loan officers at the same bank. Which of the two loan officers will respond more favorably to pay secrecy?

We argue that employees who perceive their relative pay to be closer to the top of the relevant pay distribution should have a more positive reaction to pay secrecy, so we expect LaToya to respond more favorably than Jonathan. It has been demonstrated that high performers desire pay secrecy more than low performers (Schuster & Colletti, 1973). First, since these employees believe they are being paid more than others, they may also believe that pay secrecy will prevent them from becoming targets for conflict. Second, because these employees already believe they are being paid more than others, they will be less likely to make judgments that pay levels are distributively unfair. Third, because people who are successful and paid more are more likely to attribute pay to internal causes (Miller & Ross, 1975), they will likely attribute their pay to their own superior performance and, thus, be more motivated, regardless of pay secrecy. Finally, because managers may narrow pay distributions when pay is open, as previously discussed, those who believe they are highly paid may fear that they would be paid less relative to those at the bottom of the distribution were pay to become open.

In summary, therefore, employees who perceive that they have high relative pay will tend not to suffer from judgments of unfairness or decreases in motivation under pay secrecy. Thus, because pay secrecy was described as a potential cost in the previous section, the implication is that this expectation holds for employees who view themselves as being at the bottom of the pay distribution (i.e., probably the lower performers). We predict that what previously appeared to be costs of pay secrecy—lack of fairness perceptions and lowered work motivation—would tend to occur most strongly for those employees who believe they are paid low relative to relevant others.

But does this make sense? What is it about these employees that could render pay secrecy even more negative for them? For example, we might argue that the employees who perceive themselves as making low relative pay may also perceive themselves as having low value in the organization.

In that case, they should see pay secrecy as a benefit. As one worker stated:

> *I worked in a place where a lot of people knew others' salaries.... I was humiliated when I found out that others at my title and experience level were making vastly higher amounts of money.... If management had kept that information to themselves, and discouraged discussion, they would have prevented a lot of problems (Cohen, 2003).*

The "humiliation" spoken of by this worker suggests a privacy violation: he or she experienced negative affect when allowed to compare his or her own pay with that of others. The humiliation was undoubtedly not only due to the realization that others at the same title and level of experience were making more but also that coworkers could realize that this worker was making *much less*. This type of privacy issue is the one we identified as a benefit to pay secrecy.

However, employees who perceive themselves as being paid less than others are more likely to experience an array of negative outcomes from pay secrecy for a variety of interrelated reasons that do not concern privacy. First, they will intuitively be more likely to experience conflict with decision makers about pay and perhaps other coworkers whom they perceive to be paid at higher levels—a negative factor. Second, employees who experience negative pay outcomes are more likely to perceive them as distributively unfair. It is under conditions of judgments of distributive unfairness that employees will also be most concerned about procedural fairness of pay allocation decisions (Brockner & Weisenfeld, 1996), which we have already described as tending to be negative under pay secrecy. Finally, employees who experience negative outcomes will be more likely to attribute the cause of those outcomes to external sources, such as bias on the part of the decision maker. This might increase the likelihood of conflict and reduce motivation (Miller & Ross, 1975). Thus, pay secrecy should clearly be linked to costs of judgments of unfairness and lowered work motivation in this situation.

In addition, perceptions of being paid less than relevant others could increase perceptions of mobility by making relatively low offers or lesser opportunities from the outside look more appealing than they otherwise would, particularly if the employees are attributing low pay level to unfairness or bias (Hulin, Roznowski, & Haichya, 1985). Thus, those who believe themselves to be at the lower end of the pay scale should experience pay secrecy in a more negative manner than those who believe they are at the higher end.

What Remains to be Known about Pay Secrecy?

In short, much. In this article we have entered into a discussion of pay secrecy with multiple goals in mind. The notion of pay secrecy jumped into our research minds when one of us, Asghar Zardkoohi, discussed with the rest of us a news article he had just read on the topic. As conversation evolved, we realized that we knew and had heard very little about this topic. Our own investigation of early research efforts indicated that scant scholarly work existed on this topic, and most of it had been done many years ago. It seemed that most of what we thought we knew about pay secrecy was anecdotal.

Numerous discussions later, we emerged with this framework for discussing pay secrecy. Our hope is to regenerate an interest in the topic, one that this time will engage more scholars and produce more scholarship. We hope that our framework provides many research questions that academics will find interesting. No longer need we make the intuitive jump, as many organizational researchers have, that pay secrecy is obviously bad for organizations. No longer need we embrace economists' intuitive belief that pay secrecy must be good for organizations or organizations would not use it.

In addition, we have attempted to suggest that pay secrecy is not just a human resources issue. It has individual and societal consequences that cannot be ignored, even beyond their impact on the organization. For example, the very concept of privacy is an important social value during the early twenty-first century. Pay secrecy may not only reflect this value but may be critical for promoting this value more strongly in American society. Future research could focus more generally on the role that pay secrecy in organizations plays in helping society maintain or even attain a level of individual privacy that allows American citizens or residents to live in comfort, experience important freedoms, or even achieve other goals that we, as a society, see as valuable.

What is the overall impact of pay secrecy on society? Does it maximize the differential between higher- and lower-paid employees? What is its net effect on wages? If it is true, as we have conjectured, that pay secrecy will enable supervisors and managers to create larger pay differentials among employees, then we expect that high-performing employees could make even more in wages or salary than they would tend to under pay openness. Also, the pay differential should be wider under pay secrecy, because there is less of a concern about conflict when employees do not know what others are making, as we have discussed. Thus, society could experience an even bigger gap between those who are highly paid and those who receive little pay. This topic should be of particular interest to a broad range of management scholars. For example, is it even possible for all organizations to hold pay secrecy policies at the same time in a capitalist society? What benefits would be expected to accrue to the "first mover"—the first organization to offer pay openness? What would characterize the first-mover organization?

Pay secrecy also can be important in the study of international management or cross-cultural management, as we have alluded to in this article. First, further study regarding the notion that organizations operating in a capitalistic society may nonetheless try to instill the values associated with collectivist societies is interesting to explore in and of itself.

What happens when American businesses locate in countries having cultural values different from our own? Is it true that pay secrecy has a different impact in more collectivist cultures? (Here, it might be interesting to consider whether pay openness leads those at the top of the pay distribution in Eastern cultures to be the most embarrassed for "sticking out," whereas in Western cultures those at the top may be the most proud, even if they want to avoid being the targets of conflict.) What happens when workers from different cultural backgrounds and expectations must work alongside each other in the same organization? The strategic considerations accompanying pay secrecy simply should not be ignored, but research is needed to inform us of the importance of culture to strategic decision making in this regard.

One aspect of organizational control not considered in this article is the manner in which pay secrecy is "enforced." We believe this variable falls along a continuum, from implicit to explicit enforcement. At the more lenient end is a situation where there are no explicit norms or organizational policies regarding the discussion of pay—where pay secrecy might exist only because individual employees choose not to discuss their pay with each other. At the most restrictive level—the more explicit of the two poles—there is an enforced and formal organizational policy that prohibits discussion of pay. Along the continuum are levels that include varying degrees of pay secrecy. For example, somewhat beyond the more lenient of the poles is a level where pay secrecy is enforced by group or departmental norms alone, despite no formal organizational policy existing about the discussion of pay. Closer to the more restrictive pole is a level where there are strong organizational norms or informal policies against sharing pay information—for example, a statement emphasizing that pay discussion should not take place, but without sanctions in place.

The manner in which pay secrecy is enforced is likely to affect how employees will respond to it. On the one hand, when pay secrecy stems from either individual choices or informal group norms not to discuss pay, employees are signaling that they value the privacy avoidance of conflict that they obtain from pay secrecy to a greater degree than they value information about what others are being paid. It is unlikely that this situation would arise if there were suspicions of bias in the pay distribution or if there were substantial negative fairness inferences regarding the organization. On the other hand, when the enforcement of pay secrecy is tied to the organization and is not volitional on the part of employees, employees may view this as over-reaching, providing a basis for suspicion that the organization has something to hide and may be biased and unfair. Research on this issue could help to elucidate the trade-offs employees make regarding privacy choices about their own pay, as well as shed light on broader issues of organizational control.

Certainly, strategic HR academics can pursue many research questions stemming from pay secrecy. For example, the question of internal alignment (i.e., the degree to which different HR practices fit together and work with the overall strategy of the organization) is related to compensation strategies and, thus, potentially, to pay secrecy. Corporate strategy may influence the effectiveness of a pay secrecy policy in conjunction with whether the firm is pursuing a defender strategy or a prospector strategy (see Miles & Snow, 1978, for a review of these strategies).

Gomez-Mejia and Balkin (1992) have proposed two different compensation strategies that would be appropriate for these different business strategies: algorithmic and experiential strategies. An algorithmic strategy is one characterized by pay based on individual performance, internal equity, above-market salary and benefits, and *pay secrecy*. An experiential strategy, in contrast, is characterized by pay based on level of skills, external equity, below-market salary and benefits (but salary plus incentives above market), and *pay openness*. Gomez-Mejia and Balkin hypothesized, and have found support for the idea, that defenders would use algorithmic compensation strategies, whereas prospectors would employ experiential compensation strategies (Balkin & Gomez-Mejia, 1987, 1990).

However, our analysis makes it unclear as to the extent to which these aspects of a compensation system *should occur* together if a firm wishes to achieve the benefits of pay secrecy. For example, a firm following an algorithmic strategy would appear to be attracting top employees, paying them along internal hierarchical distinctions in individual performance (which could be relatively wide), and would probably invest in firm-specific training for them. Both the relatively wide pay distribution and the firm-specific investments for the employees suggest that the employer would suffer the costs of a pay secrecy policy instead of realizing the benefits. *Pay openness* would appear to be more appropriate for firms in this situation.

If a firm followed an experiential strategy, however, it would appear to be maintaining general human capital for its employees and encouraging weaker employees to leave the organization by paying below market. The incentive pay system should lead to wider pay distributions, providing perceptions that pay is unfair and potentially leading to conflicts. Pay openness would seem inappropriate in this situation. Instead, the benefits of having pay secrecy could be achieved (privacy and lack of conflict; maintaining high-quality employees) while its costs would be mitigated (perceptions of unfairness and lack of trust; subjecting good employees to poaching). Thus, *pay secrecy and not pay openness* would be desirable in this situation. Further investigation of Gomez-Mejia and Balkin's contingency approach to compensation strategies should be conducted as a result of our research.

Additional HR strategy issues may also be generated from our work by considering pay-level secrecy in conjunction with other pay system characteristics more generally. Clearly, based on the above, HR strategy can influence the effectiveness of pay secrecy policies. We have examined pay-level secrecy in isolation from other pay system characteristics and corporate strategy (implying a "best practices" approach), but future work is needed to expand our approach.

Pay secrecy continues to be a contentious and interesting issue in our society today. Nonetheless, there has been little scholarly research over the past several decades. We hope that our efforts here will reignite research on this timely and provocative topic and serve as a guide for future research.

Source: Academy of Management Review, 32, (1), 55–71 (2007). Reprinted by permission of the CCC.

REFERENCES

Abercrombie, N., & Hill, S. 1976. Paternalism and patronage. *British Journal of Sociology, 27*: 413–429.

Ashforth, B. E., & Mael, F. 1989. Social identity theory and the organization. *Academy of Management Review*, 14: 20–40.

Balkin, D. B., & Gomez-Mejia, L. R. 1985. Compensation practices in high tech industries. *Personnel Administrator*, 30: 111–123.

Balkin, D. B., & Gomez-Mejia, L R. 1987. Toward a contingency theory of compensation strategy. *Strategic Management Journal*, 8: 169–183.

Balkin, D. B., & Gomez-Mejia, L. R. 1990. Matching compensation and organizational strategies. *Strategic Management Journal*, 11: 153–169.

Bartol, K. M., & Martin, D. C. 1988. Effects of dependence, dependency threats, and pay secrecy on managerial pay allocations. *Journal of Applied Psychology*, 74: 105–113.

BBC News. 2004. *Salary secrecy "penalises women."* http://news.bbc.co.uk/1/hi/business/3392937.stm, January 14.

Bierman, L., & Gely, R. 2004. Love, sex, and politics? Sure. Salary? "No way": Workplace social norms and the law. *Berkley Journal of Law and Employment*, 25: 167–191.

Bies, R. J., & Moag, J. F. 1986. Interactional justice: Communication criteria of fairness. *Research on Negotiations in Organizations*, I: 43–55.

Brickley, J. A., Smith, C. W., Jr., & Zimmerman, J. L. 2000. *Managerial economics and organizational architecture* (2nd ed.). New York: McGraw-Hill.

Brockner, J., & Weisenfeld, B. M. 1996. An integrative framework for explaining reactions to decisions: Interactive effects of outcomes and procedures. *Psychological Bulletin*, 120: 189–208.

Burroughs, J. D. 1982. Pay secrecy and performance: The psychological research. *Compensation Review*, 14: 44–54.

Butler, J. K. 1991. Toward understanding and measuring conditions of trust: Evolution of a condition of trust inventory. *Journal of Management*, 17: 643–663.

Cohen, S. 2003. Keeping pay details away from friends. *WSJ.com College* Journal. http://www.collegejournal.com/salaryinfo/negotiationstips/20030106-jobspectrum.html.

Colella, A., & Garcia, M. F. 2004. *Paternalism: Hidden discrimination*? Paper presented at the annual meeting of the Academy of Management, New Orleans.

Colquitt, J. A., Conlon, D. E., Wesson, M. J., Porter, C. O. L. H., & Ng, K. Y. 2001. Justice at the millennium: A meta-analytic review of 25 years of organizational justice research. *Journal of Applied Psychology*, 86: 425–445.

Danziger, L., & Katz, E. 1997. Wage secrecy as a social convention. *Economic Inquiry*, 35: 59–69.

DeNisi, A. S. 1996. *Cognitive approach to performance appraisal: A program of research.* London: Routledge.

Dornstein, M. 1989. The fairness judgments of received pay and their determinants. *Journal of Occupational Psychology*, 62: 287–299.

Fredricksburg Glass and Mirror. 1997. 323 NLRB 165.

Futrell, C. M., & Jenkins, O. C. 1978. Pay secrecy versus pay disclosure for salesmen: A longitudinal study. *Journal of Marketing Research*, 15: 214–219.

Gely, R., & Bierman, L. 2003. Pay secrecy/confidentiality rules and the National Labor Relations Act. *University of Pennsylvania Journal of Labor and Employment Law*, 6: 121–156.

Gerhart, B., & Rynes, S. L. 2003. *Compensation: Theory, evidence, and strategic implications.* Thousand Oaks, CA: Sage.

Gomez-Mejia, L. R., & Balkin, D. B. 1992. *Compensation, organizational strategy, and firm performance.* Cincinnati: South-Western Publishing.

Hrnext.com Survey. 2001. www.hrnext.com/content.

Huber, V. L., Seybolt, P. M., & Venemon, K. 1992. The relationship between individual inputs, perceptions, and multidimensional pay satisfaction. *Journal of Applied Social Psychology*, 22: 1356–1373.

Hulin, C. L., Roznowski, M., & Haichya, D. 1985. Alternative opportunities and withdrawal decisions: Empirical and theoretical discrepancies and an integration. *Psychological Bulletin*, 97: 233–250.

Jackman, M. 1994. *The velvet glove: Paternalism and conflict in gender, class, and race relations.* Berkeley: University of California Press.

Jost, J. T., & Banaji, M. R. 1994. The role of stereotyping in system-justification and the production of false consciousness. *British Journal of Social Psychology*, 33: 1–27.

Kahneman, D., & Tversky, A. 1973. On the psychology of prediction. *Psychological Review*, 80: 237–251.

Klein, H. J., Wesson, M. J., Hollenbeck, J. R., & Alge, B. J. 1999. Goal commitment and goal setting process: Conceptual clarification and empirical synthesis. *Journal of Applied Psychology*, 84: 885–896.

Klopfer, P. H., & Rubenstein, D. I. 1977. The concept of privacy and its biological basis. *Journal of Social Issues*, 33: 52–65.

Lawler, E. E. 1965a. Managers' perceptions of their subordinates' pay and of their supervisors' pay. *Personnel Psychology*, 18: 413–422.

Lawler, E. E. 1965b. Should managers' compensation be kept under wraps? *Personnel*, 42: 17–20.

Lawler, E. E. 1967. Secrecy about management compensation: Are there hidden costs? *Organizational Behavior and Human Performance*, 2: 182–189.

Leventhal, G. S. 1976. The distribution of rewards and resources in groups and organizations. *Advances in Experimental Social Psychology*, 9: 92–131.

Leventhal, G. S., Karuza, J., Jr., & Fry, W. R. 1980. Beyond fairness: A theory of allocation preferences. In G. Mikuyla (Ed.), *Justice and social interaction*: 167–218. New York: Springer.

Leventhal, G. S., Michaels, J. W., & Sanford, C. 1972. Inequity and interpersonal conflict: Reward allocation and secrecy about reward as methods of preventing conflict. *Journal of Personality and Social Psychology*, 23: 88–102.

Lind, E. A. 2001. Fairness heuristic theory: Justice judgments as pivotal cognitions in organizational relations. In J. Greenberg & R. Cropanzano (Eds.), *Advances in organizational behavior*: 56–88. Stanford, CA: Stanford University Press.

Lind, E. A., & van den Bos, K. 2002. When fairness works: Toward a general theory of uncertainty management. *Research in Organizational Behavior*, 24: 181–223.

Locke, E. A., & Latham, G. P. 1990. *A theory of goal setting and task performance.* Englewood Cliffs, NJ: Prentice-Hall.

Major, B., & Adams, J. B. 1983. Role of gender, interpersonal orientation, and self-presentation in distributive justice behavior. *Journal of Personality and Social Psychology*, 45: 598–608.

Markels, A., & Berton, L. 1996. Executive pay: A special report. *Wall Street Journal*, April 11: R10.

Markus, H. R., & Kitayama, S. 1991. Culture and the self: Implications for cognition, emotion, and motivation. *Psychological Review*, 98: 224–253.

Mashek, D. J., Aron, A., & Boncimino, M. 2003. Confusion of self with close others. *Personality and Social Psychology Bulletin.* 29: 382–392.

Mayer, R., Davis, J. H., & Schoorman, F. D. 1995. An integrative model of organizational trust. *Academy of Management Review*, 20: 709–734.

Meyer, J. P., Allen, N. J., & Gellatly, L. R. 1990. Affective and continuance commitment to the organization: Evaluation of measures and analysis of concurrent and time-lagged relations. *Journal of Applied Psychology*, 75: 710–721.

Miles, R. E., & Snow, C. C. 1978. *Organizational strategy, structure, and process*. New York: McGraw-Hill.

Milgrom, P., & Roberts, J. 1992. *Economics, organizations, and management*. Upper Saddle River, NJ: Prentice-Hall.

Milkovich, G. T., & Anderson, P. H. 1972. Management compensation and secrecy policies. *Personnel Psychology*, 25: 293–302.

Miller, D. T., & Ross, M. 1975. Self-serving biases in attribution of causality: Fact of fiction? *Psychological Bulletin*, 82: 213–225.

Mishra, A. K. 1996. Organizational responses to crisis: The centrality of trust. In R.M. Kramer & T.R. Tyler (Eds.), *Trust in organizations: Frontiers of theory and research*: 261–287. Thousand Oaks, CA: Sage.

Murphy, K. R., & Cleveland, J. N. 1995. *Understanding Performance appraisal: Social, organizational, and goal-based perspectives*. Thousand Oaks, CA: Sage.

Naylor, J. C., Pritchard, R. D., & Ilgen, D. R. 1980. *A theory of behavior in organizations*. New York: Academic Press.

NLRB v. Main Street Terrace Center. 2000. 218 F.3d 531 (6th Cir.).

Padavic, I., & Earnest, W. R. 1994. Paternalism as a component of managerial strategy. *Social Science Journal*, 31: 389–405.

Paetzold, R. L., Boswell, W. R., & Belsito, C. A. 2004. *Theorizing with the need for privacy construct*. Paper presented at the annual meeting of the Academy of Management, New Orleans.

Pappu, S. 2001. Whispered numbers. *Money*, August: 23.

Schuster, J. R., & Colletti, J. A. 1973. Pay secrecy: Who is for and against it? *Academy of Management Journal*, 16: 35–40.

Sim, V. 2001. Commentary on "When salaries aren't secret." *Harvard Business Review*, 79(5).

Steele, F. 1975. *The open organizations: The impact of secrecy and disclosure on people and organizations*. Reading, MA: Addison-Wesley.

Stone, E. F., & Stone, D. L. 1990. Privacy in organizations: Theoretical issues, research findings, and protection mechanisms. *Research in Personnel and Human Resource Management*, 8: 349–411.

Sundstrom, E. 1978. Crowding as a sequential process: Review of research on the effects of population density on humans. In A. Baum & Y. M. Epstein (Eds.), *Human responses to crowding*: 31–116. Hillsdale, NJ: Lawrence Erlbaum Associates.

Sundstrom, E., Burt, R. E., & Kamp, D. 1980. Privacy at work: Architectural correlates of job satisfaction and job performance. *Academy of Management Journal*, 23: 101–117.

Thibaut, J. W., & Walker, L. 1975. *Procedural justice: A psychological analysis*. Hillsdale, NJ: Lawrence Erlbaum Associates.

Thompson, P., & Pronsky, J. 1975. Secrecy or disclosure in management compensation? *Business Horizons*, 18(3): 67–74.

Triandis, H. C. 1989. The self and social behavior in differing cultural contexts. *Psychological Review*, 96: 506–520.

Triandis, H. C. 1994. *Culture and social behavior*. New York: McGraw-Hill.

van den Bos, K., Lind, E. A., Vermunt, R., & Wilke, H. A. M. 1997. How do I judge my outcome when I do not know the outcome of others? The psychology of the fair process effect. *Journal of Personality and Social Psychology*, 72: 1034–1046.

Vroom, V. 1964. *Work and motivation*. New York: Wiley.

Walsh, M. W. 2000. Workers challenge employers' policies on pay confidentiality. *New York Times*, July 28, accessed at http://www.nytimes.com/library/financial/072800discuss-pay.html.

Williamson, O. E. 1985. *The economic institutions of capitalism*. New York: Free Press.

READING 11.3

Navigating Shareholder Influence: Compensation Plans and the Shareholder Approval Process

Pamela Brandes, Maria Goranova and Steven Hall

Executive Overview

Corporate governance research emphasizes the influence of institutional owners on company outcomes such as strategic decisions, organizational structures, and executive compensation. However, little is known about the process companies use to gain support for management-sponsored compensation plan resolutions. This article reviews prior literature linking institutional ownership and compensation practices and investigates the little-studied process of how management tries to work with owners to secure shareholder approval of compensation plans. In addition, it provides brief cases of two Fortune *300 companies (General Mills and PepsiCo) that received positive votes on their compensation plans. The article ends with several recommendations for managers trying to gain institutional owners' approval of future compensation plans.*

Executive compensation has received a great deal of attention in the academic literature and in the mainstream press. Not surprisingly, shareholders are taking note. A recent survey by Watson Wyatt indicates that 90% of institutional investors believe corporate executives are overpaid (Watson Wyatt, 2005). This might explain, in part, the surge in shareholder activism in the past six years, which is mostly focused on executive compensation and boards (see Figure 1; Georgeson, 2000, 2005). The changing nature of ownership in modern corporations from predominantly individual to institutional ownership is giving the institutional investor greater influence over corporate governance issues. Whereas in 1965, institutional owners accounted for less than 20% of the ownership of equities outstanding, current estimates put this figure at 61.3% ($9.3 trillion) of the total value of U.S. equities outstanding (Coffee, 1991; Securities Industry Fact Book, 2002, p. 64), making institutional investors the "most ubiquitous corporate shareowner[s]" (Daily, Dalton, & Rajagopalan, 2003). Researchers are consistently looking more closely at institutional owners, investigating their impact on a variety of corporate activities, including CEO compensation, R&D intensity, innovation, international diversification, corporate venturing, and corporate social performance.

Although the role of institutional investors in mitigating agency conflicts and encouraging managers to undertake decisions that fall in line with owners' interests is well researched, the firm's response to investor preferences remains poorly understood. In particular, firms often appear as passive recipients[1] of investors' influence, and the reverse process, whereby companies actively work with shareholders and their advocates to anticipate and allay shareholders' concerns, is seldom acknowledged.

In response, this article focuses on two themes. First, we provide a brief review of the literature that details the impact of institutional ownership on executive compensation and discusses the variety of mechanisms institutional investors use to gain influence. Hence we revisit the question *how do institutional owners influence corporate compensation plans*? Second, while prior research on corporate governance has significantly advanced our understanding of the impact of monitoring and the alignment of executives' interests with those of shareholders (Beatty & Zajac, 1994; Eisenhardt, 1989; Jensen & Meckling, 1976; Tosi, Katz, & Gomez-Mejia, 1997; Zajac & Westphal, 1994), less attention has been devoted to the efforts firms make to improve communication with their shareholders. This issue is even more pertinent in light of recent changes that require shareholder approval of equity compensation plans (Borges & Silverman, 2003). This leads us to our second major question, *how do companies work with shareholders to gain approval of corporate compensation plans?*

In answering these questions, we highlight the significant players and processes through which companies seek endorsement of their compensation resolutions. Notably, we bring to light the informal processes through which companies confer with owners about their compensation plans, as well as the players involved that have so far remained largely

Special thanks to our corporate interviewees: Mike Davis, Vice President, Compensation, Benefits, and Staffing, General Mills; and Greg Smith, Senior Manager, Global Compensation, PepsiCo. The authors thank the editor and two anonymous reviewers for their insightful comments on previous drafts.

FIGURE 1 Total, Compensation-Related, and Board-Related Shareholder Proposals (1993–2005)

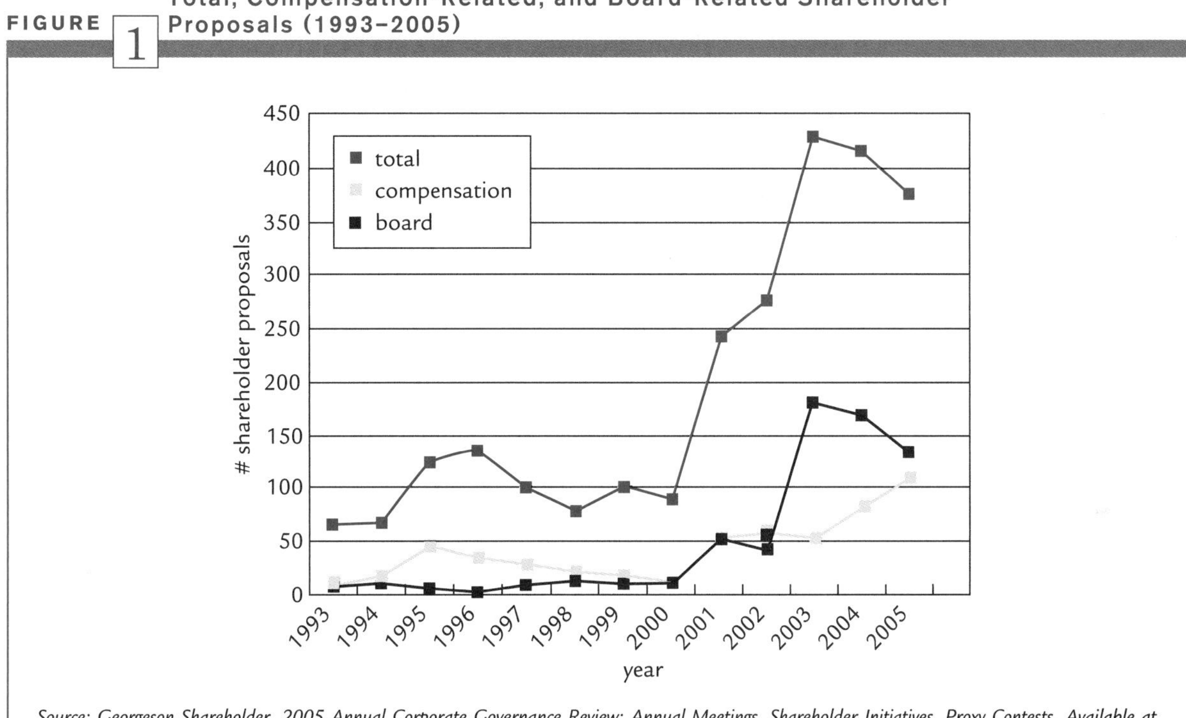

Source: Georgeson Shareholder, 2005 Annual Corporate Governance Review: Annual Meetings, Shareholder Initiatives, Proxy Contests. Available at http://www.georgeson.com/usa/download/acgr/acgr2005.pdf, accessed 1/29/2008.

unstudied. For example, while institutional shareholder advisory services such as RiskMetrics Group (the former Institutional Shareholder Services[2] [ISS]) and Glass-Lewis represent important influences on management's efforts to obtain shareholders' approval of compensation plans, their role is rarely acknowledged. We then provide cases that demonstrate two companies' experiences with the shareholder approval process. Finally, we close the article by discussing strategies firm managers could implement to create more effective working relationships with shareholders in the compensation approval process.

Institutional Owners' Influence: Effects on the Firm

Institutional investors are organizations such as banks, mutual funds, insurance companies, public and private pension funds, and investment companies (for an excellent review, see Ryan & Schneider, 2002). Their diversity drives differences in terms of their monitoring interests and ability and, consequently, organizational outcomes (Brickley, Lease, & Smith, 1988; Johnson & Greening, 1999; Kang & Sorensen, 1999). While sizable ownership, or blockholding, has emerged as the dominant proxy for the willingness of an investor to bear monitoring costs (Edwards & Hubbard, 2006; Hambrick & Finkelstein, 1995), scholars have pointed to other factors that could help explain owners' involvement, such as the importance of the firm within the investor portfolio (Ryan & Schneider, 2002), the business ties of the owner to the firm (Brickley et al., 1988), the owner's propensity to engage in active monitoring (David et al., 2001), and the owner's temporal horizon (Hoskisson et al., 2002).

Although institutional investors traditionally have been perceived as rubber stamps on managerial decisions, their power has grown rapidly in the past 20 years (Neubaum & Zahra, 2006). Increasingly, we see instances of institutional owners challenging executives' agendas and seeking to influence target firms' policies, structure, and governance (Del Guercio & Hawkins, 1999; Gillan & Starks, 2000; Wahal, 1996). Recently, researchers have linked institutional ownership to a wide variety of corporate outcomes, including CEO compensation (David, Kochhar, & Levitas, 1998; Hartzell & Starks, 2003), firm survival (Filatotchev & Toms, 2003), R&D and innovation (David et al., 2001; Hoskisson et al., 2002; Kochhar & David, 1996), international diversification (Tihanyi et al., 2003), corporate entrepreneurship (Zahra, 1996; Zahra et al., 2000), and capital structure (Chaganti & Damanpour, 1991).

Institutional Investor Effects on Compensation

Anecdotal evidence suggests that large institutional owners stand at the forefront of mitigating conflicts about executive compensation (Bebchuck & Fried, 2004). The extent to which institutional investors can monitor the process associated with evaluating and rewarding CEO performance depends on several factors. Equity-based compensation and awards can dilute shareholders' ownership rights. In response to such concerns, the New York Stock Exchange and NASDAQ mandated in 2003 that equity-based compensation plans for listed companies be approved by shareholders (Borges & Silverman, 2003). When managers seek investor approval on company compensation plans, institutional investors may use the companies' proposals as a bargaining lever. As one financial institution manager suggested: "A company may propose a new remuneration package for executives based on, say, an option scheme. We will respond by saying OK, but what about the flowback or added value for us as a result of implementing this scheme?" (Holland, 1998, p. 256).

When such plans do not benefit shareholders, investors may withhold future votes for board members who have authorized them: "We are going to hold compensation committees accountable for giving away shareholders' money in a way that provides no benefit to us" (Richard Ferlauto, director of the American Federation of State, County, and Municipal Employees [AFSCME], cited in McGregor, 2007, p. 59). Furthermore, executive pay provides a venue for principled monitoring, in which "we are careful to only attempt to influence a firm on matters of principle such as a corporate governance issue," unlike firm strategy, in which influence attempts mean the financial institution is "trying to second-guess management in its own field of expertise" (Holland, 1998, p. 251). Similarly, Hendry, Sanderson, Barker, and Roberts' (2006, p. 1113) interviews with institutional investors revealed that though they viewed managers as "dutiful, hardworking fiduciaries, running their companies as best they could in the long-term interests of shareholders," they believed CEO pay still is influenced by management's self-interest: "Management needs are often a source of conflict with shareholders.... Their requirement for income, for perks, for incentive schemes, for power, for independence of owners, can all create major conflict(s) in relations and stimulate active intervention by us" (Holland, 1998, p. 256).

To attract managerial attention, institutional investors may use a spectrum of interventions, ranging from "private club" solutions to public confrontation strategies (Holland, 1998). For instance, some shareholders have tried to informally influence corporate decisions, while others have publicly pursued bylaw amendments, "just vote no" campaigns, proxy contests, and shareholder proposals (Thomas & Martin, 1999). Although shareholder resolutions have been described as powerful tools for influencing management (Wilcox, 2001), they rarely garner majority support among voters. For example, only one of 30 resolutions raised by shareholders at Verizon in the past five years received at least 50% of the vote (Dvorak & Lublin, 2006). Even if a resolution passes with a majority, shareholder resolutions remain advisory in nature, meaning boards may ignore these statements of shareholder wishes (*The Economist*, 2006), which would force sponsors to rely on the publicity that plays out at shareholder meetings and in the business press. Such publicity can threaten executives' reputations and tenure (Neubaum & Zahra, 2006), as it did in the recent high-profile case of Home Depot's CEO, who was ousted in part because he refused to have his stock awards package reduced in light of mediocre stock price performance during his tenure (Grow, 2007).

Alternatively, institutional investors can communicate their positions on compensation directly to executives and then resort to more confrontational tactics only if management ignores their interests. Both quiet diplomacy (i.e., private negotiations, letters, regular private meetings [e.g., Carleton et al., 1998; Hendry et al., 2006]) and public activism (i.e., shareholder proposals, proxy fights, publicized letters, and target lists) thus have become increasingly commonplace.

Empirical Evidence: How Institutional Ownership Affects Executive Compensation

Empirical research largely supports anecdotal evidence that institutional investors' involvement reduces executives' power over the boards that set their compensation (see Table 1). For example, Hartzell and Starks (2003, p. 2366) found that institutional owners with large stakes lower total compensation, thus "act[ing] as a check on pay levels" and "ensuring that management does not expropriate rents from shareholders in the form of greater compensation." Similarly Khan, Dharwadkar, and Brandes (2005) found that ownership stakes by the largest owner are negatively related to CEO total pay, but the relationship is opposite for aggregate institutional ownership. Gomez-Mejia and colleagues (2003) found that institutional ownership depresses the long-term income for family CEOs, but Daily et al. (1998) did not find a more general relationship to executive compensation. Outside the United States, Cheng and Firth (2005) found that institutional ownership moderates executive compensation in Hong Kong firms. In addition to linking institutional ownership to total executive compensation, studies have found connections to options repricing (Pollock et al., 2002; cf. Carter & Lynch, 2001), use of stock options (Khan et al., 2005; Ryan & Wiggins, 2002), and perks such as personal use of corporate aircraft (Yermack, 2006).

Furthermore, researchers have pointed at the temporal orientation, pressure sensitivity, and activism of institutional owners. For example, executive compensation is lower in firms where pressure-resistant institutional investors own higher stakes (David et al., 1998), as well as in firms with higher concentrations of active institutions (Almazan, Hartzell, & Starks, 2005). Brandes and colleagues (2006) also found that institutions with longer-term horizons are more likely to expense stock options, thereby improving transparency in executive compensation.

Although influential institutional owners are well positioned to restrain executive compensation levels, they may be even more concerned about pay for performance. Hartzell and Starks (2003) indicated that large institutional owners, as more effective monitors, are associated with greater pay-for-performance sensitivity, i.e., CEOs receive greater rewards for improving shareholder value. Similarly, prior research has associated institutional activism with more salient investor demands and suggested that it relates positively to pay-for-performance sensitivity (Almazan et al., 2005).

Table 1 Institutional Ownership and Executive Compensation

Authors	Year	Journal	Findings
Almazan, Hartzell, Starks	2005	FM	Pay-for-performance sensitivity is positively related to the concentration of active institutions
Brandes, Hadani, Goranova	2006	JBR	Long-term institutional investors prefer stock-options expensing
Carter & Lynch	2001	JFE	Insignificant relationship exists between institutional ownership and option repricing
Cheng & Firth	2005	CG	Institutional ownership in Hong Kong moderates compensation but is not linked to pay for performance
Daily, Johnson, Ellstrand, Dalton	1998	AMJ	Institutional ownership is not related in a systematic fashion to CEO compensation or changes in compensation
David, Kochhar, Levitas	1998	AMJ	Pressure-resistant institutional owners are related to lower CEO compensation
Gomez-Mepa, Kintana, Mokri	2003	AMJ	Institutional ownership depresses long-term income for family CEOs
Hartzell & Starks	2003	JF	Institutional ownership concentration is positively related to the pay-for-performance sensitivity of executive compensation and negatively related to the level of compensation
Khan, Dharwadkar, Brandes	2005	JBR	Institutional ownership affects level of executive compensation, pay mix, and options performance sensitivity
Pollock, Fisher, Wade	2002	AMJ	Institutional ownership reduces the likelihood of repricing of executive options
Ryan & Wiggins	2002	FM	Institutional ownership is positively related to stock options for high-growth firms
Yermack	2006	JFE	Institutional ownership is positively related to CEO's personal aircraft use

The Company/Management Perspective on the Shareholder Approval Process

Although companies increasingly appreciate the importance of maintaining dialogue with institutional investors (Useem, 1996) and boards may be compelled to take into consideration shareholder views to ensure the passage of a proposed stock option plan (Thomas & Martin, 1999), companies rarely appear as active initiators of this communication. Instead, previous work has largely rationalized the process of owner-management interactions as a "black box," in which inputs such as ownership preferences or monitoring capabilities lead to firm actions. In answering our second question (i.e., how do companies work with shareholders to gain approval of their compensation plans?), we attempt to peer inside the black box and identify an important, yet currently unacknowledged, process. Specifically, we identify the essential parties and steps of a reverse process, in which managers work with institutional shareholders.

Thus far, companies' attempts to discern investors' preferences, such as those disclosed in proxy voting policies, as well as their attempts to work with institutional investors and the groups representing their interests, have gone largely unnoticed, even though we know managers and their firms are active players in the institutional environment and attempt to co-opt institutional investors and/or renegotiate owner expectations (Neubaum & Zahra, 2006; Useem, 1996). For example, CalPERS has been solicited by numerous firms in phone calls, letters, and personal visits from top executives (Hawley, Williams, & Miller, 1994). This influence process is even more important today, as brokers who routinely voted with management in the past cannot vote without explicit voting directions from beneficiary owners (Borges & Silverman, 2003).

Table 2 Conceptual View: How Firms Interact with Institutional Investors Regarding Compensation

		Nature of Company Response	
		Substantive	**Symbolic**
Timing	Responsive	Respond to shareholder concerns by adopting compensation policies that shareholders deem desirable	Respond to shareholder concerns by adopting, but not necessarily implementing, compensation policies that shareholders deem desirable
		Ex: Following negotiations with TIAA-REF several companies adopted confidential voting and agreed not to issue preferred stock without first securing shareholder approval (Carleton, Nelson, & Weisbach, 1998)	Ex: Symbolic adoption of long-term incentive plans without subsequent implementation (Westphal & Zajac, 1994; 1998). Symbolic adoption of stock repurchase programs (Westphal & Zajac, 2001)
	Anticipatory	Preempt shareholder concerns by undertaking compensation policies that shareholders deem desirable	Co-opt shareholders by demonstrating alignment between the company and shareholders without changing company compensation policy
		Ex: Voluntary expensing of stock options (Brandes, Hadani, & Goranova, 2006)	Ex: Announce, but do not implement, voluntary expensing of stock options

Categorizing Influence Strategies

From a practical point of view, we suggest that companies' strategies differ when they attempt to influence the shareholder approval process. We suggest that these strategies vary along two major dimensions (see Table 2). First, companies differ in terms of *when* they get involved with shareholders—firm actions range from an anticipatory to a responsive stance toward shareholder concerns. Specifically, in attempting to influence shareholders' opinions on compensation, some companies proactively scan their environments, seeking input from shareholders directly and through the use of hired intermediaries who more closely have their fingers on the pulse of shareholder concerns. Other companies, already largely confident in their compensation approach, feel that communication with shareholders regarding compensation plans is best accomplished after management's compensation resolutions have been released in company proxy statements.

The second dimension on which we categorize these strategies is the extent to which revisions to companies' compensation packages are substantive vs. symbolic. For example, Westphal and Zajac (1994, 1998) suggested that companies decouple substance from symbolism in compensation, resulting in higher pay with lower risk for executives while seeming to be responsive to owners. Managers' influence on these compensation arrangements can be problematic if it dilutes and distorts incentives, leading to reductions in shareholder value and excessive executive compensation (Bebchuk & Fried, 2004). As illustration, Westphal and Zajac (1994, 1998) suggested that organizations adopted long-term incentive plans under the typical rubric of creating incentive alignment between management and owners. However, many of these "adopted" programs were never implemented, denoting a symbolic rather than a substantive response to shareholder demands.

Identifying the Players in the Shareholder Approval Process

Before we move to our two mini-cases, we highlight the cast of players who move on and off stage over the time of the shareholder approval process. The process has evolved into a consultative one. Acting on behalf of the organization are human resource (HR) departments, particularly senior members of the compensation function and vice presidents of HR. This group is assisted by other members of the organization, including those employed in investor relations, legal and finance departments, top management, and even company controllers. Boards and the subset of directors who constitute the compensation committee represent the interests of shareholders. Furthermore, institutional owners take great interest in the compensation process; in a letter to companies in which Vanguard has substantial equity interests, the large mutual fund claimed it was pleased with its "ability to influence, in appropriate situations and in an appropriate manner, the structure of compensation programs" (Vanguard, 2002). Many institutional investors also rely heavily on proxy advisory resources, such as Glass-Lewis and ISS, for voting advice and recommendations. Compensation consultants such as Mercer and Hewitt and Associates provide benchmarking data to compensation committees, assist in compensation plan designs, and report to boards (Watson Wyatt, 2005).[3] Finally, proxy solicitors (e.g., Georgeson, D. F.

King, Morrow, etc.) assist companies in the preparation and tabulation of proxies, actively encourage owners to vote, and may provide consulting services to companies regarding owners' preferences.

Case Studies

We now turn to the experiences of two companies—General Mills and PepsiCo—to illustrate the shareholder approval process. These companies' approaches although not identical had similarities—the main one being their communication with institutional investors regarding their compensation plans. This is something that few companies do, but we expect more companies to adopt similar strategies in the future.

General Mills[4]

In compensation circles, General Mills is a leader and an innovator (Bryant, 1998). The company was a pioneer in linking pay to performance, one of the first companies to put virtually all employees on an incentive pay program, and at the forefront of providing periodic all-employee stock option grants (Davis, 2006). It also developed a very innovative approach that allows most professional employees the opportunity to receive a supplemental stock option grant in lieu of a merit increase.

Before shareholders' approval of its 2003 stock plan, General Mills had a strong ownership culture, including several all-employee stock option grants and ownership guidelines for executives and the board (General Mills, 2003). As an example of the company's commitment to its ownership culture, its 2003 proxy statement indicated that it "believes that broad and deep employee ownership effectively aligns the interests of employees with those of stockholders and provides a strong motivation to build stockholder value" (General Mills, 2003, p. 21). The company's extensive and unique use of equity incentives led to a burn rate (i.e., total number of equity awards granted in any given year divided by the number of common shares outstanding; Frederic Cook and Co., 2004) of 4.2% in 2002, which the company wanted to reduce to 1.6% (General Mills, 2003). Its stock option overhang (i.e., potential shareholder dilution)[5] was "slightly above 17% ... higher than average for the consumer products industry" (General Mills, 2003, p. 27). It also was running low on shares allocated for incentive plans and knew it would need shareholders' authorization for more at its annual meeting in September 2003 (Davis, 2004).

As General Mills considered its future incentive plan, it remained cognizant of what was going on in the compensation and corporate governance domains. Recent corporate scandals in other industries suggested more scrutiny of compensation programs in the future, and an ever-growing threat indicated that stock option expensing would become mandatory, which would eliminate the accounting advantage options provided over other equity-based rewards (General Mills, 2003). At the same time, proxy voting advisers, such as Glass-Lewis and ISS, had become increasingly vocal in advising clients about how investors should vote their company proxies to protect their interests. Nearly all of General Mills's 75 largest institutional shareholders subscribed to ISS's and/or Glass-Lewis's voting recommendations services (Davis, 2004). "Within this context, the company realized it had to change the way it dealt with its stock plan design, its proxy disclosure, and the shareholder vote" (Davis, 2004).

Before designing its 2003 approach to stock compensation, the company contacted three of its 10 largest shareholders to understand their views of the company's past practices and learn in general terms what they would like to see in a new stock compensation plan. These investors, long-term owners of the firm, were familiar with the company and its reputation as a leader in compensation practices. They also seemed appreciative of the company's attempts to engage in dialogue and understand their perspective. A major theme that emerged from these discussions was the need for the company to communicate the various aspects of the plan clearly and effectively to the investment community, as well as why the plan was appropriate given not only the overall compensation environment but also the firm's specific situation and history. This communication later emerged in the form of the company's very elaborate proxy disclosure regarding the plan, which detailed why particular aspects were in the shareholders' best interests. No further contact was made with these three investors until after the proxy had been released.

The company also contacted the corporate services arm of ISS, which, for a fee, measures how a compensation plan would fare according to ISS's proprietary Shareholder Value Transfer (SVT) model.[6] The model estimates the cost of a proposed compensation plan by assessing "the amount of shareholders' equity flowing out of the company as options are exercised," plus the cost of voting power dilution (VPD) (ISS, 2005). The company "worked very closely with ISS to help them understand [the] unique reasons why [General Mills's] overhang and run rates were high ... [and] where we were heading with run rate and overhang" (Davis, 2004, p. 34).

In three different areas of the proxy statement, the company meticulously disclosed the elements and rationale behind its plan while showcasing its long history of ownership and previous equity incentive plans. General Mills also described its selective stock buyback policy, used to reduce the dilutive effects of equity incentives. The plan included several emerging best practices supported by shareholders. For example, the company would prohibit executive loans related to option exercises (such loans are no longer permitted for named executive officers under the Sarbanes-Oxley Act of 2002), nor would it permit the compensation committee or board of directors to (a) materially change the number of shares associated with the plan, (b) issue options at less than fair market value, (c) permit repricing of outstanding options, or (d) amend the maximum number of shares permitted for any one recipient, without first having obtained shareholder approval. Other shareholder-friendly aspects highlighted included (a) eliminating the (shareholder-unapproved) 1998 Employee Stock Plan, (b) prohibiting reload options, and (c) requiring at least four years for vesting. The plan also suggested a desire to "lower share usage by shifting long-term incentive grants to a blend of stock options and restricted stock from solely stock options ... [which would] further reduce overhang, while keeping compensation levels competitive with our industry peers" (General Mills, 2003, p. 27).

Serving as the proxy solicitor, Georgeson Shareholder Communications, Inc., helped in the "preparation, printing, and mailing ... for a fee of $17,500 plus their out-of-pocket expenses" (General Mills, 2003, p. 38).[7] Georgeson also consulted with General Mills to help it better understand the compensation-related voting patterns of the 50 largest investors in the company. The proxy solicitor provided contact information for institutional investors and whether they used ISS/Glass-Lewis voting recommendations. With this information, General Mills attempted to contact its 50 largest institutional shareholders *after the release of the proxy*[8] to "discuss the plan, our past, our future, and answer questions" (Davis, 2004, p. 34). The vice president of HR and/or head of investor relations conducted these phone calls. Discussions with the investors typically were brief (15 to 30 minutes), and investors who agreed to speak with the company generally were very knowledgeable about the company's proposed compensation plan. When the proxy was released publicly, General Mills also mailed a copy to ISS and Glass-Lewis.

The company observed that it had a short window (only a few weeks) between the release of the proxy and the voting deadline and knew, according to its proxy solicitor, that most voting occurs toward the end of the voting period. Approximately a week before the company's annual meeting, Glass-Lewis and ISS issued their voting recommendations to their clients: The 2003 plan had received the support of both ISS and Glass-Lewis, and then earned an 87% affirmative vote from shareholders.

PepsiCo[9]

In 2003, PepsiCo management needed shareholder approval for its compensation plan. PepsiCo recognized the fever pitch reached as a result of corporate scandals and media attacks on incentive compensation, as well as the reality of regulations regarding disclosure and expensing (Scherb, 2004). As an innovator and leader in compensation design, PepsiCo had a long history of employee stock ownership; its well-reputed, broad-based Sharepower Global Ownership Program had existed since the 1980s (Scherb, 2004). However, three additional factors added to the urgency associated with the company's 2003 compensation plan. First, the company had recently changed CEOs. Second, an internal survey of PepsiCo executives suggested that they "perceived the value of stock options [as] lower than the Black-Scholes value" (i.e., the actual cost to the firm of providing the incentive) (Scherb, 2004, p. 5). This perception was worrying, as the Financial Accounting Standards Board (FASB) was contemplating accounting changes that would require companies to take a charge for options, thereby creating a disconnect between the cost of providing the incentive and employee preferences. Third, the survey suggested that PepsiCo employees had "concerns about [the] financial security and stock market stability" associated with their equity awards (Scherb, 2004, p. 5).

In September 2002, with the backing of the CEO and the senior team, the company took proactive steps in accordance with emerging practices in compensation and corporate governance, including stock ownership guidelines that required "certain senior executives and directors [to] own PepsiCo stock worth between two times and eight times base compensation" and an "exercise and hold" policy, both considered shareholder-friendly actions (PepsiCo, 2003, p. 7). The core project team consisted of the vice president of compensation and benefits, a team of PepsiCo compensation professionals, and a compensation consultant (Mercer), supported by the offices of the controller and the legal and finance departments. November 2002 saw a meeting of the core project team with the compensation committee of the board of directors and the CEO. At this pivotal meeting, the compensation consultant provided a presentation focused on PepsiCo's third-quartile pay, which matched the third-quartile performance among 19 of its peers over the previous three years. Also on the agenda was the company's compensation philosophy, which affirmed that the company would "achieve its best results if its executives act and are rewarded as business owners" and that owners needed to have "skin in the game" so they would "take higher personal risks for higher rewards" (Scherb, 2004, p. 11).

The company then sought input from executives through informal (staff meetings, business reviews) and formal (survey) channels. The survey, conducted by the compensation consultant, found that base pay was considered the compensation aspect most likely to "influence [employees'] day-to-day behavior," according to 55% of employees, whereas stock options were ranked most likely by only 10% (Scherb, 2004, pp. 13–14). Furthermore, 85% of employees remarked that they would "appreciate more choice in how they received their compensation (i.e., cash vs. options)," despite the additional pay complexity (Scherb, 2004, p. 15).

In turn, the company created a new executive pay plan that incorporated suggestions from the firm's leadership, market information, and employees. The specifics go beyond the scope of this paper, but it included aspects such as granting employees a choice of options versus restricted stock units (which have less risk for recipients), enhanced bonus awards (again, more cash, less risk), and other cash bonuses (Scherb, 2004, pp. 16–17). In addition, the company maintained its broad-based global equity program but reduced the size of grants, reallocating value from options to retirement programs (and thereby adding additional compensation stability) (Scherb, 2004). Finally, PepsiCo hired ISS's Corporate Services group to model the expected SVT associated with their proposed plan, but it failed to meet ISS's SVT standards, which meant ISS would recommend a no vote—though ISS had previously given PepsiCo high overall governance scores, both within the S&P

and among players in its industry (Scherb, 2004). PepsiCo's plan may not have met the SVT model standard because of its strong support of the use of broad-based options, which, though consistent with the company's compensation philosophy and ownership culture, could have led to dilution levels over ISS's SVT cap (Smith, 2006).

These results represented an important turning point in the shareholder approval process and led the company to launch a more intensive shareholder approval campaign. PepsiCo conducted its own research on institutional investors' backgrounds and preferences regarding compensation plans and found that its 50 largest shareholders not only held 50% of ownership voting rights but also that 80% of them subscribed to the voting recommendations provided by ISS's Proxy Research and Voting business unit (Scherb, 2004). PepsiCo next sought the counsel of its proxy solicitor, Georgeson, to validate its own research into owners' preferences and vote projection analysis. Knowing that so many investors would be looking to ISS for voting recommendations and that the plan did not meet the SVT model, PepsiCo's compensation staff attempted to "set realistic expectations for board members" regarding the upcoming shareholder vote by suggesting that the "vote may be closer than in the past" (Scherb, 2004, p. 20). In order to overcome the ISS voting recommendation, PepsiCo contacted its top 75 shareholders regarding the compensation plan (Smith, 2006).

In late March 2003 the company released its compensation plan to the public in its proxy statement and soon after approached institutional shareholders, some by phone and some in person, to communicate the objectives of the proposed compensation plan clearly. In these communications, PepsiCo discussed issues of dilution and equity run rates and plans for controlling them in the future—issues that would likely influence how the company's largest investors would vote. Specifically, two-person teams of PepsiCo employees (from the HR or investor relations departments) used "scripted talking points" that were "tailored for each institution based on [PepsiCo's] research" and emphasized the company's unique position in terms of its broad-based ownership culture (Scherb, 2004, p. 21).

On May 7, just a few short weeks after the release of the proxy, the plan was approved by 68% of those voting, despite ISS's negative recommendation. PepsiCo noted that 16 institutional investors that it had expected would vote no actually ended up voting for the plan, perhaps due in part to the extensive campaign the company had undertaken (Scherb, 2004, p. 22).

The Shareholder Approval Process: Comparing the Cases

Similarities. Having kept up with current trends, both companies remained very aware of the changing compensation environment and the importance of communicating with their shareholders. In addition, both General Mills and PepsiCo used their HR and investor relations functions extensively—primarily to exploit their compensation expertise, understanding of market conditions, and recognition of how to communicate the benefits of the companies' plans to shareholders. Although most companies use proxy solicitors to identify and solicit votes, these firms employed additional support from their provider to gain a sense of the voting record of their largest institutional owners, whom both expressly attempted to enlist. Their efforts to contact all of their largest institutional owners in the few weeks between the proxy's release and the companies' annual business meetings represented huge undertakings.

Differences. The importance of companies communicating to shareholders about their compensation plans is underscored by PepsiCo's ability to obtain a positive vote on its plan, even though it did not receive the sanction of ISS. However, the PepsiCo vote was closer than the General Mills vote, which suggests that institutional investors still subscribe to the recommendations of organizations such as Glass-Lewis and ISS and wait to hear their recommendations before voting. Recall that General Mills' proxy solicitor suggested that many investors would vote quite late—within the last week or two of the voting process—which matches the time that ISS and Glass-Lewis release their voting recommendations. It remains to be seen whether companies can continue to gain shareholder approval of compensation plans when they lack the sanction of these groups.

Perhaps the strong backing of PepsiCo's plan by top management; survey evidence suggesting that employees wanted less at-risk pay; and the company's extensive comments about equity burn rates, dilution, and need for broad-based incentives to sustain its ownership culture were sufficient to persuade enough investors to carry the plan through. Furthermore, the company (and therefore, many of its institutional investors) had enjoyed solid recent performance, which may have positively affected the interactions between the firm and its shareholders. For example, in its 2003 annual report, PepsiCo noted: "Over the past four years, we've grown faster than both the S&P 500 and our industry group. We improved on that strong record in 2003: volume grew 5%, division net revenue 8%, division operating profit grew 10%, total return to shareholders was 12%" (PepsiCo, 2003, p. 1).

Managerial Recommendations

Having detailed how owners affect executive compensation and introduced the roles and process of how organizations attempt to secure shareholder approval, we offer recommendations to managers wanting to facilitate future compensation approval processes. We include some observations from our case studies and the business press as illustrations.

Communicate Clearly and Carefully with Shareholders

The importance of management communicating with shareholders on compensation issues without "resorting to boilerplate disclosure" has been underscored by recent revisions of disclosure rules (SEC, 2007). Related to the topic of clarity in communications, both PepsiCo and General Mills management recognized the need to "emphasize and re-emphasize shareholder friendly aspects of compensation" in their compensation resolutions (Scherb, 2004, p. 8). General Mills's management did so by providing a very clear proxy statement that detailed aspects of the compensation plan as well as the rationale behind the various elements. Both companies undertook extensive efforts to contact their largest institutional owners. In these communications PepsiCo explicitly addressed issues of dilution and equity run rates, as well as the firm's plans for controlling them in the future.

When attempting to persuade investors of the merits of company compensation practices, managers may not disclose information that has not already been disclosed to the market at large. In line with Securities and Exchange Commission (SEC) Regulation FD (Fair Disclosure), PepsiCo suggested that there be "communicat[ion] with key shareholders early and often [but only] *where allowed* [emphasis added]" (Scherb, 2004, p. 8). In fact, Regulation FD was enacted because companies were "disclosing important nonpublic information, such as advance warnings of earnings results, to securities analysts or selected *institutional investors* [emphasis added] or both, before making full disclosure of the same information to the general public" (SEC, 2000, p. 2).[10]

Be Alert for Shifting Preferences Among Investors and Their Advocates

Managers must be attentive to the hot buttons of investors and their intermediaries. Keeping up with institutional investors' changing priorities can be a challenge. ISS's preferences regarding equity compensation have evolved significantly just over the past decade. Between 1997 and 2001, ISS put forward its SVT model (e.g., ISS, 2005; McGurn & Ranzetta, 2006) and issued voting recommendations on management compensation resolutions solely on the basis of whether it deemed the costs of a plan reasonable compared with a standard based on the firm's industry, market capitalization, and the best of its peers (ISS, 2005). The second stage (2002–03) reinforced this cost method but also included concerns about stock option repricing, which became a litmus-type test for institutional shareholders that felt that repricing can reward poor management performance while jeopardizing pay for performance. In the third stage (2004), ISS added another consideration: greater concern about pay for performance. Finally, in the last stage (2005–06) ISS focused even more on pay for performance but also on stock option burn rates (i.e., the annual rate at which shares are used for compensation purposes). Specifically, ISS wanted management to "commit to an annual burn rate equal to the mean plus one standard deviation of its GICS (Global Industrial Classification Standard) for the next three fiscal years" (McGurn & Ranzetta, 2006, p. 19). More recently, ISS has developed formulas that compensation plans must meet before it will recommend a yes vote. In fact, during the 2007 proxy season ISS recommended against 38% of equity pay plans, compared to 30% in 2006 and 31% in 2005 (RiskMetrics, 2007).

In summary, managers who are uninformed about the opinions of institutional investors and their intermediaries on compensation components may fail to incorporate aspects of compensation plans investors consider essential to creating principal-agent alignment, or may include aspects of compensation design that are anathema to shareholders. Management that overlooks shareholder concerns may encourage contentious votes and heightened scrutiny of future compensation plans.

Clarify Pay-for-Performance Issues for Shareholders

Managers must continually evaluate the extent to which pay matches performance and must communicate to shareholders the steps they have taken to ensure that pay and performance are in alignment. Previously, some institutional shareholder resolutions tried to encourage pay for performance through extremely prescriptive pay restrictions. For example, the United Brotherhood of Carpenters and Joiners of America, one of the largest pension funds, previously issued what it called "Common Sense" resolutions that restricted/capped pay (Plitch & Whitehouse, 2006). However, when these resolutions failed to garner much support, Carpenters changed its strategy, so its recent proposals regarding DuPont, Mattel, PepsiCo, and Bank of New York did not stipulate pay restrictions but instead proposed making awards contingent on outperforming competitors (Plitch & Whitehouse, 2006). Managers who fail to articulate the relationship between pay and performance in their compensation plans risk the reproach of such investors and their intermediaries. In fact, in 2004, ISS issued "cautionary notes" to 230 firms whose compensation plans had tenuous links between pay and performance.

Managers who refuse to acknowledge the importance of pay for performance for shareholders also risk drawing the ire of institutional shareholders when it's time for board elections and/or reelections. Although offering no specific guidelines as to what is "excessive" compensation, in 2005 ISS recommended withhold votes at more than 75 firms for board candidates who had previously authorized "excessive" bonuses, options, and/or severance pay (McGurn & Ranzetta, 2006, p. 13). In the same vein, two Pfizer corporate directors recently received withhold votes of approximately 21%—levels virtually unknown in the domain of corporate governance (Morgenson, 2006).[11] More recently, investors have started to withhold votes for board candidates who have ignored shareholder resolutions approved by the majority of owners in prior periods (RiskMetrics, 2007). In summary, some institutional owners blame mismatches between management pay and performance on a lack of oversight by board members and may voice their displeasure by voting down management's board candidates. Management must ensure that board candidates have a sincere commitment to issues such as pay for performance or risk prickly board elections that may be played out in the business press or at shareholder meetings.

Increase Transparency Regarding Pensions, Severance, and Perquisites

Managers are under increasing legal and institutional owner pressure to more thoroughly disclose post-employment compensation. This compensation can result from (a) retirement (i.e., pensions and other deferred compensation) or (b) the end of an employment relationship (i.e., dismissal, changes in control). Managers must be aware that institutional owners and their advocates are concerned with incomplete disclosure of post-employment payouts and/or payouts that are misaligned with performance. For example, ISS suggested that it is not the more presence of "golden handshakes" (severance agreements) that engenders its ire, but that severance plans that go beyond 299% of annual compensation should be put to shareholder vote (McGurn & Ranzetta, 2006, pp. 34–35).[12,13] Clear management disclosure about these arrangements is essential, as this better informs investors and assures then that there isn't any "hidden" compensation.

The SEC recently required "the disclosure of perquisites and other personal benefits unless the aggregate value of such compensation is less than $10,000 ... [a level that] is a *reasonable balance between investors' need for disclosure of total compensation and the burden to track every benefit* [emphasis added]" (SEC, 2006). As an example of this increased disclosure, Merck management claimed in its 2006 filings that the aggregate value of company reimbursement for financial/tax planning, the use of company planes, reimbursements for home security, and physical examinations by the company staff was less than $50,000 for each of its executive officers (McGurn & Ranzetta, 2006, p. 28; Merck, 2006). Freescale Semiconductor indicated that it would not cover its CEO's tax burden for the 50 hours of company aircraft time he is allowed for personal use but would cover his income tax expense associated with allowing his wife to travel with him on business-related trips (Freescale Semiconductor, 2006). For most investors it is less the presence of particular perquisites that upsets them but rather their excessive use or declines in company performance after their implementation (McGurn & Ranzetta, 2006, p. 26). Consequently, management must ensure that perquisites are within acceptable ranges and commensurate with performance levels. Clearly, disclosing "appropriate" compensation can engender shareholder trust regarding post-employment compensation that may carry over to other aspects of compensation.

Limitations and Conclusion

We recognize that the generalizability of our two cases and our managerial recommendations may depend on factors such as firm performance and size. For example, performance represents an important criterion when institutional investors select compensation activism targets, and firms with above-average performance may be able to garner greater institutional investor support for their compensation plans. Firm size may be an important predictor of how much investor activism management may anticipate; large firms may be better able to work with shareholders' demands, in that they can expend more resources, such as talent and experts, to address them. In contrast, smaller firms may have to rely on less-formal processes to address institutional owners' concerns.

Some question why institutional owners, with their massive, diversified portfolios invested in hundreds if not thousands of firms, would bother to get involved with firms' compensation arrangements. After all, institutional owners are not experts in compensation design, and disgruntled investors can vote with their feet by taking their investments elsewhere. However, if owners note an increasing percentage of mismatches between pay and performance among the firms in their portfolios, they may raise compensation resolutions, create voting guidelines on compensation, consult intermediary voting advisory services, vote down or offer up their own board candidates, and/or demand change in the amounts and/or disclosure of compensation. Insightful management must anticipate or respond to institutional shareholder feedback using the arsenal of internal and external support detailed in this article to ward off public criticism, or worse, negative shareholder votes, regarding company compensation plans.

Source: Academy of Management Perspectives, 22, (1), 41–57 (2008). Reprinted by permission of the CCC.

ENDNOTES

1. A notable exception is research examining the decoupling of substance and symbolism in executive pay (Westphal & Zajac, 1994, 1998; Zajac &. Westphal, 1995). We thank an anonymous reviewer for that insight.
2. In January 2007, RiskMetrics Group completed its acquisition of Institutional Shareholder Services (ISS). RiskMetrics modified the name to ISS Governance Services.
3. Recent concerns center on whether compensation consultants' independence suffers when a consultant simultaneously offers services related to executive compensation and other HR consulting. A Watson Wyatt report based on a survey of institutional investors finds that 67% of these investors "favor having independent consultants report to the compensation committee."
4. Information for this case came from "General Mills Stock Compensation: Yesterday, Today, and Tomorrow," presented by Mike Davis, Vice President, Compensation, Benefits, and Staffing, General Mills, as part of the World at Work Webinar, "Gaining Shareholder Approval in a Challenging Proxy Season" with M. Davis, K. Crean, &. P. Chingos, January 22, 2004, as well as an interview with Davis on July 12, 2006.
5. Stock option overhang is a "measure of potential dilution from stock compensation plans equal to: the number of shares in outstanding grants plus those remaining available for grants divided by common shares outstanding" (World at Work, Advanced Concepts in Executive Compensation Programs [C6A] Glossary, p. 15). High levels of overhang can dilute shareholder value, in conflict with the interests of shareholders.
6. At the time, Institutional Shareholder Services ran two separate business units. ISS Proxy Research and Voting Solutions provided voting recommendations and "corporate governance solutions that enhance the interaction between shareholders and companies, in order to help shareholders manage risk and drive value"

(www.issproxy.com/institutional), whereas ISS Corporate Services, Inc., (ICS) was a "stand-alone, wholly owned subsidiary of ISS" that provides "a suite of services designed to help companies advance their corporate governance standards in the post-Sarbanes-Oxley era" (www.isscarporateservices.com). Although ICS "has historically been managed as a separate division of ISS, operating with a staff completely apart from ISS' core institutional services division," some members of the business press note a potential conflict of interest in simultaneously "setting governance standards and helping clients meet them." See R. Hershey, "A little industry with a lot of sway on proxy votes." *New York Times*, June 18, 2006.

7. This is roughly comparable to the average solicitation fee for S&P 500 clients of $11,075 for the 1996-98 proxy season, as reported by Bethel & Gillen (2000).
8. That is, investors were approached about plan specifics *after* the proxy was disclosed. Companies cannot solicit a vote before the actual shareholder vote takes place, in line with regulation FD, which we discuss in the Managerial Recommendations section of this paper.
9. This case relies on information provided by David Scherb, former Senior Vice President of Compensation and Benefits, PepsiCo, in D. Scherb and P. Chingos, "Getting Dramatic Shift to Occur in Your Compensation Strategy," presented at the annual meeting of World at Work, May 24, 2004, in Boston. It also synthesizes information gained during an interview with Greg Smith, Senior Manager, Global Compensation, PepsiCo, November 20, 2006.
10. Specifically, "the regulation provides that when an issuer, or person acting on its behalf, discloses material nonpublic information to certain enumerated persons (in general, securities market professionals and holders of the issuer's securities who may well trade on the basis of the information), it must make public disclosure of that information" (www.sec.gov/rules/final/33-7881.htm#P12_1308).
11. Under Pfizer's election rules, candidates who receive less than 50% support among those votes cast must submit their resignation to the board, but the board still maintains discretion over accepting the resignations. In other words, the vote is only advisory.
12. Severance payouts in excess of 299% will generally result in unfavorable tax treatment under Sections 280G and 4999, which can result in lost tax deductions to the company that are believed to hurt shareholders.
13. An analysis of the *Fortune* 100 by Equilar suggested that the median compensation multiplier in the case of (disclosed) CEO severance arrangements was two times base plus bonus compensation; for executive job loss resulting from a change in control, it was a multiplier of three (McGurn & Ranzetta, 2006, p. 35).

REFERENCES

Almazan, A., Hartzell, J. C., & Starks, L. T. (2005). Active institutional investors and *costs* of monitoring: Evidence from executive compensation. *Financial Management, 34*(4), 5–35.

Beatty, R. P., & Zajac, E. J. (1994). Managerial incentives, monitoring, and risk bearing: A study of executive compensation, ownership, and board structure in initial public offerings. *Administrative Science Quarterly, 39*(2), 313–335.

Bebchuk, L., & Fried,]. (2004). *Pay without performance: The unfulfilled promise of executive compensation.* Cambridge, MA: Harvard University Press.

Bethel, J. E., & Gillan, S. L. (2000). Corporate voting and the proxy process: Managerial control versus shareholder oversight. Presented at Tuck-JFE Contemporary Corporate Governance Conference. Available at SSRN: ssrn.com/abstract=236099 or DOI: 10.2139/ssrn.236099.

Borges, M., & Silverman, C. (2003, July 7). All equity plans now need shareholder approval. Mercer *Perspective Alert!*

Brandes, P., Hadani, M., & Goranova, M. (2006). Stock options expensing: An examination of agency and institutional theory explanations. *Journal of Business Research, 59*(5), 595–603.

Brickley, J. A., Lease, R. C., & Smith, C. W. (1988). Ownership structure and voting on anti-takeover amendments. *Journal of Financial Economics, 20*, 267–291.

Bryant, A. (1998, February 1). How companies make the boss buy stock, but soften the pinch. *New York Times.* Retrieved January 16, 2008, from query.nytimes.com/gst/fullpage.html?res=9D0CE3DD123A-F932A35751C0A96E958260&sec=&spon=&pagewanted=3

Carleton, W. T., Nelson, J. M., & Weisbach, M. S. (1998). The influence of institutions on corporate governance through private negotiations: Evidence from TIAA-CREF. *Journal of Finance, 53*(4), 1335–1362.

Carter, M., & Lynch, L. (2001). An examination of executive stock options repricing. *Journal of Financial Economics, 61*(2), 207–225.

Chaganti, R., & Damanpour, F. (1991). Institutional ownership, capital structure, and firm performance. *Strategic Management Journal, 12*(7), 479–491.

Cheng, S., & Firth, M. (2005). Ownership, corporate governance and top management pay in Hong Kong. *Corporate Governance, 13*(2), 291–302.

Coffee, J. C. (1991). Liquidity versus control: The institutional investor as corporate monitor. *Columbia Law Review, 91*(6), 1277–1368.

Daily, C. M., Dalton, D. R., & Rajagopalan, N. (2003). Governance through ownership: Centuries of practice, decades of research. *Academy of Management Journal, 46* (2), 151–158.

Daily, C. M., Johnson, J. L., Ellstrand, A. E., & Dalton, D. R. (1998). Compensation committee composition as a determinant of CEO compensation. *Academy of Management Journal, 41*(2), 209–220.

David, P., Hitt, M. A., & Gimeno, J. (2001). The influence of activism by institutional investors on R&D. *Academy of Management Journal, 44*(1), 144–157.

David, P., Kochhar, R., & Levitas, E. (1998). The effect of institutional investors on the level and mix of CEO compensation. *Academy of Management Journal, 41*(2), 200–208.

Davis, M. (2004, January 22). General Mills stock compensation: Yesterday, today, and tomorrow. Presented at the World at Work Webinar, "Gaining Shareholder Approval in a Challenging Proxy Season" with M. Davis, K. Crean, & P. Chingos.

Davis, M. (2006, July 12). Telephone interview.

Del Guercio, D., & Hawkins, J. (1999). The motivation and impact of pension fund activism. *Journal of Financial Economics, 52*, 293–340.

Dvorak, P., & Lublin, J. (2006, May 3). Verizon tries to mute criticism of CEO pay. *Wall Street Journal*, p. Bl.

The Economist (2006, June 16). The shareholders' revolt, p. 71.

Edwards, F. R., & Hubbard, G. (2005). The growth of institutional stock ownership: A promise unfulfilled. In *Corporate governance at the crossroads* by D. H. Chew and S. L. Gillan (Eds.), Irwin, NY: McGraw-Hill.

Eisenhardt, K. (1989). Agency theory: An assessment and review. *Academy of Management Review, 14*(1), 57–74.

Filatotchev, I., & Toms, S. (2003). Corporate governance, strategy, and survival in a declining industry: A study of UK cotton textile companies. *The Journal of Management Studies, 40*(4), 895–920.

Frederic W. Cook and Co. (2004, December 17). ISS 2005 Policy Changes. Retrieved January 16, 2008, from www.fwcook.com/alert_letters/12-17-04%20ISS%202005%20Policy%20Changes.pdf

Freescale Semiconductor (2006, March 16). Proxy statement. Retrieved January 16, 2008, from www.sec.gov/Archives/edgar/data/1272547/000119312506051207/ddef14a.htm

General Mills (2003, August 11). Notice of 2003 annual meeting of stockholders and proxy statement. Retrieved January 16, 2008, from www.sec.gov/Archives/edgar/data/40704/000089710103000933/gm032224s1_def14a.htm

Georgeson Shareholder (2000). Corporate governance: Annual meeting season wrap-up. Retrieved January 29, 2008, from http://www.georgeson.com/usa/download/acgr/acgr2000.pdf

Georgeson Shareholder (2005). Annual corporate governance review: Annual meetings, shareholder initiatives, proxy contests. Retrieved

January 29, 2008, from http://www.georgeson.com/usa/download/acgr/acgr2005.pdf

Gillan, S. L., & Starks L. T. (2000). Corporate governance proposals and shareholder activism: The role of institutional investors. *Journal of Financial Economics, 57*, 275–305.

Gomez-Mejia, L. R., Larraza-Kintana, M., & Makri, M. (2003). The determinants of executive compensation in family-controlled public corporations. *Academy of Management Journal, 46*(2), 226–237.

Grow, B. (2007, January 15). Out at Home Depot: Behind the flameout of controversial CEO Bob Nardelli. *BusinessWeek*, 56–58.

Hambrick, D. C., & Finkelstein, S. (1995). The effects of ownership structure on conditions at the top: The case of CEO pay raises. *Strategic Management Journal, 16*, 175–193.

Hartzell, J. C., & Starks, L. T. (2003). Institutional investors and executive compensation. *Journal of Finance, 58*(6), 2351–2374.

Hawley, J. P., Williams, A. T., & Miller, J. U. (1994). Getting the herd to run: Shareholder activism at the California Public Employees Retirement System. *Business and the Contemporary World, 6*, 26–48.

Hendry, J., Sanderson, P., Barker, R., & Roberts, J. (2006). Owners or traders? Conceptualizations of institutional investors and their relationship with corporate managers. *Human Relations, 59*(8), 1101–1132.

Holland J. (1998). Influence and intervention by financial institutions in their investee companies. *Corporate Governance, 6*(4), 249–264.

Hoskisson, R. E., Hitt, M. A., Johnson, R. A., & Grossman, W. (2002). Conflicting voices: The effects of institutional ownership heterogeneity and internal governance on corporate innovation strategies. *Academy of Management Journal, 45*(4), 697–716.

Institutional Shareholder Services (2005). Setting the bar for equity-based compensation: A summary of ISS's compensation guidelines. Retrieved January 16, 2008, from www.presidiopay.com/linked%20files/news2105.pdf

Jensen, M., & Meckling, W. (1976). Theory of the firm: Managerial behavior agency, cost, and ownership structure. *Journal of Financial Economics, 3*(4), 305–360.

Johnson, R. A., & Greening, D. W. (1999). The effects of corporate governance and institutional ownership types on corporate social performance. *Academy of Management Journal, 42*, 564–576.

Kang, D. L., & Sorensen, A. B. (1999). Ownership organization and firm performance. *Annual Review of Sociology, 25*, 121–144.

Karpoff, J. M., Malatesta, P. H., & Walkling, R. A. (1996). Corporate governance and shareholder initiatives: Empirical evidence. *Journal of Financial Economics, 42*, 365–395.

Khan, R., Dharwadkar, R., & Brandes, P. (2005). Institutional ownership and CEO compensation: A longitudinal examination. *Journal of Business Research, 58*(8), 1078–1088.

Kochhar, R., & David, P. (1996). Institutional investors and firm innovation: A test of competing hypotheses. *Strategic Management Journal, 17*, 73–84.

McGregor, J. (2007, January 15). This proxy season, expect a brawl. *BusinessWeek*, 59.

McGurn, P., & Ranzetta, T. J. (2006, May 9). Point/counterpoint: What institutional investors want and how companies are responding to this new era in executive compensation. Presented at the International Meeting of World at Work (formerly the American Compensation Association), Anaheim, California.

Merck & Co., Inc. (2006, March 9). Proxy statement. Retrieved January 16, 2008, from www.sec.gov/Archives/edgar/data/64978/000119312506049692/ddef14a.htm

Morgenson, G. (2006, April 30). Can't take it anymore? *New York Times.* Retrieved January 16, 2008, from select. nytimes.com/2006/04/30/business/yourmoney/30gret.html?scp=8&Lsq=Can%92t+take+it+anymore%3F

Neubaum, D. O., & Zahra, S. (2006). Institutional ownership and corporate social performance: The moderating effects of investment horizon, activism, and coordination. *Journal of Management, 32*(1), 108–131.

PepsiCo (2003, March 24). Notice of annual meeting of stockholders and proxy statement. Retrieved January 16, 2008, from http://www.sec.gov/Archives/edgar/data/77476/000095013003002300/ddef14a.htm

Plitch, P., & Whitehouse, K. (2006, February 27). Executives' pay faces new tactics. *Wall Street Journal*, p. B3.

Pollock, T. G., Fischer, H. M., & Wade, J. B. (2002). The role of power and politics in the repricing of executive options. *Academy of Management Journal, 45*(6), 1172–1182.

RiskMetrics Group (2007, October). 2007 postseason report: A closer look at accountability and engagement. Retrieved January 16, 2008, from www.riskmetrics.com/pdf/2007PostSeasonReportFINAL.pdf

Ryan, H. E., & Wiggins, R. A. (2002). The interactions between R&D: Investment decisions and compensation policy. *Financial Management, 31*(1), 5–29.

Ryan, L. V., & Schneider, M. (2002). The antecedents of institutional investor activism. *Academy of Management Journal, 27*(4), 554–573.

Scherb, D. (2004, May 24). Getting dramatic shift to occur in your compensation strategy. Presented at the annual meeting of World at Work, Boston, Massachusetts.

Securities and Exchange Commission (2000). Final rule: Selective disclosure and insider trading. Retrieved January 16, 2008, from www.sec.gov/rules/final/33-7881.htm#P12_1308

Securities and Exchange Commission (2006, July 26). SEC votes to adopt changes to disclosure requirements concerning executive compensation and related matters. Retrieved January 16, 2008, from www.sec.gov/news/press/2006/2006-123.htm

Securities and Exchange Commission (2007, October 9). Staff observations in the review of executive compensation disclosure. Retrieved January 16, 2008, from www.sec.gov/divisions/corpfin/guidance/execcompdisclosure.htm

Securities Industry Fact Book (2002). Retrieved January 28, 2008 from http://www.sifma.org/research/statistics/other/2002Fact_Book.pdf

Smith, G. (2006, November 20). Telephone interview.

Thomas, R. S., & Martin, K. J. (1999). The effect of shareholder proposals on executive compensation. *University of Cincinnati Law Review, 67*(4), 1021–1081.

Tihanyi, L., Johnson, R. A., Hoskisson, R. E., & Hitt, M. A. (2003). Institutional ownership differences and international diversification: The effects of boards of directors and technological opportunity. *Academy of Management Journal, 46*(2), 195–211.

Tosi, H. L., Katz, J. P., & Gomez-Mejia, L. (1997). Disaggregating the agency contract: The effects of monitoring, incentive alignment, and term in office on agent decision making. *Academy of Management Journal, 40*(3), 584–602

Useem, M. (1996). *Investor capitalism: How money managers are changing the face of corporate America.* New York: Basic Books.

Vanguard (2002, December 5). Letter to the SEC. Retrieved January 16, 2008, from www.sec.gov/rules/proposed/s73602/rgbartonl.htm

Wahal, S. (1996). Pension fund activism and firm performance. *Journal of Financial and Quantitative Analysis, 31*, 1–23.

Watson Wyatt (2005). Institutional investors dissatisfied with US executive pay system, Watson Wyatt study finds. Press release. Retrieved January 16, 2008, from www.watsonwyatt.com/news/press.asp?ID=15518

Westphal, J. D., & Zajac, E. J. (1994). Substance and symbolism in CEOs' long-term incentive plans. *Administrative Science Quarterly, 39*(3), 367–390.

Westphal, J. D., & Zajac, E. J. (1998). The symbolic management of stock holders' corporate governance reforms and shareholders reactions. *Administrative Science Quarterly, 43*(1), 127–153.

Wilcox, J. C. (2001). Ending the stalemate: Take a second look at the SEC's 1997 Release 39093. *Corporate Governance Advisor, 9*(1), 1–2.

Yermack, D. (2006). Flights of fancy: Corporate jets, CEO perquisites, and inferior shareholder returns. *Journal of Financial Economics, 80*, 211–242.

Zahra, S. A. (1996). Governance, ownership, and corporate entrepreneurship: The moderating impact of industry technological opportunities. *Academy of Management Journal*, *39*(6), 1713–1735.

Zahra, S. A, Neubaum, D. O., & Huse, M. (2000). Entrepreneurship in medium-size companies: Exploring the effects of ownership and governance systems. *Journal of Management*, *26*(5), 947–976.

Zajac, E. J., & Westphal, J. D. (1994). The costs and benefits of managerial incentives and monitoring in large US corporations: When is more not better? *Strategic Management Journal*, *15*, 121–142.

Zajac, E. J., & Westphal, J. D. (1995). Accounting for the explanation of CEO compensation: Substance and symbolism. *Administrative Science Quarterly*, *40*(2), 283–308.

Labor Relations

12

Learning Objectives

- Understand the provisions of the National Labor Relations Act, which apply to all employers, regardless of whether their workforce is unionized
- Explain the reasons why employees form and join unions
- Describe the restrictions the NLRA places on union organizers and employer behaviors during organizing campaigns
- Gain an appreciation of the reasons for decline in union membership and the challenges organized labor faces in a global information-based economy
- Understand the process of collective bargaining and the various types of bargaining items
- Appreciate the role of alternative dispute resolution when collective bargaining has been unsuccessful

Labor Unrest at the New York MTA

On the morning of December 20, 2005, New Yorkers who relied on public transit to get to their places of employment or around town to complete their holiday shopping woke up to find that the subway and public bus systems had been shut down by a strike of the 34,000 workers who were members of the Transport Workers Union Local 100 of the Metropolitan Transportation Authority. Negotiations for a new contract had broken down because of a failure to agree on retirement/pension provisions and wage increases. The strike was seen as a particular hardship for lower-income residents of the outer boroughs of New York City.

While the strike itself lasted only 60 hours, it took another day to get the transit system fully up and running. Nonetheless, the strike had a significant impact on New York. Public schools were affected and had to operate on a delayed schedule, while many private schools were forced to close completely. Public safety was impacted detrimentally because of the increased congestion on streets and sidewalks. The financial impact of the strike was significant, as the city estimated that it lost more than $300 million per day and other revenues.

The strike was illegal under the New York State Public Employees Fair Employment Act, more commonly known as the Taylor Law, which prohibits municipal workers from striking and provides alternative means for resolution of labor-related disputes. This law, which had been enacted in response to a previous transit strike, which took place in 1966, also provides for criminal penalties, including imprisonment for union officials and fines to be levied against both the union and striking employees. Local 100 did not have the support of its parent union—the International Transport Workers Union—for the strike, with the parent union ordering Local 100 workers to return to work as soon as it became aware of what had transpired. As a result of the strike, Local 100 president Roger Toussaint was sentenced to ten days in jail and the union was fined $2.5 million. $300,000 in strike-related penalties were levied against union members and deducted from the paychecks of striking workers.[1] The aftermath of the strike involved a tremendous amount of published analysis of the political behavior of the union as well as local elected officials, particularly Mayor Michael Bloomberg, illustrating the politically charged realities in which organized labor operates.

Labor relations is a key strategic issue for organizations because the nature of the relationship between the employer and employees can have a significant impact on morale, motivation, and productivity. Workers who feel that the terms and conditions of their employment are less than advantageous will not be as committed to perform and to remain with an employer. Consequently, how organizations manage the day-to-day aspects of the employment relationship can be a key variable affecting their ability to achieve strategic objectives.

Workers who have unionized create special challenges for human resource management. When workers form unions, the employment relationship becomes more formal through a union contract and is subject to special provisions of the National Labor Relations Act. This act allows unions to be formed and exist as employee organizations that have the legal right to bargain with management over various terms and conditions of employment. Unions provide membership solely for employees; managers are prohibited by law from joining employee unions or from forming their own unions.

Organized labor in the United States has had a cyclical history, generally consisting of short periods of sharp growth in union membership and activity followed by extended periods of decline.[2] In the early part of the 20th century, employee-centered management practices were eroding interest in unionization. The Great Depression then ignited strong interest in unions with the resultant creation by John Lewis of the Congress of Industrial Organizations (CIO). At that time, both the CIO and the American Federation of Labor (AFL) were able to unionize large segments of the workforce. These organizing efforts were largely focused on second-generation immigrants, particularly Catholics, Italians, and Jews, as unions attempted to provide these individuals with the full benefits of working in the WASP-dominated economy.

Unions continued to enjoy increased membership until World War II. Interest in unions declined postwar until the mid-1960s, when unions began to reach out to African-Americans during the drive for civil rights and subsequently enjoyed a renewed popularity. Also at that time, Cesar Chavez founded the National Farm Workers Association, drawing attention to the plight of Latino and Filipino farm workers who had been forced to endure deplorable working conditions and substandard wages. Chavez's efforts led to a grape boycott that was observed by more than 17 million Americans and, more generally, resulted in widespread awareness and distrust of exploitation of workers by employers. These successes also led to a flurry of union organization among public sector employees that continued until the early 1980s.

August 3, 1981, is considered to be a significant day in the history of American labor. On that date, more than 12,000 employees of the Federal Aviation Administration who were members of the Professional Air Traffic Controllers (PATCO) union walked off of their jobs. When President Reagan ordered them back to work within 48 hours, 11,325 of them refused and were fired immediately, as the FAA commenced hiring permanent replacements. Since the unsuccessful PATCO strike, strikes have nearly disappeared in the United States. During the 1950s organized labor successfully orchestrated an average of 344 work stoppages annually.[3] However, post-PATCO, that number had continuously been in decline and by 2008 had dipped to just 15, with 9 of these 15 lasting for 10 days or less.[4] The PATCO strike greatly influenced public perceptions against organized labor stoppages and affirmed the right for employers to hire permanent replacements for striking workers. This shift has turned the strike into a present-day near-suicide tactic for unions.

In 2005, one of the most significant changes in the history of American labor took place with the withdrawal of seven unions from the combined AFL-CIO, which had merged in 1955. This new coalition, which called itself Change to Win, represented approximately 6 million workers at the time. Reading 12.1, "The Future of Unions," discusses some of the challenges that will face the Change to Win coalition and the weakened AFL-CIO as well as the ongoing challenges organized labor in general faces in the global economy.

Union membership in the United States has been steadily declining for a number of years. In 1970, approximately 30 percent of the private workforce was unionized, in addition to a majority of public sector employees. By 1999, the U.S. Department of Labor reported that only 13.9 percent of the workforce was unionized. Government employees were four times more likely to be union members than were private sector employees (37.3 percent versus 9.4 percent). These numbers represented declines in overall union membership as well as in both the public and private sector union density.[5]

The decline in union membership can be attributed to a number of factors. First, many workers have become disenfranchised from their unions. Allegations of union corruption and misuse of funds—combined with the fact that workers sometimes feel that the costs of union membership outweigh the benefits—have eroded union membership. Second, many organizations have moved their manufacturing and assembly operations outside the United States. Unions have traditionally had their strongest bases of support among these blue-collar workers, and the movement of those jobs overseas has hurt unions. Third, changes in the nature of work and technology have eliminated many of the traditional manual labor jobs in which union members were employed. Finally, many unions have refused to be flexible enough to allow organizations to grow and adapt in relation to the changes taking place in their industries, markets, and the technological, economic, and sociocultural environments. The traditional model of American labor unions, which guard employee rights by attempting to maintain the status quo, no longer benefits employers or employees. Unions of the future will have to be based on a different model and have different relationships with the organizations whose workers they represent—if they continue to exist.

Although overall union membership is declining it is important to understand organized labor relations for at least three reasons. First, in many industries, unionization is the norm. Many public sector workplaces are unionized. In the private sector, industries such as transportation, construction, hospitality, publishing, education, and healthcare are usually highly unionized. In fact, the transportation industry has the highest level of private sector union membership, at 25.5 percent.[6] Managers and business owners in these industries have no choice but to be well-versed on the laws that regulate the relationship with union employees. Second, competitors may be unionized, and settlements in those organizations may impact HR practices, programs, and policies needed to remain competitive in recruiting and retaining productive employees. Arguably, the most important reason for employers to have a sense of the labor relations landscape is that the National Labor Relations Act provides all employees—rather than just those who have unionized—with specific rights. Consequently, many employers who operate in nonunion environments may be unfamiliar with some of the terms and conditions of employment outlined in the act. Section 7 of the act grants all employees, including those who are not members of unions, the right to engage in activities that support their "mutual aid or protection." There are six notable provisions under this section that employers must know to avoid violations of the act.[7]

First is the right of employees to discuss employment terms. In order for employees to consider whether they wish to organize, they must be able to discuss the terms and conditions of employment, including compensation, harassment, and discrimination. This right, however, does not extend to the disclosure of confidential information, such as salaries, to which an employee might have access as part of his or her job. Second, employees reserve the right to complain to third parties, such as customers, clients, and the media, about their treatment by the employer. Again, however, the employer retains the right to prohibit disclosure of any confidential or proprietary information. Third, employees have the right to engage in a work stoppage or collective walkout to protest working conditions without fear of retaliation. Any employee who is disciplined or discharged for engaging in such behavior has a valid claim against the employer under the National Labor Relations Act. Fourth, employees have the right to honor picket lines without fear of retaliation. This is considered protected activity regardless of whether the employee is a member of the picketing union or merely sympathetic to the cause and plight of the workers on the picket line. Fifth, employees have the conditional right to solicit and distribute union literature. Such behavior can be restricted but not fully prohibited, as will be discussed shortly. Finally, employers cannot unilaterally ban employees access to the worksite while off-duty. Restrictions may be imposed that limit access to the interior of the facility if applied consistently to all employees for all purposes, but employees still retain the right to be present on company property, such as the employee parking lot, after working hours to engage in behaviors protected under the act.

It cannot be emphasized enough that non-union employees enjoy significant protection against arbitrary, capricious, or harassing conduct by employers. This standard was established by the Supreme Court in the 1962 case of *NLRB v. Washington Aluminum Co.*,[8] where the Court found that employee activity that was concerted for mutual aid or protection (in this case, walking off the job in protest of poor working conditions) was lawful. As long as the employee or group of employees actions are beyond that of a personal complaint pursued in self-interest, such behavior is protected without the presence of a formally recognized union. These rights have consistently been reinforced in numerous court cases since the initial ruling in *Washington Aluminum*.

Just because an organization is not unionized today does not mean that it may not be in the future. Managers in such organizations need to know why workers form or join unions, how the law requires the employer to behave during any union-organizing campaign and after a union has been voted in, how the collective-bargaining process is conducted, and how impasses may be settled.

The word *union* means that workers have agreed to work together in dealing with and negotiating the terms and conditions of their employment with management. The Latin root *uni* means *one*; in the sense of a union, it means that a plurality of workers has united to speak with "one voice."

Organized labor presents a number of key strategic challenges for management. First, when workers unionize, the power based within the organization is redistributed. Employers can find that their ability to manage workers at their discretion to achieve the organization's strategic objectives has been severely curtailed. Second, the process of unionization involves bringing in outside players: union representatives, who then become an additional constituency whose support must be gained for any new or ongoing management initiatives. Finally, a unionized work setting can greatly impact the organization's cost structure, particularly payroll expenses and work processes that may contribute to or retard efficiency in operations.

Why Employees Unionize

Employees usually form or join unions because of the perceived benefits that unionization might provide them. These benefits can be economic, social, and/or political. Economic benefits can result from a union's ability to negotiate higher wages, better or expanded benefits, greater job or employment security, and improved working hours and conditions. Social benefits can be derived from the affiliation and sense of community that workers share when they are unionized. Their personal issues and needs relating to their jobs and lifestyles can often be integrated within the union agenda, with corresponding support gained from coworkers. Unions also often sponsor social events for their members and their families. Is it not surprising that many unions have the word *brotherhood* in their name; this attempts to signify the family or community atmosphere the union tries to create for its members.

Political benefits can be gained through the sense of power in numbers. In negotiating with management over terms and conditions of employment, individual employees are relatively powerless. They often need the organization (to earn a living) far more than the organization needs them (individual workers can be easily replaced). When workers unionize and speak with one voice, they leverage their individual power against management and equalize the balance of power within the organization. Management may be able to do without individual employees, but they cannot do without their entire workforce. Unions can allow workers far greater say and involvement in negotiating and setting critical terms and conditions of employment and in ensuring fair treatment from the organization. Unions can often provide additional political benefits in a literal sense in that the power and strength of their united membership can be used to support and influence political races and legislation passed at the local, state, and federal levels.

No benefits come without some cost, and union membership is no exception. Union members pay at least two significant costs for their benefits. First are the economic costs of the fees or dues that unions charge their members to support the initiatives the union undertakes on behalf of its employees. Second are the political costs employees assume when they relinquish their individual freedom to deal with their employer and be represented by the union. Individual employees may not agree with the terms and conditions negotiated for them or the tactics and strategies the union uses in negotiating. Although individual employees do vote on the decision to strike, an employee who does not wish or cannot afford to go out on strike is basically stuck in accepting the majority position and then assumes any risk associated with deviating from the union majority.

The National Labor Relations Act

In 1935, Congress passed the National Labor Relations Act (NLRA), also called the Wagner Act, which gave employees the right to unionize and to regulate union/management relations. This act has been amended several times, most notably in 1947, with amendments known as the Taft-Hartley Act, and in 1959, with amendments knows as the Landrum-Griffith Act.

The NLRA created the National Labor Relations Board (NLRB) to oversee the provisions of the act. Among other duties, the NLRB is responsible for overseeing union elections, certifying a particular union as the official bargaining representative of a group of employees, and hearing allegations of violations of the act from employers, unions, and employee groups.

As a first step in establishing a union, a group of employees petitions the NLRB, often through the assistance of a union representative, to conduct an election. As a prerequisite for an election, the NLRB requires at least 30 percent of the employees to have signed authorization cards, which indicate an expressed interest in having union representation from a specific union. Most petitions to the NLRB involve the presentation of authorization cards from a far greater number of employees than 30 percent. These authorization cards are not a vote for the union; they are merely the means for establishing the level of employee interest to conduct an election. Some employees who are not in favor of union representation often sign authorization cards under peer pressure or to facilitate the election process. Union-organizing campaigns often create very stressful working conditions, and some employees who are against unionization may sign authorization cards to ensure that the election be held as soon as possible.

Once the NLRB has received the authorization cards and determined that there is sufficient interest to conduct an election, it will attempt to determine the appropriate bargaining unit. A bargaining unit is a group of employees who have similar wages, skill levels, working conditions, and/or levels of professionalism. The NLRB will determine whether the organization should have one bargaining unit that covers all employees or separate bargaining units for different groups of employees, given the differences in their jobs.

For example, airlines have separate bargaining units for flight attendants, pilots, and ramp workers, given the differences in job responsibilities, training, hours, and working conditions. Newspapers have separate unions for writers, printers, and presspeople because of similar differences. A restaurant, on the other hand, might have one bargaining unit that includes waitstaff, cooks, hosts, bartenders, and bus staff. When a unionized organization has more than one bargaining unit, each bargaining unit negotiates a contract with management separately; however, the individual units are often impacted by what the other units negotiate, and each unit often lends support to the others during periods of labor unrest.

When the NLRB conducts an election, the option that receives the majority of the votes (50 percent plus one) wins the election. There may, however, be more than two options (union or no union) on the ballot. Given that the NLRB requires authorization cards from only 30 percent of employees, it is mathematically possible for more than one union to be part of an election. This has been the case when there has been public knowledge of dissatisfied employees and thus more than one union attempted to organize workers simultaneously. If there were three options on the ballot (no union, Union A, Union B) and none of them received more than 50 percent of the initial vote, then the option receiving the least support would be dropped and a second ballot would be issued. Eventually, one option will have the support of more than 50 percent of the employees in the prospective bargaining unit.

Behavior during Organizing Campaigns

Union-organizing campaigns often present difficult working conditions for employees, who are often continuously subjected to opposing information from management, union representatives, and pro-union coworkers in support of their respective positions. In passing the NLRA, Congress determined that it should regulate the behavior of management and union representatives in union-organizing campaigns to ensure that one does not have an unfair advantage over the other in communicating positions to employees.

The NLRA outlines specific provisions pertaining to employer conduct during union-organizing campaigns in its discussion of unfair labor practices. Section 8(c) of the act provides that "the expression of views, arguments or opinions, or the dissemination thereof, whether in written, printed, graphic or visual form shall not constitute or be evidence of an unfair labor practice … if such expression contains no threat of reprisal or force or promise of benefit." Therefore, employers have free rein to communicate their position concerning unionization to employees during working hours, which is only appropriate because the employers are paying employees for that time. However, employers are forbidden from making any threat or promise pending the outcome of the election. The reason for this directive is that allowing employers to do so would give employers an unfair advantage in the election. The union does not have the power to make any such promises, so to ensure a level playing field, the NLRB also prohibits employers from doing so. Employers need to treat employees more favorably *before* the NLRB has stepped in and established employee interest in conducting an election.

The act also allows pro-union employees the full right to approach their coworkers at work and express their support of the union, as long as such contact takes place during nonworking periods in nonworking areas (such as the employee cafeteria during lunch breaks, the parking lot after leaving work, or in a restroom during a scheduled break). This is consistent with the constitutional guarantee of freedom of speech. Employers can prohibit employees who support the union from communicating this support to coworkers at any other time.

A more difficult question concerns the extent to which employers can prevent employee solicitation by union representatives at the worksite. The U.S. Supreme Court has issued several rulings in this area that continue to redefine the relative positions of unions and management. Generally, an employer can restrict nonemployee access to employees if two conditions have been met: (1) The nonemployee—in this case, a union organizer—must have some reasonable means to access and communicate with employees outside the workplace, such as electronic or print media, and (2) the employer must have a general ban on all non-employee solicitation. The latter condition is not limited to union solicitation; it might also include charitable appeals, blood drives, or employer-sponsored outings for which employees have to pay. If these two conditions are met, then the employer can restrict union organizers' access to employees.

Historically, this issue of access to employees has involved somewhat of a "chess game" between employers and union organizers. Subsequent to the Supreme Court rulings described above that restrict union organizer access to employees, unions have turned to a strategy called "salting" the workplace. Salting involves a paid union organizer applying for employment with an employer whose employees are the target of an organizing drive. The Supreme Court has held that under the NLRA, an employer cannot discriminate against a person solely on the basis of his or her status as a salt and intention to organize the workplace. Employers have since countered salting efforts through the use of restricted hiring criteria that have the effect of eliminating salts from employment consideration. The portrayal of union organizing efforts and management responses as a chess game relates to the fact that each side is attempting to develop a response to counter the other side's most recent "move" or court victory. Reading 12.2, "A Big Chill on a 'Big Hurt:' Genuine Interest in Employment of Salts in Assessing Protection Under the National Labor Relations Act," illustrates the tensions that exist between unions and employers in organizing campaigns.

Employees who are dissatisfied with their union representative may elect to de-certify the union. The process for decertification happens in exactly the same manner as certification—utilizing authorization cards and requiring a 50 percent plus one majority employee vote. The NLRA does, however, require employees to wait at least one year from certification until a de-certification election can be held. This is to ensure that the union has had appropriate time to work on behalf of the employees and to ensure that employees do not drain the time and resources of the NLRB by continually calling for certification and de-certification elections. Similarly, if a union loses an organizing campaign, the NLRA prohibits another organizing campaign and election for at least one year.

Collective Bargaining

When a union is elected to represent employees, the union representative and employer are jointly responsible for negotiating a collective-bargaining agreement that covers various terms and conditions of employment. There are no set requirements as to the term or content of any collective-bargaining agreement, but the NLRA classifies bargaining items as mandatory, permissive, or prohibited. Mandatory items must be negotiated in good faith if one party chooses to introduce them to the negotiations. They consist of many of the economic terms of employment, such as wages, hours, benefits, working conditions, job-posting procedures, or job security provisions. Mandatory items also include management rights clauses and union security clauses. The two parties are not required to come to an agreement on these items, but they are legally required to discuss them and bargain in good faith if requested by the other party. Mandatory simply means that one party cannot refuse to discuss one of these items if the other party requests to do so.

Permissive items can be discussed if both parties agree to do so. Neither party can legally force the other party to negotiate over a permissive item nor can either party pursue a permissive item to the point of impasse. Permissive items include things such as changes in benefits for retired employees, supervisory compensation and discipline, and union input in pricing of company products and services. Prohibited items are things neither party can negotiate because these items are illegal. They include featherbedding (requiring the employer to pay for work not done or not requested), discrimination in hiring, or any other violation of the law or illegal union security clauses. A listing of some of the items that fall under each classification is presented in Exhibit 12.1.

Unions often attempt to negotiate security clauses into the collective-bargaining agreement. These clauses are a mandatory bargaining item and an attempt to ensure that the union enjoys some security in its representation of employees and that the cost of the union's efforts on behalf of employees is covered. The two types of union security clauses are union shop agreements and agency shop agreements. Union shop agreements require all newly hired employees who are not union members to join the union within a specified time period after beginning employment. Agency shop agreements do not require employees to join the union but require all non-union members who are part of the bargaining unit to pay the union a representation fee, usually equivalent to the amount of dues paid by union members. The rationale for collecting such fees is that although individual employees can maintain the freedom of being non-union, as bargaining unit members, they reap the advantages of what the union negotiates. Therefore, it is only fair that they should share equally in the cost of obtaining what the union is able to achieve for the bargaining unit. Although union security clauses are a mandatory bargaining item, the NLRA allows individual states to pass right-to-work laws that prohibit union and agency shop arrangements. To date, nearly half the 50 states have passed such laws.

A third type of union security agreement that was originally allowed under the NLRA has since been outlawed. Closed-shop agreements required the employer to hire only

EXHIBIT 12.1 Types of Bargaining Items

Mandatory	Permissive	Illegal
Base wages	Union representation on board of directors	Closed-shop agreements
Incentive pay	Benefits for retirees	Featherbedding
Benefits	Wage concessions	Discrimination in hiring
Overtime	Employee ownership	
Paid time off	Union input into company pricing policy	
Layoff procedures		
Promotion criteria		
Union security clauses		
Management rights clauses		
Grievance procedures		
Safety and health issues		

applicants who were already union members. Congress found such arrangements to be detrimental to labor because individuals without income were forced to pay union dues without the benefit of any employment. There was no guarantee that an applicant who belonged to a union subsequently would be hired, so closed-shop agreements were eventually outlawed.

Failure to Reach Agreement

When the union and the employer are unable to agree on the terms of the collective-bargaining agreement, workers have the right—under the NLRA—to strike. Whether employers are obligated to rehire striking employees at the conclusion of the strike depends on the kind of strike.

An economic strike is one in which the parties have negotiated in good faith but have been unable to settle on a contract or collective-bargaining agreement. The organization has the right to continue to operate during such a strike and often does so by utilizing management employees, hiring temporary workers, and/or hiring permanent replacements. The discretion of how to proceed rests with the organization. Economic strikers cannot be terminated simply for engaging in collective strike activity. At the conclusion of the strike, they must be reinstated if two conditions are met: (1) Their individual jobs still exist and (2) permanent replacements have not been hired. Economic strikers run the risk that the employer may eliminate their jobs or hire replacements; both activities are protected under the NLRA.

An unfair labor practice strike is one in which employees strike in response to some action of management that the NLRA identifies as an unfair labor practice. These behaviors are outlined within the statute, and workers who go out on such a strike have a guaranteed legal right to reinstatement by the employer even if the employer has hired permanent replacements in the interim.

A wildcat strike is one in which workers decide not to honor the terms of the collective-bargaining agreement and walk out in violation of their obligation to the employer under the agreement. Because wildcat strikers have breached their contractual obligations to the employer, they have no right to reinstatement in their jobs. Wildcat strikes can be caused by perceived unfair treatment of an employee by management or a work-site may be perceived as hazardous or dangerous, such as those found in the mining and construction industries. In certain industries, management will attempt to resolve the issue if the claims are deemed to have merit in lieu of fighting the union in court. In addition, federal workers are prohibited by law from striking for any reason, including an economic strike. Any strike by federal employees is not protected under the NLRA, and striking employees have no legal rights to return to their jobs. Such was the case in the early 1980s when the Professional Air Traffic Controllers (PATCO) union struck, and President Reagan immediately fired and replaced the striking workers.

The incidence of labor strikes in the United States is decreasing as both employees and employers realize that everyone loses during a strike. The company gets hurt financially and in the public domain; workers get hurt financially and emotionally; customers may be hurt operationally and financially, particularly if there are no substitute providers. Organizations can prevent strike activity in two principal ways: through the use of a formal grievance procedure or through the alternate dispute resolution (ADR) processes of mediation or arbitration.

Grievance procedures are a permissive bargaining item under the National Labor Relations Act, as indicated in Exhibit 12.1. Grievance procedures outline how conflicts or disagreements between workers and management over the terms of the collective-bargaining agreement are handled. Grievance procedures are often the catalyst to resolving problems before the conflict escalates to a strike. They are also useful in helping union leaders and management identify weaknesses or oversights in the collective-bargaining agreement that can be addressed during the negotiations over subsequent collective-bargaining agreements. Grievance procedures are also useful as a means of communicating to management firsthand work-related sources of employee dissatisfaction that can hamper morale and productivity.

An increasing number of collective-bargaining agreements are calling for mediation or arbitration of labor disputes as a means of avoiding strikes. Mediation involves an outside third party who has no binding decision-making authority assisting both sides in reaching a settlement. This individual assists the two sides in finding some middle ground on which they can agree and facilitating dialogue and concessions. Arbitration works in a similar manner: It involves an outside, unbiased third party who listens to the arguments presented by both sides. However, the arbitrator renders a ruling or decision that binds both parties. Both sides agree to abide by the decision of the arbitrator prior to entering the arbitration hearing. Mediation is frequently used in public sector organizations where strike activity is outlawed at the federal level and often greatly restricted at the state and local levels. Arbitration is used quite frequently in professional sports in resolving salary disputes between union players and the owners of their teams.

Arbitration has been controversial in that it has been perceived as depriving employees of their rights to pursue claims in courts of law and have their cases heard by a jury and replacing this process with an employer-controlled system that is less likely to result in a favorable decision for the employee. However, history has shown that this is not the case. Employment-related cases heard in federal district court historically have resulted in a 12 percent rate of success for employees, while general employment arbitration has favored employees in 33 percent of cases decided, and labor arbitration—heard under a collective-bargaining agreement—has favored employees in 52 percent of cases.[9]

Unions Today

One way in which unions are attempting to maintain their viability in light of declining membership is to recruit in organizations and industries with which they have no previous affiliation. With the demise of their traditional manufacturing base, many domestic unions have expanded their missions, as efforts to recruit new members have become a top priority. Such recruiting efforts are seen as so central to the ongoing livelihood of unions that the AFL-CIO now earmarks one-third of its operating budget for organizing, compared to just 5 percent 10 years ago.[10] Consider the diversity now present in some of the leading labor unions: the United Steelworkers of America, established in 1936 to represent steelworkers, now includes employees from Good Humor/Breyers, the Baltimore Zoo, and Louisville Slugger; the United Auto Workers, established in 1935 to represent auto workers, now includes employees from Miller Beer, Planter's nuts, Kohler bathroom fixtures, Yamaha musical instruments, and Folger's Coffee; the International Brotherhood of Teamsters, established in 1903 to represent drivers in the freight-moving industry, now includes flight attendants, public defenders, and nursing home employees. There is no consensus regarding the value of such diversification by unions. Some argue that it provides more power to unions and their members by strengthening their numbers and preventing their dependence on one particular industry. On the other hand, critics argue that this prevents unions from being very influential in setting wages and policy in a particular industry, given the need to spread time and resources across multiple industries. However, given the demise of traditional manufacturing jobs from which unions originated and relied on for their support and power, unions have little choice but to reach out to new industries. The critical issue is whether this diversification is really strategic for the union or merely opportunistic.

Another new development in how unions operate is their reliance on technology. Unions have been using the Internet effectively to recruit new members, particularly those in technology-based industries, and to gain support from others in their organizing efforts. The South Bay Central Labor Council, based in California's Silicon Valley, consists of 110 affiliated unions that represent more than 100,000 employees in the area. The Council is using the Internet to communicate with and, it is hoped, organize contingent workers.[11] Similarly, the Service Employees International Union undertook a campaign to organize janitorial workers in the Silicon Valley. The union successfully used the Internet to publicize its case against Apple Computer, Oracle, and Hewlett-Packard worldwide via electronic bulletin boards that informed engineers and programmers about the wages and working conditions of those who cleaned their offices at night.[12] Finally, the Oakland-based Local 2850 of the Hotel Employees & Restaurant Employees International Union used the Internet in a campaign against software giant PeopleSoft. In attempting to organize workers from a hotel used extensively by PeopleSoft and its corporate partners and unable to gain the support of PeopleSoft, the union launched an Internet campaign that caused PeopleSoft's stock value to decline by more than $63 million, according to the company's own estimates.[13]

The NLRB has also considered the role of technology as it relates to worker rights under the NLRA. Given its charge to ensure that employees are able to communicate freely with each other about wages and all other conditions and terms of employment, the NLRB has endorsed e-mail communication between employees as a means of safeguarding those rights. Only when an employee's behavior is disruptive does NLRA protection cease. As a result, employer policies that ban all nonbusiness and/or personal use of e-mail may interfere with the right to self-organize and therefore constitute a violation of the NLRA. A key issue here is the extent to which employees normally use the employer's computer system for their regular work and communication with coworkers. Employees who normally use a computer system in carrying out their regular job responsibilities are considered differently from employees who generally do not use computers or e-mail to carry out their regular job responsibilities. In addition, the more e-mail is normally used in the workplace, the less restrictive a policy an employer can implement that regulates communication that might be considered protected concerted activity under the NLRA.[14]

Conclusion

Unions have a long and deep history in the United States and enjoy strong support under federal law. However, union membership is declining in America; unions in this country probably will not survive if they continue to display traditional adversarial relationships with employers. Traditional approaches to negotiation usually involved the union trying to gain concessions from management and winning the negotiation. To be successful in the future, unions must develop partnerships with employers and seek win-win outcomes to collective bargaining that strengthen both the union's position and employees' rights and enhance the performance of the organization. Rigid posturing by unions in attempting to maintain the status quo works against the many initiatives and innovations organizations develop at they attempt to respond to changes in their environments and remain more competitive.

Given the changing nature of organizations and work, unions clearly need to reinvent themselves. Unions need to consider that the jobs of today and those of the future are quite different from the jobs of the past. Increasing global competition, changing technology, the heightened pace of merger and acquisition activity, the move toward smaller businesses and autonomous divisions, and the increasing diversity in the workforce represent broad changes for unions in the United States. The jobs being created in our economy are more service- than manufacturing-oriented; are much more complex, multifaceted, and broadly designed; involve teams, cooperation, and working with others; and involve more self- or peer supervision than supervision by management. Countries such as Japan and Germany have extensive unionization and produce some of the highest quality, most technologically advanced products. Their unions facilitate worker involvement, development, and participation programs; also, the unions partner with employers in creating beneficial change rather than inhibiting change and attempting to ensure workers' rights by maintaining the status quo.

As unions decline in number and stature, workers become less powerful. Without union representation, employee interests can only be advanced through increased government regulation of the employment relationship or through innovative and responsive HR programs that organizations initiate themselves. Increased legislation may ensure worker rights, but it can also inhibit organizational flexibility and change. Innovative HR programs can provide workers with benefits, but usually, the organization retains power and control over the workers, who maintain their individual status in dealing with separate issues with the employer. Legislation preserves rights and empowers workers to a limited extent, but it inhibits change. Organization-designed initiatives can promote change but still leave individual workers at a disadvantage when dealing with employers on issues of equity. Hence, policymakers need to take a critical look at the institution of collective bargaining to determine whether it has lived up to the ideals Congress established for it under the NLRA. Reading 12.3, "Collective Bargaining: Keeping Score on a Great American Institution," examines the ideological and practical perspectives of collective bargaining as well as how effectively collective bargaining has served the American workplace.

Very few unionized companies have developed effective worker participation programs because unions are interested in keeping workers insulated from management issues. Ironically, however, successful employee participation programs in non-unionized organizations have actually increased workers' power and voice in dealing with management. Union leaders need to create a new model of worker representation if they plan to survive in the 21st century. This can only be done if union leaders rethink their roles and adopt collective-bargaining strategies that allow both the employees and employers to benefit. Union leaders need not only political and negotiating skills but also management skills in understanding the whole organization: strategic issues facing the employer and the organization's environment. Instead of seeing themselves as adversaries to management, they should envision themselves as facilitators and consultants. Although employers clearly need to consider labor relations from a strategic perspective, union representatives must do so even more if they are to keep their unions viable for tomorrow's organizations.

Critical Thinking

1. With unionization on the downturn, why should an organization be concerned about labor relations?
2. What benefits are received and what costs are incurred when workers unionize?
3. Describe the process by which workers unionize.
4. What are the possible outcomes of failure to reach consensus on a collective-bargaining agreement?
5. Contrast the style of labor unions in the United States to that found in other countries.
6. Does union diversification make unions stronger or weaker? How would you feel as an auto worker to see the UAW representing employees outside the auto industry?

Reading 12.1

7. What is the current status of major labor organizations such as the ALF-CIO and the "Change to Win" coalition? What strategies is each pursuing, and how effectively are they responding to the needs of workers?

Reading 12.2

8. Assess the status of employer and union recruiter behaviors in union organizing campaigns. How much access should union organizers have to employees? What new behaviors are likely from employers and union organizers in response to the actions of the other party?

Reading 12.3

9. What factors have influenced the current state of collective bargaining in the United States? What likely development will affect collective bargaining in the coming years?

Exercises

1. Locate a local unionized organization. Interview both a manager and a union employee to determine the level of satisfaction each has with the employment relationship. What types of union activity/inactivity contribute to these positions?
2. Investigate one large union, such as the United Auto Workers, United Steelworkers, or Teamsters, in depth and then examine its member base and recent activity on behalf of its members. Does it appear that diversification has made this union more or less effective?
3. Investigate the nature of collective bargaining in Australia, Canada, and Mexico and the countries that constitute the European Union and then compare and contrast the nature and state of collective bargaining in these areas as well as determine the implications this has for global business.
4. Visit the Web sites for the AFL-CIO (http://www.aflcio.org) and Teamsters (http://www.teamsters.com). What programs does each union offer its members? What are the main issues each union appears to be pursuing? Do these programs and issues appear to be well-matched to the needs of the U.S. labor force?
5. Visit the Web site for the National Labor Relations Board (http://www.nlrb.gov). Of what value is this Web site for employers? Of what value is this Web site for union leaders?

Chapter References

1. Wikipedia. 2005 New York City Transit Strike, http://en.wikipedia.org/wiki/2005_New_York_City_transit_strike.
2. Caudron, S., et al. "The Labor Movement to War," *Workforce*, January 2001, pp. 27–33.
3. McCartin, J. "PATCO, Permanent Replacement and the Loss of Labor's Strike Weapon," *Perspectives on Work*, 10, (1), Summer 2006, pp. 17–19.
4. Bureau of Labor Statistics, http://www.bls.gov/news.release/wkstp.nr0.html.
5. U.S. Bureau of Labor Statistics, Labor Force Statistics from the Current Population Survey, Union Members, http://stats.bls.gov.
6. Ibid.
7. Segal, J. A. "Labor Pains for Union-Free Employers," *HR Magazine*, March 2004, pp. 113–118.
8. 370 U.S. 9 (1962).
9. Wheeler, H., Klaas, F. and Mahony, D. *Workplace Justice Without Unions*. W.E. Upjohn Institute for Employment Research, 2004.
10. Hirsh, S. "Unions Reach Everywhere for Members," *Baltimore Sun*, January 25, 2004, p. ID.
11. Newman, N. "Union and Community Mobilization in the Information Age," *Perspectives on Work*, 6, (2), pp. 9–11.
12. Ibid.
13. Ibid.
14. Lyncheski, J. E. and Heller, L. D. "Cyber Speech Cops," *HR Magazine*, January 2001, pp. 145–150.

READING 12.1

The Future of Unions

Jennifer Schramm

The recent schism in the AFL-CIO, the coalition of U.S. unions created in 1955 when the American Federation of Labor and the Congress of Industrial Organizations merged, has brought about a renewed interest in the future of unions. For some, the split was seen as another step in the slow decline of union membership and influence, while others viewed the development of a new coalition, Change to Win, made up of seven unions and representing around 6 million workers, as an important step in the revitalization of unions in the United States. The aftermath of the union split is likely to be significant, but it is not the only factor that may influence the future of unions. For organizations operating in a global economy, some of the most important union developments may occur overseas, and the dynamics of a global economy where competition for jobs is fierce may also influence the types of workers unions target for recruitment, the formation of union alliances—both within and across nations—and the types of workers who decide to join unions.

Union Development, Union Decline

The National Labor Relations Act of 1935 gave most U.S. workers the right to join or form unions as a way for employees to bargain with employers over pay and working conditions. Union membership in the United States rose steadily over the following years but has declined in the last few decades. The AFL-CIO divide—largely a result of disagreements over the causes of this decline and what to do about it—marks a historic time for labor unions in the United States. Though there is disagreement over what direction unions will take in the future, there is somewhat more agreement both within labor leadership and among outside observers on what factors are likely to be most influenced by the split in the short term: union organizing, new member recruitment tactics and a potentially more focused approach to targeting specific companies. More long-term issues, such as the impact on political alliances, international activities and the changing demographics of union members, are less clear.

Part of the reason why there is disagreement among labor leaders over the best way for unions to move forward may be because there is still no solid consensus on why unions have declined in the United States so dramatically over the past 40 years. Critics of unions argue that they have made it more difficult to complete globally, are too politically entrenched and have created needless conflict between workers and employers that has led to declines in production and competitiveness—thus reducing the number of U.S. jobs that are most likely to be unionized. The changing nature of work and the development of employment legislation that protects workers are also often cited as key reasons why unions have declined—these developments may have led more employees to decide that joining a union was no longer necessary.

Understanding the decline in unions within the United States is made more complicated when considering that trends in union membership in many other countries have been very different. Some labor analysts argue that social and political factors play the most significant role in determining levels of union membership within particular countries. Other labor analysts focus more on the importance of economic trends, citing the growth in international competition from low-wage countries, especially in the manufacturing sector, as the main reason for the decline of manufacturing jobs, the traditional base for union recruitment. Labor analysts emphasizing the importance of economic factors in determining levels of union membership argue that countries where labor union membership remains high are simply responding more slowly than the United States to the new global economic landscape due to their more rigid employment structures.

These two views lead to different scenarios for the development or decline of unions in the United States and in nations where union membership is still relatively high. Those emphasizing the importance of social and political factors argue that union membership in countries where the underlying political and social infrastructure places a strong emphasis on collective versus individual rights and responsibilities is unlikely to shift dramatically as a result of economic factors—or only if economic imperatives are accompanied by major shifts in the political and social climate. On the other hand, those emphasizing economic conditions as the major force behind the growth of unions are more likely to argue that the underlying social and political environment in countries with high union density rates (that is, the proportion of employees who belong to unions) will eventually adjust to the new economic realities with resulting changes in unionization.

This argument is likely to continue as we move forward into a more globalized, integrated world economy because it will help explain how unions and labor laws in different countries will respond to broader economic changes. Not only will companies need to understand the legal and employment implications of different systems underlying the union infrastructure in nations where they operate, but they must also understand that the factors that are likely to influence the way these unions actually operate may also be very different—in some nations unions may take on a political role that extends far beyond the employment realm, while in others the role of unions may be limited to a very small sphere of influence.

Another important factor that labor analysts emphasize is that the rise and fall of unions seem to coincide with major events such as war and prolonged periods of unemployment. Thus, the United States saw a major increase in unions and union membership after both World War I and World War II and during the final years of the Great Depression. This is an important factor to bear in mind for companies investing in international regions—either through establishing their own operations or via their supply chains—where political instability or widespread poverty continue to be significant challenges. In the United States, some labor analysts believe that only the convergence of a number of major historical and economic events would be enough to boost union density rates significantly, and even in this case, they argue, the numbers would eventually begin to decline once again. Clearly, U.S. union leaders on both sides of the schism disagree with this assessment and believe that the decline in unions in the United States can be reversed. Where they differ is in their strategies for bringing this reversal about.

The U.S. Union Split

The Service Employees International Union (SEIU), the Teamsters, UNITE HERE and the United Food and Commercial Workers are now disaffiliated from the national AFL-CIO. The withdrawal of the unions that made up nearly a third of the AFL-CIO's membership and budget has focused a great deal of attention on the differences within the labor movement. Regardless of the reasons behind the division, the repercussions for labor are likely to be significant.

What are these changes likely to be? The top priorities of the Change to Win coalition, which is now the umbrella organization for those unions that withdrew from the AFL-CIO, give a good indication of some of the main changes that are likely to emerge in the aftermath of the split. These priorities are listed in their proposal as follows:

> *"Make it our first priority to help millions more workers form unions so we can build a strong movement for rewarding work in America; unite the strength of everyone who works in the same industry so we can negotiate with today's huge global corporations for everyone's benefit; reflect the diversity and commitment to change of today's workforce; build a growing, independent voice for working people in politics based on economic issues, not party; modernize the strategies, structure and priorities of the AFL-CIO to make these changes possible."*

With the exception of the last priority, which has already been and will continue to be influenced by the union divide itself, each of these priorities has the potential to represent a major shift in union strategy from the past decades and could have a profound impact on unions in the decades ahead.

Recruiting and Organizing

The areas most likely to be influenced by the split are the recruiting and organizing efforts of unions. The SEIU, whose leadership was among the most vocal in criticizing the AFL-CIO, is the largest and fastest growing union in North America. Its membership has grown from 625,000 in 1980 to more than 1.8 million in 2005. Much of this is likely due to the growth in the number of service-sector jobs, many of these in the public sector, which is generally considered much easier to enroll than the private sector—in 2004, 36.4% of public-sector workers belonged to a union, whereas only 7.9% of private-sector employees were union members. However, the SEIU itself credits aggressive organizing as the main reason for its growth in membership.

Organizing and Union Structure

Overall, the new coalition is likely to focus attention on organizing activity at the local, national and, in some cases, even international levels. This may put some pressure on the AFL-CIO to follow suit, so an overall increase in organizing activity may be expected. What is not yet clear is if the schism between the two groups will weaken some of these initiatives. Shortly after the split, the AFL-CIO announced that it would allow locals of disaffiliated unions to apply to be part of the central labor council or state federation through "Solidarity Charters." This represents a major shift in policy as up until now unions that left the national federation also left the AFL-CIO at the local level. The new proposals appear to be aimed at enabling local unions to work together in cities and states, regardless of which of the national coalitions they are affiliated with. However, some observers believe that animosity between labor groups could make this kind of cooperation difficult and is likely to further erode unions' bargaining power. Conversely, greater competition between unions for membership could potentially increase union activities overall and, by increasing membership, also increase unions' bargaining power.

Another potential outcome is a shift to a more centralized model of organization. This model is one that the SEIU has used for several years, and SEIU leaders credit this change as an important factor in the union's growth. However, many local union members and leaders are opposed to the centralized model. "Staffing up" with nonunion members is a key component of the centralized model. There is disagreement over whether this has created greater consistency and strength in campaigns or if it has alienated rank-and-file members. This debate appears likely to be ongoing, so for some unions a shift to the centralized model may be more difficult than anticipated.

Demographics

The types of workers that unions target for membership is likely to adjust to ongoing changes in the workforce. This will probably occur in two main ways. First, the general demographic changes that are leading to a more diverse workforce are likely to lead unions to focus more and more on recruiting women and ethnic and cultural minorities. Secondly, the decline in the types of manufacturing and heavy industrial jobs that characterized the work of the typical union member of the past is giving way to jobs in the service sector, a change that has already influenced union strategies and will continue to do so. A shift to more aggressive organizing tactics that closely target key worker demographic groups such as women, young people and racial or ethnic minorities and job types such as service workers, knowledge workers and temporary workers may therefore be one of the main outcomes of the U.S. union split.

According to a Zogby International poll, demographic factors appeared to have an important impact on whether or not someone would join a union. For example, men were more likely than women to be against unions in their workplace, and single individuals were more likely than married individuals to be in favor of unionizing. Though union membership among young people continued to decline between 2003 and 2004, other polls have found that young people are more likely than older people to support unions. These findings go against the idea that women and young people are not receptive to unionization. It is possible, therefore, that unionization efforts have not been able to connect with these target groups for reasons other than any inherent resistance to unionization within these demographics.

Traditionally women, immigrants and other minority workers were viewed as difficult to recruit into unions. However, recent trends indicate that service-sector unions, in particular, have made recruitment of these groups a central part of their organizing and recruitment strategies. One of the most important ways that unions are likely to do this is to find out exactly what kinds of issues are most likely to galvanize individuals from specific demographic groups to join a union. For example, the AFL-CIO 2004 "Ask a Working Woman Survey" aimed to find out what working women's main priorities were. Unsurprisingly, "finding and keeping a job with basic benefits in today's economy" was the top concern of the 14,000 women who participated in the online survey. Almost half of the women who responded had either been out of work themselves or had a family member or close friend who had been out of work. Around 33% did not have access to affordable health insurance. The survey also found that women who had health insurance were working in industries that were losing jobs while those who said they did not have health insurance were most likely to be working in industries that were growing. The 2005 research on job satisfaction by the Society for Human Resource Management (SHRM) also showed that benefits, especially health insurance, were the most important factor in determining job satisfaction for all workers. An ongoing decline in benefits such as health insurance and pensions could boost unions' ability to organize and recruit, but only if workers view unionization as a way to ensure access to these benefits.

Another factor that unions may emphasize in their recruitment efforts aimed at women is work/life balance. Women rated work/life balance as the single most important job satisfaction factor in SHRM's 2005 *Job Satisfaction Survey Report*. However, according to the Bureau of Labor Statistics (BLS), men are actually slightly more likely than women to have flexible schedules and an increasing number of women work evenings, nights or weekends on a regular basis. SHRM research on benefits (2005) found that, in spite of demand, there had actually been a slight decrease in some types of flexible working arrangements such as job sharing that women may seek out in order to balance work and personal responsibilities. As the costs of benefits, particularly health care, increase, employers looking to boost employee productivity as a way to offset these costs may be less likely to offer flexible working arrangements, and this could have an ongoing impact on employee work/life balance. As a result, unions are likely to continue to focus on benefits, job flexibility and scheduling in their recruitment efforts aimed at women.

The changing demographics of workers in the fastest growing areas of the economy may also drive union recruitment efforts. A good example is the Latino population, which is the fastest growing segment of the U.S. population, according to the U.S. Census Bureau, and makes up a growing proportion of service-sector employees. Unions are already targeting Latino workers in a number of ways. Many unions are providing translators for election ballots and union meetings and other services aimed at helping non-English speaking Latino workers participate more fully in union activities. These kinds of services and initiatives are likely to grow, not only for Spanish-speaking union members but for other members for whom English is not their first language. Especially in those segments of the economy where foreign-born workers make up a large proportion of the workforce, unions are likely to set aside extra resources for these types of services. And because unions are legally obliged to represent all members fairly, the availability of bilingual liaisons between non-English speaking members and their unions and other related services may be seen as a necessary way of guaranteeing that all union members are represented. At the same time, union leaders may find it increasingly difficult to bridge the language divide in some situations. This may be the case not only domestically as unions try to facilitate communication between U.S. and foreign-born members, but also in global efforts to create international labor alliances.

Another challenge for unions will be organizing the large undocumented workforce. While fear of deportation and, in some cases, the nature of the work being done will continue

Table 1 2004 Union Member Demographics

Gender	Percentage of Employees
Men	13.8%
Women	11.1%
Race	
Black	15.1%
White	12.2%
Asian	11.4%
Hispanic or Latino	10.1%
Age	
16 to 24	4.7%
25 to 34	10.6%
35 to 44	13.7%
45 to 54	17.0%
55 to 64	16.8%
65 and older	7.5%
Full-Time/Part-Time	
Full-time workers	13.9%
Part-time workers	6.4%
Public Sector/Private Sector	
Public sector	36.4%
Private sector	7.9%

Source: Bureau of Labor Statistics

Table 2 2004 Wage Differential by Union Membership

$781	2004 median weekly salary, union employees
$612	2004 median weekly salary, nonunion employees

Source: Bureau of Labor Statistics

Table 3 Union Density by State*

Four U.S. States with Highest Union Density	
New York	25.3%
Hawaii	23.7%
Michigan	21.6%
Alaska	20.1%
Four U.S. States With Lowest Union Density	
North Carolina	2.7%
South Carolina	3.0%
Arkansas	4.8%
Mississippi	4.8%

*Union density is the percentage of employed individuals who belong to a union.

Source: Bureau of Labor Statistics

to make it difficult for unions to recruit undocumented workers, falling wages may make unionization more attractive to a growing number of workers. According to a study by the Pew Hispanic Center, Latinos are the only major group of workers who have experienced wage declines in both 2003 and 2004. Labor and immigration experts believe that the growing supply of immigrant workers is likely the main reason behind the drop and that new arrivals are the most likely to experience wage decline. The growing presence of undocumented workers in the U.S. workforce makes it likely that unions will continue to take this population into account in their organizing and recruiting efforts, while lower wages among this population may make them more receptive to unions.

Location is another major demographic factor that unions are likely to continue to focus on, but unions may find it extremely difficult to organize and recruit in those states and regions where union density is currently low. Though union density varies widely depending on geographic location, within regions union density rates do not appear to have changed drastically over the past decade. States with the lowest union density rates tend to be located in the South, and of the four states that reported union membership rates below 5% in 2004, both North Carolina (2.7%) and South Carolina (3.0%) continued to record the lowest union membership rates as they have done each year since the date became available in 1995. The states with the highest union membership rates (over 20%) have also remained stable: New York, Hawaii, Michigan and Alaska have all had rates above 20% every year since 1995. Unions may attempt to step up their organizing efforts in states that currently have low union density by taking different approaches in rural and metropolitan areas, shifting resources to these areas and trying to develop strategic regional alliances.

Industries and Work Organization

Along with changing demographics that have caused unions to rethink their recruitment and organizing strategies, the changing nature of work itself has been perhaps the single biggest issue that has caused unions to reexamine the tactics they use to recruit workers. Disagreement over the implications of new ways of working and the growth of new industries may also have been the main factors behind the U.S. union split. The unions leaving the AFLCIO were

Table 4 Potential Targeted Occupations With Largest Expected Employment Growth Through 2012

Job	Current Employment (Millions)	Projected Growth*
Nursing aide	1.3	25%
Customer service	1.9	24%
Food preparation	2.0	23%
Janitorial	2.2	18%
Waiter/waitress	2.1	18%
Retail sales	4.1	15%
Cashier	3.4	13%

*Projections of job growth from 2002 to 2012
Source: Bureau of Labor Statistics

dominated by the service sector. According to some labor experts, because many service-sector jobs are not unionized and wages in many of these types of jobs are often lower than those of the more established unionized sectors, the unions made up of members in the service sector are more likely to be focused on recruitment in order to increase bargaining power and gain access to the kinds of benefits that members of the more established unions already have.

Related to industrial changes is the growth in temporary work, which may play an increasingly significant role in union strategies. Not only are unions likely to target temporary workers as potential members, but the use of temporary replacement workers to offset the threat of strikes may become much more common and could act to reduce unions' bargaining power. This recently occurred when Northwest Airlines' mechanics union, American Mechanics Fraternal Association (AMFA), went on strike. Northwest used replacement mechanics, including some former workers at major airlines who were laid off after 9/11, to continue services. The outcome of the strike, which is still ongoing at the time of writing, could impact strategies of both unions and companies. More companies may decide to put together contingency plans using temporary replacement workers in the case of a strike and, in some cases, shift to the use of temporary contract workers on an ongoing basis. For unions, the incident may lead to more mergers and consolidations. One important factor in the Northwest mechanics strike was that other Northwest unions, including those representing pilots, flight attendants, ramp workers and ticket agents, all decided not to honor AMFA's picket lines. Some observers felt this may have been due to AMFA's "go-it-alone" strategy, which may work well for skilled workers in times when the economy and labor market are buoyant, but may be less successful when the job market is slack.

This leads to the next category of workers that unions are likely to increasingly target—skilled and knowledge workers. For those skilled workers who are already in unions, like the mechanics in the Northwest strike, a more challenging global economy may lead to the consolidation of smaller unions into larger unions as a way to leverage bargaining power. For some of the larger service-sector unions, such as the SEIU and the Teamsters, this strategy of growth is viewed as the best way to deal with the growth of multinational companies that have themselves increased their reach through an ongoing cycle of mergers and acquisitions. Though many rank-and-file members may disagree with this approach, preferring looser, more democratic management structures, a growing number of smaller unions made up mainly of skilled workers may decide that their bargaining power can only be increased by joining in with larger unions, even if these are dominated by low-skilled, low-wage workers. Unions will also continue to try to recruit white-collar knowledge workers. Historically, unions have been weak among professionals in fields like accounting, banking, finance and hightech, and most experts believe that it would take a major attitudinal shift among workers in these industries for unions to make inroads in these areas. However, some believe it might be possible if large numbers of knowledge workers are eventually faced with significant wage and benefit decreases or job loss due to global competition. Conversely, the threat of offshoring could inhibit this as workers willingly accept cuts in order to keep their jobs.

Unions in a Global Economy

Changing their tactics to adjust to this shift to a global economy is one of the main issues preoccupying the unions that left the AFL-CIO. There are two main strategies that appear to be emerging: first, targeting specific multinational companies for international campaigns; and second, putting more resources into organizing workers at either targeted companies or within specific industries across the globe. For example, the SEIU has placed global issues at the center of its "Uniting Our Strength to Win Big" campaign, in large part as a response to the offshoring trend. The union explains why global strength is such a major part of its overall strategy in the following way: "Huge global service-sector companies routinely cross national borders and industry lines as they search for places where they can shift operations to exploit workers with the lowest possible pay and benefits. To confront this challenge, SEIU will step up its mutual support alliances with unions in other nations, with the goal of uniting workers who do the same type of work around the world." The aim of building transnational union alliances has been a part of the debate within labor for some time, so it is not yet clear if these new developments will have any more of an impact than past efforts. However, the offshoring trend and the use of technology to bring together groups may encourage the development of international union alliances in a new way. In addition, the shift of investment and the establishment of operations in countries such as India, China and

Eastern Europe may mean that union developments in these key offshoring destinations may have a global impact regardless of whether they are locally, nationally or internationally led.

Global Union Alliances and Federations

In 2000 the Union Network Federation (UNI) was created with the intention of building an alliance that could represent workers across many countries. According to UNI, "when companies are local, unions can be local; when companies are national, unions must be national; when companies are global, unions must be global." Apart from UNI, there are several other global trade union bodies that could have some influence on the development of unions globally in the future. There are currently 10 Global Union Federations (GUFs), which are the international representatives of unions in specific industry sectors or occupational groups. The International Confederation of Free Trade Unions (ICFTU) represents most national trade union centers or federations. Individual unions may belong to several GUFs, depending on the number of industries that belong to that union, and many relate to the ICFTU through their national trade union federation. While many of these global union bodies have been around for many years, their influence may grow if the impact of globalization leads to more union activity at the international level.

Targeting Multinational Corporations

Because the right to strike is not uniform across borders, UNI Global Union campaigns are instead limited to campaigns that focus on the image and reputation of the company in question. The development of global union alliances may therefore mean an increase in campaigns that target specific companies. These types of campaigns, usually aimed at multinationals, can include lawsuits, consumer boycotts and appeals to shareholders, community leaders and politicians. Based on current trends, the main targets for these types of actions in the near future could be multinational retailers and wholesalers. UNI has already used this tactic in campaigns targeting German and British retailers with operations around Europe. It recently announced a program to step up global organizing at Wal-Mart, focusing on new organizing initiatives in countries such as Korea, Russia and India.

Unionization in Key Offshoring Destination Countries

Multinational companies adding operations in major offshoring destinations may also be affected by national unionization trends in these countries. For example, Honda Motor recently incurred a loss of millions of dollars through lost output during a labor dispute at its unit in Gurgaon, India. India's business and political leaders were quick to label the dispute, in which some employees were injured in a confrontation with local police, as an isolated incident that had no bearing on the investment climate in India overall. But the incident served as a reminder that labor disputes in one of the world's top offshoring destination countries can have a fairly significant financial impact.

China has also recently experienced a grassroots movement to raise worker awareness of their legal rights. According to the Chinese Labor Bulletin, in 2004 alone around 3 million Chinese workers joined a total of 57,000 protests across the country. The use of technology to connect activists has played a major role in the growth of this movement, creating networks of training centers, legal aid clinics and other forms of employee support. Worker shortages in many parts of the country may strengthen this trend, particularly among workers in the manufacturing sector.

Increasingly, foreign investors will need to consider the impact of labor issues in offshoring destination countries. In democratic countries such as India, labor disputes may more quickly lead to legal changes in employment law, while in countries such as China, a growing grassroots labor movement could have a much wider political impact.

Political Implications

These and other global developments may be leading unions to rethink their traditional alliances. Not only may more U.S.-based unions begin working with international bodies such as UNI and other unions around the world, they may also get much more involved with NGOs working internationally to establish basic labor standards and to target specific companies and labor practices through protests, boycotts and other types of activism. Greater involvement in these types of initiatives may also play a role in unions' attempts to involve and recruit young people. By tapping into global causes that many students and other young people are already involved in, unions may attempt to create a bridge between these causes and the labor movement in general.

One alliance that some observers believe may weaken as a result of the union split is that between unions and the U.S. Democratic Party. Because one of the key priorities of the Change to Win coalition is to "build a growing, independent voice for working people in politics based on economic issues, not party," along with the coalition's emphasis on recruitment over political lobbying, some political observers believe that the traditional support of unions for the Democratic Party may wane. However, some union insiders predict that union donations to political campaigns will not change significantly.

Implications for HR Professionals

The divisions within the U.S. labor movement could lead unions into many different directions in the years ahead. HR professionals will need to continue to keep up to date with changes in union tactics, alliances and recruiting methods, as changes over the coming years could be significant. Worker demographics, along with the growing importance of labor disputes and alliances across the globe, will all shape the interactions between unions and employers. The philosophical divides within the labor movement itself—between those who aim to reinvent unions as centralized organizations focusing on a limited number of employment issues but on the global scale and those who see unions as a broader social movement led by decentralized, local rank-and-file members—are also likely to continue to clash. No one is sure what the main outcomes will be over the long term, but for employers and HR professionals, understanding developments in unions will continue to be critical, even as the task grows more complex.

Source: Workplace Visions, 4, (2005) Society for Human Resource Management. Reprinted by permission.

REFERENCES

AFL-CIO. (2005, August 11). AFL-CIO proposes to leadership to unite local labor movements through new Solidarity Charters [News release]. Retrieved from www.aflcio.org/mediacenter/prsptm/pr08112005.cfm.

AFL-CIO. (2004). *Ask a working woman survey report.* Retrieved from www.aflcio.org/issues/jobseconomy/women/speakout/upload/aawwreport.pdf.

Armour, S. (2005, July 25). Breakaway groups crumble labor's once-solid foundation. *USA Today.*

Baker & McKenzie. (2001). *Worldwide guide to trade unions and works councils.* Chicago, IL: CCH Incorporated.

Bernstein, A. (2005, August 8). So long, AFL-CIO. Now what? *Business Week.*

Bhatnagar, P (2005, August 24). Is India's outsourcing honeymoon over? *CNN Money.*

Burke, M. E. (2005). *2005 benefits survey report.* Alexandria, VA: Society for Human Resource Management.

Esen, E. (2005). *2005 job satisfaction survey report.* Alexandria, VA: Society for Human Resource Management.

Esen, E. (2005). *Job benefits survey report.* Alexandria, VA: Society for Human Resource Management.

Fantasia, R., & Voss, K. (2004). *Hard work: Remaking the American labor movement.* Berkeley, CA: University of California Press.

Gordon, M., & Turner, L. (Eds.). (2000): *Transnational cooperation among labor unions.* Ithaca, NY: ILR Press.

Grossman, R. (2005, May). Unions follow suit. *HR Magazine.*

Harrod, J., & O'Brien, R. (Eds.). (2002). *Global unions? Theory and strategies of organized labor in the global political economy.* London: Routledge.

Labor unrest in India: Honda loses over $27 million. (2005, July 27). *GG2.Net News.* Retrieved from www.gg2.net/viewnews.asp?nid=1216&tid=top_stories&catid=Top%20Stories.

Lawrence, J. (2005, July 26). Democrats ponder labor split's effect at election time. *USA Today.*

Lester, W. (2001, August 29). Poll: Labor unions gain sympathy. *Associated Press.*

Lipset, S., & Meltz, N. (2004). *The paradox of American unionism.* Ithaca, NY: Cornell University Press.

Lund, J. (2004, Spring). Making unions more accessible to Latino workers. *Working USA, 7,* 4, pp. 70–77.

Maher, K. (2005, August 18). Union federation gathers to draft Wal-Mart plans. *The Wall Street Journal.*

Majority of workers wouldn't join unions, Zogby poll finds. (2005, July 26). *Bloomberg News.*

Maynard, M. (2005, August 21). Well-laid plan kept Northwest flying in strike. *The New York Times.*

Nissen, B. (2003, Spring). Alternative strategic directions for the U.S. labor movement: Recent scholarship. *Labor Studies Journal, 28,* 1.

Paulson, A. (2005, July 27). Union split: sign of decline or revival? *Christian Science Monitor.*

Roberts, D. (2005, August 22). Waking up to their rights. *Business Week.*

Seyfarth Shaw LLP. (2005, August 1). The AFL-CIO schism: Why employers should care and what they should be thinking about. *Seyfarth Shaw Management Alert.*

Sirocchi, A. (2005, May 4). Latinos left behind U.S. economic growth. *Tri-City Herald.*

Soto, A. (2005, August 24). Unions plan fight against Wal-Mart: *Reuters.*

RESOURCES

www.afl-cio.org AFL-CIO

www.bls.gov Bureau of Labor Statistics

www.changetowin.org Change to Win Coalition

www.icftu.org International Confederation of Free Trade Unions

www.shrm.org Society for Human Resource Management

www.union-network.org Union Network International

READING 12.2

A Big Chill on a "Big Hurt:" Genuine Interest in Employment of Salts in Assessing Protection Under the National Labor Relations Act

Jeffrey A. Mello

Abstract

As union membership has continued to decline steadily in the US, union organizers have become more creative and vigilant with their organizing strategies. Chief among these strategies has been "salting," a process by which unions attempt to organize employees from the inside rather than the outside. The Supreme Court has ruled that, under the National Labor Relations Act, "salts" cannot be discriminated against solely on the basis of their status as salts. This paper examines employer responses to resist salting efforts, including a recent decision by the National Labor Relations Board, which redefines the landscape under which salting activities can be conducted and considered protected activity.

Union membership has been declining steadily in the US since the US Bureau of Labor Statistics began tracking such numbers 25 years ago. At that time, 20.1% of the US workforce was unionized. By 2008, only 12% of workforce was unionized with a continuous steady decline having been recorded over that time. In 2008, public sector unionization stood at 35.9% while private sector unionization had declined to 7.4%, with both percentages having each lost a full percentage point over the preceding 3 years (Bureau of Labor Statistics 2008). This steady 25 year decline, however, was not a new trend but rather the continuation of a trend that pre-dated the Bureau of Labor Statistics tracking (Curms *et al.* 1990).

This decline can be attributed to a number of factors. First, the movement of many traditionally union-held jobs to developing countries overseas to take advantage of lower labor costs has been increasingly dramatically in recent years. Second, changes in the nature of the employment relationship, including the increased transience of the workforce and the erosion of the assumption, or presumption, of lifetime employment and the growing trend toward part-time and contract employment have impacted workers' interest in being represented by unions. Third, the rise in undocumented or illegal workers who are unprotected or afraid to protest and/or organize has affected unions. Fourth, many of the jobs being created in our economy are in areas in which unions have no experience organizing, such as call centers, and involve workers who work from their homes or remote locations, rather than at the employer's physical facility. Fifth, an increasing number of employers are resisting and fighting union organizing attempts more so than in the past. More than 75% of employers confronted with union organizing campaigns now hire consultants and an entire new industry of "union avoidance firms," often consisting of former union leaders, has been established over the past three decades with anti-union success rates that generally exceed 90% (Maher 2005; Logan 2006). Sixth, unions themselves have been blamed for not keeping up with the times and failing to address the concerns of the fastest growing segments of the hourly labor force, including women, minorities and immigrants. Finally, the alleged anti-union doctrine and teachings of business schools have been cited as promoting and encouraging more adversarial relations between employers and unions (Gould 2008; Anonymous 2003).

Unions have responded to declines in membership by becoming much more aggressive in their recruiting tactics. One of the main strategies now being employed by unions is "salting," a process by which union organizers attempt to organize a workplace internally. Originally implemented in the early 1970s in the construction industry (Raudabaugh 2008), salting involves a union representative applying for and subsequently obtaining employment with the organization whose workers are being targeted for unionization. Salting provides union organizers with more direct and regular access to employees who are the target of the unionization drive that would be realized by organizing from the outside. More recently salting activity has evolved into a means of political and economic warfare against employers as the basis for unfair labor practice allegation filings with the National Labor Relations Board (NLRB). This paper discusses the legal foundation upon which salting activities are based, the recent court activity and NLRB rulings in salting cases, subsequent management reactions to curtail salting activity and the judgments on the legality of such activities under the National Labor Relations Act (NLRA; 29 U.S.C. § 151 et. seq.). These decisions have significant implications not only for unions as they attempt to maintain their viability but also for employers in ensuring that their management practices and actions do not run afoul of the NLRA.

Supreme Court Provides Protection to Salts Under the National Labor Relations Act

The Supreme Court first addressed salting in *NLRB v. Town and Country Electric, Inc.* (116 S. Ct. 459, 1995) where it found that paid union representatives who attempt to gain employment with a specific employer whose workers they are trying to organize cannot be discriminated against *solely* on the basis of their status as "salts." Even though a salt may have no intention of remaining with the employer subsequent to a successful organizing drive, the Court found that union salts are considered "employees" under the NLRA and hence, are entitled to the full range of rights expressly provided to employees under the statute. As a result, any failure to consider or hire otherwise qualified salts, as well as the decision to terminate a salt once the salt's intentions are made known or union organizing activities begin, solely based on salt status, is unlawful under the NLRA. While an employer has no per se obligation to hire a salt, no job applicant can be denied employment solely based on her or his status as a salt.

Town and Country constituted what was described as a "chess match" between employers and union organizers as each attempted to assert their rights under the NLRA (Mello 1998). A previous Supreme Court ruling, *Lechmere, Inc. v. NLRB* (112 S. Ct. 841, 1992), had strengthened management rights in resisting organizing activity by disallowing the practice of union organizers approaching employees on the employer's property; in this case, the employer-owned employee parking lot. Salting served as a union response to the restrictions placed on union organizer access to employees in *Lechmere* and the *Town and Country* decision validated the use of salting as a tactic to organize workers. While *Town and Country* was a significant victory for organized labor in prohibiting employers from refusing to hire an applicant or subsequently terminate an employee who is attempting to organize its workers, the decision didn't address the question of whether a salt can intentionally lie as part of her or his employment application process about his or her status as a salt and/or the intention to organize the workplace. More so, to the extent that *Town and Country* gave unions the upper hand in the "chess match," the decision certainly gave employers incentive to respond by monitoring more closely the specific activities of union organizing efforts.

Intentional Misrepresentation in the Employment Application Process

In 2002 the Seventh Circuit addressed the extent to which a salt may lie about organizing intentions in *Hartman Bros. Heating and Air Conditioning, Inc.* v. *NLRB* (280 F.3d 1110, 2002). Hartman Bros., an Indiana-based heating and air-conditioning contractor, hired Starnes, who had stated on his employment application that he had been laid off from his previous job which paid him $11 per hour. The truth was that Starnes had taken a formal leave of absence from his position so that he might work for a union to assist with its organizing efforts. As the position at Hartman for which Starnes had applied paid only $8.50 per hour, suspicions might have been aroused if Starnes stated that he was still employed at a job which paid $11 per hour. Immediately upon being hired, Starnes informed Hartman Bros. that he was a union salt who intended to organize the company. Hartman responded by telling Starnes to leave the workplace without formally terminating him.

The job for which Starnes had applied and been hired required driving. Consequently, as part of his application Starnes was required to provide information about his driving history and stated that he had received one speeding ticket. Hartman Bros. then informed him that its liability insurer would need to check his driving record and that Starnes would be ineligible for employment if, as a result of this investigation, the insurer refused to provide liability coverage for his driving. Four hours after Starnes had been ordered off the premises for declaring his salting intentions, the insurer contacted Hartman Bros. and disclosed that Starnes had received not one, but two speeding tickets and that he would be denied coverage. Starnes was immediately discharged as a result of this misrepresentation and his disqualification for insurance coverage.

Around the time Starnes applied for a position with Hartman, Till also applied for employment. Till, however, was accompanied by a known union organizer, who declared that he was a union organizer and wore a baseball cap with the union's logo. Hartman refused to hire Till.

The court found Hartman Bros. in violation of the NLRA in its refusal to hire Till as it found that this refusal was motivated solely by hostility toward unions. Hartman was ordered to cease and desist in its discriminatory practices against salts and other union supporters and to hire Till with backpay, in line with the Supreme Court ruling in *Town and Country.*

Starnes' case was more complicated than Till's. In justifying its decision to terminate Starnes, Hartman cited an Indiana law which prohibits any person from knowingly or intentionally making a false or misleading written statement in seeking employment. The court, however, found that if the state statute was being cited as a means for an employer to deny employment to an individual based on an applicant's lies about salt status, the statute would be pre-empted by the National Labor Relations Act. Any lie about salt status would be immaterial to the hiring decision nor to an applicant's qualifications for the job for which (s)he had applied and be based on a presumably erroneous employer assumption that the individual would not be a bona fide employee at any point in time. The court further found that criminalizing any applicant deception over salting intentions could only be a strong-arm means of discouraging salting, which would be further at odds with the Supreme Court's decision in *Town and Country.* The fact that Starnes lied about his being laid off by his previous employer would not be grounds for dismissal as it was done solely to hide his salting intentions and the NLRA would preempt the Indiana statute that prohibits individuals from making false or misleading statements as part of an employment application.

The Seventh Circuit did concur with the earlier NLRB ruling that the discharge of Starnes based on his driving record was legitimate as the action was done pursuant to a company policy that had been uniformly applied to all employees without animus toward an employee's participation with or attitudes toward unions. Hartman Bros. was, however, required to pay Starnes backpay, for the 4 h that had elapsed between his arrival at work and being sent home upon receipt of the insurance report. The court further ruled that the unfair labor practice committed by Hartman Bros. was not the discharge of Starnes but rather, sending him home and depriving him of the opportunity to begin organizing prior to the arrival of the insurance report.

Implications

Hartman Bros. dealt employers another post-*Town and Country* blow in finding that paid union organizers *can* lie on their job applications about their affiliation with unions as salts but *cannot* misrepresent facts about their credentials, skills or qualifications for employment. Lying about salt status is not material to a hiring decision because, under *Town and Country*, an employer cannot reject a job applicant solely on the basis of being a salt, union employee or union supporter. Any applicable state statutes which might make it illegal for applicants to lie or make misrepresentations on their employment applications are preempted by the National Labor Relations Act when any such lies or misrepresentations pertain to any union affiliation or activity.

The *Hartman Bros.* decision represented another victory for unions that further put employers on the defensive. Under *Hartman Bros.*, unions have less difficulty placing paid organizers in the employ of companies they are attempting to organize. To prevent unfair labor practice charges from being levied, employers need to be sure that any criteria used for screening and selection of employees is objective, valid, essential for job performance and not based, in any way, on an applicant's actual or perceived salt status. Although no cases have been heard relative to "perceived" salt status, the Seventh Circuit's ruling in *Hartman Bros.* makes it likely that those applicants perceived to be salts would enjoy the same protection as actual salts. One weapon employers might have to counter salting in light of *Hartman Bros.* would be the implementation of a policy that prohibits any employee from simultaneously holding any full or part-time employment with another employer, particularly one within the same industry. Any such policy may or may not be upheld in a given jurisdiction based on local laws and general attitudes toward labor but its chances of success are more likely if enforced in a uniform manner toward all employees.

Employers Fight Back—Use of Preferential Hiring Criteria

The Seventh Circuit provided unions with a significant victory in *Hartman Bros* which affirmed their rights to use aggressive salting tactics as a means of organizing a workplace. As unions have gained the upper hand in their "chess match" with employers, employers have not been passive in fighting aggressive union organizing efforts. A post-Hartman Seventh Circuit ruling, *Operating Engineers Local 150* v. *NLRB* (325 F.3d 818, 7th Cir, 2003), provided employers with a significant victory in their efforts to fight union salting tactics.

Local 150 involved Brandt Construction Company, an Illinois highway contractor, which provides municipal road construction, bridge building, concrete and asphalt paving, sewer and water utility work and demolition work. Brandt had utilized a long-term preferential hiring policy whereby employment applications submitted by current or former employees and those filed by individuals referred by current employees received preferential consideration over applications received from non-referred walk-in applicants. Brandt also gave preferential consideration to applicants referred by equal employment opportunity service providers under a prior conciliation agreement entered into with the US Department of Labor which required Brandt to increase the numbers of women and minorities employed on each job pursuant to federal, state and local equal employment opportunity regulations. Brandt allowed any of these applicants who receive preferential treatment to apply for employment at any time without an appointment while walk-in applications were only accepted on Mondays and only when the company was hiring.

These hiring practices and policies were formalized and posted at the time Brandt entered into its agreement with the Department of Labor. The posting noted that applications would only be "considered current for a period of two weeks......After fourteen days the employment application expires and any individual interested in employment must complete a new application, if they are being accepted. We do not accept applications when we are not hiring." The posting further specified that Brandt showed preference for applicants in the following descending order; (1) current employees of the company; (2) past employees with proven safety, attendance and work records; (3) applicants recommended by supervisors; (4) applicants recommended by current non-supervisory employees; (5) unknown (walk-in) applicants.

Shortly after the conciliation agreement and Brandt's award of a large job, Local 150 sent some of its members to Brandt to apply for employment. The union members had been told by Local 150 to apply wearing union hats or other insignia and further instructed to indicate on their applications that they were salts and had been sent by the union for the express purpose of organizing Brandt. At the same time, Brandt received 32 referral applications as well as 20 additional non-union walk-in applications. Brandt hired a total of eight applicants, all of whom had been referred. For the remainder of that year, Brandt hired 29 additional applicants, 28 of whom were referrals, from a pool of 67 referrals. Consistent with posted policy, all new hires were offered employment within 14 days of their application.

In response to the hiring, Local 150 filed an unfair labor practice charge against Brandt with the National Labor Relations Board. The union alleged that Brandt had "changed, limited and made more onerous its hiring practices and procedures with the purpose of making it more difficult for applicants with pro-union sentiments to apply or obtain employment," in direct violation of Section 8(a)(1) of the National Labor Relations Act. Several months later Local 150 filed an additional unfair labor charge against Brandt, alleging that the company refused to hire union members despite the fact that all of new hires at Brandt at that point had been former employees, referrals from current employees or supervisors or referrals from equal employment opportunity service providers and the company had also not accepted any walk-in applications. Local 150 later filed a third unfair labor charge which alleged that Brandt "has in effect and continues to maintain and apply a hiring practice of giving preference in hiring to referred applicants regardless of their skill level over walk-in or unknown applicants" and that "such policy is designed to discriminate, interfere and prevent union-affiliated applicants from being considered for employment ... and is designed to deter the effects of union organization in violation of the Act."

The court found that while Brandt's policy clearly made it more difficult for union applicants and salts to gain employment, it did not violate the NLRA as the manner in which all applicants had been hired, by referral, excluded *all* walk-in applicants, regardless of whether or not these individuals were affiliated with a union. In issuing this decision in favor of the employer the court relied on two earlier NLRB rulings. The first was *Zurn/N.E.P.C.O.* (329 N.L.R.B. 484, 1999), which held that a hiring policy which gives preference to current and former employees, as well as referrals by management, did not discriminate on the basis of union activities because "the policy does not on its face preclude or limit the possibilities for consideration of applicants with union preferences or backgrounds." The second, *Custom Topsoil, Inc.* (328 N.L.R.B. 446, 1999), held that an employer did not discriminate on the basis of union membership when it differentiated between "stranger" and "familiar" applicants as this differentiation did not involve a per se distinction between union and nonunion applicants.

In issuing its ruling favoring Brandt, the court relied on the fact that Brandt applied its preferential hiring policy in a nondiscriminatory manner with applications submitted by all walk-ins rejected under a long-standing and consistently applied policy, absent of any direct anti-union animus. The court also noted and commended Brandt for improving its employment of women and minority applicants pursuant to its conciliation agreement with the Department of Labor. The court found that the critical factor that prevented Local 150 members from being hired was the fact that they freely chose to apply as walk-ins, traditionally the applicants of last choice for Brandt under its publicized policy. Brandt gave union applicants exactly the same consideration as all other walk-in or unknown applicants and union members were in no way prevented from obtaining a referral from a preferential applicant source if they so chose.

The NLRB ruling in *Local 150* has found support in subsequent cases. The Board also ruled in favor of another employer who used preferential hiring criteria in *Ken Maddox Heating and Air Conditioning, Inc.* (340 N.L.R.B. No. 7, 2003). Maddox, an Indiana HVAC contractor, gave preference in hiring to applicants it had previously employed as well as to applicants referred by current employees and business associates, similar to Brandt. This long-standing policy was challenged when only one of 37 qualified overt union applicants was hired while 55 nonunion applicants were hired to fill 56 vacancies. The NLRB noted that because Maddox's policy had been in place for some time, this fact invalidated the allegation that the policy was specifically implemented to counter a salting campaign. The Board further found that the policy "was not inherently destructive of employee rights" or "sufficient, by itself, to establish animus." Citing *Brandt* as precedent the NLRB found that the general use of referral policies is a legitimate and justifiable employment practice. In *Maddox* the referral practice did not create a closed hiring system, which effectively screened out union applicants, nor was it applied in any kind of inconsistent or disparate manner.

Employers Find Additional Support for Their Use of Restricted Hiring Criteria

The victory for employers in *Local 150* was only the beginning as other employers have succeeded in their attempts to fight union organization and salting through the use of restricted, rather than preferential, hiring criteria. *Kanawha Stone Company, Inc.* (334 N.L.R.B. No. 28, 2001) involved an employer whose hiring policy consisted of an assessment of specific hiring needs on a particular job, based on applications filled out on the employee's first day of work. The company did not maintain any applicant pool or hiring lists unless some kind of mass hiring was being conducted. All hiring was handled by superintendents at individual job sites rather than at the main office. Kanawha's hiring criteria restricted hiring to three groups of individuals; (1) employees on temporary lay off, (2) former employees and (3) referrals from existing employees. Applicants not falling into one of these categories were not considered for employment. This long-standing policy had been in effect since the company's inception. After a group of union members applied for employment at the main office, rather than at an individual job site, and who did not fit the above criteria were not hired, the union filed charges with the National Labor Relations Board.

Refusal to hire cases are considered under a burden-shifting scheme established by the Third Circuit in *NLRB v. FES* (*A Division of Thermo Power*, 301 F.3d 83, 3rd Cir., 2002). This case established the following criteria by which refusal-to-hire cases are analyzed:

> *To establish a discriminatory refusal to hire, the General Counsel must....first show: (1) that the respondent was hiring, or had concrete plans to hire, at the time of the alleged unlawful conduct; (2) that the applicants had experience or training relevant to the announced or generally known requirement of the position for hire, or in the alternative, that the employer has not adhered uniformly to such requirement, or that the requirements were themselves pretextual or were applied as a pretext for discrimination; and (3) that anti-union animus contributed to the decision not to hire the applicants. Once this is established, the burden will shirt to the respondent to show that it would not have hired the applicants even in the absence of their union activity or affiliation.*

When the NLRB applied this criterion to *Kanawha*, it found that while union applicants were excluded from consideration for employment and some anti-union animus appeared to be present, Kanawha met its burden of proof by showing that it lawfully failed to consider the union applicants because they simply failed to meet any of its legitimate hiring criteria.

While *Kanawha* dealt with a flat-out refusal to hire, an employer in another case found a more specific means of excluding union members from consideration for employment. This criteria, refusal to hire based on wage incompatibility, was challenged in the NLRB ruling *Kelley Construction of Indiana, Inc* (333 N.L.R.B. No. 148, 2001). Kelley utilized the hiring criterion that new employees be accustomed to earning wages in line with those paid by Kelley. This policy ideally would allow Kelley to retain employees for as long as possible and minimize disruptions and costs incurred through excessive turnover. When Kelley refused to hire 27 union applicants based on this criterion, the union filed charges with the NLRB. The NLRB had previously established a precedent for wage disparity as a legitimate means of selecting applicants in the absence of evidence of disparate application to union members in *Wireways, Inc* (309 N.L.R.B. 245 1992). In *Kelley*, the Board applied the *FES* burden-shifting criterion in concluding that Kelley's hiring decisions were made without regard to the prospective salts' union affiliation because the salts did not satisfy the neutral and legitimate hiring criteria of wage compatibility.

Subsequent to *Kelley*, however, the NLRB was presented with another salting case involving wage incompatibility criteria in which it ruled that wage disparity was not a legitimate justification for denial of employment. In *Contractors Labor Pool* (CLP; 335 N.L.R.B. No. 25, 2001) the employer enforced a "30% rule," which involved rejection of any applicant whose most recent wages differed by more than 30% from CLP's starting wages. When challenged by a union, CLP's 30% rule had been newly established and based on a study of worker retention which calculated the "break point" at which employees would be less likely to remain in the employ of CLP.

The NLRB found that while CLP had shown a legitimate business reason for adopting the policy that appeared not to be motivated by anti-union animus, the policy was "inherently destructive" of employees' NLRA rights to organize as the net effect of the policy was to "disqualify automatically virtually all applicants who had recently earned union contract wages" which "directly penalizes those who have exercised their protected right to work in an organized workforce and imposes a formidable threshold barrier to protected organizational activity in the unorganized workforces of CLP and its contractor clients." The Board considered this outcome analogous to the theory of disparate impact applied to anti-discrimination cases heard under Title VII of the Civil Rights Act of 1964. In disparate impact cases, all individuals are treated the same but the treatment results in different outcomes or consequences for different groups.

While the NLRB acknowledged that the 30% policy impacted both union and non-union applicants, this fact did not mitigate the "obvious and profound discriminatory effect" it had on those who rights were "expressly protected under the NLRA." This was based on the finding that the policy, regardless of its intent, excluded virtually *all* applicants with union history while only excluding *some* applicants with non-union wage history. The outcome was that the only way to gain employment with CLP was through prior employment with another nonunion employer.

Despite the fact that the NLRB accepted the employer's legitimate business interest in employee retention as the basis for its wage compatibility policy, it held that a balancing act was necessary between the legitimate rights of CLP'S business interests and those of employees under the NLRA. Because the 30% rule was "not essential to the successful operation of CLP's business," the "destructive direct, broad, severe and enduring impact of this rule on employee rights" had to receive priority in the balancing act.

The Board did note that it was not making a blanket ruling in *CLP* on the legitimacy of any other wage compatibility rules "that may have a lesser exclusionary effect or that may be more narrowly drawn and essential to an employer's business operation." While *Kelley* provided affirmation for employer wage disparity policies, *CLP* refined that ruling by articulating the need for wage disparity cases to be examined on a case-by-case basis relative to balancing employer needs with employee rights. The end result is that while employers may be able to justify wage disparity employment screening policies, they clearly need to be able to show that such policies have a non-disparate impact on union members and/or prospective salts.

The Latest Chapter—Genuine Interest in Employment

As the courts and NLRB have ruled on wage disparity policies and clarified the criteria under which they should be considered, another issue has arisen regarding salting and employer responses to salting activities. This issue concerns whether prospective salts need to show a genuine interest in actually working for the employer to which they've applied in order to received protection of their salting activities under the NLRA.

In *Phelps Dodge Corp. v. NLRB* (313 U.S. 177, 1941), one of the first Supreme Court cases under the NLRA, it was held that the statute made it an unfair labor practice by an employer to discriminate against applicants for employment in addition to actual employees. As noted, the Supreme Court ruled in *Town and Country Electric* that job applicants who are also salts are considered "employees" under the NLRA and entitled to protection afforded by the statute, particularly section 8(a)(3) which prohibits an employer from "discrimination in regard to hire or tenure of employment or any term or condition of employment to encourage or discourage membership in any labor organization." In other words, job applicants are de facto "employees" under the NLRA. Such protection has served as the foundation for salting activities by union organizers but a new NLRB ruling, *Toering Electric Company* (Toering Electric Company and Foster Electric, Inc., and Local Union No. 275, International Brotherhood of Electrical Workers, 351 NLRB No. 18, 2007), answered the question of whether an applicant needed to be genuinely interested in employment to qualify for protection under the NLRA.

In 1987 the President of the International Brotherhood of Electrical Workers (IBEW) announced an aggressive campaign to begin targeted nonunion employers for unionization via salting. Indeed in a videotaped speech produced and distributed at that time he encouraged local unions to unite with him in "driving the non-union element out of business." In tandem with this, the IBEW issued a Construction Organizing Membership Education Training (COMET) manual, which provided guidance for local unions on how to conduct effective salting campaigns. The COMET manual emphasized organizing strategies that would cause employers to scale back their businesses, be forced to leave the union's jurisdiction entirely or even completely go out of business. The driving force behind such economic outcomes would be the filing of unfair labor practices charges against employers at every opportunity. Such charges would impose immediate and usually substantial costs on employers as they attempted to defend themselves as well as disrupt the employer's workforce and operations via a series of continuous and ongoing unfair labor practice allegations.

In 1994 Toering Electric became a target of Local 275 of the IBEW's salting campaign. IBEW filed charges alleging that Toering refused to hire or even consider any union-affiliated individuals who applied for employment, in violation of section 8(a)(3) of the NLRA. In 1995 Toering agreed to settle the allegations by offering employment to six members of Local 275 but all six failed to show up for work. Prior to the settlement, Local 275 boasted in its newsletter that it succeeded in inflicting "a big hurt" on Toering's business.

In 1996 Local 275 again targeted Toering via a salting campaign. The head of Local 275 submitted 18 resumes to Toering. Of these resumes, five contained no work history dates, five were "stale," meaning that they were not current, outdated by as much as 6 years, and one was from one of the six individuals who had failed to show up for work when hired the previous year under the settlement agreement. Because the resumes were mostly stale or incomplete, Toering declined to hire any of the individuals whose resumes were submitted by Local 275. This action prompted another set of unfair labor practices charges to be filed by Local 275 against Toering. Toering Electric argued that the applicant salts should not be entitled to protection under the NLRA as they had no intention of ever working for Toering, as evidence by the fact that none of the applicants to whom employment offers had been made the previous year ever showed up for work. Instead, Toering argued that the only purpose of the charges was to induce economic harm on Toering and such behavior should not be protected under the NLRA.

In considering the merit of Local 275's allegations, the NLRB considered that under *Phelps Dodge*, protection against discrimination is not limited to individuals who are actually employed by the employer and extends to job applicants as well. This interpretation was further reinforced by the Supreme Court in *Town and Country Electric* in 1995 in which the Court considered whether salts could receive any protection under the NLRA. In this latter case, the Court stated that the term "employee" did not necessarily exclude paid union organizers but stopped short of saying that paid union organizers enjoyed blanket protection under the NLRA. The NLRB was asked to determine in *Toering* whether in order for a job applicant to receive protection under the NLRA that such applicant have a genuine interest in employment with the employer to whom he had applied.

The NLRB found that *Phelps Dodge* was distinguishable from *Toering* as the applicants in *Phelps Dodge* were clearly interested in employment with the employer. The NLRB held in *Toering* that in order for a job applicant to receive protection under the NLRA the applicant had to be "genuinely interested in seeking to establish an employment relationship with the employer." The NLRB found that the salt applicants at Toering had incurred no harm as the employment they were being denied was not something they actually sought and that the filing party, the union, had to prove an individual's genuine interest in actually seeking to establish an employment relationship with the employer as a prerequisite for filing a charge. The Board found that it had an obligation to "allay reasonable concerns that the Board's processes can be too easily used for the private, partisan purpose of inflicting substantial economic injury on targeted nonunion employers rather than for the public, statutory purpose of preventing unfair labor practices that disrupt the flow of commerce." In considering the request for backpay for the rejected applicants, the Board found that Section 10(c) of the Act did not provide for any kind of punitive damages and was limited to effecting "a restoration of the situation, as nearly as possible, to that which would have obtained but for the illegal discrimination." Hence, there was no basis for any action or award to the salt applicants, even if Toering had been found to have committed an unfair labor practice in violation of the NLRA. The board found that "submitting an application with no intention of seeking work but rather to generate meritless unfair labor practice charges is not protected activity" under the NLRA.

Perhaps what is most significant about *Toering* is the fact that the Board realized that the automatic presumption of an applicant's genuine interest in employment with an employer is a flawed assumption. Because it had not been previously necessary to prove this as the basis for filing a charge, unions could easily inflict "big hurts" on employers by engaging in such tactics used by Local 275. Employers would indeed incur significant costs and disruption of operations. More so, the resources of the NLRB ended up being diverted to cases and protracted litigation where there was no actual loss of the opportunity to work as applicants never intended to work for the employer in the first place. Hence, in *Toering*, the Board shifted the burden of the employer needing to prove that the applicant was indeed interested in employment back to the union and applicant in requiring that this evidence of "genuine interest" be submitted in justifying the unfair labor practice allegation. Hence, the Board felt the need to "abandon the implicit presumption that anyone who applied for a job is protected" under the NLRA. Most important for employers is that the employer's motivation for engaging in the behavior that constitute the alleged discrimination act does not become relevant until the burden of proof has been satisfied that the applicant does indeed have a genuine interest in employment.

Implications

The Supreme Court decision in *Town and Country Electric* represented the beginning of a new era in labor relations in the US (Mello 2004). At the time of the decision, unions were suffering from declining memberships and finding little success as they attempted to employ more creative and aggressive organizing strategies. In its *Town and Country* decision, the Supreme Court validated the right of labor organizers to salt the workplace, handing organized labor a significant victory. As salting has become a more prevalent union organizing strategy, employers have attempted to counter salting by attempting to force salts to disclose their union affiliations if the salts have not blatantly done so and are attempting to organize in a more discreet manner. The Seventh Circuit handed unions and labor organizers an additional major victory in *Hartman Bros.*, which will bolster union efforts to continue to test the extent of their NLRA support in the courts.

These pro-labor rulings have enticed employers to devise new strategies to prevent their workplaces from becoming unionized. Chief among these have been the use of preferential and restricted hiring criteria. Employers do not appear to be in violation of the NLRA when they employ preferential hiring policies as evidence in *Local 150*, where the Seventh Circuit affirmed an employer's right to do so, as long as the policies were consistently applied to both union and non-union applicants. Restricted hiring criteria cases, heard under the FES burden-shifting scheme, are a bit ambiguous. Initially affirmed by the NLRB relative to the right of an employer to exclude non-refereed applicants from hiring consideration, those cases involving wage disparity are less clear-cut as the Board has stressed the need to consider them based on their individual facts and circumstances.

Even though employers have enjoyed some success with the use of restricted hiring criteria, such policies should be implemented with caution. While both the courts and NLRB have found that referral-only policies do not directly violate the National Labor Relations Act, such policies may violate anti-discrimination in employment provisions of the Civil Rights Act of 1964. To the extent that an employer has a homogeneous workforce, referrals may logically come from the same population, which could expose an employer to a possible discrimination charge if non-hired salts were not part of this population. Under the theory of disparate impact, all employees/applicants are treated equally but the treatment results in different outcomes for different classes of individuals.

This may be particularly true when an employer has a racially homogeneous workforce. In such case, a union might simply target employers whose workforces are entirely Caucasian by using an African–American, Hispanic–American or Asian–American salt. While the consequences of using such a strategy have not yet been tested in the courts, the civil rights of individual salts might easily trump employer rights and responsibilities under the NLRA and ultimately impede an employer's ability to use restricted hiring criteria and remain salt and union-free in the long run.

In *Toering*, the NLRB addressed the fact that union organizing campaigns in which prospective salts applied for employment had turned, in many instances, from those in which there was a genuine interest in organizing the employer's workforce, which is protected activity under the NLRA, to adversarial processes which were designed intentionally to inflict substantial harm on employers. The shifting of the burden of proof from employer to applicant under *Toering* greatly alters the landscape under which salting activities can and will be conducted in the future. Union organizers, on the other hand, will now be forced to consider salting as originally intended; a means of organizing the employer's workforce from the inside, an activity that is clearly within the protection of the National Labor Relations Act, rather than one that is used to coerce employers into responses that form the basis for unfair labor practices allegations. Ironically this "pro-employer" decision could greatly benefit unions. By realizing the limitations of the protection afforded to salting efforts to "gain entry" into an employer's workforce can allow unions to fine-tune their campaign organizing strategies.

It is also probably safe to say that the issues confronted by the NLRA in *Toering* have not been put to rest. The case was decided by a slim 3–2 margin and in a lengthy and scathing dissent the minority points out several problems with the majority's decision. First is the fact that Congress has expressly chosen not to amend the NLRA relative to the issue of genuine interest or intent of job applicants through a number of anti-salting bills which have been introduced since *Town and Country*. Second, and perhaps more notable, is concern over the difficulty of assessing "genuine interest," given the multitude of factors which enter into a job applicant's decision whether to accept or not to accept employment. Of course, the importance of such factors can vary from one applicant to another so certainly the issues addressed in *Toering* have not been fully resolved and give unions the opportunity to test the ambiguities inherent in the decision. While *Toering* constitutes a victory of sorts for employers there is no question that unions, many of whom are fighting for their livelihood, will be further resolved in their organizing efforts as a result of the decision. More so, the slim majority in this case could easily be overturned in the future by political appointees to the NLRB from another political party or even by those from the same party with different ideologies.

Organized labor in the US continues to find itself at a critical juncture. As jobs traditionally performed manually by union members have become automated, filled by undocumented/illegal workers, and/or moved overseas, unions have to be aggressive and creative in maintaining and expanding their membership bases if they are to survive. This will need to happen at the same time that many employers take actions to cut costs by eliminating positions held by union members and/or reducing benefit levels of unionized employees. The stakes are high for both sides with the parties continuing to see collective bargaining as a zero-sum game. Recent court decisions have provided both employers and unions added incentive to continue their adversarial behavior. As both sides test the limits of the NLRA, the courts and the NLRB will ultimately determine who wins not only individual battles but the ongoing war as ambiguous sections of the National Labor Relations Act are challenged interpreted. Ladies and gentlemen, the chess match is far from over.

Source: Employee Responsibilities and Rights Journal, 21, (1), 37–49 (2009). Reprinted by permission.

REFERENCES

Anonymous (2003). Special Report: Deja Vu?—Trade Unions. The Economist *367*(8327). 77–80.

Bureau of Labor Statistics (2008). Report USDL 08-092 (issued 25 January, 2008). http://www.bls.gov.cps.

Curms, M. A., Hirsch, B. T., & MacPherson, D. A. (1990). Union membership and contract coverage in the United States, 1983–1988. *Industrial and Labor Relations Review*, *44*(1), 5–33.

Gould, W. B. (2008). LERA and industrial relations in the United States. *Perspectives on Work*, *11*(2), 6–9.

Logan, J. (2006). The union avoidance industry in the United States. *British Journal of Industrial Relations*, *44*(4), 651–676.

Maher, K. (2005). Unions' new foe: Consultants. *The Wall Street Journal*, August 15, 2005, *p.* Bl.

Mello, J. A. (1998). Redefining the rights of union organizers and responsibilities of employers in union organizing drives. *Society for the Advancement of Management Advanced Management Journal*, *63*(2), 4–9.

Mello, J. A. (2004). Salts, lies and videotape: Union organizing efforts, management responses and their consequences. *Labor Law Journal*, *55*(1), 42–52.

Raudabaugh, J. (2008). National Labor Relations Board 2007 year in review: Fueling unions' demand for Euro-centric labor lab reform. *Labor Law Journal*, *59*(1), 16–25.

READING 12.3

Collective Bargaining: Keeping Score on a Great American Institution

Joel Cutcher-Gershenfeld, Stephen R. Sleigh[1] and Frits K. Pil

The decentralized approach to collective bargaining is a great American institution. Ideally, it serves four core functions in society. First, collective bargaining has been endorsed in public policy as the preferred vehicle by which wages, hours, and working conditions are to be established in the United States. Second, it provides a means to codify past workplace innovations into governing contract language. Third, it serves as a forum to signal and guide future strategic directions for workplace voice and workplace conditions. Fourth, it has taken on an emergent but major role in defending deferred claims such as pensions and retiree health care benefits.

The core thesis of this chapter is that the institution of collective bargaining is failing to deliver on its potential for codifying workplace innovation and setting future strategic directions. Further, it is experiencing great stresses and strains when it comes to delivering basic wages, hours, and working conditions, and it is finding it difficult to assure the pay-out of deferred claims. To use baseball, another great American institution, as a metaphor: It is the bottom of the ninth inning for collective bargaining as a social institution; it is down by a number of runs and at great risk if it cannot spark a rally.[2] In this metaphorical game, collective bargaining must succeed in the face of a triple threat: shifts in markets (particularly globalization, deregulation, and other factors intensifying competition), changes in the nature of work (including new technology, increased focus on knowledge and skills, and outsourcing dynamics), and the erosion of other, interwoven social institutions (including unions, employer-centered systems for health care and retirement benefits, and work–family dynamics).

The consequences of a failure to "step up to the plate" and meet the challenges are substantial. While collective bargaining once provided an important check and balance in society, ensuring fair treatment in the workplace and the distribution of earnings that fueled a growing middle class, today collective bargaining is most notable by its absence.[3] We have, for example, seen a massive restructuring of the U.S. pension system and the future retirement health benefits of younger workers. This has happened, however, not through the give and take of bargaining, but through unilateral employer announcements. Bankruptcies decimated labor agreements over a decade ago in the steel industry, and they are now having the same effect in the airline and auto supply sectors. Similarly, fair treatment in nonunion workplaces is assured only where inappropriate actions are specifically prohibited under the law (and even then only where the employee is prepared to file a complaint or a lawsuit) or where an employer chooses to support alternative dispute resolution vehicles. The increasing polarization of wealth in this country has the potential to erase many decades of gains achieved through collective bargaining, making The American Dream more distant for the coming generations (Kochan 2005). Ultimately, there is the risk of what is termed a "race to the bottom," where wages and benefits are progressively diminished as work moves to low-cost providers in this country and abroad.

Collective bargaining has not, of course, disappeared. There are still approximately 23,000 private sector labor negotiations every year in this country and at least half again as many public sector negotiations. Notable instances can be found where parties do craft innovative agreements that deliver mutual gains, some of them featured in this chapter. These are exceptions, however, and often even these important initiatives rest on fragile foundations.

Our aim is to use a combination of quantitative data and qualitative case examples to outline the full scale and scope of the challenge facing collective bargaining as an institution in the United States. The focus is not on unions—a distinct but interwoven institution—but specifically on collective bargaining. We seek to foster research, debate, and action around this important institution that is presently at risk.

Collective Bargaining as an Institution

In 1935, "encouraging the practice and procedure of collective bargaining" was declared national policy in the United States (National Labor Relations Act [29 U.S.C. §§ 151–169], Section 1. {§ 151.}). At that time, one of the architects, George Taylor, commented:

> *Our government policy is obviously to raise collective bargaining to the status of a social institution, in*

accordance with the belief that the process provides the best democratic procedure for eliminating the basis for employee grievances as distinct from treating mere surface symptoms (Shils et al. 1979).[4]

To understand collective bargaining as a social institution, consider three key properties of institutions—they are emergent, embedded, and enduring.

Like all institutions, collective bargaining achieved its status in society over time. There was collective bargaining long before the passage of the National Labor Relations Act, and there was even supporting legislation at the state level that preceded the national legislation. In this sense, the institution is emergent in nature and the particular form has not been predetermined.[5] In fact, the initial form that emerged (bargaining oriented around craft unionism) shifted and expanded to accommodate a new form (bargaining oriented around industrial unionism) that matched the rise of the industrial revolution. Today, there are aspects of unionism that are oriented around professional development, community action, and other elements of what has been termed a global and knowledge economy. It remains to be seen if new forms of collective bargaining will again emerge to reflect these new realities.

Also, like other institutional arrangements, collective bargaining doesn't stand on its own. It is embedded in a range of additional institutions, including a market economy, concepts such as freedom of speech and freedom of association, democratic principles for individual and collective expression, and others. In particular, the future of collective bargaining is interwoven with that of labor unions, which have experienced a 50-year decline in membership.[6] The two institutional arrangements are distinct—craft guilds existed long before the practice of collective bargaining, and the links between unions and political parties, as well as many other union activities, are also distinct from collective bargaining. Also, there are collective negotiations that take place all the time in workplaces even in the absence of a union. Nonetheless, as we will outline, collective bargaining can only be understood embedded in its context as we enter a new century.

While the emergent and embedded aspects of institutions clearly continue to be applicable, they are combined with a third aspect that is more complicated. This concerns the way that institutions are enduring. Our very point is that collective bargaining is at risk of not enduring—of losing its standing as a viable social institution. Much has been written on the way that institutions perpetuate themselves,[7] but it is also possible for an institutional arrangement to fail at this task—particularly when there are shifts in the larger context or when alternative institutional arrangements emerge. In the case of collective bargaining, the larger context has shifted as a result of globalization, new technology, sectoral shifts, growth in right-to-work states, and new forms of work. Furthermore, alternative arrangements have emerged in the form of nonunion human resource management practices that provide individual employees with some degree of (nonunion) voice.

Table 1 provides data on the most important forces shaping collective bargaining from the point of view of today's labor and management chief negotiators. These data are taken from a 2003 national random sample survey of matched pairs of negotiators, commissioned by the Federal Mediation and Conciliation Service (FMCS; with data from an earlier 1999 survey as a comparison).[8] The respondents were asked to indicate which of 14 different forces had directly impacted their most recent negotiation. As Table 1 indicates, fringe benefit pressures had a heavy or moderate impact on the vast majority of negotiations. Pressure on work rules and domestic competition were also highly salient factors. International competition was also mentioned, but not as frequently as the forces listed in the table (it was cited approximately 27% of the time by union respondents and 20% of the time by management). On some of the most

Table 1 Contextual Forces Moderately or Heavily Influencing Labor Negotiations Cited by Matched Pairs of Union and Management Negotiators in U.S. Private Sector Collective Bargaining

	Union, 1999 (%)	Union, 2003 (%)	Management, 1999 (%)	Management, 2003 (%)
Fringe benefit pressure	76.9	81.2	68.1	67.9
Work rule flexibility	54.4	54.1	57.7	55.6
Domestic competition	51.8	53.8	48.2	46.8
Falling real wages	72.2	62.5	37.2	31.8
Low trust	54.7	53.5	46.7	29.1
Fear of job loss	36.4	48.5	28.3	26.4
Pressure to upgrade skills	31.4	30.9	32.6	33.2

Source: Analysis conducted with data from the FMCS National Performance Review Surveys of 1999 and 2003. Access to the survey instrument and the data is available on request from the authors, with approval from the FMCS.

commonly cited forces, namely falling real wages, low trust, and fear of job loss, the views of labor and management were very different. In a number of cases parties pointed to pressure to upgrade skills as an important force.

Given the forces that are influencing collective bargaining as an institution, a key question concerns how the process will adapt. It is our belief that collective bargaining is more than just a conduit for economic and social forces—that the process does matter. Thus, this investigation into how the institution is doing in this metaphorical ball game does take into account the larger context, but we are particularly concerned with what is happening on the playing field.

Delivering on the Basics—One Foul Ball after Another

How is collective bargaining doing when it comes to delivering on the basics—agreements about wages, hours, and working conditions that maintain or improve standards of living while not impairing competition? This is the first "batter up" in our metaphorical ninth-inning stand, and things do not look good. There has been one foul ball after another when it comes to basic collective bargaining practices and outcomes.

As is documented in a companion article,[9] the 2003 FMCS survey of union and management negotiators indicates problems with the most basic of collective bargaining outcomes: whether an agreement was reached. Approximately 10% of the negotiations surveyed in 2003 failed to reach an agreement—more than double the rate in similar surveys conducted in 1999 and 1996. This number represents a dramatic increase in negotiations involving an employer that has gone out of business, a bargaining unit that has been decertified, or a negotiation that has not settled for more than two years after expiration (the cutoff in the FMCS data set for classifying a contract as not settled).

Additionally, consider the contract expiration date, which traditionally served to focus negotiations toward agreement. Over half of the negotiations in the 2003 survey had not reached agreement more than 30 days after the expiration date. Increasingly, the union is unwilling to strike, for fear of replacement workers or other adverse consequences, while management is unwilling to lock out the workforce, for fear of disruptions in service and production. The 2003 survey data on settlements are presented in Table 2, broken out by four regions (selected as representative of distinct parts of the country). Delays in settlement and failure to reach agreement are key issues on the West Coast. However, there are also delays in almost half of the negotiations on the East Coast and in the Midwest, where collective bargaining is of longer standing.

In fact, while union representation has declined from approximately 20% of the workforce in the early 1980s to 12.5% today, the decline in work stoppages has occurred at a much faster rate. Figure 1 presents data on work stoppages (strikes and lockouts) for bargaining units of 1,000 or more employees. It is clear that the role of overt demonstrations of power in collective bargaining has shifted.

Even though work stoppages are less common, negotiations are not necessarily less contentious or more productive. Indeed, there is evidence to suggest the opposite. Some of the most recent stresses in the process may reflect the cyclical pressures associated with the post-9/11 recession. For example, while approximately 95% of agreements in the 1996 and 1999 surveys included a wage increase, only 80% of the 2003 negotiations did, and there was a similar dropoff in the proportion of agreements with a benefit increase, with only about 45% of the most recent agreements featuring an increase in benefits compared to higher levels in prior surveys.[10] In the case of benefits, the pressures around health care costs and retirement benefits (pensions and other retirement benefits) are now part of a bargaining landscape that goes well beyond economic cycles.

To provide a closer look at these and other more traditional issues, we have compiled a unique analysis, which is

Table 2 Settlements Reached and Timing of Agreements, by Region, Cited by Matched Pairs of Union and Management Negotiators in U.S. Private Sector Collective Bargaining

	Union, 1996 (%)	Union, 1999 (%)	Union, 2003 (%)	Management, 1996 (%)	Management, 1999 (%)	Management, 2003 (%)
Settlements of renewal agreements (first contracts excluded)	95.5	97.8	91.4	95.9	97.4	89.5
Early agreements (more than a month before expiration)	6.8	8.3	4.1	6.0	6.4	3.7
On time (within a month before or after expiration)	59.9	68.9	44.3	55.6	64.5	42.5
Late agreements (more than a month after expiration)	29.9	22.8	51.6	37.6	29.0	53.7

Source: Analysis conducted with data from the FMCS National Performance Review Survey of 2003. Access to the survey instrument and the data is available on request from the authors, with approval from the FMCS.

FIGURE 1 Work Stoppages by Year for Bargaining Units of 1,000 or More Workers

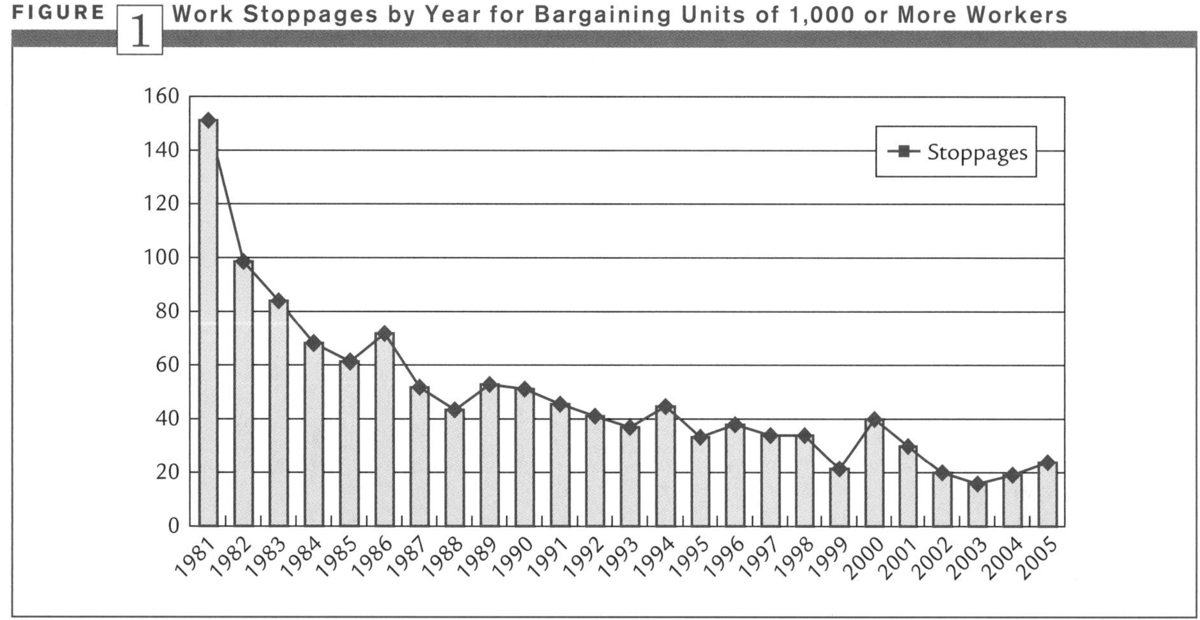

Table 3 Traditional Outcomes Reported as Having Ever Been Negotiated by Union and Management as Cited by Matched Pairs of Union and Management Negotiators in U.S. Private Sector Collective Bargaining

	Reported by Union (%)	Reported by Management (%)	Reported by Union and Management (%)
Wage reduction	17.2	12.8	2.7
Wage freeze	26.9	19.7	11.9
Benefit reduction	24.6	23.3	11.6
Wage increase	98.8	99.3	98.4
Benefit increase	57.8	73.1	44.5
Workplace safety	75.2	62.6	46.2

Source: Analysis conducted with data from the FMCS National Performance Review Survey of 2003. Access to the survey instrument and the data is available on request from the authors, with approval from the FMCS.

presented in Tables 3 and 4. Table 3 presents data on whether a given outcome is reported as having ever been negotiated and included in an agreement between the union and management matched pairs. While there is general agreement between union and management on whether there has ever been a wage increase or a benefit reduction, union respondents are almost 30% more likely to report new language on workplace safety. Management, by contrast, is more likely to report a benefit increase. There is also some variation in how the parties perceive negotiations regarding wage reductions and wage freezes.[11] The data in Table 3 are a baseline for the analysis of new agreements achieved, as presented in Table 4.

Table 4 shows the cases in 2003 in which new language on a given issue was reported as proposed (by union and by management), with a third column indicating the percentage of cases in which both parties reported a new agreement on the issue. The third column of data represents the relative efficiency of the process—the proportion of cases in which language was both proposed and achieved. Thus, over 75% of the time, when a wage increase was proposed, some wage gain was achieved. By contrast, new language on benefits (increase or decrease), safety, and wage freezes was achieved only about 30% to 40% of the time that these issues were proposed. While parties may sometimes see it in their interest to make a proposal without expecting an agreement, we assume that most of the time proposals are made with the hope of achieving some sort of agreement. While wage freezes and reductions in benefits or wages are clearly highly contentious areas where agreement may be difficult to attain, even proposals for new language on workplace safety are infrequently achieved. A well-functioning

Table 4 Traditional New Language Proposed and Achieved in Labor Negotiations, Cited by Matched Pairs of Union and Management Negotiators in U.S. Private Sector Collective Bargaining

	New Language Proposed (reported by union and management; %)	New Language Achieved (reported by union and management; %)	Negotiations Efficiency (%)
Wage reduction	3.3	0.2	6.1
Wage freeze	23.3	8.1	34.8
Benefit reduction	27.2	8.2	30.1
Wage increase	98.4	75.0	76.2
Benefit increase	73.7	25.6	34.7
Workplace safety	21.3	8.4	39.4

Source: Analysis conducted with data from the FMCS National Performance Review Survey of 2003. Access to the survey instrument and the data is available on request from the authors, with approval from the FMCS

institutional forum would be one where parties can surface issues and, most of the time, find common ground. By this standard, collective bargaining is not performing particularly well on these traditional issues.

Behind the numbers in Table 4 are intense debates on the proportions of escalating health care costs to be borne by the employer and by the employee, the increasingly strict requirements on retiree benefits accounting, the hard choices around protecting current wage and benefit levels at the expense of future hires, and the dynamics around new competitors in many industries that do not face the legacy costs carried by more established employers. These issues have resulted in recent high-profile strikes, including those at SBC Communications and the California Safeway supermarkets, as well as lockouts at Kroger and Albertsons in 2004. Tens of thousands of workers at the auto parts manufacturer Delphi are now facing a very uncertain future, with all of these tensions playing a central part in that situation.[12] None of the traditional aspects of negotiations constitute a strikeout, but neither do they represent much in the way of base hits. The process continues, but there is not much progress to report for labor or management—we are stuck with a succession of foul balls.

Enabling Innovation: Don't Count on Many Home Runs

In addition to its role in delivering traditional outcomes in wages, hours, and working conditions, collective bargaining has the potential to codify innovations that have emerged and to set the stage for new strategic directions. It is this innovative capacity that was a key focus of Kochan, Katz, and McKersie (1986), who indicated that only a combination of shop floor, collective bargaining, and strategic innovations would make it possible for industrial relations to reclaim its leadership role in shaping employment relations in this country. At the time, the alternative was for leadership to remain with a non-union human resource management (HRM) model that was playing an ever-stronger role in fostering frontline and strategic innovations. Today, both the "New Deal" industrial relations model and the HRM model are at risk in the face of what some have termed a "race to the bottom" that emphasizes the lowest common denominator for wages and benefits, with a primary focus on people as a cost to be minimized rather than as a resource that has the potential to create value and hence to be maximized.

In this context, let's consider the ability of collective bargaining to deliver agreements that are oriented around innovation and transformation. Table 5 reports baseline data on whether parties have ever reached agreements in a given relationship on potentially transformational issues important to labor and management, including work rule flexibility, new pay systems, work–family matters, joint committees, job security, employee involvement, and teams. As we saw with the more traditional outcomes, matched pairs of union and management respondents do differ in the degree that they report such agreements, with management more likely to report agreements for the first three and labor for the next three. Most of all, it is a relative minority of labor–management relationships that have provisions on any of these subjects in their agreements.

If we turn to relative efficiency of the process in delivering agreements on these issues, we see in Table 6 that most are just above a 50% level of efficiency—the parties reach agreement slightly more than half the time that these transformational issues are proposed. The record is a bit better for work–family issues (around 70%) and much worse for job security and employee involvement (around 20%). Considering that most models of workplace innovation require a coupling of all of these issues, the variation in efficiency is a concern. Further, the agreements on most of these issues

Table 5 Transformational Outcomes Reported as Having Ever Been Negotiated by Union and Management, Cited by Matched Pairs of Union and Management Negotiators in U.S. Private Sector Collective Bargaining

	Reported by Union (%)	Reported by Management (%)	Reported by Both Union and Management (%)
Work rule flexibility	47.8	57.3	34.1
Gain sharing, profit sharing	26.7	34.7	17.5
Work–family	29.0	37.1	17.1
Joint committees	37.3	25.2	17.1
Job security	34.1	20.8	10.3
Employee involvement	26.3	17.1	8.6
Teams	11.0	12.9	3.9

Source: Analysis conducted with data from the FMCS National Performance Review Survey of 2003. Access to the survey instrument and the data is available on request from the authors, with approval from the FMCS.

Table 6 Transformational New Language Proposed and Achieved in Labor Negotiations, Cited by Matched Pairs of Union and Management Negotiators in U.S. Private Sector Collective Bargaining

	New Language Proposed (reported by union and management, in %)	New Language Achieved (reported by union and management, in %)	Negotiations Efficiency (%)
Work rule flexibility	44.6	24.8	55.6
Gain sharing, profit sharing	19.2	10.1	52.6
Work–family	10.7	7.6	71.0
Joint committees	6.5	3.5	53.8
Job security	17.4	3.4	19.5
Employee involvement	10.8	2.1	19.4
Teams	1.1	0.6	54.5

Source: Analysis conducted with data from the FMCS National Performance Review Survey of 2003. Access to the survey instrument and the data is available on request from the authors, with approval from the FMCS.

have declined compared with the 1999 and 1996 surveys (the exceptions being work rule flexibility and new pay systems; also, no data were collected on work–family issues in the earlier surveys). In all, it does suggest that collective bargaining is able to generate new language on many innovative matters—so a transformation enabled by collective bargaining is possible, but in terms of our baseball metaphor, it is more likely to be a series of base hits rather than any highly visible home runs.

In order to more fully understand the transformational dynamics, consider the data presented in Table 7 on new work practices in the automobile sector. These data are based on surveys of North American auto assembly plants conducted by the International Motor Vehicle Program (IMVP) in 25 U.S.-owned car factories in North America in 1994, and 23 in 2000. While the samples are not identical, what the figures do suggest is that there has been a general dropoff in the use of teamwork, a reduction in the number of workers involved in off-line quality improvement activities, and reductions in organizational practices associated with enhanced flexibility, skill development, and quality. Competitors in other parts of the world have dramatically increased their use of these same practices in the same period. This is further evidence of a trend away from integration across what Kochan, Katz, and McKersie (1986) termed shop floor, collective bargaining, and strategic levels.

There are, of course, instances where parties have achieved important innovations at the bargaining table that are connected to innovation at the workplace and strategic levels. In our next section, we will detail two case examples involving the use of interest-based bargaining methods. In both cases, process innovations have combined with substantive agreements that do confirm that innovation is feasible—even if it rests on fragile foundations in both cases.

Table 7 Workplace Innovation in U.S.-Owned Auto Assembly Plants, 1994 and 2000

	U.S.-Owned Plants in North America	
Work Organization Measure	1994	2000
Plants in regions with teams	35%	46%
Workforce in teams	49.4%	24.6%
Workforce in employee involvement or quality circles	32.8%	25.2%
Suggestions per employee	0.3	0.2
Suggestions implemented	41.8%	31.8%
Extent of job rotation in and across work groups on a scale of 1 (none) to 5 (frequent)	2.0	1.8
Responsibility for quality inspection/statistical process control on a scale of 0 (specialists only) to 4 (production workers only)	2.4	2.1

Note: Because our 1994 and 2000 samples are not identical for these measures, the figures represent only trends.

Data sources: MacDuffie and Pil 1997; Pil and MacDuffie 1999; Holweg and Pil 2004.[13]

To conclude our look at traditional and transformational collective bargaining outcomes, consider a key overarching outcome—the direction in which the overall union management relationship is headed. As Table 8 illustrates, about a third of union–management pairs report that things are improving. However, managers are the more positive, with an increasing proportion of managers reporting improvement. While the trend line for managers is in the positive direction, an increasing number of union respondents indicate worsening relationships and a decline in relationships that are improving. Consider also that 31.3% of union respondents report, in response to a separate question, that their relationship itself is somewhat or very adversarial, while just 15.6% of their counterpart managers have the same view.

Thus, we have a number of union–management pairs who have divergent views of the current state of their relationships and the direction of change. The majority, however, report that the relationship is not changing. If the relationship is in fact serving the interests of both parties, this could be a stable, beneficial situation. If, however, there are problems, as the earlier analysis suggests, the lack of change makes things even more problematic.

The overall perceptions reported in Table 8 are broken out by region in Table 9, and the patterns are highly variable. These data, which are from only the 2003 survey, indicate a much more positive view of the direction of change by both union and management in the New England region. There are also, however, a high proportion of union leaders in New England and on the West Coast who report that things are getting worse in their relationships—a much higher proportion than their counterparts in management. One finding that is particularly interesting is the high proportion of union respondents reporting improving relations in right-to-work states. In fact, only 10.2% of the union respondents in the right-to-work states report that their relationship is somewhat or very adversarial, which contrasts with 30.8% of union respondents in New England, 40.8% in the Midwest, and 51.2% on the West Coast.

Table 8 Perceived Direction of Change in Labor–Management Relations, Cited by Matched Pairs of Union and Management Negotiators in U.S. Private Sector Collective Bargaining

	Union, 1996 (%)	Union, 1999 (%)	Union, 2003 (%)	Management, 1996 (%)	Management, 1999 (%)	Management, 2003 (%)
Relationship improving	29.0	32.7	22.0	29.0	34.5	35.7
Relationship not changing	64.0	59.5	66.6	62.0	60.5	62.8
Relationship getting worse	7.0	7.8	11.4	9.0	5.0	1.5

Source: Analysis conducted with data from the FMCS National Performance Review Surveys of 1996, 1999, and 2003. Access to the survey instrument and the data is available on request from the authors, with approval from the FMCS.

Overall, there is important variation over time in perceptions about collective bargaining between union and management and across regions. Moreover, the trends are not favorable for this institution. It is not achieving the ninth inning production needed when it comes to the basics or when it comes to innovation, our first two metaphorical batters. We now turn to our third and final player—the new challenges facing the institution.

Collective Bargaining in Challenging Circumstances: Two Whiffs, a Bunt Single, a Double, and (At Last!) a Home Run

To highlight the complex dynamics that underlie the survey data, we will focus on five very challenging circumstances that push at the limits of collective bargaining as an institution: the representation of collective workforce interests in the context of a bankruptcy, contested first-contract negotiations, the sale of assets, an interest-based approach to negotiations on health care issues, and the effort to transform the bargaining process on a massive scale. For chapter co-author Steve Sleigh, the first three situations occupy enormous time and resources for his union, the International Association of Machinists and Aerospace Workers (IAM). Case examples will be presented for each of these situations. Two represent what might be considered complete failures, where the process has struck out. In a third example, bargaining produced a better outcome than a nonnegotiated settlement but still was very difficult for all parties—in baseball terms, a bunt single, where a bad situation has been made into something at least workable. The fourth example, the interest-based bargaining and health care negotiations case, might be considered a double, and the transformation of the bargaining process on a massive scale may qualify as a home run.

Case 1: Bankruptcy Negotiations

Companies who file for Chapter 11 bankruptcy seek to reorganize and continue the business. Chapter 11 proceedings are meant to give the debtor company relief from creditors and give it time to come up with a plan of reorganization. In return, creditors, including unions with significant economic claims on the business, have privileged positions on a committee that gets to oversee the reorganization process. However, normal collective bargaining is thrown out the window by the presiding bankruptcy judge, who is charged with maximizing the value of the company as an ongoing concern. While negotiated settlements between labor, management, and other interested parties are preferred by the bankruptcy judge, the gavel belongs to the judge alone. Without a negotiated settlement the judge may terminate existing agreements and impose new terms.

Since September 11, 2001, nearly half of the commercial airlines in the United States have gone into Chapter 11 bankruptcy at one point or another. The combined effects of an economic downturn that became a recession, public fear of flying post-9/11, and the rapid rise of fuel prices created a sea of red ink that continues to hit the commercial airlines. "Bargaining" in such a situation is well described by two of co-author Sleigh's colleagues at the IAM:

> *Faced with the choice of agreeing to a pay cut and keeping the other protections of the union contract, or having the agreement abrogated and thereby experiencing a pay cut and losing all other protections of a union contract, it should not be surprising that*

Table 9 Perceived Direction of Change, by Region, Cited by Matched Pairs of Union and Management Negotiators in U.S. Private Sector Collective Bargaining

	Union, New England[a] (%)	Union, Midwest[b] (%)	Union, West Coast[c] (%)	Union, Right-to-Work[d] States (%)	Management, New England[a] (%)	Management, Midwest[b] (%)	Management, West Coast[c] (%)	Management, Right-to-Work States[d] (%)
Relationship improving	42.2	9.6	11.1	48.1	52.5	28.2	32.3	31.7
Relationship not changing	41.1	82.2	71.8	48.1	47.5	69.0	68.1	68.3
Relationship getting worse	16.7	8.2	17.1	3.8	0.0	2.8	1.6	0.0

[a]New England is defined as Connecticut, Massachusetts, Maine, New Hampshire, New Jersey, New York, Pennsylvania, Rhode Island, and Vermont.

[b]Midwest is defined as Iowa, Illinois, Indiana, Michigan, Minnesota, Missouri, Ohio, and Wisconsin.

[c]West Coast is defined as California, Colorado, Montana, Nevada, Oregon, and Washington.

[d]Right-to-work states include Alabama, Arizona, Arkansas, Florida, Georgia, Idaho, Iowa, Kansas, Louisiana, Mississippi, Nebraska, Nevada, North Carolina, North Dakota, Oklahoma, South Carolina, South Dakota, Tennessee, Texas, Utah, Virginia, and Wyoming.

Sources: Analysis conducted with data from the FMCS National Performance Review Survey of 2003. Access to the survey instrument and the data is available on request from the authors, with approval from die FMCS.

workers will "agree to" even draconian cuts in pay; the alternative is even worse (Roach and Almeida 2005).

In the airline industry, as with the steel industry earlier and auto parts manufacturing currently, Chapter 11–inspired labor cost cutting in one firm has led to a pattern of competitive price reductions that put pressure on other companies to cut their costs in order to survive. Once one firm in a competitive industry has a price advantage, others clamor for the same cuts. The spiral downward is hard to stop. After years of trying to "take wages out of competition," wages and benefits reductions are very much back in play: in baseball parlance, a strikeout.

Case 2: First-Contract Negotiations

The decline of union density is well documented, falling from nearly 40% of the private sector workforce in the 1950s to under 8% today. As a result, more and more unions have come to understand that organizing new members is imperative to survival. Organizing workers who are fearful of employer retaliation is extremely difficult. Still, many employees do exercise their fundamental right to have a voice at work and, as the labor movement has promoted it, say "Union Yes!" Unfortunately, once a majority of workers make that statement, the battle for a collective bargaining agreement has just begun. For example, in December 2003 the IAM organized and won a representation election for the nearly 600 production employees at New Piper Aircraft in Vero Beach, Florida. Negotiations for a first contract commenced immediately and continued for nearly nine months. In August 2004, the IAM and New Piper were close to an agreement, but then not one, not two, but three hurricanes passed over, around, and through the New Piper facility.

For the next four months negotiations were put on hold as the company sought to rebuild its shattered factory. Negotiations restarted in January 2005, but little progress was made over the next six months. It was clear to observers that the company had determined that the longer it took to get an agreement the less support the union would have. In June 2005, the IAM informed New Piper that they were taking the last proposal made to the membership for a vote. That little bit of leverage forced the company to bargain seriously, and it made modest improvements for a proposed three-year agreement. Just prior to sending the proposed agreement to the employees for ratification, however, a decertification petition was filed. The contract was ratified, but the National Labor Relations Board ruled that a contract bar was in force since a ratified agreement was not in place at the time the petition was filed. In March 2006, more than 27 months after the union was elected by the employees to represent them, the IAM narrowly lost the decertification election.

This is just one case example, but it vividly illustrates a combination of management delays, unfortunate business circumstances, and the limits of traditional power tactics, all of which can undermine first-contract negotiations. When these first contracts prove hard to achieve, the very ability of collective bargaining to perpetuate itself is at risk. Despite many policy recommendations on this issue,[14] there has been gridlock at a federal level for many decades. In that sense, this is a metaphorical whiff, not just for this case, but also for the efforts to constructively engage this issue at a policy level.

Case 3: Negotiating an Asset Sale

The first two examples of "bargaining" in today's environment represent misses or whiffs for the union and workers they represent. The third example is a case of taking lemons and making lemonade, or at least something closer to acceptable! In the summer of 2004 the Boeing Company announced that it was putting its largest manufacturing facility for commercial airplanes up for sale. The Wichita, Kansas, facility was the biggest in a series of asset sales that Boeing had initiated three years earlier with the sale of its St. Louis manufacturing facility. The IAM and the engineers unit of the International Federation of Professional and Technical Employees (IFPTE) represented nearly 9,000 employees at the giant aerospace manufacturing facility.

After a competitive process the sale was awarded to an investment firm from Canada, the Onex Corporation, with little aerospace or manufacturing experience. A condition of the sale was successful negotiations with the IAM and IFPTE. Another condition was very aggressive cost savings back to Boeing. To achieve those savings Onex proposed significant reductions in pay rates, more shifting of health care costs to employees, the elimination of defined benefit pensions, and a host of other concessions.

After two months of negotiations a proposal was taken to IAM members that included many of these concessions. The proposal was rejected after a raucous meeting of nearly 4,000 very angry workers who were about to become former Boeing employees. The IAM and Onex then went into extended negotiations and came up with an innovative stock option program that would offset the wage reductions, and perhaps more, if the new company met or exceeded certain financial targets. With a new proposal in hand, and with a long-term commitment by Onex to grow the business, including participation in the IAM's multiemployer pension plan, IAM members overwhelmingly ratified the new agreement. The new company, Spirit Aerosystem, is a work in progress but so far largely a positive one. This may count as a bunt single in our metaphorical ball game.

Case 4: Interest-Based Bargaining and Health Care Cost Containment

Benefits issues—particularly health care—are having a paralyzing impact on collective bargaining negotiations around the country. The issue is, of course, larger than the unionized sector of the economy. As Peter J. Hurtgen, former director of the FMCS, observed, "Don't use the word 'solution' and the words 'health care' in the same sentence." Nonetheless, parties are finding themselves having to fashion responses to these larger forces at the bargaining unit, facility, or enterprise levels. Our fourth case illustrates how these dynamics intrude in efforts to use an interest-based, problem-solving approach to bargaining.

The case involves DTE, the gas and electric utility that serves south–east Michigan and other parts of that state, which was bargaining in 2004 with Local 223 of the Utility Workers (representing over 4,700 employees in a mix of trade, office professional, and gas operations). Well in advance of negotiations, the parties agreed to approach bargaining using what is termed an "interest-based" approach—avoiding locking in on positions and instead focusing on finding mutual gains agreements that address the underlying interests of each party. The context was challenging—there had been deregulation in the utility sector of the state, three separate contracts (for the electric, gas, and office professional workforces) were being combined into a single master agreement, and health care costs had been increasing (and the represented workforces were making minimal contributions to this cost).

The interest-based approach was evident at the outset in the establishment of six joint committees: contract consolidation, health and welfare benefits, pension/savings plan, safety, sick absence, and technology and training. This approach was enabled by joint training for both bargaining committees and for other key individuals on both sides who were likely to be involved in the negotiations as internal subject-matter experts or key stakeholders. The process itself involved the use of an external facilitation team[15] and a formal structure for examining each issue that included statement of the issue, review of relevant data, brainstorming on the interests of each side, brainstorming on options to consider, and then bargaining to agreement (taking into account the interests and the options).

Using this approach, the parties achieved mutual gains agreements on issues such as job security, safety, new technology, attendance, bidding on new jobs, the operation of the grievance procedure, workforce planning, and disability/workers compensation. In exploring the attendance issue, for example, the parties surfaced a common set of interests connecting attendance to work–family issues facing a population of many younger single mothers working in telephone call centers. On the issue of job security, management had prepared for union demands to limit subcontracting, but instead found itself engaged in a dialogue introduced by the union with the following opening questions from local president Jim Harrison:

> *How can we ensure long-range workforce planning and implementation, increases in productivity, and utilization of represented employees? How can we ensure that our local union members are the workforce of priority and choice for this company?*

Instead of a positional contest around potential subcontracting restrictions, the parties talked frankly about the strengths and limitations of the represented workforce relative to contractors. This led to agreements on advance union notification and input prior to outsourcing and contracting of work regularly and customarily done in the bargaining unit, but it also led to broader dialogue and action on work rules, flexibility, and other related matters. The parties also reached agreements supporting continuous improvement on safety, advance notice and skills training on new technology, improved processes for job bidding and posting, introduction of a problem-solving oriented approach to grievances, and a commitment to hire 350 new bargaining unit employees.

The problem-solving orientation became complicated, however, as the parties took on the issue of health care. The union came into the negotiations knowing that an increased contribution would be needed from its members to help defray what had been escalating costs that were all being absorbed by the employer. Still, the long list of desired adjustments in plans, benefits, and contributions suggested by the employer was both confusing and overwhelming to the bargaining committee. They were fearful that any such agreement would not be ratifiable. Further, there were continued complications around the quality of available data on the health care costs and usage rates. All of this had the parties making little progress on this critical issue for a few days, until the union surfaced an unexpected option. They proposed that members contribute a percentage of pay (1% for single employees, 1.5% for married employees, and 2% for married employees with children)–a simple formulation that was not hard to communicate, that had an equity component and a growth component, and that generated a substantial portion of the revenue that management sought. As the current director of human relations, Dennis Dabney, commented, "This was not anything that we had considered. Even though there was hard bargaining on this issue, the idea would not have surfaced if it weren't for the interest-based process that we have been following on other issues." Additional revenues were generated with a disease management program, plan consolidation, incentives for preventive care, health education, and many other adjustments.

Still, as the contract expiration approached, management was still seeking additional savings due to the intensified competitive context, while the union felt that there was not much more to give. In one emotional moment, the union listed dozens of joint productivity initiatives over the past decade that represented many millions of dollars of savings—all of which would be at risk due to member resentment of an overly concessionary agreement. The senior vice president of operations at the time, Ron May, confirmed the validity of the savings associated with all of these projects, making the moment even more poignant. Ultimately, the parties brought the wage issue into the discussion—a risky move if an agreement couldn't be reached. At the eleventh hour, an agreement was reached that allowed for some additional employee contributions (which provided benefit savings valued by the company and which also featured caps to limit total employee liability). These contributions were offset with an additional wage increase of approximately *1%* in the first year (which was highly valued by the workforce). At this point, it was straight hard bargaining, but an agreement was finally achieved.

As an epilogue to the case, the parties found themselves six months into the new agreement, but with many provisions that were not being fully implemented. As a result, they established nine joint implementation teams and agreed that the full bargaining committees would meet every six months to take responsibility in an oversight capacity for these implementation efforts. After a year of joint implementation efforts, following a standardized joint alignment and implementation process, more than half of the agreements have been fully implemented, and the others are in various stages of review and action. The efforts have been recently complicated as industrial pressures are driving management to contemplate restructuring of some business operations. In terms of our baseball metaphor, the DTE story may count as a double—a success in applying a problem-solving process to bargaining, as well as a constructive engagement of health care issues, but continuing challenges in the linkage at strategic and workplace levels.

Case 5: Transformation of Negotiations on a Massive Scale[16]

Kaiser Permanente provides healthcare services to 8.2 million people in 18 states, which involves 30 medical centers, 431 medical offices, 11,000 physicians, and 110,000 employees who are represented by 10 different unions (with the Service Employees International Union [SEIU] being the largest). Beginning in 1996, a coalition of the unions came together with management out of recognition that deteriorating adversarial relations had the potential to be mutually destructive. A partnership was established, involving unions representing 81,000 employees (the two largest groups to stay out of the partnership are the northern California nurses and the Hawaii unions). Today, this partnership structure is organized around the framework in Figure 2.

While the initial partnership activities were not focused on collective bargaining, the 2000 negotiations were seen by both sides as a pivotal event. A comprehensive, interest-based approach was fashioned, which involved the coordination of timing for 31 separate local agreements and the establishment of a master national agreement. There were a total of approximately 200 union representatives and 200 management representatives in the subsequent 2001 negotiations. Their efforts were organized around seven major committees, each with various subcommittees. More than 20 external facilitators were engaged, some from the private firm Restructuring Associates and some from the FMCS.

The process initially faced skepticism by many on both sides, but that shifted as brainstorming surfaced many innovative options, which then led to agreements that were unprecedented in the healthcare sector. For example, the parties reached agreements on joint processes for tracking medical errors and near-misses—issues virtually taboo in the industry—as well as constructive processes for preventing recurrence. New language was agreed to on work–life issues, ongoing information sharing, technology adjustment, training and skills development, and performance sharing.

FIGURE 2 Kaiser Permanente Partnership Structure

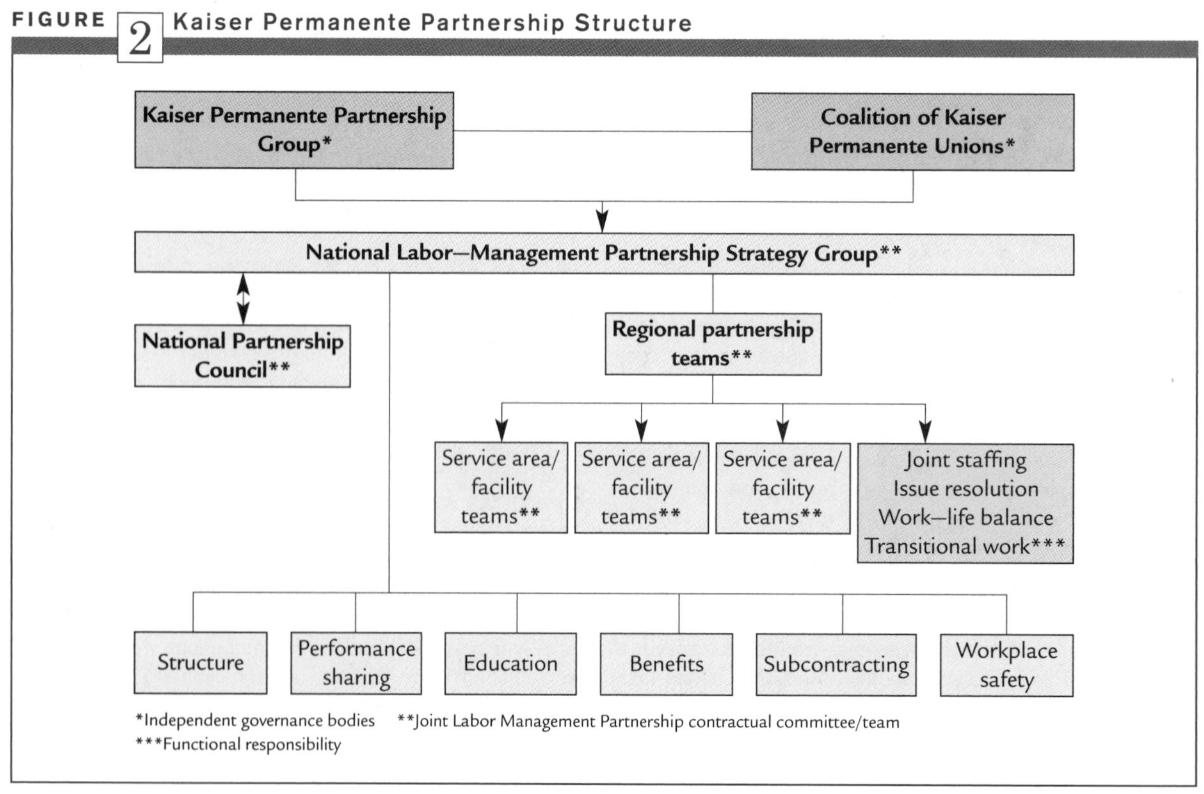

*Independent governance bodies **Joint Labor Management Partnership contractual committee/team
***Functional responsibility

FIGURE 3 A Sample of More than 300 Local Partnership Activities Identified by Kaiser Permanente and the Coalition of Unions (with Geographic Area Indicated)

Workplace Safety (all regions)	Patient Safety (all regions)
SOS Committee (most regions)	Documentation Task Force (CO)
CARS Steering Committee (CO)	Music Guidelines (CO)
Chrysler Workgroup (CO)	Local Recognition Committee (CO)
Advice LMP Committee (MAS)	Tech Training Committee (NW)
Floor Staffing (NW)	After Hours Coverage (NW)
Social Design (NW)	EVS-Dirty Linen (NW)
Attendance Project (most regions)	Ambulatory Redesign (OH)
Work-Life Balance (OH)	Violence in the Workplace (OH)
Nursing Pathways (SCAL)	Optimal Office Practices (SCAL)
Service Excellence (SCAL)	Parking Task Force (SCAL)
Nursing Quality Improvement (SCAL)	New Model of Care Team (NCAL)
Bilingual Program (NCAL)	Supply Costs/Management (NCAL)
Contact Lens Assessment (NCAL)	Organizational Pride (NCAL)

Other notable achievements in the early year of the partnership were the joint design and planning for the opening of a new hospital (Baldwin Park) below cost and on schedule; negotiation to restructure, save from closing, and turn around the performance of the Northern California Optical Laboratory; and the signing of an employment security and workforce adjustment agreement.

Following the 2000 negotiations, the parties took many of the ideas that surfaced in brainstorming during bargaining and began pursuing them as local partnership activities. Figure 3 provides an illustrative list of some of these projects. In each case, the project involves joint representatives and a structured process for problem solving. While these and other topics are highly compelling, the implementation of the 2001 agreement has been highly variable, with some projects producing notable successes and others falling short of expectations.

Negotiations of a second interest-based agreement took place in 2005, again with more than 400 representatives and the negotiation of a national master agreement, followed by various local agreements. Once again, a large group of facilitators has supported the process. This time, greater attention to implementation of provisions for improving performance, service quality, attendance, and other aspects of healthcare delivery has been integrated into the bargaining. What is most notable, however, is the continuity in approach relative to the first round of interest-based bargaining. While the ongoing relationship and negotiations will still benefit from continuous improvement efforts, the many dimensions of success lead us to classify this as a home run relative to the baseball metaphor. It may still be a long way from winning the game, but this is certainly a landmark negotiation.

Conclusions

We conclude this chapter with a final metaphorical batter still at the plate—and having a very tough at-bat. These five brief vignettes have highlighted the changed nature of collective bargaining today. In two examples, bankruptcy and first-contract negotiations, bargaining is a misnomer. There is no equality of power, no incentive for management to settle, and little reason for management to engage in the process. In the third example, an asset sale, the purchaser wanted the entity, so they were motivated to achieve a negotiated settlement. Of course the alternative for the union and workforce, a plant closure, made the union much more motivated to reach a negotiated settlement. In two additional examples we saw that innovation is possible and linkages to the strategic and workplace levels can be made.

To be clear, not all bargaining fits in these five categories. The IAM, which we drew on as a source for the first three case examples, negotiates nearly 1,000 agreements a year across a wide spectrum of industries and companies, both large and small and everything in between. The vast majority of these are not done in bankruptcy, as a first contract, or as an asset sale. While the IAM is proactive in supporting high-performance work systems where partnership structures can be established, these too do not represent the vast majority of negotiations. Still, the decline of union density, coupled with the lack of standing, experience, or enforcement of existing collective bargaining processes and the absence of a large volume of innovative efforts, has seriously eroded the institution of collective bargaining.

Public policy, in this case, has shortchanged collective bargaining. The patterns set in bankruptcy, first-contract negotiations, and asset sales impact all other bargaining.

Without proper standing in bankruptcy or a meaningful requirement to reach agreement in either first contract or asset sales, collective bargaining becomes a one-sided affair with workers and unions on the short end of the deal.

We have seen that transformation of the U.S. industrial relations system depends on a combination of innovative substantive outcomes and constructive process improvements. These are found in only a minority of labor–management relationships. The process is moderately efficient in delivering on these innovations—when they are proposed—but not sufficiently so as to drive broad-scale transformation. Regional variation suggests that there may not be one single set of problems or solutions for collective bargaining in the United States. While some of the quantitative and qualitative findings presented in this chapter are certainly a product of the recent economic downturn, there is no question that we are also witnessing deterioration in the private sector. That is not to say there are no bright spots. For example, in case 3, we highlighted the success that IAM had in negotiating novel agreements using a stock option program to offset wage reductions, while cases 4 and 5 featured innovative process and substance in two high-profile situations. Similar examples can be found (for example) in efforts by unions to get board member seats, rights of first refusal on asset sales, successorship guarantees, and related matters.[17] Time will tell whether these strategies lead to successful outcomes for workers, employers, and communities. While union membership is shrinking overall, it should be noted that unions like the Service Workers International have become increasingly successful in organizing both smaller workplaces and those sectors of the economy undergoing the most rapid growth. The success in new sectors of the economy, and workforces that historically have proven hard to unionize, may prove to be another point of growth in this institutional landscape.

The decline in collective bargaining in the private sector raises serious questions about the voice of workers in today's workplace. While it has been argued that new work practices such as team work and quality improvement activities provide alternative mechanisms for workers to exert voice in their work lives, these do not constitute the collective input or the role supported and enabled by the institution of collective bargaining. In 1951 George Taylor warned that "the successful use of collective bargaining was dependent upon union and the management voluntarily giving reasonable weight to the broad public interest.... A general 'ganging up on the consumer' would be incompatible with the development of collective bargaining as a socially desirable institution" (Taylor 1951). Taylor's concern was that the parties would become too powerful at the bargaining table. While there is still the question of the public interest, today it shows up in new ways—such as teacher agreements with school boards that specifically address ways to improve educational outcomes, or police and fire agreements with municipalities that specifically address ways to improve public safety, or industrial agreements that specifically address environmental, quality, and other concerns, or healthcare agreements that specifically address issues such as medical errors, or agreements in any sector that specifically address work–life matters. In these types of agreements, the parties are utilizing the forum of collective bargaining to reach beyond issues of wages, hours, and working conditions and signal a mutual commitment to broader social concerns. Whether by these means or other methods, the key to seeing collective bargaining come out of this metaphorical ball game a winner will be its again achieving the status that George Taylor signaled—that of a socially desirable institution.

Source: In Lewin, D. (ed.) Contemporary Issues in Employment Relations. Cornell University Press, 39–67 (2006). Reprinted by permission.

ENDNOTES

1. Steve Sleigh formerly was with the International Association of Machinists and Aerospace Workers and is currently with The Yucaipa Companies.
2. As we focus on a critical U.S. institution, we hope that the baseball metaphor adds a helpful counterpoint. We also note that for the first time since 1970, baseball players and management in 2002 reached a collective bargaining agreement without a strike or walkout—perhaps a good omen for collective bargaining as the line blurs between the baseball metaphor and the baseball reality.
3. We are grateful to Betty Barrett for her insights on the absence of unions—of which this is one part.
4. George Taylor, who went on to become a top industrial relations adviser to five U.S. presidents, made this comment at a Wharton Roundtable Conference in 1938.
5. Many historians emphasize the social construction of institutional arrangements, noting alternative paths taken in other nations with very different consequences. See, for example, the way that Thomas Hughes (1993) traces the very different approaches to electrification in the United States and England.
6. Unionization in the United States is at an all-time low of 12.5% in 2005 compared to 1953, when approximately one third of the workforce was represented by unions. The unionization rate of private sector employees is at 7.8%. (U.S. Department of Labor 2006). It is notable, however, that over 225,000 new workers were organized in 2005, stabilizing the unionization rate at the level of 2004.
7. See, in particular, Robert Michels ([1915] 1962) and the key insights from what is termed the new institutionalism literatures in organizational behavior, sociology, and economics (for example, Powell and DiMaggio 1991).
8. This portion of the chapter draws on the same data as our companion article, which come from a series *of* three stratified, national random-sample surveys of matched pairs of private sector union and management negotiators. (For final reports on the surveys, see Kochan and Cutcher-Gershenfeld 1997; Kochan and Cutcher-Gershenfeld 2000; and Kochan, Cutcher-Gershenfeld, and Ferguson 2004.) The surveys were commissioned by the FMCS and conducted using a telephone survey protocol administered by the University of Massachusetts Survey Research Center in 1996, 1999, and 2003, with the sample drawn from the 30-day notices that parties provide to the FMCS before their contracts expire. In the 1996 survey, 1,557 union and management representatives (1,050 of them matched pairs) were interviewed between October and December, with a 74% response rate. In the 1999 survey, 2,004 union and management representatives (1,654 of them matched pairs) were interviewed between July and October. A subsample of over 400 public sector negotiations were surveyed in the handful of states where federal mediators also provide mediation support for state-level public

sector bargaining units. In the 2003 survey, 1,718 union and management representatives (1,168 of them matched pairs) were interviewed between October 2003 and January 2004, with over 400 cases drawn from public sector and federal sector settings. A three-year sampling window was selected since the average contract duration is three years. In each round of data collection, we oversampled large employers and parties that had used mediation services. All results reported in this chapter are weighted to take into account the oversampling.

9. See *Collective Bargaining in the 21st Century: A Negotiations Institution at Risk*, the companion article prepared for a general negotiations audience (Cutcher-Gershenfeld et al. 2006).
10. While union and management gave similar responses on whether there was a wage increase, there was much more variation in their perceptions of whether there was a benefit increase, a perceptual difference that we examine in more detail shortly. In the 1996 and 1999 surveys, approximately 70% of union respondents and 55% of management counterparts reported a benefit increase. In 2003 the numbers were 45% and 43%, respectively—closer agreement between labor and management, but also a fall-off comparable to that found with wage increases.
11. Note that in almost all instances, there are a number of matched pairs where one side reports an outcome that the other does not. This prompted follow-up calls to respondents, through which we learned that the disparities primarily reflect different perceptions of the same agreement. For example, a union respondent may report increased job security based on some provisions that are seen as enhancing it (such as a commitment to make new investments by management), while management will report having not made any specific job security guarantee. Similar dynamics were found on many items. As a result, some analysis of the data has involved a focus only on the cases where both sides agree that a provision was in the contract.
12. The specific complications of negotiating in the face of bankruptcy will be addressed below.
13. Also note that the fraction of workforce in teams is based only on plants with teams. The extent of job rotation is scored on a 1 to 5 scale, and the rotation policies are ordered as follows: 1. Workers are trained to do one job and do not rotate to other jobs; 2. workers are capable of doing other work tasks in their work group (or teams if teams are present), but generally do not rotate jobs; 3. workers rotate jobs frequently within their group, but not outside their group; 4. workers rotate jobs within their work groups and across work groups in the same department (body, paint, and assembly), but not across departments; and 5. workers rotate jobs within the work group, across work groups, and across departments. Responsibility for quality control looks at four areas of responsibility: incoming parts, work-in-progress, finished products, and charting statistical process control (SPC) data. At one end of the spectrum, quality control staff can undertake these activities. At the other end of the spectrum, production workers (or no one) can do them. Other options include skilled trades, first line supervisors, and engineering staff.
14. See, for example, U.S. Departments of Commerce and Labor 1994.
15. Co-author Joel Cutcher-Gershenfeld served as lead facilitator, along with Betty Barrett.
16. For more detail on this case, see McKersie, Eaton, and Kochan (2003) and McKersie, Kochan, et al. (2006).
17. Examples of strategic linkages can be found, for example, in the United Steel Workers agreement with the international Steel Group. An example of the impact of parent guarantees is currently playing out with Delphi. GM consolidated its automotive components group into Delphi as a separate business unit within GM. In 1997, GM began disclosing separate financial information for the entity, and in 1998 incorporated it. GM spun off Delphi in 1999. GM's CEO at the time, John Smith, agreed to protect the interests of Delphi workers affected by the spinoff. In particular, GM provided assurances on postretirement benefits in the event Delphi ran into financial difficulty. This is proving to be extraordinarily costly for GM since Delphi entered Chapter 11 in October 2005.

REFERENCES

Cutcher-Gershenfeld, Joel, Thomas Kochan, John-Paul Ferguson, and Betty Barrett. 2006. *Collective Bargaining in the 21st Century: A Negotiations Institution at Risk.* Cambridge: MIT Working Paper.

Holweg, M., and F.K., Pil. 2004. *The Second Century.* Cambridge, MA: MIT Press.

Hughes, Thomas, 1993. *Networks of Power: Electrification in Western Society, 1880–1930.* Baltimore: Johns Hopkins University Press.

Kochan, Thomas A. 2005. *Restoring the American Dream: A Working Families' Agenda for America.* Cambridge, MA: MIT Press.

Kochan, Thomas A., and Joel Cutcher-Gershenfeld. 1997. *Final Report to the Federal Mediation and Conciliation Service on the National Performance Review Survey.* Washington, D.C.

——. 2000. *Final Report to the Federal Mediation and Conciliation Service on the Second National Performance Review Survey.* Washington, D.C.

Kochan, Thomas A., Joel Cutcher-Gershenfeld, and John-Paul Ferguson. 2004. *Final Report to the Federal Mediation and Conciliation Service on the Third National Performance Review Survey.* Washington, D.C.

Kochan, Thomas A., Harry C. Katz, and Robert B. McKersie. 1986. *The Transformation of American Industrial Relations.* New York: Basic Books.

MacDuffie, J.P., and F.K. Pil. 1997. "High-Involvement Work Practices and Human Resource Policies: An International Perspective." in T. Kochan, R. Lansbury, and J.P. MacDuffie, eds., *Evolving Employment Practices in the World Auto Industry.* Ithaca, NY: Cornell University Press, pp. 9–44.

McKersie, Robert, Susan Eaton, and Thomas Kochan. 2003. "Interest-Based Negotiations at Kaiser Permanente." MIT Sloan Working Paper No. 4312-03; Institute for Work & Employment Research Paper No. 05-2003.

McKersie, Robert, Thomas A. Kochan, Teresa Sharpe, Adrienne Eaton, George Strauss, and Mary Morgenstern. 2006. *Negotiating in Partnership: A Case Study of the 2005 National Negotiations at Kaiser Permanente.* Cambridge: MIT Sloan School of Management.

Michels, Robert. [1915] 1962. *Political Parties: A Sociological Study of the Oligarchical Tendencies of Modern Democracy.* New York: Dover.

Pil, F.K., and J.P. MacDuffie. 1999. "Organizational and Environmental Factors Influencing the Use of High-Involvement Work Practices." In P. Cappelli, ed., *Employment Strategies–Understanding Differences in Employment Practices.* New York: Oxford University Press.

Powell, Walter W., and Paul J. DiMaggio, eds. 1991. *The New Institutionalism in Organizational Analysis.* Chicago: University of Chicago Press.

Roach, Robert Jr., and Beth Almeida. 2005. "Response to *Airborne Distress.*" *New Labor Forum*, Vol. 14, no. 2 (Summer), pp. 60–62.

Shils, Edward B., Walter J. Gershenfeld, Bernard Ingster, and William M. Weinberg. 1979. *Industrial Peacemaker: George W. Taylor's Contributions to Collective Bargaining.* Philadelphia: University of Pennsylvania Press.

Taylor, George. 1951. "National Labor Policy." *Annals of the American Academy of Political and Social Science*, Vol. 247 (March), pp. 185–194.

U.S. Department of Labor. 2006. *Union Member Survey* (USDL 06-99). January 20.

U.S. Departments of Commerce and Labor. 1994. *Fact Finding Report of the Commission on the Future of Worker Management Relations.* Washington, DC: GPO.

Employee Separation and Retention Management

13

Learning Objectives

- Understand the importance of proactive management of employee separation
- Examine the alternatives employers have when considering large-scale layoffs/reductions-in-force
- Gain a sense of the costs of turnover and how to manage turnover strategically
- Appreciate the factors that influence retirement and how employers can actively and strategically manage this process
- Understand the function of and processes associated with employee retention and its critical role in strategic human resource management

Retention Management at Kraft Foods

Information technology (IT) is one of the most difficult areas for organizations to staff. The short supply of trained, experienced workers coupled with increasingly strong demand have presented almost limitless career opportunities for IT professionals. Most large organizations experience annual turnover in the 20 percent range. Kraft Foods, however, has developed a retention program that has resulted in the reduction of the turnover rate of its nearly 1,000 full-time IT professionals to a staggering 5 percent.

The program involved Kraft's chief information officer (CIO) partnering with HR to help HR understand the unique challenges being faced by IT. Kraft's retention program involves more than just the standard attractive stock options; it involves a holistic and integrated set of HR programs. Many of Kraft's IT professionals have come directly from its college internship program. Interns are given early responsibility for learning different technologies and are held accountable for rigorous performance outcomes early on. Seventy percent of IT interns who are offered permanent jobs accept.

Once hired on a permanent basis, employees are expected to engage in an objectives-based management system. Managers are specially trained to provide ongoing feedback and conduct developmental performance feedback sessions. Employees are allowed to pursue one of two career tracks within IT: technical or managerial. To assist with development, an intranet site provides learning tutorials, links to job postings, formal training courses, and both division and functional area Web sites that discuss competencies required in these areas. Consequently, employees are allowed to develop a plan for career development within Kraft. IT employees are further encouraged to devote ten working days per year exclusively to career development pursuits. In addition to in-house development opportunities, a tuition reimbursement plan is offered for outside programs of study.

Employees also become part of the IT Leadership Program, where junior employees are paired with an executive mentor. The one-year program involves about 30 days of joint work activities and provides additional exposure to leadership and technology issues.

Probably most importantly, IT employees at Kraft note the top reason they stay is the sense of family they find at work. Ideas are solicited and accepted from every level in the organization, and inclusion is a strong company value. Kraft also understands the needs of its younger workers who populate the IT division. It offers flexible hours, telecommuting and part-time work options, a casual dress code, and a new campus that includes a company store and an on-site health club.[1]

Organizations can expect continuing pressure to change and adapt. Societal changes affecting lifestyles, technology, and the economy create threats and opportunities for nearly all organizations. The organization of yesterday that was able to serve the same customers in the same markets, use the same production technology, and operate in a relatively stable domestic economic landscape no longer exists. Profitable markets invite entry of new competitors; technological changes in production impact efficiency; lifestyle changes alter preferences for certain types of products and services; and economic decisions must be made within a global context.

Contemporary organizations that wish to remain competitive need to be flexible and responsive to their environments. These organizations must develop ways to deal with increasing skill obsolescence among their employees and the labor market in general; they must also consider alternative forms of organization structure due to downsizing operations, selling off subsidiaries, and merger and acquisition options. From an HR perspective, this often involves employee training and development. In an increasing number of scenarios, however, the organization must strategically analyze its workforce and objectives and make decisions to sever relationships with employees. Similarly, employees today spend less time with individual employers than workers did in the past and make a greater number of career changes during their working years. Personal lifestyle decisions, opportunities with other organizations, and entrepreneurial motivations are causing many employees to leave their organizations.

The pressure to remain competitive and efficient—coupled with the fact that employees are less committed to individual employers than in the past—makes the process of employee separation a key strategic issue for organizations. An effective HR strategy involves managing the process by which employees leave the organization, regardless of whether such departure is by the employer's or employee's choice. Organizations can manage this separation process to ensure that transitions are smooth for both employers and employees, that operations are not disrupted, and that important professional relationships are not damaged. The three major ways that employees leave the organization are through reductions in force (initiated by the employer), turnover (initiated by either the employer or employee), or retirement. Organizations should have strategies for managing each form of separation.

Reductions in Force

Reductions in force or employee layoffs are attempts by employers to reconfigure their workforces. Reductions in force are becoming increasingly common in nearly all industries and are often caused by organizational restructuring following merger or acquisition activity. A reduction in force is sometimes used to make an organization more competitive by reducing costs.

Organizations reduce the size of their workforces for three main reasons: inefficiency, lack of adaptability in the marketplace, and a weakened competitive position within the industry. In all regards, efficiency is a major driving force: In many organizations, labor or payroll is one of the largest expenses. This is particularly true in service organizations, which are making up an increasingly significant portion of our economy and gross national product (GNP). Efficiency is sought by attempting to reduce labor costs and accomplishing more work with fewer individuals by redesigning work processes. Interestingly, an organization's stock price often skyrockets when layoffs are announced. Such decisions create expectations among investors of improved short-term financial performance.

One federal law regulates employer actions taken as part of reductions in force. The Worker Adjustment Retraining and Notification Act (WARN) went into effect in 1989 and requires employers with 100 or more employees to provide affected employees with a minimum of 60 days' written notice of any facility closings or large-scale layoffs of 50 or more employees. WARN does not apply to federal, state, or local government agencies. Employers found to be in violation of the law can be required to provide back pay, expenses, and benefits to all workers dismissed without appropriate notice in addition to fines.

Employers who conduct layoffs often provide affected employees with 60 days' notice and immediately relieve them of their job duties. The employees remain on the payroll for two months but are able to use the two-month period to adjust, seek new employment, and transition out of the organization. This not only assists the employee in his or her transition and job search, but it also helps to ensure that laid-off employees will be less likely to file for unemployment compensation insurance. State unemployment compensation insurance programs are funded by employers, with the percentage rate determined by the use of the funds by the employers' former employees. An employer who lays off a large number of employees who file for and collect unemployment compensation will have to reimburse the compensation insurance program proportionately.

To facilitate the transition (and ensure that their unemployment insurance payments remain lower), many organizations implement outplacement programs for laid-off employees. Outplacement services, which may be conducted in-house or contracted to an external vendor, assist not only with helping laid-off employees land on their feet but also serve as a public relations tool: These services help to retain the support and goodwill of remaining employees by making them feel that the organization will look out for them if future reductions are necessary. In addition to helping maintain the morale and motivation of remaining employees, outplacement programs reduce the risk of litigation by disgruntled former employees.

Realizing that in certain circumstances it might be unrealistic, impossible, or unfair to require employers to provide such written notification, Congress allowed several exceptions to WARN. These exceptions are for (1) a "faltering company" that is actively seeking capital to retain its scope of operations and reasonably believes that giving employees a warning will jeopardize the financing; (2) an "unforeseeable circumstance," such as a strike at a supplier's business; (3) a natural disaster, such as a fire, flood, earthquake, or hurricane; and (4) any operation set up as a "temporary facility," where employees who were hired were informed that the facility and employment were nonpermanent.

Layoffs can sometimes be avoided through proper planning. The main benefit of strategic human resource planning is to ensure that supply and demand of employees are equated while avoiding the costs associated with severe overstaffing and understaffing. Effective human resource planning in most instances can reduce or eliminate the need for any kind of large-scale reductions in force or layoffs. Regardless of the size of the surplus, employers must identify the real reason for the excess number to determine an appropriate response. This strategic perspective determines whether the surplus is expected to be temporary or permanent in order to assist in developing a plan of action with a corresponding time frame. For example, longer-range surpluses can often be managed without the need for layoffs by utilizing hiring freezes, not replacing departing employees, offering early retirement incentives, and through cross-training of certain employees to allow them to develop skills that the organization anticipates needing. Short-run surpluses can be managed through loaning or subcontracting employees, offering voluntary leaves, implementing across-the-board salary reductions, or redeploying workers to other functions, sites, or units.

Two more policy-oriented solutions to remedy overstaffing might involve (1) tying a greater portion of compensation to division or organization performance and/or (2) regularly staffing the organization at less than 100 percent and making up the difference with temporary employees or offering overtime. The former strategy creates a flexible or variable pay plan to control costs because payroll expenses are directly related to the organization's profitability. Therefore, overstaffing is somewhat less of a concern. The latter strategy creates a flexible or variable workforce that can be expanded or contracted to meet business needs and conditions. These strategies are summarized in Exhibit 13.1.

As part of any layoff plan, the organization also needs to develop an appropriate strategy for managing the survivors. A key management challenge that is often overlooked is ensuring that the retained employees can adjust to the changes. It should not be assumed that these individuals will automatically be relieved (and thrilled) to have retained their jobs during the layoff and will still be motivated and productive. These individuals may feel less secure about the jobs they have retained; be asked to perform

EXHIBIT 13.1 Strategies for Managing Employee Surpluses and Avoiding Layoffs

Long Run	Short Run	Policy
• Hiring freezes • Attrition • Offer early retirement incentives • Cross-training of employees	• Loaning or subcontracting labor • Voluntary leaves • Across-the-board salary reductions • Re-deploying employees	• Greater percentage of compensation tied to performance • Staff at less than 100 percent

more work than previously without a corresponding increase in pay; have lost long-term friends and coworkers; and may have damaged morale and fear that they are vulnerable to future layoffs. Consequently, they may be less loyal to the employer and have strong incentives to leave the organization. The organization needs a separate strategy in addition to its layoff strategy to ensure that these retained employees remain committed, loyal high performers. Retention of these employees and their level of productivity will probably determine whether the organization will survive. Ironically, downsizing organizations often ignore this critical fact and assume that retained workers will be happy to still have their positions and work harder than ever. Reality has shown that nothing could be farther from the truth.

Layoffs at Kodak

A critical component of the successful outcome of any layoff is the manner in which the survivors are managed. Rochester, New York–based Kodak actually had its surviving employees defend the organization's decision to lay off colleagues to the media during recent job cuts. When Kodak decided it needed to lay off 3,500 employees worldwide, it immediately considered how this decision would impact not only the employees being cut but those who were staying. One key to the positive response to the layoffs was the manner in which communications were handled. To help minimize uncertainty and anxiety, complete and honest information was provided to employees as soon as it was available. Employees were informed that details had not been worked out yet but that the downsizing was not temporary and would affect only certain, specified parts of the organization. A range of services was provided to those employees being let go, including a termination allowance of two weeks' pay for each year of employment; retained medical, dental, and life insurance for four months; outplacement counseling; and a retraining allowance of up to $5,000 for schooling. By strategically planning and implementing the layoffs, Kodak was able to enjoy the continued support of its remaining employees and customers.[2]

While the decision to lay off employees should usually be done as a "last resort," it is inevitable that sometimes an employer has no other choice. However, many layoff decisions by senior management are misguided and create additional problems for the organization. While the investment community may react to a layoff announcement with initial enthusiasm, the long-term performance results are often disappointing. One study found that employers that laid off more than 3 percent of their workforces saw little or no gain in their stock price over a three-year period, whereas those that laid off 15 percent or more of their workforces performed significantly below average over the same time period.[3] Layoffs tend to have better results when done strategically as part of a merger or repositioning rather than as a means to cut costs or impact stock price in the short term. In 2001, Sears, Roebuck & Company eliminated 2,400 jobs and closed 89 stores as part of a strategic restructuring. In the same year, Praxair, Inc., a $5 billion producer of specialty gases, eliminated 900 jobs as part of a plan to change its product mix. In both cases, the value of the company stock rose 30 percent in three months.[4] The lesson here is that layoffs alone will not turn around a company whose strategy is ineffective. However, when layoffs are conducted as part of a strategic restructuring that involves fundamental changes in the direction of an organization, they have a higher probability of success.

Unfortunately, too many layoffs are conducted as a short-term strategy to improve financial performance rather than as strategic initiatives. The majority of organizations that have undertaken downsizing initiatives have failed to report any kind of increased efficiency, productivity, or profitability.[5] A good deal of this failure has been attributed to poor management of the survivors of the downsizing[6], many of whom subsequently display behavior and attitudes that are dysfunctional to the organization's success.[7] In addition, one study found that considerable costs result from unanticipated increases in voluntary turnover that follow layoffs. Post-downsizing turnover increases can be staggering as, on average, layoffs that reduce an employer's workforce by 1 percent generally result in a 31 percent increase in voluntary post-downsizing turnover rates.[8] Reading 13.1, "Cost Reductions, Downsizing-Related Layoffs and HR Practices," addresses some of the human and social effects of downsizing and presents a framework to help organizations better understand both the consequences of and alternatives to large-scale layoffs over the short, medium, and long terms.

Strategic Downsizing at Charles Schwab

San Francisco–based discount brokerage Charles Schwab was hit hard in the early 2000s by the downturn in the stock market. However, given the cyclical nature of the economy, it was likely that many workers who were no longer needed might be needed again in the undeterminable future. In March 2001, when the company laid off 3,400 employees, each received a transition package that consisted of 500 to 1,000 stock options, cash payments to cover COBRA costs for benefits continuation, a stipend of up to $20,000 to cover tuition for schooling, and a full range of outplacement services. More important, however, was the $7,500 bonus to be provided to any employee who was rehired within 18 months of separation. This program greatly assisted in the quick rehiring of knowledgeable, trained employees when business improved, saved the organization a tremendous amount of money, and secured the goodwill of customers and remaining employees. Perhaps more important, when across-the-board pay cuts of 5 percent for rank-and-file employees were announced, it was also announced that any manager at the vice-presidential level or higher would be receiving a 25 percent pay cut. Schwab was cited as a model responsible employer within the business community and continued to be one of the most sought-after employers in the country.[9]

Turnover

Employees who leave the organization at the organization's request (involuntary turnover) as well as those who leave on their own initiative (voluntary turnover) can cause disruptions in operations, work team dynamics, and unit performance. Both types of turnover create costs for the organization. In some cases, these costs may be short term but have longer-term benefits; in other cases, the costs may be significant and longer lasting. Costs of turnover include the direct economic costs of staffing and training new hires as well as the indirect costs of the downtime needed for the new employee to gain proficiency in his or her job and to become fully socialized and integrated into the organization. In addition, those responsible for training the new employee are pulled away from their regular job responsibilities. If an organization has made significant investment in training and developing its employees, that investment is lost when employees leave. Excessive turnover can also impact the morale of employees and the organization's reputation as being a good place to work, which makes retention and recruitment more challenging and time-consuming.

The economic costs of turnover can be staggering. In Chapter 8, it was noted that one technology company calculated turnover costs to average $200,000 per employee.[10] Merck and Company, the pharmaceutical giant, has estimated that its turnover costs are between 150 percent and 250 percent of the employee's annual salary.[11] Sears, Roebuck estimated that turnover among its retail sales staff amounted to $110 million annually, which constituted 17 percent of its operating income.[12] Sears also found a strong negative correlation between employee turnover and customer satisfaction. Merck and Sears are not alone; most large employers suffer from excessive turnover costs. A recent survey found that at companies with more than 1,000 employees, annual voluntary resignations averaged 21 percent.[13] For employers with more than 5,000 employees, the rate climbed to 26 percent.

Turnover can, however, be beneficial. It can allow the organization to hire new employees with more current training who are not locked into existing ways of doing things. Fresh ideas from outsiders can be critical to organizations that have become stagnant and are in need of innovation. Turnover can also lower the average tenure of employees and translate into lower payroll expenses. Turnover also affords opportunities to promote talented, high performers. Finally, when poor performers or disruptive employees leave the organization, morale can improve among coworkers.

It may be assumed that voluntary turnover generally provides more costs than benefits and that involuntary turnover is beneficial for the organization from a cost perspective. Both of these assumptions are often false. First, voluntary turnover may allow the organization to find an even better performer than the employee who left, possibly at a lower salary. Second, involuntary turnover often results in much higher costs than training or counseling an employee with performance deficiencies.

Both voluntary and involuntary turnover can be managed strategically to allow the organization to maximize the benefits of turnover and minimize the costs incurred with the process. Exhibit 13.2 presents a Performance-Replaceability Strategy Matrix that was

EXHIBIT 13.2 The Performance-Replaceability Strategy Matrix

PERFORMANCE	REPLACEABILITY: Difficult	REPLACEABILITY: Easy
High	High performers—difficult to replace Highly Dysfunctional Turnover Retain/invest in employee: develop backups	High performers—easy to replace Dysfunctional Turnover Retain/invest in employee
Average	Average performers—difficult to replace Dysfunctional Turnover Retain/provide performance incentives: develop backup	Average performers—easy to replace Dysfunctional Turnover if Replacement Costs Are High Retain/provide performance incentives
Low	Poor performers—difficult to replace Short-Term Dysfunctional/Long-Term Functional Turnover Improve performance or terminate: develop backup	Poor performers—easy to replace Functional Turnover Improve performance or terminate

Source: Adapted from Martin, David C. and Bartol, Kathryn M. "Managing Turnover Strategically," Personal Administrator, *Volume 30, #11, November 1985, p. 63.*

developed by Martin and Bartol as a tool to allow organizations to manage turnover strategically.[14] The model on which this matrix is based argues that turnover in organizations, while unavoidable, can be strategically managed to allow organizations to minimize the disadvantages of turnover and maximize its advantages.

Martin and Bartol have classified turnover as being functional (beneficial) or dysfunctional (problematic) for an organization. Whether turnover is functional or dysfunctional depends on two factors: the individual employee's performance level and the difficulty the organization would have replacing the individual. In Exhibit 13.2, replaceability is depicted on the X axis and performance level on the Y axis. Each of the six cells is then classified as resulting in functional or dysfunctional turnover, and appropriate strategies for managing employees who fit into each of the cells are provided. Clearly, the more dysfunctional the turnover, the greater the attention that will be required by management to retain the employee. Retention strategies for such employees might involve additional career development opportunities, incentive compensation that rewards high performance, or innovative benefits that are tailored to the needs of the employee. Regardless of the performance level, backups should be developed by the organization for any employees who would be difficult to replace. Ideally, the strategy for managing turnover involves keeping high performers rewarded through innovative compensation and recognition and reward programs while engaging in human resource planning to ensure that as few employees as possible occupy positions that will make them difficult to replace.

Exhibit 13.3 presents the eventual outcomes of a successfully managed employee turnover and retention program. All employees whose turnover would be disruptive would be reclassified as easy to replace once appropriate backups had been trained. At the same time, performance incentives and counseling should be provided to low performers to encourage and motivate them to become average performers. Similar incentives should be provided to average performers to encourage and motivate them to become high performers. If these lower performers do not improve in time, they should be terminated.

EXHIBIT 13.3 Strategic Management of Turnover and Retention

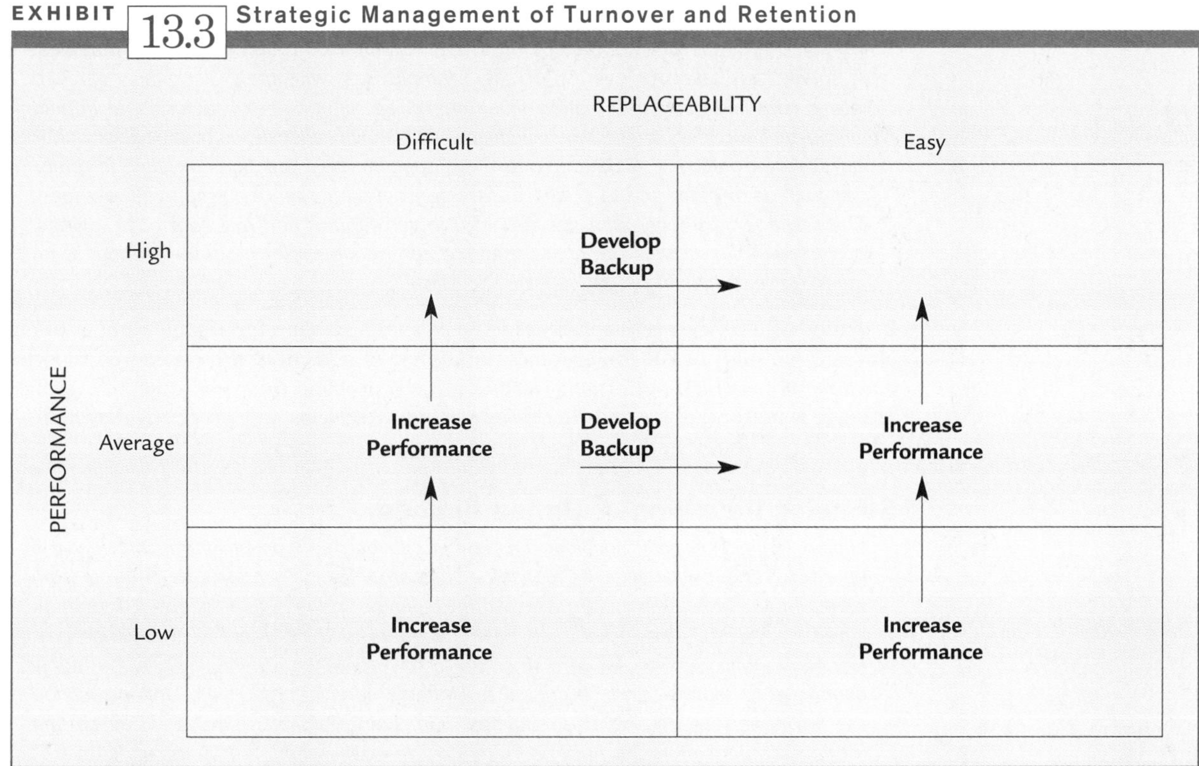

In cases of involuntary turnover or termination, employers need to have a strategy and standard policy that, if followed, would allow the employer to defend a charge of wrongful termination. In recent years, courts have been increasingly open to hearing complaints that an employer violated the public policy exception to employment at will, as discussed in Chapter 7. Although there may be no legal responsibility to continue to employ individuals, many courts have found that employers have an ethical responsibility to discharge employees only for just cause. Consequently, employers who discharge their employees should have strong evidence of just cause that has been documented and communicated to the employee over time. Otherwise, the employer could incur significant costs in defending itself against the charges or face negative publicity and dissension among the ranks of its employees. The Martin and Bartol model argues that the organization's goal should not necessarily be to reduce all turnover but to reduce dysfunctional turnover by developing appropriate human resource programs and policies.

Managing Retention at Sprint PCS

In the early 2000s, Sprint PCS, a provider of consumer cellular telephone services, suffered from excessively high turnover, which exceeded 100 percent annually. Employees were leaving faster than new hires could be brought on board. Unfortunately, many of the organization's highest-performing employees were among those departing. Sixty-eight percent of employees reported in exit surveys that the organization could have done something to retain them. To address this, Sprint developed a strategy to address retention that focused not on pay and programs but on developing managers to become "retention agents." Through survey data, Sprint learned that employees were leaving not because of issues related to compensation or benefits but because their managers were not seen as individuals who knew and understood them and therefore were deemed to be untrustworthy. Ten retention competencies were designed for managers: trust builder, esteem builder, communicator, climate builder, flexibility expert, talent developer and coach, high-performance builder, retention expert, retention monitor, and talent finder. Assessments were then done in five pilot customer contact centers to rate each manager on each of these competencies via 360-degree surveys. Each manager then received a plan that identified at least four competencies to be developed through e-learning modules. A survey was taken of over 7,000 PCS employees, with their response compiled into a database; that information illustrates three categories of factors that impact employee retention: organization-wide conditions, job conditions, and leader behaviors. Managers use this database to share specific "best practices" relative to retention with each other and to create a learning community around employee retention. The result is that every pilot site reported lower attrition and resultant cost savings, projected in the millions of dollars, than the control sites. The program is about to be rolled out to remaining customer service sites.[15]

Retention of top employees continues to be a vexing problem for a large number of employers. One study of HR professionals found that 75 percent of those surveyed reported that retention of high performers was the top HR problem they confronted.[16] A critical strategic issue for employers is the development of policies and programs that help retain high performers and/or those employees who are difficult to replace.

Strategic Retention at United Airlines

United Airlines recently developed a "key employee retention program" that focuses on 600 workers identified as critical to the organization's efforts to emerge from bankruptcy. These individuals, who were employed in the organization's information services division, received a cash payment equal to 20 percent of their base pay. Because these individuals were deemed to have highly marketable skills, be highly expensive to replace, and be critical to United's survival objectives, United justified the payments even as other employees were being laid off. Turnover rates among these technical workers had risen to 11 percent, while the company's overall turnover rate stood at 7 percent. The plan, while popular with technical employees, was criticized by United's Association of Flight Attendants, which argued that the retention bonuses would come at the expense of other workers.[17]

When attempting to retain talented employees and top performers, employers face competition not only from other organizations but also from the very employees they are attempting to retain. Particularly in service and information-related industries, startup costs for new businesses are often relatively low, creating opportunities for employees to start their own organizations. The access to information, such as client lists and marketing and strategic plans, that many employees have in the course of doing their jobs can provide strong support for such endeavors. In addition, these employees may have also built strong relationships with customers that transcend loyalty to the organization on the part of both parties. The number of lawsuits that involve employee startup companies has increased greatly in recent years, and many employers now require employees to sign "noncompete" agreements. However, such noncompete agreements frequently are not seen as legally valid and binding. For example, the courts in California, a state with some of the highest startup activity, do not recognize any noncompete agreements.

When an employee decides to engage in an entrepreneurial endeavor, an employer essentially has two ways in which it can respond: It can treat the new business as an adversarial competitor or it can attempt to enter into a partnership with the new enterprise.[18] Many large organizations, including Xerox, General Motors, Sun Microsystems, and Microsoft, have been involved in the funding of new startup organizations created by their employees. This funding, however, comes in exchange for some involvement with and control of the new enterprise.

Retaining Talent at Intel

One of the employers that not only supports but actively embraces startup operations by employees is Intel. The Oregon-based computer chip manufacturer has an internal program called the New Business Initiative (NBI) that not only funds startups but actively solicits proposals for new businesses from Intel employees. The NBI has its own staff to examine proposals and determine whether NBI will provide funding. If approved, the employee works with the NBI to develop the project, becoming an entrepreneur while still remaining on the Intel payroll. Successful new enterprises may operate as independent organizations; others may be integrated into Intel's operations. The program is consistent with Intel's innovation strategy and entrepreneurial culture and has also served very successfully as both a retention and a training and development tool. Employees who decide to abandon their projects return to their jobs at Intel with new job skills and a stronger commitment to the organization. Employees are allowed to chase their dreams as technical entrepreneurs without the financial risk of investing in the business and having to leave their full-time employment. The program has also helped the company to retain many of the employees who have come on board as part of one of the many mergers or acquisitions completed by Intel.[19]

Retention of employees, particularly in a strong employment market and for those employees who are top performers, can be a significant challenge for organizations. While many employers appropriately attempt to retain top employees by offering opportunities for growth and development, interesting work, a congenial work environment, and strong values-driven management, the reality is that many top performers still remain focused on their salary, particularly relative to the marketplace.[20] Yet, in other cases, employees may be willing to stay with an employer at a lower salary than could be obtained elsewhere because of the non-salary related factors noted above.[21] The ultimate decision for an employee to voluntarily leave an organization is a function of whether 1) the inducements to stay are sufficiently attractive and 2) the ease with which the employee could depart and is willing to sever or rearrange personal and social networks established.[22] A related factor could also be the transitions necessary for the employee's family, which might result from a decision to change employers. The significant challenge for employers in managing retention of top employees is the fact that different employees are motivated by different factors relative to their desire to stay with an employer. Hence, any retention program needs to be individualized based on the needs of the key employees who have been targeted for retention.

Smaller organizations face special challenges relative to retention of employees. Individuals who choose to work in small organizations generally do so for the unique benefits and challenges associated with small companies. Small companies offer a fast-paced work environment with less bureaucracy, near-constant change, less structure, constant interface with coworkers, including senior management, opportunities for growth and development, and the chance to shape a new organization's future. Small companies may also provide significant opportunities to share in the organization's future financial success, sometimes in tandem with a more modest starting salary. However, as smaller organizations become more successful, they change. Growth usually mandates more formality and bureaucracy which can greatly alter the work environment employees have come to enjoy. Many smaller organizations simply cannot retain many of their early employees who opt to move on to other smaller startups. Some smaller organizations attempt to become more creative as they grow and organize, with smaller units or divisions that retain the characteristics of the initial startup. Others attempt to create a strong and unique vision or mission that keeps employees engaged as the internal environment of the organization becomes more formalized. Small organizations face some unique challenges relative to employee retention and hence need to be creative in developing the necessary means to engage and retain their top performers.

One key tool employers can use to gauge the effectiveness of their retention efforts is the exit interview. Exit interviews provide employers with the opportunity to gain candid feedback from departing employees in a manner that might not be possible if conducted within the context of an ongoing employment relationship. Departing employees are more likely to be forthcoming and honest in their assessments of their employer without fear of repercussions, and assuming that departing employees have been interviewing with other organizations, they are able to provide employers with information as to how the organization compares with other employers who recruit from the same talent pool. Exit interviews can serve three purposes: 1) provide the organization with feedback to allow it to better compete in the recruiting marketplace; 2) ensure that departing employees are able to voice their concerns and respond to such to keep the employer's reputation strong; and 3) provide, in some cases, an opportunity to retain the employee by addressing concerns in a satisfactory manner.[23] Effectively conducted exit interviews can be a catalyst for maintaining an ongoing relationship with departing employees who might be recruited back to the organization at some point in the future. The data that can be obtained in the exit interview process can provide key insights as to how well an employer is doing relative to delivery of its overall HR strategy and branding initiatives. Departing employees can also influence the perceptions of others who might be possible future employees and/or customers of the organization. Employers need to be cognizant of the value of the exit interview from multiple perspectives as well as understand the role of the exit interview from the perspectives of data collection and communication.

Retirement

Employees also leave the organization through retirement. Except for certain occupations dealing with public safety (such as airline pilots), the Age Discrimination in Employment Act of 1967 prohibits an employer from setting a mandatory retirement age. Because medical advances are allowing individuals to live longer and stay healthier longer, older workers are maintaining a strong and increased presence in the workforce. Ironically, however, many older workers tend to be set in their ways and resistant to change, particularly to technological change. Employers have a distinct challenge in finding ways to keep older workers motivated and productive and ensuring that they do not violate the legal rights of these employees.

When older workers retire, the organization can hire new employees to replace older workers who may have less physical or mental energy or skills that have become dated or obsolete. These new employees may cost less than the older workers relative to salaries and health insurance premiums. Because many older workers are higher in the organizational hierarchy, promotion opportunities may be made available when they retire.

However, significant costs are often associated with retirement. Retirees who have worked for the organization for many years usually have a wealth of knowledge about the industry and the marketplace. They also have extensive historical knowledge about the organization and experience with organizational processes, politics, and culture. Although fresh ideas from outsiders can be critical to an organization, knowledge and experience can be equally important, and decision-makers need to ensure that the organization capitalizes on both to assist in meeting its objectives. The challenge again becomes how to maximize the benefits of retirement while simultaneously minimizing the costs. Reading 13.2, "Knowledge Management among the Older Workforce," presents some insights as to the needs and interests of senior employees as well as some strategies for managing both older workers and the process of knowledge management and retention.

Older workers will become more prominent in the workplace. Employers can usually not set mandatory retirement ages, force employees to retire, or treat older workers in a discriminatory manner in any employment decision. Particularly when conducting layoffs, employers must ensure that there is no adverse treatment of older employees, which would violate the Age Discrimination in Employment Act. Indeed, many large-scale reductions in force have been accompanied by lawsuits that allege discrimination based on age. This issue may be exacerbated in the very near future as the baby boom generation moves through middle age.

Older workers are becoming a reality for employers. A recent study by the American Association of Retired Persons found that 80 percent of the baby boom generation intends to continue to work during retirement.[24] This statistic helps to counteract existing fears concerning the mass retirement of baby boomers in the coming years In fact, the number of Americans age 65 and older in the labor force recently grew by 7 percent, to a total of 4.5 million individuals.[25] One survey of executives found that 44 percent intend to continue working past the age of 64, while 15 percent plan to continue working past the age of 70.[26]

In addition to the many seniors who wish to keep working, there are a number who have to keep working: Lack of adequate health insurance in post-employment years is keeping some seniors in the workforce.[27] Others feel the need to continue working because of the perceived inadequacy of their organization's retirement benefits programs, many of which have been altered in recent year because of the economic downturn.[28] Those workers who are part of the baby boom generation are also known to have a strong work ethic and, in many cases, wish to continue to contribute to their organizations. Another survey of baby boomers reported that 67 percent of this group stated that their main motivation to stay working in later years was the mental stimulation and challenge associated with work.[29] Consequently, employers may face not the anticipated worker shortage but rather an older workforce.

Many older individuals seek to cut back on their working hours in what is known as a "phased retirement" stage of their careers. Employees who opt for phased retirement show a significant lower probability of ever retiring completely compared to those who move from full-time employment to full retirement.[30] However, phased retirement can impact an employee's ability to collect retirement pensions, so it is critical that such programs be structured to benefit both the employee and the organization.[31] As part of overall human resource planning, employers need to determine how to deploy human assets for maximum organizational benefit. Assisting with retirement planning has become a critical strategic human resource function of which phased retirement programs may be a vital component.

Employers can develop programs to give older employees incentives to retire or to take early retirement as long as employees are not coerced into doing so. When older employees retire, the organization can replace them with younger workers, but the organization can lose a great wealth of knowledge and expertise. To remedy this, many employers rehire retirees on a part-time or consulting basis. This allows the organization to retain the benefits these older workers bring to the company and gives these individuals the opportunity to gradually transition into a shorter workweek or semi-retirement. Retirees can enjoy more leisure time and work at a less hectic pace but also continue to make meaningful contributions to their employers, maintain their careers, and stay alert and challenged. Reading 13.3, "Managing Older Worker Exit and Re-entry Practices: A 'Revolving Door'?" presents some findings from a study of retirees in Australia relative to their interest in and desire to gain re-employment once they have initially retired as well as some of the implications this phenomenon has for effective human resource management.

Strategic management of the retirement process results in everyone winning: Retirees gain the best of both worlds; the organization retains their knowledge and experience base; existing employees are afforded opportunities to be promoted; and new employees may be hired and learn from the experiences and knowledge bases of seasoned veterans.

Conclusion

Organizations have only recently begun to pay attention to the HR function of employee separation. The increased pace of merger and acquisition activity as well as downsizings have made HR programs and policies that address employee separation a key strategic issue in ensuring the new organizations' success.

For many years, managing turnover has been ignored, taken for granted, or assumed to be a simple process of automatically terminating poor performers and trying to fill the gaps when employees involuntarily left the organization. It was more of a coping process than any kind of active strategic management. Organizations today, however, are realizing that the effective strategic management of turnover can be a critical factor affecting overall performance.

Retirement is no longer a process of filing paperwork as employees reach mandatory retirement age. Effective management of employee retirement can provide organizations with an important competitive advantage: the means of retaining knowledge, expertise, experience, loyalty, and positive role models while simultaneously allowing an infusion of new ideas and energy. The development of creative, mutually beneficial programs and policies related to retirement will become even more critical as our population ages and baby boomers approach traditional retirement age.[32]

The reality of employee separation is that the organization relinquishes key assets. Every employee represents an investment by the organization in terms of direct and indirect expenditures relative to staffing, training, compensation, and benefits. Strategically managing employee separation entails determining the value of human assets from an investment perspective and considering the costs of discarding these assets. How this process is managed may be one of the most important investment decisions an organization makes.

Critical Thinking

1. Why is it important to manage the process of employee separation?
2. What short-run, long-run, and policy options are available to employers in lieu of layoffs?
3. Under what conditions might layoffs be advantageous to an employer?
4. What costs are associated with turnover? What benefits can be derived from turnover?
5. Explain the Martin and Bartol matrix for managing turnover. How does this relate to taking an investment approach to human resources?

6. Because workers live and stay healthy longer, the workforce is aging. How might this impact an organization's competitive position?
7. Discuss the ways an organization might attempt to retain its most valued employees.

Reading 13.1

8. Locate news accounts in both the popular and business presses of an organization that has recently implemented large scale layoffs. Apply the framework of alternative cost reduction strategies presented in the reading to determine whether any other possible solutions might have allowed the employer to avoid the layoffs/downsizing.

Reading 13.2

9. What are some of the techniques that employers can use to address the needs of senior workers, keep these individuals motivated, and also ensure effective knowledge retention and transfer from these employees?

Reading 13.3

10. What factors influence retirees' plans to remain in the workforce and how might an organization best utilize this source of labor?

Exercises

1. Calculate the turnover costs for a university professor who voluntarily resigns, retires, or is dismissed. Be sure to consider both economic and non-economic costs in your analysis. How difficult is it to gain an accurate accounting of these costs? How might you recommend to the university president that these costs be managed?
2. Select an organization of your choice and examine the extent to which it has established any processes or procedures to ensure knowledge retention of departing employees.
3. Visit the Web sites http://www.aarp.org and http://www.50andoverboard.com. What unique characteristics and needs do older workers have? What special contributions can older workers make to an organization? How might organizations best strategically employ older workers?

Chapter References

1. Melymuka, K. "Kraft's 5% Solution," *Computerworld*, 32, (44): November 2, 1998, pp. 69–71.
2. Juezens, J. "Motivating Survivors," *HR Magazine*, July 2001, pp. 92–99.
3. Jossi, F. "Take the Road Less Traveled," *HR Magazine*, July 2001, pp. 46–51.
4. Cascio, W. F. "Corporate Restructuring and the No-Layoff Policy," *Perspectives On Work*, 7, (1), pp. 4–6.
5. Glebbeek, A. and Bax, E. Is High Employee Turnover Really Harmful? An Empirical Test Using Company Records. *Academy of Management Journal*, 47, 270–286. (2004); Kacmar, K., et al. Sure Everyone Can Be Replaced . . . But At What Cost? Turnover As A Predictor of Unit-level Performance. *Academy of Management Journal*, 49, 133–144 (2006); Macky, K. Organisational Downsizing and Redundancies: The New Zealand Worker's Experience. *New Zealand Journal of Employment Relations*, 29, (1), 63–87 (2004).
6. Devine, K., Reay, T., Stainton, L., and Collins-Nakai, R. The Stress of Downsizing: Comparing Survivors and Victims. *Human Resource Management*, 42, 109–124 (2003).
7. Beylerian, M. and Kleiner, B. The Downsized Workplace. *Management Research News*, 26, 97–108 (2003).
8. Trevor, C. and Nyberg, A. Keeping Your Headcount When All About You Are Losing Theirs: Downsizing, Voluntary Turnover Rates and the Moderating Role of HR Practices. *Academy of Management Journal*, 51, (2), 259–276 (2008).
9. Jossi, F. "Take the Road Less Traveled," *HR Magazine*, July 2001, pp. 46–51.
10. Joinson, C. "Capturing Turnover Costs," *HR Magazine*, July 2000, pp. 107–119.
11. Bacarro, J. P. "The Hidden Cost of Employee Turnover," *Grant Thornton Benefits and HR Advisor*, Grant Thornton, 1992.
12. Schlesinger, L. A. and Heskett, J. A. "The Service-Driven Service Company," *Harvard Business Review*, 69, September–October 1991, pp. 71–81.
13. Barrette, D. L. "Survey Highlights Retention Concerns," *HR News*, 19, (10), October 2000, Alexandria, VA: Society for Human Resource Management, pp. 11–16.
14. Martin, David C. and Bartol, Kathryn M. "Managing Turnover Strategically," *Personnel Administrator*, November 1985.
15. Taylor, C. R. "Focus on Talent," *Training & Development*, December 2002, pp. 26–31.
16. Ibid.
17. Cole, A. "Attendants Fight United Retention Plan," CBS.MarketWatch.com, July 7, 2003.
18. Leonard, B. "Inside Job," *HR Magazine*, October 2001, pp. 64–68.
19. Ibid.
20. MacLean, B. "Rewarding Contribution, Not Job Title: A Base Pay Strategy to Retain Peak Performers," Society for Human Resource Management, article 015913, published at www.shrm.org/hrnews/published/artides/CMS Q20036.asp, January, 2007; Gurchiek, K. "Lack of Career Advancement Main Reason Workers Consider Leaving," Society for Human Resource Management, article 024814, published at www.shrm.org/hrnews/published/articles/CMS 016356.asp, February 29, 2008.

21. Branham, L. "The 7 Hidden Reasons Employees Leave," AMACOM (2005).
22. Daniel, T. "Managing for Employee Retention," Society for Human Resource Management, published at www.shrm.org/research/articles, March 1, 2009.
23. Frase-Blunt, M. "Making Exit Interviews Work," *HR Magazine*, 49, (8), August 2004, pp. 109–113.
24. Carpenter, D. "Looking Forward to a Long Goodbye," *South Florida Sun-Sentinel*, September 18, 2002, p. 10D.
25. Ibid.
26. Pomeroy, A. "They Keep Going (and Going...)," *HR Magazine*, 50, (6), June 2005, p. 20.
27. Grensing-Pophal, L. "Departure Plans," *HR Magazine*, July 2003, pp. 83–86.
28. Pomeroy, A. "They Keep Going (and Going...)," *HR Magazine*, 50, (6), June 2005, p. 20.
29. Gurchiek, K. "Workers Taking Phase Retirement: A Special Breed," Society for Human Resource Management, article 015913, published at www.shrm.org/hrnews/published/articles/CMS 016356.asp, February 23, 2006.
30. Gurchiek, K. "Workers Taking Phase Retirement: A Special Breed," Society for Human Resource Management, article 015913, published at www.shrm.org/hrnews/published/articles/CMS 016356.asp, February 23, 2006.
31. Hirschman, C. "Exit Strategy," *HR Magazine*, December 2001, pp. 52–57.
32. Leonard, S. "The Aging Workforce; As Baby Boomers Retire, Employers Will Face New Challenges," *Workplace Visions*, No. 1. Alexandria, VA: Society for Human Resource Management (2000).

READING 13.1

Cost Reductions, Downsizing-related Layoffs, and HR Practices

Franco Gandolfi

Introduction

Organizational decimation, or downsizing, has been a pervasive managerial practice for the past three decades. If a firm finds itself in financial difficulties, the widely accepted corporate panacea has been to cut personnel. While strong empirical evidence suggests that reduction-in-force (RIF) activities rarely return the anticipated economic and organizational gains (Cascio, Young, and Morris, 1997), there is increased understanding and awareness that downsized companies are forced to deal with the human and societal after-effects, also known as secondary effects, in a post-downsizing phase (Gandolfi, 2007). Research shows that the human consequences of layoffs are costly and devastating for individuals, their families, and entire communities (Macky, 2004). While workforce reductions cannot always be completely avoided, downsizing-related layoffs must be a managerial tool of absolute last rather than first resort (Gandolfi, 2006).

During an economic downturn, a company must carefully consider its options and assess the feasibility and applicability of cost-reduction alternatives prior to adopting RIF-related layoffs. While a large body of research presenting and discussing the alternatives to downsizing has emerged (Littler, 1998; Mirabal and DeYoung, 2005), there is still a lack of conceptual understanding of downsizing-related layoffs as part of an organization's cost-reduction stages (Gandolfi, 2008). It is vital for a firm to factor in the concept of cost-reduction and recognize the specific cost-reduction stage that characterizes the firms' current business position and environment. Ideally, a company should be in a position to determine the expected duration and severity of the business downturn as accurately as possible. To perform that task successfully, the executives need to know the cost-cutting phase that the firm is currently in (Vernon, 2003). A firm's cost-reduction stage refers to the time-frame the organization requires to be able to reduce operational expenditures (George, 2004). In reality, however, accurately forecasting a business downturn can be extremely difficult. Thus, firms have a natural tendency to react to rather than anticipate economic declines (Gandolfi, 2006).

The primary objective of this paper is to present a methodology enabling firms to minimize, defer, or avoid the adoption of RIF, layoffs, and downsizing-related activities. The research introduces and showcases a conceptual framework presenting the cost-reduction stages of a firm coupled with a brief introduction of contemporary human resources (HR) practices that some firms have adopted. Fundamentally, the paper builds upon Vernon's (2003), George's (2004), and Gandolfi's (2008) work of three cost-reduction stages: short-range, mid-range, and long-range phases. Technically speaking, the article constitutes a review and extension of previously published work. The underlying conceptual framework of the cost-reduction stages is depicted in Figure 1.

Cost-reduction Stages

The conceptual framework shown in Figure 1 encompasses three timeframe-related phases commanding several internal cost adjustments that have produced a variety of stage-related HR practices. It is important to note that the HR practices are cumulative. In other words, the practices in each stage are not unique to the actual phase, but applicable in subsequent phases in a cumulative fashion.

First Stage: Short-range Cost Adjustments

The first stage of the cost-reduction framework represents short-range cost adjustments in response to a short, temporary decline in business activities (Vernon, 2003). These business slowdowns are expected to last less than six months (Gandolfi, 2008). Most likely, the firm resorts to minor, moderate cost-reduction measures in this stage. These preliminary adjustments should enable the firm to shun RIF-related layoffs and involuntary cutbacks and return to normal business activity within four to six months (Gandolfi, 2008). Typically, this phase originates with an unexpected drop in sales or a decline in sales forecast. It is characterized by short-term expenditure adjustments to prevent a medium-range downturn or a more lasting, long-range decline. The immediate recognition of a temporary business slip and the resolute engagement in preliminary cost-reduction methods should allow the firm to focus its operations in a cost-sensitive mode for a quick recovery (Vernon, 2003).

FIGURE 13.1 Conceptual Framework of Cost-reduction Stages

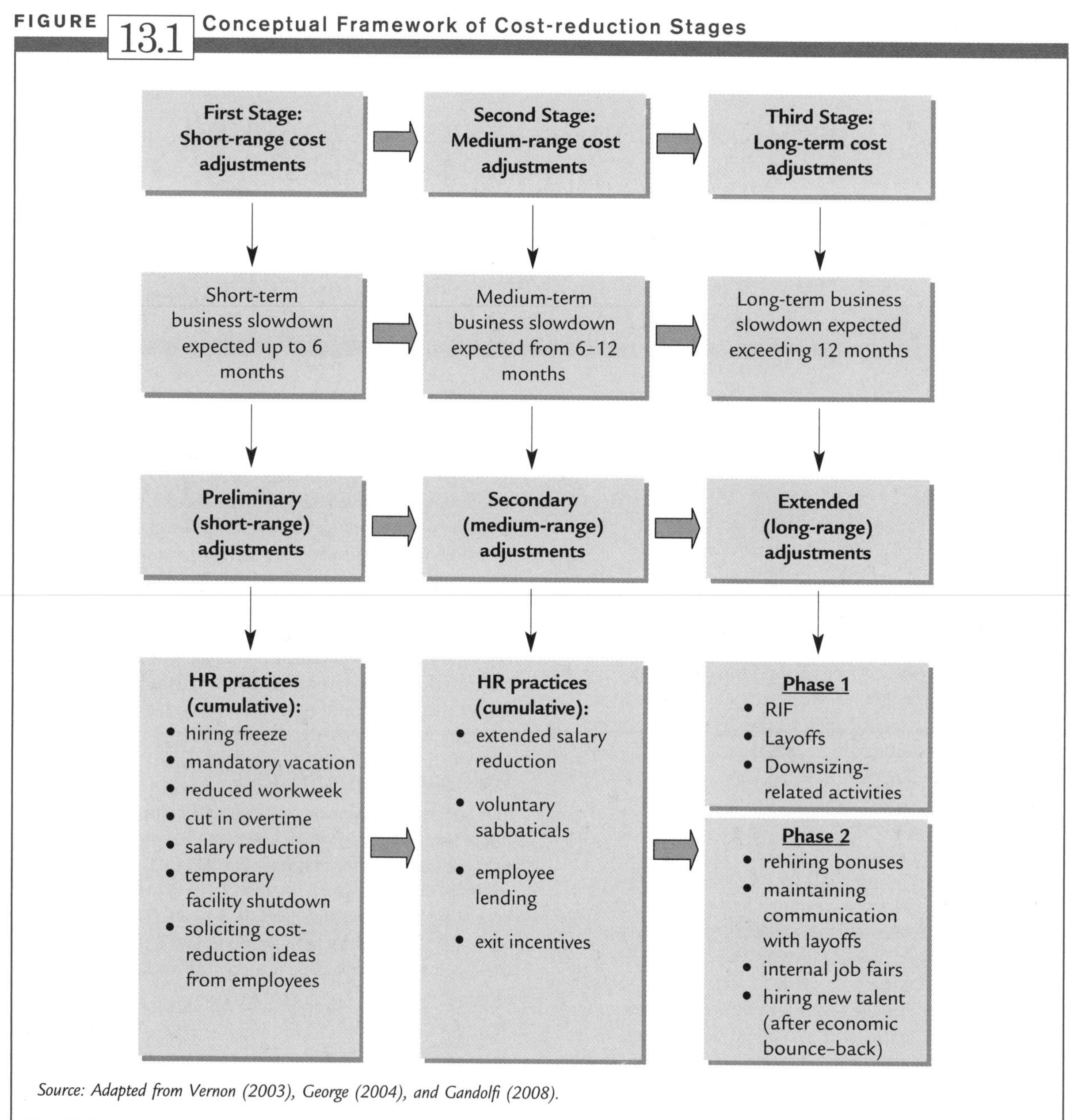

Source: Adapted from Vernon (2003), George (2004), and Gandolfi (2008).

The probability of success for the short-range cost adjustments hinges on a number of factors: First, senior management must be able to articulate the business necessity for the cost-adjustment measures effectively and stress the short timeframe of the strategy. A firm's ability to convey the message that preliminary cost-reduction measures at the present time will likely prevent RIF-related layoffs in the future is critical. Second, the HR's role is to communicate decisions made by the board of directors to the entire workforce promptly and to implement the cost-reduction methods swiftly. Third, the employees' flexibility in allowing the firm to modify cost structures increases the chance of success for the planned cost alterations. Therefore, a firm's capacity to overcome a business downturn in the first stage will depend to a large degree on its organization's ability to respond to the new environment by immediately and resolutely modifying expenditures (Vernon, 2003).

Suggested HR Practices for Short-range Cost Adjustments A review of the literature and the popular press reveals several HR-related practices that firms have implemented for preliminary cost reductions. The following is a non-exhaustive overview and explanation of some of the approaches suggested by scholars and implemented by firms in the global corporate landscape.

- **Hiring Freeze**

A hiring freeze is a mild form of downsizing that reduces labor costs in the short term (Littler, 1998). However, a hiring freeze does not imply that there is no hiring activity at all. Some firms hire new employees while cutting jobs at the same time (Vernon, 2003). While this practice may make sense in terms of supplying the firm with key personnel, it tends to send a confusing message to the workforce. As an example, in its latest attempt to fight rising jet fuel costs and a deteriorating U.S. economy, American Airlines imposed an immediate hiring freeze on all management and support staff (Maxon, 2008).

- **Mandatory Vacation**

Mandatory vacation involves requiring employees to use their accrued vacation days or requiring them to take a number of unpaid vacation days during a certain time period. While employees might not want to be told when and how to use their entitlements, they will nonetheless appreciate the reaffirmed job security (Vernon, 2003). At the time of writing, Chrysler plans a corporate-wide shutdown of its U.S. operations during two weeks in July 2008 to improve the automaker's efficiency and boost productivity (Govreau, 2008).

- **Reduced Workweek**

Firms sometimes resort to a reduced workweek. This may translate into a reduction from 40 to 35 or fewer hours, thereby reducing short-term payroll expenditures. While most employees appreciate being able to spend more time with their families, a reduced paycheck is not always welcomed. Also, employees may find that the same amount of work still needs to be performed while they spend less time on the job (Gandolfi, 2008). Nucor Steel Corporation in South Carolina has avoided layoffs for 35 years by resorting to two and three workdays for its employees during downturns (George, 2004). In a similar vein, in 2008, workers at a St. Thomas automotive parts plant in the U.K. voted a reduction in their workweek rather than see 200 employees leave permanently (De Bono, 2008).

- **Cut in Overtime Pay**

Minimizing or abolishing overtime pay for employees can be a powerful technique of reducing operational costs in the short term (Vernon, 2003). Firms may institute an across-the-board (i.e., all employees) abolition or confine the cut to selected categories, such as nonmanagerial, blue-collar, or salaried employees (Gandolfi, 2008). In 2004, GM and Ford and car-supplier Visteon Corporation slashed overtime pay for most employees indefinitely (Dybis and Garsten, 2004).

- **Salary Reduction**

Salary reduction methods have been standard practice for firms experiencing unexpected financial pressure. Whereas salary reductions mitigate financial concerns in the short run, extended salary reductions can negatively affect employee morale and loyalty. Also, while companywide salary reductions prevent layoffs, there is a clear risk that top performers will be encouraged to leave for competitors that dangle superior compensation (Gandolfi, 2008). In 2006, White Electronics Designs introduced salary reductions of 5% for salaried employees and 10% for management, while the hourly workers remained unaffected. In 2006, a collation of Intel managers agreed to take a temporary 100% pay cut to avoid permanent layoffs. Prior to that, Intel announced that it had planned to cut 10,000 employees, including 1,000 managers (Paul, 2006).

- **Temporary Facility Shutdown**

Temporary facility shutdowns occur when a work site closes for a designated period of time, while some administrative functions still perform (Vernon, 2003). A shutdown allows employees to have time off without using their vacation days. While overall company production decreases, the firm can achieve considerable costs savings, thereby avoiding layoffs. In early 2008, Aleris International shut down its rolling mill production in Virginia to align production with demand. As a consequence, production for customers was phased out and transferred to other facilities within the U.S. (Aleris, 2008).

- **Soliciting Cost-reduction Ideas from Employees**

Employees appreciate the opportunity to make a positive impact on their workplace and environment. Firms frequently solicit cost-reduction ideas from employees, who are often creative in producing such solutions. This HR practice has proven to be most effective when employees are able to make suggestions in the early stages of cost cutting (Vernon, 2003). At Martin Heyman Associates, all professional construction consultants are encouraged to contribute cost-reduction ideas. Unfortunately, many executives still do not realize that employees are the best source of such ideas because workers on the job are in a prime position to identify and recognize waste (Yorke, 2005).

This overview has shown that there are numerous HR tools at an executive's disposal to reduce short-term expenditures. While some firms have come up with innovative ideas, others have used layoffs as a very first resort. Again, it must be understood that the techniques introduced in this stage are cumulative and applicable in other stages. Moreover, the utilization of each HR practice is unique in that each selected tool will have certain consequences that need to be carefully considered by management prior to adoption.

Second Stage: Medium-range Cost Adjustments

The second stage of the cost-reduction frame-work comprises medium-term cost adjustments in response to a medium-range business down-turn exceeding six months (Vernon, 2003) and up to 12 months (Gandolfi, 2008). These secondary cost-reduction adjustments are frequently signaled through extended company-wide or industry-wide forecasts of diminished sales activity. If properly recognized and executed, the firm may be able to transition to mid-range cost adjustment and thus prevent long-term, RIF-related layoffs and forced downsizing. In this phase constituencies need to recognize that deeper cost-reduction strategies may be required to avert downsizing-related layoffs. Senior management must be able to present the purpose and objectives of the expenditure adjustments convincingly to the entire workforce. This should ensure employee buy-in and commitment. Adopting HR practices in this stage could potentially alter employees' work environment. Therefore, the HR department will play an essential role in the conduct and transition of these practices (Gandolfi, 2008).

Suggested HR Practices for Medium-range Cost Adjustments A review of the literature and the popular press reveals several HR-related practices that corporations have used trying to obtain secondary cost reductions. The following is a non-exhaustive summary of practices recommended by scholars and introduced in the corporate landscape.

- **Extended Salary Reductions**

Extending salary reductions can be a method of choice if an economic downturn exceeds six months (Vernon, 2003). While the extension of salary reductions can negatively affect employee commitment and morale, advocates stress that employees would prefer a smaller income temporarily than a permanent loss of their jobs. As with short-term salary reductions, there is a risk that high-performing individuals are encouraged to pursue external employment opportunities (Gandolfi, 2008). Firms have generally been innovative regarding altering variable pay options. Specifically, while some firms balance the reduced salaries by distributing once-a-year payments over 12 months, others substitute stock awards for variable cash payment. For example, U.S. firm 415 Production offered an overall 5% pay cut or a four-day work week reflecting the appropriate decrease in pay to its employees (Morss, 2008).

- **Voluntary Sabbaticals**

Voluntary sabbaticals, also called furloughs, allow salaried employees to take voluntary leaves for a designated period of time. Companies may offer sabbaticals with considerably reduced or no pay. Most firms continue to provide benefits during sabbaticals. Sabbaticals enable firms to reduce their medium-term expenditure and can be effective in avoiding downsizing-related layoffs (Gandolfi, 2008). While employees may feel motivated and re-energized upon their return, HR professionals point out that medium-and long-term sabbaticals may cause employees to lose their leading edge and to return with outdated skills. Interestingly, evidence suggests that firms offer generous sabbaticals during times of economic growth but refrain from this HR practice during tough financial periods (Vernon, 2003). Practical examples abound. For example, in 2001, consulting firm Accenture announced that 800 employees qualified for a special voluntary sabbatical program, while 600 employees were going to be laid off permanently (Taub, 2001). In 2001, Information and Communication Mobile, a Siemens division, offered its employees a one-year time-out at reduced pay without losing their jobs permanently (Perera, 2001). Siemens was thus able to reduce costs without losing high-performing employees during difficult economic times.

- **Employee Lending**

With this HR practice, the current employer lends an employee to another employer firm for a set period of time while continuing to pay salary and providing benefits (Vernon, 2003). The borrowing firm, which can be a competitor, in return, reimburses the lending company for part or all of the salary. While employee lending can dramatically decrease medium-range expenditure of the lending firm, some employees may not wish to work for a third party. There is also the risk that the borrowing firm decides to hire the employee permanently once the contracted period is lapsed. As a consequence, the lending firm would loose a critical knowledge base (Gandolfi, 2008). Texas Instruments engaged in lending HR staffers to vendors for up to eight months with the intention of bringing them back to their original jobs at the end of that period. The supplier reimbursed Texas Instruments for their staffers' salaries during the loan period and agreed not to offer them permanent jobs (Morss, 2008).

- **Exit Incentives**

Exit incentive options give employees the option of leaving the firm and collecting severance pay or taking early retirement (Vernon, 2003). This strategy enables firms to target jobs while recognizing employees for their service and helps the firm retain the remaining employees (Gandolfi, 2008). Exit incentives can be costly and may create an entitlement mentality for the remaining workforce in the future (George, 2004). In 2007, technology-outsourcing firm EDS (Electronic Date Systems) offered extra retirement benefits to its 12,000 U.S. employees in an offer to accept early retirement (EDS, 2007).

Corporate leaders need to be innovative about reducing medium-term expenditures. As with previous stage, some firms have demonstrated creativity and resourcefulness regarding the design and implementation of medium-range cost-reduction practices. Anecdotal evidence indicates a natural tendency for firms to resort to layoffs hastily by default without considering legitimate alternatives (Gandolfi, 2008).

Third Stage: Long-range Cost Adjustments

The third stage of the cost-reduction framework represents long-term adjustments that are necessary if a firm experiences a prolonged business downturn exceeding 12 months. This stage may be recognized through an extended decline of current and projected customer demand or extremely volatile economic conditions (Vernon, 2003). The third stage generally requires extended expenditure adjustments by the firm (Gandolfi, 2008). In this timeframe RIF, layoffs, and downsizing-related activities are frequently inevitable. The third stage has two phases (see Figure 1). Phase 1 contains workforce reduction strategies that firms commonly adopt after a prolonged business downturn. While RIF and downsizing activities should always be seen as a last resort, firms should avoid mass layoffs at all costs (Macky, 2004; Gandolfi, 2007). Companies who find themselves engaged in deep workforce cuts must adopt HR practices that instill loyalty and commitment in the remaining and exiting workforces (Vernon, 2003). In contrast, Phase 2 encompasses HR activities that aim to re-attract formerly laid off individuals and hire new employees in a post-downsizing period. This pre-supposes that the RIF have been implemented, that the business downturn has ended and reversed, and that the firm is able and willing to re-hire.

Suggested HR Practices for Long-range Cost Adjustments. Firms forced to embrace permanent RIF and layoffs have reported mixed results. While the execution of downsizing promises immediate financial relief, considerable empirical evidence demonstrates that downsizing-related strategies do not automatically translate into improved organizational performance (Littler, 1998; Macky, 2004). Such strategies have significant secondary consequences for the firm and its stakeholders (Gandolfi, 2006). While downsizing and RIF-related layoffs should always be a strategy of absolute last resort (Gandolfi, 2007), it is clear that layoffs are at times warranted, desirable, or unavoidable. Once the firm has conducted RIF-related activities, the firm will need to re-position itself to be able to re-attract those laid off or hire new employees. Again, this presumes that the economy has bounced back sufficiently and that the firm is in a position to hire again. Some firms re-hire formerly laid off employees, whereas others opt to return to the labor market and seek out new talent. How does the firm attract previous employees? The following constitutes a brief summary of three commonly-used practices.

- **Rehiring Bonuses**

While some firms provide a monetary rehiring bonus for veterans to return within a specified period, others hire laid-off employees as external consultants. In some cases, firms realize that they cut too many or the wrong employees, while in other cases management decides to hire back after the economic downturn (Vernon, 2003). Evidence suggests that employees and consultants return to the downsized firm with improved monetary rewards (Gandolfi, 2006). For instance, in 2001 and after two rounds of deep layoffs, Charles Schwab Corp. offered a $7,500 hiring bonus for any previously downsized employee rehired by the firm within 18 months following the layoffs (Morss, 2008).

- **Maintaining Communication with Laid-off Employees**

Firms frequently make a concerted effort to maintain friendly relations with laid-off employees (Vernon, 2003). Modern-day technology, including Internet forums, 24-7 hotlines, and e-mail, provides effective ways to foster and sustain positive employer-employee relationships (Lublin, 2007). This is particularly important if firms intend to rehire the former employees when the economic climate has improved.

- **Internal Job Fairs**

Firms should make every possible attempt to retain high-performing employees (Gandolfi, 2008). A powerful method is an internal job fair, where firms host events to help place and redeploy downsized employees within the company. For example, the Ford Motor Company is currently putting on internal job fairs in its U.S. plants to entice employees to find new careers beyond the assembly-line (Vlasic, 2008).

Concluding Comments

This paper has presented a methodology of cost-reduction stages enabling firms to minimize, delay, or circumvent reductions-in-force, layoffs, and downsizing-related activities. The depicted conceptual framework is an extension of Vernon's (2003), George's (2004), and Gandolfi's (2008) original work on cost-reduction stages, including an expansion of the third stage incorporating two distinct phases. The research has shown that the key to responsible cost reduction and the selection of appropriate cost reduction methods can be found in the alignment of a firm's cost reduction practices with its current cost-reduction stage. The paper has further established that it is difficult for a firm to accurately forecast the duration and magnitude of a business downturn. Consequently, firms have a natural tendency to respond reactively rather than to anticipate economic declines.

Source: SAM Advanced Management Journal, 73, (3), 52–58 (2008). *Reprinted by permission.*

REFERENCES

Aleris. (2008). Aleris announces temporary shutdown of its Richmond, Virginia, rolling mill facility. Retrieved from http://www.prnewswire.com/cgi-bin/stories.pl? ACCT=109&STORY=/www/story/02-22-2008/0004760651&EDATE=

Cascio, W.F., Young, C., and Morris, J. (1997). Financial consequences of employment-change decisions in major U.S. corporations. *Academy of Management Journal*, 40(5), 1175–1189.

DeBono, N. (2008, March 18). Presstran workers vote for reduced work week. *Sun Media*. Retrieved from http://lfpress.ca/cgi-bin/publish.cgi?p=228100&s=wheels

Dybis, K. and Garsten, E. (2004, March 18). Michigan firms cut overtime. *The Detroit News*. Retrieved from http://www.detnews.com/2004/specialreport/0403/18/a01-96041.htm

EDS. (2007, September 13). EDS offers exit incentives to 12,000 workers. *The New York Times*. Retrieved from http://www.nytimes.com/2007/09/13/technology/13data.html?partner=rssnyt&emc=rss

Gandolfi, F. (2006). *Corporate downsizing demystified: A scholarly analysis of a business phenomenon*, Hyderabad. India: ICFAI University Press.

Gandolfi, F. (2007). How do large Australian and Swiss banks implement downsizing? *Journal of Management & Organization.* 13(2), 145–159.

Gandolfi, F. (2008, July/August). HR strategies that can take the sting out of downsizing-related layoffs. *Ivey Business Journal.*

George, J. (2004). Cutting costs: should personnel be the first to go? *Employment Practices Solution.* Retrieved from http://www.epexperts.com/modules.php?op=modload&name=News&file=:article&sid=1409

Govreau, J. (2008, March 14). Chrysler announces mandatory two-week shutdown of all plans in July 2008. *Market Watch from Dow Jones.* Retrieved from http://www.marketwatch.com/news/story/chrysler-announces-mandatory-two-week-shutdown/story.aspx?guid=%7BD7228E3E-9177-4EC7-A0EB-3946EAA50A66%7D

Littler, C.R. (1998). Downsizing organisations: The dilemmas of change. *Human Resources Management Bulletin*, CCH Australia Limited, Sydney.

Lublin, J. (2007, September 24). Employers see value in helping those laid off. *The Wall Street Journal Online.* Retrieved from http://online.wsj.com/public/article/SB119058596757936693.html

Macky, K. (2004). Organizational downsizing and redundancies: The New Zealand workers' experience. *New Zealand Journal of Employment Relations*, 29(1), 63–87.

Maxon, T. (2008, April 4). American Airlines imposes hiring freeze on management and support staff. *The Dallas Morning News.* Retrieved from www.dallasnews.com/sharedcontent/dws/bus/stories/040508dnbusaafreeze.368d67e.html

Mendels, P. (2001, April 18). Downsizing pay, not people. *Business Week.* Retrieved from www.businessweek.com/careers/content/apr2001/ca20010418_060.htm

Mirabal, N. and DeYoung, R. (2005). Downsizing as a strategic intervention. *Journal of American Academy of Business*, 6(1), 39–45.

Morss, R. (2008). Creative layoff policy and alternatives to layoffs, *Salary.com.* Retrieved from http://www.salary.com/personal/layoutscripts/psnl_articles.asp?tab=psn&cat=cat011&ser=ser032&part=par276

Paul (2006). 100% pay reduction for all Intel employees. Retrieved from www.starkedsf.com/archives/100-pay-reduction-for-all-intel-employees-a-tnt-special-report/

Perera, R. (2001, August 31). Siemens offers workers 'time outs' to save cash. *IDG News Service.* Retrieved from http://www.thestandard.com/article/0,1902,28858,00.html

Taub, P. (2001, June 7). Accenture to cut 600 jobs, *CFO.com.* Retrieved from http://www.cfo.com/article.cfm/2996624?f=search

Vernon, L. (2003, March). The downsizing dilemma; a manager's toolkit for avoiding layoffs. *Society for Human Resources Management (SHRM)*, White Paper.

Vlasic, B. (2008, February 26). Ford is pushing buyouts to workers, *The New York Times.* Retrieved from http://www.nytimes.com/2008/02/26/business/26ford.html?_r=1&oref=slogin

Yorke, C. (2005). Why employees are the best source of cost-cutting ideas. Ezine Articles. Retrieved from http://ezinearticles.com/?Why-Employees-Are-the-Best-Source-of-Cost-cutting-Ideas&id=:66695

READING 13.2

Knowledge Management Among the Older Workforce

Floor Slagter

Introduction

The world is never standing still. The world is quickly changing; internationalization increases, regulations change and costumers demand flexibility, speed and quality. This makes it difficult for an organization to keep up with its environment, or even be competitive. Literature has devoted a lot of attention to these topics and new concepts made their entry, like total quality management, business process reengineering and learning organizations. It becomes more and more obvious that the optimal generation and application of knowledge is one of the most important keys to success. An organization needs to be flexible in order to keep up with their competitors and knowledge is needed to obtain that flexibility. Knowledge management is a discipline that recognizes the importance of knowledge and assists organizations in optimally using the knowledge that is present in the organization.

Another issue that is being extensively discussed in journals now a day is the ageing workforce; between 2005 and 2015 the so-called baby boomers are going to retire *en masse*. A well-planned and effective knowledge transfer between the different generations of the workforce is of great importance. Knowledge about the organization, the processes within the company, and much more critical organizational knowledge need to be transferred to the other generation of employees. If this does not happen then this knowledge will disappear and the knowledge level of many organizations will become unbalanced. Especially in knowledge intensive industries this can have disastrous consequences. Knowledge management is an activity that can help organizations to overcome these threats.

This article will bring these two topics together; the senior employee and knowledge management. First the two topics will be discussed separately in order to create clarity about their content and meaning. Secondly, the issues will be combined and aligned. Furthermore this article will provide a number of guidelines for human resource (HR) managers, which they can use as a starting point when coping with this problem.

Knowledge Management: Definition and Processes

There exists a lot of discussion about what the proper definition of knowledge management is or should be. Scholars, practitioners, and others in field of business management are still debating about the concepts and definitions related to knowledge management (KM) and its definition is currently still evolving. To give an impression of what kind of concepts are used in the different definitions, below a few of them will be discussed. One definition of KM is one by Groff and Jones (2003):

> *Knowledge management is the tools, techniques, and strategies to retain, analyze, organize, improve, and share business expertise.*

This definition places the emphasis on the KM processes that take place within an organization and especially the IT facilities that support these processes. This definition is more about managing explicit knowledge, by the use of IT. The human factor is not mentioned.

Another widely accepted definition is the following of Dr. Yogesh Malhotra:

> *Knowledge management caters to the critical issues of organizational adaptation, survival, and competence in face of increasingly discontinuous environmental change ... Essentially, it embodies organizational processes that seek synergistic combination of data and information processing capacity of information technologies, and the creative and innovative capacity of human beings (Dr. Yogesh Malhotra).*

This definition is more encapsulating the human factor that is needed to manage knowledge. This leads us to the following definition of Rastogi (2000), who really emphasizes the importance of the human factor in his definition. This definition focuses on the ability of individuals and groups to enable knowledge creation, use and sharing. The definition is:

> *Knowledge management as a systematic and integrative process of coordinating organization-wide*

activities of acquiring, creating, storing, sharing, diffusing, developing, and deploying knowledge by individuals and groups in pursuit of major organizational goals. It is the process through which organizations create and use their institutional and collective knowledge.

This article will use this definition of KM, since this definition recognizes the importance of the human factor in KM by focusing on the ability of individuals and groups to enable knowledge creation, use and sharing. This article will focus on KM among senior employees and places its emphasis on how KM can be optimized among this group of employees. The human factor is therefore very important to take into account.

Although there exist not yet agreement about what the definition of knowledge management should be, researchers agree that KM is an important activity for an organization to undertake.

But why is KM so important? To stay, or even become competitive it is extremely important for organizations to be flexible and to be able to adapt quickly. Knowledge is thereby an important factor.

Knowledge management focuses on ways of sharing, storing and maintaining knowledge, as a means of improving efficiency, speed, and competency of individuals within an organization, and therefore increasing the profitability, flexibility and adaptability.

Within literature a lot of different processes that form KM can be distinguished. However it is possible to bring these activities back to four processes in which the basic operations of KM are realized. In Figure 1 these processes are depicted.

This article is mostly concerned with the processes of guaranteeing existing knowledge and the distribution of knowledge, since these are the first two processes that come to the front when employees leave the organization (in case of this article the senior employee).

FIGURE 1 The four Basic Processes of Knowledge Management

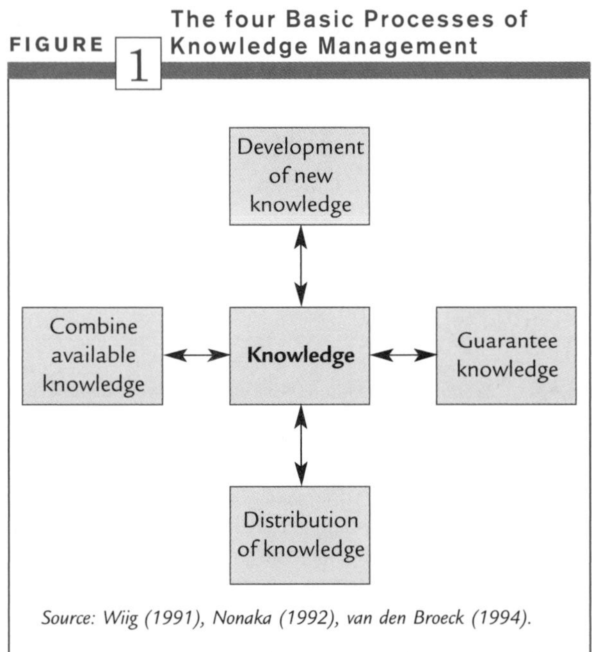

Source: Wiig (1991), Nonaka (1992), van den Broeck (1994).

The Ageing Workforce

To be able to clarify why this article is focusing on knowledge management among the senior employee and why this is becoming so increasingly important it is necessary to take a look at the recent developments within the labor force and the characteristics of the senior employee.

The percentage of employees in the age group 50 to 60 increased significantly the last ten years. The increase of senior employees within organization has certain consequences for managers, and it also means that the upcoming years many of the senior employees will retire. Most organizations are not fully aware of the serious consequences that the loss of this large source of labor can have (Ekamper *et al.*, 2001). Research has shown that individual managers do not seem to have a sense of urgency that they need to anticipate and act on this development (Ekamper *et al.*, 2001). However, there is a need to act and anticipate since these employees have a great pool of knowledge at their disposal.

After discussing these developments it is necessary to discuss how to define the senior employee exactly. This article will use the definition of employees within the age group 54–60 years. This because a lot of studies and research concerning the senor worker use the same definition and in this way it is easier to apply the knowledge gained in those researches to the problem discussed in this article.

The Managers' Perspective on the Senior Worker

There is of course no single "managers' perspective" on senior workers, and it is important to emphasize that, in all different literature that exist about this issue, there is evidence of both positive and negative images of senior workers, and of good practice and bad. However there are some themes that often come to the fore, when discussing senior workers with managers. To illustrate this, the findings in this area within the 1990s and some current findings will be discussed.

Two studies performed in the 1990s (Institute for Manpower Studies, 1990; Lynn and Glover, 1998) of manager attitudes to senior workers suggested that managers associated certain characteristics with age. These are shown in Table 1 and can be seen in both a positive and negative way.

A recent study performed by Remery *et al.* (2001) found out that a lot of managers tend to associate an increase in the average age of their workforce with higher labor costs. Managers also tended to lock upon senior staff as employees with a high level of absenteeism and a resistance to change. But managers also associate an older workforce with higher levels of experience and an increase in know-how.

These presumptions narrow the mindsets of managers; when they think mainly negatively about the senior employee, they will not initiate activities for these employees

Table 1 Positive and Negative Characteristics of Senior Employees According to Managers

Positive Characteristics	Negative Characteristics
Responsibility and maturity	Lack of flexibility
Commitment to work	Slow to adapt or resistance to change
Experience	Outdated skills, particularly in relation to new technology
"Staying put" in a job	Lack of mobility
	Difficult to retrain
	Prone to ill-health

that demand flexibility, change, etc., since managers are convinced that this age group is incapable of living up to these demands. In this way the senior employee never gets a chance to "prove" him/herself.

It might be the case that managers bring all these presumptions to the fore to cover their true reason why they do not like to employ senior employees; the high costs. But when managers want to get rid of senior employees as soon as possible, because of the high costs, they tend to overlook one important thing; by firing the employee the knowledge gained by the employee over the years go with him/her.

From the information above we can conclude that the perspective that managers have on senior employees has not changed significantly over the years. But what is actually true about these presumptions? Different studies (McIntosh, 2000; Society for Human Resource Management, 1998) affirmed that, in general, senior workers:

- had low turnover rates;
- were flexible and open to change;
- possessed up-to-date skills;
- were interested in learning new tasks;
- had low absentee rates; and
- had few on-the-job accidents.

The only area where professionals expressed their concern was the area of senior employees and new technology (McIntosh, 2000).

It is interesting to see the contradictions that exist. But how do we find out what is true? This issue will be addressed under "recommendations".

Characteristics of the Senior Employee

Senior employees have other characteristics than younger employees. This part of the article will discuss the most important differences.

Motivation and Job Satisfaction

There are a lot of theories about what motivates employees. One of the earliest ones was Maslow's (1954) theory. He explains a certain hierarchy of human needs; five levels of needs that can be visualized in a pyramid (see Figure 2).

In order to motivate employees a manager needs to satisfy their needs. The satisfaction of these needs can be realized by:

- money (material needs; level 1 and 2);
- a say in things and involvement (level 3 and 4); and
- a certain degree of autonomy or independence (level 5).

As a human being grows to maturity, the need for experiencing respect increases, implying both respect for others and self-respect. The same is true for the needs for self-actualization. Both needs function as a motivator for the senior worker (Keuning, 1998).

Also, as employees grow older, interesting work becomes more of a motivator. A report by Heymann and Terlien shows that senior employees want work that has a meaning; they want to feel useful on the work floor. These researchers also emphasize that respect and recognition are highly valued by senior employees. Managers should keep these changes among adulthood in mind, to be able to employ their employees as efficient and effective as possible through all stages of life. Research performed by Diekstra (2003) also recognizes the importance of job significance among senior employees.

Job satisfaction shows consistently that work-related attitudes are more positive with increasing age in surveys of employed adults. Senior workers may have a different perspective on work than younger adults. For senior workers, survival needs are less likely to be urgent as they will probably have reached the maximum income for their jobs. Senior workers report that job satisfaction is more closely related to intrinsic or internal rewards of work (Sterns and Miklos, 1995). This theory supports the findings of Keuning, related to Maslow's theory.

As people grow older they find it important to reach a certain balance between their work and their private life. This is also linked up with their changing needs. Senior workers demand for flexible working hours, also keeping health issues in the back of their minds. The degree to which the employer can adjust to these needs affects the level of job satisfaction of the senior employee.

FIGURE 2 Maslow's Pyramid of Needs

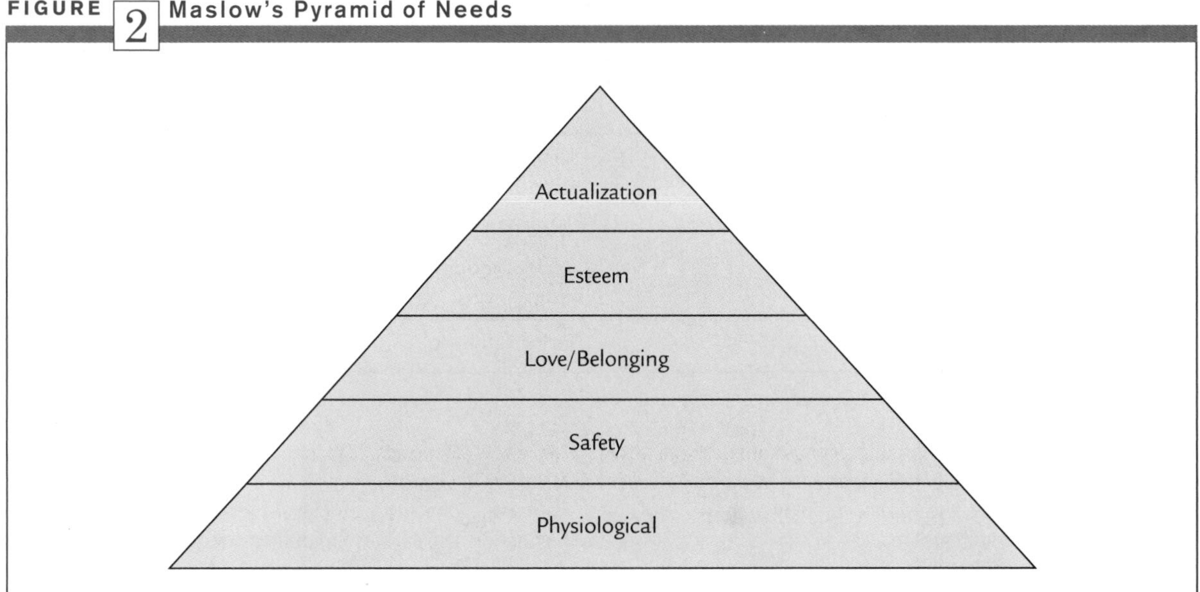

Self-development among Senior Employees

Today's society has self development high in its standard. The younger generation is used to setting goals for themselves with regard to what they want to achieve. A lot of managers are of opinion that employees are responsible themselves for their development and career. However, a lot of senior employees expect their managers to come up with initiatives concerning their development and career path (Heymann and Terlien, 2003). They are not used to taking initiative in this area. A coaching leadership style would be very appropriate for this age group. In that way the manager can show the different possibilities and the employee gets a better overview of what is possible for him/her and can subsequently make his/her decision.

Knowledge of the Senior Employee

A study of Kanfer and Ackerman (2004) explains that there exists a strong positive association between adult age and knowledge level. Tacit knowledge needs to be transferred from the senior employee to the younger one, since senior employees have built up a lot of experience and organizational know-how. Senior employees can be reticent in sharing their knowledge with younger employees, being afraid to become redundant afterwards.

Currently a lot of organizations are thinking about how to convince their senior workers to stay longer, because employers might face the loss of a significant amount of knowledge and know-how. However, several recent studies have shown (Henkens, 1998) that a vast majority of the senior workers themselves would like to withdraw from the labor force at the earliest possible opportunity. A well known question among senior employees is: "How long do you still have to work?". It is therefore important that managers start considering how they can transfer the knowledge that is present in these senior employees before they leave. This leads us to the problem definition of this article.

Problem Definition

From all the information above we can draw a couple of interesting conclusions. The first conclusion is that a lot of managers do not see the urgency of taking measures with regard to their ageing workforce and that they are not aware of the serious problems the massive retirement can cause with regard to the loss of knowledge. Another conclusion we can draw is that KM is an activity that can contribute to the preservation of knowledge and the distribution of it. When we combine these two findings we see that KM can serve as a tool to help managers to transfer the knowledge that is present in the senior employee in order to overcome the imminent loss of knowledge. The question is how this can be done adequately. To determine this, we need to take a look at the factors that determine the success of KM and how these factors can be applied to the senior employee. This brings us to the goal and problem definition of this article.

The goal of this article is to come to a number of guidelines in which the specific characteristics of the senior employee are coupled to the critical success factors (CSFs) of knowledge management. By using these guidelines as a starting point the human resource manager will be able to manage knowledge among this particular age more effectively than before.

This brings us to the following problem definition: which critical success factors of knowledge management can be aligned to the senior employee to enhance the effectiveness of this activity (among this age group)?

This problem definition is going to be discussed by using the following sub-questions:

1. What are the CSFs of KM?
2. How can these CSFs be aligned to the senior employee?
3. What are the implications for the HR manager?

Before starting to answer the problem definition, the limitations of this article need to be discussed.

Limitations

Knowledge management is a broad concept and definitions of KM are still developing. This article will focus on the human factor of knowledge management, using the definition provided by Rastogi.

A lot of studies (e.g. Abou-Zeid, 2002; Malhotra and Galletta, 2003) argue that information technology can assist KM in an important way. Although this article recognizes the importance of information systems within KM it will not address this aspect of KM. It will focus on the human and social processes of KM.

A lot of different processes are incorporated in KM; this article will focus on guaranteeing knowledge and distributing knowledge, since these are the two basic processes of KM that come to the front when employees leave the organization. These basic processes involve underlying processes, which includes knowledge sharing. Knowledge sharing is one of the most important processes when knowledge needs to be transferred, since these processes are mutually exclusive.

Furthermore it is important to stress the intention of this article. This is not to provide managers with a recipe that needs to be followed to solve the problem. Therefore organizations are far too diverse, and unique. Other limitations due to organizational culture and business sector are therefore also relevant to mention; specific organizational cultures and business sectors may require different approaches.

In addition, national or society cultures can have their influences. For example, in Asian countries senior employees are much more respected since values of respect for the elderly are ingrained in Asian cultures. While the level and forms of respect are swiftly changing, the value of older persons is still recognized in most Asian and Pacific region societies (ESCAP, 2001). These cultural differences between nations and societies can have influence on how processes of KM take place.

This article explores the opportunities for HR managers in a broad context and its intention is to provide a number of general guidelines to HR managers how they can prevent the loss of knowledge when senior employees leave the company; a starting point where they can begin to address this issue.

This article is based on extensive literature review and conversations in the field with MA M. Diekstra, she is the project leader of the project "Exploration of labor prospects by senior employees' (see Appendix for further details). This project had the main focus to develop a route for senior employees to assist them in their self development, by looking at their past experiences, discovering where they are now and where they want to go in the future.

The information from the literature review and the conversations were used to come to the characteristics of senior employees and the critical success factors of knowledge management.

Critical Success Factors of Knowledge Management

The success of a KM initiative depends on many factors, some within human control, some less or not at all. A critical success factor is a performance area of critical importance in achieving consistently high productivity. There exist two categories of critical success factors: business processes and human processes. This article will focus on the human processes.

Theorists do not completely agree on what the critical success factors of KM are. Below several views will be discussed, thereafter the final five will be presented, which will be used in this article.

Bixel's Four-pillar Model and Davenport's and Probst's List

Different theorists describe different CSFs for KM. Bixler (2002) is one of them. He developed a four-pillar model to describe success factors for KM implementation. These four pillars consist of: leadership, organization, technology, and learning. Leadership is concerned with the fact that managers develop business and operational strategies to survive and position for success in today's environment. The pillar "organization" stresses the fact that the value of knowledge creation and collaboration should be intertwined throughout an organization. Operational processes must align with the KM framework and strategy, including all performance metrics and objectives. Technology enables and provides the whole infrastructure and the tools where KM can rely on. Furthermore Bixel stresses the fact that without learning a KM strategy will not survive; managers must recognize that knowledge resides in people, and knowledge creation occurs in the process of social interaction and learning.

Davenport and Probst developed a similar, but a more extensive list of CSFs. Their CSFs are leadership, performance measurement, organizational policy, knowledge sharing and acquisition, information systems structure, and benchmarking and training.

The Five CFSs of KM

After the literature review of above and after consulting additional articles and research (Holowetzki, 2002; Chourides *et al.*, 2003) this article will use the following five CSFs that emphasize the human factor within knowledge management:

1. Coaching leadership style.
2. Structure, roles, and responsibilities.

3. Emphasis on learning and education.
4. Attention to motivation, trust, reward and recognition.
5. Establishing the right culture.

Below these different success factors will be discussed in more detail.

Coaching Leadership Style

Management support is essential for the success of KM initiatives. Coaching leadership shown by the managers enhances the value and strategic quality of KM initiatives and sends a signal to all employees that managers view KM as an important activity in their organization to undertake. It is important that the leader fosters open knowledge sharing by creating an environment that is built on trust.

Structure, Roles and Responsibilities

The organizational structure has to support sharing of knowledge. The collection and validation of knowledge, the availability of the appropriate IT infrastructure, and "help systems" that enable employees to share knowledge, all require appropriate structures within the organization. The organizational structure should also encourage the formation of teams, work groups, and communities of practice. Furthermore it is important that knowledge sharing is encouraged across role and functional boundaries.

Emphasis on Learning and Education

By focusing on (earning and education, new knowledge is created, which can help an organization to develop new innovative ideas. But during a learning process knowledge is also shared among individuals and they can learn from each other. In this way a bonding process between senior and the younger employee is initiated.

Attention to Motivation, Trust, Reward and Recognition

It is important that the contributors of knowledge and re-users of knowledge are assured that they have nothing to fear or be anxious about being discarded when giving knowledge "away" or by using "other people's" knowledge; a trustful environment is therefore an important goal to achieve. In business organization, trust has been identified as an essential condition for people to share knowledge and expertise (Nottingham, 1998).

The knowledge provider has to be specifically rewarded and compensated for doing something that is not explicitly stated in his or her contract. It is therefore important to reward sharing of knowledge. The reward system should be in balance with regard to intrinsic and extrinsic motivators.

Establishing the Right Culture

Creating the right culture for KM, considering the factors mentioned above, is very important, especially since other success factors are influenced by the organizational culture. Establishing a culture that enhances KM is a process and cannot be achieved overnight; it might take several years to adapt an organizational culture. However, when the right culture has been established KM can take place very effectively. Wah (1999) suggests that no KM program can succeed a shift in the culture of the organization.

Alignment of the Senior Worker to the CSFs of KM

In this part of the article possibilities to tailor the critical success factors to the senior employee are discussed, so that KM among this age group can take place as effective as possible.

A coaching Leadership Style

This leadership style is important for knowledge management since employees become conscientious about the fact that management values knowledge sharing. On the other side a coaching leadership style (as discussed earlier) has also a positive influence on the self-development of senior employees. When a manager sits down with his/her employee and reflects on things achieved in their lives and what is still possible in the future, senior employees can regain their enthusiasm and start to feel more committed to the organization (again). This increases job satisfaction and also benefits knowledge sharing. Career planning is often only done with younger employees (Zetlin, 1992), but this can be also an important tool to motivate the senior employee.

Structures, Roles and Responsibilities

Senior employees value the feeling of usefulness in their daily activities at work. This possibility could be created by letting the senior employee actively share their experience and know-how with younger employees. By giving senior employees responsibility and an active role in knowledge transfer and sharing they feel useful at work. This again increases the motivation (the senior employee experiences the intrinsic rewards) which also benefits knowledge sharing. By creating this opportunity the knife cuts two ways.

Emphasis on Learning and Education

Senior employees are willing to learn and want to develop themselves, but they need an active approach from their mangers, who help them to see where their area of interests lays. Most of the time this active style is absent and seniors are not offered the opportunity to engage in new projects or trainings. A lot of HR managers do not really offer senior employees educational trainings, since they do not see the benefits this can deliver to the company. This critical success factor of KM needs a lot of improvement with regard to the senior employee.

Attention to Motivation, Trust, Rewards and Recognition

Older employees are motivated in a different way, as described earlier in this article. They value the intrinsic rewards of work, life experiencing feelings of respect and recognition. This could be achieved by creating opportunities for senior employees in which they can feel appreciated and respected, for example, in a mentor relationship with a younger employee. I will come back to this possibility later on.

Trust is an important factor to reassure that people share their knowledge and know-how. It is important that the environment in which the senior employee works feels safe, so that they do not have the idea that when they share their knowledge they will became superfluous in the eyes of their managers.

Establishing the Right Culture

A senior employee needs an organizational culture where there exists trust and respect. A culture in which there are possibilities for flexible working hours and where their knowledge and know-how is recognized and appreciated. In a lot of organizations this is not the case and managers have negative images and ideas about the senior employee, this makes it difficult to create a culture that stimulates KM among this particular age group. A study performed by Taylor and walker (1998), also acknowledges the importance of establishing the right culture, since the culture of an organization acts as a key factor in shaping orientations towards senior employees.

Implications for the Human Resource Manager

In order for managers to effectively manage all the knowledge that is present in the senior worker, it is first important that these managers become conscientious of the value of senior employees. They should step out the mindset that holds all the negative images and presumptions about the senior employee. A positive vision that senior employees can still be of great importance to the organization and that they are a great value should replace the old, negative vision. Only after this goal is obtained the next (more practical) steps towards effective knowledge management can take place.

Managers should start talking with senior employees about what their self development needs are and where they want to go with respect to their careers. They should show their senior employees that they value them and encourage them to undertake new activities.

Managers should establish teams or work groups that contain both senior and junior employees. In this way the cooperation between the younger and the more experienced employee is stimulated and they can inspire each other and learn from each other, by sharing their knowledge. Developing mentor relationships is also a possibility, in these relationships specific organizational know-how can be transferred and shared.

Managers should also reward knowledge transfer between generations. This means creating confidence that experienced employees who pass on their knowledge to younger colleagues not need to be afraid of being replaced by them. This also has to do with building up a certain level of trust within the organization.

Managers must be aware of the fact that senior employees have other needs and therefore maintain a life-phase oriented HR development strategy. This strategy should make clear that senior employees have needs for flexible working hours and a balance between work and private life.

A culture which fosters the senior employee and in which KM can prosper needs to be created. Figure 3 visualizes this culture.

This culture entails factors that are important for stimulating knowledge sharing among senior employees, but also entails factors that are critical to the success of KM in general. By establishing a culture as depicted above KM can start to take place in a more effective way among senior employees.

An organizational culture is, of course, not only created by HR managers, the whole organization needs to contribute to its establishment. However, a lot of activities that are undertaken by the HR manager can add to the right culture for KM.

Conclusion

This article has quite extensively discussed the issues of KM and the developments within the workforce that took place over the last couple of years. The main reason for doing this is the lack of understanding that turns out to exist among managers about the impact the great loss of organizational knowledge and know-how, that is threatening many organizations, can have within the upcoming years. By discussing the issues in more detail the author hopes HR managers start to become conscientious about the possible problems.

In today's literature, the two topics (KM and the senior employee) discussed in this literature review, have received only little attention from researchers; this literature review is one of the first scientific articles that does explicitly link the senior employee to the process of KM.

However, some organizations are starting to understand the need for knowledge transfer among their own senior employees and the one's of their customers, like IBM (IBM Consulting Services, 2006). Several other authors address the issue of the ageing workforce and the impact on the knowledge industry (Bradly, 2005). Others stress the factors of how to deal with senior employees in terms of human resource development and training (Rhebergen and Wognum, 1997; Armstrong-Stassen and Templer, 2005).

This article has investigated how KM can take place in an effective way among senior employees, by looking at the CSFs of KM and aligning these CSFs to this particular age group. This first sub-question was: "what are the CSFs of KM?". Different theorists mention different critical success factors of KM, but when looking specifically at the ones that emphasize the human factor, five CSFs come to the fore:

1. Coaching leadership style.
2. Structure, roles, and responsibilities.
3. Emphasis on learning and education.
4. Attention to motivation, trust, reward and recognition.
5. Establishing the right culture.

The last factor comprises a significant part of the other factors; the other factors all have their influence on the organizational culture.

FIGURE 3 The Ideal Culture for Effective KM among Senior Employees

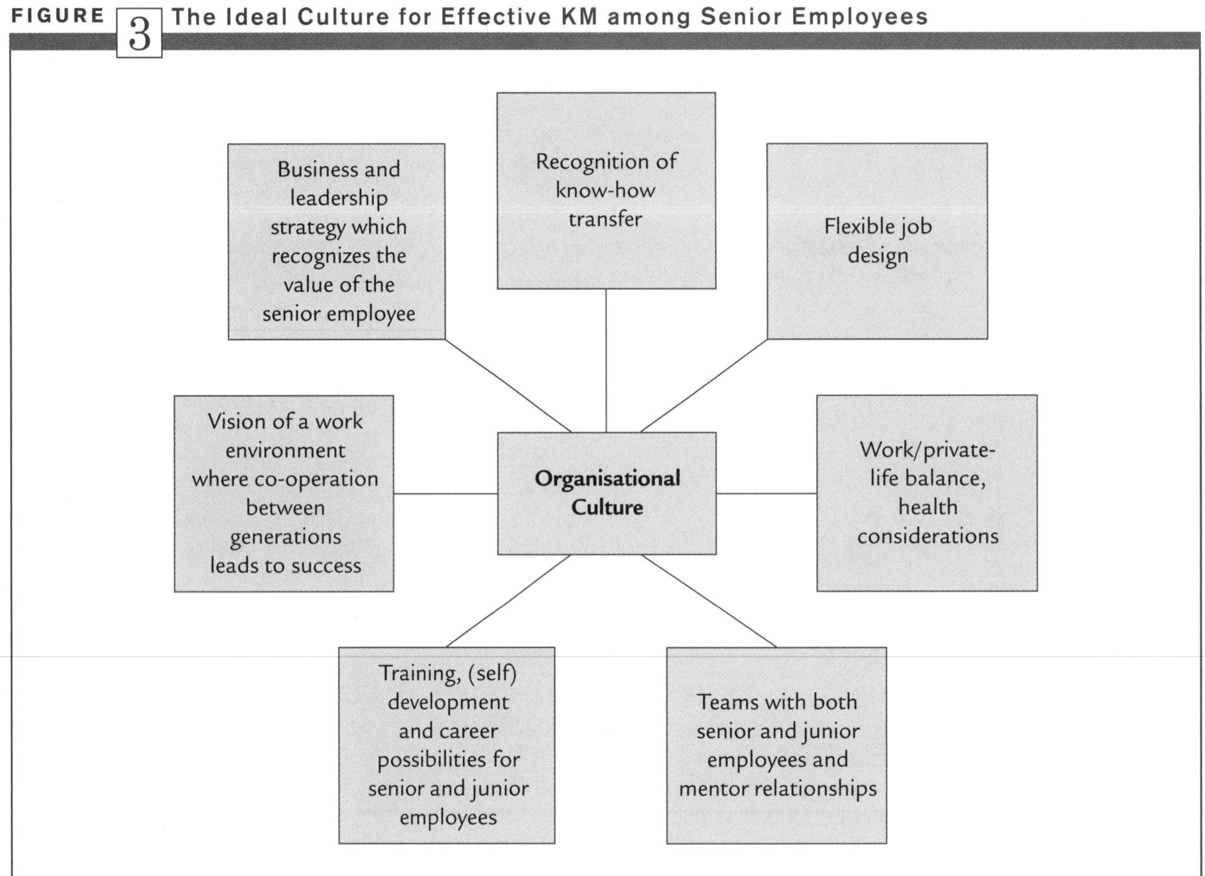

The second sub-question was: "how can these CSFs be aligned to the senior employee?". It appears to be the case that the CSFs of KM can be aligned very successfully to the senior employee. Mainly, because a lot of the critical success factors of KM contain aspects that are valued highly among the senior employee (attention to recognition, trust) or aspects where this age group can benefit by (a coaching leadership style; emphasis on learning, education; and assigning responsibility).

The third sub-question was: "what are the implications for the HR manager?". The most important implication for the HR manager is that they should take a more proactive management style towards the senior employee. They should guide them in their self-development and assist them with deciding on their goals. When this happens, the senior employee experiences the feeling of being appreciated again and than more practical steps that will benefit KM more directly can be taken.

The problem definition of this article that had to be answered was: "which critical success factors of Knowledge Management can be aligned to the senior employee to enhance the effectiveness of this activity? (among this age group)". During the writing of this article the author discovered that there exist a lot of synergetic opportunities between a more proactive management style towards senior employees and effective KM among this group of employees. Therefore, the implications and recommendations for the HR manager point mainly towards an approach that stimulates this leadership style. When this management style is initiated by the HR manager the critical success factors of KM can be very well aligned to the senior employee and the level of effectiveness of KM among this age group will be able to increase significantly. However, further research in this area is recommended, also because the level of impact can differ for each organization.

Furthermore it has become clear that there exist lot of literature that comes to a negative image of the senior employee, but also a lot that comes to a positive image. Mapping out the real situation at micro-level is therefore important.

This article is not extensively based on the direct empirical findings, therefore further research is needed to verify, falsify, specify and complete the recommendations made in this article and the conclusions that can be drawn from it. Undertaking further research in this area is strongly recommended, especially since the significant social relevance of this issue. Further (empirical) research should point out how the effectiveness of KM can be stimulated among senior employees and which theories are relevant to consult in this area. Maybe after more research and bringing the findings into practice HR managers are able to turn the question among senior employees: "How long do you still have to work?" into: "how long do you still can work?" and will it be possible to optimize the effectiveness of KM among this age group.

Recommendations

The implications and conclusions mentioned above point towards a more proactive management style; organizations should face the current developments and start to invest in their senior employees again. But how and where to start?

HR managers should start to map out the current situation in the organization in order to develop a social chart of the organization's personnel file. The company needs to get clear what kind characteristics, based on hard figures, can be assigned to the different age groups present within the organization. Managers need to look at, for example, the age structure of the organization and at retention rates and training participation of employees. When management has fulfilled this task, it should start looking at which trends can be discovered and what the backgrounds of the figures are. Based on trends and backgrounds, the organization can determine if action is needed. By doing this an honest and sincere view of the different groups of employees can be formed and presumptions that might exist can be eliminated. Management also becomes more conscientious about the situation in their organization.

The next step the HR management should take is to actively involve the employees themselves in the process. This can be done by asking them about the bottlenecks they experience and other experiences they have with regard to the management of personnel, but also by individual interviews between HR manager and senior employee in which self development issues are discussed. In this way the awareness among employees about the issue will increase and management will also demonstrate that it is undertaking some "real" action. This is also a knowledge sharing activity, which positively influences KM.

It will not be easy to establish a complete change in organizational culture. In today's society a lot of prejudices exist about senior employees and a lot of regulations are aimed at resignment of senior employees (although this currently starts to change). It is therefore important that a basis for structural cultural change is created and HR managers should take an active position in this process. They should appoint the value of senior employees, refute the presumptions that exist and change their personnel policy.

When senior employees experience that management is really changing their point of view, their trust in management increases and management can then start to implement activities that facilitate KM, like mentoring relationships and mixed teams. Subsequently, knowledge sharing and transfer can take place and the organizations can begin to work towards effective KM.

Source: Journal of Knowledge Management, 11, (4), 82–96 (2007). Reprinted by permission.

REFERENCES

Abou-Zeid, A. (2002), "A knowledge management reference model", *Journal of Knowledge Management*, Vol. 6 No. 5, pp. 486–99.

Armstrong-Stassen, M. and Templer, A. (2005), "Adapting training for older employees: the Canadian response to an aging workforce", *Journal of Management Development*, Vol. 24 No. 1, pp. 57–67.

Bixler, C.H. (2002), "Applying the four pillars of knowledge management", *KM World*, Vol. 11 No. 11.

Bradly, J. (2005), "The ageing population and knowledge work", *Foresight: The Journal of Future Studies, Strategic Thinking and Policy*, Vol. 7 No. 1, pp. 61–7.

Chourides, P., Longbottom, D., and Murphy, W. (2003), "Excellence in knowledge management: an empirical study to identify critical factors and performance measures", *Measuring Business Excellence*, Vol. 7 No. 2, pp. 29–36.

Diekstra, M.C.W.M. (2003), *Project Arbeidstoekomstverkenning Eindrapportage, ("Project Future Labour Exploration")*.

Groff, T.R. and Jones, T.P. (2003), *Introduction to Knowledge Management: KM in Business*, Elsevier, Amsterdam.

Henkens. K. (1998), "Older workers in transition: studies on early retirement decisions in The Netherlands", PhD thesis, Utrecht University, Utrecht.

Heymann, F.V. and Terlien, M.H.D. (2003), *Spelen met je toekomst, 50-plussers op weg naar zingeving, ("Playing with your future, employees who are 50 and above on their way to sensemaking")*.

Holowetzki, A. (2002), "The relationship between knowledge management and organizational culture: an examination of cultural factors that support the flow and management of knowledge within an organization", Applied Information Management, University of Oregon, Eugene, OR, available at: http://aim.uoregon.edu/research/pdfs/Holowetzki2002.pdf (accessed 1 June 2005).

IBM Consulting Services (2006), "Addressing the challenges of an aging workforce", available at: www.1.ibm.com/services/us/imc/pdf/g510-3970-aging-workforce-asia.pdf (accessed 16 May 2006).

Kanfer, R. and Ackerman, P.L. (2004), "Aging, adult development and work motivation", *Academy of Management Review*, Vol. 29 No. 3, pp. 440–59.

Keuning, D. (1998), *Management: A Contemporary Approach*, Pitman Publishing, London.

Lyon, P. and Glover, I. (1998), "Divestment or investment? The contradictions of HRM in relation to older companies", *Human Resource Management Journal*, Vol. 8 No. 1, pp. 56–66.

McIntosh, B. (2000), "An employer's guide to older workers: how to win them back and convince them to stay", US Department of Labor, Employment and Training Administration, available at: www.doleta.gov/Seniors/other_docs/EmplGuide.pdf (accessed 20 May 2005).

Maslow, A. (1954), *Motivation and Personality*, Harper & Row, New York, NY.

Metcalf, H. and Thompson, M. (1990), "Older workers: employers' attitudes and practices", Report No. 194, Institute for Manpower Studies, Brighton.

Malhotra, Y. and Galletta, D.F. (2003), "Role of commitment and motivation in KMS implementation: theory, conceptualization, and measurement of antecedents of success", *Proceedings of the 36th Hawaii International Conference on System Sciences*.

Nottingham, A. (1998), "Knowledge management as the next strategic focus", paper no. 42, *Proceedings of the 8th Annual BIT Conference, Manchester Metropolitan University*.

Rastogi, P.N. (2000), "Knowledge management and intellectual capital: the new virtuous reality of competitiveness", *Human Systems Management*, Vol. 19 No. 1, pp. 39–49.

Remery, C., Henkens, K., Schippers, J., and Ekamper, P. (2001). "Managing an ageing workforce and a tight labour market: views held by Dutch employers", *Population Review and Policy Review*, Vol. 22, pp. 21–40.

Rhebergen, B. and Wognum, I. (1997). "Supporting the career development of older employees: an HRD study in a Dutch company", *International Journal of Training and Development*, Vol. 1 No. 3, pp. 191–8.

Sterns. H. and Miklos, S. (1995). "The ageing worker in a changing environment: organizational and individual issues", *Journal of Vocational Behaviour*, Vol. 47 No. 3, pp. 248–68.

Taylor, P. and Walker, A. (1998). "Policies and practices towards older workers: a framework for comparative research". *Human Resource Management Journal*, Vol. 8 No. 3, pp. 61–76.

Wah. L. (1999). "Making knowledge stick", *Management Review*, Vol. 88 No. 5, pp. 24–9.

Zetlin, M. (1992), "Older and wiser: tips to motivate the 50s crowd", *Management Review*, Vol. 81 No. 8, pp. 30–3.

READING 13.3

Managing Older Worker Exit and Re-entry Practices: A 'Revolving Door'?

Kate Shacklock, Liz Fulop and Linda Hort

This paper reports findings from an Australian study about the post-employment experiences of older persons who had left the full-time workforce (either voluntarily or involuntarily). It examines their perceptions about seeking re-employment in terms of their desires to remain in or return to work, and what employment conditions might entice them to remain in or return to work, including how organisations might help or hinder such re-entry to the workforce. A qualitative approach using exploratory semi-structured interviews was chosen to explore this relatively under researched area. Participants from a mix of employment histories, industries, occupational categories and ages (but all over 45 years of age) formed the sample.

A key finding of the study was the lack of planning on the part of employers to consider these older workers as a potential future pool of employees. The study points to some important lessons for the management of older workers to meet the predicted looming labour shortage in Australia.

The population of Australia is ageing (Australian Bureau of Statistics 2003). In Australia, as in other western countries, the average age of people in the workforce is also increasing, with people generally living longer. Population ageing has thus become a primary focus of financial and welfare policy-makers. The Australian Bureau of Statistics (ABS) (2003) forecasts that the proportion of Australia's population over the age of 65 years would double to a quarter of all Australians by 2051. In the same report, the ABS predicted that the 15 to 64 year-old cohort (those relied upon to fund the general taxation reserve from which future welfare payments would be made) will decline by 7 percent over the same period.

Australia's ageing profile is a consequence of the post-World War II baby boom – baby boomers are those turning 65 years old between 2011 and 2031 (Productivity Commission 2005) – declining post-war birthrates, the immigration of people of working age, and increased longevity (ACIL Consulting 2000). Further, ageing largely causes a decline in workforce participation rates because, as people grow older, they tend to participate less in the labour force, through retiring or leaving the workforce – either voluntarily or involuntarily. As can be seen in Table 1, in 1984, compared to those aged 45 to 54 years (with a participation rate of 70.25 percent), the participation rate for those aged between 55 and 65 years was 42.25 percent. A similar drop was recorded in 2003 between the same age groups from 82.2 percent to 55.2 percent (ABS 2005).

Such demographic changes in Australia's future workforce highlight the need for organisations to ensure the effective management of their older workforces, including increasing the retention rates of older workers, and possibly, re-employing older people who have already left the workforce. However, little research has been conducted with individual older workers to investigate whether they want to extend their working lives, or what employment arrangements might entice them back to work (except for example: Encel and Studencki 2004; Myers 2001; Onyx 1998; Patrickson and Clarke 2001; Stein, Rocco and Goldenetz 2000). Additionally, Minichiello, Browne and Kendig (2000) commented that there was limited research into the area of how older people felt about how they were stereotypically treated. According to Glover and Branine (2001, 363), students of HRM and management 'have done little so far to understand age–employment relationships, and need to do more'. Therefore, there is a need to further explore the intentions of older workers to continue working and assist to meet the predicted shortfall of labour, and what factors might influence such intentions. This paper begins to address this important issue.

Table 1 Labour Force Participation Rates for Over-45 Year Olds

	45–54 years		55–64 years	
	1984	2003	1984	2003
Males (%)	92.2	90.2	63.6	66.7
Females (%)	48.3	74.2	20.9	43.7
Average (%)	70.25	82.2	42.25	55.2

Source: Adapted from ABS (2005).

The Australian government and policy-makers have begun the public debate, policy discussions and research into the issues of the ageing workforce and the predicted labour shortfall (Department of Parliamentary Services 2005; Department of the Treasury 2004; Equal Opportunity Commission of Victoria 2001; House of Representatives Standing Committee on Employment Education and Workplace Relations 2000; House of Representatives Standing Committee on Health and Ageing (H of R Health and Ageing) 2005; Productivity Commission 2005) in an effort to reduce negative impacts from these workforce challenges. One shared recommendation was to increase the workforce participation rates of older people, including extending their working lives. The advantages of such extended working lives include: additional productivity within the workforce; reducing the financial burden on (younger) tax payers who will be relied upon to cover health and allied care; increased tax income which will improve government budgets; and the potential for increased private financial resources (Sheen 2001).

However, the impact of the ageing population appears not yet to have been fully acknowledged by employers. Older people find it harder to get and keep jobs, are kept out of the workforce for longer, and suffer from the effects of ageism (Encel and Studencki 2004). In terms of trying to gain employment, just over one-fifth (21 percent) of Australia's unemployed people had been unemployed for 12 months or longer at July 2004 (ABS 2005). According to Hartmann (1998, 10), Australian employers have 'continued to reduce their older workforce and to disregard the advantages that these (older) people may bring'.

On the one hand, with increased life expectancy, better health facilities and medical advances, the financial need to continue to work is likely to have made changes in the retirement plans of many potential retirees. The 'older Baby Boomers are already becoming financially sandwiched in their need to provide for two other generations' (O'Neill 1998, 178). Not only are people commonly having children later in life – so that older people may still have children to educate, financially help to buy a home and so on – but also, the parents of baby boomers are more likely to still be alive and if they are, their health care costs are likely to be greater and last longer. These financial imperatives may push older people to continue working or to desire to return to the workforce. The same consequence could result from dwindling government-funded social service payments with individuals having to financially fend for themselves more than in previous decades. Some older workers will be forced to continue working because they will not be able to live on their accumulated savings, superannuation and pension (Schwartz and Kleiner 1999), and this situation is more likely to occur for women (Patrickson and Hartmann 1996; Patrickson and Ranzijn 2004) Concurring with this perspective, Gardyn (2000, 55) reported 'about 44 percent [of retirement aged American people] say they've worked for pay at some point after they retired'.

On the other hand, from a healthy older person's perspective, working may provide benefits including greater lifestyle choices, increased spending power, and greater resources to rely on for a probably extended life span. Other advantages may include greater feelings of self-worth and self-esteem, and associated psychological benefits. Many baby boomers enjoy working, according to Shoebridge and Ferguson (1997, 34), and 'will never retire; they will simply change what they do. They'll remain active and adventurous'. Furthermore, Australian research (Leonard 1999, 28) has found that many older workers were continuing to work, not because of financial needs but because their work colleagues had become like family to them, and 'their pride and self-esteem are also linked to the notion that they are making a contribution to society'. Likewise, Field (2001) and Gardyn (2000) found that the main motivator for older workers continuing to work was not to earn money, but to keep active, have social interaction, and feel productive. This is borne out in a survey of Australian managers aged 50–55 years. Participants were asked: 'if the company provided you with the option of working part-time, and arranging different ways so you can continue the knowledge transfer, would you be interested in maintaining employment? In 100 percent of cases, the answer [was] yes' (Tabakoff and Skeffington 2000, 4). In other words, many older people may enjoy working, yet desire different working circumstances than the traditional full-time standard hours. Further, from older people's perspectives, opportunities to remain in or return to the workforce may have increased, now that age-based retirement has been removed.

To summarise to this point, there is a labour shortage imperative to both retain older workers and to find suitable and attractive opportunities for older people to re-enter the workforce. While older people may financially need to continue working later in their lives, organisations may simultaneously be keen for more older people to work. However, the slim evidence in the literature suggests that alternative arrangements that might be attractive to older people have not been fully canvassed with older people.

Any solution to the predicted labour shortage based on increased employment of older people is likely to find the consequences of ageism (age discrimination) to be a hurdle. Age discrimination has been blamed as a key reason for older people not getting jobs (see for example, Bennington and Calvert 1998; Encel and Studencki 2004; Human Rights and Equal Opportunity Commission 2000; Sheen 2000, 2004; Taylor and Walker 1997; VandenHeuvel 1999) even though ageism is outlawed in Australia. Moreover, older people found it difficult to return to the workforce once they had left, tended to be out of the workforce for longer, and were less likely to be offered job-related training (H of R Health and Ageing 2005).

While there appear to be fewer current job opportunities for older people (at a time when a labour shortage is predicted), and notwithstanding the power of employers in such situations, there is a gap in the literature concerning employment arrangements that would be attractive to older people choosing to remain in, or re-enter, the workforce.

The remainder of the paper discusses the literature about whether older workers desire to continue working, followed by a description of the study undertaken, the findings and discussion from that study and, finally, the implications and conclusions.

To Work or Not to Work?

In an Australian survey of those unemployed aged 45–54 years, 29 percent reported their main difficulty finding employment was that they were 'considered too old by employers', and this rose to nearly half (46 percent) of unemployed people aged 55 years and over (ABS 2005). While the situation for older people may be improving, those who lose their jobs are likely to experience long periods without work or with marginal workforce attachment. It is these discouraged older people who may then slide into early retirement (Sheen 2000). Alternatively, some older workers may have left the workforce temporarily, only to find that when they wanted to return, or tried to find another job, the opportunities were not available (Encel and Studencki 2004), or they may have insufficient training for the available jobs (Crown, Chen and McConaghy 1996), as stereotyped by employers (Wrenn and Maurer 2004). Older people were reportedly stereotyped by employers as being less able to learn new things (American Association of Retired Persons 1992; H of R Health and Ageing 2005; Reark Research 1990), less adaptable (Steinberg et al. 1998) and less trainable (Encel 2001; Kern 1990; Steinberg et al. 1998; Taylor and Walker 1994).

A theme concerning the lack of employment opportunities for older people is consistent throughout much of the literature. For example, there were many 'job losers rather than job leavers' in the age group of 45 to 64 years who had retired from full-time work (Sheen 1999, 6). The majority retired for reasons beyond their control, citing 'significant employment problems' prior to their retirement (Sheen 1999, 8). According to Sheen, these reasons included age victimisation in the workplace, the forceful casualisation of jobs, or the perception that older workers' performance is not satisfactory. These issues are central to the apparent growing likelihood of older people finding it more difficult to keep, or get, a job.

According to ACIL Consulting (2000) and Taylor and Walker (1997), many employees would have liked to remain working (arguing that most redundancies were involuntary), and had high levels of employment commitment. Moreover, VandenHeuvel (1999) found many older people were under-employed and would prefer to work more hours. However, according to Taylor and Walker, many older people felt there were strong pressures to retire early due to social attitudes, employer preferences, and individual pension/superannuation timing advantages.

If the demographers and statisticians are accurate forecasters, the swing of the pendulum towards demand for labour should create conditions in which employers will be forced to increase opportunities for the employment of older people. However, if older people are not sufficiently healthy, or become discouraged through lack of opportunity and success at employment, they are less likely to seek (re)employment. Instead of 'does the workforce want or need older people?', the more important question may be 'do older people want or need the workforce?' The study in this paper therefore investigated older people's perceptions about seeking re-employment in terms of their desires to remain in or return to work, and what employment conditions might entice them to remain in or return to work, including how organisations might help or hinder such re-entry to the workforce.

The next section describes the methodology adopted for the study, including the participants, all of whom had left the paid full-time workforce. Many participants had voluntarily retired, with some then returning to work, while others had involuntarily left the workforce and subsequently retired.

Research Design

In-depth, semi-structured exploratory interviews were used to investigate participants' experiences of being older ex-workers, and their re-employment-seeking experiences. The issues investigated with each participant were: their work and retirement history; their current desire for paid work; their experiences of seeking re-employment; and any employment conditions or arrangements considered attractive to entice them back to work. Interviews each lasted between 60 and 125 minutes, with the majority conducted in participants' homes or offices. Pseudonyms were used to ensure participants' anonymity, and selected participants' verbatim comments are presented below to represent the views of other participants, usually for their descriptiveness or comprehensiveness. The audiotapes obtained from the interviews were transcribed using voice recognition software, which was found to be effective and resource-saving. The researchers analysed the resulting data firstly, by identifying and coding the dominant themes, and secondly, by finding supporting comments for each theme.

Twenty participants were involved in the study—ten females and ten males (see Table 2). The sample was selected using purposeful sampling (Creswell 2003, 185), as 'the idea behind qualitative research is to purposefully select participants or sites that will best help the researcher understand the problems and the research question'. The snowballing technique (Minichiello et al. 1995) was also used: the researcher sought participation from retirees from an Australian tertiary sector organisation, and these participants were then asked if they knew of other suitable older people who might be willing to participate in the study. Once the data began being repeated, the point of 'saturation' was reached and then no more participants were sought (Cresswell 1998, 57). The final number of participants was thereby determined at 20. Participants of both genders were selected with differing employment histories, age and industry type (including academia, accountancy, corporate finance, retail sales, childcare and teaching schoolchildren).

Table 2 Participant Categories and Ages

	Total Number	Average Age	Age Range	Average Retire Age	Now Working
Males	10	62.5	49–69	58.4	8
Females	10	59	46–69	57	2
Total	20	60.7	46–69	57.7	10

The sample was a mix of persons currently in the paid workforce (8 of 10 males; 2 of 10 females) and out of the paid workforce (2 males; 8 females). The majority (14 of 20) had voluntarily left the paid workforce; others had left the workforce involuntarily (6 of 20). Three of the involuntarily retired persons had continued seeking work, but had eventually become discouraged and stopped looking, declaring themselves 'retired'. Some participants (8 of 20), including three involuntarily retired participants, had 'retired' then returned to work but with different (usually contractual) working arrangements. Other participants (9 of 20) had retired with no intention of ever seeking work again. One advantage of such a variety of participants was the consequent mix of attitudes to working. However, the gender mix of working/non-working participants was noteworthy, and may represent a preference for certain types of older men and women to continue working later than others. However, gender issues were not a focus of this study and therefore further analysis along those lines was not pursued.

The age range of participants was 46 to 69 years, with the average age of participants being 60.7 years (62.5 years for males and 59 years for females). Several participants had retired many years prior to the interviews (one as long as 10 years prior), and one participant had only recently retired. The average age at retirement was 57.7 years (58.4 years for males and 57 years for the females). None of the participants reported having childcare or elder-care responsibilities to restrict their availability to work. See Table 3 for further participant details.

Table 3 Participant Details

Athena	aged 63, widow, ex-administration clerk, 'retired permanently'
Barb	aged 46, married, ex-childcare director, supported by husband, 'retired permanently'
Bill	aged 68, married, ex-salesman, involuntarily retired but returned to work several years later in similar industry
Doris	aged 60, married, ex-administration clerk, retired but returned to work part-time in similar work
Doug	aged 64, married, ex-academic, retired but returned to work in similar job on part time contract
Geoff	aged 61, married, self-funded retiree, ex-accountant, 'involuntary age-related retirement', became discouraged seeking work, now 'retired permanently'
Howard	aged 65, married, self-funded retiree, some consulting work
Jean	aged 65, married, ex-administration clerk, 'retired permanently'
Jenny	aged 54, married, ex-library clerk, 'retired permanently'
Jerry	aged 64, married, self-funded retiree, ex-academic, works as a consultant
John	aged 69, married, retired ex-senior administrator, now working as a mail delivery person
Lee-Anne	aged 49, married, ex-finance clerk, 'permanently full-time' retired
Marg	aged 67, married, ex-general clerk, involuntarily retired, 'retired permanently'
Michaela	aged 69, single, ex-academic, involuntarily age retired, and returned to work part-time in the same job
Norma	aged 60, single, ex-general clerk, involuntarily retired on a disability pension, now 'retired permanently'
Paul	aged 49, married, ex-businessman, 'retired permanently'
Sarah	aged 60, married, ex-general clerk, 'retired permanently'
Sam	aged 67, ex-academic, married, involuntarily age retired, working part-time in the same field as before his retirement
Tony	aged 55, ex-teacher, married, 'retired permanently'
Wayne	aged 63, ex-academic, married, retired but returned to work in similar job on part-time contract

It is generally accepted that 45 years of age is the benchmark for an 'older' worker (ABS 2004). Thus, 45 years was selected as the minimum age for this study. There was no maximum age as Drucker (2001) predicted that within three decades, Australia and other developed countries would have raised the minimum age of access to full retirement benefits to 75 years. At the time of the interviews, age pension access was available to males at the age of 65 years and to females at the age of 60 years. However, Australia is in the process of incrementally increasing the age of female access to the age pension to 65 years, to match that of males.

Findings and Discussion

Six dominant themes emerged from the participants' comments: 1) flexible working arrangements were considered very desirable; 2) their age was reported as the most common cause of participants leaving the workforce; 3) age was reported as a barrier to re-entry to work; 4) working with a team and other social aspects of work were seen as attractive; 5) the qualified participants wanted to continue working; and 6) self-worth and job satisfaction were important to older people. Details of comments made by participants in support of each of the six themes are provided below.

Flexible Working Arrangements

In response to questions about what kind of working arrangements older people found attractive, the majority (18 of 20) of participants reported flexible and less than full-time arrangements as the most attractive. All participants interested in working (10 of 20), irrespective of their employment history or qualifications, specified that they would prefer 2 or 3 days' work a week, or assignment-type employment. For example, Howard represented others' views with his comment, 'I wouldn't mind a job that was for three months full-time but I wouldn't like full-time for two years – but for three to six months that would be okay'. Comments associated with the attractiveness of less than full-time work included 'less pressure and stress', 'more time to do the other interests in my life', 'only accepting jobs that utilise my skills', and 'only taking jobs that I want'. Agreeing, Norma added, 'I don't mind if I could find a job for two days a week. I would be happy because I think that's all I could manage.' Lee-Anne commented that she thought 'family' was a very important part of older workers' decisions about continuing to work, and that offering employment arrangements other than full-time would be attractive to her and may entice her back to work. Soon after their leaving the workforce, the two involuntarily 'retired' participants had been keen to earn a high income and would have preferred to find full-time work. However, they had become discouraged, had stopped searching for work, and now would be willing to work part-time.

This flexible employment finding supports previous research in the USA by Maurer (2001) who found that 24 percent of organisations were offering flexible working schedules to retain workers. In New Zealand, Koopman-Boyden and Macdonald (2003) likewise found flexible working arrangements to be a successful retention strategy, and in Australia, Patrickson and Hartmann (2001) argued a similar case. This finding also supports the statistics showing older workers work fewer hours per week (ABS 2005).

Offering part-time working arrangements to older workers might prove a bonus to both organisations and individual older workers, as it suits both parties' needs in times of dwindling labour and skills supply. For employers, it may attract extra staff with specific skills who wish to reduce their hours or cease working completely. For individual older people, the opportunity to work part-time may be attractive whereas working full-time may not. In other words, extra labour may be found in addition to those already employed. However, the social justice issue of age discrimination may impinge on individual older people's expectations with regard to employment opportunities, and this is discussed next.

Age and Leaving the Workforce

A significant finding was that all participants reported age-related reasons for leaving the workforce, whether they chose to leave because they judged they were at a suitable age, or their organisation forced them to leave. Seven (of 10) males and 7 (of 10) females had retired voluntarily, citing age-related reasons for choosing to retire including, 'I had had enough – I wanted to get off the treadmill', 'I wanted to make room for the young blokes to come up', and 'I had been working for 40 years – it was time'. Of the 6 participants (3 males; 3 females) who had involuntarily retired, all reported age was the reason they were made redundant, or 'pushed' out of their last jobs. For Bill, 'we moved to the Gold Coast and nobody wants a 55 plus [years of age] person anymore'. Geoff remarked, 'it was expected that I would leave because of my age'. Jerry added that he thought older people 'have a slippery [employment] path. It doesn't take much to fall off and if you do fall off it, then pity help you, because I don't think there are very many opportunities to get back on it'.

This theme reflects older people's lack of opportunity to return to the workforce. As mentioned by the ABS (2005), age was reported as the single most important factor in older people not being able to get another job—supporting findings by Encel and Studencki (2004) that age discrimination still occurred in Australia, and Sheen's (1999) notion of 'job losers' rather than 'job leavers'. However, other researchers have argued that while ageism is widely accepted as prevalent, the causes are more contentious (for example, Duncan and Loretto 2004; Murray and Syed 2005). In other words, participants' comments lend support to the literature concerning the critical nature of age-related factors in employment decisions.

Re-entry to Work

In discussing their experiences with trying to re-enter the workforce, participants commented on a range of issues such as barriers resulting from their age, a perception by employers of their over-qualification, a lack of training of the hiring interviewers, the bias that can occur in an interview situation itself (such as lack of empathy and age differences between applicant and interviewer), an inability to provide recent references, and the process of hiring being perceived to be a farce.

Four participants had left the workforce, expecting to be able to re-enter later, but all had been unsuccessful. For example, Norma remarked, 'I went back and applied for all these jobs and you know, you go in and you could see it on their faces, in "oh gosh, she's an old biddy, and we don't want her"'. Similarly, Marg reported that having resigned from her job after the company had relocated a long distance away, she was unable to find suitable employment and was convinced this was due to her age. Geoff commented, 'why I don't think I progressed any further [in the selection process] was that I was not able to offer a current referee. They wanted a referee that you had reported to within the last 12 to 18 months'. Bill noted, 'the interviewers are always much, much younger than you, and you could always tell, in their faces, that they thought you were too old'.

One explanation of why age may be the reason reported for lack of job search success could be that 'age' is a well-known and socially accepted reason to provide others (and yourself) as to why a job search has been unsuccessful. Using this explanation could mean that no self-analysis is undertaken, as the cause for non-hiring appears beyond the control of the individual and therefore analysis of one's own comparative competence or experience seems unnecessary. Another reason could be employers' stereotypical perceptions of older people's lesser abilities and adaptability.

Eight other participants (6 males; 2 females) had left the workforce but immediately started working again, mostly in a similar role in the same organisation, but less than full-time. These participants commented that they recognised the difficulties in re-entering the workforce, and therefore most (5 of 8) had negotiated their 'return to work' prior to their 'retirement'. None of their organisations had been proactive in this negotiation; the initiative had come from the employees. Yet, according to the participants, the arrangement was successful for both parties. Six months after having retired, one female decided that she wanted to return to work and contacted her previous employer who found her ongoing part-time work. Additionally, these older workers reported high levels of satisfaction with their new more flexible, less than full-time, working arrangements.

This finding suggests the need to provide flexible working arrangements to attract older persons to either stay in or return to the workforce. If organisations are keen to retain the abilities and corporate knowledge of older workers, different proactive approaches to the exit and re-entry of older workers appear needed. However, there was little evidence of proactive approaches on the part of organisational human resource management (HRM) in this study.

The Social Aspects of Work

In terms of the employment circumstances under which they would prefer to work, most non-working participants (8 of 9 females; 1 of 2 males) commented that, having retired, they missed the social aspects of working. As Sarah said, 'I liked the company. I liked the socialising and the company at work. That's what I missed most I think when I gave up work, is the company'. Similarly, Jean remarked:

> *I liked the friendliness and the interaction with people. I'd talk to people and have a joke and walk on. I am quite happy with my own company, but after a while if I do want to meet with other people, then yes I do miss the interaction.*

John commented that his desire for social interaction was one of the reasons he returned to work after retiring 'the first time'. He reported, 'I missed the people tremendously. I really did. I would come back every two or three weeks and call in and see people and have a couple of cups of coffee'.

Participants mentioned that the social aspects of work are attractive to them, and having a pleasant social environment would assist to make working more attractive to them, and positively affect their health and well-being. Therefore, to increase retention and re-entry rates, management and HRM could increase opportunities for social interaction at work.

Qualifications and the Desire to Continue Working

Half the participants (8 males; 2 females) were working, the majority (6 males; 2 females) involved in part-time work, for example undertaking casual or contract work. They reported being content with less than full-time arrangements, commenting that they liked continuing using their skills and experience, and wanted to continue doing so for longer. Doug represented others' views when he said, 'I want to keep using my skills and knowledge for a while yet'. Yet, whether working or not, none of the qualified participants (8 males; 1 female) was interested in full-time paid work.

In contrast, the majority (7 of 8) of the non-working females, none of whom was qualified, reported that they did not want to return to work at all. The majority (6 of 8) of these females also reported they relied upon a government pension for income in their retirement. It appears that there may be a negative relationship between access to a government pension and the desire to work in later years. Five participants (2 males; 3 females), who were not qualified or financially independent, would have liked to have worked to an older age to save for their retirement, or were still interested in work to 'top up' or save more for full-time retirement. For example, Geoff said, 'but by the time you get to 60 or 70 or 80 the money can go pretty quick so I was still keen to get something to top up the money'. Further, Bill said, 'And I actively looked in the paper for positions for the first few years coming up here. No one ever asked for a 55 or 60 year-old manager to work.' Geoff concurred, 'I looked at buying a business in order to buy a job'.

However, none of these unqualified older people was successful in re-entering the workforce.

These findings suggest, perhaps not surprisingly, there may be a relationship between being qualified and having greater access to work later in life. There may also be a relationship between being qualified and wanting to continue working. Explanations could include higher levels of work autonomy and networking capabilities of qualified people, enabling higher levels of flexibility (Platman 2004).

Self-worth and Job Satisfaction

Another theme that emerged from comments by several participants (12 of 20) was the importance of job satisfaction and self-worth found from work. While not all of these participants wanted to work, they reported that if they did, such work would need to be satisfying and worthwhile. As Sam said, 'job satisfaction is probably the number one priority'. When asked what might attract him back to the workforce, Howard said, 'the most attractive thing would be being asked to do something that I felt that I had experience and competence to do better than most people'. Agreeing with the general sentiment, Bill said, 'I would rather earn money than have it give to me'.

These views support the literature about the low rates of absenteeism and turnover of older people (for example, Encel 1998; Gordon 1995; Steinberg et al. 1998; Tabakoff and Skeffington 2000). Further, perhaps some older people may be more selective when choosing to re-enter the workforce, wanting to maximise the levels of job satisfaction and self-worth.

Implications and Concluding Remarks

The comments made by the participants supported the literature in the areas of: flexible working hours being attractive employment options to older people; age being a common reason for leaving the workforce; and age being a common barrier to rejoining the workforce. New findings from this study were that: access to social aspects at work were attractive to older workers; qualified older workers were more likely to want to continue working; and older people seek self-worth and job satisfaction from working, and are less likely to accept work that does not provide both.

Some participants commented that they had found job searching to be a difficult task, and they believed their age was a significant part of the reason for their lack of success. In other words, Australian employers apparently did not value older people as new hires, supporting the literature previously mentioned. The participants' comments suggest that there are several changes that Australian organisations will need to make to reduce the apparent preference for youth as employees, as well as revising some broad policy issues, such as the taxation system, to entice people to continue to work beyond the traditional age of retirement.

However, generalisability of the findings is limited as the sample size was small and the study used purposeful and snowballing sampling techniques. While these types of sampling may introduce the possibility of bias, this study was exploratory and sought attitudes and perceptions in general, and rich descriptive material on personal perceptions of experiences. Such possible bias is thus not of great concern here. In this study, there appeared to be a gendered effect in the desire to work in retirement. The majority of males (8 of 10) wanted to work in retirement, while, only a minority of females (3 of 10) wanted to work in retirement. With a small sample size, and the differences between the employment types, levels of qualification and skill of the genders, it is not meaningful to generalise from this finding. This gendered issue was not pursued in this study, but appears worthy of additional investigation. Therefore, research would be worthwhile in broader contexts and exhausting all factors likely to influence the intention to continue working.

Overall, the findings confirm that flexible employment options are needed to attract older people to possibly return to, or stay in, the workforce, and that, depending on individual circumstances, many older people may want to continue to work. Notably, these older people commented that they were willing to learn new things, challenging employers' views about older people not being as flexible, adaptable or willing to learn as younger people.

The implications from the findings suggest the need for change if organisations/HRM wish to create an environment where older people are attracted to stay in or return to paid work. Although older workers differ from one another in their needs and desires about work, a re-entry strategy might be effective, made available to those older workers valued by the organisation. Early discussion with those considering their future working or retirement options, including the offer to continue working either immediately or at a later date, with flexible employment arrangements, could create a database of skilled and knowledgeable older people – a kind of 'grey army', similar to 'the reserves' of most military forces.

The HRM challenge in managing the exit and re-entry of older workers may be partly met by a 'revolving door' approach, whereby valued older workers may exit and re-enter the organisation many times after initially leaving. Such arrangements would need to meet both parties' needs, including performance standards and expectations. The rotating movement into and out of an organisation could include staged work, seasonal or busy period extra staff, as well as ongoing part-time roles. In summary, to meet the predicated labour shortage, organisations could offer 'revolving door' employment opportunities to older workers considering leaving the workforce, including roles that maximise job satisfaction and self-worth, flexible working arrangements and social interaction.

Finally, further inquiry would seem beneficial in the areas of gender, employment arrangements, qualification and older people's desires to continue working. The findings from this study suggest relevance within the international context, at least for other OECD countries that share the challenges of their own ageing workforces. For example, there is a suggestion that more flexible working arrangements are more attractive to older persons, who will be needed in the labour force to assist in meeting the predicted shortfall of labour. Further, the finding that age is still perceived as a barrier to employment and as a reason for retirement may be relevant to other countries in the development of public policies, and to organisations in their human resource strategies.

Source: Asia Pacific Journal of Human Resources, 45, (2), 151–167 (2007). Reprinted by permission.

REFERENCES

ACIL Consulting. 2000. *Ageing gracefully: An overview of the economic implications of Australia's ageing population profile.* Canberra: Commonwealth Department of Health and Aged Care.

American Association of Retired Persons. 1992. *How to stay employable: A guide for midlife and older workers.* Washington DC: Andrus Foundation.

Australian Bureau of Statistics (ABS). 2003. *Population projections, Australia.* Catalogue no. 3222.0. Canberra: ABS.

Australian Bureau of Statistics (ABS). 2004. *Mature age workers – Australian social trends.* Catalogue no. 4102.0. Canberra: ABS.

Australian Bureau of Statistics. 2005. *Year book Australia: Labour force participation in Australia.* Catalogue no. 6105.0. Canberra: ABS.

Bennington, L. and B. R. Calvert. 1998. Antidiscrimination legislation and HRM practice. In *Managing an ageing workforce*, eds M. Patrickson and L. Hartmann, 136–153. Warriewood. NSW: Business and Professional Publishing.

Creswell, J. W. 1998. *Qualitative inquiry and research design: Choosing among the five traditions.* Thousand Oaks, CA: Sage Publications.

Creswell, J. W. 2003. *Research design: Qualitative, quantitative, and mixed methods approaches.* 2nd edn. Thousand Oaks, CA: Sage Publications.

Crown, W. H., Y. -P. Chen, and R. W. McConaghy. 1996. The growing interest in older worker employment policy. In *Handbook on employment and the elderly*, edited by W.H. Crown, 1–14. Westport, CT: Greenwood Press.

Department of Parliamentary Services. 2005. *Research note: Australia's ageing workforce.* Canberra: Parliament of Australia.

Department of the Treasury. 2004. *Australia's demographic challenges.* Canberra: Department of the Treasury.

Drucker, P. 2001. A survey of the near future. *The Economist*, November: 3–22.

Duncan, C. and W. Loretto. 2004. Never the right age? Gender and age-based discrimination in employment. *Gender, Work and Organisation* 11(1): 95–115.

Encel, S. 1998. Age discrimination. In *Managing an ageing workforce*, edited by M. Patrickson and L. Hartmann, 41–52. Warriewood, NSW: Business and Professional Publishing.

Encel, S. 2001. Working in later life. *Australasian Journal on Ageing* 20(3): 69–73.

Encel, S. and H. Studencki. 2004. Older workers: Can they succeed in the job market? *Australasian Journal on Ageing* 23(1): 33–37.

Equal Opportunity Commission of Victoria. 2001. *Age limits.* Melbourne: Equal Opportunity Commission of Victoria.

Field, A. 2001. Work still does a body good. *Business Week*, 10 December (3761): 98–99.

Gardyn, R. 2000. Retirement redefined. *American Demographics* November: 52–7.

Glover, I. and M. Branine, eds. 2001. *Ageism in work and employment.* Aldershot: Ashgate Publishing.

Gordon, C. 1995. Continuous employability: Mature workers in the new workplace. *Management Accounting* May: 5–7.

Hartmann, L. 1998. The impact of trends in labour force participation in Australia. In *Managing an ageing workforce*, edited by M. Patrickson and L. Hartmann, 3–25. Warriewood, NSW: Business and Professional Publishing.

House of Representatives Standing Committee on Employment Education and Workplace Relations. 2000. *Age counts.* Canberra: Parliament of the Commonwealth of Australia.

House of Representatives Standing Committee on Health and Ageing. 2005. *Future ageing: Inquiry into long-term strategies to address the ageing of the Australian population over the next 40 years.* Canberra: Parliament of the Commonwealth of Australia.

Human Rights and Equal Opportunity Commission. 2000. *Age matters: A report on age discrimination.* Sydney: Commonwealth of Australia.

Kern, A. 1990. *Productive ageing: The health policy implementation of continued employment for the elderly. Report for the World Health Organisation's Program on Health of the Elderly.* Geneva: World Health Organisation.

Koopman-Boyden, P. G. and L. Macdonald. 2003. Ageing, work performance and managing ageing academics. *Journal of Higher Education Policy and Management* 25(1): 29–40.

Leonard, B. 1999. Growing number of older workers stay on in the job. *HR Magazine* February: 28.

Maurer, T. 2001. Career-relevant learning and development: Worker age, and beliefs about self-efficacy for development. *Journal of Management* 27(2): 123–140.

Minichiello, V., R. Aroni, E. Timewell, and L. Alexander. 1995. *In-depth interviewing: Principles, techniques, analysis.* Melbourne: Longman Cheshire.

Minichiello, V., J. Browne, and H. Kendig. 2000. Perceptions and consequences of ageism: Views of older people. *Ageing and Society* 20: 253–278.

Murray, P. and J. Syed. 2005. Critical issues in managing age diversity in Australia. *Asia Pacific Journal of Human Resources* 43(2): 210–224.

Myers, B. A. 2001. The lives and work experience of older workers 'across the great divide'? Paper presented at Australia and New Zealand Academy of Management conference, Auckland.

O'Neill, G. L. 1998. Managing performance and remuneration. In *Managing an ageing workforce*, edited by M. Patrickson and L. Hartmann, 170–9. Warriewood, NSW: Business and Professional Publishing.

Onyx, J. 1998. Older women workers: A double jeopardy? In *Managing an ageing workforce*, edited by M. Patrickson and L. Hartmann, 88–105. Warriewood, NSW: Business and Professional Publishing.

Patrickson, M. and M. Clarke. 2001. Voluntary redundancy: Its role in stimulating early retirement. Paper presented at Australian and New Zealand Academy of Management conference, Auckland.

Patrickson, M. and L. Hartmann. 1996. Australian gender differences in preferences for early retirement. *International Employment Relations Review* 2(1): 1–19.

Patrickson, M. and L. Hartmann. 2001. Human resource management in Australia: Prospects for the twenty-first century. *International Journal of Manpower* 22(3): 198–204.

Patrickson, M. and R. Ranzijn. 2004. Bounded choices in work and retirement in Australia. *Employee Relations* 26(4): 422–432.

Platman, K. 2004. 'Portfolio careers' and the search for flexibility, in later life. *Work, Employment and Society* 18(3): 573–99.

Productivity Commission. 2005. *Economic implications of an ageing Australia: Research report.* Canberra: Australian Government Productivity Commission.

Reark Research. 1990. *Attitudes of people aged 55–64 to employment, unemployment and early retirement.* Canberra: Department of Employment, Education and Training.

Schwartz, D. A. and B. H. Kleiner. 1999. The relationship between age and employment opportunities. *Equal Employment International* 18(5/6): 105–10.

Sheen, V. 1999. *Older Australians: Working for the future.* Melbourne: Council on the Ageing.

Sheen, V. 2000. *Older Australians: A working future?* Melbourne: Council on the Ageing and Committee for Economic Development of Australia.

Sheen, V. 2001. The economics of the ageing population: The role of mature age employment. Paper read at Committee for Economic Development of Australia seminar, 20 March, Melbourne.

Sheen, V. 2004. *Strategic ageing – working on: Policies and programs for older workers, Australian issues in ageing.* Melbourne: Council on the Ageing.

Shoebridge, N. and A. Ferguson. 1997. Rise of the baby-boom bosses. *Business Review Weekly*, 20 January: 28–34.

Stein, D., T. S. Rocco, and K. A. Goldenetz. 2000. Age and the university workplace: A case study of remaining, retiring, or returning older workers. *Human Resource Development Quarterly* 11(1): 61–80.

Steinberg, M., L. Walley, R. Tyman, and K. Donald. 1998. Too old to work? In *Managing an ageing workforce*, edited by M. Patrickson and L. Hartmann, 53–68. Warriewood, NSW: Business and Professional Publishing.

Tabakoff, N. and R. Skeffington. 2000. The wise old heads are back. *Business Review Weekly* 3 November: 1–6.

Taylor, P. and A. Walker. 1994. The ageing workforce: Employers' attitudes towards older workers. *Work, Employment and Society* 8(4): 569–91.

Taylor, P. and A. Walker. 1997. Age discrimination and public policy. *Personnel Review*, 26(4): 307–318.

VandenHeuvel, A. 1999. Mature age workers: Are they a disadvantaged group in the labour market? *Australian Bulletin of Labour* 25(1): 11–22.

Wrenn, K. A. and T. J. Maurer. 2004. Beliefs about older workers' learning and development behavior in relation to beliefs about malleability of skills, age-related decline, and control. *Journal of Applied Social Psychology*, 34(2): 223–42.

Global Human Resource Management 14

Learning Objectives

- Gain an appreciation for how global HR differs from domestic HR
- Understand different dimensions and models of national culture and how they influence effective human resource management practices
- Appreciate the challenges involved in selecting individuals for international assignments as well as the purposes of expatriation
- Describe the various levels of standardization of global HR practice and the pros and cons associated with each
- Gain an awareness of the challenges associated with repatriation and associated knowledge retention
- Understand some of the critical HR-related issues involved with doing business in select foreign countries in the European Union, North America, and Asia

Global Human Resource Management at Reebok

In 1998, athletic shoe global industry leader Nike was hit by a wave of negative publicity regarding the conditions in many of its overseas factories. Growing reports of strikes, unsafe working conditions, poor wages, worker abuse, and the use of child labor aroused a fury within the United States. Although Nike's market share remained constant, its stock price sagged with each new report of labor abuse in Asia.

Reebok, one of Nike's main competitors and a company with a history of strong support for human rights, acted quickly to ensure that there were no similar problems at overseas sites owned by Reebok or those in which subcontractors produced goods for Reebok. Reebok contracted with a respected nonprofit social research group in Jakarta, Indonesia, for thorough inspections of two of its shoe factories that employed more than 10,000 workers. The researchers interviewed and surveyed workers, performed health and safety tests, and discussed operations with managers. These audits marked the first time that a U.S. company allowed truly independent outsiders with expertise in labor issues to inspect their factories and make their findings public.

The report found a range of problems including poor ventilation, the presence of harmful chemicals, inadequate toilet facilities, and sex bias. Reebok took immediate action but found some cultural challenges in addressing the problems. These problems were largely because of the difficulty of introducing industrialized-world work and culture environments. Workers did not report sexual harassment largely because they did not understand the concept of it. There was also a thriving local market for empty hazardous chemical containers. Reebok's vice president for human rights was relentless in his attempt to force Western values on the reluctant Indonesians. Workers and managers were trained in gender awareness and harassment; requirements were set for the safe disposal of chemical containers; and workers were educated as to the reasons and personal benefits for the protective clothing they were required to wear. Reebok's two Indonesian contractors were forced to spend more than $250,000 to address these issues or lose Reebok's business.

Reebok led the way in ensuring that oppressive sweatshop operations were curtailed. Within days, both Liz Claiborne and Mattel followed suit in having outside independent agencies review their operations and those of their subcontractors. Although these initiatives clearly show good business sense, particularly in light of what happened to Nike, they also show a sensitivity to basic human rights and the ethical treatment of their global labor force.[1]

The strategic business decisions being made by modern organizations increasingly involve some plan to conduct business that was previously conducted domestically in the global arena. In some cases, this may involve a minimal physical presence in another country; in others, it may involve setting up operations that will eventually exceed the size of domestic operations. We no longer live in a domestic economy, as evidenced by diminished trade barriers and regional economic alliances, such as the North American Free Trade Agreement (NAFTA) and the European Union (EU) as well as the acceleration of global financial markets and information networks. Tremendous opportunities exist to market goods and services abroad, particularly in less-developed countries; to participate in joint ventures with foreign organizations; and to outsource operations to other countries as a means of lowering costs. When one considers that less than 10 percent of the world population resides in the United States and that many domestic consumer markets are saturated, it should not be surprising that an increasing number of organizations are developing strategies to expand internationally.

These strategic opportunities are resulting in employers' sending an increasing number of employees abroad to start up, manage, and develop their global operations. While a greater percentage of the U.S. workforce is being moved abroad, an increasing number of U.S. domestic workers are natives of other countries. These trends are not just limited to larger organizations as they once were; small and medium-size employers are taking advantage of international opportunities, and their workforces are becoming more culturally diverse.

An organization might focus on expanding globally for a number of reasons. Foreign countries may present enhanced market opportunities. In addition, expanding the scope and volume of operations to support global initiatives could result in economies of scale in production as well as in the administrative side of the organization. Competitive pressure may require an organization to enter foreign markets to keep pace with industry leaders. Finally, acquisition activity may result in the ownership of a foreign-based organization or subsidiary.

Regardless of the reasons a company may have for expanding operations globally, human resource management is critical to the success of any global endeavor. If one adopts the perspective that human resource strategy must be derived from corporate strategy and that people do determine an organization's success or failure, then the human resource function needs to be a key strategic partner in any global undertakings. Ironically, human resources is often neglected in the planning and establishment of global operations.

Strategic Global HR at McDonald's

When fast-food king McDonald's initially expanded outside the United States, it followed a very ethnocentric approach to going global. U.S. expatriates were sent abroad to develop the new sites and maintain as much consistency as possible with domestic operations. Locals were "McDonaldized"—taught the specific operations and business plans developed back in the United States. This approach has evolved over the years to one that is now very polycentric. When opening locations outside the United States, expatriates are rarely used and HR professionals at McDonald's partner closely with locals to develop an operation that fits with local culture, customs, and lifestyles. A four-phase approach is used in which HR has a specific and critical role to play at each step. The first phase, development preparation, usually begins 18 to 24 months prior to the actual opening. During this phase, HR researches issues such as compensation and benefits, considers recruiting strategies, and secures a labor attorney or consultant. The second phase, resources selection, takes place 8 to 12 months prior to opening. HR takes the information gathered in phase one and begins to develop specific HR programs and plans and determines staffing needs and compensation levels. The third phase, resource development and strategy implementation, takes place 3 to 8 months prior to opening. HR puts together employee handbooks, considers the effects of local labor laws on operations, and begins to implement its staffing plan by hiring employees. The final phase, pre-opening preparation, begins 90 days prior to opening.

Here, HR conducts training and lays the groundwork for the performance review system. McDonald's strategy for its global operations includes HR as a key strategic partner, facilitating the implementation of the human and cultural dimension of the operation for maximum success.[2]

How Global HRM Differs from Domestic HRM

Despite the fact that the core principles of strategic human resource management also apply to global human resource management, global human resources presents some unique contingencies. First, managing people in global settings requires human resources to address a broader range of functional areas. These areas include clarifying taxation issues; coordinating foreign currencies, exchange rates, and compensation plans; and working directly with the families of employees who may be accepting overseas assignments. Second, it requires more involvement in the employee's personal life. The employee is usually assisted with acquiring housing in the host country; selling or leasing domestic accommodations; locating recreational and cultural opportunities for the employee and family; arranging and paying for school for the employee's children; and locating and securing domestic help for the employee. Third, the organization must often set up different human resource management systems for different geographic locations. Fourth, the organization is often forced to deal with more complex external constituencies, including foreign governments and political and religious groups. Finally, global assignments often involve a heightened exposure to risks. These risks include the health and safety of the employee and family; legal issues in the host country; possible terrorism; and the human and financial consequences of mistakes, which may greatly exceed the costs of those made domestically.

The threat of terrorism has added to many of the anxieties employees face when considering and undertaking a global assignment. A recent survey found that expatriates need and want more support from headquarters than they are receiving regarding health and safety concerns; only 20 percent responded that their employers were keeping them sufficiently informed about health and safety issues.[3] Dissatisfied expatriates can be expensive for an organization: The average cost of a three-year assignment abroad is $1.3 million.[4] In addition, concerns about the employee's and/or family safety can diminish productivity and cause stress. Consequently, employers need to communicate with—and provide the needed support for—expatriates about their safety to ensure that the assignment is a success.

The decision to expand globally first involves determining the appropriate strategy for involvement in the host country. For example, the organization may decide to simply export its goods to a foreign country; this might require very limited presence on the part of domestic employees. The organization might also decide to subcontract or license certain goods and services to a foreign partner. On a slightly more involved scale, a joint venture might be undertaken abroad with a foreign partner. Finally, the organization could decide to establish a significant presence abroad by setting up operations in the form of a foreign branch office or subsidiary.

Assessing Culture

Several factors will influence the level of involvement an organization might choose in its foreign operations. Economic, market, social, and political conditions will certainly play a significant role in any decision to go abroad. A larger issue might be the culture of the host country and how it compares to the national culture of the organization's home. National cultures differ on a variety of dimensions, and many global undertakings fail because of a lack of understanding or appreciation of cultural differences.

One of the most popular models of cultural differences among countries was developed by Hofstede, who explained cultural differences along four dimensions.[5] The first dimension is the extent to which a society emphasizes individualism or collectivism.

Individualistic societies value the development of and focus on the individual; collectivistic societies value togetherness, harmony, belongingness, and loyalty to others. The second dimension is power distance. This dimension looks at the extent to which a society is hierarchical, with an unequal distribution of power among its members, as opposed to one where there are few distinctions and power is more evenly distributed among individuals. The third dimension is uncertainty avoidance, which refers to the extent to which the society feels comfortable with ambiguity and values and encourages risk-taking. The fourth dimension is the extent to which the society displays "masculine" or "feminine" tendencies. A masculine society is one that is more aggressive, assertive, and focused on achievements; the feminine society is one that emphasizes interpersonal relationships and sensitivity toward the welfare and well-being of others. Although many are uncomfortable with the sexist connotations of *masculine* and *feminine* and the stereotypes they encourage, this dimension does significantly explain many differences in cultural behavior in societies. Some researchers who have applied Hofstede's work have substituted *quantity of life* for *masculinity* and *quality of life* for *femininity*. Exhibit 14.1 illustrates how a number of countries fit Hofstede's model of culture.

Another well-known model that explains differences in culture was developed by Hall, who characterized culture by the patterns with which we communicate.[6] His work focused on the more subtle means by which we express and display our culture. These means might not be evident to someone from outside the culture, but they are understood and accepted by insiders. Hall's model describes culture in terms of five silent "languages": time, space, material goods, friendships, and agreement.

The language of time considers how we use time to communicate and how we use it to manage our daily lives. For example, how much do individuals in the culture rely on schedules, appointments, and deadlines? Is it considered appropriate to keep someone waiting for a meeting? Do meetings usually have a timed agenda? Are meetings and appointments scheduled with an ending time or are they open-ended?

The language of space considers how we communicate through space and distance. For example, what is considered the appropriate physical distance between two people engaged in a conversation? Friendship, formality, and even intimacy are often communicated

EXHIBIT 14.1 Examples of Hofstede's Cultural Dimensions

Country	Individualism—Collectivism	Power Distance	Uncertainty Avoidance	Quantity of Life*
Australia	Individual	Small	Moderate	Strong
Canada	Individual	Small	Low	Moderate
England	Individual	Small	Moderate	Strong
France	Individual	Large	High	Weak
Greece	Collective	Large	High	Moderate
Italy	Individual	Moderate	High	Strong
Japan	Collective	Moderate	High	Strong
Mexico	Collective	Large	High	Strong
Singapore	Collective	Large	Low	Moderate
Sweden	Individual	Small	Low	Weak
United States	Individual	Small	Low	Strong
Venezuela	Collective	Large	High	Strong

*A weak quantity-of-life score is equivalent to a high quality-of-life score.

Source: G. Hofstede, "Motivation, Leadership, and Organization: Do American Theories Apply Abroad?" Organizational Dynamics, *Summer 1980, pp. 42–63.*

by distance. How are spaces in organizations arranged to communicate rank, power, and status? Does an organization have private offices and/or designated parking spaces? Are some offices larger than others?

The language of material goods can be similarly used to signify power, success, and status. In some cultures, these indicators are of critical importance in establishing one's personal and professional identity. In an organizational setting, this language might be communicated through generous perks such as a company car and might be further evidenced by executive salaries that are many times those of lower-level workers. Organizations that establish and maintain pay compression plans are attempting to silence this kind of language.

The language of friendships considers how we form interpersonal relationships. For example, are friendships formed and dissolved quickly or are they built on a foundation over a long period of time? Is there a mutual sense of ongoing obligation in interpersonal relationships or are they more transient and maintained only as long as both parties see some benefit? Some cultures communicate status via material goods; other cultures communicate status through one's network of friends and the support this network provides.

The language of agreement considers how consensus is reached among people. For example, are formal, written contracts signed under an oath of law the norm in business negotiations or is a simple handshake sufficient guarantee? Is it acceptable to debate someone with whom you do not agree and, if so, is it acceptable to debate in front of others?

A key issue that impacts an organization's success in the global arena is an awareness of cultural differences and the development of both a business strategy and corresponding HR strategy that is consistent with the culture of the host country. Although it is beyond the scope of this chapter to detail how cultural differences might impact people management systems, a culture in which negotiations are based on trust and friendship that is built over time might pose some difficulty for an American, who might be used to getting down to business and negotiating without developing any kind of interpersonal connection. Also, the candor and outspokenness for which Americans are known could conflict with the styles of those from other cultures. In short, when cultures come together in organizational settings, special consideration must be paid to managing processes such as power dynamics and relationships, norms of participation and decision-making, and performance management and compensation systems to prevent misunderstandings. Reading 14.1, "Selected Cross-Cultural Factors in Human Resource Management," summarizes several frameworks for analyzing culture as well as how these cultural factors can influence a variety of behaviors and dynamics within organizations.

Much as societies have cultures, organizations also have their own cultures. As a result, decision-makers need to examine the interface between the culture of the organization and the culture of the host country in determining whether an appropriate fit exists and, subsequently, in developing an optimal business strategy and appropriate human resource management strategies. For example, if the organization strongly values diversity, what will be done when a host country's culture fails to support these values? In many cultures, it is acceptable to discriminate on the basis of gender, race, ethnicity, age, disability, and sexual orientation. Does the organization extend its ban on smoking to all overseas locations? Will it prohibit facial hair on employees or prohibit employees from enjoying a glass of wine with their lunches? What will happen in a culture in which bribes are an accepted and expected means of conducting business?

In going abroad, an organization needs to decide what human resource policies will be implemented in the host country and needs to make these decisions prior to arrival. These decisions will force top managers to confront a number of ethical decisions and may test the strength of the organization's culture. Conflict issues will need to be resolved relative to incompatible local and corporate cultures. Decision-makers need to understand which values the organization holds so deeply that it will not compromise, even in the face of significant financial consequences. Although these ethical decisions can present difficult choices, they can help to strengthen the organization's mission, strategy, and employment practices.

National culture can have a significant effect on an organization's ability to utilize strategic HR. A culture that is oriented toward tradition, for example, might not understand the logic of, or resist, any kind of planning. Certain cultures have stringent rules regarding staffing and may require the organization to employ individuals assigned to it by a centralized labor bureau. Individuals in some very strict hierarchical cultures would probably not respond well to upward performance feedback programs. In some cultures, it is considered inappropriate for a worker to report to a manager who is younger than the subordinate. The inappropriateness of using direct eye contact in conversation in some cultures might bias the results of the employment interview process. Where a culture fits on the individualism/collectivism continuum would influence how it defines acceptable performance and appropriate compensation. Consequently, in managing across cultures, it is critical to have a strong sense of cultural self-awareness yet remain aware that oversensitivity to cultural issues can be as detrimental as undersensitivity. Reading 14.2, "In the Eye of the Beholder: Cross Cultural Lessons in Leadership from Project GLOBE," examines the similarities and differences of the cultures of five major would countries and the implications for both American executives in each of these countries and for the development of effective global leaders.

Strategic HR Issues in Global Assignments

An organization can use several different approaches in managing the process of sending workers abroad. An administrative approach involves merely assisting employees with paperwork and minor logistics—for example, hiring movers, ensuring that taxes are paid, and obtaining a work visa for the employee and travel visas for family members. A tactical approach involves managing the risk or failure factor—for example, handling the administrative paperwork while also providing limited, usually one-day, training for the employee. This approach does only what needs to be done to prevent failure. A strategic approach to global assignments, however, involves much more support and coordination. In addition to those items cited previously, strategically managing such a process would involve adding extensive selection systems; ongoing, integrated training; a specific performance management system; destination services; and a strategized repatriation program at the end of the assignment.

A model that outlines the strategic human resource issues in global assignments is presented in Exhibit 14.2. The first step in the strategic management of global assignments is the establishment of a specific purpose for the assignment. There may be numerous reasons for the assignment, including business or market development; the setup, transfer, or integration of information technology; management of an autonomous subsidiary; coordination or integration of foreign with domestic operations; a temporary assignment to a vacant position; or the development of local management talent.

After the purpose of the assignment has been identified, the process of selecting an appropriate employee for the assignment can commence. Much as there is an organizational purpose for the assignment, there should also be an individual purpose for the assignment, as indicated in Exhibit 14.3. An employee could be chosen for and accept an international assignment to prepare that employee for a top management position, develop further technical or interpersonal skills, or allow an employee to follow a dual-career spouse/partner.

Both the organizational and individual purposes for the assignment must be identified and matched. The assignment needs to be conceptualized as a win/win proposition. There should be clear articulated gain for both the organization and the employee as a prerequisite to success on the assignment.

After an appropriate individual has been identified, it is important to assess the adaptability to the host culture of both the employee and any family members who will be accompanying the employee on the assignment. The single greatest reason for failure on an overseas assignment has to do with adaptability skills rather than technical skills and

EXHIBIT 14.2 Strategic HR Issues in Global Assignments

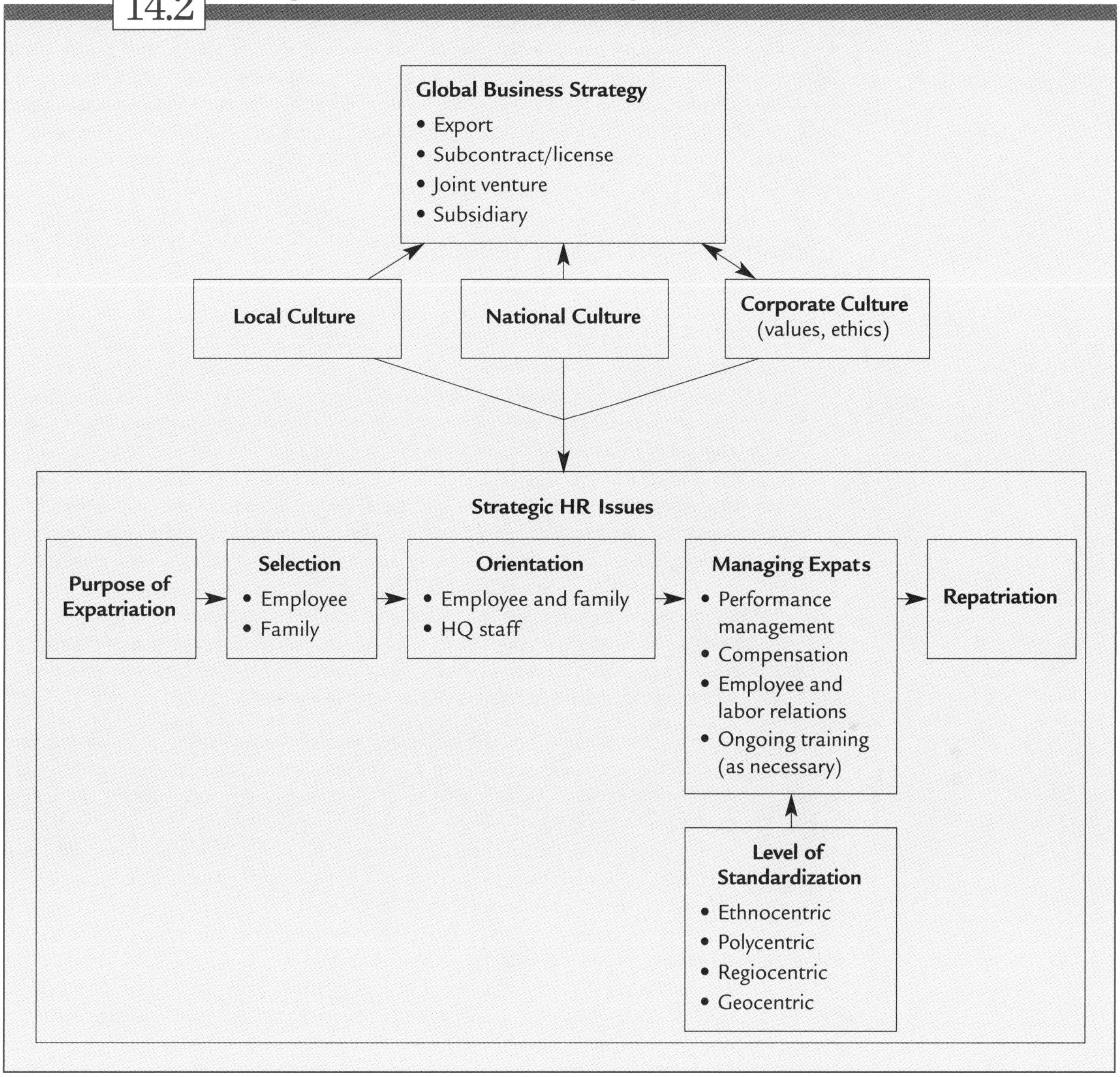

Global Business Strategy
- Export
- Subcontract/license
- Joint venture
- Subsidiary

Local Culture

National Culture

Corporate Culture
(values, ethics)

Strategic HR Issues

Purpose of Expatriation

Selection
- Employee
- Family

Orientation
- Employee and family
- HQ staff

Managing Expats
- Performance management
- Compensation
- Employee and labor relations
- Ongoing training (as necessary)

Repatriation

Level of Standardization
- Ethnocentric
- Polycentric
- Regiocentric
- Geocentric

EXHIBIT 14.3 Purposes of Expatriation

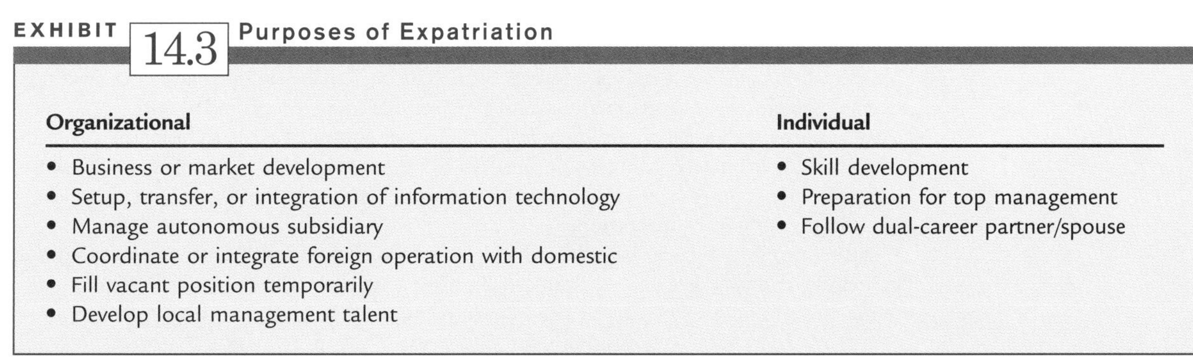

Organizational	Individual
• Business or market development	• Skill development
• Setup, transfer, or integration of information technology	• Preparation for top management
• Manage autonomous subsidiary	• Follow dual-career partner/spouse
• Coordinate or integrate foreign operation with domestic	
• Fill vacant position temporarily	
• Develop local management talent	

is usually a consequence of the adaptability of the employee's family to the host culture. Individuals and their families should be screened to determine their ability to be comfortable in the host culture. This might include sending the employee and family members to the host country for several weeks to test their adaptability. Among the areas that an organization will need to assess are the technical abilities of the employee; the adaptability, willingness, and motivation to live overseas; tolerance of ambiguity; communication skills; patience and openness to differences in others; and willingness to interact of both the employee and accompanying family members.

Expatriate Selection at Kellogg Co.

Given the high cost of most global assignments, it is critical for organizations to get some return on their investment in sending employees abroad. Battle Creek, Michigan–based breakfast cereal manufacturer Kellogg saw its turnover rate among expatriates reach 40 percent. Kellogg viewed the retention problem as being rooted in poor selection of candidates for global assignments. To remedy this problem, Kellogg first implemented a selection strategy for its global assignments, including a pilot program that identified the best candidates based on assessments from managers. HR and senior management partnered to narrow the list down to 16 individuals who were then given assessment tests that examined work styles, habits, values, interests, and lifestyles. Employee spouses were also given the assessment. Key personality traits critical to assignment abroad, such as flexibility, willingness to learn, openness, sense of humor, adaptability, ability to handle ambiguity, and interest in others, were measured. The information was then analyzed and the results given to employees and their spouses to explain potential risks and areas of concern that needed to be addressed prior to any assignment. This new process has had a 100 percent success rate for Kellogg in its expatriate assignments.[7]

Once an employee has been selected for the overseas assignment, the organization then needs to provide the appropriate training for the employee and family members. The initial training should begin at least six to nine months prior to the start of the assignment. Longer training periods will reflect the need to learn language skills necessary in the host country. Prior to departure, the employee and family, if possible, should be allowed a trial period living overseas (if this was not done as part of the selection process). Although this may involve significant costs, it should be viewed as an investment; the costs incurred for such a trip will be much less than the monetary, political, and reputation-damaging costs of a failed overseas assignment.

Also prior to departure, the employee and family should receive cross-cultural training in the norms and values of the host country, workplace and business practices, language training (as necessary), health and safety issues, and realistic expectations of what day-to-day life in the country will be like. This training should not be considered completed when the employee and family depart for the host country. A critical mistake made by many organizations is the lack of follow-up once employees have gone abroad to provide additional support to ensure that there have been no unexpected surprises or consequences.

While the employee and family are being trained, simultaneous training should be conducted for headquarters staff who will be supervising and/or interacting with the employee who is abroad. Clashes between local culture and headquarters are common on overseas assignments, and headquarters personnel should be provided with some sensitivity training. Sensitivity training will (1) help headquarters staff understand how and why local decisions are being made and (2) allow them to give the expatriate employee the necessary support and empathy while keeping the expatriate informed as to what has been happening at headquarters.

After employees have been relocated to the host country, the day-to-day issues in managing expatriates are not dramatically different from those involved in managing domestic employees. The same principles and practices of general human resource management apply with a few additional concerns. First, it is critical to assess ongoing training needs of the expatriate employee and family after they have arrived at the host country. Particularly if this is the first time an employee of the organization has been assigned to a particular country, it is likely that some unanticipated events that require additional support and training could materialize. Second, performance management will be more of a challenge; the expatriate's functional boss is usually located domestically, and others in the organization may not be aware of how economic, social, and political conditions and everyday living situations impact the expatriate's performance. Third, many aspects of employee and labor relations will be localized. The expatriate may have to manage a local workforce under far more challenging conditions than those presented domestically. The expatriate may also have to manage the dynamics of being a foreign manager of local employees. Finally, compensation for the expatriate will be different. It is costly to send an employee overseas, usually amounting to as much at three times the employee's annual domestic salary. Income tax payments for the employee may be complicated and costly. Benefits such as armed security guards or private schooling for the employee's children may be necessary. Although compensation for expatriates is often outsourced, organizations need to be very careful in this regard; compensation is a key strategic issue not only from a cost perspective but also in impacting the employee family's ability to live in the host country. Outsourcing compensation to a third party who does not fully understand the organization's overall strategy or have a holistic appreciation of all of the organization's human resource systems could result in disaster.

There are three traditional approaches to determining expatriate compensation. The first is the balance sheet method. With this approach, salary is based on home country pay, and additional expenses associated with relocation and the assignment itself are added to arrive at an overall reimbursement and compensation level. These expenses might include the cost of housing in the host country, furniture, household help, a car and driver, or spousal/partner assistance. This approach ensures that the expatriate gains a sense of equity and fairness in the compensation package; however, the local employees, particularly if they are poor, may sense some inequity. This system can be complex to administer, but it is still widely used, particularly for short-term or temporary assignments.

The higher-of-home-or-host approach takes into account the employee's salary at home and adjusts it upward, as necessary, to account for a higher cost of living in the host country. This approach is usually accompanied by standard perquisites for executives in the host country and is used most commonly for intermediate term assignments of indefinite duration.

When the employee is assigned to a host country on a permanent basis, the localization approach is usually used. Here, the employee's salary is converted to the host country equivalent. Depending on the country, salary structures, and the cost of living, this approach can initially result in a salary decrease for the employee. Localization has become an increasing popular approach for organizations, now used by upward of 78 percent of employers.[8]

Expatriate selection assignments are some of the most critical decisions that organizations make relative to their global operations. The success or failure of an expatriate assignment can easily determine the fate and success of an organization's entry into a new global market. Much of the focus of expatriation has traditionally been concerned with the selection and training of expatriates and their accompanying family members. However, this focus has been expanding to examine local factors which can impact the success or failure of a global venture. Reading 14.3 "A Local Perspective to Expatriate Success," examines these local factors and how they impact expatriate and ultimately organizational performance.

In establishing general human resource policy for the day-to-day management of all employees abroad—locals as well as expatriates—the organization also needs to make a strategic decision as to the level of standardization it desires across locations. Heenan and Perlmutter identified four different approaches an organization can take in setting and enforcing policy: ethnocentric, polycentric, regiocentric, and geocentric, as illustrated in Exhibit 14.4.[9]

An ethnocentric approach involves exporting the organization's home country practices and policies to foreign locations. This strategy is often used by organizations whose

EXHIBIT 14.4 Four Approaches to IHRM

Aspect of the Enterprise	Orientation: Ethnocentric	Polycentric	Regiocentric	Geocentric
Standard Setting, Evaluation, and Control	By home country headquarters	By local subsidiary management	Coordination across countries in the region	Global as well as local standards and control
Communication and Coordination	From HQ to local subsidiary	Little among subsidiaries, little between subsidiary and HQ	Little between subsidiary and HQ, medium to high among subsidiaries in region	Totally connected network of subsidiaries and subsidiaries with headquarters
Staffing	Home country managers	Host country managers	Managers may come from nations within region	Best people where they can be best used

Source: Heenan, D. A. and Perlmutter, Howard V., Multinational Organizational Development, *Addison-Wesley, pp. 18–19 (1979).*

competitive strategy is focused on creating an image. An ethnocentric approach can be beneficial in allowing standardization, integration, and efficiency. However, if it is forced on another culture that does not subscribe to the values on which the practices are based, there can be severe problems. Some turnover can and should be expected and even encouraged when using this approach. It can also help to make expatriate assignments more attractive to the organization's domestic employees.

A polycentric approach involves allowing each location to develop its own practices and policies that are consistent with the local culture and workforce characteristics. Management practices are localized to suit the existing needs of the marketplace, and adaptability to customer tastes is a key strategic initiative facilitated by this approach. Although this approach can be costly, it is also extremely responsive to local market and labor conditions and can help to reduce employee turnover in an acquisition, particularly if there are anti–foreign ownership attitudes among locals.

A regiocentric approach involves developing standardized practices and policies by geographic region; therefore, there is some consistency and efficiency within operations. At the same time, there is some variation among regions to support the local markets. This approach commonly involves establishing autonomously managed regional subsidiaries within a geographic region.

A geocentric approach involves developing one set of global practices and policies that are applied at all locations. This approach differs from the ethnocentric approach in that although the ethnocentric approach exports its one set of management systems based on home country culture to all locations, the geocentric approach considers the global workforce in all its areas of operations as well as the numerous local cultures in which it operates and attempts to develop practices and policies that transcend cultural differences. This approach can be very difficult to implement, given different host government policies and regulations and the need to address them simultaneously. Compensation plans and standards of living can be difficult to unify in an equitable way across different cultures.

Repatriation

The final issue in managing international assignments is repatriation of returning employees. This function is probably one of the most neglected areas in global human resource management. Ironically, it is the one that has the greatest impact on the return on investment made in employees sent abroad.

Very few companies deal successfully with the issue of repatriation. Retention rates of repatriates during the first year of return are often as low as 50 percent in many companies. This is not surprising in light of the fact that only 27 percent of expatriates are even guaranteed a position upon return from their international assignment.[10] Employers typically make no plans for any post-return assignment, and expatriates are left to fend for themselves in finding a position within or outside the organization upon their return. Despite the fact that expatriates usually undertake international assignments with career development and advancement in mind, only 33 percent of those who return to their employers are promoted. Fifty-eight percent of expatriates remain at the same level of responsibility, and 9 percent end up accepting positions with lesser responsibility.[11]

Organizations need to establish a strategy that allows them to take the valuable experience abroad and (1) integrate it with what is happening at home and (2) allow coworkers to learn of the repatriate's experience to enhance their own performance. As a prerequisite, repatriates need to be considered from an investment perspective. In many cases, the organization has invested a sizable amount of time and money in the global assignment of the employee, during which time the employee has further developed both personally and professionally. If the organization fails to develop career management programs that allow those returning from abroad to share their knowledge and insights—rather than leave the organization and share that knowledge with competitors—then the investment has a negative return. An employee who has worked in another country may be of great value to a competitor who would like to start up overseas operations.

Many repatriates return from overseas assignments and either have no job assignment waiting for them or receive a job that is considered a demotion. Expatriates often have high-ranking autonomous positions overseas and are forced to assume positions that strip them of this autonomy upon their return. It is not surprising that some expatriates choose to move to another expatriate assignment with the same employer or with a different employer rather than return to headquarters.

Any strategy for repatriation has to address the purpose of the expatriation. The process of repatriation can be greatly facilitated if a clear purpose for the assignment was established ahead of time based on the needs of both employer and employee.

A specific repatriation process needs to address several critical career and personal issues, as outlined in Exhibit 14.5. The first career issue is resolving career anxiety by helping the employee returning from abroad find an appropriate place that is connected with a career path for the future. The second career issue is the organization's reaction to the return. Is the repatriate made to feel welcome? Is any value placed on the global experience? Are new skills that have been developed being put to use? The third career issue is the loss of autonomy. In planning repatriation programs, some consideration must be given to the level of autonomy the repatriate enjoyed overseas and the correspondingly appropriate types of responsibilities, work assignments, and supervision for the return assignment. The fourth career issue is adaptation. During the expatriation period, there were probably some significant changes taking place at the home office. The repatriate needs to be provided with assistance in adapting to those changes to facilitate maximum performance in the new assignment.

On a personal level, three major issues need to be addressed in repatriation. The first is logistics. Personal savings will need to be transferred, currency converted, personal

EXHIBIT 14.5 Issues to be Addressed in a Repatriation Process

Career	Personal
• Career anxiety—current place, future	• Logistics
• Organization's reaction	• Personal re-adjustment
• Loss of autonomy	• Family re-adjustment
• Adaptation to change	

belongings inventoried and shipped, automobiles and homes possibly purchased and sold, school transfers arranged, and possibly spousal employment assistance arranged. The more logistical details with which the employee has to contend, the more he or she will be distracted from work. The second personal issue is re-adjustment and integration into the community for the employee. The third personal issue is re-adjustment and integration into the community for the employee's family. Although it may seem logical that the return home should be a welcome and easy process, experience has shown that it often is not. Much as the workplace has changed, and the community in which the employee family lives or is moving to may have changed dramatically during the time abroad. Support for such transition for the employee and family can greatly facilitate the repatriation process.

Repatriation at Colgate-Palmolive

One of the biggest problems with the traditional high attrition rate among repatriates is the loss of experience, skills, and knowledge that accompany the employee's departure. To address this, Colgate-Palmolive has established a global succession database. Used primarily for succession planning purposes, the database—available to the organization's management team worldwide—also contains information on experiences and skills related to work abroad in various cultures. Because Colgate-Palmolive operates over a widely dispersed global area, detailed information about local markets is critical to ongoing success. Seventy-five percent of the company's $9.5 billion annual sales comes from outside North America. At any time, approximately 300 expatriate global managers are on assignment. Seventy-five percent of these managers have had two or more global assignments and 40 percent of these managers have had four or more. Because foreign assignments are seen as critical to an individual's career success within Colgate-Palmolive and the necessary track to senior management, global assignments are in demand. By collecting information related to success in a particular location, Colgate-Palmolive is not only able to provide assistance to managers going on a new assignment but also ensures that its investment in skills, knowledge, and experiences stays with the organization, given the longer "shelf life" of cultural information over market data.[12]

The European Union

Employers who choose to do business in the European Union (EU) do not have the option of taking an ethnocentric approach to HR in their operations there. The European Union has a large number of umbrella employment laws, the details of which vary from country to country, that provide workers with far more protection than their counterparts in the United States. The common intent of these laws is an employment relationship that is not adversarial or confrontational but one that protects the rights of workers via more collectivist social policy.

Unlike the United States, the EU does not follow the employment-at-will policy. Terminating an employee can be a very difficult and expensive undertaking, and the laws regulating the ability to terminate, the notification period, and required severance vary from country to country. In the Netherlands, court approval may be needed to terminate an employee; even termination for cause requires very rigid and specific documentation. Germany requires three months' notification before terminations can take effect; Sweden requires up to six months' notice. In Belgium, where terminations are very difficult, employers may be required to pay up to four years' salary to an employee as severance.[13] Spain requires nine weeks of severance pay for each year of service.[14]

Other areas of the employment relationship are also regulated in various EU countries. Most require a minimum of 4 weeks of paid vacation, but France requires 5 weeks, with an additional week for employees between 18 and 21 years of age. Maternity leave in France is a minimum of 16 weeks, 10 of which must be taken after the child is born, and can extend up to 26 weeks for a third pregnancy. For any pending layoffs, Germany requires a "social plan," which outlines the specific selection criteria used and performance and education levels of workers. German employers must also report employee ages and the number of dependants, as older workers and those with more dependants enjoy a greater level of job security than others.[15]

One major way in which the employment relationship in the EU differs from that of the United States is the level of worker involvement seen in European organizations. U.S. employers generally have a unilateral right to make decisions that affect employees, but European employers are required to communicate and negotiate many of these decisions with employees as part of the EU's Directive on Information and Consultation. Works councils, composed of employee-elected worker representatives, are required to meet monthly with senior management to discuss all employment policy issues. Works councils operate at individual work sites and in Germany, France, and the Netherlands must approve many of the decisions that employers hope to implement. Employers who do not consult with their works council are subject to fines and possible recision of the decisions implemented. Germany requires works councils in organizations with five or more employees. France requires them in organizations with 50 or more employees. Larger employers, with at least 1,000 employees and at least 150 in each of two member countries, must also form an EU-wide works council. Decisions that affect workers in more than one country must be presented to these groups, which are employer-funded. U.S. employers operating in the EU are faced with a dramatically different mandate relative to how they manage their employees than what they are used to domestically. Works councils formalize the employment relationship far more than is seen with a typical collective-bargaining agreement.

Mexico and Canada

Even though Mexico and Canada are border countries with the United States and primary trade partners, human resource management in these countries is often carried out in stark difference to human resource management in the United States. Employment discrimination that would be illegal in the United States is rampant and ingrained into hiring practices in Mexico. A recent recruiting advertisement in a Mexico City newspaper for retail managers for Office Depot Mexico requested applicants who were no younger than 26 and no older than 38 and preferably married.[16] The ad cautioned that it was useless to apply if one did not meet these requirements. Despite the fact that Mexico's constitution strictly forbids such discrimination, enforcement is lax. Employers frequently mandate that applicants be of a specified age, gender, marital status, height, or satisfy other personal non-work related criteria. Female applicants are frequently asked to submit photographs as evidence that they possess a "nice appearance." Gender bias in employment runs rampant—consistent with focus on masculinity in the national culture.

On the other hand, Canada is known to vigorously enforce laws that prohibit discrimination in employment and also provide extensive protections for arbitrary or unjust dismissal of employees. While 90 percent of the Canadian population lives within 60 miles of the U.S. border, these individuals receive far more protection in the employment relationship than do their American counterparts. Canada does not subscribe to the doctrine of employment-at-will and requires reasonable notice of termination as well as legally mandated severance pay based on years of service with the employer. The usual standard is one month per year of service of notice from an employer of pending termination. This amount can be higher if a court feels that the termination was not handled fairly. Employees also are entitled to one week's severance pay per year of service. Most Canadian employers must also provide employees up to 52 weeks of parental/maternity leave; employers in Quebec must provide up to 70 weeks. Noncompete clauses for departing employees are frowned upon, as is a former mandatory retirement age of 65. The province of Quebec amended its Labour Standards Act in 2004 to prohibit bullying or "psychological harassment" in the workplace. More than 10,000 charges had been filed under this law by 2008.[17]

China

With a population of 1.3 billion people and its 2001 accession into the World Trade Organization, which eliminated the requirement that foreign organizations partner with state-owned Chinese partners, China has seen tremendous economic growth, largely through foreign organizations that have set up operations there. Those organizations seeking to take advantage of the rich economic opportunities offered by China have been confronted with significant challenges relative to human resource management. While Chinese universities produce nearly 5 million graduates annually, many of these individuals are not suitable for employment in Western-style multinational organizations. In fact, one survey found that only 10 percent of Chinese university graduates were employable in multinational organizations because of deficiencies in language, interpersonal skills, ability to work in teams, and basic literacy.[18] Even more problematic is the lack of middle and upper-level manager candidates, many of whom were victims of the Chinese Cultural Revolution that stymied the Chinese education system from 1966 to 1976.

The tremendous demand for workers capable of working in a multinational organization—combined with the short supply of such individuals—has created an employment market in which those with sufficient skills can demand high salaries and expect fast upward mobility. Expatriates typically expect very high compensation, yet many remain unaware of the key dimensions of Chinese culture that affect business relations. Recruiting returnees—Chinese citizens who have lived and/or studied abroad—allows an organization the advantage of having employees who are bilingual and bicultural, but many of these individuals have become assimilated to and enjoy Western lifestyle and culture and have no desire to return to China.[19] Even if an employer is successful in hiring qualified applicants, the strong demand for individuals capable of conducting business in China within a multinational organization makes retention of such employees an ongoing challenge.

There are a number of key factors that influence an employer's ability to retain such individuals. The first of these is supervisory relations. Because Chinese society is very hierarchical, shows respect for elders and authority, and is family-centered, employees who have good relations with their supervisors and feel that they "belong" in an organization are less prone to risk this dynamic by seeking employment elsewhere.[20] A second factor is employer prestige. Because China has such a brand-conscious culture, 75 percent of Chinese employees prefer to work for a well-known foreign organization rather than a domestic Chinese organization.[21] This brand-consciousness extends beyond consumer goods to the workplace. A third factor is development opportunities. A primary component of Chinese culture is learning and growing through one's lifetime. Chinese employees enjoy challenges and the opportunity to discuss what they are learning and projects on which they are working not only with coworkers but also with friends and family members. A fourth factor is compensation. Chinese employees with sought-after skills know their market value and expect to be compensated accordingly. While performance-based bonuses are relatively new to China, employees—particularly younger ones—have been very receptive to incentive-based compensation plans.[22] A fifth factor that can aid in retention is job title. Because the Chinese are very status-conscious, job titles—regardless of associated responsibility—are very meaningful to employees. While Chinese workers do seek opportunities for growth and development, a change in job title can often be a sufficient reward for performance.[23]

India

In some ways similar to China, with a population of 1.5 billion people and a rapidly growing economy, India has become a major player in global economic development and a target of many multinational organizations. However, India presents some significant challenges for employers related to human resource management, which distinguish it from its Asian counterpart.

Unlike China, India has a sizable population of citizens who are well-equipped to work in a multinational organization. India has more than 22 million university graduates, a third of whom have backgrounds in science and engineering, and produces 2.5 million new graduates annually.[24] Hence, India has been a leader in information technology and business process outsourcing. Despite India's large technically trained workforce, demand for skilled labor exceeds supply. Competition among employers for talent remains intense, and job-hopping and poaching of employees are standards of doing business in India.

One of the greatest challenges to doing business in India is the onerous legal system, which involves more than 100 different noncodified and ambiguous laws as well as joint federal and state government oversight of laws related to employment and labor.[25] These laws require employers to maintain registers and provide annual filings to regulatory authorities. Every employee must receive a formal letter of appointment that outlines all terms and conditions of employment and serves as a legally binding contract. Termination of employees in India can be difficult and requires that multiple procedures be followed, which include appropriate cause and notification as well as arbitration. While misconduct is generally accepted as a valid ground for termination, poor performance is not necessarily an acceptable basis. Employers are also required to provide employees with a flexible benefit plan, which accounts for 35 percent of overall compensation. Employers and employees jointly contribute to social security, called the "Provident Fund," whereby each party contributes 12 percent of the employee's wages.[26]

Employment discrimination based on religion, race, caste, sex, or place of birth is specifically banned in the public sector by India's constitution. Gender-based pay disparities are prohibited by the Equal Remuneration Act of 1948, while the Maternity Benefit Act of 1961 provides employees with 12 weeks paid maternity leave. The Shops and Establishments Act mandates paid annual leave for all employees, which can be carried forward to subsequent years.

Much as in China, retention of skilled workers in India is a challenge because of the demand that exceeds supply. India also has a pronounced shortage of sufficiently experienced and trained middle managers to oversee employees. Because the human resources function in most organizations needs to spend an inordinate amount of time on recruiting, compliance, and other associated transactional activities, there is little involvement in strategic issues.

Retention at Prudential Process Management Services

Prudential Process Management Services (PPMS) is a Mumbai, India–based organization that provides customer service for Prudential's financial services customers in the United Kingdom. With 1,200 employees, PPMS had quickly adapted to doing business in India and enjoys a 20 percent annual attrition rate in a customer service industry that has a norm of 45 percent.

PPMS's success can be attributed to its workers in India and its appropriate workplace policies and programs. PPMS hires an average of 25 employees per month but is able to streamline its hiring process so that a candidate can pass through five successive levels of screening in a single day, resulting in an offer of employment letter being extended at the end of the day. Once an employee is hired, training consumes the first 16–20 weeks on the job, where employees learn about the company history, values and culture, industry, and products. Because PPMS hires young entry-level workers with an average age of 23 at the time of hire, opportunities are provided to move laterally and cross-train in other areas of the business. PPMS also offer its own in-house MBA program, developed in partnership with top-rated business schools in India. The workplace is also literally designed to be a family-type environment where friends and family members are invited to visit employees at work. This builds the organization's culture and goodwill in the community as well as affords PPMS with an additional opportunity to recruit employees.[27]

Conclusion

Although the principles and processes of strategic human resource management are universal and apply to all organizational settings and cultures, an organization whose strategy involves multinational operations faces some additional challenges in ensuring the success of global assignments. The model for strategically managing global human resources presented in this chapter is independent of the larger model for the book for this very reason; it addresses a different set of issues and challenges that present themselves in the global arena. However, the underlying theme of strategic human resource management in looking at human assets as investments remains quite apparent when looking at global human resource management. Employees on global assignments represent valuable assets who need to be managed more systematically and strategically than they traditionally have been to ensure greater probability of success in global markets.

Critical Thinking

1. How does global human resource management differ from domestic human resource management?
2. Explain the organizational and individual purposes for expatriation. Why do these need to be incorporated as part of a strategic approach to managing global assignments?
3. Describe the four levels of standardization of global human resource practices. For what strategic objectives might each level of standardization be best suited?
4. Explain how each of Hofstede's cultural dimensions might result in specific kinds of human resource programs and practices.
5. How can employers be more successful with retention of repatriates?

Reading 14.1

6. Explain the different dimensions of culture and how each effects the development of human resource program and policies from a strategic perspective.

Reading 14.2

7. What differences need to be taken into account by American managers who oversee employees in Brazil, France, Egypt, and China, and what are the implications for American managers in each of these countries?

Reading 14.3

8. How can expatriate assignments be improved through the development of human resource programs and policies that address local staff and conditions?

Exercises

1. Examine the four dimensions of culture presented in Hofstede's framework. What strategies would you recommend in dealing with a different culture that is polar on each of the dimensions? For example, what advice would you give to someone from a culture that stresses individualism when dealing with someone from a collectivist culture?
2. What challenges does doing business in the European Union present to an employer? In small groups, have each member investigate the HR environment in a different EU country and then compare and contrast your findings, making recommendations to U.S. organizations considering doing business there.
3. Apply the concepts presented in the Javidan reading on Project GLOBE across all the countries discussed in the reading (i.e., consider the examples of one manager from Brazil, one from France, one from Egypt, and one from China operating in each of the other countries, including the United States).
4. You have been asked to design a Web site that would assist expatriates in getting ready for their overseas assignments. What kinds of information would you include on the site? Locate appropriate Internet sites that provide either useful information about culture in general or guidance in how culture affects business relationships with citizens from a particular country.

Chapter References

1. Anonymous. "Business; Best Foot Forward at Reebok," *The Economist*, October 23, 1999, p. 74; Bernstein, A. "Sweatshops: No More Excuses," *Business Week*. November 9, 1999, pp. 104–106; Gilley, B. "Sweating It Out," *Far Eastern Economic Review*, December 10, 1998, pp. 66–67.
2. Overman, S. "HR Is Partner in 'McDonaldizing' Employees in New Countries," *HR News*, May 2002, p. 7.
3. Britt, J. "Expatriates Want More Support from Home," *HR Magazine*, July 2002, pp. 21–22.
4. Ibid.
5. Hofstede, G. *Culture's Consequences: International Differences in Work-Related Values*, Beverly Hills: Sage, 1984.
6. Hall, Edward T. "The Silent Languages in Overseas Business," *Harvard Business Review*, 1960.
7. Poe, A. "Selection Savvy," *HR Magazine*, April 2002, pp. 77–83.
8. Dwyer, T. Localization's Hidden Costs. HR Magazine, 49,(6), 135–144, June 2004.
9. Heenan, D. A. and Perlmutter, Howard V. *Multinational Organizational Development*, Reading, MA: Addison-Wesley, Inc., 1979.
10. Tyler, K. Retaining Repatriates. HR Magazine, 51, (3), 97–102, March, 2006.
11. Tyler, K. Retaining Repatriates. HR Magazine, 51, (3), 97–102, March, 2006.
12. Connor, R. "Plug the Expat Knowledge Drain," *HR Magazine*, October 2002, pp. 101–107.
13. Hirschman, C. "When Operating Abroad, Companies Must Adopt European-Style HR," *HR News*, 30, (3), pp. 1, 6.
14. Falcone, P. "Learning from Our Overseas Counterparts," *HR Magazine*, February 2004, pp. 113–116.
15. Ibid.
16. Cox News Services. In Mexico, Discrimination is Ingrained. Baltimore Sun, 18 July, 2004, p.17A.
17. Hassell, J. and Poysa, S. Canadian Employment Law: A World Apart from Its U.S. Counterpart. Society for Human Resource Management, article 023972, published at www.shrm.org/hrnes/published/articles/CMS 023972.asp 24 January, 2008.
18. Fox, A. China: Land of Opportunity and Challenge. HR Magazine, 52, (9), 38–44, September, 2007.
19. Gross, A. and Connor, A. Recruiting, Retention Strategies Can Save HR Managers' "Face" Society for Human Resource Management, article 052107, published at www.shrm.org/global/news/published/XMS 052107.asp May, 2007.
20. Fox, A. Developing Managers Key Retention at Ail Levels. HR Magazine, 52, (9), 41, September, 2007.
21. Fox, A. China: Land of Opportunity and Challenge. HR Magazine, 52, (9), 38–44, September, 2007.
22. Gross, A. and Connor, A. Recruiting, Retention Strategies Can Save HR Managers' "Face" Society for Human Resource Management, article 052107, published at www.shrm.ore/global/news/published/XMS_52107.asp May, 2007.
23. Ibid.
24. Gross, A. and Minot, J. Workforce Issues in India that HR Needs to Understand. Society for Human Resource Management, article 019786, published at www.shrm.org/global/news/published/XMS_019786.asp January, 2007.
25. Iyer, R. and Shroff, V. Ensuring Compliance with Employment Laws In India. Society for Human Resource Management, article 026877, published at www.shrm.org/hrresources/lrpt published/CMS 026877.asp October-November, 2008.
26. Gross, A. and Minot, J. Workforce Issues in India that HR Needs to Understand. Society for Human Resource Management, article 019786, published at www.shrm.org/global/news/published/XMS_019786.asp January, 2007.
27. Grossman, R. HR's Rising Star in India. HR Magazine, 51, (9), 46–52, September, 2006.

READING 14.1

Selected Cross-Cultural Factors in Human Resource Management

Nancy R. Lockwood

Introduction

As a concept and as a reality, culture is broad and multifaceted. On a daily basis, culture influences who we are—as individuals, families, communities, professions, industries, organizations and nations—and how we interact with each other within and across regional and national borders. Defined as a set of values and beliefs with learned behaviors shared within a particular society, culture provides a sense of identity and belonging.[1] From language, communication styles, history and religion to norms, values, symbolism and ways of being, "culture" is everywhere.

> *Human resource management is the formal structure within an organization responsible for all decisions, strategies, factors, principles, operations, practices, functions, activities and methods related to the management of people.*[2]

In domestic and global workplace settings, people in organizations reflect their respective cultures. As shifting demographics bring together people of many cultural backgrounds, human resource management (HRM) must be thoughtfully examined—and sometimes altered—to support organizational goals. SHRM Special Expertise Panel members point out that for sustainability, organizational leaders must expand their perspectives from a local to a worldly view.[3] SHRM's 2008 *Workplace Forecast* highlights several trends in culture that will likely have a major impact on the workplace: 1) heightened awareness of cultural differences in domestic and global workplaces; 2) greater need for cross-cultural understanding/savvy in business settings; 3) managing talent globally; 4) greater emphasis on global leadership competencies; and 5) increased use of virtual global teams.[4]

Thus, HR professionals experienced in workplace diversity and cross-cultural communication are well-positioned to develop and implement culturally appropriate HRM strategies, policies and practices. While not exhaustive, this Research Quarterly focuses on selected cross-cultural factors in HRM in today's workplace and provides insights for HR to better serve the needs of the organization.

Business Case for Cross-Cultural HRM

With the advent of globalization, research on cross-cultural organizational behavior has become a pathway to understand the dynamics of multicultural domestic and international workplaces.[5] In fact, successful organizations of the 21st century require leaders who understand culturally diverse work environments and can work effectively with different cultures that have varying work ethics, norms and business protocols. Yet, diverse cultures create HRM challenges. As Lisbeth Claus, Ph.D., SPHR, GPHR, associate professor of global HR at Willamette University, points out, "the HRM challenges lie between the various types of cultures—the cultures of emerging and developed countries and the growing heterogeneity of the workforce in terms of multiculturalism."

Gaining cross-cultural competence takes time, education, experience, openness, and sensitivity. When people lack intercultural skills, miscommunications can damage business relationships, deadlines can be missed, projects may fail and talented people will go to the competition. Key HR responsibilities are to understand how cross-cultural factors interact with HRM, be the conduit for organizational learning for cross-cultural intelligence and foster cross-cultural communication throughout the organization.

Cultural Value Dimensions

Cross-cultural intelligence is the ability to switch ethnic and/or national contexts and quickly learn new patterns of social interaction with appropriate behavioral responses. This competence is essential to work effectively in multicultural environments. Thus, linking future career paths and global business success with cultural competence is important for HR to emphasize, with the goal that managers are motivated to acquire new behaviors and skills and understand the benefits of learning from different cultures.[6]

To become culturally competent, the first step is to have a solid understanding of one's own values and how they shape cultural identity. Within this process, it is also important to realize that different cultures often exhibit different

FIGURE 1 **Cultural Value Dimensions**

Edward Hall (1966)[7]	Geert Hofstede (1980)[8]	Fons Trompenaars (1993)[9]
• High- and low-context cultures • Concept of time	• Power distance • Individualism • Masculinity • Uncertainty avoidance • Long-term orientation	• Universalism vs. particularism • Individualism vs. collectivism • Neutral or emotional • Specific vs. diffuse • Achievement vs. ascription • Passage of time • Relationship to the environment

values. Cross-cultural management researchers and theorists (i.e., Edward Hall, Geert Hofstede and Fons Trompenaars) have developed cultural value dimensions, often within the realm of comparing national cultures (see Figure 1). Today, many of these terms are used to explain cross-cultural differences in the workplace.

For the purpose of discussion in this article, several major cultural value dimensions are defined below:[10]

- *High power distance* indicates that hierarchy is important.
- *Uncertainty avoidance* is achieved by behavior that results in fewer unforeseen consequences.
- *High-context cultures* rely upon an internalized social context and/or physical environment (such as body language) and face-to-face communication for all or a large part of the message (e.g., indirect, subtle, ambiguous), whereas low-context cultures rely on direct messages (e.g., clear, stated in words, with emphasis on time management, punctuality and deadlines).
- *Collectivism* refers to societies in which the group is valued over the individual and the individual's responsibility to the group overrides the individual's rights; individualism refers to societies that emphasize individual achievements and rights.
- *Long-term orientation* indicates that cultural values are future-looking, including thrift, perseverance, humility/shame, and observe hierarchical relationships, whereas short-term orientation values look to the past, such as respecting tradition.

The concept of "face" is yet another term essential for understanding cross-cultural communication. Face is a sense of self-respect in an interaction and may be related to social status, a projected identity and/or a communication phenomenon. Facework strategies include verbal and nonverbal cues, acts of self-preservation and management impression interaction.[11] In Chinese society, for example, the concept of guanxi is that of personal relationships, trust and returning favors to support a network of influence.

Through cultural value dimensions, HR will gain a greater awareness of miscommunication or cultural conflict that may occur in the multicultural workplace. Should these concepts be new to the reader, the cultural factors outlined in Figure 2 offer another way to consider key cultural differences.

FIGURE 2 **Factors in Cultural Differences**

Communication	**Verbal and nonverbal**
Concepts of time	Adherence to schedule
Group dependence	Importance of group over the individual
Hierarchy/authority	Perception of rank in relationship to others
Openness to diversity	Country of origin, religion, race, gender, language
Physical space	Space and privacy needed for personal comfort
Relationships	Importance for business interactions
Status attainment	Perceived level of "success"
Tolerance of change	Perception of control over one's destiny

Source: Adapted from Henson, R. (2002). Culture and the workforce. In K. Beaman, (Ed.), Boundaryless HR: Human capital management in the global economy *(pp. 121–141). Austin, TX: Rector Duncan & Associates, Inc.*

Corporate and Organizational Cultures

The culture of an organization's headquarters may highly influence the overall organizational culture. Specific factors determine the shape of corporate culture: 1) the relationship between employees and the company; 2) the hierarchical system of authority; and 3) the overall view of employees about the company's future, including its mission and goals, and their respective roles in the organization.[12] According to cross-cultural researchers and management consultants Fons Trompenaars and Charles Hampden-Turner, there is a link between corporate and national cultures. Organizations can be classified into four different ideal-types of corporate culture, based on their focus on tasks/relationship and the extent of hierarchy: 1) the family; 2) the Eiffel Tower; 3) the guided missile; and 4) the incubator.[13] These models of corporate culture provide insights as to why HRM policies and programs differ.

In the family model, a high-context culture, the leaders set the tone. This model gives high priority to doing the right things rather than doing things right. Pleasing one's superior, for example, is considered a reward in itself. Within this corporate model, some HRM policies, such as pay for performance, are viewed as threatening to family bonds. Countries that often use the family model include Japan, Italy, France and Spain. The Eiffel Tower model—contrary to the family model, where relationships are most important—is based on prescribed roles and functions within a rigid system (e.g., Germany). In this model, people are viewed as capital and cash resources. Typical HRM strategies in the Eiffel Tower culture include workforce planning and performance appraisal systems.[14]

The guided missile model is egalitarian, impersonal and task-oriented (e.g., United States, United Kingdom). The focus is on achieving the end goal ("do whatever it takes"), and the value of employees is in how they perform and to what extent they contribute to the overall outcome. For example, teams serve as vehicles to accomplish goals and are disbanded once the goal is reached. HRM strategies focus on management by objective and pay for performance.[15] At the other end of the spectrum, the incubator model has a different philosophy, wherein the fulfillment of individuals is more important than the organization. The structure is egalitarian, personal and individualistic, such as entrepreneurial firms in Silicon Valley in California and many Scandinavian companies, where the goal is innovative products or services. HRM strategies focus on rewards for innovation.[16]

As illustrated through these four corporate culture models, approaches to work, authority, problem solving and relationship building differ. This information provides HR with additional insight when working with companies of different corporate cultures.

Building Business Relationships

Building optimal business relationships requires global fluency. Global fluency—defined as "facility with cultural behaviors that help an organization thrive in an ever-changing global business environment"—is a competitive advantage to establish and maintain good business relationships.[17] To promote people working effectively with those of other cultures, cross-cultural training assists employees in becoming knowledgeable about cross-cultural communication in terms of their own cultural values, behaviors and assumptions, and those of other cultures. Cross-cultural communication also includes global business etiquette—from greeting behaviors, exchanging business cards and toasting at business dinners to work attitudes, appropriate work attire and nonverbal communication. To not cause offense, it is helpful to be aware of differences in greetings, such as the handshake.[18] Another differing communication style is the use of silence, a form of nonverbal communications. In high-context cultures, such as in Asian countries, silence indicates thoughtfulness in decision-making. In contrast, people in low-context cultures, such as the dominant culture in the United States, are uncomfortable with silence and tend to fill the void with 'small talk,' such as comments about the weather.[19]

People establish rapport in accordance with their cultural values. Based on social capital theory and the importance of social networks, a recent study explored intercultural communication strategies for business relationship building through interviews with business executives in China, India, New Zealand, and South Africa. The findings indicate that building a business relationship is defined within the socio-cultural and economic contexts of the respective cultures and that depending on the culture, different strategies are used to build and maintain business relationships. The following mini-case study demonstrates a success story from the viewpoint of the Indian culture.[20]

Mini-Case Study #1: "The Indian Story"[21]

A senior manager works at an Indian company that sells a broad array of products (groceries, liquor, durable goods) and describes his philosophy about relationship building with an example from his company:

"To successfully achieve our business goals, establishing and maintaining relationships with distributors is an essential strategy. Some of our customers are large firms, managed by graduates from the elite university I attended. This link creates strong networking opportunities. Once this jan pehchan *(connection) is made, it is critical to invest time in this relationship, and I always counsel my subordinates on the importance of relationship building. One employee in particular is very good at maintaining relationships. He works hard to do so, even going to the airport or train station without prior arrangement to meet clients upon their arrival, once at 5 a.m.! This effort shows that he is sincere and demonstrates how far he will go to maintain this valuable relationship. This personalized service adds to our commitment to nurture a long-term business relationship."*

Effective cross-cultural communication is necessary to build and maintain business relationships. To support their organizations, HR professionals can develop HRM practices and policies that promote cross-cultural training and reward managers for their part in educating employees on effective cross-cultural communication.

The Role of Language

Today, communicating in the global marketplace requires new perspectives and new communication skills. In fact, the appropriate use of language in cross-cultural settings often depends on the situation. Thus, when developing HRM policies, practices and initiatives, it is important to consider the role of language in cross-cultural environments. For example, to roll out new initiatives worldwide, it may be necessary (and often required by law) to translate HRM policies and programs into other languages. Colgate-Palmolive Company is an example of an organization that has effectively communicated key HRM programs to its global workforce. Keeping in mind the different languages spoken in the firm, two critical HRM core value initiatives, *Valuing Colgate People* and *Managing with Respect*, were translated into 10 languages. *Valuing Colgate People* includes a section on the company's business ethics, code of conduct and business practice guidelines. These initiatives set the stage for the organization's strategy to become a best place to work.[22]

When working with people from different cultures and/or countries, organizational leaders must know how to "read" body language, a key communication factor in high-context cultures. Misunderstanding body language can lead to inaccurate expectations. With many Western companies now doing business with India, a good example of a common cross-cultural difference is one of the head gestures by Indians. As cross-cultural trainer and management consultant Craig Storti explains, the Indian head gesture for "yes" appears similar to how Westerners shake their head to indicate "no." When seeing this gesture, Westerners may think that the Indian has disagreed, when that is not necessarily so.[23] Taking time to understand communication through body language can make the difference in a positive or negative outcome. These various points are representative of the many scenarios that require flexibility and knowledge about language and cross-cultural communication.

Finally, although the international language of business is English, not everyone speaks English fluently. When non-native English speakers come in contact with native English speakers, the result is often miscommunication. *International English*, a relatively new term, describes a mode of communication increasingly used in international business where non-native English speakers speak English with native English speakers. International English requires the avoidance of culturally laden language, such as cultural shortcuts, metaphors, jargon, slang, and idiomatic phrases. U.S. Americans, for example, often use metaphors with sports terms, such as "all the bases are covered" or "we want a level playing field," most of which are not understood by non-native English speakers. Interestingly, it takes time and practice for native English speakers to become proficient with the use of International English and to consciously avoid using phrases or terms that are culturally based.[24]

Cultural Perceptions of Organizational Justice

Regarding fairness in the workplace, organizational justice is a central theme within the employee relations domain. A fair workplace helps maintain employee commitment, contributes to job satisfaction and minimizes absenteeism and turnover. There are three broad categories of organizational justice: 1) procedural justice (fairness of methods used); 2) interactional justice (the quality of treatment); and 3) distributive justice (perception of process and fairness of the outcome).

In a culturally diverse workforce, perceptions of justice may vary due to cultural values. A recent study examined cultural factors that influence how employees form overall justice perceptions in the United States, China, Korea, and Japan. The study examined employee reactions in industry sectors such as finance, education, service, information technology, and manufacturing. According to the study, the effect of perception of fairness on turnover is greater for Americans than for Chinese or Koreans. Americans are more likely to leave their organization as a result of perceived organizational injustice than are Japanese, Chinese or Korean employees.[25] Yet, not all studies point to differences regarding justice based on country culture. The results of one study suggest that cultural dimensions should not be used as a generalization. This study considered whether individualist (low power distance) or collectivist dimensions (high power distance) had the most impact on organizational justice perceptions regarding employee work outcome relationships at a multinational bank with Hong Kong Chinese and American employees. While employees from low power distance cultures were more influenced toward perceived justice, a key finding was that the perceptions of fairness were important to both groups. This study suggests that for managing in different cultures, workplace justice and its corresponding positive effects are important, no matter a country's cultural values.[26]

Turnover is another key aspect related to organizational justice. In an increasingly diverse workforce, turnover due to unfairness in the workplace is very costly. While research on domestic and cross-cultural issues in relation to fairness in the workplace is relatively new, studies demonstrate how insensitivity can damage work relations and result in increased turnover. A recent study of U.S. employees found that more than 2 million managers and professionals leave their jobs as a result of inappropriate and insensitive comments in their organizations, costing U.S. employers $64 billion annually. The study highlights that illegal discrimination is no longer the greatest threat when it comes to attracting, recruiting and retaining talent. Rather, every-day inappropriate behaviors are the root cause of losing talented employees.[27] By ensuring that HRM policies and practices—including consequences for inappropriate behaviors in the workplace—are fair, consistently applied and culturally appropriate, HR can create a work environment that fosters respect, employee commitment and contribution. However, it should be noted that not all localized policies and practices may be consistent with corporate policies.

Cross-Cultural Decision-Making

Decisions in the workplace are influenced by cultural viewpoints, beliefs, assumptions, and values. Cultural values have an impact on why and how decisions are made and implemented. Although cross-cultural decision-making is rarely a topic of discussion, this information provides valuable insight for HR to improve communication in the workplace. Figure 3 illustrates cultural variations involved in decision-making, based on questions such as 1) do managers of different cultures view problems in similar ways; 2) do they seek out similar kinds of information to investigate problems; 3) do they come up with similar solutions; 4) are different strategies used to determine alternatives; and 5) do they implement their decisions in similar ways.[28]

Culturally influenced decision-making can be seen in various aspects of HRM. Change management is one example where culture influences decision-making. In a culture that is future-oriented, such as the United States, with strongly held beliefs about people's ability to learn and change, HR creates change management programs with the goal to be more productive and efficient in serving internal and external customers (e.g., employee training programs on new technology). In contrast, in a company with a hierarchical management style—common in Japan, for example—where major decisions are made by a senior-level manager, HR would be unlikely to promote a program that emphasizes team decision-making.

Whether in a domestic or global workplace, HR needs to be cognizant of cross-cultural decision-making and the corresponding influence on HRM. By being aware of cultural differences in the decision-making process (e.g., the reasons for making decisions, the various ways that decisions are made in different cultures, the party responsible for making those decisions—individuals, groups, various levels within the organization—and the ways decisions are implemented), HR can better gauge culturally appropriate decisions and work with managers of other cultures in the decision-making process.

Cross-Cultural Performance Feedback

Lack of cross-cultural sensitivity in the performance appraisal process can result in negative impact on communication, employee morale, teamwork and turnover. It is critical that managers be culturally appropriate when assessing performance and delivering feedback. Additionally, to get better performance results in culturally diverse employee populations, companies may need to re-examine and redefine their

FIGURE 3 Cultural Contingencies in Decision-Making

Five Steps in Decision-Making	Cultural Variations	
1. Problem Recognition	*Problem Solving* We should change the situation.	*Situation Acceptance* Some situations should be accepted as they are.
2. Information Search	*Gathering "facts"*	*Gathering ideas and possibilities*
3. Construction of Alternatives	*New, future-oriented alternatives* Adults can learn and change.	*Past-, present- and future-oriented alternatives* Adults cannot change.
4. Choice	*Individual decision-making* Decision-making responsibility is delegated. Decisions are made quickly. Decision rule: Is it true or false?	*Team decision-making* Senior managers often make decisions. Decisions are made slowly. Decision rule: Is it good or bad?
5. Implementation	*Slow* Managed from the top. Responsibility of one person.	*Fast* Involves participation of all levels. Responsibility of team.

Source: From ADLER, International Dimensions of Organizational Behavior, *5E, © 2008 South-Western, a part of Cengage Learning, Inc. Reproduced by permission, www.cengage.com/permissions*

performance standards to ensure cultural bias does not influence the performance appraisal process.[29] However, as the literature shows, performance management is originally a Western practice. When coming from an international perspective, there are complexities primarily due to cultural and structural constructs that may not directly match the Western use of performance management.[30]

Researchers Philip Harris and Robert Moran point out that at the cross-cultural level, how performance is defined and judged is "culture-bound." In an individualistic society, such as the United States, performance is judged on productivity, timeliness, quality of output, job-specific knowledge and proficiency, with emphasis placed on individual and work outcomes, not on the group and work process.[31] At the same time, culture influences the communication of performance feedback. In a collectivist or high-context culture, such as India and Japan, where in-group harmony and interpersonal relationships are highly valued, it is recommended to give feedback in a manner that is subtle, indirect and nonconfrontational. Researchers suggest that for certain feedback processes, such as 360-degree feedback, which involves explicit feedback, employees be trained to understand and utilize such feedback, particularly if it does not match their cultural orientation of communication.[32] Presented by authors Milliman, Taylor and Czaplewski, the following mini-case study illustrates a critical incident in which cultural differences in the performance feedback process contributed to an unexpected response. This situation is an example of one that may commonly occur without cross-cultural training about how feedback is perceived and received in different cultural contexts.[33]

Mini-Case Study #2: Cross-Cultural Performance Feedback[34]

Fred, a team leader in software engineering at a U.S.-based multinational enterprise, leads a virtual work group. His team is working on a new product and is under pressure to meet quality standards and get the product to the marketplace. Some of his team members are located in Malaysia. Since the team was provided with technology for global communications, such as electronic group software and teleconferencing, the company did not provide cross-cultural training. Fred writes an e-mail to his counterpart team leader, Hisham, in Malaysia to inform him that the testing process must end and the next phase of the project must now go forward. Hisham does not respond to Fred's e-mail for many days, and the Malaysian team continues to do testing on the product. For the final stage of the project, Fred flies to Malaysia. Two weeks after the U.S. deadline has passed, the project is successfully completed.

Within the company's goal to operate as a global company, one of the new practices is 360-degree feedback. In his supervisory role, Fred gathers the required feedback and then meets with Hisham. Fred informs Hisham that while he performed well on the project, there were issues upon which he could improve. Fred documents the feedback in an e-mail to Hisham, with a copy to Hisham's supervisor in Malaysia. From Fred's viewpoint, he has completed the performance appraisal in accordance with the company standards, feeling that he has been both fair and transparent. Back in the United States the following week, Fred is quite surprised to learn that Hisham, immediately following the performance appraisal meeting, applied for a transfer to another team. Fred recalls that Hisham was quiet during the performance appraisal. He thinks that the transfer is for the best, particularly if Hisham cannot deal with constructive criticism. After all, Fred knows that the success of the project is what is most important.

In this mini-case study, different cultural dimensions are involved: 1) Malaysia is a high-context culture where communication requires awareness of facial expressions, tone of voice and eye contact, and 2) the United States is a low-context culture where people depend more on words than on external expressions for meaning. Differences in collectivism-individualism also explain the miscommunication between Fred and Hisham. Collectivism emphasizes creating harmony and loyalty between people. Yet, due to Fred's direct and assertive approach in the performance appraisal, Hisham experienced individual criticism and consequently suffered a loss of "face" for his team. On his end, Fred acted within the values of his individualistic culture and emphasized individual responsibility, not group responsibility, in Hisham's performance appraisal. Clearly, Fred is unaware of the cultural context in which he spoke to Hisham.[35] Had Fred received cross-cultural training regarding the Malaysian workplace and appropriately communicated his feedback, Hisham may not have requested the transfer.

To break the cross-cultural conflict cycle, organizational learning is essential. Examples of learning mechanisms are many: 1) HR puts systems in place to catch cultural issues and then addresses them; 2) supervisors bring cultural dilemmas to the attention of HR; 3) HR learns about cultural conflicts through exit interviews; 4) progress reports sent to managers may flag cross-cultural issues; 5) HR trains managers and team members on communication-style differences between cultures; and 6) prior to sending managers to work abroad, HR provides them with cultural informants, such as mentors and/or managers with multicultural expertise, to offer support and advice.[36] As highlighted in a study on society culture and HRM practices, the methods of communication–downward and upward–are strongly linked to cultural value dimensions. This research points out that in a culture of high power distance, it is unlikely that the manager would use electronic methods in communication. Again, the lesson here is that managers be trained to be culturally appropriate when communicating performance feedback.[37]

Developing Global Mindset

The SHRM's 2008 *Workplace Forecast* cites training and developing global leaders as a global trend to which organizations are now responding.[38] In particular, intercultural competence is emerging as a key focus in global leadership development, with the critical themes of cross-cultural communication skills, developing global mindset and respecting cultural diversity.[39] In fact, global mindset has become an essential competency in global business strategy. As researchers Gupta et al. emphasize, "a deeply embedded global mindset is a prerequisite for global industry dominance."[40]

From a cross-cultural viewpoint, Paul Evans, Vladimir Pucik, and Jean-Louis Barsoux, experts in global HR management, point out that it is "global mindset"–a state of mind–that differentiates global managers. Global mindset is the ability to work effectively across organizational, functional and cross-cultural boundaries. The strongest mechanism to develop global mindset is the international assignment. HR can foster development of global mindset by ensuring that talented employees worldwide–no matter their passport country–have equal access to opportunities. Focused learning programs can also promote global mindset. Multinational corporations such as Unilever, Johnson & Johnson, and General Electric have effectively used in-house experiential action-learning programs for a broad cross-section of high-potential employees to speed up the development of global mindset.[41]

Global mindset is ongoing, driven by four factors: 1) curiosity about the world and the desire to know more; 2) awareness of one's current mindset; 3) exposure to novelty and diversity; and 4) a specific intention to develop an integrated perspective that weaves together many aspects of knowledge about different markets and cultures. Global mindset is of value for local/domestic organizations as well as companies in the global marketplace. At the local level, for instance, a company might use global mindset to benchmark product and process innovations of competitors outside its domestic borders. For organizations operating in other countries, having global mindset helps people relate to others in different cultural contexts and then develop the foundation essential for "interpersonal glue," such as in cross-border mergers (e.g., Alcatel and Lucent).[42] Ultimately, global mindset greatly fosters global learning, allowing for faster access to other markets or providing quality customer service to diverse groups. As HR supports its organization in training for global competencies, global mindset should head the list of essential cross-cultural factors in HRM.

Career Perspectives Across Cultures

Research about cross-cultural perspectives on careers offers insights on similarities and differences from cultural and national contexts. Career development, a part of human resource planning, is an HRM strategy within talent management. However, Western career attributes and definitions, which dominate the career development literature, are not always representative of how people in other cultures view and formulate careers. Proactive career behavior by individuals to promote their career plans, for example, is uncommon in high power distance cultures, where HR decisions are usually centralized. Where hierarchical status takes priority, decisions for promotions may be made by high-level executives. In contrast, HR planning in low-power distance cultures (e.g., United States, United Kingdom) often includes input from managers at many levels.[43] In high power distance and paternalistic cultures (e.g., France), employees often look to their superiors for guidance, whom they assume know what is best for their career development.[44]

Recent studies look at career beliefs, social networking and the influence of political, social and economic changes on career concepts in nations around the world.[45] One study explores career-life success and family social support among successful women in Argentina, Canada, and Mexico. In all three countries, women now consider broader measures of career success than have been traditionally viewed, such as learning and contributing to society. In Canada and Mexico, many women now see receiving recognition in the workplace as evidence of career success.[46] A study in Russia notes that new career beliefs and behaviors are emerging, in great part due to multinational corporations entering Russia and introducing

FIGURE 4 Examples of Questions of Assess Global Mindset

Individual	Organization
• In interacting with others, does national origin have an impact on whether you give equal status to them? • Does being in a new cultural setting result in fear, anxiety or excitement? • When living in or visiting another culture, are you sensitive to cultural differences, without becoming a prisoner of these differences?	• Do you recruit your employees from the global talent pool? • Do employees of every nationality have equal opportunity to climb to the top of the career ladder? • Do you perceive your company as having a universal identity or a strong national identity?

Source: Adapted from Gupta, A. K., Govindarajan, V., & Wang, H. (2008). The quest for global dominance: Transforming global presence into global competitive advantage, 2nd edition. *San Francisco: John Wiley & Sons, Inc.*

Western ideas about career development (e.g., mentoring and coaching, management education and training, professional development).[47] Yet, another study found that social or informal networks are greatly used in the job search process in both the United States and China, with a different focus by workers in each country. Social networks in the United States (an individualistic culture) are used to open doors for opportunities and gain information. In comparison, social networks in China (a collectivist culture) emphasize *guanxi* (the importance of interdependence of relationships, based on trust and expectations of returning favors).[48] Thus, research illustrates that while cultural viewpoints about career development are gradually changing, differences based on cultural values and past history continue to influence careers in today's global marketplace. This information provides HR with a broader understanding of what is valued in a career through the eyes of other cultures as well as a movement toward global career values.

In Closing

As globalization continues to expand, it is increasingly important for HR to understand the implications of HRM in a changing world. Not all HRM strategies will fit every situation. Communication styles and cultural value dimensions need to be taken into consideration when establishing or changing HRM strategies, policies, and practices. Whether in domestic or global business environments, HRM must adapt to cross-cultural factors for the success of the organization and its people.

Source: Society for Human Resource Management, Research Quarterly, Third Quarter, 2008. Reprinted by permission.

ENDNOTES

1. Bodley, J. H. (1999). *Cultural anthropology: Tribes, states, and the global system* (3rd edition). United Kingdom: Mayfield Publishing Company.
2. Society for Human Resource Management. (n.d.). *Glossary of human resources terms.* Retrieved May 14, 2008, from www.shrm.org
3. Society for Human Resource Management. (2007). *The 2007–2008 workplace trends list.* Alexandria, VA: Author.
4. Society for Human Resource Management. (2008). *Workplace forecast.* Alexandria, VA: Author.
5. Gelfand, M. J., Erez, M., & Aycan, Z. (2007). Cross-cultural organizational behavior. *Annual Review of Psychology*, 58, 479–514.
6. Alon, I., & Higgins, J. M. (2005, November/December). Global leadership success through emotional and cultural intelligence. *Business Horizons*, 48(6), 501+.
7. Hall, E. T. (1964). *The silent language.* Greenwich, CT: Fawcett.
8. Hofstede, G. (1980). *Culture's consequences: International differences in work-related values.* Newbury Park, CA: Sage.
9. Trompenaars, F. (1993). *Riding the waves of culture: Understanding cultural diversity in business.* London: Nicholas Brealey.
10. Varner, I., & Beamer, L. (2005). *Intercultural communication in the global workplace* (3rd ed.). London: McGraw-Hill Irwin.
11. Ting-Toomey, S. (Ed.). (1994). *The Challenge of facework: Cross-cultural and interpersonal issues.* Albany, NY: State University of New York Press.
12. Trompenaars, F., & Hampden-Turner, C. (1998). *Riding the waves of culture: Understanding diversity in global business*, 2nd edition. New York: McGraw-Hill.
13. Ibid.
14. Ibid.
15. Ibid.
16. Ibid.
17. Tosti, D. T. (2002). Global fluency. In K. Beaman (Ed.), *Boundaryless HR: Human capital management in the global economy* (pp. 109–119). Austin, TX: Rector Duncan & Associates, Inc.
18. Varner, I., & Beamer, L. (2005). *Intercultural communication in the global workplace* (3rd ed.). London: McGraw-Hill Irwin.
19. Martin, J. S., & Chaney, L. H. (2006). *Global business etiquette: A guide to international communication and customs.* Westport, CT: Praeger Publishers.
20. Zhu, Y., Nel, P., & Bhat, R. (2006). *A cross cultural study of communication strategies for building business relationships.* Cross Cultural Management, 6(3), 319–341.
21. Ibid, p. 339.
22. Carter, L. (2005). *Best practices in leading the global workforce: How the best global companies ensure success throughout their workforce.* Burlington, MA: Linkage.
23. Storti, C. (2007). *Speaking of India: Bridging the communication gap when working with Indians.* Boston: Intercultural Press.
24. Carobolante, L. (2005, October). *International English: A new global tool.* Mobility, 64–80.
25. Kim, T-Y, & Leung, K. (2007). Forming and reacting to overall fairness: A cross-cultural perspective. *Organizational Behavior and Human Decision Processes*, 104, 83–95.
26. Lam, S. K., Schaubroeck, J., & Aryee, S. (2002, February). Relationship between organizational justice and employee work outcomes: A cross-national study. *Journal of Organizational Behavior*, 23, 1–18.
27. Level Playing Field Institute. (2007, January). *The corporate leavers study: The cost of employee turnover due solely to unfairness in the workplace.* San Francisco: Author.
28. From ADLER, *International Dimensions of Organizational Behavior*, 5E, © 2008 South-Western, a part of Cengage Learning, Inc.
29. Moran, R. T., Harris, P. R., & Stripp, W. G. (1993). *Developing the global organization: Strategies for human resource professionals.* London: Gulf Publishing Company.
30. Claus, L. (2008). Employee performance management in MNCs: Reconciling the need for global integration and local responsiveness. *European J. International Management*, 2(2), 132–152.
31. Harris, P. R., & Moran, R. T. (1996). *Managing cultural differences, 4th edition.* Houston, TX: Gulf.
32. Aycan, Z. (2005, July). The interplay between cultural and institutional/structural contingencies in human resource management practices. *The International Journal of Human Resource Management*, 16(7), 1083–1119.
33. Milliman, J., Taylor, S., & Czaplewski, A. J. (2002). Cross-cultural performance feedback in multinational enterprises: Opportunity for organizational learning. *HR. Human Resource Planning*, 25(3), 29–44.
34. Ibid.
35. Ibid.
36. Ibid.
37. Papalexandris, N., & Panayotopoulou, L. (2004). Exploring the mutual interaction of societal culture and human resource management practices: Evidence from 19 countries. *Employee Relations*, 26(5), 495–509.
38. Society for Human Resource Management. (2008). *Workplace forecast.* Alexandria, VA: Author.

39. Rosen, R., Digh, P., Singer, M., & Phillips, C. (2000). *Global literacies: Lessons on business leadership and national cultures.* New York: Simon & Schuster.

40. Gupta, A. K., Govindarajan, V., & Wang, H. (2008). *The quest for global dominance: Transforming global presence into global competitive advantage (2nd edition).* San Francisco: John Wiley & Sons, Inc.

41. Evans, P., Pucik, V., & Barsoux, J-L. (2002). *The global challenge: Frameworks for international human resource management.* New York: McGraw-Hill Irwin.

42. Gupta, A. K., Govindarajan, V., & Wang, H. (2008). *The quest for global dominance: Transforming global presence into global competitive advantage (2nd edition).* San Francisco: John Wiley & Sons, Inc.

43. Aycan, A. (2005, July). The interplay between cultural and institutional/structural contingencies and institutional/structural contingencies in human resource management practices. *The International Journal of Human Resource Management*, 16(7), 1083–1119.

44. Aycan, A., & Fikret-Pasa, S. (2003). Career choices, job selection criteria, and leadership preferences in a transitional nation: The case of Turkey. *Journal of Career Development*, 30(1), 129–144.

45. Inkson, K., Khapova, S. N., & Parker, P. (2007). Careers in cross-cultural perspective. *Career Development International*, 12(1), 5+.

46. Lirio, P., Lituchy, T. R., Ines Monserrat, S., Olivas-Lujan, M. R., Duffy, J. A., Fox, S., et al. (2007). Exploring career-life success and family social support of successful women in Canada, Argentina and Mexico. *Career Development International*, 12(1), 28–50.

47. Khapova, S. N. (2007). Dynamics of western career attributes in the Russian context. *Career Development International*, 12(1), 68+.

48. Song, L. J., & Werbel, J. D. (2007). Guanxi as impetus Career exploration in China and the United States. *Career Development International*, 12(1), 51–67.

READING 14.2

In the Eye of the Beholder: Cross Cultural Lessons in Leadership from Project Globe

Mansour Javidan, Peter W. Dorfman,
Mary Sully de Luque, and Robert J. House

Executive Overview

Global leadership has been identified as a critical success factor for large multinational corporations. While there is much writing on the topic, most seems to be either general advice (i.e., being open minded and respectful of other cultures) or very specific information about a particular country based on a limited case study (do not show the soles of your shoes when seated as a guest in an Arab country). Both kinds of information are certainly useful, but limited from both theoretical and practical viewpoints on how to lead in a foreign country. In this paper, findings from the Global Leadership and Organizational Behavior Effectiveness (GLOBE) research program are used to provide a sound basis for conceptualizing worldwide leadership differences. We use a hypothetical case of an American executive in charge of four similar teams in Brazil, France, Egypt, and China to discuss cultural implications for the American executive. Using the hypothetical case involving five different countries allows us to provide in-depth action oriented and context specific advice, congruent with GLOBE findings, for effectively interacting with employees from different cultures. We end the paper with a discussion of the challenges facing global executives and how corporations can develop useful global leadership capabilities.

Impact of Globalization

Almost no American corporation is immune from the impact of globalization. The reality for American corporations is that they must increasingly cope with diverse cross-cultural employees, customers, suppliers, competitors, and creditors, a situation well captured by the following quote.

> *So I was visiting a businessman in downtown Jakarta the other day and I asked for directions to my next appointment. His exact instructions were: Go to the building with the Armani Emporium upstairs—you know, just above the Hard Rock café—and then turn right at McDonalds. "I just looked at him and laughed, "Where am I?"*
>
> *Thomas Friedman,* New York Times, *July 14, 1997*

Notwithstanding Tom Friedman's astonishment about the global world in Jakarta, the fact is that people are not generally aware of the tremendous impact that national culture has on their vision and interpretation of the world. Because culture colors nearly every aspect of human behavior, a working knowledge of culture and its influences can be useful to executives operating in a multicultural business environment. It is a truism by now that large corporations need executives with global mindsets and cross-cultural leadership abilities. Foreign sales by multinational corporations have exceeded $7 trillion and are growing 20 percent to 30 percent faster than their sales of exports.[1] But while the importance of such business grows, 85 percent of *Fortune* 500 companies have reported a shortage of global managers with the necessary skills.[2] Some experts have argued that most U.S. companies are not positioned to implement global strategies due to a lack of global leadership capabilities.[3]

How can companies best use the available information for executive development and, moreover, what is the validity and value of such information? U.S. and European executives have plenty of general advice available to them on how to perform in foreign settings. During the past few years much has been written about global leadership, including several books.[4] Journals are also getting into the global action as seen in *The Human Resource Management Journal* which recently published a special issue on global leadership.[5] Nevertheless, in a recent review of the literature, Morrison concluded that despite the importance of global leadership, "relatively little research has thus far been carried out on global leadership characteristics, competencies, antecedents, and developmental strategies."[6]

Advice to global managers needs to be specific enough to help them understand how to act in different surroundings. For example, managers with an overseas assignment are frequently exhorted to have an open mind and to show respect for other cultures.[7] They may also be told of the importance of cross-cultural relationship management and communication. Some will wrestle with the idea that they need to develop a global perspective while being responsive to local concerns.[8] Or they may wonder if they have the "cognitive complexity" and psychological maturity to handle life and work in a foreign setting. And they are likely to hear or read that they must "walk in the shoes of people from different cultures" in order to be effective.[9] There is nothing wrong with such advice, and the scholars and writers who proffer it have often been pioneers in the field. But it is insufficient for a manager who is likely to assume, mistakenly, that being open minded in Atlanta, Helsinki, and Beijing will be perceived identically, or that walking in someone else's shoes will feel the same in Houston, Jakarta, and Madrid. Because of the lack of scientifically compiled information, businesspeople have not had sufficiently detailed and context-specific suggestions about how to handle these cross-cultural challenges. This is a particular problem for those in leadership positions.

Although there are universal aspects of leadership, information about which will be presented shortly, people in different countries do in fact have different criteria for assessing their leaders.[10] The issue for the American manager is whether the attributes that made him or her successful as a leader in the United States will also lead to success overseas, be of no value or, worst of all, cause harm in the foreign operation. Using the findings from an extensive research effort known as the Global Leadership and Organizational Behavior Effectiveness (GLOBE) project, this article provides a few answers to the questions about the universal and culture specific aspects of leadership. We will present specific information about key cultural differences among nations and connect the "dots" on how these differences influence leadership. This information should help a typical global executive better understand the leadership challenges s/he faces while managing operations outside the United States. It will also provide suggestions on how to more effectively cope with such challenges.

To make the GLOBE findings come alive, we will follow a hypothetical American executive who has been given two years to lead a project based in four different countries: Brazil, France, Egypt, and China. This hypothetical project involves developing a somewhat similar product for the four different markets. The project team in each country is tasked with the marketing of a new technology in the telecommunications industry. The executive will work with local employees in each location. Success will be determined by two criteria: the executive's ability to produce results and to show effective leadership in different cultures and settings.

The four countries represent different continents and very diverse cultures. Brazil is the most populous and economically important South American country. France is the largest, most populous, and most economically developed Latin European country. Egypt is the largest and most populous Arab country. China is the fast growing giant economy with unprecedented growth in its economic and diplomatic power in the world. We chose these countries to provide context specific analysis leading to general recommendations for global executives. Our choice of countries was guided by our efforts to cover a wide range of cultures. Before turning to our hypothetical scenario, we will examine common cultural dimensions that characterize nations and discuss why these dimensions are important for the development of global leaders.

Common Cultural Dimensions

To be open minded and to understand the cultures of the different countries, managers need to be able to compare their own cultures with those of other countries. After a review of the available literature, especially the work of Hofstede, Trompenaars, and Kluckhohn and Strodtbeck,[11] GLOBE conceptualized and developed measures of nine cultural dimensions. These are aspects of a country's culture that distinguish one society from another and have important managerial implications. While a few of these dimensions are similar to the work of other researchers, the manner in which we conceptualized and operationalized them was different.[12] We reconceptualized a few existing dimensions and developed a few new dimensions. In all cases, the scales designed to capture and measure these cultural dimensions passed very rigorous psychometric tests. A brief description of each cultural dimension is provided below along with the basic research design of GLOBE. Further details can be found on GLOBE's website, http://www.thunderbird.edu/wwwfiles/ms/globe/.

It might be noted that the GLOBE Project has been called "the most ambitious study of global leadership."[13] Our world-wide team of scholars proposed and validated an integrated theory of the relationship between culture and societal, organizational, and leadership effectiveness. The 170 researchers worked together for ten years collecting and analyzing data on cultural values and practices and leadership attributes from over 17,000 managers in 62 societal cultures. The participating managers were employed in telecommunications, food, and banking industries. As one output from the project, the 62 cultures were ranked with respect to nine dimensions of their cultures. We studied the effects of these dimensions on expectations of leaders, as well as on organizational practices in each society. The 62 societal cultures were also grouped into a more parsimonious set of ten culture clusters (list provided in the next section). GLOBE studies cultures in terms of their cultural practices (the ways things are) and their cultural values (the way things should be). The nine cultural attributes (hereafter called culture dimensions) are:

Performance Orientation The degree to which a collective encourages and rewards (and should encourage and reward) group members for performance improvement and excellence. In countries like the U.S. and Singapore that score high on this cultural practice, businesses are likely to emphasize training and development; in countries that score low, such as Russia and Greece, family and background count for more.

Assertiveness The degree to which individuals are (and should be) assertive, confrontational, and aggressive in their relationships with others. People in highly assertive countries such as the United States and Austria tend to have can-do attitudes and enjoy competition in business; those in less assertive countries such as Sweden and New Zealand prefer harmony in relationships and emphasize loyalty and solidarity.

Future Orientation The extent to which individuals engage (and should engage) in future-oriented behaviors such as delaying gratification, planning, and investing in the future. Organizations in countries with high future oriented practices like Singapore and Switzerland tend to have longer term horizons and more systematic planning processes, but they tend to be averse to risk taking and opportunistic decision making. In contrast, corporations in the least future oriented countries like Russia and Argentina tend to be less systematic and more opportunistic in their actions.

Humane Orientation The degree to which a collective encourages and rewards (and should encourage and reward) individuals for being fair, altruistic, generous, caring, and kind to others. Countries like Egypt and Malaysia rank very high on this cultural practice and countries like France and Germany rank low.

Institutional Collectivism The degree to which organizational and societal institutional practices encourage and reward (and should encourage and reward) collective distribution of resources and collective action. Organizations in collectivistic countries like Singapore and Sweden tend to emphasize group performance and rewards, whereas those in the more individualistic countries like Greece and Brazil tend to emphasize individual achievement and rewards.

In-Group Collectivism The degree to which individuals express (and should express) pride, loyalty, and cohesiveness in their organizations or families. Societies like Egypt and Russia take pride in their families and also take pride in the organizations that employ them.

Gender Egalitarianism The degree to which a collective minimizes (and should minimize) gender inequality. Not surprisingly, European countries generally had the highest scores on gender egalitarianism practices. Egypt and South Korea were among the most male dominated societies in GLOBE. Organizations operating in gender egalitarian societies tend to encourage tolerance for diversity of ideas and individuals.

Power Distance The degree to which members of a collective expect (and should expect) power to be distributed equally. A high power distance score reflects unequal power distribution in a society. Countries that scored high on this cultural practice are more stratified economically, socially, and politically; those in positions of authority expect, and receive, obedience. Firms in high power distance countries like Thailand, Brazil, and France tend to have hierarchical decision making processes with limited one-way participation and communication.

Uncertainty Avoidance The extent to which a society, organization, or group relies (and should rely) on social norms, rules, and procedures to alleviate unpredictability of future events. The greater the desire to avoid uncertainty, the more people seek orderliness, consistency, structure, formal procedures and laws to cover situations in their daily lives. Organizations in high uncertainty avoidance countries like Singapore and Switzerland tend to establish elaborate processes and procedures and prefer formal detailed strategies. In contrast, firms in low uncertainty avoidance countries like Russia and Greece tend to prefer simple processes and broadly stated strategies. They are also opportunistic and enjoy risk taking.

Regional Clustering of GLOBE Nations

GLOBE was able to empirically verify ten culture clusters from the 62-culture sample. These culture clusters were identified as: Latin America, Anglo, Latin Europe (e.g., Italy), Nordic Europe, Germanic Europe, Confucian Asia, Sub-Saharan Africa, Middle East, Southern Asia, and Eastern Europe. Each culture cluster differs with respect to the nine culture dimensions (e.g., performance orientation). Table 1 shows a summary of how the clusters compare in terms of their scores on cultural practices. The clusters that are relevant to this paper are in bold. For instance, clusters scoring highest in performance orientation were Confucian Asia, Germanic Europe, and Anglo (U.S. and U.K. among other English-speaking countries). Clusters scoring lowest in performance orientation were Latin America and Eastern Europe. The Appendix shows the actual country scores for the six clusters in this paper.

Managing and Leading in Different Countries

Given the differences found in cultures around the globe, what does an effective American manager need to do differently in different countries? Everything, nothing, or only certain things? From a leadership perspective we can ask whether the same attributes that lead to successful leadership in the U.S. lead to success in other countries. Or are they irrelevant or, even worse, dysfunctional? In the following sections, we will answer these questions. We will examine some similarities and differences among cultures regarding management and leadership practices. We then assert that many of the leadership differences found among cultures stem from implicit leadership beliefs held by members of different nations.

Expatriate managers working in multinational companies hardly need to be reminded of the wide variety of *management* practices found around the world. Laurent, and more recently Trompenaars and Briscoe and Shuler,[14] document the astonishing diversity of organizational practices worldwide, many of

Table 1 Cultural Clusters Classified on Societal Culture Practices (As Is) Scores

Cultural Dimension	High-Score Clusters	Mid-Score Clusters	Low-Score Clusters	Cluster-Average Range
Performance Orientation	**Confucian Asia**	Southern Asia	**Latin America**	3.73–4.58
	Germanic Europe	Sub-Saharan Africa	Eastern Europe	
	Anglo	**Latin Europe**		
		Nordic Europe		
		Middle East		
Assertiveness	Germanic Europe	Sub-Saharan Africa	Nordic Europe	3.66–4.55
	Eastern Europe	**Latin America**		
		Anglo		
		Middle East		
		Confucian Asia		
		Latin Europe		
		Southern Asia		
Future Orientation	Germanic Europe	**Confucian Asia**	**Middle East**	3.38–4.40
	Nordic Europe	**Anglo**	**Latin America**	
		Southern Asia	Eastern Europe	
		Sub-Saharan Africa		
		Latin Europe		
Humane Orientation	Southern Asia	**Middle East**	**Latin Europe**	3.55–4.71
	Sub-Saharan Africa	**Anglo**	Germanic Europe	
		Nordic Europe		
		Latin America		
		Confucian Asia		
		Eastern Europe		
Institutional Collectivism	Nordic Europe	**Anglo**	Germanic Europe	3.86–4.88
	Confucian Asia	Southern Asia	**Latin Europe**	
		Sub-Saharan Africa	**Latin America**	
		Middle East		
		Eastern Europe		
In-Group Collectivism	Southern Asia	Sub-Saharan Africa	**Anglo**	3.75–5.87
	Middle East	**Latin Europe**	Germanic Europe	
	Eastern Europe		Nordic Europe	
	Latin America			
	Confucian Asia			
Gender Egalitarianism	Eastern Europe	**Latin America**	**Middle East**	2.95–3.64
	Nordic Europe	**Anglo**		
		Latin Europe		
		Sub-Saharan Africa		
		Southern Asia		
		Confucian Asia		
		Germanic Europe		

Power Distance		Southern Asia	Nordic Europe	4.54–5.39
		Latin America		
		Eastern Europe		
		Sub-Saharan Africa		
		Middle East		
		Latin Europe		
		Confucian Asia		
		Anglo		
		Germanic Europe		
Uncertainty Avoidance	Nordic Europe	**Confucian Asia**	**Middle East**	3.56–5.19
	Germanic Europe	**Anglo**	**Latin America**	
		Sub-Saharan Africa	Eastern Europe	
		Latin Europe		
		Southern Asia		

Note: Means of high-score clusters are significantly higher ($p < 0.05$) *than the rest, means of low-score clusters are significantly lower* ($p < 0.05$) *than the rest, and means of mid-score clusters are not significantly different from the rest* ($p > 0.05$).

which are acceptable and considered effective in one country but ineffective in another country. For instance, supervisors are expected to have precise answers to subordinates' questions in Japan, but less so in the United States. As another example, the effectiveness of working alone or in a group is perceived very differently around the world; this would certainly influence the quality, aptitude, and fair evaluation of virtual teams found in multinational organizations.[15] An inescapable conclusion is that acceptable management practices found in one country are hardly guaranteed to work in a different country. Titus Lokananta, for example, is an Indonesian Cantonese holding a German passport, managing a Mexican multinational corporation producing Gummy Bears in the Czech Republic.[16] What management style will he be most comfortable with, and will it be successful with Czech workers and Mexican CEOs? How does he effectively manage if a conflict evolves between managing his workers and satisfying his supervisors?

Should we, however, conclude that cultural differences are so vast that common management practices among countries are the exception rather than the rule and will ever remain so? Not necessarily. Companies are forced to share information, resources, and training in a global economy. The best business schools educate managers from all over the world in the latest management techniques. Using academic jargon, the issue of common versus unique business and management practices is framed using contrasting perspectives embodied in the terms *cultural universals* versus *cultural specifics*. The former are thought to be found from the process of cultural convergence whereas the latter from maintaining cultural divergence. Perhaps not surprisingly, empirical research supports both views. For example, in their event management leadership research program Smith and Peterson found both commonalities and differences across cultures in the manner by which managers handled relatively routine events in their work.[17] All managers preferred to rely on their own experience and training if appointing a new subordinate, relative to other influences such as consultation with others or using formal rules and procedures. However, there were major differences in countries in the degree to which managers used formal company rules and procedures in contrast to more informal networks, and these differences covary with national cultural values.[18] As another example, Hazucha and colleagues[19] found a good deal of similarity among European countries regarding the importance of core management competencies for a Euromanager. Yet there were significant differences among countries in the perceived attainment of these skills. Javidan and Carl have recently shown important similarities and differences among Canadian, Taiwanese, and Iranian managers in terms of their leadership styles.[20]

Should we also expect that leadership processes, like management practices, are similarly influenced by culture? The answer is yes; substantial empirical evidence indicates that leader attributes, behavior, status, and influence vary considerably as a result of culturally unique forces in the countries or regions in which the leaders function.[21] But, as the colloquial saying goes "the devil is in the details," and current cross-cultural theory is inadequate to clarify and expand on the diverse cultural universals and cultural specifics elucidated in cross-cultural research. Some researchers subscribe to the philosophy that the primary impact of culture depends on the level of analysis used in the research program. That is, some view the basic functions of leadership as having universal importance and applicability, but the specific ways in which leadership functions are enacted are strongly affected by cultural variation.[22] Other researchers, including the contributors to this article, question this basic assumption, subscribing more to the viewpoint that cultural specifics are real and woe to the leader who ignores them.

Do Required Leadership Qualities Differ Among Nations?

It has been pointed out that managerial leadership differences (and similarities) among nations may be the result of the citizens' implicit assumptions regarding requisite leadership qualities.[23] According to implicit leadership theory (ILT), individuals hold a set of beliefs about the kinds of attributes, personality characteristics, skills, and behaviors that contribute to or impede outstanding leadership. These belief systems, variously referred to as prototypes, cognitive categories, mental models, schemas, and stereotypes in the broader social cognitive literature, are assumed to affect the extent to which an individual accepts and responds to others as leaders.[24]

GLOBE extended ILT to the cultural level of analysis by arguing that the structure and content of these belief systems will be shared among individuals in common cultures. We refer to this shared cultural level analog of individual implicit leadership theory (ILT) as *culturally endorsed implicit leadership theory (CLT)*. GLOBE empirically identified universally perceived leadership attributes that are contributors to or inhibitors of outstanding leadership. Project GLOBE's leadership questionnaire items consisted of 112 behavioral and attribute descriptors (e.g., "intelligent") that were hypothesized to either facilitate or impede outstanding leadership. Accompanying each item was a short phrase designed to help interpret the item. Items were rated on a 7-point Likert-type scale that ranged from a low of 1 (this behavior or characteristic greatly inhibits a person from being an outstanding leader) to a high of 7 (this behavior or characteristic contributes greatly to a person being an outstanding leader). Project GLOBE also empirically reduced the huge number of leadership attributes into a much more understandable, comprehensive grouping of 21 primary and then 6 global leadership dimensions. The 6 global leadership dimensions differentiate cultural profiles of desired leadership qualities, hereafter referred to as a CLT profile. Convincing evidence from GLOBE research showed that people within cultural groups agree in their beliefs about leadership; these beliefs are represented by a set of *CLT leadership profiles* developed for each national culture and cluster of cultures. For detailed descriptions of the statistical processes used to form the 21 primary and 6 global leadership dimensions and development of CLT profiles see House et al.[25] Using the six country scenarios, in the last half of this paper we will show the range of leadership responses that should be effective in each cultural setting. The six dimensions of the CLT leadership profiles are:

1. **Charismatic/Value-Based**. A broadly defined leadership dimension that reflects the ability to inspire, to motivate, and to expect high performance outcomes from others on the basis of firmly held core beliefs. Charismatic/value-based leadership is generally reported to contribute to outstanding leadership. The highest reported score is in the Anglo cluster (6.05); the lowest score in the Middle East cluster (5.35 out of a 7-point scale).
2. **Team-Oriented**. A leadership dimension that emphasizes effective team building and implementation of a common purpose or goal among team members. Team-oriented leadership is generally reported to contribute to outstanding leadership (Highest score in Latin American cluster (5.96); lowest score in Middle East cluster (5.47)).
3. **Participative**. A leadership dimension that reflects the degree to which managers involve others in making and implementing decisions. Participative leadership is generally reported to contribute to outstanding leadership, although there are meaningful differences among countries and clusters. (Highest score in Germanic Europe cluster (5.86); lowest score in Middle East cluster (4.97)).
4. **Humane-Oriented**. A leadership dimension that reflects supportive and considerate leadership but also includes' compassion and generosity. Humane-oriented leadership is reported to be almost neutral in some societies and to moderately contribute to outstanding leadership in others. (Highest score in Southern Asia cluster (5.38); lowest score in Nordic Europe cluster (4.42)).
5. **Autonomous**. This newly defined leadership dimension, which has not previously appeared in the literature, refers to independent and individualistic leadership. Autonomous leadership is reported to range from impeding outstanding leadership to slightly facilitating outstanding leadership. (Highest score in Eastern Europe cluster (4.20); lowest score in Latin America cluster (3.51)).
6. **Self-Protective**. From a Western perspective, this newly defined leadership dimension focuses on ensuring the safety and security of the individual. It is self-centered and face saving in its approach. Self-protective leadership is generally reported to impede outstanding leadership. (Highest score in Southern Asia cluster (3.83); lowest in Nordic Europe (2.72)).

Table 2 presents CLT scores for all 10 clusters. Analysis of Variance (ANOVA) was used to determine if the cultures and clusters differed with respect to their CLT leadership profiles. Results indicate that cultures (i.e., 62 societal cultures) and clusters (i.e., 10 groups consisting of the 62 societal cultures) differed with respect to all six CLT leadership dimensions ($p < .01$).

Table 3 presents summary comparisons among culture clusters to indicate which clusters are most likely to endorse

Table 2 CLT Scores for Societal Clusters

	CLT Dimensions					
Societal Cluster	**Charismatic/ Value-Based**	**Team Oriented**	**Participative**	**Humane Oriented**	**Autonomous**	**Self-Protective**
Eastern Europe	5.74	5.88	5.08	4.76	4.20	3.67
Latin America	5.99	5.96	5.42	4.85	3.51	3.62
Latin Europe	5.78	5.73	5.37	4.45	3.66	3.19
Confucian Asia	5.63	5.61	4.99	5.04	4.04	3.72
Nordic Europe	5.93	5.77	5.75	4.42	3.94	2.72
Anglo	6.05	5.74	5.73	5.08	3.82	3.08
Sub-Sahara Africa	5.79	5.70	5.31	5.16	3.63	3.55
Southern Asia	5.97	5.86	5.06	5.38	3.99	3.83
Germanic Europe	5.93	5.62	5.86	4.71	4.16	3.03
Middle East	5.35	5.47	4.97	4.80	3.68	3.79

Note: CLT leadership scores are absolute scores aggregated to the cluster level.

Table 3 Summary of Comparisons for CLT Leadership Dimensions

	CLT Leadership Dimensions					
Societal Cluster	**Charismatic/ Value-Based**	**Team Oriented**	**Participative**	**Humane Oriented**	**Autonomous**	**Self-Protective**
Eastern Europe	M	M	L	M	**H**/H	H
Latin America	H	**H**	M	M	**L**	M/H
Latin Europe	M/H	M	M	L	L	M
Confucian Asia	M	M/H	L	M/H	M	H
Nordic Europe	H	M	H	**L**	M	**L**
Anglo	**H**	M	H	H	M	L
Sub-Sahara Africa	M	M	M	H	L	M
Southern Asia	H	M/**H**	L	**H**	M	**H**/H
Germanic Europe	H	M/L	**H**	M	H/**H**	L
Middle East	**L**	L	L	M	M	H/**H**

Note: For letters separated by a "/", the first letter indicates rank with respect to the absolute score, second letter with respect to a response bias corrected score.

H = high rank; M = medium rank; L = low rank.

H or L (bold) indicates Highest or Lowest cluster score for a specific CLT dimension.

or refute the importance of the 6 CLT leadership dimensions. Tables 2 and 3 may be used in combination to provide an overall view of how the different cultural clusters compare on the six culturally implicit leadership dimensions.[26]

Cross-cultural Leadership Is Not Only About Differences

The global and cross-cultural leadership literature is almost exclusively focused on cultural differences and their implications for managers. There is a basic assumption that leaders operating in different countries will be facing drastically different challenges and requirements. GLOBE surveys show that while different countries do have divergent views on many aspects of leadership effectiveness, they also have convergent views on some other aspects. From the larger group of leader behaviors, we found 22 attributes that were universally deemed to be desirable. Being honest, decisive, motivational, and dynamic are examples of attributes

Table 4 Cultural Views of Leadership Effectiveness

The following is a partial list of leadership attributes with the corresponding primary leadership dimension in parentheses.

Universal Facilitators of Leadership Effectiveness
• Being trustworthy, just, and honest (integrity)
• Having foresight and planning ahead (charismatic-visionary)
• Being positive, dynamic, encouraging, motivating, and building confidence (charismatic-inspirational)
• Being communicative, informed, a coordinator, and team integrator (team builder)
Universal Impediments to Leadership Effectiveness
• Being a loner and asocial (self-protective)
• Being non-cooperative and irritable (malevolent)
• Being dictatorial (autocratic)
Culturally Contingent Endorsement of Leader Attributes
• Being individualistic (autonomous)
• Being status conscious (status conscious)
• Being a risk taker (charismatic III: self-sacrificial)

that are believed to facilitate outstanding leadership in all GLOBE countries. Furthermore, we found eight leadership attributes that are universally undesirable. Leaders who are loners, irritable, egocentric, and ruthless are deemed ineffective in all GLOBE countries. Table 4 below shows a few examples of universally desirable, universally undesirable, and culturally contingent leadership attributes.

Identifying universally desirable and undesirable leadership attributes is a critical step in effective cross-cultural leadership. It shows managers that while there are differences among countries, there are also similarities. Such similarities give some degree of comfort and ease to leaders and can be used by them as a foundation to build on. Of course, there may still be differences in how leaders enact such attributes. For example, behaviors that embody dynamic leadership in China may be different from those that denote the same attribute in the U.S. Current research currently under way by GLOBE team members is focused on this issue.

Understanding Culturally Contingent Leadership

In this section, we will focus on those attributes of leadership that were found to be culturally contingent. These are attributes that may work effectively in one culture but cause harm in others. To provide an action oriented analysis, we explore differences in effective leadership attributes among the four countries in our hypothetical scenario and discuss specific implications of these differences for our hypothetical American manager. Admittedly, we are being ethnocentric using the American manager as the focal person who finds himself/herself managing in a foreign culture. Obviously, expatriate managers are found from virtually all industrialized nations; however, there are over 200,000 U.S. expatriates worldwide.[27] Nevertheless, expatriates from non-American and non-Western countries should be able to identify with cultural differences between their culture and that of the comparison countries. GLOBE cultural data for the five comparison countries can be found in Table 1 and the Appendix. Please note the United States, Brazil, and France are part of the Anglo, Latin American, and Latin European, clusters, respectively. Egypt, and China part of the Middle East, and Confucian Asia clusters respectively.

Each section below begins with a summary of how each culture cluster fares with respect to the CLT profile. We then show how the countries of interest in this paper compare on specific leadership attributes that are culturally contingent. Next, we examine in detail what these differences mean and what they imply for the hypothetical American executive.

Brazil

Brazil is part of GLOBE's Latin American cluster. Viewing Tables 2 and 3, it is apparent that the CLT leadership dimensions contributing the most to outstanding leadership in this country cluster include Charismatic/Value-Based and Team Oriented leadership, followed by the Participative and Humane Oriented CLT dimensions. Autonomous and Self-Protective leadership are viewed as slightly negative. Table 3 shows that the Latin America cluster receives the highest rank for the Team Oriented dimension, among the highest ranks for Charismatic/Value-Based leadership, and ranks lowest with respect to the Autonomous CLT leadership dimension. It occupies the middle ranks for the remaining CLT dimensions.

Figure 1 below contrasts the U.S. and Brazil on the culturally contingent leadership items. Perhaps due to their high in-group collectivism, Brazilian managers intensely dislike the leaders who are individualistic, autonomous, and independent. A Brazilian sales manager working in the petrochemical industry recently reflected this suggesting, "We do not. prefer leaders who take self-governing decisions and act alone without engaging the group. That's part of who we are." While American managers also frown upon these attributes, they do not regard them as negatively as do the Brazilians. An American manager needs to be more cognizant to make sure that his/her actions and decisions are not interpreted as individualistic. He/she needs to ensure that the group or unit feels involved in decision making and that others' views and reactions are taken into consideration.

On the other hand, Brazilian managers expect their leaders to be class- and status-conscious. They want leaders to be aware of status boundaries and to respect them. A manager in a large company in Brazil noted that blue and white-collar workers from the same company rarely socialize together within and outside of work. They expect leaders to

FIGURE 1 USA vs. Brazil

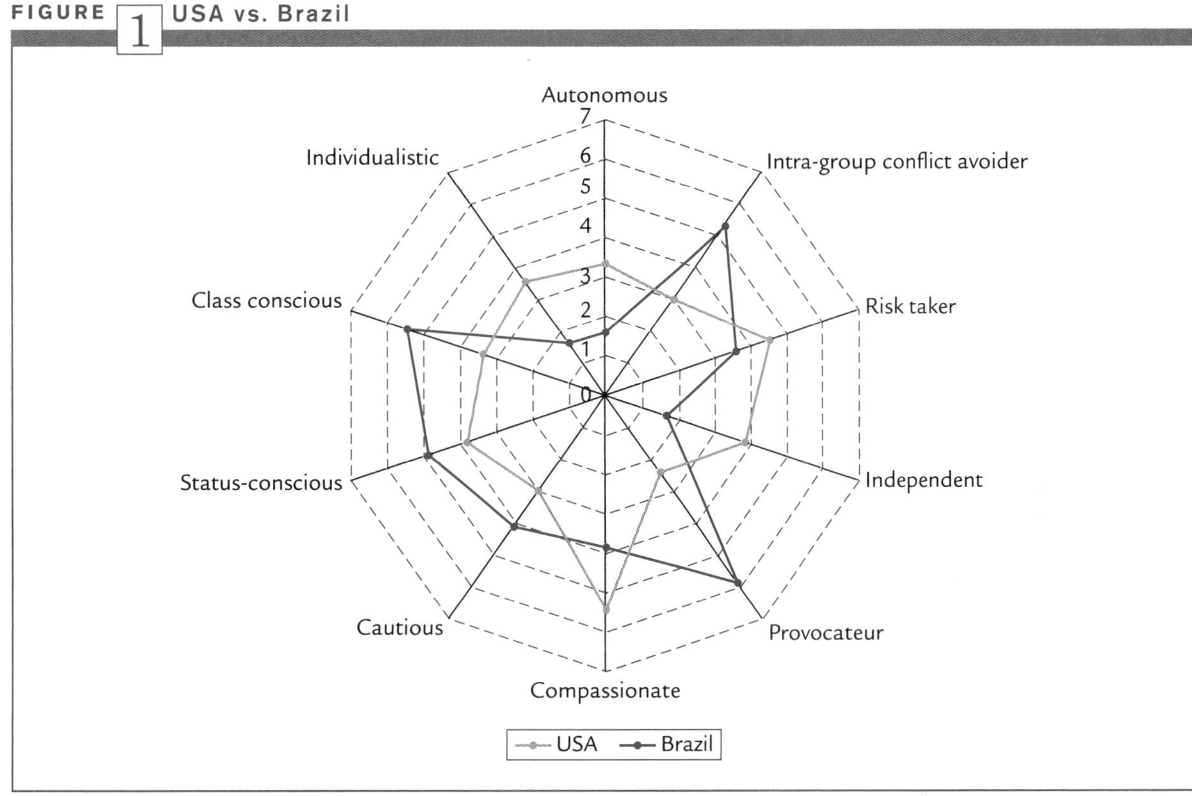

treat people according to their social and organizational levels. Perhaps due to their high power distance culture, Brazilians believe that people in positions of authority deserve to be treated with respect and deference. They prefer a formal relationship between the leader and followers. The same petrochemical sales manager told how Brazilian subordinates tend to stay outside of the perceived boundaries of their leaders and respect their own decision-making limitations. He added, "It's clear who has the most power in the work environment in Brazil, but in America this is not always the case." Americans tend to frown on status and class consciousness. Respect, to an American manager, does not necessarily mean deference but mutual respect and open dialogue. Americans tend to see formality as an obstacle to open debate. But what seems an open debate to an American manager may be viewed as aggressive and unacceptable behavior on the part of the subordinates by a Brazilian manager. So, while Brazilians do not like individualistic leaders, a typical American manager should be cautious using an open style of decision making. While it may be a good idea in an American organization to directly contact anyone with the right information regardless of their level, such behavior may be seen as a sign of disrespect to those in formal positions in a Brazilian organization.

Another important difference is that American managers prefer a less cautious approach and a greater degree of risk taking. In contrast, Brazilian managers prefer a somewhat more cautious and risk averse approach. This is consistent with the finding that U.S. culture is more tolerant of uncertainty than is Brazilian culture. Also, perhaps due to stronger assertiveness and performance orientation in American culture, U.S. managers seem to favor a speedier decision making process and a higher level of action orientation. Brazilians on the other hand, may be more sensitive to group harmony and risk avoidance. A Brazilian account manager leading a four-company consortium working on a $200 million U.S. contract with the Federal Department of Roads in Brazil realized this when a conflict occurred among the consortium players. He noted,

> *Since our contract was a long-term relationship, we could not focus only on the particular moment. I had to find a way to motivate and to build a trusting environment. The only way to do so was to promote several meetings with all the consortium members trying to find a way to put all the members back together. By doing this, I assumed this was the best action to produce results, no matter how difficult it was or how much time it required.*

Still another difference relates to the strong in-group collectivism dimension of the Brazilian culture. They expect their leaders to avoid conflict within the group to protect its harmony, but at the same time they like their leaders to induce conflict with those outside the group. A particularly successful executive working in Brazil told how Brazilians take pride in membership in small groups, especially families.

In business, he said that people who are members of the same group expect special treatment (such as price discounts, exclusivity of contracts, etc.). In fact, without these group affiliations, attracting and conducting business can be difficult. American managers seem to dislike both these attributes, perhaps due to their stronger performance orientation culture. Avoiding internal conflict, simply to maintain group harmony, even at the expense of results, is not a positive attribute to Americans. The typical American view of harmony is reflected in the following quote from the popular book *Execution* by Bossidy and Charan:[28]

> *Indeed, harmony—sought out by many leaders who wish to offend no one—can be the enemy of truth. It can squelch critical thinking and drive decision making underground. When harmony prevails, here's how things often get settled: after the key players leave the session, they quietly veto decisions they didn't like but didn't debate on the spot. A good motto to observe is: "Truth over harmony."*

Last, but not least, an important and counter intuitive finding is that American respondents have a much stronger desire for compassion in their leaders. They want their leaders to be empathetic and merciful. The Brazilian respondents, on the other hand, are quite neutral about this attribute. While this seems to go against the conventional stereotypes of Americans and Brazilians, it seems to be rooted in the fact that Brazil is reported to be a less humane culture than is the U.S. Confirming this finding, one manager stated that this reflects the expectation that people should solve their own problems, relying on help from their family or groups.

When in Brazil...

Here are a few specific ideas on what our hypothetical American manager needs to do when he starts working with his Brazilian team:

Very early on, he needs to spend time meeting with the key executives in the organization, even those who may not be directly relevant to his project. This is an important step because of high power distance and in-group collectivism in that culture. Being a foreigner and a newcomer, it is crucial to show respect to those in positions of power and to start the process of building personal ties and moving into their in-groups. Further, this step helps make sure that the other stakeholders do not view the manager's team as being insular, something that is likely to happen in high in-group cultures.

While it is important to work with the individual members of the team, it is also critical to spend as much time as possible with the team as a whole, both in formal work related occasions and in informal settings. The families of the team members should also be invited to get together on many occasions. They are an important part of the relationships among team members. The high in-group culture facilitates the group working closely together, and the Brazilians' dislike for independent and individualistic leaders means that the leader is expected to treat the team and their close families as an extended family, spending much time together.

In developing a business strategy for the team's product, it is important to keep in mind Brazil's low scores on performance orientation and future orientation and its high score on power distance. The process of strategy development needs to allow for input from the employees, but the manager needs to be patient and to make an effort to encourage and facilitate the employees' participation. The Brazilian employees will not be as forthcoming with their ideas and input as typical American employees are. At the same time, the manager will need to make the final decision and communicate it. Brazilian employees are not used to strong participation in decision making, but they also do not like leaders who simply dictate things to them. The strategy should not be seen as too risky or ambitious and should not have a long time horizon. Instead, it should consist of explicit short term milestones. It should also focus on delivering short term results to enhance employee understanding and support.

Due to the country's low score on institutional collectivism, employees will not be moved much by grand corporate strategies and visions. Instead, they would be more motivated by their individual and team interests, so the reward system should be based on both individual and team performance, although the team component should have the greater emphasis. The manager should also not be surprised if there are not many clear rules or processes and if the ones in existence are not followed very seriously. These are attributes of a society like Brazil with low levels of rules orientation. Instead, the manager needs to make it very clear early on which rules and procedures are expected to be followed and why.

France

France is part of the Latin Europe GLOBE country cluster. The most desirable CLT dimensions in this cluster are Charismatic/Value-Based and Team Oriented leadership. Participative leadership is viewed positively but is not as important as the first two dimensions. Humane Oriented leadership is viewed as slightly positive, whereas Autonomous leadership is viewed as slightly negative and Self-Protective is viewed negatively. Table 3 shows that the Latin Europe cluster is Medium/High for Charismatic/Value-Based leadership. It is in the middle rank for the remaining CLT leadership dimensions except the Humane Oriented and Autonomous dimensions where it ranks among the lowest scoring clusters.

Figure 2 below shows the contrast between French and American leadership on culturally contingent leadership attributes. The French culture is similar to the U.S on one cultural dimension, in that they both practice moderate levels of uncertainty avoidance. Although both cultures utilize predictable laws and procedures in business and society, characteristic of uncertainty avoidance cultures, France is much better known for its strong labor unions and bureaucratic formality. There are, however, significant differences between the French and American respondents on other cultural dimensions and leadership attributes. Both groups seem to like sincere and enthusiastic leaders who impart positive energy to their group, although American managers have much stronger preferences for these attributes. This

FIGURE 2 USA vs. France

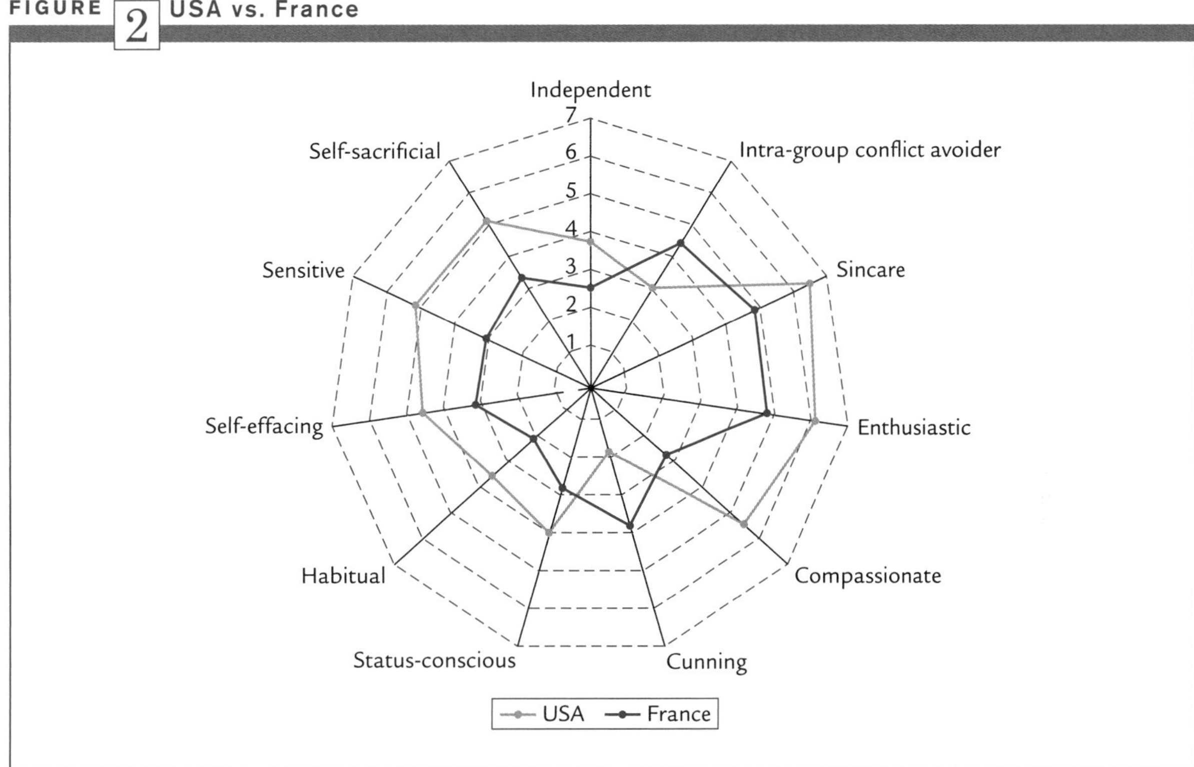

may be a reflection of the finding that French culture is not as performance oriented as U.S. culture.

Besides their dislike for avoidance of conflict within the group (as discussed earlier) American managers have a clear dislike for cunning and deceitful leaders. The French, on the other hand, are neutral about both attributes. While Americans see these attributes as dysfunctional, the French see them as a part of the job that goes with the position of leadership. Compared to the U.S., in-group collectivism is more noted in French societies in the form of "favoritism" given to people from similar education, family, social, and even regional backgrounds. This is shown in the general tension that is perceived to exist between labor and management, as well and employees and clients.[29]

American managers seem to have a strong preference for compassionate and sensitive leaders who show empathy towards others. In contrast, French managers seem to have a distinctly negative view towards both these attributes. The CEO of an international audit firm expressed this in a quality audit of a French hotel stating, "The staff had an inability to apologize and empathize. I think that could be construed as typically European, and especially French."[30] These same behaviors would be expected from their leaders. Such a large contrast can perhaps be explained by the fact that the French culture is much less humane oriented and much more power oriented. To French managers, people in positions of leadership should not be expected to be sensitive or empathetic, or to worry about another's status because such attributes would weaken a leader's resolve and impede decision making. Leaders should make decisions without being distracted by other considerations. Indeed, a very successful corporate executive in France noted that a leader should be able to handle change that affects the environment, but at the same time not change his or her characteristics, traits, and skills that put the leader in that position. In other words, they should allow no distractions.

In contrast to Americans, French respondents have a negative view of leaders who are self-sacrificial and self-effacing. They do not like leaders who are modest about their role and forgo their own self-interest. The French executive added, "A leader must be clear about his role and vision. If a leader puts himself in a compromising situation, then doubt will arise in the followers' minds about the leader and that would affect their views of the roles the followers play in the broader picture." To them, the leader has an important role to play and important decisions to make, and s/he should not minimize that. They also do not like leaders who are habitual and tend to routinize everything because that diminishes the importance of their role. They do still prefer their leaders to work with and rely on others to get things done and do not like independent leaders. A French CEO known for his corporate turnaround finesse explained that leaders should not have too much independence from their followers because otherwise this would denote lack of character from the followers. He adds that a leader should guide without having too much power over the followers' thought processes, to ensure diverse thinking critical to conserve several solutions to the leader.

To sum up, a typical American executive taking on a leadership role in a French organization will face a more bureaucratic and formal work environment with higher levels of aggressiveness and lower levels of personal compassion and sensitivity than s/he is used to.

When in France...

The American manager in our scenario will face a very different experience with his or her French team. These managers will experience much more formal and impersonal relationships among the team members. The concept of visionary and charismatic leadership that is popular among American managers may not be as desirable to the French. They do not expect their leaders to play heroic acts and, due to their high power distance, have a more bureaucratic view of leaders. So, the American manager, in contrast to his experience in Brazil, needs to tone down the personal side of relationships and be much more business oriented. The manager also has to be more careful and selective in contacting other executives and stakeholders. Their preference for maintaining high power distance may curb their enthusiasm about meeting with someone if they feel it is a waste of time and of no clear value to them. It is perhaps best for our American manager to make an offer to them and leave it to them to decide. Their low humane orientation culture may mean that they are not particularly interested in being supportive of others, even in the same organization, especially if they are from separate in-groups.

Due to lower levels of future orientation and performance orientation, grand corporate strategies and visions may be of limited value to a French team. Any strong competitive language may be seen as typical American bravado. The manager needs to develop a process for making strategic decisions about the project and get the team members involved, but he needs to keep in mind that French employees may be best motivated by transactional forms of leadership where they see clear individual benefit in implementing the team's plans. The strategy and action plans need to be simple and well planned. So, the content and process of strategy development for the French team may have many similarities with the Brazilian team, even though they are different on many other dimensions.

Egypt

Egypt is part of the Middle East cluster. There are a number of striking differences in comparison to other clusters. While both Charismatic/Value-Based and Team Oriented leadership are viewed as positive, they have the lowest scores and ranks relative to those for all other clusters. Participative leadership is viewed positively, but again scores low compared with other clusters' absolute score and ranks. Humane Oriented leadership is perceived positively, but only about equally to other cluster scores. The Self-Protective CLT dimension is viewed as an almost neutral factor; however, it has the second-highest score and rank of all clusters.

Figure 3 below shows a contrast of leadership styles in the U.S. and Egypt. The Egyptian culture is distinct by its emphasis on in-group and institutional collectivism, power distance, humane orientation, and male domination. In terms of leadership, American managers dislike autocratic leaders

FIGURE 3 USA vs. Egypt

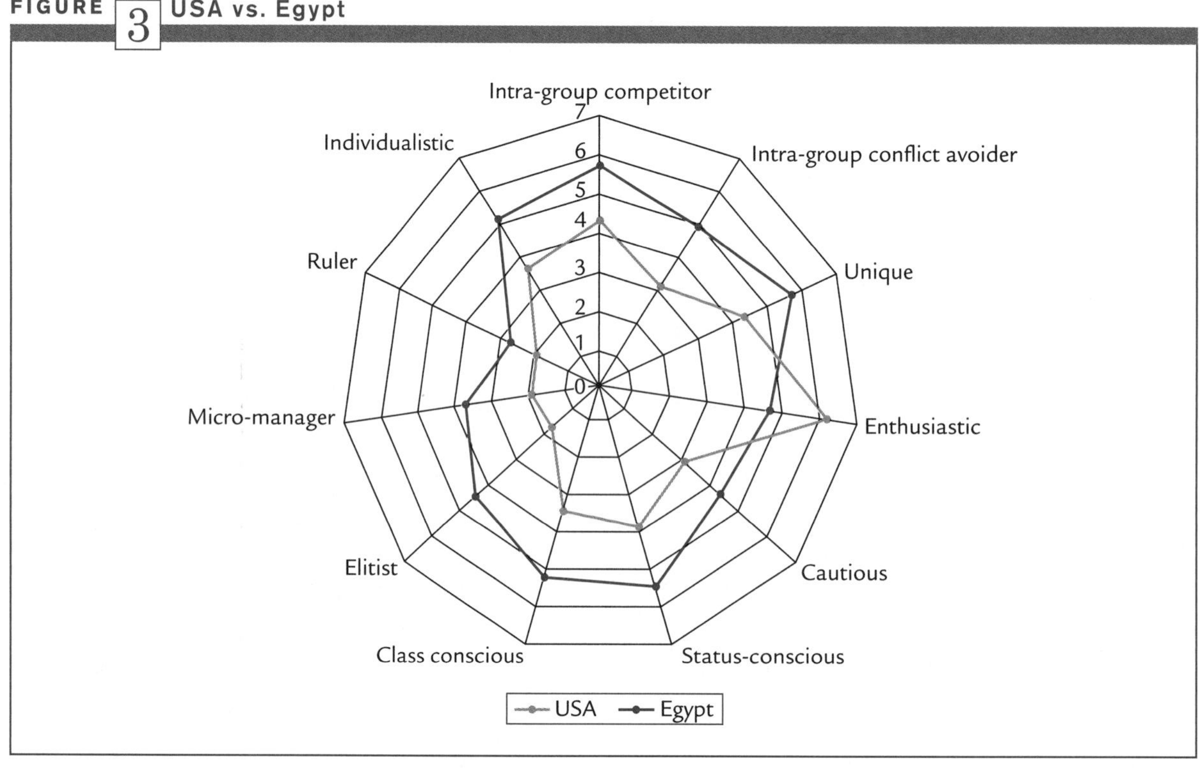

who want to make all the decisions themselves and micro-manage their employees. They do not want their leaders to suppress others' ideas, even if they disagree with them. Egyptian managers have a more temperate view of such executives, perhaps due to their strong power distance culture.

A very important difference is the image of leaders in the Egyptian vs. the American mind. Egyptian managers seem to have an elitist, transcendent view of their leaders. They view them as a distinct group and a breed apart. They want their leaders to be unique, superior, status- and class-conscious, individualistic, and better than the others in their group. They show strong reverence and deference toward their leaders. Americans, on the other hand, have a more benign and simplistic view toward their leaders. They do not see them as a breed apart or superhuman. They regard them as successful people but not extraordinary ones.

The country of Egypt has been ruled by dictators dating as far back as the time of the Pharaohs. Leaders were expected to lead by portraying a self-assured image. To maintain power, Egyptian leaders need to continuously be involved in making decisions. In the Arabic culture that is very much influenced by Islam, men do not wish to appear weak.

Despite such high level of respect for leaders, Egyptian employees, perhaps due to their very strong in-group collectivism, prefer their leaders to respect group harmony, avoid group conflict, and take caution in decision making. It is rare to see leaders, especially political leaders, come out publicly and criticize a popular belief. They tend to avoid a conflict when it is not necessary, and they often use this collectivism to build their influence and popularity.

The importance of kinship as the family is the most significant unit of Egyptian society. An individual's social identity is closely linked to his or her status in the network of kin relations. Kinship is essential to the culture. Describing the tendency toward generosity and caring in their society, an Egyptian manager told of how early Islamic authorities imposed a tax on personal property proportionate to one's wealth and distributed the revenues to the needy. This type of government behavior left a certain culture of doing business in Egypt that has a strong emphasis on harmony with the environment, the industry, and the competition.

When in Egypt...

Our hypothetical American manager will find that his experience in Egypt will have both similarities and differences with his time in France and Brazil. First, what the manager may regard as a normal informal leadership style in the U.S. may be seen as weak and unworthy of a leader. This manager (typically a male) is expected to act and be seen as distinct from the others on the team and present an image of omnipotence. In the minds of his Egyptian team members, he needs to be seen as deserving of his leadership role and status. Addressing his role as a leader, a project manager from Egypt noted that being a leader brought with it great responsibility. He was in charge of disciplining anyone that did not follow the team rules. He noted, "In order to keep the team spirit up and focused on our goals, we can't afford to have individuals deviating from what we have set out to do." This is almost the opposite of his experience in France.

The American manager will also find that due to very strong in-group collectivism, various groups inside and outside the organization tend to show in-group/out-group phenomena in decision making; i.e., strong participation by in-group members, little participation by out-group members; strong communication with in-group members, and little communication with out-group members. The extent to which Egyptians take pride in belonging to certain groups is immensely important. Families have endured through difficult times, requiring many of the members to stay together and work together. Family businesses tend to be passed from father to son without too many exceptions. Maintenance of the in-group is paramount in any decision. Leaders build their legitimacy not necessarily by accomplishing high performance but rather by forging loyalty to the group and group values. Furthermore, as a result of reliance on personal relationships, decision making criteria and processes regarding any aspect of the organization tend to be informal and unclear.

Given such cultural underpinnings, the American manager needs to do even more than he did in Brazil to build and maintain group harmony. Many informal and formal meetings are needed, but there are three important differences compared with the experience in Brazil. First, to Egyptians, the team leader is more than just an executive; he is a paternal figure who will be rather autocratic but benign. He cares about them and their families. The relationship between the boss and employees is much more emotional and personal in Egypt. The Egyptian project manager described how he helped one of his employees who had experienced some personal difficulties. Explaining that the employee's behaviour was unacceptable, the manager added, "At the same time, I tried to understand if there were any personal issues that forced him to behave the way he did. I felt an obligation to try to help him." Secondly, due to very high humane orientation in Egypt, if the family of an employee has a problem, colleagues and the boss will quickly get involved to help. Taking care of friends in need is a major element of the culture and there is very little demarcation between colleagues and friends. Third, it is easier and more acceptable for the boss in Brazil to get to know the family members and spend time with them during social occasions. It is not, however, a good idea for him to try to do the same with Egyptian families. The contact should only be with and through the employee. Egyptian families tend to be more private and inaccessible to outsiders, possibly due to the intense in-group culture. People tend to stay close to their roots and develop a very strong sense of belonging. In short, even though the American manager will spend time building personal ties and maintaining in-group relationships both in Egypt and Brazil, the nature of his behaviour will need to be somewhat different.

Like Brazil, the manager needs to pay his respects and call on the key executives in the Egyptian organization and start the process of building personal relationships. Unlike the French executives, the Egyptian executives will in all likelihood enjoy this approach and respond positively.

In developing a business strategy for the team, several cultural attributes need to be taken into consideration. The team will enjoy providing input but they expect decisions to be made by the leader. Family related activities are always celebrated and employees are often excused from work to be able to properly plan such occasions. However, leaders also tend to use the friendly environment to maintain their control and build loyalty within their workforce. Egyptian employees expect their leaders to develop and communicate heroic and grand strategies. Due to their high institutional collectivism and performance orientation, it is helpful to design and communicate ambitious strategies and put them into the broader context of the corporation. Employees will resonate to ideas that would help the corporation and the unit achieve prominence in their competitive arenas. They also like strong rhetoric and get excited by the desire to be part of the winning team. In terms of the reward system, individual performance-based financial rewards, while helpful, are not the best motivators. The system should be seen to be humane to all; it should have a strong group based component, and it should consist of a variety of benefits that are not typically offered in the U.S. Such benefits should be focused on the families of employees. For example, tuition assistance to employees' children, paid family vacation, free or subsidized toys or home appliances could be very well received. As with other Middle East countries, although it is important for the individual to be successful, it is the family or group success that is more dominant.

China

China is part of the Confucian Asia cluster. The two CLT dimensions contributing to outstanding leadership are Charismatic/Value-Based and Team Oriented leadership, even though these scores are not particularly high. Humane Oriented leadership is viewed favorably, but it is not as important as the first two CLT dimensions. Although Participative leadership is also viewed positively, it is about equal to the lowest-scoring clusters. Autonomous leadership is viewed neutrally, and Self-Protective leadership is seen as a slight impediment to effective leadership. Table 4 shows that compared to other GLOBE countries, the Confucian Asia cluster is ranked relatively low with respect to Participative and relatively high with respect to Self-Protective leadership dimensions.

As shown in the Appendix, the US and Chinese cultures are similar in terms of their performance orientation, humane orientation, and power distance. The Chinese culture seems to be less future oriented, less assertive, more collectivist, both small group and socially, and more rules oriented.

Figure 4 below shows the comparison of culturally contingent leadership attributes between American and Chinese managers. Both American and Chinese managers like

FIGURE 4 **USA vs. China**

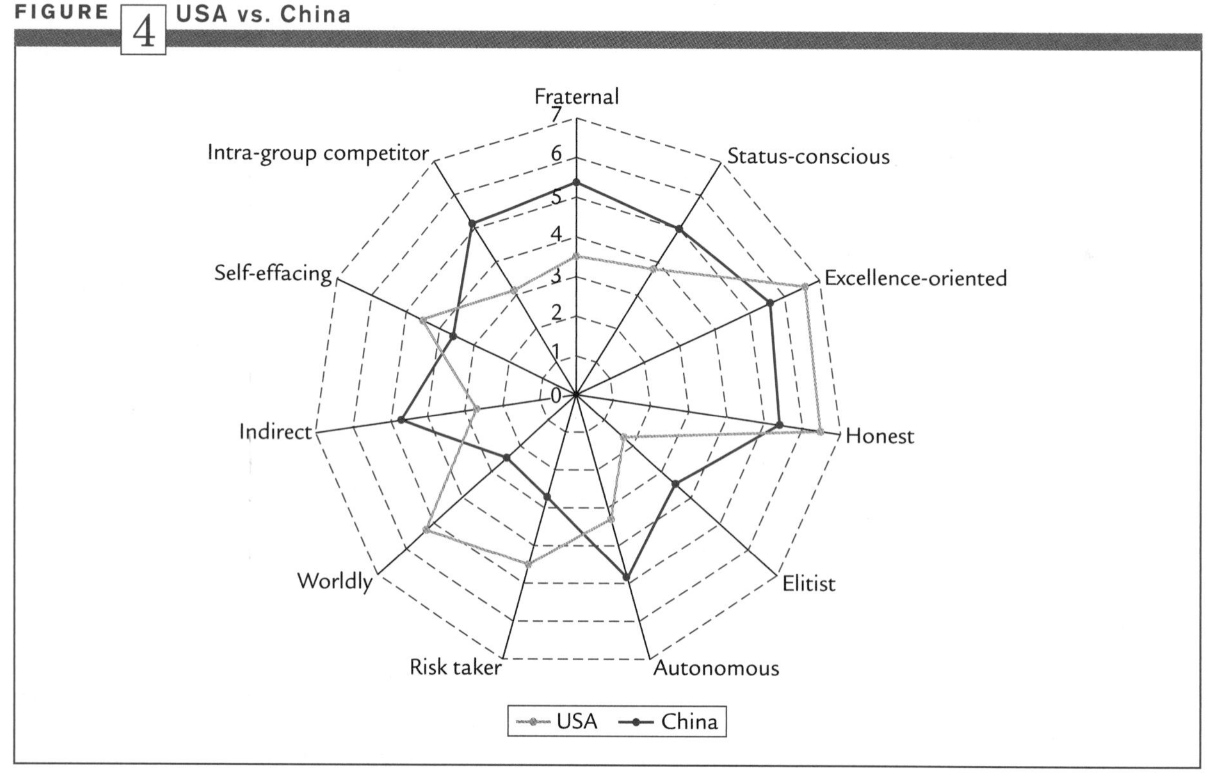

excellence oriented leaders who strive for performance improvement in themselves and their subordinates. This is probably driven by the fact that both cultures share a strong performance orientation, as shown in the Appendix. They also both like leaders who are honest. However, the figure shows that the US scores on both these attributes are higher that the Chinese scores.

Chinese managers seem to like leaders who are fraternal and friendly with their subordinates and who have an indirect approach to communication, using metaphors and parables to communicate their point. American managers have a neutral view of fraternal leadership and a negative view of indirect leadership. The difference can probably be explained by the fact that the U.S. culture is much more assertive and less in-group oriented than that in China (see appendix). In a less assertive culture like China, people tend to use nuances and a context rich language to communicate. They prefer indirect communication to avoid the possibility of hurting someone. Furthermore, in a highly group oriented culture like China, group harmony is critical and the leader's role is to strengthen group ties. As a result, leaders are expected to be supportive of their subordinates and act as good friends for them. They are expected to build emotional ties with their groups and their relationships with their subordinates go far beyond what is the norm in a country like the U.S. The leader is seen as a paternal figure who should take care of his subordinates and their families.

American managers are not excited about leaders who are status conscious and are negative towards leaders who are elitist. In contrast, Chinese managers like the former type of leadership and are neutral towards the latter. This is reflective of the importance of hierarchy in the Chinese culture. Confucianism's 'Three Bonds'—emperor rules the minister, father rules the son, and husband rules the wife—serve as the foundation of the Chinese society:

> *Chinese business structure can be directly linked to the history of patriarchy: the owner or manager plays the father's role, and the subordinates or employees play the son.*[31]

Within such a hierarchical structure, the leader tends to be authoritative and expects respect and obedience and tends to make autonomous decisions. That is why Chinese managers do not admire leaders who are self-effacing, because such leaders do not emanate confidence. A group of American managers was recently in China to discuss a possible joint venture with a Chinese company. American managers expected to spend a few days working with their Chinese counterparts to brainstorm ideas and develop action plans. After a few frustrating days, they were told that they needed to find a Chinese agent to help them implement the deal. In conversations with the Chinese agent, they learned that the Chinese counterpart's expectation from the meetings was very different. They learned that the Chinese company wanted to use the meetings to help build personal ties among the Chinese and American managers and was upset that the Americans were asking aggressive questions and were focused solely on business rather than personal matters. They also learned that the top Chinese executive had no interest in sharing decision making with any one. Instead, he wanted to use private lunches and dinners with the head of the American delegation to make serious decisions and reach agreements.

Chinese managers are very negative towards worldly leaders who have a global outlook. In contrast, Americans admire such leaders. This could be explained by the fact that the two cultures are very different in terms of in group collectivism. The Chinese culture is very high on this dimension, which means it is less interested in anything outside of their in-group. Perhaps they view the world as out-group compared to China and view it as less important.

When in China...

The Chinese culture is distinct by its high performance orientation, high institutional orientation, and high in-group collectivism. Building personal ties and relationships is reflected in the Chinese concept of "guan xi" whose loose English translation is networking. It is a manifestation of the fact that one's value and importance is embedded in his/her ties and relationships. As a result:

> *In China, the primary qualities expected in a leader or executive is someone who is good at establishing and nurturing personal relationships, who practices benevolence towards his or her subordinates, who is dignified and aloof but sympathetic, and puts the interests of his or her employees above his or her own.*[32]

Much of Chinese life and culture is based on Confucian ideas which emphasize the importance of relationships and community. Even the word "self" has a negative connotation.[33] Our hypothetical American manager needs to be careful about how his behavior and manners are perceived by the Chinese. Being polite, considerate, and moral are desirable attributes. At the same time, the American manager can get the Chinese employees excited by engaging their high performance culture. Developing an exciting vision is very effective. The relative high score on future orientation can also help the new manager get the employees motivated. But perhaps the most critical key success factor is how the manager goes about building personal ties and relationships with a wide network of individuals and groups. His "guan xi" will be the ultimate test of his success. In building guan xi with his employees, he needs to show high respect to the employees' families, keep them in mind when designing work schedules and reward systems, and make sure that employees see him and the organization as a strong supporter of their own guan xi. Perhaps a big challenge to the American executive is how to make sure his natural American assertiveness does not turn his Chinese employees and counterparts off and does not impede his efforts at building strong relationships.

Embarking on a Cross-cultural Leadership Journey

The existing literature on cross-cultural management is more useful at the conceptual level than at the behavioral level. Much of the advice offered to executives tends to be context-free and general such as "understand and respect the other culture." But the problems facing a typical global executive are context-specific; for example, how to understand and respect the Brazilian culture. In behavioral terms, understanding the Brazilian culture may be quite different from understanding and respecting the Egyptian culture because they are very different cultures.

In this paper, we have presented the cultural profiles of four countries based on a rigorous and scientific research project. We have also provided very specific ideas on the managerial implications of the different cultural profiles along with action oriented advice on how an American manager can "put himself in the other culture's shoes" and be adaptable. Besides the culture specific ideas presented earlier, we propose a two-step process for any executive who is embarking on a new assignment in a new country. Regardless of the host country, these two steps help build a positive pathway towards cultural understanding and adaptability.

First, the executive needs to share information about his own as well as the host country's culture. Most of the advice that executives receive is about how they can adapt and adjust to other cultures. We propose a somewhat different approach. When people from different cultures come into contact, they usually have unstated and sometimes false or exaggerated stereotypes about the other side. While it is important that the executive learn about the host culture, it is not sufficient. Executives need to tell the host employees about their own cultures. For example, if these executives are in Egypt, then they should show the employees how the American and Egyptian cultures and leadership attributes compare. They should show both similarities and differences. In this paper, we showed that there is a set of leadership attributes that are universally desirable and universally undesirable. Similarities represent a fertile ground to build mutual understanding. The informed executive can then use the session to discuss their implications. What does integrity mean to a French manager? Or to a Brazilian manager? The executive can also compare the findings about his or her own culture with their perceptions of American culture to dispel any misunderstandings. This exercise in mapping and surfacing cultural attributes can go a long way to build mutual understanding and trust between the players. For example, our findings show that American culture is reported to be more moderate on many cultural dimensions than it is stereotypically believed to be. One of the unique features of GLOBE is that we have taken several steps to ensure that the reports by country managers are not confounded by such things as methodological problems and represent the true broader culture of their societies.

Second, the global manager needs to think about how to bridge the gap between the two cultures. Much of the advice executives receive seems to suggest, explicitly or implicitly, that the executive needs to become more like them. We do not necessarily subscribe to this viewpoint. While it is important to understand the other culture, it does not necessarily mean that one should automatically apply their approach. For example, leaders are seen as benign autocrats in Egypt. If an American manager does not like this approach, then he should educate the employees on his approach to leadership; why it is not dictatorial, and why he prefers it. Managers need to make sure the employees understand that their approach is not a sign of weakness, but a more effective style for the manager and for the team's and organization's success. It's a judgment call to say it's a "more effective" style than what the team is used to, but it is one that they should employ with the team. The global manager needs to tell the employees what managerial functions they are willing to change and what team functions they would like the employees to change so that the team can work from, and succeed on, common ground incorporating both cultures. The manager then needs to seek their help on both approaches; i.e., each culture making changes to accommodate and strengthen the other. Both approaches can take place at the same time and with respect to both cultures, as long as the manager gets the employees involved in the process. In other words, instead of a solitary learning journey for the executive, managers can create a collective learning journey that can be enriching, educational, and productive for both sides.

Attributes of Global Leaders

The essence of global leadership is the ability to influence people who are not like the leader and come from different cultural backgrounds. To succeed, global leaders need to have a global mindset, tolerate high levels of ambiguity, and show cultural adaptability and flexibility. This paper provides some examples of these attributes. In contrast to a domestic manager, the hypothetical manager discussed in this paper needs a global mindset because s/he needs to understand a variety of cultural and leadership paradigms, and legal, political and economic systems, as well as different competitive frameworks.[34] We used GLOBE findings to provide a scientifically based comparison of cultural and leadership paradigms in the five countries. We showed that countries can be different on some cultural dimensions and similar on others. Brazil and Egypt are both high on in-group collectivism, but different on performance orientation. France and the U.S. are both moderate on uncertainty avoidance but differ on power distance. China and the U.S are both high on performance orientation but very different on in-group collectivism. Furthermore, there are similarities and differences in the countries' leadership profiles. While a leadership attribute like irritability is universally undesirable, another attribute like compassion is culturally contingent, i.e., it is much more desirable in the U.S. than in France.

Tolerance of ambiguity is another important attribute of a global leader. Every new country that s/he has to work in represents a new paradigm and new ways of doing things.

This is typically an uncomfortable position for many people to be in because it requires learning new ideas quickly and letting go of what has already been learned. Of course, in the four scenarios, we showed that there are things in common across cultures and there are portable aspects of cultural learning. But we also showed that there are differences as well. Figuring out which one is which and what to do represents potentially stressful ambiguity to an expatriate manager.

Cultural adaptability refers to a manager's ability to understand other cultures and behave in a way that helps achieve goals and build strong and positive relations with local citizens. In the country scenarios, we showed that while in France the manager should not emphasize grand and ambitious corporate strategies, he can do this in China. Cultural adaptability refers to the mental and psychological ability to move from one situation and country to another. It means the ability to do a good job of developing personal relationships while in Egypt and then doing it very differently in France. The dexterity to adjust one's behavior is a critical requirement. Not everyone can do this; to many people it may bring into question one's own identity. In some ways it is reminiscent of acting but the difference is that the global manager, unlike the actor, lives and works among real people and not other actors, so his task is more complicated.

Developing Global Leaders

As mentioned earlier in this paper, a large majority of *Fortune* 500 corporations report a shortage of global leaders. Devising programs that would develop a global mindset in leaders has been called "the biggest challenge that looms in the new millennium for human resource managers."[35] There are a variety of ways that companies can enhance their pool of global leaders. To start with, they can make a large volume of information on cross-cultural and global issues and country specific reports available to their managers. We have already referred to several books on this topic. In addition to the special issue of the *Human Resource Management Journal* mentioned earlier, there are special issues of other journals.[36] There are also a variety of software packages such as a multimedia package called "Bridging Cultures," a self-training program for those who will be living and working in other cultures. In addition, several services like CultureGrams (www.culturegram.com) provide useful information about many countries. There are also a few Internet sites providing useful information to managers[37] such as www.contactcga.com belonging to the Center for Global assignments, the CIA World Fact Book at www.odci.gov/cia/publications/factbook/, and Global Dynamics Inc.'s www.globaldynamics.com/expatria.htm.

Formal education and training can also be helpful in developing global leaders. A recent survey showed that a large majority of firms were planning to increase funding for programs that would help globalize their leaders.[38] But despite its prevalence among multinational corporations, there is general consensus among experts that it is not a highly effective source of developing global leaders.[39] It is generally best used as a component of a comprehensive and integrated development program. Work experience and international assignment is by far the most effective source for developing global leadership capabilities.[40] Some experts view long term international assignments as the "single most powerful experience in shaping the perspective and capabilities of effective global leaders."[41] Increasingly, companies like GE, Citigroup, Shell, Siemens, and Nokia are using international assignments of high potential employees as the means to develop their managers' global leadership mindset and competencies.

Appendix Country Scores on Cultural Practices

Performance Orientation	Anglo Cultures	Latin Europe	Middle East Cultures	Confucian Asia	Latin America
	USA 4.49	**France 4.11**	**Egypt 4.27**	**China 4.45**	**Brazil 4.04**
	Canada 4.49	Israel 4.08	Kuwait 3.95	Hong Kong 4.80	Bolivia 3.61
	England 4.08	Italy 3.58	Morocco 3.99	Japan 4.22	Argentina 3.65
	Ireland 4.36	Portugal 3.60	Qatar 3.45	Singapore 4.90	Colombia 3.94
	New Zealand 4.72	Spain 4.01	Turkey 3.83	South Korea 4.55	Costa Rica 4.12
	South Africa (W) 4.11	Swiss (French) 4.25		Taiwan 4.56	Ecuador 4.20
	Australia 4.36				El Salvador 3.72
					Guatemala 3.81
					Mexico 4.10
					Venezuela 3.32

Future Orientation	Anglo Cultures	Latin Europe	Middle East Cultures	Confucian Asia	Latin America
	USA 4.15	**France 3.48**	**Egypt 3.86**	**China 3.75**	**Brazil 3.81**
	Canada 4.44	Israel 3.85	Kuwait 3.26	Hong Kong 4.03	Bolivia 3.61
	England 4.28	Italy 3.25	Morocco 3.26	Japan 4.29	Argentina 3.08
	Ireland 3.98	Portugal 3.71	Qatar 3.78	Singapore 5.07	Colombia 3.27
	New Zealand 3.47	Spain 3.51	Turkey 3.74	South Korea 3.97	Costa Rica 3.60
	South Africa (W) 4.13	Swiss (French) 4.27		Taiwan 3.96	Ecuador 3.74
	Australia 4.09				El Salvador 3.80
					Guatemala 3.24
					Mexico 3.87
					Venezuela 3.35
Assertiveness Orientation	Anglo Cultures	Latin Europe	Middle East Cultures	Confucian Asia	Latin America
	USA 4.55	**France 4.13**	**Egypt 3.91**	**China 3.76**	**Brazil 4.20**
	Canada 4.05	Israel 4.23	Kuwait 3.63	Hong Kong 4.67	Bolivia 3.79
	England 4.15	Italy 4.07	Morocco 4.52	Japan 3.59	Argentina 4.22
	Ireland 3.92	Portugal 3.65	Qatar 4.11	Singapore 4.17	Colombia 4.20
	New Zealand 3.42	Spain 4.42	Turkey 4.53	South Korea 4.40	Costa Rica 3.75
	South Africa (W) 4.60	Swiss (French) 3.47		Taiwan 3.92	Ecuador 4.09
	Australia 4.28				El Salvador 4.62
					Guatemala 3.89
					Mexico 4.45
					Venezuela 4.33
Societal Collectivism	Anglo Cultures	Latin Europe	Middle East Cultures	Confucian Asia	Latin America
	USA 4.20	**France 3.93**	**Egypt 4.50**	**China 4.77**	**Brazil 3.83**
	Canada 4.38	Israel 4.46	Kuwait 4.49	Hong Kong 4.13	Bolivia 4.04
	England 4.27	Italy 3.68	Morocco 3.87	Japan 5.19	Argentina 3.66
	Ireland 4.63	Portugal 3.92	Qatar 4.50	Singapore 4.90	Colombia 3.81
	New Zealand 4.81	Spain 3.85	Turkey 4.03	South Korea 5.20	Costa Rica 3.93
	South Africa (W) 4.62	Swiss (French) 4.22		Taiwan 4.59	Ecuador 3.90
	Australia 4.29				El Salvador 3.71
					Guatemala 3.70
					Mexico 4.06
					Venezuela 3.96
In-Group Collectivism	Anglo Cultures	Latin Europe	Middle East Cultures	Confucian Asia	Latin America
	USA 4.25	**France 4.37**	**Egypt 5.64**	**China 5.80**	**Brazil 5.18**
	Canada 4.26	Israel 4.70	Kuwait 5.80	Hong Kong 5.32	Bolivia 5.47
	England 4.08	Italy 4.94	Morocco 5.87	Japan 4.63	Argentina 5.51
	Ireland 5.14	Portugal 5.51	Qatar 4.71	Singapore 5.64	Colombia 5.73

	New Zealand 3.67	Spain 5.45	Turkey 5.88	South Korea 5.54	Costa Rica 5.32
	South Africa (W) 4.50	Swiss (French) 3.85		Taiwan 5.59	Ecuador 5.81
	Australia 4.17				El Salvador 5.35
					Guatemala 5.63
					Mexico 5.71
					Venezuela 5.53
Humane Orientation	Anglo Cultures	Latin Europe	Middle East Cultures	Confucian Asia	Latin America
	USA 4.17	**France 3.40**	**Egypt 4.73**	**China 4.36**	**Brazil 3.66**
	Canada 4.49	Israel 4.10	Kuwait 4.52	Hong Kong 3.90	Bolivia 4.05
	England 3.72	Italy 3.63	Morocco 4.19	Japan 4.30	Argentina 3.99
	Ireland 4.96	Portugal 3.91	Qatar 4.42	Singapore 3.49	Colombia 3.72
	New Zealand 4.32	Spain 3.32	Turkey 3.94	South Korea 3.81	Costa Rica 4.39
	South Africa (W) 3.49	Swiss (French) 3.93		Taiwan 4.11	Ecuador 4.65
	Australia 4.28				El Salvador 3.71
					Guatemala 3.89
					Mexico 3.98
					Venezuela 4.25
Power Distance	Anglo Cultures	Latin Europe	Middle East Cultures	Confucian Asia	Latin America
	USA 4.88	**France 5.28**	**Egypt 4.92**	**China 5.04**	**Brazil 5.33**
	Canada 4.82	Israel 4.73	Kuwait 5.12	Hong Kong 4.96	Bolivia 4.51
	England 5.15	Italy 5.43	Morocco 5.80	Japan 5.11	Argentina 5.64
	Ireland 5.15	Portugal 5.44	Qatar 4.73	Singapore 4.99	Colombia 5.56
	New Zealand 4.89	Spain 5.52	Turkey 5.57	South Korea 5.61	Costa Rica 4.74
	South Africa (W) 5.16	Swiss (French) 4.86		Taiwan 5.18	Ecuador 5.60
	Australia 4.74				El Salvador 5.68
					Guatemala 5.60
					Mexico 5.22
					Venezuela 5.40
Gender Egalitarianism	Anglo Cultures	Latin Europe	Middle East Cultures	Confucian Asia	Latin America
	USA 3.34	**France 3.64**	**Egypt 2.81**	**China 3.05**	**Brazil 3.31**
	Canada 3.70	Israel 3.19	Kuwait 2.58	Hong Kong 3.47	Bolivia 3.55
	England 3.67	Italy 3.24	Morocco 2.84	Japan 3.19	Argentina 3.49
	Ireland 3.21	Portugal 3.66	Qatar 3.63	Singapore 3.70	Colombia 3.67
	New Zealand 3.22	Spain 3.01	Turkey 2.89	South Korea 2.50	Costa Rica 3.56
	South Africa (W) 3.27	Swiss (French) 3.42		Taiwan 3.18	Ecuador 3.07
	Australia 3.40				El Salvador 3.16
					Guatemala 3.02
					Mexico 3.64
					Venezuela 3.62

Uncertainty Avoidance	Anglo Cultures	Latin Europe	Middle East Cultures	Confucian Asia	Latin America
	USA 4.15	**France 4.43**	**Egypt 4.06**	**China 4.94**	**Brazil 3.60**
	Canada 4.58	Israel 4.01	Kuwait 4.21	Hong Kong 4.32	Bolivia 3.35
	England 4.65	Italy 3.79	Morocco 3.65	Japan 4.07	Argentina 3.65
	Ireland 4.30	Portugal 3.91	Qatar 3.99	Singapore 5.31	Colombia 3.57
	New Zealand 4.75	Spain 3.97	Turkey 3.63	South Korea 3.55	Costa Rica 3.82
	South Africa (W) 4.09	Swiss (French) 4.98		Taiwan 4.34	Ecuador 3.68
	Australia 4.39				El Salvador 3.62
					Guatemala 3.30
					Mexico 4.18
					Venezuela 3.44

Source: Academy of Management Perspectives, 20, (1), 67–90 (2006). Reprinted by permission.

ENDNOTES

1. House, R. J., Hanges, P. J., Ruiz-Quintanilla, S. A., Dorfman, P. W., Javidan, M., Dickson, M., et al. 1999. Cultural influences on leadership and organizations: Project globe. In W. F. Mobley, M. J. Gessner & V. Arnold (Eds.), *Advances in global leadership* (Vol. 1, pp. 171–233). Stamford, CT: JAI Press.
2. Gregersen, H. B., Morrison, A. J., & J. S. Black. 1998. Developing leaders for the global frontier. *Sloan Management Review*, Fall: 21–32.
3. Hollenbeck, G. P. & McCall, M. W. 2003. Competence, not competencies: Making global executive development work. In W. Mobley & P. Dorfman (Eds.), *Advances in global leadership* (Vol. 3). Oxford: JAI Press.
4. Black, J. S., Morrison, A. J., & Gergersen, H. B. 1999. *Global explorers: The next generation of leaders.* New York: Routledge; Rheinsmith, S. H. 1996. *A manager's guide to globalization.* Chicago: Irwin; Osland, J. S. 1995. *The adventure of working abroad: Hero tales from the global frontier.* San Francisco: CA: Jossey-Bass, Inc.; Black, J. S., Gergersen, H. B., Mendenhall, M. E., & Stroh L. K. 1999. *Globalizing people through international assignments.* Reading, MA: Addisson-Wesley; Mobley, W. H. & Dorfman, P. W. 2003. *Advances in global leadership.* In W. H. Mobley & P. W. Dorfman (Eds.), *Advances in global leadership* (Vol. 3). Oxford: JAI Press.
5. Gergerson, H. B., Morrison, A. J., & Mendenhall, M. E. 2000. Guest editors. *Human Resource Management Journal*, 39, 2&3, 113–299.
6. Morrison, A. J. 2000. Developing a global leadership model. *Human Resource Management Journal*, 39, 2&3, 117–131.
7. Kiedel, R. W. 1995. *Seeing organizational patterns: A new theory and language of organizational design.* San Francisco: Berrett-Koehler.
8. Pucik, V. & Saba, T. 1997. Selecting and developing the global versus the expatriate manager: A review of the state of the art. *Human Resource Planning*, 40–54.
9. Wills, S. 2001. *Developing global leaders.* In P. Kirkbride & K. Ward (Eds.), *Globalization: The internal dynamic.* Chicester: Wiley, 259–284.
10. Bass, B. M. 1997. Does the Transactional-Transformational Leadership Paradigm Transcend Organizational and National Boundaries? *American Psychologist*, 52(2), 130–139.
11. Hofstede, G. 1980. Culture's consequences: International differences in work-related values. New Bury Park, CA: Sage; Hofstede, G. 2001 Culture's Consequences: Comparing values, behaviors, institutions, and organizations across nations. 2nd ed. Thousand Oaks, CA: Sage; Trompenaars, F. & Hamden-Turner C. 1998. *Riding the waves of culture.* 2nd ed. New York: McGraw-Hill; Kluckhohn, F. R. & Strodtbeck, F. L. 1961. *Variations in value orientations.* New York: Harper & Row.
12. House, R. J., Hanges, P. J., Javidan, M., Dorfman, P. W., & Gupta, V., & GLOBE Associates. 2004. *Leadership, culture and organizations: The globe study of 62 societies.* Thousand Oaks, CA: Sage Publications, Inc.
13. Morrison, A. J. 2000. Developing a global leadership model. *Human Resource Management Journal*, 39, 2&3, 117–131.
14. Laurent, A. 1983. The cultural diversity of western conceptions of management. *International Studies of Management and Organization*, 13(2), 75–96; Trompenaars, F. 1993. Riding the waves of culture: Understanding cultural diversity in business. London: Breatley; Briscoe, D. R., & Shuler, R. S. 2004. *International human resource management.* 2nd ed. New York: Routledge.
15. Davis, D. D. & Bryant, J. L. 2003. Influence at a distance: Leadership in global virtual teams. In W. H. Mobley & P. W. Dorfman (Eds.), *Advances in global leadership* (Vol. 3, pp. 303–340). Oxford: JAI Press.
16. Millman, J. Trade wins: The world's new tiger on the export scene isn't Asian; it's Mexico. *Wall Street Journal*, p. A1. May 9, 2000.
17. Smith, P. B. & Peterson, M. F. 1988. *Leadership, organizations and culture: An event management model.* London: Sage.
18. Smith, P. B. 2003. Leaders' sources of guidance and the challenge of working across cultures. In W. Mobley & P. Dorfman (Eds.), *Advances in global leadership* (Vol. 3, pp. 167–182). Oxford: JAI Press; Smith, P. B., Dugan, S., & Trompenaars, F. 1996. National culture and the values of organizational employees: A dimensional analysis across 43 nations. *Journal of Cross-Cultural Psychology*, 27(2), 231–264.
19. Hazucha, J. F., Hezlett, S. A., Bontems-Wackens, S., & Ronnqvist. 1999. In search of the Euro-manager: Management competencies in France, Germany, Italy, and the United States. In W.H. Mobley, M.J. Gessner & V. Arnold (Eds.), *Advances in global leadership* (Vol. 1, pp. 267–290). Stamford, CT: JAI Press.
20. Javidan, M. & D. Carl. 2004. East meets West. *Journal of Management Studies*, 41:4, June, 665–691; Javidan, M. & Carl, D. 2005. Leadership across cultures: A study of Canadian and Taiwanese executives, *Management International Review*, 45(1), 23–44.
21. House, R. J., Wright, N. S., & Aditya, R. N. 1997. Cross-cultural research on organizational leadership: A critical analysis and a proposed theory. In P. C. Earley & M. Erez (Eds.), *New*

perspectives in international industrial/organizational psychology (pp. 535–625). San Francisco: The New Lexington Press.

22. Chemers, M. M. 1997. An *integrative theory of leadership.* London: Lawrence Erlbaum Associates; Smith, P. B. & Peterson, M. F. 1988. *Leadership, organizations and culture: An event management model.* London: Sage.
23. Shaw, J. B. (1990). A cognitive categorization model for the study of intercultural management. *Academy of Management Review*, 15(4), 626–645.
24. Lord, R. G. & Maher, K. J. 1991. *Leadership and information processing: Linking perceptions and performance* (Vol. 1). Cambridge, MA: Unwin Hyman.
25. House, R. J., Hanges, P. J., Ruiz-Quintanilla, S. A., Dorfman, P. W., Javidan, M., Dickson, M., et al. 1999. Cultural influences on leadership and organizations: Project GLOBE. In W. F. Mobley, M. J. Gessner & V. Arnold (Eds.), *Advances in global leadership* (Vol. 1, pp. 171–233). Stamford, CT: JAI Press.
26. In addition to the aggregated raw (i.e., absolute) scores for CLTs provided in Table 2, we also computed a response bias corrected measure as an integral part of the analysis strategy. We referred to this measure as the relative measure because of a unique property attributed to this procedure. These relative CLT scores indicate the relative importance of each CLT leadership dimension within a person, culture, or culture cluster. This procedure not only removed the cultural response biases, but it also had the advantage of illustrating the differences among the cultures and the clusters. Along with ranking the clusters with absolute CLT scores, we used this relative measure to compare the relative importance of each CLT dimension among cultures. Ranking of clusters using both types of scores are presented in Table 3. We should point out that the correlation between the absolute and relative measures is close *to* perfect—above .90 for all of the CLT leadership dimensions. Computational procedures for this measure are detailed in House et al. 2004.
27. Cullen, J. B. 2002. *Multinational management. A strategic approach.* (2nd ed.). Cincinnati, OH: South-Western Thomson Learning.
28. Bossidy, L. & Charan, R. 2002. Execution: *The discipline of getting things done.* New York: Crown Business Books. p.103.
29. Hallowell, R., Bowen, D., & Knoop, C. 2002. Four Seasons goes to Paris, *Academy of Management Executive*, 16(4), 7–24.
30. Hallowell, Ibid.
31. Dayal-Gulati, A. 2004. Kellogg on China: Strategies for success, Northwestern University Press.
32. De Mente, Boye Lafayette. 2000. *The Chinese have a word for it: The complete guide to Chinese thought and culture.* Chicago, IL. Passport Books.
33. Rosen, R. Global *Literacies.* Simon and Schuster, 2000.
34. Black, J. S. & Gergersen, H. B. 2000. High impact training: Forging leaders for the global frontier. *Human Resource Management Journal*, 39 (2&3), 173–184.
35. Oddou, G., Mendenhall, M. E., & Ritchi, J. B. Leveraging travel as a tool for global leadership development. *Human Resource Management Journal*, 39, 2&3, 159–172.
36. Dastmalchian, A. & Kabasakal, H. 2001. Guest editors, special issue on the Middle East, *Applied Psychology: An International Review.* Vol. 50(4); Javidan, M. & House, R. Spring 2002 Guest editors, special Issue on GLOBE. *Journal of World Business*, Vol. 37, No, 1; Peterson, M. F. & Hunt, J. G. 1997. Overview: International and cross-cultural leadership research (Part II). *Leadership Quarterly*, 8(4), 339–342.
37. For more information, see Mendenhall, M. E. & Stahl, G. K. Expatriate training and development: Where do we go from here? *Human Resource Management Journal*, 39, 2&3, 251–265.
38. Black, J. S., Morrison, A. J., & Gergersen, H. B. 1999. *Global explorers: The next generation of leaders.* New York: Routledge.
39. Dodge, B. 1993. Empowerment and the evolution of learning, *Education and Training.* 35(5), 3–10; Sherman, S. 1995. How tomorrow's best leaders are learning their stuff. *Fortune*, 90–106.
40. Conner, J. Developing the global leaders of tomorrow. *Human Resource Management Journal*, 39, 2&3, 147–157.
41. Black, J. S., Gergersen, H. B., Mendenhall, M. E. & Stroh, L. K. 1999. *Globalizing people through international assignments.* Reading, MA: Addisson-Wesley.

READING 14.3

A Local Perspective to Expatriate Success

Soo Min Toh and Angelo S. DeNisi

Executive Overview

Many expatriate human resource (HR) policies, particularly in the area of compensation, remain rooted in the past because they continue to favor the expatriate over local staff and do not take into account the increasing qualifications and aspirations of these local employees. Inequitable treatment leads to low commitment and poor work performance among local staff. More importantly, inequitable treatment creates tension between local and expatriate employees and causes the local staff to be less willing to be cooperative or supportive of the expatriates with whom they have to work. Without local support, expatriates may experience greater difficulty adjusting to their new jobs and the new environment, which is a contributing factor in the failure of expatriates. To minimize these problems, HR practices of expatriating organizations should focus on providing more equitable compensation for local and expatriate employees, selecting expatriates who are truly worthy of the higher pay, and increasing the transparency of pay practices so that local employees can see the linkage between work inputs and compensation more clearly. Managers at the local organization should emphasize favorable referents for local staff, breed organizational identification among the employees, prepare the local staff for incoming expatriates, and encourage them to assist and mentor incoming expatriates. It is critical that multinational companies (MNCs) are aware that some existing HR practices have potentially unintended negative consequences and that neglecting the impact of these practices on local employees hurts the effectiveness of the organization as well as the ability of expatriates to succeed in their assignment.

A Local Perspective to Expatriate Success

With increasing foreign revenues, multinational companies' (MNCs) need for expatriate assignments shows little signs of slowing down. Maintaining an expatriate is a costly and often complicated process – and if the expatriate fails in his or her assignment, the expatriate exercise becomes even more costly for all involved. Losses and damages resulting from expatriate failure include loss of business and productivity, damage to other employees and relationships with customers, suppliers, and host government officials, as well as the financial and emotional costs borne by the expatriate and his or her family.[1] Given these potential costs, it is imperative that expatriate assignments are managed effectively.

A recent survey released by the U.S. National Foreign Trade Council reported failure to adjust to the foreign cultural environment as a key reason for expatriate failure.[2] MNCs' records for providing sufficient pre-departure training for expatriates and their families have been poor. Expatriates often complain that they are not well prepared for the challenges they face on the assignments. Selection practices have also frequently been criticized for emphasizing technical competence and neglecting critical success factors such as relational skills and cross-cultural competence. Therefore, in addition to providing attractive expatriate packages, many MNCs have worked to improve training and orientation programs for expatriates, and to fine-tune the selection criteria to better match identified critical success factors.

Clearly, the onus for completion of a successful assignment has been primarily on the expatriate, as well as the parent company, whose responsibility has been to engage in various activities that are deemed to facilitate the adjustment of expatriates Whereas these efforts have been met with measured success, many MNCs have overlooked the potential of yet another important avenue to facilitate adjustment. This potential lies in the local or host country staff with whom the expatriates work closely while on assignment. Traditionally, local employees were the expatriate's subordinates, but they are increasingly the coworkers and supervisors of expatriate assignees as well. As we will discuss in the present paper, local staff could be the expatriate's best on-site trainers as expatriates wade in possibly treacherous cultural waters. In the same vein, local staff could also seriously jeopardize the expatriate's ability to carry out his or her assignment by engaging in various counterproductive behaviors at work. Yet, with few exceptions, multinationals overlook the socializing potential of local staff in aiding expatriates in their adjustment and are not cognizant of how the very practices meant to ensure the success of expatriates can also inadvertently lead to their failure.

Given the potential importance of local staff to any multinational, the present paper has three main objectives. First, we identify the HR practices in MNCs that may adversely affect the organizations' effectiveness. Certain types of expatriate HR practices, especially ethnocentric ones, can be perceived as inequitable by local staff and create unforeseen (and unwanted) effects on the local staff's work attitudes and behaviors. Lowered commitment and job satisfaction, as well as counterproductive work behaviors such as absenteeism and turnover, are potential outcomes of ethnocentric HR practices, and can ultimately hurt the effectiveness of the multinational. Second, we demonstrate how violating equity between local and expatriate employees is detrimental to expatriate adjustment. The fates of the two groups of employees are often inextricably linked – the expatriates cannot be successful if their host country counterparts are not. In fact, it seems obvious that expatriates will find it much more difficult to succeed in their assignments without the support of local staff. Unfortunately, ethnocentric HR practices do not create the conditions that would cause such support to be forthcoming. Last, we propose several alternative interventions adopted by companies that have been relatively successful at managing expatriate assignments, which multinationals should consider as means to motivate and retain local staff as well as to better harness the important socializing potential that local staff can offer to expatriates. Hence, our recommendations for the design of HR practices consider their larger effects on all employees in the organization and not merely on any particular subset of employees in the organization. Throughout, we highlight real-life issues faced by multinationals, provide real-life solutions adopted around the globe, and report relevant findings of organizational research.

Local Employees Are Important Too

A critical factor often considered by MNCs when making decisions about where to locate overseas subsidiaries is the availability of qualified local workers. MNCs depend on a qualified local workforce to be effective and this dependence amplifies significantly if it is the MNC's aim to completely localize its overseas subsidiaries. Siemens AG, for example, locates itself worldwide and relies heavily on local workers to achieve its goals – in the U.S. alone it employs over 60,000 Americans, and hires more than 20,000 personnel in China. New research also suggests that local managers can offer more control to the MNC than expatriates can in situations where cultural asymmetries between the headquarters country and the host country are high and the operating environment is risky.[3] Furthermore, if the market that the MNC enters is one where its existing personnel have little relevant knowledge or expertise to effectively run the local subsidiary, local human capital would be especially useful because the local managers speak the local business language and also understand the country's culture and political system better than most expatriates sent to perform the job. Local staff are thus often better equipped than expatriates to penetrate the target market. The experience of MNCs in China, for example, has demonstrated that capable local managers and professionals are indispensable for the success of MNCs because expatriates continue to flounder in unfamiliar territory. Hence, there is little dispute that capable local employees are strategic assets to a MNC.

It is also in host countries like China that we find much discontent among local staff and resentment towards expatriates because often inept expatriates are ostensibly treated as superior relative to the locals in terms of their compensation, benefits, and developmental opportunities.[4] This is especially so when expatriates do not have a clear advantage over the local employees in terms of work qualifications, expertise, or experience. Local staff may feel that they are treated like second-class citizens when working alongside expatriates in their own country, and may resent that fact. They may also perceive expatriates as being sent to be "watchdogs" for headquarters instead of value-added resources. Clearly, this mistrust of and dissatisfaction with the expatriate and the multinational set the stage for a whole host of negative consequences for the multinational, such as lowered productivity and effectiveness and higher rates of turnover and absenteeism. When resentment is high, more extreme counterproductive work behaviors may also ensue, such as theft and sabotage. It is clear that multinationals truly cannot afford to be insensitive to the feelings and opinions of the local staff in their organization.

However, local staff have yet another important part to play. It lies in their potential significance as a valuable socializing agent and facilitator of the expatriate's role in the host unit organization. Most of us are probably able to recall that time when we first started a new job: adjusting to the new environment, new responsibilities, and new relationships were probably made easier if we had received some guidance and support from someone in the early transition stages of our job. This person (or persons) probably had more experience and greater knowledge of the job and environment we were entering into than we did. This person was also often someone holding a similar or higher post than us, who had been in the organization longer than us, and had sufficient history with the organization to understand how things worked or how best to get things done. Organizational research corroborates these experiences by showing very clearly that the stresses related to starting a new job can be assuaged by supportive relationships within the work organization (e.g., coworker, supervisor, mentor). Hence, many organizations apply this principle by adopting mentoring and buddy systems to orient new employees in domestic operations, and the effects have often been very positive. For example, Sun Microsystems Inc. in Palo Alto, California, pairs newcomers with more experienced "SunVisors," while the New York office of PriceWaterhouseCoopers uses a buddy system, as well as more senior coaches, to supplement their formal training and orientation programs.

In some companies, peers and designated mentors are also put through training programs to become effective coaches, and hiring managers attend workshops on getting ready for new employees joining the unit. A U.S.-based company, National City Corp., uses a similar training program where managers are trained to communicate effectively and create supportive environments, and reports that the training is highly successful. Specifically, they report decreased turnover and absenteeism rates and higher productivity, which resulted in annual savings of over a million dollars after implementing the program.[5]

The same principles could and should be applied more widely to the context of the host unit organization where an expatriate assignee needs to learn the ropes of being a new member of the host subsidiary despite possibly having had experience in the parent company. He or she must also quickly become proficient in the performance of his or her job, while at the same time adapting to the unfamiliar surroundings and culture. MNCs like SAS Institute and Intel recognize the importance of expatriates gaining the cooperation of their local counterparts, loyalty from their subordinates, and the trust of their supervisors. Instead of placing the onus solely on the expatriate to develop effective working relationships and strong bonds with the local staff, these organizations adopt buddy systems where local peers act as ad hoc trainers for the expatriate. They also encourage and prepare the receiving managers and local teammates of the expatriate to ensure that the newcomer expatriates are assimilated quickly. Intel, for example, trains managers who are about to receive an expatriate. The training emphasizes ways to integrate and work with groups of people of other cultural backgrounds. With this training, local managers are better equipped to interact with expatriates and are less likely to find expatriates foreboding. Faced with more approachable local counterparts, expatriates are less likely to be isolated by the local staff, and have greater opportunities to learn from them and develop effective work relationships with them.

We will return later to other steps MNCs can employ to help insure that local employees contribute more fully. Before we do, however, we need to address how local staff can contribute to the adjustment and success of expatriates through the informational support, cooperation, and emotional support they provide to those expatriates.

Informational Support

Expatriates face substantial uncertainty regarding their new role in the organization when they first arrive in their new location. They must figure out how things work and what the best way is to approach problems that they may encounter. Any information the expatriates gain regarding the new job, the organization, and the larger cultural environment will help them learn what to expect, how to interpret various stimuli they encounter day-to-day, and what the appropriate behavior is in a given situation. In most situations, expatriates need to have a working knowledge and good understanding of the cultural mores of the organization and the national context in order to be effective. This need is especially critical when the job is novel and challenging for the expatriate, when the culture of the organization and the country is unfamiliar, or when sources of information which the expatriate relied upon in his or her home country are not readily available.

Informational support is also important if the expatriates are sent to host subsidiaries to acquire knowledge and gain cultural competence. Such assignments are increasingly popular as MNCs recognize the importance of gaining international experience among their employees. For example, ABB (Asea Brown Boveri) rotates about 500 managers around the world to different countries every few years to develop a cadre of managers with a global outlook.[6] Similarly, expatriates who are sent to the host location to set up "greenfield" operations will also need to acquire rich local knowledge in order to find sources for raw material, human resources, potential business associates, and potential customers. This necessity has been encountered by many companies that have tried to set up shop in China and found it to be a culturally challenging environment and impossible without local "guanxi," because these social networks are also very rich informational networks. The expatriates may be left out of important decisions and information if they are unable to penetrate existing informational networks.[7]

Of course, the local employees at the host organization would have these different types of information. By virtue of being born and raised in the host country and having been members of the host organization longer than the expatriate, local staff possess the additional experience and understanding of the culture and the organization, and also have developed the necessary network of relationships that could facilitate the conduct of many of the expatriates' tasks. The local staff's advantage is even greater in new markets for the multinational where expatriates are likely to be treading in unfamiliar political, economic, and social waters. If local staff are willing to share their intimate local knowledge with the expatriates, expatriates can set up shop in the host country or learn what they were sent to learn much more successfully. Local staff also possess critical information regarding the cultural mores of the workplace.[8] For example, many Western managers in Beijing report the Chinese culture as being quite incomprehensible and they have great difficulty operating effectively in the Chinese context. Sharing insights about the cultural norms and idiosyncrasies with fledgling expatriates will help them better establish the necessary networks within the organization and facilitate their adjustment to the new organizational and national culture. Knowing what is culturally acceptable and appropriate behavior is also critical for expatriates to avoid offending local coworkers, subordinates, and supervisors. As in the case of a *Fortune* 100 company, it was reported that its expatriates across 19 worldwide locations demonstrated greater adjustment to their work and social interactions when they had access to on-site host country mentors.[9] Clearly, the informational support from local staff is integral to an expatriate's ability to succeed.

Paradoxically, informational support from local staff most critical to the successful experience of the expatriate is also likely to be more difficult to gain. Many local staff have traditionally expected to learn from expatriates, because the expatriates are often viewed to be the experts with specialized knowledge, sent to the host unit to lead local staff rather than to learn from them. When these expectations are coupled with the fact that expatriates often earn much more than the local staff, the local employees may feel resentful. This resentment may be expressed by shutting out expatriates from informational networks since they may feel that doing so, and helping expatriates out, are not really part of their job requirement. As a result, the expatriates and the organization lose a valuable source of country and organizational information. Thus, it is important that the practices of the multinational do not breed resentment, but encourage the sharing of information between local staff and expatriates.

Cooperation

Expatriates sent to lead subsidiaries in various capacities will find gaining the local staff's cooperation indispensable to the performance of their job. Without the following of local subordinates and the cooperation of other local managers – neither of which expatriates should erroneously take for granted – expatriates may find their leadership role seriously frustrated and undermined. Those sent to manage local employees quickly lose credibility if they appear to have little local understanding or lack endorsement from other local staff managers. Also, if expatriates do not become part of the social network, decisions may be made without the full input and acceptance of the local employees. With the increased use of teams, expatriates who are not well integrated and accepted by their local staff colleagues are less likely to perform the job well or be satisfied with work relationships within the team. In the case of expatriates sent to transfer knowledge and expertise to local staff and train future local managers, these expatriates will not be successful if local staff are not receptive to their presence in the host organization and are unwilling to learn from them.

Poor expatriate-local relations may also lead to other counterproductive work behaviors ranging from tardiness and absenteeism to more extreme behaviors such as insubordination, withholding of vital information, and even sabotage. For example, local American executives admit that they would continue to produce data with errors because they are not willing to work around the clock to make it error free no matter what their Japanese bosses say; and local Chinese managers deliberately exclude the expatriate manager whom they view as an outsider in the making of major decisions.[10] A top manager from a Swedish-Swiss MNC recounts how Singaporean employees deliberately did not alert an expatriate manager of a bad decision because the expatriate simply "should know better." These problems could have been avoided if expatriates had been able to gain the local staff's cooperation or if the organization had ways in which to encourage and reward cooperation.

Emotional Support

Whereas the importance of the spouse's emotional and moral support has been recognized in research and practice, the role of local staff as a source of emotional support for expatriates has not been widely regarded as important. However, research in newcomer adjustment finds unequivocal evidence for the importance of supportive work relationships as well. Emotional support helps a person to believe that he or she is cared for, esteemed, valued, and belongs to a network of communication and mutual obligation.[11] It includes the friendships that provide emotional reassurance, or instrumental aid in dealing with stressful situations. No doubt, being a newcomer in a new organization or a newcomer in a foreign country can be a highly stressful experience. But with the support of others in the organization, the newcomer can better make the transition to the new job and situation. We see evidence of this in a group of expatriates in Hong Kong, where expatriates' level of adjustment was significantly higher when support was available from their local coworkers than if such support was not available.[12]

According to existing research, even if actual support is not needed or sought after, the mere knowledge of the existence and availability of such support for the newcomer can be quite reassuring, and in turn can reduce the level of stress experienced by the individual. Thus, although the expatriate may never encounter the need to confide in local staff, just knowing that local staff are available and willing confidants alleviates some of the stress the expatriate faces. Furthermore, having supportive relationships in the organization can create a stronger sense of belonging for expatriates. Expatriates feel like they "fit in" with their local colleagues better and thus enjoy greater levels of work satisfaction and commitment to the host organization. The lack of such support could, on the other hand, hinder the expatriate's adjustment. Expatriates in U.S. and Europe based multinationals reported lower levels of commitment and adjustment when they felt that they were being ostracized by their local colleagues.[13] The lack of deep friendships is especially disappointing for expatriates of more relationship-oriented cultures. For example, Korean expatriates in the U.S. find their American counterparts friendly on a superficial level, but quite unwilling to develop stronger relationships. This often results in hurt feelings, disappointment, and a sense of isolation. The expatriates, in turn, become reluctant to socialize with the native-born Americans because they feel that they do not understand them and therefore seek solace through the friendships with the other expatriates.[14] The distancing of expatriate groups ultimately hurts the overall adjustment of expatriates, and also negatively affects their job performance and their ability and willingness to learn from their local counterparts.

However, just as is the case with informational support and cooperation, providing care and support to another employee is not usually specified in one's job description.

Forming supportive relationships or friendships with the expatriates they work with is not required by local staff's jobs and would have to occur on their own initiative. Given suitable circumstances, local staff may be willing to go out of their way to support expatriates and help socialize them during their time of transition along the dimensions discussed. Unfortunately, several conditions are prevalent in multinational organizations that could cause local staff to be unwilling socializing agents. We discuss these factors next, and highlight how HR policies can inadvertently discourage the socializing role of local staff.

HR Practices that Discourage the Socializing Role of Local Employees

What would determine whether local staff chose to exhibit or withhold critical socializing behaviors? Empathy is a critical driving force for an employee's decision to help a fellow coworker.[15] Employees who like and care about their coworker are more likely to provide help on their own accord, whenever help is needed by the coworker. Employees in cohesive work groups, or groups with enhanced positive relationships among members, are more likely to spontaneously help out than employees in less cohesive groups. Similarly, local staff who empathize and have positive feelings towards their expatriate coworkers will be more willing to help expatriates in the course of their work if expatriates appear to need it.

Many HR practices adopted by MNCs have the potential to indirectly hurt the establishment of cohesiveness and rapport between expatriates and local staff. Ethnocentric HR practices that favor the expatriate over local staff, whether intentionally or unintentionally, send a message to local staff that they are less valued than the expatriates. As a result, local staff are less likely to feel friendly or supportive towards expatriates who receive favorable treatment for reasons that may not always seem obvious or acceptable. The inequitable treatment also draws clear lines between local staff and expatriates, creating an intergroup mentality where local staff view expatriates as "outsiders" and expatriates remain in their exclusive expatriate cliques. The clear differentials could reinforce us-versus-them stereotypes, increase friction and frustration, and could create further misunderstandings and conflict.[16] All of these factors would make it unlikely that local staff will feel empathetic towards their expatriate counterparts or go out of their way to help them out when needed. These differentiating HR practices, which we will discuss, include compensation, selection and promotion, and training.

Compensation

A potentially long-standing sore point between expatriates and local staff has been the way both parties are compensated relative to each other. Many multinational organizations seek to minimize expatriate failure by providing expatriates with enough incentives to take on and remain on the assignment until the task is completed. When expatriates are transferred to the host country organization, they expect that the relocation will not be disadvantageous to them in any way, and may in fact be beneficial to their future with the company. According to the 1997–98 North American Survey of International Assignment Policies and Practices published by Organization Resources Counselors Inc. (ORC), the most popular approach to compensating expatriates is still the "balance-sheet approach." The balance sheet approach sets salary according to the base pay and benefits of their home country, plus various allowances (e.g., cost-of-living, housing standard, hardship) and tax equalization. With the inclusion of the various allowances and benefits, the relocation usually results in a financial gain for expatriates, especially if the relocation involves moving to a host location with a higher cost of living.

Even though the balance sheet approach has several advantages, it is particularly problematic for maintaining internal equity among local staff and expatriates in the host unit organization. Expatriates who come from a country of higher standards of living are likely to have a base pay that is much higher than that of the local staff, in addition to the various allowances and incentives awarded to the expatriates for taking on the assignment. When expatriates are moved to a destination with a high cost of living such as Tokyo or London, MNCs usually make significant adjustments to the expatriates' total compensation package to allow the expatriate to maintain a standard of living comparable to that which they would have enjoyed in their home country.

Few companies attempt to replicate local peers' pay in the assignment location, and expatriates are often lavishly rewarded with various perks that are not available to the locals. Consequently, it is not unusual to find cases of differentiation where a local manager's total compensation forms only a fraction of the expatriate's pay package.[17] For example, expatriates of a German chemical company in China are paid an average of $300,000 a year, including salary, housing, education of children and other benefits, but the local managers are paid only 10–20 percent as much.[18] Such significant wage discrepancies will not be viewed as justified by the local staff if they do not view the expatriates as being more qualified and deserving of higher pay. These discrepancies can lead to strained relationships between the two groups of employees, making it unlikely that the local staff will go out of their way to help out an expatriate who may be having difficulties adjusting to the new job and environment. Worse, these discrepancies can result in resentment, leading the local staff to be unwilling to cooperate with the expatriate on any aspect of the assignment, and potentially frustrating the expatriate's efforts to be successful. Thus, the very compensation practices often put in place to help ensure expatriate success may actually jeopardize it instead.

Selection, Promotion, & Training

Ethnocentric HR practices can also be found in selection, promotion, and training. In many MNCs, the staffing of top positions in overseas units continues to be reserved for individuals from the parent country company. This is especially true when headquarters believes that having a parent country expatriate at the helm has some strategic value. Frequently, for control purposes, parent companies prefer their own nationals to hold those positions whether or not they are the necessarily the best-qualified persons for the job. It becomes frustrating for local staff when they view expatriates getting choice positions while a similarly qualified local gets passed over. Singaporean managers, for example, often report being disadvantaged when competing against parent company expatriates for opportunities in training and promotion.[19] Local managers in Japanese corporations' overseas subsidiaries recognize that they would have to be exceptional to be selected over a Japanese manager for a high level post. Such ethnocentric practices often come at the expense of the promotion and development of capable local staff, further perpetuating the large wage discrepancies between local staff and expatriates and creating resentment among them.[20] Feeling like they have little future in an organization that treats them as second-class citizens, local staff display little loyalty towards the host organization and are more likely to leave when better job opportunities arise elsewhere.

So What Has Changed?

The HR practices we have described have generally been in place for quite some time, yet they have not always resulted in the negative consequences we are suggesting in this article.[21] The reason for this is that many aspects of globalization have changed, but the HR practices have not changed accordingly. One thing that has changed is the relative competence of expatriates versus local staff.

The basis for much of the global economy has it roots in colonialism. From the earliest days of colonization, the home country was significantly more developed and had superior resources relative to the overseas host (colony) destinations. This easily led to the practice whereby managers from Western multinationals were sent to Asia, South America, and other locations to fill needs in foreign operations that could not be satisfied with local labor, and provide a source of much desired control over the foreign operations. Local staff would have been unlikely to view themselves as comparable to expatriates because of the vast differences in backgrounds, qualifications, and experience. Thus, local staff were more accepting of expatriates being managers and of the privileges they enjoyed.[22] They may also have already been quite satisfied with the relatively favorable remuneration they received compared to their previous job or their present alternatives. One study found that Chinese managers felt fairly treated by their organization because they perceived themselves to be better off compared to other locals in the same company or in other international joint ventures, even though they were worse off than the expatriates in their organization.[23] We also find this situation outside multinational organizations – in universities, for example, among professors and trainers who are sent to places such as Asia to team-teach courses where they receive much higher salaries than their local counterparts.[24]

The new reality, however, presents quite a different scenario. Popular host countries in the Asia Pacific region, such as China, India, Malaysia, and Singapore are no longer merely sources of cheap labor, but the homes of some of the most competitive workforces in the world with high work aspirations.[25] The gap between the parent and host countries in terms of level of economic development has narrowed and the local staff are often trained in many of the same institutions as the expatriates. They are increasingly similar to expatriates in qualifications, and thus are more often coworkers, rather than merely subordinates, of expatriates. These locals are progressively more fluent in English, are trained in the West or in Western managerial ideology, and on top of that have an advantage over expatriates with their intimate understanding of the local culture and practices.[26] They are also less likely to encounter the adjustment and commitment issues faced by expatriates. Accordingly, their perceptions and expectations of how they should be treated by the organization change. Many Russian managers feel that they are generally better educated and cultured than their Western peers and expect to be treated similarly to the expatriates. As a result, the acute pay discrepancies that traditionally occur are now quite unacceptable in far more situations than before.

In addition, international assignments are increasingly treated by MNCs as a key developmental activity for their personnel and future executives. Expatriates are posted overseas to gain international experience and learn new processes that are unique to the host organization.[27] This could be a form of on-the-job training for expatriate managers as they learn how to operate effectively in a different environment. Thus, these expatriates are sent to learn from the local staff. When local staff perceive expatriates as not possessing any unique or specialized skill above what they themselves possess, or may in fact know more about the task that the expatriates and end up being the person the expatriate has to lean on to perform the expatriate's job, the large wage discrepancies between them quickly become objectionable.[28] In other words, if expatriates are viewed to be less qualified than the local staff in the organization, the extra privileges awarded to them will be viewed by the local staff as unfair and unacceptable.

Interestingly, despite the changes that have been occurring, we find that cultural differences sometimes mitigate the problems we highlight in this article, i.e., the reaction to inequity is not universal. Cultures differ in their sensitivity to inequity. Fairness is defined differently by people of different cultures. Some cultures, such as many Asian and Latin cultures, prefer rewards to be allocated based on seniority or need, rather than equity.[29] The importance and value placed on various forms of rewards also differs. Monetary rewards are often not necessarily the most valued. Thus, salary differences, per se, may not be as important to local staff as significant differences in status or other benefits such as housing, medical, and transportation. In certain economies, such as that of Russia, where commodities are often more valuable than money, differentials in salaries are likely to be less undesirable and offensive than differentials in prized commodities. In collective societies, harmony may take precedence over pay equity. We often find that the assumed "same job same pay" mentality is not prevalent among local staff in the organizations of various host countries. As such, local staff's reactions to compensation differentials and differences in treatment and opportunities vary according to the cultural values that they hold and the problems that we suggest to result from differential treatment are not necessarily universal.

What Can Organizations Do?

Thus far, we have described a situation where expatriates need the help and support of local staff, but where multinational HR policies may be working to reduce the willingness of the local staff to do so. Although there may be exceptions, as noted above, any such unwillingness on the part of local staff will certainly be unacceptable in the long run. But, even in cases where local staff are sensitive to pay differentials, there are some steps a multinational firm could take to minimize this problem. Specifically, we propose seven recommendations for MNCs to consider (see Table 1): 1) change existing compensation practices; 2) select expatriates more carefully; 3) use transparent procedures to determine pay and promotion; 4) emphasize favorable comparative referents; 5) breed organizational identification; 6) prepare local staff; and 7) use and reward local staff buddies or mentors. We will discuss each of these in greater detail.

Change Existing Expatriate Compensation Practices

As noted, many multinational firms have adopted HR practices that serve to differentiate expatriates from local staff which are often inequitable from the perspective of the local staff. Clearly, if a firm minimizes the differential treatment between expatriates and local staff, the perceptions of inequity are likely to diminish. However, less than generous incentives for expatriates may deter employees from taking on overseas assignments, and thus expatriate packages are quite resistant to change. Many of the large MNCs, such as the traditional manufacturing enterprises, have become too large, complex, and entrenched in their existing practices to effect changes to compensation policies easily. Thus, even though the benefits of a more flexible approach are widely recognized, a 2000 PriceWaterhouseCoopers survey of 270 European multinational organizations reported that only 7 percent of the companies surveyed adopted such an approach. Furthermore, expatriates still tend to expect favorable compensation packages for their relocation. For example, expatriate managers of 49 Taiwanese multinationals reported that the compensation package was the most important factor in deciding whether or not to relocate internationally.[30] Without favorable remuneration, organizations will have trouble finding enough interested employees to take on overseas postings.

In time, change should become easier as expatriates come to view overseas assignment as a valuable part of their portfolio and become willing parties to the assignment even without lavish compensation packages. However, many expatriates still have concerns over their career progression while they are away on assignment, as well as having a suitable job and promising career upon repatriation.[31] The truth of the matter is, most multinationals do not guarantee a job upon return and do not counsel repatriates when they come home.[32] Hence, we find that employees sometimes view overseas assignments as a career graveyard, and that organizations are forced to provide attractive incentives to convince employees to accept long-term overseas assignments. If, however, MNCs develop better strategies for managing the careers of expatriates, including specific plans for repatriation prior to the assignment, expatriates may be more willing to forego lavish compensation packages and view assignments as a benefit by itself.

More companies have also turned to paying expatriates at host country levels (localization) or adopting more flexible approaches for compensating their employees in order to reduce their wage bills and lower pay discrepancies between expatriates and locals.[33] Many companies, such as Nokia Asia Pacific, localize their expatriate employees after a certain number of years in the host country whereby the employee takes on the same pay package as would a local employee. Companies like Deloitte & Touche, National Semiconductor, and Towers Perrin have also started on paying for performance programs, varying compensation packages based on assignment length and type, and using more sophisticated measures to calculate cost-of-living differences.[34] As a result, discrepancies between expatriates and local staff may be reduced. Also, more and more multinational companies are using short-term assignments and extended business trips, as opposed to long-term expatriate assignments, thus avoiding the need to pay excessive benefits and adjustments to the expatriate. We see this trend as being quite positive, and as having the potential to truly reduce resentment among the local staff.

Yet we recognize that there is only so much an organization can do to adjust these HR policies, especially in the short run, since most organizations must still somehow induce managers to accept overseas assignments, or at least assure them that they will not suffer as a result of those assignments. Eventually, salary localization policies and increased reliance upon short-term assignments may make it easier to adopt HR practices that treat expatriates and local staff the same. Expatriates sent overseas for developmental reasons should not necessarily expect a significant pay adjustment since the stint is usually short-term and potentially beneficial for the employee. For now, though, expatriate HR practices, especially in the area of compensation, will probably continue to favor expatriates over local staff. As such, MNCs must turn to other means to overcome the negative effects of internally inequitable expatriate compensation packages.

Select More Carefully

One alternative to changing compensation practices in order to reduce problems caused by perceived inequity is to

Table 1 How to Improve Expatriate-Local Relations

At the headquarters of the organization:

1. *Change Existing Compensation Policies* – Pay expatriates salaries more in line with local employees. But, in order to do this, the organization should:
   a. Develop better plans for repatriation to assure expatriates that they will get comparable jobs upon return.
   b. If overseas assignments are truly valued as a developmental activity, include procedures so that they can be rewarded.
– In the end, the real question is "Will managers still accept expatriate assignments?" If the answer is "no," then the organization must consider alternatives.

2. *Select More Carefully* – Ensure that expatriates are qualified to perform the jobs expected of them at a level consistent with the pay they will receive. But this will require the organization to:
   a. Make sure that expatriate managers have social as well as technical skills needed.
   b. See if there are local employees who are equally qualified. If so, are they paid comparably?
   c. Communicate performance expectations and criteria for success clearly to the expatriate.
– There will be fewer problems if host country nationals can see clear evidence that the expatriate is "worth" what he or she is paid.

3. *Use Transparent Pay and Promotion Policies* – Develop pay policies that are viewed as fair and that are clear to all involved. But this requires the organization to:
   a. Actually develop pay policies that can stand scrutiny by local employees as well as by home country employees.
   b. Communicate pay policies as well as the basis for expatriate compensation rates (clear statement of hardships and barriers to overcome).
– If host country nationals come to see that the fact that they are paid less than expatriates is based on fair procedures, they will be less resentful.

At the host country site:

4. *Emphasize Favorable Referents* - Identify alternative referent persons for host country national comparisons instead of the expatriate manager. But this requires that the organization should:
   a. Determine that such reasonable comparison others exist and make them public.
   b. Work to make expatriates less salient as referents.
– If host country nationals can be convinced to compare their pay (and treatment) to other employees in their country, instead of expatriates, they will be more satisfied with their conditions.

5. *Breed Organizational Identification* – Build a single organizational identity instead of allowing an "us vs. them" mentality to develop. But, for this to happen, the organization must:
   a. Develop a superordinate corporate identity strong enough to overcome identification based on nationality.
   b. Insure that host country nationals have access to various organizational "symbols" such as a company car or parking spaces.
   c. Increase the number and frequency of experiences that expatriates and host country national share.
   d. Develop common goals for host country nationals and expatriates to work towards.
– If host country nationals develop a strong corporate identity they will work harder towards company goals and be less concerned about comparisons within the company.

6. *Prepare Local Staff* - The local employees should be trained and oriented to deal with the incoming expatriates in much the same way as expatriates are often trained to deal with locals. But this would require the company to:
   a. Spend resources on training and orientation for employees who usually do not receive such attention.
– The entire expatriate assignment process requires adjustment and consideration on the part of everyone involved, and if local employees could be trained to know more about the culture of incoming expatriates, this would make the process easier.

7. *Use and Reward Local Mentors* - Identifying mentoring expatriates as part of the local employee's job, and then rewarding such behavior will make it more likely to occur. But this would require the company to:
   a. Recognize the important role local staff play in the success of expatriates.
   b. Recognize that, normally, local staff behavior aimed at helping expatriates adjust, is exhibited on a purely voluntary basis.
   c. Actually reward local staff for behaviors that help expatriates succeed.
– This lies at the heart of our arguments about the importance of local employees. They are critical to expatriate success, but this fact must be recognized by organizations and encouraged as well as rewarded.

ensure that the expatriates MNCs send overseas are in fact suitably qualified to perform the job in question and deserving of any higher pay they receive. As noted, expatriates encounter resentment if they are viewed as overpaid by local staff (i.e., being equally or under qualified for the position they hold in the host unit, but at the same time being paid more than a local holding the same position). If expatriates demonstrate competence worthy of higher pay, local staff will be less dissatisfied. Many experts suggest that it is important to select expatriates who not only have the technical knowledge, but also the social and cultural skills needed to be effective in a different culture. Expatriates equipped with good communication skills will be able to integrate themselves better into the new culture and work more effectively with local staff. The European division of ICI, a British chemicals company, selects individuals who are good at getting along with colleagues at home because this is usually a good predictor of how much effort they will put in building understanding and trust with local staff.[35] Thus, adopting selection techniques that takes into consideration these "soft skills," and prepare expatriates adequately for the assignment and all the challenges that it entails is a highly pertinent measure that MNCs could take.

At the same time, MNCs should make the criteria and procedures for selecting candidates to hold high level positions in the host unit as clear as possible. Unambiguously stated criteria and procedures could reduce perceptions of nepotism. Seeking and utilizing input from local staff in making assignment decisions can be helpful for selecting the appropriate candidate, and could increase the legitimacy of the expatriate assignee in the local staff's eyes. Where suitable, other qualified local staff should also be allowed to compete for promotions alongside expatriates. This creates opportunities for local staff to gain desirable jobs within the organization and debunk any views of favoritism in the organization. Local staff who do compete for the promotion should be kept informed throughout the process. Transparency of the selection and promotion procedures is especially important if the local employee is not selected because local staff might feel that they have been unfairly rejected. In such instances, it is especially imperative that management treats the rejected applicant with much sensitivity and dignity to avoid hurt feelings or misunderstandings.

Use Transparent Procedures to Determine Pay

In addition to using open and rigorous selection procedures, MNCs should also ensure that the procedures used to determine pay packages for expatriates and local staff be transparent and fair. If local staff view the procedures used to arrive at the pay packages (and selection, promotion, and training decisions) as legitimate, receive reasonable explanations and justifications for the discrepancies, and feel that their concerns and needs are treated with care and sensitivity by the organization, their dissatisfaction with any inequity may be reduced.[36] Local staff often do not realize the challenges faced and sacrifices made by expatriates. To that effect, multinational organizations should be proactive in explaining the purpose of sending expatriates and establishing and communicating clear and fair procedures to local staff. If reward discrepancies have to persist, then it is imperative that organizations make an extra effort to be sensitive to the reactions of the local staff and also to treat them with the necessary dignity and respect.

Emphasize Favorable Comparative Referents

Organizations can also reduce the negative perceptions held by local staff by emphasizing the ways in which local staff are better off compared to other groups of employees. As mentioned earlier, one study found that locals in a Hong Kong joint venture were not disturbed by having lower wages than expatriates because they were cognizant of how much better off they were compared to other Chinese employed by local firms. Often, even though local staff feel disadvantaged relative to the expatriates in their organization, they may still regard their higher wages, greater autonomy, and better opportunities for career development as very attractive aspects of being employed by a MNC. Furthermore, if expatriates are a less prominent comparative referent in local staff's minds, and local staff are satisfied with other aspects of their jobs, local staff react less negatively to the inequity between themselves and the expatriates. MNCs can redirect local staff's attention away from expatriates by publishing statistics that emphasize the advantages these employees have in terms of their pay packages, investments in training and development, and other employee benefits relative to employees of other local organizations or other industry competitors. In general, MNCs have access to a large pool of resources to make more investments in their human resources, which are not matched by local enterprises. Clearly, some careful impression management goes a long way in helping multinational organizations avoid the negative consequences we have suggested.

Breed Organizational Identification

Us-versus-them perceptions by local staff can be minimized by emphasizing the corporate identity to local staff so that expatriates are viewed less as outsiders, but fellow members of the larger, more inclusive organizational group. This process is known as "recategorization," where enhancing the prominence of an overarching identity reduces the prominence of a lower level group identity. In the case of the host unit, emphasizing organizational identity over national identity may reduce the local staff's likelihood of viewing an expatriate in the organization as someone they are competing against for organizational rewards.[37] Emphasizing the superordinate identity has another advantage of raising organizational commitment, and drawing attention away from contentious tendencies within the organization to focus on extra-organizational referents, such as the organization's competitors. In other words, intergroup comparisons can be diverted to occur across organizations (e.g., industry competitors), rather than within the organization between the local staff and the expatriates. As far as possible, organizations should minimize referring to expatriates as a separate group from local staff. Distinctions in day-to-day operations should be avoided and expatriates integrated to the local unit as much as possible so that they are perceptibly less different from the local staff. Organizational symbols, such as office space, parking spaces, common cafeterias, and informal socializing grounds act as subtle yet strong signals to local staff about how much distinction the organization makes between the two groups, and thus should be minimized.

Organizational identification can also be developed by putting both local staff and expatriates together in orientation and training programs. The shared experiences help develop a sense of cohesiveness. Examples of this type of socialization include McDonald's policy of having all restaurant managers attend Hamburger University, or joint training exercises for NATO military units. In each case, the process builds a strong corporate identity that could transcend other types of group identities (e.g., nationality) by putting employees through similar socialization experiences.

Increasing the interactions between expatriates and local staff as well as emphasizing common work goals can also breed organizational identification and minimize the perception of expatriates as outsiders. By having more frequent interactions with their expatriate colleagues, local staff have more opportunities to learn about each expatriate personally and develop more accurate understanding of the expatriates with whom they work. In this way, pre-existing stereotypes may be refuted and the locals can come view expatriates more as "one of us" rather than "one of them." Organizing expatriates and local staff in teams, working together to achieve common objectives, can help local staff and expatriates be more attuned to a common fate shared between them. When local staff perceive themselves and the expatriates to be working towards the same overarching goal(s), the prominence of the national boundaries may diminish and the perception of expatriates as part of the organization may heighten. As local staff begin to view expatriates as part of their ingroup, they will also be more likely to support and cooperate with them.

Prepare Local Staff

MNCs should also provide both expatriates and local staff adequate training in cross-cultural communication and understanding. Being able to communicate effectively with each other is a key step in developing supportive relationships. Local staff, as well as the expatriates, need to be equipped with the necessary knowledge and skills to interact and work effectively with foreign nationals. Research suggests that large cross-cultural differences pose significant obstacles to the effective transfer of knowledge between locals and expatriates.[38] Thus, when Tellabs acquired Helsinki-based Martis Oy, all foreign executives underwent training on conducting business meetings, developing supervisory-subordinate relationships, and communicating effectively. Many Finnish engineers were also sent to headquarters to learn how to interface with their American colleagues and other employees.[39]

People make assumptions about an individual's intelligence, competence, and even social class based on how the individual speaks and carries him or herself. Cultural sensitivity training will help avoid misunderstandings, educate both local staff and expatriates on the appropriate behaviors, and dispel whatever negative stereotypes and assumptions they have about each other. In an experimental study of American host country managers confronted with Japanese managers, it was found that the extent to which the American managers' expectations of the Japanese managers' behaviors were met influenced subsequent intentions to trust them and to associate with them.[40] The researchers concluded that it is important to equip receiving local managers with realistic expectations of foreign managerial behavior in order for more positive relationships to be developed between them.

Some MNCs make the mistake of not carrying out cultural training based on the fact that the host country and the expatriates share the same language. However, even if expatriates and local staff speak the same language, misunderstandings can still occur. The director of an international provider of international assignment support programs recounts how a Texan in the UK came across to her British colleagues as arrogant and vulgar because she talked too loud and slowly, and was prematurely familiar with her colleagues both verbally and in her body language.[41] As a result, she was unable to fit in with her work group. It is important that organizations do not overlook the significance of preparing both the expatriates and the local staff for cross-cultural encounters at work.

Use and Reward Local Buddies or Mentors

As noted before, there is often no formal requirement or reward for local staff to facilitate the adjustment of expatriates and thus helping expatriates out or being cooperative needs to stem from their own initiative. To avoid leaving such behaviors to chance, MNCs could provide formal incentives to local staff for displaying cooperative and supportive behaviors towards expatriates. MNCs could pair up expatriates with local staff for a period of time and reward local staff involved in socializing newcomer expatriates, or for participating in some sort of buddy program that facilitates the expatriate's entry to the host unit. In this way, local staff's socializing behaviors are formalized and rewarded, and the help that expatriates need from local staff is better ensured. MNCs should also make efforts to involve local staff in the planning and facilitation of an expatriate's transition. This not only boosts local staff morale but also improves the chances of expatriate success.[42] Getting the local staff involved in the process also increases the transparency of the policies surrounding expatriation and the local staff who themselves are interested in developing their international experience could gain from being in continuous contact with incoming expatriates. This informational exchange greatly benefits both parties.

To ensure that information is shared with expatriates, SAS Institute's regional headquarters in Heidelberg, Germany, assigns insider buddies to expatriate newcomers to help the newcomer to be self-sufficient and reach high levels of productivity as quickly as possible. These buddies are volunteers with no explicit or formal obligations. They help listen and answer simple questions expatriates may have, offer simple advice, and help point expatriates in the right direction on work and non-work matters. Similarly, at Korean multinational semiconductor manufacturer Samsung's Texas computer memory chip factory, each incoming expatriate is paired with an American counterpart upon arriving at Austin. These "buddies" help the Korean expatriates with work and with their downtime. The locals take the Korean workers on nights out, lunch meetings, and weekend trips.[43] With the help of local staff who are willing to share information with expatriates, the expatriates enjoy greater success in their efforts to adjust to their work demands and cultural challenges.[44]

The Local Perspective

In this paper we have discussed how HR practices designed to help and encourage expatriates can produce negative reactions by the local staff. We believe that this possibility has been largely overlooked because multinationals have tended to focus more on the expatriates than on the locals. We also believe, however, that the changing competitive landscape, the development of human capital in local markets, and the importance of cooperation and teamwork in a global economy, all point to a need to increase the attention paid to the local workforce. No global organization can hope to be truly competitive unless it fully utilizes its entire workforce. Furthermore, as we have pointed out in this paper, local staff are important, not only in their own right as potentially productive members of the organization, but also as a source of support and help for expatriate managers sent to their country.

What does this mean? It means that multinational organizations must pay attention to and gather information on the attitudes, goals and feelings of the local staff. It also means that organizations need to develop programs to increase the motivation and commitment of those local employees. Many managers of MNCs view local staff as dispensable – perhaps more so now than before. Local staff are still likely to believe that the multinational pays better and treats employees better than the alternatives, and would still be motivated and committed to the organization. However, we believe that a local perspective means that the MNC will no longer take those things for granted. Instead, the MNC will recognize that the local staff have alternatives in third-party countries, or with other MNCs, and that the organization needs to work at motivation and commitment of the local staff. Of course, this perspective would also require the MNC to consider the impact upon local staff of any proposed policy, and weigh this impact when deciding whether or not to implement these programs. We believe it is critical that MNCs adopt such a perspective in order to be successful in the future.

Conclusions

The present paper represents a call for attention to be paid to local staff. We began by pointing out how, although local staff employees are increasingly well-trained and well-educated, many HR policies for expatriates still favor expatriates over local staff, and so do not recognize these accomplishments. We also discuss how local staff could compare their outcomes to those of the expatriates and how this could result in local staff believing they are being treated unfairly. These beliefs could then result in those local employees withholding advice and support which, while not required as part of the local employee's job, are important for the ultimate success of the expatriate.

But, as we also note, a number of global companies are coming to recognize the importance of local staff, and are implementing programs designed to improve commitment and perceptions of fairness by those local employees. We also suggest a number of other interventions and programs which might help local staff feel appreciated, fairly treated, and committed to the larger organization. Several of these suggestions mirror those implemented by some more innovative multinationals, and we discuss these examples as well.

Therefore, we end by reiterating the message that local staff is important and must be recognized as such by MNCs. We believe that many organizations are coming to recognize this and act accordingly, but we also believe that there is much more that can be done. We believe that it is increasingly clear that the effective management of local staff will be a key component of effective competition in the coming years.

Source: Academy of Management Executive, 19, (1), 132–146 (2005). Reprinted by permission.

Acknowledgements

We thank the Editor Bob Ford, Jim Wilkerson, Sonia Chainini, and the two anonymous reviewers for their input.

ENDNOTES

1. Vatikiotis, M., Clifford, M., & McBeth, J. 1994. The lure of Asia. *Far Eastern Economic Review.* 157(5): 32–34.
2. Cited from Swaak. R. A. 1995. Expatriate failures: Too many, too much cost, too little planning. *Compensation and Benefits Review,* 27(6): 47–55. Over 90 percent of the respondents cited failure to adjust as the key reason for expatriate failure.
3. Volkmar, J. A. 2003. Context and control in foreign subsidiaries: Making a case for the host country national manager. *Journal of Leadership and Organizational Studies,* 10(1): 93–105.
4. Li, L. & Kleiner, B. H. 2001. Expatriate-local relationships and organizational effectiveness: A study of multinational companies in China. *Management Research News,* 24(3/4): 49–55.
5. Hammers, M. 2003. Quashing quick quits. *Workforce,* 82(5): 50.
6. Deresky, H. 2002. *Global management: Strategic and interpersonal.* Upper Saddle River: New Jersey. Prentice Hall.
7. Bjorkman, L. & Schaap, A. 1994. Outsiders in the Middle Kingdom: Expatriate managers in Chinese-Western joint ventures. *European Management Journal,* 12(2): 147–153.

8. Black, J. S., Mendenhall, M., & Oddou, G. 1991. Toward a comprehensive model of international adjustment: An integration of multiple theoretical perspectives. *Academy of Management Review*, 16(2): 291–317.
9. Feldman, D. C. & Bolino, M. C. 1999. The impact of on-site mentoring on expatriate socialization: A structural equation modeling approach. *International Journal of Human Resource Management*, 10(1): 54–71.
10. Li & Kleiner, op. cit.; Bjorkman & Schaap, op. cit.
11. Fisher, C. D. 1985. Social support and adjustment to work: A longitudinal study. *Journal of Management*, 11(3): 39–53; Kirmeyer, S. L. & Lin, T. R. 1987. Social support: Its relationship to observed communication with peers and superiors. *Academy of Management Journal*, 30(1): 138–151.
12. Aryee, S. & Stone, R. J. 1996. Work experiences, work adjustment and psychological well-being of expatriate employees in Hong Kong. *International Journal of Human Resource Management* , 7 (1): 150–162.
13. Florkowski G. W. & Fogel, D. S. 1999. Expatriate adjustment and commitment: The role of host-unit treatment. *International Journal of Human Resource Management*, 10(5): 783–807.
14. Solomon, C. M. 1997. Destination USA. *Workforce*, April: 18–22.
15. Barr, S. H. & Pawar, B. S. 1995. Organizational citizenship behavior: Domain specifications for three middle range theories. *Academy of Management Best Paper Proceedings*, 302–306.
16. Schneider, S. C. & Barsoux, J-L. 2003. *Managing Across Cultures.* 2nd Edition. Essex: England. Prentice Hall.
17. For more on expatriate pay policies, how they are developed and what they mean for pay differentials, see Beamish, P. 1998. Equity joint ventures in China: Compensation and motivation. *Ivey Business Quarterly*, 63(1): 67–68; Dowling, P., Welch, D. E., & Schuler, R. S. 1999. *International human resource management: Managing people in a multinational context.* Cincinnati, South-Western College; Hodgetts, R. M. & Luthans, F. 1993. U.S. multinationals' expatriate compensation strategies. *Compensation & Benefits Review*, 25(1): 57–62; Peters, S. 1994. Expatriates' pay exceeds nationals' in Central and Eastern Europe. *Personnel Journal*, 73(5): 19–20.
18. Hagerty, B. Executive pay (A special report) – Asian Scramble: Multinationals in China hope lucrative compensation packages can attract the local executives they desperately need. *Wall Street Journal*, 10 April 1997, R12.
19. Hailey, J. 1996. The expatriate myth: Cross-cultural perceptions of expatriate managers. *The International Executive*, 38(2): 255–271.
20. Further discussions of multinational policies regarding opportunities for local staff versus expatriates can be found in Geringer, J. M. & Hebert, L. 1989. Control and performance of international joint ventures. *Journal of International Business Studies*, 20(2): 235–254; Hamill, J. & Hunt, G. 1996. Joint ventures in Hungary: Criteria for success. In Arch G. Woodside and Robert E. Pitts (Eds.) *Creating and Managing International Joint Ventures*, 77–106. Wesport, CT: Quorum Books; and Shenkar, O. & Zeira, Y. 1987. Human resources management in international joint ventures: Directions for research. *Academy of Management Review*, 12(3): 546–557.
21. Leung, K., Smith, P. B., Wang, Z., & Sun, H. 1996. Job satisfaction in joint ventures hotels in China: An organizational justice analysis. *Journal of International Business Studies*, 27(5): 947–962.
22. Hailey, op. cit.
23. Chen, C. C., Choi, J., & Chi, S. C. 2002. Making justice sense of local-expatriate compensation disparity: Mitigation by local referents, ideological explanations, and interpersonal sensitivity in China-foreign joint ventures. *Academy of Management Journal*, 45(4): 807.
24. Bates, R. A. 2001. Equity, respect, and responsibility: An international perspective. *Advances in Developing Human Resources*, 3(1): 11–25.
25. For example, Delisle, P. & Chin, S. 1997. Remunerating employees in China – The complicated task faced by foreign firms. *Benefits & Compensation International*, 24(2): 16–20.
26. Hailey, op. cit.; Vatikiotis et al., op. cit.
27. For example, Carpenter, M. A., Sanders, W. G., & Gregersen, H. B. 2001. Bundling human capital with organizational context: The impact of international assignment experience on multinational firm performance and CEO pay. *Academy of Management Journal*, 44(3): 493–511; Hailey, op. cit.; Solomon, C. M. 1995. Global compensation: Learn the ABCs. *Personnel Journal*, 74(7): 70–75; Torbiom, I. 1994. Operative and strategic use of expatriates in new organizations and market structures. *International Studies of Management and Organizations*. 24(3): 5–17.
28. Semeneko, I. 2002. Study: Expat managers ethical but big headed. *Moscow Times;* Hailey, op. cit., 263.
29. Clearly, the relationship between culture and fairness models is more complicated than we can discuss here. More extensive treatments of the relationship between fairness models and nationality are provided by Kim, K. I., Park, H-J., & Suzuki, N. 1990. Reward allocations in the United States, Japan, and Korea: A comparison of individualistic and collectivistic cultures. *Academy of Management Journal*, 33(1): 188–198; and Mueller & Clarke, op. cit. A more detailed discussion of culture and sensitivity to differential outcomes is provided by Chen, C. C. 1995. New trends in rewards allocation preferences: A Sino-US comparison. *Academy of Management Journal*, 38(2): 408–428; Chen, C. C., Meindl, J. R., & Hui, H. 1998. Deciding on equity or parity: A test of situational, cultural and individual factors. *Journal of Organizational Behavior*, 19(2); 115–129; Chen, Y., Brockner, J., & Katz, T. 1998. Toward an explanation of cultural differences in in-group favoritism: The role of individual versus collective primacy. *Journal of Personality and Social Psychology*, 75(6): 1490–1502. Several other authors have addressed cultural differences in the importance attached to inputs versus outcomes for deciding upon fairness. These include Beamish, op. cit.; Huo, Y. P. & Steers, R. M. 1993. Cultural influences on the design of incentive systems: The case of East Asia. *Asia Pacific Journal of Management*, 10(1): 71–85; Leung et al., op. cit.
30. Huang, L-Y. 2003. Attitudes toward the management of international assignments – A comparative study. *Journal of American Academy of Business*, 3(2): 336–344.
31. Yan, A. M., Zhu, G., & Hall, D. T. 2002. International assignments for career building: A model of agency relationships and psychological contracts. *Academy of Management Review*, 27(3): 373–391.
32. GMAC Global Relocation Services. 2002. *Global relocation trends 2002 survey report.* February 2002.
33. Milkovich, G. T. & Bloom, M. 1998. Rethinking international compensation. *Compensation and Benefits Review*, 30(1): 15–23.
34. Mervosh, E. M. 1997. Managing expatriate compensation. *Industry Week*, 246(14): 13–16; and Barton, R. & Bishko, M. 1998. Global mobility strategy. *HR Focus*, 75(3): S7–S9.
35. Schneider & Barsoux, op. cit.
36. Chen, et al., op. cit.; Kickul, J., Lester, S. W., & Finkl, J. 2002. Promise breaking during radical organizational change: Do justice interventions make a difference? *Journal of Organizational Behavior*, 23(4): 469–488.
37. Toh, S. M. & DeNisi, A. S. 2003. Host country national (HCN) reactions to expatriate pay policies: A proposed model and some implications. *Academy of Management Review*, 28(4): 606–621.
38. Bhagat, R. S., Kedia, B. L., Harveston, P. D., & Triandis, H. C. 2002. Cultural variations in the cross-border transfer of organizational knowledge: An integrative framework. *Academy of Management Review*, 27(2): 204–221.
39. Solomon, C. 1995. Learning to manage host-country nationals. *Workforce*, 74(3): 60–67.
40. Thomas, D. C. & Ravlin, E. C. 1995. Responses of employees to cultural adaptation by a foreign manager. *Journal of Applied Psychology*, 80(1): 133–146.

41. Melles, R. 2003. 'They speak the same language so I'll be ok.' Not so fast. *Canadian HR Reporter*, September, 23, 11–12.
42. Ashamalla & Crocitto, op. cit.
43. Gallaga, O. M. Welcome to Austin: Samsung helps new employees feel at home. *Austin American Statesman*, 6 August 1997, DI.
44. Aryee, S. & Stone, R. J. 1996. Work experiences, work adjustment and psychological well-being of expatriate employees in Hong Kong. *International Journal of Human Resource Management*, 7(1): 150–162.

SUBJECT INDEX

A

B

C

D

E

F

G

H

I

J

S

T

U

Z

COMPANY INDEX

H

I

J

K

L

M

N

P

Q

R

S

T

U

V

Z

NAME INDEX